The Student's Guide to Careers in the Law

2009

Published by Chambers and Partners Publishing
(a division of Orbach & Chambers Ltd)
23 Long Lane, London EC1A 9HL
Tel: (020) 7606 1300 Fax: (020) 7600 3191
email: info@ChambersandPartners.co.uk
www.ChambersandPartners.com

Our thanks to the many students, trainees, pupils,
solicitors, barristers and graduate recruitment personnel
who assisted us in our research. Also to Chambers and
Partners' recruitment team for their knowledge and
assistance and to the researchers of *Chambers UK 2009*
from which all firm rankings are drawn.
Copyright © 2008 Michael Chambers and
Orbach & Chambers Ltd

ISBN: 978-0-85514-311-4

Publisher: Michael Chambers
Managing Editor: Fiona Boxall
Editor: Anna Williams
Deputy Editor: Michael Lovatt
Writers: Abigail Andersen, Alexis Hille,
Christopher Nichols, Colin Warriner, Dana Seay,
Jenna Course-Choi, Lauren Bennett, Phil Roe,
Richard Simmons, Russell Bramley, Samantha Rose
Database: Andrew Taylor
A-Z Co-ordinator: Gemma Buckle
Production: Jasper John, John Osborne,
Paul Cummings, Pete Polanyk, Robert Howe
Business Development Manager: Brad D. Sirott
Business Development Team: Neil Murphy,
Richard Ramsay, Bianca Maio, Gita Mohan
Proofreaders: Jennifer Gallagher, Nicholas Widdows
Printed by: Butler Tanner & Dennis

So you want to be a lawyer...

Welcome to the 2009 edition of Chambers and Partners' *Student's Guide to Careers in the Law.* We've written this book to give you the information, tools and confidence to help you make a sound career decision.

This Guide is the only publication to offer these three key ingredients:

- The True Picture: an insight into the training schemes at 150 law firms, based on in-depth interviews with hundreds of trainees. The trainees were selected by us, not by their law firms, and they to us spoke freely and frankly under the protection of anonymity.
- Chambers Reports: a look at life inside 25 barristers chambers. These reports were written after visits to each of the sets and interviews with pupils, barristers and clerks.
- Law School reviews based on feedback from students who have completed courses at each of the schools, plus interviews with course directors.

Chambers and Partners publishes guides to the legal professions around the world. You will benefit enormously from using our *Chambers UK* guide to refine your search for a law firm or chambers to train with. The best performing firms and sets in over 65 areas of practice are identified by way of league tables in *Chambers UK,* and you can get all this information online, for free, by visiting www.chambersandpartners.com.

All the guides we publish have one thing in common – they are independent. In a market flooded with publications for law students we take great pride in this fact. No one's money influences what we say about them.

This book could be the most useful thing you read this year, so get stuck in and we wish you great success for your future career.

The Student Guide team
September 2008

Contents

- **This guide, if used properly, can greatly ease the process of pursuing a career in the law**

- # Use this book in conjunction with www.chambersandpartners.com to find your perfect traineeship or pupillage

Chambers and Partners publishes a suite of legal guides that you should find helpful in your search for a training contract or pupillage.

- **Chambers UK** is the product of interviews with solicitors, barristers and their clients. It identifies the leading firms, sets and players across the full sweep of legal practice in the UK.

- **Chambers Global** sets out the results of our research into legal jurisdictions worldwide from Australia to Zambia. If you are considering a training contract with an international law firm, it's a must-read resource.

- **Chambers USA** provides a more detailed analysis of the performance of the best firms across all US states.

- **Chambers Asia** covers 23 countries in one of the world's most dynamic legal markets.

- **Chambers Europe** looks at the leading law firms and individuals from Albania to Ukraine.

- **Chambers Latin America**, first published in 2008.

These guides can all be read online for free at
www.chambersandpartners.com

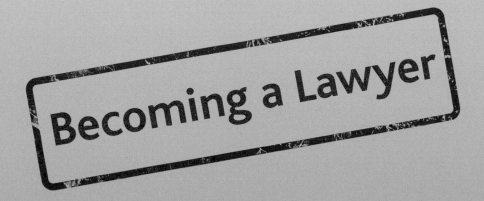

Becoming a Lawyer

- **Procrastination is the thief of time:** Plan well ahead to ensure against missing deadlines for vacation scheme and training contract applications.

Calendar of events 2008-2009

Law Fairs

October 2008

16	Northumbria University
23	University of Nottingham
28	University of York
30	University of Cambridge (Solicitors); Queen Mary, London

November 2008

3	University of Leeds
4	University of Leeds; University of Liverpool; University of Cardiff
5	City University London; University of Reading; Queens University Belfast
6	University of East Anglia
11	University of Sussex; University of Leicester; University of Essex; SOAS
12	University of Bristol; University of Hull
13	University of Bristol
15	University of Oxford
17	University of Newcastle
18	University of Warwick
19	University of Birmingham
20	University of Manchester; University of Southampton
24	University of Durham; UCL
25	University of Durham; UCL; LSE
26	University of Exeter; University of Sheffield
27	LSE

December 2008

| 1 | Kings College, London |
| 2 | Kings College, London |

February 2009

| 5 | University of Cambridge (Barristers) |

Vacation Scheme Deadlines

October 2008

31 Allen & Overy (for Winter 2008)
Jones Day (for Winter 2008 (non-law))
Norton Rose (for Christmas)

November 2008

10 Herbert Smith (Christmas)

11 Lovells (Christmas)

12 Stephenson Harwood (Christmas)

14 CMS Cameron McKenna (Christmas)

15 Clearly Gottlieb Steen & Hamilton (Christmas)

21 Denton Wilde Sapte (Christmas)

December 2008

31 Latham & Watkins (for Easter)

January 2009

12 Skadden

16 Allen & Overy
Freshfields

28 Cleary Gottlieb

30 Barlow Lyde & Gilbert   Dechert
Dundas & Wilson   Shoosmiths
Reynolds Porter Chamberlain

31
Addleshaw Goddard	Kirkland & Ellis
Ashurst	Latham & Watkins
Baker & McKenzie	Lawrence Graham
Berwin Leighton Paisner	Lewis Silkin
Bird & Bird	Lovells
Clyde & Co	McGrigors
Davenport Lyons	Mills & Reeve
Dewey & LeBoeuf	Mishcon de Reya
Dickinson Dees	Norton Rose
DLA Piper	Olswang
DMH Stallard	Pinsent Masons
Eversheds	SJ Berwin
Farrer & Co	Taylor Wessing
Field Fisher Waterhouse	TLT Solicitors
Government Legal Service	Travers Smith
	Walker Morris
Hammonds	Weil, Gotshal & Manges
Herbert Smith	White & Case
Ince & Co	Withers
Jones Day	

Vacation Scheme Deadlines

February 2009

1 O'Melveny & Myers

6 Denton Wilde Sapte

8 Nabarro

11 HBJ Gateley Wareing

13 CMS Cameron McKenna (for Easter/Summer)
Speechly Bircham

14 Holman Fenwick Willan

15 Stephenson Harwood
Manches
Forsters

19 Bates Wells & Braithwaite

20 Pannone (for Easter)

22 Watson, Farley & Williams

27 Clarion Solicitors
Edwards Angell Palmer & Dodge

28
Arnold & Porter	Macfarlanes
Bristows	Michelmores
Capsticks	Paul Hastings
Covington & Burling	Shadbolt
Dechert	Vinson & Elkins
Halliwells	Ward Hadaway
Hay & Kilner	Wedlake Bell

March 2009

1 Geldards
Trowers & Hamlins

31
Bevan Brittan	Laytons
Coffin Mew	Lester Aldridge
Foot Anstey	Penningtons
Hill Dickinson	Pricewaterhouse-Coopers
Hugh James	

April 2009

30 Howes Percival
Morgan Cole

May 2009

15 Edwards Angell Palmer & Dodge
(for open days)

July 2009

6 Brabners Chaffe Street

10 Pannone

Training Contract Deadlines

January 2009

16 Allen & Overy (non-law)

31 Bristows (Feb interviews)

February 2009

18 Baker & McKenzie (non-law)

27 Clarion Solicitors

May 2009

31 BP Collins (for 2010)

June 2009

30 Finers Stephens Innocent
Freeth Cartwright
Campbell Hooper Solicitors

July 2009

1 Maxwell Winward
Michelmores

6 Brabners Chaffe Street

10 Pannone

12 Blake Lapthorn

19 Weightmans

24 DWF

30 Davenport Lyons

31
Addleshaw Goddard	Eversheds
Allen & Overy (law)	Farrer & Co
Anthony Collins	Field Fisher Waterhouse
Arnold & Porter	Foot Anstey
asb law	Forbes
Ashurst	Forsters
Baker & McKenzie (law)	Freshfields
Berwin Leighton Paisner	Geldards
Bevan Brittan	Government Legal
Bingham McCutchen	Service
Bircham Dyson Bell	Halliwells
Bird & Bird	Hammonds
Bond Pearce	Harbottle & Lewis
BPE Solicitors	Hay & Kilner
Bristows	HBJ Gateley Wareing
Browne Jacobson	Henmans
Burges Salmon	Herbert Smith
Charles Russell	Hill Dickinson
Clarke Willmott	Holman Fenwick
Cleary Gottlieb	Howes Percival
Clyde & Co	Hugh James
CMS Cameron McKenna	Hunton & Williams
Cobbetts	IBB Solicitors
Coffin Mew	Ince & Co
Covington & Burling	Irwin Mitchell
Cripps Harries Hall	Kirkland & Ellis
Dechert	K&L Gates
Denton Wilde Sapte	Latham & Watkins
Dewey & LeBoeuf	Lawrence Graham
Dickinson Dees	Lester Aldridge
DLA Piper	Lewis Silkin
DMH Stallard	Lovells
Dorsey & Whitney	Lupton Fawcett
Dundas & Wilson	Mace & Jones (2010)
Edwards Angell	Macfarlanes

Training Contract Deadlines

July 2009

Manches
Martineau
Mayer Brown
McDermott, Will & Emery
McGrigors (for 2010)
Mills & Reeve
Mishcon de Reya
Morgan Cole
Nabarro
Needham & James
Norton Rose
Olswang
O'Melveny & Myers
Orrick, Herrington & Sutcliffe
Osborne Clarke
Pannone
Paul Hastings
Penningtons
Pinsent Masons
PricewaterhouseCoopers
Pritchard Englefield
Reed Smith
Reynolds Porter Chamberlain
Salans
Shadbolt
Shearman & Sterling
Sheridans

Shoosmiths
Sidley Austin
Simmons & Simmons
SJ Berwin
Skadden
Speechly Bircham
Stephenson Harwood
Taylor Wessing
Teacher Stern
Thomson Snell & Passmore
Thring Townsend
TLT Solicitors
Travers Smith
Trethowans
Veale Wasbrough Lawyers
Walker Morris
Ward Hadaway
Warner Goodman
Watson Burton
Watson Farley & Williams
Wedlake Bell
Weil, Gotshal & Manges
White & Case
Wiggin
Wilsons Solicitors
Withers
Wragge & co

August 2009

1   Beachcroft   Trowers & Hamlins
    Gordons   Thomas Eggar
    Payne Hicks Beach

3   Maclay Murray & Spens

14   Prettys

18   Higgs & Sons

31   Barlow Lyde & Gilbert   Jones Day
    Capsticks   Laytons
    Ford & Warren   Mundays
    Hewitsons   Vinson & Elkins

September 2009

30   Stevens & Bolton   Winckworth Sherwood

October 2009

31   Wollastons (for 2010)

What kind of lawyer do you want to be?

Let's start with one of the most basic questions – do you want to be a barrister or a solicitor? Here we give a simple description of each.

Barrister

Ask a solicitor about the key difference between the two sides of the profession and they will probably tell you it's the size of your average barrister's ego. At first sight the role of a barrister certainly looks a lot cooler than that of a solicitor. Even if you've only ever seen fictitious ones in TV dramas, you know the deal – it's all about striding into courtrooms, robes flowing; tense moments waiting for missing witnesses; and razor-sharp cross-examinations. Glamorous? It's downright sexy! The truth is there's a great deal more to the job than looking good in a wig and gown…

> **Essentially barristers do three things:**
>
> - **appear in court to represent others**
> - **give specialised legal advice in person or in writing**
> - **draft court documents**

How much of these a barrister does depends on the type of law they practise. Criminal barristers are in court most of the time, often with only an hour or two's notice of the details of their cases. By contrast, Chancery barristers spend most of their time in chambers writing tricky opinions and advising in conference on complicated legal points.

Barristers must display the skill and clarity to make complex or arcane legal arguments accessible to lay clients, juries and the judiciary. Their style of argument must be clear and persuasive, both in court and on paper. It has been some time since barristers have had exclusive rights of audience in the courts. Solicitors can, and some have, become accredited advocates in even the higher courts. This blurring of the distinction between the two halves of the profession hasn't been an utter disaster for the Bar, although solicitor advocates are undertaking a lot more of the most straightforward cases. When it comes to more complicated and lengthy matters, barristers are usually still briefed to do the advocacy, not least because this is often the most cost-effective way of managing a case. As a point of interest, solicitor advocates do not wear the wig and gown and are referred to as 'my friend' rather than 'my learned friend'.

Solicitors value barristers' detailed knowledge of the litigation process and, as a result, their ability to assess and advise on the merits and demerits of a case. A solicitor will pay good money for 'counsel's opinion'.

Certainly in the area of commercial law, a barrister must understand the client's perspective and use their legal knowledge to help construct a solution that makes business or common sense as well as legal sense. If you're hoping a career as a barrister will allow you to remain at the top of an ivory tower, you should consider life as an academic.

Most barristers are self-employed. This is why you hear the expression 'the independent Bar'. A minority are employed by companies, public bodies or law firms, and they make up 'the employed Bar'. To prevent independence from turning into isolation, barristers work in groups called sets, sharing premises and professional managers, etc. Barristers do not work for their sets, just at them, and as 'tenants' they contribute to the upkeep of their chambers and give a percentage of their earnings to their clerks and administrators. Unlike employed barristers and solicitors, those at the independent Bar get no sickness pay, holiday pay, maternity leave or monthly salary. What they do get is a good accountant.

To enter practice, LLB grads need to complete the Bar Vocational Course (BVC) before starting a much sought-after year of 'pupillage'. At the end of that it's a case of finding a set that wants you to join them as a member of their chambers – this is called 'tenancy'. Once you have that then the legal profession is your oyster.

Being a barrister is a great job, but the competition is fierce. If your appetite has been whetted you will find much more information in the final section of this book, where we have detailed the recruitment process and laid bare some of the more obscure practices and terminology. We have also tried to give a fair assessment of some of the difficulties that aspiring barristers may encounter. The Chambers Reports give invaluable insight into the lives of pupils and junior barristers at some of the best sets.

The Bar's professional body is the Bar Council, and it is regulated by the Bar Standards Board.

Solicitor

Most budding lawyers qualify as solicitors. Their role is to provide legal services directly to lay clients, who could be individuals, companies or public or other bodies. In short, clients come to solicitors for guidance on how to deal with their business or personal proposals and problems. These could be anything from drafting a will to defending a murder charge or buying a multibillion-pound business. The solicitor advises on the steps needed to proceed and then manages the case or the deal for the client until its conclusion. They will bring in a barrister if and when a second opinion or specialist advocacy is needed. The solicitor's role is much more like that of a project manager than the barrister's.

There are over 100,000 solicitors in England and Wales with practising certificates issued annually by the Solicitors Regulation Authority (SRA). The majority of them are in 'private practice' in solicitors' firms, though many thousands work in-house for companies, charities or public authorities. In the last 30 years the number of practising solicitors has risen by an average of 4% per year.

Most readers will be well aware that after the degree, law school awaits. Law grads need to take the Legal Practice Course (LPC). Non-law grads must first complete a law conversion course before being eligible for the LPC. Next comes the practical training. The most common way of qualifying is by undertaking a two-year training contract with a firm of solicitors, law centre, in-house legal team or public body. Much of the rest of this book deals with the nature of training contracts at different firms and how to procure one. The SRA's website gives all the fine detail you could wish for as to the requirements for training.

There's a big change on the horizon though. The profession is about to enter a new era in which it could also become possible to qualify as a solicitor without a traditional training contract, instead clocking up relevant work-based learning experiences. A pilot programme started in September 2008, full details of which can be found on the SRA's website at www.sra.org.uk/students/work-based-learning.page. The plan is that this second qualification route could dovetail with a new option to take the LPC in two parts, perhaps blending study and work. More on the LPC changes later.

Upon satisfactory completion of their training contract (or work-based learning) and the mandatory Professional Skills Course (PSC), a person can be admitted to the roll of those eligible to practise. In plain English that means they are then fully qualified. There are enrolment ceremonies for anyone who wants to give mum and dad a day to remember and a new photo for the mantelpiece.

Exactly when you should apply for a training contract depends on the kind of firm you hope to join. If you are studying for a law degree and you want to work in a commercial firm, the crucial time for research and applications is during your penultimate year at uni. If you are a non-law student intending to proceed straight to a law conversion course before going to a commercial firm then you'll have to juggle exams and career considerations in your final year. Students wanting to enter high street practice usually don't need to worry about training contract applications quite so early. Unlike commercial firms, which generally offer contracts two years in advance of the start date, smaller firms do so closer to the start date, and possibly after a trial period of work as a paralegal. We discuss the role of paralegals on page 24.

Larger commercial firms commonly offer their future trainees scholarships to cover law school fees and other basic expenses. Public sector organisations, eg the Government Legal Service, may also come up with some cash. Students hoping to practise in smaller firms soon learn that financial assistance is highly unlikely and this can make law school an uncertain and expensive endeavour. Reading our Funding section on page 80 may help.

Needless to say, your choice of training contract will determine the path (and perhaps also location) of your future career. A firm's clients, its work and its reputation will determine not only the experience you gain, but probably also your future marketability as a lawyer. At Chambers and Partners, we've made it our business to know who does what, how well they do it and what it might be like working at a particular firm. Our parent publication *Chambers UK* will be an incredibly useful resource for you. Its league tables show which firms command greatest respect from clients and other professionals in different areas of practice right across the country. You can read the entire thing for free at www.chambersandpartners.com and use it to create a shortlist of firms to apply to.

In the True Picture section of this book we've profiled 150 firms in England and Wales. This section of the book should help you understand what kind of firm might suit you and the kind of work you can expect to undertake when you get there. It is the product of many hundreds of interviews with trainees and we think you'll really benefit from making it your regular bedtime reading.

It may help you to understand the extent and nature of the solicitors' profession by grouping law firms into the following categories, starting with the biggest.

Magic circle

The magic circle is traditionally defined as Allen & Overy, Clifford Chance, Freshfields Bruckhaus Deringer, Linklaters and Slaughter and May. To those for whom bigger is better (bigger deals, bigger money, bigger staff numbers and bigger billing targets), these firms are the be-all and end-all. Corporate and finance work is central at these firms, as is international business. By organising their training on a massive scale, these firms can offer seemingly unlimited office facilities, great perks, overseas postings and excellent formal training sessions. Although these five giants top many lists, not least for revenue and partner profits, consider carefully whether they'd top yours. Training in a magic circle firm is CV gold but bigger is not better for everyone. One factor to consider is the requirement to work really long hours. Big profits and big international deals equate to one dreaded thing – a major intrusion into a trainee's personal life.

London: large commercial

The top-ten City of London firms (including the magic circle) offer around 1,000 traineeships between them each year, representing approximately a fifth of all new training contracts registered with the SRA. There's not such a huge difference between the magic circle and 'silver circle' firms such as Herbert Smith, CMS Cameron McKenna, Lovells and a few others. Training contracts at these chasing-pack firms are strongly flavoured with corporate and finance practice and, again, international work. The salaries match those paid by the magic circle, which is only fair given that the lawyers work equally hard. As a trainee you can expect to assist on big, high-value deals and cases, although you certainly can't expect to be conducting particularly challenging duties all the time. If you are working against a deadline then you will be expected to stay until it is finished. This can mean working through the night and coming in at weekends from time to time.

London: American firms

Since the 1990s, there has been a steady stream of firms crossing the Atlantic to take their place in the UK market. Currently more than 40 of them offer training contracts to would-be UK solicitors. New training schemes are popping up all the time, so if you've revolutionary leanings stay eagle-eyed if you want to be the first to jump on the bandwagon. At the risk of over-generalising, these firms are characterised by international work (usually corporate or finance-led), smaller offices, more intimate training programmes and rather long hours. On the other hand they usually give trainees a good amount of responsibility and many of them pay phenomenally high salaries. Lawyers at the hotshot US firms frequently work opposite magic circle lawyers on

deals; indeed many of them were magic circle and top-ten firm partners or associates before they joined a US firm. The arrival of the US firms has had a knock-on effect on City law, not least on City salaries, which have soared in the past decade.

London: mid-sized commercial

Just like their bigger cousins, these firms are almost entirely dedicated to business law and business clients. Generally, they don't require trainees to spend quite so many hours in the office; however, some of the most successful mid-sizers – eg Macfarlanes and Travers Smith – are giving the big boys a run for their money in terms of profitability, so trainees can expect their share of late nights. Ostensibly, the size of deals and cases on which these firms work means trainees can do more than just photocopying and bundling documents. The atmosphere in these firms is generally a bit more intimate than at the giants of the City and there is a greater likelihood of working for partners directly.

London: smaller commercial

For those who don't mind taking home a slightly more modest pay cheque in exchange for better hours, these firms are a great choice. After all, money isn't everything (note: if you don't agree with that statement, look above and read no further). Usually these firms will be full-service outfits, although some may have developed on the back of one or two particularly strong practice areas or via a reputation in certain industries. Real estate is commonly a big deal at these firms. Along with commercial work, these smaller firms often offer private client services to wealthier people. If you train at one of these firms, both partners and family members are more likely to recognise your face.

Niche firms

London abounds with firms specialising in areas as diverse as aviation, media, insurance litigation, shipping, family, intellectual property, sport... you name it, there's a firm for it. Niche firms have also sprouted in areas of the country with high demand for a particular service. How about equine law in Newmarket? If you are absolutely certain that you want to specialise in a particular field – especially if you have already worked in a relevant industry – a niche firm is an excellent choice. As well as making sure your heart is set on a niche area, you need to be able to back up your passion with hard evidence of your commitment. Some of these firms also dabble in other practice areas, but if any of these firms try to woo you by talking at length about their other areas of work, ask some searching questions – they're called niche for a reason.

Regional firms

Many of you will agree that there is more to life than an EC postcode. In the regions, there are some very fine firms acting for top-notch clients on cases and deals the City firms would snap up in a heartbeat. There is also some international work going on outside the capital. The race for training contracts in the biggest of these firms is just as competitive as in the City, and some regional firms are even more discerning than their London counterparts in the sense that applicants may have to demonstrate a long-term commitment to living in the area. These firms hardly want to shell out for training only to see their qualifiers flit off to the capital. Trainees at smaller regional firms tend to focus on the needs of regional clients and would therefore suit anyone who wants to become an integral part of their local business community. Salaries are lower outside London, in some cases significantly so, but the cost of living is generally more reasonable. There's a perception that working outside London means a chummier atmosphere and more time for the gym/pub/family of an evening, but do bear in mind that some of the biggest and most ambitious regional players will expect you to work longer hours than others.

National and multi-site firms

Multi-site firms are necessarily massive operations, some of them with offices spanning the length and breadth of the country and overseas. To give you just three examples, Eversheds has nine branches in England and Wales plus several overseas; DLA Piper has eight in England and Scotland and many more overseas; Shoosmiths mostly operates in smaller cities and towns from the South Coast up to Nottingham. These firms attract students who want to do big-ticket work outside London, but their national spread can sometimes mean that trainees in regional offices do London levels of work for a lower salary. Some of these firms allow trainees to be based in one office, whereas others expect them to move offices at the drop of a hat. Make sure you know the firm's policy or you could end up having a long-distance relationship with friends, family and your significant other while you move to a new town for six months... or get up at 5am to sit in traffic on the M62. The work on offer is mostly commercial, although some private client experience may be available.

General practice/high street

These range from substantial, long-established firms in town centres to sole practitioners working above shops in the suburbs. They act for legally aided clients, individuals funding themselves and local businesses. Staple work includes landlord and tenant problems, conveyancing, personal injury, employment, family, wills and probate, and crime. Given the changes to legal aid funding, these firms are having to take on more privately paying and commercial clients just to stay afloat. Be prepared to earn considerably less than your peers in commercial practice, and don't expect there to be an abundance of amenities or resources in the office. Excessively long hours are unlikely unless you're on a rota for police station duty, in which case you'll be paid extra for that. If you want to grow up fast as a lawyer and see how the law actually affects individuals and the community in which you practise, then this is the kind of firm to go for. Larger firms may take up to ten or so trainees a year; the smallest will recruit on an occasional basis. It is in this part of the profession where salaries are the lowest, often the minimum required or recommended for trainees by the SRA.

- Minimum salary Central London = £18,420 pa
- Recommended salary Central London = £18,870 pa
- Minimum salary elsewhere = £16,500 pa
- Recommended salary elsewhere = £16,790 pa
  As of 1 August 2008

Anyone thinking of entering the legally aided sector should be aware that dramatic changes are affecting the public funding of legal services. Read the following section **How legal aid works.**

How legal aid works

Created in 1949, legal aid recognises the idea that equality of access and right to representation before the law are fundamental to a just society. Initially managed by the Law Society, since 2000 the system has been run by the Legal Services Commission (LSC).

Who gets legal aid?

The LSC funds solicitors and other agencies to provide advice to people facing civil and criminal problems such as family breakdown, debt, detention in police stations and those needing representation in court who could not otherwise afford it. Solicitors enter a contract with the LSC to provide services to clients and are subject to an annual audit to ensure their files are run correctly. The CLS (Community Legal Service) administers funding for civil matters, and to be eligible individuals must satisfy both means and merits tests. The CDS (Criminal Defence Service) administers funding for defendants who must satisfy an interest of justice test and, if the case is in the magistrates' court, a means test. There is talk of introducing the latter to Crown Court cases too.

Legal aid transformation

The legal aid system has been under review throughout its history, but in the last few years that scrutiny has intensified. The primary driver is the size of the annual spend, which has risen from £1.5bn to £2.1bn over the past nine years. In July 2005 the DCA published 'A Fairer Deal for Legal Aid', setting out the government's long-term legal strategy. Lord Carter of Coles was instructed to review procedures and practices to devise new, more efficient models. The Carter review was published in 2006 and the government's response – 'Legal Aid: A Sustainable Future' – set out the ways in which reform of funding for criminal, civil/family, and immigration and asylum matters would function, as well a reform of the contracting regime. While some of Carter's recommendations have been followed, others have not been reflected in subsequent policies. In the broadest of terms, the government is keen to open legal aid procurement to market forces via competitive tendering (Best Value Tendering or BVT) by solicitors. Many in the legal profession see this approach as fundamentally flawed. Recent successful court action by the Law Society against the LSC's Unified Contract for civil work has seen the introduction of BVT significantly delayed in both criminal and civil matters.

Reforms in relation to crime

- Defence services in magistrates' courts and now also Crown Courts are paid for under a newly revised systems of graduated fees.
- Panels of firms work to strict cost and case management rules to provide defence services in Very High-Cost Cases (VHCC).
- BVT by solicitors is still under consultation and will be the subject of a pilot scheme before any roll-out.
- All requests for publicly funded police station work must be made through the Defence Solicitor Call Centre (DSCC) and fees are now fixed.
- CDS Direct, a telephone advice service trialled by the LSC during 2008, is now rolling out across the country. Detainees for less serious offences may in the future only be eligible for this service rather than seeing a solicitor in person.

Reforms in relation to civil/family

- A fixed fee scheme has been introduced for areas such as housing and debt advice.
- New graduated fee schemes have been introduced for private law family cases and in-court child care cases.
- BVT by solicitors is still under consultation and will be the subject of pilot schemes before roll-out. This will not happen for mainstream civil Legal Aid services until 2013, with pilots proposed in some areas from 2010.
- Community Legal Advice Centres (CLACs) are being set up by the LSC and local authorities to provide a one-stop shop integrated social welfare law provision. Five are currently up and running following a tendering process and a dozen more are in negotiation.

The response of the professions and their concerns

Legal aid practitioners are, to be frank, pissed off about the reforms, the manner of their implementation and the LSC's perceived disregard for the recommendations of consultations. There have been demonstrations outside Parliament and the Law Society launched a campaign called *What Price Justice?* supported by a wide range of organisations such as MIND, Shelter and the Refugee Council. So what are people concerned about?

- Competitive tendering is dependent on having sufficient numbers of firms to engender competition, and there just aren't that many in certain areas, like Wales and East Anglia. It could lead to those making the lowest bid getting the work and this will not necessarily mean higher quality.
- Fixed-fee systems will benefit larger firms that can handle a high volume of straightforward cases. They could endanger specialist firms by discouraging them from taking on complex cases. A 'one size fits all' standard service incapable of addressing client needs could emerge. Fixed fees may also see solicitors doing the minimum amount of work for the price.
- Practitioners argue that as the LSC is a monopoly purchaser, the idea of free market forces is redundant, and that the government simply wants more for less. They point to evidence from the USA indicating that competitive tendering drives down standards and lowers the quality of representation.

There is also concern that there will be reduced access to justice:

- Many firms have closed down their legal aid criminal departments because they no longer pay their way.
- Opponents fear that consolidation will lead to blackspots of meagre or no provision in some areas.
- The 'fewer firms doing more work more economically' argument for BVT doesn't take into account representation of black and minority ethnic (BME) clients or other vulnerable groups (disabled clients, children) who are often advised by small firms of specialist or local practitioners. Making practice uneconomical for such lawyers may decrease access to justice for such minorities.
- There is some apprehension that disabled clients will be indirectly discriminated against. As the solicitors of such clients often incur additional expenses, which

will not be met in fixed-fee arrangements, there may be less economic incentive to take cases on.
- The Bar Council observes that if legal aid is less accessible there will be an increased number of litigants in person.
- There are fears that CLACs are not sufficiently independent of funding bodies to avoid conflicts of interest, especially in areas such as housing. The fact that CLACs effectively become monopolies in their areas is also perceived as potentially unfair.
- Economic strictures may see firms cutting costs in areas like training, meaning fewer legal aid practitioners in the future.
- The Bar Council and the Law Society fear that top-quality students will be driven away from legal aid work by low remuneration.

The future of the legal aid landscape

Students, trainees, pupils, barristers and lawyers committed to legal aid work have never been in it for the money, but the current state of affairs is giving many ideologically dedicated practitioners and would-be practitioners enormous cause for concern. Uncertainty as to quite how and when legal aid reforms will go forward means a number of firms have held off from offering training contracts in the past couple of years. It seems unlikely that legal aid will die a death any time soon, but regardless of the exact form ongoing changes take, the trend for greater economic pressure and consolidation/reduction in the number of firms will continue. If you have a burning desire to enter any publicly funded area of practice, none of this will stop you, but we'd advise anyone considering a legal aid career to research the practice area, the firms and the current state of reforms as thoroughly as possible.

For more news on this subject check out:

- www.legalservices.gov.uk
- www.whatpricejustice.lawsociety.org.uk
- www.barcouncil.org.uk

- **Start early:** Some kind of legal experience, whether it's involvement with a student law magazine or shadowing your aunt's neighbour's lawyer friend, is pretty crucial since you need to convince potential employers that you're serious about the profession, not just following an adolescent fantasy.

Some other career options

There are a number of different organisations and roles to look at other than becoming a solicitor or barrister in private practice. Here are a few of the main ones.

Working in-house for a company

A number of large companies offer training contracts and/or pupillages. In-house lawyers populate the banking, utilities, telecommunications and entertainment industries, to name but a few. There is no easily accessible comprehensive list of organisations offering training contracts, so for further information, aspiring solicitors should contact the Commerce & Industry Group (www.cigroup.org.uk) and aspiring barristers should contact the Bar Council. It's also worth keeping an eye out in the legal press and in *The Times* on Thursdays to see who is recruiting.

We spoke to one recently qualified solicitor who trained in-house with an international bank. He had already built up experience of the financial sector through working as a transaction manager in a bank and eventually asked the head of the legal department if they would be willing to fund him through part-time GDL and LPC courses and provide him with a training contract. The proposal was feasible as the bank was already an accredited training provider and had a solicitor with sufficient experience (and interest) who was happy to take on the role of training supervisor. The only thing the bank couldn't provide was sufficient contentious training and so it arranged a secondment to one of the law firms on its legal panel.

Our source felt his training was as good as, if not better than, anything available in private practice. 'I was given my own work to manage and had a great deal more latitude than in a conventional training contract. I got responsibility earlier and a lot less grunt work to do.' In-house trainees certainly develop very marketable skills because almost everything they do has a practical application and their sector knowledge is immense. Cold-calling heads of legal at banks or companies you're interested is not recommended. Unless the organisation publicises vacancies, usually its trainees will be recruited after having already worked there in some other capacity, and even then 'you have to exercise discretion in trying to obtain a contract.' A softly-softly approach usually works best.

Most in-house lawyers started out in private practice, switching to the role some time after qualification. They do so because of a general perception that the rewards are good and the hours more manageable than in a law firm. In-house lawyers don't lose touch with private practice; indeed part of the job involves selecting and instructing law firms to provide specialist advice to the company. This part of the job ensures the in-house lawyer plenty of invites to parties, lunches and sporting events as the different law firms curry favour.

Law Centres

From its roots in North Kensington in 1970, the network of UK Law Centres has grown to around 60 today. Law Centres are members of the not-for-profit sector and are registered as charities and companies limited by guarantee. All of them have local management committees. Advice and representation is provided without charge to the public with funding from their local authority, contracts from the Legal Services Commission (LSC) and some of the major charities, such as the Big Lottery. Recently many have received additional funding from the new Equality and Human Rights Commission.

The legal problems handled may vary from one Centre to another, but those who work in them can all be described as social welfare law specialists. Community care, all types of discrimination, education, employment, housing, immigration, asylum and public law form the caseload. In a recent development, crime has become a specialty for one Law Centre and family advice for another.

Law Centres see themselves as more than just providers of legal advice to the public; their horizons are broader than those of the Citizens Advice Bureau and they tend to take on cases with a wider social impact. A client with a consumer dispute is less likely to be taken on than someone who is affected by, say, a local authority's decision on rent arrears because Law Centres have noted an alarming trend for social landlords to bring ever increasing numbers of rent arrears cases. Identifying such trends is part of their job. From there, it's a case of using little matters to change the big picture, perhaps by way of a test case that makes it to the House of Lords, the European Court of Justice and the broadsheets. And because Law Centres are also eager to involve the community they operate within, providing legal training and education. A job in this field can also take you down the local comprehensive to offer up your legal know-how to young teenagers.

Recent reforms to the provision of legal aid have required Law Centres to become more target-oriented, but there is still a strong political commitment to the sector. Because of the quality and range of services provided by Law Centres, they should become even more embedded in the provision of legal services as the LSC continues to develop the Community Legal Service. Recent Law Centre highlights include the Streetwise Law Centre based in Bromley that ensures that young people have access to justice; Hammersmith and Fulham Law Centre's successful challenge brought under the Human Rights Act against the controversial Section 55 of the Asylum and Immigration Act; and the Butterfly Project at Avon & Bristol Law Centre which is funded by the Big Lottery to assist migrant women to gain better access to services.

Most Law Centres employ 10-15 lawyers and, if you're attracted to working with colleagues who share your ideals and social conscience, you may want to investigate a career in the sector. Routes to a career are as varied as the work. Newly qualified solicitors with relevant experience in private practice are recruited; so too are those who have worked as paralegals for non-profit agencies and have gained supervisor level status. A career may also begin at a Law Centre itself. Each year the LSC provides funding to support trainee solicitors. Law Centres can apply for 50% of a trainee's salary, and in the past many have been successful in gaining this support. Mirroring a training contract in private practice, the trainee will experience different branches of law, learning from specialists in each area. Law Centres often liaise closely with local firms to ensure that trainees get a wide experience of different areas of law.

Concern with the 'Greater Good' comes with a caveat. As a trainee and a newly qualified solicitor your salary will roughly match private practice on the high street – £24-30,000 or more in London. However Law Centres tend lose their competitive edge when seeking to appoint more experienced lawyers. Without wishing to sound trite, what you lose in the bank you gain in the soul. Law Centres operate along different lines to private practices: less hierarchy, more of an equal say for staff at all levels (some even operate as collectives with all staff drawing the same salary). Terms and conditions at work emulate those in local government and, as such, pension and holiday provisions, etc. are good, while flexible and part-time working is common. Law Centres are keen equality and diversity employers and encourage trainees from their local community. You will need to be flexible and willing to accept new challenges. It is an exciting environment and many lawyers have gone on to take up influential roles outside of the movement.

Candidates will only be considered if they respond to an advertisement. Look for these in *The Guardian* (Wednesdays), local newspapers, a monthly publication called *Legal Action* (your university law library should have it), and the Law Centres Federation website www.lawcentres.org.uk (updated daily).

To enhance your prospects you should be able to demonstrate your interest in social justice. Earn some stripes on committees or community groups; working in a local authority while studying a CPE/LPC part-time will give you a taste of the fields Law Centres plough. While at law school take advantage of any schemes that bring you closer to working for social justice. Some volunteers are accepted by Law Centres to help with administration and (if accredited) translation work. Volunteers usually come via other non-profit agencies so don't expect to just walk into a Law Centre and be accepted as a volunteer. A voluntary role with a Citizens Advice Bureau is easier to get hold of and would prepare you well for the type of clients served by Law Centres.

Government Legal Service

Lately between 20 and 30 trainee solicitors and pupil barristers have been recruited each year by the Government Legal Service (GLS) to work within different government departments and offices. At one end of the scale there are full-time litigators, and at the other people drafting new legislation or advising ministers. We'd recommend anyone applying to the GLS to have a long think about the role government lawyers take, particularly considering how law and politics interact, and the impact that they can have on life and society in the UK, whether this is by bringing about the prosecution of drugs smugglers or human traffickers, or drafting new sexual offences or employment legislation. If the idea appeals, read our True Picture and Chambers Reports features on GLS training contracts and pupillages. The GLS A-Z is on page 738.

Local Government

Roughly 4,000 solicitors are employed in local authorities across the UK. Each authority acts as a separate employer; some offer training contracts, but there's no central list of vacancies and no single recruitment office. Finding out about training contract opportunities is a challenge in itself, as is finding out which few councils offer sponsorship for the GDL and/or LPC. A good starting point for research is www.lgcareers.com. Click on 'career descriptions' and then head for 'supporting your community'. Also have a good rummage through the information at Solicitors in Local Government www.slgov.org.uk, where you can find several testimonies from qualified solicitors and trainees of their day-to-day experiences. Most authorities advertise in the Law Society's *Gazette* and *The Lawyer*. You can also try the law and public service job ads in *The Times*, *The Guardian* and *The Independent*, or even approach local authorities directly.

Solicitors in local government advise elected council members and senior officers on a wide variety of topics, ranging from employment to land purchases and even the prosecution of rogue traders and suppliers. This breadth of practice is particularly true of solicitors in small authorities, while those in larger ones usually specialise in a particular area, such as housing, planning, highways, education or social services. Duties include keeping councils on the straight and narrow, making sure they don't spend their money unlawfully and advising councillors on the legal implications of their actions. The typical salary for a local authority solicitor is £29,700-£39,900.

Trainees usually follow the same seat system that prevails in private practice, but for local authority trainees there is the added bonus of having rights of audience in civil and criminal courts and tribunals that outstrip those of peers in private practice. Trainees shadow solicitors and gradually build up their own caseload, acting for officers from different departments of the local authority. If you want a sneak preview of what it's really like before you take the plunge then some authorities offer paid summer placements. Others will arrange an informal unpaid attachment during vacations. Contact the head of legal services at a local authority to ask about these.

Be prepared to wade through the bureaucratic bog and at times be driven to distraction by the slow machinations of local government. However, the benefits of a great training contract, variety in your day-to-day work, flexible hours and a sense of serving the community often outweigh this. The best way to climb up the ladder is by hopping from one authority to another, and many local authority chief executives trained as solicitors. Training in local government also opens doors to careers in private practice, the Crown Prosecution Service and the GLS.

Crown Prosecution Service

If you have a passion for criminal law, and the idea of billable hours and contract drafting leaves you cold, the Crown Prosecution Service (CPS) may appeal. The CPS is the government department responsible for bringing prosecutions against people who have been charged with a criminal offence in England and Wales. It handles all stages of the process, from advising the police on the possibility of prosecution right through to the delivery of advocacy in the courtroom.

The CPS employs over 2,700 lawyers in England and Wales to handle more than 1.2 million cases in the magistrates' and Crown Courts. CPS prosecutors review and prosecute criminal cases following investigation by the police. They also advise the police on matters of criminal law and evidence, some working from Criminal Justice Units, which have been established within police stations to combat the problem of failed prosecutions. Lawyers here advise the police on the appropriate charge for the crime, spending one day in the office preparing cases and the next in the magistrates' court dealing with administrative matters relating to each case. Lawyers in the Trials Unit handle Crown Court cases, including murder, rape and robbery.

CPS prosecutors can expect to come into contact with 30 or 40 cases each day in the magistrates' courts. Many Crown Court trials are conducted by self-employed barristers; however, there are increasing opportunities for CPS Crown Advocates. The Director of Public Prosecutions, Sir Ken Macdonald QC, is keen to improve and modernise the service offered by the CPS, and an essential part of this is the development of in-house advocacy, such that the CPS will routinely conduct a large proportion of its own cases in all courts. Although prosecutors don't have the same intense client contact as defence lawyers, they do interact with everyone from magistrates, clerks, solicitors and probation and police officers, to civilian and expert witnesses. They also liaise with racial equality and victim support agencies as well as victims and witnesses themselves. For example, where a prosecution is abandoned, the prosecutor will inform the victim of the reasons.

Competition is fierce for training contracts and pupillages with the CPS, but once you get in, unless something goes wrong, you are guaranteed employment on qualification. 'Strong communication and sound decision-making skills and advocacy potential' are just some of the attributes you will need to apply, according to Head of Legal Development Lesley Williams. The service is looking for those with 'commitment – not necessarily for a lifetime with the CPS, but those who at least see their next few years here.' Some lawyers give up lucrative careers in the private sector to join the CPS, taking pay cuts in return for a family-friendly working environment with good training opportunities.

Trainees liaise closely with supervisors to determine what they should be working on, sometimes on a daily, often on a weekly basis. All supervisors volunteer for the task, so you can be sure that they are willing participants in the relationship. Although they can state three preferences, trainees must be prepared to work anywhere within the region to which they apply. Expect to be shadowing prosecutors, observing or even assisting with pre-charge advice, assisting busy colleagues and interacting with the police on a day-to-day basis.

As well as learning everything about criminal litigation within the CPS, there are opportunities in the form of three-to-four month secondments in private practice, the GLS or local government. There have even been opportunities to do placements at organisations such as the BBC.

At around the 16th month, trainee solicitors have the opportunity to begin a two-week course to become Associate Prosecutors, so that they have limited rights of audience in the magistrates' court.

While still a CPS trainee, Sibylle Cheruvier set up the Legal Trainee Network, which aims to connect the trainee solicitors and barristers scattered throughout in the service's different offices across the UK. Socials, a mentoring and buddy scheme and an online discussion board are just some of the benefits. It's 'a way to link trainees together to share knowledge, experience or good news,' she told us.

Opportunities for training places in the CPS are advertised on the website www.cps.gov.uk. This is also the starting point for vacation placements and work experience. Vacancies may also appear in the legal, national and local press. The CPS will be advertising its 2009 campaign for legal trainees from October 2008 and places will be open to internal and external candidates. The CPS expects all trainees to have completed and passed the LPC or BVC before taking up a post. A trainee's salary starts at £18,425 nationally and £19,441 in London. Salaries for newly qualified lawyers start at £26,000 nationally and £28,662 in London.

The traditional LLB to LPC/BVC route is by no means the only route into the CPS. Many CPS trainees have juggled work and part-time study; some have entered the service sideways, having left school with few qualifications. CPS caseworkers are the beneficiaries of the service's eagerness to grow talent from within. This being so, perhaps becoming a caseworker is the way forward for future trainees. They assist prosecutors by researching cases and making recommendations on information required and charges to be brought. Beyond these duties, they liaise with advocates, witnesses, police and court staff; provide support to witnesses and victims; and additionally attend court to assist counsel on a regular basis. Impressive organisational skills and an ability to relate to people are essential. Remuneration runs between £18,425 nationally and £19,441 in London. Theoretically you could start anywhere within the CPS and end up as a prosecuting lawyer.

Legal executive

If you haven't found a training contract or are thinking about moving sideways into a legal career, you could consider the Institute of Legal Executives (ILEX) course. Those who complete the course become legal executives – qualified lawyers who are sometimes known as the 'third branch' of the legal profession. The work they do is similar to that of a solicitor but, as a rule, legal executives will deal mainly with low-value, high-volume cases such as residential conveyance work and personal injury claims, although it is possible to climb higher with experience.

There are over 24,000 legal executives and trainee legal executives across the country. No prior legal training is required to enrol on the course, which makes it suitable for school leavers, new graduates or those already engaged in a career and looking to branch out. It can be taken on a part-time basis, giving trainees an opportunity to combine study with practical experience. Trainees initially study for a Professional Diploma in Law, which takes about two years part-time. The course includes an introduction to key legal concepts as well as legal practice and procedure and can be examined either by the mixed-assessment route (a portfolio, case studies and one end of course examination) or the examination route (four papers). Trainees then progress to the Professional Higher Diploma in Law, which allows them to specialise in a particular area of practice, usually guided by the job the trainee is doing at the time.

On completion, trainees become members of ILEX. To become a fully qualified ILEX fellow, it is necessary to gain five years of qualifying experience in a legal background (at least two after completing the exams) and be over the age of 25. Law graduates are exempt from the academic part of the course and can take examinations solely in legal practice, enabling the qualification to be gained in a little over twelve months. For those without a law degree, the professional qualification will usually take three or four years to complete while in full-time employment. There is no set time to complete the examinations, so trainees can work at their own pace.

Once qualified, ILEX graduates end up in employment across the full spectrum of legal services from private practice to government departments and the in-house legal teams of major corporations. Some ILEX fellows continue studying and eventually become fully qualified solicitors. Most can seek exemption from the GDL, having already covered the core subjects, and move straight on to the LPC. They may also be exempted from the two-year training contract.

Although ILEX can provide a useful route to becoming a solicitor, it is by no means the quickest. However, positions for trainee legal executives may be available when solicitors' training contracts are not and, crucially, the route does enable the student to earn whilst studying. A full list of colleges offering the course (including via distance learning) is available at www.ilex.org.uk.

Paralegal

If you have time to fill before starting your training contract or you are yet to be convinced you want to spend time and money on law school, paralegal work can provide a useful introduction to legal practice. There is no single job description: some experienced paralegals may run their own cases; others with little to offer by way of experience may end up doing very dull document management tasks for months on end. Employers view time spent paralegalling favourably as it demonstrates commitment to the profession and enables candidates to gain valuable experience and commercial or sector insight. Some firms and companies – though not all – offer traineeships to the most impressive of their own paralegals, but you should always keep in mind that the job is a valuable position in its own right. Guard against giving the impression that you will leave as soon as something better crops up.

The paralegal market is competitive, so those with no legal qualifications or practical experience may find it harder to secure a position. Indeed, some top City firms require all paralegal applicants to have completed the LPC. When starting out, it may be necessary to work a number of short-term contracts until one firm decides it wants you on a long-term basis.

Some firms insist that prospective trainee solicitors complete a trial period of paralegalling before offering them a contract. This practice is widespread and does sometimes lead to allegations of exploitation by firms. Should you find yourself in a position whereby you think a firm has taken advantage of you the best organisation to contact is the Junior Lawyers Division of the Law Society.

Paralegalling can be a career in its own right, and experienced paralegals with specialist skills can make a very decent living. If you're thinking about becoming a career paralegal you should take a look at the National Association of Licensed Paralegals' website at www.nationalparalegals.com. For information on current vacancies, check the legal press or register with a specialist recruitment agency. You should also find out if your law school's careers office has contacts, and regularly check the websites of any firms in your area. Some firms employ paralegals from among those who write to them on spec.

Her Majesty's Court Service

Her Majesty's Court Service is an executive agency of the Ministry of Justice responsible for the daily business of the civil, family and criminal courts in England and Wales – right up to the Court of Appeal. Its stated aim is 'to ensure that access [to justice] is provided as quickly as possible and at the lowest cost consistent with open justice and that citizens have greater confidence in, and respect for, the system of justice.'

HMCS is responsible for the management of 725 properties and 591 court buildings, including the modernisation of their physical appearance. It deals with the timetabling of hearings and ensures there are always ushers to manage the process. On a lighter note, the service is even responsible for making courts available as filming locations. Many HMCS jobs are administrative in nature; however, the service recruits Judicial Assistants (JAs) three times a year, with each successful applicant assigned to one of the Court of Appeal's senior judges for a period of between three to 12 months. Duties include legal research, advice and providing assistance in drafting judgements, and JAs may also help define the shape and nature of appeals in less well-presented cases. A former JA asserts that 'whether you're a barrister or a solicitor, just before or after qualification is probably the best time to do it.' There are usually ten positions available at any one time. Applicants must be qualified lawyers who have or are about to complete pupillage or traineeship; have proved their intellectual ability by achieving a first or 2:1 at degree level; and have the ability to work under pressure as part of a team. As and when they become available, positions are advertised in *The Times* and the *Law Society Gazette*, as well as on the HMCS website: www.hmcourts-service.gov.uk.

Those looking for a long-term career might consider the roles of administrative officer, bailiff and county and Crown Court ushers or clerks. Court clerks do not have a legal advisory role and do not need legal qualifications. Their responsibilities include maintaining the records of a court and administering oaths to witnesses and jurors. Magistrates' clerks do give legal advice to lay magistrates on issues like self-defence, identification of suspects and inferences from the silence of defendants after arrest. All court clerks need to be able to think on their feet and deal confidently with people. Very occasionally they need to exercise the power to order individuals into custody for contempt of court, although the clerks we spoke to indicated that the vast majority of defendants treat them with respect.

A shift in recruitment policy has seen the traditional route (by which those without degrees could train while studying for the Diploma in Magesterial Law) overtaken by the recruitment of LPC and BVC graduates as trainee court clerks. As the individual progresses through a structured training programme, the number and complexity of their court duties will increase until ultimately they are advising lay magistrates on points of law and procedure. Most courts operate nine or ten sessions a week, and most clerks will be in court for the majority of these. The remaining time will be spent exercising powers delegated to them by the magistrates, such as issuing summonses. For more information about careers with the magistrates' courts or any other part of HMCS, visit its website.

The Law Commission

Many laws are the product of centuries of precedent; others arise from little more than political expediency. Constant reform is needed to ensure that the law is fit for purpose in the modern age; however, the government is not always best placed to see where reforms could be made. The Law Commission, an advisory non-departmental public body sponsored by the Ministry of Justice, was set up by Parliament 43 years ago to review the laws of England and Wales and propose reform where necessary.

It is not just a case of repealing laws which are clearly archaic; it's equally important not to accidentally remove the legal basis for someone's rights. The commission employs around 15 researchers every year to help it fulfil its remit, and as a researcher you would analyse many different areas of law, identifying defects in the current system and examining foreign law models to see how they deal with similar problems. You may also help to draft consultation papers, instructions to Parliamentary Counsel and final reports.

The commission is engaged in about 20 projects at any one time. Among the topics it set out to examine in its most recent reform programme were the extremely complex laws controlling the UK's railway level crossings; the status of the insanity defence; the possible abolition of the common law offence of public nuisance; and treason – an area where the criminal law could be simplified and pruned.

Researchers are normally law graduates and postgraduates, those who have completed the LPC or BVC, or people who have spent time in legal practice but are looking for a change. The job of research assistant involves some fascinating (and less fascinating) subjects and is intellectually challenging. Candidates should have a First or high 2:1 along with a keen interest in current affairs and the workings of law.

The job suits those with an analytical mind and a hatred of waffle. They must also love research because there's a lot of it, be it devising questionnaires and analysing the responses, studying statistics or examining court files. So far, more than two-thirds of the commission's recommendations have been implemented by the government – for example, wide-ranging reform of homicide law has just been announced following a 2006 report – so you will get the satisfaction of seeing your work put into practice. Another plus point is that if you go on to train as a solicitor or barrister, you will be streets ahead of your peers in terms of your research skills and knowledge of how statutes work. For further information on 12-month contracts and long-term careers, check out www.lawcom.gov.uk. The recruitment drive for research assistant positions commencing September 2009 starts in December 2008, with the closing date for applications in January 2009.

Legal Services Commission

This government body was created by the Access to Justice Act 1999 and replaced the Legal Aid Board in 2000. It employs nearly 1,700 staff and operates from 15 offices across England and Wales. Its HQ is in London. Helping around two million people every year, it manages the distribution of public funds for both civil legal services and criminal defence services. The work of the LSC is essentially broken down into two departments covering these areas: the Community Legal Service and the Criminal Defence Service. Both are undergoing transformation, so keep your eyes and ears open as to what is happening.

In the Community Legal Service (CLS) caseworkers assess the merits of applications for legal funding and means test applicants. They also assess and authorise claims for payment for legal services. Working with legal aid solicitors, Citizens Advice Bureaux, Law Centres, local authority services and other organisations, the CLS ensures people can get information and advice about their legal rights and help with enforcing them. Recent reforms have seen the CLS working with local authorities to create Community Legal Advice Centres in a bid to provide a more integrated service in relation to social welfare law.

The Criminal Defence Service (CDS) organises the supply of legal advice to those accused of crimes through the use of local solicitors who are accredited by the service. The CDS also performs an audit role in relation to authorised providers of criminal legal advice. Part of the CDS's work is the Public Defender Service (PDS). Set up in 2001, its four offices are staffed by solicitors and accredited representatives who are directly employed by the LSC but required to provide independent advice. These offices employ their own lawyers to advise members of the public 24 hours a day, seven days a week, in what the LSC believes to be a more cost-effective and efficient way. A recent independent report said the PDS racked up substantially higher costs than other criminal defence providers during its formative years, but the PDS anticipates that as it grows it will become more cost-effective. The report also referred to a peer review of the PDS, which found that the quality of its work was roughly equivalent to or better than private practice criminal defence firms in most areas.

The Contracting Sections of both the CLS and the CDS audit claims for Legal Help, the funding used for preliminary and basic advice on how individuals might be represented. The Planning and Partnership Sections of both departments employ consultants and executives in order to better understand how the LSC should spend funds and place its resources.

Jobs at the commission are advertised in local and/or national newspapers, as well as online. A first point of contact is www.legalservices.gov.uk. A few work-experience placements crop up, usually in the CLS, and these tend to last about six weeks.

Patent attorney

The profession in the UK numbers some 1,700 attorneys, virtually all registered with the Chartered Institute of Patent Attorneys (CIPA). Patent attorneys can work in private firms, the patent departments of large companies or in government departments. It is their job to obtain, protect and enforce intellectual property rights for their owners. In short, a patent is a right conferred by the government to an inventor, which prevents others from exploiting the invention for a certain amount of time. In return, the inventor gives public disclosure of their invention.

The website www.cipa.org.uk has a useful careers section, but to summarise it takes four or five years to become a UK Chartered Patent Agent and/or a European Patent Attorney. All candidates must have a scientific or technical background (usually a relevant degree such as science or engineering) and the aptitude for learning the relevant law. Attention to detail, good drafting skills and a logical, analytical mind are essential and, increasingly, a knowledge of French or German is seen as key due to the international dimension to the work. The traditional route is to work and study for professional exams simultaneously. It is also an option to take the Certificate or Master's courses in intellectual property.

Once qualified, there is the opportunity to obtain a further qualification to become a Patent Attorney Litigator entitled to conduct litigation in the High Court, although all patent attorneys have the right to conduct litigation and to appear as advocate in the specialist Patents County Court. In order to become a European Patent Attorney, candidates must complete another set of examinations. See *Inside Careers'* useful guide to the patent attorney's profession: www.insidecareers.co.uk.

Trade mark attorney

A trade mark is a form of intellectual property used to distinguish a manufacturer or trader's particular brand from its competitors. It can be anything from a logo, a picture, a name or even a sound or smell. There are about 530 fully qualified trade mark attorneys in the UK, all registered with the Institute of Trade Mark Attorneys (ITMA). Most work for large companies, or at firms of patent and trade mark attorneys. Their role is to advise clients on all aspects of trade mark registration, protection and exploitation in the UK and Europe, liaising with counterparts in other parts of the world whenever necessary.

Good communication and drafting skills are required, but a degree is not a prerequisite to qualification. The minimum educational requirements are five GCSEs (grade A-C) and two A-Level passes in approved subjects. The road to qualification involves passing the exams set for ITMA. Candidates with certain degrees, such as law, may be exempt from some foundation papers. It is most common for aspiring practitioners to study while learning on the job as a trainee. With no central admissions procedure, students need to approach firms or in-house trade mark departments directly. www.itma.org.uk has a helpful careers page.

Compliance officer or analyst

Banks and other financial services companies are eager to recruit law and non-law graduates into their compliance units, which take on the vital role of advising senior management on how to comply with the applicable laws, regulations and rules that govern the sector. They also ensure that the banks' own corporate procedures and policies are followed. Other functions relate to the handling of complex regulatory and internal investigations and examinations. Due to the proliferation of financial regulation, the importance of compliance departments has grown enormously, so that in larger banks they are often equivalent in size to in-house legal teams and offer equally solid career prospects.

Through compliance risk management banks improve their ability to control the risks of emerging issues, thus helping to protect the organisation's reputation. The role of compliance officer or analyst requires astute advice, clear guidance, reliable professional judgement and the ability to work in a team. Attention to detail and a determination to see the consistent application of compliance policies and practices are essential. The extent of reliance on compliance teams means regular exposure to senior management occurs much earlier for trainees in this area than for trainee solicitors at law firms. A minimum 2:1 degree is standard for successful applicants, and salaries are typically comparable with other graduate trainees in the City. With some compliance teams numbering more than a hundred staff, in the longer term there is plenty of scope for career development.

Several banks run a two-year compliance analyst training scheme, over the course of which a trainee will gain a broad base of business knowledge and technical experience. It is not usually necessary to have completed the GDL, LPC or even a law degree before undertaking a graduate scheme, although those with a mind to move across to an in-house legal role later in their career would need to find the time to qualify as a lawyer. Being legally qualified opens up the door to general counsel work and it is not uncommon for a bank's head of legal to also lead the compliance team.

How suitable are you and what do recruiters want?

In the race to secure a training contract or pupillage, you need to stand out from the crowd, by which we mean impress recruiters with a plethora of interesting talking points, not flail about in a clown suit. The road to success is smoother for some than others, but a few nips and tucks to your CV and a healthy dose of self-confidence can work wonders.

Hitting a redbrick wall

So you've not got a law degree. So what? From the top sets at the Bar to the little-known solicitors' firms on the high street, non-law graduates are just as able to secure training positions as their LLB peers. In the few cases where employers prefer law grads they will specify this, so unless you hear differently, conversion route applicants may proceed with confidence. More and more trainees are telling us that they were advised by friends in the law to do a first degree in a subject they were passionate about and convert to law later on, and indeed many recruiters tell us just how highly they regard staff with language skills and scientific or technical degrees, particularly where their clients' businesses will benefit. Humanities degrees require many of the same research and analytical skills that lawyers need, and believe it or not, being able to discuss literary criticism with your clients could come in handy, since clients – just like lawyers – are people too.

It's a fact of life that many solicitors' firms and barristers' chambers subscribe to the idea of a pecking order of universities. It's not quite as widespread as it once was, but it's still there. Go to some firms in the City and around half the trainees will have attended Oxford or Cambridge University. A tour of the university law fairs – held over the autumn and spring terms – quickly shows which other universities are regarded as the richest pools for recruitment. Among the best attended by recruiters are Bristol, Nottingham and Durham. You can't change the identity of your university, so if you perceive it may put you at a relative disadvantage, make sure you get the best degree possible and work on enriching your CV in other ways.

Your degree result is perhaps the single thing on your CV that has most impact. Net a First and you'll impress all and sundry (at least on paper); walk away with a 2:1 and your path to employment will be made smoother; end up with a 2:2 and you're going to have to perform some fancy footwork to get a training offer. In exceptional circumstances, the effect of a poor degree result can be softened by a letter from your tutor stipulating the reason why you underachieved. Alas, it's rarely relevant that you just missed a 2:1 by a percentage point or two; however, if you were a star student who suffered a serious accident or illness as finals loomed, confirmation of this (perhaps also by way of a doctor's letter) should assist. Having spoken to a number of trainees and a couple of pupil barristers who left university with 2:2s, we would never presume to discourage anyone from applying for a training position, but these people all had other impressive qualities and/or CV-enhancing experiences. If you find yourself at the back of the job queue, think hard about what you can do to overcome that 2:2 – a year or more in a relevant job, a further degree, a commitment to voluntary work perhaps.

Possibly unaware that they could be applying for training contracts and vacation schemes in their second year, many new undergraduates are lulled into a false sense of security concerning their academic performance in the first year. If the only marks you have to show recruiters are amazing thirds, you'll struggle to make headway. As obvious as it may sound, working for good results throughout your degree is crucial. At the very least, doing so will maximise your chances of a great final result.

Get up, stand out

Resist the urge to become an expert on daytime telly. Jeremy Kyle, the Loose Women and – much as it pains us to say it – Dick van Dyke in the role of Dr Mark Sloan have nothing to offer you. Face it, even *Neighbours* has gone downhill since Harold left. Instead, take advantage of your freedom and the practically unlimited opportunities on offer. Almost every university has a wide range of societies, meeting groups and sports clubs. Pursuing your interests will give an extra dimension to both your university experience and, crucially, your CV.

Some kind of legal experience, whether it's involvement with the student law magazine or shadowing your aunt's neighbour's lawyer friend, is pretty crucial since you need to convince your prospective employers that you're serious about the profession, not just following an adolescent fantasy. You can also acquire this later on, through open days and vacation schemes, but it's never too early to start. Non-legal extracurriculars can be just as useful to show that you play well with others. It also gives you something to write about when an application form asks 'Discuss a time when you worked with a group to achieve a common goal.'

Relevant work experience is vital to almost every successful job application, so keep your eyes open for suitable positions and use them to test your own ideas of what you would like to do. Many universities run law-specific career seminars in association with solicitors' firms or barristers' chambers. Be savvy, go along and find out as much as you can by talking to trainee solicitors and recruiters. A bit of networking never ever goes amiss.

Do remember that only a minority of law firms and chambers throw drinks parties – the legal profession is not limited to the folk who've actually stood you a beer. Build up a decent understanding of the structure of the profession before deciding what kind of lawyer you want to be and which firm you want to work for. Many graduates adopt a scattergun approach of applying to as many firms as possible and seeing what comes back. While there's nothing wrong with this strategy per se, simply sending the same covering letter to 50 firms will do you no favours. Recruiters can tell very easily which applicants have a genuine interest in their firm and which have put minimal effort in. Research, research and research some more. Demonstrating your understanding of what the firm is about, what the work will entail and being able to explain honestly and realistically why you want to do it will be among the most important things to get across. Advice on how to do this can be found later section on applications.

Read all about it

If you want to become a commercial lawyer, you'll need this thing they call commercial awareness. We're not suggesting you become a mini-Murdoch, rather that you should gain a sense of what's going on in the commercial world. Unless you've been living in a box, in a cave, on Mars, you'll be aware that we're all doomed, doooomed, because of the credit crunch. The legal sector hasn't escaped its effects and many partnerships, particularly ones with big finance, real estate and construction briefs, are starting to feel the pinch. But what other themes should you be aware of? Gain some understanding of the attraction of India and the Gulf States as international marketplaces, the convergence of media technologies, big issues in the oil and gas sector. If you have zero interest in all this stuff, what makes you think commercial law will

interest you? Why not read the *Financial Times* now and again or find a website that will give you headline bulletins in bite-sized chunks? Keep up to date in a way that suits you, and make sure you're not oblivious to the events going on around you at national and international level.

Students looking to go into criminal law should be aware of recent legislation, like the Violent Crime Reduction Act 2006. Future family lawyers should be able to discuss the major cases that have hit the headlines, including Miller, McFarlane and Charman. Needless to say, anyone interested in human rights issues will have a full-time job keeping up to date with all the cases and developments arising out of the war in Iraq and anti-terror measures here in the UK.

Time out

A candidate who has wanted to be a lawyer since the age of five and shot straight through without stopping to breathe may be dedicated but is potentially less attractive to recruiters. If you've itchy feet and if you haven't already been out there for a look-see, then follow your heart – the career can wait. As well as giving you more confidence, navigating your way around a foreign country will develop your organisational and problem-solving skills. It also gives you another fertile ground of conversation. Recruiters do appreciate that not everyone has the desire or, more importantly, the money to swan off on a gap year to count fish or turtles or whatever. If travel is the last thing on your agenda, don't stress about it or feel you're going to be marked down for being a stay-at-home.

With the advent of new legislation, an employer discriminating against candidates on the grounds of age is officially a thing of the past. Nevertheless, some mature applicants still worry that their years will disadvantage them. Remember (if you still can), with age comes experience and probably an impressive set of transferable skills. You already know how to work, your people/client-handling skills are doubtless better developed and you may even have relevant experience. We've chatted with successful barristers and solicitors who've done everything from secretarial work, pub management and film production to policing and soldiering. But when is old too old? If you're still in your 20s, get over yourself – you're still a kid. If you're in your 30s, ask what it is you can offer a law firm that will make your application stand out. And if you're older still? Never say never. We have run into a small number of 40-something trainees, all of whom were glad to have made the career change. Given that each year after qualification a certain percentage of the UK's lawyers move firms or even drop out of the profession for good, the argument that employers expect 30 years of service from new recruits simply doesn't hold water. Of greater relevance is the adage concerning old dogs and new tricks, so if your coat is greying, consider carefully how you'd cope with being asked to revert to puppyhood.

Inclusively yours

Despite the legal profession being more diverse than ever before, for students with mental or physical disabilities things are not straightforward. In the experience of the Group for Solicitors with Disabilities (GSD), many students with disabilities have great difficulty in securing work placements and training contracts. The good news is that there are sources of advice and assistance available and the GSD has been actively involved in approaching law firms to set up designated work placement schemes for disabled students. The group also provides a forum in which students and practitioners can meet in order to share experiences and provide one another with guidance and support. Would-be barristers should refer to the Equal Opportunities (Disability) Committee of the Bar Council. GSD's website is www.gsdnet.org.uk.

Show me something different

Gone are the days of firms and chambers populated exclusively by white men smoking fat cigars. Not only has the smoking ban put paid to the Cubans but women and ethnic minorities are now firmly ensconced in the profession. In the course of our research more than 150 firms provided us with lists identifying their trainees. In most firms the girls outnumber the boys, something we would expect to see given that more women have gone into the profession than men for well over a decade. The names on most of these lists also reflect a healthy spread of ethnic backgrounds. It is worth mentioning, however, that female and non-white trainees still have too few senior role models and there are always a small number of law firm sex or race discrimination claims going through the employment tribunals.

On the subject of sexual orientation, we know scores of gay and lesbian lawyers for whom their lifestyle choice is entirely a non-career matter. This subject sparked debate in mid-2006 when a Law Society report criticised law firms, and in particular those in the City, for having non-gay-friendly working environments. It's fair to say that the report was widely viewed as way off the mark and the weeks following its publication saw many gay and lesbian City lawyers refute the claims and question the sampling methods used.

A number of diversity-related organisations have sprung up and you may see evidence of them at your university. Without doubt anything that encourages genuine diversity in the workplace is to be commended, but before signing on the dotted line with any intermediary – especially if you are asked to hand over any money for their services – make sure you know you are dealing with a respected organisation. Ask if they are affiliated with particular law firms and if so, how.

The topic of diversity covers more than just ethnicity; if you think your accent or upbringing or a disability could stand in your way then find out if there is anything these organisations can do for you. If you know your university gets less attention from law firms than, say, Oxford or Durham, then a diversity-related organisation may well be just what you need to get your foot in the door. One reputable organisation is the City Solicitors' Educational Trust (CSET), which runs summer schools designed to help students not studying at one of the top UK universities, or who might not have excelled in their A-levels, pursue a career in law. More information is available at www.cset.org.uk.

Stranger in a strange land

London attracts professionals from all over the world, so you can skip this bit if you're a Brit intending to work in the capital. If you hold an EU passport or have a pre-existing right to live and work in the UK and you are following the appropriate path to qualification, you should also proceed with optimism. Applicants who tick none of these boxes may find doors are easier to push open if they apply to firms with business interests in the country or region from which they come. This is because law firms have to show sound reasons why an overseas applicant is worth employing over someone who needs no work permit. Generally, the people we encountered who were neither EU nationals nor had a permanent right to live and work in the UK were training in City firms with international business. Additionally, a number of barristers' chambers take pupils who then return to practise in their home jurisdiction. In all cases, excellent written and spoken English is essential and you will need a convincing reason why you have chosen to commence your career in the UK.

Regional firms and sets are sometimes more comfortable recruiting candidates with a local connection, be this through family or education. Quite simply, they want to know that whoever they take on will be committed to a long-term career with them. They are wary of having their brightest and best skip off to higher-paying jobs in London on qualification. The picture across the UK is a variable one: some firms clearly state their preferences for local lads and lasses; others tell us that most of their applicants do have links with the region but that they are happy to consider anyone.

Keep it in perspective

What with studying hard, reading the *FT*, helping out at the CAB, captaining the university rugby and netball teams, debating, acting as student law society president and attending all the careers events that crop up, you'll hardly have time for a pint, let alone the ten that students supposedly put away in between lectures. But blow us down and slap us with a wet kipper if you're not demonstrating excellent time-management skills – a phrase that may serve you well when it comes to filling in applications. Ultimately, your years at university are supposed to be fun, and developing your interests and friendships is important because these can last far longer and be more rewarding than any career.

- **It always takes longer than you think:** However long you reckon it will take to complete something, double your estimate (and then add some more). You can always go to the pub if you finish early.

Pro bono and volunteering

The idea of providing free 'pro bono publico' legal advice for the public good has been ingrained in the legal profession for centuries.

In 1594 the Lord Chief Justice explained to newly qualified barristers that the 'two tongues' of linen hanging from counsels' shirt collars in court, and which appear to this day, 'signifie that as you should have one tongue for the rich for your fee… so should you also have another tongue as ready without reward to defend the poor and oppressed.' In the UK many lawyers have always responded to the pro bono call in a very British, quiet way, but the last five or six years have seen the rise of structured pro bono programmes at law firms, law schools and universities. National Pro Bono Week (10-15 November 2008) is now in its seventh year, and two years ago was moved from the exam season in June to November to enable more students to take part.

The bigger picture

The value of doing pro bono work isn't simply CV points. Far from it, as Kara Irwin, director of the BPP Pro Bono Centre, emphasises: 'Of course undertaking pro bono work is good to gain practical experience and learn new skills, and of course employers love to see it on applicants' CVs, but the key point about pro bono work is that it gives students an understanding of the role of law and the legal profession in society and access to justice issues.' The onus is (or should be) on lawyers, as the gatekeepers of justice, to constantly question issues and make sure justice is accessible to all, not just those who can pay for it. 'It's easy for students to become so focused on completing assignments,' Kara continues, 'that they lose the big picture – what is the nature of the legal system they are studying and the profession they are joining? Is it a fair system that provides justice to all? Is the legal profession doing all it can to ensure that the system is a fair and just one? Pro bono work provides students with the opportunity to develop an educated perspective on these issues.'

Many firms now have formal pro bono relationships with community organisations, such as Citizens Advice Bureaux and law centres. Arguably the increased scope and visibility of pro bono work is in part due to the influx of US law firms into the UK market, as typically American lawyers have placed a greater emphasis on pro bono advice than UK lawyers. More of our UK firms now recognise the business case of doing this kind of work: as well as the PR benefits of telling the world what a caring organisation it is, a commercial firm might well find some of its larger corporate clients ask for details of its pro bono activities. This sort of information is certainly attractive to students.

Real life

There are opportunities aplenty for law students through programmes operated by law schools. BPP, for example, aims to provide work that matches its students' interests and commitment. Programmes include the Employment Telephone Advice Line, the Legal Advice Centre, in which students interview and advise members of the public on their legal problems, and Streetlaw, where teams of students research and deliver presentations on legal matters to community groups including schoolchildren, prisoners and the homeless. Teams are often comprised of students from the BVC, LPC and GDL courses, giving them a rare opportunity to work together. There are various national prizes on offer for students including the Law Society's annual Young Lawyer Pro Bono Award. This year's winner's pro bono work included assisting housing clients facing eviction who needed a lawyer fluent in Arabic; helping an elderly, unwell council tenant to obtain compensation for defective central heating; and winning an unpaid wages claim for another client.

At university level, student pro bono opportunities have been more limited, largely because it's too risky for inexperienced undergrads to provide real-life legal advice. This is changing as undergraduates are receiving more support. In October 2007 the Law Society funded the appointment of a full-time project manager for students and law schools. He is Martin Curtis at LawWorks, which is the operating name of the Solicitors Pro Bono Group, a charity that encourages commitment across the profession. Martin's role is to advise universities and law schools on how best to establish pro bono initiatives. He identifies lawyers to supervise students and strengthens existing opportunities by facilitating new partnerships and contacts. Look out for the LawWorks Student Conference at Nottingham Law School (1 November 2008), to which speakers will come from around the country.

If you hope to go to the Bar or become a solicitor specialising in any contentious area of law, then you should seriously consider becoming a ratified member of The Free Representation Unit (FRU), a charity founded in 1972 to provide legal advice, case preparation and advocacy for people who aren't able to claim Legal Aid. Kara Irwin says: 'Undertaking real work for a real client who will be relying on the service provided is a far more engaging and stimulating way of learning than attending a lecture or even than partaking in classroom role-plays.'

There are countless organisations with which students can get involved. Here are just a few ideas to get you started:

www.probonouk.net

This site will identify the organisations working in your area. It has a section devoted to students.

LawWorks

A good source of advice and information. It now has a dedicated student officer. www.lawworks.org.uk.

A4ID

Advocates for International Development facilitates free legal assistance to civil society, developing country governments and social organisations to help achieve the UN Millennium Development Goals. Research-based opportunities exist for students. www.a4id.org.

Amicus

Charity providing assistance to US attorneys working on death row cases. Provides training and arranges unpaid internships in the USA for UK postgraduates. As only a limited number of scholarships exist, applicants should have a self-funding plan. www.amicus-alj.org. Another similar organisation is **Reprieve** www.reprieve.org.uk.

The AIRE Centre

Provides European human rights information and advice. It also offers direct legal advice and assistance on a case-by-case basis to legal practitioners or advisers. Internships are available for students with a good working knowledge of human rights law and EU law. European language skills are an advantage. www.airecentre.org.

Bar Pro Bono Unit

Established in 1996, the unit matches individuals in need with barristers in private practice. Opportunities are available for students to provide administrative support on a part-time basis. www.barprobono.org.uk.

Citizens Advice Bureau

CAB provides free advice from 3,300 locations. Those with real commitment can take its Adviser Training Programme to gain a widely recognised qualification that may subsequently enable your law firm training contract to be reduced by up to six months. Other less time-consuming work is also available. Debt, benefits, housing, employment, consumer issues, family matters and immigration are the most commonly raised problems. www.citizensadvice.org.uk.

Independent Custody Visiting

Independent custody visitors work in pairs, conducting regular unannounced checks on police stations to monitor the welfare of detainees. Anyone over the age of 18 can apply to become an ICV. www.icva.org.uk.

Law Centres

Law Centres provide free, independent legal services to people who live or work in their catchment areas. Some accept student volunteers to provide administrative support and casework assistance. www.lawcentres.org.uk.

Liberty

Provides advice and representation to groups and individuals in relation to domestic law cases involving the Human Rights Act. Liberty has opportunities for a small number of students to provide general office assistance and help with casework. www.liberty-human-rights.org.uk.

National Appropriate Adult Network

Under 17s and adults who are considered to be mentally vulnerable must have an 'appropriate adult' with them when they are interviewed by the police. Organised groups of trained volunteers carry out this important role. www.appropriateadult.org.uk.

Prisoners' Advice Service

Provides free advice and assistance on an individual and confidential basis, taking legal action where appropriate. www.prisonersadvice.org.uk.

Refugee Council

The Refugee Council is largest refugee agency in the UK. It provides advice on the asylum procedure, support and entitlement. Volunteers can offer their assistance in three areas: direct services, office-based and community-based. www.refugeecouncil.org.uk. See also Bail for Immigration Detainees – www.biduk.org.

Victim Support

The Victim Support Witness Service operates in every Crown Court, providing guidance and support to witnesses, victims and their families before, during and after court proceedings. www.victimsupport.co.uk.

Youth Justice Board

The YJB oversees the youth justice system. Contact your local board. www.yjb.gov.uk.

Vacation Schemes

You wouldn't rent a flat without looking around it first, so why jump into a career without testing the waters? Vacation schemes are an ideal solution to several problems: lack of knowledge, lack of certainty and lack of CV material.

Vac schemes teach you what goes on inside the offices of a law firm, provide hard evidence that you are committed to a career in law and can iron out those 'am I doing the right thing' niggling fears. Even if you're not sold on a place or practice area at the end of a couple of weeks, you'll know why and be able to search out firms of a different size or orientation.

Welcome to the real world

You can pick up a lot about a firm at interview and on assessment days, but do remember that these are often conducted in stylish client suites that give little away about a firm's true character. Even the interviewers may be putting on an act, be it good cop, bad cop or yeah-I've-got-that-on-my-iPod-too cop. Spending an extended period of time in a place reveals the reality of working there. All around you, deals will blow, people will stress, crises will be averted and people will bitch. Believe us, a lawyer is not going to postpone a rant or a resignation just because a student is in the office and might hear about it. Watching how lawyers interact with clients, with each other and with support staff, seeing how work is distributed and handled, even observing who makes the tea can be pretty enlightening.

> 'It is clear from speaking to trainees, associates and partners that everyone works very hard. My impression, however, is that it's only done when necessary, everyone preferring to go home by around 7pm or 8pm. Although one of the trainees I spoke to had just done an 85-hour week, she had been given a week off in lieu.'

Playing your part

Reading about law firms' latest work on websites and perhaps even the national press makes it all sound rather exciting. How are these big deals and cases actually conducted? Attending a vacation scheme can be a useful way of understanding how court battles and M&A deals are broken down into component stages, as you are likely to be given files to read through. Do your best to understand the key steps and any major problems within a file as you will probably be asked for your opinion and possibly asked to prepare a note on a particular aspect of the file. Another typical vac scheme exercise is to conduct research that will better inform the solicitors on a particular topic. Vac schemers are likely to be invited along to meetings, both internal and with clients, and court visits are also possible at some firms, either to watch an application on an actual case, or for an arranged tour. In short, the tasks you will be given may contribute in some small way to live files, but you won't do anything too significant. Finish your assignments quickly and you might heed the advice of one recent schemer: 'I never just sat there and doodled, I'd go up to people and ask if I could help in any way.'

> 'I took my jacket off and was informed about the fire rules and confidentiality of all case files. After that, POW! I was given a new case to deal with, no intro. Within one hour I was expected to give my thoughts; within three hours I had to come up with a plan of how to win it.'

Bad manners

Aside from such exercises and other watch-and-learn type activities, the graduate recruitment team will commonly arrange talks about the firm's key departments and how its training contract is organised. There'll also likely be plenty of social events, both to leave you with good memories of a fun working environment and to look at your social skills. While buying the rounds, recruiters and trainees will also be looking out for vaccies who revert to student union bar mode once the beer starts flowing. Best behaviour is advised at all times; bad-mouthing the firm, flirting with the HR assistant and throwing up on the pavement are not. There's a trend among City firms for taking groups of vac schemers to fancy clubs. Should anyone invite you to a strip joint, however, you should feel no compunction about declining. If strip clubs are your thing, well, you can probably look after yourself without any advice from us. And while we are on the subject of vac scheme etiquette, even if you are given your own

Outlook account, we recommend you resist sending e-mail funnies across the intranet. We also recommend that you switch off your mobile phone when in the office.

> 'I was given some really interesting (completely confidential) pro bono stuff. Everyone else on the scheme was really, really bright, which was a bit intimidating. It was brilliant fun and the evening entertainment was very impressive – dinner at The Criterion followed by a private booth at Boujis nightclub was a highlight.'

Under pressure

If a vac scheme confirms that you have found your ideal firm, you'll be happy to hear that your time there can act as a useful foot in the door. Just don't overestimate the size of your shoe. Even though many firms have a fast-track application process for vac schemers, a training contract interview – never mind a job offer – is not guaranteed. Many firms place their vacation schemes at the heart of the recruitment process, taking the lion's share of their trainees from the scheme. Does this make a placement a fortnight-long interview? Effectively, yes. It will serve you well to go in with the attitude that your actions will be scrutinised at all times and by anyone, including current trainees and secretaries. Don't get paranoid; just be yourself. The impression you want to leave people with is that you're polite, willing to put effort into whatever tasks you're asked to perform and confident enough to approach people in the office. Take your lead from how trainees interact with more senior colleagues, but don't get cocky. Any familiar behaviour you witness is likely to have developed after a period of assimilation into a team.

It's a numbers game

So, vacation schemes are a great idea, but it's not always easy to get your hands on one. The strongest candidates always manage to secure a clutch of vac scheme offers and a few become serial schemers, perhaps tempted by the money on offer – as much as £250-£350 per week at City firms. Don't feel too disheartened if you don't manage to secure a place on an organised scheme; it doesn't mean you'll never get a training contract. After all, those serial schemers can only accept one training contract. Try to build up your CV in other ways. Firms look favourably on candidates who have gained other experience – perhaps in another legal or commercial environment or with a voluntary organisation.

Another thing to bear in mind is the timing of your application. Schemes are frequently targeted at penultimate-year law grads and final-year non-law grads, which can leave other students frustrated. The simple fact is that law firms most want to see those people who are ready to apply for training contracts. The law firms' literature should make it clear if applications are sought from particular groups of students.

Take care with application forms and prepare for interviews and assessment days as thoroughly as for a training contract. For tips on how to prepare refer to pages 40-43. The following table and the **calendar** at the front of the book show vac scheme application deadlines.

The quality of vac schemes and how much of a 'real' trainee experience they offer can vary enormously. Here, one of our researchers in search of a training contract sums up two very different weeks spent at two similar-sized firms.

Firm one

- Only vac schemer that week.
- No set tasks; work included sitting in on meetings and admin jobs for paralegals.
- Brief contact with qualified solicitors.
- Structure of days left up to me.
- One arranged event, an informal lunch with three current trainees.

Firm two

- Part of group of vac schemers.
- Tasks included research assignment, group activities and department-specific work. Given sample pieces of work to do for current trainees.
- Lots of contact with partners and associates.
- Informal meeting with grad recruitment team to talk through the process of getting a training contract with the firm.
- Three social events: two lunches and a night out with current trainees where I could ask questions in a neutral environment.

> 'I did a vac scheme with a magic circle firm. The interview was quite straightforward, provided you know a bit about politics and commerce. The proportion of Oxbridge students on the scheme was about half, and the same was true of the law/non-law split.'

Vacation Schemes

Firm name	Number of Places	Duration	Remuneration	Deadline
Addleshaw Goddard	90	1, 2 or 3 weeks	Not known	31 January 2009
Allen & Overy	100 – winter (grads & final year non-law); spring/summer (penult year law & non-law)	Not known	£250 p.w.	Winter: 31 Oct 08 Easter/summer: 16 Jan 09
Arnold & Porter	8	2 weeks	Not known	28 February 2009
Ashurst	Easter (grads & final year non-law); summer (penult year law)	Easter: 2 weeks summer: 3 weeks	£275 p.w.	31 January 2009
Baker & McKenzie	London: 30 international: 3-5	London: 3 weeks Lon/o'seas: 8-12 weeks	£270 p.w.	31 January 2009
Barlow Lyde & Gilbert	Yes, plus open days and drop-in days	Not known	Not known	30 January 2009
Bates Wells & Braithwaite	12	1 week	Not known	19 February 2009
Beachcroft	Summer	Not known	Paid	Not known
Berwin Leighton Paisner	Easter (final year law grads); summer (penult year & above)	Easter: 1 week summer: 2 weeks	Not known	31 January 2009
Bevan Brittan	40 across 3 offices	Not known	Not known	31 March 2009
Bird & Bird	20	3 weeks	£275 p.w.	31 January 2009
Bond Pearce	Summer	2 weeks	Not known	Not known
Boodle Hatfield	10	2 weeks	Not known	Not known
Bristows	Yes	Easter: 1 week summer: 2 weeks	£250 p.w.	28 February 2009
Burges Salmon	40 plus open days	2 weeks	£250 p.w.	Not known
Capsticks	Yes	2 weeks	Not known	28 February 2009
Clarion Solicitors	24	1 week	Not known	27 February 2009
Cleary Gottlieb Steen & Hamilton	5 at Christmas, 10 at Easter & 20 in summer	Not known	£500 p.w.	Easter/summer: 28 January 2009 Christmas: 15th November 2008
Clifford Chance	Christmas, Easter and summer (some overseas)	Christmas: 2 days others: 2-4 weeks	£270 p.w.	Not known
Clyde & Co	20	2 weeks	Not known	31 January 2009
CMS Cameron McKenna	60, Christmas, Easter and summer	2 weeks	£250 p.w.	Christmas: 14 Nov 08 Easter/summer 13 Feb 09
Coffin Mew	Open week in July	1 week	Not known	31 March 2009
Covington & Burling	24	Not known	Not known	28 February 2009
Davenport Lyons	Yes	Not known	£200 p.w.	31 January 2009
Dechert	Easter and summer aimed at penult year law	Not known	Not known	28 February 2009
Denton Wilde Sapte	Open days in December and summer scheme	Not known	Not known	Open days: 21 November 2008 Summer: 6 February 2009
Dewey & LeBoeuf	20	Easter: 1 week Summer: 2 weeks	£400 p.w.	31 January 2009

Vacation Schemes

Firm name	Number of Places	Duration	Remuneration	Deadline
Dickinson Dees	40	1 week	£200 p.w.	31 January 2009
DLA Piper	200	2 weeks	£250 p.w (London) £200 p.w (Others)	31 January 2009
DMH Stallard	Yes	1 week	Unpaid	31 January 2009
Dundas & Wilson	Yes	4 weeks	Not known	30 January 2009
DWF	50	1 week	Paid	Not known
Edwards Angell Palmer & Dodge	10	2 weeks	Not known	27 February 2009
Eversheds	Summer: 100 Easter: in some offices	1 or 2 weeks	£240 p.w. (London) £175 p.w. (Regions)	31 January 2009
Farrer & Co	30: Easter and summer	2 weeks	£250 p.w.	31 January 2009
Field Fisher Waterhouse	Yes	2 weeks	Not known	31 January 2009
Foot Anstey	Yes	Not known	Not known	31 March 2009
Forsters	Yes	Easter: 1 week Summer: 2 weeks	£250 p.w.	15 February 2009
Freshfields Bruckhaus Deringer	80	3 weeks	£825 total	16 January 2009 (earlier apps recommended)
Geldards	Yes	Not known	Not known	1 March 2009
Government Legal Service	60	2-3 weeks	£200-250 p.w.	31 January 2009
Halliwells	75	2 weeks	£210 p.w.	28 February 2009
Hammonds	64	2 weeks	£230 p.w. (London) £180 p.w. (Regions)	31 January 2009
Hay & Kilner	Yes	Not known	Not known	28 February 2009
HBJ Gateley Wareing	Yes	2 weeks	Not known	11 February 2009
Herbert Smith	130: some o/seas (winter: non-law only)	Not known	Not known	Winter: 10 Nov 08 Spring/summer: 31 Jan 09
Hewitsons	Yes	1 week	Not known	Not known
Hill Dickinson	24	1 week	Not known	31 March 2009
Holman Fenwick & Willan	Yes	2 weeks	£250 p.w.	14 February 2009
Howes Percival	Yes	1 week	Not known	30 April 2009
Hugh James	Yes	2 weeks	Not known	31 March 2009
Hunton & Williams	Yes	Not known	Not known	Not known
Ince & Co	15	2 weeks	£250 p.w.	31 January 2009
Irwin Mitchell	70	1 week	£100 p.w.	Not known
Jones Day	20 at Christmas: non-law 10 at Easter: non-law 40 in summer: law	2 weeks	£400 p.w.	Christmas: 31 Oct 08 Easter/summer: 31 Jan 09
K&L Gates	Yes	2 weeks	Not known	Not known
Kirkland & Ellis	20	2 weeks	£300 p.w.	31 January 2009
Latham & Watkins	Yes	Easter: 1 week Summer: 2 weeks	£300 p.w.	Easter: 31 December 2009 Summer 31 January 2009

Vacation Schemes

Firm name	Number of Places	Duration	Remuneration	Deadline
Lawrence Graham	32: Easter and summer	2 weeks	£250 p.w.	31 January 2009
Laytons	6	1 week	Not known	31 March 2009
Lester Aldridge	8	2 weeks	£125 p.w.	31 March 2009
Lewis Silkin	12 plus open days	2 weeks	Not known	31 January 2009
Linklaters	30: Christmas (non-law) 80: in summer (law) some o/seas	Christmas: 2 weeks summer: 2 or 4 weeks	Not known	Not known
Lovells	90: Christmas, Easter and summer	2 or 3 weeks	£300 p.w.	Christmas: 11 Nov 08 Easter/summer: 31 Jan 09
Macfarlanes	75	2 weeks	£250 p.w.	28 February 2009
Manches	24	1 week	Under review	15 February 2009
Mayer Brown	36	Easter: 2 weeks Summer: 3 weeks	Not known	Not known
McGrigors	16	3 weeks	£250 p.w.	31 January 2009
Michelmores	Yes	1 week	Not known	28 February 2009
Mills & Reeve	Yes	2 weeks	Not known	31 January 2009
Mishcon de Reya	15	2 weeks	£250 p.w.	31 January 2009
Morgan Cole	Yes	Not known	Not known	30 April 2009
Morrison & Foerster	10	2 weeks	Travel + allowance	Not known
Nabarro	65	3 weeks	Not known	8 February 2009
Norton Rose	20 at Christmas 40 in summer plus open days	Christmas: 2 weeks summer: 4 weeks	£250 p.w.	31 October 2008/09 31 January 2009
Olswang	Yes	2 weeks	£275 p.w.	31 January 2009
O'Melveny & Myers	Yes	2 weeks	Not known	1 February 2009
Osborne Clarke	20: Easter and summer	1 week	Not known	Not known
Pannone	112	1 week	None	Easter: 20 February 09 Summer: 10 July 09
Paul Hastings	7	2 weeks	£500 p.w.	28 February 2009
Penningtons Solicitors	Yes plus information days	Not known	Not known	31 March 2009
Pinsent Masons	150	2 weeks	Not known	31 January 2009
Prettys	Yes	1 day	Not known	Not known
PricewaterhouseCoopers Legal	Yes: Summer and winter	2 weeks	Not known	31 March 2009
Reed Smith	25	2 weeks	Not known	31 March 2009
Reynolds Porter Chamberlain	Easter: 12 Summer: 24	Easter: 1 week Summer: 2 weeks	£275 p.w.	30 January 2009
Shadbolt	6	2 weeks	£200 p.w.	28 February 2009
Shoosmiths	Yes	2 weeks	Not known	30 January 2009

Vacation Schemes

Firm name	Number of Places	Duration	Remuneration	Deadline
Simmons & Simmons	Yes	Not known	Not known	Not known
SJ Berwin	Yes	Not known	Not known.	31 January 2009
Skadden	Yes: Easter and summer	2 weeks	Paid	12 January 2009
Slaughter and May	Yes	1-2 weeks	£275 p.w.	Not known
Speechly Bircham	20	3 weeks	£275 p.w.	13 February 2009
Stephenson Harwood	40	1-2 weeks	£260 p.w.	Easter & Xmas: 12 Nov 2008 Summer: 15 Feb 2009
Stevens & Bolton	8	1 week	£200 p.w	Not known
Taylor Wessing	40	2 weeks	£275 p.w.	31 January 2009
Teacher Stern	25	Not known	Not known	Not known
Thomas Eggar	Yes	1 week	Travel expenses	Not known
TLT Solicitors	40	1 week	Paid	31 January 2009
Travers Smith	Christmas: 15 Summer: 45	2 weeks	£250	31 January 2009
Trowers & Hamlins	38 plus open days	2 weeks	£225 p.w. (London) £170 p.w. (Manchester)	1 March 2009
Veale Wasbrough	Yes	1 week	Not known	Not known
Vinson & Elkins	Yes	2 weeks	Not known	28 February 2009
Walker Morris	48	1 week	£250 p.w.	31 January 2009
Ward Hadaway	Yes	1 week	Not known	28 February 2009
Watson, Farley & Williams	40	2 weeks	£250 p.w.	22 February 2009
Wedlake Bell	8	3 weeks	£200 p.w.	28 February 2009
Weil, Gotshal & Manges	20: Easter and summer 5: New York	Not known (NY: 3 weeks)	Not known	31 January 2009
White & Case	Easter: 20-25 Summer: 40-50	Easter: 1 week Summer: 2 weeks	£350 p.w.	31 January 2009
Wilsons Solicitors	Yes	1 week	Not known	Not known
Withers	Yes: Easter and summer (plus Milan for Italian speakers)	2 weeks	Not known	31 January 2009
Wollastons	Yes	Not known	Unpaid	Not known
Wragge & Co	Yes	Easter: 1 week Summer: 2 weeks	£220 p.w.	Not known

How to make successful applications

Recruiters can afford to be choosy, so don't assume that a CV filled with any old guff will secure you a training contract. Completing application forms is both an art and a science: the sooner you develop the right techniques the better.

www

Who? Why? What? Narrowing down the list of the firms you'd like to work for, assessing whether the firm's a good cultural match for you and making sure they do the kind of work you want are good starting points.

- The **Solicitors' Practice Areas** and **Practice Areas at the Bar** sections of this book summarise the main types of work for solicitors and barristers. Our parent publication *Chambers UK* identifies and ranks all the best firms and chambers in over 60 areas of practice. Make sure you use it to identify the key players in your chosen field and find out more about the work they do. Just log on to www.chambersandpartners.com and click onto our UK guide.
- Look at firms' and chambers' own websites and those of the legal press – *The Lawyer* (www.thelawyer.com), *Legal Week* (www.legalweek.com) and the Law Society's *Gazette* (www.lawgazette.co.uk) are useful weeklies.
- The **True Picture** and **Chambers Reports** sections of this book will give you a sense of a firm or set's culture, the specifics of what work current trainees or pupils have experienced and how easy they found it to get the experiences they wanted.
- Better still, take a vac scheme or mini-pupillage and sample the work yourself.
- Once you've narrowed the field, remember to do a quick idiot check: Do your qualifications and experiences fit what the firm or set wants?
- And when is the application deadline? Most commercial firms recruit two years in advance. A few of the big City firms have even earlier application deadlines.
- Smaller firms recruit one year in advance, sometimes even closer to the start of the contract. Some firms may offer a paralegal position for a trial period before a training contract is discussed.
- Most barristers' chambers stick with the OLPAS timetable, others recruit earlier.

Mailshotshy

Word and mailmerge may enable you to fire off 100 applications in a day, but it's not the right approach. Targeted and carefully reasoned CVs, letters and application forms stand out. Here are a few tips:

- Don't put anything in your CV or form unless you can expand on it at interview.
- Avoid chronological gaps in your experience: if you've taken time off, put it down and be prepared to explain why.
- CVs are a chance to make your achievements shine: keep them to two, possibly three, pages max and make the most of your strengths by effective use of headings, bullets and bold text.
- Covering letter: unless stated otherwise, always include one with your CV. It's a chance to expand on why you want to work for a firm and what experience/interests fit you for a firm, as well as giving the reader a more personal insight into your qualities. One page should do.
- No gimmicks: avoid photos, bizarre fonts or lurid colours, bribes or jokey applications.
- Spellcheck: thers nothing moor distratcing ad unproffesional than mistakes.

Good form

If firms and chambers don't ask for a CV, they'll want you to complete an application form. Remember:

- Forms take way more time than you'd imagine: start early and get them in on time. We've heard of online applications being rejected because they were submitted just two minutes past a deadline. Construct a table of the firms or sets you are applying to, their deadlines and where you are with your application to each.
- Practice makes perfect: photocopy any form that needs to be handwritten and prepare a rough draft. Tipp-Ex and different colours of ink look shabby.
- Read the questions carefully: make sure you're answering the question posed, not the question you want to answer. Plan each response and make sure

that however little you have to say, you fill much of the box available. Acres of white space look bad.

- Keep to the word count if one is given.
- You will be able to recycle some of your answers as firms and chambers tend to ask roughly the same sorts of things. Take care that any re-used answers are a good fit for each set of questions and be prepared to modify them as necessary.
- Make sure you use the questions to cover your whole range of skills and attributes. Demonstrate your personal qualities through your achievements and language. You can claim to be a team player, but it's far better for this to be obvious to the reader from the experiences you relate.
- You can allow some of your personality to show through, so long as you don't come across as too gushing or a wisecracker. If you read a completed form and it looks like an automaton filled it in, this is when you should consider revealing more of your personality and motivations. Let your experiences and language do the talking for you.
- Include a covering letter if the mode of application makes this possible. Your letter should highlight the best aspects of your application.
- Keep a copy: weeks later you may struggle to remember what you wrote.
- Increasingly, firms are making application forms available to only those who perform well enough on online tests, sometimes verbal reasoning, sometimes numerical. There are books and websites with sample tests and helpful hints on how to perform well. Get in some practice ahead of time.

Show 'em what ya got

- Qualifications, gap year conservation work, 17 A*s at A-level, endless vac schemes: applicants must show high levels of academic and personal achievement. The top applicants will always reap a sheaf of offers, but care and attention can go a long way.
- Applications should demonstrate teamwork and problem-solving skills as well as a commercial outlook and commitment to becoming a lawyer. Never underplay your work experience or vac schemes and try to speak to lawyers wherever you can; it all helps to show that you understand the reality of practice. Explain to the reader what you learned from your experiences rather than just listing them.

How many applications should you make? That's difficult one. Some people are so employable they may only need to fill in a small handful of forms. Most people need to make considerably more applications because, like it or not, securing a training place is a numbers game. Even if you're a good candidate you may still need to turn out 15 or 20, and some people could end up making a hundred. The Barristers section discusses OLPAS applications in more detail.

How to succeed at interviews and assessment days

Dress smartly. Think about what you might be asked. Don't act like a complete mug.

As simple as this advice may seem, recruiters are still occasionally confronted by hopefuls with wild hair and scuffed shoes who, when questioned, seem to have got their knowledge from the *Ladybird Book of Legal Practice*. Maybe nerves get the better of these people, but more likely what they are suffering from is a simple lack of preparation. And, as everybody knows, if you fail to prepare, then you prepare to fail. There. We've said it.

Interphew!

Having secured an interview, make sure you prepare, prepare, prepare. After all, you wouldn't qualify for the Olympics, then laze around eating cheeseburgers until the day of the race. Detailed preparation helps boost confidence and gives weight to your answers. No one likes a bluffer.

- Be up to date with legal news and current affairs: the law doesn't exist in a vacuum. Useful publications and websites include *The Lawyer, Legal Week, The Law Gazette,* Thursday's law supplement in *The Times.*
- Study the firm's own literature just prior to interview. If you know which partner will be interviewing you, research him/her.
- Practise answering questions, even the most obvious ones. Can you actually justify why you want to be a lawyer? Don't find out that the answer is 'no' in your interview.
- Remind yourself of what you wrote on your application form/covering letter, as interviewers are likely to bring up things you mentioned. If, for example, they asked you to write 400 words on a civil rights case that has been in the media recently, it would be wise to check up on the most recent developments.

Into the belly of the beast

Interviews are a two-way process: remember the experience is also a chance to assess the firm, its people, atmosphere and whether you'd like to work there. You

must avoid appearing arrogant, but you have every reason to be confident and not awestruck. Here are some general tips:

- Arrive early. If you're late, in a rush or pouring with sweat, you're liable to flummox yourself, make a bad impression, keep partners waiting and undo all that hard prep. Arriving early to sit in a nearby cafe and review your application is a much better way to go. Keep the firm's phone number and a contact name on you in case you are genuinely delayed.
- Dress appropriately. Casual dress won't convey the right message, nor will anything too racy or alternative. Even if you hate the idea, suits for men and something equally formal for women is the safest choice. The law is a profession based on sober suits, so turning up in anything too natty could mark you out as dangerously avant-garde.
- Be polite to everyone you meet: don't take your nerves out on the receptionist and be careful what you say to those friendly trainees you meet. Bad impressions travel fast.
- Everyone gets nervous, but if you've prepared properly you should be able to stave off the worst of it. If you're particularly prone to the jitters, research some calming techniques and if they help, employ them before you go in.
- It's possible to establish a connection or even a rapport with an interviewer. A firm handshake and maintaining eye contact (as far as possible without scaring anyone) helps create a good first impression. If they ask you how you are, ask the same question in return. Look like you want to be there.
- Don't be afraid to smile!
- If more than one person interviews you: try to speak to everyone on the panel. When asked a question, direct your response at the person who asked it, but if it's a long answer, don't forget that the other people in the room exist.
- Listen carefully and think clearly before answering questions.
- Expect to be tested: if your answers are challenged, don't get defensive or aggressive. Asking their opin-

ion once you have given your own is a good way to turn an interrogation into a conversation.

- Interviewers want you to shine, not trip up: difficult questions are designed to test your reactions so try not to freeze.
- Any questions? Prepare a couple of sensible questions for the end of the interview.

Assessment days

Many firms put candidates to the test via written assignments, negotiation exercises and group tasks. These sessions tend to be firm-specific and can change year on year, but your LPC or GDL provider may have a back catalogue of student feedback on different firms' assessment days. Many trainees we spoke to praised the precedent bank of the College of Law careers service as a particularly fine example of this.

Psychometric tests, beloved of American firms, are gradually catching on over here. Some say they're pseudo-scientific quackery, others that they are a useful indicator of an applicant's aptitude and personality. Such tests can be hard to prepare for, because the companies who supply firms with papers guard their secrets carefully. Some law firms will post sample papers out in advance and your careers service may have a back catalogue.

The Watson Glaser and SHL tests are common ones. These tend to feature multiple-choice, reasoning-based questions centred on snippets of information. Some tests look for business awareness and intellectual rigour. Some need to be completed in a given time; others assess speed by having too many questions. Make sure you know which kind you're sitting.

You may also be asked to write a letter or summarise a piece of research. Such tasks are normally equally accessible to law and non-law students. CMS Cameron McKenna's grad recruitment officer Vicky Wisson says: 'Whatever exercise you are asked to complete make sure you plan your time effectively. Failure to do so can result in large gaps in your reports or tasks and the assessors cannot mark what isn't there. Communicate your ideas professionally, and evidence your points using the information received.'

Don't forget to ask around. A friend who attended the same assessment day can brief you on what to expect. Equally, don't hang all your hopes on insider tips as firms may vary their assignments.

The I in Team

Group exercises determine how well you play with others. There's a fine line to walk here. Show-offs, shouters and bossy boots won't impress, but neither will blushing wallflowers. The best advice is to be yourself. If you have a nat-

urally dominant personality then you may feel most comfortable setting the agenda at the beginning of the task, and that's fine – just be aware that people will be looking for your listening skills as well. If, like most of us, you aren't that person then Vicky Wisson suggests: 'Rather than leading a group discussion, try to be the facilitator, ensuring everyone gets their chance to speak and you settle on ideas amicably and whole-heartedly.' Don't simply jockey for position: listen to others, pick up on what everyone is saying and make your own comments on their suggestions. In at least one assessment day we heard of, they make you mark your own performance after the group exercise to see if you can recognise your own strengths and weaknesses.

Don't relax too much if there's a social event as these can be just as important when it comes to making a good impression. Some firms have lunches where you sit round with three or four partners and a handful of other applicants and make small talk over the duck à l'orange. Who will your prospective supervisor want to hire? The girl who kept her eyes on the plate for the entire meal and whispered unintelligible answers to every question? The chap who drank too much of the Bourgogne Pinot Noir and spent most of the evening calling him buddy? Or the nice young man who made some pertinent observations on the rise of the Gulf economies and showed an interest in his taxidermy hobby? Similarly, a drink with the firm's trainees is an opportunity to strike up a rapport with them, not to start making comments about how your vac scheme at Norton Rose was so much better.

The hardest word to say...

No one likes being rejected but, if things don't work out and you do get the PFO (please f*** off) letter in the post, don't let it get you down. Just because you aren't suited to one firm doesn't mean you won't fit in elsewhere. When we ask trainees why they chose their firm, the single most common response we get is, 'I walked out of my interview and it just felt right.' Your perfect firm is out there somewhere, and the whole point of the *Student Guide* is to help you find it.

If you just can't understand why you were rejected, bite the bullet and phone up to ask. However hard it is to hear, finding out your strengths and weaknesses will help you. Should you reapply to a firm that has rejected you the year before? It may work for some candidates, especially if they got through to a later stage of the process, but many firms will not want to revisit your application.

And finally...

We've told you to shine your shoes. We've given you the old 'prepare to fail' line. We've reminded you not to get trollied in front of your prospective colleagues. Now it's up to you. With common sense and a healthy dose of confidence, you'll go far.

Managing job offers

After all the hard work involved in securing a training contract offer, you'll need to know what to do when you actually land one.

The Solicitors Regulation Authority publishes its 'Voluntary Code to Good Practice in the Recruitment of Trainee Solicitors' at www.sra.org.uk/documents/students/training-contract/voluntarycode.pdf and we recommend you read through these guidelines if at any stage you are in doubt as to what you should do. The guidelines address the conduct of both recruiters and students.

On offers, the guidelines say:

- If you're still an undergrad, an offer of a training contract cannot be made before 1 September in your final undergraduate year. If you've impressed the firm during a vacation scheme or period of work experience, the firm must wait until this date before making you an offer.
- At an interview, you will be told if there is a further stage to the selection process. You should also be told within two weeks of reaching the end of the process whether or not you have been successful.
- Offers should be made in writing. If you receive an offer by phone you don't need to say yes or no: you can ask the firm to send a formal offer in writing for you to consider.

On deadlines, the guidelines say:

- No deadline should expire earlier than four weeks from the date of the offer. If you need more time to consider an offer, firms are supposed to consider your request 'sympathetically' provided you have a good reason. No definition of 'good reason' is given in the guidelines.
- If a firm is going to pay your law school fees, it should set out the terms and conditions of the arrangement in the training contract offer letter. The firm's willingness to provide financial assistance should not affect the time limit for accepting the contract.
- If you feel you need more time, you will have to enter into diplomatic discussions with the law firm, telling them how much longer you need. Make sure you get written confirmation of any extension to the deadline as simply asking for it won't be enough.

You may want to hang on to an offer from one firm while you pursue applications with others. This is okay, but you must bear in mind the following:

- You should not hold more than two (as yet unaccepted or declined) offers at any one time.
- Students are supposed to respond promptly to a firm that's made an offer, either by accepting or rejecting it. The word 'promptly' is not defined in the code.
- Because offers can and will be made with time limits for acceptance, do guard against allowing a deadline to elapse. The stupidity tax you may otherwise pay doesn't bear thinking about.
- Once your preferred offer has been accepted in writing, you must then confirm to everyone else that you are withdrawing your application. This is only fair to busy recruiters and other applicants who may suffer if you clog up a shortlist.

The guidelines are silent on the issue of what happens if a student changes their mind after accepting an offer. It's a rare firm that will be particularly sympathetic to a post-acceptance withdrawal but, on occasions, these things do happen. We can give no general advice on this subject, as each individual case will have its own merits. What we can say is that the whole trainee recruitment market relies on all parties playing by the above 'rules'. So what if a law firm puts pressure on you to accept an offer earlier than the guidelines say they should? Again, there is no simple answer as the SRA's code of conduct is voluntary. If this situation arises you will have to enter into delicate negotiations with the law firm. We also recommend that you report the problem to your university or college careers adviser and ask if they can recommend a course of action.

The recruitment market summarised

With the economic crisis dominating headlines in the legal as well as national press, you'd be forgiven for thinking the profession agreed with the conclusion of Private Frazer from *Dad's Army* – 'We're doomed!' A closer look reveals it's not all grey skies ahead for aspiring solicitors, but you should still carry an umbrella...

Keep the bubbly on ice

The last few years were a really good time to be looking for a training contract. A buoyant economy kept law firms busy with new work, more and more training places were offered and salaries climbed ever higher. Ah, halcyon days! Now we hear again and again that the huge transactions that had so many lawyers raising their glasses of Moët are thinner on the ground. The troubles in the housing market mean real estate lawyers have become the first to go since firms have started to tighten their belts. The formerly cutting-edge high-finance field of securitisation is, to put it plainly, blunted.

For a segment of our readership, snagging a contract in 2009 will still be a walk in the park; however, the pinch that's been hurting the markets since August 2007 is liable to leave a lot of firms taking a more cautious approach to the 2009 recruitment round. The last time the deals market went quieter, quite a few commercial law firms deferred the arrival of some of their new trainees, and we've already started to see the first instances of that happening this time around. Granted, it's impossible to make accurate predictions, either about the economy or the demand for new recruits. All we can say is that it is possible for law firms' requirements for trainees to go down as well as up.

Lessons learnt

Now the good news. This year (at least), while some firms we've looked at are advertising for slightly fewer recruits, others are increasing their cohorts, perhaps banking on either the market levelling out or their own ability to weather the storm. Last time the markets dipped and trainee numbers were cut, many firms were left with too few junior lawyers when the economy picked up. Firms will want to avoid making this mistake again.

As for those with contracts already, there's a sense that in boom times a so-so performer could slip through the net and land an NQ job. Now that trainees have to work that little bit harder to impress, underperformers are finding themselves without offers from their firms that they might previously have taken as guaranteed. Those approaching qualification in September 2008 were less confident than their predecessors and we noted a realistic awareness of the fact that there weren't as many real estate or niche jobs around.

Never had it so good?

Aside from a few high-profile examples trumpeted in the legal press, NQ retention rates across the market were fairly good in 2008. At the 150 firms we looked at this year for the True Picture, 2,144 of the 2,612 qualifiers stayed on at the firm that trained them. This equates to 82.08%, which is actually slightly higher than we've seen before. It is likely that the next couple of years will see lower retention. You can see the statistics going back to 2000 on our website and compare firms' retention rates year on year.

In looking at trainee and NQ salaries, it might be worth dusting off that old Harold Macmillan line about never having had it so good. This year has generally seen the rate of increase in salaries at City or big regional firms slow, and in many cases halt. Crucially, lawyers' pay hasn't yet fallen and remains at the highest level it has ever been, especially in London. Law school sponsorship has also remained much the same as last year, following large increases in 2006. Minimum trainee salaries are set by the Solicitors Regulation Authority: trainees in central London must receive no less than £18,420 pa. and those elsewhere £16,500 pa. Undeniably there are plenty of people who would welcome a training contract at any price, simply because the number of student hopefuls outstrips the number of training opportunities.

And finally...

While the factors affecting the number of training positions are many, all stem from the financial considerations which law firms face, be these general economic conditions or changes in legal aid rates and coverage. The market is going to be difficult for a while, so be prepared to work a little harder for that training offer and/or NQ job.

Contacts

The Law Society
113 Chancery Lane,
London WC2A 1PL
Tel: 020 7242 1222
E-mail: contact.services@lawsociety.org.uk
www.lawsociety.org.uk

Solicitors Regulation Authority
Tel: 0870 606 2555
E-mail: contactcentre@sra.org.uk
www.sra.org.uk

Junior Lawyers Division
The Law Society
113 Chancery Lane,
London WC2A 1PL
Helpline: 08000 856 131
E-mail: juniorlawyers@lawsociety.org.uk
www.juniorlawyers.lawsociety.org.uk

The Bar Council
289-293 High Holborn
London WC1V 7HZ
020 7242 0082
www.barcouncil.org.uk

Bar Standards Board
289-293 High Holborn
London WC1V 7HZ
020 7611 1444
www.barstandardsboard.org.uk

Gray's Inn, Education Department
8 South Square, Gray's Inn,
London WC1R 5ET
Tel: 020 7458 7965
E-mail: quinn.clarke@graysinn.org.uk
www.graysinn.info

Inner Temple, Education & Training Department
Treasury Building, Inner Temple,
London EC4Y 7HL
Tel: 020 7797 8208
E-mail: ffulton@innertemple.org.uk
www.innertemple.org.uk

Lincoln's Inn, Students' Department
Treasury Office, Lincoln's Inn,
London WC2A 3TL
Tel: 020 7405 0138
www.lincolnsinn.org.uk

Middle Temple, Students' Department
Treasury Office, Middle Temple Lane,
London EC4Y 9AT
Tel: 0207 427 4800
E-mail: members@middletemple.co.uk
www.middletemple.org.uk

The Institute of Legal Executives
Kempston Manor, Kempston,
Bedfordshire MK42 7AB
Tel: 01234 841000
E-mail: info@ilex.org.uk
www.ilex.org.uk

The National Association of Licensed Paralegals
73 Shenley Road,
London SE5 8NE
Tel: 020 7252 7545
www.nationalparalegals.com

Government Legal Service
Chancery House,
53-64 Chancery Lane,
London WC2A 1QS
Tel: 020 7649 6023
E-mail: glstrainees@tmp.com
www.gls.gov.uk

Crown Prosecution Service
50 Ludgate Hill,
London EC4M 7EX
Tel: 020 7796 8000
E-mail: recruitment@cps.gsi.gov.uk
www.cps.gov.uk

The Law Commission
Steel House
11 Tothill Street
London SW1H 9LJ
Tel: 020 3334 0200
E-mail: communications@lawcommission.gsi.gov.uk
www.lawcom.gov.uk

Head Office, Myddelton House,
115-123 Pentonville Road,
London N1 9LZ
Tel: 020 7833 2181
Volunteer Hotline: 08451 264264
www.citizensadvice.org.uk

Legal Services Commission
Head Office, 85 Gray's Inn Road,
London WC1X 8TX
Tel: 020 7759 0000
www.legalservices.gov.uk

Chartered Institute of Patent Agents
95 Chancery Lane,
London WC2A IDT
Tel: 020 7405 9450
E-mail: mail@cipa.org.uk
www.cipa.org.uk

The Institute of Trade Mark Attorneys
Canterbury House, 2-6 Sydenham Road, Croydon, Surrey CR0 9XE
Tel: 020 8686 2052
E-mail: tm@itma.org.uk
www.itma.org.uk

**The Institute of Chartered Secretaries
and Administrators**
16 Park Crescent,
London W1B 1AH
Tel: 020 7580 4741
E-mail: info@icsa.org.uk
www.icsa.org.uk

The Law Centres Federation
293-299 Kentish Town Road,
London NW5 2TJ
Tel: 020 7428 4400
E-mail: info@lawcentres.org.uk
www.lawcentres.org.uk

Free Representation Unit
6th Floor 289-293 High Holborn
London WC1V 7HZ
Tel: 0207 611 9555
E-mail: admin@freerepresentationunit.org.uk
www.freerepresentationunit.org.uk

The Bar Lesbian & Gay Group
(BLAGG) www.blagg.org
Lesbian & Gay Lawyers Association
C/o Alternative Family Law
3 Southwark Street
London SE1 1RQ
Tel: 020 7407 4007
E-mail: info@blagg.org
www.lagla.org.uk

The Society of Asian Lawyers
c/o Saima Hanif
4-5 St Gray's Inn Square
Gray's Inn
London WC1R 5AH
E-mail: info@societyofasianlawyers.com
www.societyofasianlawyers.com

Society of Black Lawyers
11 Cranmer Road
Kennington Park
London SW9 6EJ
Tel: 020 7735 6592

The Association of Muslim Lawyers
PO Box 148, High Wycombe
Bucks HP13 5WJ
E-mail: info@aml.org.uk
www.aml.org.uk

The Association of Women Barristers
187 Fleet Street
London EC4A 2AT
E-mail: chambers@187fleetstreet.com
www.womenbarristers.co.uk

Group for Solicitors with Disabilities
c/o Judith McDermott
The Law Society, 113 Chancery Lane
London WC2A 1PL
Tel: 020 7320 5793
E-mail: Judith.McDermott@lawsociety.org.uk
www.gsdnet.org.uk

LPC Central Applications Board
PO Box 84, Guildford,
Surrey GU3 1YX
Tel: 01483 301282
www.lawcabs.ac.uk

CPE Central Applications Board
PO Box 84, Guildford,
Surrey GU3 1YX
Tel: 01483 451080
www.lawcabs.ac.uk

Online Pupillage Application System
Technical Assistance
E-mail: pupillages@gtios.com
www.pupillages.com

Career Development Loans
Tel: (freephone) 0800 585505
www.direct.gov.uk

- **Be spontaneous:** Remember that it's important not to sound over rehearsed at interview. Sufficient practice can make perfect, but rote recitation of answers will bore both you and the panel.

Law School

Solicitors' Timetable

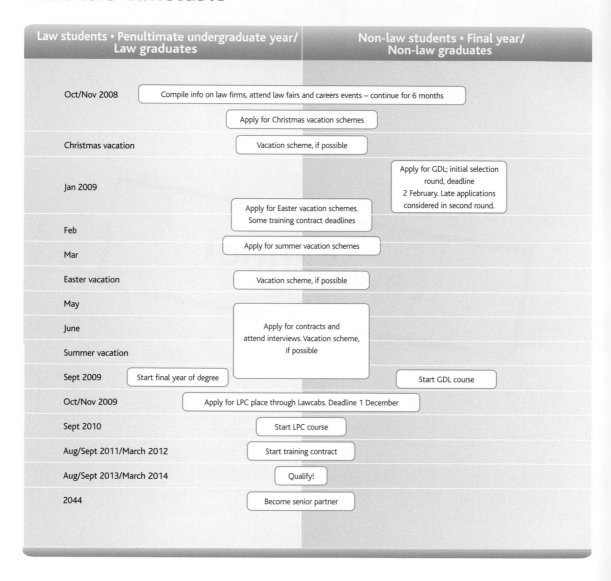

Law students • Penultimate undergraduate year/ Law graduates		Non-law students • Final year/ Non-law graduates
Oct/Nov 2008	Compile info on law firms, attend law fairs and careers events – continue for 6 months	
	Apply for Christmas vacation schemes	
Christmas vacation	Vacation scheme, if possible	
Jan 2009		Apply for GDL; initial selection round, deadline 2 February. Late applications considered in second round.
Feb	Apply for Easter vacation schemes. Some training contract deadlines	
Mar	Apply for summer vacation schemes	
Easter vacation	Vacation scheme, if possible	
May		
June	Apply for contracts and attend interviews. Vacation scheme, if possible	
Summer vacation		
Sept 2009	Start final year of degree	Start GDL course
Oct/Nov 2009	Apply for LPC place through Lawcabs. Deadline 1 December	
Sept 2010	Start LPC course	
Aug/Sept 2011/March 2012	Start training contract	
Aug/Sept 2013/March 2014	Qualify!	
2044	Become senior partner	

Notes

1 It is important to check application closing dates for each firm as these will vary.

2 Some firms will only accept applications for vacation schemes from penultimate-year students, whether law or non-law. See A-Z pages for further information.

3 Some firms require very early applications from non-law graduates. See A-Z pages for further information.

4 The timetable refers primarily to those firms that recruit two years in advance. Smaller firms often recruit just one year in advance or for immediate vacancies.

Barristers' Timetable

Law students • Penultimate undergraduate year	Non-law students • Final year
Throughout the year	Start thinking about getting some relevant work experience. Do plenty of research into chambers/mini-pupillages
By the end of January 2009	Apply for the GDL
By the end of April	Apply for a pupillage under the year early scheme on OLPAS
May	Apply for a GDL scholarship from an Inn of Court. If successful, join that Inn
June to September	Do pre-GDL mini-pupillages
September/October 2009	Start final year of degree · Start GDL
November	By November apply through BVC Online for the BVC. Apply to an Inn of Court for a scholarship
During final year/GDL	Apply for pupillage to non-OLPAS sets. Do mini-pupillages
April/May	Before 1st May apply for pupillage through OLPAS
June	Apply for Inn membership
September 2010	Start the BVC. Apply for the September tranche of OLPAS; make further pupillage applications to non-OLPAS sets
April/May	If unsuccessful last year, apply for pupillage before 1st May
June	Finish BVC
September	Apply for pupillage through OLPAS if you have yet to be successful
October 2011	Start pupillage
Summer	Be offered tenancy at your pupillage chambers or apply for tenancy or a 3rd six elsewhere
October 2012	Start tenancy
2042	Be appointed to the High Court Bench
2052	Get slapped on the wrist by Ministry of Justice for falling asleep in court

- **It doesn't matter what you studied at university:** A high proportion of solicitors and barristers did not study law as a first degree. Lawyers come from any and every academic discipline.

The Graduate Diploma in Law (GDL)

If you opted to spend your time at university reading great books, perfecting your Ancient Greek or divining the inner workings of the human body, you can still come to the law via a one-year conversion course known as the Graduate Diploma in Law (GDL). You may also see the course referred to as the CPE (Common Professional Exam) or PgDL (Postgraduate Diploma in Law).

The GDL will bring you up to a required standard in the seven core legal subjects that are typically taught in the first two years of an LLB. Because skills like textual analysis, research, logical argument, writing and presentation can be acquired in a whole range of disciplines from archaeology to zoology, legal employers tend not to make a distinction between applicants with an LLB and those with the GDL.

The standard requirement for admission is a degree from a university in the UK or Republic of Ireland. It is possible for non-graduates to get onto a course if they've shown the requisite drive and determination, and have exceptional ability in some other field. Such candidates – and those with a degree from an overseas university – must obtain a Certificate of Academic Standing from the Bar Council or Law Society before enrolling on the GDL.

The course is no easy ride. Taken full-time it lasts a minimum of 36 weeks, during which you'll be expected to undertake 45 hours of lectures, tutorials and private study each week. It is possible to take the course part-time over two years. Assessment tends to be by written exams, with regular coursework and an extended essay thrown in. Depending on the institution you attend, there will be more or less emphasis on academic essays, written problem questions or practical preparation of debates for the classroom. Because the institutions that offer the GDL vary in perceived quality, their approach and the composition of their student bodies, it is well worth doing your research before you apply. City University and Nottingham are renowned for offering more academic courses, often attracting a large number of students headed for the Bar. In London, BPP, for example, is packed with City types and there are reams of paper and manuals that need to be consigned to memory.

The GDL gives a grounding in core legal principles and statutes and exposes students to the key case law in each area. Legal reasoning is, for the most part, an exacting discipline – there is not much room for posturing, even if the opinions of some esteemed judges may defy any conventional standards of logic. Lord Denning's judgments, in particular, should be worth a chuckle or two, although some of his more convoluted legal inventions, like promissory estoppel, may make your head ache. English Common Law is an intriguing amalgam of cold logic and a concern for justice to be done – a combination of metaphysics, logic and ethics, with a good bit of policy (and arguably prejudice) thrown in.

- There's a huge amount to take in, so get into a good study routine early on.
- You're there to learn a set curriculum, not to think outside the box. Probably the best use of your creativity is to come up with amusing ways of remembering case names.
- Attend classes!

Land Law

The favourite subject at many a dinner party, the saleability of property is more crucial to the functioning of society than you might expect. Some academics even argue it's the reason the institution of marriage was created. Land law is dominated by checklists, which are used to determine everything from the existence of an easement to the identity of Equity's Darling. You can pick up several useful tips to apply to your own life, including how to ensure you're not screwed over if you decided to buy a house with a friend, how to claim a right of light when a new housing development blocks out the sun from your greenhouse and how to prevent the bank foreclosing on your mortgage. Finding the answers to these involves some mind-numbing jargon, and it's safe to say that at times the subject feels drier than the Sahara. But for the technically and metaphysically minded, it's like getting under the bonnet of an antique car with a box of medieval tools. Words to try and work into dinner party conversation: overreaching, chattel, fee simple, flying freehold, socage, bona vacantia.

EU

The law of the European Union is massively important, since the European Court of Justice (ECJ) is effectively the highest court of appeal for all its member states. This course studies the institutions, sources and underlying principles of the EU system and substantive European law. Big subjects include the establishment of a free market, the free movement of workers, competition policy and the freedom of establishment, as well as the incorporation of the European Convention on Human Rights into our national law. For Europhiles it is a fascinating mix of politics, history, economics and comparative jurisprudence, but its case law contains some of the longest and most tongue-twisting names you're likely to see. Some of it can be quite dry, particularly when dealing with the free movement of goods, where every answer seems to be 'labelling' or 'a certificate of safety.' Much more amusing is the case of Van Duyn, which established that the UK could bar a Scientologist from entry into the country. This is the source of competition law, an enduringly popular area of commercial practice, particularly for those with a love for Brussels.

Equity and Trusts

The uninitiated (and fans of Dickens) would be forgiven for thinking that trusts are the preserve of tax-evading toffs. The truth of the matter is that the 'trust' (the legal arrangement whereby one person holds property for another) has a multiplicity of uses. It has applications in the worlds of high finance and charity as much as in providing a nest egg for a beloved grandchild. The trust is a key contribution made by 'equity' – a rather opaque term for a line of law that calls upon ideas of fairness to remedy any injustices brought about by the strict application of black letter law. Although some of it is tricky to get your head round, the subject is filled with plenty of gems of cases involving wealthy eccentrics. You'll learn how the courts decided the fate of little Penelope Pilkington and why a fat cat should never use the words 'our yacht' in front of his mistress. The course deals with how to set up trusts for illegitimate kids without your wife knowing and what happens in fiendishly complicated financial transactions when someone tries to establish a trust to avoid tax (the name Vandervell will haunt you for years). Equity is the bread and butter of Chancery practice, which preoccupies some of the biggest brainboxes at the Bar. The subject also crops up in solicitors' practice through anything from complex financial transactions to advice to individuals. For those destined to cater for the *Sunday Times'* Rich List, studying equity provides you with the basic tools which you'll later use to crack the taxman's safe.

Contract

The law of contract governs when an agreement becomes legally binding and enforceable. The principles you learn here underpin any commercial agreement you'll have to draft, peruse or persuade someone to sign. You'll learn how to tell when a contract is formed, the required formalities, permissible terms and what happens if the seller has neglected to tell you the Jackson Pollock you've just bought is actually a product of his son's finger-painting. Interesting issues include how you can avoid paying a debt by giving the creditor 'a horse, a hawk or a robe' instead, why a little notice saying 'see back' is all-important on a ticket and why you might still be bound by a contract to sell your favourite guitar even if the buyer's letter of acceptance gets lost in the post. Armed with your knowledge of the Sale of Goods Act, you may find yourself bringing any number of small claims against the high street retailers whose products fall apart the minute you get them home.

Crime

Some people think the law begins and ends at crime. Perhaps they watch too much *CSI*. In terms of human interest this subject reaches parts that the others don't even know exist. Whether your interest is in policy or in the gruesome things that people do to one another, the crime course should provide plenty to engage and surprise. The syllabus touches on all the usual suspects: sexual offences, theft, assault and homicide as well as more philosophical discussions, like what amounts to a 'reasonable man' in the eyes of the law. Also covered are the liability of secondary parties, attempts, affirmative and capacity defences and fraud, which is defined so broadly that almost any lie can be a crime (so watch your p's and q's). You'll find out just how much of your body you need to get through a window in order to count as a burglar and why epileptics are deemed insane. By the end of the course you'll also be in a better position to explain why it's okay for a wife to consent to her husband branding his initials on her backside, but not for grown men to allow each other to whip their genitals with stinging nettles.

Tort

The law of civil wrong covers anything from tripping on a wonky paving stone to kicking a football into your neighbour's garden or publishing salacious celebrity gossip on your website. Fault is measured in terms of loss to the victim and damages payable by the 'tortfeasor'. The big subject here is the tort of negligence, but also covered on a typical course are a veritable ragbag of wrongs ranging from defamation, occupier's liability, employer's liability and liability for defective products. The common thread is working out who is to blame for a chain of unfortunate incidents leading to some kind of injury – either physical or financial. The most famous case, Donoghue v Stevenson, involves a lady finding a snail in a bottle of ginger beer. Other intriguing problems are whether the fire brigade has a duty of care to answer an emergency call, what happens if you suffer some kind of psychiatric illness from witnessing a horrific accident and how much the law says your arm is worth. This is the field which fuels the so-called compensation culture and gives lawyers a bad name. You'll hear stories about people being impaled, trampled and crushed, so try to cultivate an iron stomach or a gruesome sense of humour.

Public Law

Studying the nature of the UK constitution (hint: yes there is one, albeit unwritten and composed of several parts) and the process of judicial review is a far cry from learning about contractual terms or mortgages. The first part of the course is an accelerated study of the functioning and evolution of the Houses of Lords and Commons and the impact of the EU on UK law. Those with politics degrees will have a running start, and you're more likely to enjoy the constitutional bit of the subject if you're a history buff. When in doubt, questioning the strength of Parliamentary supremacy, the rule of law and the Royal Prerogative should suffice to convince the tutor you've done your reading. After the academic bit is over and done with, a large chunk of the rest of the course is devoted to judicial review, the process by which the courts can challenge the decisions of public bodies. The shift from constitutional to administrative topics is probably the most pronounced on the entire GDL, so those who don't enjoy thinking about how the Jackson case, concerning the fox hunting bill, highlighted the modern state of Parliamentary supremacy can instead focus on why a local authority can't compulsorily purchase your house just because you haven't paid your council tax. The last part of the course teaches you about the freedoms of speech and assembly, as well as the nitty-gritty of exactly how much force the police can use when they throw you in the back of their van.

All GDL applications are made through the Central Applications Board (www.lawcabs.ac.uk). It's worth getting your application in as early as possible if you have your heart set on a particular institution. Applications for first-round 2009/10 applications must be made by 2 February 2009. The institutions will consider these and make offers from 9 March. Applications made from 2 February until April 17 will be considered from 17 April. Later applications will be considered as and when they are received. In short, the later you apply the more flexible you may have to be about where you study. Applications for part-time courses should be made directly to the providers.

If you intend to do an LPC or BVC at a very popular institution you might stand a better chance if you choose it for your GDL as many providers guarantee LPC places to their GDL graduates. The GDL is now offered at around 39 different universities and law schools in England and Wales. Our website has a table detailing course providers, fees and other useful information.

The GDL Providers

University of Birmingham (ft)
Birmingham City University (ft/pt)
Bournemouth University (ft/pt)
BPP Law School, Leeds (ft/pt)
BPP Law School, London (ft/pt)
BPP Law School, Manchester (ft/pt)
University of Bradford (ft/pt)
University of Brighton (pt)
Bristol Institute of Legal Practice (ft/pt)
Brunel University (ft)
University of Central Lancashire (ft/pt)
The City Law School (ft)
College of Law, Birmingham (ft/pt)
College of Law, Chester (ft/pt)
College of Law, Guildford (ft/pt)
College of Law, London (ft/pt)
College of Law, Manchester (ft/pt)
College of Law, York (ft/pt)
De Montfort University (ft/pt)
University of East Anglia (ft)
University of East London (ft)
University of Glamorgan (ft/pt)
University of Hertfordshire (ft/pt)
Holborn College (ft/pt)
University of Huddersfield (ft/pt)
Kaplan Law School (ft)
Keele University (ft/pt)
Kingston University (ft/pt)
Leeds Metropolitan University (ft/pt)
University of Lincoln (ft)
London Metropolitan University (ft/pt)
London South Bank University (ft/pt)
Manchester Metropolitan University (ft/pt)
Middlesex University (ft/pt)
Northumbria University Law School (ft/pt)
Nottingham Law School (ft/pt)
Oxford Brookes University (ft/pt)
University of Plymouth (ft)
Sheffield Hallam University (ft/pt)
Southampton Solent University (ft/pt)
Staffordshire University (ft/pt)
Worcester College of Technology at Worcester (pt)
University of Sunderland
University of Sussex (ft)
Swansea University (ft)
Thames Valley University (ft/pt)
University of Westminster (ft/pt)
University of Wolverhampton (ft/pt)

The Legal Practice Course (LPC)

The LPC exists in that grey area between university life and the dreaded real world. You're still a student but the delightful vagaries of undergraduate study have been replaced by procedural drudgery. Taken full-time over one year or part-time over two, the LPC aims to mould unformed students into sharp legal minds ready for practice.

As one pragmatic tutor told his class, on the LPC 'there are no marks for original thought.' Best get your head down, start checklisting and realise that the course is a necessary, if sometimes tedious, hurdle in the race to becoming a solicitor. After slogging through double-entry bookkeeping, board meeting sandwiches and the Civil Procedure Rules, you may find that you come out the other side having learnt more than you think. And it has its amusing points – when participating in mock advocacy and having to refer obsequiously to the assessor in front of you as 'master,' you may feel less like a lawyer and more like Darth Vader in a suit.

Since LPC students spend a significant amount of time learning how to fill in forms rather than philosophising about jurisprudence, the course is generally seen as an easier ride than a law degree or the conversion course. Unless, of course, you're on a firm-specific LPC, which could see you saddled with a heavier workload than your chums on the regular LPC, including specialised modules relevant to your future firm. Future Linklaters trainees get extra lessons on derivatives; future A&Oers reportedly spend Friday afternoons doing African drumming. Whichever LPC route you take, you will generally be provided with every single flowchart, precedent and random piece of paper you need, and then some. These, combined with the beloved PERC approach (principle, explain, relate, conclude), will see you through the exams.

The year begins with the compulsory subjects, which include company, partnership and insolvency law, conveyancing and civil and criminal litigation. Spicing up (or complicating, depending on your viewpoint) your timetable will be lessons in skills deemed central to the profession, including interviewing, advocacy, drafting, letter writing and legal research. Tax, accounts, professional conduct and money laundering regulations are also on the set menu. The profession is particularly keen on drilling FSMA (Financial Services and Markets Act

2000) into students' brains, perhaps to counteract a hitherto unreported trend of unregulated trainees flogging life assurance policies to clients? We can only speculate.

After the compulsory subjects are examined in February, the remaining months are taken up with three elective subjects. Future Gordon Gekkos tend towards acquisitions, debt finance and equity finance, while wannabe Erin Brockoviches go for family or personal injury and clinical negligence. Presumably those who choose the private client elective enjoy watching Stephen Fry in *Kingdom*? There is a smorgasbord of electives to choose from, with slight variations among providers, including the odd media or charity law option. For a full list of who offers what, refer to our website.

The LPC doesn't quite teach you BlackBerry etiquette or how to bundle documents for court, but it is chock full of handy tricks and tips for the pragmatic solicitor, including: the difference between a balance sheet and a profit and loss account; how much income tax HMRC will take from your first pay cheque; how to determine whether the tenant or the landlord is responsible for fixing a hole in the roof; whether a company can loan money to a director's wife; what documents you do and don't need to disclose to the other side in a dispute; why personal representatives in the UK might need to take out an ad in Australia; who you can act for and who you can't; and your duties to the court.

The Solicitors Regulation Authority (SRA) is transforming the structure of the LPC to widen access to the profession by providing greater flexibility. From September 2010, all LPC providers will have to adopt the new structure, but some have applied to the SRA for validation of their new-look LPCs for the 2009/10 academic year. The biggest change is the separation of the compulsory subjects from the electives, into Stage One and Stage Two, to complement the SRA's proposed work-based learning model as an alternative to securing a training contract. Widening access to the profession is undoubtedly a worthy goal, but there is a danger that a two-tier system could be created. The old and new LPC formats can't be combined, so if you fancy splitting your compulsories from your electives, you'll have to wait until at least 2009 to begin. Subject to any further changes, the plans are for the LPC to change as follows:

Compulsory subjects

- All providers will continue to offer courses in Business Law and Practice, Property Law and Practice, and Litigation.
- If they wish, providers will be able to tailor the compulsory subjects. For instance, a City-style provider could teach the criminal element of litigation in the context of white-collar crime.
- **Pros:** The distinction between providers would be more obvious so students could make more informed choices. Students could undertake an LPC more relevant to their chosen type of practice.
- **Cons:** Initially the distinction will only be theoretical, as most providers will continue to offer a balance of everything.

Electives

- Currently students complete their electives immediately after their compulsory subjects. This has the benefit of cohesion and enables students to use skills developed during the earlier part of the LPC.
- Students will be able to separate their electives from their compulsories. The full-time LPC could be six months long and the electives could be taken during the training contract. Although it seems the SRA doesn't want to promote this as a rule, its proposal suggested some universities could create subjects for law students to take during the final year of their undergraduate course to fulfil the elective requirement. It also means students could study their electives with different providers.
- It would no longer be a requirement that students complete electives before their traineeship is registered.
- Firms could create tailored firm-specific electives to be taught to trainees in-house.
- Students would still have the option of doing the full-time LPC in one year, with electives immediately following compulsories.
- **Pros:** The course would be more flexible, so potentially students and firms could save time and money.
- **Cons:** It might cause confusion as to which areas should be dealt with on the Professional Skills Course and which should be electives. Feedback from law firms suggests that most would still prefer for their trainees to do things the old-fashioned way.

Timing

- The current LPC takes one year to complete full-time and two years if studied part-time. There will be no required length for the new-look LPC, just a minimum number of 'notional' study hours.
- This means the course could be accelerated for those who want to get it over quickly or protracted for those with financial constraints or other commitments.
- Although providers will have to offer some face-to-face contact, they could ramp up e-learning significantly, which will please some and frustrate others.
- The entire LPC must be completed within five years.
- **Pros:** Flexibility, flexibility, flexibility.
- **Cons:** Although an accelerated LPC is theoretically possible under the new system, it is unlikely to be offered any time soon.

Overall LPC pass rate, 2007: 75.7% (7,830 students)
- **Pass with Distinction: 28%**
- **Pass with Commendation: 33.2%**
- **Pass: 14.5%**
- **Refer/resit/defer/fail: 24.4%**

Figures published by the Law Society

The LPC table on our website will reveal that the cost of taking the course is substantial. This is of most concern to the many students who self-fund because there is no financial support from the type of law firm in which they intend to practise. Since the Access to Justice Act 1999, the government has promised to fill the massive gaps in the coverage of legal services in the UK, yet less than 0.4% of public spending currently goes on these services. The number of students training to provide advice to legally aided clients is shrinking and so the Legal Services Commission (LSC) has in the last few years set aside an annual figure of £3m to help fund students who agree to go into legally aided practice for at least two years after qualification. With only around 150 students benefiting each year, each grant covers 60% of the cost of the LPC. The grants are awarded via law firms so don't think about applying to the LSC direct. If you want to know which law firms will have available funds, this information will be posted on the LSC website. To ensure good use of the funds, the LSC requires beneficiaries of the grant to take elective subjects that are pertinent to smaller and high street firms, law centres and local authority practice.

At the other end of the spectrum, students going to the country's biggest and most profitable law firms benefit from generous law school sponsorship packages. These rarely come without conditions; indeed with each passing year the conditions become more stringent. Ten years ago few firms cared which LPC provider you chose. Now, more and more are signing up to firm-specific LPCs or requiring their future trainees to attend a sole provider. This has been criticised as creating a two-tier LPC, limiting choice and stifling diversity, since students headed for corporate giants won't interact very much with other students headed for different kinds of practice. However, law firms like it because it means they get more for their money; future trainees get into the mindset of the firm, learn the firm's internal day-to-day procedures and start to understand the firm's areas of expertise sooner.

The two front runners in the rapidly changing race for LPC supremacy are BPP Law School and the College of Law. Each is signing deals with large law firms to provide either tailor-made electives or entire bespoke courses. For example, if you choose Linklaters for your training contract you must study a Linklaters LPC at the COL's new Moorgate branch. The same goes for students headed to Allen & Overy and Clifford Chance. Choose Weil Gotshal, Berwin Leighton Paisner, Barlow Lyde & Gilbert, Baker & McKenzie, Cobbetts, Halliwells or Wragge & Co and you must take the new LPC+ which contains elective subjects designed by the firms in collaboration with COL. Sign with Addleshaw Goddard, Simmons and Simmons, Macfarlanes, CMS Cameron McKenna, SJ Berwin or Jones Day and you must take a standard LPC course with commercial electives at one of BPP's three schools in Manchester, Leeds or London. Norton Rose, Slaughter and May, Freshfields, Herbert Smith and Lovells also send their future trainees to BPP. In 2007 Kaplan Law School secured an exclusive mandate to provide the LPC to future Mayer Brown trainees. Students on firm-specific courses sometimes say it makes them feel hot-housed and worry that it will cause problems for them if they want to go to a different firm on qualification. However, as these marriages of convenience between law firms and LPC providers are gradually becoming the rule rather than the exception, it looks as though students with City training contracts must resign themselves to a more tailored LPC experience.

Another product of the increasingly competitive LPC market is the introduction of MBA-style modules onto the course. Behind this is the idea that young lawyers need a greater awareness of the business context in which their clients operate. If you think that as a crime or family lawyer such knowledge will be superfluous, think again. As a partner in a law firm, you too may one day be running a business of your own.

Yet another recent development in the fast-changing LPC arena is the use of e-learning. Instead of sitting in large lecture theatres with 200-odd other students being taught in real time by real people, students at some course providers now assimilate lecture information via online tutorials and CD-ROMs. Students still benefit from human contact by attending their small group tutorials. Some argue that e-learning is beneficial to students because it allows them to learn in their own time and at their own pace, rewinding bits that are unclear until understanding sinks in. However, others who have had a taste of e-learning see it as a money-making exercise in amateur dramatics and criticise the way in which it prevents students from asking questions and experiencing the dynamics of a live lecture. While the more cautious providers have introduced online lectures as an addition to live lectures, others have gone the whole hog and scrapped live lectures altogether. Only time will tell whether e-learning prevails over the old-fashioned combo of podium and PowerPoint.

How to apply

The Central Applications Board (www.lawcabs.ac.uk) administers all applications for full-time LPCs. Applications for the 2009/10 full-time course received by 1 December 2008 will go into the first round and offers will be made from 2 February. Later applications will be processed in a second round with offers made from 20 March. Applications received any later than 20 March will be processed as and when they are received. Later applicants' chances of securing a place at a popular provider are reduced, but be aware that, nationwide, there are more validated places than enrolled students on both full and part-time courses. Applications for part-time courses should be made directly to the providers.

There are plenty of things to consider when choosing a law school, so be sure to arm yourself with as much information as possible. Request prospectuses, attend open days, chat to representatives visiting your university, talk to current students and ascertain your priorities.

Career issues

Your future employer may well specify where you go and at the very least they should be able to give you advice. If you don't yet have a training contract, look into the range of extra-curricular activities, clubs and societies on offer that may help you improve your CV. Also think about the quality of careers advice available at each institution. Have they got a good record of getting students placements and training contracts?

Electives

Your future employer may steer you towards particular electives. Otherwise, find out which course providers offer the electives best suited to the type of practice you want to move into. If all else fails, pick the one offering the electives you fancy; although most offer a pretty standard package, some also have the odd media or charity law elective. Some may have restrictions on elective combinations or run electives only when there is sufficient demand. Our website gives a full run-down on who offers what.

Assessment grades and pass rates

Pass rates are published on the SRA's website each autumn, but be aware that direct comparisons are impossible as each institution examines and marks independently of the others. The SRA visits and inspects each institution and then publishes a report.

Teaching and assessment methods

Most institutions timetable around 14 hours of classes per week, but there uniformity ends. If you have travel plans, you may want to check term dates, as these can vary between institutions by a couple of weeks. Similarly, if you are going to have a long commute to classes, or are hoping to fit in part-time work, check the timetabling of classes. Some places will fix you up with neat morning or afternoon timetables and a day off mid-week; others will expect you to hang around between classes that are spread throughout the day. Consider whether you are self-disciplined enough for e-learning or better suited to attending lectures in person. Whereas some institutions only permit a modest statute book and practitioner text to be taken into the exam room, others hold open-book exams leading to students precariously balancing files and books Jenga-style on tiny exam desks.

Facilities

For every school where students must search plaintively for a quiet study corner, there is another where they can spread out in blessed peace in their own 'office'. Take the LPC course at a university and you'll belong to a proper law faculty (complete with Klix coffee machine and last week's *Independent*); elsewhere, leather sofas and acres of plate glass may convince you you've strayed into the offices of a City firm. Given the importance of IT to the LPC course in general, consider whether the institution offers endless vistas of the latest flat screens or a few dusty typewriters in a basement. A large institution may appeal to students keen to be streamlined through the system while maintaining desired anonymity. Conversely, the intimacy of smaller cohorts and easily accessible tutors may tip the scales in favour of a smaller institution.

Atmosphere and direction

Some institutions are known to attract Oxbridge types destined to be City high-flyers, while others cultivate the talents of those headed for regional practice. Still others purport to offer a mix of students, so the commercially minded can mingle with future high street solicitors. Consider which flavour of LPC you're after. Some providers offer LPCs with a noticeably corporate slant, both in the electives available and the manner in which the compulsories are taught; at other providers you can experience an LPC more suited to the high street. Elsewhere, several choices of direction are offered all under one roof.

Tactics

Some of the most popular institutions must be placed first on the LawCabs application form. This type of information is in the LPC Providers table on our website. Check also whether your university, GDL provider or law firm has an agreement or relationship with a provider.

Money

Fees vary and so do the institutions' policies on the inclusion of the cost of textbooks and Law Society membership, etc. Even if you have sponsorship, living expenses still need to be taken into account. The cost of living in London especially can be a nasty shock.

Location

Plenty of students find that tight finances restrict their choice of school. Living at home will save you a packet... if you can stand it. If you're able to strike out on your own, it's worth considering what you like or don't like about your university or GDL provider and whether you want to prolong your undergraduate experience or escape it. Be aware that certain LPC providers are dominated by graduates of local universities. When weighing up providers in large cities, find out whether the campus is in the city centre or out on the ring road. In London, consider whether you'd prefer to be near the buzz of Soho or the distinguished fields of Gray's Inn.

Social mix and social life

Studenty cities such as Nottingham and Bristol are always a lot of fun, but the bright lights of the capital may be irresistible. Experience tells us that compared to those in other cities students in London tend to slink off the moment classes end.

LPC provider reports

There are now so many places to take the LPC, so how do you pick the best course for you?

In past editions we chose to write features on those LPC providers that were rated as 'Excellent' or 'Very Good' by the Law Society. The Solicitors Regulation Authority (SRA) is now responsible for monitoring visits and no longer assesses providers using a simple, single grade (from 'Excellent' down to 'Satisfactory'). Instead providers are graded on six different elements, with marks ranging from 'commendable practice' through 'confidence in the provision' to 'failure to meet the required level of provision'.

The new grades will not be known for all providers for another year, effectively leaving students still looking at two different grading systems. To add to the confusion, it looks as though the 'new' grading system will fade away once the new LPC arrives. We have decided not to use SRA grades to identify the best providers for inclusion in the guide this year. Instead, we have included detailed features on the biggest providers, with 150 or more total LPC students, and shorter snapshots of smaller providers.

On our website you will find a table detailing all providers and allowing a comparison of their fees, student numbers, available option subjects and useful tips for applicants.

Birmingham City University

Number of places: 120 full-time, 40 part-time

The LPC at Birmingham City University (formerly the University of Central England) has received 'commendable' ratings across the board from the SRA and its significantly lower fees should appeal to students on a tighter budget. In exchange for saving almost £2,000, students at BCU trek to the City North campus three miles outside the city centre, but there are local buses and half-hourly trains to Perry Barr from Birmingham New Street. Once on campus, students have rigorously enforced access to a careers tutor as well as a personal tutor, but the pride and joy of the school – especially for those without training contracts – is a mentoring scheme that pairs students with local solicitors at all levels of the profession. BCU doesn't hide the fact that it aims to send its alumni to high street firms or small or medium-sized commercial firms in Birmingham, and around half the students leave the

The LPC Providers
Aberystwyth University (ft)
Anglia Ruskin University (ft/pt)
Birmingham City University (ft/pt)
Bournemouth University (ft)
BPP Law School, Leeds (ft/pt)
BPP Law School, London (ft/pt)
BPP Law School, Manchester (ft/pt)
Bristol Institute of Legal Practice at UWE (ft/pt)
Cardiff Law School (ft)
University of Central Lancashire (ft/pt)
The City Law School (ft)
College of Law, Birmingham (ft/pt)
College of Law, Chester (ft/pt)
College of Law, Guildford (ft/pt)
College of Law, London (Bloomsbury) (ft/pt)
College of Law, London (Moorgate) (ft)
College of Law, Manchester (ft)
College of Law, York (ft/pt)
De Montfort University (ft/pt)
Kaplan Law School (ft)
University of Glamorgan (ft/pt)
University of Hertfordshire (pt)
University of Huddersfield (ft/pt)
Leeds Metropolitan University (ft/pt)
Liverpool John Moores University (ft/pt)
London Metropolitan University (ft/pt)
Manchester Metropolitan University (ft/pt)
Northumbria University Law School (ft/pt)
Nottingham Law School (ft/pt)
Oxford Institute of Legal Practice (ft/pt)
University of Plymouth (ft)
University of Sheffield (ft)
Staffordshire University (ft/pt)
Swansea University (ft)
Thames Valley University (ft)
University of Westminster (ft/pt)
University of Wolverhampton (ft/pt)

course with a training contract. Its broad spread of electives reflects this tendency to look beyond big City law. Students can choose from commercial electives like mergers and acquisitions and commercial property, as well as non-commercial ones like welfare and immigration. There is also an EU law elective on offer, and changes to the LPC structure mean there may be even more to choose from in the future. Some parts of the campus are WiFi-ed, and students can access some course materials online through BCU's e-learning platform, Moodle. Podcast lectures are available to supplement group sessions, but the faculty takes pride in keeping the emphasis on face-to-face teaching and a level of care and attention that it believes elevates it above some of its larger local competitors.

BPP

BPP's reputation as the Big Kahuna of City-orientated LPC providers is well founded. Students' first impressions are of a 'very professional,' 'slick operation,' as evidenced by the wireless networking and laptop loan system. All this impressive kit must cost a bundle, and unsurprisingly, since BPP is the priciest of LPC providers, students were quick to note that the course is 'very expensive.' Its price tag clearly isn't a problem for the City firms that send their trainees exclusively to BPP's Holborn campus. These include Macfarlanes, Simmons & Simmons, Freshfields, Norton Rose, Slaughter and May, Herbert Smith and Lovells. In addition, BPP's high-flying atmosphere often attracts swathes of Oxbridge graduates and future corporate legal eagles. Teachers wear suits and so do a number of students. BPP in London does deserve its City reputation, but in Leeds and Manchester the student population is noticeably more diverse in career aspirations. Although BPP offers a good range of non-commercial electives, students confirm that its feet stand firmly in the commercial camp. Not only is BPP noticeably commercially focused, its LPC course is very much in the business of getting students over the exam hurdle: 'They prepare students to pass exams. They don't stimulate people to think or analyse things too much.' In the midst of all this 'slick machinery,' students are provided with 'everything you need,' including copious handouts, textbooks, manuals and DVDs. The course is so slick that one of our sources said it is 'a bit too seamless; there's no character or fun about it at all.' Unfortunately, it is doubtful whether there is much fun to be had on any LPC course, given the 'formulaic' nature of its procedural aspects. Overall, students are happy to be 'spoon-fed' by 'intelligent lecturers.'

BPP trialled 'optional lectures' on the LPC course last year. Students could still attend live lectures, but performances were also available via MP3 download. Looking ahead, BPP expects most students will still choose to attend lectures, and will view downloaded lectures as a godsend for going over tricky bits and at revision crunch time. Students have classes four days a week, timetabled between 9am and 5.30pm, with one day off for private study or, for the less diligent, watching daytime telly. Closed-book exams mean students 'very much have to understand and really get to grips with the issues.' 'It forces you to learn things.' BPP expects the learning to start straight away; before students even finish their pre-LPC holidays they have a whopping 100+ pages of reading. For the majority of the year no one's left to contemplate the impact of the Companies Act 2006 alone, as each student is allocated a personal tutor at the beginning of the year. In the spirit of its results-focused mentality, BPP offers mock tests and revision classes before exams, 'which basically tell you what will be in the exam,' so by the time the real thing rolls around, students feel well prepared.

Among those without City training contracts or deep pockets, a lucky few can profit from BPP's scholarships for disadvantaged students. If you don't have a training contract and don't manage to secure one of these sought-after awards, you can still benefit from BPP's dedicated careers service, which seems to have developed rather an obsession with securing training contracts for students. According to our sources, 'they go out of their way completely to ensure that students find contracts.' BPP also offers an unusually broad range of pro bono activities, including a legal advice clinic, a human rights unit and IP projects which run out of all four centres. Apparently, if you have a particular yearning to engage in pro bono in an area not currently covered by BPP, the director of the programme will find you a project, even in something as out-there as space law. To further beef up your CV, BPP introduced an LLM programme in 2008, so your LPC can be topped up either full-time over the summer or part-time over a longer period.

BPP Law School, Leeds

Numbers of places: 342 full-time, 90 part-time

BPP's LPC at Leeds draws a lot of praise for its impressive facilities (including an 'excellent' if 'a bit small' library) as well as its 'great location' five minutes from the central train station. According to students, 'lots of tutors are ex-commercial practitioners' and provide 'top-notch teaching.' BPP's Leeds centre has bounteous pro bono schemes and boasts the North's only IP Centre of Excellence, in which students can assist local businesses and individuals to protect their IP rights. Socially, it is far from grim up North. The city of Leeds has plenty of after-hours fun to offer, such as shopping in the Victoria Quarter (the Knightsbridge of the North), the largest collection of 20th century art outside London, countless trendy bars and nightspots and the Yorkshire Dales and Brontë Country on its doorstep. Unsurprisingly, the tight social group of Leeds students make the best use of their day off each week.

BPP Law School, London

Number of places: in Holborn 1,080 full-time, 288 part-time; in Waterloo 230 full-time, 76 part-time

The SRA recently bestowed 'commendable' ratings on BPP Holborn across the board, but the Waterloo site failed to reach top marks in the 'learning resources' category on the SRA's grading visit in 2006. Most LPC students study at Holborn, but those who apply late are sometimes allotted to Waterloo. Although BPP is the most expensive LPC provider, 'you can really see where your money's going.' The glass-fronted Holborn building can't be cheap, and there are leather sofas and orchids in reception. Although 'slightly cramped' at peak times, the computer facilities and library also look reassuringly expensive. Some find BPP's 'regimented,' 'spoon-fed' approach 'patronising,' but there's no doubt 'it gets you through a lot of information quickly.' Students' impressions of BPP are of 'a large law factory which produces lots of law-shaped sausages,' but it is a 'very business-like, professional course.' In emphasis, BPP's LPC seems 'geared more toward hardcore City firms.' Although there are non-corporate/commercial electives available, BPP frowns upon students who want to take a combination of mainstream and non-mainstream options. Generally, you can only mix and match if your sponsoring firm contacts BPP directly.

Some think BPP's closed-book exam policy 'turns the exams into a memory test instead of a test of analytical skills,' and rumours abound over BPP's draconian and rather bizarre rules on exactly how students are allowed to annotate books. Apart from 'a couple of dodgy tutors,' the standard of teaching is 'brilliant.' Tutors 'don't beat around the bush' and 'do the best they can with boring material.' In addition to the pro bono projects offered at all of BPP's centres, London has an environmental law clinic, a programme for students to shadow solicitors at local law centres and projects enabling students with foreign language skills to provide legal translation services. As Waterloo students are more likely to be commuters, the Holborn bunch are generally more social. They tend to favour the Square Pig as their local, but they also drift over to Pagliacci's on Kingsway and to the profusion of other local establishments around Red Lion Street.

BPP Law School, Manchester

Number of places: 360 full-time, 108 part-time

Having opened in September 2005, it is testament to the 'strength of the legal community' in Manchester and BPP's drive that the 360 full-time places are now fully subscribed. This vigorous health and demand certainly explains why the school has no fears about the College of Law's Manchester opening in 2009. Situated in the middle of town, around 35% of students arrive at BPP's swish premises with a training contract, but 'strong connections with the local legal community' and a 'great careers service' mean that figure 'increases greatly over the year.' Unsurprisingly for what is an institution with a 'highly commercial outlook,' many students will be heading off to big northern outfits or national firms like DLA Piper, Pannone or Cobbetts. Despite the school's insistence that it should appeal to all varieties of intending lawyer, someone we spoke to observed: 'If I had my time again I might go elsewhere; there are the elective options but it's so commercially driven that the emphasis of resources and mindset is on those areas.' The building is fully kitted out, business-like and buzzy, and students say: 'The facilities are excellent in terms of technology but it's quite cramped.' There was agreement that 'e-lectures are good' and marked enthusiasm for 'being taught by people who have just come out of practice,' not least because 'you learn skills for business.' A student cafe is the perfect place for pre-lecture chat, and proximity to the redeveloped heart of Manchester, with its wealth of bars, music venues, shops and restaurants, means social escapades are near at hand. The situation also allows students to take advantage of the city's excellent transport system. All in all, this branch of BPP offers a fresh and commercially driven approach to legal training in the North.

Bristol Institute of Legal Practice at UWE

Number of places: 400 full-time and part-time

All providers claim to listen to students, but Bristol seems to walk the walk. Based on student feedback, Bristol has decided to axe the undersubscribed local government elective and instead split the current commercial law elective into two separate options on commercial contracts and IP, respectively. With a total of 15 different elective options, including charity law, media and entertainment, banking and capital markets, Bristol does 'seem to have the best range of electives' of any provider. The 'very enthusiastic staff' are raring to introduce their version of the new-look LPC from September 2009. The biggest changes will be a more regular timetable, with options to have classes two days, four mornings or four afternoons a week, and slightly shorter workshops (down from a hefty three and a quarter hours to a more usual two and a half). Students will still have the option to attend lectures, but individual tutors will also develop alternatives to attending each lecture, in the form of handouts, podcasts or interactive online lectures. Bristol is adamant that as each lecturer will be able to choose which alternative format best suits the material, the course won't fall victim to the 'spoon-fed, flat-packed' approach of other providers. Tutors are 'approachable' and 'very on the ball,' and Bristol is very keen on active personal tutoring, allocating a 'supervising principal' to each student. Students work within small groups and each group is given its own 'office' for the year for workshops, studying or procrastinating. Each office has a mini-library and four computers, and the main UWE library is excellent. Bristol places a much greater emphasis on the use of primary sources than other providers, so students are expected to get comfortable thumbing through the white book instead of relying on edited versions of the Civil Procedure Rules. Bristol has close contacts with several big local firms, and students go on to train at a very broad range of practices, from City and large commercial players to niche and high street firms. Students can top up their LPC with an LLM. Although the M4 location can make students 'feel stranded,' many do live in the city centre and there are organised LPC social events in town.

Cardiff Law School

Number of places: 180 full-time

Cardiff's LPC is a natural choice for students fresh from the city's university, those moving home and those intending to practise in Cardiff or Bristol. Indeed its top-rated course is broad enough to cater for most students. There is no denying Cardiff's strong Welsh theme: students can even take a short course on advocacy in Welsh. There are 'a handful of students going to London, but the majority of people tend to have training contracts in Cardiff, Bristol or more regional firms.' Cardiff has established links with local legal organisations, and every year about 50% of students take advantage of short work placements with employers ranging from commercial firms like Eversheds to government offices to high street firms. By the time students finish the LPC they feel they 'already know half the lawyers in South Wales.' A 'sizeable minority' of students participate in Cardiff's pro bono opportunities, which include an Innocence Project and a programme to help people obtain NHS continuing care. Most of the teaching rooms, along with the library and computer facilities, are situated in a purpose-built extension of the Law School. The refurbished Graduate Building houses additional teaching rooms, a mock courtroom and a student common room. Classrooms are equipped with hi-tech interactive smartboards, which save what is written on them and can link to websites to illustrate the discussion. Tutors are 'excellent' and 'approachable,' and small class sizes mean students benefit from 'more one-on-one time.' The administration seems to genuinely listen to students, not least via the medium of the staff/student panel, which meets three times a year and provides a forum for student concerns. The LPC intake is small

enough that 'the whole year can go out together' to one of the plethora of Cardiff drinking establishments. With balls, pub quizzes and dedicated LPC rugby, netball, football and cricket teams, no wonder students say 'the social life is so good.' Cardiff gives precedence to applicants who list it as their first choice.

City Law School

Number of places: 176 full-time

Since its inception seven years ago, City's LPC has consistently been ranked as 'excellent' and, most recently, 'commendable' by the Law Society/SRA. City (formerly Inns of Court School of Law) is perhaps better known for training would-be barristers, but it also wants to attract 'free-thinking' future solicitors who 'won't follow the herd' to BPP or COL. City's historic Gray's Inn location is a far cry from the leather and glass boxes of other providers. Note, however, that the cost of City's LPC, while cheaper than BPP, is slightly pricier than COL. Those who choose City are attracted to its 'more intimate atmosphere' and lack of 'conveyor-belt feeling.' Students come from 'a varied range of backgrounds' and go on to train at City firms, small commercial and high street firms and even the Government Legal Service. Tutors are equally diverse, with one who sits as a district judge. Teaching is 'generally really good,' with few exceptions. The timetable for the compulsory subjects allows students to choose between morning or afternoon sessions and gives them at least one day off a week. Although not extensive, the elective choices include the unusual e-commerce option and a new advanced criminal procedure elective is in the works (to be introduced spring 2009). Exams are open book. City's pro bono offering is impressive, with options for LPC students to participate in Streetlaw, the Blackfriars Settlement clinic, the Liberty letters clinic, general evening and employment advice clinics and a partnership programme with a range of legal advice centres and charities. City intends to improve its pro bono initiatives even further by hiring a dedicated pro bono director. Studying the LPC within a university has its perks, and City students have access to commercial awareness lectures via Cass Business School. Students can now convert their LPC into an LLM, and City plans to launch a part-time LPC from September 2009.

College of Law

Progressive to a fault, the College of Law seems to be driving the bandwagon that other providers are keen to jump on. It casts the widest geographical net of all, with branches in Birmingham, Chester, York and Guildford, as well as two in London. In 2009 it will extend its reach into Manchester. As the longest running provider of vocational education to prospective solicitors, it is well respected and has consistently garnered high rankings from the Law Society and the SRA. On the back of its prestigious reputation, COL was given degree-awarding powers in 2006. Students who complete both the GDL and LPC at COL now receive an LLB, and LPC students can top up their qualification with an LLM.

The College of Law is thought to provide a more diverse LPC because it caters for students of varying legal persuasions, offering corporate, commercial and private and public legal services study routes. Each route features the same law and procedure, but with case studies relevant to the particular route and with a variety of applicable electives. COL also runs the LPC+ programme, which offers firm-specific electives to future trainees of Baker & McKenzie, Barlow Lyde & Gilbert, Berwin Leighton Paisner, Weil Gotshal, Cobbetts and Halliwells. Allen & Overy, Clifford Chance and Linklaters all send their trainees to complete a tailored firm-specific course at COL's Moorgate branch.

COL's 'flat-packed' approach to teaching the LPC can instil a sense of being 'just a student number,' but of course the 'be-all and end-all is getting through the exams.' And although it might not be the most enjoyable year, COL does at least do what it says on the tin. Its LPC is also cheaper than BPP, City or Kaplan. Students have ten hours of small-group workshops each week to elaborate on material introduced in online lectures, which are supposed to be viewed for four to six hours per week, depending on how often you pause the program to jot down some notes or make a cup of tea. In addition to a large slice of preparatory reading, group assignments and research, students complete online multiple-choice exercises before each tutorial, which are 'a slight pain the neck' to some, but valuable revision tools to others. Opinion is divided as to how the online lectures, called I-tutorials, compare to standard lectures. Some feel that 'with what you pay in fees, you expect to be able to chat to someone rather than sit down and watch a video.' Completing a large chunk of the course in front of a screen is 'not very good socially' and 'your motivation isn't as good as when you're in a room and someone can bring it to life.' However, COL maintains that students learn more effectively through I-tutorials, and they are definitely here to stay. At least they're useful for revision and for getting your head round trickier subjects like accounts and tax.

COL clearly thinks that modularised, online courses are the way of the future, and from 2009 it will offer a new 'S-mode' part-time LPC, which will be done entirely by distance learning, with attendance only required on campus for an introductory programme and skills assessments. In case you're wondering, the S stands for supervision. By providing S-mode students with one-on-one supervision via regular e-mail and online contact, the

COL thinks that students will get the best tuition without having to trudge into campus. Of course, many people already averse to the idea of I-tutorials will be put off by an LPC with no meaningful face time, but it will doubtless be useful for those with serious childcare or work commitments, or maybe even people who live on desert islands… so long as they have broadband.

Back in real life, COL places a rather tedious emphasis on whiteboard work, which involves 'getting groups to give you the same answer ten different times.' At least most students love the open-book exams. The largely excellent careers service organises a broad programme of talks from external speakers. Befitting its status as a registered charity, COL boasts a well-developed pro bono programme offering students a variety of rewarding and potentially CV-enhancing opportunities. Options vary by location, but usually include advice centres, not-for-profit placements and Streetlaw.

College of Law, Birmingham
Number of places: 528 full-time, 200 part-time

COL set up shop in Birmingham less than ten years ago, so the 'brilliant facilities' still seem 'modern and new.' Ignore the graffiti at the school entrance: the area in which it's located – the Jewellery Quarter – is quite nice. Students say the 'fantastic teaching staff' are 'really approachable' and networking opportunities are excellent because of the school's links with local legal organisations. Many students go on to train at national firms with Birmingham offices, while others head to Midlands firms. Students can participate in pro bono placements at the Birmingham Employment Rights Advice Line and the Refugee Council. Birmingham also operates a French legal exchange with L'Ecole d'Avocats in Lyon. On the social front, there are numerous organised activities, including quiz nights, pub crawls, bowling nights and a table tennis society.

College of Law, Chester
Number of places: 600 full-time, 160 part-time

The Chester campus is in a 'fairly remote position in a little village' two miles outside Chester proper. Although this can make it feel 'quite insular,' the campus's tranquil beauty makes it an 'idyllic place,' complete with 'little bunny rabbits hopping across the grass.' The lack of nearby distractions makes Chester 'quite conducive to studying,' although there is a pub nearby. Wealthy Chester itself is 'really lovely,' with good shops and cafes, and plenty of WAGs to gawp at. Many students commute from Manchester, Liverpool and North Wales. A significant percentage of people who begin the LPC at Chester don't yet have training contracts, so the 'fantastic careers service' is a big help. After the LPC, many students end up training at national, regional and local firms, although a few head down to the hustle and bustle of London. On the pro bono front, students can train to become Mackenzie Friends to support victims of domestic abuse in court. There are also schemes to assist witnesses to give evidence in court and a telephone employment hotline manned by student volunteers.

College of Law, Guildford

Number of places: 720 full-time, 240 part-time

Guildford offers the best of both country and city life. With a campus built around an old manor house, studying the LPC at Guildford can feel a bit like 'being tutored in a stately home,' yet the capital is only a short train ride away. The 'collegiate atmosphere' is evident among the groups of students lolling about the campus's grassy knolls or playing hockey or tennis on the grounds. Some lucky students are even invited to lunch at tutors' homes. While a fair proportion of students are 'prospective City firm trainees' who simply want to avoid the congestion and expense of London for as long as possible, others head to firms in the regions, the Home Counties and the South Coast. Both the setting and the teaching style make students feel 'more relaxed,' which becomes important when exam stress looms. Tutors teach to 'a very high standard' and many have come from City practices. Smaller classes mean tutors can take a personal interest in students. We heard no complaints about the library or the all-important computer facilities. Although Guildford 'doesn't have quite the same distractions as London,' students still manage a 'great social life' thanks to the many pubs and restaurants in town.

College of Law, London (Bloomsbury and Moorgate)

Number of places: 1,200 full-time, 360 part-time (Bloomsbury); 1,040 full-time, 100 part-time (Moorgate)

The London branches of the College of Law and BPP are seen by many City-bound students as the only two viable options among LPC providers, if only because they are the most well known and should therefore theoretically be the best. Those who plump for COL do so because they think it offers 'a wider range of options and a less corporate focus.' The sheer number of students, coupled with the 'pre-packaged' nature of the course, can make it feel like a 'conveyor belt.' Clearly the Bloomsbury branch at Store Street will outgrow itself soon (some would say it already has, given the crowded computer rooms and 'dated' premises), but the College plans to cram a few more in before it moves on to bigger pastures. Any squeeze on IT resources is more noticeable at COL

because of the emphasis it places on I-tutorials. At least there's a nifty screen in the foyer indicating which computers in the building are free. When in a classroom, students generally find teaching 'excellent,' with a few exceptions. Pro bono opportunities are extensive, and last year a group of students performed a comedy musical at nearby RADA. Some social butterflies venture out to the bars and clubs of Soho, but most are content to have a drink with the younger teachers and other students from their workshops at the nearby College Arms.

Two miles and a world away from the commercial and private client and public legal routes at COL Bloomsbury, the exclusively corporate Moorgate centre is a snazzier affair. Although the interior is admittedly rather heavy on the grey tones (perhaps to subconsciously acclimatise students to their office-bound futures), there is a Costa Coffee in-house and a lovely view of Bunhill Fields. Most of the LPC students milling about the leather sofas in reception are headed to top 50 firms, apart from the pesky part-timers who show up on Thursdays. COL devotees Linklaters and Weil Gotshal are conveniently (or disconcertingly) nearby. Local entertainment options also have a decidedly corporate flavour. All Bar One, anyone?

College of Law, York

Number of places: 504 full-time, 160 part-time

York is the smallest of the COL centres and students appreciate the 'less pretentious' and more intimate atmosphere. The course feels 'less London-focused,' and most students go on to train at national, regional or local firms. Students also say that training at York is a great way to build contacts in the Leeds area. For those without training contracts, the York careers service is reportedly 'brilliant' at jazzing up CVs and interviewing skills. The 'very supportive' atmosphere extends to the teaching staff, many of whom are fresh from private practice. In addition to the college-wide pro bono opportunities, York offers the chance for students to shadow advocates in court, advise asylum seekers and participate in a mock criminal trial in the Crown Court organised by Eversheds. Many students live in the nearby South Bank area, which livens up their journeys to class: 'You have to cross the racecourse to get to college. It's brilliant.' During the year, the student social committee organises events like racing on the Knavesmire, trips to pantomimes and an Easter ski trip. York itself is a medieval beauty that offers 'a really nice, easy lifestyle.'

De Montfort University

Number of places: 110 full-time, 130 part-time

For those who can't bear to leave Leicestershire, or who simply want an inexpensive LPC near to home, De Montfort's 'small but beautifully formed' course is a popular choice and 'attracts people from the North and the South.' On its last monitoring visit, De Montfort received grades of 'commendable practice' in all categories except learning resources, but the LPC's upcoming move to new city-centre premises in September 2009 should see improvement in that area. The faculty has had a lot of input into the planning for the £35m project, complete with a massive new energy-efficient building, which will house the entire Faculty of Business and Law and host a dedicated LPC library and common room, mock courtrooms and interview rooms. De Montfort relies on Blackboard e-learning to provide students with extra practice questions for technical subjects like accounts. It has incorporated online multiple-choice questions into its workshops and is considering the use of sound files and podcasts in some subjects. De Montfort is particularly well known for its large cohort of part-time LPC students, who usually make up around half of the entire LPC population and are taught by the same staff as the full-time students. The part-time course is conducted via open learning, which is run in conjunction with ILEX and sees students visiting the campus for one three-day weekend each month. For those students without training contracts, there is a mentoring scheme to pair them with local solicitors, as well as several practitioner evenings each year for networking with practising solicitors and trainees who previously studied at De Montfort. There's a strong pro bono presence, so students can practise giving advice at a law clinic, get involved with Streetlaw or take advantage of a few summer placements with the city council.

Kaplan Law School

Number of places: 300 full-time

Kaplan arrived on the London scene in 2007 through a partnership with Nottingham Law School. Essentially, Nottingham is primarily responsible for providing the course structure, materials and tutors; Kaplan is the moneyman behind the project. The aim of the joint venture is to provide an alternative player in the City LPC market to rival COL and BPP. From the testaments of the first students to undertake Kaplan's LPC, we think this new LPC entrant is off to an excellent start. Kaplan has the top-rated resources of Nottingham's course, combined with a swanky new central London building and a small intake to 'foster a community feel.' Kaplan even bought its students dozens of pizzas for defending its reputation on rollonfriday.com. The London Bridge campus is dangerously close to the gastronomic delights of Borough Market, so it's lucky that Kaplan is generous with its funding for student sports and societies. Last year students and staff burned off the calories together in a mixed netball game, which admittedly caused a few minor injuries to the slower members of staff. Such antics illustrate the real benefit of studying the LPC in a

'close-knit community.' Of course, students applying for the LPC may be wary of choosing the newest kid on the block, but Kaplan's LPC has been endorsed by Mayer Brown, which sends all its future trainees here. The student body is 'a really mixed bag,' with many going to major City players and 'a fair few going to high street practices.' There are also some mature students whose academic backgrounds may have caused them to slip through the nets of bigger providers, but as Kaplan reads every application form thoroughly it can root out diamonds in the rough. Kaplan allows students to tailor their LPC via one of three routes—corporate/commercial, litigation and public services, which includes immigration, housing and family electives. Having Mondays off is 'very useful for study time' or for recovering from the weekend. Overall, teaching is 'first class,' and students feel their learning is 'geared towards our time in practice, not towards passing the exams.' Mirroring the realities of practice, only primary sources like Butterworth's are allowed in the exam. Notes and manuals are a no-no.

Leeds Metropolitan University

Number of places: 105 full-time, 45 part-time

Despite Leeds Met's 2005 move to modern new premises in the city's business district, the SRA's last assessment of its learning resources (in 2006) said improvements could be made regarding the number of computers and up-to-date library books, the amount of study space and availability of an LPC common room at Cloth Hall Court. However, the inspectors did bestow 'commendable practice' grades in the other five categories, and former LPC students say that Leeds Met's LPC is 'very good' and 'a brilliant course.' Apart from those few practical issues, Leeds Met offers a solid LPC for students wedded to the city or attracted by 'fees over £2,000 cheaper than the College of Law.' Furthermore, those who do the GDL or LLB at Leeds Met get a 10% loyalty discount on LPC fees. Befitting the ambitions of many of its students, Leeds Met offers a roughly 50-50 mix of non-commercial and commercial electives. Most of the tutors were local practitioners, and students praise them as being 'very friendly.' Students can also benefit from a professional mentor scheme, which partners students with solicitors from firms in Leeds and West Yorkshire, including Pinsent Masons, Eversheds, Irwin Mitchell, Walker Morris, Lupton Fawcett, Cobbetts and Ford & Warren. The criminally minded can be paired up with a solicitor in the local Crown Prosecution Service. As an added CV bonus, students can top up their LPC with an LLM by completing a dissertation.

London Metropolitan University

Number of places: 154 full-time and part-time

As one of the largest universities in the UK after its 2002 merger, London Met is a big player in the London LPC provider stakes for professional and vocational qualifications, and its philosophy is to widen participation in the legal profession as much as possible. Many students who want to be in London during their LPC, but don't want to fork over quite so much money, choose to study at London Met. The course is run from the Goulston Street campus in Aldgate East, where there are classrooms aplenty, a mock courtroom, a 175-seat lecture theatre and WiFi. The law library is located in nearby Calcutta House. London Met's part-time LPC is big business for the uni, as it typically accounts for around two-thirds of the annual intake and is offered on both day and evening bases. In September 2007, after realising that a lot of its part-timers were mature students (half its students are over 35) working around the Docklands and commuting into the City, it began a part-time evening LPC at Canary Wharf. Both Aldgate East and Canary Wharf are home to a multitude of City law firms, but London Met doesn't favour any one route and students often go on to other types of training contracts at West End or high street firms or in local government. LPC diplomates can top-up their qualification with an LLM by studying for an additional year on a part-time basis.

Manchester Metropolitan University

Number of places: 164 full-time, 68 part-time

On the other side of the Mancunian Way from BPP, MMU offers a cheaper, university-affiliated LPC that's rated 'commendable' across the board. MMU has proved that Manchester can sustain more than one LPC provider and is now carving a niche for itself as the one offering a cheap and cheerfully intimate course. Among the new bells and whistles to be introduced lately are pro bono initiatives with Partners of Prisoners (POPs) and death row charity Amicus, online lectures for tricky subjects like accounts and revenue law, an online 'firm' for students to use as a single entry point to a wide range of resources, and podcasts from potential employers. It's now considering how to implement the coming changes to the LPC, with an even wider range of electives one possible outcome. The facilities are impressively futuristic: skywalk bridges stretch across a central atrium to reach double-height lecture theatres. In addition to the full-time LPC, MMU is keen to bulk up its part-time spaces as much as the SRA will allow. Full-time classes are generally run over four full days a week and a morning-only timetable is available to people with childcare issues or an especially long commute. The £500 fee discount for MMU alumni is effective persuasion for many students. At the end of the course, 90% of students find gainful employment in a legal field, with well over half of those going on to training contracts. To help them along the way, students have access to a dedicated careers adviser. Socially, there's 'a city centre-based environment,' and the student body is integrated with the rest of the university, so there is no shortage of social and sporting opportunities to tap into. There is also a joint LPC/BVC social committee that organises charitable events, as well as the odd drinks night. MMU has close links with the Black Solicitors' Network and the local Junior Lawyers Division, both of which sponsor social and professional events throughout the year.

Northumbria University Law School

Number of places: 120 full-time, 50 part-time

Northumbria is one of only two institutions to offer a degree that exempts students from the LPC. Instead, students on Northumbria's four-year LLB (Hons) course cover the LPC subjects during their degree so they are qualified to begin training contracts straight after graduation. This path comes highly recommended as a money-saving option by former students, though top-up fees may yet shift the balance. Of those who choose to go down the traditional route, many students are initially attracted to Northumbria's LPC because it's still one of the cheapest providers to have scored 'commendable' ratings from the SRA across the board. Even though the course fees are relatively easy on the wallet, the School of Law, buoyed by university backing, has invested serious money to bring the facilities bang up to date. In September 2007, the entire school moved to impressive purpose-built premises in central Newcastle – or as the uni's own website puts it: ' A 21st century design for a 21st century university for those who wish to experience 21st century learning.' What this amounts to is WiFi, high-spec mock courtrooms and a brand new cafeteria and library. The course tries to cater for a wide variety of people, and while it is a good choice for future commercial solicitors, some former students told us they'd found it 'more useful for high street training.' This broad spectrum approach exposes students to several areas of law and a diverse mix of people, but it occasionally means 'you spend time doing things that aren't very relevant to you.' Subject to validation, Northumbria plans to run parallel commercial and general practice routes for stage one of the new LPC from September 2009. In addition to a good range of commercial and high street electives, there's the CV-bolstering student law office, or SLO. Those who opt for it (and it is extremely popular so be aware you might not get it) will have a 'very hands-on' experience advising law centre clients, drafting court documents and briefing counsel in lieu of sitting in lectures. Instead of an exam, students submit a portfolio of practical work. Conscious of the need to help its students compete in the crowded legal marketplace, Northumbria offers a top-up qualification in the form of an LLM in Legal Practice.

Nottingham Law School

Number of places: 650 full-time, 90 part-time

When asked for his views on what's new for Nottingham this year, Bob White, the rather colourful course director, was quick to point out that 'there hasn't been a murder in Nottingham for a while, and there are fewer knives and guns than last year.' While Nottingham does have a somewhat rough reputation, its students are savvy enough to steer clear of 'dodgy areas.' Instead, students can spend their evenings in the pro bono clinic, interviewing and writing letters for 'real people.' Once students have enough experience under their belt, they can move forward to hearings. For students who prefer the *FT* to the *Big Issue*, Nottingham also offers a commercial pro bono clinic, in which student volunteers assist start-up businesses. Although Nottingham adamantly insists on students 'being taught by humans,' it recently began videoing its lectures and posting them online immediately afterwards to give students the opportunity to watch lectures online either in lieu of live lectures or for revision purposes, as 'you can go through the whole course in a couple of hours.' However, given Nottingham's insistence on face-to-face tuition, it seems unlikely that online lectures will become anything more than secondary additions to the live delivery of lecture material. Bob White charmingly expressed Nottingham's stance on the e-learning issue: 'Around here it's not a ghost town because we're all out watching our computer screens at home. There's an indefinable but crucial feeling of community.' That sense of community extends to the 'wicked' social scene. Nottingham's heady social brew seems to be based on the combination of 'a university feel' and the fact that 'it's a reasonably compact city' with 'a million places to go as a student.' Even though Nottingham is a relatively cheap city, the drinks budget goes even further because 'lots of people have already got training contracts with big firms in London, so they have a bit of money to spend.' Students readily acknowledge 'a high density of Oxbridge students' on the course, as well as 'lots of like-minded people who work hard and play hard.' Perhaps it is the students themselves, as much as the course structure, that give Nottingham's LPC 'a good feel – it's professional but not too pressurised.'

Oxford Institute of Legal Practice

Number of places: 300 full-time, 50 part-time

OXILP takes full advantage of its location to attract students from all over the Thames Valley and former Oxonians who still want to dawdle amid the dreaming spires. Since 1 August 2008 Oxford Brookes bought Oxford University out of its joint ownership of the institute and now the course will be taught from Headington

Hill Hall, a short bus ride (or uphill bike ride) from the city centre. With Brookes undergoing a renovation programme, OXILP is gaining dedicated skills suites, cameras with which to practise interviewing and – subject to validation – the chance to top up the LPC to an LLM. Never fear, though: Oxford University will continue to validate the diploma and LPC students will still have access to its careers service, sports facilities and the Bodleian Library. OXILP was divested of its formal links with City firms in 2006, so now it offers a broad commercial LPC taught by a mix of ex-City and ex-regional practitioners. With around two-thirds of its students securing training contracts by the time they leave, OXILP sees most of its alumni head to large regional firms like Burges Salmon and Shoosmiths, as well as a few of the smaller City firms. Nine electives are offered, two-thirds of which are commercial. Students have four days of classes, the exact times of which change week on week. At OXILP, students are expected to be more autonomous than at other more 'spoon-fed' providers, but some alumni told us this meant 'it wasn't very hard-working.' Our overall impression from students' comments is that teaching standards vary. While some claimed that tutors could be 'just appalling,' others said teaching quality was 'really good' and singled out lecturers for high praise – particularly the head of private client studies David Day. Overall, 'a more academic environment' delivers a course where 'it's nice being a student instead of pretending you're already a lawyer.' A handy tip for those who fancy OXILP: it gives priority to applicants who put it as their first choice on the application form.

Staffordshire University

Number of places: 150 full-time and part-time

Given 'commendable' ratings all round by the SRA, Staffordshire offers a solid course with a good range of commercial and non-commercial electives, all for relatively low fees. It is especially popular with locals who want to take advantage of a smaller intake and capitalise on the opportunity to save a few bob by living at home. The really practical course is good at gearing you up for the profession, past students tell us. There are mock courtrooms, IT facilities and simulated solicitors' offices aplenty, as well as a useful practitioner mentoring scheme that connects students with solicitors. A new pro bono clinic and advice centre is being launched this year to complement Staffordshire's thriving Streetlaw scheme, which sees groups of students visit schools, prisons, housing associations and drug rehab units. LPC students can also upgrade their diploma to an LLM. The campus is located in Stoke-on-Trent, and while the city isn't the liveliest of places, the campus is near to the nightclubs, bars and restaurants of Hanley, and Alton Towers and the Peak District are only a short drive away – as is Manchester Airport.

University of Sheffield

Number of places: 180 full-time

This provider prides itself on giving its LPC students a university experience. Many of them attended Sheffield Uni or Sheffield Hallam, and last year's move to new premises across the street from the main university facilities in the city centre means the school is even more closely tied-in to student life than before. Students have 24/7 access to an ultra-modern library ('The Information Commons') where they have a dedicated area and the use of 'so many computers you don't know what to do with them.' Lectures are held on Monday mornings, and Sheffield is one of the few providers to offer students the choice of morning or afternoon group sessions. Because of its small size, 'the staff-student ratio is quite good' and Sheffield students enjoy a lot of contact with personal tutors. The 'very well structured' course is geared towards allowing students to steer themselves in the direction best suited to their chosen area of practice. As such, Sheffield offers 'a good mix of electives' for aspiring commercial and high street solicitors. The teachers, who come in for high praise from former students, have previously practised in high street, regional and national firms – over a third of them at partner level. Open-book exams mean students can take in a lever arch file crammed full of notes, study packs, manuals and core texts. One alumnus told us 'not that many people went there with a view to going to London,' but Sheffield is one of the institutions DLA Piper recommends its future trainees attend, and over half of the students end up in training contracts at a huge range of firms. A careers service is available to those who don't snare a contract by the course's end for a further three years after finishing, perhaps explaining why the eventual success rate is around 90%. Students have plenty of scope to try pro bono work, such as the Innocence Project and Irwin Mitchell-sponsored Pro Uno. An up-and-coming cultural hotspot, Sheffield has no shortage of music venues or trendy, dimly lit bars and boasts the largest theatre complex outside London. If students tire of the urban scene, the Peak District and the Pennines are on their doorstep.

University of Westminster

Number of places: 120 full-time, 64 part-time

The University of Westminster has a distinctly special feel to it, and it isn't just the shopaholic-friendly location just above Oxford Circus. We don't know whether the Oxford Street sales have gone to the administrators' heads, but Westminster offers £500 off its already inexpensive course fees to all students who passed the LLB with a 2:1 or above or the GDL with a commendation or above. Students get a further 5% off if they pay their course fees in full by the end

of September. Such deals are enough to entice many a would-be solicitor, but there is much more on offer at this little West End gem that sends a lot of its graduates to smaller firms. First off, the course received top marks across the board on its latest SRA visit. With a small intake (by London standards) the course is cosier and more collegial, and students get lots of one-on-one time with teachers who are 'always enthusiastic and fresh.' Westminster has rolled out Blackboard e-learning facilities, and students can borrow laptops from the LPC-exclusive resource room. Classes are generally held from Monday to Thursday from 10am to 4pm. Subject to demand, Westminster offers a broad range of electives, including the rather unusual options of entertainment and media law and e-commerce. Students can impress prospective employers by gaining experience in the Pro Bono Clinic, which is planned to have its own elective when the new LPC comes into force and takes on projects dealing with land registration, disability discrimination and IP among others. A unique selling point for hopeful high street solicitors is that students who take the immigration law elective can also study and sit for Level 1 of the Immigration Accreditation Scheme. Last but not least on the rather long list of Westminster's fringe benefits, LPC diplomates can also receive an LLM in Legal Practice upon completion of some taught modules and/or a dissertation.

Snapshots of the smaller providers

Midlands and East

Anglia Ruskin University

Number of places: 70 full-time, 40 part-time

Anglia Ruskin scored 'commendable' grades in five out of six areas on its last SRA visit. The part-time course is run in Cambridge, while full-timers study in a brand-new faculty building in Chelmsford. Given the relatively small LPC intake, large group lectures can be delivered to all students at once, and small groups normally contain around 15 students. Each student also has a personal tutor to provide pastoral care. Ten percent of LPC places are initially reserved for disabled students, and the LPC provides credits that can be used towards an LLM qualification. An LPC team competes in the National Client Interviewing Competition every year, and after winning it for the fifth time, the 2007/08 students managed to reach the International semi-finals in India.

University of Hertfordshire

Number of places: 64 part-time

Hertfordshire offers the LPC on a part-time basis (though there are tentative plans for a full-time course), and this specialisation has enabled it to perfect its LPC, which received 'commendable' grades across the board from the SRA. The six elective options are geared to students heading for high street or local commercial practice. Classes are held one full day per week for two years, on which students are also able to meet with their personal tutors. Located in the centre of charming and well-to-do St Albans, the law school has a strong sense of community and the university has invested heavily in its bespoke e-learning platform, StudyNet. There are also various pro bono projects on offer, including a law clinic where students are able to give legal advice to clients and pursue Streetlaw community initiatives.

University of Wolverhampton
Number of places: 60 full-time, 30 part-time

Students heading to law firms with office park locations can acclimate to park life early, since Wolverhampton's LPC is taught at the Wolverhampton Science Park, one mile outside the city proper. The purpose-built facilities include lots of high-spec technical equipment, including interactive whiteboards, DVD recorders and laser printers. Students use the 'WOLF' e-learning platform, which also hosts the virtual town of New Molton. Those with physical or learning disabilities receive dedicated support from the university. There is also an established mentoring scheme, a student law clinic run in conjunction with Irwin Mitchell and the LPC Plus programme, which invites speakers to describe what life as a solicitor is like in practice.

North

Liverpool John Moores University
Number of places: 72 full-time, 72 part-time

On its last SRA visit, John Moores' LPC scored 'commendable' grades in four out of six areas. Full-time course classes are held Monday to Friday for around 15 hours per week, while part-timers come in on Tuesdays and Wednesdays for six hours. Days are 'very regimented,' with small group sessions at 9.30am and lectures at noon, with more workshops in the afternoon. Roughly half of full-timers attended the university as an undergraduate, but there's also a noticeably large Irish contingent. The part-time student population is a mix of students who are working full-time, those doing a part-time training contract and legal executives and magistrates' clerks. The course is now taught in a purpose-built section of the John Foster building in the city centre. A solicitor mentor scheme provides 'good contacts that can get you work experience.'

University of Central Lancashire
Number of places: 80 full-time, 48 part-time

UCLan's LPC is one of the cheapest in the North West, but the smaller price tag doesn't come at the expense of quality teaching, a good range of electives and access to mock courtrooms and the latest IT facilities. One of its best features is its small class size of around 12 students per small group. UCLan also has a pro bono clinic and is developing a shadowing programme with local solicitors. Many students were undergraduates at UCLan and were probably keen to receive the 20% reduction in LPC fees offered to them. The rest of the student body tends to come from universities all over Lancashire or have ties to the area.

University of Huddersfield
Number of places: 40 full-time, 35 part-time

In September 2007, Huddersfield expanded its postgraduate legal training by offering a new four-year Masters of Law and Practice degree, which exempts students from the LPC. For those who don't want to boldly go where no man has gone before, it still offers the standard LPC in full and part-time options. Elective choice is limited to seven options, which roughly balance general commercial subjects with non-commercial subjects. The course is taught on the Firth Street campus in central Huddersfield. Affordable fees, state-of-the-art IT facilities and a mock courtroom are all well and good, but we think the most impressive and pub-worthy Hud goss is that the Chancellor is none other than the erstwhile *Star Trek* captain and Shakespearean supremo Patrick Stewart.

South

Bournemouth University
Number of places: 96 full-time

Bournemouth's small LPC, taught on the Talbot Campus in Poole (two miles outside Bournemouth city centre) received five 'commendable' rankings from the SRA last time. Many students go on to regional or high street firms and the available electives reflect this, with one graduate saying they'd 'thrived on the practical nature of [the course].' In addition to hardship grants and bursaries, several scholarships are available for any postgraduate course, including the LPC, and it's not only the brightest who can benefit. As well as an academic scholarship, there are scholarships for citizenship, musical and sporting prowess, so all those South Coast aspiring solicitors who also happen to be musical virtuosos or crack clay pigeon shots can get a little help with Bournemouth's already moderately priced LPC fees.

Thames Valley University

Number of places: 40 full-time

On its last SRA visit, TVU's LPC received four 'commendable practice' grades. It currently takes only full-time students, but there are hopes to bring back a part-time offering in the near future. Electives are geared towards the high street and include immigration, housing and family. Through a mentoring scheme, students can take placements with local firms or see magistrates' courts at work. Further networking opportunities come from a new law fair and the Middlesex Law Society, whose lectures students and staff can attend for free. The student population reflects the university's impressive diversity, and the Ealing campus is within reach of Central London and Berkshire, but it's easiest to get to for students who live in West London. From this year, students can top up their diploma with an LLM.

University of Plymouth

Number of places: 120 full-time

Plymouth took over Exeter Uni's LPC in 2006. The merged course received four grades of 'commendable practice' from the Law Society and offers a balanced choice of commercial and non-commercial electives and 'lots of staff support.' The course is very much a part of the university, and is run from the Cookworthy Building on campus. Exeter and Plymouth LLB or GDL graduates receive a 10% discount. In addition, up to five high achievers per year (with one place reserved for a Channel Islander) receive a £2,000 Saltram scholarship to assist with fees. A top-up LLM is available on completion of a dissertation or workplace-based project and is normally undertaken part-time.

Wales

Aberystwyth University

Number of places: 100 full-time

Although Aber has the oldest law department in Wales, it only began offering the LPC in 2006. The location is clearly dear to many students' hearts and the Penglais campus, overlooking Aberystwyth and Cardigan Bay, reportedly boasts some of the best views of any British university. The tutors are qualified solicitors, although some members of the university's academic staff are guest-speakers during electives. For students aiming to practise in Welsh courts, advanced criminal advocacy in Welsh is on offer.

Swansea University

Number of places: 100 full-time

Set in parkland and right by the beach in an area taking off as a popular surf spot, Swansea University recently won an award for its student experience, so it's no surprise its LPC attracts a lot of former Swansea undergraduates who don't want to leave. Those who did their LLB or GDL at the university get a discount on their LPC fees. Swansea has strong links with the local community and offers a broad range of electives suitable for the mix of high street and large commercial firms its graduates go on to. There's also a good range of CV-boosting opportunities, including an established student-run pro bono clinic and work experience placements at local firms. Swansea's LPC can be upgraded to an LLM in Legal Practice and Advanced Drafting.

University of Glamorgan

Number of places: 140 full-time and part-time

The law school recently hopped across the River Taff to a specially designed location in a renovated Victorian building on the main university campus in Treforest (birthplace of the legendary Tom Jones). The move has also brought the added benefit of greatly improved IT facilities. The full-time course involves 18 hours of lectures and workshops each week, or eight to nine hours part-time. The number of electives is relatively small but encompasses a range of options, from wills and the elderly client to mergers and acquisitions. It's not unusual for students to take advantage of an optional work placement scheme that operates between February and May.

- **General advice for life:** Carpe diem; neither a borrower nor a lender be; no one ever went broke by underestimating the intelligence of the American public; carpe noctem; never play cards with anyone called Doc; brevity is the soul of wit; never believe mirrors or newspapers; DON'T PANIC; oranges are not the only fruit; courtesy costs nothing; if it ain't broke, don't fix it; faint heart ne'er won fair lady; to err is human, to forgive divine.

The Bar Vocational Course (BVC)

The BVC is the one-year vocational training course for barristers in England and Wales. It can also be taken part-time over two years. Eight law schools are permitted to teach the course at locations in London, Bristol, Cardiff, Leeds, Manchester, Newcastle and Nottingham.

Applications are made online at www.bvconline.co.uk and the first application round opens on 3 November 2008. There is no cap on the number of schools you may apply to but during the first round only your top three choices will look at your application. These providers will be able to see where they have been ranked on your form. Exact dates were not available from the Bar Standards Board at time of going to press, so check the BVC website, but the deadline for first-round applications is usually in early January and offers are made from early March. The acceptance period for these offers ends around the end of March. Any unsuccessful applications then go into a clearing pool, along with late applications. This pool will open in early April and close to new applicants in mid July. Offers can be made until the end August.

Make a considered decision

Before firing off an application ask yourself: have you really got what it takes to succeed at the Bar? As the table on page 847 shows, around one in four BVC students gain pupillage and even then there is no guarantee a tenancy will follow. Course fees of nearly £15,000 in London (and not much under £10,000 elsewhere), not forgetting living expenses to be rustled up, make the BVC an expensive undertaking.

Trying to address the oversupply of BVC students has led to some disagreement between the Bar Council and the Bar Standards Board, but the recommendations of a 2008 working group report have largely been positively received and it seems likely that some, if not all, will be adopted. Instead of seeking to put a cap on the number of BVC places, the key idea is to introduce a new aptitude test for students wishing to start the course. There are also plans to update the course in a variety of ways, including centrally set and marked exams. Furthermore, in the process of being reaccredited, schools may have to justify their fees. The course may even be renamed The Bar Professional Training Course. Quite how and when changes will be introduced remains to be seen, but we'll update our website as more details emerge.

Currently, people are 'called' to the Bar and may refer to themselves as barristers following completion of the BVC. A proposal to delay 'call' until after 12 months of pupillage was rejected after extensive consultation in 2007. While there's minimal benefit in the UK in being a barrister without a pupillage, the title confers greater advantage to overseas students due to its wide international recognition. Such students form about 30% of the total BVC intake each year, and at the Bristol Institute of Legal Practice, some 95% of these students have pupillage or the equivalent arranged in their home jurisdictions by the end of the course.

Money matters

If you decide to go ahead you should do some serious number crunching and work out exactly how you are going to raise the necessary cash. The main funding options are BVC scholarships from the Inns of Court (see their websites for details), career development loans, bank loans and – if you're fortunate – the Bank of Mum & Dad. The Inns and the Bar Council have also negotiated with HSBC's London Barrister Commercial Centre in Fleet Street to offer to favourable loan terms for BVC students (see Bar Council website for details). It's worth contacting your local education authority just in case it can help. For more information on funding see page 80.

Securing a place

When it comes to getting a place on the BVC, don't underestimate the competition. While the Bar Council's criteria isn't (currently) onerous – you need to be a member of an Inn and have a 2:2 LLB or GDL pass – real entry standards are slightly higher and academic grades do matter. BPP, for one, has upped the ante by formally requiring a 2:1, although the 'save in exceptional circumstances' get-out clause seems to stretch to a fair number of people. At all providers, course directors emphasise that they want to see evidence of commitment to the Bar, be it through mini-pupillages, paralegalling or pro bono experience. Some experience in public speaking, mooting or debating helps an application, but don't panic: you don't need to be a high-powered debater at university to be assessed well under this heading. Check out the individual application criteria on each course provider's website or send off for a prospectus so that your application is well targeted. Most providers focus on those who have listed them as their first choice. Cardiff Law School tells us: '95% of our offers are taken up by candidates who have put us in first place.' Competition for places can't disguise the fact that, according to our research, the academic standard of your classmates speaking is likely to be patchy. Although proposed changes aim to counter this problem, for now schools can and do take on students who are frankly not up to the course or have no real chance of a career at the Bar.

Choosing a provider

Research thoroughly what each institution has to offer by reading prospectuses, attending open days and – if you can – chatting to past and current students. As a guide, we've covered some of the basic points on the following pages. Current Bar Council rules mean course content, class sizes and assessment vary little, but there are still considerable differences between schools that could make or break the year. Here are some things to think about:

- **Cost:** Some providers and locations are significantly cheaper than others. London is the priciest but even here there is variation. If you're an international student, look at the differential in price. Part-timers should note whether fees increase in the second year;
- **Success Rate:** Ask providers what percentage of their students pass the BVC, what percentage have to re-sit modules and what percentage of their students gain pupillage;
- **Location:** Regional providers are the best option for those looking for pupillage on the circuits, not least because of strong links and networking opportunities with the local Bar. London students meanwhile benefit from proximity to the Inns of Court and more easy access for pupillage interviews, however, through compulsory dining and advocacy training courses in the Inns, regional students are able maintain their links with the capital;
- **Size:** Smaller providers pride themselves on offering a more intimate and collegiate environment. Student feedback indicates that this does make a difference and the friends you make on the BVC will be a source of support during the search for pupillage and beyond. There's definitely a different feel to the providers which are run as companies (the College of Law and BPP are both plcs), as opposed to those which are universities;
- **Facilities:** Students can tap into a far wider range of support services, sports and social activities by taking the BVC at a university. Library and IT resources vary from one institution to the next, as does the level of technology used in teaching – some places make it a key feature of the course;
- **Option subjects:** Available option subjects vary. For example, although judicial review and immigration are popular, they are not offered everywhere. The BVC Providers table on our website sets out what's on offer at each place. This table also compares fees and offers provider-specific application tips;
- **Extra-curricular English lessons:** If you are an international student, find out whether these are included within the course fees. At some providers they are compulsory for anyone whose language ability does not meet a certain standard;
- **Pro bono:** Opportunities range from minimal to superb across the eight providers.

What can you expect from the course?

During the BVC the spotlight is on developing the skills of advocacy, drafting, opinion writing, conferencing, negotiation, case analysis and legal research. In terms of substantive knowledge, students are required to familiarise themselves with study manuals outlining civil and criminal litigation procedure and the rules of evidence. Learning for the multiple-choice tests used to examine this component is a time-consuming part of the course, but only counts for 15% of the final mark. It is only in the final term that students have some choice, picking two option subjects in areas where they might see themselves specialising. These can provide a real confidence boost when encountering tricky research assignments during pupillage. Most teaching is delivered to groups of 12, with the rest tackled in classes of six or fewer for practical skills such as advocacy and conferencing. Methods vary slightly between providers, but learning is commonly by way of case studies that track the litigation process. Written-skills classes often involve interactive drafting exercises using multimedia such as electronic whiteboards. Oral skills classes make increasing use of video-recording equipment in role plays. The skills acquired are then tested in over a dozen assessments in the second and third terms. Written skills are tested through a mix of unseen, seen and take-home tests, while professional actors are drafted in to take part in oral assessments.

Course directors tell us the BVC is a tough course, so students have to work hard. Student opinion differs. Some report that the BVC experience is not a particularly testing year, although we suspect that a certain amount of bravado is attached to such claims. We think students tend to fall into three groups: those who struggle; those who rest on their laurels a bit because they already have a pupillage offer; and those who throw themselves into the course to achieve high marks and impress chambers' recruiters.

Making the best of it

Whatever critics say, there's no doubt that the BVC provides a vital impetus to 'snap out of the academic mind-set and into a practical one' – a transition every fledgling barrister must make. It's a great year for mooting and other advocacy competitions, while most providers also have their own pro bono units. On top of this, the Inns provide opportunities to socialise with barristers, judges and other students at compulsory dinners, lectures and advocacy training weekends, as well as running their own mooting and debating competitions. During holidays and reading weeks, grab the chance to squeeze in mini-pupillages or court marshalling, or try and get some hands-on experience in a Citizens Advice Bureau or through FRU. These experiences could be the difference between receiving a big pile of rejection letters or being invited to interviews.

The BVC Providers

BPP Law School, Leeds (ft/pt)

BPP Law School, London (ft/pt)

Bristol Institute of Legal Practice at UWE (ft/pt)

Cardiff Law School (ft)

The City Law School (ft)

College of Law, Birmingham (ft)

College of Law, London (ft/pt)

Manchester Metropolitan University (ft/pt)

Northumbria University Law School (ft/pt)

Nottingham Law School (ft)

'ft' = full-time
'pt' = part-time

BVC provider reports

Which of the law schools teaching the BVC will be right for you?

BPP Law School, London

Number of places: 264 full-time, 96 part-time
Contact time: 12-16 hrs/wk on 4 days f/t,
1 w/e a month p/t

BPP is not just a professional education provider, it's a public company with a website providing as much information about corporate governance and share performance as careers guidance. If the school's motto – Serving the Client – isn't enough of a giveaway, its swanky glass and steel building should leave you in no doubt that this school 'takes itself very seriously.' With state-of-the-art facilities, including a series of mock courtrooms, nothing is spared to make the experience as realistic as possible. Students are even required to wear suits on certain days. Competition for places is intensified by the minimum requirement of a 2:1 which, save in 'exceptional circumstances,' forms the school's admissions policy. Once there, students describe the BPP experience as 'a very time-intensive course… they keep you busy with exercises and a structured schedule.' Although the place is generally 'very attentive to students,' tuition is arguably geared towards those who may have difficulty passing the course. Said one source: 'They are very professional about getting you to pass if you're struggling.' While most end up feeling 'comprehensively prepared for pupillage,' on the downside brighter sparks may experience frustration. Advocacy, negotiation and conference skills are the mostly highly praised parts of the course, and these are taught by practising barristers in court dress. A total of nine electives are offered including Judicial Review, Company Law, Property and Chancery. There are more hours of advocacy per week than at any other provider, and each student is required to complete five hours of pro bono activities over the year, not to mention plenty of mooting. Everyone wishes the 'significantly high' fees were less so, but then this was the only London BVC to be unconditionally revalidated by the Bar Council for a full six-year term. Those who complete the BVC can undertake additional study in the months after the course to obtain an LLM in Professional Legal Practice.

BPP Law School, Leeds

Number of places: 48 full-time, 48 part-time
Contact time: 12-16 hrs/wk on 4 days f/t,
1 w/e a month p/t

BPP jumped at the chance to exploit the northern market by opening a brand-new BVC programme in Leeds in September 2006. Closely following the London approach, there is an almost identical course structure and equally modern facilities in Leeds, but the fact that the course is so much smaller means that 'each student knows everyone on the course' and at meet-and-greet sessions with the local Bar 'the chances of being able to network and make those connections is much better.' A BPP London advocacy tutor spent time in Leeds in the first year to ensure continuity with the quality of teaching in the capital, while two practising barristers and a series of professional actors helped students perfect their skills in time for their final assessments. To assist with dining requirements and save the trip to London, a black-tie dinner organised in Leeds was a storming success. For mooting, while Leeds has its own competition, a team also enters the London-wide mooting competition. Pro bono opportunities are available. Heavy involvement from members of the Northern Circuit and fees significantly lower than in London have ensured high application numbers. Experience already shows that successful candidates invariably put BPP as their first choice. Those who complete the BVC can undertake additional study in the months after the course to obtain an LLM in Professional Legal Practice.

Bristol Institute of Legal Practice at UWE

Number of places: 120 full-time, 48 part-time
Contact time: 15 hrs/wk f/t, 11 w/e per yr plus
week induction course p/t

If you're drawn to the South West, competitive prices and strong connections with the Western Circuit make this course well worth considering. Although stats show fewer traditionally well-qualified students are attracted to Bristol than some of its rivals, the institute responds by pointing out that a 'less traditional intake' does not prevent the course from scoring highly in terms of added value. Course director Stephen Migdal believes 'passing the BVC at

UWE is something that has to be earned, but thereby provides a real sense of achievement.' Students work in groups of 12 or fewer for 90% of the time and are given a base room complete with their own set of keys, to which they have access seven days a week. These rooms are equipped with books and IT facilities and become 'a second home' to many students. There's also a dedicated practitioner library. The commitment and dedication of staff is 'constantly remarked upon by students,' leaving us in no doubt that Bristol is working hard to achieve its goals. All students take to their feet in the second term to compete in three complete one-day mock trials – one civil and two criminal. They also commented on the 'strong sense of community.' Students can use pro bono work for FRU, alongside two weeks of compulsory work experience, to fulfil both of their optional modules. A new initiative also enables students to attend inquests, represent juveniles at police stations and carry out prison visits: vital preparation if you're thinking of going into criminal practice. Members of the local Bar assist in advocacy teaching, something students practise during three full trials, while the provision of digital cameras facilitates sometimes excruciating self-scrutiny. Inns of Court requirements are met by the introductory weekend, two Education Days in London and a university-based educational dinner. The location of the university off the M4 is a bit of a downer. Said one student: 'I didn't realise how far away from the city centre it was.' However, ample campus facilities mean students have full access to a range of sporting and social activities.

Cardiff Law School

Number of places: 72 full-time
Contact time: 16-20 hrs/wk f/t

Course leader Jetsun Lebasci sums up the BVC at Cardiff as 'an intense year where high standards are expected, but that is ultimately vastly rewarding.' If you're looking for a well-established, university-based law school you'd do well to give Cardiff some thought. But make sure you put it as your first choice – '95% of our offers are taken up by candidates who have put us in first place.' Located on a campus that is 'green, pleasant and seconds away from the city centre,' the law school is small enough for staff and students to know each other by name, indeed the BVC cohort is one of the smallest going. This gives the school the 'chance to change, adapt and be flexible in a way that other providers can't.' While a number of students are from Wales, many come from other parts of the UK and around 25% are international students who benefit from compulsory two-hour TEFL sessions on a weekly basis if the school judges that it would be in their interest. The school prides itself on the 'quantity and quality' of its skills teaching (advocacy, negotiation and conferencing) and goes beyond the mandatory syllabus, with tuition for these modules delivered to groups of four or six students. Coming in both written and oral form, feedback on students' complete performance over the two hours is extremely thorough. In turn, students are encouraged to complete anonymous online questionnaires to ensure any problems are quickly addressed. Jetsun explained that there is still a strong emphasis on the knowledge-based subjects during the first two terms as 'we feel that they need this to underpin the other skills.' Having said that, the course is now 'less front-loaded than in the past' and a regular dialogue between the school and local practitioners ensures that the materials used are of an appropriate nature. Mini-pupillages and court marshalling are organised for students during two placement weeks. Other extracurricular activities include the Innocence Project, a scheme that involves students with long-term prisoners who maintain their innocence.

The College of Law, London

Number of places: 240 full-time, 48 part-time
Contact time: 12-16 hrs/wk on 4 days f/t, regular w/e p/t

From its Bloomsbury branch situated just off Tottenham Court Road, the College of Law is a thoroughly well-established supplier of legal education in the capital. It has recently gained new degree-awarding powers, meaning students who complete the GDL and BVC here will automatically gain an LLB. An LLM is also available if you're willing to put in extra time at the end of the year by completing three additional modules and an assignment. The teaching on the course follows the litigation process, meaning the timetable 'is never the same from week to week.' Everything is done through classes, as opposed to lectures, a unique feature among London providers that students really appreciate. These are based on groups of 12 students (or as small as four per group for certain oral skills sessions) who work together until their optional subjects start in the final term. Judges and practitioners visit the college to give students feedback on advocacy and preside over mock trials. There are also after-hours speaker programmes on subjects such as commercial awareness and justice, which 'draw in high-profile lawyers and professionals from the business world, and provide plenty of opportunity for mingling afterwards.' Such is the wealth of opportunity that 'you only have yourself to blame if you don't get advocacy practice.' Many students get involved in the Tribunal Representation Service, which provides opportunities to appear at the Leasehold Valuation Tribunal around the corner from the college. Some become panel members with the Youth Offending Service. Students have also been able to handle small claims, social security and employment cases. Two teams enter the National Negotiation Competition each year; mooting is encouraged at all levels of proficiency, and for the last two years the college has organised prison visits. 'Our extensive extracurricular activities are one aspect of the course that we're immensely proud of,' says course director Jacqueline Cheltenham. In turn, students praise what they feel is 'a more friendly environment than at other London providers,' even if 'you are surrounded by thousands of LPC students.'

College of Law, Birmingham

Number of places: 96 full-time
Contact time: 12-16 hrs/wk on 4 days

Having started in September 2007, the College of Law's Birmingham course is identical in content and structure to that offered in the capital. Located in the historic Jewellery Quarter close to the city centre, COL's Brum outpost is typically modern, with state-of-the-art facilities, a decent library and plenty of study space, not to mention the swish, dedicated 2nd and 3rd floor BVC rooms. Strong links with local megaset St Philip's Chambers – one of the largest barristers chambers in the country – and other regional practitioners means plenty of networking opportunities with the local Bar. A well-developed pro bono capacity allows students to get involved with groups like Birmingham Employment Rights Advice Line, Birmingham Employment Advice Clinic and The Refugee Council, as well as represent clients before the employment and social security appeals tribunals. Training with the Youth Offending Service is also possible. On both the London and Birmingham courses, a 2:2 is the minimum required degree grade, although the grading system used by the college still gives more marks to a 2:1 applicant. The GDL and LPC have long been available in this city, and the arrival of the BVC means students can take advantage of already well-developed social activities, whether formal events, or simply chewing the cud with contemporaries in Chompers, the onsite student cafe.

City Law School
(formerly the Inns of Court
School of Law)

Number of places: 575 full-time, 75 part-time
Contact time: 12-14 hrs/wk on 4 days, 2 evenings/ wk p/t

Once upon a time this was the only BVC provider. The school developed the course and is still author of a series of manuals that are used by many students elsewhere and even those starting out in practice. Sited at the edge of Gray's Inn, the school has occupied a position in the heart of legal London for a very long time and, despite the undermining of its hegemony, City still makes much of its longevity and traditional appeal. It educates more full-time BVC students than the other two London providers combined. Some question the school's ability to deliver the best course because of the sheer size of the student body, but City/ICSL points out that the majority of classes take place in groups of 12 (six for advocacy) and that students are split into four manageable cohorts, each with a course director. The course does include some larger group sessions, albeit that these make full use of some pretty smart facilities in the interactive lecture theatre. There's also the stimulation of being a part of what one recent graduate called 'a real cauldron of

the talents atmosphere.' Students also form a 'very supportive' network. Pro bono opportunities are plentiful as the school enjoys links with numerous organisations across the capital, including FRU (with which students can complete one of their two option subjects). Relationships with practising barristers and judges are strong, and practitioners visit regularly for a variety of evening events. Keen students can choose to tack an LLM in Professional Legal Practice onto their BVC.

Kaplan Law School, London

BVC scheduled to commence 2010

Manchester Metropolitan University

Number of places: 108 full-time, 48 part-time
Contact + study time: 9-4 on 2 days, 9-7 on 2 days f/t, 2 days per month p/t

Renowned for its close involvement with members of the Northern Circuit, MMU is a cracking choice for anyone wanting to break into the Bar in this part of the country. The strength of its professional links are impressive: at least seven two-hour advocacy master classes per year see local barristers coming in to give students feedback, and professionals also get involved in MMU's practitioner-mentor scheme, offering useful careers and study advice. Another way to rub shoulders with potential recruiters is attendance on the Additional Professional Programme, involving a series of extracurricular lectures from practitioners. The BVC is taught at the university's six-year-old law faculty building and MMU adopts a 'syndicate group' approach, organising its students into groups of 12 with their own rooms with IT facilities and core texts, designed to be like mini barristers' chambers. Apparently students 'absolutely love it,' and while there are course-wide social events, 'most socialising is with that group, they become great friends.' MMU is massively oversubscribed: course director Alan Gibb informed us that for the 108 full-time places on the 2007/08 course there were 220 applicants who put MMU as their first choice. It allows the university to be picky, usually taking only those with a 2:1, sometimes offering places to candidates with a 2:2 but otherwise remarkable CVs. Those who pass muster on grades still have to produce an impressive application detailing 'clear, articulate reasons' for wanting a career at the Bar. Gibb advises students to 'approach the application form as if it were an application for pupillage, making sure it is word-perfect.' What will not count against you is a lack of northern soul: 'We are happy to take people from anywhere as we know that students put us first because they want to practise on the Northern Circuit.' Around 10% of students intend to return to practise overseas. Typically around 20% of domestic students will have gained pupillage by the time they finish the course, and 40% will have secured a pupillage within two years of commencing the BVC. In 2007 the university appointed a pro bono director who has been busy initiating programmes for students: schemes include advising families of prisoners. All in all, competitive fees, good facilities and those all-important links to professionals make this provider stand out up north.

University of Northumbria, Newcastle

Number of places: 128 full-time, 48 part-time + 40 on exempting LLB
Contact + study time: 9-6 Mon-Thur, plus Mon eves

In addition to its conventional BVC, Northumbria offers an integrated LLB and BVC programme carried out over four years. Students apply for a place on this 'exempting degree' during the second year of their undergraduate LLB and, if successful, spend the following two years combining undergraduate options with components of the BVC. A parallel LLB/LPC course is also run. There are some very practical benefits to combining the two courses, not least a saving in cost, and students are generally able to extend their student loan to cover all four years. For those who are too late to take advantage of this programme, there are still benefits in taking the conventional BVC at Northumbria, which has additionally offered 48 part-time places since 2007. The well-respected course recently moved into a swish £70m purpose-built building in central Newcastle, complete with mock courtrooms and live video-link equipment. Its nationally recognised Student Law Office has also benefited from the extra space, which allows even more students and members of the public to benefit from the free advice clinics on offer. Having five practising barristers teaching on the course is an undoubted asset, yet with only a handful of sets based in Newcastle, staff encourage students to be realistic about their prospects of gaining pupillage in the city. 'We never mislead people at law fairs… they need to look beyond Newcastle.' Networking opportunities arise at guest lectures, moots, mock trials and Wednesday evening 'practitioner sessions'. In terms of structure, the course is described as 'short and fat,' with all the teaching squeezed into the first two terms. This allows the whole of the summer term to be spent on revision. The university provides a series of revision lectures and seminars and is relaxed about giving students free time to organise their own revision schedules. Take a few extra months to complete a research project and you could bag yourself an LLM in Advanced Legal Practice or an MA in Legal Practice & Policy.

Nottingham Law School

Number of places: 125 full-time
Contact + study time: 9am-6pm Mon-Fri

Part of Nottingham Trent University, NLS offers a challenging BVC that competes well with its London rivals. Twice as many first-round, first-choice applications are made to NLS as there are places available and this allows the school to only take people with a fighting chance of gaining pupillage. On average 50% of enrolling students will have secured one by the March following the end of the course. To stand a chance of getting onto this BVC you'll need a 2:1, good A-levels or a good postgrad degree, evidence of interaction with the legal profession (usually a minimum of three weeks' pupillages or vac schemes) plus evidence of public speaking and initiative (eg through positions of responsibility). Students come from all over the UK and enter practice across England and Wales. In the city of Nottingham itself there are only four or five pupillages a year. NLS has a relatively low intake of international students – usually less than 10%. By keeping student numbers down and having a dedicated BVC building, staff and students can get to know each other well. The school's director James Wakefield reveals: 'Staff meet every month to decide which students need pressure put on them or taken off them… this is not a place to come to be anonymous.' The BVC year is judged by students to be a demanding one and they know they are expected to spend five full days a week on their studies, with most sessions taught in groups of 12 or six. Skills and knowledge learning focus on the seven briefs that are followed throughout the year. Criminal advocacy sessions are held in courtrooms at Nottingham's old Guildhall. The appointment of a full-time pro bono co-ordinator and a public-access advice clinic at NLS have enhanced the range of real-life experiences open to students, and there is no shortage of links with professionals in London and the Midlands. Barristers and judges present guest lectures on a regular basis, and there are sponsored plea-in-mitigation and mooting competitions plus a marshalling scheme. A pupillage interview training day assists those who've not yet secured training and, to help students keep contact with their Inns in London, there are coaches to the capital for qualifying sessions. NLS can also dangle the carrot of an LLB for all those who successfully complete the GDL and BVC, and students can also tap into the social, sporting and other facilities offered by the university.

How to fund law school

Details of what solicitors are now offering their future trainees are given in the Salaries and Benefits table on page 660. Further information about the funding of pupillages is given in the Bar section.

Training as a lawyer is an expensive caper. Fortunately many of the students who secure training contracts or pupillages before commencing their studies will receive funding to cover their course fees and some living expenses. But what if you're not that lucky?

Taken for granted

There's a super-slim chance your local education authority (LEA) may come to the rescue with a grant or allowance – assuming you have the stamina to make it through the forest of application forms. We contacted a number of different LEAs and encountered vastly different responses from each, from a flat 'no, we do not offer assistance for students undertaking the LPC' through to a much more positive 'send in an application and see.' It is definitely worth a quick phone call or e-mail to get the lay of the land. You can track down the contact details for your LEA at www.studentsupportdirect.co.uk. If this doesn't bring much joy then there are a couple of other possibilities. An organisation called the Educational Grants Advisory Service (EGAS) can carry out a charity and trust search on your behalf. Visit their website www.egas-online.org.uk for more helpful information. Also see www.support4learning.org.uk. Additionally, the Law Society has various schemes and bursaries that are worth looking into.

Bank loans

Already got a huge overdraft? No problem. You could still qualify for a special package from a high street bank. Interest rates are relatively low and the repayment terms usually favourable, but sniff around to see what different banks are offering. A number of banks such as NatWest, Lloyds TSB and HSBC have graduate loan schemes tailored to the needs of the legal profession and will, for example, regard pupillage as a formal part of the training when it comes to determining the time for repayment. Intending barristers can now take advantage of special terms agreed by the Bar Council and the four Inns with HSBC's Fleet Street-based Commercial Barrister team (see Bar Council website for details). Whichever loan you take out, remember that as repayments are delayed interest accrues and the sums involved can be sizeable.

Career development loans

Barclays Bank, The Co-operative Bank and RBS provide these on behalf of the DfES. Full details can be found at: www.direct.gov.uk/en/EducationAndLearning/AdultLearning/CareerDevelopmentLoans. These allow you to borrow up to £8,000 to fund up to two years of study but are only available for the LPC not the GDL, which is deemed an academic course not a vocational one.

Surf the internet for scholarships

Here are some of the funds we found:

- BPP Law School offers seven scholarship awards, set by key members of staff; each one has its own criteria, eg the applicant must be the first lawyer in his/her family.
- City Law School has six awards of £1,500 for students on the GDL. Each of the four Inns of Court nominates one candidate and the university selects the recipients of the other two once the course commences.
- The Law Society Bursary Scheme is open to GDL or LPC students.
- The Law Society Diversity Access Scheme supports talented people who face obstacles to qualification.
- Inderpal Rahal Memorial Trust supports women from an immigrant or refugee background.
- The Kalisher Scholarship works with each of the BVC providers to ensure that every year one talented but financially disadvantaged student has a free place on the course.
- The Leonard Sainer Foundation provides financial assistance in the form of interest-free loans of £7,500 each, to help fund either the LPC or BVC. For further information go to www.dechert.com.
- The Student Disability Assistance Fund can award up to £500 for students who are studying on a full-time or nearly full-time basis. See www.bahshe.demon.co.uk.
- Universities and publicly funded colleges have discretionary college access funds available to assist especially hard-up students.

The Inns of Court

Pupil barristers and Bar students can apply for a range of scholarships from the four Inns of Court. Most awards are given to students on the BVC, but the Inns also have funds available for those on the GDL. Indeed, 25% of students studying for the BVC have managed to secure some funding from the Inns, and many base their choice of Inn on the likelihood of getting their hands on some of the £3.5m-plus that is paid out each year. Some awards are merit-based; others consider financial hardship. They range from £100 up to £20,000. During their pupillage year all pupils must be paid no less than £833.33 per month plus reasonable travel expenses. Some sets pay far more and allow students to draw on these awards while on the BVC.

Part-timing and the four-letter word

If a decade of loan repayments doesn't appeal then you must do as fools and horses do – work. If you go for this option, bear in mind that full-time study and earning money are uncomfortable bedfellows. Should you be studying part-time instead? This is an important question, particularly as engaging in part-time work while studying for a full-time course is increasingly frowned upon by the providers and the law firms that might be paying the bill for the fees. When asked about the fact that no student can be guaranteed morning or afternoon classes, the College of Law told us that if students can't commit a full working week to the course they should be taking advantage of the available part-time options.

For those fresh from undergraduate life, part-timing might seem like an affront. What's more it may force them to mingle with mature students, men and women with wives, husbands, kids, mortgages... bald spots even. We say revel in the difference – it will be good practice for when you are a lawyer. Studying part-time may also allow you to work in a more rewarding job and perform better at college. For LLB grads or students who have completed the GDL, paralegalling may be an option. Indeed, there are many options on the periphery of the profession, from commercial contracts negotiation and transaction management to social policy or other research. Several of the researchers here at Chambers and Partners are part-time law students. Whatever job you do, working while studying brings with it a commodity to be traded on – respect.

If the part-time option is really not for you then why not consider an evening or weekend job, but be realistic in the number of hours you do. The GDL and LPC are not designed to be a walk in the park and too much work (like too much play) can see your studies suffer.

Capital concerns

Newsflash: London's streets aren't paved with gold, just concrete, pigeon droppings and chewing gum. Rent and living costs in cities like Sheffield, Nottingham and Cardiff are far lower. Don't assume, though, that out of London automatically means within your price range – Guildford, for example, is as pricey as it is pretty.

Before taking any further steps, sit down and add up what you think you'll need and then add some more. If you intend to study for the GDL and LPC or BVC, and you do so at the most expensive places, course fees could cost you around £19,000 (GDL/BVC) or £17,000 (GDL/LPC). Do so at the least expensive schools and these figures could be reduced to around £10,000 and £12,000 respectively. It's worth thinking about if money is the main sticking point.

Benefits, benefactors, begging...

Living at home while you study may not sound that appealing but sometimes needs must. Forget ideas of declaring bankruptcy to evade student debt; consider other creative ways to ease the debt burden.

- A student card will get you low-cost travel, discount haircuts, cinema tickets and drinks in some places. If nothing else, you will be a cheap date.
- Websites such as www.studentbeans.com has discounts and deals for meals, entertainment and more.
- Law books are pricey so don't go on a spending spree before term starts. College libraries will have the core texts and we guarantee you'll find former students with books for sale. Check out notice boards for second-hand tomes.
- A number of law schools, chambers and solicitors firms run competitions. Do a Google search to find them.
- Market research focus groups will pay decent money for an hour or two of your time.
- In terms of more clinical options... consider carefully any decision to become a human guinea pig in a medical trial. And gents, if you choose to make a 'special donation' remember that one day a stranger might knock on your door and call you dad.

- **Pace yourself:** The way to climb a mountain is step by step. The LPC is just the same. Keep going at a steady but determined pace and you'll make it to the end.

A-Z of Universities
& Law Schools

BPP Law School

68-70 Red Lion Street, London, WC1R 4NY
Tel: 0845 075 3522
Email: admissions@bpp.com   Website: www.bpplawschool.com

College profile

BPP is a leading provider of professional legal education, located in Leeds, London (Holborn and Waterloo) and Manchester. BPP's programmes are flexible, providing more study modes than any other leading provider and several ways of viewing lectures, meaning that you can study at a time and in a way that is convenient for you. BPP has the skills and resources to offer the individual support needed to prepare you for the realities of legal practice. This is achieved using a unique mix of academic and practitioner tutors, first-rate facilities, award-winning pro bono projects and a specialist Careers Service. This distinctive blend of knowledge and experience ensures that you are fully equipped with the knowledge and support needed to secure a training contract or pupillage.

GRADUATE DIPLOMA IN LAW (GDL) (full-time, part-time and distance learning - Leeds, London (Holborn and Waterloo) and Manchester)

BPP's 'Distinctive GDL' is designed to help you make the transition from undergraduate study to the practice of law. Taught using a practical, student-focused approach to learning, the GDL provides an invaluable foundation for practice. BPP offers you a one-hour tutorial to every one-hour lecture – the best ratio of any leading provider. BPP's GDL is the only programme in the country to feature the optional 'GDL Extra' and Company Law module, giving you the opportunity to specialise early. Although competition for places at BPP is intense, BPP GDL graduates are guaranteed a place on the LPC and intending barristers can apply to join the BVC. In addition, you have the opportunity to convert your GDL to an LLB by completing two additional modules via a combination of face-to-face and distance learning or solely distance learning. The conversion programme can be done during the summer after you finish your GDL and before you commence your LPC or BVC, or you could spread it over more time – up to five years after you complete your GDL.

LEGAL PRACTICE COURSE (LPC) (full-time and part-time - Leeds, London (Holborn and Waterloo) and Manchester)

BPP's LPC is designed to prepare you for practice. The LPC reflects the growing role of lawyers as business advisers, and contains 'MBA-style' training in business and finance using simulated client portfolios and specific client relations sessions. Taught by experienced solicitors from a variety of practice backgrounds using a high number of small group sessions and live lectures, you will benefit from a programme designed in close collaboration with leading law firms. BPP offers a wide range of electives, ensuring you can study the area of legal practice that interests you.

BAR VOCATIONAL COURSE (BVC) (full-time and part-time, Leeds and London (Holborn))

BPP's BVC is highly regarded by the profession and is designed to prepare you for a career at the Bar. Studying the BVC at BPP allows you to concentrate on developing the essential skills of drafting, legal research, opinion writing, advocacy and negotiation. These skills will be refined in groups as small as six students alongside practising barristers, who will sometimes act as your opponents in our realistic mock courtrooms.

At BPP, by completing two additional modules you can convert your LPC or BVC to an LLM in Professional Legal Practice. The conversion programme is flexible and can be completed full-time during the summer after you finish your LPC or BVC and before you commence your training contract or pupillage, or alternatively you could do it part-time and spread it over more time - up to seven years after you register on the LPC or BVC.

Other programmes include LLB in Business Law*, LLM in Commercial Law, LLM in International Business Law and Law Summer School. Scholarships are available. Please visit www.bpplawschool.com/funding_and_scholarships for more information.

Contact
Admissions
to apply:

Full-time GDL and LPC
www.lawcabs.ac.uk

Full-time and part-time BVC
www.bvconline.co.uk

Part-time GDL and LPC. LLB, LLB in Business Law*, LLM in Professional Legal Practice, LLM in Commercial Law, LLM in International Business Law and Law Summer School
www.bpplawschool.com/apply_now

*Subject to validation

BPP
LAW SCHOOL ®
preparing you for practice

Cardiff Law School

Cardiff Law School, Cardiff University, Museum Avenue, Cardiff CF10 3AX
Tel: (029) 2087 4941/4964 Fax: (029) 2087 4984
Email: law-lpc@cf.ac.uk or law-bvc@cf.ac.uk
Website: www.law.cardiff.ac.uk/cpls

Contact
LPC: Byron Jones
Tel: (029) 2087 4941/6660
Email: law-lpc@cf.ac.uk
BVC: Lucy Burns
Tel: (029) 2087 4964
Email: law-bvc@cf.ac.uk

Other postgraduate law courses:
The Postgraduate Office
Tel: (029) 2087 4351/4353

University profile

Cardiff Law School is one of the most successful law schools in the UK and enjoys an international reputation for its teaching and research. In the most recent assessment of research quality conducted by the Higher Education Funding Council, Cardiff achieved a grade 5 rating, placing it in the top law schools in the country. Cardiff offers opportunities for students to pursue postgraduate study by research leading to the degrees of M.Phil and Ph.D. In addition, taught Masters degrees in the areas of canon, commercial, European legal studies and medical law are offered in full and part-time mode.

Legal practice course and bar vocational course

A part of the Law School, the Centre for Professional Legal Studies is the leading provider of legal training in Wales and is validated to offer both the Legal Practice Course and the Bar Vocational Course. Students are taught by experienced solicitors and barristers who have been specifically recruited for this purpose. The Centre prides itself on its friendly and supportive teaching environment and its strong links with the legal profession. Placements with solicitors' firms or sets of Chambers are available to students pursuing the vocational courses, while students studying the Bar Vocational Course additionally enjoy placements with Circuit and District Judges.

In 2005 Cardiff's Legal Practice Course once again achieved the highest rating following the Law Society's assessment visit. The course has consistently been rated "Excellent" by the Law Society; one of the few providers of this course to hold the top ranking. The Law Society praised the challenging learning environment and stimulating range of activities. The LPC nationally is changing and Cardiff intends to take advantage of the new flexibility while continuing to provide its excellent hands-on teaching experience. Please see the Law School website for further details.

Pro bono

The Cardiff Pro Bono Scheme has two distinct elements: The Innocence Project, which deals with cases of long-term prisoners maintaining their innocence; and the general Pro Bono Scheme, which assists members of the community and vulnerable groups where legal aid is not available. The scheme enables students to experience the law in action, work alongside volunteer legal professionals and develop transferable skills to add to their CVs.

Facilities

The Law School has dedicated accommodation for the vocational courses which houses a practitioner library, fixed and moveable audio visual equipment for recording practitioner skills, inter-active teaching equipment and extensive computer facilities. In addition, the main law library contains one of the largest collections of primary and secondary material within the UK. The Law School is housed in its own building at the heart of the campus, itself located in one of the finest civic centres in Britain and only a short walk from the main shopping area. The Law School has its own postgraduate centre, together with a full range of sports and social facilities. Cardiff is a vibrant capital city with excellent cultural, sporting and leisure activities.

The City Law School

City University London, Northampton Square, London, EC1V 0HB
Website: www.city.ac.uk/law

College profile

Located in the heart of legal London, The City Law School is one of London's major law schools and offers an impressive range of academic and professional courses. We're the first law school in London to educate students and practitioners at all stages of legal education.

The school's exceptional legal courses are fully accredited by the relevant professional bodies and are developed and delivered by its team of highly respected practitioners and academics. The school takes a personalised approach to your learning experience and aims to develop you into the professional, dynamic, highly motivated, "practice-ready" lawyers of the future.

Graduate Diploma in Law/CPE (full-time)

Started in 1976, this internationally renowned course was the first of the Common Professional Examination (CPE) programmes for non-law graduates. The course is designed to provide you with the knowledge and skills traditionally gained from an undergraduate law degree in just one year. The school teaches you the seven core legal subjects through a variety of lectures, tutorials and seminars. At The City Law School you also have the unique opportunity to convert your GDL into a full LLB degree by taking additional units.

Legal Practice Course (full-time)

The school's LPC has repeatedly been awarded the highest possible grading by the Solicitors Regulation Authority (SRA, formerly The Law Society). The course is skills-based and replicates the demands and disciplines of practice through realistic exercises fully preparing you for professional legal life. You are taught in small groups by qualified solicitors on a wide range of specialist subjects. At The City Law School you can add value to your LPC by completing an additional research project to be awarded an LLM in Professional Legal Practice.

Bar Vocational Course (full-time and part-time)

The school's BVC has been designed to meet the demands of the modern legal profession. Its teaching is practically oriented and student centred, you are taught in small group sessions of no more than twelve and interactive large group sessions. The school has excellent links with the profession and count amongst its staff a number of leading authors in the field. At The City Law School you have the unique opportunity to convert your BVC into an LLM in Professional Legal Skills, by taking an additional dissertation on a personally selected area of legal practice.

Masters Degrees (LLMs)

The school offers LLMs in a number of distinct areas, giving you the opportunity to develop your understanding and expertise in a specific area of law. Developed in direct consultation with the profession, the school's high quality master degrees include: LLM in International Commercial Law; LLM in Housing and Land Law; LLM Media Law and LLM in Criminal Litigation. Each LLM is offered on a full and part-time basis, giving you the freedom to fit your study in around work, family or other commitments you may have.

The College of Law

Admissions, Braboeuf Manor, Portsmouth Road, Guildford GU3 1HA
Freephone: 0800 328 0153
Fax: (01483) 577045
Email: admissions@lawcol.co.uk
Website: www.college-of-law.co.uk

Contact
GDL/LPC/BVC
Freephone:
0800 328 0153
Overseas:
+44 (0)1483 216500
Email: admissions@lawcol.co.uk
LL.M
+44 (0)1483 216500
Website:
www.college-of-law.co.uk

College profile

At The College of Law you'll get the best possible start to your legal career. With centres in Birmingham, Chester, Guildford, London, Manchester and York, the College is the UK's leading provider of legal education. It's innovative courses are designed and taught by lawyers, with a clear focus on building the practical skills, commercial awareness and independent thinking you'll need to succeed. This is supported by an award-winning pro bono programme, the largest and best-resourced careers service in UK legal education and excellent tutor support.

Graduate Diploma in Law (full-time/part-time)

Designed to build knowledge and skills that more than match a law degree – with a clear focus on preparing you for life in practice. Academic training is built around real-life examples and case studies, and you'll be given research assignments that directly reflect the way you'll work as a lawyer. Students who pass the College GDL are guaranteed a place on the College LPC, and if you go on to successfully complete your LPC or BVC at the College, you'll graduate with an LL.B law degree without the need to study or pay for additional modules.

Legal Practice Course (full-time/part-time)

The College LPC is rigorous and practical – equipping you with the skills you need to succeed. It has the widest selection of vocational elective subjects available and uniquely offers three different LPC routes, allowing you to specialise in your chosen field: corporate, commercial & private and public legal services. The majority of teaching is in small, student-centred groups and the course features extensive use of multi-media learning resources. Students who complete this LPC will be a third of the way towards the College's LL.M in Professional Legal Practice.

Bar Vocational Course (full-time/part-time)

The College BVC has been designed to resemble practice as closely as possible. Study follows a logical, realistic process from initial instruction to final appeal, and learning is based around the seven core skills and three knowledge areas stipulated by the Bar Standards Board. Most of your learning will be in small groups, and you'll have plenty of opportunities to put your learning into action through: practitioner evenings, mock trials, court visits, mooting, negotiating and advocacy competitions, and pro bono. Students who complete this BVC will be a third of the way towards the College's LL.M in Professional Legal Practice.

Master's Degrees (supervised online/blended learning)

The College's LL.M Master's degrees are truly professional qualifications and reflect cutting-edge approaches to legal practice. They offer a wide choice of flexible, specialist modules to suit your area of interest and enhance your expertise. These can be studied via supervised online modules, or by blended learning modules that combine online and face-to-face teaching. This will lead to an LL.M in either Professional Legal Practice or International Legal Practice.

Open days

Find out more about The College of Law and its courses by attending an open day or arranging a centre visit. For further details and to book a place, visit www.college-of-law.co.uk/comeandmeetus

Kaplan Law School

Nottingham Law at Kaplan Law School
Palace House, 3 Cathedral Street, London SE1 9DE
Tel: (020) 7367 6400
Email: admissions@kaplanlawschool.org.uk
Website: www.nottingham-kaplan.org.uk

College profile

Kaplan Law School (KLS) offer Nottingham Law School's market leading courses at its central London campus. KLS achieved the highest ratings from the Solicitors' Regulatory Authority (SRA) in its first validation, reflecting the success of the partnership with Nottingham Law School (NLS) and the quality of training provided.

Kaplan is the world's largest diversified training company and provides education to over 48,000 students in the UK every year through 30 national centres.

The Law School faculty are qualified lawyers with a proven record in practice and legal education. They work in close collaboration with NLS faculty to ensure the delivery of a consistently excellent student experience.

The London campus overlooks the River Thames and has been custom-built with state of the art facilities designed to optimize the student and teaching experience. The South Bank location provides excellent transport links, proximity to the City's legal hub and a great social and cultural community.

All students benefit from a proactive and dedicated careers service and pro bono schemes.

GDL: Graduate Diploma in Law (full time)

This one year intensive course is designed for any non-law graduate who intends to become a solicitor or barrister in the UK. Delivered with the same high standards that ensure the NLS 90% pass rates, the KLS GDL effectively covers the core of an undergraduate law degree in 36 weeks. Face to face tuition is a priority and the course is taught through interactive small group sessions and small lecture cohorts.

The KLS GDL also places the academic subjects into a work related context (for example through its Business Enterprises module) so that students are more prepared for practice. All students who successfully complete the GDL will be guaranteed a place on the KLS LPC.

LPC: Legal Practice Course (full time and part time)

The NLS LPC has long been regarded as the industry leader and is the only LPC to receive the SRA's highest rating every year since its inception. KLS offer the same rigorous, professional standards of course design and delivery, reflected in the same highest rating received from the SRA in 2007. The LPC is taught in a practical, experiential method in small group sessions and small lecture cohorts.

From September 2009, the KLS LPC will give you a choice of broad-based or specialist pathways through your LPC. Once you join KLS you can choose to tailor your LPC to a particular area of legal practice. Kaplan Law School also aims to get you ready to practice through its Bridge to Practice programme.

BVC: Bar Vocational Course

KLS plan to offer the NLS Bar Vocational Course (BVC) from September 2010. See www.kaplanlawschool.org.uk/bvc for more information.

Summer School

KLS runs a highly successful Summer School to introduce potential GDL, LPC and BVC students to the skills sets necessary to become a transactional lawyer.
See www.kaplanlawschool.org.uk/summerschool for more information.

Scholarships

Kaplan Law School award two annual scholarships on their LPC or GDL courses. See www.kaplanlawschool.org.uk/scholarship for more information.

Contact

GDL and LPC full time:
apply to: Central Applications Board
Contact:
admissions@kaplanlawschool.org.uk

LPC part time:
apply to: Nottingham Law at Kaplan Law School
Contact:
admissions@kaplanlawschool.org.uk

NOTTINGHAM LAW
KAPLAN
LAW SCHOOL

Nottingham Law School

Nottingham Law School, Belgrave Centre, Nottingham NG1 5LP
Tel: +44 (0)845 845 9090
Email: nls.enquiries@ntu.ac.uk
Website: www.ntu.ac.uk/nls

Contact
Nottingham Law School
Belgrave Centre
Nottingham NG1 5LP
Tel: +44 (0)845 845 9090
Email: nls.enquiries@ntu.ac.uk
Website: www.ntu.ac.uk/nls

Nottingham Law School has partnered with Kaplan Law School to offer NLS's Legal Practice Course and Graduate Diploma in Law from a central London campus as well as from Nottingham.

Legal practice course

The School's highly regarded Legal Practice Course has received the highest possible rating in every Law Society assessment. The LPC is offered by full-time and part-time block study. This course has been designed to be challenging and stimulating for students and responsive to the needs of firms, varying from large commercial to smaller high street practices.

The School is designing a new offering for the Legal Practice Course from 2009 onwards. The programme will allow you to select pathways that lead to a specific type of practice, or maintain a broad based professional legal education if you are not sure yet what type of practice you intend to move to. In addition to the School's broad based LPC, it is planning to offer corporate, commercial and public funding pathways. Nottingham's Legal Practice Course allows you to select your pathway after you get here, rather than having to sign up for a particular route in advance.

Graduate diploma in law

The GDL is offered full-time or by distance-learning. Nottingham Law School's GDL is designed for any non-Law graduate who intends to become a solicitor or barrister in the UK. The intensive course effectively covers the seven core subjects of an undergraduate Law degree. It is the stepping stone to the LPC or BVC, and a legal career thereafter.

GDL students who embark on Nottingham Law School's LPC or BVC will also be eligible for a full LLB on successful completion of that professional course.

Bar vocational course

Nottingham Law School has designed its BVC to develop to a high standard a range of core practical skills, and to equip students to succeed in the fast-changing environment of practice at the Bar. Particular emphasis is placed on the skill of advocacy. Advocacy sessions are conducted in groups of six and the School uses the Guildhall courtrooms for most sessions. The BVC is taught entirely by qualified practitioners, and utilises the same integrated and interactive teaching methods as all of the School's other professional courses. Essentially, students learn by doing and Nottingham Law School provides an environment in which students are encouraged to realise, through practice and feedback, their full potential.

LLM professional practice

Students who complete Nottingham Law School's LPC or BVC can choose to 'top up' to an LLM. The university will award you 90 credit points towards the 180 credits required for the LLM. You will need to complete both a week long summer school programme in June after you have completed your LPC/BVC, and a Professional Practice Dissertation (20,000) on a subject relevant to professional practice in the legal services sector. Students who have not completed their professional studies with Nottingham Law School are still eligible to take this qualification, please contact the university prior as you may need to complete additional modules or provide evidence of learning.

NOTTINGHAM
LAW SCHOOL
Nottingham Trent University

Northumbria Law School

City Campus East, Newcastle Upon Tyne, NE1 8ST
Tel: 0191 227 4433   Fax: 0191 227 4561
Email: nb.admissions@northumbria.ac.uk
Website: www.northumbrialawschool.co.uk

Contact
Law Admissions
Tel: 0191 227 4433
Email:
nb.admissions@northumbria.ac.uk

College profile

Renowned for excellence in learning and teaching and offering an innovative portfolio of programmes at undergraduate, postgraduate and professional levels, Northumbria Law School really is at the forefront of legal education.

The Law School benefits from a well-rounded mix of academics and practitioners, both solicitors and barristers, from the public and private sector and maintains connections with legal practitioners locally and nationally.

Graduate diploma in law (GDL)- full-time/ distance learning/ e-learning

The GDL provides the academic stage for non-law graduates who intend to practise law. Successful Northumbria GDL students are guaranteed a place on Northumbria's LPC and are entitled to a £1,000 discount off LPC or BVC fees (must be studied over consecutive years).

Legal practice course (LPC)- full-time/ part-time

The LPC provides vocational training across a range of subjects and skills, enabling students to learn how to apply their legal knowledge in a practical context. Northumbria Law School was awarded the 'commendable practice' rating across all areas of assessment by the Solicitors Regulation Authority. The school plans to offer the new LPC from September 2009 (subject to validation).

Bar vocational course (BVC) – full-time/part-time

Northumbria Law School is one of only six institutions outside of London to offer the BVC. Lectures which focus on key areas of practice are delivered regularly by senior practitioners in modern, purpose-built accommodation.

LLM – full-time/distance learning

The Law School offers a range of distinctive and innovative Masters programmes which focus on the practical operation of the law.

Facilities

In September 2007 the Law School relocated to a stunning £70m development in the heart of Newcastle, boasting state-of-the-art teaching and learning facilities.

northumbria
UNIVERSITY
Law School

Weightmans is a top 60 law firm with a national presence offering real experience across 17 practice areas.

Our aim is to be both the law firm and employer of choice.

With a reputation built on an open culture, solid values, trust and reliability Weightmans recognises the importance of a happy and well motivated workforce.

Unlike many firms we offer our trainees real legal experience during their training contract, including attendance at court and client meetings. Challenged from the outset, our trainees have the opportunity to demonstrate their talents across a range of seats following a focused training plan.

The quality of our training is an important commercial investment. Our retention rate is high and we want today's trainees to remain at Weightmans and be leaders in our future.

For further information, please visit www.weightmans.com or contact James See on 0151 242 7989

Deadline for applications is 19 July 2009

www.weightmans.com

Birmingham Leicester Liverpool London Manchester
Weightmans is an equal opportunities employer
Weightmans is a limited liability partnership

Solicitors' Practice Areas

Banking and finance

In a nutshell

Banking and finance lawyers may work in any one of the specialist areas described below, but they all deal with the borrowing of money or the management of financial positions. They advise on the legality of an investment (or borrowing) proposition, document the parties' contractual relationship, negotiate with the other party and discuss potential outcomes if problems arise. It's a complex and jargon-heavy area of law.

Straightforward bank lending: a bank lends money to a borrower on documented repayment terms. **Acquisition finance:** a bank lends money to a corporate borrower or private equity sponsor in order to fund its acquisition of another company (read our corporate law section). **Property finance:** a loan is made to enable (usually) a property acquisition or development. It will commonly be backed by the security of a mortgage deed binding property assets but could also involve other types of security. **Project finance:** the money required to allow a project (eg a road or a hospital) to be started, continued or completed. Could be backed by mortgages on property, other assets, rights over company shares or other types of security. **Asset finance:** allows the purchase or leasing of things such as ships, aeroplanes and machinery. The lender normally takes security over the assets in question. **Capital markets:** the borrower issues bonds to investors. Bonds are listed, traded debt instruments. Unlike loans they are actively traded on a market, similar to the way shares are issued and traded. **Securitisation:** essentially this is where a lender wants to sell its loans. It does so by selling them to a shell company, which then issues bonds to the markets. Bond investors get paid from the interest and principal on the loans owned by the shell company. **Islamic finance:** many borrowers, lenders and investors in Muslim countries only participate in transactions if they are Shari'a-compliant. This usually involves specific structuring; for example, payment of interest is not permitted under Shari'a law. Usually a Shari'a scholar must confirm that the product is Shari'a-complaint before it is sent to investors. **Derivatives:** at its most basic, this product lets a company or bank deal with a mismatch between incomings and outgoings. For example, if a UK company sells most of its products to French customers, its income will be in euros but most of its expenditure will be in sterling. A derivative will allow it enter into a swap with a bank to fix the euro/sterling exchange rate for the year so that it does not lose out if the value of the euro goes down against the pound. Derivatives can be used to hedge against, or bet on, almost anything, from foreign exchange and interest rates to the weather.

What lawyers do

- Meet with clients to establish the commercial context of a deal and to understand the specific requirements of the client.
- Negotiate with other lawyers and their clients to agree the terms of the deal and record them accurately in the loan/security documentation. Lenders' lawyers usually produce initial documents. Many deals do not veer far from standard-form documentation, but borrowers' lawyers try to negotiate more favourable terms for their clients. Lawyers on both sides must know when to compromise and when to hold out.
- On complicated or ground-breaking financings, assist with the structuring of the deal and ensure innovative solutions comply with all relevant laws.
- Carry out due diligence – an investigation exercise to verify the accuracy of information passed from the borrower to the lender or from the company raising finance to all parties investing in the deal. If financial instruments, such as bonds, are being offered to investors, the report will take the form of a prospectus and must comply with the requirements of the EU prospectus directive and rules in other countries where the bonds are sold. This can involve onsite meetings for a few days with management of the company, so lawyers learn how their clients' businesses work.
- Gather all parties to complete the transaction, ensuring all agreed terms are covered in the written documents and that all documents have been properly signed and sealed. Just as in corporate deals, many decisions need to be made at properly convened board meetings and recorded in written resolutions.
- Finalise all post-completion registrations and procedures.

The realities of the job

- City firms act for international banks, whereas the work of regional firms is generally simpler and mostly domestic in nature, usually for UK banks and building societies or companies they lend to. If you want to be a hotshot in international finance then it's the City for you. There are plenty of finance jobs that involve international travel, but remember short business trips leave no time for exploration.
- Lawyers need an understanding of where the client wants to be and the legal risks involved in getting

there. This may involve the movement of money across borders and through different currencies and financial products. International deals have an additional layer of difficulty: political changes in a country can render a previously sound investment risky.

- Clients can be demanding and the hours can be long. On the plus side your clients will be dynamic and just as smart as you. It is perfectly possible to build up long-term relationships with investment bank clients, even as a junior.
- Working on deals can be exciting. The team (the lawyers, the client and any other advisers) plus the other side are all working to a common goal, often under significant time and other pressures. Deal closings bring adrenalin highs and a sense of satisfaction.
- Banking and finance requires hard graft and teamwork. There are peaks and troughs as deal flow depends on the buoyancy of the economy.
- You need to become absorbed in the finance world. Read the City pages in your daily newspaper for a taster.

Current issues

- The banking and finance world was in a halcyon period before autumn 2007, with banks lending freely and many law firm finance teams turning in best ever turnover. The credit crunch (call it 'liquidity crisis' – bankers prefer that) has brought a sharp correction to the market. Many major financial institutions have written off billions of pounds of bad debt in 2008 due to exposure to the US sub-prime mortgage crisis so are now more cautious; credit control is tighter and there's much less lending.
- You'll appreciate from the dire reports in the press that bank lending is way down on last year. Deals are still being done, though banks are far more cautious than before. The sorts of mega-deals handled by magic circle or big City firms are currently less common, and even mid-market and regional finance deals are affected.
- Property finance seems to be the area hit hardest by the liquidity crisis. Project finance remains buoyant and property funding in relation to sectors like healthcare or education continues unabated for now.
- The London banking market is more competitive than ever. Once-loyal relationships between clients and their lawyers can no longer be depended upon.

- In big City firms you'll become specialised early on. This may or may not appeal to you, and if it doesn't then a smaller or regional firm may be a better choice.
- Secondments to banks are available, even for trainees. Subsequent moves in-house are common, especially for capital markets work or compliance roles to ensure that banks do not fall foul of financial services regulations.
- If you're interested in banking and finance, read our True Pictures on…

Read our True Pictures on...

Addleshaw Goddard • Allen & Overy • asb law • Ashurst • Baker & McKenzie • Barlow Lyde & Gilbert • Beachcroft • Berwin Leighton Paisner • Bevan Brittan • Bingham McCutchen • Bird & Bird • Blake Lapthorn • Bond Pearce • Brabners Chaffe Street • Browne Jacobson • Burges Salmon • Charles Russell • Cleary Gottlieb Steen & Hamilton • Clifford Chance • Clyde & Co • CMS Cameron McKenna • Cobbetts • Dechert • Denton Wilde Sapte • Dewey & LeBoeuf • Dickinson Dees • DLA Piper US • DMH Stallard • Dundas & Wilson • DWF • Eversheds • Farrer & Co • Field Fisher Waterhouse • Foot Anstey • Freeth Cartwright • Freshfields Bruckhaus Deringer • Geldards • Halliwells • Hammonds • Hay & Kilner • HBJ Gateley Wareing • Herbert Smith • Hill Dickinson • Holman Fenwick Willan • Howes Percival • Hugh James • IBB Solicitors • Ince & Co • Irwin Mitchell • Jones Day • K&L Gates • Latham & Watkins • Lester Aldridge • LG • Linklaters • Lovells • Lupton Fawcett • Mace & Jones • Macfarlanes • Manches • Martineau • Mayer Brown • McDermott Will & Emery • McGrigors • Michelmores • Mills & Reeve • Morgan Cole • Nabarro • Norton Rose • Olswang • Orrick, Herrington & Sutcliffe • Osborne Clarke • Pannone • Pinsent Masons • Reed Smith • Salans • Shoosmiths • Sidley Austin • Simmons & Simmons • SJ Berwin • Skadden, Arps, Slate, Meagher & Flom& Affiliates • Slaughter and May • Speechly Bircham • Stephens Scown • Stephenson Harwood • Stevens & Bolton • Taylor Wessing • TLT • Travers Smith • Trowers & Hamlins • Veale Wasbrough Lawyers • Walker Morris • Ward Hadaway • Watson Burton • Watson, Farley & Williams • Weil, Gotshal & Manges • White & Case • Wragge & Co

Competition and antitrust law

In a nutshell

It is the job of the UK and EU regulatory authorities to ensure that markets function effectively on the basis of fair and open competition. The competition rules in the UK and EU are substantially similar, but the UK bodies concentrate on those rules that have their greatest effect domestically, while EU authorities deal with matters where the rules affect multiple member states. The UK regulators are the Office of Fair Trade (OFT) and the Competition Commission; on matters also affecting other EU countries, it is the European Commission. Additionally, there are industry-specific regulatory bodies, such as Ofcom for the media and telecoms industry.

Competition authorities have extensive investigative powers – including the ability to carry out dawn raids – and can impose hefty fines. The OFT for one has become more proactive and litigation-minded in recent years: in 2008 it scored a High Court victory in the ongoing, prominent bank charges case – an investigation into major lenders like Abbey, Barclays, Clydesdale Bank and HSBC – not to mention handing out the largest ever charge for a competition law infringement, when it fined British Airways £121.5m for colluding with Virgin Atlantic over the price of long-haul passenger fuel surcharges. Meanwhile the European Commission had success at the European Court of First Instance, when it upheld the Commission's decision that Microsoft abused its dominant position by refusing to supply interoperability information to its competitors and tied its Windows Media Player to its Windows PC operating system. This result will probably encourage the pursuit of dominance cases in the future.

What lawyers do

- Negotiate clearance for acquisitions, mergers and joint ventures.
- Advise on the structure of commercial or co-operation agreements to ensure they withstand a competition challenge.
- Deal with investigations by the regulators into the way a client conducts business.
- Bring or defend claims in the Competition Appeal Tribunal (CAT).
- Advising on cross-border trade or anti-dumping measures (preventing companies exporting a product at a lower price than it normally charges in its home market).

- Regulators investigate companies, bring prosecutions and advise on the application of new laws and regulations.

The realities of the job

- You won't get much independence; even junior lawyers work under the close supervision of experienced partners. In the early days, the job involves a great deal of research into particular markets and how the authorities have approached different types of agreements in the past.
- You need a genuine interest in economics and politics.
- The work demands serious academic brainpower twinned with commercial acumen so as to understand how clients run their businesses.
- As a popular area of practice, it's hard to break into. Competition-specific studies – say a master's degree – will enhance your prospects.
- Advocacy is a relatively small part of the job, though in time you could end up appearing in the High Court or CAT. Advocacy skills can also be honed on paper.
- In international law firms you will get to travel abroad and may even work in an overseas office for a while, perhaps in Brussels, which is the hub for European competition work. Fluency in another language can be useful.

Current issues

- On 1 May 2004, when ten new member states were admitted to the EU, antitrust enforcement ceased to be the monopoly of the European Commission and European Court. An EC modernisation regulation effectively handed more power back to member states with respect to the enforcement of Articles 81 and 82 of the Treaty of Rome. Domestic authorities are definitely upping their game and in 2007 as many as 90% of cases applying these principles came from national competition authorities.
- Following the liquidity crisis and a slowing of M&A deal activity, abuse of dominance (like the Microsoft example above) and cartel investigation work is more common than merger control work.
- The remit of the CAT has been widened to allow claims for damages brought by third parties. Private enforcement can be a useful tool for competitor businesses and consumer groups, but thus far has not been extensively utilised, perhaps due to concerns over the cost of proceedings.

- Competition investigations by sector regulators are on the rise, with a substantial increase in appeals of OFT decisions and sector regulators in front of the CAT. The most prominent sector inquiries are in the energy, pharmaceutical, financial services, transport and insurance sectors.

- Regulators now have the power to impose criminal sanctions. This has forced solicitors' firms to consider how they will advise clients on the white-collar crime element of competition law. A few have started to employ specialists; others have formed close ties with boutique white-collar crime firms.

- US-style class actions are appearing and US plaintiff firms are setting up in the UK. Law firms traditionally associated with white-collar crime, such as Peters & Peters and Kingsley Napley, are increasingly involved in criminal cartel defence work.

- There are increased opportunities to work for the regulatory authorities; the OFT, for example, employs many more investigators than before. There is also a trend for lawyers to switch between private practice and working for the regulators.

Read our True Pictures on...

Addleshaw Goddard • Allen & Overy • Ashurst • Baker & McKenzie • Berwin Leighton Paisner • Bird & Bird • Bond Pearce • Burges Salmon • Cleary Gottlieb Steen & Hamilton • Clifford Chance • CMS Cameron McKenna • Denton Wilde Sapte • Dickinson Dees • DLA Piper US • Dundas & Wilson • Eversheds • Field Fisher Waterhouse • Freshfields Bruckhaus Deringer • Herbert Smith • Latham & Watkins • Linklaters • Lovells • Macfarlanes • Martineau • Mayer Brown • McDermott Will & Emery • McGrigors • Nabarro • Norton Rose • Osborne Clarke • Pinsent Masons • Reed Smith • Shoosmiths • Simmons & Simmons • SJ Berwin • Slaughter and May • TLT • Ward Hadaway • Wragge & Co

Construction & projects

In a nutshell

Construction

Construction law can broadly be divided into non-contentious and contentious work. The first involves lawyers helping clients at the procurement stage, pulling together all the contractual relationships prior to building work; the second sees them resolving disputes when things go wrong during or after the build. In the past, the relatively high monetary stakes involved in big projects and the industry trend for recovering building costs through the courts made construction a lengthy litigation-happy practice. About ten years ago a new trend began to take hold and today most new contracts contain a mandatory arbitration procedure to be adopted in case of dispute. Adjudication of disputes has become the industry norm and these follow a swift 28-day timetable. Since the Technology & Construction Court introduced its Pre-Action Protocol many more disputes are resolved through mediation. All this has changed the way lawyers must operate and had a knock-on effect at the contract-drafting stage. Some disputes are so complex that the parties do still choose to slug it out in court.

Projects

Specialist construction lawyers work hand in hand with finance and corporate lawyers to enable projects to come to fruition, whether it's an oil pipeline in Azerbaijan or a new prison in South Wales. A few City firms and the largest US practices dominate the biggest international projects, but there's work countrywide. In the UK the Private Finance Initiative (PFI) – an aspect of Public Private Partnerships (PPP) – is an important source of work, introducing private funding and management into areas that were previously the domain of government. Some law firms consistently act for the project company, usually a 'special purpose vehicle' (SPV) established to build, own and operate the prison or power station or whatever it may be. Often the project company is a joint venture between various 'sponsor' companies – for example the manufacturer of the gas turbines installed in a power station, the construction company that will erect the plant, and the power company that will buy the electricity. An SPV could also be partially owned by a government body or banks. Other firms consistently act for the project promoters, the organisations that commission projects – for example an NHS trust that wants a new hospital. Then there are the firms that act purely on the finance side for banks, guarantors, export credit agencies, governments and international funding agencies.

What lawyers do

Construction: procurement

- Negotiate and draft contracts for programmes of building works. Any such programme involves a multitude of parties including landowners, main contractors, subcontractors, engineers, architects and others.
- Work in conjunction with property lawyers if the client has invested in the land as well as undertaking the building project. Together, lawyers seek and obtain all the necessary planning consents as well as local authority certifications.
- Liaise with the owner's solicitors over matters such as stage payments, architects' certificates and other measures of performance, if the land is not owned by the developer.
- Make site visits during development.

Construction: disputes

- Assess the client's position and gather all related paperwork and evidence.
- Extract the important detail from huge volumes of technical documentation. This evidence is vital in proving the client's case, whether through mediation, arbitration or litigation.
- Follow the resolution methods set out in the contracts between the parties; the TCC Pre-Action Protocol leads to negotiations at an early stage.
- Where a settlement is impossible, issue, prepare for and attend proceedings with the client, usually instructing a barrister to advocate on the client's behalf.

Projects:

- Too varied to list. The field has specialists with excellent drafting and organisational skills in the areas of funding, construction, real estate, planning, energy, telecoms and all aspects of the public sector, including health, education and housing.

The realities of the job

- Drafting skills require attention to detail and careful thought.

- It's essential to keep up to date with industry standards and know contract law and tort inside out.
- People skills are fundamental. Contractors and subcontractors are generally earthy and direct; structural engineers live in a world of complicated technical reports; corporate types and in-house lawyers require smoother handling. You'll deal with them all.
- The construction world (if not construction law firms) is often perceived as a male-dominated environment, but while some clients might see a visit to a lap-dancing club as par for the business entertainment course, there are many successful female construction lawyers, architects and engineers in the business who easily avoid such activity.
- Most lawyers prefer either contentious or non-contentious work, and some firms like their construction lawyers to handle both aspects, so pick your firm carefully.
- A background in construction or engineering is a major bonus because you'll already have industry contacts and chances are you'll be able to combine legal know-how with practical advice – you'll know how the client thinks.
- Projects work demands lawyers who enjoy the challenge of creating a complex scheme and figuring out all its possibilities and pitfalls. Projects can run for years, involving complex, multidisciplinary legal work spanning finance, planning permissions, construction, service and employment issues.

Current issues

- While property finance has been hit hard by the liquidity crisis, investment in public sector public infrastructure projects continues unabated. The length of ongoing projects means there's a lag before any economic downturn hits.
- While health sector investment continues apace in things like complex hospital projects, the popularity of education project PFIs is waning. Nevertheless, urban regeneration is dominating the work of many firms up and down the country, and many local authorities are choosing to shop locally for legal services.
- Lawyers are beginning to see an influx of disputes from the PFI sector. Only ten years old as a model of investment, inadequate original planning and unforeseen problems are generating contentious work.
- New London rail link Crossrail is currently in the planning and development stage, and contractors are eyeing up the construction work. Lawyers are also gearing up for the slew of work, both contentious and non-contentious, that will emanate from the construction of the 2012 Olympic Village, the modification of rail links and general infrastructure redevelopment. It will be interesting to see the effect of EU procurement directives on the tendering process.
- A long list of other major projects – the Broadgate Tower, the Heron Tower, the Shard of Glass and others – point to the next few years being interesting ones for the sector.
- Nearly all international construction and engineering projects are governed to some extent by English or New York law, so experience in this field is internationally marketable. American law firms, in particular, are recruiting experienced English lawyers, so international projects lawyers can command whopping salaries. Top-level arbitration lawyers can expect to work in Singapore, Hong Kong and the Middle East. There are also ample opportunities to work in-house for large construction companies.

Read our True Pictures on...

Addleshaw Goddard • Allen & Overy • Anthony Collins Solicitors • Ashurst • Baker & McKenzie • Barlow Lyde & Gilbert • Beachcroft • Berwin Leighton Paisner • Bevan Brittan • Blake Lapthorn • Bond Pearce • Brabners Chaffe Street • Browne Jacobson • Burges Salmon • Campbell Hooper • Charles Russell • Clifford Chance • Clyde & Co • CMS Cameron McKenna • Cobbetts • Cripps Harries Hall • Davies Arnold Cooper • Denton Wilde Sapte • Dewey & LeBoeuf • Dickinson Dees • DLA Piper US • DMH Stallard • Dundas & Wilson • DWF • Eversheds • Forsters • Freeth Cartwright • Freshfields Bruckhaus Deringer • Geldards • Halliwells • Hammonds • HBJ Gateley Wareing • Herbert Smith • Hill Dickinson • Holman Fenwick Willan • Hugh James • Hunton & Williams • Ince & Co • K&L Gates • Latham & Watkins • Lester Aldridge • Lewis Silkin • LG • Linklaters • Lovells • Mace & Jones • Macfarlanes • Martineau • Maxwell Winward • Mayer Brown • McDermott Will & Emery • McGrigors • Michelmores • Mills & Reeve • Morgan Cole • Nabarro • Norton Rose • Olswang • Osborne Clarke • Pannone • Pinsent Masons • Reynolds Porter Chamberlain • Shadbolt • Shoosmiths • Simmons & Simmons • SJ Berwin • Skadden, Arps, Slate, Meagher & Flom & Affiliates • Slaughter and May • Speechly Bircham • Stephens Scown • Stephenson Harwood • Taylor Wessing • Thring Townsend Lee & Pembertons • TLT • Trowers & Hamlins • Veale Wasbrough Lawyers • Vinson & Elkins • Walker Morris • Ward Hadaway • Watson Burton • Watson, Farley & Williams • Wedlake Bell • White & Case • Wragge & Co

Corporate

In a nutshell

The work of the corporate lawyer is the buying and selling of businesses, business assets or business equity and the arrangement of the finance to carry out these activities. Here are some of the other terms you'll encounter:

Mergers and acquisitions (M&A): deals involving one company buying or joining with another. Depending on the relative size or strength of the businesses it might be seen as a takeover (acquisition) or a fusion of the two businesses (merger). **Corporate restructuring:** involves changes to the composition of the businesses in a company's portfolio or the disposal of certain assets a company no longer requires. Perhaps it wants to concentrate on more profitable parts of its business; perhaps certain activities are no longer seen as acceptable to the general public or will fall foul of regulations. **Stock exchanges:** where companies generate income by making their own shares available for sale and where trading in those stocks and shares are carried out. On the London Stock Exchange (LSE) there's the Financial Times (FTSE) list of companies, the Alternative Investment Market (AIM) and others. New York lists include the Dow Jones and NASDAQ, and there are many exchanges and lists worldwide. **Private equity:** refers to the holding of stock in unlisted companies (those not listed on a stock exchange). Private equity houses or companies offer alternative sources of transaction-funding money to traditional bank lending. (In)Famous private equity houses like Blackstone Capital Partners, 3i and Alchemy Partners provide money for various activities, such as new business start-ups, the expansion of operations, the purchase of a company or management buyout (MBO – when a group of employees/managers decide they want to buy, own and run their company). **Private equity companies:** usually manage multiple funds and invest in numerous businesses simultaneously. Many well-known UK businesses have turned to private equity investment, including DIY retailer Wickes, Legoland Parks, The AA and shoe maker Jimmy Choo. PE companies usually require some money from banks and in the aftermath of the credit crunch, the latter are in a stronger position to dictate terms, meaning the rate of PE-funded deals has slowed. **Venture Capitalists:** smaller-scale version of PE houses, these are individuals or companies looking for a good return by investing in a fledgling or growing business. The BBC2 show *Dragons' Den* is a good example of how this works.

What lawyers do

- Negotiate and draft agreements – this will be done in conjunction with the client, the business that is being bought or sold, other advisers (eg accountants) and any financiers.
- Carry out due diligence – this is an investigation to verify the accuracy of information passed from the seller to the buyer, or from the company raising money to the funder. It establishes the outright ownership of all assets; the status of employees; whether there are outstanding debts or other claims against the company; any environmental or other liabilities that could reduce the value of the business in the future, etc. If shares or bonds are being offered to the public, the report will take the form of a prospectus and must comply with statutory regulations.
- Arrange financing – this could come from banks or other types of investor; they will wish to have some kind of security for their investment, eg owning shares or bonds, taking out a mortgage over property or other assets.
- Gather all parties for the completion of the transaction, ensuring all assets have been properly covered by written documents that are properly signed and sealed. Company law requires that decisions are made at properly convened board meetings and recorded in written resolutions.
- Finalise all post-completion registrations and procedures.

The realities of the job

- Large companies listed on major stock exchanges tend to use the services of large City firms and American firms in London. These firms will also take a large share of the international deals and compete with smaller City and regional firms for business from AIM-listed or privately owned companies.
- Your experiences will be affected by the type of client your firm acts for. Publicly listed companies, major private equity houses and the investment banks that underwrite deals have different demands and attitudes to risk than, say, rich entrepreneurs, owner-managed businesses (OMBs) and small to medium-sized enterprises (SMEs).
- Corporate lawyers need to be conversant in a variety of legal disciplines and know when to refer matters to a specialist in, say, merger control, employment, property or tax.
- This is a very practical area of law, so commercial acumen is a must. The work is largely paper-based, so

you need to be well organised and have good drafting skills.

- Long hours arise through client demand, and their expectations have risen even further with instant communication via mobile phones, e-mail and BlackBerrys. Being surrounded by busy, intelligent, high-achieving people is half the appeal.
- Corporate lawyers work in teams; indeed at times team spirit and adrenaline will be the only things that get you through yet another 20-hour day. It takes time to learn your craft, however, and in the beginning the most junior member of a deal team can get stuck with boring or unrewarding tasks. The banes of the corporate trainee's life are data room management (putting together and caretaking all the factual information on which a deal relies) and bibling (the creation of files containing copies of all the agreed documents and deal information).
- A robust and confident manner is typical; stamina is a must. You have to keep pushing yourself because deals wait for no one.
- The fortunes and schedules of corporate lawyers are tied to the general economy. Corporate lawyers are more likely to experience feast or famine than a steady flow of deals year after year. It is not unheard of for them to experience burnout after a few years.
- You need to become absorbed in the corporate world. Get a taster by reading the City pages in your daily newspaper and if you don't pick up an interest, choose another area of practice pronto.

Current issues

- The liquidity crisis – or credit crunch – has significantly affected the market in 2008. Banks are hesitant to lend except on their own strict terms, so private equity houses are sitting on their funds waiting either for more favourable economic conditions or for things to worsen so they can snap up businesses at cut-price rates. UK mid-market and regional deals are less affected, but few big deals are going ahead in private equity or other spheres.
- Many UK corporate practices are relying on emerging markets – think India, China and energy work in Central Eastern European countries. This is heightening the cosmopolitan nature of much M&A work, with multi-jurisdictional co-ordination of key importance. Because they are largely unaffected by economic variation, many firms are also targeting sovereign wealth funds in the Middle East.
- Sarbanes-Oxley regulations in the USA made London an increasingly attractive financial centre. This is best illustrated in the success of the LSE's AIM market,

although again the area is currently notable mostly for Russian, Middle Eastern or Chinese company flotation.
- The weak dollar means Indian and European companies are picking up bargains in the US market.
- A sound grounding in corporate finance makes an excellent springboard for working in industry. Lawyers move in-house to major companies, tempted by decent hours. Some go to banks, usually as in-house lawyers, occasionally as corporate finance execs or analysts. Company secretarial positions suit lawyers with a taste for internal management and compliance issues.

Read our True Pictures on...

Addleshaw Goddard • Allen & Overy • asb law • Ashurst • Baker & McKenzie • Barlow Lyde & Gilbert • Bates Wells & Braithwaite • Beachcroft • Berwin Leighton Paisner • Bevan Brittan • Bird & Bird • Blake Lapthorn • Bond Pearce • BPE Solicitors • Brabners Chaffe Street • Browne Jacobson • Burges Salmon • Charles Russell • Clarion Solicitors • Cleary Gottlieb Steen & Hamilton • Clifford Chance • Clyde & Co • CMS Cameron McKenna • Cobbetts • Coffin Mew • Covington & Burling • Cripps Harries Hall • Dechert • Denton Wilde Sapte • Dickinson Dees • DLA Piper US • DMH Stallard • Dundas & Wilson • DWF • Edwards Angell Palmer & Dodge • Eversheds • Farrer & Co • Field Fisher Waterhouse • Finers Stephens Innocent • Foot Anstey • Forsters • Freeth Cartwright • Freshfields Bruckhaus Deringer • Geldards • Gordons • Halliwells • Hammonds • Harbottle & Lewis • Hay & Kilner • HBJ Gateley Wareing • Henmans • Herbert Smith • Hill Dickinson • Holman Fenwick Willan • Howes Percival • Hugh James • Hunton & Williams • Irwin Mitchell • Jones Day • K&L Gates • Latham & Watkins • Lewis Silkin • LG • Linklaters • Lovells • Lupton Fawcett • Mace & Jones • Macfarlanes • Manches • Martineau • Mayer Brown • McGrigors • Michelmores • Mills & Reeve • Morgan Cole • Morrison & Foerster • Nabarro • Norton Rose • Olswang • Orrick, Herrington & Sutcliffe • Osborne Clarke • Pannone • Penningtons Solicitors • Pinsent Masons • Prettys • Reed Smith • Reynolds Porter Chamberlain • Salans • Shadbolt • Shoosmiths • Sidley Austin • Simmons & Simmons • SJ Berwin • Skadden, Arps, Slate, Meagher & Flom& Affiliates • Slaughter and May • Speechly Bircham • Stephens Scown • Stephenson Harwood • Stevens & Bolton • Taylor Wessing • Thomson Snell & Passmore • Thring Townsend Lee & Pembertons • TLT • Travers Smith • Trowers & Hamlins • Veale Wasbrough Lawyers • Walker Morris • Ward Hadaway • Watson Burton • Watson, Farley & Williams • Weil, Gotshal & Manges • White & Case • Wilsons • Wragge & Co

Crime

In a nutshell

Criminal solicitors represent defendants in cases brought before the UK's criminal courts. Lesser offences are commonly dealt with exclusively by solicitors in the magistrates' courts; more serious charges go to the Crown Courts, which from an advocacy perspective are essentially still the domain of barristers, not least because most defendants still prefer this. Everyday crime is the staple for most solicitors – theft, assault, drugs and driving offences. Fraud is the preserve of a more limited number of firms. Fraud cases aren't all as long-winded and complicated as the infamous Guinness trial, but they do require a different approach from, say, crimes of violence. Criminal practice is busy, often frantic, with a hectic schedule of visits to police stations, prisons and magistrates' courts, meaning plenty of face-to-face client contact and advocacy.

A summary of the work of the Crown Prosecution Service is given on page 23.

Details of the Public Defender Service are given on page 26.

The criminal courts of England and Wales

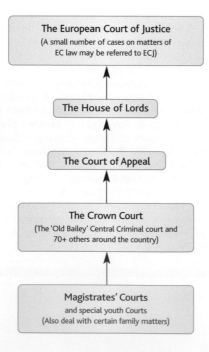

The European Court of Justice
(A small number of cases on matters of EC law may be referred to ECJ)

The House of Lords

The Court of Appeal

The Crown Court
(The 'Old Bailey' Central Criminal court and 70+ others around the country)

Magistrates' Courts
and special youth Courts
(Also deal with certain family matters)

What lawyers do

- Attend police stations to interview and advise people in police custody.
- Visit prisons to see clients on remand.
- Prepare the client's defence using medical and social workers' reports, liaising with witnesses, probation officers, the CPS and others.
- Attend conferences with counsel, ie barristers.
- Represent defendants at trial or brief barristers to do so.
- Represent clients at sentencing hearings, to explain any mitigating facts.
- Fraud solicitors deal with a considerable volume of paperwork and financial analysis. They also need a head for business.

The realities of the job

- Hours are long and can disrupt your personal life. Lawyers who are accredited to work as Duty Solicitors will be on a rota and can be called to a police station at any time of the day or night while on duty.
- Confidence is essential. Without it you're doomed.
- In general crime you'll have a large caseload with a fast turnaround, but this means plenty of advocacy.
- The work is driven by the procedural rules and timetable of the court. Even so, recent figures show that almost a quarter of trials do not proceed on the appointed day, either because defendants or witnesses are absent, or at the request of the CPS.
- Your efforts can mean the difference between a person's liberty or incarceration. You have to be detail-conscious and constantly vigilant.
- You'll encounter horrible situations and difficult or distressed people. Murderers, rapists, drug dealers, conmen, football hooligans, paedophiles. If you have the ability to look beyond the labels and see these people as clients who are deserving of your best efforts then you've picked the right job. Some will have drug or alcohol problems, others will be mentally ill, others just children.
- It can be disheartening to see clients repeat the same poor choices, returning to court again and again.
- Public funding of criminal defence means there's a good helping of bureaucracy. It also means you'll never be a millionaire.
- Trainees in fraud find the early years provide minimal advocacy and masses of trawling through warehouses full of documents. Caseloads are smaller but cases can run for years.

Current issues

- Huge changes in legal aid funding are ongoing and many firms that have previously excelled in crime are moving out of the area entirely or no longer taking publicly funded work. Read page 18 for more detail.

- A change in police station procedures means police are cautioning more and charging less in an effort to meet government targets. This obviously has a knock-on effect on the number of cases available.

- The nationwide roll-out of the LSC's Criminal Defence Service Direct in April 2008 is also affecting the amount of work available for solicitors. The CDS is now providing telephone advice to those detained at police stations over less serious offences – eg drink driving, non-imprisonable offences, breach of bail and warrants.

- In the past, victims have been seen as merely witnesses. Not so since the introduction of the Victim's Personal Statement (VPS). A new victims' advocate scheme has been piloted in the Old Bailey and Crown Courts in Birmingham, Cardiff, Manchester and Winchester.

- The Criminal Justice Act contains provisions concerning the possible abolition of juries for serious fraud cases. Not yet engaged, the proposal was forced onto the back burner as it was met with huge resistance from practitioners, though it will no doubt rear its head again.

- There is an increase in the number of terrorism-related cases.

- More fraud cases are popping up, and with authorities pushing for criminal charges for competition regulation violations, corporations are facing greater criminal liability (see our Competition and antitrust feature on page 96). This kind of work tends to go to the firms that have traditionally handled white-collar crime.

- Check out www.clsa.co.uk for other news and discussion on major developments in criminal practice.

Read our True Pictures on...

Blake Lapthorn • BTMK Solicitors • Clarion Solicitors • DLA Piper • Fisher Meredith • Foot Anstey • Forbes • Herbert Smith • Hugh James • IBB Solicitors • Irwin Mitchell • Pannone

Employment

In a nutshell

Employment lawyers guide their clients through the ever-growing area of workplace-related legislation and are intimately involved in the relationship between employers and employees. The divide between employers' and employees' lawyers is often clear-cut, although many firms do act for both types of client. A few are known for their union connections. Always remember that the nature of a firm's clientele determines on which side of the fence its lawyers end up. Usually the job includes both advisory work and litigation, but when choosing a training contract you may wish to check that this is the case, or if the two roles are split.

Disputes are almost always resolved at an Employment Tribunal, or before reaching one. Tribunals are far less formal than a court, so barristers do not wear wigs or robes and modify their performance, while individuals will often be unrepresented. In these situations the tribunal panel usually forgives their inexperience and may expect the employers' representatives to do so too. Appeals are heard at the Employment Appeal Tribunal (EAT). The grievances leading to litigation fall into the following broad categories: redundancy, unlawful dismissal, breach of contract, harassment and discrimination. This latter category can be brought on the grounds of race, religious or philosophical belief, gender, sexual orientation, disability and age.

What lawyers do

Employees' solicitors

- Advise clients on whether they have suffered unlawful or unfair treatment at work and establish the amount to be claimed. This will either be capped or, in the case of discrimination, can include additional elements to cover loss of earnings, injury to feelings and aggravated damages.
- Gather evidence and witnesses to support the claim.
- Try to negotiate a payment from the employer or take the matter to tribunal. If there is a breach of contract element to the claim, it might be heard in a court rather than a tribunal.
- If the matter does reach tribunal, the solicitor may conduct the advocacy themselves.

Employers' solicitors

- Defend or settle the sorts of claims described above.

- Negotiate employment contracts or exit packages for senior staff.
- Negotiate with unions to avoid or resolve industrial disputes.
- Formulate HR policies and provide training on how to avoid workplace problems.

Realities of the job

- You quickly develop an understanding of human foibles. By their very nature employment cases are filled with high drama.
- Clients may assume your role is to provide emotional support as well as legal advice, so you need to take care to define your role appropriately.
- Acting for employers, you won't always like what you hear, but you still need to protect the clients' interests. Soon enough you'll see the advantage of preventative counselling and training programmes.
- Solicitors who want to do their own advocacy thrive here, although barristers are commonly used for high-stakes or complicated hearings and trials.
- The work is driven by the procedural rules and timetable of the tribunals and courts.
- The law is extensive and changes frequently. You'll read more than your fair share of EU directives.
- Newspapers regularly report the detail of high-profile cases, so it's easy to familiarise yourself with the area.

Current issues

- In October 2006 the Employment Equality (Age) Regulations came into force and will undoubtedly prove significant, and not just for the 'stale, pale males' who will finally have a chance to bring a legitimate grievance. Thus far there has been no avalanche of claims, but businesses have been reviewing their employment policies to ensure compliance, especially in the areas of performance management, training, benefits, retirement and redundancy. One particular area of concern will be recruitment, where job descriptions should not indirectly discriminate. Looking for an energetic graduate for a funky, young firm implies that older candidates need not apply, while requiring a mature person with gravitas and ten years' experience rules out younger applicants. Proving that ten years' experience is strictly necessary for the job may be difficult. Likewise, rejecting a candidate for being overqualified could be discriminatory. Some law firms are dropping the use of the term

PQE (post-qualification experience) in favour of competency-based measures.

- The value of discrimination and harassment claims rises with no sign of abatement, particularly in relation to highly paid City executives at big banks. These cases carry substantial risk to the banks' reputations and illustrate the decision taken by a significant number of companies to fight claims. Disputes over bonuses are also increasingly common, especially in the light of the credit crunch.

- The growth of in-house legal teams in large organisations means employer-led law firms need to specialise and offer added value to their clients. Many companies believe solicitors are too expensive and, privately, some solicitors acknowledge that they are indeed losing work to clients' in-house legal teams.

- Equal pay in the public sector is a big issue and claims against the NHS are on the rise.

- There is huge competition amongst trainees for employment seats, and even more for NQ-level jobs. Consider applying to train at specialist or employment-heavy firms if this is your intended field. In many mainstream firms, gaining exposure to employment work can be a lottery.

Read our True Pictures on...

Addleshaw Goddard • Allen & Overy • Anthony Collins Solicitors • asb law • Ashurst • B P Collins • Baker & McKenzie • Barlow Lyde & Gilbert • Bates Wells & Braithwaite • Beachcroft • Berwin Leighton Paisner • Bevan Brittan • Bircham Dyson Bell • Bird & Bird • Blake Lapthorn • Bond Pearce • BPE Solicitors • Brabners Chaffe Street • Browne Jacobson • Burges Salmon • Charles Russell • Clarion Solicitors • Clifford Chance • Clyde & Co • CMS Cameron McKenna • Cobbetts • Coffin Mew • Cripps Harries Hall • Dechert • Denton Wilde Sapte • Dickinson Dees • DLA Piper US • DMH Stallard • Dundas & Wilson • DWF • Eversheds • Farrer & Co • Foot Anstey • Ford & Warren • Freeth Cartwright • Freshfields Bruckhaus Deringer • Geldards • Gordons • Halliwells • Hammonds • Harbottle & Lewis • Hay & Kilner • HBJ Gateley Wareing • Henmans • Herbert Smith • Higgs & Sons • Hill Dickinson • Howes Percival • Hugh James • IBB Solicitors • Irwin Mitchell • Jones Day • Latham & Watkins • Lester Aldridge • Lewis Silkin • LG • Linklaters • Lovells • Lupton Fawcett • Mace & Jones • Macfarlanes • Manches • Martineau • Mayer Brown • McDermott Will & Emery • McGrigors • Michelmores • Mills & Reeve • Morgan Cole • Nabarro • Norton Rose • Olswang • Osborne Clarke • Pannone • Pinsent Masons • Prettys • Reed Smith • Reynolds Porter Chamberlain • Salans • Shadbolt • Shoosmiths • Simmons & Simmons • SJ Berwin • Slaughter and May • Speechly Bircham • Stephens Scown • Stephenson Harwood • Stevens & Bolton • Taylor Wessing • Thomson Snell & Passmore • Thring Townsend Lee & Pembertons • TLT • Travers Smith • Trethowans • Veale Wasbrough Lawyers • Walker Morris • Ward Hadaway • Warner Goodman • Watson Burton • Watson, Farley & Williams • Wedlake Bell • White & Case • Wilsons • Withers • Wragge & Co

Environment

In a nutshell

Environmental lawyers advise corporate clients on damage limitation, pre-emptive advice and defence from prosecution; the majority of private practitioners work for, rather than stick it to, big business. Opportunities do exist to work in-house for organisations like Greenpeace and Friends of the Earth or for niche public interest firms but these jobs are highly sought after. Another non-commercial option is to work for local authorities, government departments such as the Department for Environment, Food and Rural Affairs (Defra) and regulatory bodies like the Environment Agency.

Environment law overlaps with other disciplines such as property, criminal law, corporate or EU law. Will your client's new housing development destroy a colony of rare newts? Does the manufacturing business your client is buying have a history of environmental problems? Environmental issues can be deal breakers, especially in the modern era of corporate social responsibility. However, the small size of most law firm environmental teams, and the need for practitioners to keep extra strings to their bow, means there are relatively few pure environmental lawyers around.

What lawyers do

Lawyers in private practice:

- Advise on the potential environmental consequences of corporate, property and projects transactions – in effect environmental due diligence.
- Advise on compliance and regulatory issues to help clients operate within regulatory boundaries and avoid investigation or even prosecution by the Environment Agency or other authorities.
- Defend clients when they get into trouble over water or air pollution, waste disposal, emission levels or health and safety. Such cases can involve criminal or civil actions, judicial reviews and even statutory appeals. They may also be the subject of damaging media coverage.

Lawyers working for local authorities:

- Handle a massive variety of work covering regulatory and planning issues plus waste management and air pollution prosecutions.
- Advise the authority on its own potential liability.

Lawyers working for Defra:

- Responsible for litigation, drafting of subordinate legislation, advisory work and contract drafting on any of Defra's varied mandates, be it access to and the protection of the countryside or the maintenance of good water quality and water environments.
- Defra employs over 80 lawyers including trainees on GLS-funded schemes. Broadly it aims to promote sustainable development without compromising the quality of life of future generations.

Lawyers working for the Environment Agency (EA):

- Prosecute environmental crimes, requiring the gathering evidence, preparation of cases and the briefing of barristers.
- Co-operate with government lawyers on the drafting and implementation of legislation.
- The EA has lawyers in Bristol and eight regional bases and is responsible for protecting and enhancing the environment. It also regulates corporate activities that have the capacity to pollute. As such the scope of work stretches from waste management to flood defence, from air quality to environmental impact assessment, from contaminated land to climate change.

The realities of the job

- In this competitive and exacting field, all-round skills are best complemented by a genuine interest in a specific area, say renewable energy, conservation or water pollution. The way in which environmental law spans disciplines requires commercial nous and a good understanding of corporate structures.
- Excellent academics are a must to help wade through, extrapolate from and present research and complex legislation; so too are sound judgement, pragmatism and a sense of improvisation in offering clients the most practical solutions.
- A basic grasp of science helps.
- If you want to change environmental laws or crusade for a better planet, then nail your colours to the public mast. A life in private practice, trying to get a company off the hook for having accidentally discharged three tonnes of mercury into a river may not be for you.
- Client contact is a big feature of this work and relationships can endure over many years. Environmental

risks are inherently difficult to quantify and clients will rely on your gut instincts and powers of lateral thinking.

- What with visits to waste dumps or drying reservoirs, and a workload that can span health and safety matters, corporate transaction and regulatory advice all in one day, this is neither a desk-bound nor a quiet discipline.
- Research constantly advances and legislation is always changing in this field, so you'll spend a lot of time keeping up to date.
- An interest in European law is increasingly useful as more and more EU directives prescribe the boundaries of environmental law in the UK.

Current issues

- Changes in environmental law are coming thick and fast; keep on top of them via websites like www.endsreport.com. You should enhance your CV and prime yourself by joining organisations such as the Environmental Law Foundation (ELF) and the UK Environmental Law Association (www.ukela.org). Most environmental lawyers are members of UKELA and students are welcome to attend events across the country. Look out for UKELA's annual essay and mooting competitions. The charity ELF (www.elflaw.org) provides a referral service for members of the public, organises lectures in London and produces regular newsletters for its members.
- Swathes of new EU Directives are currently impacting the UK.
- The Contaminated Land Regime, introduced in England and Wales seven years ago, means clients acquiring sites can be liable for historic pollution. Now local authorities have woken up to the idea of taking action, the effects of the regime are starting to bite.

- Climate change isn't just for academics any more. Businesses need advice on how to navigate the EU Emissions Trading Scheme and the mechanisms for reducing emissions provided for under the Kyoto Protocol. Environmental lawyers in the top-flight firms are encountering this type of work more and more often. International issues in general are coming to the fore with initiatives like the Equator Principles and Corporate Social Responsibility prominent.
- Finally, energy. We all need it and there isn't going to be enough of it. Scores of renewable energy projects have led to environmental lawyers working alongside planning and project finance colleagues. Oil and gas schemes continue unabated and the prospect of new nuclear installations is also hot.

Read our True Pictures on...

Addleshaw Goddard • Allen & Overy • Ashurst • B P Collins • Baker & McKenzie • Barlow Lyde & Gilbert • Berwin Leighton Paisner • Bircham Dyson Bell • Blake Lapthorn • Bond Pearce • Browne Jacobson • Burges Salmon • Clifford Chance • CMS Cameron McKenna • Denton Wilde Sapte • Dewey & LeBoeuf • Dickinson Dees • DLA Piper US • DMH Stallard • Dundas & Wilson • DWF • Eversheds • Freshfields Bruckhaus Deringer • Geldards • Hammonds • Herbert Smith • Hill Dickinson • Hugh James • Hunton & Williams • Irwin Mitchell • Jones Day • K&L Gates • LG • Linklaters • Lovells • Macfarlanes • Manches • Mayer Brown • McGrigors • Mills & Reeve • Nabarro • Norton Rose • Osborne Clarke • Pinsent Masons • Simmons & Simmons • SJ Berwin • Slaughter and May • Stephens Scown • Stephenson Harwood • Stevens & Bolton • Taylor Wessing • Thring Townsend Lee & Pembertons • Travers Smith • Walker Morris • Watson Burton • Wragge & Co

Family

In a nutshell

Family lawyers deal with almost every aspect of family life – in one or two cases even the moment of conception itself. Day-to-day matters include the legal mechanics and complications relating to marriage, divorce, disputes between cohabitants, inheritance disputes between family members, prenuptial and cohabitation agreements, all matters relating to children and issues arising from registration of same-sex unions under Civil Partnership legislation. Whether working in the family department of a general high street practice with a large caseload of legally aided work, or for a specialist practice dealing with big-money divorces and complex child or international matters, family solicitors are on their feet in court a good deal and fully occupied back in the office.

There is effectively a division within family practice between child law and matrimonial law, with many practitioners devoting themselves exclusively to one or other. Some do plant a foot in each.

What lawyers do

Matrimonial lawyers

- Interview and advise clients on prenuptial agreements, cohabitation arrangements, divorce and the financial implications of divorce. This can involve issues like inheritance and wills, conveyancing, welfare benefits, company law, tax and trusts, pensions and even judicial review (particularly when it comes to public funding issues).
- Prepare the client's case for divorce and settlement hearings, including dealing with witnesses and providing summaries of assets/finances. As such, accountants, financial and pensions advisers, and family lawyers from overseas jurisdictions are familiar faces.
- Attend conferences with counsel – ie meetings with barristers.
- Represent clients in hearings or brief barristers to do so.
- Negotiate settlements and associated financial terms.

Child law lawyers

- In private cases – interview and advise clients (husbands, wives or cohabitants) on the implications of divorce with regard to child contact and residence. In many instances this will result in court action. Deal with disputes between parents or other family members over the residence of, and contact with, children.
- In public cases – represent local authorities, parents, children's guardians or children themselves on matters such as children's care proceedings or abuse in care claims. Social workers, probation officers, psychologists and medical professionals will also be involved in cases.

The realities of the job

- When it comes to relationships and families, no two sets of circumstances will ever be the same. Advocacy is plentiful.
- You will encounter a real mix of clients, some at a joyful moment in their lives, others facing deeply traumatic times or personal problems. A good family law practitioner combines the sensitivity, trustworthiness and capacity for empathy of a counsellor, with the clarity of thought, commercial acumen and communication skills of a hard-nosed lawyer. Your client may treat you as a shoulder to cry on, but you need to retain detachment to achieve the result they need.
- Tough negotiating skills and a strong nerve are must-haves because your work has immediate and practical consequences. How often your client gets to see their children, what happens to their home, their family or their livelihood are all in your hands. The prospect of telling a client that they've lost a custody battle does much to sharpen the mind.
- A pragmatic and real-world outlook is useful, however you'll also need to spend time keeping abreast of legal developments. The Human Rights Act opened up new legal ground, while action groups like Fathers4Justice have intensified the scrutiny on child residence and contact issues. Even matrimonial cases continually push at the boundaries.
- On publicly funded matters you'll face your share of bureaucracy and you'll never earn mega-bucks.

Current issues

- London is arguably becoming the divorce capital of Europe. In the biggest cases, the wealth and assets involved far outstrip the reasonable needs of the parties, and lawyers are glad to now have precedents. The House of Lords' decisions in Miller, where the issue is how to deal with a short marriage, and McFarlane, where the wife had given up a career to raise a family, have provided clarity but left certain issues cloudy. In 2007 the High Court awarded a massive £48m to the wife of insurance magnate John Charman when they divorced. The Court of Appeal upheld the award.

- Cases such as these help explain increased interest in prenuptial agreements. Everyone's heard of a 'pre-nup', but since the arrival in 2005 of same-sex civil partnerships there is also the 'pre-cip'. Lawyers are interested to see how the courts will handle the division of assets following the breakdown of a civil partnership.

- Collaborative law is a new buzzword. For some lawyers it is the way forward for family disputes; others say they've seen it all before with mediation. In short it takes a round-table approach to resolving marital settlements. It doesn't suit every case, and if it doesn't work, the parties must change to new solicitors if they subsequently litigate. The take up of collaborative law is strong in some cities (eg Cambridge and Bath) but negligible elsewhere.

- These are challenging times for the publicly funded lawyer. Many firms are feeling the squeeze and some are choosing to limit, or even cease, legally aided work altogether. This is the case with both matrimonial finance cases and child care proceedings, although some firms have stuck with the latter due to idealistic

commitments. In 2008 the government's implementation of Care Proceedings Reforms, aiming to speed up the resolution of cases involving children and avoid court, caused further consternation. For details see www.justice.gov.uk/guidance/careproceedings.htm

Read our True Pictures on...

Anthony Collins Solicitors • Anthony Gold • Blake Lapthorn • Boodle Hatfield • Brabners Chaffe Street • Burges Salmon • Charles Russell • Clarion Solicitors • Coffin Mew • Collyer Bristow • Cripps Harries Hall • Dickinson Dees • DWF • Farrer & Co • Fisher Meredith • Foot Anstey • Forsters • Gordons • Halliwells • Hay & Kilner • Henmans • Higgs & Sons • Hill Dickinson • Hugh James • IBB Solicitors • Irwin Mitchell • Lester Aldridge • Lupton Fawcett • Mace & Jones • Manches • Michelmores • Mills & Reeve • Morgan Cole • Pannone • Prettys • Reynolds Porter Chamberlain • Speechly Bircham • Stephens Scown • Thomson Snell & Passmore • TLT • Ward Hadaway • Watson Burton • Wilsons • Withers

Intellectual property

In a nutshell

Intellectual property lawyers help protect their clients' highly valuable IP assets in several ways. Acquiring a patent provides the proprietor of a new, industrially applicable invention or process with the exclusive right to work it for a certain period. Acquiring a trade mark provides its owner with a limited monopoly to use the mark on certain goods or services, and a registered design provides the exclusive right to use the design. By contrast, copyright exists as soon as material is created, without the need for any registration: it covers things like music, paintings and drawings, works of literature or reference, databases and web pages. Increasingly the work of IP lawyers is crossing over with other disciplines, not simply IT and life sciences, but also areas such as competition and employment law.

What lawyers do

- Search domestic, European and international registers of patents, trade marks and registered designs to establish ownership of existing rights or the potential to register new rights.
- Take all steps to protect clients' interests by securing patents, trade marks and registered designs; appeal unfavourable decisions; attack decisions that benefit others but harm the lawyer's own client.
- Write letters to require that third parties desist from carrying out infringing activities or risk litigation for damages and an injunction.
- Issue court proceedings and prepare cases for trial, including taking witness statements, examining scientific or technical reports and commissioning experiments and tests. In the world of brand protection, junior lawyers may find themselves conducting consumer surveys and going on covert shopping expeditions.
- Instruct and consult with barristers. Solicitor-advocates can appear in the Patents County Court, but usually recognise the advantages of having a specialist IP barrister for higher court hearings.
- Draft commercial agreements between owners of IP rights and those who want to use the protected invention, design or artistic work. The most common documents will either transfer ownership of the right to another party or grant a licence for them to use it.
- Work as part of a multidisciplinary team on corporate transactions, verifying ownership of IP rights and drafting documents enabling their transfer.

The realities of the job

- Lawyers must be able to handle everyone from sophisticated or pushy company directors to mad inventors and quirky artistic types. Clients come from manufacturing, the hi-tech sector, engineering, pharmaceuticals, agrochemicals, universities and scientific institutions, media organisations and the arts.
- A degree in a relevant subject is common among patent lawyers. Brand and trade mark lawyers need a curiosity for all things creative and must keep up with consumer trends. Both types of IP lawyer need to have a good sense for commercial strategy.
- Attention to detail, precision and accuracy: words are important and you must be meticulous in their use, particularly when drafting.
- In patent and trade mark filing, everything has a time limit. You will live by deadlines.
- The volume of paperwork involved can be huge on patent matters, though on the upside you'll visit research labs or factories to learn about production processes, etc.
- You'll learn that the development of new drugs and inventions is motivated more often by profit than philanthropy. Success or failure in litigation can dramatically affect a company's share price.

Current issues

- The liquidity crisis, coupled with a general growing awareness of intellectual property as a valuable asset has given rise to a renewed interest in protecting IP and led to an increase of work on the transactional side.
- In the UK courts, pharmaceutical patents continue to be heavily litigated along with an increasing number of telecoms patents. The constant battle between innovative pharmaceutical companies and generic ones continues, with patent entitlement being a hot topic.
- In the trade mark arena clients seek strategic advice and want to tackle the growing problem of counterfeit goods. On the contentious side there are more cases involving domain names.
- Convergence between different forms of media and technology is giving rise to sensitive issues of data protection.
- The trend of digitalisation is bringing online copyright issues to prominence.
- Manufacturing, pharmaceutical and research companies employ patent specialists and there are in-house

legal teams at all the large pharmaceutical companies. In the media, major publishers and television companies employ in-house IP lawyers.

- The name of the Patent Office has been changed to UK Intellectual Property Office (UKIPO) to reflect its broader functions.

- European patent attorneys and trade mark agents work as a parallel profession. You can find out more about what they do on our website. There are early signs of convergence between the legal profession and these other professions. Some law firms provide in-house trade mark and patent-filing services, allowing clients to sidestep patent and trade mark attorneys.

Read our True Pictures on...

Addleshaw Goddard • Allen & Overy • Arnold & Porter • Ashurst • Baker & McKenzie • Beachcroft • Berwin Leighton Paisner • Bird & Bird • Blake Lapthorn • Bond Pearce • Brabners Chaffe Street • Bristows • Browne Jacobson • Burges Salmon • Charles Russell • Clarion Solicitors • Clifford Chance • CMS Cameron McKenna • Cobbetts • Coffin Mew • Covington & Burling • Cripps Harries Hall • Davies Arnold Cooper • Dechert • Denton Wilde Sapte • Dickinson Dees • DLA Piper US • DMH Stallard • Dundas & Wilson • DWF • Eversheds • Field Fisher Waterhouse • Finers Stephens Innocent • Foot Anstey • Freeth Cartwright • Freshfields Bruckhaus Deringer • Geldards • Gordons • Halliwells • Hammonds • Harbottle & Lewis • Herbert Smith • Hill Dickinson • Howes Percival • Irwin Mitchell • Jones Day • K&L Gates • Lewis Silkin • Linklaters • Lovells • Lupton Fawcett • Macfarlanes • Manches • Martineau • Mayer Brown • McDermott Will & Emery • McGrigors • Mills & Reeve • Morgan Cole • Morrison & Foerster • Nabarro • Olswang • Osborne Clarke • Pannone • Pinsent Masons • Reed Smith • Reynolds Porter Chamberlain • Shadbolt • Shoosmiths • Simmons & Simmons • SJ Berwin • Slaughter and May • Speechly Bircham • Stevens & Bolton • Taylor Wessing • Thring Townsend Lee & Pembertons • TLT • Walker Morris • Ward Hadaway • Watson Burton • Wedlake Bell • White & Case • Wiggin • Withers • Wragge & Co

- **Changing times:** In a less buoyant economy the volume of litigation generally increases. We should see an increase in the number of claims made in the UK courts, and by way of other methods of dispute resolution.

Litigation/dispute resolution

In a nutshell

Litigation solicitors help their clients resolve disputes, either at trial or by reaching a settlement before a matter gets anywhere near court. Commercial disputes range from unpaid bills or unfulfilled contract terms to problems between landlords and tenants, infringement of IP rights, construction-related claims, the liabilities of insurers, shipping cases, defective products cases, media and entertainment industry wrangles… the list is endless. Confusingly, there are two divisions of the High Court – the Chancery Division and the Queen's Bench Division – and each hears different types of case. The following diagram shows the court system in England and Wales, and the Bar section of this guide summarises the differences between the QBD and Chancery Divisions on page 849.

Unless settled by initial negotiations, disputes are concluded either by court litigation or some alternative form of dispute resolution, hence the interchangeability of 'litigation' and 'dispute resolution' as names for departments within law firms. The most common of these other methods are arbitration and mediation, the former often being stipulated as the preferred method in commercial contracts, the latter commonly achieved through structured negotiations between the parties, overseen by an independent mediator. Even alternative methods have problems: mediation is not necessarily adequate for complex matters, and there's a perception that opponents can use it as a means of 'bleeding' money from each other or a covert form of interrogation.

What lawyers do

Claimants' lawyers

- Advise clients on whether they have a valid claim.
- Gather evidence and witnesses to support the claim.
- Where correspondence with the prospective defendant does not produce a satisfactory result, issue court proceedings or embark on a process of alternative dispute resolution.
- Represent clients at pre-trial hearings and case management conferences.
- Attend conferences with counsel (ie barristers) and brief barristers to conduct advocacy in hearings, trials and arbitrations.
- Attend trials arbitrations and mediations with clients; provide assistance to barristers when they are being used.

Defendants' lawyers

- Advise on the validity of a claim brought against a client, making recommendations as to whether to settle or fight.
- Prepare defences, including gathering all evidence and witness statements.
- Represent clients at pre-trial hearings and case management conferences.
- Attend conferences with counsel and brief barristers to conduct advocacy in hearings, trials and arbitrations.
- Attend trials, arbitrations and mediations with clients; provide assistance to barristers when they are being used.

The realities of the job

- The work is driven by the procedural rules and timetable of the courts. Good litigators understand how best to operate within the system, while also developing winning case strategies.
- Litigation generates a phenomenal amount of paperwork and young litigators spend much of their time sifting through documents, scheduling and copying them in order to provide the court and all other parties with an agreed bundle of evidence.
- Litigators need to express themselves concisely and precisely.
- Unless the value of a claim is small, the solicitor's job is more about case preparation than court performance. Solicitor-advocates are gaining ground, and once properly qualified they can appear in the higher courts; however, barristers still dominate court advocacy.
- Trainee workloads largely depend on the type of firm and the type of clients represented. Big City firms won't give trainees free rein on huge international banking disputes – they might not even go to court during their training contract – but they will be able to offer a small contribution to headline-making cases. Firms handling much smaller claims will often expect trainees to deal with all aspects of a case, from drafting correspondence and interim court applications to meetings with clients and settlement negotiations.
- There are a number of litigation-led law firms that handle cases of all sizes and these represent the best opportunities for a litigation-heavy training contract.

Current issues

- The Solicitors Regulation Authority requires all trainee solicitors to gain some contentious experience

The civil courts of England and Wales

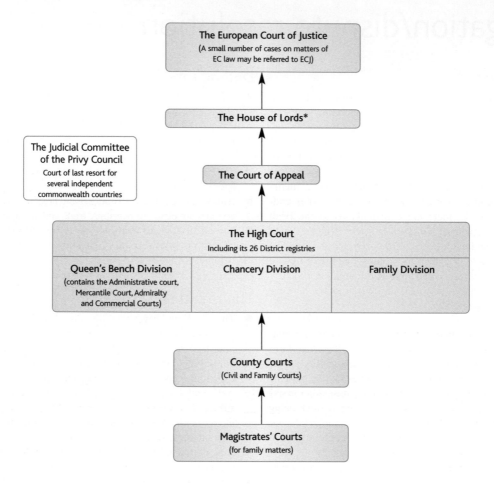

Other Specialist Courts

Employment Tribunals

Lands Tribunals

Leasehold Valuation Tribunals

VAT and Duties Tribunals

General and Special Commissioners (Tax)

Asylum & Immigration Tribunals

Europe

ECJ: Any UK court can refer a point of law for determination if it relates to EU law. The decision will be referred back to the court where the case originated.

European Court of Human Rights: Hears complaints regarding breaches of human rights.

* Following the constitutional reform Act 2005, a supreme court for the UK is being established to replace the House of Lords as the last appeal court. Opening at Middlesex Guildhall in Oct 2009, the intention is to legally and physically separate the judiciary from the legislature with judges no longer being members of the House of Lords.

and people tend to discover early on whether they are suited to this kind of work. Increasingly in big City firms, this contentious requirement can be fulfilled by a litigation crash course.

- The competition for litigation jobs at NQ level in large firms is fierce. Consider litigation-led firms if you are certain of your preference for this type of work.

- Despite a few firms like Herbert Smith and Hammonds starting up in-house advocacy units, the courts are still dominated by barristers, who are still felt to have the edge when it comes to the skills and expertise needed to advocate. If you are determined to become both a solicitor and an advocate, certain areas of practice have more scope for advocacy – eg family, crime, employment and lower-value civil litigation.

- In general there is now less domestic commercial litigation, but more international litigation and arbitration, often from Russia and Eastern Europe. London is a popular forum for international arbitration.

- The economic downturn has seen an increase in general disputes, especially financial and property. Fallout from the credit crunch may also lead to banks suing each other or being sued by hedge funds.

- Banking/finance and regulatory litigation is expected to increase as a consequence of an agreement between the Securities & Exchange Commission (SEC) and the Financial Services Authority (FSA). Also starting to bite are the corporate governance provisions contained in the Financial Services and Markets Act 2000 (the UK equivalent of Sarbanes-Oxley legislation in the USA), designed to counteract Enron-like corporate skulduggery.

Read our True Pictures on...

Addleshaw Goddard • Allen & Overy • Anthony Collins Solicitors • Arnold & Porter • asb law • Ashurst • B P Collins • Baker & McKenzie • Barlow Lyde & Gilbert • Bates Wells & Braithwaite • Beachcroft • Berwin Leighton Paisner • Bevan Brittan • Bingham McCutchen • Bird & Bird • Blake Lapthorn • Bond Pearce • Boodle Hatfield • BPE Solicitors • Brabners Chaffe Street • Bristows • Browne Jacobson • Burges Salmon • Charles Russell • Clarion Solicitors • Clifford Chance • Clyde & Co • CMS Cameron McKenna • Cobbetts • Collyer Bristow • Covington & Burling • Cripps Harries Hall • Davies Arnold Cooper • Dechert • Denton Wilde Sapte • Dewey & LeBoeuf • Dickinson Dees • DLA Piper US • DMH Stallard • Dundas & Wilson • DWF • Edwards Angell Palmer & Dodge • Eversheds • Field Fisher Waterhouse • Finers Stephens Innocent • Foot Anstey • Forbes • Ford & Warren • Forsters • Freeth Cartwright • Freshfields Bruckhaus Deringer • Geldards • Gordons • Halliwells • Hammonds • Hay & Kilner • HBJ Gateley Wareing • Henmans • Herbert Smith • Hill Dickinson • Holman Fenwick Willan • Howes Percival • Hugh James • IBB Solicitors • Ince & Co • Irwin Mitchell • Jones Day • K&L Gates • Latham & Watkins • Lester Aldridge • Lewis Silkin • LG • Linklaters • Lovells • Lupton Fawcett • Mace & Jones • Macfarlanes • Manches • Martineau • Mayer Brown • McDermott Will & Emery • McGrigors • Michelmores • Mills & Reeve • Morgan Cole • Nabarro • Norton Rose • Olswang • Osborne Clarke • Pannone • Penningtons Solicitors • Pinsent Masons • Prettys • Reed Smith • Reynolds Porter Chamberlain • Salans • Shadbolt • Shoosmiths • Simmons & Simmons • SJ Berwin • Skadden, Arps, Slate, Meagher & Flom& Affiliates • Slaughter and May • Speechly Bircham • Stephens Scown • Stephenson Harwood • Stevens & Bolton • Taylor Wessing • Thomson Snell & Passmore • Thring Townsend Lee & Pembertons • TLT • Travers Smith • Trethowans • Trowers & Hamlins • Veale Wasbrough Lawyers • Walker Morris • Ward Hadaway • Watson Burton • White & Case • Wilsons • Withers • Wragge & Co

Personal injury and clinical negligence

In a nutshell

Personal injury and clinical negligence lawyers resolve claims brought by people who have been injured, either as a result of an accident or through flawed medical treatment. Injuries can be as simple as a broken wrist resulting from tripping over a wonky paving stone, or as serious as a fatal illness caused by exposure to dangerous materials. Clinical negligence cases could result from a failure to treat or diagnose a patient, or treatment going wrong, be it a botched boob job or a baby born brain-damaged.

The claimant lawyer usually acts for one individual, but sometimes a claim may be brought by a group of people – this is a class action or multiparty claim. The defendant lawyer represents the party alleged to be responsible for the illness or injury. In most PI cases the claim against the defendant will be taken over by the defendant's insurance company, which will then become the solicitor's client. Local authorities are common defendants for slips and trips, and employers end up on the hook for accidents in the workplace. In a majority of clinical negligence cases the defendant will be the NHS, although private medical practitioners and healthcare organisations are also sued.

What lawyers do

Claimant solicitors

- Determine the veracity of their client's claim and establish what they have suffered, including how much income they have lost and any expenses incurred.
- Examine medical records and piece together all the facts. Commission further medical reports.
- If the defendant doesn't make an acceptable offer of compensation, issue court proceedings.

Defendant solicitors

- Try and avoid liability for their client and, if and when this looks unachievable, resolve the claim for as little as possible.
- Put all aspects of the case to the test. Perhaps the victim of a road traffic accident (RTA) wasn't wearing a seatbelt; perhaps the claimant has been malingering.

Both solicitors

- Manage the progress of the case over a period of months, even years, following an established set of procedural rules.
- Attempt to settle the claim before trial.
- If a case goes to trial, brief a barrister and shepherd the client through the proceedings.

The realities of the job

- The work is driven by the procedural rules and timetable of the court.
- There is a mountain of paperwork to manage and produce, including witness statements and bundles of evidentiary material.
- You can't be squeamish and must deal with medical issues and records.
- Claimant lawyers have face-to-face contact with large numbers of clients. Good people skills are needed.
- Defendant lawyers build long-term relationships with insurance companies.
- PI lawyers have large caseloads, especially when dealing with lower-value claims.
- There is some scope for advocacy, although barristers are used for high-stakes or complicated hearings and trials. Solicitors appear at preliminary hearings and case management conferences.

Current issues

- Conditional Fee Agreements (CFAs) – commonly known as no-win, no-fee agreements – continue to be hotly debated and, despite changes to simplify their application, are not always popular with solicitors.
- The Compensation Act 2006 contains new provisions relating to the law of negligence and breach of statutory duty.
- You may have seen claims management companies – sometimes derided as claims farmers – advertising on the TV. Despite some degree of regulation being introduced, they cause concern to lawyers because they can sometimes adopt unscrupulous tactics. The practice of claims farmers selling cases on to solicitors is under intense scrutiny.
- The sector is awaiting a Ministry of Justice report that could have far-reaching effects – especially for lower value PI claims – by upping the lower limit of compensation that can be given.
- The recent House of Lords ruling that pleural plaques (caused by asbestos) claims are non-compensatable

has invalidated huge numbers of cases. If an appeal in Scotland is successful, it may have knock-on effects south of the border.

- A number of claimant law firms, including several of the most well known in the field, have come under fire for their part in the distribution of a £7bn government-backed compensation scheme for sick miners. At least 50 firms of solicitors have been referred to the Solicitors Regulations Authority and 17 firms to the Solicitors Disciplinary Tribunal.

- If, as envisaged by the Legal Services Act, companies such as Tesco enter the market for legal services, they are likely to have a big impact.

- Opinion is split as to whether there is a growing compensation culture in Britain. Those who recognise one say CFAs must shoulder much of the blame; those who don't, say that increased difficulties in securing legal aid have led to a reduction in the number of claims brought.

- Clin neg lawyers are concerned about the likely effects of the NHS Redress Act 2006, which gives the power to introduce a scheme allowing lower-value claims to be handled by the NHS without going to court. Obviously this would cut away some of the lawyers' bread-and-butter work.

Read our True Pictures on...

Anthony Collins Solicitors • Anthony Gold • asb law • Barlow Lyde & Gilbert • Beachcroft • Bevan Brittan • Blake Lapthorn • Bond Pearce • BPE Solicitors • Browne Jacobson • Capsticks • Charles Russell • Coffin Mew • Davies Arnold Cooper • DLA Piper US • Dundas & Wilson • DWF • Eversheds • Field Fisher Waterhouse • Foot Anstey • Forbes • Ford & Warren • Freeth Cartwright • Halliwells • Hay & Kilner • HBJ Gateley Wareing • Henmans • Hill Dickinson • Hugh James • IBB Solicitors • Irwin Mitchell • Michelmores • Mills & Reeve • Morgan Cole • Nabarro • Pannone • Penningtons Solicitors • Reynolds Porter Chamberlain • Shoosmiths • Stephens Scown • Thomson Snell & Passmore • Thring Townsend Lee & Pembertons • Trethowans • Veale Wasbrough Lawyers • Ward Hadaway

Private client and charities

In a nutshell

You have money. Perhaps a mountain of cash or maybe a carefully accumulated nest-egg, but either way you need to know how best to control it, store it and pass it on: enter the private client lawyer. Solicitors advise individuals, families and trusts on wealth management; whilst some offer additional matrimonial and small-scale commercial capability, others focus exclusively on highly specialised tax and trusts, or wills and probate.

Whether it's for a multinational organisation such as the Red Cross, or for a slightly more local concern such as The Whitley Bay Fund for Disadvantaged Minors, specialised charities lawyers advise on all aspects of a not-for-profit organisation's activities.

What lawyers do

Private client lawyers

- Draft wills in consultation with clients and expedite the implementation of wills after death. Probate involves the appointment of an executor and the settling of an estate. Organising a house clearance or even a funeral is not beyond the scope of a lawyer's duties.
- Advise clients on the most tax-efficient and appropriate structure for holding money. If trusts are held in an offshore jurisdiction, lawyers must ensure their clients understand the foreign law implications.
- Advise overseas clients interested in investing in the UK, and banks whose overseas clients have UK interests.
- Assist clients with the very specific licensing, sales arrangement and tax planning issues related to ownership of heritage chattels (individual items or collections of cultural value or significance).

Charities lawyers

- Advise charities on registration, reorganisation, regulatory compliance (such as Charities Commission investigations) and the implications of new legislation.
- Offer specialist trusts and investment expertise.
- Advise on quasi-corporate and mainstream commercial matters; negotiate and draft contracts for sponsorship and the development of trading subsidiaries; manage property issues and handle IP concerns.
- Charities law still conjures up images of sleepy local fundraising efforts or, alternatively, working on a trendy project for wealthy benefactors. In the wide middle ground you could be working with a local authority, a local library and four schools to establish an after-school homework programme, or you could rewrite the constitution of a 300-year-old church school to admit female pupils. Widespread international trust in British charity law means that you could also establish a study programme in Britain for a US university, or negotiate the formation of a zebra conservation charity in Tanzania.

The realities of the job

- An interest in other people's affairs is helpful. A capacity for empathy, coupled with impartiality and absolute discretion are the hallmarks of a good private client lawyer. Whether it's little old ladies with their savings in a stocking, well-heeled, excessively moneyed City gents, or fabulously flash celebrities, you'll need to be able to relate to and earn the trust of your clients.
- Despite not being as helter-skelter as some fields, the technical demands of private client work can be exacting and an academic streak certainly goes a long way, especially when it comes to tax and accounts matters.
- An eye for detail and a rigorous approach will help you see through the mire of black letter law (and regular new legislation) so as to spot the loopholes and clever solutions that will save your clients most money.
- The 'green wellies, two smelly Labradors and a 1950s Land Rover' stereotype of the typical client is far from accurate: lottery wins, property portfolios, massive City salaries and successful businesses all feed the demand for legal advice.
- The combination of practical, technical and social skills means it is a testing discipline. If you are wavering between private clients and commercial clients, charities law might offer a nice balance.

Current issues

- The private client world is becoming increasingly internationalised. Wealthy people are selecting a wider geographical spread of assets and London has become a hub for the management of these assets. Many clients come from Russia, the Middle East, the USA, India and France.
- HMRC is clamping down on tax avoidance and the role trusts can play in inheritance tax planning. Ever-increasing property values mean that, on death, more and more little old ladies' assets are getting caught in a net really intended to catch bad guys.
- A Charities Bill is currently held up in the House of Commons, following its successful trip through the

Lords in 2005. Charity lawyers are frustrated at the delay, but are for the most part anticipating a Bill that will clarify and simplify the registrations and incorporations of new charities.

- After an interminably long wait, the Charities Act 2006 was finalised. The Act addresses fundamental questions about what constitutes a charity and what 'public benefit' means. It also provides for greater regulation in some areas, and greater freedom for charities in others.

- Firms right across the country bemoan a dearth of young lawyers who can claim to be true private client specialists. It looks like a good time to put your hand up and be counted!

Read our True Pictures on...

Addleshaw Goddard • Allen & Overy • Anthony Collins Solicitors • asb law • B P Collins • Baker & McKenzie • Bates Wells & Braithwaite • Berwin Leighton Paisner • Bircham Dyson Bell • Blake Lapthorn • Boodle Hatfield • Brabners Chaffe Street • Browne Jacobson • Burges Salmon • Campbell Hooper • Charles Russell • Clarion Solicitors • Clifford Chance • Cobbetts • Collyer Bristow • Cripps Harries Hall • Dickinson Dees • DMH Stallard • Farrer & Co • Foot Anstey • Forsters • Freeth Cartwright • Geldards • Gordons • Halliwells • Harbottle & Lewis • Hay & Kilner • HBJ Gateley Wareing • Henmans • Herbert Smith • Higgs & Sons • Hill Dickinson • Howes Percival • Hugh James • IBB Solicitors • Irwin Mitchell • Lester Aldridge • LG • Lupton Fawcett • Macfarlanes • Martineau • Michelmores • Mills & Reeve • Morgan Cole • Osborne Clarke • Pannone • Penningtons Solicitors • Pinsent Masons • Speechly Bircham • Stephens Scown • Stevens & Bolton • Taylor Wessing • Thomson Snell & Passmore • Thring Townsend Lee & Pembertons • Trowers & Hamlins • Veale Wasbrough Lawyers • Ward Hadaway • Watson Burton • Wedlake Bell • Wilsons • Withers

Property/real estate

In a nutshell

Property lawyers are essentially transactional lawyers. They have fairly similar jobs to their corporate law colleagues; the only real difference is that real estate deals require an extra layer of specialist legal and procedural knowledge and there aren't quite so many regulatory authorities breathing down their necks. The work centres on buildings and land of all types – cinemas, supermarkets, churches, million-pound mansions, farms, factories, housing estates – and even the most oblique legal concepts have a bricks-and-mortar or human basis to them, for example, you can physically see and touch a right of way or a flying freehold. It is common for lawyers to develop a specialism within this field, say residential conveyancing, mortgage lending and property finance, development projects, retail or office leasing, social housing, agricultural land or the leisure and hotels sector. Most firms have a property department, and the larger the department the more likely the lawyers are to specialise. As for the difference between 'property' and 'real estate', there isn't any; the terms are entirely interchangeable.

What lawyers do

- Negotiate sales, purchases and leases of land and buildings, and advise on the structure of deals. Record the terms of an agreement in legal documents.
- Gather and analyse factual information about properties from the owners, surveyors, local authorities and the Land Registry.
- Prepare reports for buyers and anyone lending money.
- Manage the transfer of money and the handover of properties to new owners or occupiers.
- Take the appropriate steps to register new owners and protect the interests of lenders or investors.
- Advise clients on their responsibilities in leasehold relationships, and how to take action if problems arise, eg non-payment of rent or disrepair.
- Help developers get all the necessary permissions to build, alter or change the permitted use of properties.

The realities of the job

- Property lawyers have to multi-task. A single deal could involve many hundreds of properties; a filing cabinet could contain scores of files, all of them at a different stage in the process.
- As the work is so paper-based you must be well organised.
- Good drafting skills require attention to detail and careful thought. Plus you need to keep up to date with industry trends and standards.
- Some clients get stressed and frustrated; you have to be able to explain legal problems in lay terms.
- While there will be site visits, this is mainly a desk job with a lot of time spent on the phone to other solicitors, estate agents, civil servants and technical consultants.
- Most instances of solicitor negligence occur in this area of practice. There is so much that can go wrong.
- Your days will be busy, but generally the hours are predictable. You'll rarely be called into a meeting in the wee hours.

Current issues

- The increasing sophistication of the UK real estate market means more deals involve complex funds or joint ventures. It is not uncommon for high-value deals to be structured as corporate transactions, so that a buyer can acquire a company that owns property rather than the property itself.
- A lack of UK property for domestic and overseas investors to target has encouraged the development of more sites for resale at a profit. Until the credit crunch there was definitely more interest in investment and development and investors were getting bored of paying silly money for UK property when they could get a better deal elsewhere, say in Germany, France or Eastern Europe. Since the credit crunch activity has started to drop off and property lawyers have begun to worry about the deal flow turning into a trickle.
- The domestic and European hotels and leisure sector has witnessed an increasing amount of consolidation, and there has been a lot of money chasing the best-performing assets.
- London for sale! A number of trophy properties were sold in the past year or so – the Gherkin for £600m; CityPoint for £650m and HSBC's HQ for a staggering £1.09bn.
- Urban regeneration projects have featured high on the agenda along with Olympic preparations. The London Olympics and Paralympic Games Act 2006 created the Olympic Delivery Authority, responsible for building and delivering the 2012 Games.
- Real Estate Investment Trusts (REITs), originally developed in the USA, have become a useful means of channelling investment into real estate. Several of the

UK's biggest property companies have taken advantage of the system and converted to REIT status.
- Procedures are becoming increasingly streamlined and managed electronically.
- Having previously undergone recruitment drives, UK law firms must now face the prospect of making residential conveyancers and commercial property lawyers redundant. The process has already started.

Read our True Pictures on...

Addleshaw Goddard • Allen & Overy • Anthony Collins Solicitors • Anthony Gold • asb law • Ashurst • B P Collins • Bates Wells & Braithwaite • Beachcroft • Berwin Leighton Paisner • Bevan Brittan • Bircham Dyson Bell • Bird & Bird • Blake Lapthorn • Bond Pearce • Boodle Hatfield • BPE Solicitors • Brabners Chaffe Street • Browne Jacobson • Burges Salmon • Campbell Hooper • Charles Russell • Clifford Chance • Clyde & Co • CMS Cameron McKenna • Cobbetts • Coffin Mew • Cripps Harries Hall • Davies Arnold Cooper • Dechert • Denton Wilde Sapte • Dickinson Dees • DLA Piper US • DMH Stallard • Dundas & Wilson • DWF • Eversheds • Farrer & Co • Field Fisher Waterhouse • Finers Stephens Innocent • Fisher Meredith • Foot Anstey • Forsters • Freeth Cartwright • Freshfields Bruckhaus Deringer • Geldards • Gordons • Halliwells • Hammonds • Harbottle & Lewis • Hay & Kilner • HBJ Gateley Wareing • Henmans • Herbert Smith • Higgs & Sons • Hill Dickinson • Howes Percival • Hugh James • IBB Solicitors • Irwin Mitchell • Jones Day • K&L Gates • Lester Aldridge • Lewis Silkin • LG • Linklaters • Lovells • Lupton Fawcett • Mace & Jones • Macfarlanes • Manches • Martineau • Maxwell Winward • Mayer Brown • McGrigors • Michelmores • Mills & Reeve • Morgan Cole • Nabarro • Needham & James • Norton Rose • Olswang • Orrick, Herrington & Sutcliffe • Osborne Clarke • Pannone • Penningtons Solicitors • Pinsent Masons • Prettys • Reed Smith • Salans • Shadbolt • Shoosmiths • Simmons & Simmons • SJ Berwin • Slaughter and May • Speechly Bircham • Stephens Scown • Stephenson Harwood • Stevens & Bolton • Taylor Wessing • Thomson Snell & Passmore • Thring Townsend Lee & Pembertons • TLT • Travers Smith • Trethowans • Trowers & Hamlins • Veale Wasbrough Lawyers • Walker Morris • Ward Hadaway • Watson Burton • Wedlake Bell • White & Case • Wilsons • Withers • Wragge & Co

Public interest

In a nutshell

Human Rights lawyers protest injustice enshrined in law and fight for principle at the point of intersection between a state's powers and individuals' rights. Cases usually relate in some way to the UK's ratification of the European Convention on Human Rights (the Convention) through the Human Rights Act 1998 (HRA) and crop up in criminal and civil contexts, often through the medium of judicial review, a key tool in questioning the decisions of public bodies. Civil contexts include claims regarding the right to education or community care under the Mental Health Act, cases of discrimination at work and, because the Act enshrines in law the right to family life, even family issues. Criminal contexts could relate to complaints against the police, prisoners' issues, public order convictions arising out of demonstrations, or perhaps extradition on terror charges.

Immigration lawyers deal with both business and personal immigration matters, the former having been embraced by the present government in its quest to manage economic migration. In this more lucrative area, lawyers assist highly skilled migrants to obtain residency or leave to remain in the UK, and help non-nationals to secure visas for travel abroad. They also work with companies that need to bring in employees from overseas. Personal immigration lawyers represent individuals who have fled persecution in their country of origin, and for whom return could mean death or torture. They also take on cases for people whose right to stay in the UK is under threat or indeed entirely absent.

What lawyers do

Human rights lawyers:

- Advise clients (predominantly individuals but sometimes groups in class actions) on how to appeal a decision made or action taken by a public body, whether an institution such as the police, a local authority, a court, or a branch of government.
- Collect evidence, take witness statements, prepare cases and instruct barristers.
- Pursue cases through the procedural stages necessary to achieve the desired result. The final port of call for some human rights cases is the European Court of Justice (ECJ), so lawyers need to be fully conversant with both UK and European laws.

Business immigration lawyers:

- Advise and assist businesses or their employees in relation to work permits and visas. They need to be fully conversant with all current schemes, such as those for highly skilled migrants and investors.
- Prepare for, attend and advocate at tribunals or court hearings, where necessary instructing a barrister to do so.

Personal immigration lawyers

- Advise clients on their status and rights within the UK.
- Secure evidence of a client's identity, medical reports and witness statements and prepare cases for court hearings or appeals. Represent clients at these hearings or instruct a barrister to do so.
- Handle an immense amount of unremunerated form filling and legal aid paperwork.

The realities of the job

- A commitment to and belief in the values you're fighting for are essential in this relatively low-paid area. Work in the voluntary sector for orgnisations like the Refugee Council, or taking on important cases pro bono, can provide the greatest satisfaction.
- Sensitivity, empathy and sympathy are absolutely essential qualities because you'll often be dealing with highly emotional people, those with mental health issues or those who simply don't appreciate the full extent of their legal predicament.
- Strong analytical skills are required to pick out the legal issues you can change from the socio-economic ones beyond your control.
- In the battle against red tape, bureaucracy and institutional indifference, organisational skills and a vast store of patience are valuable assets.
- Opportunities for advocacy are abundant, which means that knowledge of court and tribunal procedures is a fundamental requirement. Often cases must pass through every possible stage of appeal before they can be referred to judicial review or the ECJ.
- There's enormous competition for training contracts in the field. Voluntary work at a law centre or specialist voluntary organisation (eg the Howard League for Penal Reform), or membership of Liberty or Justice will help.
- Because much of the work is funded publicly, the firms who specialise in these areas of work don't usually offer attractive trainee salaries or sponsorship through law school.

Current issues

- Issues of asylum and people seeking permission to stay in the UK on human rights grounds never cease to arouse strong opinions.
- The advent of the Freedom of Information Act, and increased transparency in the public sector in line with Article 6 of the Convention, mean law firms have seen a greater willingness from the public to challenge the decisions of public authorities.
- The interface between terrorism and public law, and between public law and the HRA, has become even more acute, as evidenced by the furore surrounding the Counter-Terrorism Bill and its 42-day detention clause.
- The Convention continues to have a serious impact on coroners. The number of inquests continues to proliferate, with prison deaths and military deaths dominating the field.
- Because of the surplus of asylum and special educational needs cases in the Administrative Court, urgent healthcare cases are now taking weeks to get to permission stage, a significant problem for the NHS.
- Following the Freedom of Information Act 2000 and the Environmental Information Regulations 2004, the development of information rights continues to be a major feature both for businesses and pressure groups.
- In immigration law there have been many modifications of late, with rules and regulations affecting the highly skilled migrant programme and people applying for leave to remain or settle in the UK. A new points-based immigration system is effective from late 2008.
- Legislative change, which will transfer responsibility for processing and granting work permits to employers' HR departments, is likely to create more advisory work for lawyers.

Read our True Pictures on...

Addleshaw Goddard • Allen & Overy • Anthony Collins Solicitors • Ashurst • Baker & McKenzie • Barlow Lyde & Gilbert • Bates Wells & Braithwaite • Beachcroft • Berwin Leighton Paisner • Bevan Brittan • Bircham Dyson Bell • Bird & Bird • Blake Lapthorn • Bond Pearce • Browne Jacobson • Capsticks • Charles Russell • Clifford Chance • Clyde & Co • CMS Cameron McKenna • Cripps Harries Hall • Denton Wilde Sapte • Dickinson Dees • DLA Piper US • DMH Stallard • Dundas & Wilson • Edwards Angell Palmer & Dodge • Eversheds • Farrer & Co • Field Fisher Waterhouse • Fisher Meredith • Freshfields Bruckhaus Deringer • Geldards • Herbert Smith • Irwin Mitchell • Latham & Watkins • Lewis Silkin • LG • Lovells • Manches • Martineau • McGrigors • Mills & Reeve • Morgan Cole • Nabarro • Norton Rose • Olswang • Pannone • Penningtons Solicitors • Pinsent Masons • Reynolds Porter Chamberlain • Simmons & Simmons • Slaughter and May • Speechly Bircham • Stephenson Harwood • Taylor Wessing • Trowers & Hamlins • Veale Wasbrough Lawyers • Walker Morris • Wragge & Co

Shipping

In a nutshell

Shipping lawyers deal with the carriage of goods or people by sea, plus any and every matter related to the financing, construction, use, insurance and decommissioning of the ships that carry them (or sink carrying them, or are arrested carrying them or are salvaged carrying them). Despite being centred around specialist firms, or relatively self-contained practices within larger firms, the discipline offers varied challenges. The major division is between wet work relating to accidents or misadventure at sea and dry work that involves the land-based, commercial and contractual side of shipping. Wet work is broadly speaking tort-based, concerning disputes arising from collision, salvage, total loss and modern day piracy, while dry work relates to contracts like charter parties, bills of lading, ship construction or refitting, sale of goods agreements or ship financing. In extension, disputes or litigation relating to contracts means there is also a contentious side to dry work. While some lawyers in the area may be generalists, it is more common to specialise.

What lawyers do

Wet lawyers

- Act swiftly and decisively at a moment's notice to protect a client's interests and minimise any loss.
- Travel around the world to assess the condition of a ship, interview crew or witnesses and prepare a case.
- Handle court and arbitration appearances, conferences with barristers and client meetings.
- Take witness statements and advise clients on the merits of and strategy for cases.

Dry lawyers

- Negotiate and draft contracts for ship finance and shipbuilding, crew employment, sale and purchase agreements, affreightment contracts, and the registration and re-flagging of ships.
- May specialise in niche areas such as yachts or fishing, an area in which regulatory issues feature prominently.
- Deal with similar tasks to wet lawyers as relating to contractual disputes.
- Are less likely to jet off around the world at the drop of a hat if focusing on non-contentious dry work.

The realities of the job

- Wet work offers the excitement of international assignments and clients, so lawyers need to react coolly to sudden emergencies and travel to far-flung places to offer practical and pragmatic analysis and advice.
- Despite the perils and pleasures of dealing with clients and instructions on the other side of the world, back in the office shipping law has little of the all-night culture about it. Hours are likely to be steady beyond those international-rescue moments.
- Non-contentious work touches on the intricacies of international trade, so it's as important to keep up with sector knowledge as legal developments.
- Dealing with a mixed clientele from all points on the social compass, you'll need to be just as comfortable extracting a comprehensible statement from a Norwegian merchant seaman as conducting negotiations with major financers. Shipowners, operators, traders and charterers, P&I clubs and hull underwriters will all come onto your radar.
- Contentious cases are driven by the procedural rules and timetable of the court or arbitration forum to which the matter has been referred. A solid grasp of procedure is as important as a strong foundation in tort and contract law.
- Some shipping lawyers do come from a naval background or are ex-mariners, but you won't be becalmed if the closest comparable experience you've had is steering Tommy Tugboat in the bath, as long as you evince a credible interest in the discipline.
- Though not quite 'no place for a lady', parts of the shipping world are still male dominated. Women lawyers and clients are more commonly found on the dry side.
- If you decide to move away from shipping law, non-contentious experience should allow a transition into asset or more general finance. A few years of contentious shipping law should leave you with a solid grounding in commercial litigation.
- In the UK, shipping law is centred around London and a few other port cities. Major international centres include Pireaus in Greece, Hong Kong and Singapore. Some trainees even get to work in these locations.

Current issues

- Increasingly there is a crossover between shipping, energy and international trade. Liquefied natural gas (LNG) is a big driver, with Floating Production, Storage and Offshore Loading (FPSO) taking much of the limelight. FPSO installations are big news in the Caspian Sea, the Middle East, West Africa and the Far East. One knock-on effect is the extent to which UK firms are now working with lawyers in these regions, and sending their own lawyers to work overseas.

- The rise of China as an economic power is impacting on the cargo market, on shipbuilding and on financing. Most shipyards are fully booked for the rest of this decade.
- A boom in shipping has led to increased levels of resales of ships.
- P&I clubs are beginning to employ more in-house lawyers.
- Super yachts! Despite the credit crunch, the wealth of Russian oligarchs and Middle Eastern families keeps the international luxury yacht market hot.

Read our True Pictures on...

Allen & Overy • Barlow Lyde & Gilbert • Berwin Leighton Paisner • Clifford Chance • Clyde & Co • Denton Wilde Sapte • DLA Piper US • Eversheds • HBJ Gateley Wareing • Hill Dickinson • Holman Fenwick Willan • Ince & Co • Linklaters • Norton Rose • Prettys • Reed Smith • Shoosmiths • Simmons & Simmons • Stephenson Harwood • Watson, Farley & Williams

Sports, media and entertainment law

In a nutshell

Advertising and marketing lawyers offer advice to ensure a client's products or advertisements are compliant with industry standards, plus general advice on anything from contracts between clients, media and suppliers, to employment law, corporate transactions and litigation. Entertainment lawyers assist clients in the film, broadcasting, music, theatre and publishing industries with commercial legal advice on contract, employment litigation and intellectual property law, among other things. Strictly speaking, sports lawyers work in an industry sector rather than a specific legal discipline, and firms draw on the expertise of individuals from several practice groups. Sports lawyers may represent clubs, individual sportspeople, governing bodies or companies interested in offering sponsorship or funding. They may work in-house at a sports broadcaster. Advice encompasses regulatory matters, media issues, advertising and image rights, plus general corporate and commercial wisdom. Reputation management lawyers advise clients on how best to protect their own 'brand', be this through a defamation claim or an objection to invasion of privacy.

What lawyers do

Advertising and marketing lawyers

- Copy clearance to ensure advertising campaigns comply with legislation such as the Consumer Protection Act or regulatory codes controlled by the Advertising Standards Agency or Ofcom.
- Advise on comparative advertising, unauthorised references to living persons, potential trade mark or other intellectual property infringements.
- Defend clients against allegations that their work has infringed regulations or the rights of third parties. Bring complaints against competitors' advertising.

Entertainment lawyers

- Offer production companies advice on every stage of the creation of programmes and films, from research and development, to production and marketing, sponsorship and tie-ins.
- Assist on the complicated banking and secured lending transactions that ensure financing for a film.
- Help engage performers; negotiate a multitude of ancillary contracts; negotiate distribution and worldwide rights; and manage defamation claims.

Music lawyers

- Advise the three key components of the music industry: major recording companies, independent labels and talent (including record producers and songwriters as well as artists).
- Advise on contracts, such as those between labels and bands, or between labels and third parties, eg websites selling downloads and ringtones.
- Offer contentious and non-contentious copyright and trade mark advice relating to music, image rights and merchandising.
- Offer criminal advice when the things get truly rock 'n' roll.

Theatre and publishing lawyers

- Advise theatre and opera companies, producers, agents and actors on contracts, funding and sponsorship/merchandising.
- Advise publishing companies and newspapers without an in-house legal team on contractual, licensing, copyright and libel matters.

Sports lawyers

- Assist on contract negotiations, be they between clubs and sportspeople, agents and players, sporting institutions and sponsors, broadcasters and sports governing bodies.
- Handle varied employment law issues.
- Advise on corporate or commercial matters such as takeovers, public offerings, debt restructuring and bankruptcy, or the securing and structuring of credit to finance stadium redevelopments.
- Enforce IP rights in the lucrative merchandise market and negotiate on matters affecting a sportsperson's image rights.
- Work on regulatory compliance issues within a sport or matters relating to the friction between sports regulations and EU/national law.
- Offer reputation management and criminal advice.

Reputation management

- Claimants' lawyers advise individuals – commonly celebrities, politicians or high-profile businessmen – on the nature of any potential libel action or breach of privacy claim, usually against broadcasters or publishers, before it either settles or goes to court.

127

- Defendants' lawyers advise broadcasters and newspapers or other publishers on libel claims brought against them. With the burden of proof on the defendant, the lawyer's job is to help prove that what was published caused no loss to the claimant or was not in fact libellous.
- Help clients stay out of trouble by giving pre-publication advice to authors, editors or production companies.

The realities of the job

- Advertising lawyers must have a good knowledge of advertising regulations, defamation and intellectual property law. The work is real world and fast-paced – a campaign that comes out today might need to be pulled tomorrow for legal reasons.
- Clients are creative, lively and demanding. The issues thrown up can be fascinating and must be dealt with creatively.
- Many advertising disputes will be settled via regulatory bodies but some, particularly IP infringements, end in litigation.
- Entertainment lawyers need to be complete immersed in their chosen media and have a good grasp of copyright and contract law.
- Clients look to you for the rigour and discipline they may rarely exercise themselves. This is a sector where who you know makes a big difference, so expect to put in serious time getting your face known.
- Sports lawyers need to be proactive, passionate and creative and have bags of commercial nous. They must be able to deal with people involved at all levels of all sports. Some organisations may be institutionally conservative or structurally opaque and suspicious of outsiders.
- Reputation management lawyers need a comprehensive understanding of libel laws and a willingness to think laterally.
- Individual claimants will be stressed and upset, so people skills, patience and resourcefulness are much needed.
- Solicitors prepare cases but barristers almost always get the glory attached to presenting cases in court.

Current issues

- There have been developments in libel law. The 'qualified privilege' defence previously established in 2001 in Reynolds v Times Newspapers was re-examined when George Galloway MP sued *The Daily Telegraph*. Time will tell just how much impact the decision in Max Mosley's privacy case against the *News of the World* will have on what newspapers feel they can publish.
- The popularity among claimants of no-win, no-fee agreements has led to an increase in the number of privacy and defamation claims brought.

- In the world of sport, the 2012 Olympics are keeping lawyers busy and football has filled the headlines. The sale of the Premier League's television and radio rights achieved a higher than ever figure and these were separated into a number of different packages and sold separately, both domestically and internationally. Several Premier League clubs have been the subject of corporate takeovers.
- Although record companies' profits are on a downward spiral, consumer enthusiasm for new music and back catalogues has never been higher. Lawyers are busy working on rights issues, as file sharing and illegal downloading cause headaches for those trying to turn a profit. Live events are the biggest money spinners these days, while artists like Radiohead have embraced new technology to sell their albums directly to fans and Prince actually gave his latest album away free with a national newspaper.
- Broadcasting is changing rapidly, and with the number of media growing, content providers are falling over themselves to reach their target audiences, whether it's content on TV, Internet repeats, downloading online, mobile phones, Apple iPods or on-demand systems.
- The book-publishing sector is tentatively embracing the digital age, having been stung by the CD ROM flop in the 90s. With Google digitising entire libraries and the gradual launch of the e-book, things are set to change.
- New tax credits for the financing of films have resulted in less collaboration between British filmmakers but bigger budgets for projects.

Read our True Pictures on...

Addleshaw Goddard • Allen & Overy • Arnold & Porter • Baker & McKenzie • Bates Wells & Braithwaite • Berwin Leighton Paisner • Bird & Bird • Blake Lapthorn • Brabners Chaffe Street • Bristows • Campbell Hooper • Charles Russell • Clifford Chance • CMS Cameron McKenna • Collyer Bristow • Denton Wilde Sapte • DLA Piper US • Dundas & Wilson • Eversheds • Farrer & Co • Field Fisher Waterhouse • Finers Stephens Innocent • Freshfields Bruckhaus Deringer • Geldards • Halliwells • Hammonds • Harbottle & Lewis • Herbert Smith • Hill Dickinson • Hugh James • K&L Gates • Lewis Silkin • LG • Linklaters • Lovells • Macfarlanes • Manches • Mayer Brown • McDermott Will & Emery • Morgan Cole • Olswang • Osborne Clarke • Pinsent Masons • Reed Smith • Reynolds Porter Chamberlain • Sheridans • SJ Berwin • Slaughter and May • Taylor Wessing • Teacher Stern • Travers Smith • Walker Morris • Wiggin • Wragge & Co

Tax

In a nutshell

Tax lawyers ensure that clients structure their business deals or day-to-day operations such that they take advantage of breaks and loopholes in tax legislation while staying on the right side of the law. Although predominantly an advisory area of practice, on occasion matters veer into the territory of litigation.

What lawyers do

Tax lawyers in private practice:

- Handle tax planning for clients, making sure they understand the tax ramifications of the purchase, ownership and disposal of their assets, including advice on structuring corporate portfolios in the most tax-efficient way.
- Offer transactional advice when working with corporate and other lawyers on, say, the structure of an M&A deal, a joint ventures or the acquisition of a large property portfolio.
- Deal with investigations or possibly litigation resulting from prosecution by HM Revenue & Customs (HMRC) for not paying enough tax. Litigation is always conducted against or brought by the government.

HMRC lawyers:

- Investigate companies and bring prosecutions.
- Advise on how new laws apply to different situations.
- Defend cases brought against the government.

The realities of the job

- This is an intellectually rigorous, even cloistered area of law and ideally suited to the highly intelligent.
- Corporate tax lawyers are very well paid, treated respectfully by their colleagues and find intellectual stimulation in their work.
- Clients demand that their lawyers not only have the ability to translate and implement complex tax legislation, but can also advise how to structure deals in a legitimate and tax-efficient way that avoids trouble from HMRC.

- If you don't already wear specs, you will after a couple of years of poring over all that black letter law. The UK has more pages of tax legislation than almost every other country. The law also changes every year.
- Extra qualifications, such as the Chartered Tax Adviser exams, will be useful.
- It is not uncommon for lawyers to switch between government jobs and private practice. A number of tax barristers were once solicitors.

Current issues

- Since the Inland Revenue and HM Customs & Excise merged to form HMRC, there has been a more assertive approach to clamping down on tax avoidance. HMRC also revised its Litigation and Settlement Strategy, reducing the frequency with which it offered deals to avoid litigation. Consequently, firms with once purely transactional tax practices are now building their litigation capabilities.
- Real Estate Investment Trusts (REITs) now allow property portfolios to be invested in trusts to, among other things, avoid capital gains tax, meaning tax lawyers need to get their teeth into the complex tax structuring surrounding these vehicles.
- In the current cautious economic conditions big deals are less common, but companies feeling the pinch are keener than ever to save money on the most tax-efficient structuring possible. This means tax lawyers are coming to the fore on deals.
- Following Marks & Spencer's landmark win against HMRC in 2005 (finding that some aspects of UK tax legislation do not comply with European law), tax lawyers are more likely to advise litigation against HMRC to recover overpaid tax.
- Law firms have come into their own in relation to tax advice. Before Enron it looked like accountancy firms were taking over. Companies now prefer to take advice from advisers who are separate from their auditors.

Read our True Pictures on...

Addleshaw Goddard • Allen & Overy • Ashurst • Berwin Leighton Paisner • Blake Lapthorn • Browne Jacobson • Burges Salmon • Charles Russell • Cleary Gottlieb Steen & Hamilton • Clifford Chance • CMS Cameron McKenna • Dechert • Denton Wilde Sapte • Dickinson Dees • DLA Piper US • Dorsey & Whitney • Dundas & Wilson • Eversheds • Field Fisher Waterhouse • Freeth Cartwright • Freshfields Bruckhaus Deringer • Hammonds • Herbert Smith • Irwin Mitchell • Jones Day • Latham & Watkins • LG • Linklaters • Lovells • Macfarlanes • Mayer Brown • McDermott Will & Emery • McGrigors • Mills & Reeve • Nabarro • Norton Rose • Olswang • Osborne Clarke • Pannone • Pinsent Masons • Reynolds Porter Chamberlain • Sidley Austin • Simmons & Simmons • SJ Berwin • Skadden, Arps, Slate, Meagher & Flom& Affiliates • Slaughter and May • Stephenson Harwood • Taylor Wessing • Travers Smith • Walker Morris • Weil, Gotshal & Manges • Wragge & Co

Technology, telecoms and outsourcing

In a nutshell

Technology lawyers differ from general commercial advisers because of their specific industry know-how. They combine a keen understanding of the latest developments and advances in various technologies with a thorough knowledge of the ever-changing law that regulates, protects and licenses them. As forms of media and new technologies converge – eg on-demand TV, football highlights on mobile phones – clients have come to rely on technology lawyers' skills of innovation and imagination in offering rigorous legal solutions to maximise and protect income and ideas. There are plenty of job opportunities and the majority of the top 50 firms possess dedicated groups of lawyers. Even within many smaller commercial firms there are specialists and a number of niche firms have emerged.

What lawyers do

- Advise on commercial transactions and draft the requisite documents to implement them. There is a heavy emphasis on risk management, such as advising on the way in which a software agreement can prevent potential litigation in the future.
- Assist in the resolution of disputes, commonly by arbitration or other settlement procedures as this is a court-averse sector. Many disputes relate to software or hardware that doesn't do exactly what it says on the tin, or simply doesn't work at all.
- Help clients police their IT and web-based reputation and assets. Cyber-squatting, ownership of database information and the Data Protection Act are common topics.
- Give clients mainstream commercial, corporate and finance advice.
- Specialised outsourcing lawyers represent customers and suppliers in the negotiation and drafting of outsourcing agreements for the provision of IT or other services by a third party.

The realities of the job

- You need to be familiar with the latest regulations and their potential impact on your client's business. How do you make the purchase of a ringtone by text a legally binding contract? Does a website need a disclaimer? What measures should your client take to protect data about individuals gathered from a website?
- You need a good grasp of the jargon of your chosen industry, firstly to write contracts, but also so you can understand your clients' instructions. You have to know your WLAN from LAN, your 3G from GPRS and your ISPs from your SMSs. Read trade journals like *Media Lawyer* and *Wired*, or magazines such as *Computer Weekly* or *New Scientist*.
- The ability to think laterally and creatively is a must, especially when the application of a client's technology or content throws up entirely new issues.
- In this frontier world, gut instinct matters. One in-house lawyer made what looked a risky move from BT to little-known internet auction site eBay. Six years later he moved to head up the legal team of eBay's broadband-based phone service Skype, a perfect example of the convergence of internet and telephone technology that is forcing companies like BT to rethink strategy.
- In the outsourcing arena, high-end private sector work involves complex, high-value and increasingly multi-jurisdictional outsourcings, and such deals are mostly handled by larger law firms. In the public sector, deals involve UK government departments, local authorities and the suppliers of services to those entities.

Current issues

- Digital convergence throws up many legal problems, as the business opportunities created by new technologies move beyond the capacity of existing legal or regulatory structures to contract or protect. Copyrighted content being transferred onto handheld devices like mobile phones or mp3 players, film or TV programme downloads from the internet… the list is practically endless.
- Legislation and regulations, such as those upholding the freedom of information regime and the waste electronic and electrical equipment disposal regime, are also creating work, not least after high-profile public and private customer data loss scandals in the past year. Cross-border issues relating to data protection are becoming more common.
- IT outsourcing began in the late 1980s, followed by business process outsourcings (BPOs) that involve handing responsibility to third-party service providers for functions like human resources, finance and accounting. Smart outsourcing – the concept of outsourcing parts of a company, one part at a time, often using different suppliers – is in vogue at present, while Eastern Europe is the hot new offshoring location.
- Vtesse Networks is taking a case to the European Court to discover whether the preferential rates paid

by BT for its broadband cable amounts to illegal state aid. If successful it could end up transforming the prices internet providers pay for broadband cable.

- The NHS Connecting for Health national database project is rumbling on: Accenture pulled out and then the project waved goodbye to Fujitsu, which is likely to be replaced by BT.

Read our True Pictures on...

Addleshaw Goddard LLP • Allen & Overy LLP • Ashurst • Baker & McKenzie • Barlow Lyde & Gilbert LLP • Beachcroft LLP • Berwin Leighton Paisner LLP • Bevan Brittan LLP • Bird & Bird • Blake Lapthorn • Bond Pearce LLP • Bristows • Burges Salmon LLP • Charles Russell LLP • Clifford Chance LLP • Clyde & Co LLP • CMS Cameron McKenna LLP • Covington & Burling LLP • Dechert LLP • Denton Wilde Sapte • DLA Piper US LLP • DMH Stallard • Dundas & Wilson • DWF LLP • Eversheds LLP • Field Fisher Waterhouse LLP • Foot Anstey • Freshfields Bruckhaus Deringer LLP • Geldards LLP • Halliwells LLP • Harbottle & Lewis LLP • Herbert Smith LLP • Hugh James • Hunton & Williams LLP • Jones Day • K&L Gates • Latham & Watkins LLP • Linklaters • Lovells LLP • Manches LLP • Martineau • Mayer Brown LLP • McGrigors LLP • Mills & Reeve LLP • Morgan Cole • Morrison & Foerster LLP • Nabarro LLP • Norton Rose LLP • Olswang • Osborne Clarke • Pinsent Masons • Shadbolt LLP • Shoosmiths • Simmons & Simmons • SJ Berwin LLP • Slaughter and May • Speechly Bircham LLP • Stephenson Harwood • Stevens & Bolton LLP • Taylor Wessing LLP • Travers Smith • Wedlake Bell • White & Case LLP • Wragge & Co LLP

The True Picture

The True Picture reports on 150 firms in England and Wales, ranging from the international giants to small regional practices. Most handle commercial law, although many also offer private client experience.

The True Picture

We're bored by the same tired lines used in many recruitment brochures. You know, the ones that tell you Smashing, Great & Partners is different from all the other firms because of its friendly culture in which everybody is down-to-earth and where approachable partners operate an open-door policy...

How we do our research

Every year we spend eight months compiling the True Picture reports on 150 firms in England and Wales, ranging from the international giants to small regional practices. Our purpose is to get to the heart of what you need to know about a prospective employer – what it can really offer you in terms of work and working environment. You'll want to know how many hours a day you'll be chained to your desk, the tasks that will keep you occupied during those hours and who you'll be working with. Importantly, you'll want to know about a firm's culture and whether colleagues will turn into party animals or party poopers come Friday night.

Most of our chosen firms handle commercial law, although many also offer private client experience. There are a few general practice firms offering publicly funded advice to their local communities. To take part in the True Picture a firm must provide a complete list of its trainees. After checking the list is complete, we randomly select a sample of individuals for telephone interviews. Our sources are guaranteed anonymity to give them the confidence to speak frankly. The True Picture is not shown to the law firms prior to publication; they see it for the first time when this book is published.

Trainees tell us why they chose their firm and why others might want to. We put on our serious faces and talk about seat allocation, the character and work of different departments, the level of supervision and what happens to people on qualification. And we flirt shamelessly to get the gossip on firm politics, office oddities and after-hours fun. We look for the things trainees agree upon, and if they don't agree we present both sides of the argument. We have no axe to grind – our only agenda is to give you the fairest and most detailed view there is. That's why we call it the True Picture.

What kind of firm do I choose?

Your choice of firm will be based on location, size and the practice areas available... then it's a matter of chemistry.

Some firms are stuffier, some are more industrious and some are very brand-aware and involve trainees heavily in marketing activities. Some work in modern open-plan offices; others occupy buildings long past their sell-by date. Some focus on international business; others are at the heart of their local business communities. Some concentrate on contentious work, others transactional. The combinations of these variables are endless.

What we found out this year...

Despite the economic downturn, retention rates for the class of 2008 have not been too bad at most firms. Usually, around 80% of qualifiers stay with the law firms that trained them, and 2008 was no different. We try not to concentrate too much on current market conditions when writing the True Picture as we recognise that things may have changed by the time our readers start their training. However, we also recognise that the climate of 2008/09 affects the fortunes and market positions of law firms, and this in turn has a bearing on what firms will be like in 2011 and beyond. Just days before this book went to print investment bank Lehman Brothers and Bradford & Bingley became the latest casualties of the credit crunch. Wiser minds than ours are uncertain as to where current market conditions will lead us, so we've no hesitation in saying it's impossible to predict which firms will tighten their belts and make redundancies and which will take a long-term outlook and carry on hiring. Of course one man's misfortune is another man's gold rush, and while real estate and corporate or finance-focused firms will feel the pinch, insolvency lawyers and litigators are set for a busy few years.

If you intend to use retention rates as a determining factor in your choice of firm, do be wary of the statistics being bandied around. Law firms make their own rules on how to calculate retention rates – you may not be getting a full picture from them. For this reason we collect our own statistics and include them in each law firm feature. We have collated statistics since 2000 and publish them on our website.

The other things we just can't predict are law firm mergers or closures. Thankfully, the latter are rare, but mergers are a regular thing in the profession these days. When firms merge, trainees' contracts are honoured, though of course it does mean that new recruits find themselves in a different firm to the one they signed up to.

...and across the board

- Some seats are more popular than others. The perfect example is employment law.
- Levels of responsibility vary between departments. In property you might have your own small files. In corporate you will generally work in a very junior capacity as part of a team.
- The experience in litigation depends entirely on the type of cases your firm handles; usually a trainee's responsibility is inversely proportionate to the value and complexity of a case. If your firm handles personal injury claims you may have conduct of matters yourself. If your firm goes in for long-running financial services litigation or multi-jurisdictional matters you could be stuck for months on document management jobs.
- In times of plenty, corporate and finance seats mean long hours, commonly climaxing in all-nighters. The size and complexity of a deal will determine your role, but corporate and finance usually require the most teamwork.
- Most firms offer four six-month seats; some offer six four-month seats and others operate their own unique systems. Trainees switch departments and supervisors for each seat. Most share a room and work with a partner or senior assistant; others sit open-plan, either with the rest of the team or with other trainees. Occasionally trainees have their own room.
- All firms conduct appraisals: a minimum of one at the conclusion of each seat, and usually halfway through as well.
- Client secondments help you learn to understand clients' needs. They can be the highlight of a training contract.
- The Solicitors Regulation Authority requires all trainees to gain experience of both contentious and non-contentious work. Additionally most firms have certain seats they require or prefer trainees to try. Some firms are very prescriptive, others flexible. Remember, a training contract is a time to explore legal practice to see what you're best at and most enjoy. You may surprise yourself.

Jargonbusting

- Agency work – making a court appearance for another firm that can't get to court

- Associate – a term used to denote solicitors who are not at partnership level but are more senior than an assistant solicitor
- Bundling – compiling bundles of documents for a court case
- Bibling – putting together sets of all the relevant documents for a transaction
- CMC – case management conference
- Counsel – a barrister
- Coco – company-commercial department/work
- Data room duty – supervising visitors to rooms full of important documents, helping them find things and making sure they don't steal them. With electronic data rooms the job becomes more of a desk-top exercise
- Dispute resolution – litigation, mediation, arbitration, etc
- Due diligence – the thorough investigation of a target company in a deal
- Equity partner – a partner who receives a contractually agreed share of the firm's annual profits. A part owner of the firm
- Grunt work – also known as donkeywork, monkey work or even document jockeying. Administrative (and boring) yet essential tasks including photocopying, bundling, bibling, paginating, scheduling documents, data room duties and proof-reading or checking that documents are intact
- High net worth individuals – rich people
- Infant approvals – court authorisation for a settlement involving a minor
- Limited Liability Partnership (LLP) – a way of structuring a professional partnership such that no partner is liable to any of the firm's creditors above and beyond a certain sum
- NQ – a newly qualified solicitor
- PQE – post-qualification experience
- PSC – a compulsory course taken during the training contract
- Salaried partner – a partner who receives a salary but has no contractual claim on the firm's profits. They are not equity partners and so do not own the business
- Seat – a spell working in a department, usually four or six months
- SRA – Solicitors Regulation Authority
- Training partner – the partner who oversees the training scheme
- Trainee partner – a trainee who acts like a partner
- Verification – the aspect of a deal in which lawyers ensure stated information is accurate

And finally...

We hope the True Picture will help you decide which firms to target. No matter how hard or how easy securing a training contract is for you, you'll want to end up with the right one.

Firms by size in the UK

	Firm	London	S & Thames Valley	South West	Midlands	East	Yorkshire & NE	North West	Wales	Trainees	True picture	A-Z solicitors
1	Eversheds	●			●	●	●	●	●	160	309	726
2	Government Legal Service	●						●		36	351	738
3	DLA Piper	●			●		●	●		188	289	720
4	Pinsent Masons	●		●	●		●	●		132	515	794
5	Linklaters	●								278	429	764
6	Allen & Overy	●								240	143	676
7	Clifford Chance	●								260	245	706
8	Addleshaw Goddard	●					●	●		95	139	675
9	Herbert Smith	●								184	375	745
10	Freshfields	●								200	341	735
11	Berwin Leighton Paisner	●								81	179	686
12	Beachcroft	●	●	●	●		●	●		69	175	685
13	Lovells	●								155	432	765
14	CMS Cameron McKenna	●								124	252	708
15	Slaughter and May	●								166	557	809
16	Norton Rose	●								114	487	785
17	Ashurst	●								105	161	680
18	Hammonds	●			●		●	●		81	359	740
19	Wragge & Co	●			●					63	648	839
20	Bond Pearce	●	●	●						27	201	692
21	Nabarro	●					●			70	479	783
22	Mills & Reeve	●			●	●	●	●		46	469	778
23	Denton Wilde Sapte	●	●							75	279	717
24	Halliwells	●					●	●		76	355	739
25	SJ Berwin	●								98	549	807
26	Shoosmiths	●	●		●					36	539	804
27	White & Case	●								55	635	833
28	McGrigors	●						●		24	463	776
29	Simmons & Simmons	●								100	545	806
30	Irwin Mitchell	●			●		●	●		46	404	755
31	Hill Dickinson	●						●		30	381	748
32	DWF	●					●	●		34	302	724
33	Osborne Clarke	●	●	●		●				40	497	789
34	Olswang	●	●							48	491	786
35	Burges Salmon			●						43	227	699
36	Mayer Brown	●								62	455	774
37	Charles Russell	●	●	●		●				40	236	702
38	Dundas & Wilson	●								18	299	723
39	Baker & McKenzie	●								77	165	681
40	Barlow Lyde & Gilbert	●								41	169	682
41	Field Fisher Waterhouse	●								41	315	728
42	Taylor Wessing	●				●				48	575	814
43=	Clyde & Co	●	●							49	249	707
43=	Cobbetts	●			●		●	●		47	257	709
45	Reynolds Porter Chamberlain	●		●						33	527	799
46	Blake Lapthorn	●	●							32	197	691
47	Reed Smith	●			●					59	523	798
48	Travers Smith	●								41	593	820
49	Trowers & Hamlins	●		●				●		40	601	822
50	HBJ Gateley Wareing	●			●					22	368	743

Notes: Firms are listed in order of size as measured by UK partner and solicitor figures provided to Chambers and Partners.

Firms by size in the UK	London	S & Thames Valley	South West	Midlands	East	Yorkshire & NE	North West	Wales	Trainees	True picture	A-Z solicitors
51 Macfarlanes	●								53	441	769
52 Pannone							●		37	504	790
53 Bevan Brittan	●		●	●					33	182	687
54 Dickinson Dees						●			38	285	719
55 Lawrence Graham	●								45	417	763
56 Morgan Cole		●	●					●	20	475	780
57 Watson Burton	●					●			20	621	828
58 Bird & Bird	●								33	193	690
59 Dewey & LeBoeuf	●								27	282	718
60= Browne Jacobson	●			●					24	220	698
60= Withers	●								32	645	837
62= Speechly Bircham	●								18	561	810
62= Walker Morris						●			37	611	825
64= Jones Day	●								30	407	756
64= Stephenson Harwood	●								31	569	812
66 Freeth Cartwright				●			●		15	337	734
67 Latham & Watkins	●								18	414	759
68 Holman Fenwick Willan	●								30	385	749
69 TLT	●		●						21	589	819
70 Brabners Chaffe Street							●		22	213	696
71= Martineau	●			●					20	448	772
71= Ward Hadaway						●			22	615	826
73 Foot Anstey			●						21	324	730
74 Davies Arnold Cooper	●	●					●		17	272	715
75 Sidley Austin	●								18	542	805
76= Manches	●	●							20	445	771
76= Penningtons Solicitors	●	●							22	510	793
78 Farrer & Co	●								20	312	727
79 Geldards				●				●	16	345	736
80 Hugh James	●							●	17	391	751
81 Bircham Dyson Bell	●							●	17	189	689
82= K&L Gates	●								16	411	757
82= Lewis Silkin	●	●							11	424	762
84 Thring Townsend Lee & Pembertons	●		●						14	585	818
85 Skadden	●								9	552	808
86 Ince & Co	●								24	401	754
87 Michelmores	●		●						9	466	777
88 Dechert	●								23	275	716
89= Howes Percival		●		●	●				25	388	750
89= Watson, Farley & Williams	●								26	625	829
91 Gordons						●			16	348	737
92 DMH Stallard	●	●							19	292	721
93 Weil, Gotshal & Manges	●								23	631	832
94 Veale Wasbrough			●						16	604	823
95 Wedlake Bell	●								14	628	830
96= Cripps Harries Hall	●	●							15	269	713
96= Mace & Jones							●		11	438	768
98 Forsters	●								13	334	733
99= Anthony Collins				●					17	146	677
99= Stevens & Bolton		●							8	572	813

Notes: Firms are listed in order of size as measured by UK partner and solicitor figures provided to Chambers and Partners.

Firms by size in the UK

	Firm	London	S & Thames Valley	South West	Midlands	East	Yorkshire & NE	North West	Wales	Trainees	True picture	A-Z solicitors
101	Cleary Gotlieb Steen & Hamilton	○								14	242	705
102	Forbes						○	○		11	327	731
103=	Boodle Hatfield	○	○							13	204	693
103=	Coffin Mew		○							17	260	710
105=	Capsticks	○			○					10	233	701
105=	McDermott Will & Emery	○								7	459	775
107	asb law		○							10	157	679
108	Bates Wells & Braithwaite	○								10	172	683
109	Bristows	○								13	217	697
110	Salans	○								10	530	800
111	Harbottle & Lewis	○								9	362	741
112=	Lester Aldridge	○	○							13	420	761
112=	Stephens Scown			○						9	564	811
114=	Finers Stephens Innocent	○								12	318	729
114=	IBB Solicitors		○							12	398	753
116	Fisher Meredith	○								20	321	n/a
117	Thomson Snell & Passmore		○							10	581	817
118	Wilsons			○						10	641	835
119	Campbell Hooper	○								10	230	700
120	Collyer Bristow	○								8	263	711
121	Maxwell Winward	○								7	451	773
122	Henmans		○							6	371	744
123	Higgs & Sons				○					10	378	747
124	Lupton Fawcett						○			6	435	767
125	Morrison & Foerster	○								6	472	781
126=	BPE			○	○					9	210	695
126=	BTMK					○				5	223	n/a
126=	Orrick	○								18	494	788
129	BP Collins		○							8	207	694
130	Shadbolt	○	○							8	533	801
131	Trethowans		○	○						8	596	821
132=	Needham & James				○					6	482	784
132=	Warner Goodman		○							7	618	827
134	Clarion Solicitors						○			10	239	703
135=	Dorsey & Whitney	○				○				8	295	722
135=	Ford & Warren						○			7	331	732
137	Teacher Stern	○								7	578	815
138	Hay & Kilner						○			10	365	742
139	Covington & Burling	○								8	266	712
140	Prettys					○				12	518	795
141=	Anthony Gold	○								12	150	n/a
141=	Edwards Angell	○								15	305	725
143	Sheridans	○								2	536	803
144	Wiggin	○		○						8	638	834
145	Paul Hastings	○								7	507	791
146	Bingham McCutchen	○								4	185	688
147	Arnold & Porter	○								2	153	678
148	Hunton & Williams	○								5	394	752
149	Palmers					○				6	500	n/a
150	Vinson & Elkins	○								8	607	824

Notes: Firms are listed in order of size as measured by UK partner and solicitor figures provided to Chambers and Partners.

Addleshaw Goddard

the facts

Location: Manchester, Leeds, London

Number of UK partners/solicitors: 189/532

Total number of trainees: 95

Seats: 4x6 months

Alternative seats: Secondments

Extras: Pro bono – Manchester Uni and Springfield Legal Advice Centres

For the last three years the firm has featured in the *Sunday Times'* '100 Best Companies to Work For' league table, leaping from 94th to 40th place in 2008.

National firm Addleshaw Goddard is pursuing a dream of being the best in the country outside the magic circle.

Ag-a saga

Addleshaw Goddard was formed in 2003 when northern powerhouse Addleshaw Booth scooped up prestigious but slightly troubled London outfit Theodore Goddard. This move gave the northerners critical mass and established relationships in London, while the Londoners were introduced to more decisive leadership. It can be a challenge to blend northern no-nonsense and City swagger but AG has been on a roll ever since. It now employs well over 700 lawyers across its three UK offices and is a top 15 UK firm by turnover, billing £195m in 2007/08. AG advises private and public sector clients up and down the country, and according to the *Chambers Client Report FTSE Survey* only five other UK firms represented more FTSE clients in 2007. The firm's neatly balanced practice makes it a good choice for those seeking a broad commercial training.

AG has real ambition for the future and a defined goal: 'not to be a magic circle firm but to be in the pool of firms just outside it.' Transactional departments are seen as the way forward, and following the departure of its family team the majority of remaining private client work is based on high-end trusts and private capital. The northern arms are 'definitely involved in the growth process, and the heads of practice groups are not necessarily based in London.' With those northern offices already pre-eminent in their markets, AG in the capital still has some bulking up to do and 'there's no disputing the fact it wants to increase its presence in London.' 'We're moving towards being a City firm,' confirmed one interviewee, 'even though there are no alpha males wandering around

and people don't show off about how many hours they work.' Nevertheless, the plan does rest on the full integration of the three offices, so much so that there's a rallying slogan 'Three Offices, One Team' (abbreviated to TOOT). TOOT clearly works better in some departments than others, but the firm dreams of providing identical service in each of its offices.

Smells like keen spirit

'Most trainees end up doing two transactional seats,' with corporate, banking, projects and real estate all capable of ticking the box. The corporate team works for an impressive list of clients including 3i Group, Interflora, Capita and BT. In the past year it advised Tiscali on its £187m purchase of Pipex's broadband division and BA on the sale of its UK regional business to Flybe. 'Keenness' wins corporate trainees better work. 'There was a progression,' confirmed one, 'from more mundane things like checking documents to highbrow pieces of work and I felt a part of the team.' At times it's necessary to put in some really long hours, and despite the firm's flexible working initiative 'a lot of the work in corporate isn't transportable.'

The banking and finance practice is another of the firm's main planks. This group (especially its London team) has seen some of the strongest growth in the firm (up 30% nationally and 46% in London), due to instructions from Citi, Abbey, Nationwide, HSBC and Deutsche Bank among others. We can't say if this level of activity is sustainable, or if the seat's 'reputation for incredibly long hours' could become a thing of the past. Busy or not, trainees are monitored closely. Said one source: 'They must look at everyone's timesheet because [during one hectic period] a partner pulled me off one deal and gave it to a trainee who wasn't so busy.' These seats allow trainees to explore their drafting abilities and attend completion meetings, while 'dealing with large national and international banks' and racking up 'lots of contact with local authorities and contractors on PFI matters.' In both corporate and finance seats, 'when you're working hard on a transaction you have to do things quickly and show your skills. If you do a good piece of work, they tell you so.'

Two other main transactional areas are projects and real estate. The latter is a popular option as the lawyers are 'helpful and supportive' of trainees. 'The people chosen to be supervisors take training very seriously,' said one; 'they listen to what you want to achieve over the months.' Of course it's a two-way process: 'You have to build up the relationship with people you're working for.' As well as working on large files, trainees commonly control smaller deals so they can learn how to draft basic documents and structure transactions. Some less happy sources perhaps didn't get such experience, feeling they were 'doing things that were useful and necessary, but wanted to be more involved.' No matter which office you take a property seat in, there is 'a broad geographical spread' of work for 'large, national clients' like Standard Life Investments, Sainsbury's, British Land, Phones4U, Travelodge and the MoD. Helping to earn the real estate department a crust, lawyers worked on the sale of Europe's largest sandwich-making factory for Matrix Securities. Busy in all three locations, this is a department where you're likely to work with lawyers in the other offices and hours are fairly consistent.

Keep an open mind

For the most part trainee grumbles are limited to seat allocation and the transparency of the system. One or two people sniffed favouritism, telling us 'there are certain people who get every seat they ask for.' We asked the firm about this and they were keen that readers know they treated the fair distribution of seats as a priority. Realising some trainees may simply be more adept than others at working within the system, we sought top tips for getting what you want. One: recognise that 'not everyone can do everything they want.' Two: remember to back up a non-transactional top choice seat with a preferred transactional second choice; after all, 'if someone puts down four niche or popular seats they're bound to be disappointed.' Corporate or banking take masses of trainees, so if your ambitions lie there you're laughing. In general the best advice came from the trainee who said: 'Don't come in with preconceptions about the work you'll do – what I think I'd enjoy changes all the time.'

Chambers UK rankings

Advertising & Marketing • Agriculture & Rural Affairs • Asset Finance • Aviation • Banking & Finance • Banking Litigation • Charities • Competition/European Law • Construction • Corporate Finance • Data Protection • Defamation/Reputation Management • Dispute Resolution • Education • Employee Share Schemes • Employment • Environment • Financial Services Regulation • Fraud: Civil/Criminal • Health & Safety • Healthcare • Information Technology • Insurance • Intellectual Property • Life Sciences • Local Government • Outsourcing • Partnership • Pensions • Planning • Private Client • Private Equity • Product Liability • Projects, Energy & Natural Resources • Public Procurement • Real Estate • Real Estate Finance • Real Estate Litigation • Restructuring/Insolvency • Retail • Social Housing • Sports Law • Tax • Telecommunications

A contentious seat is obligatory and then there are various choices for the remaining fourth seat, such as IP, sports law, construction, pensions and commercial. The latter can expose trainees to 'some glam clients' in Manchester and is popular. As are certain client secondments, some of which (like Diageo) involve travel overseas. 'There are usually a few people from the London office doing them and there's always someone at AstraZeneca from Manchester.'

Those who show independence seem to get the most out of their contracts and this philosophy of assertiveness can even influence your work hours. Said one old hand: 'If you say you're leaving by 7pm, nobody seems to mind, so long as you're prepared to do something the following day.' Generally, trainees' hours are reasonable; this obviously fluctuates according to department, so expect to see more of your desk in corporate and banking seats. Then again, trainees' bonuses are partly calculated by reference to their hours (bill 1,000 hours in a year and the bonus is triggered) and partly on the strength of appraisals.

The indisputable top dog

Trainee integration starts long before the contract with future joiners herded together at one of BPP's branches for their LPC. Many also spend a week together in Romania building houses, said to be an 'outrageous and fun' way of bonding. Throughout the training contract they meet again at inter-office departmental jaunts and an annual trainee conference. The firm permits inter-office trainee moves, though it's more usual for northerners to want to visit London. Moves the other way are being encouraged.

Are the northern and southern trainees different? It depends who you ask. Most people think not; some find the London trainees 'more competitive between themselves.' Certainly most Leeds and Manchester recruits have connections to the regions and it's clear why they flock to the firm – AG is indisputably at the top of the pile. In London it attracts 'people who are top tier academically but who are not gung-ho enough to go to the magic circle.' The words of one trainee said it all: 'In the North, we're the top dog. In London if you want to be top dog you go to Slaughter and May.'

Paradise gained

However the firm's UK strategy is likely to make the London office ever more appealing to students, and all our sources were clued up. 'We're focusing on the FTSE 350, as opposed to the 100. We're differentiating ourselves from the magic circle and the strategy has become more aggressive as we see an opportunity to break into the top ten.' Internationally, the firm has been slow off the mark, but it's now time to accept that 'to further [the domestic] goal we need a strong international presence.' Hence a drive to establish a network of preferred referral firms in different jurisdictions.

We heard a lot about AG's mantra for winning 'more better work'. No points for grammar, but you get the message. Another thing that got trainees talking was 'The AG Way', five values that require staff to be open, honest, led by teamwork, dynamic and business-focused. There are branded nick-nacks ('I've got a Rubik's cube on my desk') and awards to recognise tireless AG Way Champions. The subject provokes mixed reactions. Some trainees are cynical, telling us: 'People generally laugh when you mention it;' others are wholeheartedly behind the scheme. Apparently 'everyone would agree that AG has the values it espouses, but some would be uncomfortable with documenting them.' Something must be working because for the last three years the firm has featured in the *Sunday Times'* '100 Best Companies to Work For' league table, leaping from 94th to 40th place.

Leeds and Manchester are each based in a single office, but London remains split between three until its new Milton Gate premises are completed, hopefully in September 2009. 'It looks like the office of a firm with rallying ambition,' thought one Northern source after a peek at the plans. 'The move is going to excite everybody... we might have a Milton Gate effect up here!' Trainees certainly feel it will be real evidence of the firm's achievements in London.

Within each office trainees socialise together and every branch has its favourite local bars and group socials. 'There isn't really a stereotypical trainee in terms of background or type of person. You have your rugby-playing public schoolboys and people who've worked their way through. Everyone is keen and you've got to be optimistic about things.' Trainees commend the firm's recruitment process: a high proportion of our interviewees had completed the vac scheme and they also believed that 'as a firm we're quite innovative in terms of grad recruitment.' In their eyes 'the thing that sets AG apart is the sense of optimism and enthusiasm that the people here have for the firm and for each other. They don't regard work as a bind. They are proud to work here.' In 2008 34 of the 43 trainees chose to stay on after qualification.

And finally...

Many trainees find that first-hand contact sways them AG's way, so we recommend you try its vacation scheme. One last piece of advice, which fits the application process as well as the training: 'Go in with enthusiasm and you'll reap the rewards.'

Start at the top
A Career in Law

ALLEN & OVERY

When it comes to eggs, it's more than just a question of etiquette. Edward VI certainly thought so. That's why he decreed that any person found breaking a boiled egg at the sharp end would be sentenced to 24 hours in the village stocks.

☐ Law or ☐ Non-law?

Law and business are full of surprises. Whether you are exploring the modern implications of existing laws, or working to find legal solutions to new situations, you'll need to be open-minded, creative and commercial. At Allen & Overy, we are working at the forefront of today's evolving legal landscape, helping to shape and frame the environment in which business, and life itself, is conducted.

Breaking with tradition

You don't need to have studied law to become a lawyer, but business sense curiosity and a commitment to excellence are essential.

Answer: Non-law

www.allenovery.com/careeruk

Allen & Overy means Allen & Overy LLP and/or its affiliated undertakings

Allen & Overy LLP

The facts

Location: London

Number of UK partners/solicitors: 212/675

Total number of trainees: 240

Seats: 3 or 6 months long

Alternative seats: Overseas seats, secondments

Extras: Pro bono – Liberty, Battersea Legal Advice Centre; language training

> Deals often make newspaper headlines and colleagues muck in together with a supportive, let's-get-this-done mentality.

Squeaking past the billion-pound revenue barrier this year, global force Allen & Overy is a heavyweight in high finance and a master of all things commercial.

Deal me in

Allen & Overy started its legal life as a plucky Holborn firm created by two men who'd dashed from their old employer with a cab full of files. One was the darkly handsome George Allen; the other Tom Overy, who reportedly had the sort of face that scares small children. The new firm quickly built an impressive client list, famously including Edward VIII, whom Allen advised during his affair with Wallis Simpson and resulting abdication. Almost 80 years on, A&O has metamorphosed into a global legal presence so massive it is 'kind of like a machine.'

Among offices in 21 countries, 'London is the mothership,' and the firm's star turn is its unsurpassed finance division. Lawyers acted on the $55bn facility to finance mining giant BHP Billiton's $147bn bid for rival Rio Tinto, which is thought to be the largest financing ever. A&O reigns supreme in project financing, thanks in part to a strong flow of instructions from the Middle East – the team advised on 36 deals worth a total of £15.2bn during the first half of 2008. Project finance lawyers are currently involved in Saudi Kayan Petrochemical ($10bn) and the $6bn Jubail refinery in Saudi Arabia, as well as the Burgas-Alexandroupolis Pipeline in Russia. The debt finance team put together a €2.475bn package for ABN AMRO, Barclays, Credit Suisse, Goldman Sachs, Lehman Brothers and Merrill Lynch to finance an investment consortium's takeover of Endemol. The debt and equity finance teams were recently instructed by the lead arrangers of InBev's successful $52bn bid for Anheuser-Busch, creating a global beer giant. The international capital markets division (ICM) is equally important, and here lawyers assisted Sumitomo Mitsui Banking on its £500m investment in Barclays. They also helped Morgan Stanley, National Bank of Abu Dhabi and Standard Chartered Bank on the first ever Shari'a-compliant mandatory exchangeable sukuk issue. These jargon-heavy deals don't need to make sense to you yet, but if they send a shiver of fear rather than excitement up your spine, best to look elsewhere.

Although finance brought in 44% of revenue in 2007/08, corporate added a healthy £335.3m to the coffers. The M&A team has run some impressive deals of late: it represented Alliance & Leicester on its much-publicised acquisition by Banco Santander, and has assisted Iberia in relation to merger talks with British Airways. Private equity lawyers meanwhile have advised infrastructure investment consortium Greensands on its £4.195bn agreement to acquire Southern Water, and Charterhouse Capital Partners on its purchase of TSL Education Holdings, publisher of the Times Educational Supplement.

Together, finance, ICM and corporate account for three-quarters of the firm in London. The remainder encompasses dispute resolution, tax, employment and benefits, real estate and private client, all of which get up to some pretty interesting work. The dispute resolution team is representing HBOS in the much-publicised overdraft charges litigation. Although not technically part of the disputes division, the antitrust team is advising BSkyB on its dispute with the Competition Commission over the size of its shareholding in ITV. When Emap decided to sell to a private equity investor, the company asked A&O's incentives team to deal with employee share scheme issues.

Standard bearers

When trying to pinpoint why trainees choose A&O over others, we heard the usual mentions of 'genuine friendliness,' 'international deals' and the 'kudos' of working at a place with a 'huge reputation.' Delving deeper, one recruit reasoned: 'If you're going to be a lawyer, you want to be a good one.' To A&O trainees, being a good lawyer comes from exposure to 'the self-proclaimed best training in the City' and working with 'people who are the best at what they do and who you genuinely want to spend evenings with.' The trainees we chatted with were too well mannered to say it plainly, but the unspoken implication was that it doesn't get any better than 'the A&O standard,' for which they felt 'real pride.'

Beyond the healthy Oxbridge contingent, trainees come from a range of good universities. They say A&O is 'trying to reinforce change' in its recruitment policy 'rather than sticking to old traditions. Among the partners now there are very few women and ethnic minorities, but over time that will change.' The trainee intakes boast a respectable range of nationalities and ethnicities, and a roughly equal gender balance. Said one source: 'It makes conversations more interesting if people are from different countries. They think about things in a slightly different way.' Paradoxically, 'because there are so many trainees, you're going to find someone who's like you.' Future trainees have plenty of time to get chummy on a bespoke LPC at the College of Law. Although the hot-housed students risk developing 'a cliquey, one-firm view,' having already formed 'fully fledged groups' means the first day in the firm is 'more comfortable and not a big scary step up.' Once the LPC is finished, about half opt to jump straight into their contracts, with the others taking six months out (perhaps to travel) before starting in March.

Planes, trains and jumbo deals

Everyone spends at least 12 months in the banking, corporate and/or ICM departments. While the sheer variety of seats that fall within these core areas means 'no one should be put off by the 12-month requirement, it's obviously worrying if you don't have an interest in any of them.' Finance seats range from banking, leveraged finance and asset finance to projects, restructuring, regulatory and global loans. Don't worry if you can't differentiate between them just yet: each practice group gives a

Chambers UK rankings

Administrative & Public Law • Asset Finance • Banking & Finance • Banking Litigation • Capital Markets • Charities • Climate Change • Competition/European Law • Construction • Corporate Finance • Data Protection • Dispute Resolution • Employee Share Schemes • Employment • Environment • Financial Services Regulation • Fraud: Civil/Criminal • Information Technology • Insurance • Intellectual Property • Investment Funds • Life Sciences • Media & Entertainment • Outsourcing • Partnership • Pensions • Private Client • Private Equity • Projects, Energy & Natural Resources • Public International Law • Public Procurement • Real Estate • Real Estate Finance • Real Estate Litigation • Restructuring/Insolvency • Shipping • Social Housing • Tax • Telecommunications • Transport

presentation to newbies, followed by a mix 'n' mingle over drinks. Banking trainees 'manage conditions precedent, co-ordinate international advice, organise powers of attorney and keep everyone updated on the transaction.' The asset finance team 'mainly acts for financiers providing funds for companies who are purchasing planes, ships or trains.' In addition to the standard 'big banking element,' restructuring seats also involve 'some black letter law, like dealing with insolvency and the appointment of administrators.' Recently the team advised Ernst & Young as the PPP administrators of Metronet, which overspent by millions in a failed attempt to maintain and upgrade two-thirds of the London Underground network.

ICM seat options include general securities, derivatives and structured finance (DSF), debt, equity, securitisation and corporate trustee work. The general securities team is 'happy to get junior people involved at an early stage,' perhaps because 'there's a know-how system where you can plug in different bits and suddenly you have an agreement in front of you to tailor to what the client needs.' Although this can get 'quite repetitive,' it makes it easier for trainees to take on a 'sink or swim' level of responsibility. We couldn't get A&Oers to shut up about how much they 'absolutely loved' the derivatives side of a DSF seat. This 'wonderfully abstract' and 'sexy' field involves 'swapping fixed or floating income.' Although it takes a while to get to grips with it, eventually 'you handle your own mini negotiations.'

A corporate trainee's role involves 'verification of documents, setting up shelf companies, filing at Companies House and drafting board minutes.' Also making an appearance are 'mundane due diligence' and 'data room' tasks. If you go into corporate hoping for a 'really hardcore' experience, you won't be disappointed. Describing the long hours, one trainee admitted: 'The worst was not going home at all and then being called in at the weekend.' On the plus side, deals often make newspaper headlines and colleagues muck in together with a 'supportive, let's-get-this-done mentality.'

Priority boarding

Beyond the mandatory time in core areas, trainees have a guaranteed 'priority seat', usually in a more specialised department. Certain areas like the 'very female-dominated' private client team and econ-heavy antitrust seat inspire 'fierce' competition, so the former only lasts three months and the latter is sometimes only available for three months. There is a 'great range of experience' available in real estate and the employment team is 'very pastoral. They don't use you as a photocopying machine.'

One trainee admitted: 'You don't think about litigation as A&O's strong point;' however, experience of this team offers the chance to get involved in 'real law' and remind yourself that 'there are actually courts,' even if you only see one via a tour at the start of the seat. A lucky few get to 'actually sit in court and feel involved in the case, which is the most exciting bit.' Die-hard transactional lawyers can instead attend a litigation course run by Nottingham Law School.

For their final seat, many trainees go on international or client secondments. Most offer a greater level of responsibility, to the extent that some secondees felt they 'made the jump to associate six months early.' Hong Kong and New York are the most hotly contested; for a full list of options see page 670. Apparently, the Champions League final in Moscow and the Beijing Olympics prompted a sharp increase in applications for those destinations. Like all foreign secondees, trainees in New York live in a rather swanky apartment in a luxury high-rise with Hudson River views. Irrespective of the destination, there's a salary uplift and perks like 'people to pack up and ship your stuff.' Those going to non-English speaking countries also have language tuition. Client secondments include Barclays Capital and the human rights organisation Liberty.

The credit crunch made qualification at most firms a slightly more uncertain prospect, and A&O didn't escape the effects either. Some qualifiers praised the firm for being 'very good at managing people's expectations. If you've got some outlandish hopes the partners are good at tempering your suggestions and showing you other options.' Others found the process 'very stressful... even after the jobs are published you sense it's slightly changeable and you may need to move to another area.' Indeed, A&O did reshuffle some lawyers from quieter departments into busier ones, in lieu of making redundancies. In

2008 a slightly lower than usual 92 of the 120 qualifiers stayed with the firm, the majority going into finance, corporate and ICM teams.

The travelling classes

According to trainees, 'it's impossible to summarise an A&O type.' We'll give it our best shot. The majority are quietly ambitious and relish challenges, so long as they feel 'the security of being well supervised.' Trainees are mostly 'international in some way,' whether by birth or in attitude. Continuing with the globetrotting theme, A&Oers are reportedly 'of the social and educational background which would allow one to travel for a year,' so maybe it's just as well qualifying trainees get six weeks' unpaid leave at the end of their contracts. Sensibly, most joined with an expectation of working long hours, but the reality properly sinks in when trainees find themselves occasionally 'watching the sun rise from the office.' Although everyone we spoke to had muddled through 'times when you need to put a fair amount of hours and graft in,' this was balanced by quieter periods of leaving 'at 7pm or 8pm.'

A&O's £108m Foster-designed Spitalfields offices are 'amazing.' The gym has classes and is big enough to play football in, and in the evening the sixth-floor coffee stand transforms into a subsidised bar with 'a really fabulous roof terrace.' The local area is awash with good bars, not least in Brick Lane and Commercial Road. Some departments, notably projects, have Friday cakes paid for by partners. One trainee said, half sympathetically and half gloating: 'It's sad for the departments that don't have cakes.' The social committee has previously spent its annual budget on masquerade and 1920s-themed trainee balls. Senior partner David Morley even hosted a summer party at his home, with 100 invitations determined by ballot. One lucky winner recalled: 'People with power seem so distant, but he was really down to earth.' There is an A&O choir and orchestra, and sports opportunities galore. The A&O team ethic is perhaps best exemplified by this anecdote – 'People talk about how busy they are and then a partner will organise for us to go to a rugby match and suddenly everyone can make it!'

And finally...

Top-tier deals, unbeatable training and a name that will make your CV sparkle – if the magic circle's on your mind and you're a fan of finance, what are you waiting for?

Anthony Collins Solicitors LLP

The facts

Location: Birmingham

Number of UK partners/solicitors: 21/71

Total number of trainees: 17

Seats: 4x6 months

Alternative seats: None

Extras: Pro bono – St Basil's legal Advice Centre

> The initial cover letter is the stage at which most people fall. If you haven't demonstrated you've got a handle on what the firm's about in the letter, you might as well not bother.

Anthony Collins has gained a reputation as a law firm that operates with integrity, excellence and a keen interest in improving society.

To Birmingham and beyond

The eponymous Mr Collins who founded this Birmingham-based concern in the early 1970s retired a couple of years ago, but his legacy lives on. The firm may have relocated to a flash city centre building, but it shows every sign of staying true to its roots. Its three main areas of practice are commercial services, private client and something called 'Transformation'. The commercial practice encompasses coco, dispute resolution, commercial property, employment and licensing law, and Anthony Collins has several Midlands stalwarts on its books, including Goodyear Dunlop, the NEC Group, Birmingham Hippodrome and Twycross Zoo. It also acts for a handful of national organisations, notably La Tasca Restaurants and The Restaurant Group (the company behind Frankie & Benny's, Chiquito and Garfunkel's).

Commercial law may be where the money's at, but the much-praised Transformation team is a standout performer. This department specialises in the regeneration of communities, working on behalf of local authorities and registered social landlords (housing associations and the like). Again, clients range from local organisations like Midland Heart and Walsall Housing Group, to those elsewhere in the country, including the city councils of Manchester and Southampton. The team is also working as an independent consultant for local residents groups on a West London estate that is being completely redeveloped.

Last and by no means least is the private client division offering family and clinical negligence services that are among the best in the Midlands. These teams handle some worthy cases, such as one involving the abuse of an elderly pensioner in her own home by her professional carers. Another case dealt with a complex road traffic accident involving two claimants who suffered very serious and lasting head injuries. A million-pound settlement over future loss of earnings was achieved just before the case reached trial.

Community service

In the four-seat training contract second-years are given priority when seats are being doled out. Before that there's a good chance that a first seat will be taken in the licensing or property teams, as the firm views these as good starting points. Licensing law is not something you'll find in many firms, certainly not on the scale to be found at AC. Having built on its Brummie client base over the years, it is now the biggest player in the West Midlands. 'It basically involves smoking, gambling and drinking,' said one trainee before adding: 'That might have come out a bit wrong.' What they meant, of course, is that the work consists of dealing with the law relating to smoking restrictions, the sale and consumption of alcohol and the Gambling Act 2005. What with 'applying for new operating licences for all our clients,' plus sorting out standard liquor licence applications, it's a busy seat. Because 'you can get to grips with it all quite quickly,' trainees soon take on files of their own, perhaps for large national chains. 'I'm probably on the phone for five hours a day, chasing documentation,' explained one source. If you're wondering whether this is the most exciting first seat, just listen to the perks: 'We visit a lot of clients around Birmingham, and if we're successful we often get free drinks there the next day.'

The housing team offers a similarly good starter seat as there are a fair number of simple claims for the possession of properties. As well as 'having a go on low-value, straightforward files,' it provides 'a useful first taste of advocacy... it's basically just going to the judge and saying, 'These guys haven't paid their rent' and the judge saying back to you, 'Yeah, I can see that.' It builds your confidence for later on.' The commercial property team, however, is not seen as such a desirable place for a newbie to end up. It has a heavy workload and a reputation for throwing trainees in at the deep end, combined with 'not much of a support network' compared to other seats.

For second-years commercial dispute resolution (CDR), employment and personal injury are the hip places to be. CDR in particular is 'perceived to be quite glamorous because it has some high-value cases.' One of the big cases of 2008 was a construction dispute involving a large organisation running a service contract with a contractor to do housing association repairs. 'Problems with the contract have meant that both parties find it unworkable, but only our client wants to terminate it,' explained one source. With millions of pounds in penalties to pay if the contract is binned without justification, the litigators have been trying to mediate a resolution. Another case involved 'a property dispute in which the other side have drawn out the process so much that the original issues have become clouded.' Again, mediation is the key. The role of the trainees in all this is to compile the necessary files of documentary evidence. 'There are literally dozens of lever arch files,' sighed one of our contacts, 'and it's a question of trying to find the relevant documents within them.' Trainees also attend mediation and telephone conferences and sit behind barristers at hearings. In addition to helping out on other cases, it's the job of the two CDR trainees to run all simple debt recovery files.

Transformation appeals to trainees with an interest in improving communities. For those unclear as to what it entails, a fine example of the team's work is its involvement in the government's Guide Neighbourhoods initiative, designed to allow greater participation from residents in run-down districts. There have been some astounding success stories, with 'several areas that were rubbish turned into places where people are really involved in their community.' There are non-lawyers within the department in the form of community regeneration workers, and 'the lawyers here don't just talk law,' said one trainee. The firm also represents several housing associations, and 'if an organisation is having a tricky time, say the council is giving them grief, we're very good at negotiating.' Trainee tasks include constitutional matters, such as preparing memoranda and articles, filing returns and writing agendas for board meetings. And vis-

---

Chambers UK rankings

Charities • Clinical Negligence • Construction • Dispute Resolution • Employment • Family/Matrimonial • Licensing • Local Government • Private Client • Public Procurement • Real Estate • Real Estate Litigation • Social Housing

---

its to clients are 'the really exciting part of the job because you get to see the changes that are being made.' The team represents several charities, including Tearfund, Spring Harvest, The Royal Society for the Prevention of Accidents, Mind, Groundwork UK, The Baptist Union and the Fellowship of Independent Evangelical Churches.

Holy acceptable

Which brings us to the side of AC that everyone always remarks upon – the Christian leanings of its founder and a number of the current partners and staff. 'Yeah, we get jokes from the trainees at other firms,' said one source. 'Things like, 'Do you pray before meetings?' and so on.' To be honest, none of our contacts felt the Christian ethos of the firm impinged significantly on their daily lives, and all were keen to stress that 'we have people here of all faiths and none.' Given that the Transformation team has many of the firm's committed Christians, and not every trainee takes a seat there, it's no surprise that this aspect of the firm's character doesn't dominate. Nevertheless, it was agreed that religion was 'there in the background... it informs the way people behave towards each other, but I wouldn't say it was intrusive. You can either choose to get involved or not.' In short: 'It's very important to the partners, as that's where the firm came from and they want to stay true to that.'

As the firm has grown, it has evolved. It is now pushing 'seven focus themes,' with partners acting as 'theme enthusers' in an attempt to encourage a cross-departmental attitude and give more clarity as to what the firm stands for. None of our contacts could name all seven themes – the one with the best memory managed to reel off four – but then it is still early days. For your information, those seven themes in full are enterprise, entertainment and leisure, transforming communities, adult health and social care, children and young people, faith communities and housing.

Love thy neighbour

Anthony Collins is known to be a place where everyone is incredibly nice to each other. Any trainee celebrating qualification or a birthday can expect to receive a present from the others. 'It's so sweet, isn't it?' remarked one source without a hint of irony. The partners are easy to approach: 'In the lift at the end of the day I might be standing next to a senior fee earner I've never spoken to before and he'll chat with me and ask me how my day has been,' another trainee confirmed. A quick glance at the profiles on the firm's website, in which every single partner sports a cheesy grin and an endearing haircut, confirms that you can't help but trust these guys.

A couple of mature trainees add a touch of sophistication to the ranks, but other than that there's no typical Anthony Collins trainee, nor does the firm expect applicants to have a prior commitment to the West Midlands. Here's a useful tip: 'They get hundreds of applications and I'm told the initial cover letter is the stage at which most people fall. If you haven't demonstrated you've got a handle on what the firm's about in the letter, you might as well not bother.' Don't let those words of warning put you off, though. 'I was applying to all sorts of firms,' said one source, 'and as the months went on I was phoning them all and updating my details. Anthony Collins remembered me every single time I rang, and they always had my details to hand. I seemed to have a connection with them.'

We're told the firm pays 'more than lip service' to the concept of work-life balance: for example, 'no one would raise an eyebrow if I left at 5.15pm. And by 6pm people are coming round asking, 'Why are you still here?'' An active social scene involves going out for drinks 'every Friday except the one before payday,' summer and Christmas parties, trips to Alton Towers, plus greyhound racing and the cinema. The girls play netball and the boys have recently set up a five-a-side football team, finishing third (of eight) in the league in their debut season. The firm also recently ran a Celebrating Enterprise event in its office, inviting some of its bigger clients and putting on little shows in every room. So-called stress angels gave massages ('because Anthony Collins takes the stress out of dispute resolution'), a jazz band played on the top-floor balcony ('beautiful views of Birmingham') and a bar served cocktails in AC colours (ie, green). Trainees admire the firm's commitment to corporate social responsibility issues and to staff welfare and they throw themselves into charity events and fundraising.

And finally...

All our interviewees hoped to stay on after finishing their traineeships and in 2008 all five qualifiers did so.

- **Practical experience can be the most eloquent and essential aspect of your CV:** As a leading human rights lawyer told us 'People always ask me, how do I show an interest in human rights law? but that's the wrong way round. People who are genuinely interested will already be involved.'

Anthony Gold Solicitors

The facts

Location: London

Number of UK partners/solicitors: 18/22

Total number of trainees: 12

Seats: Flexible

Alternative seats: None

Extras: Pro bono – Association for the Victims of Medical Accidents, Families Need Fathers advice clinics, Grandparents Association, CABs

Settling cases for kids that have been brain-damaged at birth is really quite important stuff to be doing, and Anthony Gold has a great track record in intricate cases such as these.

Equally at home on the gritty streets of South London or among the skyscrapers of the City, Anthony Gold acts for rich and poor without discrimination.

Good as gold

Most firms out there don't actually put down on their website in black and white the phrase 'we're not just in it for the money', but then Anthony Gold isn't most firms. True, it has a thriving commercial practice and produces reams of tax, trusts and wills advice for wealthy individuals, but it also has particular expertise in acting for the socially excluded, and is well known to the tired, poor and huddled masses of South London for its legal aid work. This duality is reflected in its offices. 'Plush' new headquarters in London Bridge will house the firm's main money-spinners: commercial dispute resolution, family, PI and clin neg, while two satellite offices in Streatham and Walworth are 'high street' in both location and outlook. Geared towards community work, they offer social housing and property litigation services, along with wills, probates and conveyancing. It's also worth noting that the firm claims particular experience in advising gay and lesbian clients and has actively pursued the pink pound in recent years.

Given the nature of the majority of its work, it should come as no surprise to find that the type of people who are attracted to Anthony Gold are those who like their law up close and personal, 'dealing with real people's lives' and helping clients sort out problems that cause them real distress. Most of our interviewees came to the firm knowing of its reputation and hoping to gain experience in one of its star departments. They know that their salary will never be on a par with their friends at the big commercial firms (£21,200 for a first-year at last check, rising to £23,200 and then £30,400 on qualification), but 'the benefits we get make it a good trade-off.' The hours are acknowledged as 'brilliant' – 9.30am to 5.30pm is standard – and trainees feel their varied and interesting caseload beats the kind of mundane tasks allotted to their contemporaries in the City.

The structure of the training contract is somewhat out of the ordinary. Operating a three-seat system, the firm asks what area each trainee has a particular interest in and gives them a year there along with two other shorter seats, the nature of which are often dictated by business needs. In practice we found that while most trainees did indeed expect to visit three departments, the length of time they spent in each varied hugely. Some had a first seat lasting five months, while for others it was eight or nine. The shortest amount of time we heard of in any one department was three months, the longest over a year. The arrangement seems to work, however, and we heard no grumbles about seat allocation. The majority of the dozen or so trainees are based at London Bridge, although there will usually be two or three out in the Streatham and Walworth offices at any one time.

Fares fair

Everyone knows that 'personal injury lawyers get a bad rep as ambulance chasers,' and indeed, one PI trainee attempted to bring a tear to our eyes by telling us stories of being mocked in bars for revealing what her job was. Never afraid to pose the difficult questions, we hardened our hearts and asked her why we should sympathise. Her response was difficult to argue with – 'Settling cases for kids that have been brain-damaged at birth is really quite important stuff to be doing.' Anthony Gold has a great track record in 'intricate' cases such as these. In 2007 it secured £7.5m, one of the highest ever lump sum settlements of a birth injury claim, for an eight-year-old boy who suffered cerebral palsy caused by negligence on the part of the consultant who was delivering him. The department handles everything from high-value cases like this right down to simple slip-and-trip claims. 'At the moment we have a trial for a young lady who fell off the back of a Routemaster bus when it went over a hole in the road too fast.' Perhaps Boris Johnson should think twice about reintroducing them: the firm won nearly £600,000 for another client who fell from the back of a bus after drinking. Tasks for trainees 'vary quite significantly. You are not just doing the same things over and over again.' Fielding new enquiries and keeping existing clients up to speed on what's going on are two of the most common responsibilities, along with research, drafting and taking witness statements. 'The aim of the game is to settle before it goes to trial,' so trainees will often sit in on round-table negotiations. When things do go all the way to trial they will be involved there too. Supervisors provide 'a balance between giving responsibility, breathing space and regular support.' For example, one trainee informed us: 'If they know I've done something like a schedule of special damages before, it won't be checked in any great detail.' While a seat in PI isn't compulsory, it's the largest team and the firm recommends trainees take the relevant elective on the LPC.

The family crew 'are very much resolution lawyers.' Kim Beatson, a well-known name in family law circles, heads the department and 'is not interested in clients who want to pick at each other.' She was one of the first solicitors in the country to qualify as a family mediator and has chaired Resolution, an organisation that promotes a non-confrontational approach to family problems. Of course there are 'hugely rich clients who can afford to argue,' and another senior partner has handled many high-value cases, working in the past for City professionals and celebrity clients, including several Chelsea footballers. Trainees work on all sorts of cases, including divorce settlements, pre-nups and, since 'one solicitor here is up on international law,' even a child abduction case that stretched across two jurisdictions. A commercial dispute resolution seat also brings a variety of files to a trainee's desk. 'You start off dealing with new client calls and graduate up to dealing with clients... taking on a small caseload of your own.' Among other things the department covers are domain name disputes, insolvency, debt collection, employment law and disputes between company directors.

Chambers UK rankings

Clinical Negligence · Family/Matrimonial · Personal Injury · Social Housing

Where there's a will there's affray

We mentioned interesting and varied work: let's explore that in a bit more detail. Here are a couple of case studies from the traditionally dry area of law that is wills, trusts and probate. Example 1: Anthony Gold challenged a will drawn up by a reclusive Norfolk farmer who had died bedridden, having just made a series of wills to various people. Records showed that he thought he had a non-existent nephew; that he believed his neighbours had poisoned his cat (which he claimed was 36 years old); that he did not appreciate the extent of his estate; and that he had fired his shotgun at trick-or-treaters. Despite a rebuttal by the solicitors who drew up the will, and a lack of medical records due to the farmer not having seen a doctor for 40 years, the firm was able to establish a strong enough case to take the matter to ongoing mediation. Example 2: advising on the validity of a will where the executor had fraudulently removed money from the estate and the deceased had five wives and 38 children in Africa. Yep, that's varied all right.

Things are just as interesting in the social housing and property litigation seat, although here it can be shocking to see how the other half live. Dealing with disrepair of council properties – 'leaks, cracks, subsidence, infestations' – is a large portion of the work. 'One client came in and offered to show me the jar of bed bugs he had collected,' winced a trainee. Another represented a tenant whose flat was frequently flooded by sewage, resulting in mushrooms sprouting up everywhere. 'We got an injunction to stop that and compensation to help her.' The firm also appeals for individuals in homelessness cases when the council has refused accommodation, for example, or when they have been unlawfully evicted. 'We got a young single mum back into her house within a week recently,' said one trainee. 'It's quite rewarding though you need to be that way inclined.' It's a 'very busy' team and responsibility comes from day one. Trainees are allocated days when they are in charge of taking new enquiries, 'maybe 15 or 20 a day,' and other tasks include completing legal aid forms, going to court for hearings, drafting witness statements, preparing claim forms and, especially for elderly or sick clients, the occasional property visit.

The sad fact is that it's getting harder to obtain funding for this sort of work due to changes in the way legal aid is provided (see page 18 for details). Anthony Gold is 'one of the fewer and fewer firms that do housing.' Trainees are well aware of the changes being made and do notice an increasing focus by the department on the type of cases for which they are more likely to get funding. Nevertheless, while other departments will always be more profitable, Anthony Gold's high street operation remains an important area of practice for the firm.

Writ large

The firm's impending move to an office with '50% more space' leads us to draw the obvious conclusion: it intends to hire more (or maybe just bigger) staff. Beyond that, our interviewees remained hazy on future plans. 'Do what we do, better', was the gist of their comments. Anthony Gold will certainly continue to hire trainees that fit its 'people firm' ethos. Asked if there were any other trends among trainees, one said: 'I would have said that we are all a couple of years older,' before adding, 'but we have a new starter who's come straight through from university and law school so that defeats my theory.' Undoubtedly a few months' work experience in the area of law you are most interested in would help you impress at interview here.

Some felt the social scene 'has been a bit disjointed in the past,' but trainees seem to have got their act together and Friday night drinks in the bars of the South Bank are now a regular fixture. Girls dominate the current cohort, so perhaps it's no surprise the most recent outing was to the Take That musical *Never Forget*. 'Someone was trying to organise a netball team,' one of the ladies told us; apparently the gents make 'sporadic attempts at five-a-side.' It should be said that staff don't shirk when it comes to good causes and are involved with charity events – in recent months moonwalking through London for breast cancer and abseiling off The Gherkin.

And finally...

Trainees commonly choose Anthony Gold for its ethical stance and its expertise in family law and personal injury, but its commercial work shouldn't be ignored. We see this as a very likeable firm and clearly qualifying trainees agree: in 2008 all five stayed on after their training.

Arnold & Porter

The facts

Locations: London

Number of UK partners/solicitors: 16/17

Total number of trainees: 2 (as of Sept 2009)

Seats: 4x6 months

Alternative seats: Brussels

Extras: Pro bono – eg LawWorks, Caribbean death row appeals

> A&P's London pharma practice is run by a top-notch team of lawyers who are always winning awards and between them could probably start their own drug company.

New to the True Picture this year, leading US regulatory and litigation firm Arnold & Porter is restarting its London training scheme in September 2009 after a couple of years' break.

Pret a Porter

Arnold & Porter was founded in Washington, DC in 1946 by three government insiders, Thurman Arnold, Abe Fortas and – the following year – Paul Porter. True to a firm founded by veterans of the New Deal, its profile was first raised through its pro bono work, for example the 1963 case of Gideon v Wainwright, a landmark decision that affirmed a defendant's right to counsel and was later turned into a movie starring Henry Fonda. Abe Fortas, the partner on that case, was two years later appointed to the US Supreme Court. The firm also represented the survivors of one of the worst mining disasters in US history and several victims of Joseph McCarthy's 'loyalty review boards' in the 1950s. But don't think A&P only represents the little guy. In the States its impressive regulatory, litigation and corporate practices have represented CBS, Philip Morris, Random House, US Airways and the Venezuelan government.

In contrast to its celebrated American history, A&P is still largely unknown in the UK legal market, but in the areas in which it is known it is fêted as one of the best. *Chambers UK* places the firm's life sciences practice in the top tier in London, while its IP/media and product liability teams are listed as among the most impressive nationwide. Now there are rumblings from DC that the firm is looking to expand its operations and make London central to its future plans. The firm is 'recruiting very heavily,' our sources confirm: indeed high-profile hires have strengthened and diversified the London office, taking it beyond its traditional comfort zones in pharmaceuticals and publishing.

Everyone we spoke to told us the firm was eager to hear the pitter-patter of trainees' feet in the corridors after a couple of years' silence. A&P attributes its decision to temporarily ice its training programme to 'caution' and its determination to keep every recruit it took on. Elaborated one of our interviewees: 'The firm wouldn't want to have to hire when it knew it wouldn't be able to offer full support to a trainee.' As it stands, A&P will now take trainees on a biannual basis, starting from September 2009, so bear that in mind.

Pharma chameleon

All trainees do seats in corporate, IP, pharmaceuticals ('pharma' to insiders) and a shape-shifting commercial seat that can encompass anything from competition to data protection and includes three months in A&P's Brussels office. That may not seem like a lot of choice on paper, but interviewees assured us that 'because the firm only had a few trainees, we were able to discuss the areas of most interest to us and be allocated to seats that would best appeal.' It's a small firm, though, so wherever you end up 'you will have to help out where you're needed and do things you don't want to do.' 'The philosophy that comes from the USA is that lawyers aren't only going to work in one area.'

A&P's London pharma practice is run by a top-notch team of lawyers who are 'always winning awards' and between them could probably start their own drug company. Six have medical, toxicological or pharmacological qualifications and two sit periodically as deputy coroners. The group acts for clients at the top of the industry, such as Alcon, AstraZeneca, Bayer and Pfizer, and covers 'a huge range of work – from litigation when the drugs go wrong to questions of distribution and communicating with regulators.' Notable instructions last year included advising the Juvenile Diabetes Research Foundation and Cambridge University on the clinical development of an artificial pancreas, advising Smith & Nephew on the issues surrounding the collection and use of human tissue, acting for manufacturers in judicial review proceedings against the National Institute for Health and Clinical Excellence (NICE), the UK Licensing Authority and the Secretary of State for Health, and defending companies against a host of large multi-claimant litigations. The seat is 'always busy' and trainees should anticipate a lot of disclosure and case management for hefty ongoing instructions as well as some juicier drafting.

A&P has also acted on behalf of pharma clients in IP matters, such as GlaxoSmithKline's patent licence dispute with Abbott Laboratories. In this sense there's a neat overlap with the firm's other flagship practice. Unless you live in a cave, the IP group's clients should be immediately recognisable: A&P has handled regular work for Sony, Orange and Disney, as well as a host of matters arising from the rebranding and relaunch of Virgin Media. A&P's media lawyers notably represented Random House and Dan Brown, the publisher and author of *The Da Vinci Code*, when they were sued for copyright infringement by the authors of *The Holy Blood and the Holy Grail*. The prolonged litigation (and its famously playful judgment) was a major breakthrough for A&P, and trainees were on the frontline as it happened. Our sources raved about their time in IP, where 'the partners are particularly good at getting you involved' and always invite recruits to hearings or trials.

The corporate team has been increasing its influence in London. Last year it represented Veolia Transport on a number of matters, including a potential acquisition of a major transport company, as well as some pharma clients, major lenders and the governments of Brazil and Israel. Trainees are likely to set up shelf companies and conduct research as well as performing all the usual document management tasks that come with the territory. The highlight of a commercial seat is the opportunity to spend three months with the competition team in Brussels, described as 'sort of an island in the murky waters of EU competition law.' Fluency in French might lead to a wider variety of work.

Chambers UK rankings

Intellectual Property • Life Sciences • Media & Entertainment • Product Liability

Small is beautiful

Formal provisions for pastoral care are pretty loose. 'It's up to you to monitor your own workload' and 'it's not always easy to say no [to more]'– but it's never sink or swim and our sources had not felt out of their depth. 'You can make of it what you want, but you've got a structure where people look after you.' Trainees sit with 'protective' associates, a mentoring scheme is often called on only for the 'free lunch' and 'everyone's got to keep their doors open.' There are 'sporadic' internal training sessions, but the firm pays for trainees to go on any relevant training courses they feel they'd benefit from.

Our interviewees valued working in a relatively small office, where 'there's a lot more personality that might get lost in bigger City practices.' Birthday cakes in the kitchen are testament to a friendly and familiar atmosphere. Work hours are variable but fair: 'That can mean you're substantially busier than your contracted hours, but also means that leaving at 5.30pm is an option when there's not a lot on.'

Small offices are a hallmark of most American firms in London, but otherwise A&P's transatlantic origins might be hard for the newcomer to spot. 'Most of our work is sourced in the UK,' our sources said, all agreeing that the office didn't just feel like an outpost of the USA HQ. They also pointed to A&P's Washington origins, 'which means it's not a bill-as-much-as-you-can and destroy-your-soul firm.' Its size and standing in the States means it receives instructions 'out of proportion' to its size in London, and it has document production and typing teams in the USA ready to do London's bidding. 'All the new joiners get to go see the mothership,' when they attend the new associates' retreat. As for A&P's Stateside reputation for being a bit left-of-centre or 'liberal with a small L' (eg lobbying work for the Democratic Party and progressive causes), there's no such political culture in the London office.

Rooms with a view

So who does A&P recruit? Usually it's people from top-end universities with impressive academic records. 'The USA has to look at CVs and give final approval, though I can't think of any circumstance where they'd say no,' revealed one source. Anyone who's interested is advised to thoroughly research the kind of work the firm does and clearly state why they're interested in those areas, so 'maybe it's not the best firm for people who aren't really sure what they want to do.' It's perhaps worth knowing that a science background is 'not uncommon' and 'a lot of the partners are qualified medical doctors.' As one source explained: 'Some of the most experienced pharma lawyers have no science background, but if you're looking for that kind of work it can add much more to your understanding.'

There are no trainee-specific social events organised by the firm, although new joiners get a budget allocation to take 'pretty much anyone they like' out to lunch. Instead, a social committee organises firm-wide initiatives. The long gaps between the annual Christmas and summer parties are filled with Thursday 'Garden Room' drinks, named after a tradition started in the firm's very first office in DC. A monthly staff lunch involves games, prizes, raffles and themed non-alcoholic cocktails. New starters all spend a long weekend in DC getting to know the firm, and if you're lucky enough to be in a department at the right time you might be invited on a week's retreat in Virginia.

As might be expected from this firm, pro bono opportunities are plentiful. One source explained the process: '[Pro bono matters] are offered around the office. If there's something the co-ordinators think a particular person will do well at, they ask them to do it.' Recent matters have included advising international student organisation AIESEC, Liberty, Fair Trials Abroad and PIPLinks, which supports the human rights of indigenous peoples in the Philippines. The firm sets a minimum-hours target for pro bono work and it's taken into account when calculating bonuses. And all this from A&P's eyrie on the 30th floor of Tower 42, where 'we possibly have the best views of any office in the City!'

And finally...

A&P's training programme will be biannual for the time being, but if its mix of commercial, pharmaceuticals and IP practice intrigues you, it could be worth the wait. Try the vac scheme: They've really thought it out. You'll know at the end of those two weeks if you want to work here.

- **Take a chance:** Places on training schemes can open up even if quotas were originally filled. A firm might decide to expand or recruits might drop out, so if you're looking for a training contract to start early, it's worth asking your firm if it has any sudden openings.

  If you're asked to defer the start of your contract, ask yourself 'would that be so bad?' There's a lot you can achieve in a year.

asb law

The facts

Location: Crawley, Maidstone

Number of UK partners/solicitors: 36/47

Total number of trainees: 10

Seats: 4x6 months

Alternative Seats: Occasional secondments

The aviation practice ranks as among the best in the UK and has grown rapidly over the past year in terms of the work undertaken.

A force in the South East, asb law has been reshaping its business of late. It offers quality regional work across a broad range of areas of practice.

Less is more

In 1999 the euro was introduced, Britney Spears dominated the airwaves and we were all preoccupied with the impending Y2K disaster, not that it was ever that problematic. It was also the start of asb law as we know it. The firm emerged as a fusion of Maidstone's Argyle & Court, Stonehams of Croydon and Burstows, which had offices in Brighton, Horsham and Crawley. The world did not end with the millennium, but for asb things have not always gone entirely to plan: there was a phase of partner losses and poor financial results. Undeterred, the firm resolutely looked to a brighter future and, under new stewardship, is now reconfiguring its once-diffuse network of offices. Trainees tell us they 'feel confident in where the firm is going.'

Now pursuing a three-year strategy to boost profitability and improve turnover by more than a third to £25m by 2010, asb moved into new premises in Maidstone in 2006 and displayed a shift in focus towards its new Kent stronghold. 'asb aspire' was launched as a separate business handling residential conveyancing, personal injury and uninsured loss recovery. The latest development sees the firm closing its Brighton, Horsham and Croydon offices to concentrate solely on Crawley and Maidstone. The idea was that most fee earners from the other three would be consolidated into Crawley, however there have been redundancies, some of them voluntary.

Summing up, trainees tell us that 'convergence is at the forefront of the change' to bring both the commercial and private client aspects of the firm under one roof.

Understandably, 'there are a few people who don't agree, but I can generally see the long-term reasons,' one trainee commented. Actually the changes barely affect the trainees, who for the past year have only done seats in Maidstone and Crawley.

At the same time as the restructuring, the firm also appears to be targeting larger corporate commercial transactions and private client work for higher net worth individuals. When asked if they were in the loop in terms of where the firm was going, trainees' overall opinion was that they were, but 'sometimes the flow of information could be better as you hear on the grapevine what is going on then the official announcement comes.'

Diamond deals

Crawley was one of the six original New Towns created by the post-war Labour government to offer a better life away from smoggy and overcrowded London. Today it is far from countrified calm and not many people's idea of the des res of their dreams. From a business perspective it is viewed entirely differently. Crawley sits at the heart of the business-rich Gatwick Diamond (the region stretching from London down to Brighton and from Horsham over to East Grinstead), which explains the 'all bells and whistles for Crawley' approach – 'it just makes strategic sense.' Asb follows a sectoral approach to business, targeting areas such as aviation, technology, travel and charities. As one source said: 'We are proud of this approach as it stands us apart, but it's unlikely these areas will be focused on to the detriment of others.' The travel team draws in fee earners from a number of departments and works for clients such as Virgin Holidays, Sunsail and TUI Travel Group (formerly First Choice and Thomson Holidays), which it recently advised on the employment aspects of its creation. As you can imagine, when two major tour operators with a total of 19,000 employees combine there are going to be many issues to settle. The aviation practice ranks as among the best in the UK and has grown rapidly over the past year in terms of the work undertaken. The sort of things the team is involved in are the purchase and sale of passenger planes and private jets, and one client that recently benefited is Transaero – a fast-expanding Russian airline – which bought a number of planes from South African Airlines. Other work includes chartering and hiring agreements, maintenance agreements and agreements with tour operators and travel agencies.

Asb has a sterling reputation in corporate finance and this wins it a number-one spot in *Chambers UK* for the South. The team worked on some 70 deals valued at £600m last year, sits on the legal panels of Lloyds TSB and HSBC and undertakes regular work for Svenska Handelsbanken, Fortis, HBOS and Vanquis. Assisting the team on management buyouts and shareholder agreements, trainees get good experience in the corporate seat. Asb also has a successful commercial litigation department that offers what can be a 'hectic' seat. Our sources got to experience High Court trials, met barristers, created court bundles and interviewed witnesses around the country. Said one: 'It was very hands-on.' Aside from the big cases there is always a range of smaller files, such as partnership disputes or debt recovery claims on which trainees can take control of the day-to-day running. Another well-visited seat is tax, trusts and probate, where the occupant is never left wanting client contact. The clients are small estates as well as wealthy individuals, and here trainees occupy their time 'drafting wills, completing inheritance tax papers and managing Court of Protection work (when people became mentally incapable of controlling their funds).'

Pick 'n' mix

There's a vast array of practice groups on offer in this firm and no compulsories. Options fall into two strands: either commercial (corporate finance, commercial litigation, commercial contracts, commercial property/planning, insolvency and employment) or private client (tax, trusts and probate, family and personal injury, mainly of the defendant variety). We're told that in the first year 'you get what you're given,' with second-years being asked to give five preferences for their third and fourth seats. 'It's best to push for the ones you want and make your interests known from the start, otherwise you may miss out,' came their advice. Most people get their first or

Chambers UK rankings

Aviation • Banking & Finance • Corporate Finance • Dispute Resolution • Employment • Personal Injury • Private Client • Real Estate • Restructuring/Insolvency • Travel

second choice 'for at least one of these last two seats, and the fact that first-years have no choice means you have a better chance.' Exactly which seats are offered at each rotation depends on business needs, but departments such as commercial litigation and corporate are always available. Not all seats are offered at both offices, so 'it is always on the cards that you may have to move.' Some people do manage to avoid one or other location, not that it's a major drama to commute to either and a travel allowance is available.

Generally trainees felt they had lots of responsibility, something which caused one source to admit: 'I panic for five minutes that I can't cope, then realise they believe you can do it. And if you get stuck everyone is so friendly you can ask anyone for a hand.' Both offices are open-plan, which creates an atmosphere in which trainees feel able to shout up if they have too much or too little work. 'Even if the senior partner asks you to do something, you never feel you can't say no if you are at maximum capacity.' Something trainees also buzzed about was the fact that 'people recognise you have a life outside of work, as they do too – lots have young families or have things organised for their evenings.' Trainees are spared 'horrid City hours' and most are at their desks for a steady nine to five. At times, there will be 'the odd late one, depending on the deals going on.' In 2008 four of the five qualifiers stayed with the firm.

Speak up

Many people apply to asb for its location and our sources sensed the firm does look for trainees with a local connection, or at least 'enthusiasm for and commitment to the South East.' Another similarity between the trainees this year was the fact that all were women. We're reassured that the new intake in 2008 has two boys and more will follow. The firm appears to welcome applicants who have taken an alternative route to a training contract, resulting in 'a really good mix of people and certainly no single type' However, over the years we've learned that this is the sort of place where you need to speak up to get on, or as one interviewee summed it up: 'If you don't ask you don't get.'

Socially, your diary won't be blocked out for two years. In terms of Friday drinks, 'Crawley is not that nice a place to go out, but they are knocking areas down as we speak, so it may improve!' As for Maidstone, the office is out of town so 'most people drive to work and then just head straight home.' There was some regret about the closure of the Brighton office as it was always such a good town for out-of-hours fun. Luckily, following a realisation 'that things were slow on the social scene,' both Maidstone and Crawley now have a social committee and, thankfully, 'what they do, they do well.' We heard about bowling nights and theatre trips, and the Maidstone office hosts an annual summer BBQ with a rounders game thrown in for added laughs. The event is open to people's families too. One trainee did indicate that 'the distance between the two offices is a shame, as it is a bit of a blockade to the social side of the firm.' The only joint event is the summer party – generally a dinner and disco – but trainees do occasionally organise a group get-together. Young Professionals Network events are a good opportunity to mingle with other lawyers and accountants from the area.

Lunch is the best time to catch up with colleagues and we heard the break-out/kitchen area in the Crawley office has a Wii for healthy midday competition. A host of real sporting options are on offer, including a few more unusual things such as beach volleyball and dragon boat racing. Trainees are 'not hugely involved in client entertaining,' however when seminars are organised by the firm they are encouraged to go along and chat to clients. Our sources were pleased to tell us that they do get to celebrate with the rest of their team after deal closures, court wins or simply when a department thinks it deserves a pat on the back. Such perks have included a trip to London for some embarrassing karaoke, a weekend to Cambridge for a spot of punting and a black-tie ball.

And finally...

Asb has plenty of experience in a good spread of practices. If you can show a commitment to the South East, are not afraid to voice your opinion and don't mind moving around, then this is one for the short list.

Forget the competition

At Ashurst we work as a team, which means less competition and more communication.

If you've got team spirit call Stephen Trowbridge, Graduate Recruitment & Development Manager, Ashurst LLP, on 020 7638 1111, email gradrec@ashurst.com or visit www.ashurst.com

ABU DHABI BRUSSELS DUBAI FRANKFURT LONDON MADRID MILAN MUNICH NEW DELHI NEW YORK PARIS SINGAPORE STOCKHOLM TOKYO

Ashurst LLP

The facts

Location: London

Number of UK partners/solicitors: 136/333

Total number of trainees: 105

Seats: 4x6 months

Alternative seats: Secondments, overseas seats

Extras: Pro bono – Islington & Toynbee Hall legal advice centres, Disability Rights Commission, Business in the Community, Death Row Appeals; language training

> There are no wallflowers among Ashurst trainees; naturally, some are more studious than others, most people are game for a laugh.

The Ashurst website may be decked out in rainbow hues, but it's the colour of money that stands out at this successful City firm.

Ashurst and the amazing techni-colour dream

Not so very long ago, Ashurst had a reputation as a bit of a rah place. An old-school City firm founded by a bona fide Victorian eccentric and other Establishment figures, Ashurst Morris Crisp was the place where posh Oxbridge graduates went to train. Following a rebrand, during which it lost its Morris Crisp and adopted all the colours of the rainbow as its livery, that stuffy image has melted away to the extent that the trainees we spoke to sounded decidedly nonplussed when we brought it up. 'You've got to have the right academic record,' said one, but a 'conscious policy decision' has been made to widen the net. These days only about a quarter of recruits come from Oxbridge, although the majority do still hail from established universities like Bristol, Durham and Edinburgh rather than post-1992 foundations.

Three sets of abandoned merger talks back at the turn of the century convinced the partners that 'organic' growth was the best option for Ashurst, and it was probably at this stage they decided to shake up the firm's image. This in turn helped reinvigorate partners and staff such that by 2006 the firm had nudged its way over the £200m annual turnover mark. Some two years later and it has smashed through the £300m barrier, pulling in fees totalling £323m for the last financial year. It's no wonder, then, that trainees see a rosy future for the firm, saying that 'the focus is more and more on results and profits, but our strong point is that this is still a fun place to work.'

Like so many of its City rivals, Ashurst has cast itself as a corporate and finance firm, and our parent publication *Chambers UK* ranks it highly in both these fields. Also worthy of note is a litigation department that is 'underrated,' even within the firm. Its product liability unit in particular is superb, and it counts Imperial Tobacco as a major client. Ashurst's corporate/finance fixation extends to the training contract, where in a four-seat system trainees must visit both of these core areas. Seat allocation has proved tricky of late: there was a certain amount of dissatisfaction among fourth-seaters this year, after many of them went unwillingly into finance teams for their final seat. 'I think the firm were surprised by the strength of our reaction,' said one affected party. We sense that, despite not being an entirely perfect system, this particular problem was a one-off and things should get back to normal.

At the oche

One of the reasons so many fourth-seaters ended up in finance recently was an attempt to end something of a tradition of putting first-seaters in the department. Almost everyone we spoke to had started their contract in one of the three major finance teams (real estate finance, leveraged finance and securities and structured finance [SSF]), and naturally partners and associates were getting a little tired of taking in hordes of wet-behind-the-ears newbies. Ashurst's finance lawyers handle substantial deals: the leveraged and real estate finance teams recently joined forces to act for Odeon in a major restructuring to allow the cinema chain's refinancing without damaging its operational viability. They also represented Bank of Scotland, RBS and Barclays on the £1.44bn acquisition of one of BUPA's holding companies. Real estate finance trainees get stuck into 'a lot of Form 395 applications, run conditions precedent lists, update all the parties concerned as to the status of a transaction... managing deals from the bottom basically.' Leveraged finance brings a similar type of work. More responsibility is forthcoming in the 'very niche, very academic' SSF team; 'a great group of people who take a lot of interest in training.' As befits 'a growing and busy area,' the firm has ensured there is good admin support from paralegals and proof-readers, and paper bibles are now a thing of the past here so trainees are spared that drudgery. Instead, 'you manage your own stuff, and day to day there's a lot of drafting.' On the downside, the hours 'can be brutal,' so it's great to hear that 'the people in finance are a warm team, and it's not a department where you would get shouted at.'

Ashurst's excellent corporate department frequently scoops mandates that might otherwise have gone to the magic circle firms and it is especially fêted for its private equity expertise. Life in the corporate department means an up-and-down schedule. At the time we called, the lawyers were experiencing a quiet patch, although a period of 'very intense' work was still fresh in our contacts' minds. Most of them had worked on one of two massive deals: the first was the acquisition of the digital TV company Sparrowhawk Holdings by American media giant NBC Universal, in which Ashurst advised the British company's shareholders. The second was the £2bn merger of Merlin Entertainments (the company behind Alton Towers, the London Eye and Legoland) with Madame Tussauds. This deal was backed by private equity company Blackstone. In a major coup for Ashurst, hedge fund Cerberus turned to its lawyers when it decided to bid for Northern Rock. On such deals, 'you can write off your social calendar... I still liked the atmosphere though, even if it took me a while to get used to it.'

There are a few moans about corporate seats however. 'I think trainees are sometimes treated a little too much like paralegals,' said one source. It is true that there's a lot of due diligence, verification, 'data room after data room,' taking minutes at board meetings and 'all the things you'll hear a thousand trainees talk about,' however, people seem to appreciate that 'the work gets better as you move up.' The ultimate test comes at qualification, and there is always competition for NQ jobs in corporate. Furthermore the corporate team is 'prone to giving you time off' after a busy period and there are dartboards dotted around the office to help relieve stress. Despite the high-pressured nature of the department, no one has succumbed to temptation and scored a bull's eye in a colleague's head. Believe us, we asked.

Chambers UK rankings

Banking & Finance • Banking Litigation • Capital Markets • Competition/European Law • Construction • Corporate Finance • Dispute Resolution • Employee Share Schemes • Employment • Environment • Financial Services Regulation • Fraud: Civil/Criminal • Insurance • Intellectual Property • Investment Funds • Life Sciences • Local Government • Outsourcing • Pensions • Planning • Private Equity • Product Liability • Projects, Energy & Natural Resources • Real Estate • Real Estate Finance • Real Estate Litigation • Restructuring/Insolvency • Tax • Telecommunications • Transport

Oil right

'Historically, Ashurst has not been perceived as a litigation firm,' nevertheless it has good cases, covering everything from international arbitration to banking, real estate, defamation, IP and fraud. With clients like FTSE 100 mining company Vedanta Resources, O2, Motorola, BAE Systems, Royal & SunAlliance, IBM, Canary Wharf, Goldman Sachs, Abbey and Tesco, this is not a department to be ignored. Once again trainees can expect their share of less glamorous work and 'stinking great bundles' of court documents, however most enjoy the research aspect. 'One of the shocks of litigation is actually having books on your desk again,' said one who had almost forgotten what studying law was like. The biggest case of the moment is the litigation arising from the explosion at the Buncefield oil storage depot in December 2005. Similarly, real estate is often overlooked, which is a shame given that trainees who spent time there are quick to praise the team. 'You really run a lot of cases on your own,' said one, mentioning the leasing and management of individual retail units in a shopping centre as a common way for trainees to get involved. Ashurst is on board with the plans to develop the Shard of Glass skyscraper at London Bridge, and was behind the joint venture between PropInvest and Derek Quinlan to acquire the Citi building in Canary Wharf for £1bn.

Energy, transport and infrastructure (ETI) is another popular team and an important earner for the firm. Its domestic and international work 'spans everything from oil and gas projects to building schools and hospitals. They try to put you in different areas to get a chance to see the full range of things.' The firm's relationships in the rail sector are particularly strong, and it has acted for Transport for London on several major projects, including the £100m extension of the Docklands Light Railway to Stratford International and the largest proposed transport infrastructure project in the world – Crossrail.

Client secondments are available to the likes of IBM, Citi, JPMorgan and Merrill Lynch. 'It really takes the blinkers off,' said one trainee. 'You suddenly realise your client's interest is really not all about the law.' The firm also sends people to some of its numerous international outposts. Ashurst is particularly strong in Europe, where it has branches in Brussels, Frankfurt, Madrid, Milan, Munich, Paris and Stockholm. Further afield it operates from Dubai, New York, Singapore, New Delhi and Tokyo. 'They won't be rushed by anyone,' one trainee said of the Paris office. 'They love lengthy debates on moot points of law – London is perhaps more pragmatic.' Don't be fooled; international seats can be as hard as any but give 'an unprecedented opportunity to get to know a region and to see how different offices work.' In all seats there are standard appraisals every three months and each trainee also has an annual review with the HR team.

The law of the jungle

At law school, many of our contacts had heard that Ashurst was a 'friendly and sociable' place to work, and were keen to inform us that the reputation was well deserved. There is even a widely held belief that March intakes tend to be more sociable than September ones. An explanation was offered: 'The September intake have usually come straight from law school, while people in the March group have often taken seven months off to go travelling and are still buzzing and keen to make friends.' From talking to a range of trainees we did note that the Marchies had more to say about the social life of the firm.

Friday night drinks in Exchange Square is a regular fixture, and among the big organised events is 'a summer ball at an old manor house with all sorts of theme park rides.' There's a definite fitness vibe: a three peaks challenge had just been completed by some of the trainees, and one has even been granted time off to go and climb Everest. Most settle with 'going to the gym together' or joining the firm's 'fairly decent' rugby and football teams.

There are 'no wallflowers' among Ashurst trainees; naturally, some are more studious than others, 'most people are game for a laugh.' Dressing up seems to be a running theme, for example at the intriguing black-tie 'with a twist of grrr' themed party at London Zoo, one trainee interrupted the speeches by 'dancing in an all-in-one leopardskin catsuit to the tune of *In The Jungle*.' Another came into work dressed in his Christmas party elf costume after a partner promised to make a donation to charity. Trainees can't even do something simple like dragon boat racing without feeling the need to dress up as 'Jane Fonda-type 80s aerobic instructors.' More seriously, many get involved with the firm's various charitable activities.

And finally...

Ashurst has an ambition to be 'the biggest law firm in the UK outside the magic circle.' Its focus on private equity, its growing hedge funds experience and its interest in shareholder activism and sovereign wealth funds are perfectly in tune with a changing corporate market.

Your perspective × Our world

Multiplying
your potential

"It's exactly how I wanted my career to develop. I'm working in a global, multi-cultural setting, on high quality deals with blue-chip clients, and all within a welcoming and supportive environment. It's about helping me to develop my experience and enabling me to be the best lawyer I can be."

Emily Carlisle, Associate, Corporate

Do you want to multiply your potential?
www.multiplyingyourpotential.co.uk

Baker & McKenzie LLP

The facts

Location: London

Number of UK partners/solicitors: 84/209

Total number of trainees: 77

Seats: 4x6 months

Alternative seats: Overseas seats, secondments

Extras: Pro bono – eg Waterloo Legal Advice Centre, Caribbean death row appeals, Prisoners Abroad; language training

The classic Baker Mac London trainee has gone to a top university and is academically strong. People tend to be quite commercially minded and interested in business, and a few arrive with other career experience.

After prize-fighting his way through university in Chicago, all-round hero Russell Baker founded a law firm in 1949 with a man he'd met in a cab a year earlier. Their vision was to create a truly international business. Intrigued? Either buy yourself a copy of *Pioneering A Global Vision: The Story of Baker & McKenzie* or read on...

Around the world in 60 years

Baker & McKenzie has grown to a whopping 3,600 lawyers in 70 offices across 38 countries stretching from Tijuana and Taipei to Bangkok and Baku. Trainees are acutely aware that this makes it one of the biggest firms on the planet; indeed it is this aspect that drew them to B&M in the first place. Although global domination is not usually the domain of the liberal, the firm has somehow managed to maintain a philosophy of equality across the network and allows a degree of autonomy for each office. There is apparently 'no dominant nationality' at the firm, so while the firm's chairman is based in Chicago and 'the odd internal procedure may be dealt with out of the States,' trainees were emphatic that 'we certainly don't answer to them.' The stats back them up: the London branch opened in 1961, has grown to become the biggest office in the network, and is increasingly one of its most profitable. 'The partners here are nearly all British,' confirmed sources, before assuring us that the work isn't: 'The firm's international scope is evident in almost all of what you do.'

By way of proof, London lawyers have recently assisted on the complex restructuring of three multibillion-dollar global businesses for American Standard Companies Inc, which works in 50 countries worldwide. They assisted MerchantBridge, as part of a consortium with Qtel and AsiaCell, on its $1.25bn acquisition of an Iraqi GSM licence and advised Daiwa SMBC Principal Investment on the ¥16bn buyout of HMV Group's Japanese business. It's not only the work that's international but also the way the lawyers work in 'truly European practice groups,' so that even trainees 'speak to people all over the world.' Putting faces to familiar voices, they're also invited to attend international departmental conferences or jollies: 'The property department went skiing this weekend and met up with property people from Milan.'

Brand loyalty

Baker & McKenzie has its fingers in an awful lot of pies and a breadth of practice in the London office, which naturally benefits trainees. Each is given one preferred seat, which can be more or less guaranteed at some point over the two years, and as payback,' they try to steer you towards the corporate and finance departments, which are the biggest.' Corporate is actually compulsory and quite often crops up in the first year, if not as a first seat. The experience is good for showing you how the firm fits together, as it is the department with the most obvious international reach and trainees are perpetually 'picking up the phone and speaking to counterparts in Mexico or Korea.' Despite corporate having a reputation for long hours and hard graft, our sources hadn't been worked to the bone. Said one: 'I had two or three weeks where I was working really hard and only one all-nighter. Apart from that it was fairly steady.' It sounds as if there's every reason to enjoy the experience: 'At times I got a lot of responsibility – on a company reorganisation I drafted all the documents and I helped on a private equity deal.' Banking and finance has been a growing area of practice in London in recent years and the firm is proud to represent major banks such as Citi, Dresdner Kleinwort, HSBC and ING. Despite the pressures and the occasional long nights and early mornings, the department is welcoming. It is split into two teams – one dealing with securitisation and capital markets, the other with banking and acquisition finance.

Trainees say that even in a quieter transactional market, B&M can rely on its 'extras' to attract new trainees. In other words, 'its international, standalone niche areas,' such as IP/IT, pensions, competition and employment. The strength of these non-transactional departments means 'you get excellent exposure to specific advisory work and they are not just corporate department satellites.' Work with the IP lawyers for example and you'll be introduced to the likes of Apple, Accenture, Arts Council England and AstraZeneca: that's only the clients beginning with the letter A. By the time you've reached Vodafone and Yahoo! you'll have advised half the best-known brands on the planet. And then there's the 'intellectually stimulating' competition law department, which challenges trainees' research skills. 'It's a mixture of merger control and contentious antitrust work involving EU cartel cases.' Apparently it 'also advises on trade issues, which can mean giving advice to clients on the application of sanctions on different regimes.' Lawyers here have lately acted for Mitsubishi Electric in a number of European Commission cartel investigations; advised the BBC Trust (which replaced its governors in 2007) on competition, state aid and regulatory matters; and provided general counsel to Sony, Seiko, Sharp and Timex.

Dispute resolution seats are prized because trainees are 'not just treated as a bundler or photocopier' but see 'real variety of work from fraud to arbitration to construction to general commercial matters to trust litigation.' They might even be 'let loose on some small matters.' Property seats definitely involve running your own files. Eye-catching clients include Borders, Cisco Systems, eBay, Levi Strauss or Versace, and jumping from one matter to another, speaking to clients or answering queries from the Land Registry and Companies House is the daily fare.

Niche and easy

The popularity of those excellent niche areas means qualification decisions sometimes aren't easy. It sounds as if the firm has tackled this problem head on and we hear that an increasing number of new recruits arrive with interests in finance and corporate. 'The emphasis has

Chambers UK rankings

Administrative & Public Law • Advertising & Marketing • Banking & Finance • Banking Litigation • Capital Markets • Climate Change • Competition/European Law • Construction • Corporate Finance • Data Protection • Dispute Resolution • Employee Share Schemes • Employment • Environment • Financial Services Regulation • Franchising • Fraud: Criminal • Immigration • Information Technology • Intellectual Property • Media & Entertainment • Outsourcing • Pensions • Private Client • Product Liability • Professional Discipline • Projects, Energy & Natural Resources • Public Procurement • Telecommunications

changed since I applied,' confirmed a source; 'there is now a pull to corporate and to portraying the firm as a big corporate and banking player. This is realistic and it makes sense.'

One thing that hasn't changed is the tendency for trainees to visit an overseas office or try a client secondment. The latter are viewed as a 'refreshing' change, and for one of our interviewees it meant feeling 'really important to the team' with a 'constant stream of work, all within my comfort zone so I could turn it around rapidly.' Overseas seats were the highlight for others. The trick is to decide which practice area you want then find out which offices can offer you a space. Hong Kong is a good choice for property; Sydney does a nice line in IT; for corporate there's Chicago, Moscow, Sydney or Melbourne, while Washington and Brussels are the places for competition/antitrust. With the firm organising accommodation, flights and visas, the transition couldn't be easier, and if the three-month trainee posting is just too short, once qualified it's possible to transfer to another office for up to two years.

Back at home the training scheme runs smoothly. As well as 'positive and encouraging supervisors,' there are junior and senior associates who are 'ridiculously good at what they do' to 'watch and model yourself on.' Of course, a training contract is a time for learning and making mistakes and there's 'constant feedback, with departments telling you how you've done and giving you scores to let you know how you can improve.' We hear that the graduate recruitment team is clear about 'where you're going and they will tell you if something is a popular choice and you should look elsewhere.' It goes without saying that 'you'll never have a problem getting something in corporate and banking.' In 2008 20 of the 24 qualifiers stayed on with the firm, the largest number going into corporate.

Low-pressure cookers

B&M is 'somewhere where you feel motivated but can also have a giggle,' although some people are more stiff-collared than others: 'I went to a vac scheme evening out and changed into my jeans but was told it would have been better to stay suited.' Hours are determined by department, so somewhere like pensions might require you from 9am to 6.30pm, whereas in a busy period in corporate you could be in until 8pm consistently and occasionally much later. Get into a department where you want to impress and there might be some self-imposed pressure to stay late. 'I threw myself into one seat and used to stay until 8pm or 9pm regularly,' admitted one trainee who thankfully 'got the recognition for it.' We hear that a weekend spent working is 'a one-off rather than an occupational hazard.'

The classic Baker Mac London trainee has gone to a top university and is academically strong. 'People tend to be quite commercially minded and interested in business,' and a few arrive with other career experience, so there is usually a mix of interests and age groups. An international outlook is essential and the firm is said to want 'co-operative individuals – there's a great sense of things being done together in departments or even globally, not single-handedly churning out work.' What this produces is an atmosphere in which 'there's no snobbery or old-school-tie culture and not too much hierarchy.' The office itself is well appointed with a 'brilliant' subsidised staff canteen outsourced to 'really creative' caterers. 'At any time of day you can get everything from a yoghurt to a tub of dried apricots or a latte.'

On the second Friday of every month there are drinks for all London staff. First-seat trainees take on bar-tending duties, which can be a good way to get to know everyone. Sports are another option. The men's football team competes each year in the Baker Cup European tournament at which 'the Germans are renowned for their competitiveness and the Frankfurt office normally fights us for the cup.' For the Manches Cup sailing regatta, 'you don't have to prove you've sailed the Atlantic five times to get in a team.' Classic venues are chosen for the big office-wide parties – a black-tie Christmas ball at The Savoy and a garden party in one of the Inns of Court. Not everyone loves the City's 'work hard, play hard ethos' that is 'as pervasive here as everywhere,' but 'most of the trainees get on well and go out on a regular basis.' Of course, future intakes of trainees will already know each other, having met at law school on the B&M LPC+ course run by the College of Law in London.

And finally...

If you want to work for a massive international firm but you don't fancy walking into a huge office then Baker & McKenzie is ideal. We strongly recommend you investigate its cracker of a vacation scheme, which offers up to three months of experience in both London and an overseas office.

BARLOW LYDE & GILBERT

www.blg.co.uk

For more information please contact Caroline Walsh, Head of Graduate Recruitment and Trainee Development

Barlow Lyde & Gilbert LLP
Beaufort House
15 St Botolph Street
London EC3A 7NJ

Telephone 020 7643 8065
Facsimile 020 7643 8500

grad.recruit@blg.co.uk

Barlow Lyde & Gilbert LLP

The facts

Location: London

Number of UK partners/solicitors: 78/209

Total number of trainees: 41

Seats: 4x6 months

Alternative seats: Hong Kong, Singapore, secondments

Extras: Pro bono – Toynbee Hall Legal Advice Centre, Caribbean death row appeals

> The vacation scheme is central to BLG's recruitment process and approximately 75% of trainees secure their contracts this way.

City-based Barlow Lyde & Gilbert LLP is home to one of the UK's largest and most prominent litigation and dispute resolution practices and sits on the front row when it comes to insurance and professional indemnity. If you want to litigate, arbitrate and mediate on a huge range of disputes, then read on.

Litigreat!

The majority of BLG lawyers work within its mighty dispute resolution team. Having been involved with the insurance sector pretty much since it was created in non-marine form, BLG's collective expertise covers everything from marine, aerospace, energy and transport cases through to personal injury and police authority matters. The firm has a peerless reputation for professional negligence litigation, and in the field of clinical negligence it sits on the all-important NHS Litigation Authority legal panel. Prominence in insurance has also attracted big names from other sectors, among them Rolls-Royce, British Airways and Deutsche Bank. And how could we not mention BLG's involvement in the truly enormous Equitable Life case that dominated the litigation landscape during the early noughties.

After some lean years in its core insurance and litigation markets, and a spate of high-profile departures from the partnership, among them Clare Canning who led a team to success on that mammoth Equitable Life case, BLG appears to be staging a recovery. The bounce back could be credited to a number of things: a resurgence of litigation instructions following the credit crunch, recent partner-level hires or the efforts of a PR firm to push BLG as a place for commercial litigation as well as insurance cases. Whatever the cause, a 7% increase in annual turnover to more than £80m and rising internal promotions are all healthy signs, and a record eight home-grown associates were made partner this year.

Three out of four seats in a BLG training could be contentious, so 'if corporate is your main interest, then this is not really your firm.' Given the size and prominence of the professional and financial disputes and commercial litigation and arbitration teams (PFD & CL), most trainees spend time in one or both. Until last year the teams were joined as one mammoth department, but the firm's desire to 'sell itself more widely than simply for insurance' and pursue general litigation work meant a split was sensible, so trainees can now spend time in various seats within each.

Blgging it

PFD is the 'flagship insurance department.' It advises the insurance companies of top-end professionals who come unstuck, and the roll call of clients is impressive: PwC from the world of accountancy, DTZ from surveying, and a gazillion solicitors' firms from the silver circle right through to the high street. PFD offers 'very good experience,' even if on the more complex cases 'running into millions' responsibility is fairly low. Trainees' days are occupied with taking attendance notes at client meetings, researching tricky points of law and preparing written updates on things like changes in FSA rules. On smaller files, trainees say supervisors 'just let you run with them if you can.' Professional liability is likely to be a busy field in coming years. Already many cases relate to the construction world and the architects, engineers and other professionals operating within it. The Olympics, Crossrail and various other major developments are expected to generate disputes and divert resources away from other projects, which in turn could lead to difficulties and litigation on these other projects. The credit crunch may also lead to funding problems for large construction projects, in turn fuelling the number of claims. Another type of case that is making a comeback is disputes between mortgage companies and surveyors concerning the over-valuation of properties. Such cases were common following the early 90s property crash.

CL can also mean big-ticket litigation: working on the huge British Energy case in the Court of Appeal, then spotting it in *The Times* brought a 'cool, I worked on that' glow to one source. That case involved option rights for the coal-fired Eggborough Power Station, but others in 2008 included a successful tax registration appeal for DSG (formerly Dixons Group). Lawyers have also been appointed as investigators of alleged undisclosed receipt of share options by senior employees of Max Petroleum, and most recently the Inner London South District Coroner's Court appointed BLG as official solicitors to the inquest into the death of Jean Charles de Menezes. Naturally trainees take a lesser role on high-stakes cases, but it's worth knowing that both CL and PFD have large paralegal teams to absorb more tiresome tasks. 'I don't think I did any bundling in my seat,' sighed one source happily, though this isn't true across the firm. The department's 'trainee pool' system, which allows trainees to indicate their capacity (or lack thereof), is widely accepted to be a good way of achieving an even distribution of quality work.

Insurance may be big, big, big at BLG, but don't worry if 'third party, fire and theft' is the extent of your expert knowledge. Recruits now follow a specific College of Law LPC+ route with a specialised insurance module, meaning by the time they start at the firm the lingo comes naturally. Departments like reinsurance – traditionally less popular with trainees – clearly hope this will help counteract avoidance 'purely due to fear of not knowing anything about the area.' There's certainly no reason to miss this market-leading, 'challenging but fun' team, which acts on cases like the recent Lloyd's £350m Commercial Court claim against a major insurance/reinsurance broker and is 'very vibrant with lots of nights out.'

Men in uniform

The 'fast-paced' casualty and commercial risk (CCR) team defends claims for personal injury at work, cases

Chambers UK rankings

Aviation • Banking Litigation • Clinical Negligence • Commodities • Construction • Corporate Finance • Dispute Resolution • Employment • Environment • Financial Services Regulation • Health & Safety • Insurance • Outsourcing • Personal Injury • Police Law • Product Liability • Professional Discipline • Professional Negligence • Real Estate Litigation • Restructuring/Insolvency • Shipping • Transport • Travel

involving firemen and clinical negligence issues for the NHSLA. Trainees manage to gain 'an element of control over their own matters' in this seat, spending their time attending court, drafting instructions to counsel and working on letters of claim. 'It's also good because you get out of the office on site investigations and taking witness statements.' High Court visits to make simple applications before masters are memorable for some trainees, and one spent a day interviewing firemen... perhaps not a career ambition but certainly enough to arouse envy among quite a few colleagues.

Smaller, niche areas of litigation are also open to trainees, including aerospace, and marine, energy and trade, which offer a greater sense of intimacy and involvement. Recent highlights include defending the UK Civil Aviation Authority in High Court proceedings arising out of a fatal gyroplane accident, and the London market hull and machinery insurers on the total loss of the cruise ship 'Sea Diamond' while berthing at Santorini in Greece. There are always a few trainees who find their feet in 'wet and dry shipping cases' or 'commodities trading in grain and sugar.'

Trainees were keen to stress that the non-contentious side of the firm is 'not just a sideline.' Tax, property, employment, commercial technology and straight corporate all fall under the coco umbrella and are flourishing. Particularly eye-catching are several recent billion-pound transactions for the corporate team in the food manufacturing and healthcare sectors. Corporate trainees manage the due diligence for company purchases, prepare minutes and resolutions for board meetings and generally help smooth transactions to a conclusion. 'Comm Tech' is a popular seat covering data protection, outsourcing and competition issues. Since suffering a number of departures a couple of years ago, the team is now rebuilding its numbers and client base. However, employment was this year's 'real hot spot;' it's a 'thriving' team where trainees are 'very much in demand.' These non-core departments obtain much of their work from insurance companies through internal referrals but do also have their own impressive clients, including Tesco, mobile phone company 3 and the consumer's champion *Which?*

Hong Kong dingdong

Most sources had been able to gain experience in their preferred departments, even if it meant biding time elsewhere first. In all seats, trainees sit with their supervisor and receive work from across the department. 'It's a good way to get your name known,' and so long as the system of monitoring workloads is working well, variety of experience follows naturally. Supervisors are deemed 'very supportive' and, following a few grumbles from past years' trainees, we hear that the amount and timing of feedback is sufficient. As one trainee put it: 'The people who now supervise trainees are those best suited for the job.' As well as formal end-of-seat appraisals with HR, mid-seat reviews with supervisors allow trainees to 'get an inkling of how we're getting on and how to improve.'

There always used to be a bit of a tussle for seats in the Hong Kong office, which offers a contentious and non-contentious option, but this year also saw the introduction of a contentious seat in Singapore, easing competition. The feeling is 'if you ask twice you are likely to get it.' One trainee speculated that expansion in Asia is likely to continue as the firm is 'developing a local client base.' If spending six months away from the office appeals then a client secondment might be just the ticket.

Lettuce play

BLG is a sociable place and recruits are invariably 'the type who are up for going out and keen to get involved in the wider social aspects of being a trainee.' As is common to litigation-led firms, the hours are 'pretty decent,' so knocking off around 7pm allows plenty of social time. The nearby Slug and Lettuce has always been the trainees' favourite after-work venue, though they also join in organised wine tasting events and go for curries. Actually there's plenty of firm-wide socialising: regular meet and greets in the reception area or roof garden encourage departments to span the divisions created by

the firm being spread over the third, seventh and eighth floors of its building. There are also departmental events, such as PFD karaoke and a fancy dress summer party at which 'people really got into dressing up.' Every Friday afternoon a drinks trolley is delivered to each department offering 'a good reason to stop for the day and relax.' Trainees are also included on the guest list at client events and can join one of the BLG sports teams – cricket, rugby sevens, football. The brave, fit or insane can sign up to BLG's annual London-to-Brighton cycle race team.

As for grumbles, we heard the odd comment about 'pretty revolting' sandwiches and 'slightly cramped offices,' and there was an element of frustration that on the admin front 'trainees are generally the last to be consulted.' These aside, the people we spoke to were happy. Fourteen of the 19 qualifiers stayed on with the firm in 2008, most going into litigation teams.

The vacation scheme is central to BLG's recruitment process and approximately 75% of trainees secure their contracts this way. Most applicants have no experience of the insurance world, however if you have spent time working within it this will allow you to stand out. The only other tip trainees have is to leave any attitude at the door – 'If you are arrogant then you just won't fit in.'

And finally...

Barlow Lyde & Gilbert is a long-time litigation heavyweight. Its training contract packs powerful contentious punch while also giving exposure to transactional work.

Bates Wells & Braithwaite LLP

The facts

Location: London

Number of UK partners/solicitors: 26/56

Total number of trainees: 10

Seats: 2x6 + 3x4 months

Alternative seats: None

Extras: Pro bono – Blackfriars Legal Advice Centre, St Bartholomew's free will service, LawWorks; language training

> Working with interesting and inspiring people who are so committed to their sector that you can't help but be impressed breeds loyalty. So too does an inclusive environment populated by liberal-minded people.

Bates Wells & Braithwaite is that rarest of rare specimens, the lesser-spotted City firm with a conscience.

Charity begins at home

Distinguishable for its charities, administrative, employment and immigration law expertise, BWB has been busy acquiring sports and media/defamation abilities to match, but above all this is a place where a commercial outlook doesn't come at the cost of principles. 'One of our slogans is 'The City firm with a difference'. We have the feeling and professionalism of the City, but equally you can't put a tag on us, the firm is unique.' We'll not argue. Where else in the Square Mile could you work on theatre and defamation law matters while also finding such a 'strong commitment to the third sector' that charity clients receive a substantial discount on fees? Where else could trainees expect to become charity trustees or sit on the boards of trusts? Nowhere else is the simple answer.

Clearly many people are drawn to this aspect of the firm – it has, after all, the UK's top charity law team. 'It's not because it's all good in a holier-than-thou way, but good because you're making a difference, for example in the regulatory area, you're working at the intersection of law with politics and government.' Charity and social enterprise issues undoubtedly 'drive the firm,' however BWB is definitely more than the sum of its charitable parts. Our sources had observed 'more value being put on other types of work,' pointing out by way of example that 'we've traditionally worked for public health sector clients and now we're trying to generate work in the private sector.' A 2006 management overhaul has proved profitable in all senses, and the subsequent hire of sports law partner Mike Townley and media/defamation experts

Rupert Earle and Martin Kramer from Addleshaw Goddard has provided clout and synergy across the administrative, litigation and charities fields.

It's important to understand that 'the third sector is changing and Bates Wells is at the centre of that change.' These days many charities are 'massive organisations run on a commercial, professional basis, not the woolly, cardigan-wearing stereotype of the past.' But any fears about the erosion of what makes BWB so distinctive were quickly pooh-poohed: 'There's still the feeling of the old tribal Bates Wells; we might have taken on a more commercial approach but this will never make us a cut-throat firm.'

Pick your own

The breadth of the training reflects the firm's eclectic strengths and its unique seat structure of two six-month placements in the first year (chosen from immigration, charities, coco or 'first-year litigation'), followed by three four-month seats in the second (chosen from real estate, 'second-year litigation', administrative law, private client, employment and the occasional sports law, theatre and arts seat). Seat allocations are decided by trainees 'sitting down and trying to work out who wants to go where.' As you might imagine, people tend to behave well throughout this process. No matter where they seat themselves, a characteristic feature of BWB work is that 'you're involved in headline stuff, the pure law where the firm is acting to push the boundaries of the law or clear up points for clients.' As such, it's worth considering the practice areas in turn.

The charities department is 'really busy, incredibly colourful work-wise' and thrives on 'being the best.' Modern charities are 'run as complicated corporate structures' and require their legal teams to be as on-the-ball as those serving big City institutions. 'You meet the chief executives of charities on a daily basis and they are formidable business people,' sources explained. By way of illustration, recent cases include the merger of John Grooms Housing Association with The Shaftesbury Society, creating a new charity with 2,000 employees and turnover of approximately £50m, and advising multinational Amnesty International on its application for charitable status. Other major clients include the Rugby Football Union, Diabetes UK, National Council for Voluntary Organisations, Countryside Alliance Foundation and The Samaritans. It adds up to 'lots of responsibility because the team really needs you' and, when occasion demands, 'staying very late.' By way of compensation, trainees end up with 'the kind of work you'd never dream you'd get' and note how 'people are very grateful for what you do.' Typical tasks include 'setting up charities and making sure they're acting within their objects,' as well as assisting on 'setting up all the necessary contracts to carry out aid work in Africa' or helping to resolve trustee disputes. The 'big-team feel' finds its counterpart in the voluntary work that trainees can get involved in, perhaps a spot of campaigning for the voluntary sector that might take them as far as Parliament. 'If you want to be a charity lawyer, you want to be in on the policy side of it all too,' enthusiasts explained.

Wheels in motion

BWB has set up a number of client-facing groups to service sectors such as education, carbon trading and trade associations, and consequently, trainees can engage with a broad spread of matters even within seats. The coco team, for example, represents clients in the television, sports, film and theatre worlds, as well as charities and any number of other bog-standard corporates. It counts Friends of the Earth and Ethical Investment Research Services as clients and recently worked on the sale of bike chain Cycle Surgery to Snow & Rock Sports and the substantial sale of Challenger Security Services (provider of DX document exchange service). Meanwhile, the arrival of top sports law practitioner Mike Townley has brought in new clients and plenty of fresh instructions. In the short term, trainees taking a seat in the charities department will be able to pick up some arts, media and sports work. Perhaps trade mark, IP and other rights/obligations with regard to the London 2012 Olympics for the International Paralympic Committee. Or maybe they'll help with matters for sporting regulatory bodies – BWB recently acted for 16 of the Trinidad & Tobago Football World Cup squad in relation to unpaid World Cup bonuses and helped the ECB form the England and Wales Cricket Trust. New sports clients include the Football

Association, Premier League, IFSA Strongman (World's Strongest Manrights owner) and MotorSport Vision.

BWB's litigators handle 'a real mixed bag' of claims relating to anything from the position of a hedge to IP infringements. In this smaller department trainees get 'real responsibility, maybe handling a small contractual dispute yourself for a charity or commercial company.' They could also get a front-row seat on 'a dispute between theatres or a high-profile judicial review.' Recent media/defamation work includes acting for *The Times* in a successful Freedom of Information Act case, which forced HM Treasury to disgorge information relating to Gordon Brown's 1997 withdrawal of tax credits for pension funds, and The Sunday Times' Information Tribunal appeal concerning cost allowance claims by MPs. New partners have strengthened the administrative law practice, with Rupert Earle advising the Advertising Standards Authority on numerous judicial review threats. As the sole legal adviser to premium rate telephone industry regulator PhonepayPlus, the firm handled matters such as the *Richard & Judy* and GMTV premium rate call cases. Depending on business need, paralegals may or may not be around, so a trainee may be required to shoulder administrative tasks. Those completing a second-year stint can expect 'applications in the county courts and in the High Court before a master.'

Not dogg EAT dog

The immigration team's work helps set the agenda in the UK. Trainees are exposed to both corporate immigration matters for companies like Tesco, Endemol and Nike and fee-paying asylum seekers. One recent instruction saw lawyers successfully appeal the decision not to grant Snoop Dogg a visa to enter and perform in the UK. It was also busy in the run up to the implementation of a new points-based immigration system for the UK, handling a key judicial review challenging Home Office rule changes relating to the Highly Skilled Migrant Programme. One trainee recalled how 'my supervisor said, 'Get the file, do the letter... this is what you need to tell the Home Office, then go to the tribunal to represent us.''

A small property team with a predominantly residential conveyancing caseload is a quieter destination, as is an employment team that is nevertheless handling some landmark cases. Having secured the first-ever reference to the European Court of Justice on the Disability Discrimination Act, BWB received a verdict of discrimination by association for a legal secretary client, Sharon Coleman. Trainees find 'the short timescale of many matters means a lot of contact with clients' and there's a good amount of attendance at EAT tribunals. Finally, there's the three-lawyer private client team, which assists social entrepreneurs and new-money folk and includes secondments to the likes of the Tate Modern.

Just the ticket

The systems for seat allocation and NQ recruitment haven't always been the most cleanly run; however, 'fantastic new trainee partner' Dinah Tuck seems to have upped the consultative ante. Reflecting on this change in emphasis, trainees say: 'You feel as if you're really well looked after,' one adding: 'It's made an impact on me; you really feel a part of the firm, which wasn't quite how it was when I joined.' In 2008 all five qualifiers took up NQ positions. In instances where there is a mismatch of jobs and qualifiers' preferences, BWB's cross-sector approach can be helpful and the firm has a good record for 'being sympathetic to the specific areas you're interested in – they have the flexibility to build a role.' Working with 'interesting and inspiring people' who are 'so committed to their sector that you can't help but be impressed' breeds loyalty. So too does an inclusive environment populated by 'liberal-minded people.' While some – including consultant Andrew Phillips who is a Liberal Democrat Lord

– make that Liberal with a capital L, not everyone is so inclined. 'We've got the full spectrum of opinions here, so there are some healthy debates while you're making tea.' Nevertheless, regular 'talks on what partners have been doing in the voluntary sector' do highlight the firm's nature, so you'd be daft to come here without sharing its ideals and outlook. Trainees suggest 'a few of us had previous voluntary experience,' but say 'an interest that goes outside the legal work you do' is the way to endear yourself to recruiters rather than endless volunteer stints.

As 'people seem to have quirky hobbies' and full lives outside work, this is 'not the kind of firm where everyone goes out on a Friday night together.' There are 'well-attended boardroom drinks once a month' and trainees sometimes repair to a bar below the office. Plenty of theatre clients mean tickets to West End shows and 'organised fun' is catered for by 'a pub quiz that's become quite competitive' and 'wonderful' summer and Christmas parties.

And finally...

Bates Wells & Braithwaite's new commercial appetites and tasty sector specialisms are a potent blend. Don't expect to be the only one attracted to this City training with an ethical twist.

Beachcroft LLP

The facts

Location: Birmingham, Bristol, Leeds, London, Manchester, Winchester

Number of UK partners/solicitors: 137/440

Total number of trainees: 69

Seats: 4x6 months

Alternative seats: Secondments

Extras: Pro bono – eg Prince's Trust

> Although people here are good at what they do, they dont have big egos. There's not a City-firm vibe where everyone is determined to work late and not enjoy life.

Even with 1,400 staff on the books, this traditionally modest national giant is sometimes overlooked by students simply because 'it's not a big-stomping-feet law firm.' It is best known for insurance and health sector work and also offers a range of corporate and commercial services.

New stomping grounds

Since rebranding as Beachcroft LLP in 2006 the firm has been 'working on promoting itself, as it hasn't always done so as well as other firms.' Even so, 'many people's views are stuck on the firm being mainly insurance litigation and public sector work, especially health sector.' Until recently we would have agreed with trainees that such pigeon-holing was unfair, and the firm was justifiably 'trying to gain the recognition it deserves as a full-service firm,' however as recently as summer 2008 Beachcroft's management openly acknowledged these core client sectors are at the heart of the firm's business strategy. It's not that Beachcroft wants to underplay the progress it has made in the private sector – after all its employment group recently scooped McDonald's as a client – it's more about choosing to play to existing strengths. One way in which it does so is by leveraging its public sector prowess in the transactional sphere, recently bagging a role advising the Ministry of Justice on its £2.5bn property portfolio. In true Beachcroft fashion, while trying to become more of a full-service operation changes have been made in a subtle and considered way, 'keeping in mind the feelings of staff.' By not going all-out for change the firm may have saved itself the agony of too many redundancies in a tightening corporate market. So far the only casualties we've heard about are a handful of internationally focused lawyers in Beachcroft's London office.

Risky business

Choosing the right office is key when applying here, as each has its own character and seat options, and trainees are expected to stay in one place for both years. Bristol has the largest intake (ten per year) and here 'a new managing partner and new office have everyone very excited about where we are going.' That new office has 'floors the size of a football field and all mod cons such as paperless filing, etc.' A Bristol training contract is certainly not for the risk adverse, as the firm's traditional insurance industry focus remains central. Clients like Zurich, AXA and Norwich Union send through high-value claims as well as an ample supply of run-of-the-mill small matters to the injury risk, professional risk and commercial property risk teams. In these popular seats trainee experiences range from 'liaising with counsel in the week leading up to an insurance recovery case that went all the way to the Court of Appeal' to 'running a number of lower-value road traffic claims on my own.' Given the size and reputation of the insurance group, trainees' claims to be 'doing London work in the regions' is somewhat justified. Nowhere is this more true than in the clinical risk department, which the NHS instructs on the type of cases that few other firms can handle. These include such weighty clinical issues as consent to treatment, confidentiality, access to medical records and mental health law.

Further exposure to the NHS comes in the property, corporate and employment seats, but as the firm develops these areas it is also beefing up its roster of commercial clients. The employment team, in particular, has done well, winning instructions from such names as Capgemini, the global consulting company, MITIE, which provides staff and services for Heathrow T5, Sodexho, RWE npower, DHL and Egg. Trainees don't mind the extra hours or fast pace required in the commercial seats: 'I got to do advocacy in tribunals, client meetings, interviewed witnesses and prepared witness statements,' chirped one employment law fan. In corporate, trainees picked up on a cultural shift, telling us: 'No one wants to be the first to leave the office, even if they are not that busy.' This usually results in a battle of wills with the stomach which lasts 'until people are too hungry and have to go home.'

Other popular seats include commercial property, which involves 'a lot of landlord and tenant matters and drafting leases and licences.' Commercial services is described as 'a dynamic department with big technology, outsourcing and procurement projects and plenty of demanding work for trainees.'

Capital gains

London attracts eight new trainees every year and offers them a similarly wide range of seats. Most will spend at least six months in the firm's Eastcheap office, working for the renowned insurance group. The office may be described as 'quite subdued' and 'not exactly Fun Central,' however the work is extremely well received. 'If you're interested in litigation it's a fantastic seat as it gives you all the practical basics.' These include 'everything from boring bundling to drafting pleadings, letters of advice and a lot of reports to insurers.' Trainees are given 'as much client-facing time and court exposure as possible,' with professional indemnity proving especially popular and invoking tales of large trials and multidefendant mediations.

In the Fetter Lane office trainees choose from corporate, financial services, commercial services, public law, a whole host of litigation seats and excellent property and employment departments. In almost all these areas trainees frequently encounter public sector clients, although the corporate group is becoming the exception. The diet of 'mid-sized M&A deals and AIM and PLUS listings' hadn't convinced our sources that Beachcroft is the perfect place for corporate hotshots, but they did tell us the seat is consistently oversubscribed. 'It's clearly not as big as insurance litigation or employment, but everything you hear is positive and it's definitely a department on the up.' A secondment to Unilever is even more popular: 'You get to work autonomously on small litigation matters, contract drafting and analysis, etc. It's great in-house experience and a good company name for your CV.'

Chambers UK rankings

Administrative & Public Law • Banking & Finance • Clinical Negligence • Construction • Corporate Finance • Debt Recovery • Dispute Resolution • Education • Employment • Financial Services Regulation • Franchising • Health & Safety • Healthcare • Information Technology • Insurance • Intellectual Property • Licensing • Local Government • Outsourcing • Personal Injury • Product Liability • Professional Discipline • Professional Negligence • Projects, Energy & Natural Resources • Public Procurement • Real Estate • Real Estate Litigation • Restructuring/Insolvency • Retail

Food for thought

Leeds recruits six people per year, and as personal injury is big business 'most trainees are likely to do the injury risk seat.' Those with an academic bent can get stuck into 'legal research on a diverse range of topics to work out if there was negligence in each case,' while outdoor types will find gratification in regular court visits. Once again the NHS dominates the client roster: it accounts for around half of the employment group's work ('the public sector element adds another dimension and further interest to an issue') and also fuels the dedicated healthcare group. This team's work includes 'juicy clinical issues like whether you can force feed an anorexic,' as well as 'commercial contracts between NHS trusts and GPs or dentists, and the disputes that arise out of these.' Other options include professional risk, commercial and property risk, projects, construction and property.

Manchester also recruits six per year and offers a slightly more rigid contract – first-years are guaranteed time in the injury risk and property departments. The former includes work for 'heavyweights' Zurich, Chubb and AXA, and trainee tales include 'running case management conferences on my own, attending court, a lot of witness contact and going on site to factories where people have had their hands cut off and the like.' Property can be similarly active, with site visits and client meetings par for the course. Indeed one trainee said they'd been given so much responsibility that 'most clients didn't even realise I was a trainee.' Second-years choose between employment, property litigation, commercial litigation, professional indemnity and a seat in the two-partner corporate team, where there are plenty of tasks to keep a trainee busy. 'A lot of it was drafting minutes or researching, but I also got to undertake huge disclosure and due diligence exercises alongside big firms.' The major downside is that 'it all needs to be done yesterday.'

The price of a life

Trainees wax lyrical about Beachcroft's 'understated' charm. 'At the recruitment fair they stood back and let you go to them rather shoving pamphlets in your hand. It made me think that they were more down-to-earth,' recalled one source. The firm has catholic tastes when it comes to recruiting: our sample included young and less young, local and international, and law and non-law graduates from a genuinely broad spread of universities. That said, they do all display modesty, and appreciate this quality in others. 'Although people here are good at what they do, they don't have big egos,' said one, while another ventured: 'There's not a City-firm vibe where everyone is determined to work late and not enjoy life.'

On this front we have sorry news to report from Manchester, where trainees confessed that their office had slipped off the perch as the social centre of the firm due to a lack of inspiration and funds within the social committee. Undeterred, trainees have made their own fun, thanks to the proximity of the St Ann's Square office to numerous bars. 'One drink can often end up as a story of turning up to a club at 3am with a kebab in one hand, having lost your keys and phone.' Classy. Leeds trainees were more upbeat about firm-sponsored events, having followed one *X-Factor*-themed Christmas party with a girl-boy, *Grease*-style dance-off at the end of 2007. Subscription to the office's Hundred Club brings curry nights and trips to the races, as well as entrance to a monthly cash prize draw.

Bristol trainees spoke of the obsession for karaoke that has swept through their office. After 'copious amounts of singing, drinking and dancing on stools,' trainees have ample opportunities to work off the calories from Friday drinks in Toto Bar or 'the best bacon and brie sandwiches in the world' at The Bridge Inn by joining one of several sports teams. In the capital, the glamorous 2007 black-tie summer ball at the V&A Museum left trainees eagerly anticipating the Thames boat cruise planned for 2008. Five-a-side football, quiz nights, ice skating and bowling events crop up throughout the year, while Café 100 in the Fetter Lane office is a great spot for 'breakfast, coffees or trainee lunches,' especially in December when the firm subsidises a three-course Christmas dinner. The White Swan pub is 'conveniently built into the side of our office,' which makes it a popular destination at the end of a hard day.

As all of these tales of revelry suggest, across the offices the hours are 'pretty reasonable.' According to trainees, this fact goes some way to justifying unspectacular wages: 'Our pay has always been just that bit lower than the market we compete with, but I can leave at 5.30pm if I need to, whereas a lot of people elsewhere wouldn't dare. It's less money, but they compensate with a work-life balance.' The exception, as always, is the corporate department. The balance must be right for most trainees because 31 of the 38 2008 qualifiers stayed with the firm.

And finally...

Beachcroft attracts trainees very much in its image, so if you're looking for a large firm with a heavy emphasis on litigation and/or health, and you're more of a reliable Ford than a flashy Ferrari, go and grab one of those Beachcroft brochures.

- **Phone a friend:** The Junior Lawyers Division of the Law Society runs a telephone helpline providing useful advice to trainees and solicitors up to five years qualified. You can find details at http://juniorlawyers.lawsociety.org.uk

Berwin Leighton Paisner LLP

The facts

Location: London

Number of UK partners/solicitors: 181/480

Total number of trainees: 81

Seats: 4x6 months

Alternative seats: Brussels, secondments

Extras: Pro bono – eg Sonali Gardens Legal Advice Service

> Trainees' mentors are all senior partners, often practice group heads. It is fantastic to have someone of that stature going in to bat for you if you have a problem.

This City firm is home to a flock of extremely contented trainees, but can training with an expanding top 20 player such as Berwin Leighton Paisner really be an idyllic experience?

Blooming Leighton Paisner

During the past seven years since Berwin Leighton wedded Paisner & Co, it has spared neither time nor effort in becoming a force to be reckoned with. The firm's name will always be associated with its flagship real estate department, however it has significantly bolstered other teams. Since the beginning of 2007, the firm has tempted more than 30 partners away from competitors such as Clifford Chance and Herbert Smith, as well as from in-house sources including Goldman Sachs. This strategy has had a particularly advantageous effect on the real estate, corporate and tax groups, the latter having grown to a notable 13 partners.

BLP's expansionary tactics have paid dividends, and despite announcing a 6% dip in profits for the last financial year (a fact the firm partly attributes to the refurbishment of its London office, adeptly described by one of our more sardonic sources as resembling a 'newly Ikea-ed showroom'), BLP remains justifiably confident. Turnover increased by a whopping 82% over the past five years.

Aside from the surge in the firm's status in the City, BLP trainees were attracted by its character. Said one: 'It's a decent City firm where you'll get good work without being made to feel like an anonymous individual who is just a small part of a monolithic trainee intake.' Another who'd completed a vacation placement here had quickly picked up on 'a buzz about the place; a feeling that people liked coming to work in the morning, which wasn't commonplace at other firms that I went to.' They can't have been the only ones to feel this way about the firm: in 2008 BLP made its debut in the *Sunday Times'* 100 Best Companies to Work For survey.

Citius, altius, fortius

Despite significant strides in other practice areas, the firm is undoubtedly still best known for real estate; indeed *Chambers UK* confirms there is no better firm for major property deals of all kinds. The department's sparkling client list includes Canary Wharf, Great Portland Estates, Land Securities, Morgan Stanley Real Estate Fund and key client Tesco, for which it has done a phenomenal amount of work over the past 30 years. Lawyers recently assisted Tesco on the real estate aspects of the Competition Commission inquiry into the groceries market. By setting up a large team of 30 paralegals and a database of over 900 properties, the firm was able to respond quickly to the client's queries. Meanwhile, the Olympic Delivery Authority has been using the firm in relation to the Olympic and Paralympic Games site, which includes a Wembley-sized stadium, aquatics centre, velodrome, international broadcasting and press centre, six other sporting venues, 100ha of parkland and hundreds of residential units. As you might imagine, BLP's crack team of planning lawyers is fully involved in this project.

The real estate finance team is a market leader too. It works on the full range of financing transactions from straightforward debt facilities to structured pan-European, tax-driven facilities and capital markets deals. Lawyers recently acted for Barclays Capital on the financing of Sweden's largest property deal to date. We should mention the firm's approach to international work at this juncture. In short it is winning a lot more business for overseas clients, and services them through a network of 'best friend' firms in other countries. From a trainee's perspective this means no vast network of foreign BLP offices and only one overseas seat – competition law in Brussels.

It's a rare trainee that doesn't take a seat in real estate. Here they take responsibility for their own files (mainly small leases and licences) as well as assisting on the larger projects. 'Whilst you are running files by yourself, you always have your supervisor on hand and never feel that you're left paddling on your own,' explained one interviewee, another adding: 'It's a great training opportunity and a big confidence boost when you realise that you can handle work by yourself.' Real estate has the additional advantage of offering 'really decent hours – 9am until 7pm would be an average day' and 'rather than having peaks and troughs, there is a steady stream of work so you can plan your life and the things you want to do outside the office.'

Aiming for the top

The corporate team was one of the first to establish itself in the AIM market and enjoys an enviable reputation in this area. In late 2007 BLP acted on its first Indian AIM admission, floating the Isle of Man holding company of DQ Entertainment and raising approximately £27m. It also has a strong following for mid-market M&A and recently advised Balfour Beatty on its £33m acquisition of Covion from its management and private equity investors. Almost all trainees take a corporate seat: as well as shouldering some of the usual grunt work, they are kept busy drafting ancillary documents, articles of association and simple share purchase agreements. Although this 'sometimes seemed a bit daunting,' most were reassured by good levels of supervision. As is often the case, the corporate department brings the longest hours, and talk of 1am finishes was not uncommon. Having said that, 'if things are quiet then you really can leave as early as 5pm. There is no culture of hanging around the office and partners will often just tell you to go home.'

Trainees are spoilt for choice when it comes to contentious seats; possible contenders include employment, commercial litigation, tax, construction, planning and sometimes EU/competition. In a real turnaround from a few years ago, contentious seats are now among the most popular, perhaps because the departments are 'smaller and friendlier' than the major transactional groups. Commercial litigation trainees experience wide-ranging

Chambers UK rankings

Asset Finance • Banking & Finance • Banking Litigation • Capital Markets • Charities • Commodities • Competition/European Law • Construction • Corporate Finance • Dispute Resolution • Employment • Environment • Financial Services Regulation • Franchising • Information Technology • Insurance • Intellectual Property • Investment Funds • Licensing • Local Government • Media & Entertainment • Outsourcing • Parliamentary & Public Affairs • Pensions • Planning • Private Client • Private Equity • Projects, Energy & Natural Resources • Public Procurement • Real Estate • Real Estate Finance • Real Estate Litigation • Restructuring/Insolvency • Retail • Shipping • Tax • Telecommunications • Transport

tasks, including 'doing research, writing letters of advice and instructing counsel.' A seat in employment involves 'going along to case management discussions and employment tribunals,' and sources noted that 'even when the cases were quite high-value and I couldn't take a leading role, I was always involved and allowed to go along for the experience.' Very occasionally some trainees are able to sidestep a contentious seat by taking a two-week litigation course.

There are a host of appealing options to occupy trainees' remaining six months. Of these, tax, competition, planning and BTS (business and technology services) stand out as the most popular. BTS offers the possibility of a three-month secondment to a client, where trainees can see things from the client's perspective. The competition team also allows its trainees out of the office, usually on secondment to the BLP office in Brussels. Competition is 'a technical, research-based seat,' nonetheless the training is 'excellent and you may get the chance to fly to the European Court of First Instance, which is fascinating experience.' Thanks to BLP's recent spate of hiring, the tax department has become one of the most exciting places to be. A seat here brings 'a really good mix of things, from writing tax opinions to helping with transactional work.' The seat is quite challenging, which is perhaps why it's not available to first-seaters.

Monumental fun

The pattern of one real estate, one contentious, one corporate and one more specialist seat is followed by the vast majority of trainees. The popularity of particular departments ebbs and flows, either due to the changing tastes of each new intake or driven by word of mouth. 'If someone has a particularly good seat and they are quite loud about it then it becomes popular.' The qualification process meets with widespread approval. It's quite quick and hopefully painless – 'a bit like taking a plaster off' – despite the need to interview for positions. In 2008 27 of the 31 qualifiers stayed with the firm.

Trainees benefit from 'a huge support network.' In addition to seat supervisors ('as a rule they are extremely open and supportive') and the HR department ('absolutely fantastic during the qualification process'), there are mentors and buddies. The mentors are all senior partners, often practice group heads, and on the whole trainees don't find them at all intimidating; indeed 'it is fantastic to have someone of that stature going in to bat for you if you have a problem.' Trainees themselves act as buddies, offering advice to those who have yet to start their contracts.

The departments form the core of the trainees' day-to-day social lives: 'There are usually drinks in the departments on a Friday, as well as regular birthday celebrations and six-monthly parties to welcome and say goodbye to each round of trainees.' There are also department outings, for example, punting in Cambridge or a weekend in Paris. Trainees will often organise their own nights out: 'We tend go to wherever is closest, usually The Monument or The Fine Line.' The highlight is the firm-wide Christmas party – 'your typical extravagant black-tie affair.' Should you crave something more active, there is a full raft of sports teams. 'I would say one of the nicest moments that I have had at the firm was when we beat Freshfields 4-2 at football,' one still-jubilant player admitted.

All pluses, no minuses

The current trainee group represents a range of ages, universities and law/non-law degrees, and they commend BLP for 'being open to people who haven't taken a traditional route into law.' If we were to hazard a guess what the recruiters look for, it would probably be people who are 'pretty friendly and down to earth' and 'definitely lacking an excessive ego – there are no personality clashes among the trainees.' The September 2007 intake guinea-pigged the firm's new LPC+ at the College of Law in Moorgate. 'It was a good way of meeting fellow trainees before starting with the firm' and 'the talks from BLP and regular trips to the office certainly eased anxieties about starting.' Despite the fact that participants don't have any say about the electives they take, trainees were happy with the rationale, commenting that 'we do the electives that are going to be most pertinent to our training, which is great as you want to feel as prepared as possible.'

'I would say that BLP is a great firm to train at,' concluded one typical source; 'people are encouraging and supportive, and even though they are ambitious there is still a healthy respect for having a work-life balance.' After speaking to trainees we seriously questioned whether they had a critical bone in their collective body – they failed miserably to think of any aspect about the firm they'd improve. 'I would have said that the coffee could be better,' posited one, 'but they have recently changed that and it is really good now… perhaps they could increase the variety of biscuits on offer.'

And finally...

So there you have it. If a highly respected City firm with an amenable working environment appeals to you, and you are not too fussy about your biscuits, Berwin Leighton Paisner could be your ideal match.

Bevan Brittan LLP

The facts

Location: Bristol, Birmingham, London

Number of UK partners/solicitors: 58 /156

Total number of trainees: 33

Seats: 4x6 months

Alternative seats: Secondments

Extras: Pro bono – ProHelp

> Trainees say the firm looks for people who can shoulder a bit of responsibility.

Bevan Brittan is a three-office outfit with significant historical involvement in the public sector and a persistent itch to do more in the private sector. These days the balance between the two sides of the firm is roughly equal, and at the intersection of the two we find PFI and PPP projects – some of BB's most interesting work.

Going solo

Two decades ago in the West of England, Bevan Hancock merged with Ashford Sparks & Harwood to become Bevan Ashford, only to split again after some years of chaste, arms-length union into Bevan Brittan and Ashfords. More an annulment than a divorce, we'd say. Able to rely on a client list heavy with NHS bodies, local government and public authorities, BB did the classic post-break up thing and threw itself energetically into something new, namely getting a bigger piece of the lucrative private sector. It grew in its Bristol homeland, doubled in size in London and opened up in Birmingham.

Close involvement with the health sector is one of BB's distinguishing features. It is one of just 11 firms on the legal panel of the NHS Litigation Authority, the service's centralised clinical negligence claims handler. And the NHS' endless legal needs mean there's not a single department at BB that doesn't represent the service in some way, be it for hospital trusts, primary care trusts or local health authorities. This experience has been crucial in the firm winning work from private healthcare providers like BUPA Insurance and Spire Hospitals.

Knowing the public sector well has also enabled BB to target education clients and various other public services. In the age of PFI and PPP, this means vast and complex projects, and yet again the firm has cunningly used its experience with the public sector to gain instructions from the construction companies and banks that build and help finance public-private projects. Recent work includes advice to Birmingham City Council on one of the largest BSF (Building Schools for the Future) schemes undertaken to date, acting for Cyclerval UK and a consortium in relation to the Telford and Wrekin waste scheme, and advising West Sussex, Hampshire and Southampton councils on their £230m street lighting procurement. UK-based projects are just the start: BB has broken onto the international scene, lately working on bids in Poland, Greece and the Republic of Ireland.

Healthy appetites

If you like the sound of this public-private blend, you'll want to know what's on offer in each of the offices, the biggest being Bristol, followed by London and then Birmingham. The seat options available in each are clin neg/NHS claims, healthcare, projects, public sector/local government, coco, employment and property. Bristol and London also offer comlit and construction; Bristol alone has IT/IP. While there are no compulsory seats, trainees will definitely spend time working for healthcare clients. Moves to another office are unusual, although client secondments are not uncommon. Apparently 'very few people have the same transition through their contract.'

Some of this year's interviewees weren't enthused by seat allocation, and the firm is aware of this, as partner and solicitor departures have shifted its resource requirements recently. 'There doesn't seem to be a clear-cut system and there sometimes isn't much rhyme or reason,' said one source, another adding: 'I think there needs to be more liaison between the partners and HR.' Of course this is less important to trainees who choose the firm for its core work. 'I was attracted by the public sector aspects' was a sentiment more than half our sources expressed, some even wanting to 'make a difference to the NHS.' Whatever seats they'd done, there was general agreement from our interviewees that 'the quality of work is great.' Said one trainee: 'I have never been stuck behind a photocopier for very long. I've found a real willingness to get me involved.' Supervisors are picked from among the assistants and associates, with partners designated overall control. 'Some partners you see more of than others, but you sit next to or in the same area as your supervisor.' No matter the location, BB is not known for excessively long hours. Even in London the average trainee goes home between 6pm and 7pm.

Passion fashion

Lawyers in the high-earning projects department are said to be 'knowledgeable and passionate, incredibly open to guiding trainees.' An abundance of training helps people – especially first-seaters – get to grips with a complex area in which 'projects go on for a substantial amount of time, so you might see the first three months of one and the close of another.' Arguably this is the area where trainees can make the least impact as the work is complex; even so it's worth trying as the firm has big plans for the group. 'At the moment it is a hugely expanding area and we are at the forefront of PFI matters. We were involved in Pathfinder, LIFT and BSF from the start... involved in the thinking. As the waves roll out we will still have involvement but will be looking towards international markets and energy projects.'

The partner-heavy healthcare department has two strands: pure commercial work and regulatory and general inquiries. On the commercial side, trainees learn about general NHS contracts, the process of granting foundation trust status to hospitals and GP contract issues. In the other seat there will be inquests, mental health issues and inquiries concerning fertility regulations. Recalling their time in the seat one source told us: 'I would look at a case to find out what had happened and summarise it all in a report. I'd then go along to the inquest.' A workload 'dictated by the NHSLA' brings many cases relating to brain-injured infants. 'To begin with you see families going through trauma and babies with severe ailments and you

Chambers UK rankings

Administrative & Public Law • Banking & Finance • Clinical Negligence • Construction • Corporate Finance • Dispute Resolution • Education • Employment • Healthcare • Information Technology • Licensing • Local Government • Personal Injury • Planning • Professional Discipline • Projects, Energy & Natural Resources • Public Procurement • Real Estate • Real Estate Litigation • Restructuring/Insolvency • Social Housing

do find it quite disheartening.' In time professional detachment develops, making it easier to cope. The firm is involved in some high-profile cases, including one that could save or lose the NHS about £2bn. Currently awaiting its turn in the House of Lords, Thompstone v Tameside and Glossop Acute Services NHS Trust relates to the indexation of annual payments for future care awards.

Other seats receiving favourable reviews include comlit in Bristol, where 'claims are worth into the hundreds of thousands of pounds.' Unfortunately two of the team's four partners left shortly after our interviews, but we liked the sound of the regulatory department, where 'the work involves regulating professional people and services providers such as children's homes and care homes.' Primarily a contentious seat, many of the cases lead to tribunal hearings for which trainees interview witnesses, draft statements and sometimes see criminal proceedings in the magistrates' and Crown Court. 'It is one of the areas they are trying to expand here, and in fact in the profession as a whole it is a growing area.' Corporate seats can often take on a projects flavour; meanwhile banking in London involves 'a complete range of project finance, property finance and corporate finance.' Among the clients offering secondments to trainees are Orange, Zurich, Motorola, Costain, WiDiP, BUPA and the NHS.

Changing faces

BB has some pretty swish open-plan offices, the newest of which is 'head and shoulders above other law firm offices in Bristol.' After an initial rent-free period, it is also said to be rather costly, which leads us to one of the big themes in our interviews. Ever since it pulled away from Ashfords, BB has aimed for growth and increased profitability by getting more private sector work, but it hasn't been entirely successful in this aim. Net profits at the firm dropped by 36.5% from £9.6m in 2006/07 to £6.1m in 2007/08. Our sources admitted: 'There are half as many trainees in our year compared with the year above,' and NQ retention has not been the best lately. 'In the last 18 months to two years they cut back and I think it's because they struggled to find work for people on qualification.' A string of departures at both assistant and partner level, with Bristol especially hard hit, meant some trainees went so far as to say: 'The firm has struggled post-demerger for longer than it had hoped.' Naturally the firm is working hard to address this and, among other developments, recently overhauled its management structure.

So, what's been going on? Strides have been made in certain areas: 'The corporate team is clearly going from strength to strength in Bristol, up from a few earners to about 12 now. It is targeting lower-level work that London firms would turn away.' By contrast, the Bristol property team was said to be 'depleting,' while some lawyers from the pensions team in Birmingham, the insolvency team in Bristol and the IP team in London have all made swift exits. There has definitely been a shuffling of the pack. 'Some partners jumped and some were pushed,' revealed one source. Most trainees see this as 'a part of the transition of Bevan Ashford to Bevan Brittan' that will level out in time. One source concluded: 'There is definitely a culture shift from being nicey-nice to more corporate-oriented and the atmosphere has changed a lot from being buzzing to being quite… well, not cut-throat, but there's been a shift.' While 'some people don't like it,' one or two of our interviewees suggested the firm could go further in its drive to become more commercial and focused on the private sector. 'There is something about this place that is a bit dual-personality,' we heard. 'They don't seem to have the conviction of actually doing what they want to do.' Clearly it will be worth keeping an eye on the legal press to monitor further changes. If you've already been watching the press, you'll be aware that BB has also brought in new partners from industry and government as well as private practice.

Dimsumthing for the weekend

All new recruits attend a week-long induction in the Bristol HQ and further training sessions then crop up 'about every three months.' Bristol, Birmingham and London trainees otherwise keep in touch by phone or e-mail. Within each office there's a good social atmosphere. 'There's always someone going for a drink in The Bridge on a Friday,' explained a Bristol source, while in London the local is Jamie's wine bar below the office. The Birmingham crowd have a new favourite, Must, which peddles chi-chi dim sum and cocktails. Each office hosts month-end drinks to coincide with a dress-down day, and for the first time in a while the firm will bring everyone together for a firm-wide 2008 autumn party – autumn rather than the summer holiday season so that as many staff as possible can attend.

We asked trainees to ponder the firm's recruitment preferences. 'They look for people who can shoulder a bit of responsibility,' said one; 'I know trainees in magic circle firms and our responsibility levels far exceed theirs.' Currently, many trainees start at BB after a period as a paralegal or in another career, but this may change with the introduction of a vac scheme. NQ retention was poor in 2006 and 2007. Apparently 'some people moved on because they wanted to specialise in areas the firm couldn't offer jobs in; others wanted more money.' The news in 2008 was that nine out of 14 qualifiers stayed on at the firm.

And finally...

Whether the volume of private sector business will ever outweigh that of public sector business isn't clear. What we can say is that Bevan Brittan is a good work in progress. Although there is a lot to be done still, it is there to be achieved. One to consider if you have leanings towards the public sector.

Bingham McCutchen (London) LLP

The facts

Location: London

Number of UK partners/solicitors: 11/21 + 2 US

Total number of trainees: 4

Seats: 4x6 months

Alternative seats: None

Extras: Pro bono – LawWorks

To make it onto the scheme you're going to need to demonstrate an interest in financial institutions. If you aren't into the work it will be very obvious.

Bingham McCutchen proves that when you hear the words 'Boston' and 'law firm' you shouldn't just think of Ally McBeal. It only started its London training scheme in 2006, so it's not yet well known among students; however its focus on financial restructuring puts it in a prime position right now.

From New England to old

Founded in Boston in 1891, multi-office US firm Bingham Dana merged with San Francisco-based McCutchen, Doyle, Brown & Enerson as recently as 2002. This was just one of a string of mergers for Bingham, in fact there have been nine in the past 11 years. Employing around 1,000 lawyers, the Bingham network now stretches to 11 US offices plus Tokyo, Hong Kong and London.

Bingham is no newcomer to the UK, having opened for business in London as early as 1973. Since the millennium it has come into its own and now hosts around 40 lawyers, most of whom are UK-qualified. The introduction of the training scheme reflects the importance Bingham head honchos place on London business. Indeed if you want to hear more about the firm's broader development and plans then watch Chairman Jay Zimmerman's video clips on its website. A careful London strategy centres on big financial institutions and funds, assisting them with sizeable workouts and restructurings across Europe. In particular the financial restructuring group (FRG) has an excellent reputation and is ranked as among the best in London by *Chambers UK*. Once a relatively quiet area in the UK, restructuring is now hot, hot, hot. 'People are expecting FRG to get a lot busier,' warned one source.

Another area in which the office is truly impressive is financial regulatory advice, and again *Chambers UK* ranks it as one of the best firms in the country for contentious matters in this field. The lawyers assist UK and US-based clients with all aspects of the UK financial services regulatory framework, and the team includes two former heads of enforcement departments at the FSA. All Bingham trainees take seats in FRG, finance, corporate and litigation. There's no formal request and allocation system, so 'the order of seats is pretty much chosen for trainees.' Whichever seat they're in, trainees receive work from the whole team and during quieter periods 'are expected to go and have a chat with people to find out what they're up to.' While it's unlikely any department will lack suitable trainee tasks, typically the further from the main areas of practice you go, the less intense the seat.

The frg prince

Before we give more details of some of the seats, you might want to note that Bingham's website gives pride of place to images from a recent marketing campaign in the USA. Featuring zebras chasing lions and paragliding elephants, the images sparked a fair amount of comment. One of the most striking – a grizzly bear cradling a human baby – is supposed to symbolise a safe pair of hands and the ability to balance aggression with delicate handling. This image is the one that best fits the London FRG practice, which has received some significant instructions lately. It represented creditors of Northern Rock, the bondholders in the €358m restructuring of international

IT consultants Damovo Group and the official committee of unsecured creditors of Sea Containers during its restructuring and subsequent filing for Chapter 11 bankruptcy. It also worked on the £100m restructuring of Focus DIY following a partial buyout by Apax and Duke Street Capital. As the firm's signature department, FRG is 'continually busy' and trainees can expect to be challenged in many ways. Their days are likely to be filled by drafting 'quite lengthy e-mails, going into some detail' and taking part in intense conference calls with clients and other lawyers. If you want to understand why Bingham looks like a top choice right now you have to know a little about how the restructuring market has evolved to respond to changes in the lending and investment market.

Since the entry of hedge funds, proprietary trading desks and the investment arms of investment banks, traditional bank restructurings have been superseded by large bondholder restructurings of major listed companies. Until recently credit was incredibly cheap and then when liquidity peaked in 2007 a number of private equity buyouts were left in real financial bother. Whereas they might previously have been saved by something called distress refinancing, now there is often little choice but to opt for complete financial restructuring. Banks, having increasingly become minority debt holders, also found themselves short on usable funds and much more cautious about lending what they did have. And let's not forget the sub-prime market itself. Structured investment vehicles (SIVs) invested in credit market instruments, such as US sub-prime mortgage-backed bonds and collateralised debt obligations. Since this market went pear-shaped a number of participants have required considerable assistance. Bingham's financial restructuring practice has lawyers with the knowledge and experience to deal with these changes in the market and they have become known for their representation of creditors in all manner of sticky situations. It won't come as a surprise that impenetrable jargon is a feature of complex areas of finance and restructuring law, so the firm is keen to get trainees up to speed as soon as possible. It sends them on a training course run by BPP and requests attendance at internal lunchtime sessions. Ultimately, to make sure you know what's going on around you, 'you have to be quite proactive.' Often this means 'going away from a meeting you've not understood and looking things up yourself.'

In the finance seat trainees raved about the 'huge amount of responsibility, if you're willing to accept it.' In this small department their role includes bibling, conditions precedent, drafting securities and loan agreements, and being taken to client and committee meetings with partners. Finance is the only seat where recruits sit with a partner – all others have them sitting with associate-level supervisors. Understandably there is considerable overlap with the work done in FRG.

Chambers UK rankings

Banking Litigation • Financial Services Regulation • Restructuring/Insolvency

If you can't stand the heat...

The litigation team assists on FSA investigations and works closely with FRG, providing strategy advice on major restructurings and situations where companies are in default or heading towards bankruptcy. One 'really complex' instruction came from bondholders of the Polish conglomerate Elektrim, which successfully pursued the company for over 500m. Most of the trainee's work here is research-based, although they can expect to do some drafting and document review, while also gaining a little court experience and a good amount of client contact, mostly via conference calls. In-house training consists of fortnightly lunchtime meetings where everyone chats about ongoing cases and listens to presentations. The corporate department also works in conjunction with FRG, but has a nice line in M&A. Before ex-Thai PM Thaksin Shinawatra bought Manchester City, Bingham gave advice on the hostile takeover bid that was backed by SISU Capital. It also advised that client on its bid for Coventry City. The opening of the Hong Kong office in 2007 brought an Asian dimension to the team's caseload and made it possible for trainees to ask for a six-month corporate secondment. Anyone hoping to work in Hong Kong and then qualify into corporate in London may have to take a UK corporate seat as well as the one in Asia.

Our interviewees were keen for students to understand that training here does not require people to devote their every waking hour to the job. They know many American firms are reputed for their long-hours, but say: 'Maybe because Bingham is a Boston firm this applies less.' Getting into the office by 9.30am and leaving by 6pm is not uncommon during quieter periods; when the going gets tougher 'the average leaving time is maybe 8pm,' and there can be quite a few later nights when you'll definitely miss last orders. The payback comes in the form of a nice fat salary. At trainee level it's chunky enough and then on qualification it leaps to £94,120. London salaries are tied to New York rates.

... get out of McCutchen

In 2008, Bingham was placed 41st in the FORTUNE list of the 100 best companies to work for in America. This was the fourth year in a row it had been fêted by the American business bible, so the firm was understandably proud of its achievement and laid on 'a whole month of treats' for everybody. Like many American firms, Bingham takes workforce diversity seriously and each year London associates are sent to Boston so they can report back on new diversity initiatives. Women not only make up a fair proportion of the London partnership but a majority of the associates and 'of counsel' as well. Bingham's trainees reckon the firm stands out from other US players in London, not least because it is very English. Certainly, the office at 41 Lothbury, near the Bank of England, is 'a nice old building rather than a big glass tower.' Furthermore, 'around 90%' of its work in London is sourced from the UK.

If you want to succeed here you'll have to be up for a challenge. The small trainee intake means 'you're not going to be able to melt into the background' and 'people will notice you and your work.' To make it onto the scheme you're going to need to demonstrate an interest in financial institutions. Essentially, 'if you aren't into the work it will be very obvious.' As the training scheme is still in its infancy, to some extent our sources viewed themselves as 'guinea pigs.' It is evolving so, for example, provisions for pastoral care have been improved. Aside from the regular feedback given by supervisors there are monthly meetings with HR and second-year trainees each take a new recruit under their wing. Our interviewees thought the high degree of flexibility in the scheme was utterly appropriate at this early stage, even if they saw it as inevitable that 'it will continue to become more structured.' The qualification process, having only gone through one cycle, is still informal. Both of the qualifiers stayed at the firm in 2008, going into the corporate and restructuring teams.

Trainees aren't totally subsumed by their jobs: on occasion they can be found in one of the City's many bars and they know how to make use of a decent budget for trainee and associate nights out. One evening a large conference room was turned into The Bingham Arms for the night, and professional quizmasters were brought in to run a proper pub quiz. Somewhat apt for a firm that's as big in Japan as Bingham, 'certain associates have a penchant for karaoke,' and periodically partners take groups of lawyers and trainees out to a restaurant just to chat and get to know each other. The annual Christmas party is well attended, and a summer ball, held at Somerset House, doubles as a client event.

And finally...

For such a new training scheme, Bingham offers a notably stable environment: barring a few tweaks here and there, there's no sign the system will need to change much, even if the financial restructuring practice goes into overdrive.

It's not just our business that's diverse

Based in London we are a leading law firm offering a broad range of legal services with groups providing expertise in Major Projects, Real Estate, Corporate & Commercial, Employment, Litigation, Private Client and Charities.

Our approach and track record have enabled us to attract some of the brightest people in the profession, in an environment that encourages talent to flourish.

We aim to give everyone the opportunity to realise their full potential. Discover yours by visiting www.bdb-law.co.uk

Bircham Dyson Bell

Bircham Dyson Bell

The facts

Location: London, Cardiff, Edinburgh

Number of UK partners/solicitors: 50/72

Total number of trainees: 17

Seats: 4x6 months

Alternative seats: Secondments

Extras: Language training

> If you are looking for huge deals then you would be better suited to Canary Wharf, however if you like the idea of getting stuck in with high levels of responsibility and a rounded training contract then you're a classic BDB type.

If you find the inner workings of government stimulating rather than soporific, and you fancy being involved in some of the largest and most politically sensitive projects of the day, then Bircham Dyson Bell may well be your firm.

Up your street?

Don't be fooled by its 'elegant, old-school façade,' this Westminster firm is on a mission. It has doubled in size over the past five years and its long-term aim is to achieve a £50m annual turnover and make it into the UK's top 50 firms by 2011. Well known for its parliamentary and charities work, the list of public sector and charities clients is impressive and includes names such as the London Development Agency, Arts Council England, St John Ambulance, Centrepoint Soho, War on Want, the Met Police and English Heritage. Among the firm's recent mandates was advice to long-standing client TfL on the planning aspects of the £500m Victoria underground station redevelopment, and the Law Society's challenge to the Legal Services Commission's right to unilaterally amend the controversial unified contract for civil legal aid. The firm's corporate/commercial offering is thought to be 'on the up' and here BDB has relationships with National Express, Virgin Trains, Mitsubishi, Orient-Express Hotels, Qantas and AIG. Its highly ranked private client department, meanwhile, enjoys the patronage of fabulously wealthy individuals from around the world.

All the trainees we interviewed spoke of the attraction of the firm's PPP (parliamentary, public affairs and planning) department. 'No other firm can offer anything quite like it,' explained one enthusiastic source. And they are right: BDB occupies something of a rarefied position as one of just six law firms employing 'Roll A' Parliamentary Agents (four of whom are based at the

firm). These agents are licensed to draft, promote and also oppose bills, orders and other forms of legislation, and the firm enjoys a stellar reputation for its work in this area. In fact it is also the only law firm in the country to offer political consultancy services. This vaunted status has led BDB to become involved in some pretty high-profile projects. One interviewee told us he had made his application to the firm after 'I had read about the work that it had done on Crossrail and thought it sounded like it would be up my street.' BDB lawyers represented more than a quarter of the objectors to the £13bn Crossrail scheme, and this is indicative of the size and import of the work that trainees will be exposed to. Current projects include advising Docklands Light Railway on the public consultation stage of its eastern extension to the line, the fourth time it has been extended, and the London Gateway Port/Shellhaven project, which received approval from the Department for Transport in 2007. Client DP World will now spend £1.5bn over the next ten to 15 years constructing a deep-water container port and a ro-ro facility at a former Shell oil refinery near Thurrock in Essex.

An average day in the PPP department would consist of 'attending a select committee meeting at the House of Lords' or 'spending time researching an issue in the Parliamentary library.' As exciting as this may seem, the size and lifespan of projects is such that six months in the department gives trainees only 'a brief window on the issue.' It also makes it hard for them to take ownership of files or have a great deal of client contact. 'I think I only had two or three meetings in the entire time that I was there,' admitted one source. Nonetheless our interviewees found the experience exhilarating and 'really enjoyed the political aspect of the department.' So much so that four trainees applied for only two NQ PPP positions in 2008, leaving two disappointed.

Send in the bailiffs

Even when handling work for commercial clients, the stormy world of politics is never far away. The employment department has nurtured an impressive industrial relations specialism, as illustrated by the firm's work for Royal Mail during its dispute with the Communication Workers' Union, which included obtaining an injunction against the union. Employment has proved a particularly popular seat with trainees, and seeing as the team can only accommodate one trainee at a time, competition is fierce. If you do triumph over the opposition and secure a seat, you should brace yourself for 'a very busy six months' of running files and have a fantastic amount of client contact. 'I became the first port of call for many clients,' explained one trainee. You'll experience a wide range of matters from drafting staff handbooks through to high-profile disputes. An unfair dismissal claim for the former chief exec of an FSA-regulated fund turned on a public interest disclosure aspect. The claim was heard over six days in the Cardiff Employment Tribunal and resulted in a substantial compensation settlement for BDB's client.

Litigation is another top choice. After 'being thrown in at the deep end with armbands,' trainees get stuck into landlord and tenant cases (at their most dramatic requiring the trainee to accompany bailiffs on early morning visits to errant tenants). The firm has developed expertise in relation to leasehold disputes on the big London estates and has been instrumental in achieving some landmark rulings. As well as general commercial disputes there are also family law and contentious probate cases. There is some photocopying and bundling to be done, but one source said: 'It was more a case of helping out rather than it being delegated to me.' Such drudgery is more than compensated for by the chance to try advocacy, which our sources generally found 'scary but exhilarating.'

All hands to the pump

Consisting of just two partners and five other fee earners, the successful charities department is one of the smallest in the firm. 'Everyone is really friendly and passionate about their work.' Clients range from 'massive international charities down to inspired individuals operating out of lockups,' and trainees enjoy the variety that this offers, especially as the volume and diversity of the work allows them to run some of their own files. Private client is the

Chambers UK rankings

Administrative & Public Law • Agriculture & Rural Affairs

• Charities • Education • Employment • Environment •

Local Government • Parliamentary & Public Affairs •

Planning • Police Law • Private Client • Transport

most traditional department. While some found it 'quite a stuffy place to work in' others enjoyed 'the old-school atmosphere.' A trainee's workload encompasses tax planning and a fair amount of probate. It may not be the sexiest part of the firm, however it is a significant part of BDB's business, so applicants should be mindful of the fact that they are highly likely to take a seat in this area. Some trainees also spend time on secondment to a client, most commonly with Esso.

Mid and end-of-seat appraisals are reasonably relaxed. 'It's just you and the supervisor and they have a pro forma list of things to go through, like your phone manner and drafting skills. Really it depends on your supervisor as to how useful the appraisals are.' As for who trainees get work from and report to, primarily this is their official seat supervisor, however we did hear about a few confusing incidents from various trainees. 'Other fee earners are supposed to go through your supervisor, but sometimes they do try to give you work directly. On one occasion in real estate, nobody really wanted to take responsibility for a piece of advice and I needed somebody to talk to, but generally it is okay.' In another slightly awkward situation, a second trainee in another department felt their supervisor resented other fee earners trying to give them work, even though they had the capacity and the desire to accept it.

Blades of glory

BDB has always recruited a 'mixed bag' of trainees and is 'definitely open to people that have had a previous career.' Nonetheless if you can clearly explain your reasons for applying to the firm, it is completely open to applications from undergraduates and new graduates. It's very obvious that 'if you are looking for huge deals then you would be better suited to Canary Wharf,' however if you like the idea of getting stuck in with high levels of responsibility and a rounded training contract then you're a classic BDB type. While you may be attracted by the firm's niche departments, say the PPP team, it is important that you are 'prepared to do a bit of work that you aren't interested in as a trade-off to get the seats that you really do want.'

One thing that isn't in doubt is that if you plump for BDB you'll have time for a life outside the office. The firm has 'genuine commitment to its staff maintaining a work/life balance,' so while one source admitted to 'a couple of midnight finishes,' 6pm departures are regular. Although the social life is 'probably a lot more relaxed than at some of the larger firms,' it is certainly not the case that the trainees are left twiddling their thumbs of an evening. 'You can usually find some of the younger staff going out on a Friday' and there are several sports teams, including one that plays in the London legal softball league. 'We are by far the smallest firm in the league and the American firms always hammer us!' There is also an annual Christmas party and summer rowing regatta for which 'each department gets together a team of four people to learn to row.' This energetic event takes place one Friday night on the Thames at Putney and apparently the different departments are well matched, although 'PPP got really competitive and well organised last year, so they won it by a mile.' Following the race, friends and family join rowers and other staff for a barbecue.

One area that has caused some upset amongst trainees is the way that the firm has handled job applications for newly qualifieds. Last year trainees 'kicked up a slight fuss,' as they felt the rigmarole of having to send in a CV and covering letter and then go through two interviews for an NQ position made them feel like external candidates. They were also concerned that the process happened too late for them to look for an alternative position should they be unsuccessful in their application to BDB. The firm responded to the criticism and in 2008 the process was brought forward significantly and the second interview was dropped. The trainees still dislike the system: 'The downside is that the interviews took place one week into the fourth seat and so in terms of choosing an NQ role the fourth seat is almost redundant,' explained one exasperated source. And despite the fact that the process is slightly less formal than last year, they still have to submit a CV with covering letter – 'quite daft.' In 2008 six of the seven qualifiers stayed on.

And finally...

BDB wants to be come a larger, more profitable business by expanding its commercial pratices. For some, change isn't happening fast enough; others say the changes are eroding the cosy side of the firm's character. Unless it leaves its Westminster location this firm will always stand out from the City crowd.

At Bird & Bird you'll always hit the ground running

As a trainee at Bird & Bird we'll provide you with first-class learning and development opportunities, including practical workshops and the chance to work with some of the world's best lawyers and clients. This will give you an excellent foundation from which to choose the area of law you'd like to specialise in.

With us, you'll get comprehensive and individual support to ensure you'll always hit the ground running.

www.twobirds.com/graduates

BIRD & BIRD

The perfect trainers

Bird & Bird

The facts

Location: London

Number of UK partners/solicitors: 64/116

Total number of trainees: 33

Seats: 4x6 months

Alternative seats: Overseas seats, secondments

Extras: Pro bono – Toynbee Hall Legal Advice Centre, The Prince's Trust, Own-It IP advice, LawWorks; language training

Will the firm ever stop growing? On 1 October 2008 it merged with 30-lawyer London firm Lane & Partners, a specialist in aviation, construction, fraud and travel law.

With an intellectual property practice that rules the roost, Bird & Bird has plenty to crow about. The past decade has seen it transform from a mainly domestic operation to a 19-office business spanning Europe, China and Hong Kong.

Big birds

The firm traces its origins back to 1846, not that you'd guess. Today it is defined by deep involvement in technology, life sciences and other 21st century industries, such as aviation and sport. Although London is still the largest office, more than half the firm's lawyers now work elsewhere. The growth can't continue at its current pace for much longer – if it did there would be a branch on Mars by 2015 – but even as recently as September 2008 the firm announced four new nesting places in Prague, Warsaw, Budapest and Bratislava.

Bird & Bird came to the fore primarily because of its superb IP practice, which *Chambers UK* ranks in a class of its own. Such effusive praise does something of a disservice to other teams however: sport, IT, telecommunications and data protection issues are all areas in which Bird & Bird excels, and it performs well in mainstream areas such as employment and corporate. The corporate department recently helped Mattel buy the entire issued share capital of Origin Products, owner of IP rights to the 2D Polly Pocket image. It also enabled client Eurofins to buy a food and environmental testing company in East Anglia and a €50m laboratory testing business from Southern Water.

There are no compulsories in the four-seat traineeship, but most people spend time in the extensive commercial division. Most also go to IP, though be warned – while the firm is 'more than happy for you to do a seat there, since the majority of the practice is patent litigation it's tough to qualify into that area if you don't have a hard science degree.' For this reason, many Bird & Bird recruits are science graduates, and the only 'soft' IP seat, handling non-scientific matters like copyright, trade marks and design rights, is incredibly popular among those who aren't.

Wise old birds

The IP team could be seen as 'a firm within a firm.' It is based in a separate building just down the road from the central London HQ in Fetter Lane, and this physical detachment is mirrored in the more academic, intellectual aura of the place. 'Because it has such a strong reputation it can do its own thing,' one source surmised. 'Sometimes you get the feeling that if the rest of the firm disappeared no one in IP would notice.' Nonetheless, trainees relish the opportunity to work with 'gurus in the field.' Among several internet and software clients are Yahoo!, Adobe and, new this year, Facebook. The department has been working on two major telecommunications cases for Nokia and Ericsson, which are both embroiled in multi-jurisdictional patent disputes. Working on these massive cases can be 'a blessing and a curse, as your input as a trainee is usually in inverse proportion to the size of the case.' Trainees who turn up halfway through the process can find it 'quite challenging to stay motivated after a lot of fairly monotonous tasks.' Those arriving later in proceedings might at least get to see the case go to trial. 'I was making sure witnesses were in the right place at the right time,' said one contact. 'It doesn't sound glamorous, but if I had stopped doing it everything would have gone pear-shaped pretty quickly.' Among the many pharmaceuticals and life sciences companies that use the firm are Reckitt & Coleman, sanofi-aventis subsidiary Rhone-Poulenc Rorer, generic drug producer Actavis and Dutch pharma company Synthon.

Partners are aware that six months of bundling isn't going to be educational, so they do involve trainees in smaller cases with more responsibility. One source reviewed a herbal medicine company's product portfolio 'to make sure their ads and labelling complied with the regulatory legislation. I reviewed their product range, and looked at how their products were marketed in store, then went back to the client with recommendations.' Another worked on trade mark infringement of domain names: 'I compiled evidence with the client, put together a cease and desist letter, and then dealt with the ongoing correspondence.' The partners expect results, so trainees end up working 'above and beyond' in terms of hours. Generally they remain stoic about their role, pointing out: 'You are working at the cutting edge of IP law, so it's got to be worth it.'

The early bird catches the work

'Everyone wants to do the commercial seat' and fortunately the department takes three trainees at a time, so their chances are good. Located in Bird & Bird's newest and smartest building, 'you get the feeling of working in a powerhouse department that's at the top of its game.' The department strikes trainees as being 'more open than IP – there's no academic barrier to qualification,' and they like its 'huge variety of work.' An IT team is currently advising BT on a gargantuan £2.6bn upgrade of NHS systems that will hopefully lead to massive savings across the health service. Telecommunications is another big area, and the outsourcing team advised T-Mobile on a collaboration with 3UK to create the world's largest known 3G network sharing agreement. As in IP, when trainees work on a huge matter they can find themselves knowing a lot about it but still doing 'general dogsbody' tasks. Again, more engaging tasks come from smaller files. One source especially enjoyed a deal for a computer games manufacturer that was raising finance for a couple of new products. 'I was working in a small team, so I was heavily relied upon to the extent that I was negotiating directly with the other parties, drafting agreements and talking to the clients regularly.' The commercial department also houses a renowned data protection practice.

The sports law team is among the best in the country. Formerly known for its sponsorship and merchandising

Chambers UK rankings

Aviation • Banking & Finance • Competition/European Law • Corporate Finance • Data Protection • Dispute Resolution • Employee Share Schemes • Employment • Immigration • Information Technology • Intellectual Property • Life Sciences • Media & Entertainment • Outsourcing • Private Equity • Product Liability • Public Procurement • Real Estate • Real Estate Finance • Restructuring/Insolvency • Sports Law • Telecommunications

advice, it recruited a large part of the Hammonds sports team and these new lawyers specialise in regulatory and contentious work. A growing list of clients includes governing bodies, clubs, individuals, broadcasting networks, sponsors and kit manufacturers. Even a partial list is impressive: the International Olympic Committee, FIFA, UEFA, The FA, Sport England, the International Cricket Council, the Lawn Tennis Association, the British Darts Association, Chelsea FC, Tottenham Hotspur FC, the British Lions, Andy Murray, Nike, Wembley Stadium and the London Organising Committee for the 2012 Olympics have all sought the firm's advice. This glamorous seat is much sought after, although one insider tried to shatter some illusions by saying: 'The people who say the sport seat is sexy haven't done it – it's bloody hard work.' Trainees don't grouse about it: they understand that at the bottom of the food chain there's a lot of disclosure and bundling, and they know that come tribunal time they'll be preparing evidence and liaising with QC on exciting cases. One recent highlight was the representation of The Football League when Leeds United challenged the 15-point deduction that was imposed following its insolvency. If you really want to try sports law make your interest known early and keep pushing for the seat.

Away from these prestigious niche teams, Bird & Bird has several other successful departments, including employment, real estate, corporate and dispute resolution. They tend to be less popular among trainees. 'People come here to do certain seats and corporate isn't one of them,' one source announced bluntly. Nevertheless, these departments win great work and offer decent levels of responsibility. 'It was a nice contrast to IP, where I had a limited role,' said one trainee of their dispute resolution seat. 'The work is of a smaller magnitude and as a trainee you have a much better chance of getting involved.' The department has 'a nice buzz to it, one where you don't quite know what's going to happen next.' Likewise, in employment there is good client contact and trainees can deal with smaller matters themselves, preparing documents, drafting witness statements and writing letters of advice. The employment team's clients include BAE Systems, Nokia, Yahoo! and Albert Popkov, owner of Russia's most popular social networking site.

With the notable exception of IP, our sources hadn't felt especially connected to other Bird & Bird offices. A few do get the opportunity to fly the nest – to Madrid and Hong Kong most recently – but 'practically it's not always possible.' To gain an overseas seat you might need to put forward a good business case, otherwise wait until after qualification when further opportunities arise.

Birds of a feather

'It's so nice when your work colleagues become your friends,' enthused one interviewee, mentioning that some of the gang had taken a ski holiday together. Trainees meet for lunch in the canteen (official name: The Bird Table) and there are plenty of visits to local pubs, including The Swan. The office has numerous sports teams and plays in an annual football tournament against the other European offices. Summer and Christmas parties are always a laugh, and if you're a member of the IP team you might get to meet the overseas lawyers at the annual departmental retreat, last time held in Marbella. If it all gets too much at work, why not relieve stress on one of the table football sets dotted around the office? Do heed the cautionary tale of the trainee who 'once beat a partner ten-nil. It was a result he described as career limiting!' Fortunately, when dealing with those further up the pecking order, trainees say: 'Bird & Bird is friendly – for a law firm anyway.' In their view 'the overwhelming majority' of partners are easy to deal with and won't expect any-thing unreasonable. Trainees are rarely night owls. Said one typical source: 'I've only had three or four really late finishes, and less than ten after 7pm.'

The firm doesn't send its grad recruitment team out to that many universities, so don't necessarily expect them to come knocking; however, it is clearly looking for bright and capable candidates. Science and technology graduates have obvious appeal, though law and arts grads also do well. Those who make it to the finish line in the training contract race are looked after: before starting their contract an extranet site puts them in touch with other successful candidates and on arrival they are assigned a buddy to show them the ropes. In 2008 12 out of 15 qualifiers stayed with the firm, just one of them going into an IP job.

And finally...

If you have a keen interest in IP then you must apply here. Bird & Bird is also worth considering for its general commercial practice and its specialist areas like sports law or telecoms. You'll need to be a high-flyer to impress, so make the application a good one.

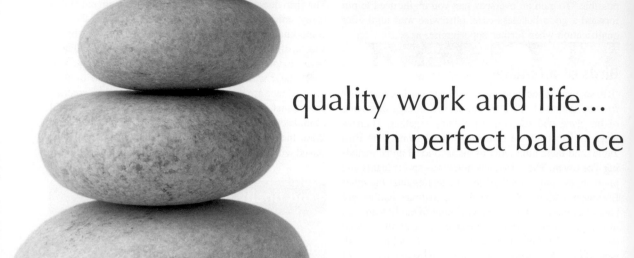

quality work and life...
in perfect balance

As the South East's premier law firm also in the heart of London, Blake Lapthorn has ambitious plans for the future, and you can be a part of it!

Our reputation, range of practices and locations in Southampton, Winchester, Oxford, Portsmouth and London make the firm a very attractive place to work.

Equally important are the calibre and variety of our clients, who find our commercial and friendly approach a vital ingredient in choosing us to work with them. With more than 100 partners and 800 staff, we provide a full range of legal services for business, the not-for-profit sector and the private individual.

We are looking for bright individuals to become the future partners of the firm and at all stages of your career we will be looking for evidence that you have the breadth of ability one day to take that step.

Why not visit the graduate recruitment section on our website for further information:

www.bllaw.co.uk/recruitment

the natural choice in law

Blake Lapthorn

The facts

Location: Southampton, Portsmouth, Oxford, Winchester, London

Number of UK partners/solicitors: 107/156

Total number of trainees: 32

Seats: 4x6 months

Alternative seats: Secondments

> The supervision has been just excellent. I've sat with partners who had bad experiences with supervisors when they were trainees and they're keen to be better than that.

Originally confined to Southampton and Portsmouth, after a period of rapid expansion Blake Lapthorn has become the largest firm in the South East.

The name game

Blake Lapthorn has changed its name more often than Sean 'P. Diddy' Combs/Puff Daddy/Puffy/Diddy. Since 2003 it has merged with Oxford's Linnells, Winchester's White & Bowker and London's Tarlo Lyons, eventually ending up with the name Blake Lapthorn Tarlo Lyons. Realising that this was something of a mouthful and discovering that 'when we answered the phone people would stop listening halfway through the name,' it has come full circle and started using the name Blake Lapthorn again.

Clearly a firm with national ambitions, Blake Lapthorn has not yet finished growing. In an impressive prediction based on 'opinion persuaded by gossip,' one trainee even claimed they would be 'flabbergasted' if it didn't join forces with a certain large northern practice in about five years' time. For the foreseeable future, 'consolidation' is the watchword, and predicted one soothsayer: 'In the short term we will ride out the recession.' Blake Lapthorn is not resting on its laurels as the credit crunch begins to bite: there has been restructuring at the higher end with partner-level departures. Trainees don't see this as necessarily a bad thing: 'After all the mergers it's more a case of getting rid of the dead wood. In the current financial climate it's better to act now than regret it later.' Cutbacks have not extended to trainee level; the firm is still recruiting as many as ever.

Blake Lapthorn is the epitome of a full-service law firm. *Chambers UK* ranks it among the best in the country in such diverse fields as charities, partnership law, education, professional discipline and rail work, and it has large mainstream commercial teams. There are also substantial numbers of fee earners dealing with high-volume, low-value personal injury, conveyancing and debt collection. Among the clients are South West Trains, the Daily Mail Trust, Deutsche Bank, Fujitsu, Goldman Sachs, Ministry of Sound, Morgan Stanley, Prudential, the Royal British Legion, the Society of London Art Dealers, the universities of Surrey and Reading, and Trinity Corporate Finance. Each office has its own specialities. BL Southampton is one of the best in its region for insolvency and IT; the Oxford office comes top in the Thames Valley for planning, crime and construction work; while in London the firm leads the way in licences for gambling.

Trainees mostly stick to mainstream areas of practice during their four-seat training, with some branching out into more niche areas. They can apply for contracts in Oxford, London or Hampshire, although those who want it can opt to flit between the offices. Blakes is also keen to send trainees out to work with clients, so there are secondments available to the General Teaching Council and Air Traffic Systems, among others.

X-Men (and women)

London trainees can sit in the coco, property, contentious employment, insolvency, commercial litigation and recruitment teams. This last one is 'a mix of corporate, tax and employment work, all geared towards the recruitment sector.' The office was formerly a separate firm – Tarlo Lyons – and it's the most recent addition to the Blakes family. Since the tie-up, London trainees have noticed a renewed 'vibrancy' in the office: the merger has revived fortunes somewhat and the plan is to expand in the capital and grow a family team here too.

Trainee opinions are divided on how successful Blake Lapthorn has been in combining so many firms into one business. Those who were completing their training in one location felt it was fairly unified, while those who had moved around took a slightly different view. 'Does it feel like one firm? No. The IT systems are different in every office, for one thing. And people treat each other differently.' For example, Oxford is considered to be the most relaxed, and 'the hub of all gossip.' Staff get a 75-minute lunch break and many leave at 5.15pm, 'which is a Linnells legacy.' On the other hand, the Portsmouth team is in an X-shaped building: 'It's like four different offices because you never see anyone outside of your wing.' Most of our contacts agreed that despite their differences, 'offices do cross over quite a lot. We can farm London work off to Southampton or elsewhere, which makes it cheaper for our clients. We win a lot of work that way.'

Fishermen's friends

Oxford has a flourishing private client practice and anyone interested in 'dealing with people and individuals rather than with companies' problems' should be well served by it. The private client seat essentially involves the administration of estates and allows 'a lot of client contact and the ability to run your own files.' Cases can range from the simple to the complex. 'We did the will of one lady who said she had no foreign investments,' said one trainee. 'When she died it turned out that she had forgotten about a load of properties that she owned in France, so I was liaising with the land registry and our team on the South Coast to track down exactly what she possessed.' Property is another area large enough for most Oxford trainees to end up there at some point, either in a residential or a commercial seat. Blake Lapthorn acts for many of the Oxford colleges, a couple of major national residential developers, Cotswold Water Park, Abbey, NatWest and Bank of Ireland.

Talking about their experience here, one interviewee said: 'It was kind of a halfway house between being a solicitor and a secretary.' On the solicitor side, 'you get a great opportunity to run your own files' – one of our contacts had acted on the sale and purchase of pubs, while another did some work for the commercial team, dealing with the property aspect of a company sale. 'It was unclear who owned what. Our client had paid no rent and had no paperwork and that made it very complicated.' Added another: 'I did some interesting research involving drainage. I know that sounds dull but it was really good; it was something where there was no right or wrong answer that was readily apparent.' On the secretary side, there's a huge amount of preparing and filing forms ('leg-

Chambers UK rankings

Agriculture & Rural Affairs • Asset Finance • Banking & Finance • Charities • Clinical Negligence • Construction • Corporate Finance • Crime • Debt Recovery • Dispute Resolution • Education • Employment • Environment • Family/Matrimonial • Franchising • Information Technology • Intellectual Property • Licensing • Media & Entertainment • Partnership • Pensions • Personal Injury • Planning • Private Client • Professional Discipline • Real Estate • Real Estate Litigation • Restructuring/Insolvency • Tax • Transport • Travel

work stuff'), which trainees say is 'very good for learning diary management.' Oxford trainees can also take seats in non-contentious construction, family, employment, commercial litigation, IP/IT and corporate tax.

A Hampshire training contract is split between Southampton, Portsmouth and Winchester, and between them they offer a plethora of seats including insolvency, corporate, pensions, environment, banking, construction, private client, property and property litigation. The ever-popular employment team is praised ('They give you so much support') as are many of the niche departments. A charities seat, for example, 'sounds nice and fluffy but gives you a really strong commercial training, It's basically coco work for charities.' The team recently acted in the merger of the Fleetwood Fishing Industry Benevolent Fund and the Hull Fishermen's Trust Fund with the Shipwrecked Fishermen and Mariners Society. Lawyers have also advised a university on the structuring of a prize fund, and a military charity during a dispute with a family over a gift of a Victoria Cross. Other clients include the Royal Agricultural Benevolent Institution and the Portsmouth Roman Catholic Diocese. The regulatory team deals with 'any breach of regulation that leads to a criminal sanction,' which could be anything from corporate manslaughter to money laundering, animal cruelty or people trafficking and international prostitution. 'Every day was so different,' a trainee enthused. 'There's not much responsibility because all the cases are very serious, but I got exposed to so much. There was one case that was on the front page of the paper for weeks, but I couldn't discuss it even with other people in the firm because it was so confidential.' Clients we can mention are the General Teaching Council, the General Optical Council, the Chartered Institute of Public Finance Accountants, the General Osteopathic Council and the Association of Accountancy Technicians.

Raiders of the lost files

Recently one of Blake Lapthorn's specialist teams encountered a problem. They were finding it hard to recruit young solicitors. Trainees would come and do six months and then want to qualify into trendier departments like corporate or employment. In an attempt to address this situation, the team came up with a novel plan. There was a paralegal working within its ranks in whom they had great faith but who didn't meet the required criteria to be accepted for the standard training contract. Instead, the lawyers in the team offered the paralegal a bespoke contract with two years of training that met the SRA's requirements but was heavily geared towards their area. It was a win-win situation. The paralegal got the chance to qualify and the team got a loyal, fully qualified solicitor. Both parties were so happy that some other teams within the firm are now following suit. The process is ad hoc rather than a formalised scheme, but it serves as a reminder that not securing a training contract when you first start applying isn't necessarily the end of the world.

When it comes to training, this firm is rigorous to say the least. 'The supervision has been just excellent,' said a satisfied customer. 'I've sat with partners who had bad experiences with supervisors when they were trainees and they're keen to be better than that.' This sentiment was echoed by virtually all our contacts. Nor does the firm stint when it comes to appraisals: 'four in six months' isn't out of the ordinary. A three-month review with the seat supervisor is usually followed a couple of weeks later by a chat with the trainee's mentor. We were very excited to learn that all trainees are trained as dawn raid assistants, the firm figuring that they are the people it's most efficient to deploy at short notice in such a situation. 'I took part in a raid on a bankrupt's business,' said one intrepid crime fighter. 'The main objective was to obtain information regarding his affairs that it was feared he might try to conceal.'

The London office has all the bars of Farringdon on its doorstep, but elsewhere socialising poses problems. Southampton's lawyers have just relocated from the city centre out to Chandler's Ford near Eastleigh and are hoping the move to distant suburbia won't have too bad an effect on their previously lively social scene. The Portsmouth office is in a business park with only 'a Beefeater, a Pizza Hut and the Costa Coffee in Tesco within walking distance.' The South Coast offices are the sportiest, with the most established football team and several sailors among the trainee ranks. Despite being a long way from the city centre, the Oxford staff have several pubs to choose from. The Fishes is 'the posh one' and does excellent food, while the Seacourt Bridge is 'the rough one' favoured by trainees for its low prices. Our contacts complimented the firm on the size of the trainee social budget, which allows for a firm-wide get-together every three or four months. On the other hand, they grumble that the salary hasn't grown at a fast enough rate, calling it 'appalling for a firm this size.' This didn't stop 11 out of 14 qualifying with the firm in 2008. Anyone who declines an NQ job offer is required to repay law school sponsorship

And finally...

Outside London Blake Lapthorn is the King Kong of the South. It would be practically impossible to not find an area of practice to suit here.

Bond Pearce LLP

The facts

Location: Bristol, Plymouth, Southampton, London, Aberdeen

Number of UK partners/solicitors: 76/350

Total number of trainees: 27

Seats: 4x6 months

Alternative seats: None

Trainees say Bond Pearce is a strong commercial firm with big aspirations, but despite this it really understands that lawyers are people and not robots.

Stretching from Devon in the West to Hampshire in the South, and now with branches in Aberdeen and London, this mid-sized commercial firm has an excellent client base and allows trainees to strike a very decent work-life balance.

Power to the people

Representing the likes of Carlsberg, Shell, Marks & Spencer and Hilton UK, Bond Pearce competes with London outfits for some of the top clients and serves smaller local clients as well. As a measure of its success, it has 17 FTSE 100 companies and 16 FTSE 350 companies on its books. Some trainees do wish though that the firm had a bigger profile: 'It just doesn't shout loud enough about how good it is!' As one lamented: 'A lot of my London friends don't know the name or brand. It's not fair.' Trainees do credit the firm for 'investing in its image' and are proud of its packaging. Said one: 'We look fresh and modern and a lot less fuddy duddy than some established firms.' As Bond Pearce 'keeps working on giving a consistent image to the outside world,' its trainees are assisting in any way they can, for example by attending marketing and networking events such as the Law Society dinner and employment clubs. In fact, it seems that trainees were the major impetus behind getting Bond Pearce back in this book after several years' absence. Nice going!

So down to business. What's Bond Pearce all about? Well, it offers clients the full scope of corporate, commercial, property and dispute resolution services, and it's particularly well known for its work in the education, energy, retail, real estate and insurance sectors. 'If you aren't sure what area you'd like to go into this firm is large enough to give you a choice,' say trainees. Generally people are able to try the seats they most want, 'although this usually doesn't happen the first seat around… it's on the second and third seats that you get given the most preference, which is perfect because in the first seat you're still getting used to the firm and by the fourth seat you've already decided where you want to qualify.'

Maybe you know exactly what you're into, and if it's energy then Bond Pearce is an obvious choice as 'energy and environmental services are definitely a specialty of the firm.' It takes on the gamut of oil and gas, electricity and renewable energy matters. Newly opened in May 2008, an office in Aberdeen focuses on oil and gas and has space for one trainee on secondment from England. Because of its focus, this office turns out 'a really high level of work,' offering trainees exposure to such major matters as a $20m hydrocarbon royalty dispute. Elsewhere, the firm advises on significant M&A and financing deals for clients in this sector, including Renewable Energy Systems, RWE npower, Ecotricity and ScottishPower.

From BBC to BCC

The real estate department incorporates teams for commercial property and planning and is always a popular choice among trainees. According to our sources, 'the main advantage of a seat in real estate is the amount of client contact; it's quite lively.' *Chambers UK* consistently gives Bond Pearce tier-one rankings in real estate-related areas, and this shows in the firm's impressive roster of clients: Virgin Group, BBC and Bristol City Council to name just three. In 2007 the group represented the pub, bar and hotel business Eldridge Pope in its disposal of a 152-property estate to Marston's for a whopping £155m. Not bad stuff to be exposed to as a trainee. The planning seat is actually 'quite specialised' and you can expect to do a lot of work with those big energy companies, particularly in relation to the wind farms that have become a Bond Pearce specialism. Given that opposition to such developments is commonplace, it can be 'incredibly entertaining at times: you go to inquiries and sometimes have drunk people storming about.'

If contentious work turns out to be your bag you'll fit right in doing professional indemnity litigation for the likes of insurance companies AIG, Zurich Professional, QBE and Aon Claims Solutions. This is a great seat because 'you look at so many different areas of law, getting really interesting and broad experience' from a range of industries, most notably surveying, accountancy and law. 'The underlying stories in cases are really fascinating in themselves... and there's a strong analytical element to the work,' explained one source. Another seat option, employment law, is 'a really busy department' where you'll find yourself working for national clients such as Royal Mail and Princess Yachts. For instance the group recently successfully represented Specsavers in the defence of a whistleblowing claim, a brand-critical and sensitive case made more complex by the death of one of the key witnesses before trial. Trainees reported involvement in 'every element of running a file' and one told us: 'I came out feeling like I knew every aspect of the role; if I took an employment job next week I could definitely hold my head above water.'

Across the offices the full seat list is: commercial; commercial property; planning; corporate; professional indemnity; commercial litigation; property litigation; retail litigation; liability claims; employment; banking and insolvency; corporate finance; property finance; construction; tax and pensions; environmental and oil and gas. Phew! The Bristol office takes the most trainees and therefore has the most seats on offer.

Shipshape and Bristol fashion

The firm tends to keep trainees in their home office and this comes as a relief to those who would 'hate to move around.' It's perfectly possible to request an office move though, as the firm prides itself on its flexibility. A move is especially likely if a seat is only available elsewhere, or if you want to do a client secondment as these take place out of the Southampton office. According to trainees, 'the firm is trying to make this home-office policy clearer from the get-go now' because, as with most matters, 'it really does listen to complaints and concerns.' In fact

Chambers UK rankings

Banking & Finance • Competition/European Law • Construction • Corporate Finance • Debt Recovery • Dispute Resolution • Education • Employment • Environment • Health & Safety • Information Technology • Intellectual Property • Licensing • Local Government • Personal Injury • Planning • Professional Negligence • Projects, Energy & Natural Resources • Real Estate • Real Estate Litigation • Restructuring/Insolvency • Retail

'there's a forum for trainees that takes place in the Southampton office every three to six months.' According to sources: 'It really works and things do get changed.' In each office there is a partner and an associate assigned to trainees, and that's in addition to seat supervisors. New recruits are also hooked up with a buddy from the year above.

The majority of Exeter staff recently relocated to Plymouth or Bristol following the closure of their branch, leaving Bond Pearce with only a touchdown facility in that city. Reactions to the change were mixed: some trainees viewed it as a major inconvenience, whereas others were more than happy to integrate with colleagues elsewhere. After all, 'being in the Bristol office has its advantages.' Unofficially known as the head office, 'a lot of the firm's resources are in Bristol and there are lots of available seats. Last time round there were more seats than people.' In all, 13 trainees will work in Bristol from 2008. This branch is also notable for all of its 'weird and wonderful technology,' including teleconference facilities, digital temperature controls and the like. Even though there's a brand spanking new building in London (which will host one trainee beginning in September 2008), the Bristol office is generally viewed as 'the newest and the nicest.' The Plymouth office meanwhile is situated just on the dockside and 'has amazing views out to sea.' It was the workplace of seven trainees in 2008. Another seven work in the half open-plan Southampton office, which is close to the main railway station.

Just be yourself

The recruitment process involves an assessment centre with group exercises, presentations and individual interviews, all designed to 'filter out the good from the bad' and to 'find out if you've got the intellectual capacity to hold your own.' Sources say the process is 'gruelling.' For one trainee the process included 'acting like a lawyer while one of the partners played the part of a horrible client. He completely went to town with it – it really stretched me.' So what illuminating advice do current trainees have? 'Don't bullshit and don't be too arrogant or cocky. They're looking for people who are down to earth but have a bit of personality.' Plenty of Bond Pearce trainees have ties to their respective local areas and a good number of them are undertaking law as a second career. Quite a few trainees are recruited from among the firm's paralegals too; four of the current 27 trainees got their contracts this way. The firm definitely has its eye on people who will stick around. A recent review of career structure at Bond Pearce has created new roles in the firm, including the titles of senior associate and senior counsel, all geared towards keeping you on side if you make it to associate. As a final sweetener the firm offers funding for both the GDL and LPC, including a £6,000 bursary for each year.

Trainees say Bond Pearce is 'a strong commercial firm with big aspirations,' but despite this 'it really understands that lawyers are people and not robots.' Work-life balance is carefully maintained such that 'your weekends are your weekends and if you work late during the week it's acknowledged… it's not simply the expected thing.' In terms of the social life 'people aren't out every night or even every Friday, but there is a good cross-section of people who do go out and you can take part if you choose.' The trainees have their own social budget to keep them going throughout the year. It kicks off on 31 July, with a rather interesting day-long event for new trainees. 'You have lunch then there's a bunch of events including a speed dating-like game and a friendly *Dragons' Den* event. We were all sceptical about the speed dating but in the end we had to hold our hands up and admit it was really great! Afterwards they provided dinner then we all went out to the pub and a club after.' Future trainees and first-years from all of the offices are invited to take part in this bonding experience. There's also a shared training session in Bristol but, these events aside, trainee socialising is normally an office-by-office thing. A highlight for some

was a recent surfing trip to Devon. Back on home territory, the quality of nearby pubs is quite mixed. In Bristol it's not uncommon to end up at the local Wetherspoons or Toto's, a popular choice with local lawyers. 'It's next to the old office so it's kind of a tradition left over from that.' Next door to the Southampton office is Jo Daflo's, a converted church that's a popular choice for drinks. It took quite a bit of prompting to get the name of this one though, because trainees are 'usually through the door too quick to even notice the name.' If you're apprehensive about launching into your Friday night straight after work, never fear because dress-down Friday is something 'everyone takes part in.' Some trainees see this as 'a blessing and a curse' because 'it can be so hard figuring out what to wear.'

None of the trainees we spoke to could avoid mentioning Bond Pearce's 'brilliant! Absolutely brilliant!' Christmas party. The firm goes the whole hog, transporting everyone to the location, providing a three-course meal, entertainment, 'the works,' and even forking out on a hotel for the night. The party 'really breaks down barriers and you dance with whoever you like.' A good job too as it's one of the only times the entire firm gets together.

And finally...

These trainees are a distinctly happy bunch. They say: It's the quality of the work you get and the quality of life outside of work that makes Bond Pearce a smart choice for a training contract. In 2008 17 of the 21 qualifiers stayed on, five in Southampton, eight in Bristol and four from Plymouth.

Boodle Hatfield

The facts

Location: London, Oxford

Number of UK partners/solicitors: 29/57

Total number of trainees: 13

Seats: 4x6 months

Alternative seats: None

Extras: Pro bono – Fulham Legal Advice Centre

How is this firm like Stephen Fry? Trainees say it's accessible to that kind of tweedy, Wodehouse generation who like that quaintness, but also really intelligent and quite flippant about it in a QI kind of way.

London firm Boodle Hatfield, snugly perched in Mayfair's elegant terraces, has provided legal services to an impressive roster of private and commercial clients for nearly three centuries.

Get into the Grosvenor

Despite its traditional reputation for private client work, the biggest practice area at Boodle Hatfield is property. In fact, 'property is probably more dominant than necessarily comes across.' According to official stats that department accounts for just over 40% of the firm's turnover (around half of that coming from large property estates), so maybe it's understandable that the property team is the 'largest by far.' Within this department – and certain others for that matter – trainees 'mostly work for Grosvenor,' which is a vast estate that is privately owned by the Duke of Westminster. With £3bn worth of assets under management in London alone, Grosvenor is the largest urban landowner in Britain. The connection with this client goes back to the 18th century and the firm's origins as estate managers, but even though Boodle is sometimes 'very much overshadowed' by the relationship, it's not the sole focus of its endeavours. 'They're a very important client but we still have plenty of other clients as well,' including Bedford Estates, Marriott Hotels and Nationwide.

Obviously Boodle's standing as 'a long-established firm' appeals to some applicants, but we would be remiss if we left things at that. 'To say it has an established client base and is very old doesn't define the firm, as it doesn't just look to the past.' Though they don't know many specifics about the firm's plans for the future, tainees do have a 'general feeling' that it is 'trying to branch out and expand our appeal,' and gradually become 'a more cutting-edge firm.'

The first of a trainee's four seats is allocated to them on arrival, though at the interview stage 'they do ask you where your particular interests lie.' Subsequent seats are 'all mapped out' for recruits, but it is sometimes possible to 'negotiate a bit as you go along.' Usually trainees spend time in the large litigation and private client departments, and 'inevitably everyone does a property seat because of the size of the department and nature of the firm.' Often two property seats are taken. Recruits share an office with a supervising partner, which usually facilitates regular feedback, though obviously 'for some people it's in their nature to give feedback as they go along and some people you have to ask.' More formal appraisals are held every three months.

The work can vary greatly between seats, as the size and demands of departments dictate. In particular a seat in the 'really, really busy' property department can land a recruit at the forefront of Boodle's practice. It is certainly 'one of the busiest departments to be in,' and there's scope within it for a range of occupations. Take a construction seat and you'll work with the team that's been assisting Grosvenor with the £920m Liverpool One development. This project has required a great deal of document negotiation. For a trainee 'it does make you a hell of a lot more confident on the phone,' through 'ringing up people to make sure they sign stuff.' Over in the estates team, one trainee recalled being 'confronted with a cupboard full of my own files' only to really enjoy the process of 'having to push things forward myself.' More than in most others, the experiences of a property seat is 'more akin to being a qualified solicitor.' Other major deals have included a 70,000 sq ft redevelopment at 70 Chancery Lane for Ebble Developments and the £20m development of Cirencester Town Centre for Wildmore Properties.

The whole kit and caboodle

In Boodle's 'quite small' corporate department, trainees can often find themselves supporting other teams. Still, one described it as a 'pleasant surprise,' probably because of its 'nice mix of full-on corporate work and commercial matters.' Recruits do everything from liaising with clients to writing board minutes. 'You do get the whole package,' said a source. The litigation department is divided into commercial, matrimonial, property and employment teams. Three trainees broadly help a team or two each, and can potentially work for all four. Deemed 'a really good seat to start out in,' the trainee's role encompasses research, collating documents and drafting letters of claim. They are rarely short of client contact and at meetings 'you get to see how the advice is structured and how to elicit as much information from a client as possible.' With property being Boodle's bag, rent arrears claims are two a penny and trainees often run these, taking them all the way 'from inception to potentially enforcing judgment.' Other duties include runs to the Royal Courts of Justice and the Central London County Court. While they might have to 'read the material on the tube on the way down,' trainees appreciate the opportunity to 'go out and represent the firm.'

Although the private client department might not be as big as property, it will 'always be a really defining feature' of the firm. The tax and financial planning (TFP) seat is 'very much biased towards research' and offers contentious as well as non-contentious experiences. One interviewee told us contentious wills were 'the most exciting area of law I've done so far.' Hardly surprising when you see some of the unseemly things people will do to get their hands on a dead relative's cash. Issues in tax planning can get pretty complicated; indeed the Boodle lawyers have been doing a lot of work lately on the impact of the Finance Act 2006, which made sweeping changes to the inheritance tax treatment of trusts. Again, there is a lot of client contact for TFP trainees.

It's worth mentioning at this point that Boodle has an office in Oxford dedicated to private client and matrimonial litigation. Let us not forget that there are 'a lot of wealthy individuals around there who need the same service as they do in London.' The London-based trainees will have contact with this office from time to time, but people are only sent there on request. Boodle encourages recruits to go, so if you have an urge for a spell amid the dreaming spires you might be in luck. As an added incen-

Chambers UK rankings

Agriculture & Rural Affairs · Family/Matrimonial · Private Client · Real Estate · Real Estate Litigation

tive the firm may even pay your rent and some other expenses.

Boodle-y functions

We go from one Oxford to another, as Boodle's New Bond Street office sits on the corner of Oxford Street. While the shopping opportunities might appeal to some, more than one of our sources confessed they hated the street, especially around the busy Christmas season. 'I try to get away as fast as possible,' confessed one grinch. The social scene fits the Mayfair location. Clients sometimes take trainees to meals or comedy clubs, and there are 'loads of barristers' garden parties' at which 'partners will introduce you to everyone.' Naturally, 'at some point you always have contact with Grosvenor's own trainees,' a situation the firm is 'very keen' to encourage and provides a budget for. Boodle recruits know that they 'need to take an active part in marketing' and that it is 'healthy for the client-firm relationship going forward.' More informally, as the two sets of trainees so often work together, 'it's good to have met them in a social context.'

Boodle trainees will usually meet up for drinks at the end of the week at Bond's just around the corner, or any of the other 'nice bars and pubs' in the West End. Attendance isn't consistent throughout the year (certain departments 'tend to go out more than others') and there isn't 'a massive party atmosphere.' The firm itself organises some events, with the Christmas party being the highlight. Last year it was held at a 'really posh' venue near Hyde Park Corner and 'carried on well after we left the official party.' Cricket is played against the Longford Estate team at Longford Castle in Wiltshire and the firm also competes in dragon boat racing. We say 'competes', but as one pointed out: 'We used to come last every year so the wooden spoon they give people is called the Boodle.' There's also an eleven-a-side football team, joint with Grosvenor.

The luck of the Fryish

Who, then, is the typical Boodle lawyer or trainee? While we heard the usual comments about people being 'grounded' and 'not purely about work,' a few more distinctive qualities also came to light. For one, regarding Boodle's long-standing clientele, 'you have to be able to speak to these people and elicit the information you need.' It takes a certain finesse and 'essentially you have to be quite a charming person' to convey the sense of a personal service. Secondly, brightness is 'probably one of the most important things.' Partners are 'fantastically clever' and 'shamelessly intellectual,' and one interviewee claimed: 'This is the closest I can get to being an academic and earning decent money.' The same source compared the firm to Stephen Fry: 'Accessible to that kind of tweedy, Wodehouse generation who like that quaintness, but also really intelligent and quite flippant about it in a QI kind of way.' That told us.

Boodle's trainees certainly appreciate its differences from big City firms. Some thought smaller, West End firms could accommodate 'eccentrics' and allow one to 'have a lot more fun actually doing law.' More relaxed work hours are another benefit and coming in on weekends 'feels very strange.' Even during the week 'you start getting strange looks from the cleaners if you're around later than 8.30pm.'

And finally...

Satisfaction runs high among trainees. 'Not for all the money in the world would I go to a different firm to train,' declared one. In 2008 three out of six took jobs. There were no property vacancies, so two went into corporate and one into litigation.

B P Collins

The facts

Location: Gerrards Cross

Number of UK partners/solicitors: 20/30

Total number of trainees: 8

Seats: 4x5 + 1x4 months

Alternative seats: None

> Shuddering at the idea of being a just a number in the big City, trainees wanted somewhere that was a nice size; small enough that you get to know almost everybody but big in personalities.

Small firm, big personality. Attracting business from both London and the Home Counties, B P Collins mixes commercial deals with high-worth private client advice.

Village people

The little village of Gerrards Cross might seem an unusual location for a firm with such a good reputation. In fact it makes great sense because, despite having a name like an angry Scouser, it's one of the most exclusive and expensive places to live in the entire country. As well being home to the odd celebrity, it's where bowler-hatted, pinstripe-suited company directors retire to when they've finished being captains of industry. When they arrive, they need a law firm to help them sell their old home, sort out their will, trade in the wife and challenge all the parking fines they've accumulated. But that's not all B P Collins can do. The firm works for many companies in the Thames Valley/Northern Home Counties area, a fertile land of airports and business parks, with Pinewood Studios one of the most prominent local clients.

B P Collins kicked off in 1966, when the eponymous Mr C started his high street firm above a butcher's shop. The business has come a long way since then, and along the way it has acquired several escapees from much larger City firms. Its aim now is to achieve further growth and higher profitability by getting more work rather than charging higher fees. After all, say trainees: 'What attracts people to us is that we do incredibly good work but don't charge London prices.'

The sincerest form of flattery

A slightly unusual seating system sees trainees do four seats of five months each, followed by a final four months in the department into which they hope to qualify. Seats are available in coco, employment, litigation, property, family and private client, and departments have very different working practices. 'As I was leaving my first seat I was told that it can almost be like moving to a different firm,' said one trainee. 'That's a little harsh because there's a lot of crossover, but certainly the individual partners have imprinted their own personality and way of doing things on each department.' Adding to this feeling is the multi-site nature of BPC. It has two buildings separated by a short walk along Gerrards Cross High Street. In each department trainees sit with their supervisor and have two reviews per seat. There's also an overall training partner with whom monthly meetings are scheduled.

Litigation is a seat where 'they do expect a lot from you, but if you get something wrong they are always there to help and to tell you how you can be better next time.' The open-plan department is divided into four pods of property litigation, commercial litigation, shareholder disputes and general litigation. BPC also handles some intellectual property matters, despite the loss of its specialist lawyer to a City firm. The firm is currently deciding how to rebuild its IP practice, and it might want to start by looking at the promotional material on the graduate recruitment pages of its own website. The 'so you want to be a lawyer' page bears uncanny similarities to a section from previous editions of the *Student Guide*. Rather than draft a cease-and-desist letter, we'll just suggest a credit be given next time.

Recent litigation highlights include defending Persia International Bank against a substantial claim brought against it, and bringing one forward on behalf of Continental Tyres against a logistics company. Defamation issues occasionally pop up: 'One case that was in the papers recently was a woman who was getting divorced from her husband and took their kid to his parents. There was an altercation and she claimed the father-in-law had hit her. He was a local magistrate and he sued her.' Trainees tend to work on three or four of their own small files, particularly 'debt recovery claims or people with parking issues.' The 'very good client contact' in this seat goes some way to countering tasks involving disclosure list and bundles ('normally a couple of hours a day'). They are 'quite careful not to overload you, but sometimes needs must.'

Waste not, want not

The largest department, property is split between residential and commercial matters, with trainees mainly working for the commercial team. BPC is known for its connections in the gravel, waste and recycling industries, and other clients include Bonsoir (owners of the Lacoste clothing label), several property developers and vehicle rental company Sixt Kenning, which has an extensive roadside property portfolio. Lawyers recently acted for City & Provincial Properties during its disposal of parts of a portfolio of 14 former industrial sites. Its efforts here motivated another company, MP & G Trading, to transfer a significant portion of its work to the firm, beginning with the acquisition and leaseback of a call centre facility in Yorkshire. On the residential side, Gerrards Cross is one of the most expensive places in Britain to buy a house, so trainees handle sales and purchases at the top end of the market. Compared to the 'focused and intense' litigation team, property is 'slower-paced, the days are shorter and you have more time to stop and chat.' Property trainees are normally out by 6pm, whereas those in litigation sometimes hang around for an hour or two longer.

'Coco is a really good seat as it provides a general background for wherever you end up.' BPC has considerable experience in waste-to-energy sector deals. In 2007 it advised client Summerleaze on the £80m sale of an electricity generation business to private equity firm Infinis and a successful tender to supply a new development with power from renewable sources. Another client, NTR UK Waste, is a major international operator in renewable energy and sustainable waste management. The firm has worked on all its UK acquisitions, four of which completed during 2007, including the acquisition of Verdant Group, a supplier of waste services to local authorities.

Often working in tandem with coco is the employment team. On the Verdant deal these lawyers performed a due diligence exercise relating to over 1,200 staff, plus pen-

sion and share schemes. In contentious matters, one client – a regulatory manager for leading healthcare company Roche Products – was dismissed for whistle-blowing and her case became widely reported. Also working alongside the coco team are charity lawyers, whose clients include The National Society for Epilepsy, religious charities such as Biblelands (which works in Israel and the Occupied Territories, Lebanon and Egypt), RSPCA and Nordoff-Robbins Music Therapy.

Even though 'the trainee in the department at the moment raves about it,' family has traditionally been a less popular seat. 'A lot of people just aren't interested in it in the first place. It's seen as a bit girly by the male trainees, and helping with divorces you see the worst in people.' The team's bread and butter are financial relief claims for and against wealthy local residents, some of them in the public eye. Not too long ago the firm was instructed by a professional football star and, separately, by the wife of a published author of fictional thrillers. It's not all about splitting the dosh; there's 'a small amount of child work, a bit of cohabitation, and pre-nups and civil partnerships are on the up.' Family is a department where you are chucked in at the deep end, though 'there's a very good training principal who explains things' and is infinitely preferred to her predecessor. The private client seat covers wills, probate, tax and estate planning. 'I really enjoyed the work, trying to find loopholes and problem solving,' said one trainee. Unsurprisingly, the seat involves a lot of drafting and witnessing of wills, plus liaising directly with clients. Recently trainees dealt with 'hundreds and hundreds' of Enduring Powers of Attorney, as clients rushed to beat a change in the law (EPAs have been replaced with Lasting Powers of Attorney, a far more complex document).

Buns in the oven; mince pies on the wall

We won't pretend Gerrards Cross is the entertainment capital of the universe; indeed it's not even the entertainment capital of South Bucks (that title goes to neighbouring Dorney, where the first pineapple in the UK was grown). Fortunately, London is but a brief train journey away, close enough for some trainees to commute from the metropolis every day. Since 'people don't really live round here,' pub lunches rather than after-work drinks are the norm, although trainees will sometimes go out together in London. When we rang to speak with them, theatre trips and a boat cruise down the Thames were on the agenda for the summer, and there are football and rounders teams to get involved with. Don't be fooled by sleepy Gerrards Cross: BPC folk can party with the best of them. The litigation department has the biggest 'play hard' ethic, and their Christmas revelries are 'notorious for food fights.' Apparently they got into 'a bit of trouble at a medieval banquet' two years ago. A more dignified firm-wide event is also held at Pinewood Studios.

Day to day, the trainees' main social venue is the post room, where they have the task of opening the mail every morning. After extensive talks, 'an 8.45am instead of an 8.30am start has been negotiated.' BPC is clearly a firm that understands the importance of work/lie-in balance. It's also a good place to be a young parent. Last year we reported pregnancies and maternity leave left, right and centre, and we are pleased to report the steady production of babies shows no sign of abating. Though there are 16 male partners to five females, at associate level women outnumber the men and this gives it the feel of a young, family firm. Indeed, the family atmosphere is why most of the trainees we spoke to chose BPC: shuddering at the idea of being a just a number in the big City, they wanted somewhere that was 'a nice size; small enough that you get to know almost everybody, but big in personalities.'

The office at Collins House has had a refurb and now looks very professional. The town has had a makeover too – not only is there a new Marks & Spencer Simply Food, Waitrose is on the way. A word of warning to those who intend to drive to work: the local car park 'costs a fortune.' Some staff park further down the road, which has provoked the wrath of residents but has the bonus of being free. Trainees may commute from London, however the salary is definitely regional, even after a 'decent' pay rise. Still, if you're considering BPC after reading this, the chances are it's never been about the money for you. In 2008 three of the four qualifiers stayed with the firm, each going into corporate.

And finally...

'People are attracted by the firm's proximity to London, but the pace of life of a regional firm.' If you get what they're talking about, give B P Collins a close look.

BPE Solicitors

The facts

Location: Cheltenham, Birmingham

Number of UK partners/solicitors: 24/28

Total number of trainees: 9

Seats: 4x6 months

Alternative seats: None

> Last year five trainees climbed the highest mountain in North Africa – Morocco's Mount Toubkal – to raise money for National Star College, a school for disabled children in Cheltenham.

Don't imagine for a second that an address in refined and peaceful Cheltenham Spa gives BPE lawyers a life of quiet rural bliss. BPE is one of the largest commercial law firms in Gloucestershire and it has made good inroads into the Birmingham market.

Cheltenham races

BPE was formed in 1989 from the merger of established Cheltenham firms Bretherton Price and Elgoods. Property and development have long been mainstays of the firm's business, and its clients including Chelsea Building Society, Countrywide Estate Agents, Twyning Developments, Clydesdale Bank and Lloyds TSB. Its property expertise now stretches beyond its established patch to the M4 corridor, Somerset, Northants and even as far as Yorkshire, where it acted for Golden Tulip, the North Yorkshire-based hotel development and operating company (now owned by Whitbread) in its acquisition of a site in York. The commercial property team also advised long-term client Blooms of Bressingham on the property aspects of its £30m takeover by Sir Tom Hunter's West Coast Capital.

In 2007 BPE achieved significant client wins across all departments, and in corporate, construction, and consumer and asset finance the firm had its most successful year ever. The employment practice has grown fivefold in the past three years and, according to one source, 'the firm is looking to grow even further.' Back in 2002 when it opened a Birmingham office, it perhaps didn't realise just how rapidly that side of the business would expand. The Brum branch had to move into bigger premises in 2006, this time to a 'bright, modern' open-plan office in a converted bank near New Street. Word is this 'very progressive, innovative firm' remains 'on the lookout for new business areas' and is 'open to suggestions.' All this growth, our sources say, 'has to be good for trainees.'

Corporate's record-breaking results came from a raft of deals including AIM floats, takeovers, M&A and complex commercial contracts. The eight-strong team completed over 55 deals with an aggregate value of more than £250m last year. Many of the deals were for BPE's nine AIM-listed clients (among them Mears Group, Maxima Holdings, The Jelf Group and Hexagon Human Capital). Mears also instructs the employment team, as does logistics specialist Howard Tenens and Coventry City Football Club. The firm also recently advised Active Private Equity on its acquisition of a £35m majority stake in high street chain Evans Cycles. Active is run by former Goldman Sachs economist and BBC chairman Gavyn Davies. In dispute resolution, clients include The Bolton Pharmaceutical Company 100, Bowmore Estates, RBS, Cintec International and Evesham Vale Growers. In the consumer and asset finance team, and more than £1.5m worth of debts were recovered for banks and motor finance clients last year. People say clients choose BPE because its style is 'friendly, approachable and has a definite common-sense edge.'

A good vintage

BPE allocates your first three seats and you choose the fourth, which all being well will be in the practice area you want to qualify into. BPE can offer trainees a broad range of experiences – corporate (including employment), commercial property, insolvency, private client, personal injury, finance, dispute resolution and construction. 'If you have a particular bias towards one area you'll be moved in that direction.' This is particularly true for mature trainees who may have spent time working in the real world. BPE, we hear, is 'quite happy to talk to potential trainees who are older,' something which some of our sources still sensed many other firms were hesitant about, despite recent age discrimination legislation. Naturally clients – and the firm itself – benefit from recruits who bring industry knowledge, and it is canny about how it fits them into the business. For example, 'if you have worked for years in a credit and asset finance house then it is highly likely your training seats will be skewed in this direction.' The construction team, meanwhile, has quite a few people with an industry background.

Naturally what you get depends on what's available because, like anywhere, 'they're juggling seats and people.' There wasn't a consensus as to which seats are loved and which are loathed – 'it depends on the individual.' Some trainees 'had been dead against property but came out really enjoying it,' and while employment, commercial dispute resolution and corporate are 'quite popular for some, they aren't for others.'

In the hefty commercial property department 'you get a lot of responsibility,' and experience all aspects of a transaction from its earliest stage talking to a client about a potential opportunity, right through to filling out post-completion forms. Trainees do all the usual tasks – drafting leases, checking deeds, overseeing the exchange of contracts and completion of transfers, liaising with clients and dealing with Land Registry enquiries. Our sources had enjoyed 'the nitty-gritty of buying and selling property.' Among the clients are Innsworth Technology Park, Pizza Hut, Bathstore.com and Llanelli Scarlets RFC, for whom lawyers sold land at the Stradey Park ground for development by house builder Taylor Wimpey. As in any seat, 'a judgement call is made by your supervisor about the level of your responsibility' and 'they make sure you're okay with what you're doing.' Grunt work amounts to 'the odd bit of photocopying' – more so in Birmingham at the time we interviewed, as the team was without the same level of backroom support as the Cheltenham office.

Suited and booted

In commercial dispute resolution, trainees experience everything from 'from taking instructions, reviewing paperwork, drafting defences, reviewing the viability of claims and general legal research, to attending court and enforcing judgment.' On the insolvency side of the team the focus is on 'researching legislation, drafting appoint-

Chambers UK rankings

Corporate Finance • Debt Recovery • Dispute Resolution • Employment • Personal Injury • Real Estate • Restructuring/Insolvency

ment documents for administrators, making sure cases are filed in court by the appropriate dates and checking the validity of transactions made before administration dates.' The credit and asset finance seat is a common one, and can also count as a trainee's mandatory litigation seat because of the recovery element to the work.

While the firm encourages as much communication and interaction between Cheltenham and Birmingham as possible, it seems there's a slightly more formal vibe in Birmingham. For example, the dress code in cheerful Cheltenham is 'smart casual,' whereas Birmingham staff are strictly 'suited – you can take your tie off but that's about it.' One trainee in Cheltenham recalled that when starting his contract 'half a dozen people bought me ties… but then I realised I was the only one wearing one.' Additionally, Birmingham is 'more heads down and get on with it,' whereas Cheltenham has a more relaxed style. The firm aims for seamless working between the two offices and the commercial dispute resolution team, for example, does regard itself as a single unit with colleagues separated solely by geography. They communicate via video link when they need to and the train takes 40 minutes between Cheltenham and Birmingham. 'Quite a few' of the current Birmingham staff trained with the firm, some moving across from Cheltenham; others were lateral hires. In both offices, the working hours are very reasonable. Even in corporate 'they aren't manic.'

To keep everyone on point, training days are held in both Cheltenham and Birmingham. These are supplemented by regular talks on developments in the law; for example, 'when there was a new consumer credit act, a credit and asset finance partner gave a talk and an e-mail went out inviting all the trainees. Those with an interest in this area went along.' As for appraisals, 'at the end of every seat you'll sit down with your supervisor for a two-way discussion to make sure you've covered everything you're supposed to have done.' The system is deemed to work well.

Star trekkers

Trainees praise BPE for being 'a very open firm… you feel comfortable speaking to anyone.' Last year the Birmingham office introduced a suggestion box to encourage feedback from employees and 'a small prize is given for the best suggestion – vouchers or something like that.' We hear that trainees are positively encouraged to participate in marketing efforts, so this gives them early exposure to 'networking functions, drinks do's with local professionals and charity sports events.' Our sources felt that BPE genuinely wants to retain as many people as possible on qualification, and this year only one person left out of five, for 'relocation reasons.' Of the others, one was hired into each of the construction, employment, litigation and corporate teams.

The imaginative extra-curricular scene includes regular charity fundraisers. 'BPE encourages trainees to do fundraising' and last year five of them climbed the highest mountain in North Africa – Morocco's Mount Toubkal – to raise money for National Star College, a school for disabled children in Cheltenham. 'We organised the route and put a case to the board asking for some funding and time off work,' explained one adventurer. BPE was very supportive. 'It's up to trainees if they want to do something similar this year,' although when we spoke to them they'd so far opted to make and sell bacon butties every week (cream teas during Wimbledon weeks), with the money again going to the Star College.

Work hours are reasonable – 'typically 8.30–9am to 6–6.30ish.' The only real complaint we heard about the firm was that 'the coffee is crap, despite the expensive machines.' Friday Friendlies are popular monthly knees-ups, when both BPE offices put the company platinum card behind the bar at a local watering hole. These may be preceded by afternoon seminars in some departments. In addition trainees might organise their own thing every couple of months, alternating between Cheltenham and Brum. When it comes to sports and games, a table football crew called Nosh & Becks is 'massively popular' and some staff play netball. This year's Christmas party was a 1940s evening in The Daffodil, a stunning converted art deco cinema in one of Cheltenham's popular backstreets. 'People dressed up in army uniforms, as land girls, in French berets…' The firm-wide summer bash was a less sophisticated rodeo affair. Up in Birmingham, trainees take full advantage of the city's famous curry houses.

And finally...

As one trainee told us: 'I chose BPE not because I wanted an easy life outside London but because I wanted the right firm.' This place should satisfy anyone with an appetite for both commercial law and Cotswold life.

Brabners Chaffe Street

The facts

Location: Liverpool, Manchester, Preston

Number of UK partners/solicitors: 62/89

Total number of trainees: 22

Seats: 4x6 months

Alternative seats: Secondments

Extras: Pro bono – Liverpool University Law Clinic

> The commercial and sports department regularly advises Manchester United, in particular taking responsibility for dispute resolution and real estate, as well as some aspects of the company's commercial activities.

Operating from three locations across the North West, Brabners Chaffe Street has marked itself out as a firm to watch. If your heart belongs to this part of the country, you can't afford to ignore it.

Best foot forward

When Liverpool's Brabners merged with Manchester's Chaffe Street in 2001 it marked the beginning of an enormously successful union that was buttressed further when in 2006, James Chapman & Co. dissolved and its commercial arm joined forces with Brabners. Expansion continued into 2007 when the firm added senior lawyers to its Manchester-based property practice from local rivals, including Halliwells and Eversheds, as well as supplementing its employment team. In 2008 the firm leapt an impressive 40 places up the *Sunday Times'* '100 Best Companies to Work For' table, making it the second-highest placed law firm on the list.

Property is a particularly strong sector for the firm, contributing around a third of the annual revenue. Recent work in this area includes negotiating the development agreement for the £100m New World Square project in Liverpool on behalf of the Princes Dock Development Company. Brabners' corporate division is another very successful part of the firm, thanks to its concentration on mid-market companies and a strong following among local businesses. This focus appeals to the trainees who 'enjoy working for smaller, North West-based companies,' as they 'like the size of the clients, often get to meet the MDs and get a real feel for the businesses.' A good example of the firm's core clients are the shareholders of Liverpool computer software developer, Bizarre Creations, who the team advised during the company's sale to US software publisher Activision.

All trainees take a seat in the property department and they're very likely to spend six months in corporate. Contentious training requirements can be satisfied by either the employment or litigation departments, and then in the remaining six months trainees can opt for a more niche department, perhaps the commercial and sports team, private client, banking or a secondment with a major client, the Mersey Docks & Harbour Company. Alternatively the firm is open to trainees returning to a seat that they have particularly enjoyed and want to gain more experience of. 'I had a fair idea of where I wanted to qualify,' explained one source, 'and so I asked whether I could stay on in the department and they were fine with me doing that. They are very flexible as they want you to be happy.'

Cider with Brabners

Interviewees concede that the first few weeks in the property department can be a challenge, despite the fact that it is an 'extremely supportive environment' where you are sat with a partner 'who will go through everything with you so that you don't feel under pressure.' As if that weren't enough, 'you're surrounded by really helpful one, two and three-year qualified solicitors who are more than happy to assist.' Once settled, trainees can really get stuck in on their own files. 'I started off doing Stamp Duty Land Tax forms and towards the end of the seat I was doing my own conveyancing, from negotiating the contract to completion.' Importantly, the hours are 'really reasonable' and the grunt work is minimal thanks to 'a fantastic support team.' Among the firm's major deals are the £10m purchase of 82 off-plan apartments over three sites in Manchester's Trafford and Hulme districts, and the £3.2m sale of Greenfield Bowling Club's land in Oldham for property development. Another similar deal saw a developer buy the site of a former fabric printing mill in Strines, near Stockport for £14m. Last year the firm created a new unit to bring together lawyers in Liverpool and Preston who have experience working for agricultural land owners. They deal with both contentious and non-contentious rural issues, including environmental law, development, tourism, estate planning and employment.

The busy corporate department presents an opportunity for confident trainees to take a degree of control in transactions. 'I was thrown in at the beginning of the seat,' explained one interviewee, 'but it is when you are given that kind of responsibility that you learn the most.' The firm's core clientele ensures that the work is varied, so 'you are dealing with small businesses and you often have to consider all aspects for them, including the employment and property considerations thrown up by a transaction.' Among the largest transactions handled by the team are the 'white knight' rescue and restructuring of the Kwik Save group of companies and Q Group's £38m cider mill joint venture with Scottish & Newcastle.

Footballers and wives

In the smaller Preston office the commercial litigation and employment departments are combined and trainees feel this 'gives you a good overview of the law rather than a specific area.' In the larger Liverpool and Manchester offices the departments are separate. Six months in employment exposes trainees to a broad palette of work from high-level compromise agreements with company directors, to unfair dismissal claims. The firm is best known for its work on behalf of employers, however it will also take on individuals' cases. Our sources seemed to have thrived on the nature of the work here: 'Employment law often marks out the boundaries of what society is prepared to accept,' explained one enthusiastic source; 'there is never a dull day.'

If you decide against a return trip to a favoured department, the remaining seat options include some glamorous choices. Perhaps first among these is the commercial and sports department, which regularly advises Manchester United, in particular taking responsibility for dispute resolution and real estate, as well as some aspects of the company's commercial activities. The lawyers also recently advised Blackburn Rovers on former manager Mark Hughes' move to Manchester City. A seat in this Manchester-based department is naturally sought after, and not just because of the nature of the clientele. One source reported having 'plentiful responsibility and client

Chambers UK rankings

Banking & Finance • Charities • Construction • Corporate Finance • Defamation/Reputation Management • Dispute Resolution • Employment • Family/Matrimonial • Intellectual Property • Private Client • Real Estate • Real Estate Litigation • Social Housing • Sports Law

contact without ever feeling out of my depth or isolated.' Furthermore, as it is one of the smaller departments 'people are always on hand and open and friendly.'

Finally, we mustn't forget the firm's private client activities. It has built up a good clientele of wealthy individuals, among them an increasing number of professional sportspeople, some of whom seek advice on divorce and prenuptial agreements. There have even been cases relating to child abduction, the law on which is usually governed by the Hague Convention. Both the private client and family departments are highly ranked by *Chambers UK*.

Northern souls

Brabners' trainees tend to be 'sociable and gregarious types' and the vast majority have strong links to the North West, having either grown up in the region or studied there. 'They are keen to hire people with a good sense of humour and so perhaps it's just that northerners are better fun to be around,' suggested one interviewee. Before they start their training contracts, trainees are asked to choose which office they would like to be based in. As a rule they will stay there for the whole of the two-year contract, and yet it's clear that if someone is keen to take a seat in another office the firm is open to them moving. Certainly, when it comes to applying for NQ positions, trainees are welcome to try for a role in any of the three offices.

Although there are several opportunities throughout the year for the trainees to get together, their day-to-day social lives are governed by their choice of office. 'A similar attitude and culture pervades all of the offices,' yet in Preston trainees said that 'from what we hear of Manchester and Liverpool we suspect that it is not quite as lively here.' They don't miss out on all the fun: 'Now and again someone will send an e-mail around and we'll go for lunch or organise a day out kart racing or even crown green bowling' and 'with it being a smaller office, it feels like you are more of a team.' The office is based in the heart of Preston's professional quarter, an area dominated by solicitors and accountancy firms. In addition to their firm-based frolics, trainees are involved with the local Young Professionals Group, which organises regular drinks and events.

Both the Manchester and Liverpool contingents have recently moved into new offices so that all staff in each location are now finally under one roof. Each office is 'right in the centre of town, so we don't have far to go of an evening.' In Manchester 'almost the whole firm descends on The Thai on a Friday,' whereas in Liverpool it could be one of a handful of favourite bars. The Living Room is a popular Thursday night location for trainees. There are plenty of healthy activities to keep trainees busy: last year the firm entered several teams into the Great Lakeland Challenge, which involves canoeing across Lake Windermere, followed by a 28-mile cycle and an ascent of Scafell Pike. The event took a killer 12 hours to complete and it was a team from the Liverpool office that scooped the first prize. The Manchester office fights back on the footie field; its 11-a-side team is currently arranging games with staff from Manchester United. Once a year at the staff conference the whole firm gets together for a weekend in a hotel in Cheshire. There's another mass gathering for the Christmas party, organised by a team of trainees. The trainees also meet as a group twice a year to host future joiners at dinner or drinks. All agree: 'It makes it a lot easier to start if you know some people already.'

I got chills...

Trainees are kept informed of changes at the firm and feel they are 'listened to and considered during the decision-making process.' This impression is reinforced by a number of internal newsletters and a monthly statement from the managing partner that helps to keep everyone up to date. Another lubricating factor is money: 'substantial bonuses' go some way to making up for trainee salaries that are 'probably slightly below larger firms in the region.'

With their packed social calendars and claims to have made 'some of the best friends that I have got,' it's not a surprise that trainees are usually in no rush to leave on qualification. The firm sends around a list of available positions and trainees are then expected to write a letter expressing their interest in each department and explaining what they would add to the team. Depending on the competition for each team, there may or may not be an interview. Despite their enthusiasm for the firm it would seem that the recent economic slowdown scuppered several trainees' plans to stay, especially in the corporate department where competition for places was fierce. In 2008 only six of the 11 qualifiers were retained.

Throughout our interviews the only grumbles we could discern were targeted at the overzealous air conditioning in the new Liverpool office ('it's either boiling when it is off or arctic when on'). Assuming this substantial hiccup can be smoothed out in time to accommodate future starters, we'd wholeheartedly recommend Brabners as a top alternative to the giant-sized national firms.

And finally...

Brabners Chaffe Street not only has real character and 'a fun and stimulating environment,' it provides a well-rounded training, complete with 'excellent partner-led mentoring.'

TOGETHER

If you're one of the handful of graduates who join Bristows each year, you'll be exposed to top tier work right from the start. You'll also be surrounded by some of the most respected lawyers in their fields. This is a firm where you'll learn fast and be stretched, but you'll also get plenty of support and encouragement along the way. There's no over-hiring of trainees, either. We're particularly proud of the fact that so many of the lawyers who trained with us have gone on to become partners.

If we sound like the kind of firm for you and to find out more, please visit www.bristows.com/trainingcontracts

BRISTOWS

Bristows

The facts

Location: London

Number of UK partners/solicitors: 27/54

Total number of trainees: 13

Seats: Seats of 3 to 6 months

Alternative seats: Secondments

Extras: Language training

> Considering it has no fancy overseas offices, a surprising amount of Bristows' work is international, largely attributable to the legwork lawyers have put in over in the USA, Japan and Korea.

Bristows is a king in intellectual property law. You don't have to be a sciences graduate to work here, but if you are then you might want to make a beeline for this cracking firm.

Bits and iPieces

Bristows was founded in 1837, though you'd struggle to find much detail about its august past on its new website. Actually, if you look closely at the homepage you'll spot a few clues – the web boffins' clever design emphasises Bristows' industry-spanning IP capabilities. Some of the world's largest (and smallest but most innovative) pharmaceutical, life sciences, biotech, telecoms and computer companies regard Bristows as the perfect partner to help protect their ideas and products. Bags of media companies and brand owners flock to the firm to keep their trade marks and copyrights unsullied. If we tell you the client list includes the BBC, French Connection, Sony, Honda, MTV, Diageo, Cadbury, Philips, Freeview, Samsung and British Airways, you'll get the picture.

Bristows' crafty rebrand is well timed. Late 2006/early 2007 was not brilliant for the firm as five partners from its core IP litigation team left to set up their own boutique, Powell Gilbert. Around the same time turnover dropped slightly to £20m for the year, making it an annus relativus-averagus to say the least. Quick to seek a cure, Bristows acquired 11 new IP associates (including a lawyer bouncing back from Powell Gilbert), made four internal promotions to partner, hired from Finers Stephens Innocent and the European Medicines Agency, and carried on business as usual. New client wins since then have included UCB Pharma, Cisco Systems, T-Mobile and Yell.com. Not bad.

Trainees say 'the firm has been sharpened by the reality of the partners leaving but hasn't changed in outlook.' Some observed a 'small change in ethos' in the sense that the 'determination to ride on the back of our IP litigation experience, maintain it and move it forward' is matched by a new desire to 'allow smaller departments to grow.' In other words, 'being more of a full-service firm that happens to have a specialist expertise.' All that said, trainees assure us: 'We'll never be a corporate-heavy City firm.'

Will you click?

The training contract reflects the existence of the other departments. Sure, six months in IP litigation is guaranteed, but there's usually also six in corporate or commercial property and time in non-contentious IP too. Better still, Bristows' seat system makes three-month stints possible, which allows even the most science-oriented trainee to broaden their experience by visiting the competition/EU, trade marks, commercial litigation and employment departments. Also offered, client secondments are guaranteed to be 'great experience and completely different to private practice.'

Considering it has no fancy overseas offices, a surprising amount of Bristows' work is international, largely attributable to the legwork lawyers have put in over in the USA, Japan and Korea. Big companies such as Hitachi, Mitsubishi, Canon, Sony, Toshiba and Fujitsu rely on the firm to defend and enforce their IP rights; for example,

Bristows helped Korean electronics giant Samsung on the UK aspects of a worldwide scrap with Ericsson and Sony-Ericsson regarding mobile telephony equipment. The dispute involves 15 separate patents and four actions before the High Court. In the pharmaceuticals/life sciences sector, lawyers are acting for Medtronic/Evysio in relation to patents for stents, a multibillion-pound product that can be described as scaffolding for arteries and other passageways in the body. In support of that beleaguered species, the smoker, Bristows is helping British American Tobacco oppose Philip Morris' European patent application for the use of carbon beads in cigarette filters. In the equally important field of laminate flooring, it continues to support one of the world's largest manufacturers in litigation against products infringing its glue-less 'click' joint. You may snigger, but continued success in this case helped the client add enormous value to its business, and it was recently bought for €2.2bn.

An IP litigation trainee gets to do an awful lot of document bundling, so they take great pleasure in drafting 'expert reports that may even get used in trial' and dealing with barristers. Take a seat when a case is going to court and there's the thrill of witnessing 'the barrister using your notes to make a point.' It's a pleasure also to be enjoyed in the 'soft' IP department, which deals with copyright, trade mark and design rights disputes across a wide variety of sectors from fashion to software. The team advises Freeview on its trade mark portfolio and has long protected the BBC's extensive portfolio.

The BBC also took advice from the firm on a number of discrete issues concerning the new digital iPlayer, an instruction that highlights Bristows' sizzling non-contentious commercial IP/IT abilities. The department acts for a ridiculously good-looking roster of clients, including French Connection, Tetley, MTV and Diageo, on an array of stuff, be it licensing, merchandising or on-pitch advertising. Diageo, which owns brands like Guinness, Smirnoff and Baileys, has recently instructed the firm on contracts for celebrity endorsements. Working on 'a big data protection transaction' might sound like the less interesting end of the spectrum, but 'the pan-European scope' adds interest to all the proof-reading.

Is there a doctor in the house?

The continuing pre-eminence of IP and the prevalence of 'clients with a tech-sector edge' means sciences will continue to be helpful to Bristows trainees. If you're sat there wondering whether to continue life as a library/lab geek, Bristows could well be your escape route. Nearly all its IP lawyers have further degrees in related fields and quite a few are PhDs. In 2008 only three of the 14 trainees came from a straight law or humanities background. Be it a science, engineering or computer sciences degree, this is a

Chambers UK rankings

Data Protection • Dispute Resolution • Information Technology • Intellectual Property • Life Sciences • Media & Entertainment • Partnership

place where 'you can take pride in your qualifications, make an asset of them' and 'work alongside some of the cleverest people in their fields.' Frighteningly clever sometimes: 'I feel in awe of partners and associates,' admitted one source.

If your scientific education stopped when you took your GSCEs or A-levels, the firm could still have room for you. 'A science background is not necessary and you can do the work without it,' our sources insisted. Then again, 'if a task resonates with your background it does give you a slight edge and generates interest.' Perhaps it's best to conclude this discussion by saying that, particularly in IP litigation, you have to work very hard to understand both the complex law and the highly specialised fields to which cases relate.

Thank goodness there's more to Bristows than brain-boggling patents. Life in corporate is largely about 'small-scale work for clients with a technology edge,' such as an 'equity group that invests in pharma products.' This 'sometimes hectic' seat is a winner, even if one trainee's abiding memory was 'a very complicated share purchase agreement that meant I was there until the early hours.' One of the most rewarding aspects of the seat is 'attending meetings with magic circle lawyers on the other side.' The competition/EU, commercial litigation and employment teams are popular with second-years, while the commercial property seat 'tends to be taken early because it's good for picking up transferable skills.' Last year the lawyers added Moss Bros and the Honourable Society of Lincoln's Inn to a client list that already includes Gillette, the National Portrait Gallery and Kodak. 'You don't always get as much drafting as you might like,' although 'in terms of client exposure it's good. I trooped off to a meeting with the client and other side on my own.'

'Talk of semi-informal mid-seat appraisals' has not yet become a reality, so end-of-seat appraisals must serve all purposes. In addition to seat supervisors, trainees have senior associates as mentors, so no one lacks support. For the most part they're kept in the loop with developments at the firm, and should they need scientific or technical assistance on a piece of work there's always an expert on hand.

Bespoke tailoring

Bristows has settled into plush new accommodation in the Unilever Building on the Thames Embankment. 'It's a bit of a change from the quaint Lincoln's Inn offices' that had been its home since the year dot. We were always tempted to link the cosy gentility of that location to Bristows' 'atmosphere of mutual respect that allows people of whatever level to get on and do things well.' But maybe moving to a modern des res is just what the firm needed to dispel the impression that it might be 'stuffy, traditional or genteel.' In the words of one trainee: 'The move is about us putting on a new suit of clothes' and the new office is 'a projection of the way we see ourselves, not a fundamental change in personality.' The 'smart, clever geography teacher in a jacket with leather elbow patches' image has been replaced by that of a 'smarter, suited professional.'

The identity beneath the new suit is a 'co-operative and courteous' one in which 'people help each other out rather than seeking to progress themselves.' Trainees are happy to slip on this mantle. 'We're quietly unassuming,' they explained; 'determined, but not competitive in a backstabbing way.' They all possess the capacity to 'get on with things and not let things ruffle us,' and we'd add that those we interviewed were notably intelligent, articulate and perceptive. One trainee mused that 'the reputation for gentility probably relates to the fact we don't get ground into the dust' and work 'pretty good hours.' The average trainee will experience 'a couple of late nights and busy periods,' but generally gets out by 6.30pm. Proof that everyone pulls together came for one trainee when on Christmas Eve 'even the managing partner stayed to help with bundling on a big case.'

Full house

The Unilever building boasts impressive facilities, some of which trainees can use and others they can only look at. 'Unilever has a fifth-floor restaurant and a gym, but they're off-limits,' sighed one source. Instead they must make do with 'fancy bike racks' and a ground-floor cafeteria. The north bank of the Thames has replaced Bristows' old social hotspot – Lincoln's Inn Fields – and a common room called The Hub is the venue for 'drinks put on by the partners on the last Friday of every month.' An annual black-tie bash at a swanky location is well attended and 'pretty glitzy – you can make a fool of yourself and no one minds.'

The trainees are 'reasonably sporty and do socialise together' but 'don't live in each other's pockets.' Some are on the firm's social committee; others are happy to assist in the quest to find a worthy new local pub. 'There are plenty nearby, but it's whether they have character and are interesting enough,' reflected one source. There was much to celebrate when we interviewed trainees in April 2008: all eight second-years had just accepted NQ jobs.

And finally...

A top destination for anyone fascinated by IP work, Bristows is basically a great place to work. Whether you're shedding a lab coat or a wodge of dog-eared foolscap on the way, you'll need to shine to get in.

Browne Jacobson

The facts

Location: Nottingham, Birmingham, London

Number of UK partners/solicitors: 50/127

Total number of trainees: 24

Seats: 4x6 months

Alternative seats: None

Extras: Pro bono – CAB, ProHelp, Prince's Trust, Criminal Injuries and Compensation Scheme

> One of Browne Jacobson's strengths is its multiplicity of specialist sector teams. Trainees have access to all areas of work.

Central Nottingham outfit Browne Jacobson has been committed to the Midlands since 1832, when it was founded by a former city coroner. Its appetite for growth has seen it quadruple in size over the past decade.

Coming on strong

True, 14 years ago the firm opened a small London branch, but beyond its Nottingham homeland the greatest changes have taken place in Birmingham, where a tiny office has mushroomed into a 14-partner, 100-staff, full-service operation since 1999. As an indication of the scale of that growth, the firm has launched a Birmingham-based training contract in addition to its main Nottingham scheme, and our sources easily envisaged a time when this branch will match the HQ in size. 'By 2011 Nottingham and Birmingham will be as important as each other and we may well have new office buildings,' said one trainee. And from another: 'I think we will be more commercially focused – commercial is where our marketing is going.'

Across the Midlands, the modern Browne Jacobson has been best known for its litigation focus and involvement with the insurance sector. In the dash for more commercial work, it 'doesn't seem likely that insurance will disappear;' indeed insurance, professional indemnity (including clinical negligence) and personal injury litigation still account for almost half of revenue, with still more income derived from commercial and other litigation. There are other strings to BJ's bow: its local authority team acts for over 200 of the 400 authorities in England and Wales, the corporate/commercial side of the firm is developing apace, and the property department has been going great guns. There's even a sports practice that represents the RFU and several county cricket clubs and football teams in the Midlands. Just in case the idea of major change doesn't appeal, it's worth heeding the trainee who told us: 'BJ is not the sort of firm to do anything rash. Things are a long time coming here, and you see them coming.'

As you might gather, one of Browne Jacobson's strengths is its multiplicity of specialist sector teams. Beyond the insurance, local authority and sports groups mentioned above, others focus on health, social care, education, retail, environment, fire services, food and drink, regulatory and charities. Trainees have access to all areas of work, including an array of contentious seat options to tempt even the most transactionally minded new lawyers. Nottingham offers the broadest selection of seats – though Birmingham is catching up – and trainees who opt for a six-month trip to London are given a wide-ranging role helping several fee earners. Usually one trainee visits the capital at each rotation, and it's a great experience, even if our sources felt it would be even better if the seat was tailored to a single area chosen by the visiting trainee.

Give blood?

The core insurance division, where trainees all spend at least one six-month seat, is organised into specialist teams for social care and education; health (including clinical negligence work from the NHS Litigation Authority); environment and advocacy; claims defence (much of this is motor claims referred by big insurers) and technical claims (PI and stress-at-work cases). The social care and education team, despite its interesting cases, 'doesn't tend to be a popular choice… it is quite gritty.' We also hear that unless you're proactive you might end up doing more 'monotonous tasks' like listing documents, managing disclosure and dealing with costs – 'a lot of that filters down to trainees.' Show promise and you'll get 'the run of a file – almost.' The social care lawyers handle group actions relating to historical cases of abuse. Said one source: 'From a litigation perspective I am glad I did it as it taught me a lot about group orders and putting claims together, and always being mindful of the costs.' The education team acts exclusively for education providers, not individuals, working on failure-to-educate cases and issues such as the organisation of school trips. In this context, lawyers represented the National Association of Head Teachers and the London Borough of Lambeth in relation to the drowning of a pupil while on a school trip to France. At other times, boards of governors seek guidance, perhaps on how to set up trust schools or the tricky subject of what schools can and can't do in terms of uniform policy.

Clinical negligence cases flood in from the NHSLA, the Medical Defence Union and a host of hospitals and trusts. One of the team's proudest achievements has been the development of an alternative dispute resolution process for managing over 500 claims relating to the misdiagnosis and mistreatment of epilepsy at the University Hospitals of Leicester NHS Trust. More broadly, healthcare clients need assistance in relation to things like inquests and questions of consent to treatment. An out-of-hours helpline is available to doctors faced with dilemmas over lack of consent. In one such case an emergency declaration was obtained from a High Court judge in the middle of the night to permit doctors to give a blood transfusion to a 14-year-old Jehovah's Witness against her parents' wishes.

Les e-zee riders

The commercial litigation and insolvency department has quite different cases and can be an interesting place to put to good use the procedural lessons learned in the insurance division. The work of the team is extraordinarily broad – defending Environment Agency prosecutions, representation at public enquiries before the Traffic Commissioner, product recalls, defamation, commercial disputes for foreign clients, training clients on how to deal with dawn raids by the OFT. You name it, BJ does it.

In corporate terms, you won't have heard of most of the firm's work, as it tends to be small to medium-sized deals for regional businesses rather than big plcs. That said, one recent highlight was its representation of Loomis (formerly Securitas) on the purchase of the UK cash-handling business of Brink's. The broad business services seat satisfies the curiosity of many a trainee. 'While there always seems to be seats open in all the departments, if you

Chambers UK rankings

Administrative & Public Law • Banking & Finance • Clinical Negligence • Construction • Corporate Finance • Debt Recovery • Dispute Resolution • Education • Employment • Environment • Healthcare • Intellectual Property • Personal Injury • Planning • Private Client • Professional Negligence • Public Procurement • Real Estate • Real Estate Litigation • Restructuring/Insolvency • Social Housing • Tax

couldn't get into, say tax, you could go into business services and they would involve you in the tax practice there.' For others the seat was a good place to pick up IP experience. The employment team keeps a foot in both the public and commercial camps: it does a lot for fire service and healthcare clients, as well as Midlands businesses and national retailers like TK Maxx.

The real estate department has grown considerably in recent years and focuses on specific client sectors, namely retail, health, development and public authorities, and substantial experience with public/private sector partnerships should really help it in this flatter market. Recent deals include Avon Cosmetics' acquisition of new UK warehousing facilities and the extension of Wilkinson's distribution hub in Gwent. Flash retail clients include LVMH, Prada and biker-chic French boutique Zadig et Voltair.

Home is where the start was

BJ trainees learn by doing, not dabbling. 'Positively discouraged' to spend time photocopying or typing their own letters, they are instead expected to utilise support staff in the same way a qualified solicitor would. We did hear calls for more specific training at the start of a new seat. 'It would have been helpful,' said one source; 'you are mostly left to find your feet.' No complaints about salaries though: 'We are paid towards the higher end of the Nottingham market,' said one; 'I suspect only Eversheds pay higher.' Comparisons with Eversheds came up repeatedly in our interviews: BJ trainees say they get a higher degree of responsibility and like the fact that Nottingham is the firm's 'flagship office, whereas Nottingham isn't even one of the main Eversheds offices, it's just a satellite.' They also believe BJ is less of a 'people factory.' For the most part trainees enjoy regular hours (9am until 5pm in some departments) and 'no one is doing anything exceptional,' apart from 'one or two people who have stayed until 11pm in corporate.'

Trainees are also proud of being 'a Midlands firm for Midlands businesses.' 'We're not trying to be City,' they explained, describing instead the push they observe to 'be one of the best law providers in the region.' We could hear the conviction in the voice of the person who told us: 'We know where we grew up, we know our roots and we remember who our key clients are. It's all about not forgetting that there are plenty of brilliant clients right on our doorstep.' Consequently our sources urged anyone considering training in the region to 'think beyond the big names.' 'At other firms you might work obscene hours, get depressed and burn out... this firm is a prime example of how you can get everything right.'

So what type of person is BJ looking for? 'Good academics are taken as read; everyone knows you need to be sharp,' otherwise the ideal applicant is someone who'll fit into an environment that is described as 'relaxed though not informal.' A good indication of potential fit is whether you're the sort of person with the comfortable self-confidence to 'start up a conversation in the staff restaurant,' because this is a firm where 'you can walk into any department and talk to any partner.' But, given this is also a Midlands firm through and through, does BJ only want to recruit Midlanders? Ideally, yes. If you were born and bred in the region, great. If you attended university locally, equally great. And yet despite its attraction to locals the firm also has a track record of recruiting people without a strong connection, so long as they tick all the other boxes.

Doing it for the kids

Whether you're chatting to partners or merely sipping a latte, staff fuelling station Café 44 is the stop-off point for mid-work relaxation. After 5pm, it's all about The Kids though, and by that we mean The Royal Children pub just over the road. 'Incoming trainees find out about it and want to uphold the tradition,' an old hand explained the firm's loyalty to this hostelry; 'otherwise we go to The Castle.' Essentially the first pub is exclusively frequented by BJ staff and cheap, while the pricier Castle is always full of lawyers from Eversheds and Berrymans. 'We go to The Kids first as there will always be partners to buy drinks. The unspoken rule is that trainees don't pay for anything.' A budget is available for trainee socials, some of which are open to future recruits while they're still at law school. Favourite events include quizzes, a Christmas party and a round-Nottingham treasure hunt that has proved so popular that the Birmingham office now runs one of its own. In 2008 five out of eight qualifying trainees took up positions at the firm, going into Nottingham teams.

And finally...

Browne Jacobson's vision for the future involves Midlands-focused expansion via a virtuous circle in which a positive working environment attracts good lawyers and in turn keeps clients loyal. Sign up here if you see the breadth and potential in that vision.

BTMK

The facts

Location: Southend-on-Sea, Chelmsford

Number of UK partners/solicitors: 15/37

Total number of trainees: 5

Seats: Flexible

Alternative seats: None

Extras: Chelmsford and Southend CABs

In 2008 BTMK received the accolade of being appointed to the national Very High Cost Criminal Cases panel.

When Essex firms TMK and Bates Travell merged in 2005 they became the biggest fish in the legal pond in Southend-on-Sea. Full-service BTMK's broad and detailed training programme offers flexible short seats plus an enviable level of responsibility for trainees.

Mike'll fix it

Typically trainees told us: 'I'm from Southend and wanted to avoid London. BTMK has the best reputation in the region.' Indeed the firm has made a very good name for itself: *Chambers UK* ranks BTMK in the top tier for crime in its region. Not that this firm is all about crime – there's a wealth of different departments for trainees to sample during their contracts. 'You can pretty much do anything you like,' chirped one grateful source, and while this was something of an exaggeration, there's no denying that training partner Mike Warren makes a big effort to listen to trainees' preferences. Said one: 'Mike's really accommodating. He's had quite a bit of input into my training and I can call him up any time.' If you're dead against a particular seat, chances are you can do something else. 'If you're not really keen on, say, criminal law you can avoid it.'

Notionally, trainees spend six months in their first seat, then three months each in a succession of departments until their final seat, where they spend a bit longer again. 'The rationale of structuring the seat programme this way is to give you six months of stability on first joining to settle into one department, then have a succession of short three-month seats to give you a broad range of experience. This helps you choose what you want to specialise in.' In practice things are a bit more fluid, and the trainee group we spoke to had done different combinations and lengths of seats, ranging from a mere month to over eight

months and all possibilities in between. 'You can chop and change – all the trainees have done a different combination of seats.' As if this weren't 'accommodating' enough there are also 'split seats' (allowing trainees to spend time with two departments). All this flexibility is especially helpful when finalising qualification decisions. Said one source: 'It was totally up to me whether I wanted to do more split seats or spend longer in the seat I wanted to qualify into. It really encourages trainees to make informed decisions.'

All the seats on offer tend to fall under the categories of family, civil litigation, company commercial (which includes some private client work) and personal injury. In addition, there are options in employment (part of civil) and crime, and if you're keen to gain experience in the many other areas of law BTMK offers advice in, such as conveyancing or debt recovery, then you just need to ask Mike. 'It's a small firm so everyone knows each other,' our sources reminded us. Because of this, seat-change nerves are virtually non-existent – 'When I moved to my second seat, I already knew most of the team here.'

Legal aids

While crime and family are strong departments at BTMK, trainees are wary of qualifying into them despite enjoying their time with these teams. As one explained it: 'The legal aid cutbacks mean there aren't great prospects of employment; most firms are stream-lining.' Admittedly in crime there's another key disincentive: 'I don't want to be on call 24/7 – weekends and Christmas!' There was one fan of crime last year but none this year, although the firm will continue to offer opportunities to trainees in this practice group. 'The seat was great,' said someone who'd spent time there. 'We attended Crown Court hearings and I was always out in the car meeting barristers or listening to interview tapes. It's nice to get out of the office.' One recent highlight case was a week-long drugs trial in Canterbury. It's not all excursions in the motor though; 'there's lots of clerking too.' Anyone who's interested would be offered the chance to complete the Police Station Accreditation Scheme, which gets them on the rota for out of office call-outs to the cop shop and can be a good source of overtime pay. At BTMK cases range from local drunks up on an assault charge at 4am right through to the most serious and complex criminal cases that are prosecuted in the Crown Court. In April 2008 BTMK received the accolade of being appointed to a national panel to deal with such cases, the Legal Services Commission's Very High Cost Criminal Cases panel. The work sounds really interesting to us, so it's a shame the changes in the funding regime are putting off so many people from qualifying into a life of crime.

'Legal aid difficulties have affected family law as well as crime,' according to other sources who have grappled with the dilemma of whether to qualify in that area. Family is one of the bigger practices at BTMK, with eight fee earners, two of them partners. Our source explained: 'It's very busy and cases are publicly funded so you have to do a lot of work. It was a big change of pace for me compared to my last seat.' Naturally some cases can be eye-opening. 'I went to court nearly every day. There are lots of divorces, children's contact and custody cases, etc, and clients are often emotionally distressed.' The trainee will typically 'draft divorce petitions, financial statements and letters to the other side's solicitors, all fast-moving same-day stuff.' Our sources didn't know what the future would have in store for the department, but were positive that 'the changes in legal aid haven't affected the firm yet – the family department is facing it head on and there are weekly meetings [to address issues].' Trainees valued their time here even if they didn't plan to qualify in it: 'I learnt a lot of stuff – it's useful to know about family law whatever your future career.'

Civil litigation trainees get work from everyone in the team and not just their principal. 'You're thrown in at the deep end, dealing with clients straight away, attending minor hearings at court, along with the usual trainee stuff. There's a nice mix.' The cases range from small landlord and tenants disputes in which 'people are chucked out of their homes' through to commercial litigation in which 'big businesses sue non-payers.'

Chambers UK rankings

Crime

Trainees were pleased to have enjoyed client contact and advocacy, but needless to say were less enthralled doing 'your fair share of photocopying.' Civil is 'quite a big department – two partners, three fee earners' and includes 'a good bit of employment law too.' The small employment team is likely to 'thrive' in the current economic climate and is already doing 'lots of unfair dismissal work, race discrimination and redundancy.' The CAB refers people with general civil disputes to BTMK, which holds a weekly two-hour surgeries in both Chelmsford and Southend.

The commercial seat brings trainees into contact with local businesses, estate managers, 'affluent people with big property portfolios' and a few national companies. The work is 'very varied and includes landlords and tenant issues, shareholder agreements, sales and purchases of companies, preparing loan notes, giving undertakings, drafting statutory declarations, etc.' Strangely this is also the seat to gain experience in probate matters, an area where there's lots of client contact. Personal injury seats meanwhile involve drafting witness statements for clients and, rather gruesomely, 'working out the value of certain injuries.' In addition, 'there's a lot of looking through files and preparing chronologies – not the most fun work, but it needs to be done.'

The dog ate my homework

Some trainees have already worked as paralegals with BTMK; others will have completed work experience there. All praised the hands-on training they received and the supportive environment of the firm. 'The training is all-inclusive – you do the work a solicitor does, interview the client, etc. Not just photocopying – on my first day I went to court with a solicitor and took instructions from the client. I've had loads of client contact.' Another agreed: 'People are really helpful to trainees and there's always someone to ask. If you make any mistakes they explain why. You're developing so rapidly. Every week or two I got to go through everything with my supervisor and the secretaries are invaluable for helping you too.' Trainees are also encouraged to do plenty of advocacy – 'you go to court with your supervisor, get everything explained to you, then off you go.' Appraisals differ from one department to another, with some providing day-to-day feedback and others adopting more formal arrangements. The family department, for example, even sets homework to be completed and discussed with the supervisor. Crime is another of the stricter departments when it comes to formal assessment.

Training contracts are centred on the main County Chambers office in Southend. 'Some departments are open-plan, and no offices have closed doors. They are older buildings with a modern take on them – nice, clean, laminate flooring.' Overall trainees say BTMK is 'very modern but with traditional values.' In terms of future growth, they believe 'the firm will react to what is happening in the local economy.' Right now, for example, 'debt recovery and employment are on the up because of the credit crunch. There's a downturn in conveyancing, obviously, but trainees have very little to do with this department anyway.'

'You don't have to come from Essex or have gone to a certain university to work here,' but the truth is most trainees do come from Southend or nearby. When we rang, only one of the batch of four was an outsider and they were from Enfield, a not-very-distant 40 miles away. 'It's a young firm, very sociable. There's no stuffiness and you'd feel as comfortable having a beer with a partner as a trainee.' Sport, it's fair to say, isn't high on the list of leisure activities at BTMK. If you're an Olympian athlete/god seeking like-bodied hearties to play with during every non-working moment, we suggest you look elsewhere. Team BTMK manages a family fun run once a year, followed by a huge barbecue and bevvies. BTMK's sponsorship of this popular Southend event reflects the firm's central position in the local community. 'The more athletic staff do the run and it's very competitive because everyone's names and finishing times are printed in the local paper.' As for other sports, 'some of the men play golf,' but 'attempts to start a five-a-side team have fallen on deaf ears.'

The Mews is the pub of choice – it's a quaint gastropub, which as you'd expect from an eaterie-on-sea has plenty of seafood on the menu. The firm recently organised a day at the races for staff at Newmarket and there's an annual Christmas party, the location of which seems to be 'a closely guarded secret.' Perhaps the most eagerly anticipated event of the year is the summer barbecue held in the large garden at the back of the main office to celebrate the passing out of newly qualified solicitors and arrival of new trainees. 'The whole firm's invited and it's quite a tradition. It's talked about all year because it's good fun and has cringe-worthy speeches. Then there's the Ceremony of the Pen…' In this ceremony newly qualifieds are presented with 'a posh pen – a Mont Blanc or something like that.' It's known unofficially as the pen of doom. In 2008 one of the two qualifiers stayed on.

And finally...

It's easy to understand why BTMK commands great loyalty from its trainees. If you want a flexible Essex-based training contract in which the structure and support are 'flawless', look no further.

sardines

salmon

After a long day at work, where would you rather be? Battling through the rush hour on the tube, or sipping a drink at one of Bristol's many waterfront restaurants and bars?

And it's not just our quality of life that speaks volumes about us...

"The firm has managed to win work that other national rivals would kill for... with client wins such as EMI Group, Reuters and Coca Cola HBC, Burges Salmon has quietly built the elite firm outside London" LAWYER AWARDS.

"Work on deals of all sizes and complexity is praised as 'impeccable' by a client base that appreciates the firm's blend of technical excellence and commercial nous" LEGAL 500.

For further information, please contact our trainee solicitor recruitment team on 0117 902 7797.

www.sardinessalmon.com

Burges Salmon LLP

The facts

Location: Bristol

Number of UK partners/solicitors: 72/238

Total number of trainees: 43

Seats: 6x4 months

Alternative seats: Secondments

Extras: Pro bono – Bristol Law Clinic, CAB, Environmental Law Foundation; language classes

> Big-name clients like Coca-Cola, First Group, Orange, RBS, Reuters, Shell, Samsung and the MoD make this an incredibly attractive prospect for anyone ambitious but with a dislike for City life.

A flashy sports car zooms westward through the picturesque countryside. The well-heeled young lawyer driving it smiles knowingly as the wind whips through his hair and his tie flutters over his shoulder. Not for him the daily sweat of the Northern Line. He works for Burges Salmon.

In the pink

Or at least that's the scene as Burges Salmon's marketing team would like you to believe. In recent years they have been enthusiastically courting City types with the promise of London-quality work and a countryside quality of life. The strategy seems to be paying dividends. One trainee put it bluntly: 'For me it was a very simple decision. I didn't want to be in London. I looked for the single best firm outside of London. It was obviously Burges Salmon.' Our colleagues at *Chambers UK* are pretty happy with this bold statement: the Bristolian outfit ranks among the best in the UK for health and safety, asset finance, transport, contentious tax and environment work to name just a few – not bad for out in the sticks. What's more, Burges Salmon has a portfolio of clients that any London firm would be proud of, doing work for the likes of Coca-Cola, First Group, Orange, RBS, Reuters, Shell, Samsung, the MoD and The Crown Estate. Big names like these make it an incredibly attractive prospect for anyone ambitious but with a dislike for City life. The firm also seems to be shedding a reputation for stuffiness. A recent spate of promotions means that for the first time younger partners outnumber those from the old school. 'They've seen us weather some storms with a conservative attitude, but I get the impression that the handbrake is coming off,' mused one trainee. One thing that won't be changing is BS's famous pink writing paper. Nor will the policy of sticking to a single site; everyone is 'absolutely resolute' about that. However, there will be relocation to a brand new Bristol office in 2010, a move eagerly anticipated by trainees. 'We've no air conditioning,' they chorused on the hot May afternoon when we called. 'Nor have we,' came our reply. When pressed, they did concede that the firm provides free ice creams.

Burges Salmon's core practices are corporate, commercial, banking and property, and then there's an endless number of smaller, specialist teams dispensing advice on everything from agriculture, environment and renewable energy to nuclear energy, rail transport and Islamic finance. Thanks to a six-seat system, trainees get a chance to sample several of these practice areas. Property is compulsory, and after that there are a range of either/or options; one seat must be in either commercial or corporate, one in commercial disputes and construction (CDC) or agriculture, property litigation and environment (APLE), and one in employment, pensions and incentives (EPI) or tax and trusts. For their fifth seat they get a free choice, while the final seat is normally the one that the trainee is due to qualify into. And speaking of qualification, yet again BS did very well: 19 of the 20 2008 qualifiers stayed with the firm.

Super-pfalzflugzeugwerke-expialidocious

Property is Burges Salmon's largest department. It's also the seat trainees look forward to least, but only because 'since all lawyers are stubborn egocentric bastards, we automatically don't want to do anything that's compulsory.' Once they get into it, property trainees find themselves gaining 'great experience of client management. You really learn how to deal with people.' They also pick up case management skills and benefit from 'a very interesting supervision pattern.' The trend is for trainees to spend the first two months in the seat doing isolated jobs and feeling the work is bitty, but realising in the second two months that they have done every task involved in running a file, 'but in bits so you can't muck up any whole case. In the second half of your seat, you put it all together, run the whole file and manage matters all by yourself.' Among the firm's most notable property instructions have been the compensation and temporary accommodation of First Capital East during the compulsory acquisition of its main bus depot on the site of the future Olympic village, various big restructuring deals for RBS and a swathe of deals for land-rich National Grid Property Holdings. The files that trainees manage by themselves are naturally smaller – things like drafting lease renewals and negotiations between landlords and tenants.

A seat in corporate can be a rollercoaster ride of weeks of all-nighters followed by a succession of early finishes and lazy evenings on the waterfront. Anyone who can handle pressure and the up and down nature of the work will thrive. Said one source: 'Everyone is heading towards the same goal and the camaraderie is amazing.' As in property, trainees will help on huge deals and also get the chance to manage much smaller files of 'only £1.5m or so.' Said one interviewee: 'I turned up at a client meeting expecting to take notes, and the partner left me to get on with it myself.' Corporate clients include Nationwide Building Society, Wolseley UK and tongue-twisting German company Pfalzflugzeugwerke GmbH. In terms of deals, lawyers have lately been busy with the proposed merger of Milklink with FirstMilk to create the UK's largest dairy farmer co-operative and the country's largest cheese maker, with a turnover of over £1bn. And then there was advice to the independent directors of Newbury Racecourse plc on a hostile offer to acquire all of its issued share capital for £33.5m. It's worth knowing that when it comes to deals in the agricultural sector, BS is frequently the top-choice firm, especially in the south of England.

For those less addicted to adrenalin there are seats with more of a steady workload; even so it's clear that BS isn't afraid to hand trainees plenty of early responsibility. In construction, for example, one long-running case saw four trainees come and go, 'but we knew the documents better than anyone. It was great to get to know a case in such detail.' Likewise, in tax and trusts trainees will work on cases for wealthy clients, helping to arrange their assets in trust structures, some of which are incredibly complex. In this academic area of the law research takes

Chambers UK rankings

Agriculture & Rural Affairs • Banking & Finance • Charities • Competition/European Law • Construction • Corporate Finance • Debt Recovery • Dispute Resolution • Employment • Environment • Family/Matrimonial • Health & Safety • Information Technology • Intellectual Property • Investment Funds • Partnership • Pensions • Planning • Private Client • Private Equity • Projects, Energy & Natural Resources • Public Procurement • Real Estate • Real Estate Litigation • Restructuring/Insolvency • Tax • Transport

up a lot of time, with drafting trust documents and tax reports filling much of the rest.

Tricks of the trade mark

The commercial department spans such a wide variety of things that it's difficult to generalise about the nature of the work, especially since trainees can choose to either concentrate on one area within the department or gain a broad overview. The IP team litigates and negotiates on trade mark disputes. One of its major clients is Harrods, and so the trainee will become used to 'policing the Harrods brand' on both the high street and the internet. The firm has been involved in more than a dozen disputes over Harrods-related domain names and, so far, has won all of them. On another occasion the firm acted for a company opposing a trade mark newly registered by another company on the grounds that it was too similar to their own. The trainee researched the claim, at one point touring the shops in order to get examples of the two trade marks, and then wrote up a witness statement. In the area of debt recovery 'often clients will have my number rather than my supervisor's,' said one trainee. It's interesting work that is often more complex than it first appears. 'Cases that may come in as a simple debt collection claim get more complicated as things start to come to light.'

BS currently works in an advisory capacity for several major organisations: the Nuclear Decommissioning Authority on the closure of its obsolete nuclear reactors, the Avon & Somerset Police Authority on the outsourcing of its IT services and the MoD and Department for Transport on their joint Private Finance Initiative for the procurement of search and rescue helicopters. Trainee tasks for these clients have included drafting schedules, attending negotiation meetings and going through contracts to evaluate risk and make amendments when necessary.

The employment seat has a good reputation among trainees and is consistently popular. The department mainly focuses on representing employers and has a number of big-name clients on the books. We're talking about Reuters, BAE Systems and Bank of Ireland, for example. One recent case involved defending a claim brought against a company for discrimination against an employee: the firm won the case on every point. The team does represent employees on occasion, for instance giving advice to a group of high-ranking executives who wanted to move from one company to another as a team. As well as the usual tasks of collating relevant documents and drafting witness statements, this seat can also offer a taste of advocacy.

Sing a song of salmon

It's clear from their adverts that Burges Salmon 'wants to attract the same brains, if not necessarily the same personalities' as the magic circle. After a quick examination of the facts we noted that the class of 2008 trainees hailed largely, if not exclusively, from Oxbridge and the top redbricks. The firm is also fond of second-career applicants and there were a fair few over 30 in the mix. Recruitment marketing may be geared towards a work-life balance, but our contacts told us not to expect an easy ride. 'Work-life balance doesn't equal easy option, it means being sensible not lazy.' It works both ways though, and 'people who work too hard might be surprised to find their colleagues expect to have a life outside the office.' The trainee group gets on like a house on fire and often organises impromptu weekend trips. 'Most of us went to a cottage on Exmoor last weekend,' revealed one interviewee. Other visits that brought back fond memories were shopping in Portsmouth, champagne tasting in Reims and frolicking in Bruges. A trip to see Cirque du Soleil at the Royal Opera House was already being planned months in advance. Everyone throws a couple of quid a month into the social committee pot to fund events.

BS lawyers must be some of the healthiest in the country, as the firm manages to field football, netball, cricket, rugby, hockey, basketball, sailing and softball teams, and it has squash and tennis ladders and 'quite a few surfers.' Trainees recently pushed their bodies to the limit in a sponsored 24-hour row – oh, and did we mention that one of them is an Olympic gold medal winner? As if this wasn't enough, BS harbours a multitude of musicians. Have their talents no end? A battle of the bands has been arranged, again in the name of charity, to pit the firm's wannabe rock stars against one another. 'It's called Fishstock,' intoned one trainee happily.

And finally...

There's no denying our admiration for this firm. With a new office and new partners, the wind is changing. 'Its certainly a new era for the firm and a good time to be here,' said a trainee with what we assumed would be a knowing smile, just before he jumped in his salmon pink sports car.

Campbell Hooper

The facts

Location: London

Number of UK partners/solicitors: 26/37

Total number of trainees: 10

Seats: 4x6 months

Alternative seats: None

Most apply to Campbell Hooper for the challenges and variety of a London career without the big-firm drawbacks.

Campbell Hooper has historically taken a low profile. So much so that one of its trainees admitted: 'I didn't realise until I got here how good we are.' A rebrand and a more ambitious outlook could mean this ancient West End firm should soon stop blending in with the wallpaper and start standing out more on London's legal landscape.

The past is history

Campbell Hooper is justly proud of its past and trainees told us: 'A consultant who has been at the firm longer than any of us have been alive gives a talk every now and then on the history going right back into the mists of time.' In brief, by the end of the 18th century CH was already an amalgam of several firms – one specialising in services to theatre clients, another with a strong property law pedigree. The firm has built on these historical strengths and developed new areas of expertise such that it's become a good all-rounder. Its goal is to continue expanding in all directions, but 'not just off the cuff... it's more strategic than that.' The 'rolling three-year plan' is to increase revenue and 'move away from relying on just one or two big clients.' Recognising that the firm's image was 'not quite uniform' in appearance, a 'refreshing of identity' was effected with the intention of making the CH brand appear more modern. An overhaul of the website ('everyone's been ashamed of it') and a lick and a spit for the previously 'slightly shabby' offices have trainees excited at the prospect of greater visibility for the firm.

In work terms, enhancing existing strengths is the name of the game. Campbell Hooper is organised into five main departments: corporate and commercial (including media and comlit), real estate, construction, employment, and private client and family. All departments have client lists scattered with well-known names; the real estate department, for example, works for Bellway Homes and Countryside Properties. This last client is one of the firm's biggest and is served by several departments. The corporate team assists all sorts of businesses from Jimmy Choo to banking giant Citi.

All mapped out

When trainees arrive, all four of their seats have already been selected on the basis of 'the interests you expressed during interview.' It's an approach that 'takes the stress and competition out of seat allocation' and meets with recruits' approval. No seat is compulsory, but as the largest departments by number of fee earners and revenue it would be 'rare to miss out on real estate and corporate.' Real estate trainees sit either in the commercial or the regeneration team, the former handling investment deals, developments and landlord and tenant matters. Here, trainees attend client meetings, draft documents and investigate title, as well as take part in negotiations and managing their own small leasehold files. 'Lots of responsibility' is counteracted by more tedious form filling for the Land Registry and Companies House. 'I do a lot of registration applications for other people,' muttered one source.

The regeneration team developed out of the firm's long involvement in the house-building sector and is now led by a former Pinsent Masons partner. Campbell Hooper has worked on inner-city redevelopments across the Thames Gateway and the South East for Barratt, Bellway, Berkeley, Countryside and Taylor Wimpey. We're talking about places like Greenwich Millennium Village, New Haddo, Tavy Bridge, Gillingham Riverside, Gravesham Basin, Reading Town Centre and Ebbsfleet. Elsewhere in the country there have been developments in Salford and Rugby Town Centre. On these large projects, trainees pick up useful tips when accompanying colleagues to client meetings and site visits, and they learn that lawyers need to be expert problem solvers. Regeneration lawyers have a fair degree of contact with colleagues in the construction department. Although not a huge team it is really well respected, not least by *Chambers UK,* which lists the firm as among the best in the country. The lawyers advise contractors and developers, particularly on residential building projects. On construction disputes, trainees help gather and process evidence; on the non-contentious side they help prepare the collateral warranties used to support major contracts.

Trainees say real estate and construction are busy seats, but the other big revenue generator – corporate – earned mixed reviews. For some 'it can be crazy with so many deals going on,' for others 'rather quiet.' Whatever the pace, the trainee's job is to draft board minutes, undertake due diligence and generally provide background support for deals. One recent highlight was acting for the shareholders of The Copyrights Group, which until recently managed the licensing of characters and brands including Beatrix Potter, Peter Rabbit, Paddington Bear, Raymond Briggs' The Snowman, Jacqueline Wilson, Flower Fairies, Rough Guides and Marie Claire. Another was the creation of FeelGood Media, a merger between independent media agency Target Media and brand communication and designs consultancy OTM (UK).

Console yourself

Some years back Campbell Hooper's media team suffered a mass exodus and is only now resurrecting itself with new partners, new clients and a brand new reputation in the field of computer games and gambling. As of this year, *Chambers UK* ranks Campbell Hooper as one of the best advisers to this industry, and it has an extensive gaming clientele. The firm's historical connection with the theatre also continues and it recently advised on the stage production of *Lord of the Rings.* Trainees in the media seat are additionally involved with trade mark applications, copyright infringement and brand protection. They might find themselves working for a cosmetic company or games developer one day and a betting sponsor or the owner of a website 'designed to help millionaires find

Chambers UK rankings

Charities · Construction · Media & Entertainment · Real Estate

love' another. As the department is still trying to find its feet, at times 'you feel a little thrown in at the deep end.'

Charities law is another of the firm's specialisms and it acts for some small charities, as well as larger well-known national outfits such as Barnardo's, for whose staff it provides a legal help line. The charities team sits within the broader private client department, which also deals with wills, trusts and estates. It also has a family team that has doubled in size over the past two years, a mental capacity team and a residential conveyancing team.

The employment department is headed by a former Campbell Hooper trainee – no small incentive to work hard. It acts for a range of clients from senior CEOs to companies and has a nice line in legal and accountancy firm disputes. Discrimination, victimisation, harassment, age claims and equal pay disputes for international and magic circle law firms or associates are common, and on such matters trainees might compile witness statements, prepare bundles for tribunals or court and attend hearings. They can also have a stab at drafting employment contracts, handbooks and redundancy polices.

Lazarus plays goal attack

Trainee life is undoubtedly 'very dependent on your supervisor, how good they are and their personality,' but the firm does seem to have picked them well. Our interviewees told us theirs had been 'open' and 'never made you feel in the least bit stupid for asking probably obvious things.' Even since an overhaul of the appraisal system following a request by trainees, there is some suggestion of room for a 'little more structure to be put in place.' That said, a monthly 'surgery' with the training principal for each trainee provides a welcome opportunity for a 'completely confidential' discussion and 'a fresh perspective on issues.' For their part, supervisors provide useful mid-seat reviews and are generally happy to accommodate requests for specific types of work.

The vibe at Campbell Hooper is 'friendly but not overly social,' which equates to people making 'a bit of an effort to mix' at quarterly drinks and low-key trips to the nearest pub – The Two Chairmen. Trainees have their own social budget, which lately has been used for ice-skating, a trip to the Comedy Store and meals out. They're also 'positively encouraged' to attend client events, which could be anything from 'a swanky party at the Gherkin to go-karting or pub drinks.' Sports teams are few and far between. 'The netball team has been resurrected and there is talk of setting more up,' otherwise the only option is a team that took part in the The King Sturge Property Triathlon, raising money for Cancer Research and The Children's Trust. Still, the firm's proximity to St James's Park means a lunchtime run or a sandwich-fuelled doze are equally possible.

Most people apply to train at Campbell Hooper because they want the challenge and variety of a London career, without the big-firm drawbacks. Said one trainee: 'You can get some great experience that you might not at a bigger firm.' If you 'like that everyone knows your name and who you are' and 'don't want to feel bottom of the pile,' this could be a perfect choice. Trainees themselves are apparently 'not too competitive and there's certainly no back-biting.' In fact the word 'nice' was used so often by our interviewees that, without a hint of irony, we'll sum this place up as nice people working nice hours of 9am to 6.30pm and handling some rather nice deals and cases. In 2008, three out of four people stayed with the firm and one left to go to a larger City player.

And finally...

Campbell Hooper is an august West End firm stirring itself to meet new goals. It offers a broad training without City excesses, topped off with a rich dose of history.

Capsticks

The facts

Location: London, Birmingham

Number of UK partners/solicitors: 30/54

Total number of trainees: 10

Seats: 6x4 months

Alternative seats: Occasional secondments

Extras: Pro bono – Wandsworth Law Centre

In late 2008 Capsticks moved to the UK's second city when it opened a Birmingham office.

Look at *Chambers UK* and you'll see just how big a player this firm is when it comes to healthcare. The firm is ranked in the top tier in our 'Best of the UK' tables for both defendant clinical negligence and health and social care – no mean feat when you consider the firm is a sprightly 27 years old and operates from a single location in West London.

A healthy prognosis

Capsticks evolved from a small provider of specific clinical negligence advice to its current status as an eminent legal adviser to a vast NHS. As the needs of that organisation and the wider healthcare sector have proliferated, so too have Capsticks' capabilities. Alongside major clinical negligence claims and advisory work, it now handles employment matters, commercial advice on major transactions, LIFT schemes and property issues, as well as general commercial litigation and professional misconduct prosecutions. Client statistics are impressive: as well as acting for almost half of the country's primary care trusts (including all but one in London), the firm advises five out of the nine healthcare regulatory bodies in the UK, including the General Dental Council and the Nursing and Midwifery Council. Among strategic health authorities and other healthcare bodies, an increasing proportion of clients come from the voluntary and private sectors. Charities include the Healthcare Commission and the Terrence Higgins Trust, while private sector providers include Partnerships in Care, Alpha Hospitals and Affinity Healthcare. Whether it's policy advice, help on the impact of EU legislation, next-generation public-private partnership funding, commercial contracts with suppliers or public inquiries on hospital closures, Capsticks will, can and does it.

Clearly already at the top of its game, we wondered how Capsticks will approach the future. 'I don't think we'll be branching out of healthcare, but we're always looking to develop and expand,' commented one source. 'It might look as though we have all our clients' needs covered now, but healthcare is always changing so rapidly. We certainly can't rest on our laurels and expect to stay at the top.' One thing, at least, is clear: Capsticks likes its independence and intends to keep it that way. 'I can't imagine us ever merging and becoming one department of a huge firm.'

Trainees are likely to sample at least four of the firm's five departments in their six-seat traineeship. Clinical negligence, commercial, property, employment and dispute resolution are the options, and a repeated seat is designed to add weight to a push for qualification into a favoured area. Our sources were entirely happy with the seat allocation process – after a randomly selected first seat, it's not hard for them to end up where they want. 'Even if you don't get your seats in the exact order you'd like, you know you'll get them at some point. Most people are pretty open-minded anyway because all the seats are interesting.'

Testing times

The clinical department is split into two distinct sections: the clinical negligence group and the advisory group. 'If one aspect particularly interests you, I'd imagine there is scope to specify which group you'd like to work for. Otherwise, it pretty much depends on what your supervisor is up to.' In the former group, main client the NHS Litigation Authority, as well as primary care trusts, health authorities and private healthcare providers, seek the firm's advice and counsel. A recent case involved allegations that a trust's urologists negligently failed to investigate whether a claimant had a cancerous tumour in his left testicle. The chap alleged that with proper investigation, it would not have been necessary to remove said testicle, which was subsequently found to be non-cancerous. 'Reading the cases and learning about the medical side of things is fascinating,' but as a trainee, 'this seat can't offer as much responsibility as others. You tend to have huge bundles of documents to analyse and scores of medical records to go through.' While most disputes settle, the occasional trial offers 'brilliant exposure, and inquests can be very juicy.'

More general in scope, the dispute resolution team 'seems to move faster than other departments – perhaps it's the court deadlines.' Trainees enjoy the mix of 'hard work and good fun' to be had in a team that's 'always up for a laugh.' Although the practice incorporates 'any contentious issue that falls outside of clin neg, including property, fraud and commercial disputes,' much of the work comprises professional regulatory matters for key clients such as the General Dental Council. 'If a claim comes through against a health professional who is regulated by our client, it's our job to put forward a best-case scenario and to suggest an appropriate penalty.' Described as 'mini trials in a regulatory forum,' these cases enable trainees to play a larger role than in clin neg matters. 'There has been no bundling,' declared one interviewee triumphantly. 'You can have quite a heavy caseload, which is fantastic. I've been drafting advice and gathering evidence, and there is a lot of contact with individuals. I've had a few people cry on me – the issues can be sensitive – but you get used to it.' The department has been advising the Nursing and Midwifery Council on investigations, which can get 'quite gossipy. You're looking into the naughty conduct of nurses and midwives, it's quite outstanding what some people get up to, whether it's stealing money from patients or working while claiming benefits.'

In the property department, assignments can range from 'acting for charities that want to lease out a floor in a building, all the way to main lease agreements for large-scale NHS LIFT projects.' On smaller matters, trainees handle their own files – 'an agreement for the provision of short-term accommodation, that sort of thing.' Bigger files such as the sale of a hospital entail a fair bit of research and Land Registry form-filling, as well as site visits and drafting. 'My supervisor was brilliantly supportive and the whole group takes care to involve you in everything. I was taken along to meetings and given qual-

ity work to do.' The employment team is similarly 'lovely – it's a growing, youngish group and the work is so varied. I was out and about taking witness statements, attending tribunals and really getting stuck into the cases.' In addition to unfair dismissals and breaches of contract, there are always requests for general advice from HR professionals. 'It's everything from maternity leave and holiday issues to use of the internet and Facebook.' The odd bit of advocacy and case management conferences can be 'nerve-racking, but you feel great afterwards.'

Constant restructuring in the NHS keeps the commercial group busy, so hours can be longer here than elsewhere. 'There is a City element to this part of the firm,' said one trainee. 'There's more wining and dining of clients, and it has a work-hard, play-hard feel to it. You certainly get a buzz when you've closed a deal and the champagne is out.' Our sources were pleasantly surprised by the amount of responsibility given to them: 'I was doing quite a bit of drafting on big lease agreements and PFI contracts,' said one. Towards the end of a seat trainees can even handle their own files, perhaps 'specific contract terms to advise on, procurement of services and general tender issues, that kind of thing.' In fact, although it might be easier for non-contentious departments to let trainees get stuck in, across all the seats our interviewees emphasised that 'every group does its best to give you quality work. There's no department where you get stuck photocopying.'

Everything in moderation

With such an emphasis on all things medicinal, it's fitting that staff exhibit a healthy approach to their work. 'I feel right at home here,' said one happy trainee. 'People have a good work-life balance and your colleagues are your friends as well. Although you work hard, it's a real team effort. I have to admit working here is actually kind of fun.' It doesn't take long to notice that many people are passionate about what they do. While some new recruits have had prior experience in the medical profession, 'really what the firm looks for are personable people – we're not hugely loud or terribly serious. Everybody has their own idiosyncrasies, so we're not a bland lot, that's for sure.' The Capsticks vacation scheme is a sure fire way to see if you'd fit in, and a key recruiting method too.

Capsticks is sociable 'but without that City mentality of everyone drinking themselves stupid.' Instead people enjoy their lunches out, trainees and paralegals often go for a few drinks at the end of the week, and there are a number of organised events. 'At least once a month we'll go to a quiz or a comedy night, and we've been to a wine tasting and a rugby game recently.' The 'mysterious and exclusive' social committee ('you have to be asked to join') sweats over Christmas party plans for weeks, and the event inevitably includes 'a huge venue, a black-tie dress code and gorgeous food. There's always a horrible rumour each year that the trainees will have to do a skit, but it hasn't come to anything… yet.'

Brew ha-ha

West London-based Capsticks currently inhabits a building in Putney that 'ironically looks a bit like a hospital.' Putney is an 'admittedly unusual' location, but one which suits the firm. Most staff choose to live nearby, meaning that walking or cycling to work is an option. 'We don't head into central London for drinks very often, which is a shame, but then you do get to avoid nightmare commuting on the Tube.' Although the office is nearing full capacity, trainees assure us the firm wouldn't move too far, saying: 'Our location is part of our identity now.' Trainees share an office with a supervisor, which they feel is 'a really good way for you to learn as there's always someone right there who can answer your questions.' Opposite the office, a much-frequented greasy spoon café provides sustenance. Sadly, back in the office the 'amazing tea ladies' have been replaced by vending machines. The ladies sometimes used to bring round slices of birthday cake with the afternoon brew, something the machines are unlikely to ever master.

When it comes to qualifying, recent trainees have done well. In 2008 'people have gone for different departments, and so this year all four of us are staying on.' The firm tries hard to retain qualifiers, but even when the job offers and requests don't match all is not lost. 'You don't have to be scared that you're specialising too early. Yes the clients are all in the healthcare sector, but with things like property, commercial and employment, the law is transferable regardless of the industry.'

And finally...

Capsticks certainly isn't your average firm. It offers a vastly different experience from the City, so anyone wanting ridiculously long hours and inflated salaries should look elsewhere. If you want a single industry firm then tailor your application here carefully and get on the vac scheme.

Charles Russell

The facts

Location: London, Guildford, Cheltenham, Oxford, Cambridge

Number of UK partners/solicitors: 103/204

Total number of trainees: 40

Seats: 4x6 months

Alternative Seats: Bahrain, secondments

Extras: Pro bono – LawWorks, Bethnal Green Legal Advice Centre, Surrey Law Centre

---

If you're wondering whether you're Charles Russell's type, you need to know about the famously quirky questions on the application form. Past applicants have been asked what film star or animal they would be.

Centuries-old Charles Russell is determined to show that you can succeed in balancing private client and commercial practice.

The Russell brand

This firm has been a bastion of private client and family law practice forever. It's also a smart cookie on the commercial side, offering a full service to many mid-market companies, some huge ones and a smattering of media and telecoms organisations. The evolution of the firm's commercial clientele now means it accounts for around 70% of business and 'this percentage may be skewed a bit further in years to come.' The corporate and litigation departments each bring in about a quarter of the annual revenue; the former has an excellent reputation for AIM transactions and is ranked highly by *Chambers UK*. Last year's glittering successes included advice to Yamana Gold, Aricom and GEM Diamonds (Canadian, Anglo-Russian and African mining operations, respectively) on their moves from AIM to the FTSE list. Among the firm's other clients are Zurich Group, Kookaburra Sports, Sotheby's, The RAF Benevolent Fund and the government of the Falkland Islands. For the most part trainees like the balance that has been struck between the commercial and the private, and many are attracted to the firm precisely because they can sample two distinct styles of practice. They say Charles Russell is 'not a jack-of-all-trades, master of none, but a master of all.'

The firm has five UK offices and two overseas. The oldest are London, Cheltenham and Guildford (all of which take trainees); Oxford and Cambridge are recent additions and the latter has just taken its first trainee. A Geneva office has become a good source of wealthy private clients, which is perhaps why the firm has also decided to set up shop in Bahrain. The London, Cheltenham and Guildford offices are full-service operations, Oxford focuses on corporate finance and IP, while Cambridge was given a kick-start by the arrival of the employment team from East of England firm Hewitsons.

Most trainees are London-based, while there are a few in Guildford and usually just a couple in Cheltenham. London trainees can work in almost any of the disciplines practised at the firm (the main ones are private client, family, employment, litigation, coco and property, and then there are specialist seats in corporate tax and media). In Guildford trainees can choose between the same main seats, plus niche options in property litigation and insolvency. The choice is narrower in Cheltenham, where it's basically private client, property, coco and litigation. 'Playing an increasing part in the training contract' are secondments to clients such as Arcadia, and there's now an opportunity to spend a seat in Bahrain.

easyDeals

Comfortably entrenched in the mid-market, in 2007 the corporate team in London completed 82 deals, together worth £3bn. Lawyers in Cheltenham – the other office for meaty corporate work – handled transactions worth another £1bn. It's only to be expected that trainees have limited involvement in really big deals; they'll commonly prepare board minutes, sift through documents and have a stab at drafting ancillary agreements. Thankfully 'it never feels static or like you're just going through the motions.' The team (including a partner who is 'a real weirdo but the clients love him') is 'awesome' and makes an effort to 'offer you experience in everything.' Sometimes after a hard day's work the final task is to drag team-mates to the pub; mostly people just like to get home at a decent time. Though not a place for extreme workaholics, 'when the work is here you will be too.'

Contentious seats are highly prized by trainees. Property litigation is 'an intense experience, especially in Guildford,' as the steep learning curve requires trainees to manage files with relatively little supervision. The commercial dispute resolution (CDR) team also likes to put them through their paces. Shareholder disputes are its bread and butter, with contract claims, insolvency and IP also cropping up. The 'catch-all' litigation and dispute resolution group (LDR) covers clinical negligence, contentious probate, insurance, international arbitration and a few other areas. Trainees get plenty of court experience, and one gleefully told us of a time they had 'personally summonsed a witness and took her statement.' Defamation cases are glamorous, though admittedly these are few and far between. Keep your eyes peeled for any particularly malicious football gossip: Charles Russell has been retained to advise Fabio Capello. Other libel-magnets arc the Conservative Party, the Catholic Church of England & Wales and Chris Tarrant. Overall, the litigation client roster includes some impressive household names – Virgin Media, Fiat and Pfizer to name just three.

'The real hot-to-trot department' is employment, which brings in over 10% of the firm's income through relationships with the likes of easyJet, Kangol and Westminster Abbey. In this consistently oversubscribed seat 'no two days are the same.' Trainees draft contracts and termination agreements, man the telephone helpline used by clients' HR departments, draft witness statements and attend tribunals. 'There was so much work,' gasped one interviewee; 'you don't leave at 5.30pm, that's for sure.'

Who wants to be a billionaire?

Still 'one of the biggest departments,' the private client group looks after mega-rich folk. According to Forbes these individuals are believed to have a combined net worth of $40bn. They fall into two groups: 'The landed gentry – people with titles and tracts of land and lots of art' – and international clients, often from the Middle East and Russia, frequently drawn in by the Geneva and Bahrain offices. Wealthy foreign nationals may need help with the legal and tax regimes of several jurisdictions; domestic clients, meanwhile, may have heritage property to manage or sell. Last year lawyers arranged the sale of a collection of paintings, including works by Degas and Delacroix, and negotiated on the loan of Jane Austen's family library to a specialist study centre. Trainees get involved with smaller pieces of tax advice and trusts administration, often running their own files. With at least two or three meetings a week there is 'more client contact in this seat than any other.'

Chambers UK rankings

Agriculture & Rural Affairs • Banking & Finance • Charities • Clinical Negligence • Construction • Corporate Finance • Data Protection • Defamation/Reputation Management • Dispute Resolution • Education • Employment • Family/Matrimonial • Insurance • Intellectual Property • Media & Entertainment • Outsourcing • Personal Injury • Planning • Private Client • Professional Discipline • Professional Negligence • Projects, Energy & Natural Resources • Public Procurement • Real Estate • Real Estate Litigation • Restructuring/Insolvency • Sports Law • Tax • Telecommunications

The family team is one of the best in the UK for matrimonial finance and it handles expensive, sometimes international divorces. From time to time cases make the papers and the law reports, which trainees reckon is 'quite exciting in a geeky way.' Divorce lawyers get a bad rap, but one recruit was happy to defend the team's honour: 'People can't believe it when you say you want to do divorce law. They think it makes you an evil person, but essentially you are just trying to help someone, even if no one sees it like that!' Unfortunately we can't name clients here, so you'll have to take our word for it that the quality of the cases is very good.

No of-fence intended

A few trainees admitted they didn't always feel integrated with their colleagues in other offices. It's uncommon to do a seat elsewhere; in fact one person indicated that certain Guildford partners 'possibly see it as a slur if you want to go to London.' This issue only concerns London and Guildford; Cheltenham recruits just carry on with their traineeships 'not feeling cut off at all.' The problem could be one of 'snobbery,' ventured one partisan: 'A lot of people in London don't even know where Guildford is.'

There is no barrier to qualifying away from your original office and Charles Russell's 'one firm' policy aims to ensure 'there are no fences up between the offices.' Marketing and know-how meetings are shared via telephone or videoconference facilities, and 'there's fluid movement of ideas, help and support.' The regional offices undoubtedly benefit from the presence of the large London HQ, as it helps convince people that the firm 'has the clout to attract great clients.' Vodafone, Hugo Boss, Nationwide and Credit Suisse all use the firm outside

London, and the construction department is based in Guildford not the capital. Rather than providing a lesser experience, a regional traineeship offers 'the best of both worlds' to those who prefer a country life. Trains between Cheltenham and London take just over two hours. Guildford is far closer to the capital and a few Guildford trainees even choose to live in South London. If you're thinking of one of the two smaller trainee bases, a regional connection will be a bonus as 'it helps to have an idea of how Surrey or Gloucestershire works.'

As the end of the traineeship approaches, a formal interview process gives a genuine sense that 'everyone is judged on their merits.' Said one source: 'I've got friends at other firms who were approached over a quiet drink or while standing at the water cooler – not here.' There were more jobs than applicants in 2008. Unfortunately departments like employment and CDR had around two applications for every position, so some people were disappointed. In the end 12 of the 16 qualifiers stayed on, one each in Guildford and Cheltenham and ten in London.

Stars in their eyes

If you're wondering whether you're Charles Russell's type, you need to know about the 'famously quirky' questions on the application form. Past applicants have been asked what film star or animal they would be. 'People are terrified they have to write something fantastic, but there is no right or wrong answer – that's the point.' It might amuse you to know this book was compiled by Meg Ryan, Natalie Portman, David Niven, Humphrey Bogart, a meerkat and a couple of horses. It's easy to spot trainees' shared characteristics. Everyone is determined not to become part of a large 'faceless' organisation, and 'there are no real introverts.' With private client and family being 'quite human subjects,' recruits commonly tend to be 'a bit more caring,' lacking the overly competitive edge needed in some of the bigger firms. It goes without saying that everyone wants to avoid seriously long City hours.

Sport is a big thing here, and no great skill is needed. As well as male and mixed football teams there's netball, cricket, tennis and the occasional dragon boat race. January's sports ball (black tie, posh frocks) is 'the biggest social event of the year' and open to even those whose achievements go no further than *Championship Manager*. Trophies are awarded and the managing partner reads a speech that 'takes the piss out of everybody.' Staff from around the firm enjoy major parties in the summer and at Christmas, though we hear they are 'tame by comparison' with the January bash. On any given Friday night London lawyers are to be found in nearby Bertolucci's, while Guildford trainees enjoy regular drinks evenings and departmental away days. The Cheltenham recruits have several entertainment options within striking distance of their beautiful Regency style office and they also enjoy the town's numerous festivals and beautiful Cotswold scenery.

Charitable and pro bono initiatives are encouraged and staff can take two days paid leave for CSR activities. In the past year trainees redecorated a care home, were given a day off to repaint a charity shop, baked and sold cakes, organised raffles and cycled between Oxford and Cambridge to raise money for the Make-A-Wish Foundation, the firm's chosen charity.

And finally...

It's all very well being 'an old aristocratic law firm' if you're dealing with wealthy scions of ancient families, but with corporate clients you have to offer something different. Charles Russell manages to do this rather capably.

Clarion Solicitors LLP

The facts

Location: Leeds

Number of UK partners/solicitors: 14/32

Total number of trainees: 10

Seats: 4x6 months

Alternative seats: Secondments

Extras: Pro bono – Harehills & Chapeltown Law Centre

> The thorough rebrand has rejuvenated our image and the atmosphere here is more upbeat and excitable.

Clarion may be a new name on the Leeds legal block but its face is a familiar one. Before its trip to the deed poll office, it was known as McCormicks and headed by eminent lawyer Peter McCormick.

Born again

The old firm had a kid-brother of an office in Harrogate and a glitzy sports and media practice. In February 2007, when six of the firm's partners decided to buy the Leeds operation lock, stock and nearly the whole barrel, Peter McCormick and two other partners moved into the Harrogate office, leaving the newly renamed Clarion Solicitors to forge its own future. There were no dramatic changes at Clarion following the buyout. 'It's still relaxed and professional,' said one source; 'I think what has evolved is the market's perception of us.' The thorough rebrand has 'rejuvenated our image, and the atmosphere here is a little more upbeat and excitable.' Everyone we spoke to agreed that the change was a good one to make and was optimistic about the years ahead. 'There are definitely plans to grow the firm. I'd say litigation, corporate and property are the core areas…' So that's growth across the board then.

In addition to the three main practice groups, the firm has teams working on corporate recovery, business crime/regulatory and private client/family law. All these areas can be explored. Seats almost always last six months, but can be shorter if there is excess demand for a particular department. New recruits don't tend to have much of a say about where they first sit ('I think I was told where I was going a week before I started') but once they become established it's up to them to make their preferences known. 'Don't sit on the fence, get in early and say what you want,' recommended one old hand with a good grasp of Clarion etiquette.

Moody blues

Although corporate is an important and growing practice, we hear it's also been the least popular of late. 'Nobody has wanted to do corporate this year or last year,' admitted one trainee. 'It's all been about family and litigation.' Nevertheless with the corporate and commercial department absorbing up to four trainees at each rotation, it's fairly likely you'll end up here. 'It's a busy department and a good learning experience,' a source summed it up. Recent instructions have included advising HSBC as finance provider on the management buyout of Onyx Scientific, and clients include Just Trays, which we're told is the UK's leading shower tray manufacturer; Winners Amusements; private equity fund Viking; and nightclub operator Nexum Leisure, which owns the Escapade and Zanzibar venues. When it's quiet, 5.30pm finishes aren't out of the ordinary; during busy periods chucking out time might be closer to midnight. Trainees are occupied with due diligence for the sale and purchase of businesses and shares, and on the banking side they learn how to draft facility agreements and loan documents. The main complaint is a common one for this area of law: 'I would have liked more responsibility. It's difficult to envisage being an NQ in that department because I didn't feel I got a complete handle on the work.' One thing is undeniable, the experience 'teaches you how to organise yourself and manage your time.' At present the coco department is somewhat segregated from the rest on the other side of the office building. Its open-plan layout came in for criticism: 'It's quite loud and can be difficult to concentrate. And as you're sitting in a corridor as a trainee, if certain fee earners are in a mood you can bear the brunt of it.'

The allied commercial team handles non-contentious IP issues and drafts terms and conditions for businesses. 'I received great training in that department,' reported one trainee. 'I would be given whole agreements to draft and then a partner would sit with me for a couple of hours and go through it.'

See you on the other side

The other part of the building 'gets locked up at about 7.30-8pm,' which gives some indication of the hours involved. A stint in the business regulatory unit introduces trainees to white-collar fraud and general criminal cases. As a member of the Legal Services Commission's Complex Crime Panel, the team covers an enviable range of cases and recently had a client in a four-month trial involving alleged conspiracy to defraud with terrorist links. The lawyers also represented a care home owner who was prosecuted for alleged sustained breaches of Health and Safety over a six-year period. Other cases have related to murder, rape, serious sexual offences, death by dangerous driving, possession with intent to supply and robbery. 'To be honest, I didn't know we did so much general criminal work,' a trainee confided. 'There's so much client contact and responsibility, pretty much from day one.' Trainees also tout the seat as a good confidence builder: 'You go to police stations to interview clients on your own, and you're in either the magistrates' or Crown Court most days sitting behind counsel and taking notes.' There is plenty of support from the team, and those of you who are wary of prison visits can rest assured that 'it's obviously very secure.' If you're up for it, there's ample opportunity to try some advocacy on bail applications and pre-trial reviews.

The family team tackles divorce and childcare issues. Trainees get 'a fair bit of independence. You write letters and phone clients, and the hours are very regular. The latest I've ever stayed is 7pm.' Expect your own files in private client, property and insolvency seats, the former involving simple will drafting and probate. Property seats see trainees preparing reports on title and lease reports, and drafting simple agreements and licences. A stint in insolvency will be spent working for all six fee earners in the department. 'There were lots of court applications and dealings with the Land Registry, primarily acting for trustees, administrators or liquidators. The responsibility increases as you go on and towards the end I did a few of my own bankruptcy hearings. They were fairly straightforward matters but it still felt like an achievement.' Commercial litigation trainees also work for several lawyers, which allows exposure to 'contract disputes, professional negligence, property issues and banking litigation, as well as a little bit of defamation and IP.' The latter

Chambers UK rankings

Charities • Corporate Finance • Crime • Dispute Resolution • Employment • Family/Matrimonial • Fraud: Criminal • Intellectual Property • Restructuring/Insolvency

area in particular sees some well-known clients coming through its doors, including the FA Premier League and Liverpool and Arsenal football clubs.

Bowling for Clarion

Attracting impressive work and clients requires considerable and consistent effort in the form of promotion. As one source explained: 'Marketing is very important at the moment, so we're all required to pitch in and help get the firm's name out there – possibly more than I had expected.' Generally this isn't viewed as a chore. 'As trainees we probably do a lot more than at other firms, but it's good. You're out speaking to clients, making those contacts.' When client events involve activities such as bowling, people tend to have fun. Inevitably this aspect of the job suits some people more than others, so it's little surprise to find that 'the firm likes outspoken people. I'm not saying we're a stroppy bunch, but we'll say what we think.' Some life experience helps as well. 'Although some people have come straight through the system, most have had a year out or a job elsewhere.'

Paralegalling at the firm won't guarantee a training contract, but neither will it hurt your chances. 'In my intake there were two paralegals, and in the year below I think there might be three,' said a second-year. 'It's a great way to get yourself noticed.' In past years we've commented on the presence of many more female than male trainees, so we're happy to report that the latest intake comprised two boys and three girls. 'From the outside looking in it's a good thing that the situation has been redressed, particularly as there's only one female partner at the top. Then again, at law school the girls were always much better than the boys.' No comment from us! Finally it seems that links to the area are becoming less of a factor in the recruitment process and we learned this year that 'quite a few of the first-years aren't tied to the region at all.'

So many vibrant personalities have produced a hectic social life at Clarion. Trainees go out for lunch and drinks, and then there are the departmental and external events with clients. 'The firm is great for that sort of thing,' chirped one trainee. 'On the last Friday of the month there are free drinks for all in a bar in town. They must spend an awful lot of money on us.' Nights out are not limited to trainees. 'The partners are more outgoing and friendly than you might expect and we have a lot of contact with them from both a professional and social point of view.' The firm gives staff gym membership discounts, organises fitness sessions, charity runs and football and cricket games. Last year, we even discovered a penchant for mid-week dodgeball in a local gym. This year's interviewees, however, were a grave disappointment: 'I'm not sporty at all,' admitted one. 'I think dodgeball still happens,' ventured another, 'but I'm not actually a member of any of those exercise groups.' The Christmas party does at least live on. 'Last year there was a 50s glamour theme, and there was all kinds of nonsense going on, partners strutting their stuff on the dance floor, etc.' Much better. A social committee organises yet further events such as pub quizzes and a Halloween party, and there's a networking group called ClarioNet, which runs events for younger clients and contacts.

More to come

Last year's proposal to introduce a mentoring programme has not yet come to fruition. 'There was talk of that but with a firm of our size there were issues over how confidentiality would be maintained.' It's fortunate then that 'there's always someone you can go talk to informally.' A new performance management and development programme for all staff is up and running and the process of assigning qualification jobs has been given a makeover. 'There used to be a formal application form, now it's more about approaching the head of a department and seeing if there's a job for you.' The firm tells us it is keen to maintain dialogue with trainees regarding qualification from early on in their training. Disappointingly, in 2008 just two of the five qualifiers stayed on. The firm normally retains most people.

And finally...

Trainees point to the people, the variety of work and the social aspects of the firm as its best strengths. 'You get exposure to clients and good work, but there's also a sense of unity and sticking together.'

Cleary Gottlieb Steen & Hamilton LLP

The facts

Location: London

Number of UK partners/solicitors: 16/48 + 27 US

Total number of trainees: 14

Seats: 4x6 months

Alternative seats: Overseas seats

Extras: Pro bono – LawWorks, Liberty; language training

Some American firms set foot in Europe with the alacrity of a cat facing a bath – reluctantly and as a grim inevitability. Cleary Gottleib showed no hesitation.

Truly transatlantic Cleary Gottlieb has big plans for London. Great news for any top-grade applicant who's hungry for capital markets, finance and M&A experience and ready for seriously hard graft.

European unions

Some American firms set foot in Europe with the alacrity of a cat facing a bath – reluctantly and as a grim inevitability. Cleary Gottleib showed no hesitation, perhaps because practically from the day of its founding in New York in 1946 its vision was to open itself up to business from around the world. Europe was in its sights as early as 1949, when it opened a Paris office and took the significant step of training up local counsel to become equal partners. Founding partner George Ball worked closely with Jean Monnet (later a prime mover in the creation of the European Community) on the implementation of the USA's post-war Marshall Plan aid package. Being well versed on Europe's legal and economic structures has allowed Cleary to take advantage of developing trends. For example, opening an office in Brussels in 1960 gave it an edge in regulatory and competition law that it still enjoys today. Since then many more offices have sprung up, including London (1971), Hong Kong, Rome, Frankfurt and Moscow. The latest office to open – Beijing – took the tally to 12 branches, only two of which are in the USA.

London's story is one of four core practice groups: M&A, private equity, finance and capital markets. Each of these practice groups intersect with their counterparts in other locations, so 'you feel like an international lawyer,' trainees said. The idea is a simple one: 'The firm sees its international capacity as a major competitive advantage, so tends to bid for and get that work.' Consequently, in London there are 'few UK-specific deals,' and when they're not jetting off to 'Russia, India, Kenya or Stockholm,' even the humblest trainee is likely to be 'dealing with Dutch, Belgian, German, US, Cayman, Swedish and Danish counsel all on one transaction.'

In the brave, borderless noughties, every firm with an ounce of ambition claims to have global capacity and it can be difficult to distinguish truth from hype. Even a brief assay of Cleary London's workload reveals this is 24-carat international office. In capital markets it acted for Nova Kreditna Banka Maribor and the Republic of Slovenia on the €260m offering of NKBM shares – the first ever Slovenian IPO. Cleary was English, Russian and US counsel, both to JSC Uralkali in its $1.07bn Reg S/Rule 144A IPO and to Sberbank in its $8.85bn Reg S offering of shares, the first public equity offering by a Russian bank. Proving it is also adept in the UK, Cleary represented the sponsor Deutsche Bank and joint bookrunners, Credit Suisse Securities, Morgan Stanley Securities and ABN AMRO Rothschild on a $2.7bn IPO for Eurasian Natural Resources Corporation. Meanwhile banking lawyers represented long-time client Citi on the financing for Terra Firma Capital Partners' £3.2bn cash buyout of EMI Group, helped a consortium of Spanish and international private equity firms in a take-private bid for Iberia Airlines and another consortium on an $8.75bn offer for Australian airline Qantas. Not be outdone, private equity lawyers joined forces with four other Cleary offices to advise Euronext on the substantial reduction of its stake in LCH Clearnet, and represented the same company on its $11.3bn merger-of-equals with the NYSE Group, creating the first transatlantic securities exchange company. They also acted as counsel to J.C. Flowers in the proposed €3bn sale of NIBC to Kaupthing Bank and showed credit crunch beating clout in assisting Helios Investment Partners with its acquisition of a 24.99% stake in Kenya's Equity Bank for $165m. It's okay if you don't understand what all this means, though hopefully the numbers and complexity of the deals will excite you.

Chambers UK rankings

Banking & Finance • Capital Markets • Competition/European Law • Corporate Finance • Private Equity • Tax

No limits

Beyond these core areas, London Cleary advises on tax, competition law, IP and IT issues. No practice is off limits to trainees, and that's partly because of the firm's non-departmental approach to practice. This approach is seen in all offices and allows lawyers to handle a variety of work within the main practice groupings. In Cleary's words, it allows them to develop as 'multi specialists.'

Trainees rotate through four six-month seats, technically under the supervision of partners with specialist knowledge of different types of deals and cases. The reality is that there's 'total flexibility within seats in terms of the work you do.' By way of illustration, one of our sources (in a nominally corporate seat) was handling 'a 40-40 split of private equity/corporate and capital markets work, with the other 20% in competition and finance litigation.' Recognising that 'some will prefer a more rigid approach,' trainees suggest applicants 'make sure the system is for them' and emphasise its inherent demands. 'You've got to think on your feet and be confident,' they told us. 'You can't lie low and let your training go past' because 'you will get work that is interesting and pushes you to the limit.' Unsurprisingly, there are times 'it can be overwhelming,' not least when 'you think, 'I'm just a trainee,' and there's no one to turn to except the partner who is very busy.' However, 'self-confident, self-starters' soon 'learn incredibly quickly' and come to value the 'flexibility to run matters yourself.'

Cleary definitely offers a degree of responsibility far above that experienced by the average London trainee. We're not sure there are many other firms where a trainee would be able (or even allowed) to bill more in a month than the partners, as sources confirmed had actually once happened. That's a highly unusual incident of course; more usually the trainee will tuck themselves into a deal team and get stuck in. This might mean 'working with just a senior associate on a transaction and managing the disclosure letter,' taking '20 hours of meetings with just me and the clients' or 'being the lead point on negotiating with the other side.' As a first-seater working on capital markets deals, one source had 'single-handedly drafted the listing particulars for securities in an IPO.' It's common that 'as a deal goes on, you get more responsibility. I started one in

finance with an associate and partner, now I'm running it practically myself.' In short, the only limits are the ones set by the trainees themselves, and striking out for greater responsibility or variety brings quick rewards for those who prove themselves capable. One interviewee told us their request for employment law experience, made 'a few days ago,' had quickly led to them being asked to draft employment contracts for a CEO.

Great expectations

'This isn't the most structured of training contracts' and it has its ups and downs. Experience of competition, tax or employment law will fulfil SRA requirements for contentious experience, but disputes might pop up from unexpected quarters. 'I've had a lot of contentious experience in finance,' volunteered one trainee, emphasising the sometimes unpredictable nature of the non-compartmentalised approach. Assuming you like the idea of freestyling your way through seats, consider whether you'd cope with light-touch supervision. While there is a formal system to monitor trainees' workloads, some we spoke to were 'not wholly certain it changes how much work you get.' It's not unusual for 'people to underestimate how much time it takes trainees to do things' and 'it can be difficult to say no, or to know when it's okay to stop and go home.'

Such comments were observations rather than complaints. Cleary trainees expect to work hard and recognise that at a firm where everybody is 'close to flat out' there isn't always the time for detailed feedback, even if there is a 'general recognition' of the importance of helping trainees develop. No one we interviewed had ever been turned down when asking for help, but they'd grown adept at 'knowing when to ask.'

Cleary is a lifestyle choice. The heavy workload comes with the all the trimmings – massive salary, laptop, BlackBerry, corporate Amex card and mighty leather chair. These perks exist to smooth the edges, not as unearned treats. Working until 8pm or 9pm is fairly normal, and the trainee who spoke of being 'slaughtered with working until midnight most days' took consolation in 'doing a few hours at weekends, not the full weekends some friends are doing.' Another laughed: 'I could wish more people thought it an imposition to work on Saturday and Sunday, rather than taking it as read.' The international nature of deals is a major contributory factor 'because you're trying to sync with the USA or other jurisdictions in different time zones.' That same factor allows trainees to enjoy foreign travel, be it for one of 'three European practice seminars a year,' short hops overseas or a longer stint, say in the arbitration team in Paris or for a seat in Brussels, New York, Hong Kong or Moscow.

Gold star diggers

Having decided to grow its London office, Cleary is in the process of increasing its trainee population and setting up arrangements with the College of Law for all its GDL and LPC teaching. Competition for a place at Cleary has always been phenomenally fierce and trainees don't imagine that a need for more recruits will ease the firm's thirst for the very best candidates. 'Everyone is extremely intelligent and a bit older than the average trainee,' we heard, but beyond that putting a finger on common characteristics proves difficult. We'd say Cleary trainees tend to be super-high achievers – perhaps they've a Masters degree from an American University, probably they hold the very best UK academic credentials, definitely they are incredibly determined and certainly they 'arrived via a conscious decision.' The recruiters are undoubtedly looking for 'a fit for the office,' in other words those who display an 'unusual work ethic,' who are 'able to take the initiative' and 'do the digging for themselves without being told.' The best advice trainees could give was to 'come on

the vac scheme – the firm likes to recruit from it because they get a better idea of whether someone makes the grade.' This point cannot be overemphasised – in the last round of recruiting, only one successful candidate had not been on the vac scheme.

In recent years the vast majority of qualifiers have stayed with the firm and in 2008 all five accepted jobs (and the very handsome £92,000 salary). Time will tell if long-term matches are equally possible with larger trainee intakes. Some qualified solicitors choose to work overseas for a while, and one option involves qualifying at the New York Bar once they've some experience under their belt.

Is Cleary is all work and no play? Not really. Trainees meet for lunch in the 'heavily subsidised' staff canteen, often sitting with partners and associates. If they fancy a drink 'there's always someone from the firm in the Corney & Barrow most nights.' A recent pub quiz for lawyers, support staff and vac schemers was won by a table including the librarian, secretaries and HR people. The fact that there weren't too many questions on capital markets deals would explain the result. Post-deal drinks aren't quite so common: the in-joke is that 'if you're the only person working on a deal it makes for quite a poor party.'

And finally...

To train at Cleary Gottlieb you need to be better than the best, not just the rest.

Clifford Chance LLP

The facts

Location: London

Number of UK partners/solicitors: 228/540

Total number of trainees: 260

Seats: 4x6 months

Alternative seats: Overseas seats, secondments

Extras: Pro bono – various law centres; death row appeals; language training

> You have to commit to such an extraordinary level, it's like being an Olympic athlete.

As the world's biggest and most profitable, Clifford Chance is the law firm that most people outside the legal profession have heard of. Say trainees: 'It likes to be the biggest and the best and the first to do everything.'

The sun never sets...

After exponential growth around the turn of the century through a merger with New York firm Rogers & Wells, CC has become the big boy of the magic circle. Abu Dhabi is the latest addition to its international roster of 29 offices in 21 countries – there's now a CC in practically every time zone. Having established its global network, the firm 'now needs to build up its practices in those offices.' To that end, in 2008 it made the majority of its partner promotions overseas and bulked up its Indian practice group with the hire of an Indian-qualified partner into its Singapore office.

CC's dominion over the finance world is well known. The banking department's turnover recently leapt ahead of its nearest rivals, increasing the firm's lead from a £2m margin last year to a reported £34.5m margin this year. The biggest law firm naturally attracts the biggest banks, and it would be quicker for us to list those it doesn't act for. In the world of leveraged acquisition finance CC recently advised UBS in relation to the acquisition of The Jimmy Choo Group, acted for CVC and Permira on the financing of the merger between Saga and The AA, and assisted the mandated lead arrangers (including JPMorgan, HSBC and RBS) on the investment consortium acquisition of Southern Water. Meanwhile, in Islamic finance, CC advised Investment Dar on its £479m acquisition of Aston Martin. CC's corporate lawyers also work on massive deals and are particularly adept at cross-border matters. Lately they advised Reuters on its £8.7bn takeover by Thomson and acted for Barclays on its £67.5bn-rated, unsuccessful attempt to merge with ABN AMRO.

In the lap of the gods

On paper, CC is a multifaceted firm, but there's no denying that banking and finance, capital markets and corporate dominate proceedings. Some trainees are undoubtedly 'banking people through and through.' These recruits enjoy their stint in 'the engine room of the firm,' relishing the sense of belonging to 'a department at the peak of its powers.' In a banking seat, 'all trainees end up doing transaction management and conditions precedent.' It's not all 'mundane tasks,' however; they also learn how to draft ancillary documents like board minutes, side letters to facility agreements and directors' certificates. While finance has a reputation as 'a lively, boisterous, ambitious department,' capital markets is slightly less beloved. For the uninitiated, capital markets involves a hotchpotch of interrelated finance work, including debt, equity, securitisation and derivatives: CC's team has a reputation for being rather hardcore. Apparently 'some people won't apply for a securitisation seat because they're afraid it will give them wrinkles.' One unblemished fan countered that 'the nature of the work is really exciting,' although also admitted to working '80 to 100 hours a week.'

Although corporate deserves its reputation for occasionally 'hideous' hours, it is generally seen as a good first seat, as relatively low levels of responsibility allow newbies to 'get used to the systems and the way the business works, rather than being baffled with mind-boggling work.' A hefty chunk of due diligence is normal, which can be 'incredibly boring,' but at least trainees aren't 'shafted' by grunt work. While the main corporate department 'can come across as being quite macho,' the regulatory issues-focused financial institutions team is 'very family-oriented' and 'a majority of the partners are women.' Communications, technology and media is also a corporate seat and it's a popular spot. Here trainees encounter 'lots of due diligence,' albeit 'more interesting media due diligence, which is all to do with TV programmes you've heard of.'

As well as being the biggest transactional law firm in the world, CC is rather handy at litigation and top-ranked by *Chambers UK* for high-value disputes and international arbitration. This department deals with everything from insurance matters to defamation to regulatory investigation; it continues to advise Multiplex on claims relating to Wembley Stadium and claimants in their attempts to overturn the Hunting Act 2004. The team has also been representing the Conservative Party in the 'cash for honours' investigation and an investment bank in relation to the collapse of Parmalat. The massive size of the disputes CC handles means cases can take years from start to finish. As such, trainees 'get the best and the worst work – from analysing complex problems and drafting advisory notes to sticking numbers at the bottom of pages.' Exceptionally lucky trainees may get involved in public law issues; the firm advises clients like Save the Children, Amnesty International and the Chagos islanders over their claim to return to their homeland.

Although most trainees sit in general litigation, seats are also available in insurance litigation, insolvency litigation, IP litigation and public policy litigation, as well as one 'very competitive' seat in international commercial arbitration. Trainees can choose from a standard six months in litigation, a litigation course, or a split seat with three months spent on secondment at Liberty or Law4All, where they encounter housing, benefits and employment queries. The litigation department has a 'more formal,' 'hierarchical' vibe, complete with ties for men. Trainees' opinions on their supervisors here were mixed. One painted a rather colourful picture in which 'the trainees are scum, the partners are gods and the associates run round trying to appease them.' Others appreciated 'constructive criticism' and supervisors who helped them to see 'the bigger picture.' Clearly the good points must outweigh the bad, as litigation is consistently oversubscribed for NQ jobs.

Chambers UK rankings

Administrative & Public Law • Asset Finance • Banking & Finance • Banking Litigation • Capital Markets • Climate Change • Commodities • Competition/European Law • Construction • Corporate Finance • Data Protection • Defamation/Reputation Management • Dispute Resolution • Employee Share Schemes • Employment • Environment • Financial Services Regulation • Fraud: Civil/Criminal • Immigration • Information Technology • Insurance • Intellectual Property • Investment Funds • Media & Entertainment • Outsourcing • Parliamentary & Public Affairs • Pensions • Planning • Private Client • Private Equity • Product Liability • Professional Negligence • Projects, Energy & Natural Resources • Public International Law • Real Estate • Real Estate Finance • Real Estate Litigation • Restructuring/Insolvency • Retail • Social Housing • Tax • Telecommunications • Transport

Popularity contest

Beyond the main money-spinning departments, trainees can go to real estate (including general real estate, real estate litigation, environment and planning, real estate funds and real estate finance) or the tax, pensions and employment group. Then there are 'cross-area seats', which include construction and IP, and a raft of client secondments. All seat options are described in a helpful trainee-produced guide for new starters.

The chance to experience an overseas seat is a major draw. New York, Hong Kong, Tokyo and Singapore are the most popular kids in the secondment playground. Moscow, Dubai and Frankfurt tend to be last picked. The capital markets seat in New York is 'known for being really intense,' although market conditions have rendered it quieter of late. The office 'has a more dog-eat-dog atmosphere.' NYC secondees lunch with associates at the MOMA restaurant and the 'banker-heavy' China Grill, no doubt on company plastic. CC is 'really working to build up its reputation in New York,' but in late 2007 the structured finance team laid off six NY associates, which possibly explains why at the time of writing there was just one seat in NY. Trainees share flats in Singapore, New York and Dubai, which is a 'sore point' among the ranks. The Singapore accommodation 'leaves a bit of a bad taste in the mouth' when 'after working so hard you get home and the A/C is broken.' Then again why would Singapore secondees want to stay at home when they can take full advantage of the chance to 'travel to just about anywhere in South-East Asia for the weekend.' In the city itself, outdoorsy activities like 'wakeboarding and mountain biking' abound and a 'lavish brunch' in one of its many fine restaurants is the perfect post-workout relaxation. A full list of CC's overseas options is on page 670.

Rites of passage

Trainees mentioned a sense of 'arbitrariness' in the allocation of seats and international secondments, several suggesting the rationale behind decisions could be better communicated. This problem is not uncommon in large firms but sources suggested that a 'high turnover of staff in HR' exacerbates difficulties. Other trainees had sympathy for the difficult task HR had on their hands, assuring us 'they are trying to make it more transparent.' Indeed it sounds as if they are: the HR team has expanded and turnover is now lower.

Trainees may arrive 'expecting to pick and choose from the international opportunities,' but in reality are often limited by the languages they speak. Several we interviewed felt 'forced' onto secondments they were less keen on because they had a smattering of the relevant language. With six seats to fill, Frankfurt is the most likely destination for a decent German speaker, no matter how much they want to see the bright lights of New York or Hong Kong. In addition to linguistic ability (or lack thereof), an international background and willingness to go the extra mile to make ambitions known seem to help secure the most competitive overseas placements.

An ambitious nature also helps one cope with the inevitable long hours. A trainee's first all-nighter is a 'rite of passage,' and 'when the adrenalin is pumping it's not as bad as it sounds,' particularly with 24-hour onsite catering. Usually 'the best quality of work comes with the worst hours,' although 'there is the odd occasion when you're kept back to proof-read from 6pm to 6am.' Depending on the department, some trainees are given time off in lieu 'to recharge batteries.' Time will tell whether CC's recent expansion of its India outsourcing programme will have a noticeable impact on trainees. The strategy certainly 'saves the firm money, but at the moment when you deal with [the paralegals in India] it's a call centre experience.'

Many current trainees employed a 'start at the top of the table' approach to training contract applications and never got past the first name on the list. Others jumped at CC for the international opportunities and the 'door-opening' name on their CV. Lest you fear that you won't fit in among such first-rate colleagues, rest assured 'there are the odd nutcases who actually enjoy working more than living, but the majority are really down to earth.' Whatever high-flying matters trainees may be privy to, at lunchtime they are 'more likely to have conversations about Amy Winehouse than private equity.' With so many foreign nationals among the intakes, including 'many Antipodeans and Canadians,' there is certainly no shortage of conversation. CC undoubtedly boasts an impressively diverse group of trainees: by our reckoning, roughly a quarter come from minority ethnic backgrounds.

Going for gold

The London office's Canary Wharf location is close to key banking clients but pretty far from anything else. No matter – CC's skyscraper houses everything you'd ever need, and then some, which leaves staff feeling 'spoiled.' Top of the favourites list is the firm's gym, complete with swimming pool. Leave your inhibitions in the changing room, as its glass doors make things 'very public.' On the bright side, 'it's a very levelling experience seeing partners totally naked.' The new intakes tend to be 'more cliquey' because the majority have already spent a year together on CC's LPC at the College of Law. This chummy bunch travel together, live together... we're already envisaging an MTV series of *Real World: Clifford Chance.* Everyone socialises at the office summer party, the 'pretty damned good' summer and winter trainee balls and the in-house Budgie Bar of a Friday evening. For the sporty, there's hockey, football, cricket, netball, rugby and softball. Rather like Freshers' Week, at the start of their training contracts new intakes are given a presentation about each sport.

Our interviewees emphasised the importance of behind-the-scenes networking to the qualification process. Said one: 'The people who didn't get their first choices were a bit complacent. I tried to make all the partners aware that I was keen.' As in many other firms, the economy did affect CC's qualification process this year: 'In key areas like real estate and tax there weren't many jobs going at all, so people had to make compromises' or find a job elsewhere. Whatever the backstage drama, CC put on an impressive performance in 2008, with 126 of the 132 qualifiers being offered jobs and 119 accepting them. Positions were available in all departments, although naturally predominantly in the finance, capital markets and corporate teams. Among our interviewees, most intended to stay at CC for a while, although few saw themselves as future partners because 'you have to commit to such an extraordinary level, it's like being an Olympic athlete.' Several had their eyes on international careers, public sector work and even politics.

And finally...

Rather like a high-quality sports car, whether you buy into the brand or the horsepower under the bonnet, Clifford Chance can take you pretty much wherever you want to go. Just don't expect too many rest stops along the way.

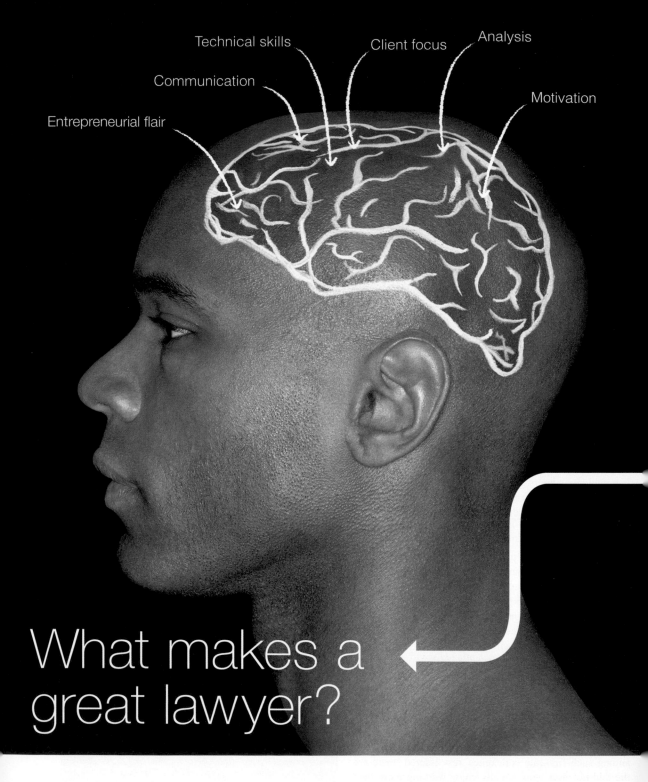

Entrepreneurial flair

Communication

Technical skills

Client focus

Analysis

Motivation

What makes a great lawyer?

At **Clyde & Co**, we believe that a variety of different qualities combine to make a really great lawyer. So if you've got what it takes, we'll provide the rest: first-class training and top-level exposure at an internationally renowned firm.

In terms of a career choice, we think it's a **no-brainer.**

Email us at: theanswers@clydeco.com

Apply at: www.clydeco.com/graduate

Clyde & Co LLP

The facts

Location: London, Guildford

Number of UK partners/solicitors: 96/174

Total number of trainees: 49

Seats: 4x6 months

Alternative seats: Overseas seats, secondments

Extras: Pro bono – RCJ CAB, Law Centres at Lambeth, Brent, Surrey and Holborn; Streetlaw

International jetsetter that it is, Clydes sends trainees to all sorts of places from Abu Dhabi to Hong Kong.

Traditionally known for its shipping and insurance practices, Clyde & Co attracts trainees looking for something a little different from run-of-the-mill Big City law.

A voyage of discovery

Clydes is a vast firm with 1,200 staff in 18 locations, just two of them here in the UK. Its international network has taken it into Europe, North and South America, Asia and the Middle East; indeed in this last region it has become a major player. Shipping and insurance is only part of the story; the firm also performs well in aviation and aerospace; energy, trade and commodities; non-marine transport and logistics; general commercial dispute resolution and international arbitration; corporate and commercial matters; EC/competition law; employment and real estate. Trainees complete four six-month seats with no department compulsory.

Chambers UK confirms the firm can't be beat for insurance and reinsurance law. It is also justly famed for its shipping practice, which with nearly 150 lawyers is the largest in the world. Many graduates turn up at Clydes thinking that shipping sounds quite interesting but not knowing quite what to expect as so little of it is taught at university or law school. To combat this, shipping department newbies go through a week's induction to learn all the basic concepts and terminology. After this they generally can't wait to get stuck in to one of the firm's 'meaty' areas. The department has several teams, each concentrating on a different aspect of marine law. The cargo team deals with two kinds of contentious work – wet and dry. Dry cases usually relate to contractual disputes; for instance 'if someone breaches a contract to supply goods or defaults on a hire agreement.' Wet cases deal with problems encountered at sea, be it salt-water damage to cargo or the loss of goods in a collision. The firm mainly acts for insurers, which pay out to the party that has lost the cargo and then pursue the ship owner for the money. A perfect example is the case of MSC Napoli, the ship that ran aground off the coast of Devon in 2007. You may remember that members of the public made off with the cargo that washed up on the beach, including cases of wine, car parts and a couple of motorbikes. Clyde is taking instructions from over 70 insurers regarding claims totalling $75m.

While a trainee's role on larger cases is 'document heavy,' elsewhere in the department they can get 'generous levels of responsibility,' spending about half their time running lower-value files. Shipping really is 'a whole other world,' full of unusual research (why do bananas ripen early; who is the best person to talk to about peaches in South Africa) and unique challenges (trawling through the temperature records of frozen herring cargoes; interviewing crew members who don't speak English). When a case involves a collision, trainees might dig out navigational charts and take a short voyage down the corridor to consult one of Clydes' in-house master mariners. These old sea dogs are more than willing to share their knowledge and 'show you their scars from when they were attacked by pirates.' If you thought piracy was a thing of the past, think again.

The jet set

'Easily the busiest department at Clyde' is the aviation finance team. A 'hectic' place for a trainee, long hours are often required when doing business with both America and the Far East. 'I worked weekends for six weeks, often not leaving until midnight or later,' said one source before revealing that this remains a popular department thanks to its team spirit. 'The drafting is really legalistic, so it's a lot harder for trainees to do the scary stuff, but our role is still massively important. If you miss an error in a document that's the deal down the toilet.' Trainees are quite capable of amending standard documents to suit straightforward deals, and they field calls from airlines asking how to go about financing aircraft. In the last year Clydes acted for several banks giving secured loans for the purchase of corporate jets, and for Singapore Airlines on the short-term lease of five Airbus A380s.

The aviation litigation team defends airlines from simple trip-and-slip and lost baggage claims, right up to major crashes. On smaller files, trainees look at issues of liability, draft advice and issue Part 36 offers (that's a specified method of case settlement, if you haven't read your White Book lately). Because courts only open during the day, the hours are more predictable than on the finance side of the department and 9am to 6pm is standard. This split between contentious and transactional hours is the same right across the firm and has caused 'a little bit of friction,' with some NQs aggrieved at doing more work for the same pay as their colleagues. We're told this is being addressed.

Boys' Own

Since you can insure pretty much anything, Clydes' insurance department covers a huge range of issues. As well as marine and aviation matters, the following are all covered: contingency; energy; engineering and construction; fine art; healthcare; negligence; political; product liability; professional indemnity; and corporate and regulatory insurance. To take just one as an example, political risk insurance covers 'CEND; that's confiscation, expropriation, nationalisation and deprivation.' It basically involves providing insurance to foreign investors in unstable countries, 'where the laws may be slightly arbitrary' or where there is political unrest. For instance, if a mobile phone company was to agree a contract in such a country, and the government suddenly decided to nationalise the telecommunications industry, the insurers would pay out. Research tasks can be really interesting here: 'It's all about munitions, terrorism; the stuff that's in the news. You read a lot of Jane's Defence Weekly during the seat.' Just in case you don't know, this magazine reports on military and corporate affairs and isn't some twisted cross between *Bunty* and *Guns & Ammo*.

Chambers UK rankings

Asset Finance • Aviation • Commodities • Construction • Corporate Finance • Dispute Resolution • Employment • Financial Services Regulation • Fraud: Civil/Criminal • Immigration • Information Technology • Insurance • Product Liability • Professional Negligence • Projects, Energy & Natural Resources • Real Estate • Restructuring/Insolvency • Retail • Shipping • Transport

A major part of Clydes' insurance work involves reinsurance, which is essentially how insurance companies protect themselves against potential losses. Three years down the line the firm is still dealing with the damage caused by Hurricane Katrina, and it's rare for the firm not to be involved in a major world disaster in some way or other. 'Big, big cases' are common here, and 'the word to the wise is that the firm is gearing up for ever larger insurance litigation. They have dropped a lot of the smaller claims that trainees could get involved in.' This is not ideal, as long-running monster-sized cases involve trainees in 'a huge amount of bundling and cross-referencing.' At least supervisors try to involve them as much as they can, as this trainee's description of their role in a big case confirms: 'I reviewed the files, picked out important documents and provided support to the supervisor. I was at all the meetings with the client, and did first drafts of correspondence at every stage.'

International jetsetter that it is, Clydes sends trainees to all sorts of places from Abu Dhabi to Hong Kong. The most likely destination for a secondment is Dubai, which takes five trainees at a time. Clydes is one of the Emirate's biggest law firms and 'it is desperately trying to increase the number of staff there, pushing for more and more business.' Trainees may liken the city to Disneyland, but the work is not Mickey Mouse and staff often graft for long hours. Since Dubai is stuffed full of ex-pats, there's a lively social scene and 'Clyde trainees probably get treated the best out of all of them.' Cars, phones and luxury apartments are handed up to compensate for the fact that they have to spend six months in a rich man's paradise where the sun always shines.

Around every silver lining is a cloud, and for many trainees this is the mandatory seat in the Guildford office. Opinion is divided here. 'It's known as a bit of a thorn in the side – trainees always moan about it,' said one, adding: 'My sympathy is short. It's made pretty clear from the outset that you'll have to go there, and yet some people still come to the firm with the express aim of not doing a seat in Guildford.' The work and the pay, should you be wondering, is exactly the same as in London, and once they are out there prejudices commonly break down. 'I found it a nice break. It's an excellent working environment, plus there's good shopping at lunchtime,' said a recent convert. The office is substantially better than the one in London's Eastcheap, which is acknowledged as 'a bit gothic and grim.' One source confessed: 'I do get a little embarrassed bringing clients in and saying, 'So, this is Clyde.'' Thank heaven for the sandwich trolley that rattles round the building three times a day: 'It can be a lifesaver.' The second London office at the Corn Exchange is much nicer we hear. What never fails to impress in any of the offices is Clydes' commitment to training: 'There are lunchtime seminars and events practically every day, and we can pick and choose the ones that are useful to us.'

Free spirits

Clydes' website claims you can ask any of its lawyers what characterises the firm and they will answer 'entrepreneurialism.' Naturally, we put this to the test. When trainees summed up the place, we got a variety of answers: 'positive,' 'motivated' and 'international' were some of them. Just as we were about to brand Clydes' marketing team as filthy stinking liars, we came across a trainee who did say 'entrepreneurial,' adding: 'I think that's the polite way of saying that each partner is given free rein so long as it makes the firm money.' If true, it certainly seems to be working. Clyde reported revenue of £157m in 2008, a 17% increase on the previous year.

The website also boasts that these lawyers are individualistic, and trainees agree. 'There are certainly a lot of characters… they are eccentric in a good way,' said one source, though we did hear reports of one or two partners who had been 'promoted for making money rather than for their man-management skills.' If the partners are individualistic, are the trainees the same? On the whole, yes. They come from all over the world and a number have already worked in other industries. 'I'm in the minority having done law at university,' said one interviewee. As for their social lives, in London The Ship and Balls Brothers are the bars of choice, while The Tup attracts the Guildford crew. The Christmas party is a high point: 'It's great seeing all your fellow trainees there. We carried on until six in the morning last time. Aah, so many stories of partners falling down stairs…' Say no more.

And finally...

Our contacts say: Clyde will never relinquish its marine practice, but is starting to realise the benefits of transactional work. 2008's NQ retention stats back this up: 17 of the 23 qualifying trainees stayed with the firm, with only six going into contentious areas of practice.

CMS Cameron McKenna LLP

The facts

Location: London

Number of UK partners/solicitors: 133/371

Total number of trainees: 124

Seats: 4x6 months

Alternative seats: Overseas seats, secondments

Extras: Pro bono – Islington Law Centre, ProHelp Bristol, Advocates for International Development, LawWorks; language training

A secondment to one of the former Soviet bloc capitals is extremely likely for CMS trainees.

Sometimes perceived as the 'cuddly' City firm, those snuggling up to CMS Cameron McKenna should be able to reap the benefits of foreign travel, big-ticket deals and perfect posture.

Diagnosis mergers... more of them

In our interviews, Cameron McKenna recruits agreed that, 'in the past we may have been seen as a bit of a soft touch' and debated whether 'we've underperformed in recent years.' Tapping CMS's knee and checking its pulse, one amateur physician came up with a diagnosis: 'I call it mid-marketitis.' However, new managing partner Duncan Weston appears confident that no major surgery is required and that a good working environment doesn't have to conflict with a more aggressive business strategy: 'It's been made clear that he wants the firm to be up with the big boys.' The boss has certainly won over the trainees: 'Duncan has a real vision for expansion, he's prepared to take risks,' several of them swooned. 'He's very charismatic, a real leader, very inspiring,' Not content with charming our interviewees with his winning ways, Weston has set out to exceed the firm's previous goal to boost turnover to £250m by 2009. Recent results suggest it is well on its way to smashing this target, and there's no secret as to how it's being done.

Corporate and banking have become the firm's big growth areas and it wants to continue to expand them further. Here in the UK, some of the corporate and banking departments' clients are HSBC, Lloyds TSB, Bank of Ireland, BP, Royal Mail, insurance brokers Heath Lambert, Nuffield Hospitals, Wellcome Trust, National Grid, Galliford Try, John Laing/Henderson and Blockbuster. It's worth noting the presence of a number of clients that are from sectors important to the firm – construction, life sciences and insurance. Other departments act for the likes of Cancer Research UK, Procter & Gamble, Microsoft and Elvis Presley Enterprises. Clients come from the UK and overseas, reflecting the firm's sphere of influence and international perspective.

Over the course of four seats trainees will visit corporate (or banking), a litigation department and, often, one of the firm's other offices. This leaves one last seat, during which most people try one of the firm's highly rated niche practices. *Chambers UK* ranks the firm among the best in the country for pensions law, but the most popular department by far is energy. The introduction of a 'priority' seat request should ensure that everyone gets to work in their first-choice department at some point. Places are also available in immigration, real estate, employment, SHEP (safety, health, environment and product liability in name, but 'mostly environment these days'), IP/IT and insurance, tax, construction and EU competition.

In all seats trainees report to a partner, usually receiving at least some work from others in the team. Supervision is described by some as 'fantastic – detailed feedback is always forthcoming,' and by others in less glowing terms. 'Truthfully, the quality of the supervision varies enormously. The official line is that we should have a catch-up every month. I personally haven't had an appraisal in nine months.' It's broadly agreed that the quality of feedback is heavily dependant on individual supervisors, with pensions singled out for particular praise: 'I could have sat down with them every week if I'd needed to.'

Fast cars and slow trains

'If you show enthusiasm and you put yourself forward you will get NQ-level work,' one trainee said of corporate. The only compulsory seat, it never used to be that popular, perhaps because of the risk of long hours. It's an increasingly desirable stop on the training route, as the firm invests more resources into the department. Deals from the past year include Alfred McAlpine's £572m takeover by Carillon, and Informa's £502m takeover of Datamonitor. One of the biggest deals was the sale of BP Nederland Energie to TAQA (the Abu Dhabi National Energy Company) for nearly £700m. On bigger deals, trainees are involved with 'the obvious tasks of proof-reading, basic company searches, quite a bit of drafting, writing research memos and managing data rooms.' Major benefits of the seat are an abundance of client and lawyer-to-lawyer contact ('I was on the phone across Europe') and the chance to take a decent role on smaller transactions.

The corporate recovery team comes into its own when companies or individuals get themselves into trouble, and it doesn't take a genius to see there's a fair amount of this on the horizon. The work might involve restructuring a business in financial difficulty or selling off the assets of an insolvent company. 'We do a lot of security reviews – that's when a bank calls and asks us to check if the security they have taken is valid.' Such work can be a loss leader; 'we're hoping that if the company does go under, the bank will come to us for the necessary advice.' Trainees in this seat learn how to review security documents and even run a few small files themselves. Contentious lawyers within the team represented Ferrari against McLaren in the wake of the big Formula One spying scandal of 2007 that saw McLaren disqualified from the Constructor's Championship with a £50m fine.

The much sought-after energy department is split into two parts. The oil and gas work is 'extremely topical.' 'We are currently working for a major North Sea oil company that is selling off parts of its oilfields,' explained one trainee. The other side of the department deals with the 'very complicated' electricity sector. 'It might help if you had an engineering degree before you get on to the legal aspects of it,' suggested one source. It does take time to get used to the department, which is perhaps why many of the tasks are classic admin chores, such as running data rooms and 'reviewing documents to check clauses within them.'

Running in tandem with the energy team is the projects team. If you've ever been stranded at Walthamstow Central because of the upgrades currently being made to the Victoria Line, rest assured that Cameron McKenna's lawyers are behind the project, doing their best to ensure

the Tube runs smoothly. Rail is an important area for the team; clients include Metronet and the Department for Transport in matters regarding Eurotunnel and the Channel Tunnel Rail Link ('I drafted my own statutory instrument to do with that,' said one source proudly). Road projects are important too, for example the FLOW consortium consulted the firm on the widening of the M25. And then there are waste projects: the firm is acting for Bank of Ireland, which is helping to find the Green Power Generation biomass project in St Helens. Other projects relate to education, defence and health. 'I went to a lot of client meetings when we were negotiating the contracts with companies that wanted to build hospitals,' said one trainee.

Flock to the bloc

In 1946, Winston Churchill spoke of an iron curtain descending across Europe, behind which 'Warsaw, Berlin, Prague, Vienna, Budapest, Belgrade, Bucharest and Sofia, all these famous cities and the populations around them lie in what I must call the Soviet sphere.' Fast forward to 2009, and it's like communism never happened. Cameron McKenna or one of its CMS allies now operate in every one of the Eastern European cities on Churchill's list, and more besides. Camerons opened up in Moscow in 1992, barely two years after the Berlin Wall fell. Stalin might as well have stuck to grooming his moustache.

Why the history lesson? Because a secondment to one of the former Soviet Bloc capitals is an extremely likely prospect for CMS trainees. The firm is very keen for second-seaters to do a stint at one of its other offices. Anyone who doesn't fancy this should bear in mind that 'having a girlfriend in London probably won't be seen as a valid excuse not to go,' but also take heart from the fact that the trainees we spoke to described their European experience as 'awesome,' 'amazing,' and 'X-rated' (they wouldn't be drawn into clarifying that last one). Be warned though; some locations are oversubscribed and you might apply for Moscow and end up in Aberdeen, or put down Prague and wind up in Warsaw. Don't let this put you off, as we didn't speak to a single trainee who hadn't loved their experience. The firm provides intensive language training and we even managed to get some Russian tutoring from one of the trainees, who taught us how to order a beer.

Cameron McKenna does realise there are people who 'don't neccessarily want to go to the arse end of Europe,' and for those who can't bear to tear themselves away from loved ones for six months, there are options nearer to home. At 530 miles from London, Aberdeen is barely closer than Prague but at least you don't have to cross the sea to get there. Edinburgh is a little nearer, and Bristol is closer still, although if even that is a suspension bridge too far, the firm has secondments to clients within the capital, including AIG, Exxon and the Wellcome Trust.

The little big firm

Cameron McKenna's size really appeals to its trainees. Smaller than the magic circle firms, yet larger than most of its mid-market rivals, it attracts applicants who want a big-name law firm without a sense of anonymity or frequent punishing hours (though on rare occasions they can be as long as any in the City). The firm recruits from a healthy mix of nationalities, backgrounds and universities, but a trainee who attended the firm's 'excellent vac scheme' noticed that, either by accident or design, 'the sociable ones from it get hired.'

There are enough events and activities to keep party animals happy once they arrive. One or two sore heads were in evidence the day we called, as a number of our interviewees had been taken to Lords to watch the cricket before (we guess) continuing on somewhere afterwards. The CMS football team can hold its collective head high, having held Slaughter and May until the last minute of extra time in the final of this year's Legal Cup. Netballers, golfers and skiers add to the sporting picture. There's a big firm-wide party in October and departmental jollies at Christmas, but the trainee bash to welcome future joiners is acknowledged as the most fun. The trainees' own social budget is put towards events like bowling, and recently a roller disco. Much of it also goes on drinks evenings, the shabby Hand & Shears pub being the venue of choice for regular nights out.

One bemusing management decision is the ballerina-themed motivational posters that are springing up around the office. Working out how slogans like 'Trust', 'Candour' and 'Stretch' relate to law is proving a bit of a stretch for trainees, who describe them as 'a complete and utter enigma.' CMS sponsors the English National Ballet, though rumours that dancers have been brought in to help partners improve their posture are unconfirmed. 'I'm looking through my window and I can see a lot of people slouching,' a trainee chuckled.

And finally...

Last year we called this firm the Goldilocks of the City – not too corporate, not too finance, not too contentious, just right. And just right is how most trainees found it in 2008, when 48 of the 58 qualifiers took up permanent positions.

- **Vicky Wisson**, CMS Cameron McKenna's Graduate Recruitment Officer, has the following assessment day tip: 'Whatever exercise you are asked to complete, make sure you plan your time effectively. Failure to do so can result in large gaps in your reports or tasks and the assessors cannot mark what isn't there.' For more of her wisdom, see our article on interviews.

cobbetts | graduate recruitment

FUTURE PROOF

At Cobbetts LLP, we're developing the next generation of legal talent.

Our partners and solicitors have the expertise to turn our trainees into confident and capable newly qualified solicitors. Future proof your future and let them release your potential.

With over 90 partners and 750 staff, we are a leading full service law firm with offices in Birmingham, Leeds, London and Manchester. No hard sell, no exaggerated promises.

Apply on-line for training contracts and easter and summer vacation placements. Visit www.cobbettsgraduate.com for more information, plus blogs, videos and trainee profiles.

YOUR FUTURE STARTS HERE...

Cobbetts LLP

The facts

Location: Manchester, Birmingham, Leeds, London

Number of UK partners/solicitors: 97/173

Total number of trainees: 47

Seats: 4x6 months

Alternative seats: Occasional secondments

A direct consequence of Cobbetts' 'one virtual office' ethos is that each of its swish new offices in Manchester, Birmingham and Leeds are practically identical in layout and decor.

Historically property-driven, Cobbetts is gradually shedding a nicey nicey reputation in favour of a more business-oriented, more corporate outlook. We're not exactly talking cut-throat, but Cobbetts is definitely acquiring an edge.

Nice but noughtier

Cobbetts originally hails from Manchester, then a pell-mell series of mergers in the early noughties saw it expand into Leeds and Birmingham, living the national law firm dream seemingly without suffering any adverse cultural effects from rapacious growth. To trainees and lawyers, it seemed to offer the perfect combination of work-life balance, ambition and quality clients. However, come 2005/06, average partner profits were hovering around a low £190,000 per year and the firm took decisive – somewhat uncharacteristically steely – action. It axed some 20 partners in a move to rectify over-population in some areas and then a number of others left of their own accord. In response, profits shot up and revenue hit a respectable, if not breathtaking, £59.3m for the last financial year. If the partner cuts were a seismic quake for a firm that had previously defined itself via a very human approach, a second partnership shake-up in 2008, aimed at driving forward the firm's performance, was an aftershock to demonstrate that the cultural landscape had altered for good. In the latest round of changes a two-partner, five-strong property finance team quit for Halliwells and a four-partner social housing team transferred to Shoosmiths. In summer 2008 the firm announced the likelihood of redundancies from the real estate division.

Having arrived 'after the big cull,' our interviewees were pretty dispassionate on the subject. 'The years since we've arrived have been transitional ones for the firm,'

they told us; 'the impression you get is that the aim was to shed the reputation as being more parochial, big but not a 'proper' national firm.' Fully aware of 'some general bad press and morale problems a few years ago, especially in Birmingham,' this new generation of Cobbetteers were fully on board with the new plan 'to expand more into the corporate field, to try and acquire more trophy clients and get our property clients to use the other teams.' Said one typically pragmatic type: 'We've seen the family team go and a big social housing team rationalisation; that sort of thing doesn't concern us day to day.'

The unveiling of a small corporate-focused London office in 2007 was of much more interest. Trainees believe it will 'open more people up to considering us' and 'funnel work to Birmingham and Leeds, bringing in some international instructions.' In general they like the idea of a leaner, meaner, more modern Cobbetts that is 'ready to step up a gear.' To them, Cobbetts has 'invested in all its offices, got itself in good shape and wants to move forward.'

A different same

As to where this change in emphasis leaves Cobbetts culturally, we're told: 'It's like the work-life balance was over-egged in the past' and 'this isn't a nine-to-five place any more.' The current state of the economy is causing many firms to examine business practices; at Cobbetts this kind of self-analysis is now a well-established part of working life. 'The partner departures have got people more focused on business development' and 'there's been more pressure in terms of fees and billing.' It all points to the firm having 'more of a business head than it had four years ago,' and with a staff forum having fallen into cessation of late, 'perhaps the management is more externally focused rather than internally putting energy into listening to staff.' Despite all this, core 'Cobbetts Values' are still in evidence and trainees thoroughly approve of the firm's 'non-hierarchical team approach,' which makes it possible to 'talk to anyone across levels.' Said one: 'Sure we want to be as professional and business-oriented as Eversheds and DLA, but we pride ourselves on being less faceless than them.'

The training scheme at Cobbetts is under review and the seat pattern will be changing in September 2009. For now it runs a four-seat system that is free of compulsory elements. Having said that, it would be strange not to visit the property and corporate departments. In Manchester, property has always been the driving force, while Birmingham is the more corporate-led of the two. Leeds is a much smaller operation and London hosts just one trainee at a time. Experiences are similar across locations, with 'quality of work, a great deal of responsibility and the opportunity to run your own files' in the majority of seats. A broad range of seats is available in sub-departments of five core areas: banking, corporate, commercial litigation, real estate and employment.

Building for the future

Property continues to be 'the heartbeat' of the firm, generating a hefty proportion of its income. A roll call of national clients (Whitbread, De Vere, Matalan, Sports Direct, Barracuda Group), North West clients (landlords and investment companies like Peel and Bruntwood) and telecoms companies (Orange, 3 and Pipex Wireless) make the property department an exciting place to be, and many of those who hated the subject at law school are soon 'totally won over.' Cobbetts also represents a swathe of public sector clients, among them the Metropolitan Borough Councils of Bury, Oldham, Rochdale and Stockport, and has put significant effort into developing its housing and urban regeneration capacities. Notable work includes advice to local authorities within the Merseyside Consortium and a leading role assisting Peel Holdings on the £400m, 200-acre, hi-tech creative hub MediaCity:UK in Manchester. Trainees are exposed to 'the full remit of the team's work,' assisting on both 'massive financings of projects' and 'running our own files for leases, licences and the like.' Some take particular pleasure in the 'tangibility of the work: you can say, 'I worked on that development or on that shop.' Others relish 'ready client contact – I'm calling the top brass at one of our biggest clients all the time.'

Chambers UK rankings

Banking & Finance • Charities • Construction • Corporate Finance • Debt Recovery • Defamation/Reputation Management • Dispute Resolution • Employment • Healthcare • Intellectual Property • Licensing • Pensions • Planning • Private Client • Real Estate • Real Estate Litigation • Restructuring/Insolvency • Social Housing

Departures from the social housing department have seen the firm lose its place on the legal panel of The Housing Corporation (the government agency that regulates and partly funds affordable housing). However Cobbetts has beefed up its Leeds planning department by pinching a partner from Eversheds. The popular planning seat gives access to 'large infrastructure projects and public inquiries on things like the underground storage of gas or wind farms.' Property litigation offers a good degree of responsibility on boundary disputes, landlord and tenant issues and housing authority matters. Despite its stature, time in property 'doesn't make you feel like you're in an enormous team because you work with and for specific groups of people.'

Mines of information

The banking teams introduce trainees to 'big national lenders like Barclays, RBS and Bank of Scotland.' The first thing trainees appreciate is that 'the drafting is complicated and more of a challenge.' The corporate finance lawyers, with their niche energy and mining expertise, are prospering, particularly through 'the foothold of the London office.' Independent oil and gas company Enegi Oil turned to them for its joint admission to AIM and the Luxembourg Stock Exchange, and Qatar construction company Panceltica sought assistance on a £236m AIM listing. The lawyers have also advised Russia's Highland Gold Mining on a £196m investment, and then there's been a plethora of regional UK MBOs and acquisitions. Whether corporate trainees focus on regional, national or international clients depends on 'how the penny falls.' One source had the pleasure of working on 'a single massive project for the entire six months – the acquisition and restructuring of a big company – that meant dealing with people in the pensions, employment and property departments across the firm.'

Contentious experience can be had in the property, banking, employment and commercial litigation departments. This last one gets trainees tackling 'huge disclosure exercises,' but also 'small debt recovery cases and charging orders for city councils.' The value of 'the full experience of running a case from start to finish' shouldn't be underestimated. Employment trainees get 'plenty of client contact' and a fair amount of corporate support tasks. One lucky so-and-so had 'had an EAT case all of my own – under supervision anyway.' Meanwhile, the business restructuring services team offers 'great court experience on charging orders, personal insolvency and repossessions,' and its overlap with banking litigation puts bigger matters within reach. 'I was involved on the bank charges litigation, defending a major bank from en masse claims for repayment of fees.' Among a few secondments is a posting to a Brussels law firm. Mid and end-of-seat appraisals, not to mention monthly 'welfare one-to-ones' with members of the HR team ensure that trainees never lack support.

In the region of national

A direct consequence of Cobbetts' 'one virtual office' ethos is that each of its swish new offices in Manchester, Birmingham and Leeds are 'practically identical in layout and décor.' Having visited the Manchester HQ, we can attest that the pastel colours, acres of glass and smooth wooden furniture make for a pleasant working environment. Having all locations the same definitely helps blur the boundaries, but how cross-office a trainee's experience is does depend on the team they enter. 'Litigation in Leeds is quite self contained,' whereas links between property teams are obvious; employment sees 'endless exchanges of people and e-mails' and there's a bustling corporate thoroughfare between London, Leeds and Birmingham.

It is possible, though uncommon, for trainees to switch offices. That doesn't prevent a welter of contact between different locations. A trainee committee organises social events that rotate around the three main sites and there's a sports day at Sale Cricket Club near Manchester for 'all trainees and future joiners.' 'Trainees really get on with each other,' said one source, perhaps referring to an ongoing cross-Pennine romance between two recruits in Leeds and Manchester. Each office also fields football, cricket and netball teams, and trainees in all locations can put their business development skills to the test at networking events run by the Cobbetts Young Professionals group.

Manchester's 'brilliant' social club costs a paltry £2 per month and the city's nightlife is just a short walk from the office. The Leeds canteen receives plaudits and consequently trainees regularly meet there for lunch. The wealth of 'new riverside bars and restaurants' near their office are reserved for post-work socialising. In Birmingham All Bar One is still the staple choice, even though Colmore Square isn't lacking in bars. The fact that the working day seems to be lengthening across the offices doesn't faze anyone – 'The firm pays the market rate, so it's fair enough.' Trainees take a similarly pragmatic stance on NQ recruitment. In 2008, 18 out of 25 qualifiers stayed with the firm.

Our sources detected a new hunger in the firm for 'people who are more interested in corporate work… which no one wanted in our year.' Beyond this there's clearly a tendency for recruits to have a local family or study connection to the office of their choice. Our top tip would be to try and get onto the vac scheme as the firm would like up to 80% of future recruits to come through this route.

And finally...

By toughening up over the past few years Cobbetts is in better shape. It offers an excellent training across a broad commercial spectrum and is one to put on the shortlist with other national firms.

Coffin Mew LLP

The facts

Location: Southampton, Portsmouth, Fareham, Gosport

Number of UK partners/solicitors: 29/57

Total number of trainees: 17

Seats: 6x4 months

Alternative seats: Occasional secondments

Extras: Pro bono – CAB

Coffin Mew's social housing department is one of the largest in the country, and *Chambers UK* ranks it as top dog in the South of England.

Down on the South Coast, Coffin Mew must be watching the expansion of Blake Lapthorn with interest. Not because it wants to follow suit, but because it realises that its rival's national ambitions will leave a gap in the regional market.

Coff mixture

With offices in Southampton, Portsmouth, Fareham and Gosport, and a name that is well regarded thanks to the efforts of its various private client and commercial teams, Coffin Mew is in a good position to plug any gap. You might think that a firm with such a quaint name and a history going back to the 1800s would be rather set in its ways. You'd be wrong. Trainees find this 'a modern firm with forward-thinking ideas.' Nowhere is this more apparent than in the structure of the training contract, which is akin to a bespoke suit – perfectly tailored to fit each person. The firm is uncannily good at its tailoring, partly due to a six-seat system that allows trainees who are still unsure of their style to try a whole wardrobe of options until the eureka moment strikes. At that point, 'once you take an interest in an area, they will tailor your contract.' We heard, for example, of a trainee who took to trusts law having a secondment to the HSBC Trust Company specifically arranged for him. It was a success, so the firm is now keen to explore further client secondments. Another point worth mentioning is that if the firm thinks a trainee hasn't done a seat that might be useful to them, it will organise a masterclass in that area of practice.

That's not to say that trainees can do whatever they like – some flexibility on their part is required too. More often than not it comes in the form of a willingness to commute between Southampton, Portsmouth and Fareham, depending on where their current department is located. To be

clear: journeys up and down the M27 are standard, not optional, in this training contract. More than that, 'you should be prepared to go to any department for a seat and get stuck in even if you're not interested in the work.' The firm makes no bones about the fact that trainees are judged on how they perform in their least favourite seat.

We normally shy away from bigging up individual partners, but we'll make an exception in this case since it's clear that one man is central to the Coffin Mew training experience. Half training partner, half favourite uncle, Malcolm Padgett (aka 'The Padge') is 'only ever a phone call away.' Our sources tell us 'he's a great support' and a great raconteur: 'If you go to him with a question he'll inevitably get distracted and start telling you stories about life in the law.' Just in case any of his colleagues read this and feel jealous, we should mention that they get rave reviews too. 'I was surprised and impressed by all the partners,' said one trainee. 'When you think how busy they are and how valuable their time is, the fact that senior-level partners will sit down with me and explain my questions in detail is amazing.'

Crack troops

Coffin Mew's social housing department is one of the largest in the country, and *Chambers UK* ranks it as top dog in the South of England. The team helps registered social landlords (RSLs) chase rent arrears and tackle antisocial behaviour, in one recent case assisting a housing association in its bid to obtain a crack house closure order in a rural area where the use of Class A drugs was seriously affecting the community. With bags of cases to choose from, trainees are given the opportunity to do as much advocacy as they like. Arguing rent arrears cases in front of a district judge in the county court can be a daunting prospect, 'as some of the judges can be pretty tough,' yet our sources grew accustomed to things quickly, some doing up to 15 hearings in four months. 'At the start of the seat everyone is asked how comfortable they'd be doing advocacy,' and for those who don't fancy it so much, the amount of court time is cut down. The social housing team has plenty of non-contentious work on land purchases and regeneration projects, so if drafting and research is more your thing there's no need to worry.

The expansive commercial services department also splits into contentious and non-contentious sections as well as being divided along office lines. As well as corporate transactions and general business advice, the department encompasses IP, IT and competition law, 'there's a partner who deals solely with care providers and RSLs, and another who does charities law and community work.' The flexibility of the training contract is fully visible here as 'every Monday everyone in the department touches base with each other, which gives trainees a chance to shout out about where they want to be this week.' In this way, trainees can either gain a general overview of the department or gravitate to the area that interests them most.

One of our sources described their involvement in a merger between two charities that were set up in different ways. One was an industrial provident society and one was a company limited by guarantee. The trainee in question 'drafted all the documents involved in the one being subsumed into the other.' Appropriately enough for a Portsmouth establishment, the firm has also recently acted for The Merchant Navy Welfare Board. Already registered as an English charity, regulators declared it needed to be registered as a Scottish one as well, an action that required major amendments to the Welfare Board's governing document. Charity law is a complex area of practice that requires specialist knowledge and training, so if you've an interest in it then take heart that Coffin Mew committed itself to forming a dedicated team of specialists back in 2005. Its clients include YMCA Thames Gateway (South), The Lions Hospice and The English Blind Golf Association.

House calls

Some sources deemed private client as 'the most hands-on department.' It thrusts new recruits onto the front line from the word go. 'You get so many enquiries from people just ringing up, even at the start of your training,' recalled one interviewee. Another concurred: 'It's a fan-

tastic early seat because of the client contact. And it's not too scary because it's generally old people rather than some company director.' Trainees appreciate being let loose on the public and running their own files from beginning to end. They draft wills and powers of attorney, set up small trusts, help on Court of Protection matters, make home visits to clients and conduct 'in-depth research on probates that span different jurisdictions.' Work comes mainly from one supervisor, but the trainee sits in an office with a couple of paralegals. 'It's nice because with three of you together you can have a bit of a giggle... while still working hard of course!' Of course.

Trainees can visit most of the firm's other departments, including family, employment, corporate, commercial property, and one of the region's leading claimant personal injury teams, which specialises in serious head injuries. In the current economic climate the insolvency team is starting to grow, and those who take a seat there will be exposed to both contentious and non-contentious work. This could mean drafting a contract to sell a business at short notice or advising a woman who doesn't want to lose her home because her husband has gone bankrupt. Apparently some of the best times are spent 'having a good argy-bargy with creditors and the like.'

Throwing it out there

'The firm's keen to think that if you sliced us trainees through the middle there'd be a slice of Coffins in there,' said one interviewee. We didn't offer to try due to the criminal charges that would inevitably follow. Our sources certainly had a clear image of themselves – we're 'down to earth' and 'level-headed,' they told us. One went further, saying: 'Coffin trainees are determined and always try to give themselves a standard to reach. They've got a bit of personality about them, they're not afraid to speak up and say what they think about things.' Chips off the old Padge, perhaps. 'I know they look for people who are good enough to work in London but have a good reason not to be there,' said another source, opening the door to an interesting question – why are most trainees female? Are they less attracted to the hard slog of the capital and more committed to a better work-life balance? Don't be fooled into thinking this contract is an easy ride – it's not – but the hours are certainly reasonable, if generally longer than nine to five. The gender question can't be answered simply, but it is true to say that here (as in most firms) girls outperform boys on paper and at interview.

The distance between offices proves no obstacle when it comes to socialising. Trainees meet up quite regularly as a group and are happy to experiment when it comes to nightspots, be they in 'Southampton, Pompey… and one of us lives in Winchester so we all went on a night out there last week.' We didn't hear much about competitive sport: this lot seemingly prefer more casual forms of exercise. 'We play rounders after work, and someone got the Frisbee out in the park this lunchtime.' Group outings are equally casual – a hoedown at a village hall, a visit to a local theme park, and day to Go Ape in the New Forest (that's negotiating a tree-top adventure course, in case you were wondering). As for big events, the funfair at the last Christmas party was well received, if a bit chilly, and when the firm recently converted to Limited Liability Partnership status, one wag decided that LLP stood for

LookaLike Party and arranged an event accordingly. Hannibal Lecter and Marilyn Monroe were among the attendees. Coffin Mew's marketing department is clearly having fun making puns on the initials LLP, but seems to be having trouble thinking up good ones: the website has the frankly rubbish offering of 'It aLL Points to quality.' We suggest they give us a call; we'll be happy to heLLP.

And finally...

There's no mystery about Coffin Mew: its a straightforward firm with a well-earned reputation. If you're fond of sand dunes and salty air, this outfit is well worth further consideration. All five of the 2008 qualifiers stayed with the firm.

Collyer Bristow

The facts

Location: London

Number of UK partners/solicitors: 32/28

Total number of trainees: 8

Seats: 4x6 months

Alternative seats: None

Extras: Pro bono – CAB, BPP legal advice clinic, Caribbean death row cases; language training

In the past year Collyer Bristow was referred work from 42 English law firms, including three in the magic circle.

At more than 250 years old Collyer Bristow is a well-respected London firm with a twist. Celebrity clients from the worlds of sport and music give the firm a touch of glamour and ensure it a place in the niche media market. Don't get star-struck though, as this is just one of the strings to the firm's bow.

Mum's not the word

This isn't a firm to make headlines of its own: there have been no recent mergers, takeovers or major shake-ups to rock its world, in fact despite a dip in turnover lately, quite possibly due to the loss of some key partners, the firm is a constant and stable player in the London mid-market. On closer inspection though, CB has some unusual features, giving it a slightly quirky reputation in legal circles. The foremost of these is its extensive list of media and sporting clients, including members of ancient rock band Status Quo (in a long-running dispute over royalty payments), Sony Pictures and Working Title Films (soundtrack agreements for the films *Casino Royale* and *Hot Fuzz*), top golfer Ernie Els, Olympic gold medallist Ben Ainslie and busty temptress Katie Price.

If you're reading this and dreaming of handling Jordan's assets, don't get your hopes up. Though the media connections permeate the firm, it's not the main thrust of CB's work and most of the current trainees chose to join for more practical reasons, namely the size of the firm and the range of work it handles. This isn't to say that a trainee in the right place at the right time won't get a glimpse of the media action. One lucky so-and-so flew out to Milan to have lunch with Marco Materazzi and his wife. Materazzi, you'll remember, was the Italian footballer on the receiving end of Zinedine Zidane's infamous

head butt in the 2006 World Cup final. The *Daily Star* alleged that Materazzi had insulted the Frenchman's mother, and Collyer Bristow represented him in the ensuing libel action. The newspaper was forced to apologise, so for the record Materazzi did not call Zidane's dear old mum a terrorist whore. He actually said something to the effect of 'I prefer your whore of a sister,' which of course is entirely different.

Such playground squabbles are the exception and most trainees find themselves working on more mainstream cases in the family, dispute resolution and private client fields in which CB has built such an excellent reputation. After the first seat, all the departments are up for grabs and trainees decide among themselves who goes where. The broad-based dispute resolution team covers IP, employment, property lit and insolvency cases as well as business disputes. As the firm's largest department it occupies two floors within the office and 'usually takes two trainees, who swap floors half way through to see the full range of work.' Early on, 'they want to see how capable you are' and, once you've earned your stripes researching and drafting claim forms, there's a chance to grab more responsibility. 'I got to go to trial and do a bit of advocacy myself,' recalled one source. A lot of cases come via other law firms; in fact in the past year CB was referred work from 42 English law firms, including three in the magic circle. Among its top cases are the proceedings brought by the President and Government of Equatorial Guinea relating to the alleged coup attempt in which Mark Thatcher was implicated. CB represents one of the defendants mixed up in the affair, who was supposedly motivated by the prospect of benefiting from oil revenues. The case involves elements of civil conspiracy but also the ability of a foreign government to sue in the UK. Having been successful both at first instance and in the Court of Appeal, CB's client was due to face a hearing in the House of Lords in front of a full panel of nine judges; however the Law Lords have refused to hear the case because the defendant has been imprisoned in Equatorial Guinea and cannot meet with his lawyers. Another headline-hitting case is for the family of Gordon Gentle, a soldier serving in Basra, in Iraq, who was killed by an explosion at the age of 19. His family was unsuccessful in their Court of Appeal application for a public inquiry into whether the government had taken reasonable steps to be satisfied that the invasion of Iraq was lawful under public international law. However, CB succeeded in obtaining an inquest verdict that Gordon was unlawfully killed. Other clients include Air France, the Bar Council, Camelot, easyGroup, Hugo Boss, the League Against Cruel Sports and Philip Morris.

Yacketty yacht

We can't divulge the names of CB's private clients, but suffice it to say it's not Joe and Jane Bloggs of Croydon. The firm specialises in high and ultra-high net worth individuals (we're talking billions of dollars in some cases), many of them from overseas, especially Eastern Europe and Latin America. That CB also staffs a Geneva office is another clue as to the identity of its clients. 'I hadn't appreciated the range of work they did before I started,' said one trainee. Common tasks include drafting wills and deeds of trust, and dealing with grants of probate. Those loaded clients pop up again in the family seat, this time usually in the context of divorce cases. The department's reputation can perhaps be measured by the fact that much its work comes from personal referrals. As you read this there's probably a couple of oil barons lounging on a yacht somewhere, with one saying to the other, 'Hey, you know who I go to for all my pre-nups…'

The property team acts for house builders, retail sector tenants and investors, and from what trainees tell us the shrinking availability of mortgages has impacted on the team's workload. Nevertheless, they did see property as a 'useful' seat, as they can get 'early responsibility' and 'a good range of work.' Not everyone takes to this type of practice though; some people find it 'quite dry' with too many 'tick-box exercises,' searching through files and chasing banks about mortgage applications. And then there's the coco seat where tasks include 'helping out with corporate transactions, private acquisitions and copyright issues on websites. There's a lot of document management and e-mailing clients' as well as 'a fair share' of pagination chores and putting together files of documents. In truth every seat has an element of this, especially if there's a big deal or case on. Among the corporate clients are Bovis Homes, Hertz, Lion Capital, Middlesex University, Miss Sixty, Sagatiba (the trendy cachaça people) and a whole bunch of Spanish, Portuguese and Brazilian banks, courtesy of a partner with Latin American connections.

Chambers UK rankings

Family/Matrimonial · Private Client · Real Estate Litigation · Sports Law

Yeah but, no but

CB is loaded with partners – 32 partners to 28 solicitors at the last count, and that top-heavy structure means most work for trainees is likely to come from a partner. 'Because you get used to receiving work from them you don't get that intimidated,' said one source, though another claimed: 'If you're not sure you what you're doing it's difficult because you don't want to be bothering them.' As in so many firms 'you always get some partners who dump work on trainees,' but it's never too much to cope with. 'I don't feel like I'm drowning,' one trainee reassured us.

Partners may get their own office while solicitors and trainees share, but they aren't aloof. 'There are a couple of people who are very willing to teach me, not just answer queries when asked, but actually teach,' one source said of the private client team. All our sources admired Clive Woolf, recently given an OBE and now in semi-retirement, but who is still 'very eager' to offer trainees a taste of his work. Because this involves pro bono advice to death row prisoners in Trinidad and Tobago, over the years several trainees have had the privilege of attending Privy Council hearings.

There were some criticisms of the appraisal system. 'We were told appraisals were going to be quite formal,' and in theory they're supposed to take place every three months, however 'by the time my appraisal got done, my seat was over. My supervisor was like, 'Yeah, you were fine.' I suppose it was nice to know I wasn't terrible, but it wasn't very constructive.' Some departments, such as dispute resolution, are better than others at giving feedback. On the plus side, all trainees have a personal mentor who takes them for lunch and is open to questions and moans.

In the nick

In keeping with its slightly offbeat atmosphere, CB likes to hire slightly offbeat people. Academic qualifications are important, of course, but 'HR told me that they look for somebody a bit different,' confided one trainee. Frustratingly no one was willing to be more specific, though we did note the current trainee group includes a former Swiss banker, an ex-TV producer, someone who appeared on *They Think It's All Over* in the Feel the Sportsman round and an avid street hip-hop dancer. Why not brush up on those alligator-wrestling skills you've let slip?

Despite talk of a clique among some of the younger crowd, most people agree that CB is a friendly firm with an inclusive social scene. Friday nights are spent in The Old Nick, which is according to one source 'a bit of an old man's pub – don't say I said that, they'll be so offended.' In the spirit of research, we popped along one lunchtime and can report that while said boozer is certainly from the traditional mould, the clientele was of all ages and the food smelled appetising. Careers advice *and* pub reviews – you don't get that in *Lex 100*. At end-of-month drinks partners take it in turns to put a credit card behind the bar and a social committee organises quizzes, bowling and one-off events such as a trip to see the Terracotta Army at the British Museum. Summer and Christmas parties (at The Clink prison with 'busty medieval serving wenches' last year) are well attended. Finally, there's the CB art gallery housed in the firm's Georgian Bedford Row office. Every Christmas trainees man the sales desk as artwork is sold for charity.

The work-life balance is good and 'they don't expect you to work stupid hours just for the sake of it,' so 9.30am to 5.30pm is not unusual. While this is reflected in a lower salary than top London firms, trainees were pleased to report that recent grumbles about pay were addressed in the last salary review. All three trainees took up positions in 2008, going into IP, employment and private client.

And finally...

Collyer Bristow needs a replacement partner in sports law if it's to maintain its position there. However, in the wake of the credit crunch, it has taken the brave decision to litigate against banks, which indicates this refreshingly quirky outfit still has its eye on the ball.

Covington & Burling

The facts

Locations: London

Number of UK partners/solicitors: 13/26 + 3 US-qualified

Total Number of Trainees: 8

Seats: 4x6 months

Alternative seats: Secondments

Extras: Pro bono – eg FRU, ProHelp; language training

Chambers UK ranks Covington among the very top London firms for life sciences and product liability instructions, and it is placed highly nationally for data protection advice.

'People have either heard of Covington and are impressed by it or don't know what the hell it is,' said one of our interviewees at the small London office of this pre-eminent American firm. We thought it was about time we introduced it to our readers...

See you later, regulator

Covington & Burling was founded in Washington, DC in 1919, and swiftly got itself noticed by the Kingdom of Norway, which it represented opposite the United States in an arbitration in The Hague. Despite this seemingly unpatriotic move, the firm's soul has always stayed close to the seat of US government: Covington's real rise to prominence came out of the demand for regulatory advice following the waves of New Deal legislation in the 1930s and one of its first associates became Secretary of State. The firm is proud of its distinguished history, and the narrative on its website is full of endearing tales. Mixing an esteemed patrician background with sometimes iconoclastic politics is something at which Covington excels.

The year 2008 was the 20th anniversary of the firm's arrival in London, and its office on the Strand is now home to more than 40 lawyers. *Chambers UK* ranks it among the very top London firms for life sciences and product liability instructions, and it is placed highly nationally for data protection advice. While regulatory work is still big business, Covington is looking to improve in other areas like litigation and corporate, and has lured a corporate partner away from Herbert Smith. Elsewhere in the world, the firm has just launched its first Asian office in Beijing.

It's a wonderful life

Covington's regulatory-based practice and its life sciences and product liability groups set it apart from the majority. As one recruit reminded us: 'Only a few firms in Europe – let alone London – do this kind of work.' The client list is the envy of firms many times its size – Merck, AstraZeneca, GlaxoSmithKline, Procter & Gamble, Genzyme, GE Healthcare and Pfizer all come calling. Much of the work is highly sensitive, so our sources couldn't tell us anything too specific, but they were only too happy to elaborate on what goes on in the practice. 'We advise on everything to do with food and drugs: labelling, promotion, safety issues, adverse event reporting.' Covington has also represented clients in defending risk-shared schemes with the government, prised retractions from tabloids for inaccuracies about a product and applied for judicial reviews concerning approvals for drugs to enter the market. 'You will do everything,' pledged a typically fervent recruit, who described their workload as 'womb-to-tomb stuff,' meaning that they followed matters from inception, through researching the relevant points and preparing memos for partners or clients on how best to proceed.

Although life sciences and IP/IT both have a regulatory focus, the two groups are 'very different.' The IP team's patents practice represents companies in the communications and electronic arts field and gets a good look at 'growing technology in its infancy.' One such development is 3DTV, so the first time you watch international football being played on your kitchen table, you'll know who to thank! Covington is well known for its IP policy advisory practice, in which it guides key clients like Microsoft and the Business Software Alliance (BSA) through the ever-growing maze of EU initiatives. Trainees find it 'intellectually stimulating' being asked to look at 'interpretations of the law – clients are always interested to discuss your view on something. They'll always have one too, so it's much more collaborative and you feel you're working with a client to get to a compliant position under the law.'

The data protection team, under the stewardship of the 'fascinating' and 'extremely articulate' lawyer Dan Cooper, advises clients like the World Anti-Doping Agency on global privacy, data security rules and transborder data flow. Last year Covington helped Privacy International file an amicus brief in a high-profile case concerning the retention of fingerprints and DNA samples of unconvicted persons, the ultimate outcome of which is expected to shape UK policy. Trainees have excellent prospects for client contact, advising them on the ramifications of new directives and offering risk evaluation of non-compliance. Meanwhile, a secondment to a pharmaceutical company gives trainees a broad mix of commercial experiences.

Fits like a glove-ington

The firm's commitment to broadening its practice is shown in the requirement that trainees do seats in corporate and litigation. Life sciences is understandably a sought-after option, but with such a small trainee group, 'to an extent you're free to do what you want' for the remaining two seats.

Bolstered last year by the arrival of a partner from Freshfields, the litigation team handles contractual disputes, occupational health claims and copyright litigation among other things for clients like Merck, Chiron/Novartis, Harley Davidson, British American Tobacco, Goodyear, Bacardi and ExxonMobil. Trainees told us: 'The scope of work here is amazing.' They loved 'responding to letters, discussing strategy with the partner and being given scope to make your mark.' Our sources had been given their own projects to handle and made trips to court to sit in on hearings, file orders and appear before masters. Just be aware: 'It's a small team and you're quite exposed, so if you're not comfortable with the work it shows quite quickly.'

Employment sometimes requires that 'you tread carefully,' especially if 'you have an individual on the phone trying to save his livelihood.' Because the law changes so frequently, it's 'one of those areas where it helps if you go to

employment tribunals, go to external training, read journals and do everything you can to understand the field.'

Trainees generally delegate more mundane tasks to paralegals or secretaries: 'You don't do any photocopying here, we're too busy finding the answers to deal with some of the more administrative functions.' Supervisors act like gatekeepers to monitor the flow of work, but ultimately 'it all boils down to how much responsibility you want.' Trainees can pursue areas that interest them, and all our interviewees felt their input was truly valued. 'You get the feeling,' elaborated one, 'when you're asked to do some research, you have to come up with a view. You will be asked to defend it, but more often than not, that's the view that goes out to the client.'

Each department has an internal training programme offering 'a great primer' on that area of law using lectures, seminars and teleconferences with the DC office. Recruits can choose the courses they want on the PSC, which is a good example of the flexibility of a firm where 'you can plan your contract around what you're interested in.' The training scheme structure is 'pretty fluid,' and Covington is 'happy to listen to concerns.' One of the only regrets we heard was that there's no formal programme of overseas seats. Qualification is a typically uncomplicated process and so far the retention rates have been perfect. All four of the 2008 qualifiers stayed on in their first-choice departments.

Knowledge is power

Covington strikes us as a measured but industrious and intellectual place, where people genuinely appreciate the value to clients of the things they work on. A great deal of attention is paid to the quality of writing, and our interviewees had a tendency to rhapsodise about 'eloquent' drafts or their supervisor's latest memorandum being 'in a league of its own in the thoroughness, perspicacity and experience it contained.' Does this mean flashbacks of school days as you get handed back a draft covered in red ink? It happens sometimes, sources say, but they remain sanguine: 'We're in a profession where our product is what we produce on paper. I'd much rather write something that reads well than knock out three papers in a day that don't.'

When you apply for a contract, interviewers 'spend the whole day with you and take you out to lunch. They don't try to throw you off with questions to see if you're quick-witted but try to go a bit deeper.' It's difficult to say who fits the profile of the ideal Covington candidate. There are a few from Oxbridge and London universities, but the firm's recruiting arm extends beyond those places. A significant number of people at the firm are from 'scientific backgrounds,' although we're assured this isn't a prerequisite. Choosing Covington, our sources say, is 'all about choosing a firm that's not going to zap you and take away your life.' By and large, working hours are reasonable, though 'you're sometimes here until 10pm with your partner or boyfriend ranting at home.' Trainees say: 'As long as you're producing good-quality work and meeting deadlines they're happy for you to come and go almost as you please.'

While it doesn't quite match the steroidal pay packets of some US firms, Covington offers £80,000 to new qualifiers, which is significantly higher than the magic circle. The firm is committed to pro bono work and in this respect there are some genuinely exciting opportunities for recruits to suggest and get involved with important causes. Recently it has begun helping the Sikh Coalition in its fight against America's policy of screening all men wearing turbans arriving at airports. Another pretty cool example was the new qualifier who went to Beijing to assist the International Paralympic Committee with its anti-doping efforts.

Saints alive!

Our interviewees pointed out that Covington's focus on writing quality is a peculiarly US import ('The Americans have been to law school longer than we have and they get taught very particular ways of writing'), so we wondered which side of the Pond the firm's culture best reflects. There are certainly 'a lot of American voices' in the office; however the office is increasingly sourcing work from out-side the USA and none of our sources felt like they were working in a satellite of DC. This balanced character is revealed in the social life of the office. There's a Thanksgiving lunch ('I was pretty ignorant about it – my knowledge of it came from *The Fresh Prince of Bel Air* – but they went through all the history so we knew what we were celebrating') and a Fourth of July celebration. But lately, to address the fact 'the Americans have so many more holidays than we do,' the firm 'seems to be getting into the pattern of celebrating saints' days – St Patrick's, a Burns Night for St Andrew's day, and this year we had a St George's Day event with Morris dancing.' Really? That stuff with the sticks and pig's bladder? 'We're an eccentric bunch... we like the weird and wonderful.'

Other events include the annual Christmas party, an 'absolutely fantastic' five-day trip to DC for second-years to meet the rest of the firm, a retreat in Geneva and a monthly drinks trolley. Involvement in inter-firm softball is 'more about fun than competition.' Less gung-ho perhaps than some of their opponents across the pitcher's mound, Covington trainees are never anything but 'comfortable with who we are.'

And finally...

One source described their early impressions of Covington as both John Grisham-esque and Ally McBeal-esque, so clearly the firm defies easy pigeonholing. While it sounds a fantastic fit for academic law types, plans to widen the scope of practice may also appeal to keen transactionalists.

Cripps Harries Hall

The facts

Location: Tunbridge Wells, London

Number of UK partners/solicitors: 40/54

Total number of trainees: 15

Seats: Commonly six of varying length

Alternative seats: None

Our sources all rated Cripps' location as one of its best features and none complained about working too many late nights.

Spa town Royal Tunbridge Wells is a genteel place. Its Georgian architecture and proximity to the countryside reek of refinement, and for many years – around 156 at the last count – local firm Cripps Harries Hall has been perceived as belonging to a similar oeuvre. No longer, according to Cripps' trainees. There's 'no sense of it being quaint,' they said; 'maybe it used to be, but certainly not any more.' Do they protest too much? Let's see.

Births, mariachis and deaths

For many years the firm's private client practice was a cornerstone of its identity. It's still one of the things that 'leaps into people's minds' when they think of Cripps. 'Private clients are still incredibly important and we have a very big department,' one source reassured us. Indeed, 'wherever there are good fees coming in, the firm is going to keep those departments.' Evidencing its ongoing commitment to private clients, Cripps hired the former managing partner of a top-20 accountancy practice to run the division. The clients are wealthy individuals, including – as the firm puts it – 'ultra-high net worth individuals and household names, both UK and non-UK domiciled.' Last year's biggest matters were the restructuring of a £20m trust and the variation of a £14m estate with assets on the Isle of Man and involvement with the Court of Protection. One tax planning case for the owner of a £100m company involved a Monaco-based trust.

The other half of the story concerns Cripps' commercial successes, of which there are many. The weighty real estate department has plenty to brag about. It attracts clients such as Fix-UK, the largest owner of trade parks and centres in the UK, the UK government (its panel lists just six preferred firms for property matters), British Land,

Wagamama and PricewaterhouseCoopers. Indicating just how significant the housebuilding sector has been to the firm, it recruited two new lawyers from in-house roles at Bovis and Redrow Homes. A fruitful relationship with City law firm Lovells and its major client Prudential Property Investment Managers (PruPIM) has also been incredibly important over the past four years. Through the Mexican Wave scheme, PruPIM's lower-value work is subcontracted by Lovells to a small handful of trusted regional firms. The arrangement has done wonders for Cripps' reputation. As have the UK government's many instructions, one of which was to help the Department for Culture, Media and Sport dispose of a large city-centre site to be used as a £90m commercial development.

Vive la France et up le duff

The corporate team has a good grip on regional business and even wins instructions from France, probably because it had the foresight to find itself a dual-qualified French-English partner. Clients include leading French food company Groupe le Duff, Air Atlanta Icelandic and EDF Energy (South East) plc. In 2007 the lawyers completed over 50 transactions with a combined value in excess of £175m. Examples include advice to a private equity house on funding arrangements for a £120m waste to energy plant, the sale of The Spa Hotel in Tunbridge Wells and the purchase of a number of specialist magazine titles for Kelsey Publishing.

Trainees do five seats, sometimes six if they exit the last seat early to return to the department into which they will qualify. The full two years' seat allocations are decided before the contract begins, which isn't necessarily as limiting as it sounds as the firm is flexible to the extent that 'if you feel you don't get enough of a bat at one seat and the department is able to help you out they will try to.' Time in the real estate division is almost certainly going to be on the cards. 'You might be able to avoid it,' said one source, but given its prominence 'it'd be a bit weird that you came to Cripps.' Indeed, 'there's a fairly, majorly strong chance you're going to end up with a couple of property seats.' Those seats include real estate, farms and estates, development, and property dispute resolution, which is 'something they give to second-year trainees, as they like people to have done a real estate seat beforehand.'

The other seat options are construction, commercial dispute resolution, corporate, employment, family and private client. The experiences vary by department. For example, commercial dispute resolution requires 'lots of bundling' but 'you do get to see a full range of litigation.' While one trainee 'really loved it,' another pointed out that as it covered 'big cases that had been going for years' there was 'less chance to get involved at a practical level.' Real estate, conversely, involves 'more substantive work,' as does corporate. Employment allows 'a lot more client contact' than most, with both employers and employees calling upon the lawyers' services. Family is 'quite popular but notoriously hard work.'

Wanting to have your cake and eat it

Above all, trainees stressed the 'transferable skills' they had gained. 'As I've moved through my training contract I've been able to build up skill sets,' said one. 'Supervisors make a real effort to try to expose you to the work you need to be doing to learn.' Cripps, we heard, is 'a pretty great place to grow as a lawyer.' In theory, appraisals should take place 'around once a month during a seat and at the end,' though how often they are completed in practice varies by department. Real estate was singled out as giving 'really good feedback,' while other departments operate 'more on an ad hoc basis.' Appraisals are generally constructive and 'there's not too much focus on the level of billable hours you're recording.'

Cripps recruits find it easy enough to interact with partners. 'Beyond the fact that you would save your dumb questions for more junior members of staff,' said one, 'I have never found myself thinking I had to communicate differently with the partners.' Yet there are still some areas in which 'a higher level of consultation would be good.'

Chambers UK rankings

Agriculture & Rural Affairs • Charities • Construction • Corporate Finance • Debt Recovery • Dispute Resolution • Employment • Family/Matrimonial • Intellectual Property • Licensing • Local Government • Partnership • Planning • Private Client • Real Estate • Real Estate Litigation • Social Housing

One of the perennial problems is the salary. 'It is the worst thing about working here,' a typical source said without any hesitation. 'If they want a reputation as a serious firm then they need to pay their trainees accordingly.' For one interviewee 'opening up the first wage packet' was the low point of their time at the firm. To make matters worse, Royal Tunbridge Wells has 'high living costs.' People do have a sense of perspective on the matter. 'I appreciate we're not in London,' one said. For its part, the firm is not oblivious to all this and does regularly review the salary issue. Working outside of London might hit the pocket, but the trade-off is the hours and the lifestyle. Our sources all rated Cripps' location as one of its best features and none complained about working too many late nights.

Those who have attended Cripps' Ten Year Vision talks report that it is 'trying to encourage Tunbridge Wells as an alternative to London' and 'bring bigger clients out this way.' Trainees tell us the firm is 'aiming towards more and more corporate clients,' 'big projects with government departments' and generally 'modernising and trying to attract more London companies.' So what is the firm's big selling point? Simple: 'offering the same quality of work for a lot less money.' Everyone's doing their bit for the campaign, not least the partners and associates who have written a raft of articles for legal and other publications, ensuring Cripps a bit of publicity in the process. The Ten Year Vision talks seem to encourage transparency within the firm and trainees say they are 'encouraged to have some input.' Right now there's talk of 'looking for a big site for the firm to be in' rather than the smaller offices it currently occupies. So long as this wouldn't involve a move from Tunbridge Wells or to 'a faceless modern building,' our sources were all for the idea. Everyone seems keen for Cripps to 'keep its badge of identity.'

Well-adjusted of Tunbridge Wells

Netball, football, rugby, dragon boat racing and bowling are all on offer after work. A cricket team is mustered each summer, 'which is brilliant, though the standard is appalling.' We also heard that 'a lot of people ride,' a rumour about someone pulling together a polo team and that 'quite a few people enjoy country pursuits.' Equestrian passions are by no means universal. 'The very concept of me riding a horse is a bad idea,' one source confessed. To those recruits who secretly yearn for a bit of alpine recreation, Kent may lack mountains, but does have the distinction of having the first curling rink in England. When two departments held a curling night there last year it went down a storm.

On the nights when they're not breaking the cleaner's brooms out of a cupboard and sneaking off to the ice, old favourite Sankey's wine bar 'still continues to draw the regular crowd,' with Davinchi's/Beluga reserved for 'the more debauched evenings.' Now if you're beginning to think Tunbridge Wells sounds like a kicking kinda place, sadly we must disappoint. 'It's not the most happening town in the world,' one source confessed. Cripps does at least make an effort with its office jollies. Each department has its own Christmas party and the second-year trainees happily organise other nights out, including a summer ball, wine tastings and a Burns Night supper.

Charity endeavours are encouraged and all staff are allowed to spend one paid day on such activities. In 2007 trainees helped a local charity set up its Christmas decorations and raised money for Kent Air Ambulance. None of this is surprising – the typical trainee is 'enthusiastic and confident' and 'willing to muck in.' In 2008 all seven qualifiers elected to accept permanent jobs, allowing the firm to keep its excellent retention record.

And finally...

Cripps Harries Hall wants to be in Tunbridge Wells, not of it, but perhaps it should be more realistic. As one recruit put it: 'If they want to stay in Tunbridge Wells they have to accept that people are going to make judgements.' Among trainees that judgement is certainly a positive one.

Davies Arnold Cooper

The facts

Location: London, Manchester, St Albans

Number of UK partners/solicitors: 69/74

Total number of trainees: 17

Seats: 4x6 months

Alternative seats: None

Extras: Pro bono – RCJ CAB; language training

The firm is expanding again after its nip-and-tuck years and now has branches in Manchester, Madrid, Mexico City and St Albans.

Let us introduce you to Davies Arnold Cooper, a London mid-sizer that's all about real estate and dispute resolution. And cake.

It's been a while

It's been some years since DAC last featured in the True Picture. In 1999 the firm went through a radical reorganisation; staff numbers were slashed as whole departments were cut. DAC went from being an all-rounder type of outfit to one that concentrated on two key areas: insurance and property. The last time we checked in with them, back in 2002, morale among the trainees was pretty low as they'd signed up to a much broader training than what they were then offered. Back then we couldn't help but wonder what lay in store in the years ahead. Yet the firm never went away and, like Gandalf the White triumphantly returning to Middle-earth after his epic struggle with the Balrog, so DAC makes a welcome return to these pages.

The basics first. DAC is one of the smaller London mid-sizers in terms of numbers, with around 150 fee earners. It operates out of headquarters just off Fleet Street, with another insurance-focused office some three Tube stops away on Gracechurch Street. Insurance remains a core area, and DAC now markets itself as expert in dispute resolution and real estate. Anyone wishing to specialise in either of these areas would be well advised to give it a closer look. Among its property clients are Arab Investments, Barratt Homes, Bioregional Quintain, EDF Energy, Ericsson, Galliford Try and Persimmon. An excellent product liability department is ranked in the top tier by *Chambers UK*, and GlaxoSmithKline is just one of the big pharmaceutical companies represented by this team. DAC also scores highly in the field of construction law.

The firm is expanding again after its nip-and-tuck years and now has branches in Manchester, Madrid, Mexico City and St Albans – the latter recently acquired after a takeover of KSB Law in early 2008. This added 60 extra fee earners (including four trainees) at a stroke, and DAC sees the new St Albans office as a way to tap into some of the big construction companies in the South East. Despite the boost in staff, trainees say the firm remains 'top-heavy,' with almost as many partners as associates. 'In most other firms the work goes from partner to associate to trainee,' explained one contact. 'Here, it goes to the partner – and then if they're busy, it's me.'

Twelve seats are currently available to trainees, and in the four-seat system only real estate is compulsory. There are six different real estate seats, then there's commercial litigation, personal injury, employment, contentious construction, reinsurance and professional indemnity (RAPI) and property and construction insurance. This choice is set to increase along with trainee numbers from 2008, when the firm will take on ten new recruits. 'I don't know where we'll find the space,' mused a current trainee.

Pinnacle of success

The six real estate group seats are all different – they are residential, commercial, property finance, planning and litigation, corporate, and finally non-contentious construction. The residential lawyers work for house builders and developers, 'buying up brownfield sites and industrial land.' They've also been advising on the development of Brighton & Hove Albion FC's proposed 'community stadium' – a football ground with facilities for community education underneath the terraces. Again in Brighton, the One Planet Living scheme is a sustainable development project that will see affordable apartments powered by solar panels and wind turbines. The commercial team gets meaty instructions from across the country. Geordie readers will be familiar with The Gate leisure complex in Newcastle: DAC advised Land Securities on the £76.5m freehold sale of that property. Those from the North West may know about the planned redevelopment of Bolton's Market Hall Shopping Centre, and Londoners should be impressed that DAC is acting for Arab Investments on the development of The Pinnacle, the helter-skelter shaped skyscraper due to appear on the capital's skyline. Arab has also instructed the property litigation team on this project. In a noisy neighbour dispute writ large, insurance company Hiscox, whose offices are right next to The Pinnacle's Bishopsgate building site, complained that construction work was causing serious disruption to life in their own building and applied for an injunction to limit noise and vibration levels within working hours. Trainees involved in that case drafted witness statements and attended court hearings.

Though the nature of the work varies between each of the real estate seats, across the board trainees have plenty of responsibility while running their own files and assisting with bigger deals. Away from the Pinnacle case, property litigation trainees have been involved with landlord and tenant and right-of-way disputes, doing background research, drafting without-prejudice letters and attending planning inquiries, an important job since it can involve 'translating what's going on to the client.' Similarly, in the residential seat 'you get client contact every day. You are taken to meetings and go on site visits to absorb the experience.' Several trainees in the commercial real estate seat had good work to do on a multibillion-pound property portfolio of a major pensions fund: 'The partner is very good at delegation,' said one. Supervision across all seats is highly commended. Partners are as 'knowledgeable' as you would hope for, but tend to let trainees stand on their own two feet. 'They are always there for you, but they won't spoon-feed you too much. If you need help it's always best to have already done some research into your question.'

A finger in every PI

Commercial litigation trainees benefit from working in 'a close-knit, dynamic team' on 'fairly high-value, high-profile cases.' Examples include 'a very large and very complicated case concerning the fraudulent writing of construction bonds.' The team is also currently defending a financial institutions professional indemnity claim for Pritchard Stockbrokers. It's alleged that the defendant mishandled client funds in

Chambers UK rankings

Construction • Dispute Resolution • Health & Safety • Insurance • Life Sciences • Personal Injury • Planning • Product Liability • Professional Negligence • Real Estate • Transport • Travel

an account in Spain, so London lawyers are working closely with their colleagues in Madrid. There's a lot of good work to be had in this department if you know where to look. It's possible to get involved with the research for cases, draft letters and court documents, attend meetings with counsel and clients and, of course, go to trials. We heard of trainees compiling and reviewing documents with an expert to help him produce a report, and there are also opportunities for small bits of advocacy. On the downside, as a junior fee earner it's your job to do the bundling and pagination, and some sources felt 'a little bit like a glorified secretary' at times. Speaking of secretaries, trainees don't get their own, and cadging the use of one can prove problematic, as they can be 'quite territorial – they don't like working for just anyone.'

Interestingly, the PI team's work is split roughly 50/50 between claimant and defendant clients. 'It's like a different hat you put on,' said a contact explaining the mental process involved in switching between the two. 'I think it's very good to do both because you learn to recognise the flaws in your own arguments.' The claimant side ('the expanding area in this department') is dominated by catastrophic accidents: a five-year-old who suffered spinal injuries in a car crash bringing a claim against the driver, her mother; a 40-year-old badly injured by a bouncer as she was ejected from a nightclub; and a 17-year-old who broke her back falling through a rotten roof panel on a building site. Some defendant lawyers are embroiled in the litigation over the Buncefield oil depot explosion, representing Total. Others are defending a claim of illness caused by exposure to tetrachloroethylene (TCE), the symptoms of which are similar to those of alcoholism, from which the claimant suffers, so expert evidence from neurologists and psychiatrists is likely to prove crucial. Product research, drafting claim forms and letters to experts and the other side, and interviewing witnesses are all tasks that trainees can expect. Meanwhile, the product liability team represents GlaxoSmithKline in issues related to the MMR vaccine, and the National Blood Authority and various NHS trusts against claims alleging hepatitis B and hepatitis C were contracted from blood transfusions and organ transplants.

In case you were wondering about the corporate and employment teams, 'corporate is of a size that is capable of taking work of its own, but is mostly a support for property' and the employment lawyers also mainly serve the clients of the core departments. Those posted to the smaller insurance-only office at Gracechurch Street find they need to dress slightly smarter to match the City-style outlook of the office, although it is still said to be 'quite a jovial place where everyone mucks in.'

Taking the cake

DAC seems to have an affinity with applicants who've taken 'a slightly more tortuous route to law' and counts an ex-doctor and ex-City trader among its current intake. 'They don't just want stereotypical trainees,' we were told. 'You need to be able to think on your feet and take off on your own.' The firm is described as 'relaxed but quite dynamic' – don't forget it had the balls to undergo that big shake-up and take a chance on a substantial merger. At the same time, DAC has 'a fairly good sense of community – it's trying to build departments where people have good working relationships and departments don't jostle against each other.' Job prospects are rosy, with all seven qualifiers staying on in 2008. Anyone who turns down a job offer on qualification is asked to repay their law school funding.

Chi, a 'backstreet noodle bar' that does happy hour drinks, is a popular venue for trainees when they're ready to escape the pressures of the office. No foreign secondments are available as yet, but London staff are on close terms with their Madrid counterparts, and men's and women's football teams fly over to Spain to compete in an annual challenge match. You'll be unsurprised to learn that the Spanish won both games this year. No greater success was forthcoming in the Manches Cup sailing regatta off the South Coast. It's a popular event with law firms and DAC enters 'a serious boat and a not-so-serious boat,' though sadly neither sailed to victory. Still, 'fun was had,' and that's the main thing.

Maybe this lack of sporting prowess is due to staff eating habits. It's well known that lawyers have an unhealthy obsession with biscuits, but there is such a thing as over-doing it. We're told that on arrival in one department, along with the usual paperwork trainees are issued with a 'cake protocol.' Apparently, this is a list of criteria 'for when you are on cake duty. You know, what sort of cakes are acceptable to buy and what aren't.' Any excuse is used as an opportunity to whip out the Battenberg: at the time of our interviews trainees were munching it down to celebrate the Spanish victory in Euro 2008.

And finally...

Property, litigation and insurance are Davies Arnold Cooper's three pillars of strength. Unlike the people we spoke to in 2002, the trainees of today have no reason to be disappointed with what the firm can offer them. Anyone interested in one or more of its core areas should be in their element.

Dechert

The facts

Location: London

Number of UK partners/solicitors: 37/60 + 12 qualified elsewhere

Total number of trainees: 23

Seats: 6x4 months

Alternative seats: Overseas seats, secondments

Extras: Pro bono – North Kensington Law Centre, RCJ CAB, FRU, Justice, LawWorks; language training

> The first thing trainees do when starting at the firm is jet off to Philadelphia.

Today's Dechert is the product of a cross-Atlantic love affair. In 2000, after a respectable period of courtship, a mid-sized London firm merged with Philadelphia-based Dechert Price & Rhodes. Since then it's not all been plain sailing for the London office as priorities changed in the aftermath of the union, but it does looks like things are finally settling down.

Welcome to Americana

The London office's once-broad practice profile has shifted, and financial services and corporate work now dominate the agenda. What was a typically British business, with all its quirks and characters, has become a slicker operation with a sharper focus on the bottom line. On this point trainees told us: 'People hear that it's a US law firm and get scared that it's going to be all American. It is true that there are Americans here, and policy decisions do come from America, but I'd say this office is still very British.' Of course there are late nights 'but there isn't the billing-is-everything philosophy you hear about in American firms.' In fact, unlike some of their predecessors, the trainees of 2008 struggled to think of a negative side to the transatlanticism of Dechert London and certainly don't hark back to the way things were. 'It's offered everyone a lot more opportunities. There's a bigger knowledge base, more resources and the possibility of placements in other offices.' Having said that, firm-wide e-mails (cue American accent: 'To all attorneys, please welcome Brad to our Palo Alto office') don't add a lot to your day. One source admitted: 'I think the guys over there sometimes forget they actually have European offices.' For the record those Euro offices also include Brussels, Luxembourg, Munich and Paris. There are 11 offices in the USA, a new branch opened in Hong Kong in 2007 and another office is expected in Beijing.

Play to your strengths

Now that the firm's new priorities have had a chance to take root, the London office has a clear identity. Contributing some 26% of the UK turnover, the financial services department is at the core of the London business. This practice has made remarkable strides in its work for investment funds and sits comfortably at the top end of the rankings in our parent guide *Chambers UK*. For hedge fund work you can't do better than go here. Without doubt, it's complicated stuff. On the contentious side Dechert is particularly hot at advising on regulation and enforcement by the FSA, SEC and other bodies.

For those who start off in financial services, a little trepidation is understandable. 'Obviously that's an area you don't encounter in your studies, so I had absolutely no idea what I'd be doing,' confessed one trainee. 'But they didn't expect me to know it all, they give us all the training we needed.' The seat involves a lot of documentation as 'FS produces a large paper trail.' Rest assured that it's far from boring: 'You're exposed to a massively broad range of work and fantastic people; you feel like your input is valued.' The hours here depend on the work coming through the door. 'Clients tend to have strict deadlines, so it can be quiet until you get a call and suddenly you're in the office for a week straight.'

The other major focus – corporate and securities – can also give newbies the jitters. 'At law school people say, 'Oooh, you'll end up in corporate,' as if it's an awful threat.' Like several of the trainees we spoke to, you might be pleasantly surprised. 'I didn't expect to enjoy that seat but actually really did,' acknowledged one. 'The department is friendlier than you might expect and the work is interesting.' Trainees' days are filled with reviewing documents, drafting board minutes, verifying information and making calls. If there's a big deal on 'you get very involved. I was taken along to all the meetings and they let me loose on the client quite a bit.' Again, the hours do vary: if it's quiet, they can be 'pretty forgiving,' but if you join at a busy time you could be leaving after midnight and coming in early. 'There's a lot of excitement surrounding a big deadline, and because people are in late there's very much a team feeling – you bond over the long hours.' Among recent deals was a £200m joint venture between The Wellcome Trust and Quintain Estates to establish the iQ Property Partnership Fund, the sale of Web 2.0 company Last.FM to CBS Corporation for $280m and V&S Vin & Sprit's multibillion-euro privatisation by the Kingdom of Sweden.

Land of the FRE

The financial services and corporate departments host up to five trainees at a time, so it's more than likely all recruits will spend some time in one, if not both. There's still plenty of scope to see other areas – finance and real estate, IP, employment, tax and dispute resolution are all on the cards. By organising the training contract around a six-seat system the firm can allow people to try a bit of everything or rack up double or sometimes even triple seats in an intended qualification department.

Finance and real estate are bundled together into the FRE department and here there are seats in straight finance, straight real estate, or a bit of both. Since the merger the property team has tilted more towards finance instructions, but continues to enjoy a long list of prominent clients from Blackfriar Investments and The Crown Estate to Southend Football Club and Wagamama. Trainees unanimously declare property and planning seats to be 'much more relaxed and laid back than corporate and FS,' and for every person who find it 'lacks excitement' there's one who appreciates it for being 'the friendliest department in the firm.' Working on a large number of smallish files, trainees end up dipping in and out of a variety of matters. On the finance side of the department, they get stuck into property finance, securitisations, bank lending and acquisition finance. Dechert is doing really well in the increasingly influential area of Islamic finance, recently seeing off competition from the magic circle to advise on a $2bn Middle Eastern bond issuance. Unfortunately the firm had to implement a small redundancy programme in its Stateside FRE department in

February 2008. We noted no such moves in London; indeed, the UK team recruited an extra partner recently.

While Dechert is undoubtedly more focused on the finance and corporate side of things, we're assured that 'the smaller departments are still integral. If you're working on a fund launch you need tax advice; and if you're selling a company, there will always be employment issues.' A seat in employment offers 'some contentious work and quite a lot of research.' It proves popular with those who appreciate 'the human element' in the subject matter, but that's not the only plus. Trainees go along to tribunals and can end up taking on real responsibility. That's something perhaps lacking in the litigation seat, which 'inevitably involves a lot of donkey work. I've been copying, bundling and doing a lot of walking to court,' sighed one source. If you're into spontaneity then head for the IP team. 'You don't really know what you're going to be doing when you arrive in the morning.' As well as helping out on disputes, trade mark registrations and commercial contracts, a lot of time is spent researching quite random pieces of law – and we mean random. 'One day it's medical trials, the next it's looking up the legalities of pubs in Jersey, and the day after you're getting clued-up on Australian DVD regulations.'

Overall, trainees are highly satisfied with their experiences. 'Not once have I felt overwhelmed,' declared one. 'The supervisors are supportive and encouraging' and all agreed 'you get a lot of responsibility if you're willing to take it.' While there is inevitably the odd bit of mindless work ('I must admit I have done quite a bit of photocopying in the last few days'), 'a training contract here is remarkably light on that sort of thing on the whole.'

Philadelphia stories

The first thing trainees do when starting at the firm is jet off to Philadelphia to join all the other newbies for an orientation event. In addition to this being 'an important bonding session,' trainees are also reminded of 'just how major Dechert is in America. You kind of forget it's a huge international firm.' During the trip they sit around a table to work out what their first seats will be. 'I really like that we had input – other firms just throw trainees in, whereas we got to decide ourselves.' We imagined a spot of arm wrestling. 'Actually it's remarkably civilised and uncontroversial. You don't have to battle it out because with six seats rather than four there is that much more flexibility.' The six-seat system proves popular because 'you can take more of a risk, knowing that you'll only be in a department for four months.' If that doesn't seem long enough, the firm does its best to let you repeat a seat. Not that it tends to be a problem: 'The training is so good that you immediately get to grips with things... They don't keep you on the outside looking in.'

Socially, trainees often go out together on a Friday night. The firm is also pretty good at organising departmental shindigs, admittedly 'mostly alcohol-related,' but frankly that's the way of things in the City of London. In the financial services group trainees go round collecting funds from associates and partners to purchase drinks and snacks and then at 5.30pm sharp on Friday everybody downs tools. Depending on who you speak to it's either 'all about fostering departmental spirit' or 'a reward for busting your gut the rest of the week.' The corporate team has been known to go ice-skating and 'there was an empty space on the third floor where we set up a table tennis table.' The summer party has been the key annual event in recent years, in part because it has sometimes coincided with the arrival of US summer associates in the London office.

Trainees are adamant there is no Dechert type. Some recruits arrive straight from university, others after a career change. 'There isn't a massively high Oxbridge percentage, though everybody has done well at good universities.' The firm's relatively small size in London makes it suited to those who are happy to take on unfamiliar challenges in plain view of experienced lawyers. As a reward, the trainee salary matches those paid in the magic circle, and for those who qualify into the hothouse of the financial services department it can be even higher. In 2008, seven of the 12 qualifiers stayed with Dechert.

And finally...

Dechert's transformation in London over the past eight years has been major. At times, especially when the firm was shrinking, people questioned the wisdom of it all, but it looks as if the plan has paid off.

DentonWildeSapte…

Wherever we
are in the world,

we're down
to earth.

Graduate Opportunities

The world might not know your name. Yet. But we will.
All of us, from partner to trainee. Perhaps more
importantly, you'll know theirs, whatever their level.
That may not sound like a lot. But think about it.
It's symptomatic of our lack of hierarchy.

It's demonstrative of a culture built on trust. It's about
being in it together. And believe us, you won't find an
environment like that in every major City law firm –
whether that city is London, Moscow, Paris, or Dubai,
for example.

Denton Wilde Sapte

The facts

Location: London

Number of UK partners/solicitors: 135/255

Total number of trainees: 75

Seats: 4x6 months

Alternative seats: Overseas seats, secondments

Extras: Pro bono – Poplaw, Whitechapel Mission; language training

DWS recently became the first international law firm to have 100 lawyers in the Middle East.

Internationally minded Denton Wilde Sapte has proved itself to be hard-working and resilient and now looks like a great option for students of a similar disposition.

Powering up

It's fair to say Denton Wilde Sapte was in the wars not so long ago. There were casualties: 70 redundancies in 2003. There were strategic withdrawals: the closure of Asian offices the following year. And there were defections: 40 media and IP lawyers joined DLA Piper in the biggest ever team walkout. Though the firm lost some battles it didn't lose the war. The DWS generals have nursed the business back to health and opened up a new front in Africa. Very decent, if not spectacular, financial results were recorded in 2008, so is it really fair to keep banging on about problems of five years ago? 'It's like some embarrassing cousin in the family that you can't ignore,' suggested one source. 'It's sad because the firm is working really hard to get away from that, but the DLA defections won't be forgotten because it was such a big story.'

Enough of such gloomy talk. What you should know is that DWS has a good reputation in the four key industry groups around which operations are now centred – financial institutions; real estate and retail; energy, transport and infrastructure; and technology, media and telecommunications (TMT). Impressive deals are coming its way, such as Sainsbury's £1.2bn property joint venture with British Land and building company Newlands Enterprises' major hotel and residential development opposite the Houses of Parliament on the South Bank of the Thames. Cadbury Schweppes used the firm to buy Turkish sweet manufacturer Intergum, as did News Corporation when it acquired major Turkish television broadcaster Huzur Radyo TV. Back in the UK, Manchester City PLC sought advice on its prospective takeover by UK Sports Investments, just like Sir John Hall when he sold his £55m stake in Newcastle United. Among the DWS energy sector clients are British Energy, Centrica, EDFE/Thames Water, Gazprom, Shell Windpower, npower, Veolia and Total. Energy lawyers have been advising Fluor-Toshiba on its bid for the £17bn Sellafield nuclear decommissioning contract.

Undeterred by its setback in Asia, DWS kept its offices in Russia and the Middle East and has taken advantage of the relatively unexploited African market through a network of associated firms. It recently became the first international law firm to have 100 lawyers in the Middle East, where it works from Abu Dhabi, Cairo, Doha, Dubai, Dubai Internet City, Istanbul, Muscat, Amman, Riyadh and Kuwait – these last three being associate firms. It has more than 25 lawyers in Kazakhstan and Uzbekistan and is firmly established in Russia. In 2007 the London office worked on 26 corporate deals in emerging markets, a third of them in Africa. The firm's international credentials mark it out from many and arguably make it an attractive merger proposition. Said one source: 'It could happen. The partners have always said that the firm would never merge unless it was in a strong bargaining position, and I think our position is getting stronger all the time.' We've nothing concrete to reveal here, just in case you were wondering.

Flyboys

The firm operates a system of four six-month seats, with trainees expected to visit both the banking and real estate departments. This first department covers a wide array of teams and of these asset finance is the one that consistently earns rave reviews. 'I wouldn't say a bad word about my time there,' said one trainee. 'The people all work very hard, but they are very willing to help and encourage the trainee, more so than in any other department.' These lawyers work on shipping, film finance and credit card deals, although their main focus is aviation, acting for banks or airlines financing the purchase of aircraft. Trainees start by doing 'the normal stuff, Form 395s, preparing bibles and so on,' and then progress to more substantial tasks, becoming 'the initial point of contact for most queries with solicitors on the other side.' They are also entrusted to deliver planes. 'I flew to Europe to hand over an Airbus to the client,' said one source nonchalantly. 'It was just four stewardesses and me on board, so happy days!'

The corporate seat prompted mixed reactions from our interviewees. Some described it as 'run of the mill' with 'a lot of what you might politely call document management;' others enjoyed 'pretty good work – drafting documents, attending meetings and corresponding with clients.' We suspect the fairly even split between the two camps reflects the difference between working in a supporting role on a large deal and getting more input on smaller deals. 'I think [your enjoyment] depends how much you want to get involved,' concluded one source, who had put in long hours.

Financial services may be the most prestigious department, yet real estate is just as big and is also doing well. It's a 'baptism of fire' for first-seat trainees because they can be managing up to 50 files from day one. 'We handle matters from opening to closing,' said one contact, before talking about grants of licences, alterations to leases, client meetings and site visits. One of the department's many big retail clients is Sainsbury's, and lawyers recently advised the supermarket giant on its plans to relocate its head office to the massive King's Cross railway lands development. On the contentious side, they also successfully settled Sainsbury's claim against the landlord of its Bournemouth store after the structural failure of the car park in December 2005. Planning law is another of the team's strong suits. In this 'lively area of law' trainees can attend public inquiries and listen to architects explain their case for new buildings. The firm acted for the Commission for Architecture and the Built Environment during the Walkie Talkie Inquiry. The Walkie Talkie is the nickname for the new skyscraper to be built at 20 Fenchurch Street, which attracted opposition from locals concerned that views of St Paul's Cathedral would be ruined.

Chambers UK rankings

Administrative & Public Law • Asset Finance • Aviation • Banking & Finance • Banking Litigation • Capital Markets • Climate Change • Commodities • Competition/European Law • Construction • Corporate Finance • Data Protection • Employment • Environment • Information Technology • Intellectual Property • Local Government • Outsourcing • Pensions • Planning • Projects, Energy & Natural Resources • Public Procurement • Real Estate • Real Estate Finance • Real Estate Litigation • Restructuring/Insolvency • Retail • Shipping • Social Housing • Sports Law • Tax • Telecommunications • Transport

Training the gossip hounds

In recent times TMT has been a problematic area for some trainees. Many of them applied to the firm because of its media law reputation, only to be dismayed by the loss of so many lawyers to DLA. As a result TMT seats have been hugely oversubscribed: 'You have to market yourself and fight tooth and nail to get the seats you want,' said someone who'd missed out. This problem should become a thing of the past as new intakes have been recruited with different expectations of the firm. The TMT department is by no means down and out: 'It's not so much shrunk as refocused and I believe it's actually making more profit than before the walkout,' confirmed a source who'd worked there. IP is nominally a litigation seat, but in this team trainees encounter both contentious and non-contentious issues, including acting for publishers with gossip magazines: 'We get sent the proofs and make sure there's nothing libellous in them.' Design rights cases can be interesting, for example when they relate to the copying of clothing and other fashion goods. Among the team's clients are literary and talent agency Curtis Brown (which signed a groundbreaking co-agenting deal with US firm, International Creative Management), publishers Macmillan and Reed Elsevier, and satellite TV company Al Jazeera.

The TMT department's data protection team works for companies including Honda and Delta Air Lines, and there's also a large telecommunications practice thanks to the firm's Middle Eastern and African connections. For example, the lawyers have been advising on a $100m contract to deploy a new mobile phone network in Uganda, and on Zain's acquisition of Westel, the second national operator in Ghana. It is currently involved with the EASSy Project, one of the largest submarine cable projects in the world. The IT lawyers have some impressive clients, including Microsoft, Intel, Teletext, T-Mobile and Shell.

For their contentious seat trainees can also go into the main dispute resolution department or the employment team. And then there are the overseas seat options – Muscat, Abu Dhabi, Dubai and Moscow. Client secondments are also offered to the likes of Total, Goldman Sachs, Citi and Shell, and for one trainee who visited a bank, 'sitting on the trading floor advising 400 people' was a real highlight. 'There was no time to get things checked, I had to make judgement calls on queries. It's definitely made me a more independent worker.'

They aim to misbehave

Trainees describe DWS as a 'civilised and human' place to work, where 'people are good at saying thank you.' Said one source: 'At my interview I was asked how I would handle a stressed partner. So far I haven't come across one.' Another (who hadn't been offered a job on qualification) added: 'I haven't encountered any archaic, scheming old partners here.' Admittedly trainees find some departments more transparent than others – asset finance for example is good at this, real estate less so; however the managing partner gives a breakfast talk every fortnight to provide updates to staff. The firm's good-chap credentials are also boosted by its environmental working group, which has introduced recycling incentives. On the subject of NQ retention, qualifiers' prospects have improved steadily in the past four years to the point that 25 out of 31 people stayed with the firm in 2008.

After work, the pub of choice used to be The Puzzle, located right underneath the office on Fleet Place, but apparently 'they have put their prices up and now it's real-ly expensive.' Loyalty has been transferred to Firefly on Old Bailey, which does two-for-one cocktails during happy hour. As at so many law firms, 'trainees tend to bunch with trainees,' and one even admitted: 'We sometimes act a bit like schoolchildren.' Well-behaved if boisterous schoolchildren, rather than the sort you're scared to sit near on the bus. Another interviewee spoke of 'a team mentality within the group. We'll always help someone out across departments if they're getting snowed under.'

An active social committee organises all sorts of events from bowling and karaoke to a summer hog roast and a roller disco. For sports fans, the rugby team is particularly active, whereas the softball team is a little less competitive. 'There's nothing like standing in the outfield on a Monday night with a cold beer and missing a catch.' The annual firm quiz 'can get a bit raucous and there's always a bit of rough and tumble to get to the chilli con carne afterwards.' DWS also has an am dram society, but we're told that no trainees are currently involved with it, which we think is a shame, since overacting is an important part of becoming a successful litigator. We learnt that from watching *The Devil's Advocate*.

And finally...

A good range of seats, opportunities for travel, a friendly place of work and great clients, Denton Wilde Sapte will appeal to many who want to work in the City but not in the magic circle. Best chosen for its finance and real estate prowess, its sector specialities or its overseas network.

Dewey & LeBoeuf LLP

The facts

Location: London

Number of UK partners/solicitors: 49/130

Total number of trainees: 27

Seats: 4x6 months

Alternative seats: Overseas seats, secondments

Extras: Pro bono – Liberty Advice Line, FRU, East London Small Business Centre, The Medical Foundation, LawWorks; language training

> The firm intends to expand London to a sizeable 300 lawyers, all ready to mine the seam of UK-based instructions flowing from fast-growing economies like Russia, the Middle East and China.

In October 2007 two New York giants LeBoeuf, Lamb, Greene & MacRae and Dewey Ballantine came together to create a mighty 1,400-lawyer firm with offices in 14 countries and a combined revenue topping $1bn.

Continental drift

Was the union of these two firms inevitable? They were similar in their profitability and size; they had compatible practice strengths, minimally overlapping international networks and an appetite for substantial growth in New York and Europe via London. In fact Dewey had been looking for a partner for some time and earlier in 2007 had withdrawn from advanced talks with Orrick, Herrington & Sutcliffe. In some quarters then the perception was that expansion-minded LeBoeuf was the dominant party in the D&L deal, and the installation of LeBoeuf chairman Steve Davies at the helm didn't discourage such talk. Whatever the truth Dewey & LeBoeuf (pronounced 'LeBuff') has become an impressive organisation with significant capacity in NY, a formidable international network, turnover to match the biggest international players and ambitious plans for the future. Already a Dubai office has opened and the firm intends to expand London from a joint total of 200 lawyers to a sizeable 300, all ready to mine the seam of UK law-based instructions flowing from fast-growing economies like Russia, the Middle East, India and China. There have been casualties at D&L however – smaller offices in three US cities are set for closure as they do not feature in the new order.

We spoke with trainees just six months after the merger, still 'pretty early to assess the success of integration,' but 'as pre-merger matters close and combined teams start pitching for deals there's much more blurring of Dewey and LeBoeuf into Dewey & LeBoeuf, if you get my drift.' Fulfilling plans, London will require everyone – including trainees – to pull together. Said one: 'In the time I've been here entire new departments like environment, competition, tax, IP and employment have sprung up, and we've grown dramatically in size.' Another added: 'The merger provides great opportunities for us. Dewey used its London English-law M&A expertise to generate work in Italy, and now it's got our Paris office too; our Moscow office was wanting to develop a German desk and now it's got access to offices in Germany, Poland and Italy.'

Time will judge the success of this continental drift strategy, but working in 'the second-largest office after New York' and knowing that London is central to future plans gives trainees confidence that 'we're not just a satellite.' Strength and independence in London matters to trainees who 'don't feel too American because we're well established, and although we do work with the USA we generate a lot of our own instructions.' Consequently there were some strong opinions about a new management structure that sees London and New York without office managing partners, power devolving instead to multiple transatlantic department heads. 'It needs a UK lawyer on the ground to manage this office,' stressed one source, while another suggested: 'People think it should change or we might lose our way.' For its part, the firm is staking its money on cross-jurisdiction management as the way forward.

There will be oil, coal and LNG

LeBoeuf trainee life was always characterised by international work and that doesn't look like changing now that D&L has offices in Frankfurt, Warsaw, Rome, Paris, Brussels, Moscow, Almaty, Milan, Beijing, Hong Kong, Dubai, Riyadh and Johannesburg. Nor do the central tenets of an old scheme that was dominated by insurance and energy work and plenty of litigation experience. It's still the case that two categories of seat are available – corporate and litigation. Corporate choices include M&A, capital markets, energy, banking and finance, insurance regulatory, employment, tax, real estate and competition law. The litigation options are commercial/insurance litigation and international arbitration. Do bear in mind that 'things will probably change quite a bit by the time [current applicants] arrive. I mean the trainee population has gone up enormously even while I've been here.'

D&L's significant energy practice is active in Africa, Russia and China, and the London office works closely with its Moscow counterpart. 'Your days are very international and you're dealing with things from all over the place.' Lawyers recently acted for ArcelorMittal, the world's largest steel company, on the $720m purchase of three Russian coal mines, AES/South African Peaker Projects on a 760 MW power project being developed by AES and its Black Economic Empowerment (BEE) partners in KwaZulu-Natal province, the project consortium in the development of the $7bn Angola LNG project, and SOCAR on financing its $2.05bn acquisition joint purchase of Petkim Petrokimya, the Turkish state-owned petrochemical company. Geographical diversity coupled with the specialist aspects of energy law (particularly public law elements) make a trainee's life 'interesting to say the least.' Not just for purely legal reasons – 'because of the kind of regions we work in, say Russia, you've got to be aware of the political factors and that can be annoying to some people. You might have everything legally sound but you get stuck by not having the right contacts in the Kremlin.'

The combination of Dewey's M&A and fund formation experience with LeBoeuf's energy and insurance corporate/capital markets skills is bearing fruit, guaranteeing trainees 'a lot of responsibility and exposure to a little bit of everything.' Said one: 'I touched on domiciled funds in Bermuda, capital markets transactions, AIM and IPOs.' Many of the European M&A and private equity transactions are supported through the debt capital markets practice. Showing its muscle, in the last year the firm advised on the £467m listing of Russian port operator Novorossiysk Commercial Sea Port on the LSE, Russian Trading System stock exchange and MICEX stock exchange. It also acted in all three sovereign bond issues that took place in the MENA region (Lebanon, Morocco and Egypt), with a combined value exceeding $3bn.

Meanwhile, the synthesis of the two old firms' abilities was evident as new client Summa Capital, backed by a Russian oligarch, instructed on the establishment of a Cayman Islands fund with a Jersey manager and advisory companies in London and Moscow. Getting involved in 'transactions crossing London, Moscow and Azerbaijan' is undoubtedly exciting, but trainees also enjoy a few domestic matters, such as 'the AIM work where I was talking to the directors of the company, in and out of their offices.' Good responsibility necessitates long hours, 'especially towards the end of a transaction when you'd be in every night until the small hours.' At least the fact it is 'a pleasant team' to work with 'makes a big difference.'

Off-the-wall litigation

A stellar insurance clientele is a major reason why the D&L training contract can offer so much contentious experience, both international and domestic. Royal & SunAlliance, Aegis and Lloyd's syndicates are just a few of the big hitters that turn to the firm. Lawyers are currently acting for reinsurers Swiss Re and Global Re in a drug liability coverage dispute that is the subject of arbitration in Bermuda. As well as handling Hurricane Ivan and foot and mouth issues, they are also advising several insurers following the collapse of The Accident Group. Trainees certainly 'experience a lot of insurance and reinsurance litigation, but it's not all insurance.' In fact the breadth of cases on offer impressed our sources, who spoke of 'attending hearings to take notes' and performing detailed research 'which places a lot of responsibility on you – you get stuck into the law and there's reliance on what you find.' The international arbitration lawyers manage sensitive disputes across Africa and Russia, and have been up to their necks in a claim concerning one of Russia's largest oilfields. The general commercial litigators are no less active for the likes of Bank of Georgia, Shell, Investcom, ArcelorMittal, Russia Partners and Alfa Bank. Oh, and Michael Jackson, who has instructed them to defend a claim made by a member of the Saudi royal family concerning a recording and entertainment contract.

International deals and cases mean travel, whether it's a few weeks in Bermuda on a closing or a dash to Ukraine to collect papers. 'There are whole spates of e-mails that come round saying we need someone to go to x, anyone free? I was gutted when I missed going to Baku [the Azerbaijani capital], when else would you get to see it?' Longer stints overseas come via seats in Paris, Moscow and Dubai. 'Generally, they don't want people to go before they've done a corporate seat as both offices are corporate-focused and you have to hit the ground running.' Described as 'amazing, it really pushes your level,' one trainee returning to London from Moscow found that the close relationship between the two meant 'several matters followed me back.'

Dewbudding talent

People used to choose a LeBoeuf training because of the potential for 'visibility as a trainee.' The growth of the London operation and its ambitious plans post-merger mean the office is changing and the small annual intake will be more like 10-20 when current readers arrive. Of course that's still well below the hundreds of trainees recruited into the biggest firms in the City, but the training scheme is bound to evolve, for example: 'HR is now catching up with training provision and procedures to fit our size.' If a greater degree of institutionalisation is to be expected, hopefully this won't affect the nature of what has always been an exacting but rewarding training. A pleasingly titled mentor scheme assigns trainees a LeBuddy (sounds better than DewBuds), and although 'some supervisors are jealous of your time' trainees tend to work for 'a number of associates and partners,' which means they're exposed to several influences at the same time.

As their numbers have increased trainees have noticed how 'more seem to have come straight through from uni and law school, whereas in my year the shared characteristic was previous work experience.' Language skills – particularly French, Russian, Arabic or Chinese – will undoubtedly continue to be attractive to the firm. Possibly an influx of younger recruits will invigorate a trainee social scene that until now has reflected the fact that 'people have their own lives' and in some cases young families. A flurry of post-merger social events, including an Oktoberfest evening, has 'died down a bit,' but there are 'firm drinks at various venues every other month,' a few trainee-organised shindigs and an annual Christmas 'black-tie bash.' In addition there are 'any number of impromptu Friday drinks.'

In 2008 all seven qualifiers accepted permanent positions with the firm.

And finally...

Change is in the air at Dewey & LeBoeuf and there's never been a more exciting time to start here. London is now at the heart of the firm's plans, due to the aim to become a dominant transatlantic – as opposed to American – player.

Dickinson Dees

The facts

Location: Newcastle-upon-Tyne, Stockton-on-Tees, York

Number of UK partners/solicitors: 38/175

Total number of trainees: 38

Seats: 4x6 months

Alternative Seats: Brussels, secondments

Many a London practice casts covetous glances at the national work and clients coming the way of this heavyweight.

Northumbrian giant Dickinson Dees has it made in the North East. Its breadth of expertise sees it ranked in some 27 sections of the *Chambers UK* guide, many of these placing the firm in the top tier.

From A to T

Dickinson Dees' name and reputation not only carries clout in the North East but also across the UK. Many a London practice casts covetous glances at the national work and clients coming the way of this heavyweight, as it simultaneously maintains a full commitment to its region. Just a few of the companies convinced by its 'regional fees and City-standard advice' formula include English Partnerships, US chemical group Huntsman, CostCutter supermarkets, shipping line Maersk, the Universities of Durham, Northumbria and Teesside, Nike, and a gazillion local authorities, NHS bodies and hospitals. The firm powers ahead in the transport sector; when GoVia entered into its £1.1bn West Midlands Rail Franchise acquisition, it naturally took advice from Dickinson Dees, following in the footsteps of Arriva, Southern Railway, London Central Bus Company, London General Transport Service, Manchester Airport Group and The Go-Ahead Group.

Matching its commercial prowess is Dickie Dees' stellar private client practice: 'It's the largest of any law firm in the North, so it constitutes a sizeable chunk of our work.' The firm represents 'traditional agricultural clients and also entrepreneurs, people who have worked hard for what they now have and appreciate a frank discussion,' offering trainees exposure to an array of great-quality work.

Whether private or commercial, most of the action is in Newcastle, where the majority of the firm's 900-plus staff is based. Two smaller offices in Tees Valley and York now recruit their own trainees so inter-office postings are no more. Rotation demands three of four seats within the coco, litigation and property groupings, with the fourth in private client or back in one of the three commercial divisions. 'Mainly they try to put you where you want to go;' but each office has its specifics. Newcastle offers the full alphabet of seats: agriculture and rural affairs, banking and finance, charities, competition law, construction, corporate finance, education, employment, energy, family, financial services, IT, IP, insolvency, licensing, litigation, local government, pensions, planning, private client, property, social housing, tax and transport. In York the options are presently property, commercial litigation and corporate, while the Tees Valley office also offers family and employment. With York in particular singled out for growth, the range of options will increase as the employment, banking and private client teams expand. All trainees can be considered for a secondment to a client (including Huntsman's office in Basel, Switzerland) or a six-week placement at a Brussels law firm.

Ain't nothing like a hound dog

In all three locations, rooms are shared either 'with your supervisor' or 'a solicitor with four or five years' experience.' A trainee's work is 'never just for the supervisor' and, despite the odd late night, the average day is 9am to 6.30pm. 'There was only one time when I was in until 4am,' a source told us, another adding: 'They want you to work your hardest but not kill yourself.' In return, trainees enjoy rewarding experiences: 'I've never been the photo-copy hound. I've always been given meaningful and con-structive work.'

Corporate seats expose trainees to various types of deals, including management buyouts, share sales and asset sales, not infrequently with a big City player on the other side. 'When you tell people that you work for Dickinson Dees, they do raise their eyebrows,' reported one happy interviewee. Newcastle's corporate clients range from 'the man who has set up a small company, through to AIM-listed companies and a few FTSE-listed ones.' As well as those big transport sector names we mentioned earlier, there's Reg Vardy plc, Northumbrian Water Group plc, Daily Mail Group and holiday company Parkdean Group. In York, 'the head of the office is very established in the area... he knows everyone,' and corporate work continues to be as important as it was to Philip Ashworth & Co before it became a part of Dickie Dees in early 2007. 'Cross-office working' and 'daily contact' mean Yorkies feel a part of the larger firm. Naturally, the change of ownership has meant 'new expectations to be met,' but 'I've never been too pressured,' one trainee assured us.

Back in Newcastle, in banking 'we have our own distinct deals but also an ancillary role working with property and corporate.' Clients include the University of Northumbria, which the firm assisted in the negotiation of £96m worth of lending facilities to develop the new City Campus East. A trainee's time is split between registering documents at Companies House, project management on deals and sim-ple drafting. 'We have standard documents on the system that we tailor to each deal.' A commercial seat, mean-while, brings general contract advice, a spot of IP and finance contracts.

A load of bokloks

Have you ever wandered around IKEA testing out the Klippans and Jokkmokks, musing over what it must be like to live in an entirely IKEA world? The reality is here. Live Smart @ Home, the property company that has the exclusive licence to build IKEA's BoKlok properties in the UK, has been developing its first site at St James Village, Gateshead, and Dickie Dees has assisted on the scheme. Despite 70 residential conveyancing team redun-dancies, property is still a big department. It incorporates housing investment, investment property and social hous-ing and finance teams. The latter represents both local authorities and housing associations, tackling rather large projects. The investment property team also works on big developments and has a good relationship with regional

development agency, One Northeast. 'We do quite a lot of work for local authorities and public sector clients and are seen as a leading firm nationwide for them. That's per-haps why private sector clients have noticed us and our practice has developed.'

Litigation experience can be gained with one of five teams – commercial disputes, employment, property lit, construction ('my supervisor there was excellent and I can't praise him enough') and environment. Of their time with the commercial litigation team, one trainee told us: 'I have worked on small claims and on a multimillion-pound case, so the seat has been quite varied.' For some, the highlight is a solo trip to court to make an application.

In the successful PFI/projects team, attending meetings means 'you see what the different parties want out of negotiations.' Much of the time trainees help out with ancillary documents 'and run data rooms, making sure that all the relevant documents in a transaction are avail-able for examination.' Get your head around the acronyms and specialists terms and the projects seat could end up one of the most interesting. 'The work is quite relevant to day-to-day life and I really liked the people,' one source concluded. Recent projects have included the £600m Tyne and Wear Metro Reinvigoration and the refurbishment of 13 Gateshead and South Tyneside schools through a Building Schools for the Future scheme, an area in which Dickie Dees has excelled. Instructions now come in from funders as well as public bodies and include NHS LIFT, schools, fire, housing, hospitals and street lighting proj-ects. 'We're looking more at private sector instructions at the minute,' explained a clued-up source.

It's not Terry's, it's ours

In a city with some fairly young commercial firms Dickinson Dees is a grand old 200 years of age. It has also clung on to its traditional practices in the private client sphere and maybe this is why 'people seem to think we are stuffy.' Insiders disagree. 'It is definitely not true: people are quite down to earth here.' Whichever way you jump, it sounds as if a new broom is sweeping through the firm. 'Our new managing partner, Jonathan Blair, is an insolvency partner and a lot younger than his predecessor, who was a private client partner: I think he will be more progressive,' one trainee told us. The plans for the York office are clear: 'They want to have a big presence in Yorkshire and are hoping to expand rapidly in all practice areas.' Our sources also saw scope to grow the Tees Valley, which we heard described by trainees as 'a little power house of an office where you get loads of partner contact.' Some wondered if it is now time to permanently staff the London office, which is presently just a meeting facility.

The large Newcastle operation is run from the St Anne's office on the banks of the Tyne and the Trinity Gardens office close to Newcastle's law courts. Now nearly 40-people strong, the York branch has moved into the former Terry's chocolate factory next to the College of Law and the racecourse, where it will remain until even bigger – if less chocolatey – premises are ready.

Bob the fundraiser

The typical trainee attended a Russell Group university or one of the others in Yorkshire or the North East. They grew up in the North of England or became a committed Geordie while at university. As well as good academics, successful applicants tend to have an easy way of dealing with people. And why do these bright young things choose Dickinson Dees? 'It is by far the biggest and best in Newcastle' comes the reply; 'other firms around here are improving but they have a long way to catch up in terms of size and quality of work.'

Favoured Newcastle bars for Friday-night revelries are The Pitcher & Piano and The Waterline. 'Or if you want to stretch your legs then The Cluny, which has live music.' While it tends to be trainees and NQs together in the pub, the wider social scene also glitters. Staff and partners let their hair down at an annual dinner dance at St James' Park and 'there are always stories to tell afterwards.' Then there's the office pantomime, which raises money for charity. Speaking of which, we should give a shout out to BOB, the new 'face of the firm' in relation to all things worthy, and 'a corporate social responsibility drive that is gathering momentum.' When it comes to sports, the netball team is top of its division and the cricket, football and tennis players are active.

After all the positives, there were consistent moans about one thing – Newcastle sources thought their salaries ought to reflect the firm's status as the biggest and best-regarded in the North East. 'If you are going to advertise yourself as such then you should pay more than other firms,' we were told in no uncertain terms. In York the only downside is that despite the city being reputed to have 365 pubs, the office has no real evening scene. 'We have been out a few times, but there's not a regular thing on Fridays.' This should change as the office grows, and already a tradition of lunching in The Woodman in Bishopthorpe on Fridays is emerging. Traditionally almost all qualifiers stay with the firm; in 2008 12 of the 14 did so.

And finally...

To its admirers Dickinson Dees is 'the Rolls-Royce of law firms,' offering a breadth and sophistication of experience that make it an obvious choice for a North East training. And should the time ever come to fly the nest, DD on the CV is a quality hallmark that opens doors anywhere in the country.

BE LOCAL – GO GLOBA

At DLA Piper, becoming the leading global business law firm depends on our most important asset – our people. That's why we take so much care in recruiting and retaining the best.

We offer exceptional worldwide career opportunities in a collaborative environment that is challenging, rewarding and truly different from that of our competitors. In the legal services sector, DLA Piper really is a different kind of business.

DLA Piper offers around 100 training contracts a year across our eight UK offices and our trainees have the opportunity to apply for secondments to our offices in Abu Dhabi, Dubai, Hong Kong, Moscow, Singapore and Tokyo.

Our broad range of departments allow us to offer a diverse training contract, with our commitment to developing each trainee being paramount.

Approximately 200 summer scheme places are available each year allowing you to find out for yourself why we're different.

For more information visit: **www.dlapiper.com**

DLA Piper UK LLP

The facts

Location: Birmingham, Leeds, Liverpool, London, Manchester, Sheffield, Scotland

Number of UK partners/solicitors: 330/802

Total number of trainees: 188

Seats: 4x6 months

Alternative seats: Overseas seats, secondments

Extras: Pro bono – eg Central Library Legal Advice Centre (Birmingham), St Hilda's Legal Advice Centre (London), The Prince's Trust

> So long as you pick the right office, you can cut the cloth to suit. If you want to be domestic or local or international, you can make a good career.

'We're taking over the world,' say trainees at DLA Piper, the Anglo-American behemoth. Having amassed a globe-spanning network of 3,700 lawyers in 64 offices across 25 countries, the organisation clearly believes this is the DLAge.

Bigger is better

The DLA Piper colossus was formed in 2005 through the triple-whammy merger of US firms Piper Rudnick and Gray Cary Ware & Freidenrich and the UK's own DLA. None of the triumvirate were strangers to aggressive expansion, and they saw no reason to tinker with a working formula. Extra teams of lawyers joined in the CIS, Germany, Italy and the UK, and management has worked non-stop to plant the DLA flag all over the world, sometimes through allied firms. Many believe the task now is 'to consolidate and let the firm catch up with itself,' certainly in a slowing economy.

In the UK, some people take a pop at DLA Piper and its rapid progress. 'Maybe they see us as upstarts, barging our way in,' ventured one bemused recruit. We even heard a report of DLA trainees being booed as they collected prizes at a raffle held by a trainee solicitors' group. 'I don't think it was particularly malicious, just a case of 'Oh, it's DLA again.'' Where it counts, the firm is respected, and in some regions 'it's the biggest firm by a long way.' Besides, there's so much good work being done that jeers slide off trainees like water off a duck's back. Last year's highlights include a multibillion-pound project to provide the UK with search and rescue helicopters, a $5bn proposed acquisition of Lear Corporation in over 30 jurisdictions by American Real Estate Partners, and the defence of Electronic Data Systems against £700m of claims brought by BSkyB.

A king of the mid-market, DLA Piper is ranked top for corporate deals in this sector by *Chambers UK*. Applicants eyeing the firm outside London needn't miss out on the good stuff, as 'regional offices can offer the same standard of work' because often clients don't want to pay higher City rates. Birmingham's corporate team oversaw the £250m admission of Accident Exchange Group to the Official List, while in Liverpool real estate lawyers aided the construction of Liverpool FC's new stadium. New clients taken on by Leeds and Sheffield's property teams include Mothercare and the London Boroughs of Hackney and Tower Hamlets. As well as handling public-to-private buyouts such as that of Crest Nicholson for £1.1bn, Manchester and Liverpool finance lawyers last year oversaw the £100m buyout of British Salt by Lloyds TSB.

Piper view

With so much on offer, there's no uniform training experience, although the firm likes everyone to try either corporate or finance. The corporate team is particularly dominant in the Birmingham office. This varied seat offers 'everything from public corporate law right through to private M&A,' if often through 'quite menial' tasks like proof-reading and data room management. The trade-off for long hours ('once it was out at 4am and back in at 8am') is a 'collegial atmosphere.' The finance and projects division has several subsections. The property finance seat receives some criticism for showing 'a reluctance to pass work onto trainees' other than archiving documents and title deeds, however the leveraged finance team earns glowing praise for allowing trainees to liaise with clients and other lawyers on corporate refinancings and buyouts. This 'fast-paced' seat 'makes you really organised – you work under pressure and rely on your secretary as you haven't got time to do everything.' In short, it is 'probably one of the seats in which you feel most valued and part of the team.' Because everything in projects is 'very long-term,' that seat is usually 'either crazy or quiet.'

Real estate is the other big department, and it's especially important in the North. In a core real estate seat trainees do get 'dogsbody' Land Registry searches and photocopying, but most assured us they'd also been 'stretched' by lease negotiations and drafting. Property litigation trainees run small cases solo and experience client contact and court visits. Construction seats also fall under the real estate umbrella, and here the firm represents clients like Boeing, Virgin Atlantic, National Express and NatWest. Despite its Bob the Builder image, the team has a 'pretty relaxed' atmosphere with 'no macho hours.'

Depending on your supervisor, the technology, media and commercial seat will mean IT outsourcing, advising TV channels on their sports coverage or high-profile IP. When trainees see the IP team's presentations, 'their mouths drop open' – Honda, Sony, Random House, Harrods and easyJet are all on the roster. The perennially popular employment team is grouped with the pensions and benefits team, so 'unfortunately some people request employment and get stuck in pensions.' At least the good hours soften the blow. Meanwhile a stint with the fraud and asset-tracing specialists in commercial litigation is exciting and broad enough that 'you're not pigeonholed.'

It bears repeating that trainees' experiences vary hugely. Some have issues with seat allocation, others receive their first choice every time. Being proactive helps: 'People get a bit wily, and if they're interested in something they'll put their face about.' Levels of supervision vary: some trainees are closely managed, while others sit with partners 'notorious for really dropping you in it.' Our interviewees had usually been given decent responsibility, although a few complained that in quieter groups 'not a lot of work is passed down, as associates want to keep hold of something to bill.' Nor is there any definite policy on where trainees get their work. Some supervisors put recruits at the disposal of an entire team; others can be 'incredibly possessive.' Thankfully, while certain senior partners can be 'on their own wavelength and a bit removed from trainees,' most fee earners are extremely approachable.

Chambers UK rankings

Administrative & Public Law • Advertising & Marketing • Asset Finance • Aviation • Banking & Finance • Banking Litigation • Competition/European Law • Construction • Corporate Finance • Data Protection • Dispute Resolution • Education • Employment • Environment • Financial Services Regulation • Franchising • Fraud: Criminal & Civil • Health & Safety • Information Technology • Insurance • Intellectual Property • Investment Funds • Local Government • Media & Entertainment • Outsourcing • Parliamentary & Public Affairs • Pensions • Personal Injury • Planning • Private Equity • Product Liability • Professional Negligence • Projects, Energy & Natural Resources • Public Procurement • Real Estate • Real Estate Finance • Real Estate Litigation • Restructuring/Insolvency • Retail • Shipping • Sports Law • Tax • Telecommunications • Transport

Hot to globetrot

Essentially, trainees stay in their home office for two years. Those desperate to see another city can try for a client secondment (ICI, Carillion, Barclays, the LSE) and there are now postings to Hong Kong, Singapore, Dubai, Abu Dhabi, Moscow, and Tokyo. Interested parties must submit a business case and CV. Having waited so long to send trainees abroad, DLA Piper makes sure they have a good time. In Singapore there's a 28th-floor apartment and daily living allowance. In Moscow one source was given more M&A work than they could expect in a similar English seat and offered 'a stab at drafting – substantial stuff, not minor like in the UK.' Someone else raved that overseas seats were 'amazing from every perspective – work, social, travel – I can't recommend them highly enough.'

In a drive for firm-wide unity, DLA Piper is emphasising its international nature. A two-week induction brings together trainees from across the UK, Europe and Hong Kong, there are regular talks from partners about the international state of the firm and 'more and more e-mails from America about integrating the different arms.' Several trainees were pretty excited to qualify into overseas offices in 2008, six going to Dubai, one each to Abu Dhabi, Tokyo and Moscow. This represented a significant departure from the previously domestic-only NQ career path. The qualification procedure can feel 'cloak and dagger,' partly because 'throughout the contract everyone is friends and then you're all in a run-off together.' Some qualifiers found jobs in other UK offices this year and retention across offices turned out quite uneven; for example, everyone stayed on in Leeds but only five of the 12 stayed on in Manchester. Nationally, 64 out of 77 were retained.

Everything matters

In the past the unremitting positivity of trainees has led us to speculate that DLA Piper is 'cult-like,' not least because of the apparent reverence for charismatic CEO Nigel Knowles. Our interviewees laughed about 'Nigel Knowles worship,' which they claim is just a big in-joke. Still, it wasn't all in our fevered imagination. 'Slightly cheesy' mottos like 'Everything Matters' are 'splashed across our desktop wallpaper' and 'they confiscate your mouse mat if it says the firm's old name.' There's even a Facebook-style website for new and incoming trainees called Inside DLA Piper. Some trainees embrace the party line, believing 'it makes you feel part of something.' Others resent being 'forced under the banner.' Nevertheless, even the most cynical recruit understands why it's necessary if DLA Piper is to reach its (modest) goal of becoming the world's biggest law firm. After all, 'the top level does need all its employees singing from the same song sheet.' Since the firm altered the pay scales for associates there have been a few dissenting voices suggesting the firm is trying to economise by stepping away from automatic annual uplifts and standardised rates.

What we find interesting is that different offices still serve different kinds of client. London wants cross-border instructions from the likes of Kraft, GE Capital, Halliburton and Lockheed Martin. To a lesser extent the Yorkshire and Midlands offices are also seeking a greater international role. Birmingham's construction team advises clients in Saudi Arabia, while Leeds has strong ties to the Russian offices and has an associate exchange with St Petersburg. By contrast, the North West isn't quite on the international bandwagon, and – particularly in the case of Manchester – is focusing on local clients. 'I can't really say where we fit in the global scheme of things,' said a Manchester trainee, 'but we're able to offer local knowledge and expertise to businesses.' Reluctant to pass up any source of work, 'Everything Matters' really is the firm's ethos. The upshot is that within DLA Piper, so long as you pick the right office, 'you can cut the cloth to suit. If you want to be domestic or local or international, you can make a good career.'

Corrie and curry

In Birmingham socialising is at its warmest when the weather's coldest – there's a massive ski trip organised for January 2009, and the city's German market tempts trainees with glühwein and bratwurst. In Liverpool there are 'drinks and nibbles' every first Friday after payday and a social club with a nominal members' fee. Manchester's team spirit runs high, with a staggering 115 people joining in a local 10 km run for charity. Managing partner Simon Woolley puts on monthly free drinks at local Rain bar for the whole office. Another favourite venue is the Manchester Press Club, 'a dive where you show a business card to get in. You get Coronation Street stars and other C-listers in there – to be honest I think you can get in with a Blockbuster card.'

Sheffield trainees frequent Ha!Ha! and the Leadmill, while their Leeds counterparts regularly go to the 'suits bars' on Greek Street and Call Lane. For sporting prowess, London leads the field with football, netball, sponsored walks and runs, discounted gym membership and the Three Peaks Charity Challenge. Following the example of the Edinburgh office, which for years has invited trainees from across the UK to a traditional Burns Night supper, this year the Liverpool lot organised a trip to Aintree for the Grand National, and Birmingham brought people together for a curry night, albeit one with a chef and flowing champagne.

DLA recruits claim not to be workaholics, despite needing to pull long hours in some seats. They invariably have well-developed social skills and 'a 2:1 from a decent university.' As for differences between people in different locations, 'you could substitute somebody from Leeds with someone from Manchester and there wouldn't be a difference.' Most people have some relevant regional connection, probably because the firm wants people who will want to stay put and not try to sneak into London by the back door. Loyalty is important at DLA: to the firm, your region and your fellow trainees, who are, ultimately, 'your friends and allies more than they are your colleagues.'

And finally...

Graduate applications have risen by a massive 40% in the past two years and trainees say: 'The firm is attracting higher-quality candidates.' The vac scheme has become a crucial recruitment tool, so if you're serious about training here and you want an edge you'd be advised to apply for it.

DMH Stallard

The firm helped Anna Ryder-Richardson adjust to life after *I'm a Celebrity* by acquiring a zoo in Wales.

Another year, another merger. DMH Stallard's relentless expansion shows little sign of abating as the firm continues its assault on the London market. Where will it end?

Fish pie

DMH was hatched back in the 1970s, when three old Sussex firms merged to create Donne Mileham & Haddock. After 20 years by the seaside in Brighton, it developed an almighty hunger that just couldn't be satisfied by a diet of private client, property, litigation and fish 'n' chips. Keen for a bigger piece of the South East pie the firm headed north, its destination Crawley. Close to Gatwick airport, the new office in Crawley was conveniently located to service the growing number of technology and transportation companies in the area, and DMH (as it became known) acquired a taste for the commercial. Keen for more, its belly led it to the capital and a merger with Stallards Solicitors in 2005. Rumours started to circulate about another London tie-up, and in 2008 became a reality when the firm merged with small commercial outfit Courts & Co.

So what exactly has the firm achieved? The short answer is a top-100 firm with over 260 staff across three locations and turnover in excess of £20m. Yet beneath the surface bubbles an interesting debate about how the firm sees itself. Last year, trainees expressed the opinion that theirs was essentially still a regional firm with a presence in the City. Following the Courts & Co merger and a move to 'image-enhancing' new premises in London (with plenty of space for further growth) a new consensus is slowly emerging. 'I think we hope to grow and establish ourselves more in the London market so that

we become known more as a London firm with offices in the regions,' said a typical source this year. The relocation of managing partner Tim Aspinall to the new office was the clincher in the eyes of many, and they didn't rule out further London mergers, if his ambitious plans to double turnover within the next five years are to be realised.

For the meantime the majority of the firm's revenue is still earned in the two offices in the South East, and we sense it has no intention of releasing its grip on this market. Merger talks may have dominated the headlines in the past year, however the firm has quietly affirmed its commitment to Crawley by acquiring new premises that significantly increase its capacity. Seats have been filled by some big-name lateral hires, most notably Jonathan Grant (previously head of corporate finance at regional rival asb law) and new head of banking and finance Gwen Godfrey (previously with London firm Barlow Lyde & Gilbert). There has also been a transfer of a number of the commercial teams that had previously resided in Brighton. This move has cemented Crawley's status as the largest office in the network and DMH Stallard's engine room, while its childhood home in Brighton has been relegated to the role of 'private client wing.' Brighton still commands a loyal local client base, and many trainees believe the firm's heart at least is still by the seaside: 'It's where it all began for the firm and people know us there.'

Wanna be like you-oo-oo

DMH Stallard offers trainees a multitude of seat choices, but for their part trainees must be prepared to move between its three offices. Following the downsizing of Brighton, this office is now only likely to feature in the schedules of trainees taking claimant personal injury or private client seats. The former means taking responsibility for a huge number of your own files and requires familiarity with a case management system that keeps supervisors aware of all deadlines. 'It's a steep learning curve but a very useful basis for any other litigation you do afterwards.' The private client seat breaks down into family law, trusts, tax and probate. However the mix pans out, trainees can expect 'loads of client contact through home visits or interviews in the office.' The Brighton offering is completed by a real estate asset management seat, although trainees are more likely to be stationed in London or Crawley when they satisfy the firm's expectation that they should sample some kind of property seat.

Most trainees view a commercial property seat as a chance to work for a real mix of clients from heavyweight public sector bodies such as the London Development Agency and the London Borough of Croydon, to wealthy individuals like Anna Ryder-Richardson. The firm helped her adjust to life after *I'm a Celebrity* by acquiring a zoo in Wales. Typical trainee duties include 'post-completion registration of interests and charges' and 'investigating stamp duty issues on various land purchases.' In the planning sphere the firm achieved something of a coup in summer 2007 when it finally secured permission for Brighton & Hove Albion FC's new 22,500-seat stadium in Falmer, following a six-year war with Lewes and Falmer councils and some cheesed-off conservationists. Trainees really value the exposure a planning seat provides to 'inquiries, planning appeals, High Court applications and judicial reviews.'

Haute couture

One of the most popular seats is in the corporate/commercial department, which has expanded at a rapid rate. New hires in Crawley have seriously beefed up the client roster, and on the finance side this now includes meaty names such as Allied Irish Bank, Bank of Scotland and Clydesdale Bank. In spite of this – and the threat of longer hours – London is regarded as the Holy Grail by many corporate-minded trainees, meaning there are not always enough seats there to meet demand. Those lucky enough to bag a spot in the capital will work for 'pretty big plcs and some quite large private companies, but not necessarily household names.' One of the best features of the seat is that 'everyone takes time out of their day to let you know what is going on and explain the context behind a task.' For one trainee, such tasks included 'drafting verification notes, stock transfers, assisting on the sale of a

company, advice on consultancy agreements for a Brazilian contract and working out if a debt was a loan or equity or goodness knows what.'

Employment was another exceptionally popular seat among our sources. The Crawley office has 'a large and very well-run department' that handles advisory and contentious work for a client list heavy with local authorities. The smaller London team also 'touches on immigration,' although the recent relocation of Crawley department head Rustom Tata is expected to pump up the City practice. On the dispute resolution front, property litigation is prominent, and there's the full gamut of business disputes for public and private sector clients. Another major string to the firm's bow is its Crawley-based technology and media group. According to one enthused trainee, the department 'gets all the sexy work.' Recent examples include protecting the Topshop, Miss Selfridge, Burton and Dorothy Perkins brands for client Arcadia. Clearly adept at chasing skirt retailers, the group also represented ISSA Couture in design and copyright enforcement proceedings against high street shops alleged to have infringed distinctive dress prints.

Money mule

To prepare for all the office swapping, many trainees base themselves either in Brighton or London. For the most reluctant travellers, the advice is simple: 'Being close to Clapham Junction can be really handy as you have a good connection to all three offices.' After nominating a base office, trainees have their travel costs covered by the firm for the duration of any seat at another office. However, for some even this is not enough to take the sting out of a placement in Crawley ('a typical sterile commuter town where everyone is just there for a purpose,' sniped one trainee). The swanky new open-plan office at Gainsborough House has clearly improved morale and there were even murmurs of a 'slowly improving' Friday night drinks scene. This, coupled with the favourable hours and good quality of work, was enough to win over some of the Brighton-dwellers, although those who were commuting out of London seemed more reluctant to look on the bright side of Crawley.

This was clearly not helped by the fact that they were reverse commuting away from a swish open-plan London office on New Fetter Lane. This had only just opened when we spoke to trainees, but already it was being hailed a huge success. 'The distinction between Stallards and DMH is dissolving, and the atmosphere has changed dramatically from traditional to a more modern and younger feel.' It's amazing what a bit of glass panelling can achieve! Trainees characterised New Fetter Lane as the most 'hectic' office, although considering hours are 'not that bad at all' we suspect this title has been gained by comparison to the firm's other offices rather than its City counterparts. Brighton sets the bar high in terms of work-life balance. It's pretty rare to have an office described as 'relaxing,' but then there are few offices that house a reception area art gallery. Easy hours leave plenty of time for post-work beverages in one of the many pubs within easy reach of its front door, or even beach volleyball if the weather permits. It seems that the loss of the managing partner to London and the commercial departments to Crawley have done little to affect the office's position as social centre of the firm. Come February, staff from all offices descend on Brighton for the AGM, at which everyone is addressed by the managing partner before being treated to a three-course meal. There's more fun to be had at the trainees' Christmas party, when the firm stuffs a wad of cash in the pockets of one lucky trainee with a view to covering the expenses of a night out on the tiles for all current and future trainees. We were disappointed to hear that following last year's session, which spilled from The Quadrant bar into Funkyfish on the seafront, the mule woke up with £50 still in their pocket to return to the firm's coffers. Our sources put this down to a poor turnout from 2008 new starters and assured us that it would not happen again.

Keen to retain as many of its qualifying trainees as possible, the firm announces NQ vacancies extremely early. In 2008 eight of the ten qualifiers stayed with the firm.

And finally...

DMH Stallard is 'a progressive and ambitious firm' and recommended as a top choice for commercially minded trainees who will share its competitive spirit and vision of growth. Despite the shift from the coast to more lucrative corporate centres, Brighton retains its symbolic importance.

Dorsey & Whitney

The facts

Location: London, Cambridge

Number of UK partners/solicitors: 13/32

Total number of trainees: 8

Seats: 4x6 months

Alternative seats: Secondments

Extras: Pro bono – LawWorks

> Most trainees love getting stuck in and appreciate how, if you've got potential and are willing to work hard, you'll get great work.

A seat in Dorsey & Whitney's London office will provide you with exposure to the commercial work of an international firm in the comfortable setting of a small office.

Top marks (& sparks)

With over 600 lawyers in 19 offices across the States, Canada, Asia and Europe, US law firm Dorsey & Whitney has been a presence in London since 1986 and more recently in Cambridge as of 2004. Further expansion is in the works as the firm plans to open a Sydney office at the end of 2008 to act as a base for its work in Asia, which mostly consists of capital markets deals in India. The international reach of Dorsey & Whitney is clearly one of its greatest draws for trainees, who found it to have 'a small-firm feel but the resources and quality of work of a big firm.' Trainees were also drawn to the perks that come with a US firm, including 'a relaxed, friendly culture' and, of course, the fact that 'US firms pay exceptionally well.' Trainees get plenty of cross-border experience, handling 'more than just Euro-centric work,' including a heavy dose of instructions for US clients. It's definitely not all about the USA though, as 'the firm has a strong base of UK clients too.' To these it provides services in a wide range of areas – capital markets, M&A and real estate transactions, IP, tax and general commercial litigation are the most prominent. Because the majority of work is 'UK relevant,' trainees often don't feel like they're working for a US firm at all; 'it acts just as a UK firm would, except for when we need to get permission from the mothership on certain things.'

Trainees are required to do seats in both of the firm's core areas of expertise: transactions and advocacy (in other words corporate and litigation), though quite how seats get assigned was a bit of an enigma to the trainees we spoke to. 'You're just put into your first seat and then you talk to the trainee co-ordinator and he schedules you in for the rest.' Our sources said they'd appreciate 'more structure in seat allocation,' but did admit that 'because it's a small office you can pretty much do what you want, it's just a question of when you'll get it.' Looking further down the line, in years past the retention of English-qualified partners has been a source of concern for those hoping for careers in US firms in the UK. Of Dorsey, trainees say: 'If there was an imbalance in the past it's been addressed now,' pointing to the healthy number of UK partners and 'only one US partner in the office.'

Dorsey's tax team is one of its strongest and it has long been a market leader in this field, particularly in disputes with HM Revenue & Customs. It made a name for itself working on such headline-grabbing cases as the landmark Marks & Spencer claim against the Inland Revenue in 2006, and more recently the team represented a group of 13 large manufacturing companies led by Mars and members of the Scotch Whisky Association in a case challenging policy decisions of HMRC. It's no wonder then that *Chambers UK* has given Dorsey top marks for contentious tax matters for two years running, not bad at all considering the office only added a tax litigation group in 2003. That said, the team has had some ups and downs, most notably being raided by DLA Piper and Berwin Leighton Paisner in 2007. Though the group is a compact one with just seven lawyers, it is nonetheless an impressive one; among these seven is Paul Farmer, a well-known European and international tax lawyer, and Michael Anderson, who re-joined Dorsey & Whitney in the autumn of 2007. Interestingly, both Farmer and Anderson left Dorsey to work at DLA Piper in the previously mentioned raids but have since returned. Trainees say this small team runs like a well-oiled machine: 'The group is fantastic and is really well organised; the delegation from the partners down to the rest of the team is absolutely brilliant.' Working in tax means you'll be dealing with such household names as American Express, Ford, Ladbrokes and PepsiCo. Luckily 'the people in charge in this group are very aware of each trainee's capabilities, so you're never overwhelmed and there's always someone to ask for help.' Tax isn't for everyone, though, as this is 'a complicated seat that's not very enthralling if it turns out not to be your cup of tea.'

High flying

Corporate, particularly AIM work, is another of the firm's key strengths and is often a popular choice for trainees; in fact, everyone in the 2008 batch was keen on this area. With 20 lawyers devoted to corporate work, this is a real emphasis of the firm. In addition to a standout global M&A practice, the firm also has a strong mid-market private equity practice in the USA and the UK. Its clients include a number of banks that are active in the mid-market, The Local Radio Company, which owns and operates 28 independent radio stations across the UK and independent production and distribution company Shed Media, which produces a bevy of hit television shows including *Footballers' Wives* and *Who Do You Think You Are?* Dorsey also names Inland, a land purchase and enhancement company, among its clients; in March 2007 it advised the company on its £82m flotation on AIM. A seat in corporate offers the opportunity to get your hands dirty and gain client contact. For one trainee this even meant a flight to India to carry out due diligence. If jet setting crops up in your time at Dorsey, you can expect 'an eye-opening experience –you get a first-class flight, five-star hotel, the works. It's quite cushy. It's also a non-stop, hectic experience and you come back feeling exhausted.' Another way of getting out of the office is a client secondment; currently slots are available with Honda and Innovation Group.

'They say at Dorsey your training contract is what you make of it,' and trainees confirmed that this is not just marketing hype. 'You can just do what your supervisor gives you and cruise, but you can also ask for the work you want… they'll give it to you but they won't force it on you.' Most trainees 'love getting stuck in' and appreciate how 'if you've got potential and are willing to work hard, you'll get great work.' Luckily, 'though the hours can be harsh they aren't consistently so, and you can usually see it coming and structure your life around it.' Even better,

'when things are quiet you can leave at 6pm on the dot or even take a four-hour lunch and no one's going to say anything; they're reasonable in their approach to hours.' One trainee put things even more pragmatically still, saying: 'We get paid quite well so you expect to work hard.'

When it comes to more administrative tasks, 'you work with paralegals who aren't beneath you but rather work alongside you.' Apparently 'there's no strict hierarchy' at the firm, which goes a long way towards explaining its atmosphere. The small size helps keep things intimate, too, so for example, 'partners organise drinks and snacks once or twice a month in the boardrooms downstairs.' The office's small size also means your voice is more easily heard. 'Partners and associates treat you like an adult and are very open to your suggestions.'

Coming of age

Though everyone conceded that 'there may be times when you feel like you don't know what you're doing,' there's always someone at hand to help. You're given a supervisor, usually a partner, and also a mentor to chat through any stresses or worries. On top of that 'everyone is very approachable and won't judge you for asking silly questions.' The main HR department is located in the States, but trainees don't see this as a problem. For the most part the systems work. Once a year there's a Stateside gathering to which second-years are invited so they can see Dorsey's Minneapolis digs first-hand and get a closer look at how the US-UK relationship works.

The London office is conveniently located equidistant between Moorgate and Liverpool Street, and according to some looks 'quite slick' thanks to a recent refurbishment which updated its former '1970s-ish' look. In truth, not all trainees were so glowing about the building, with one admitting: 'The whole brown marble thing just doesn't do it for me. It's just… so brown.' Most lawyers work in really big offices, and some trainees even get their own room for their last seat.

With just four trainees recruited per year, Dorsey likes to fill its vacancies carefully, choosing 'people that have gone over and above… they like people with a variety of different experience and areas of expertise to create a diverse pool of lawyers.' This includes experiences both 'academic and practical;' everything from postgrad study to time spent abroad. The interview process takes place in two stages: the first is all about you as a person and the second gives you a practical example to work through, always one in which no prior legal knowledge is necessary. As academic qualifications have become universally high, the firm is really looking for trainees who will be able to interact with clients right away. While it is 'a close-knit and sociable group,' the firm's attraction to candidates that are 'mature, independent and self-sufficient' might have something to do with the relatively quiet social life. 'It's quite ad hoc and Friday night drinks aren't a mainstay,' but trainees do make the effort to meet up as often as they can. The office is in 'a brilliant location for after-work drinks,' though trainees rarely venture further than Bangers, a small pub just across the road. The celebration of the London office's 21st birthday (technically it was the 22nd birthday but there wasn't time to celebrate last year) was anticipated to be a blowout with plenty of partners from the USA turning up for the occasion. Hints of the firm's American-ness are evident in the Fourth of July date for the annual summer drinks party, to which future joiners are invited. In years where the summer drinks don't fall on this date the American holiday is still acknowledged, thanks in part to the efforts of managing partner Paul Klaas, whose giant inflatable Uncle Sam is known to make an appearance. American partners stop by throughout the year, including a visit in 2008 from senior counsel Walter Mondale, best known as a former Democratic nominee for President of the United States and a former Vice President under Jimmy Carter.

And finally...

If you're willing to put in the work, a training contract with Dorsey & Whitney has a lot to offer, not least in its strongest practice areas here in London. Sadly in 2008 just one of the four qualifying trainees stayed on, as they were all vying for the single vacancy in the firm's corporate department.

- **Challenge your preconceptions:** Great training isn't the preserve of the magic circle – don't apply to them just because you're a high flyer and you feel it's expected of you. Conversely, don't ignore the most prestigious firms because you don't think you have a chance. You might be surprised.

Dundas & Wilson LLP

The facts

Location: London, Edinburgh, Glasgow

Number of UK partners/solicitors: 85/216

Total number of trainees: 18

Seats: 4x6 months

Alternative seats: Occasional secondments

> The capture of top real estate litigator Martin Thomas from Herbert Smith is a real statement of intent from the firm.

Premier Scots firm Dundas & Wilson first took the long road to London back in 2002. Expansion in the capital has been meteoric, and in six short years D&W has risen from being a relatively unknown quantity in England to become a real player in the corporate mid-market.

Tartan invasion

Dundas & Wilson's star is still very much in the ascendant in its Caledonian heartland. The firm is the chief adviser both to the consortium that has won the contract for the £4.2bn Forth Crossing project, one of the country's largest ever civil engineering projects, and on Transport Scotland's £1bn railway investment programme. Dominant though it is in Scotland, there is a feeling that 'the firm has done as much as it can there – the market is starting to become saturated.' London is seen as the way forward and trainees make it clear that their office at Bush House on the Aldwych is no token presence, saying: 'We are pretty much our own firm.' That's quite literally true: for legal reasons the Scottish and English branches of D&W are separate entities.

The firm feels 'quite Scottish, but gradually less and less so,' even if politically and administratively 'much is still done from Scotland.' London doesn't do the billing, for example, nor does it have its own dedicated HR team. However 'lots of lateral hires' from City firms are making the office ever more independent and 'smaller departments are growing into medium-sized departments, and medium-sized ones are growing into large ones.' The largest departments are currently corporate and property. In the four-seat system, while no one is forced to go anywhere, it would be an unusual trainee who didn't spend time in at least one of these two departments. Previously litigation was not a major aspect of the training scheme,

now though this is 'one of the fastest-growing areas,' and the firm is seeking to transform the department from a small team into a major operation. Other seats are available in banking, contentious construction, IP/IT and employment, and new options are coming on stream as the office hikes its trainee numbers. To give an example, the environment lawyers, who occasionally used to share a trainee with the property team, now have enough work to host a trainee of their own.

Where there's muck there's brass

It might be forging its own way in the world but D&W's London corporate department makes full use of its Highland connections to win work. Scottish Widows, Bank of Scotland and Scottish & Southern Energy all use the office for various ventures – notably Scottish & Southern's disposal of £79m worth of assets to Wireless Infrastructure Group. The department has picked up plenty of clients south of the border as well and *Chambers UK* now ranks the London team as a force to be reckoned with in the lower end of the mid-market. The deals they have been involved in include the £95m sale of Broker Network Holdings to Towergate Partnership, the sale of footwear manufacturer Stead & Simpson to Shoe Zone and Thames Water's £2.5bn Tideway Tunnel project, which will see the creation of a super sewer in an attempt to clean up the Thames. A number of AIM-listed clients are also on the books.

A training mentor (normally a more junior associate) is assigned in each seat 'to fight for your cause.' There are no issues with the levels of supervision, but the type of work that trainees see 'depends on your partner – I can't stress that enough.' Said one envious trainee: 'My friend got to draft an SPA themselves. That's a… Something Purchase Agreement. A Special Purchase Agreement? I do know what it's called, I'm just quite tired at the moment because I've been running to deliver some documents.' As we're sure our contact knew really, it's a share purchase agreement, and their experience sums up the lot of a corporate trainee fairly accurately – drafting combined with legwork. It might not be SPAs every time, but our interviewees told us that on smaller matters 'drafting most of the ancillaries' is not uncommon. The legwork consists not just of running around but also the usual bibling tasks and a lot of case management, especially at completion – 'making sure the right people have been booked for completion meetings, working out who's able to sign which document, drawing up powers of attorney if they can't make it…' As with corporate departments everywhere 'you tend to go through something of a fallow patch and then it all goes, for want of a better word, a bit mental.' Everyone we spoke to had experienced a few late nights but normally left by 7pm when deals weren't in their final stages.

Squat thrust

Not very long ago D&W's litigation department was practically non-existent in London. It has grown exponentially in the past year and 'half the team is newer than I am,' said one source. The capture of top real estate litigator Martin Thomas from Herbert Smith to head up the unit is a real statement of intent from the firm. Now eight strong, the team divides its resources between contentious property work and general commercial litigation. Trainees tend to concentrate on one side or the other, depending on their interest. Highlights of the past year include defending the Drapers Livery Company against a claim for misrepresentation that arose out of the sale of premises in the City and acting for Biffa Waste Services for a fire damage claim at a Leicester recycling plant. We were informed that trainees 'start off checking court bundles, maybe doing a little photocopying, and gradually get given more and more, say, drafting the start of the defence or a chronology.' There is also a 'heavy emphasis' on research. 'One of our clients had a disused site that was occupied by squatters,' explained one trainee. 'I had to speak to the client, find out how long they had been there, how they got in, how many there were, and then draft witness statements and an injunction to get them out.' Court time is to be expected and some trainees even 'bit the bullet and did some solo advocacy. I'd never say it was easy, but it helps if you are prepared.'

Chambers UK rankings

Administrative & Public Law • Banking & Finance • Clinical Negligence • Competition/European Law • Construction • Corporate Finance • Dispute Resolution • Education • Employee Share Schemes • Employment • Environment • Financial Services Regulation • Franchising • Immigration • Information Technology • Intellectual Property • Investment Funds • Local Government • Media & Entertainment • Outsourcing • Parliamentary & Public Affairs • Partnership • Pensions • Personal Injury • Planning • Professional Negligence • Projects, Energy & Natural Resources • Real Estate • Real Estate Litigation • Restructuring/Insolvency • Sports Law • Tax • Transport

Property is the largest team, with National Grid and Land Securities two of the major clients. In the past year, D&W was behind the £2.5bn sale of National Grid Wireless. Trainees get good work on smaller files, especially compulsory purchase orders, and are charged with the responsibility for going through leases and producing reports on titles. 'When someone was purchasing land I was researching ownership issues, easements, whether hazardous substances had been stored near the site, and so on.' Overlapping with property is environment, an area of practice that is 'picking up rapidly.' The team acts for the Environment Agency on several matters, including its flood alleviation proposal for Banbury and improvements tothe Ely Ouse-to-Essex Water Transfer Scheme. There is also work for waste companies interested in government grants available for recycling. In this seat, there's 'a lot of research into who owns what,' plus the excitement of 'site visits where you get to go out and stick up notices.' The niche IP/IT department is always popular, and here the firm has Tesco Personal Finance and RBS on its books. London takes in a handful of Scottish trainees every six months, but since the increase in their own trainee numbers office swaps depend increasingly on business needs.

Adrift in the lift

We're informed that the Edinburgh office is known to be 'very conservative and hardcore,' while the smaller Glasgow team is the complete opposite. London comes somewhere between the two, with a 'relaxed but smart' dress code that requires that 'the boys keep an emergency tie in their desks.' As a rule trainees seem to find the smaller teams more sociable to work in; with so many new faces in the larger groups, 'they are no less friendly, but it is taking a while for everyone to settle in.' Among the trainees, we were assured that 'nobody is boringly lawyerly through and through,' and the firm does seem to like 'people who are not completely green' – even if it's just a gap year somewhere along the line.

Dundas & Wilson doesn't do things by halves when it comes to the big social events. In the summer the staff enjoyed both a trip up to 'a fancy hotel in Scotland' and a barbecue in Lincoln's Inn Fields, while the Christmas party was held at the fancy Waldorf hotel close to the office. The tradition of trainees putting on a Christmas revue is still just about hanging on but sadly not everyone entered into the spirit of the thing last year, as some refused point blank to get involved in the 'spoof carol-singing-slash-dance-routine' that was proposed. 'People said it was good,' said one participant. 'Really terrible' was the verdict of another source who declined.

For the rest of the year the firm is less good at organising events. 'They sponsored a Young Lawyers Ball in London but forgot to invite us,' said one incredulous contact. It's usually left to trainees make their own entertainment and one regular event is a dinner to welcome every new bunch of Scottish secondees. After-work drinks are also common: the property department's 'beer o'clock' is about as sophisticated as it sounds, and local pub The Devereux is the usual destination. For sports fans there's a football team, and as part of the Deloitte network, the firm is invited to enter a team in an annual tournament, this year in Marseilles. Real fitness fanatics might be interested to know about the opportunities for climbing. Bush House's ancient lifts are listed, 'so they can't be replaced no matter what goes wrong.' This invariably means 'ending up on a different floor from the one you've pressed the button for,' not to mention the ever-present risk of getting completely stuck in a 5ft square box with only the managing partner for company. Best just to take the stairs, we say.

The natural consequence of growth in London is that space is running out in the office and D&W is now in occupation of four cramped floors while it waits for others to become available. In the meantime, the small seating area where trainees used to go for lunch has become an extension of the print room, much to their chagrin. Nor is there a kitchen on all floors so 'you have to swill out your mug in the toilets'… if you know what we mean.

And finally...

In 2008 Dundas & Wilson's sole qualifier took a job in the real estate department. Should they stay on, the seven trainees who qualify next year, and the ten the year after that, should benefit from being at the firm at a time when it is coming into its own in London.

DWF LLP

The facts

Location: Liverpool, Manchester, Leeds, Preston, London

Number of UK partners/solicitors: 128/203

Total number of trainees: 34

Seats: 4x4 +1x8 months

Alternative seats: Occasional secondments

Extras: Pro bono – eg CAB

> DWF trainees genuinely feel that a lot of investment, time and effort is put into people.

DWF has gone a long way to achieving its stated ambition of becoming a top 30 firm by 2010. *Pssst!* We heard on the grapevine the expansion means there may still be trainee vacancies for 2009.

Raw ambition

Founded in Liverpool in 1977, DWF moved into Manchester and more than doubled in size between the millennium and 2007. Then a merger with Ricksons added another £21m of annual turnover plus additional offices in Preston and Leeds. DWF's ambitious nature was a big draw for our trainee interviewees. 'The firm is on the up,' they said. True enough: turnover jumped last year to over £55m and the firm aggressively hired partners and solicitors across the board. According to our sources, DWF is 'looking to grow further, though this has been somewhat tempered by the credit crunch.' In June 2008 the firm recruited a leading insurance and catastrophic injury lawyer to open a London office, but around the same time managing partner Andrew Leaitherland announced that further expansion would indeed be put on hold given the economic climate.

Trainees take four four-month seats followed by one of eight months to give them extra experience in their preferred qualification area. Reflecting the broad spread of practice at the firm, seats are available in the following departments: banking and finance; corporate; insurance litigation; real estate; commercial litigation; business recovery; family, private client and employment. 'We're lucky because there's such a wide range of departments,' reflected one appreciative trainee. As the largest offices, Liverpool and Manchester currently take the bulk of each new intake.

The insurance division's many sub-departments employ well over a third of DWF's 900-strong workforce and the firm was named *Insurance Times*' Insurance Law Firm of the Year 2007. A seat within this group 'invariably involves some form of PI or catastrophic injury – for example, acting for companies that have poured concrete on people or run them over with cranes.' There's 'quite a lot of responsibility. They give you files and client contact as soon as you join to get you up the curve ASAP.' As well as assisting on large cases, there's a 'high volume of small files, like simple slips and trips worth less than £5,000.' A trainee will typically spend their time 'on the phone speaking to witnesses and the insured clients, drafting witness statements and doing everything the case requires. There is start-to-finish exposure.' One source had especially enjoyed court visits and praised the seat as 'one of those where you can really get involved.' Among the clients we can name, there's Admiral, Brit Insurance, Capita, Norwich Union, Motor Insurers' Bureau, Blackpool Borough Council and British Railways Board. As an indication of the calibre of the team, *Chambers UK* ranks DWF top for PI in the North West.

A day in the life

The corporate department is 'shrinking a bit' in that 'a partner who left hasn't been replaced yet. They need to recruit;' and given the recent hiring frenzy the firm no doubt will in due course. It's in the nature of corporate work that the department experiences 'big peaks and troughs,' though this hadn't dampened our sources' enthusiasm for the work. We heard about trainees 'drafting documents and researching the new Companies Act,' as well as gaining 'lots of client contact,' not least on 'London trips with partners.' All in all they were 'made to feel part of the machine.' If busy, people sometimes stayed in the office 'until 10pm or 11pm – but only if necessary.' Admittedly some people were 'a bit disappointed not to see any completions' during their four months. 'The seats are too short. I would have loved to do a completion but didn't get the chance. Just as you're starting to get to grips with a department you're moved on.' Lately DWF acted for Burton's Foods on its buyout by Duke Street Capital and on the £30m MBO of Esterform Packaging, backed by Gresham. The Leeds team advised Andinsure on its sale to Swinton and the Liverpool team assisted on Iceland's £370m refinancing.

What's the story?

Real estate trainees manage some of their own files, working on 'a bit of everything – leases, sales, purchases, conveyancing, property financing with the banks, legal research and drafting.' In short, 'there's a good balance between plenty of work to do and enjoyable work to do.' Recent transactions include letting distribution warehouses and office accommodation in Trafford Park to adidas and the subsequent forward sale to NFU Mutual for £33.3m. Showing its ability to lure lawyers away from well-known firms, DWF recently hired a Hammonds real estate team into Leeds.

In commercial litigation you're likely to get your own caseload of small claims and assist a partner on bigger files. There are 'plenty of meetings with counsel and you get to go to court, which is good for confidence and advocacy. Trainees sometimes have the opportunity to address the judge.' There's certainly more responsibility than in corporate, where 'they can't exactly leave you in charge of a deal.' For some, comlit is a 'very tough seat' and the non-stop pace means 'you get home knowing you've done a day's work!' Even if the hours are a very reasonable 9am to 6pm, 'each day is completely full.' The department's larger clients include Allianz Cornhill, John Moore's University, Iceland and the Catholic Archdiocese of Liverpool.

The commercial/IP seat involves 'drafting contracts, terms and conditions, licences and supply agreements, then working with a partner to amend them.' The IP side of things is 'mainly trade mark infringement and competition stuff,' with the occasional *Sweeney*-style 'dawn raids on businesses.' Highlights include advising the 10,000-seater Arena and Convention Centre Liverpool on sponsorship agreements in the run-up to the Capital of Culture Year and Liverpool department head Laurence

Chambers UK rankings

Asset Finance • Banking & Finance • Construction • Corporate Finance • Debt Recovery • Dispute Resolution • Employment • Environment • Family/Matrimonial • Health & Safety • Information Technology • Insurance • Intellectual Property • Partnership • Personal Injury • Real Estate • Restructuring/Insolvency

Pritchard walking off with the Lawyer of the Year award at the Liverpool Professionals Awards 2008.

Among the other seats, in banking and finance 'you can work on the property side too if you want.' The 'old team left to join Eversheds and there's a new team led by a partner poached from Cobbetts.' Take an asset finance seat and you'll encounter specialist aviation finance, representing the banks. 'There's not as much responsibility as in insurance seats – the documents can be complex – so you work in the background, shadowing more.' The smaller financial litigation team helps banks recover money from loan and mortgage defaulters, often when fraud is suspected. The department recently hired a couple of new lawyers 'and will probably take on more – it will prosper in the credit crunch.' The employment team, meanwhile, is 'always busy.' Said one fan: 'I pushed for a lot of responsibility and got it. I conducted my own hearing and cross-examined witnesses myself.'

People power

Broadly speaking, trainees land most of their preferred seats, though a few told us 'seat allocation could be better' and didn't believe it was entirely transparent. One told us quite simply: 'I was proactive in trying to make it work for me; if you don't say anything you get what you're given. You stand a chance if you put in a shout.' And never underestimate 'a bit of back-scratching' – for example, the two Manchester trainees who volunteered to fill gaps in Leeds were hopefully treated favourably when their next seats were allocated – 'the firm will probably see them right. There is room for discretion.'

As in all firms, the quality of the feedback in appraisals depends on your supervisor. If yours is 'hot on admin then you get your appraisal quickly and can send it to HR. Associates and senior solicitors tend to get it done quicker than partners.' Supervisors are 'happy to sit with you for a couple of hours;' the issue can be getting everything typed up promptly. To be fair, HR is trying to address niggles on this issue and recently initiated a supervisor/trainee workshop to ensure everyone knows what they should be doing and when.

DWF trainees genuinely feel that 'a lot of investment, time and effort is put into people.' Regular in-house training is provided and 'client satisfaction surveys are done by an external consultancy to extract genuine feedback' on lawyers' performance. 'There's lots of internal training for everyone – for example, a partner or associate from business recovery might give a presentation on receivership and video link in the other offices.' There's also a 'monthly-ish 8am breakfast briefing' where one practice group presents to others. Some clients have even given briefings to DWF staff to communicate their expectations. Trainees from all offices take their PSC course together in Manchester, although at trainee level inter-office interaction 'becomes less frequent as time goes on.' Liverpool and Manchester trainees try to 'catch up socially every couple of months.'

Some, but not all, of the trainees we spoke to had done vacation work experience with DWF when they were students. They sang its praises: unlike at certain other firms where they felt like a 'burden,' at DWF 'people made an effort to talk to you about what they do day to day.' Academic achievement isn't the be-all and end-all when it comes to a successful training contract application, though our sources did point out that paradoxically the minimum entry criteria has gone up in past years. If you're a southern softie, DWF will probably press you at interview on why you want to work up north and 'how you can guarantee you won't disappear to London at the first headhunter's call.' Make sure you have a convincing argument is all we can say. Mature students are more than welcome to apply and the firm has lately taken on people who worked in the media and for a police force. From now on, office hopping is highly unlikely during the contract and 'you'll train in the office you apply to.'

Just chill...

Extracurricular activities are encouraged – there's a running club and teams for football, netball, rugby sevens, sailing and cricket. Sports events are a 'great opportunity for trainees to come into regular contact with clients' and 'people come over to Liverpool from all the offices for cricket matches.' One-off team-building events have included The Chill Factor in the Trafford Centre, the biggest indoor real-snow ski centre in the country, and a trip to Haydock races. Each department has its own community day. This year trainees renovated a school garden near Manchester and litigators had a go at dry-stone walling. There will be a firm-wide Christmas party this year for the first time, complete with employee awards. The venue at the time of writing was a closely guarded secret and no one even knew 'what side of the Pennines it would be.'

DWF Liverpool has just moved into its 'new shiny office' in Old Hall Street, the swanky business district in Liverpool. Perhaps it felt the need to keep up with the Joneses – this summer the Leeds staff also moved to stunning offices in Bridgewater Place, the Leeds skyscraper. Their neighbours include Eversheds. After work, Liverpool trainees frequent Rigby's, 'the oldest pub in town,' and for posher joints head down the Albert Dock for a sesh in trendy Ha! Ha!, Pan American or babycream. You might find Manchester trainees at The 'Crombie, or bar crawling the fashionable Deansgate Locks, once home to the legendary Hacienda club. In Preston the bar of choice is the Forum, which hosts a regular night for IT professionals called GeekUp. Maybe local lawyers should petition for their own version. The 'Friday Fridge' is an event in the Leeds office every last Friday of the month, when staff down tools at 4.30pm and dash to a booze-stocked chiller.

And finally...

If you want to join a northern firm with ambitious national plans, challenge DWF to take you on. In 2008 it performed excellently in the NQ retention stakes with 14 of the 15 qualifiers taking up jobs.

Edwards Angell Palmer & Dodge UK

The facts

Location: London

Number of UK partners/solicitors: 21/19

Total number of trainees: 15

Seats: 4x6 months

Alternative seats: Possible overseas seat, secondments

Extras: Pro bono – RCJ CAB, LawWorks, Fair Trials International

Sources tell us private equity is high on the agenda for the rapidly transforming London office. If you're interested in this, it could be a great time to join a new team with momentum behind it.

EAPD UK was created on 1 January 2008 following Boston-based Edwards Angell Palmer & Dodge's takeover of Kendall Freeman, one of the UK's leading insurance practices. What follows is a snapshot of the London business today. As to how it will ultimately develop, no one can be 100% sure.

From KF to EAPD

The excitement and uncertainty that accompany any merger are both present here, and while the firm has already announced a raft of initiatives and expansion plans, it only kept on two out of seven trainees in 2008. How much this can be put down to market conditions, and how much to a refocusing of the business, remains to be seen. What we do know is that there are likely to be opportunities for trainees in new practice areas – such as IP and private equity – that didn't exist before.

Since the merger the firm has hired a partner to launch an IP and life sciences practice in London. In the USA intellectual property law is a strong suit of the firm and EAPD wants to replicate this success in London. It hopes to create a trainee seat in IP 'in the not too distant future.' Sources tell us private equity is also high on the agenda for the rapidly transforming London office, and one trainee points out: 'If you're interested in this, it could be a great time to join a new team with momentum behind it.' The firm has also hired a partner to launch a European patent prosecution practice called EAPD Innovations, with an annexe in Southampton to support it. And the firm recently partnered with anti-corruption agency Amicus, which adds a new dimension to the commercial litigation group's international asset recovery expertise. Trainees find this aspect of the firm's work 'fascinating' as there's every chance of acting for governments around the world and international anti-corruption commissions.

In March 2008 EAPD was the very first UK firm to announce a move into Bermuda, after it signed a co-operation agreement with local firm MD&M to help it establish an insurance and reinsurance practice on the island and refer work to London and the US offices. Bermudan laws are strict and a UK firm can't just set up shop, so this innovation 'is a clever way to have a presence without having a presence.' According to one source: 'Other firms may follow EAPD's lead.' In truth, relatively tiny Kendall Freeman had always done a lot of international business; it now has scope to do so much more since linking with a firm with offices all over the USA. Furthermore, EAPD announced soon after the merger that it plans to open in Hong Kong (and maybe even Tokyo) – another development with obvious appeal for travel-bugged trainees.

Learn the lingo

The fact that most trainees do insurance litigation in their first or second seat is utterly indicative of Kendall Freeman's old strengths. 'Insurance has a language of its own and it'll take you the first three months to get to grips with it,' warned one source. Opinion is split regarding the remaining three months: for one the seat was 'as dull as it sounds,' while another was 'very surprised to find myself enjoying it. After a couple of months I really found my feet.' Document management 'can be quite heavy but you need to get your head round it if you want to go on to do insurance law.' Tasks for trainees include writing articles, research memos and case reviews; even writing a senior partner's speech for a conference. Basically it's a case of 'helping fee earners with whatever they ask you to do.' The sensitivities of high-stakes litigation mean 'you're held back to a degree' because the partners can't risk 'a trainee messing something up.' By contrast, in other seats partners 'can afford to let trainees loose a little.'

Recent work includes acting for Centre Re (a Swiss Re company) in a £500m cross-border asbestos liability dispute, and a multimillion-pound offshore energy case. 'Insurance sounds really dry,' according to one source, 'but half the trainees grew to love it and wanted to qualify into it. It's always presumed to be a bum seat but people get into it. Admittedly it is contract-heavy, but the facts can be interesting and you soon realise it underpins a huge proportion of transactions.' More than one source told us they 'didn't realise the firm was so heavily into insurance' before joining. 'Any student needs to think seriously about whether they want to be an insurance lawyer.' Trainees in the past year or two have found insurance 'a pretty quiet department,' the company line being the market itself has been relatively quiet. Most said they were regularly out of the office by 6pm.

Like insurance litigation, 'commercial litigation is pretty much compulsory.' This department shares a floor with the Public International Law (PIL) team and together they are the most popular seats, along with secondments to Shell, Harrods and – for the first time this year – New York. In commercial litigation you may genuinely find yourself fighting international terrorism as the asset recovery/anti-corruption part of the practice advises foreign governments on recovering looted state assets which might otherwise end up in dangerous hands. 'There's a lot of variety work-wise,' a trainee assured us. Lawyers are also acting for one of the main defendants in the litigation following the Buncefield Oil Storage depot explosion, a company owned by Total and Chevron. And they continue to advise the Federal Republic of Nigeria on various matters including a series of asset recovery suits against former governors. Other clients include Fulham Football Club, Reed Elsevier, Corus, Textron Inc and Mohammed Al Fayed.

Trainees in these litigation seats value the fact that partners give them a relatively long leash, for example to speak to counsel and attend client meetings. One source enjoyed 'drafting witness statements one on one with the client.' Another had gained a lot of client exposure as his partner was away for a couple of weeks and trusted him not to mess up. Another did libel work and took on quite a lot of responsibility, including drafting letters and speaking to the lawyer on the other side. 'I wasn't given total free rein but I really enjoyed it.' There will be the inevitable bundling for court hearings and arbi-

Chambers UK rankings

Aviation • Corporate Finance • Dispute Resolution • Fraud: Civil • Insurance • Public International Law • Restructuring/Insolvency

trations, though 'there is a balance – it's not like all you do is photocopying.'

Borderline disputes

PIL is equally if not more 'fascinating' and EAPD is one of very few firms to have this kind of practice in the UK. The team engages with a range of subjects, including international boundary disputes (land and sea), both between countries and within countries. It also works for energy companies regarding oil and gas deposits on or straddling international boundaries – highly confidential stuff owing to extreme geopolitical sensitivity and the vast reserves of natural resources at stake. 'You might be working on state litigation, speaking to beneficiaries, drafting letters – this is ongoing work the firm's been doing for years.' There's some commercial litigation crossover and you might, for example, review documentation in conjunction with a US office on a cross-border executive investigation. 'Then there's pro bono work for states looking to establish themselves as independent entities, where you might be drafting documents on their behalf.' How many trainees in other firms can claim to have redrawn the map of the world? There are various clients we can't mention; those we can name check are the Nigerian government, the Central Bank of Nigeria and the National Accountability Bureau of Pakistan.

The remaining seat options are corporate, employment (currently 'rammed busy because of the redundancies in the City'), insolvency and now, hopefully, IP. The secondment to New York has a Manhattan apartment thrown in so no guesses as to which is going to be the most popular of the three secondments; however the Shell and Harrods postings provide 'genuine hands-on commercial experience.' Back in the home office there are frequent lunchtime training sessions and 'a stream of feedback' about your performance. Trainees typically sit two to three to a room with an assistant and/or partner. 'The atmosphere is friendly, and if not friendly, civilised.' There were mixed reviews for the seat allocation process however. A pastoral meeting with the trainee principal is the time to indicate your preferences and make a good case. 'It involves a lot of brown-nosing,' said a cynical source. 'People lobby for the best seats' and try to cut deals, revealed another of a system described as 'dog eat dog.' How much this lobbying achieves is questionable, and it's also worth asking how much our sources were still smarting over the low NQ retention rate this year.

Not-so-blind date

Many trainees have taken some kind of gap year or even had a previous career before joining; they are all 'sociable types.' Apparently the firm 'has a reputation as a dating agency because marriages have happened, either between current and/or former employees.' In this small office 'everyone knows each other' and 'there've been some good stories flying around about people after a night out.' Regular impromptu Friday drinks are well attended: 'around a quarter of the partners turn up and there's little hierarchy.' Organised social events include a summer party for staff and one for clients, an annual trainee party plus various sports events such as softball versus clients. El Vino's across the street is a popular venue, while the Blue Anchor is a favourite for a spot of Friday-night karaoke. The downside of it being a close firm is that 'you can't get away with anything!'

It's generally perceived that US law firms are much more aggressive than British firms. 'They pay you twice as much and work you four times as hard,' was the theory put forward by one source. Trainees don't believe a massive cultural shift is likely, instead they hope the EAPD bigwigs in the USA will simply want to build on Kendall Freeman's good name in the City of London. For now EAPD looks like it will stay put in Kendall Freeman's mid-market slot, although we suspect the office's new masters have plans, not least to fully utilise those London lawyers who have been too quiet of late. 'There is a work-life balance here,' said one interviewee a touch euphemistically, 'because there hasn't been enough work recently.' Looking forward, trainees sense the firm is 'definitely going somewhere; there will be growth but not uncontrolled growth' and 'they want to keep the culture British rather than go overtly American.'

And finally...

Chambers USA recommends EAPD in some 20 practice areas and it's a well-known name stateside. EAPD may be relatively unknown on this side of the Atlantic, but this could well be about to change. Watch this space!

WANTED:

RARE TALENTS

The best lawyers are multi-faceted; they combine wit with wisdom and drive with diplomacy. They're competitive but controlled; single-minded yet team oriented.

They're Rare Talents and we're searching for the next generation of them – the Eversheds lawyers and partners of

Eversheds

The facts

Location: Birmingham, Cambridge, Cardiff, Ipswich, Leeds, London, Manchester, Newcastle, Nottingham

Number of UK partners/solicitors: 333/1056 (2007 figs)

Total number of trainees: 160

Seats: 4x6 months

Alternative seats: Overseas seats, secondments

Extras: Pro bono – various projects, eg Mary Ward Centre; language training

Eversheds was often cited by trainees as the only firm in the area where you can do national and international quality work whilst staying in the regions.

Eversheds is one of the UK's largest law firms. Its staff work across three regional groups: Wales and the Midlands; London and the East of England; and the North.

Thinking big

This legal giant has some top-grade clients such as DuPont, Centrica, GlaxoSmithKline, Nokia, Royal Mail, Transport for London, Tarmac and Legal & General, and its most recent priority has been to develop its international presence. It now works in 37 locations – both its own offices and those of closely allied firms – some 33 in Europe and others in Kuala Lumpur, Shanghai, Johannesburg and Abu Dhabi. There are further plans for international expansion in Russia, Romania and Ukraine. Also in Eversheds' 2009-2012 strategy is a commitment to develop London as the firm's hub and to try and improve work-life balance for staff.

Eversheds competes well on price and cuts cost for clients by outsourcing work to less expensive offices, even alliance firms, sometimes undertaking, for example, due diligence, drafting and document checking for key client Tyco, which uses Eversheds for all of its legal requirements in Europe in exchange for a combination of fixed fees and target-led fees and bonus payments. Speaking of such arrangements with major clients, trainees were well aware of Eversheds' 'great focus on networked law,' which means using skills and capacity from various offices as needed, and targeting large national or multinational clients wherever possible. While everyone we spoke to saw the logic in this approach, some worried that it took emphasis away from local lawyer-client relationships.

Trainees in London found it 'an interesting time to be at the firm.' Determined to show that it is a law firm for the 21st century, Eversheds has spent millions in the capital on its shiny new 'office of the future – now.' This office is going all-out in a bid to be seen as a credible alternative to the magic circle, and trainees say: 'It's not a place to go for a nine to five – the firm is changing its attitude and actively recruiting people who understand that; people here will be pushed harder in years to come.' Far from being bitter about the heavy London focus, regional trainees understand that 'pumping money and resources into London means increased exposure for the firm and guarantees the quality of work for us in the regions.' Our sources hoped that, post-credit crunch, clients looking for cheaper legal advice will be more than happy to see their London work go to Eversheds' regional offices. Some in the regions even said the London office had 'injected energy and excitement' into the firm. Indeed, Eversheds was often cited by regional trainees as 'the only firm in the area where you can do national and international quality work whilst staying in the region.' Again, a few did say that for those students looking for local work, Eversheds was not necessarily the best choice.

Here, there and everywhere

Most applicants have an office or region in mind. Those who win a place in East Anglia rotate between the Cambridge and Ipswich offices (Norwich closed recently)

and it's not unusual for them to do some work in London, or even to qualify into the capital. By contrast, trainees in other regions tell us there is little scope for moving during the contract, even if the official line is that all trainees are given the chance to move offices. The best advice is to choose your location wisely, even if most seats are available in most places. Looking at just some of the regional offices, we can say that in Cardiff our sources spoke convincingly of the fact that Eversheds is 'head and shoulders above the rest in exposure to quality work and clients.' International clients are passed over from London and trainees also have exposure to heavyweight Welsh work. The office has made inroads into the renewable energy sector, particularly in the planning, corporate and construction departments. Among recent deals was the £50m sale of Scottish Resources Group's renewables interests to Infinis.

In Birmingham, where the firm comes top for planning, real estate, product liability and restructuring/insolvency, trainees say they are 'stretched and challenged.' Senior staff are praised for being 'accessible and appreciative – you're not made to feel like the most junior person around, and if you're doing a good job they let you know, which is a real confidence boost.' Among the office's highlights is the £450m Ventureast development scheme, run as a joint venture between Goodman, Advantage West Midlands and Birmingham City Council. The Nottingham office has a great reputation for corporate finance and real estate, and trainees spoke of 'a great office atmosphere with no horrible crusty partners.' As one of the smaller branches, it's easier to get to know people in Nottingham and trainees described it as 'a perfect training contract setting.'

As well as boasting top-ranked IT, corporate finance, dispute resolution, tax, real estate litigation and competition/EU law teams in Yorkshire, the Leeds office also sits with the best in the country on administrative/public and local government law. Although the computer and phone systems crashed on the day we spoke to trainees, the 'swish' new open-plan office is expected to inject a 'new lease of life' into the Leeds branch. The IT department here has some superb private sector clients and also handles impressive public sector work, such as the reprocurement and restructuring of the East Midlands' schools network (EMBC), which provides broadband connectivity and related services to over 2,500 schools. Meanwhile, Newcastle trainees claim their office has 'the best atmosphere and office culture,' as well as 'very reasonable hours.' It ranks top for employment law in the North East and a seat here can mean getting involved in cutting-edge equal pay litigation for public sector clients. The shipping team is also 'superb – these international clients expect absolute quality and are happy to pay for it, so you immerse yourself in the work and make it perfect, which is extremely satisfying.'

Chambers UK rankings

Administrative & Public Law • Asset Finance • Aviation • Banking & Finance • Banking Litigation • Climate Change • Clinical Negligence • Competition/European Law • Construction • Corporate Finance • Data Protection • Debt Recovery • Defamation/Reputation Management • Dispute Resolution • Education • Employee Share Schemes • Employment • Environment • Financial Services Regulation • Franchising • Health & Safety • Healthcare • Information Technology • Insurance • Intellectual Property • Investment Funds • Licensing • Local Government • Media & Entertainment • Outsourcing • Parliamentary & Public Affairs • Partnership • Pensions • Pensions Litigation • Personal Injury • Planning • Private Equity • Product Liability • Professional Discipline • Professional Negligence • Projects, Energy & Natural Resources • Public Procurement • Real Estate • Real Estate Finance • Real Estate Litigation • Restructuring/Insolvency • Retail • Shipping • Social Housing • Tax • Telecommunications • Transport • Travel

Socially all the offices are active, from Monopoly nights in Cardiff to dragon boat racing in Nottingham, cocktail workshops in Manchester and bhangra dancing in Birmingham. If you want to do charity work, activities such as painting school playgrounds or homeless shelters are always on offer. Most offices have an annual Christmas celebration: in London people were relieved when the firm brought glamour back with a Bond-themed bash after a less enjoyable smoothies-and-crudités party.

In the hot seat

With its renewed focus on corporate and an excellent reputation for mid-market deals for clients such as Citi and BAE Systems, this is a good place for budding corporate lawyers. Trainee tasks cover everything from grunt work (such as disclosure and bundling) to working all hours on completions, which could mean staying overnight in a swanky London hotel. This department is 'notoriously busy' in all locations, with the possible exception of Newcastle, where trainees said they were fighting for work.

Some of our sources felt they had 'come on in leaps and bounds' during their property seat. They get to run their own small files, particularly in regional offices. A seat in the contentious regulatory team is 'really exciting' and involves corporate criminal defence. Tasks include visits to court, 'police-style' interviews and presentations to clients. The ever-popular employment seat sees trainees assisting with tribunals for, say, sexual orientation or age discrimination claims. They also become familiar with drafting contracts and giving general advice to employer clients. In Cardiff seats are available with the 'legal systems' group that handles lower-value personal injury and mortgage repossession cases. In this group trainees are 'treated as a solicitor straight off' and can open, run and bill their own files, get great client exposure, draft advice and go to court regularly. Although some people sniff at this seat, it actually provides extremely useful experience.

The Eversheds contract is not overly prescribed: the firm suggests that everyone does a seat in real estate and one in company commercial, but beyond that there is 'a lot of choice and flexibility.' A few lucky trainees will swing a seat in Paris. You don't need to be an expert linguist as the firm provides refresher lessons. There are also seats in Shanghai and Qatar plus secondments to clients around the UK.

With so many variables in terms of location, department and the individual personalities of supervisors, it's little wonder our sources had encountered everything from 'spoon-feeding to letting you run with things.' They say supervisors are 'strategically picked so you can always ask them questions' and were mostly happy with their hours. The average day is 8.30am to 6.30pm, although it can extend considerably in core corporate or banking seats, where trainees in some regional offices described the regime as 'hideous' and 'London-style.' Many in the regions think they work longer hours than their peers in neighbouring firms, and this accords with what we hear from other firms. Meanwhile, London Eversheds is seen by its regional trainees as an easier deal compared to other City outfits. London trainees generally feel they 'get a lot less crap to do than at the magic circle.'

Down to earth with a bump

Our sources had one thing in common: they were down-to-earth and enthusiastic but not cut-throat ambitious or especially self-asserting. One seemed to hit the nail on the head: 'Eversheds trainees tend to be very, very hard-working people – not necessarily the kind who'll stand up for themselves, but those who will produce a high standard of work, do what they're told and are more team players than team leaders.' One even pleaded for the firm's recruiters to 'inject a bit of soul' into the hiring process. Actually the process has changed recently. Academics are still one of the selection criteria, but the firm is 'taking a more holistic view' these days.

At qualification time this year, many trainees were surprised to find that there were insufficient jobs available in the departments they wanted. They told us these included real estate, commercial and employment. The firm rather confusingly informed us that this was not the case, but also stated: 'In departments where there was a huge demand, there will never be enough jobs.' The process was described by various trainees as 'choppy,' 'unsettling,' 'fraught' and 'a nasty wakeup call.' The disappointment was greatest in Manchester, where morale was low among our sources. One trainee from another office commented: 'They messed them around no end in Manchester and then when someone had the balls to send an e-mail round they got hauled over the coals, which left a bad taste.' We were told by trainees that three out of ten stayed on in that office. Following our request for clarification, we were given the vague response – 'No, there were more trainees than three who stayed from Manchester.' A number of our sources were more confused than anything else. And frankly we were not surprised. When asked to clarify whether it was true that 65 of the 89 qualifiers stayed on across the firm in 2008, the firm merely stated that 'over 65' people had stayed. We can only hope that trainee applicants get clearer information from the firm than we did.

No matter how much they might enjoy their quality of life in the regions, pay is definitely a factor for some, who 'can't say hand on heart' that they 'won't be drawn to brighter lights and more money in London.' Said one source: 'Working hard on a regional salary tends to grind people's spirits down.' To be fair, salaries are a hot topic at other firms, as are examples of 'credit crunch belt-tightening.' In Eversheds' case measures range from the trivial – different biscuits for internal and external meetings ('the lesser biscuit is not great for feeling valued') – to the more noticeable. For example, Eversheds recently shut up shop in Norwich and postponed its pan-office AGM, which normally doubled as a Christmas party. 'They are well within their rights to save money,' said one trainee, 'but when it means sacrificing team morale for profit, it's not good.'

And finally...

Eversheds wants to be a greater corporate force in London and internationally, and believes it can use its national firm structure to help achieve this. It's worth taking the time to understand Eversheds' bigger goals, as these will determine the style and nature of work in regional offices.

Farrer & Co

The facts

Location: London

Number of UK partners/solicitors: 67/63

Total number of trainees: 20

Seats: 6x4 months

Alternative seats: Occasional secondments

Extras: Language training

> 'I think we are genuinely the most loved, cosseted and cotton wool-wrapped trainees in London.'

At more than 300 years old, Farrer & Co has a client list that pre-dates the proverbial hills. Less well known is its success in welding its sterling reputation among long-standing private clients to a thriving practice for businesses and new-money entrepreneurs.

Will conquerors

According to Farrers' own website (which is jam-packed with historical titbits) its tale stretches all the way back to 1701. The first Mr Farrer joined in 1759 and within a short time the firm quickly became a favourite of the aristocracy, royalty and various town corporations. Then in 1790 the lawyers moved into their current address at 66 Lincoln's Inn Fields. It's hardly surprising the name Farrer & Co is now synonymous with the Establishment and a certain kind of student is drawn to Farrers' seemingly unlimited list of well-heeled private clients and venerable institutions... the royal family, of course, being an example of both. These more traditional clients are 'still hugely important,' and if it's what you're passionate about then absolutely you must apply.

When it comes to clients – and trainees – it's 'not just the landed gentry' who come to Farrers nowadays. As well as entrepreneurs and investment bankers there are 'pop stars and Russian oligarchs.' Just like the old landed families, these clients want tax planning and trusts advice to help them preserve their wealth for future generations. Regardless of whether the money being handled is new or old, the firm regularly deals with trusts and estates running into hundreds of millions of pounds. Often the clients are foreign or non-dom, or there are assets held abroad. Over in the contentious side of the practice there are some fabulous cases: last year the firm successfully resisted an application from a man claiming to be an illegitimate son of Princess Margaret, calling for the unsealing of two royal wills.

Dirty sexy money

Farrers' impeccable reputation among private clients is certainly deserved but by no means the only ace up its sleeve. What are the chances of this old-school player being a solid favourite of the tabloid newspapers? Pretty slim, huh? Hardly. Farrers' media lawyers represent News International Limited (*The Sun, News of the World, The Times* and *The Sunday Times*) and Associated Newspapers (*Evening Standard* and *Daily Mail*) whenever they get into hot water. In the past year they've also dealt with an action concerning nude photographs of Sienna Miller and libel actions brought by Heather Mills-McCartney, Roman Abramovich, Ashley Cole, Kieren Fallon, Gary Lineker and Sharon Osbourne. One case that became the subject of huge interest was Max Mosely's claim that the *News of the World* breached his privacy by publishing details of his prison-themed S&M exploits with five women. The firm also advises media organisations on Freedom of Information Act issues and reporting restrictions. Recent examples include the Levi Bellfield murder trial and the case of a juror listening to her iPod under her hijab during another murder trial.

The training programme incorporates both these areas of practice and much more besides in a successful six-seat model. Each recruit spends time in charities or private client; commercial (where options include banking, IP, financial services, corporate and employment); property (commercial property or estates and private property, which includes agriculture and residential) and litigation (family, media or general disputes). The sixth and final seat is taken with the group into which the trainee hopes to qualify. Our interviewees assured us the potential downsides of packing up and moving on after just four months in a seat are outweighed by the opportunity to sample so many practice areas and be better able to 'put the pieces together.' Asked one: 'How can you fail if you're having such a varied training contract?'

Under a Blunkett of secrecy

Private client seats require trainees to do plenty of research, not least because the lawyers and their clients are involved in a never-ending game of cat and mouse with the Chancellor of the Exchequer. Drafting and practical administration skills will also be tested and we hear that the volume of work a trainee can expect can increase in the winter, 'which is when lots of people die.' There's a happy thought. Just like the private client team, the charities group is one of the best in the country and is also ranked in the top tier by *Chambers UK*. Trainees say it is 'like a corporate seat in disguise,' as there is company law involved as well as specific charity law when 'you're playing around with constitutional structures.' Trainees draft deeds of trust and correspond with the Charities Commission on behalf of independent schools, Oxbridge colleges and London-based higher education institutions, including London Business School and Imperial College. Also on the books are Victim Support London, United Synagogue, BBC World Service Trust, the Independent Schools' Bursars Association and nearly all of the national museums in England.

The perennially popular but 'incredibly emotional' family seat nicely complements a private client seat. Back in 1785 the firm advised the Countess of Strathmore on her divorce from her cruel adventurer second husband, who subsequently kidnapped her. There's not as much high drama these days, but post-separation matters are still at the fore of the practice. Following a spate of big-money divorces here in the UK this busy group has done a roaring trade in prenuptial agreements for high net worth couples. Another development was the hire of barrister Jeremy Posnansky QC from 1 Hare Court. He has acted in several important cases, including McFarlane v McFarlane in the House of Lords in 2006 and Blunkett v Quinn, the proceedings between the former Home Secretary and Kimberley Quinn. Farrers is happiest when it keeps its clients out of the papers, and this can be difficult for some

Chambers UK rankings

Agriculture & Rural Affairs • Charities • Corporate Finance • Defamation/Reputation Management • Education • Employment • Family/Matrimonial • Financial Services Regulation • Media & Entertainment • Partnership • Private Client • Professional Discipline • Real Estate • Sports Law

trainees. 'You want to go shouting from the rooftops who you're working for… you read about your clients in the papers all the time and you can't really say anything.'

The price of loyalty

Commercial practice 'doesn't jump into people's heads when they think of Farrers,' trainees admit, though the corporate team has talent. In the past year it carried out 29 transactions with a combined value of over £780m, and recent lateral hires have been made from Norton Rose and Orrick. Its clients are typically small to medium-sized businesses going through sale, restructuring or private equity investment, and the firm takes special interest in entrepreneur-led companies, particularly those with links to other departments in the firm. In 2007, for example, it acted for Sir Keith Mills (the man who's ultimately the reason why all Sainsbury's checkout staff now ask you if you have a Nectar Card) on the sale of Loyalty Management Group to Aeroplan for approximately £368m. Financial services is 'another lesser-known team,' but one that's 'blossoming' and 'looking to make a name for itself,' predominantly by advising on regulatory issues. While 'not the most glamorous of areas,' the trainees we spoke to enjoyed the client contact and were appreciative of people's willingness to explain a complex area of law. As for client secondments previously offered to trainees (eg Lawn Tennis Association, a couple of London museums), these are now usually reserved for those with a little post-qualification experience under their belts.

In 2008 Farrers' new senior partner announced a cross-practice strategic review, hoping to promote interconnectivity between departments. The trainees we spoke to could see no need for such a review beyond clarifying points of contact for a client. Most told us they had always worked in conjunction with other departments and had no problem asking for help beyond their immediate team. 'Perhaps,' speculated one, 'it's more about how it looks outwardly than works inwardly' – a statement that reveals much about the firm generally.

Farrer figures

Trainees find it 'frustrating' that the firm is perceived as 'stuffy,' telling us the office isn't covered with 'that layer of dust that accumulates on ancient deeds' and they don't spend their days 'rattling around in boxes of family jewels.' Nor do they see themselves as posh and tweedy. And yet the firm doesn't go out of its way to actively dispute these ideas. Aggressive marketing campaigns and corporate rebranding just aren't its style; it plans to continue growing at its own pace and 'responding appropriately to market conditions' with the same modesty and discretion that have characterised the firm for centuries.

The typical trainee is someone who 'didn't just apply to any old law firm,' but rather someone who had done a little delving themselves and decided they 'wanted to come here for a specific reason.' The vac scheme is the ideal way of comparing expectations with reality and, as one trainee put it, a great opportunity to 'feel the love factor early on.' Our sources characterised themselves as 'great communicators' and 'bright without being nerdy.' One typically modest interviewee emphasised they didn't want 'to give an impression that we're all sickening overachievers,' but the fact remains that trainees here are 'seriously capable characters' and the kind to excel at whatever they turn their hand to. Everyone assured us the firm definitely didn't want 'law clones,' 'automaton lawyers' or 'drones' because 'our clients want people they can chat to.' Past and present trainees have included former teachers, journalists, those who've worked in the film and fashion industries and a criminologist. Reasonable hours – meaning you're almost always out by 7pm – make it feasible to keep up interests outside work, and many people play sports and music. Said one interviewee: 'My hobbies are important to me and make me a happier and more motivated person.'

There is a work social scene for those who want it. The Farrer & Co choir performs a Christmas concert in Lincoln's Inn Chapel and cricketers can dirty their whites at an annual weekend fixture in Sussex. Rugby is played against Coutts bank. A Christmas revue, penned and performed by the trainees, is 'inscribed in the firm's traditions.' All the comedy is based on the partners and 'everyone takes it very well.' Besides all the organised activities, trainees will often meet up for drinks or meals, even cooking for each other. We're already imagining an episode of *Come Dine With Me.*

Since Farrers got its CSR committee up and running, trainees have been allowed to take a day's leave per year for associated activities and the firm is taking suggestions for events and recipients. Overall support for trainees is said to be 'incredible' and the HR team is open to suggestions as to how to improve the contract. There are appraisals halfway through and at the end of every seat, as well as breakfast meetings with the management board three times a year. 'The training partner,' one source confided, 'is very much on our side.' This kind of environment might not be for everybody, but one source was clearly very happy to say: 'I think we are genuinely the most loved, cosseted and cotton wool-wrapped trainees in London.' Maybe this is why so many stay on qualification: in 2008 seven out of eight did so.

And finally...

In a rather fitting metaphor relying heavily on secret worlds beyond mothballs and ancient fur coats, we're told Farrer & Co is 'like Narnia – there's always something going on if you look a little deeper.'

Field Fisher Waterhouse

the facts

Location: London

Number of UK partners/solicitors: 101/183

Total number of trainees: 41

Seats: 6x4 months

Alternative seats: Secondments

Extras: Pro bono – Queen Mary University Legal Advice Centre; language training

> You can visit FFW without ever leaving home if you're one of Second Life's several million residents.

Field Fisher Waterhouse is one of many mid-sized London firms that attract students who're missing the hardcore-City gene. What marks it out is a collection of interesting niche practices and a growing appetite for adventures in continental Europe.

Pros and continent

FFW must have been doing something right as the size of the partnership has risen dramatically and it has now set itself a huge target of billing £200m in 2012. That's more than double today's revenues. It has its eye on more business from Asia and the USA, and already earns 40% of its fees from international work. Many of its clients fall into the sexy bag – Apple, Viacom, Tottenham Hotspur – and it has the ear of government through its advice to the Home and Foreign Offices, as well as other public sector bodies. Not only is growth a stated aim, FFW is keen to convince the world of its talents in areas other than those with which it is typically associated. For example, our interviewees conceded that 'from an outside perspective our IP and trade mark departments are probably the most well known,' yet they were keen to talk about other practice areas they felt deserved a share of the limelight. Niche? 'That's not what they want to be at all.' Instead, FFW wants to be recognised as 'an all-rounder,' as a firm where, in particular, corporate is 'just as strong' as IP.

The firm's European presence used to mean a network of allies. That network has been dismantled in favour of co-branded operations with associated firms in Spain and Italy. FFW has additionally opened offices of its own in Brussels, Hamburg and Paris after luring partners away from its former allies in those cities. Clever. In particular the Brussels office, home to a competition team, is 'flying' since its opening in 2007 and the number of partners has tripled. Our sources speculated that future trainees might be offered secondments in the continental offices. For now client secondments are the trainees' passport to the outside world. Take a technology seat, for example, and 'chances are you'll get seconded' to one of the department's government clients or somewhere in the private sector. The most popular is MTV, a 'very media-esque' assignment that allows the lucky recipient to 'stroll up to Camden Market at lunchtime in their jeans.' Let's hope it won't be too long before they can once again have a pint and a gawp at Johnny Borrell in the Hawley Arms.

Crocodile tears

Field Fisher trainees typically do six seats of four months each, with the final seat in the department where they hope to qualify. It's not a perfect system (if you don't get your first choice, you're promised a crack at it next time round, which unsurprisingly has 'a knock-on effect') but there's a trainee committee to voice concerns to the administration. Speaking in defence of shorter seats, one trainee argued: 'It can never harm you to move on after four months,' especially if you would otherwise face six months somewhere you didn't enjoy. Of course it's not always ideal that a seat 'flies by,' so it's perhaps best to take the view that a training contract is all about getting a taster of different areas of law.

Whereas in previous years FFW trainees displayed a reluctance to try corporate seats, they seem to jump at them now. 'My year all came here wanting to do corporate work,' one source reassured us. Good job too as a seat in either corporate or commercial is compulsory. The corporate department deals with capital markets, M&A and public sector transactions, and it's heartening to learn that trainees felt more involved in partners' work during this seat than in most others. As well as proof-reading and undertaking long verification exercises, recruits learn valuable lessons, such as how to deal with demanding clients. In 2007 it acted on ten AIM flotations and a further 40 transactions for AIM-listed companies, with a total deal value of over £900m. The lawyers advised Red and White Securities on the acquisition of a stake in Arsenal Holdings for £75m and were instructed by Viacom on a television, film and digital media joint venture with Indian media group Network 18. Finance seats concentrate on either general banking or derivatives and it's worth having a chat with colleagues before deciding which to opt for. The firm represents some 50 banks and financial institutions from around the world, among them Citi, Europe Arab Bank, Danske Bank, AIB and Bank of Ireland.

The number of specialist seats on offer allows trainees to pursue work that isn't necessarily available at other firms of a similar size. Take aviation, for example: the team is a small but growing one which last year advised on over 50 deals with a combined value of more than $4.5bn for clients such as Citi, JPMorgan and the Department for Transport. Primarily a transactional seat, there is some litigation thrown in. IP remains a popular practice area for recruits. This team protects some of the world's biggest brands, including Dell, Warner Bros., Agent Provocateur, Hamleys, Twentieth Century Fox, MySpace, Laura Ashley and Apple. Something for every taste, you could say. Although free iPods aren't the order of the day, we hear there are 'plenty of chargers lying around.' Believe it or not the department teaches trainees how to spot fake iPods. 'They looked at mine,' said one interviewee, 'and luckily it wasn't.' The downside to the seat is a hefty dollop of document shuffling and bundling, but there's also plenty of research and investigation required. In the trade mark team especially there's fun to be had with fake goods. At one stage the office was inundated with 'mock Crocs,' aka counterfeit versions of one client's signature footwear.

Commercial litigation is a large department. Along with the insolvency, travel and claimant personal injury teams, it accounts for a third of the firm's turnover. To say the trainee's job has variety is probably an understatement: any given day could be taken up with a court appearance, hours of research or 'looking through someone's bank details to see where they may have defrauded a company.' Seats are also available in real estate, competition,

Chambers UK rankings

Administrative & Public Law • Advertising & Marketing • Asset Finance • Aviation • Banking Litigation • Capital Markets • Clinical Negligence • Competition/European Law • Corporate Finance • Data Protection • Employee Share Schemes • Financial Services Regulation • Franchising • Information Technology • Intellectual Property • Investment Funds • Media & Entertainment • Outsourcing • Partnership • Personal Injury • Planning • Professional Discipline • Public Procurement • Real Estate • Real Estate Litigation • Retail • Sports Law • Tax • Telecommunications • Transport • Travel

employment, construction, personal injury/ clinical negligence, the professional regulatory group and technology. Just in case we've forgotten any others you can check out the full array of practice areas on the firm's tasteful purple and yellow website. The only teams that don't currently offer seats are pensions, corporate tax, franchising and insolvency.

We ffw, we happy ffw

The firm is demonstrably willing to be flexible with its training programme and we heard of seats being extended when departments wanted to keep a trainee for a little longer or the trainee wanted a deeper experience. It listens to suggestions, as evidenced by the provision of language lessons and fresh fruit twice weekly, though you might only get a piece 'if you're quick.' Each trainee is assigned a mentor from among the solicitors and a second-year 'buddy' in their first week. Appraisals are held at the end of every seat with the supervising partner and/or assistant. Mid-seat appraisals are more ad hoc. In other words you may or may not get one.

When it comes to social events the firm takes a backseat approach. Aside from the annual summer barbecue and Christmas party, trainees are left to organise their own jollies. Said one: 'HR thought it was better that we decide what we wanted to do and they just wave the credit card.' If recent events are anything to go on, you can expect to ice skate, fritter your money away on greyhounds, eat curry and hang out in pubs. Sadly the recently refurbished Mary Janes gets 'too packed since it was mentioned in *London Lite*,' so trainees now head to the Slug and Lettuce. Some departments are more up for going out than others, with employment and commercial litigation leading the way. FFW's football tcam plays in a London law firm league and the office squash courts have reopened after several years, so there's really no excuse for allowing the tikka masalas and beer to win the battle of the bulge. The fact that there's plenty of socialising fits with what trainees told us about their decent work hours. One claimed: 'If you're staying for no reason you look a bit of an idiot.' After 9pm FFW provides taxis for those left in the office, and there's a small budget for takeout food.

Kaleidoscope for improvement

You can visit FFW without ever leaving home if you're one of Second Life's several million residents. It became the first major law firm to open an office in the virtual world, not that all our interviewees were especially impressed by this. 'It's got the firm publicity, so it seems to have worked,' one conceded. The virtual office projects a sleek, ultra-modern ideal self, which is quite a contrast to the real-world offices. These, we're assured, are 'better on the inside than the outside.' We use the plural deliberately as trainees can find themselves in one of three buildings depending on the department they work in. We did hear some criticisms that the office layout, especially in the main site, is 'corridor-ish' and 'higgledy-piggledy,' and the kitchen areas need 'better tea and coffee machines.' Apart from its low ceilings and a lack of sunlight our interviewees were generally grateful for the quaintly named bolthole in the basement. This common room has sofas, computers with Hotmail access, a kitchen, television and a pool table. Other features include the squash courts and a section of Roman London's city walls. We did sense a genuine affection for the offices and their location near Brick Lane, Spitalfields and Fenchurch Street. Then again we also detected a desire to move under a single, sleek, ultra-modern roof. Hmmm…

Each office has a different atmosphere, partly because of layout and partly because of the departments they host. One astute trainee noted that 'the division between the three isn't good for creating a united firm.' This, then, is the crux of the matter. Different offices, different approaches to appraisals, different attitudes to socialising, even different policies on interviewing NQ applicants. In the past it's been said (by us, if you must know) that FFW was a patchwork of independent-minded departments. To an extent this remains the case, though the firm is aware of the need to take steps to work in unison towards a common goal. Unsurprisingly, since the expansion into Europe 'there's been a real drive to show some collective identity' and much greater 'concern about branding.' Cue inter-departmental lunches, softball tournaments and big client events, including a party at the British Museum at which visiting soldiers from the Terracotta Army were the guests of honour.

And finally…

Despite a stated aim to develop its corporate practice and European business, our interviewees weren't overly concerned that the essential character of their firm would be lost. There's still scope for qualifying into its many niche teams. In all, 16 out of 18 took NQ jobs in 2008.

Finers Stephens Innocent

The facts

Location: London

Number of UK partners/solicitors: 36/40

Total number of trainees: 12

Seats: 4x6 months

Alternative seats: None

Partner Mark Stephens is such a well-known legal commentator that he even has his own *Spitting Image* puppet.

Since the 1999 merger between property firm Finers and high-profile media specialist Stephens Innocent, FSI has broadened its expertise. It now wishes to enter the UK top 50.

Reach for the stars

FSI has eight core departments: corporate, property, IP and media, dispute resolution, family, private client, personal injury and employment. Its enviable client list includes movie stars, pop stars, world-renowned writers, business leaders, SMEs and large international conglomerates. Trainees are invariably drawn to the firm by its medium size ('I didn't want to be a cog in a big City machine'), varied business practices, famous private clients and location ('the West End atmosphere translates into the workplace'). Commercial property remains FSI's largest department and it's a mandatory seat for trainees along with corporate and litigation, so be warned against applying here 'if all you want to do is IP and media because a seat there is far from guaranteed.' Owing to FSI's stellar reputation in media law, 'some trainees are disappointed not to get to do it, though this is made clear during the application process.' According to one source, 'IP and media sparkles for trainees at first, but they soon realise there's lots of exciting work throughout the firm.' Many initially became aware of the firm because of partner Mark Stephens, a regular talking head on TV. Indeed Stephens is such a well-known legal commentator that he even has his own *Spitting Image* puppet.

Property, which accounts for over a third of FSI's revenue, is split into three teams: development, retail and leisure, and investment. Following 15% growth in 2007 the department has 'outgrown the existing building' and taken on additional office space across the road at 180 Great Portland Street. The team includes fully integrated specialists in several property-related disciplines including construction law, planning, litigation, finance and tax, giving clients a full-service experience. This year FSI advised P-Y Gerbeau's fast-growing leisure brand X-Leisure on its £39.5m acquisition of the Cardigan Fields complex in Leeds from British Land. It also assisted Tragus Group on the property aspects of its £140m acquisition of Strada Restaurants. Other clients include Technicolor, D&D Restaurants (formerly Conran Restaurants), Monsoon Accessorize, Littlewoods, Pizza Hut and the Barclay Brothers, owners of *The Daily Telegraph*. The construction team has also been advising Tragus on a corporate concession agreement with Center Parcs. Given the general malaise in the building sector in 2008, it's a good thing that FSI had seen an increase in the number of instructions from the education sector, which has not been as affected as other areas such as house building.

According to one source: 'Departments have very different personalities. Property is friendlier than, say, coco on the whole.' A partner and consultant host weekly training seminars which teach, in detail, 'what actually happens when you're negotiating a lease.' There are also monthly trainee lunches with talks given by the training partners, sometimes on soft skills such as letter-writing and grammar, sometimes on hard legal topics. In the property seat you are 'responsible for your own files, do lots of landlord and tenant matters and sales and purchases. It's all commercial deals; generally speaking trainees won't do residential work.'

AIM high

FSI's corporate department has a 'well-developed AIM practice,' which in 2007 advised on over 12 fundraisings and was retained by 22 AIM-listed clients. It is also recognised for its M&A, IPO, advisory work and MBO expertise, and has a number of active clients from the USA and Israel. Corporate's strengths reflect the general activity of the AIM market, so it has clients in the mining, leisure, hotels and media sectors. Deals include advising Interactive World, a provider of adult content for mobiles, on its £50m acquisition of the *Daily Sport* and *Sunday Sport* to create Sport Media Group. Apparently FSI embraced its new client so whole-heartedly that it displayed the saucy red tops in its foyer for a while. Trainees gain experience of a wide range of corporate transactions 'including share purchase acquisitions, acting for vendors and purchasers. There's a plethora of AIM work, such as verification, and when you're acting for the banks, drafting security documents.' As in most other seats 'the more responsibility you ask for, the more you get as the teams are quite small.'

IP and media clients range from major international groups through to individual artists and entrepreneurs. They include broadcasters and newspapers, publishers and distributors, dotcoms, schools and universities, museums and galleries, artists, designers, photographers and photographic agencies, telecommunications companies and celebrities. FSI has experienced a big increase in regulatory work for major broadcasters since our last edition, particularly in light of the premium rate phone-in scandals. The team additionally provides advice on all aspects of publishing from negotiating and preparing contracts to freedom of information issues, unpaid royalties, copyright infringement, obscenity and privacy issues. Digital developments in the sector (such as streaming novels onto mobile phones) have provided a raft of new business opportunities. Clients include CNN, Express Newspapers, The Killers and quite a few names we're unfortunately not allowed to mention. As one trainee put it: 'Interesting clients make for an interesting work day.'

The private client practice has also grown its stable of celeb clients, among them musicians, composers and media and sport personalities – some of them bona fide A-listers. The firm has attracted authors and artists in connection with wills and estate planning, and regularly lectures on this topic. Quite a few of the clients are non-UK domiciled, and given the controversy surrounding non-doms' taxation, FSI surely has its work cut out. The family/matrimonial department shares clients with this team, drafting prenups for the rich and/or famous and

Chambers UK rankings

Corporate   Finance   •   Defamation/Reputation

Management • Dispute Resolution • Intellectual

Property • Media & Entertainment • Partnership •

Real Estate

helping with divorces, child disputes and even international abductions.

The commercial dispute resolution team posted a 25% increase in turnover last year. Recent cases have included a £750m recovery of trust assets being litigated in London, Anguilla and California. Another ground-breaking case was defending anti-corruption organisation Global Witness against a claim brought by the President of Congo-Brazzaville's son to prevent publication of allegations of corruption. The case was raised in both Parliament and the US Senate. In another well-publicised matter, FSI acted successfully on behalf of the Russian government against Shell over the company's activities in the far east of the country. The department's diverse and expanding client base includes *The Times*, CNN, Bloomberg, *The Wall Street Journal*, *The Washington Post* and *The Spectator*. Some 'hefty disputes, several worth many millions with an international dimension,' can run and run for years so FSI tries to involve trainees on smaller debt collection cases too.

Make your case

The seat allocation process is reasonably transparent and entails e-mailing the training partner explaining why you want to do your preferred next seat. 'He'll then allocate according to the case you make. There are rarely any grumbles,' apart from the fact that despite the many different areas of law practised by the firm 'you should know before you join that you'll definitely do property and probably coco, so don't think you can come here and choose the four seats you want.' Which seats are most popular? 'It depends... this year three trainees are interested in employment and two in family.' The working day is typically 9am till 6.30pm, and although 8.30am to 8.30pm isn't uncommon during busy periods, one source emphasised that there 'isn't a long-hours culture and if it's quiet I'll leave at 5.30pm.'

Trainees say FSI is very partner-led and that they enjoy working directly for partners. The main advantage is that 'if you show you can do well you'll be treated like an associate.' Trainees are not generally expected to do grunt work like photocopying. In fact one told us he was 'told off in two appraisals for not using my secretary enough.' Trainees attend monthly financial meetings where their figures are examined and they tell us that the partners want 'people who can hold themselves in an adult commercial setting.' From the trainees' perspective 'it's easy to build relationships with partners who want to see trainees enjoy their work and take responsibility.'

Celebs ahoy!

Since early 2008 the firm has been going open-plan floor by floor. Our sources were happy about this as 'the building was old and falling apart' and the meeting rooms were tired. FSI now wants to appear 'more modern' and grow each of its business areas. 'They don't want to be known as just a property or media firm and they don't, for example, want employment to be just an ancillary of corporate.' The new open-plan offices have 'worked well;' although some of the older partners are 'struggling slightly' without their own office, 'they are making an effort to tone down their voices.'

Recently the managing partner has taken it upon himself to have lunch with all the associates and NQs, four or five at a time, using the meetings as an opportunity to ask them what should be changed about the firm. 'Not much,' our sources thought, apart from a little more interaction between the managing partner and the trainee group. They also suggested that better and more regular communication about where the firm is headed would benefit everybody, although they pointed out that management seemed to agree with this point and was already trying to implement change. The office expansion and its renovation have been mirrored by other developments too. 'There's a new head of training for the whole firm who is particularly focused on improving soft skills training.' 'The firm is full of interesting characters,' we were told, 'and it encourages people to be themselves.' In the five minutes before meetings start, for example, 'it's not uncommon

for people to have a laugh. People try to be as human and relaxed as possible, given the situation.'

Of the 11 trainees at the firm when we interviewed, five were on their second careers. As one trainee's testimony on FSI's revamped website states: '[The firm] really values people who already have some work and life experience under their belt. My intake included a former bank manager, a legal secretary, me, a marketer of health and beauty products, as well as two more conventional graduates, who are as wise and well-travelled as anyone.' Trainees arrange their own social activities from time to time – a trip to the theatre, a darts night, drinks in local pubs such as the Mason's Arms, the Yorkshire Grey or the Albany. When partners tag along they usually insist on going to the more upmarket Villandry, which is fine by trainees as they can indulge in a bit of celeb-spotting. There's always a big summer party, and this year's pirate-themed bash was held at a boat club in Pimlico. A charities committee is now in its second year, the chief beneficiaries of fund-raising activities being the NSPCC and Helen & Douglas House, which provides respite care for young people with life-shortening illnesses. There's a popular annual quiz night and, best of all, 'pre-start trainees are invited to all social functions, which gives them a great opportunity to meet everyone in a relaxed setting before they start.'

And finally...

FSI's blend of commercial and glamorous private client assignments is especially interesting and trainees invariably find this a rewarding environment. In 2008 three out of five qualifiers stayed with the firm, one joining the property team, one becoming a litigator and one going into employment law.

Fisher Meredith

The facts

Location: London

Number of UK partners/solicitors: 18/55

Total number of trainees: 20

Seats: 4x6

Alternative seats: Client Secondments

> The work you do means a roof over someone's head or not, so it's an amazing feeling when it's a success.

Based in Kennington in South London, Fisher Meredith works for both privately paying and legally aided clients. Strong legal skills and a big heart are the prerequisites for a successful training here.

Committed to the cause

If you have an interest in legal aid it's likely Fisher Meredith is already on your radar as it's undoubtedly one of the biggest and best names among rights-based law firms. Founded in 1975, its focus in the early days was to service its local communities in South London, mainly Kennington, Stockwell and Brixton, providing high-quality legal services to those who couldn't otherwise afford them. To this day the firm's mission hasn't changed, though the scope of its practice has; over one half of the work it does is for clients receiving legal aid, but it is also increasingly attracting instructions from fee-paying clients, as well as a growing number of institutional clients including small and mid-sized businesses, charities, unions and foreign embassies. Helping people is what it's all about, but the commercial side of practice isn't ignored either.

Fisher Meredith has a strong reputation in a number of disciplines, including family law, children's law, mental health, community care, immigration, police law, housing and employment. For the most part a specialist litigation firm, Fisher Meredith has also been handling an increasing amount of transactional work, in part because of the impending demise of the firm's criminal legal aid practice, which will cease from 18 April 2009. Everyone agrees 'it's a real shame' as this has long been one of the firm's strongest departments. The group has been involved in a number of key cases, including representing detainees of the 21/7 attempted bombings in London and one of the youths acquitted of murdering Damilola Taylor. The group's demise comes as a result of the state of the market, specifically the Carter reforms, which severely cut legal aid funding. Fisher Meredith is 'still very committed to doing the work its reputation is based on' and is beefing up its public services law department, which covers immigration, police law, family law, welfare issues concerning vulnerable and incapacitated adults, judicial reviews of decisions made by education authorities and a niche area representing young people in care. The firm is currently being instructed by the British Family Public Association and individual claimants in relation to decisions by a primary care trust to terminate funding for homeopathic treatment.

The right stuff

At Fisher Meredith none of the seats are compulsory, so you can shape your training contract to reflect your interests, which is especially good if you have specific aims. 'You generally just get put into your first seat and then e-mail your preferences to the managing partner and HR manager, who do their best to make sure you get what you want.' The prison and police law group is 'an excellent department to train in, particularly as a first seat, because people really invest time in the trainees there.' It's a young team that has been making waves in the market, as evidenced in the group's top-tier ranking in *Chambers UK*. In the police half of the seat, you'll be acting for individuals suing the police, usually for wrongful arrest, false imprisonment, assault or malicious prosecution. 'It's an eye-opening experience: horrible things have happened to people. The seat shows you what Fisher Meredith does very well.' The emphasis on litigation also means the skills you pick up are 'very transferable.' The other half of the seat is prison law, which involves helping prisoners secure and exercise their rights. In this 'interesting and very varied' field there's a lot of travelling to prisons. The group had a recent success on behalf of a client who was handcuffed while being given life-saving chemotherapy. It was ruled to be inhuman and degrading treatment as he posed no risk to the public and there was no risk of escape.

Lean on me

The family law department deals with divorce and domestic violence cases for both high net worth individuals and those on legal aid. Court appearances and client contact are frequent, as is the satisfaction when trainees get to see a case from beginning to end. As one source explained after obtaining a non-molestation order and having a violent husband kicked out of his home: 'It was absolutely amazing seeing the immediate positive impact I had on a person's life.' Trainees who completed a seat in the housing department expressed a similar sentiment, saying: 'The work you do means a roof over someone's head or not, so it's an amazing feeling when it's a success.' Representing mostly tenants and occupiers, this group deals with repossessions, illegal evictions, disrepair and homelessness. Clients are often 'very vulnerable: they're people with mental health problems or who come with a history of being in and out of prison or growing up in care. They're very fragile which makes the help they need even more important.' It's no wonder then that 'you have to move as quickly as possible in this seat,' and there can be a lot of pressure. Immigration and Asylum is yet another popular seat choice because 'there's a lot of litigation and really meaty law involved; you're given a lot of responsibility.' Going to hearings as a trainee is a big perk. Said one source: 'I went to a bail hearing that I'd prepared – it was an amazing experience feeling the atmosphere change as we began to gain the upper hand.'

Most trainees have worked with individuals in need in one form or another before and thus knew what to expect when they started. They say the client contact is 'very welcome and definitely the best thing about the job.' Supervisors generally accompany trainees to client meetings in the beginning, and then they're given more one-on-one contact. As one trainee explained: 'There are cases where, in name, my supervisor runs them, but really I'm the one making the decisions.' It's vital that you have good people skills if you want to work at Fisher Meredith. 'You deal with some difficult personalities and people with mental health problems. Or clients might be distressed,

Chambers UK rankings

Administrative & Public Law • Civil Liberties • Education • Family/Matrimonial • Immigration • Police Law • Social Housing

not very well educated or not English speaking... what the client wants is not always immediately obvious. You have to be a good listener but also get the job done and not just turn into a counsellor.' Another tough part of the job is informing people that they aren't eligible for legal aid. 'It's hard telling someone who really needs help and is far from rich that they have to pay for a solicitor.'

While they're busy providing support to clients there are people at the firm for trainees to lean on. In addition to seat supervisors, there are three non-partner solicitors known by the (rather naff) title of 'pastoral carers', with whom trainees can confidentially discuss any problems they may have. 'They've all been trainees at Fisher Meredith, so they have insight into the process.' There's also a newly launched buddy system between trainees. The firm is well aware of the pressures they face given the nature of Fisher Meredith's work, but everyone we spoke to agreed that 'the results you obtain keep you up. It's worth dealing with the pain.'

Taking care of business

Working at Fisher Meredith isn't all group hugs and saving the world; there's also a lot of paperwork. 'It would be seriously wrong to suggest we do loads of photocopying,' one trainee clarified, 'but the amount of admin definitely does vary between departments.' Expect your fair share of bundling if you land in a team without a secretary, and there are quite a few that lack these. This leads us to the general economic climate of the firm. For some trainees 'the worst thing about the firm is the lack of resources.' The firm does have its financial constraints, exacerbated by the massive cuts in legal aid and trainees say this anxiety means 'it's hard to get anything like a photocopier that doesn't break all the time and we have to cut corners by recycling folders and things like that.' More seriously, 'some people are worried as to whether we can actually make a successful business out of legal aid work anymore.' The raison d'etre of the firm goes a long way towards battling these worries: 'We have a dedication to helping people; that's why we're here. So many people here are incredibly qualified and could be earning whatever they wanted, but they're here because of our common intention.' So what is the trade off in salary for following your passion? Trainees said their relatively low salary (actually somewhat above the recommended minimum for Central London) is 'pretty much par for the course' for this line of work, but admitted 'it does get wearing and can be hard to live on.' There are ways to compensate though, such as 'living a bit further out, not going out so much… and having a rich partner always helps.' Apparently, this last option is quite popular.

In the fight to keep legal aid services alive, Fisher Meredith is in it to win it. This is a firm of 'scrappy people who like a fight; people that will argue endlessly for their clients.' While some called this bunch 'earnest,' others emphasised the sense of humour that's necessary in this line of work. Most trainees have had voluntary sector experiences before joining the firm – as one trainee put it (showing off a sense of humour in the process): 'Everyone here has travelled to a small African country and saved an entire village, personally.' Jokes aside, prospective candidates would do well to rack up experiences working for a similarly focused firm or an NGO, either in the UK or abroad. Of course, 'there are some people who come from a more commercial background,' and as the firm places greater emphasis on its commercial side perhaps you shouldn't let your many dissimilarities to Mother Theresa put you off considering the firm. It's nice to hear that 'the firm's very good at marketing itself to students, and once you get here there are no surprises; what the firm says about itself is never far off the mark.'

Though a social bunch, the trainees have proved themselves quite unimaginative, ending up at local pub The Dog House more often than not. It's just around the corner from the office, which is 'very modern compared to most legal aid firms.' It's a custom-built, air-conditioned affair that's been home to the firm since 2004. It's located 'half-way between two Tube stations, near a nice row of restaurants and bars.' Trainees say: 'The office is quite funky and really shakes off the image that legal aid firms have grotty, high street offices.' The open-plan set-up is a hit because 'it makes it much easier to build a rapport with your colleagues.' About once a month the office has drinks in the boardroom ('the best part of which is everyone going out together afterwards') and there's also a staff away-day every summer. In 2008 this was spent in Cambridge, punting and having a barbecue.

And finally...

'Fisher Meredith is a really fun and rewarding place, but bear in mind that the money isn't great so you should only join if you really have a passion for the work.' In 2008 three out of six qualifiers stayed on with the firm, all going into the public services law department.

Foot Anstey

The facts

Location: Plymouth, Exeter, Taunton, Truro

Number of UK partners/solicitors: 47/97

Total number of trainees: 21

Seats: 4x6 months

Alternative seats: Secondments

A merger in Truro with Cornwall's Hancock Caffin has meant Foot Anstey is now the largest law firm in Devon, Cornwall and Somerset.

Gradually taking over the West Country, this ambitious firm seeks like-minded trainees to propel it upwards and onwards. It offers all the breadth you could hope for, from a strong corporate commercial practice to an expanding private client side and a secure legal aid team.

Best foot forward

For several years we've been giving annual updates on Foot Anstey's expansion. There has always been some development to report: in 2005 it was the breakout from Exeter and Plymouth, which saw the firm march into Somerset through a merger with Taunton's Alms & Young. Next, it adopted Clarke Wilmott's new homes and bulk conveyancing team and a family law unit, and in our last edition there was the merger with ten-lawyer Plymouth firm Serpell Eaton Solicitors. So what's new this year? Never one to disappoint, the firm has done it again. As of 1 December 2007, a merger in Truro with Cornwall's Hancock Caffin has meant Foot Anstey is now the largest law firm in Devon, Cornwall and Somerset.

Trainees are proud of all these developments. Said one: 'I find all the big plans very encouraging because you know they want trainees to stay and be the partners of the future.' The word 'progressive' was used by our interviewees a lot. 'It pretty much sums up our attitude,' explained one source. 'Everyone is just so focused and determined and forward thinking, and doing all they can to help the firm grow.' The latest merger brings the total number of partners to 47 and can only add to the firm's income, which had swelled to £20m by the end of the 2007/08 financial year. It also gave the firm a presence in Cornwall for the first time in over a century.

Growth has not been limited to a particular area of practice and all parts of the firm have plenty to crow about. The agricultural team advises numerous West Country estates as well as The Royal Cornwall Agricultural Association and Devon County Agricultural Association. The corporate practice contributes about half the firm's income and represents an eclectic group of clients. Last year, for example, the lawyers acted for the management team on the MBO of regional specialist chimney and flue suppliers Jarrett Collins, and they have long-standing relationships with The Wrigley Company, NatWest and Northcliffe Newspapers, which they advised on the disposal of 60 retail newsagents. Staying with newspapers, the firm advises some 400 regional titles on defamation and other related issues. Indeed, Foot Anstey's renowned media and publishing team has just completed its first year as editorial advisers to *Which?*, the consumer magazine that invokes the occasional wrath of manufacturers whose products receive poor reviews. Not to be outdone, the crime team has recently won a Legal Services Commission contract for high-cost cases across the region, and is also one of the only three regional firms to prosecute on behalf of the Health and Safety Executive in Wales and the West.

Pick your own

As these varied highlights would suggest, Foot Anstey offers its trainees an impressive range of experiences. It has seats in coco, commercial property, property litigation, planning, insolvency, employment, family, charities, crime, private client, media, IP, personal injury and clinical negligence. Be aware that crime is only available in Plymouth and Taunton; and IP, property litigation, insolvency, charities, contentious private client and media are only available in Exeter. Before starting at the firm trainees are asked via e-mail about their seat preferences. 'And then given one they don't want,' added one trainee dryly. Rather than being a deliberate policy, it's more the case that 'second-years get priority and the firm's needs have to be taken into account as well.' For one source 'it worked out very well. I'd never have chosen the first seat I was given in a thousand years, but it was great. New trainees should be open-minded. You'll get the opportunity to do your first choice later on.' For later seats, the training principal goes round in the fourth month asking about people's choices, although super keen (and perhaps a little panicky) first-years have been known to approach partners directly. Coveted seats are more likely to be gained if you're prepared to move around the different offices, and a bit of commuting carries the added bonus of getting to know more people. The firm contributes to any extra travel expenses, 'so the only thing it costs you is time in bed.'

In past years, private client, family and clinical negligence have proved most popular with trainees, but the latest intake reports 'about a 50-50 split between preferences for those areas and commercial.' This creeping commercial interest is no coincidence. 'It does seem the firm is leaning towards more commercially minded people,' observed one trainee, while another mused on whether it might become more of a factor in the recruitment process. So what might a coco seat actually involve? 'Obviously you're dealing with fairly large transactions so you tend to just assist. I was looking at certain clauses, writing up minutes, drafting supporting documents and helping with due diligence.' A few weeks into the seat and you might get to work on smaller partnership deeds on your own. The hours are regular: 'There were a couple of 8-9pm nights, but mostly you're out the door by 6pm.' Not bad at all, and other seats are even better. 'There just isn't the pressure to stay to look good,' explained one trainee. 'Everyone else leaves at 5pm, so you look silly sitting there by yourself.'

Young and hip

A stint in commercial property will see you working with investor clients on matters ranging from landlord and tenant portfolios to development work for 'very decent-sized developers.' If you're up to it there's the potential to run files yourself. The employment group has got a new client enquiry line to keep trainees busy. 'People ring wanting free advice, which we don't give! The line is just to see if they should come in.' When the phone isn't ring-

ing, there are tribunals to attend and case management discussions. Clients include Odeon Cinemas, Screwfix, South Devon College and the Royal Shakespeare Company. 'It's a very young team and they're all really helpful and supportive.' Commercial litigation gets 'a little bit hectic at times.' Trainees attend conferences with counsel and put in groundwork for mediations. If there are smaller matters, they may even be able to conduct advocacy themselves. The team is growing at an impressive pace: 'Every time we have a team meeting, there's another new face.'

Private client trainees start off shadowing a partner, sitting in on client meetings and familiarising themselves with files. Later on the responsibility increases. 'I now run estate files on a day-to-day basis and deal with all the correspondence. I also draft basic wills and there are always client meetings to go to. It's a nice seat and you see a lot of files open and resolve.' Clin neg, by contrast, has matters that go on for years. Always 'interesting and challenging,' there are meetings to go to, witness statements to draft and letters of instruction to send to experts. The caseload includes 'lots of high-value birth injury cases; cerebral palsy for example, where the damages go into the millions.' The firm works on plenty of cases relating to older people too: it represented eight women in claims against Plymouth Hospitals NHS Trust after unsatisfactory hip replacement surgery.

Day-glo memories

Some of the offices can feel quite separate and trainees are aware of the need for 'firm-wide consolidation and cohesion to make sure it really does feel like one firm.' At the moment the Taunton and Exeter offices are similar in design, open-plan and modern, while the 'tired' Plymouth office sticks out a bit. A new seven-storey building on the harbour (complete with roof terrace) will be available in early 2009, until which time Plymouth staff will stay put in a former television studio. 'I'll miss the fluorescent green stairs,' sighed one trainee. Management is making an effort to foster links between the different offices. 'There's certainly a lot of travel between Plymouth and Exeter, and people are starting to go down to Truro too.

Some departments meet up once a month, others use video conferencing.'

The social life is inevitably affected by the geographical spread. 'Trainees try to arrange things but it's difficult to meet up when we're all far away from each other.' Office-wide activities are more successful: all the branches have Friday-night drinks events every couple of months. 'The firm puts money on the tab – to a point – so you can mix with other teams from your office.' There is only one annual firm-wide event, and trainees are told about it on their very first day in September. 'The Christmas party,' intoned one source; 'it was fabulous last year. There was an Oscars theme with a red carpet, a sit-down meal in a hotel, a live band, a disco and discounted room rates for staying over.' Things are somewhat restrained until the partners leave, 'but the senior ones know that and are very obliging – they leave after the main meal.' For fairness' sake the event is based in Torquay ('so everybody has to travel') and apparently involves so much organisation the firm doesn't have time to lay on any other parties during the year.

All are agreed on Foot Anstey's warm atmosphere and think this unlikely to change, even as the firm grows. 'The managing partner knows everybody by name and walks round the offices saying hello. Everyone is willing to talk and answer questions, and it's not an intimidating sort of place.' As for the trainees, the only common trait is some kind of link to the South West. 'Even then, there are people whose only connection is that they went to Exeter Uni. You don't have to prove you're a fourth generation local.'

It must be said that there are rather more girls than boys in the trainee group, but apart from that it's a mixed bunch, with some straight out of uni and others in their thirties. 'I actually think they're open to anyone who is bright and sociable,' commented one source. We have news regarding the notorious *X-Factor*-style Foot Anstey recruitment day. 'The format has changed – it's now one day, all day, and people don't get kicked out at lunchtime anymore. There's no more psychometric testing either.' The drill is simple: ten people are all asked to prepare a presentation and there are trainees on hand to guide but also observe the group. After a lunch, each applicant is interviewed by a panel and trainees are invited to say which candidates they preferred.

In 2008 the firm produced perfect retention stats: all six qualifiers stayed on, spreading themselves across the different departments.

And finally...

If you're looking for a cosy, small, high street firm where you know the name of all the partners' dogs, you won't find that here. The firm is only going to get bigger and the impressive choice of seats should prove popular. Add in a great work-life balance, and you have a pretty good package.

Forbes

The facts

Location: Blackburn, Preston, Accrington, Chorley, Manchester, Leeds

Number of UK partners/solicitors: 32/55

Total number of trainees: 11

Seats: 4x6 months

Alternative seats: Secondments

Extras: Pro bono – Saturday drop-in clinic

> The buzz in crime comes from turning around a case when the entire weight of evidence is against your client but you know they are innocent.

Forbes is taking care not to forget the clients of the crime and personal injury departments on which its reputation was built as it continues to expand into commercial law.

Hotpot hot shots

Forbes has eight offices west of the Pennines, plus a far-flung outpost over the other side in exotic Leeds, so you could say it is a quintessentially North-Western firm. 'It's difficult to walk around Blackburn without recognising faces we've represented,' confirmed one source from the firm's heartland office.

The firm was founded Way Back When as a crime practice, and arguably its crime and PI teams are still the star performers today. However, as changes in legal aid funding bite and the threat from Tesco Law looms, Forbes has encouraged a slow but steady expansion of its commercial litigation, property, business law and defendant insurance departments. In fact if you look at Forbes' commercial client list it's quite impressive: there's conservatory manufacturers Ultraframe Plc, Blackburn Rovers and Burnley football clubs, Zurich Municipal Insurance, Pennine 2000 Housing Association, Horners Motor Group, Northcote Manor and the intriguingly named Bong UK which, rather disappointingly, manufactures envelopes. Public sector clients include the Lancashire Fire and Rescue Service, the city councils of Leeds and Preston, the district councils of South Lakeland and Wakefield and the borough councils of Wigan and Scarborough.

Anyone worried that Forbes is pursuing profit at the expense of the little guy can rest easy. Crime is still paying enough to keep the firm interested, and this department is as busy as ever. 'The recent adjustments to public funding and legal aid mean many smaller firms are having to drop crime and family because it's not profitable, but Forbes is large enough to withstand such changes.' In fact, Forbes has one of the largest criminal practices in the region and was part of the Legal Services Commission's preferred supplier pilot scheme. It was one of only 25 firms chosen to take part in the scheme out of 4,000 possible choices nationwide. And just look at the prison law team, which now has hundreds of clients, having started from scratch less than two years ago. Meanwhile, the firm also runs a legal clinic in Bolton, and rumours abound of a possible new office there. 'They are testing the waters to see what sort of clients they get and if it's going to be worthwhile,' revealed an informant.

Trainees on tour

The upshot of this private/commercial mix for trainees is that there's a veritable smorgasbord of seats to choose from. That 'Forbes offers quite a mixed bag' makes it particularly appealing for those who don't yet know what area they want to specialise in. And, of course, the buffet table of offices across the region assures it wide recognition among potential applicants from the North West.

Seating is arranged into four slots of six months. The first is allocated arbitrarily, and after that trainees usually get to go where they like, as long as they do at least one non-contentious seat along the way. It's not unusual for trainees who've decided what area they want to qualify in to go back and do a second stint in their preferred department. The multiple offices means it's likely that trainees will work in several locations. The head office in Blackburn is made up of three terraced houses knocked through and the set-up in Chorley is similar. Preston is 'a typical city centre office block' of five storeys, where you might never meet someone from the ground floor if you're based on the fifth. The Preston office has the widest range of departments and offers seats in crime, family, PI, prison law, wills and probate, housing, business crime, commercial property and commercial litigation. Between them, Blackburn's three offices have crime, family, PI, housing, commercial property, commercial litigation, business law, employment, defendant insurance and health and safety. Accrington's two buildings hold crime, family, PI and clinical negligence teams, Chorley is crime and family only, while fledgling offices at Leeds and Manchester deal fairly exclusively in defendant insurance work for commercial clients.

The buzz in crime comes from turning around a case 'when the entire weight of evidence is against your client, but you know they are innocent. It's six people working against the entire police force and Crown Prosecution Service.' Those considering a career in this field must sign up to the Police Station Accreditation Scheme, which requires a minimum of six months' experience and eventually allows the trainee to go on a rota to advise clients in custody at the station outside normal office hours. Not everyone is cut out to deal with assaults, gun crime, rape and attempted murder, nor 'getting a call at 3am from a client being very difficult,' so it goes without saying that 'a tough character is needed.' The firm has developed a reputation for handling business crime and represents company directors when they fall foul of the regulatory authorities. The lawyers successfully defended a company executive on a charge of manslaughter after he admitted a breach of health and safety regulations. They also represented several company directors facing charges relating to immigration and customs breaches.

In clinical negligence a typical starting point would be to assist a partner working on catastrophic injury cases by instructing experts, reviewing medical reports and drafting witness statements. By the end of the seat trainees might get their own files: 'I was the first point of contact for some smaller cases,' confirmed one happy source. Indeed, there's plenty of client contact in most seats. One of our interviewees said of defendant insurance work: 'A big part of my job was prepping witnesses for trial... I did 20 trials in six months.' One recent trial dealt with an employer's liability for injury after a milkman slipped on his float. The judge found in favour of Forbes' client after rejecting the claimant's allegation that the anti-slip chequer-plate metal flooring was worn out. Another success-

Chambers UK rankings

Crime • Dispute Resolution • Personal Injury

ful defence involved a claim brought by a motorcyclist against a highways authority for alleged breach of its statutory duties. The claimant alleged that ruts which had developed in the tarmac were dangerous and had caused him to lose control of his bike. The judge found that the condition of the road was not so defective as to constitute a danger to traffic.

What a way to make a living

In the family seat a common task is explaining the legal process to clients in mixed marriage cases. 'A lot of the time you have an English Asian marrying someone from an Indian or Pakistani background who doesn't understand the complexities of English law... that's quite interesting.' There are around a dozen solicitors in the department, acting for wealthier clients as well as those without a penny to their name. In one case the firm acted for an Eastern European woman who'd been trafficked into prostitution in England. She already had two children and a third child was born as a result of her situation in the UK. The police involved the social services, who then did everything to avoid accepting responsibility to house or financially support the children. As the woman was an EU national and couldn't claim asylum the situation became rather complicated and there was even talk of invoking the witness protection scheme. Forbes' job was to get social services to meet their duties, and this involved liaising with a number of agencies and the local MP. Eventually the client was housed and given some financial support.

Commercial seats are becoming increasingly popular with trainees and provide frequent interaction with clients. There's even the possibility of going on secondment to a client, which is great for 'getting their perspective.' In all seats supervision is usually close, 'but not to the extent that you're not allowed to do anything.' Work will come from the principal supervisor initially (and since in employment there's just the one partner in the office, this means 'shadowing him and dealing with all the cases he deals with'). Elsewhere, two or three partners might pass on work to a trainee and in all seats in all locations 'there's always someone to approach' with queries.

The firm mostly adheres to nine to five working hours, and although these might stretch at busy times, there's certainly no all-nighter ethos. Trainees hungry for extra experience can sign up to voluntary Saturday morning advice clinics to see new clients who walk in off the street.

Rovers and ravers

Forbes trainees commonly have a Lancashire background. We're not suggesting you have to go all trouble at t'mill for your interview, but it's certainly considered 'a big plus' to have a commitment to the North West. Trainees are drawn from an even mix of fresh-faced external candidates straight out of law school and internal candidates who've cut their teeth as paralegals. The main difference between the two is that the internally recruited trainees often have a good idea of where they want to qualify, while the externals like to dip their toes into several departments before deciding.

The geographical spread of the firm throws up logistical problems when it comes to socialising, 'though we all e-mail each other all the time.' Partying tends to be broken down into smaller groups: Blackburn trainees have more of a lunchtime scene, while the Leeds posse let their hair down on a Friday night. Forbes is generous with travel expenses for those who commute to Leeds, though some trainees do move there for six months. The main social event is the firm-wide Christmas party, held at Blackburn Rovers' ground. On the sporting front, the Forbes football team is going strong. 'They keep trying to get me to join, but I'd like to get fit first,' said one trainee who can presumably be identified by a 40-a-day habit and beer belly. A netball team is also doing nicely and there are some keen golfers at the firm. For the less athletic, Forbes has joined the Young Professionals scheme, which means its trainees can meet up with others from firms across the region to compare experiences. Trainees are kept in the loop on firm-wide developments through regular e-mails, and to encourage them to get involved, gift vouchers are offered for good suggestions.

Everyone we spoke to this year hoped to stay on after qualifying and they hinted that the system was a bit of a nudge-nudge, wink-wink affair. 'There isn't any clear process at the firm, but they will try to let you know as soon as possible, depending on the department.' Forbes has a pretty decent record of retaining qualifiers and in 2008 seven out of ten stayed on. According to one source, many people stay with Forbes for their whole career and 'that seems an indicator of a good firm.' Trainees praise its meritocracy, describing it as 'one of those firms where you could start as an office junior and work your way right to the top.'

And finally...

This unpretentious, hard-working firm is well placed to cope with changes in the profession and we'd certainly recommend it to unpretentious, hard-working applicants.

- **Friend of Desmond?** A 2:2 degree isn't the end of the road for your legal ambitions, especially if there's some context to the result. One source who'd successfully gained a training contract said: 'My advice to trainees is don't give up. Search out the firms that look for something else. Look for the firms with different application forms; that have questions you really need to think about and will let you show your qualities.'

Ford & Warren

The facts

Location: Leeds

Number of UK partners/solicitors: 21/24

Total number of trainees: 7

Seats: 4x6 months

Alternative seats: None

> It's nice to walk into a place where everybody says good morning to you and when you get into a lift with a senior partner they know who you are and ask how you're doing.

You may not have seen much of F&W other than its website, so here's the inside track on a firm that's more straightforward than two slide rules in a row.

Ford's focus

We have to admire F&W's simple plan – to stay in Leeds, focus on doing good work for existing clients and trust that this will bring in more business. This approach has served the firm well and earned it a good reputation, particularly in several areas of litigation, private client practice, licensing and advice to the road and rail transport sector. Indeed the firm is so good in this last area that *Chambers UK* ranks it as among the best in the country for regulatory advice on freight and passenger road transportation. Its clients include Balfour Beatty, the Road Haulage Association, Eddie Stobart, National Express, Norbert Dentressangle Group and First Group. F&W lawyers gave crucial advice and representation to Veolia Environmental Group when the company needed to ensure its activities would remain outside the scope of the Department of Transport's drivers' hours and tachograph rules. As a result, local authorities and domestic refuse collectors saved millions of pounds. In another case two partners acted in manslaughter proceedings on behalf of a lorry driver convicted of careless driving. Ironically for a firm with such a pedigree, F&W's office car is decidedly underwhelming. 'It's no Ferrari,' sighed one source. There is no dedicated seat in the transport team as the 'very niche' instructions can be complicated, however keen trainees can sometimes get small tasks from one of the partners.

F&W recruits take four seats of six months, with their final seat usually the area in which they want to qualify, meaning it's quite common for the second year of the training contract to be spent with one department. This shouldn't limit the scope of trainees' experiences as they are encouraged to take on work from teams other than those they're assigned to. The system suits people who are willing to be proactive and 'go out onto the floor, approach people and ask them for work.' The open-plan layout of F&W's city centre office fits the system well. Trainees sit together in banks of desks on each of the floors and the whole set-up seems to foster a good sense of teamwork.

Getting back on track

Among the various contentious options is the popular finance litigation seat. It's common for this to be taken early on in the training contract so newbies can work under partner John Flint, who is also in charge of the training programme. The team's clients include BMW Finance and the trainees have responsibility for many of the applications for court orders requiring the return of vehicles from people who've failed to keep up with payments. While most cases 'go through without hiccup… when things do go off that track they get a bit more interesting.' The seat can sometimes leave you 'swamped by civil litigation procedure,' but there's no way you can finish it without learning a thing or two. One trainee praised debt recovery work as a great way to develop advocacy skills and improve knowledge of insolvency 'tenfold, which I know will be really helpful in the future.'

The insurance seat involves defending companies like Groupama Insurances, Heath Lambert and Amec/AIG Europe from claims in relation to accidents at work and on the roads. Some claims turn out to be fraudulent, such as one from a golfer who alleged he'd been injured when a ground-working vehicle overturned in a bunker. He tried to claim substantial lost professional golf earnings from the club. The rise in motor fraud rings has led to some exciting cases for the team, one of which reached the Court of Appeal recently. The commercial litigation team handles contract disputes, some sports and defamation matters, regulatory issues, construction, white-collar crime and crisis management. Lawyers recently represented a client on a corporate manslaughter trial in Middlesbrough and have been running a series of High Court claims brought against the present owners Leeds United by a former director of the club. These include a £2m contract claim and a defamation action. One of the firm's best-known clients is Dwain Chambers, who has been seeking advice in his long-running fight to save his athletics career.

Last orders

The large and 'fast-paced' property litigation group handles disputes for local authorities across the country. Even relatively southern councils (eg Hounslow and Stratford-upon-Avon) send work F&W's way. The team also receives repeat landlord and tenant-based instructions from pub owners such as Greene King and Admiral Taverns. In fact the firm estimates it acts for companies controlling almost one third of the pubs in England and Wales. Trainees raved about a team of 'guys you really respect,' and who make sure 'you're never hungry for work.' Apparently the lawyers' commitment to providing a great service 'really rubs off on you.' Trainees get stuck into drafting instructions to counsel and making requests for warrants for possession.

It's worth knowing that F&W does a lot of work for companies in the licensed and leisure industry. As well as main client Punch Taverns, the licensing team represents a number of local pub companies and helped the Federation of Irish Societies in relation to the organisation of Birmingham's St Patrick's Day parade. Trainees have 'a massive amount of contact' with licensing department head John Coen and enjoy 'watching him in action at hearings.' Many get the chance to conduct hearings themselves after a spot of 'barrister-style advocacy training.'

The perennially popular and 'thriving' employment group is one of the bigger departments in the firm. It acts for clients in the public and transport sectors, including train company c2c, National Express Group, First Great Western, Arriva Trains, Yorkshire Ambulance Service and several Yorkshire NHS trusts. 'The main thrust of work is for employers,' perhaps in discrimination cases or advis-

Chambers UK rankings

Debt Recovery • Dispute Resolution • Employment • Insurance • Personal Injury • Transport

ing on ballots for industrial action. Leeds City Council recently sought representation on two claims of race and sex discrimination, while another client needed help defending a race/religious belief discrimination claim brought by an HGV tanker driver. The team is 'keen on a hands-on approach from trainees,' so they'll 'try to get you to run some of the cases yourself rather than just giving ad hoc pieces of work.'

Moving away from contentious practice, the commercial property team also has several large pub and restaurant chains on its books and as a result completes scores of leases each year. Other seats are available in corporate and private client, and occasionally in family. Across the firm, work hours aren't excessive and trainees can 'normally leave before 6pm.' A few sources admitted they were 'sometimes put under pressure to meet difficult deadlines.'

Good old boys?

There are a few things about F&W that imply that it's an old-fashioned sort of place. For example, the formal dress code is strictly enforced and being well presented is 'something they judge you on in appraisals.' At partner level the women still have some work to do: just two of the 21 partners are female. And then there's a general dislike of marketing and flash branding. The firm may be about to celebrate its 130th anniversary, but trainees vehemently reject the idea of it being old school. They told us about F&W's 'great IT facilities' and unique project management system and dismissed the notion that the gender imbalance at the top was meaningful, pointing out that the numbers are more even below partner level and that the trainee intake stands at about 50-50 men and women. One source nicely summed up why holding out against current marketing trends is 'not old-fashioned, but speaking to our principles.' F&W trainees seem to buy into the firm's value-for-money ethos and spoke enthusiastically about its 'competitive' rates and how fee earners 'bend over backwards to do what the client wants.' This makes sense at a firm that relies on a high volume of repeat work from large clients.

It's hard to say what kind of trainee F&W looks for. Not one of our sources believed there was a specific type of person who'd fit and we heard suggestions ranging from 'bullish' to those 'more suited to research and head-in-book law.' Some go to F&W straight after law school; others have come from previous careers. The only things that united all successful candidates, it seems, are a willingness to work hard and loyalty to the firm. Oh, and almost everyone's a proper Northerner.

Leeds the way

As part of a small trainee group, 'people recognise you and see the work you're doing' so there's no prospect of 'sitting down and stamping forms all day' or being 'stuck at the photocopier or making tea.' Said one source: 'It's nice to walk into a place where everybody says good morning to you and when you get into a lift with a senior partner they know who you are and ask how you're doing.' Our sources spoke of a 'dynamic work environment' in which people don't stand on ceremony. Everyone's ready and willing to get their hands dirty – quite literally sometimes. 'Solicitors will roll up their sleeves if it's necessary to get something finished or even get down on the floor to look at plans.'

Trainees attend appraisal meetings with the training partners every three months for a dose of 'frank discussion' and 'constructive criticism.' By contrast, the qualification process is unstructured in the sense that it's up to the individual to 'get a feel for whether they have a chance of going to a department' and then manoeuvre themselves into position. There are no formal interviews unless two or more people want the same job. Things usually turn out well and it's common for F&W to retain 100% of its trainees on qualification. True to form, in 2008 all three qualifiers stayed on.

The firm's 'grand' office is nicknamed 'Ford & Warren Towers' by some inhabitants. It is located at the top of The Headrow, across the road from the courts and within easy reach of 'great shopping and nightlife.' On most Friday nights people from all levels of the firm go out together to Greek Street. The current favourite destination is Sam's Chop House because it's 'not too loud and busy.' The trainees are actively involved with the Leeds' Junior Lawyers Division, which organises various social and educational events, and anyone can join one of the firm's football teams or the newly formed netball squad. If you're more a domestic than sporting god or goddess, staff on the first floor have a weekly baking day, which is 'quite competitive and really good fun.' The social events organised by the firm typically include year-end celebrations, a summer barbecue and Christmas parties. The F&W band usually plays at the big Christmas bash.

And finally...

Litigation-driven Ford & Warren is a hard-working firm with a good sense of camaraderie. It will suit someone without pretensions and who likes being part of a smaller crowd.

Forsters LLP

The facts

Location: London

Number of UK partners/solicitors: 33/60

Total number of trainees: 13

Seats: 6x4 months

Alternative seats: None

Extras: Language training

Given its clientele it's only fitting that Forsters should occupy premises of note, and fortunately it passes this test with flying colours. The firm has made its home in a fine eighteenth-century townhouse in Mayfair's Hill Street.

Now ten years old, this West End firm continues to punch above its weight, particularly in the private client arena and all things property-related.

A fresh start

Forsters was created by a breakaway faction of property lawyers from Frere Cholmeley Bischoff after they decided not to join the rest of their colleagues in merging with Eversheds' London office. You'd hardly guess that Forsters is a relatively new player on the scene, thanks to its core of established and prominent partners. The firm quickly built a reputation for its property work and then expanded into private client, family, employment and commercial practice.

Property remains at the core of the firm's success, with public bodies, private developers and property investors all seeking its advice. Last year lawyers acted for the investment partnership Etonfields on a series of purchases worth £55.5m, including the purchase of three properties from Eton College. They also scored their first major instruction from Center Parcs, advising on a proposed £160m development of a holiday village in Bedfordshire. The firm continues to handle an impressive variety of property transactions for funds managed by Invista, the largest listed real estate fund management group in the UK. For instance it worked on a £73m town centre redevelopment project in Carmarthen, including the construction of a major development with over 275,000 sq ft of retail and leisure space.

The firm has considerably upped the ante of its private client offering recently, having poached two partners from Withers – Patrick Harney and Charles Pike – just before going to press we also heard that they were taking another four Withers partners. This is huge news for Forsters

and naturally Withers was not best pleased. The team covers personal tax, trusts and probate work, heritage property and charity advice for wealthy entrepreneurs, traditional landed estates, foreign nationals, private banks and trust companies, and individuals from the entertainment industry. As such a range suggests, there are varied and interesting experiences to be had here, whether it's advising a wealthy philanthropist on the gift of a major library to a UK university or acting for the beneficiary of a major landed estate regarding the possible removal of trustees for malpractice.

Leasehold files and country piles

It seems that Forsters' six-by-four-month seat structure appeals to trainees more than supervisors. 'Some of the partners would like the trainees to stick around for six months, as we're of more use to the department towards the end of a seat.' From the trainees' perspective six seats are best because 'you get to see five areas rather than four, and most of us spend a second seat in the area we'd like to qualify into, which means you get eight months there. It's win-win for us.' Seats are available in employment, commercial litigation, corporate, company-commercial, family and private client, as well as commercial property, residential property, construction and property litigation. Occasionally available, a seat in the growing property finance team could present a second chance to get stuck into some corporate-style work, if that's your cup of tea, while the construction group is worth keeping an eye on as another growth area. 'The firm does its best to make the process fair' and we heard no complaints about the system. 'If you haven't managed to get a seat you want in your first year, they definitely accommodate you in your second.' Everyone must take at least one seat in a property-related area but 'given the nature of the firm that's no surprise to anyone.' Because of Forsters' prominence in the field, property seats tend to be popular anyway, as do private client postings. 'That's not universal though, one of us is super keen on family.' Just bear in mind that it may be 'more of a waiting game if you're after some of the smaller seats.'

The commercial property department is divided into two groups. They do similar work but for different categories of client – 'institutional investors on the one hand, family funds or estates on the other.' You can expect to be busy whichever group you're sitting with. 'There's great experience on offer here,' said one excited source. 'Right from the start you're often working on deals where the other side is second tier or magic circle.' Trainees additionally have their own portfolio of property management files involving licenses to assign or underlet leasehold property, lease reports and Land Registry applications. The partners are all said to be incredibly helpful and 'there's a definite buzz in that group; it's the social hub of the firm.'

Despite often being 'slightly overlooked in favour of commercial property,' the residential property department is also busy. Its trainees want you to know that 'it's extremely good at what it does. We work on some very big purchases and sales in London, as well as fancy country estates. It's great looking through the sales brochures of all these beautiful properties.'

Post haste

Take a seat in commercial or property litigation and you're likely to have less responsibility than in other seats. The firm's contentious capabilities are growing however, particularly on the property side. 'There's a steady flow of lease renewal and claim forms, seven-day letters and the odd petition to the House of Lords,' explained one past occupant of the seat. Trips to court crop up, 'mostly for admin-type tasks, but occasionally possession hearings where trainees do their own advocacy. There's definitely the opportunity to do that if you want.' Client contact should also be forthcoming and the work incorporates both residential and commercial disputes so there's a good variety of subject matter. Best of all, the working hours are pretty constant: 'A lot of things are sent by post to court, so if you miss the post at the end of the day there's not a lot more you can do.'

Sources describe corporate as 'tough but enjoyable,' with the department offering trainees good exposure and plenty of support. 'I didn't particularly know what I was doing to start with, but the assistants talk you through it all.' The clients are mostly entrepreneurs or investors and busi-

Chambers UK rankings

Agriculture & Rural Affairs • Construction • Corporate

Finance • Family/Matrimonial • Planning • Private Client

• Real Estate • Real Estate Litigation

nesses in the property sector. Although the work ebbs and flows; 'when there's a lot on your input is high because it's a small group.' You may find yourself as part of a team of three against a much bigger team on the other side – 'and I doubt the opposing side's trainee gets as much experience as we do.' In the past trainees were expected to take on a fair bit of admin, however the addition of company secretarial support to the team has put an end to this, leaving trainees to concentrate on more substantive deal tasks. 'There are lots of little files – you can run some by yourself – and then there's due diligence, accounts and drafting on the bigger deals.'

Family and employment similarly offer decent responsibility and plentiful contact with clients. Although private client was reportedly 'a bit quieter than other areas' when we spoke to the trainees, 'things are set to change with the arrival of the Withers partners. The emphasis will also be more on trusts and tax planning than wills and probate, which is more exciting.' Throughout the two-year contract, trainees generally share a room with three or four fee earners, including partners and assistants. While there are supervisors who take charge of appraisals, they won't necessarily monopolise a trainee. 'Work comes from anyone in the department, and the firm trusts the trainees to manage their own workloads.'

We need to talk

Given the nature of the clientele we think it's only fitting that Forsters should occupy premises of note, and fortunately it passes this test with flying colours. The firm has made its home in a fine eighteenth-century townhouse in Mayfair's Hill Street. It's a building that's redolent with history, charm and tradition and 'you don't feel like you're working in a normal office.' Imagine the scene: 'There are fireplaces and high ceilings, and when you step outside for lunch you can forget you're in the middle of London.' Fortunately the grand airs begin and end with the décor. 'It's a very friendly place, and the partners are young at heart. Even the most senior people are remarkably approachable, and we're not scared to joke with them or mock them a little.' In the first year, shared training sessions with other West End firms Boodle Hatfield and

Bircham Dyson Bell give trainees an opportunity to 'nosey in on them. You get the impression that other firms have a more structured hierarchy, but I like it better this way.'

Reasonable working hours make it possible to participate in out-of-work activities. 'There's a book club, a film group, a theatre group; bowling nights, softball in the summer and yoga classes in the evenings. If you're keen to do something and you can whip up interest, the firm is happy to accommodate you.' The book club is popular: 'There are usually about 20-25 people at the monthly discussions and we read all sorts of books. At the moment it's *Cranford* because of the recent TV series, but before that it was *We Need To Talk About Kevin*.' Anyone can lead the discussion, from the senior partner to HR to trainees, and we hear there's always a nice spread to satisfy grumbling stomachs. Yoga sessions take place in 'a very peaceful room with a Grade I-listed ceiling. People just go in and lie on the floor in funny positions,' explained a source who was clearly guessing rather than speaking from experience. During the summer, staff can take full advantage of a lovely roof terrace ('the Mayfair Residents' Association lets us stay out there until 9pm') for barbecues, quizzes, and last year even breakfasts during the Tour de France. Worryingly, one source spoke of a karaoke movement, 'which originated in the commercial property department and is slowly spreading.' Perhaps the Forsters' Festive Carols evening should be blamed.

As you might gather from the long list of social activities, people at this firm are 'a little bit extrovert.' Interestingly, we heard that lately the firm has had its eye on more Oxbridge recruits ('there is more of a push to target top academic people') and this observation is certainly supported by an open day solely for Oxbridge applicants. It marks a change from past recruitment: 'No one in my year is from there,' and a 2:2 was not necessarily a barrier in the past. We asked the firm about this and it told us that while the firm's website does indicate minimum requirements of a 2:1 and 320 UCAS points, it is aware that some good candidates do not have these because of extenuating circumstances. As for where people attended university, the firm insists this does not matter.

It can be hit or miss for Forsters when it comes to retaining qualifying trainees, and recent years' stats have swung between 100% and 25% retention, depending on whether the available jobs matched qualifiers' preferences. In 2008 three out of four people stayed on in qualified-solicitor roles.

And finally...

Trainees were hard-pushed to think of any aspect in which the Forsters experience failed to impress. 'I wouldn't come here if you aren't interested in property or private client,' admitted one, 'but if you are then it's fantastic – it's an extremely friendly firm that stands out for its atmosphere.'

Freeth Cartwright LLP

The facts

Location: Nottingham, Leicester, Derby, Birmingham, Manchester

Number of UK partners/solicitors: 79/89

Total number of trainees: 15

Seats: 4x6 months

Alternative seats: Secondments

Extras: Pro bono – Nottingham Law Centre

Trainees say that getting into the *Sunday Times* "100 Best Companies to Work For' survey in 2008 speaks volumes about the atmosphere at the firm.

An East Midlands institution, Freeth Cartwright has its headquarters in Nottingham and sizeable branches in Leicester and Derby. More recently the firm has opened satellites in Manchester and Birmingham, and depending on their success, London may be on the cards some day. For now Freeth has consolidation on its mind.

Something to get your Freeth into

Once best known for major class action litigation, the firm has adjusted its priorities over the past decade. It dropped its crime practice, veered away from the high street and now concentrates on commercial work. There is still a red-hot product liability practice specialising in claims over allegedly faulty products like breast and hip implants, salmonella-contaminated Cadbury's chocolate and the anti-psychotic drug Zyprexa, which is argued by some to cause diabetes. Lawyers here represented claimants in relation to the infant MMR vaccine and recently brought actions against a doctor who negligently treated hundreds of children. *Chambers UK* ranks Freeth as one of the top four in the whole of the country in relation to product liability work and the firm also scores very highly for more conventional clinical negligence actions. All this said, personal injury and clinical negligence have become 'sidelines that the firm wants to hold onto rather than big profit makers.' Seats are available in both areas, but qualification opportunities may be limited in future years. Instead, 'the vision for Freeth is to become one of the top firms in the UK serving private companies,' one of our insiders said. 'That ties in with commercial, property, construction – all the areas we are building up.'

Trainees aren't yet being recruited to the two newer offices, so the contract is definitely an East Midlands deal. Most recruits work in the Nottingham mothership. By far the largest of the offices, it supports teams in all areas of practice, although seats are available in Leicester and Derby. There's no compulsion to visit these other cities, but they always need extra bodies and if one particular seat is oversubscribed in Nottingham, one of the other offices may be able to take the overflow. The Leicester team has moved to swish new premises in the business quarter, while one over-enthusiastic trainee described the Derby office as 'the best place in the entire world.'

Fairy tales

In particular, property is the area that has really grown – the value of deals completed in 2007 was more than £1.5bn. The East Midlands property team is huge, and this area (along with property finance, planning and construction) was the initial focus of the new Birmingham office. The firm represents big-name developers Barratts and Bellway, as well as an eclectic mix of housing associations, corporates, retailers and local authorities, among them MFI, Habitat, JD Wetherspoon, Gala Group, Nottinghamshire County

Council and Loughborough University. In a four-seat system, there are no compulsory destinations, but since 'half the staff in the firm' work in this department, a visit to property is all but certain. Nominally divided into four teams, in practice most trainees receive work from all corners of the department. As the place has been 'very, very busy,' there's 'not an awful lot of hand holding' and some of our interviewees occasionally felt 'a little out on a limb.' Others revelled in the challenges, saying: 'They encourage you to make decisions and do the research yourself, but they are there for you.'

The firm has been assisting Bildurn Properties on two major projects in Nottingham city centre: The Pod, a £25m leisure and retail scheme on Bottle Lane, and the £10m Lace Market Square development that will see luxury apartments and shops built around a new piazza. For Nottingham County Council, it was behind a £7m acquisition of premises in Wollaton, which was then leased back to the seller, and the disposal of some of the council's investment property elsewhere in the country, including office premises in Bristol and a £6.8m ASDA distribution depot in Wigan. 'The big chunky stuff stays within reach of the partners,' and trainees for the most part are involved with the purchase and sale of houses and land for development. 'From day one I had loads of responsibility and client contact,' enthused a source. Tasks include running negotiations to buy sites, bearing the weight of completion procedures, registering land and dealing with clients: 'When they were asking me questions, my partner just let me get on with it.'

Across the firm, grunt work is usually kept to a minimum. Since some trainees seem to believe that 'little magic fairies' do the printing and photocopying, we'll assume the reprographics team does a good job. In the corporate finance department 'data rooms are where you start;' it's one of many essential elements in smoothing a deal towards completion. 'The thing with corporate finance is you have to do whatever it takes to get the deal done. I've been scanning stuff late at night with my sleeves rolled up and everyone else from the partner down doing the same thing alongside me. That's what I love about it,' declared one fan of the seat. Just like the property department, the corporate team is ranked in the top tier in the East Midlands by *Chambers UK*. It represents blue-chip and AIM companies, notably Experian, the FTSE 100 global credit information organisation behind most of the world's credit cards. Freeth acted for Experian during the acquisitions of N4 Solutions (one of the company's biggest-ever UK purchases) and Hitwise Inc, a $240m deal. All up, in 2007 the lawyers completed 12 deals worth £30m or more, three of them valued in excess of £100m. The firm is developing a notable specialism in care home sector deals and this is likely to keep growing.

Chambers UK rankings

Banking & Finance • Clinical Negligence • Construction • Corporate Finance • Dispute Resolution • Employment • Intellectual Property • Licensing • Personal Injury • Private Client • Product Liability • Projects, Energy & Natural Resources • Real Estate • Real Estate Litigation • Restructuring/Insolvency • Social Housing • Tax

Arch enemies

For those who don't fancy pure corporate finance, the business services team works on smaller commercial matters and deals that are described as 'less significant in the grand scheme of things.' One matter was a multimillion-pound company reorganisation involving 'a lot double-checking of documents and files.' The case had been going on for a number of years, so it was a question of 'getting your head around nearly 15 lever arch files' worth of documentation.' At the other end of the spectrum there is 'small-scale company secretarial work' (allocating shares, setting up new companies) and advice to clients on distribution agreements and in-store advertising.

Employment and construction are two areas that complement the firm's major departments, and both have contentious and non-contentious aspects to the work. The employment team's clients include E.ON, HMV Group, Center Parcs, De Montfort University, The British Psychological Society and Derby County FC, and it has defended several district councils against discrimination and unfair dismissal claims. Trainees work on both sides of the team, running meetings, preparing witness statements and doing small bits of advocacy, as well writing staff handbooks, contracts of employment, and health and safety updates. In construction, opportunities for contentious experience are more limited. The team acts for the likes of Balfour Beatty and ASDA, but 'the heavyweight work is not seen by trainees,' who mainly deal with small warranty documents and agreements for the appointment of contractors.

Freeth chief instils belief

Freeth Cartwright's slogan is 'A Different Kind of Law Firm.' This sounded familiar, so we did some research and it turns out that it's also a catchphrase used by Clifford Chance. And Dundas & Wilson. And Burton & Burton, Bells Solicitors and Butera & Jones LLP of Wayne, Pennsylvania. And... well, our Google search turned up 5,100 results for the phrase so we won't go on. This exercise tells us a couple of interesting things. The first is that law firms are actually rather predictable. The second is that they are all keen to tell the world that times have changed and contrary to popular belief, law firms can be pretty cool places to work.

With so many firms keen to show their caring-sharing/cool place-to-be credentials, can Freeth Cartwright justifiably claim to stand out? Maybe. It was, after all, named in the *Sunday Times'* '100 Best Companies to Work For' survey in 2008. To their credit, trainees don't bang on about this, but they do say that 'getting into the top 100 speaks volumes about the atmosphere at the firm.' Praise must go to Colin Flanagan and Peter Smith, the firm's head honchos and the people we suspect are behind it all. One of chairman Flanagan's skills is his capacity for 'banter,' while trainees say of CEO Smith: 'I don't think there are many firms in these parts where trainees would be happy to go and knock on the chief executive's door.' *The Sunday Times'* ranking was not the only gong that Freeth won in 2008. The firm also scooped an award for the quality of the content on its website. RSS Feeds, eBrochures, client extranet facilities, blogs and podcasts are the kind of fancypants technology you might expect on the website of a trendy niche firm, not an unpretentious regional outfit, but Freeth sees itself as a firm looking to the future.

Freeth in the night

The trainees we spoke to were a chatty lot and suggested 'individuality' and 'eagerness' as key Freeth traits. Out of hours there is a 'relaxed kind of approach' to socialising. The Castle pub is Nottingham's main lawyer hangout and here staff rub shoulders with Evershedders and Browne Jacobeans on Friday nights. Amongst themselves, trainees have organised trips to watch greyhound racing, bowling nights, karting and virtual golf. 'I think I managed to hit the ball three times all night,' chuckled one novice. Reality sports are available in the form of football, crick-

et and touch rugby, and some of the top bods got on their bikes recently for the inaugural Great Notts Bike Ride Corporate Challenge, a 50-mile cycle for charity. Less strenuous are the client networking events at the firm's corporate box at Leicester Tigers' Welford Road stadium. We are sorry to report, however, that responsibility for the annual Christmas pantomime has been lifted from the shoulders of trainees. They still aren't sure why after their *Strictly Come Dancing*-themed effort last year: 'I thought we were fantastic,' said one modestly.

After two years, most qualifiers are keen to continue their careers at the firm. 'I was doing a completion meeting and I was pretty much running it,' a source told us. 'There was this moment when everyone was signing the documents and it was going so well and I just thought, 'I love this.' I knew then that this was where I wanted to be.' All seven qualifiers stayed with the firm in 2008. The method of allocating jobs is 'not very regimented' and 'puts the onus firmly on trainees to get themselves out there.' The process was variously described as 'discussing things with the person you want a job with' and 'nods and winks and chatting people up.' This approach isn't a bone of contention among trainees, who describe it as 'fair.'

And finally...

Freeth Cartwright's easy-going nature and working environment is charming. Its commercial teams are doing well and its private client practice is alive and kicking. For those who fit here, this is a great place to be.

Freshfields Bruckhaus Deringer

The facts

Location: London

Number of UK partners/solicitors: 160/540

Total number of trainees: 200

Seats: 3 or 6 months long

Alternative seats: Overseas seats, secondments

Extras: Pro bono – RCJ CAB, Tower Hamlets Law Centre, Liberty, FRU, US death row appeals; language training

In this big beast of a corporate firm 650 lawyers work in corporate worldwide and the division generates around 30% of revenue.

More than two centuries old, Freshfields' proud history is still an important influence on the magic circle firm. It helps explain its present-day excellence and its characterful yet gentlemanly approach to business.

Pedigree chums

In 2000 Freshfields merged with two heavyweight German law firms and added the Bruckhaus Deringer to its name. Apart from giving switchboard staff a real mouthful to get through, the merger created a giant 2,400-lawyer organisation with 26 offices in 15 countries. Yet, despite its size, reach and prowess, Freshfields has always resisted the sort of 'glitz-and-glamour approach of other firms,' presenting itself as a conservative, collegiate workplace. Even old dogs can learn new tricks. As part of 'a genuine push to move into the 21st century in profile and accountability,' Freshfields acquired a sleek, 'modern and user-friendly' website to replace a somewhat staid creation. And perhaps prompted by a recent (successfully defended) age discrimination claim, it now fully outlines its diversity policies and statistics and has created the role of international HR partner. For once it caught the rest of the magic circle napping by being the first international firm to publish an externally verified corporate social responsibility report and the only magic circle firm to promote Fairtrade Fortnight.

The firm whose approach to recruitment was always understated suddenly has a bells-and-whistles graduate website with slickly produced videos, glamour shots of a diverse group of trainees and arty photos of the Fleet Street premises. An angel logo derived from the Freshfield family crest still oversees everything, and those videos stress the firm's long-standing excellence ('We've been advising some of our clients for cen-

turies…'), so there's an element of why fix what isn't broken? One of those age-old clients, The Bank of England, instructed Freshfields on its £50bn joint attempt with the US Federal Reserve and other state banks to provide much-needed liquidity in the global financial markets.

Freshfields is a master of big deals. It advised Porsche as it moved to take a €10bn majority stake in Volkswagen, Pearl Group on a £4.9bn unsolicited cash offer for Resolution, and Citi Infrastructure on the £3bn take private of Kelda. Meanwhile, the real estate team helped US investment company Lone Star on the €1bn purchase of 1,300 properties from Deutsche Post. And proving that the credit crunch doesn't have to be bad news for everyone, Freshfields advised Northern Rock when it became a takeover target, helped state-owned KfW and a pool of German banks put together a £5.8bn rescue fund for trouble-struck IKB, and scored a number of significant Chinese instructions including a $1.9bn IPO for China SOHO.

The long and the short of it

Freshfields' training involves a recommended initial six-month seat followed by stints of either three or six months. Essentially trainees extend the three-month seats they most enjoy, unless it's an oversubscribed niche seat. No seats are compulsory, but the size of the corporate and finance divisions mean that most trainees will visit both. The system gets a big thumbs-up: 'You can sample areas you're not sure about' or 'broaden your understanding, maybe doing a real estate seat to back up corporate.' The downsides are 'more for the firm than trainees,' although 'it can be frustrating that you leave a team just when you've got going.' This becomes more apparent in a department in which you hope to qualify, especially if it's a niche area. The firm's insists that three-month seats don't compromise qualification prospects and there is anecdotal evidence to support this view. It's also fair to say that HR does very well at placing 200-odd trainees in new seats.

In this 'big beast of a corporate firm,' 650 lawyers work in corporate worldwide and the division generates around 30% of revenue. Whether in a general M&A seat or one more focused on private equity, there's no escaping the common denominator of 'spending 60-70% of your time managing a data room and things arising out of that... answering queries, finding documents, attending to schedules of documents.' Here the definition of a relatively small deal is something like Guardian Media Group's £1bn recommended cash offer for the business-to-business arm of publishing giant Emap. Defenders of drudge work say it teaches 'management skills and discipline;' it certainly makes more engaging tasks all the sweeter. For those who 'prove reliable' there's the prospect of 'reviewing documents with a senior associate and being fully integrated into the team.' One hard worker remembered 'doing a restructuring for a very well-known company where I was getting work similar to that of a newly qualified associate.'

Five into two does go

Freshfields recently restructured its finance division in a manner best described as clinical. After the departure of 30 older partners following changes to the pension scheme, in 2007 more than 50 others left, many of them finance lawyers. This purge had some claiming that Freshfields no longer valued finance work, however the recent hire of crack lawyers Maurice Allen and Mike Goetz from White & Case tells a different story. Five largish finance divisions have become two broad groups covering structured and asset finance, and banking and restructuring respectively. Our sources had noticed 'downtimes and uncertainty in some teams,' but also that 'the atmosphere in finance is much improved.' They understand the firm's strategic aims: 'It's a back-to-basics approach; we're very much a corporate giant and we're trying to generate the work from corporate clients.'

Contentious, moi?

Getting in touch with one's inner litigator is relatively easy. There's a two-week litigation course for hard-nosed transactional types, but thanks to three-month seats and a healthy dispute resolution division, even they can give in

Chambers UK rankings

Administrative & Public Law • Asset Finance • Banking & Finance • Banking Litigation • Capital Markets • Competition/European Law • Construction • Corporate Finance • Data Protection • Dispute Resolution • Employee Share Schemes • Employment • Environment • Financial Services Regulation • Fraud: Civil • Information Technology • Insurance • Intellectual Property • Investment Funds • Media & Entertainment • Outsourcing • Pensions • Private Equity • Product Liability • Projects, Energy & Natural Resources • Public International Law • Public Procurement • Real Estate • Real Estate Finance • Restructuring/Insolvency • Retail • Sports Law • Tax • Telecommunications • Transport

to secret urges. 'Personally I think it's a bad idea not to have any experience of litigation,' said one source; 'you see how things end up if it all goes wrong.' Freshfields' Paris office takes some beating in the international arbitration arena, and London is no slouch. Getting involved with a large case at the right time means 'awesome experience.' Said one trainee: 'A very big case came in a month after I started so I attended court, drafted instructions to counsel, went to all the client and strategy meetings and became a real part of the team.' Another had 'spent a lot of time working with a senior associate and the New York office on a long-running arbitration in the Czech Republic.' The habit of encouraging a change of supervisor after three months also helps combat responsibility deficiency.

Because this department is 'heavily oversubscribed in the rotation and qualification cycle,' making your mark is crucial. 'It's simple, you know you need to be doing certain types of work to have a chance of qualifying there,' a pragmatic bod explained. 'When someone tried to borrow me for a mundane task I had no hesitation pointing out to my supervisor that I'd done lots of that already and he stuck up for me.' Disputes is the only area where trainees detect a whiff of 'manoeuvring when it comes to qualification. It's not backstabbing, but having worked for the right partners and associates really helps.'

With this choice, you are spoiling us...

There are a swathe of seats in smaller departments like IP, competition, employment, environment, real estate and tax. Offering 'intimacy and friendliness,' such teams handle interesting work, although time is also given to bigger transactional departments. It seems the perils of big-case syndrome aren't unique to those bigger departments. One competition law trainee 'worked almost exclusively for Tesco on the market investigation by the Competition Commission. I was just reviewing documents and evidence…'

Most trainees go overseas or to a client, usually in their final seat. Going abroad can apparently 'make you feel like you're an ambassador for London visiting a Freshfields colony,' although we do wonder what the Paris arbitration team, the New York office, the German arms and other Freshfields notables might make of that description. Quite apart from the location-specific delights of working abroad ('fewer staff, less supervision, more freedom') many offices offer a welcome dose of 'added responsibility.' Client secondments are secured via 'informal interviews with associates in related departments to make sure you aren't particularly incompetent,' and returning trainees definitely feel the benefit of 'added commercial savvy.'

On-the-job training starts as early as the 'simulated office' exercises on Freshfields' tailored LPC, where you get to pretend you're a trainee lawyer shortly before becoming one. It continues with a fortnight's induction at the start of the contract, which includes an infamous talk on the dress code. This is seen as 'mostly harmless,' even by those 'who don't wear make-up and object to being told it helps you be more successful.' Trainees say the firm's gentlemanly reputation is fair. 'It is exactly that. There's a good atmosphere without barriers between people, and while different teams have their own nuances they all fit into that ethos.' The atmosphere is collegial and 'partners try not to come across like scary head teacher figures.' One trainee recalled how 'on one long case my supervisor said, 'Let's go out for a drink,' and it was nice to talk about what he was doing with his kids instead of work.'

Because trainees work for a variety of partners and associates in each seat, developing a 'self-assured ability to manage your time' and 'getting along without constant feedback' becomes important. Appraisals are for the most part 'taken very seriously,' even if the logistics of collating comments from everyone and finding time in a partner's diary can be tricky. As a team resource 'you need to learn to say no, otherwise you'd sink.' Department managers 'watch your workload' and supervisors help to keep 'mind-numbing tasks to a minimum.' One source was e-mailed by HR to check they were okay after it was noticed they'd done several 60 to 70-hour weeks. Most of our interviewees had worked 'regularly to 10pm,' even if '9am to 7pm or 8pm' is an average day.

Fresh recruiting

Since becoming trainee recruitment partner, corporate rainmaker Mark Rawlinson has enlisted the help of 14 new partners (from a broad spread of universities). Even so, trainees foresee little change to the firm's essential requirements: 'They recruit people who are understated, not flashy,' one reflected; 'the general sense of my intake was a bunch of people who didn't talk too loudly and went about their business.' The 'blues and blondes' stereotype of yore still holds some truth (the Oxbridge bit anyway), with 44% hailing from that background. However, recruiters now engage with many more universities. In summer 2008 around 20% of trainees were from ethnic minority backgrounds and 53% were female.

The firm routinely retains most of its qualifiers and in 2008 kept on 85 out of 90. After qualification the road to partnership is too long for most: 'I want to spend more than a couple of years here, but it's not good for your health to look at partner prospects,' indicated one typical source. Recognising this problem, Freshfields introduced an 'of counsel' career path, and has been engaging with associates via away days and consultations. We'll leave you to do the maths, but this year 25 associates were made up to partner worldwide, eight of them in London.

With around 100 new trainees arriving each year, the social scene starts with a bang before 'tailing off as everyone becomes more established,' though there are more than enough 'impromptu Friday or Thursday drinks' to satisfy those who feel 'it's important to socialise with colleagues.' There's also just about every sort of sports team and even an on-site gym with an instructor who doubtless approves of the free fruit offered throughout the building. The highlights of the trainee year are the summer and winter balls, while departmental bashes have included such glitzy events as 'a party at the flight deck of the Science Museum – good fun, fantastic food, everyone mucking in.'

And finally...

At times Freshfields will demand considerably more than you could imagine. Yet the rewards – financial and otherwise – are absolutely huge and if you train here you'll be able to write your own ticket in the future.

Words our Trainees use to describe us (in no particular order)...

Easy-going
Inspirational
Competitive
Invigorating
Well-balanced
Friendly

For more information visit our website or contact our Graduate Recruitment Team on 029 2039 1495

www.geldards.com

Geldards L

Geldards LLP

The facts

Location: Cardiff, Derby, Nottingham

Number of UK partners/solicitors: 55/74

Total Number of Trainees: 16

Seats: 6x4 months

Alternative Seats: None

> In terms of getting the best work, the trainees' advice is to pipe up and show people early on you are enthusiastic and willing.

Geldards is a firm of two halves. In Wales it stomps over most of the competition, winning hefty instructions from leading Welsh clients. In England it has a pair of offices in Derby and Nottingham and competes well against the East Midlands pack.

Divided unison

Previously known as Edwards Geldard, in 2005 the firm abbreviated its name and converted to LLP status. A management shake-up followed in 2007 and the firm has now refashioned itself along more commercial lines. Its debt collection team has been downsized and trainees no longer undertake seats in personal injury or private client practice. Our parent guide *Chambers UK* puts the Cardiff office in the top tier in Wales for corporate finance, IP, employment and commercial litigation, and as our sources were quick to point out, it's one of the best known and most accomplished of the Welsh firms. In the East Midlands, Geldards is not quite the king of the hill, but it does rank very highly in areas such as employment, construction and real estate. As trainees pointed out: 'On our deals we are usually on the other side of the region's big names.'

Aside from an induction week together (including a tour of each other's offices) and then 'the occasional phone call,' there is not much contact between the two halves of the firm as far as trainees are concerned. Recruits train in one region or the other, although from what we can tell they find a remarkably similar ideology and an 'excellent quality of work' in each. In Cardiff, the firm's client roster runs from small local start-ups to some of the biggest legal instructors in the country – Geldards sits on one of the biggest public sector legal panels in the history of Wales, a panel that combines the legal spends of numer-ous government bodies including The Welsh Assembly, The Countryside Council for Wales, The Arts Council for Wales and the Sports Council for Wales. Also on the client roster are Admiral Insurance, TV channel S4C, car dealer Pendragon, numerous county councils and RBS.

Over in the East Midlands, the firm acts for the likes of Midland Mainline, ntl:Telewest and Balfour Beatty, and recently advised the shareholders of Derby City Football Club on its takeover. The East Midlands offices also boast a German law team and a growing international caseload for clients in India, Eastern Europe and North America. For example, lawyers advised North American-based Tesla Exploration on its multimillion-pound acquisition of IMC Geophysics International.

Six-seat settlement

Training works on a six by four-month seat rotation, the appeal of which is 'always up for debate – some people love the choice they get, others feel they are just getting settled before they have to move on.' Said one source: 'Seats can be over so quickly that it's hard to work out what you are good at.' The system is fairly straightfor-ward: trainees have no say as to their first two seats; everyone must try corporate, litigation and commercial property at some point; and the norm is for trainees to spend the sixth seat in the department where they want to qualify. At seat selection time trainees in both regions 'sit down and have a chat together first, so in case there are any clashes we can work it out before we go to HR.'

East Midlands trainees move between Derby and Nottingham. It doesn't seem to cause any fuss as it's only a 16-mile journey by car or train and 'both offices are on business parks within walking distance from the station.' All three offices offer seats in commercial property, employment and corporate, and then each has its own specialities. Nottingham is the place for business recovery and insolvency, and the chance to work your language skills in the German team. Derby has commercial litigation, construction and commercial contracts and utilities. Cardiff also boasts a good litigation team, as well as a highly respected planning, development and public law department and a crack IP team.

A fair day's work

Commercial property seats give trainees good experience of all the basics – 'post-completion stuff, searches, leases and transfers,' while working for a varied clientele. In Cardiff, recent deals included advising Associated British Ports on a series of property transactions including a biomass power station, a biodiesel refinery and a five-site wind turbine project. Also in Cardiff is the popular commercial litigation seat. The work in this busy department ranges from judicial reviews to IP cases to contractual disputes and 'everyone visits the RCJ in London at some point.' In both Cardiff and Derby, litigation trainees learn how to draft claim forms, defences and witness statements, and tell us that luckily 'you don't spend hours bundling.' One recent case handled in Cardiff was the substantial shareholder dispute relating to Neath Rugby Limited; over in Derby the team acted for a large motor retailer defending claims in excess of £2m.

Derby's commercial contracts and utilities team covers 'anything and everything contract-wise,' and under the guidance of partner Roman Surma trainees are exposed to a large amount of rail, transport and utilities work, which typically means 'researching into water or electricity distribution licensing.' Employment law is popular in both regions and the employment team in Cardiff has 'grown massively' in the past few years. The firm now advises 12 local authorities in Wales and three in England in relation to equal pay issues and other strategic work. All up it has handled more than 6,000 claims and provides strategic advice to authorities on the implementation of revised pay structures. For example it has been defending Coventry City Council in tribunal hearings in connection with more than 500 equal pay claims.

Less popular is the planning, development and public law department, which has 'a reputation for being a bit slower with lower-quality work for trainees' involving 'a fair bit of form-filling and lots of research.' The complex

Chambers UK rankings

Administrative & Public Law • Banking & Finance • Construction • Corporate Finance • Debt Recovery • Dispute Resolution • Employment • Environment • Information Technology • Intellectual Property • Local Government • Media & Entertainment • Planning • Private Client • Real Estate • Real Estate Litigation • Restructuring/Insolvency

nature of files may well be what causes the trainees' sense of impotence, however they do get the thrill of attending 'huge planning inquiries, site visits and client meetings.' Some trainees are wary of the corporate department because it can be either 'manic or dead – it all depends on the deals.' This means some people have to work late nights and weekends while others 'manage to get out the door at 5pm at times.' Recent East Midlands deals include Pendragon's acquisition of businesses in the Dixon Motors chain from the administrators and a series of care homes acquisitions for Ross Healthcare. Over in Cardiff the team was reappointed to the RBS and Lloyds TSB panels for corporate transactions, and last year was responsible for more than 30 deals worth over £600m.

Trainees in the East Midlands and Cardiff attend monthly meetings at which the CEO updates everyone on the state of play. 'They talk about the good and bad, which is important,' a source told us. The flow of information also works the other way and in both regions there have been forums at which a spokesperson put forward the trainees' views to HR, the training principle and the CEO. An upgraded intranet has also been used to improve communication by 'getting departments to write about the big deals and cases they are working on.'

Crazy crazy nights?

Although experiences are similar in both regions, the levels of responsibility are 'a little department dependant,' with the smaller ones generally giving more. 'They build you to a position where they can trust you' before you are given anything too demanding, and this trust clearly comes faster in some areas than others. One trainee spoke about being thrown into court on their own on the second day of their seat. In terms of getting the best work, the trainees' advice is to 'pipe up and show people early on you are enthusiastic and willing, then they give you more.' Hours are 'never crazy' with all our interviewees averaging 9am to six-ish. Trainees' desks are usually positioned with support staff in open-plan parts of the offices, but not always; 'you can be in with a partner.' Supervisors, along with everyone else, are said to be more than happy to help whenever you get unstuck: 'You can just walk into an office if you have a question.' On the downside, in both regions we did hear a few mutterings that the appraisal system could be better. There is always a formal end-of-seat review meeting and some people suggested there was a formal mid-seat one too. Others were under the impression that the mid-point appraisal was more of an informal chat, but either way 'you don't always get it as it can depend on how busy the team is.' This is deemed to be 'a shame, as it helps to know how you are doing when you are still in a seat.' One source thought HR could perhaps 'police the system more strictly.'

Although 'in practice the two regions work as separate firms in two different market places,' we observed many similarities. As is typical of regional firms, in each location most trainees had a strong local connection, be it through family or study. A number of Cardiff staff speak Welsh and some clients like to deal mainly in the local tongue. Apparently 'it can be can be difficult when proofreading.' When asked what sort of new recruits the firm is looking for, our sources insisted: 'It's not just about grades.' The ideal candidate is said to be 'a well-rounded person with a bit of character.' The firm clearly chooses well – in 2008 all four qualifiers stayed in Wales and three of the four did so in the East Midlands.

The social scene is 'pretty busy.' In Derby, people frequent Old Orleans ('we never seem to make it past there'), while the venue of choice in Cardiff is Bar 33 ('on occasion partners do buy the drinks'). Cardiff hosts bi-monthly drinks in the office and these 'can end up becoming a crazy night in town.' Each region has a Christmas and summer party, and the sports and social committees also organise events such as trips to Go Ape and *Dancing on Ice* in the East Midlands, and paint balling and comedy nights in Wales. One high point was the Three Peaks Challenge, which a team of six took on to raise money for charity. The CEO gave up his whole weekend to be the team's driver.

And finally...

A good way to get a feel for the firm is through the summer vacation scheme. Although 'a tough week,' as trainees visit a different department each day, it should enhance your chances of securing a contract.

Gordons LLP

The facts

Location: Bradford, Leeds

Number of UK partners/solicitors: 40/64

Total number of trainees: 16

Seats: 4x6 months

Alternative seats: None

Last year Gordons adopted the phrase 'Let's get down to business' as its strapline and that's exactly what it's doing.

Following a series of mergers, Gordons is becoming one of Yorkshire's hottest independent law firms. Valuing its connections in the local area and its people, this firm has strong commercial expertise as well as services for the individual.

No place like home

Originally from Bradford, over the last 100 years Gordons has grown through mergers, most recently with Leeds-based Nelson & Co in 2004 and Bradford firm David Yablon in 2007. Given that Leeds is the legal hub of the North East, the Bradford merger highlights the firm's commitment to the city of its roots. It was also a smart move in terms of new clients – David Yablon represented FTSE 250-listed retailer Findel and Britannia Developments.

As most have grown up in the area trainees are usually drawn to Gordons for its location. They value the firm's dedication to the region through its commitment to local clients – both companies and individuals – and its support for local charities. One of its solicitors currently holds the post of vice-president of the Bradford Law Society. The firm is equally keen on recruiting local lads and lasses, and attends university recruitment fairs 'mostly on the northern circuit, such as Leeds, Northumbria and Sheffield universities.' As of 2008 this list includes Birmingham, Manchester and Warwick unis too.

Last year Gordons adopted the phase 'Let's get down to business' as its strapline and that's exactly what it's doing. Our parent guide *Chambers UK* rates the firm in a number of areas, including corporate, real estate and private client, and weekly industry mag *The Lawyer* has it at the top of its Rising 50 table. Turnover has increased over the past five years and the average annual profit per equity partner sits at a very healthy £547,000. That's as high as some major City of London firms. As part of its growth strategy, the firm is investing in new business areas, in the past year establishing new teams in the areas of corporate banking, contentious wills and trusts and insolvency. With clients such as Morrisons (which the firm advised during its billion-pound buyout of Safeway), American brewer Coors, the Solicitors Regulatory Authority (SRA) and LA Fitness on its books, Gordons is moving into the territory of the region's Big Six law firms – Addleshaws, DLA Piper, Eversheds, Hammonds, Pinsent Masons and Walker Morris. It is poaching lawyers from their ranks too.

A tale of two cities

The training contract follows a standard four-seat rotation with trainees 'encouraged' to complete seats in commercial property, corporate and litigation. They experience both the Leeds and Bradford offices, however the majority of seats are offered in Leeds. When we asked why, none of the trainees could put their finger on it: 'It's not because of numbers or skills; the firm is split about 50-50 across the two sites and the work is the same in each.' The Bradford office does tend to focus on Bradford-based clients, and maybe this is why the offices 'do feel slightly different.' One source admitted that Bradford can be 'a culture shock' compared to Leeds. Who knows, perhaps it's all down to feng shui. Bradford operates out of a 'lovely historic building, but as it is all rooms and corridors it is a bit like a rabbit warren,' whereas the Leeds office building, adjacent to the canal, is very modern and everyone sits open plan.

Commercial property is the firm's largest department, lately contributing around 30% of annual turnover. Handling transactions from across the region, the department has particular strength in the retail sector through its well-established links with Morrisons. It also represents numerous financial institutions, such as Alliance & Leicester and Anglo Irish Bank, and has acted on a large number of acquisitions and subsequent disposals of residential developments by companies including Orion Homes and Northern Eye. The trainees' work is varied, with one source having the 'interesting but time-consuming' task of trying to prove a client owned its land before it could sell it as all the deeds had been lost. Another reported 'lots of lease work – drafting extensions and the related landlord and tenant issues.' The 'young team' provides its trainees with a full inbox and is 'easily approachable' when they become unstuck. There's also a seat in the residential property department, working for mortgage companies and on referrals from estate agents. It was one of the first teams in the region to offer advice on alburaq mortgages, which are a Shari'a-compliant alternative to a traditional mortgage. Fridays are a big day in this department as 'everyone wants to complete then, so they can move at the weekend.' Ensuring things run smoothly for D-day, trainees get the chance to run their own caseloads as well as assisting the rest of the team.

The other big department – corporate – was described as having 'a good team that really makes the effort to get you involved and explain things to you.' As a result trainees enjoy their time here, even though they may need to endure one or two all-nighters. As one put it: 'I guess you have to get your battle scars as a trainee.' The department, which offers seats in Bradford and Leeds, advises big and small businesses on deals right across the North of England. Trainees help draft terms and conditions, work on disclosure and assist on share purchase agreements, and then there's also the 'more basic work of form-filling, preparing bibles and lots of due diligence.'

I heard it in the post room...

With your first two seats selected for you (usually corporate and property), the second year is the time for pushing for your preferred departments. Up for grabs are private client, risk and compliance, family, construction, commercial litigation and employment. Litigation-based seats at Gordons see trainees spending a fair amount of time in court or tribunal, maybe even trying your hand at some advocacy. Trainees usually get their preferred seats, unless

Chambers UK rankings

Corporate Finance • Dispute Resolution • Employment • Family/Matrimonial • Intellectual Property • Private Client • Real Estate

they go for something that's way oversubscribed. Last year that meant employment, this year it's been family.

The employment department focuses on more profitable respondent work, advising larger international employers and smaller local businesses on their contracts of employment, disciplinary and grievance procedures and redundancies. Working for the team, a trainee's day could be spent conducting witness interviews, visiting clients, drafting particulars of claim or attending tribunals. With the opportunity to see a file from instruction through to tribunal or even appeal, one source cooed: 'By the end I was doing everything.'

Private client work is referred to as 'personal law' at Gordons. Some of the clients are very wealthy and a few are worth in excess of £50m. At the other end of the scale there are 'locals who have been with us since the word go.' The job inevitably entails will drafting and power of attorney applications, as well as some reasonably complex trusts assignments. Trainees join supervisors at meetings with clients and may then be asked to carry out the instructions themselves, 'under supervision, of course.' The new contentious probate team has some interesting Inheritance Act cases arising out of situations 'when the recipients of legacies challenge how much they have been left in a will.' The family team handles all aspects of divorce and separation for a range of individuals from landed gentry and farmers to business owners. Lastly, the Bradford-based risk and compliance department undertakes work for the SRA, investigating solicitors' conduct following complaints of poor service. When things get really bad an intervention takes place, meaning that Gordons swoops in to 'sort out the mess' after a failing firm is identified.

Basic trainee experiences are common across departments and we heard about helpful supervisors and 'good systems in place.' In most departments trainees take work from the whole team, so 'if you have an issue you can always speak to someone, even if it is not your supervisor.' We heard very few grumbles from our sources, although one felt that on occasion they'd had to 'push' for responsibility, which was 'frustrating, as the rest of the department was really busy... it just didn't feed down to me.' Although trainees 'usually manage to avoid photocopying,' they do have the chore of post duty, which requires them to be in work for an 8am start every other week. This aspect of the job is made less tedious simply by virtue of the post room being 'a hub for gossip.' Appraisals take place at the end of each seat and involve the current supervisor and the one assigned for the next seat. This doesn't mean trainees lack feedback in between. Far from it: 'We have meetings on a fortnightly basis with supervisors to check our training and discuss any issues.'

Beers, balti and Basil

Trainees' impressions of Gordons' culture were favourable. As one put it: 'Although there is the work of a bigger firm, there is a family mentality... I like the fact the senior partner says hello to me.' In general 'people are sociable and up for some fun' and they've no shortage of options come Friday night. Leeds has endless bars, clubs and restaurants, although sadly one of the trainees' favourite locals closed down recently. Staff in Bradford also like a drink at the end of the week, however it's common for the trainees doing a seat over there to jump on the train to join their peers in Leeds, as 'it's only 20 minutes away.' Partners regularly put their cards behind the bar and in Leeds 'the hardcore go on into town to Call Lane.' When it comes to organised events 'we are very much one firm,' so the social committee organises events for both sets of staff, most recently greyhound racing, curry nights, wine tasting and go-karting. There is a big annual party (last time taking a New York theme), complete with dinner and disco. 'Everyone looks forward to it' and future trainees are

invited along. Trainees like the fact that they're also welcome at client events and lunches, and willingly help out at seminars. One trainee even took a starring role as a Basil Fawltyesque character in a construction department seminar video.

Believing that healthy minds require healthy bodies, some staff practise yoga each week in one of the meeting rooms. This takes place in both Leeds and Bradford so there's no need to miss out by being in the wrong office. 'In Leeds people often go for a run along the canal' and there are sports teams for netball (including a mixed team), cricket and football. The football team is particularly popular and very proud of its achievements – 'there are always e-mails going round about what they are up to.' Football fixtures include local league games, a yearly five-a-side charity tournament hosted by Gordons, and a game or two against clients. Earlier we mentioned the firm's interest in local charities: each year the firm selects one to support and it also gets involved with events such as the Leeds Legal Clean Up, whereby deprived areas around the city are spruced up to improve the environment.

And finally...

All in all, the trainees at Gordons are content with their lot. Said one source: 'Gordons has the same idea as me – that the North is fantastic and worth committing to.' It seems they're not alone: all five qualifiers stayed with the firm in 2008.

Government Legal Service

the facts

Location: London, Manchester

Number of lawyers: 1,194 (74% solicitors)

Total number of trainees: 36 (trainee solicitors)

Seats: 4x6 months

Alternative seats: None

Extras: GLS Pro Bono network; language training

> GLS lawyers take a holistic view of the law. In private practice its all about specialisation. The government absolutely doesn't want that kind of lawyer and you're expected to be a good generalist.

The GLS is the UK's largest employer of lawyers, yet it's often unnoticed amid the deluge of free pens and assorted shiny detritus distributed at careers events by private practice firms. Those who do find it, and don't enjoy the idea of 'spending the whole day working so the partner can holiday in Mauritius for three weeks,' invariably thank their lucky stars they made this career decision.

On Her Majesty's legal service

The GLS ostensibly has only one client – she lives in a really big house and wears a sparkly hat. In practice 'the client' includes all the policymakers and managers within government departments. They seek advice on how to legally put policy into practice, how to interpret changes in European law, how to comply with treaties the government might become party to and a million other problems. Government lawyers additionally handle contentious matters as and when they arise... which is basically all the time. This is a truly unique training contract and 'the stuff you do affects everyone.'

Before you can have a shot at it all there's a 'long and complex' application process. The usual civil service nationality requirements apply (see www.civilservice.gov.uk for details) and you'll need to have a 2:1 at minimum. Beyond this, your background and university details will not be considered when your application is assessed. First there's an online verbal reasoning test and an application form of only one question, set with non-law students in mind. It poses a hypothetical scenario 'tangentially connected to government or politics' and your job will be to advise what should be done. There are no soft-focus questions about why you want to be a lawyer, as a couple of years ago the

GLS decided it didn't want 'casual applicants' giving 'stock answers.' The new and more challenging format has caused the number of applications to fall considerably and the standard to rise. Those invited to the assessment day face a group exercise, another written exercise and an interview panel. The highest-scoring candidates are awarded the contracts.

The GLS tries to break down distinctions between trainee solicitors and pupil barristers. They're all trainees together and their experiences share a great deal of common ground. You can even apply as 'either' if you're not yet sure which path you want to take. You might want to also take a look at our GLS pupillage feature on page 872.

Magical ministry tour

Trainees work for specific government departments. Applicants indicate their preferred one or two, though there's no guarantee of receiving an offer from them, as departments are left to select the candidates they want. Wherever they end up, trainees report to a training principal, who oversees the whole contract and decides which seats they'll do, a line manager to monitor workload and meet with them once a week, and a team supervisor. In this heavily structured system, 'you're trusted to learn and manage things yourself,' and while everything is checked, trainees are 'treated like actual lawyers.' Four six-month seats are taken within a department, or in other departments if one can't provide the relevant contentious or advisory experience mandated by the SRA.

The biggest departments are the Treasury Solicitor's (TSol), Her Majesty's Revenue & Customs (HMRC), the Department for Business, Enterprise and Regulatory Reform (BERR) and the Department for Work & Pensions/Health (DWP/H). Some, such as the Department for Community and Local Government (DCLG) and the Ministry of Justice (MoJ) regularly accept trainees. Others – the Home Office, Department for Transport (DfT), Office of Fair Trading (OFT), Department for Environment, Food and Rural Affairs (DEFRA) and Health & Safety Executive (HSE) – recruit more infrequently. For international experience, BERR for example, has branches dealing with European affairs and world trade.

Every department has a wide remit. DCLG covers housing, planning, regeneration, employment and constitutional law, while BERR, in addition to energy, insolvency, regulatory reform and freedom of information work, gives its trainees a free trip up Big Ben to hear it chime (earplugs included). Do you need a grasp of economics to survive the tax-heavy HMRC? Not at all. 'You just need the ability to read something and apply it legally.' Supplemental training covers the rest. Our HMRC mole explained more pressing necessities: 'You've got to get used to people pulling funny faces when you say where you work, and you find yourself telling friends that, no, you can't do their tax returns.' To learn more about the work of each department go to www.gls.gov.uk.

TSol takes by far the biggest number of trainees. Almost exclusively contentious in its remit, it supplies legal teams to handle the broad litigation needs of departments like the Attorney General's Office, the Cabinet Office, the MoD and DfES. Cases involve everything from personal injury, judicial review, pensions, companies, immigration and almost anything else you can think of. Our interviewees had 'hugely positive' experiences in contentious seats, which they could only imagine left private practice in the shade. 'On my first day I had a caseload of about 30 matters,' crowed one; 'at its maximum that went up to 70.' Contact with clients and barristers is regular, as is attendance at court, if not advocacy. One trainee was surprised by 'how many people – not just employees – get hurt in government buildings.' Judicial review, as you may know, is 'a method of holding public bodies accountable,' and as the process has to be started within six months of a decision, 'it's very fresh and quick.' Reviews range from big-picture issues such as the decision not to hold a referendum on the Lisbon Treaty, to individual social care decisions. A secondment to the Crown Prosecution

Service is possible for those who think 'criminal's way more interesting than civil litigation.'

The 'confusingly named' Strategic Litigation and Special Investigations team in HMRC 'basically covers tax avoidance – it's the typical civil service way of never saying what you mean.' The work has an inherently academic quality, as 'you can spend hours cross-eyed with half a page of legislation,' and often requires trainees to pop out to the House of Lords. A 'ridiculous rule book' covering the binding, referencing and scheduling documents to be handed to the Lords means the experience can be a bit 'bonkers,' but 'you do actually feel you're a part of it rather than just an admin monkey doing all the boring bits.'

Some good advice

All trainees must experience at least one advisory or policy seat, and realistically this type of work is a government lawyer's bread and butter. What with changes in government policy, the breadth of departments and a constant revolving door of cases, no two trainees' experiences will be the same. There's satisfaction to be gained from drafting answers that may be heard in Parliament or seen splashed across the news. For example, the MoJ has given advice on everything from the implementation of the UN convention against torture, to judicial reviews on the legality of the war in Iraq. Trainees help prepare ministers' briefs for appearances before select committees and seek out test cases in which to put forward the government's position. The Cabinet Office co-ordinates matters of state aid, pensions, civil contingencies, emergency planning and charities. Sources in the Treasury let slip a few whispers of their role in drafting statutory instruments and checking over legislation designed to protect financial stability amid the credit crunch. BERR also got in on the act with analysis of the insolvency regimes for new-build nuclear reactors.

The workload can get pretty intense (think Treasury just before budget time), but the work is so satisfying that our interviewees could think of nothing negative to say. We asked if being face-to-face with the people running the country was ever intimidating, and while we didn't get any juicy political scandal, we did hear that one prominent former officeholder was 'very engaging and friendly.'

At all levels of government, civil servants are encouraged to move jobs once every three years or so and it's no different for qualified GLS lawyers. At the root of this idea is a holistic view of the law: 'In private practice it's all about specialisation. The government absolutely doesn't want that kind of lawyer and you're expected to be a good generalist.' Employment on qualification isn't officially guaranteed, but there's a tacit awareness that 'you'd have to do something really silly not to get a job.' Last year's 90% retention was lower than usual. Trainees are never in competition with one another, so 'we feel we're all working towards a common goal.'

Public servants

'This probably isn't the place to come if you're interested in a specialist area of law.' Flexibility is key if you want to succeed, and when it evaluates applicants the GLS believes 'it's more important how your mind works rather than what experience you have.' Those called to public service come from a wide variety of backgrounds and most are 'intimidatingly' bright and articulate. The civil service once was a bastion of Oxbridge graduates, whereas the GLS now takes people from a wider range of universities than most City firms. There's an excellent diversity policy and flexible working conditions that are very much designed with parents in mind. More than one of our sources revealed that a 'mid-twenties crisis' had made them ditch the money-first lifestyle of the private sector. 'I was willing to accept I'd make less money,' said one, with a classic commitment to public service. The chance for a genuine work-life balance and an 'incredibly interesting role' is enough for those who really do 'give a shit about how the country works.'

You can't escape the political nature of the GLS, however it's not a good place to try and advance any particular agenda. You needn't leave all your convictions at the door, and campaigning for quasi-political organisations like Friends of the Earth or Amnesty International is normally acceptable. Guidelines for such things become more restrictive as you rise up the ranks: at trainee level you can belong to a political party, though stumping for them might get you taken aside for a quiet word. Discretion is supremely important, and even when you have to work on some 'loathsome' policies, a consistent level of professionalism is expected. When all is said and done, the lawyers are 'there to put together the policy, not agree with it.'

On benefits

'Sometimes you feel you're part of such a big machine you're not really being listened to as much as you'd like. You question where in the grand scheme of things you fit. You're told trainees are important, but sometimes things happen that make you think you verge on cheap labour.' What this person was referring to was the new practice of designating solicitors 'legal officers' for their first year after qualification. The title has a correspondingly lower salary and this has left some feeling frustrated. At least there's a decent pension at the end of your tenure. After qualification there's even the possibility to work from home or through a compressed timetable, and a 30-day holiday allowance, bank holidays, civil service holidays (choose one of two extra days to celebrate the Queen's birthday) all add up to a nice package. Mostly, trainees seem more prone to celebrate the advantages they've been given than dwell on those benefits they've been denied: 'Do I wish I could get paid more? Definitely. Do I wish I could do another job as a result? No, I do not.'

Trainees would rarely see their cohorts if it weren't for the efforts of the GLS social committee and the Legal Trainee Network. Every third Thursday there's a trip to a different historic pub; other events include ice-skating at Somerset House, wine tasting, and pub quizzes. A football team from BERR won the civil service shield last year.

And finally...

Far from being a pinstriped prison, the GLS offers a unique contract with outstanding work. Where else could you find yourself 'writing the word 'we' and knowing you're talking about the country?'

Halliwells

Magic...
outside
the Circle

Halliwells is a UK top 30 law firm with offices in Manchester, London, Liverpool and Sheffield. Join Halliwells and you will be part of one the fastest growing, most progressive and financially successful legal practices in the UK.

For more information contact
Ekaterina Clarke, Graduate Recruitment Manager
ekaterina.clarke@halliwells.com

www.halliwells.com/graduates

Halliwells LLP

The facts

Location: Manchester, Liverpool, London, Sheffield

Number of UK partners/solicitors: 154/231

Total number of trainees: 76

Seats: 5x21 weeks

Alternative seats: Secondments

Extras: Pro bono – Manchester and Liverpool Universities legal advice centres; language training

Trainees were unequivocal that this ambitious firm favours self-starters. If you are meek no one will rescue you.

One of the most ambitious law firms in the UK, Halliwells has evolved from a Mancunian commercial player into a four-office heavyweight aiming for the UK top 25. Its story is one of growth, hard work and sheer determination.

So far, so fast

Since the mid-1990s this 40-year-old firm has followed a strategy of growth and diversification that has earned it a reputation as a driven, profitable, swashbuckling business. From Manchester it branched into Sheffield and then London. Its latest adventure was the establishment of a Liverpool office in 2004, achieved through the takeover of property firm Cuff Roberts. Since then it has been adding to all four offices, for example hiring the bulk of the insurance-heavy firm James Chapman & Co in Manchester and building a corporate department in Sheffield. Up north, partner hires have been made from the likes of DLA Piper, DWF, Keoghs, Hill Dickinson and Cobbetts. Down south, London partners have been drawn in from Reed Smith, Charles Russell and Clyde & Co. Halliwells' transformation can also be measured in the rapid expansion of its training scheme, which has grown in the last five years from 23 trainees to more than 80.

This is essentially a commercial firm, although Liverpool has a private client department. Beyond this you should know that Halliwells is equally strong in corporate, real estate and litigation, and as such no area need dominate the training contract. The firm's five-seat training model is popular because 'you get more experience and losing a month off each seat doesn't seem to matter.' Even within departments, trainees' experiences are broad as they usually work for a number of partners and senior lawyers rather than becoming overspecialised. The firm likes all trainees to try corporate and property as well as some

form of litigation. A return visit to one's hoped-for qualification department is the norm.

Manchester: spin city

As the heart of the firm the Manchester office has the widest seat selection. Litigation seats can be spent in property lit, commercial lit or the insurance department, which involves defending insurance companies, councils and supermarkets against employers' and occupiers' liability and personal injury claims. 'You get some interesting claims: people allege things they never reported at the time, like a finger being chopped off in an accident.' Trainees handle discrete matters then 'talk about the next stage with the partner or solicitor.' Property lit incorporates mortgage repossession cases, often referred from Halliwells' sister conveyancing firm, HL Interactive.

Corporate seats can be demanding. Initially they involve 'assisting associates and partners on due diligence and disclosure;' during a second seat responsibility levels climb and trainees can be 'drafting key documents and negotiating points.' Most deals and clients are based in the North West and Halliwells is one of the UK's best firms for AIM matters, having lately broken into the Asian market. 'We're doing capital markets deals in China and the firm is happy to send trainees over to China for verification exercises.' Such deals include advice to China Central Properties on its £250m admission to AIM. This department can bring long hours: 'Over ten months I did

20 late nights, some only 9pm or 10pm, but others much later.' Most trainees accept this with good grace, pointing out 'there is no attitude of 'We will flog you whether you like it or not.''

Real estate seats can be taken in the investment, retail or development teams and there are also options such as banking, employment, IPCT (intellectual property, commerce and technology) and corporate recovery. The latter is a 'brilliant' split contentious/non-contentious posting that could land you in a search and seize operation. 'I found myself sitting in a car outside an industrial estate waiting to serve some guys with something,' recalled one trainee who'd worked long hours. Unfortunately, due to the decline in the property market, Halliwells has had to make real estate redundancies.

In 2007 Manchester staff moved to the Spinningfields area of the city and became neighbours of RBS, Manchester Evening News and the new Civil Justice Centre. A free bus from Piccadilly makes it easily accessible, although 'in the cold weather people don't go out very much.' The summer looks better for 'picnics on the many grassy areas.' The new office is an eight-floor glass triangle with a 'grotesquely huge lobby' and a top-floor staff canteen offering 'stunning views towards Old Trafford,' subsidised meals and an in-house Starbucks. Trainees say bringing everyone together into the same building was essential, even though the move has also brought a switch to formal business attire.

Friday night drinks are an institution. Even senior figures pop along, so 'when you bump into people in the office, it's someone you may have had a drink with, not just a name on the intranet.' Bar Ha!Ha! is the most frequented, although trainees also venture to the 'less expensive' Grapes.

Liverpool: Cuff mixture

In Liverpool commercial litigation and insurance litigation are combined so trainees experience a mix of cases including 'shareholders disputes, contractual disputes and some mediations.' A trainee can take over files from qualified fee earners and even make applications at court. Said one fan: 'I only did a couple of late nights, usually it was 9am until 6pm.' Property seats are similarly broad in scope. One of the office's recent highlights was relocating Everton Football Club's training ground. Since the Cuff Roberts days this department has always been the big cheese in the Liverpool office; the other seat options are corporate, IPCT and employment. In this last seat trainees can handle lower-value cases and quickly learn time management skills when 'working towards a tribunal.' One seat you might not expect to see is family, but a stint here introduces you to a well-respected private client team that generally represents wealthy individuals.

Liverpool hours are fine ('In the down times you leave at 5.30pm, sometimes you stay until 7.30-8pm') though the office is 'a bit shabby.' Apparently 'we were supposed to be moving but that fell though; we are expanding and need more room.' While the more relaxed Cuff Roberts culture has been retained, 'the arrival of DLA partners has been great for us, especially in corporate. They have had a real influence in getting the office moving.' Trainees think 'our corporate department is driving us forward now.'

Sheffield: do you want blood?

The Sheffield office was once used only for volume insurance litigation. Now it is growing into a full-service operation and took its first externally recruited trainees in August 2008. Before that all trainees had been paralegals at the firm, meaning they could talk us through how things have changed. 'We just started a corporate team by bringing in a partner from DLA; we also now have employment, real estate, an expanded corporate recovery team and commercial litigation, and there's a new clinical negligence team from DLA.' The employment department is working for the British Medical Association and British Dental Association, so trainees encounter all sorts of health professionals in sticky situations. Apparently 'psychiatrists are the most mad.'

The 150-strong staff has spread across three floors of Halliwells' old building. 'You know everybody here and that is one of the things I love,' a source explained. 'The partners are a hoot and everyone is happy to go out for a drink together.' Trainees feel their office is 'vibrant and varied' and it has at least two things in common with Manchester. 'Both offices are near a blood donation centre and an All Bar One.'

London: all at sea?

The London dispute resolution group (DRG) takes on insurance and reinsurance matters, commercial litigation and shipping cases. With two or three trainees at any one time, it is about the same size as the corporate and real estate departments. Feedback on DRG seats was positive: 'On one case I was sent to help run counsel through all the documents, and I went to a number of case management conferences and a Court of Appeal hearing.' Some trainees absolutely love the generalist corporate department in London where 'it matters who you sit with, for example one partner specialises in Far East AIM flotations and another has Israeli entrepreneurial clients.' The bad news is that the department may have overestimated the amount of business coming through, so two partners have left and there have been redundancies among solicitors and support staff. As well as real estate, other seats include banking, pensions, corporate recovery and client secondments to the likes of InBev and Cable & Wireless. The generalist approach can 'make it difficult to concentrate on a particular type of law, say securitisation or distressed debt,' but trainees agree 'that's the nature of a mid-sized firm.'

The London trainees are proud Halliwellsians, but believe the London office to be lighter on its feet than the Manchester HQ, certainly in relation to training scheme issues. 'There are so many more trainees in Manchester that they need more rigid processes. My impression is that London just tries to get things done quickly and Manchester sometimes takes its time before rubber-stamping the decisions.' They say there's a difference in the office character too: 'We are a smaller fish in a bigger sea and have to be a bit more entrepreneurial.' The source who did '300 billable hours in a month' certainly felt London hours are longer, but there is a good social life. 'Trainees go out together for drinks, mostly to Abacus, the Pitcher & Piano and the Jamaica Wine Lodge.' There's also an 'atmosphere of equality' that means 'you can go to the pub with the head of a department.'

The meek shall inherit nothing

Trainees were unequivocal that 'this is an ambitious firm and favours self-starters. If you are meek no one will rescue you.' The self-starters the firm recruits tend to come from universities like 'Manchester and Sheffield, Oxford and Cambridge' and around 40% complete the vac scheme. During training, those who had 'deliberately sought out the seats that would challenge' noticed 'Halliwells is still quite aggressive so you have to be able to hold your own.' Not that anyone's set adrift. An initial objectives meeting is the precursor to mid and end-of-seat appraisals featuring an A-D grading system that is not uniformly popular. All trainees attend a two-week induction in Manchester, but then meet only occasionally for training events. At present, all future trainees attend Chester College of Law for the LPC, and while this sounds like a great idea for trainees headed to offices in the North West, for others there are definite drawbacks. As for inter-office moves, these do happen but not regularly.

As to Halliwells' future, opinion was split between those who foresee continued growth in all locations and those who feel Manchester has peaked. 'Halliwells is the Clifford Chance of Manchester,' concluded one trainee who saw plenty of scope for the London office to improve its market position. 'It is the nature of the London office that it is sales-driven and you are encouraged to get into that from the start.' Having spent a packet on its Spinningfields HQ and with an economic slowdown in progress, financial prudence could well have been behind 2008's lower NQ retention figures: of the 40 qualifiers, 30 stayed on.

And finally...

'Ambition is the thread that joins Halliwells together,' so be sure that its modus operandi will suit you. At times training here can be a stomach-twisting rollercoaster of a ride, which is exactly how your classic Halliwells trainee likes it.

Be involved

Paris. One of six challenging seats. International transactional work and great use of my French law qualification. Total involvement – every day.

JENNA CARR | TRAINEE SOLICITOR | MANCHESTER

0800 163 498
hammonds.com/trainees
Hammonds LLP is an equal opportunities employer

Hammonds

Hammonds LLP

The facts

Location: Birmingham, Leeds, London, Manchester

Number of UK partners/solicitors: 151/297

Total number of trainees: 81

Total number of trainees: 81

Seats: 6x4 months

Alternative seats: Overseas seats, secondments

Extras: Pro bono – various, eg Paddington Law Centre

> As befits a firm with a strong northern heritage, the sort of applicant who will fare well is generally driven and straightforward and down to earth.

Following explosive national and international growth, Hammonds had a torrid start to the new millennium. As it pulls out of these stormy waters, its trainees are keen to sing the praises of 'good-quality work at a firm on the up.'

Have we got really old news for you

Bradford minnow Hammonds burst onto the national legal scene in the 1990s, when it went merger-crazy creating a network of offices incorporating Leeds, Manchester, Birmingham and London. Brimming with confidence, it launched an assault on the international market, opening offices across Europe and Asia. Unfortunately, this all proved too much too soon and growing pains turned into financial problems. These, and much-publicised discontent among partners, left the path to the door a well-trodden one and the floodgates of bad publicity wide open. Many of our second-year interviewees had applied to the firm before the bubble burst and confessed a certain 'apprehension' at starting their training contract in light of the 'absolute pounding' the firm took from the legal press. However the rewards for ignoring the tales of doom and gloom and the ribbings of their law school classmates became apparent after starting at the firm. They found a markedly different organisation to the one they expected. Said one source: 'It was really heartening to get in and see the air of positivity and what was being done to right things.'

The turnaround in the firm's fortunes since 2005 has been achieved under the stewardship of managing partner Peter Crossley. Following an overhaul of the management structure, cost-cutting redundancies and a 14-month equity partner lock-in, the lawyer exodus has all but ended and profits have bounced back. And the firm has bagged some meaty new clients: Tesco, Honda and British Energy all joined its roster in 2007, while in 2008 it was retained by National Grid and Royal Mail after panel reviews. Hammonds has won some massive instructions. For example, it acted for the management team on their £783m buyout of affordable housing specialist Keepmoat, one of Yorkshire's largest deals in recent years. Hardly surprising then that trainees are a little weary of people harping on about its troubled past. Quipped one: 'We're on the way up – it's boring to keep talking about the bad times.' True enough, but as a potential employee we figured you'd want to know.

Looking to the future, trainees say Hammonds has 'no aspirations to become like the magic circle,' instead it wants to 'focus on the things it does best, nurture the clients it already has and reach out to new ones.'

Northerly winds

Hammonds trainees undergo a rapid-fire six-seat rotation which 'gives a snapshot of plenty of different areas and allows you to repeat a seat if you really enjoy it.' Compulsory corporate, property and litigation assignments do not detract from a very broad offering, the only slight reservation being that in transactional seats 'the chances of seeing something through to completion in four months is slim.' Although trainees are based in one office for the duration of their contract, cross-office departments mean experiences are similar regardless of where a person is stationed. Regional trainees benefit from instructions 'shipped out here from London,' although for a bona fide City experience they can also request a seat in the London office.

To tick the corporate box, trainees can specialise in corporate finance, banking, asset-based lending or tax, and they enthuse about the 'well-known energy and utility company clients' that are keeping many of the corporate lawyers busy. A look at recent AIM work also reveals the benefits of Hammonds' international presence, with IPOs handled for Madara Bulgarian Property Fund and China Medical System Holdings. What this means for trainees is a range of experiences from 'working for partners on the bigger deals, staying late into the night when you can start to believe you are just a paper merchant, to smaller deals when you get huge responsibility.' Despite its share of 'menial' Companies House filings and document bibling, trainees felt 'challenged and pushed to the next level' in corporate. A strong sense of camaraderie pervades here 'because you know when it comes to the crunch you will be in late having takeaway together.'

Property seats get trainees working on all stages of transactions 'from purchases and developments to sales or leases of properties.' To make sure it all runs smoothly they are tasked with 'searches, putting together document bibles, checking completion documents and post-completion registration… and a lot of research.' This side of the business has seen a few partner departures, yet the firm retains a strong national reputation. Nowhere is this more true than in the energy and renewables sector, where Hammonds' planning expertise has secured key roles advising E.ON on windfarm projects near Doncaster and Tyneside. In 2008 the firm also gained ministerial approval for the £200m Griffin Wind Farm in Scotland. Planning is a popular option. Much to the amusement of peers, who happily retold the story, an unsuspecting trainee was even spotted on *BBC News at Six*, striding purposefully past protestors to enter a public inquiry.

Energy sector deals are just as prevalent in the construction seat, although the mix of contractual and contentious work handled by the group means projects 'are never the same.' For authentic contentious experience, the commercial and disputes resolution seat is a must. Our sources had busied themselves with 'day-to-day research, attending client meetings and drafting particulars of claim and witness statements.'

And now for something completely different

One of the outstanding features of Hammonds' training contract is the scope for real variety over the two years. As well as choices within each compulsory area, trainees

Chambers UK rankings

Advertising & Marketing • Banking & Finance • Construction • Corporate Finance • Dispute Resolution • Employment • Environment • Health & Safety • Intellectual Property • Media & Entertainment • Pensions • Pensions Litigation • Planning • Private Equity • Projects, Energy & Natural Resources • Real Estate • Real Estate Litigation • Restructuring/Insolvency • Sports Law • Tax

have a range of niche options open to them. The firm-wide pensions group acts for 13 FTSE 100 companies and provides 'a highly technical, research-heavy seat' in which 'you have to hit the ground running or you'll fall behind.' Employment is held in equally high esteem and is a chance for trainees to make contact with big clients. Said one: 'It made me giggle when the HR director of one of our clients, a man in his fifties with 30 years of experience, was phoning me up directly to ask my advice on his restructuring plan.' The London-based sports law team is 'a dream seat for sports-mad fans.' It represents almost half of the Premier League's clubs on regulatory, contentious and commercial matters. Recent highlights include advice to the International Tennis Federation and Formula One Management, as well as the representation of UK Sports Investments (the buying vehicle set up by former Thai PM Thaksin Shinawatra) on its acquisition of Manchester City FC and the subsequent signing of Sven-Göran Eriksson as manager.

As in any decent international firm, there are opportunities for budding Michael Palins. Trainees with a second language to degree level can travel to the firm's Paris, Berlin, Turin or Madrid offices, while no such barriers stand in the way of a trip to Brussels or Hong Kong. What's more, 'you don't have to fight and claw your way to the front of the list to get these seats.' The diverse training contract menu is completed by a healthy number of client secondments including regular placements to marauding events company Live Nation, as well as ad hoc opportunities that have seen trainees join the in-house teams at The Co-operative and Barclays. It's not easy to generalise about work hours, though one source spoke for many when they said their typical day ran from 8.30am to 6.30pm. 'The latest I've stayed is 9pm, but those occasions are few and far between rather than the rule. You take your chance and leave if you've no urgent work.'

Back to college

Hammonds is very keen to promote a one-firm mentality across its network. Some second-years were a little sceptical of what they saw as 'spiel,' but a newly introduced three-week greeting in Oxford for all trainees should ensure everyone is on-song from day one. The event takes place each August (Hammonds only has one intake per year) and in 2007, the first year of this initiative, it was hailed a huge success. Aside from the necessary training sessions, a crammed schedule included meals, plays and enough black-tie dinners in Oxford colleges to test your table manners to their limits. 'You get to know everyone as a group without even knowing particularly what office people are going to train in,' confirmed one recipient of all this corporate hospitality. By the end, trainees have numerous new friends to call upon for assistance when dealing with another office. A three-day return to Oxford halfway through the year ensures faces and names are not forgotten.

Otherwise, opportunities to cement bonds are constrained by geography, although during our interviews there was plenty of hype about a trainee-organised night out in Birmingham. The Midlands hosts had a night of 'food, drink and dance' planned for their visitors at the super-trendy Jam House (where patron Jools Holland is musical director). This choice of venue is a telling one from a bunch of trainees who feel the ongoing £9m redevelopment of their office is 'repositioning us in the Birmingham market – it's saying, 'We're Hammonds, we're here, we're smart and we mean business.''

Down in London, Hammonds is located in Devonshire Square, just a stone's throw from Liverpool Street. The fast pace within this corporate-driven office is remedied on a Friday night when 'everyone piles into the pub.' The smaller Manchester office lagged somewhat behind London in tales of post-work socialising, although trainees did speak of monthly 'curries, comedy clubs and Japanese meals.' The office in Manchester is undergoing a facelift that will bring the back room in line with the 'immaculate foyer and client area.' During our research period trainees were preparing for a cross-Pennines football match against their counterparts in Leeds. Their opponents' preparation for this big clash seemed to consist of regular trips to local bars Prohibition and The Waterhole.

So they're obviously a smart bunch, but what else does Hammonds look for in its trainees? As befits a firm with a strong northern heritage, the sort of applicant who will fare well is generally 'driven and straightforward' and 'down to earth.' Our sources spoke of applicants needing some kind of commercial understanding, adding that knowing cases and the law is not enough. 'The recruiters seem not to lean towards super-technical people without social skills or the personality to go out and speak with clients.' The reason for this is simple: 'This is a commercial firm with a business slant to everything it does, so they really look for commercial awareness.'

Hammonds tries to make the run-up to qualification as painless as possible. 'Once the job list is posted it all happens quickly,' explained a source. 'Everyone fills in a CV template and then has two days to choose the jobs they want. There's a week for interviews and within ten days you'll know if you got the job. It's all done at a pace.' In 2008 some 31 of the 38 qualifiers stayed on.

And finally...

According to current trainees, Hammonds offers a great opportunity for 'people who want to make the training contract their own and look for every opportunity. It's not for anyone who just wants to go through the motions.'

Harbottle & Lewis LLP

The facts

Location: London

Number of UK partners/solicitors: 24/55

Total number of trainees: 9

Seats: 4x6 months

Alternative seats: Secondments

> Every day staff sit down together for a free lunch, which is great for making friends and contacts when you first arrive.

Founded in 1955, this media and entertainment law firm promises a friendly culture, heaps of responsibility and little admin drudgery. Although life might appear to be a constant merry-go-round of A-listers – *Star Wars* billionaire George Lucas is just one celeb client – life as a trainee is rather more down to earth.

May the law be with you

The media and entertainment sector remains Harbottles' bread and butter. Its corporate department recently advised MAMA Group on its 70% acquisition of Angel Music, the owner of dance clubs like Godskitchen and festival brands including Global Gathering. Our parent publication *Chambers UK* celebrates Harbottles' top-ranking interactive entertainment work each year: it acts for clients including Atari, Virgin PLAY, SEGA and Yahoo! and advised on the acquisition of leading video games publisher Zoo Digital, creator of the *Premier Manager* series and other best-selling games. Music lawyers represent a leading opera, ballet and classical music promoter and successfully defended Procol Harum in its widely publicised copyright battle over the organ bits of *A Whiter Shade of Pale*. From the film/TV industry, Target Entertainment sought help on its acquisition of Greenlit Rights, an independent production company whose portfolio includes *Foyle's War*. And how about a dozen Olivers and Nancys? The winners and finalists of BBC1's *I'd Do Anything* trooped to the firm's West End offices for representation, no doubt after a backstage tip from the Josephs and Marias from *Any Dream Will Do* and *How Do You Solve A Problem Like Maria?* Harbottle has built a name for advising contestants in talent and reality shows and has also worked in relation to programmes such as *Cape Wrath*, *The Charlotte Church Show* and *Stuart: A Life Backwards*.

Who ate all my pies?

The training contract offers a total of seven seat options and trainees have to do four. The firm allocates these, though 'it does listen and will try to take into consideration your history and declared preferences.' Our sources say you'd be well advised to make your desires known during the interview process, particularly if you really want to do the secondment to major client Virgin. Quite naturally, the most popular are the seats in the film, TV and theatre team (FTT) and the music, IP, interactive entertainment and sports teams (MIPIES, pronounced 'my pies'). Litigation is a must, and for full-on commercial training there's a corporate seat and the posting to Virgin Atlantic's HQ near Gatwick Airport.

MIPIES is described as 'an incredible seat with amazing variety like you'll get at no other firm.' Because there's only ever one trainee here at a time you'll get work thrown at you left, right and centre, and 'because there are so many sectors you'll be asked what your interests are, and to an extent you can choose the type of work that will be dumped on you.' This contrasts with a seat like litigation, which by its very nature is more procedural, the result being 'you'll be allocated work and just told to get it done.' Harbottles' litigation department now hosts three trainees at a time. It's more pressurised here than in other seats, partly because there are more partners and fewer juniors than elsewhere. Recent highlights include George Lucas suing a British designer for allegedly making and flogging stormtrooper outfits without a licence. If you get to work on a similar case 'you'll probably be in court a lot' and there may be a few late evenings spent preparing court bundles. The lawyers also give advice to the Royal Household and Clarence House regarding documentaries about the Royal Family. You'll remember the brouhaha about the infamous faked promotional material showing the Queen supposedly storming out of a filming session. On smaller, less-sensitive cases, there is an opportunity for trainees to try a spot of advocacy before a High Court master.

Flights of fancy

The corporate seat involves 'actively assisting larger media companies on some big deals' and 'it's quite hands-on. There's naturally some low-level work, but more client contact than you might expect.' Harbottles represents both large and small charities in the arts and other sectors, and work for this type of client falls within the corporate department's remit. There's also general commercial advice ranging from 'drafting confidentiality agreements to working with a glamorous fashion celebrity client.' Corporate department clients include Channel 4, easyJet, Really Useful Group, Penguin Books, Tiger Aspect and several Virgin Group companies. Despite property not being the top option, it's far from loathed. Early-seat drudgery such as post-completion dealings with the Land Registry eventually pays off, so that by the end of the seat trainees will have a caseload of their own files with 'lots of research and client contact.' The Central School of Speech and Drama, The Institute of Contemporary Arts, Northampton Theatres Trust and The Freedom of Speech Foundation are among the clients.

Employment is 'a good seat to start in and get a grounding' as the partners and associates are 'very good at checking you're okay.' Along with research, writing memos, attending tribunals and putting together bundles for hearings, there's also some basic drafting and reviewing confidentiality agreements. Again, trainees told us their workload was surprisingly light on boring admin. Last year employment advice was given to Visit London, Comic Relief and Ministry of Sound among others. The Virgin secondment, meanwhile, allows trainees 'to put everything learnt at law school into practice in a real business setting.' Virgin's in-house team is stuffed with ex-Harbottles lawyers, so it will feel like a home from home to an extent. Tasks include reviewing commercial con-

Chambers UK rankings

Advertising & Marketing • Aviation • Charities • Corporate Finance • Defamation/Reputation Management • Employment • Information Technology • Intellectual Property • Media & Entertainment • Private Client • Real Estate • Sports Law

tracts – lots of them. The main downside is having to walk through Gatwick Airport past crowds of holidaymakers about to jet off to the sun – 'particularly galling on a freezing winter Monday morning.'

As a relatively small firm you get to know others quite quickly. 'There are some amazingly wacky creative types around,' said one source, and 'people have a real interest in their jobs.' Aside from the fact that many are drawn in by Harbottles' reputation as a media and entertainment specialist, it's difficult to put a finger on the type of trainee it hires. 'Some are trendy arts types, some sporty and others are straightlaced lawyers.' Some have time off before joining the firm; others come straight from law school. People generally choose Harbottles because they feel they'll fit better in a smaller, less City-oriented firm. The small trainee intake guarantees decent responsibility from day one, yet because of the nature of Harbottles' work, trainees are unlikely to be in the office until 4am. The working hours are 'fine' compared to big City firms and partners 'don't breathe down people's necks the whole time. There's not a massive hierarchy.'

Harbottles 'won't suit conventional types' who have their hearts set on City slick, endless training sessions and an army of support staff. 'It's not that you aren't given enough support or that training is unstructured, it's just that by necessity you do more of your own stuff, roll up your sleeves and get stuck in.' Trainees said they feel they can say no to more work if they're swamped, though most prefer to just get it done 'naturally prioritising partners' work.' No one goes short on training: individual departments organise sessions to update staff on recent cases and legal developments, and external speakers (maybe a leading barrister or representatives from clients like Virgin or 19) are invited in for presentations. Weekly Friday breakfast sessions were recently instigated. In addition to seat supervisors, all trainees are allocated a mentor from among the associates. The mentors are independent of the appraisal process, which involves the overall training partner checking in with seat supervisors and trainees twice every six months.

Bottling it

Harbottles' Hanover Square office was refurbished three years ago and now has a trendy glass reception area and hi-tech gizmos in meeting rooms. Because the building's quite old the office isn't open-plan and people share rooms, normally two to three at a time. Trainees typically sit with an associate who's five or six years qualified and the office vibe is 'laid back and fun... at least in the context of law firms.' New staff sports teams have sprung up, encouraged by the partners' willingness to bankroll them. In the old days, cricket matches were organised from time to time, mainly for business development purposes, now juniors and trainees regularly play football, netball and tennis.

Every day staff are encouraged to sit down together for a free lunch, which is not only 'a nice touch' but also great for making friends and contacts when you first arrive. The culture of the lunch room reflects the informal atmosphere within the firm as a whole: there are seven big tables 'and no mahogany!' Friday nights in a local pub are a regular feature and the firm stages drinks evenings every three months or so (basically whenever someone gets round to organising one). In the summer of 2008 the favourite staff watering hole, The Last Bid, bade its farewell after many glorious years. Rumours are it may turn into yet another gastropub. If the new pub isn't up to scratch the nearby Slug & Lettuce will have to suffice for future generations of Harbottlers. The Christmas party is always a good event and future recruits are usually invited.

Qualifying trainees understand that there isn't always room for everyone to do exactly what they want. If the firm really likes a trainee, 'they might say, 'We don't have a space here because it is only a team of three... but we can offer you a job in corporate.'' It's sensible to keep talking about your career aspirations throughout the training because 'partners do take a real interest and will try to help you.' Typically the majority of qualifiers stay on, and in 2008, two out of three did so.

And finally...

The partners are keen to stay ahead of the game and promote the firm as modern and forward-thinking. In business terms, it's likely to continue developing expertise in digital media and at the cutting edge of copyright, where it continues to be a very exciting time for the music industry.

Hay & Kilner

The facts

Location: Newcastle

Number of UK partners/solicitors: 21/22

Total number of trainees: 10

Seats: 4x6 months

Alternative seats: None

H&K remains for the moment an exceedingly local firm, with almost all trainees Geordies born and bred. Efforts to widen the intake have begun

'There are six serious commercial firms in Newcastle, and we are one of them.' So said one of Hay & Kilner's partners to *Chambers UK*. Having investigated the firm for the first time this year, we reckon he had good reason to sing its praises. And our *Chambers UK* colleagues agree.

The Hay team

This firm was formed in 1946 by a Mr Hay and a Mr Kilner. Both have now achieved the ultimate partnership at that great law firm in the sky, and Young Mr Kilner, the original's son, reached retirement age a few years ago. Over the years H&K partners and staff have worked hard to develop an impressive reputation in many areas from personal injury/clinical negligence, crime and family law to corporate, employment, real estate, banking and insolvency law. And they've done it all by keeping client care a priority. Trainees say the firm wants every client to feel they have a personal relationship with their solicitor, even as the firm continues on its growth trajectory.

Compared to the biggest firms in Newcastle, H&K is still a petite operation. It's a diverse one though, which may well swing it for you if you want your traineeship to have genuine variety and you're not yet sure what kind of clients you'll prefer. The firm organises itself into teams for commercial services, private client matters and litigation, and there's a linked but separate business called Wallers that handles mortgage recoveries and sales, home equity release and right-to-buy sales for banks, building societies and local authorities. Most staff work from an office on Cloth Market, leaving a smaller branch office in Wallsend to the crime and motoring offences team. This team defends clients accused of everything from Saturday night scuffles and health and safety prosecutions to business crimes. It doesn't often take trainees from the Newcastle office, though it sometimes hires one of its own as and when the need arises.

In the main Newcastle HQ, regular seats are available in coco, clin neg/PI, property, commercial disputes, and wills and probate. The employment and family teams didn't host trainees in 2008, but have done in the past, and with an increase in trainee numbers on the cards, a wider choice of seats will be needed. In the meantime, the close-knit nature of the firm means trainees often get handed work from these other departments anyway.

Drafting wills to pay the bills

The excellent clin neg unit is led by incredibly experienced lawyer David Bradshaw. 'We watch, listen and learn,' a source said of him admiringly. A large part of the caseload involves birth injuries: the team is currently acting for several clients with cerebral palsy, most claims being made against the NHS. Other situations involve delays in diagnosing cancer and meningitis, and there is one catastrophic injury case involving a client who may have had negligent treatment over 40 years ago. The firm is authorised by the Legal Services Commission to conduct certain multiparty actions, for example there's one for clients who have had problems with breast implants. Trainees speak of 'a good deal of responsibility' in this seat. Although unlikely to get their own files, they're busy 'researching potential grounds for claims' and 'drafting witness statements, particulars of claims and letters to the NHS.' More routine work includes contacting experts for reports and creating trial bundles. The seat also introduces them to personal injury cases, an area in which H&K has acted for a professional goalkeeper involved in a road traffic accident, for an airhostess injured when she fell onto the runway after the steps were removed from her plane, and for the family of a soldier who died in Oman. The firm works for defendants as well as claimants and represents insurers and blue-chip companies from the North East.

When Eversheds closed its private client practice in 2001, the entire team simply nipped round the corner to join Hay & Kilner. In this department, trainees essentially do the same tasks as qualified solicitors. There are wills to draft, meetings to run, applications for grants of probate and house clearances to organise, as well as learning how to give inheritance tax planning advice to some of the region's wealthier folk. Occasionally there will be 'little old grannies who've died with millions of pounds hidden under the mattress.' One or two trainees have also had the chance to help out on contentious probate cases in the past. The family department represents clients from all walks of life: salaried professionals, a few fat cats of industry and parents and children involved in child care proceedings funded by the public purse.

A commercial success

Property trainees' work comes directly from a partner who has a vast following of loyal clients. The firm represents landlords and developers on shopping centres and housing estates and recently advised Eton Square Healthcare on its £60m acquisition of a nursing home group. The transaction included the acquisition of seven existing properties and five under development. H&K is gaining quite a reputation in the nursing homes sector and in relation to pension fund clients. Trainees spend time 'reviewing, drafting and negotiating commercial leases,' as well as dealing with complexities such as rights of way over land. If commercial deals are not your bag, try residential conveyancing. Not everyone takes to the work, as it's 'fairly procedural, often less legal,' though some trainees relish the chance to manage their own files.

H&K is largely secretive about its litigation clients, but we can tell you it represents a couple of big-name companies and lately handled cases relating to the railway industry and financial institutions. 'You never know what's going to land on your desk next,' said one source; others gave a few clues as to what had crossed their desks. Between them trainees had been involved in 'boundary disputes, debt recovery, intricate contractual disputes and a gambling application for a long-standing client.' Time is spent drafting claims, meeting clients and witness, and

Chambers UK rankings

Banking & Finance • Clinical Negligence • Corporate

Finance • Crime • Debt Recovery • Dispute Resolution •

Employment • Family/Matrimonial • Personal Injury •

Private Client • Real Estate • Restructuring/Insolvency

even undertaking advocacy, mostly 'limited stuff in judges' chambers in Newcastle County Court, things you might do in the Professional Skills Course.' Occasionally cases might involve a trip down to London. That Professional Skills Course is taken at the University of Northumbria and shared with four other local commercial firms – Sintons, Muckle, Watson Burton and The Endeavour Partnership.

Commercial clients provide a steady stream of corporate transactions and commercial agreements. Mostly these come from regional owner-managed businesses and there's a decent amount of activity in the healthcare and pharmaceutical sectors. One of the most-prized instructions of late came from local entrepreneur Alex Holliday, who sold his HF Healthcare and Healthcare Plus chain of 25 pharmacies and wholesale business to Alliance Boots. Holliday started the company in 1995 and expanded it into a £30m-a-year-turnover, 250-employee operation. The H&K team has been joined by Jim Lowe, someone you might know if you studied law at Northumbria University any time between 1970 and 2006. The associated insolvency law team does a good job for individuals and companies that get into trouble. Let's hope they don't have to work too hard as the economy slows down. Another team that works closely with the corporate group is employment.

Eggheads and biggbrains

Hay & Kilner remains for the moment an exceedingly local firm, with almost all trainees Geordies born and bred. Efforts to widen the intake have begun and applications are encouraged for the summer vacation scheme. This lasts for a week and gets students into a different department every day. Of the group we spoke to in 2008, two trainees came through this scheme, while the remaining three had started as paralegals at the firm. Coincidentally, all five were female, so group dynamics this year may be slightly different from normal. Higher up the firm, just over 20% of the partners and more than 40% of the qualified solicitors are female. Unfortunately we have no NQ retention figures for 2008 as no one had finished their training contract by the time we went to press.

Hay & Kilner trainees tell us they're happy with their training, their hours and their salary, which 'competes with the biggest firms in the area.' The working day runs from 9am to 5pm, with most people tending to stay a little later than that. Not much later, however. 'I heard that Eversheds trainees sometimes have to stay until 8pm,' gasped one source. At H&K 6pm seems to be the cut-off point, and a 1am finish to close the big HF Healthcare deal was seen as an unusual and exciting oddity. Once the working week is done, trainees and partners head off to the pub. The office is located just off Newcastle's notorious Bigg Market, but trainees say categorically that the firm is 'not boozy' and most people make an exit 'before the charvers arrive on a Friday night.' The more refined surroundings of Popolo on Pilgrim Street have greater appeal. A Christmas party at St James' Park is the big event of the social calendar, and last year saw the firm cover itself in glory by winning the inaugural Marie Curie North East Brain Game quiz. The event was hosted by Edwina Currie and raised £30,000 for Marie Curie Cancer Care. And H&K's secret for success? According to one of the partners it was the team's 'perfect blend of youth and experience.'

And finally...

The fact that this very Northumbrian firm packs a punch in so many different practice areas makes it a canny choice for any student with their heart set on the North East.

HBJ Gateley Wareing

The facts

Location: Birmingham, Leicester, Nottingham, London, Scotland

Number of UK partners/solicitors: 102/137

Total number of trainees: 22 (English)

Seats: 4x6 months

Alternative seats: None

Extras: Language training

> Time will tell whether the firm will start to recruit different kinds of trainees, but for now at least boffins are avoided.

When Birmingham independent Gateley Wareing raised its periscope above the competitive waters of the Midlands legal market, the first thing it spied was Scottish top-ten outfit Henderson Boyd Jackson. In 2006 they joined forces to created a nationally minded law firm that now has its sights on international business.

Onwards and upwards

Trainees are recruited into HBJ GW's English and Scottish offices, although this feature focuses on the English training scheme.

The Gateley Wareing side of the firm started as a small city-centre high street practice, which steadily morphed into a commercial player by targeting small and mid-sized Midlands business clients. Offices were added in Nottingham and Leicester, and in time it began to win bigger and better business away from major Midlands law firms. It also managed to pluck partners from the likes of Eversheds, Wragges and Hammonds. Never imagine that Birmingham will be forgotten in the bid for national success: south of the border, this firm's veins course with pure balti sauce.

The Anglo-Scots merger was designed to do several things: to beef up the firm's ability to serve national clients, to generate work through cross-referrals and to 'get the firm onto more banking panels.' RBS and Bank of Scotland were already clients; indeed, legend has it the merger was originally the suggestion of RBS. After a relatively smooth transition period, in May 2007 HBJ GW merged with London-based shipping and transport experts Shaw & Croft, creating instant synergy between shipping lawyers in Scotland and London. At the same time the merger gave 'a London foothold for the corporate teams' and boosted existing plans to grow the corporate and finance practices nationally. A move into London could have been predicted. Not so the next decision. In August 2007 the launch of a brand new office in Dubai took most people by surprise, including trainees. 'It does make sense though,' they concluded; 'Dubai is the fourth fastest-growing economy in the world and the current aim is to serve existing shipping and construction clients out there.'

GW's speedy transition from the Midlands-based firm to which most of our sources had applied must have been dizzying, however the events have not utterly transformed life for Midlands trainees. 'We've been up to Edinburgh to play sport, but apart from that I can't say anything has changed too much,' said one. Trainees see the firm as 'steadily progressing' and 'ambitious but careful about that ambition.' They judged the firm to now be 'consolidating on what has been achieved, while steadily expanding in London.'

The windmills of change

In the four-seat English training scheme everyone does a seat in corporate. Many of the clients are the owner-managed businesses on which the firm's success was built, although a roster of national companies (including some plcs) is growing. Among the best known of the big names are BT, recruitment specialists Pertemps and insurance company Allianz. The corporate lawyers recently acted on the AIM admission of Network Group Holdings, the only IPO of a West Midlands-based company in 2007. They also advised HBoS in the financing of a cross-border acquisition by Staffordshire's Dechra Pharmaceuticals, helped Warwickshire-based private equity fund GIL Investments on its acquisition of a division of Akzo Nobel and assisted the owners of activity holiday company PGL in the sale of the group to Holiday Break. Corporate trainees 'get a good feel for everything that's going on,' although the scale of larger transactions can mean they're stuck 'mostly on the ancillary documentation, doing the board minutes and Companies House filings, and liaising with other departments for due diligence.' Smaller deals bring the satisfaction of 'seeing the whole process... on one deal I attended the initial meeting with clients and was there at the closing.' The London corporate and finance team is growing and 'new partners are starting to see things take off.' A London corporate seat is likely to be available in the future.

Real estate is another major area for the firm. Trainees can sample commercial and residential transactions, as well as contentious and non-contentious construction law. Real estate seats always mean 'a lot of responsibility,' much of the time 'acting for big developers buying huge plots of land, then building houses and selling them.' While it would be rare to handle the initial purchase of a tract of land, trainees can expect to be in charge of plot sales or perhaps a residential conveyancing file for a company director. Either way, 'dealing with clients on a daily basis and negotiating agreements' is a standard experience. Many of the transactions and projects are relatively local, such as the £360m Coventry regeneration programme being run by a consortium including Bovis Homes and Persimmon. Instructions come in from 'some of the top house builders in the country' like Taylor Wimpey and Barratt, so let's hope the market for new homes doesn't stall for too long. Old friend BT also calls in regularly to discuss its real estate needs, and we can see the beginnings of an international practice. Lawyers recently assisted Vestas Celtic, a leading supplier worldwide of wind turbine generators, on projects in the Republic of Ireland and the UK. They even advised on a £235m landmark development in Qatar.

Dubai it or build it?

The contentious real estate and construction team received a boost when in 2007 a barrister – a QC no less – joined from Birmingham superset St Philips Chambers. The team has been representing a main contractor client in a multimillion-pound arbitration of claims concerning the construction of a cross-country jet fuel pipeline in Dubai;

Chambers UK rankings

Agriculture & Rural Affairs • Banking & Finance • Commodities • Construction • Corporate Finance • Debt Recovery • Dispute Resolution • Employment • Personal Injury • Private Client • Real Estate • Restructuring/Insolvency • Shipping • Social Housing • Transport

they've also defended a large Dubai real estate developer in adjudications concerning the construction of a 42-storey tower block and advised a major UK specialist subcontractor on a multimillion-pound dispute regarding a hospital development. That new Dubai office is clearly paying its way already. The lawyers out there are lucky enough to be able to rely on the support of new colleagues in London: in May 2008 HBJ GW snaffled Simmons & Simmons' head of construction Robert Bryan.

Trainees say that many of the departments 'throw you in at the deep end,' and it's no different in the construction and real estate disputes seats, where there's 'sometimes almost too much responsibility,' be it on small issues of 'neighbour disputes and trespass claims' or larger cases. The safety net of 'all your work having to be signed off by a partner or senior associate before it goes out' keeps anyone from making truly dreadful mistakes.

In addition to these key areas it's worth knowing that corporate recovery/insolvency is 'pretty important to the firm.' Working for a team of 14 lawyers, trainees soon learn that the heavily technical and deadline-driven nature of the area can make for an intense seat. 'I worked pretty hard,' said one trainee. 'When there were big pieces of litigation on, and I was heavily involved, the pace could be relentless.' Just as in corporate or property, 'the occasional very late night' or 'a period of later finishes' must be expected. The seat has its rewards though: there are always small-scale bankruptcies and administrations on which it's easy enough to grab court time and advocacy.

Other seats on offer include banking, tax, commercial and employment, the latter involving 'a lot of research for the team, updating our employment law website' and 'going to tribunal, drafting meeting notes and doing corporate support.' When it comes to picking seats, Birmingham, Nottingham and Leicester offer the full range, while London has corporate and property, plus wet and dry shipping. The majority of English trainees are Birmingham-based, though they have the option of visiting elsewhere. The other three English offices recruit between one and three trainees of their own and it's perfectly possible for these trainees to spend time in

Birmingham. One Brum trainee was in no doubt as to the wisdom of visiting the main HQ: 'The partners on the board are based in Birmingham so if you want to get known in the firm then coming here gives you more options, especially when you consider that Leicester and Nottingham have more limited qualification opportunities.' This view may change as the other offices grow. It looks to us as if trainee mobility is on the increase, not least because English trainees can also go to Edinburgh for a seat. Naturally 'everyone is hoping there will be seats in Dubai!' Well done to HBJ GW: our sources had only good things to say about seat allocation. 'It's worked well,' they explained; 'your first seat is chosen for you but afterwards you get to choose and it's a balance of business needs and you completing your training checklist.' Just as there's every chance you'll secure a longed-for seat in, say employment, 'HR might also point out that your research skills are undercooked and suggest a stint in tax.'

Huhbuhjuh! Huhbuhjuh!

The English side of HBJ GW was always characterised by its relatively compact size and well-defined work-hard, play-hard ethos bequeathed by its early partners. It took pride in being the best among the mid-tier Midlands firms, and its reception areas were filled with awards for this, that and the other. No longer the plucky bantamweight, 'the firm now thinks of itself more as a big player in the Midlands and nationally' and consequently 'salaries and benefits are up there with the big Midlands firms.' Time will tell whether the firm will start to recruit different kinds of trainees, but for now at least they resemble their predecessors in character: boffins are avoided in favour of 'non-lawyery lawyers.' The firm likes down-to-earth people with the confidence to mingle with clients and carry a heavy work burden. As one observant source put it:

'Characterful partners define the firm today and you can see among the trainees the characterful partners of the future.' On this point most trainees agree HBJ GW is a firm to stick with and that 'you can plan a career here and grow with the firm.' Eight out of the nine English qualifiers took NQ jobs in 2008, joining the four out of nine who did so in Scotland. Recent trainees have definitely felt the benefits of the mergers, perceiving there to now be 'many more opportunities on qualification.'

This was always a place where people had fun so we weren't surprised when one source confessed: 'I thought I'd enjoy socialising with trainees, but I didn't expect it to fill my weeks.' There are 'one or two networking or client events a week in some departments' and most people get involved with social committee-organised events. The committee's substantial budget runs to quiz nights, karaoke-fests, Xbox-themed drinks evenings and much more. The undoubted highlight is the September Welcome Night for new trainees. 'Nearly everyone turns up' for this ancient ritual, though with 'HR and the employment lawyers looking over our shoulders, it's a bit less humiliating than it used to be.' Thank goodness for that.

And finally...

HBJ Gateley Wareing is a firm on the rise. For the time being it remains a great choice for strong characters willing to push themselves and be more than 'a worker ant.' Arguably it doesn't get better than this in the Midlands, only bigger.

Henmans LLP

The facts

Location: Oxford

Number of UK partners/solicitors: 24/32

Total number of trainees: 6

Seats: 4x6 months

Alternative seats: None

Extras: Pro bono – Oxford CAB

> An enthusiastic bunch, Henmans trainees are keen to embrace their seats and make the most of the experience.

Henmans is a cracker of a law firm. If the Thames Valley is in your mind then get it on your list.

Night at the museum

In 2007 the firm decided it was time for a change. It packed its bags, moved out of two offices in Woodstock and central Oxford and set up shop in a business park just inside the ring road near Cowley. The view might not be as pretty but according to trainees that's about the only downside to the slick new open-plan digs. For a start it's easier to get to and the ample free parking is 'so much better than the park and ride buses you have to take to get to Oxford High Street.' Once at your desk the improvements continue. 'It's a much better working environment now,' a source enthused. 'There's more interaction between the departments. You get to meet more people and you can keep up those relationships because you're always bumping into them.' Even the partners have embraced open-plan working, which means 'trainees can absorb a great deal just from overhearing phone calls.' The social side of things has improved as well. 'The firm has retained the supportive, friendly atmosphere it always had, but now we have a café downstairs there are even more lunches within departments.'

The move also conveys the firm's commercial aspirations. 'We have grown and are more forward-facing. There's a business feel to the place now that you find in larger firms. And the office here is only about two thirds full at the moment, so it's definitely going to grow further.' To pursue its expansion plans the firm is throwing itself into marketing and client events. 'There are lots of drinks parties in Oxford and we sponsor exhibits at the Ashmolean [Museum of Art and Archaeology] so we had a nice client

do there.' If Ashmingling with clients sounds nerve-wracking, rest assured 'the training partner keeps an eye on you and helps you at first. To be honest they're quite enjoyable events because we have nice clients.'

Funnel vision

Change is also afoot in the training programme – the second-years we spoke to perceived an improvement in the seat allocation system since they arrived. 'When we started we had no say at all in the first two seats,' commented one. 'You'd just get a letter saying, 'See you on the first of September. Oh, by the way, you're in property.' Now 'they get in touch with new joiners at an earlier stage to find out what they're interested in and what LPC electives they've done.' Newbies are also invited into the office before the start of the contract. While first seats are likely to remain the firm's pick, it's worth remembering that there are only six trainees for six seats, 'so the chances are you will get the things you want.' In fact it's often possible to bag a second seat in your potential qualifying department.

The choices are personal injury (incorporating clinical negligence), professional negligence and commercial litigation, private client (incorporating charities), property and a new combined corporate/employment seat. No matter which seats you get, 'not only is help always there should you need it, but your supervisor is aware of how much work you have and the quality and range of it. They're always tweaking your caseload, acting as a funnel to make sure you get a broad experience.'

Family circus

Henmans' private client practice impresses our colleagues at *Chambers UK* so much that it sits at the top of their Thames Valley league table. In the past year it has taken on four new assistant solicitors and an additional probate manager, making it the largest team in Oxford. Will drafting, tax and probate files (some with 'huge estates') occupy the bulk of a trainee's time. 'The head of department often gave me complex tax research assignments which, bizarrely, I enjoyed,' one source recalled. With 15 fee earners in the team, it's easy to pick up a broad range of work and the team is divided into pods, each with different specialisations, so you always know who to ask for advice. 'It was the seat that gave me the most responsibility,' commented one interviewee. 'I ran simple probate files on my own, and it's great working alongside different people – you learn the nuances, the little differences in the way people do things.' Trainees also gain access to the 'really interesting' work of the highly regarded charity law practice. The firm successfully tendered for the RSPCA's legacy administration and contentious probate portfolio; other prestigious clients include Barnardo's, Battersea Dogs & Cats Home, Oxfam, the Princess of Wales Memorial Fund and Shelter. The work can be challenging at times, such as 'when you are dealing with the relative of a recently deceased person whose estate is going to charity.'

Family law had proved extremely popular with recent trainees so in a sense it's a shame it's no longer offered as a seat option. Given that it had such good feedback we'll give a name check to the team and mention that it has some interesting clients, including one who instructed them on a super-confidential matter connected to the royal family. In its place is the new corporate/employment option which we look forward to reporting on next year.

The PI team covers both claimant and defendant angles as well as clinical negligence. The department also features a recently created sports and leisure injury team which deals with claims stemming from locations ranging from cricket grounds to circuses. On the claimant side one recent case involved a severe head injury and ongoing disability arising from a fall from scaffolding on a construction site. Liability issues were complicated by the fact that there were two potential defendants. Although it's not for everyone ('I'm hideously squeamish, I couldn't qualify there') the lawyers are 'lovely' and the seat teaches useful skills. 'It helps with your file management, your confidence, your drafting skills and your client relationships.' The trainee in this seat also gets to do some agency advocacy work. 'Because of our location other firms sometimes get us to go to court for them. You get instructions in the morning and off you go.'

Chambers UK rankings

Agriculture & Rural Affairs • Charities • Clinical Negligence • Corporate Finance • Dispute Resolution • Employment • Family/Matrimonial • Personal Injury • Private Client • Professional Negligence • Real Estate • Real Estate Litigation

The well-established professional negligence group deals with complex cases from multimillion-pound property fraud and construction claims against architects to regulatory complaints against professionals and policy coverage disputes between insurance companies. One claim for over £3m arose out of the poor drafting of a deed of trust prepared by a firm of solicitors to provide for the future needs of a child with cerebral palsy.

First serve, second helpings

An enthusiastic bunch, Henmans trainees are 'keen to embrace their seats and make the most of the experience. We're all very conscientious, sociable and confident in what we do.' With only six trainees 'you're guaranteed a lot of attention. Partners here give you quality work because they need to use you as a trainee, not for admin. I've never done any photocopying or collating documents in my entire time here.' It bodes well for an easy transition into the role of NQ, something which two of the three 2008 qualifiers chose to do, with the third relocating to elsewhere in the UK. While we feel it necessary to point out that all six of the 2008 trainees were female, we were assured that 'there is a chap starting next year. It's obviously not a policy to only recruit girls.' The trainee group generally includes both those who've come straight through from uni and those who've switched from other careers. 'I've met the prospective candidates for two years' time, and the firm has shortlisted some really interesting people,' one source revealed, adding: 'There are quite a lot of older people in the mix.'

Bearing this in mind, it makes sense that 'there is not a lot of wild partying going on' after work. 'Partly it's our location – everybody drives – and then a lot of people have young children. So no, there's no heavy drinking on a Friday, everybody just goes home.' Far from this being an issue, trainees appreciate Henmans' 'real respect for home life.' No one's claiming this is a social cul-de-sac. 'There are cakes for birthdays and teams often have lunches. Family used to take their trainee out for a meal when they join or leave the group, and property has a bowling trip planned for next week.' The 'lovely' in-house chef provides themed lunches every so often, even going to the trouble of decorating the café to suit the occasion. 'We had Chinese New Year, an Indian meal and I think we're due a British one soon,' salivated one bon vivant. Last Christmas the office doors were slammed shut for an afternoon and everyone hopped on a bus for a late lunch at one of the Oxford colleges. The firm's founder, Anthony Henman, is father of tennis-playing Tim and we rather like the way Henmans celebrates its links with the game – every once in a while table tennis is set up in the office.

And finally...

If your dream involves high finance and corporate gun-slinging in the City, keep looking. This firm is still at the stage of growing its modest corporate and commercial department, though it clearly sees the importance of doing so. If you're attracted by the variety of seats on offer, apply now.

Legal Career *or* Life Investment

Do you want your legal training to turn you into a good lawyer or an exceptional talent?

For more information on our training programme and vacation schemes, and for details on how to apply, please visit our website at:

www.herbertsmithgraduates.com

Invest in yourself

Herbert Smith

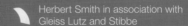 Herbert Smith in association with Gleiss Lutz and Stibbe

Herbert Smith LLP

The facts

Location: London

Number of UK partners/solicitors: 172/531

Total number of trainees: 184

Seats: 4x6 months

Alternative seats: Overseas seats, secondments

Extras: Pro bono –Whitechapel Legal Advice Centre, RCJ CAB, FRU, A4ID, Liberty, death row appeals; language training

Fans of *The Apprentice* will be happy to hear that 'Suralan' thinks Herbies has what it takes.

While continuing its reign in the City as 'the absolute best for big-ticket litigation,' Herbert Smith has also redefined and broadened its business. It now has a corporate practice that is flying high and a finance practice coming on in leaps and bounds.

Tata for now

So where's the firm at? As one of our sources mused: 'We seem to have some trouble with defining exactly what our brand is – magic circle, silver circle, international firm?' In Chambers and Partners' assessment Herbert Smith slots in just behind the magic circle and is almost certainly the best-performing member of the chasing pack. Diversification has seen the corporate department grow substantially, such that it contributes around half of the firm's overall revenue. The firm's early bid for international expansion put it in a good position and it has sustained its appetite for growth overseas.

Herbies' European practice received a boost when it entered into formal alliances with German firm Gleiss Lutz and Benelux practice Stibbe in 2001, and following a 2006 strategy review the firm decided to focus on key emerging markets in India, Russia, China and the Middle East. This decision paid off and it now has well-established offices in both Moscow and Hong Kong. More recently it opened an office in Dubai, and in April 2008 it established a formal alliance with Saudi Arabian firm GPA. The firm counts Indian giant Tata among its clients and in April 2007 it advised Tata Steel on its £6.2bn acquisition of Corus, following this deal with work on the two largest transactions involving Indian companies in 2007. Another corporate group highlight includes advising a syndicate of seven banks including Deutsche Bank and Bank of America, which provided equity finance for a consortium led by KKR and Stefano Pessina to bid £11.1bn for Alliance Boots. The deal was the largest leveraged buyout in the UK, making KKR the first private equity house to acquire a FTSE 100 company. Lawyers also advised First Choice Holidays on its recommended £1.8bn merger with TUI AG's tourism division. Using the words of one trainee: 'This firm is not just about litigation anymore.'

Of course Herbert Smith is delighted to still have a reputation as the place to go for heavyweight dispute resolution. It is currently acting for various companies in the MG Rover group (including parent company Phoenix Venture Holdings) and over 20 present and former directors and officers of these companies during the ongoing government investigation into the collapse of MG Rover. Lawyers are also representing Glacier Re in connection with reinsurance claims in excess of £10m made by Rosemont Re arising out of Hurricane Katrina and Hurricane Wilma losses.

Wish you were here?

Every trainee must take a seat in corporate, one in dispute resolution and another in either finance or real estate, leaving them with six months in which they can either go away on a secondment or experience a more niche area of practice, for instance the 'enormously popular' tax or competition departments. Luckily the fashionable overseas seats can count towards the compulsories, although trainees caution that 'you shouldn't expect to get more than one seat in a specialist area, an overseas placement or client secondment.' Overall people seem happy with their lot, telling us: 'If you are really keen to do something then you are likely to get it at some point.' We did hear a few grumbles about seat allocation decisions that 'seemed completely random,' and it sounds as if some trainees try to employ sophisticated tactics in order to work the system. 'You have to stay focused on the area that you think you want to qualify into from the very beginning,' explained one Machiavellian interviewee; 'and it is important to strike a balance between declaring your interest in a niche area, which you must do early on, and trying to avoid being put in your favourite department for your first seat when you are still a bit wet behind the ears.' There's no winning strategy, so the best advice is probably to work hard in your current seat and try to develop a good reputation. Said one observant source: 'The people who have had the best appraisals seem to get more first choices when it comes to allocation. You can't expect your ideal seat to be dropped in your lap as if from Father Christmas.'

A seat in the corporate department may involve working with holiday companies, but it is certainly no vacation. It is the worst culprit when it comes to serving up long and unpredictable hours. 'Sometimes, although not too often,' revealed one source, 'things were very quiet and I was just sat reading the *FT* in the afternoon and leaving at 5.30pm. Then when we were busy I never left before 10pm and regularly stayed as late as 2am, with a few 48-hour shifts.' Administrative tasks are rare thanks to 'a superb support staff and a dedicated reprographics team,' however our interviewees did admit that on larger projects they were often 'working on small self-contained tasks without necessarily knowing about the background to them or the end product that we were contributing to.' The smaller the deal the larger the trainee's role – drafting and verifying documents such as service agreements and prospectuses; managing data rooms and sometimes 'being properly briefed in advance and then left in charge of making sure that the deals are closed properly.' This aspect of the job can be 'hair-raising and exciting' and some trainees did admit to 'feeling out of my depth at times.' As one sage interviewee told us: 'I think that's a good thing – if you're not in deep enough water then you'll never learn to swim.'

You're hired!

Fans of *The Apprentice* will be happy to hear that Suralun obviously thinks Herbies has what it takes. In October 2007 the *Evening Standard* published an article about Sugar's former involvement at Tottenham Hotspur FC. The article contained a number of defamatory allegations and the firm successfully secured an apology from the

Chambers UK rankings

Administrative & Public Law • Banking & Finance • Banking Litigation • Capital Markets • Climate Change • Competition/European Law • Construction • Corporate Finance • Data Protection • Dispute Resolution • Employee Share Schemes • Employment • Environment • Financial Services Regulation • Fraud: Criminal & Civil • Health & Safety • Information Technology • Insurance • Intellectual Property • Investment Funds • Life Sciences • Local Government • Media & Entertainment • Outsourcing • Partnership • Pensions • Pensions Litigation • Planning • Private Client • Private Equity • Product Liability • Professional Discipline • Professional Negligence • Projects, Energy & Natural Resources • Public International Law • Public Procurement • Real Estate • Real Estate Finance • Real Estate Litigation • Restructuring/Insolvency • Retail • Sports Law • Tax • Telecommunications • Transport

newspaper, an undertaking not to repeat the allegations and a substantial award of damages, which Sir Alan donated to charity. Not all cases are so exciting and a trainee's role in the department will also include dull tasks. Such as? 'Deeply tedious updating of legal precedents' and 'quite a bit of document processing and putting together bundles.' As time goes on things become more interesting, perhaps involving juicy research or drafting witness statements. According to one source: 'While everyone is proud of the firm's strength in litigation, if you are set on becoming a litigator then Herbies might not always be the best place to train as the work is so big trainees can't be trusted with substantial roles.' This is a valid point if you're taking a short-term view; others playing a longer game disagree. The only place trainees are given the opportunity to handle any of their own advocacy is in the firm's innovative advocacy unit. This was founded in 2004 when Herbies recruited directly from the Bar in order to create its own in-house chambers. Described by trainees as 'litigation without the dull bits,' the unit draws instructions from different parts of the firm and gives trainees excellent insight into what's happening across the departments, as well as allowing them to get on their feet in court. Unfortunately it's not possible to qualify directly into the advocacy unit as the firm likes people to have built up experience in general litigation first. One word of caution: interviewees tell us that within the litigation department there is 'a core of somewhat redoubtable partners' who are among 'the most conservative and hard to approach in the firm.'

The best of the rest

'It is true what they say about seats in real estate – you do get a lot of responsibility.' So say those with time under their belts in this part of the firm. Trainees run their own small files and conduct lease negotiations; they also take charge of the due diligence on some of the larger projects as well as shouldering the responsibility for that old trainee favourite – colouring in plans. Tax has been a particularly popular destination of late and our sources said they'd thrived on a good deal of black letter legal analysis. 'Disputes can turn on a particular statutory interpretation and so I would often look through *Hansard* to see what was said when a particular act was going through Parliament,' one fan recalled. Trainees are also able to take the initiative in answering clients' queries as a lot of tax questions are discrete from larger matters.

Client and overseas secondments are 'sometimes significantly oversubscribed, in particular the Singapore and Tokyo offices.' Getting out of Herbies' Exchange Square offices usually heralds two significant changes. Whether they had been based with a client (eg BP, Coca-Cola or BSkyB) or in a smaller overseas office, our interviewees felt they were 'treated much more like a junior associate than a trainee – the levels of responsibility really rocketed and you have to think on your feet more than usual.' Understandably 'quite daunted at first,' the bright sparks at Herbies quickly adapted and felt they 'really improved as a result of the experience.' They also noticed a change in culture when it came to hours. There are more regular hours when with a client and, if abroad, 'you just have to fit in with the culture of the city you are in – for me it meant later starts and long lunches but significantly later nights.' We recommend you look at page 670 for all the overseas options as the firm now encourages everyone to spend some time abroad.

Brief encounter

A definite trend towards wannabe litigators on the firm's vac scheme ('people seem to be trying to decide between Herbies or the Bar') doesn't result in similarly minded intakes of trainees. 'There's even the odd person who tries to wriggle out of doing a proper litigation seat by doing something like corporate recovery,' divulged one interviewee. It's no longer easy to define the Herbert Smith type. 'There is a huge range of people that end up coming here,

including a 6'7' guy who plays for the Swedish rugby team and a girl who left to set up her own lingerie business.' Nevertheless we did notice a preponderance of graduates from Oxbridge and Russell Group universities.

Among the larger September intake there isn't a huge feeling of camaraderie; 'it is quite difficult to get all 60 of us together that regularly,' a source explained. The March intake 'is much more closely knit' and 'easily fits around a table' for regular nights out. The firm makes an effort to get new recruits mixing, giving each intake a budget for socialising and organising a trainee ball every two years. This glam event was held at Kensington Roof Gardens last time. Each department organises its own socials ranging from bowling to family-friendly garden parties at partners' houses. The corporate team is reputed to party hardest. At the firm-wide Christmas jolly held at Billingsgate Market, black tie is encouraged; however, there are always dedicated folk who come straight from the office in what they're wearing, leading to 'a strange mix of ball gowns and suits amongst the girls.'

Most of our interviewees felt that Herbies had 'very much lived up to expectations, particularly in relation to variety of work and good supervisors.' There are inevitably low points, they told us, 'and you know that you will have to do some fairly dull work occasionally, but overall people feel the emphasis has been on helping us learn.' After 'quite a formal and drawn-out process,' 68 of the 76 qualifiers secured jobs in 2008, spreading themselves across the departments.

And finally...

Herbert Smith trainees talk of a bright future in which the firm's international practice will continue to expand, opening up even more overseas seats. They also see the scope and reputation of the corporate and finance departments continuing to grow to match the firm's litigation prowess.

Higgs & Sons

The facts

Locations: Brierley Hill, Stourbridge, Kingswinford

Number of UK partners/solicitors: 29/26

Total Number of Trainees: 10

Seats: 4x4 + 1x8 months

Alternative seats: None

> In keeping with a firm where many people stay for the rest of their career, NQ retention rates are usually good.

Describing Black Country stalwart Higgs & Sons, one of our interviewees told us: 'The more you hear about it, the more you love it.' Read on to test their theory.

Paint it black (country)

When Joseph Higgs established his legal practice in 1875, his timing was brilliant. A boom in mining and metalworking in the Black Country meant businesses were springing up all over the shop. Higgs built up strong relationships with industrialists and their families, some of which survive to this day. Not only are there descendants of Higgs' original clients still instructing the firm's lawyers, remarkably there is still a Higgs or two working at the firm. This is a place that feels like 'everyone is family,' and not only because you might bump into someone with their ancestor's name above the door. People tend to join the firm and stick with it – no fewer than 12 of Higgs' 15 equity partners trained at the firm back in the day.

So is Higgs just a local shop for local people, or should it be viewed as a competitor of the Birmingham Establishment? Our sources mulled over this idea. 'The other big West Midlands firm is George Green, and I suppose there are some other firms that offer similar services to us. Not Wragges or people like that, but Shakespeare Putsman, who also have a family department,' said one. Another explained: 'I think we're the largest firm in the Black Country and we reach over into Worcestershire and Birmingham. Yes, we are trying to compete with some of the larger Birmingham firms.' Certainly Higgs has won some notable clients outside its traditional purview of Black Country owner-managed businesses. For example, last year it acted for Edgbaston-

based Claimar Care in its acquisition of Acorn Home Care's entire issued share capital for £10.25m. Both companies are domiciliary care providers in the Midlands and the North. Among its other commercial clients are Computeach (you'll have seen the TV ads), Ronson the lighter manufacturer, Smethwick-based confectionery importer JTS and several high-street banks.

You'd have to conclude that Higgs' ambitions are modest. 'It's not going to veer off anywhere, but rather broaden its base,' explained one interviewee. 'Each department is growing in its own way.' For example, the private client team is setting up a practice in reclaiming fees for continuing care from the NHS. Wherever Higgs' future lies, Birmingham itself doesn't loom that large. Residents of the Black Country have historically refused to be lumped in with the UK's second city, and despite living adjacent to it they even have a different accent. The firm's leaders have taken this to heart, apparently ruling out a Brummie office. 'I don't see why they would move to Birmingham,' said a loyal recruit, 'especially if you can get the clients from there anyway. You'd be wiping away all that history, cutting your nose off to spite your face if we lose that Black Country base.'

Higgs likes trainees who are dedicated to the region, and most successful applicants (though not all) haven't come from too far away. It's not just regional bias: there's practical reasoning behind such a preference. Locals 'know the people and they know the area. If clients come in, a friendly local accent helps,' so start practising those flat West Midlands vowels. With so many partners having trained there, it's no surprise Higgs is 'looking for people who want to go forward with the firm.' Higgs does state on its website that it prefers applicants to have taken the LLB route, but above all a successful application 'rests on your personality and the attributes they think you have when they're chatting away with you.' Informal interviews are followed by a tour of the office, and sources say: 'You can tell if a person's going to get the job when you see how they act on the tour.' In this gregarious, close environment, 'if you haven't got the social skills, you're not going to be very happy.'

Four play

The training scheme is four seats of four months followed by an eight-month stint in the department into which you hope to qualify. This could give someone a really useful 12 months' experience in a chosen area. 'After four months you've had a good enough taster,' said one source. 'You know what to do, how it works, and if you like it.' There is a small chance you may get a seat that's not your cup of tea, because seat allocations are 'mapped out for you when you start,' but the firm tries to be flexible and 'there is some leeway to chop and change and maybe add a fifth seat.'

Private client is Higgs' largest department. Headed by the eminent Bob Leek, who is ranked as one of the best in his field in the Midlands by *Chambers UK*, the team brings in a quarter of the firm's income, last year earning more than £2m. They're an enthusiastic bunch: 'You can see their eyes light up when they talk to you about something – it helps you enthuse about it too.' Split across all three offices, trainees have an opportunity to try out will drafting, tax planning and preparing powers of attorney, especially in Kingswinford, the smallest of the three offices and the most high-streety branch. 'There are always clients coming in off the street' and trainees quickly learn how to deal with their needs from beginning to end. The varied clientele includes everyone from 'regular Joe Bloggs off the street' to high net worth individuals. Some come from just down the road, others 'from the other end of the country.' A seat in the separate family law team offers a similarly enviable level of client contact, and deals primarily with divorce or cohabitation issues. 'I was concerned it would be really depressing meeting clients going through a difficult time, but it's different when you actually come face to face with them. A lot of them are very positive and it's actually nice having a lot of client contact, discussing what they expect in the process. Clients are often surprised at the length of the process and how complex it can be.'

Commercial property is another large department. Here, trainees work on the top floor of the Brierley Hill

HQ, drafting leases and filling out Land Registry forms for mostly local properties and clients. Meanwhile, the coco team has been quietly expanding, handling 90 transactions with an aggregate value of £85m in the past year. Higgs is on the panel of McDonald's and Thorntons for franchising advice, and receives instructions from a number of banks including NatWest, RBS and Co-op Bank. Personal injury is seen as a good introductory seat, as it's 'quite structured as to what you have to do and by when.' There are two teams – accident and injury, and clinical negligence – and recruits usually spend time with both. They meet clients and barristers, sometimes at court appearances or inquests, sometimes at conferences. There are always medical reports to wade through and research to be done into the likely value of injuries. 'The employment department gets all sorts of claims: sexual harassment, age discrimination, unfair dismissal...' A dedicated HR advice service was set up in 2006 to help clients like Warwickshire County Cricket Club deal with its staff. Seats in dispute resolution and residential conveyancing are also offered, as is the possibility of some time with the firm's two criminal lawyers working on motor offences and for privately paying clients.

Higgs' policy of delegating decent responsibility goes down well. 'I'm tested,' said one source, 'but not left to sink or swim.' As well as a seat supervisors, trainees all have partner-mentors who 'take you out for lunch once a seat and check how you're getting on.' There's no consistently popular department, although residential conveyancing is considered a short straw. One of our interviewees offered an interesting, if perhaps unreconstructed, theory on seat preferences: 'Girls like family; boys like their dispute resolution and coco.' In keeping with a firm where many people stay for the rest of their career, NQ retention rates are usually good. Both of the qualifiers stayed on in 2008.

Olymp-higgs

Of Higgs' three offices, Kingswinford is home to the residential conveyancers and some private client lawyers. Most trainees work in Stourbridge, which has four departments, and the main Brierley Hill site. 'Moving offices is how you meet everyone,' and with each so compact, after one seat you'll know the entire building. The premises are at best described as 'not so plush' and at worst as 'pretty dire.' Perhaps this is why Higgs has been looking for a new site to bring everyone under one roof.

A nine-to-five working day leaves plenty of time for outside interests. Trainees are rarely together in one place, but when they do manage to congregate it tends to be in Stourbridge in 'a nice little pub called The Swan.' There's fun at the annual Christmas and summer parties, and impromptu departmental pub trips should never be counted out. Events organised by the Birmingham Trainee Solicitors' Society (BTSS) are 'a good opportunity to see each other,' and Higgs takes charity to heart, supporting a different organisation each year by way of race nights, dress-down days, quizzes and other fundraisers. One remarkable offer came from the firm's finance director a couple of years ago – he declared he would auction his BMW for charity if the firm failed to meet its annual financial targets. Apparently he still has the car.

For the last few years, trainees have also taken part in a charity Olympics, which is more egg-and-spoon and wheelbarrow races than modern pentathlon. 'Sports are taken fairly seriously' at Higgs. One former trainee used to be Wolfie, the Wolverhampton Wanderers mascot, and each year the firm plays David against Goliaths like Hammonds, Wragges and Eversheds when competing for the BTSS inter-firm sports trophy. As well as regular football matches against other local firms and clients, there are golf events and an annual partners-versus-everyone-else cricket match.

And finally...

Higgs is ideal for someone looking for a mix of commercial and private client experience in a traditional and respected West Midlands firm. It is consistently popular with local applicants, and an increase in trainee numbers suggests it wants to become even more dominant in its local area.

Hill Dickinson

The facts

Location: Liverpool, Manchester, Chester, London

Number of UK partners/solicitors: 152/185

Total number of trainees: 30

Seats: 4x6 months

Alternative seats: Piraeus, occasional secondments

> As you might expect, Hill Dickinson's pedigree in shipping law is impressive.

For many, the name of Hill Dickinson is synonymous with shipping law, and with good cause too. No need to turn the page if the most nautical thing you've ever done is crash a pedalo – the firm has plenty more to offer trainees.

All aboard

Since the firm's inception in 1811 it has played a major role in matters maritime. For instance, long before Celine Dion began warbling about her heart going on, Hill Dicks was playing a key role in the inquiry and legal repercussions that resulted from the Titanic's brief but consequential encounter with an iceberg. In the late 1980s a decision to push non-shipping practices in insurance litigation and general commercial law caused most of the partners in firm's smaller London practice to jump ship and rechristen themselves as Hill Taylor Dickinson. This left the larger, northern Hill Dickinson with four offices: minnows in London and Chester, and whoppers in Liverpool and Manchester.

More recently the trend for consolidation in the legal market has seen Hill Dicks absorb smaller Manchester practice Gorna & Co and Liverpool property boutique Bullivant Jones, while branching out into construction, professional indemnity, fraud, environment and clinical negligence. Meanwhile, the chaps down at HTD continued to service their shipping clients from the capital and a small office in the major Greek port of Piraeus.

Then in 2006 the two firms reunited, pooling their resources to better serve large international litigation clients, consolidate their shipping strengths and increase the claim to 'national firm' status. 'While it may not have been inevitable, it was hardly a surprise. There are still

HTD people here who were with the firm when it was Hill Dickinson the first time round so it feels like the firm has come full circle.' Only this time it's bigger and better. The reunion instantly created a top-40 firm when its turnover jumped by 31%. Today Hill Dicks has clear aims for the future. 'It's very ambitious, particularly in Manchester. In Liverpool you sense that it has already got to where it wants to be and just has to maintain that, but in Manchester there is more scope for growth – every practice division there has high goals.' In London things are gradually bedding down after the Hill Dicks folk moved into the HTD building. 'We were in a state of flux at first,' said one southern trainee; 'some of the groups are now getting an overhaul and we're all adjusting to procedural changes.' All new trainees take their initial induction sessions together and the London lot are ferried to Liverpool for the Christmas party 'so the firm does make an effort to bridge the divide, even though the distance can make it difficult.'

Getting your bearings

Currently trainees are recruited for either northern or London contracts. Up north they spend the greater part of their time in Liverpool, with one or two seats in Manchester or Chester. Most enjoy 'the benefits of experiencing a different city and office.' If you've just bought a house you might not be so keen, 'but they do try to match people to location and it's easy enough to commute.' With Manchester growing rapidly, a training scheme based solely in Manchester could be on the cards. Those applying to the capital spend their two years in London unless they opt for a shipping seat in Piraeus. Thus far nobody from the North West has taken a seat in London, however, the firm is open to this idea.

Trainees have no formal input into their first seat allocation, though we hear that pre-training contract social get-togethers present an opportunity 'to have a chat with the partners who allocate things.' After that the firm does its best to accommodate preferences. The seat list includes general shipping litigation, yacht finance, yacht litigation, coco, property, private client, employment, insurance, insurance litigation, personal injury, cargo freight commodities, professional risk, IP/IT and construction.

Drives you crazy

Contentious types will thrive on all the litigation options from professional negligence and fraud to construction and commercial claims. The employers' liability and disease group, for example, deals with claims of hand-arm vibration syndrome and repetitive strain injury. Trainees assist with cases at an individual level and with the bigger picture by 'helping companies to manage their systems to defend such claims. It gave me a really broad understanding of client issues and all the elements they have to be aware of,' explained one source. As the seat progresses the challenges increase. 'By the end I was doing full reports to clients, including what the legal issues were and what our suggested steps forward would be.'

The fraud team handles public sector and health sector fraud as well as insurance fraud involving staged accidents, which sounds devilishly interesting. 'Either one party deliberately gets in an accident with an innocent bystander or two parties stage something,' explained our source. 'They write off some clapped out car and sometimes you have five people in each vehicle claiming for whiplash.' It's a trainee's job to instruct experts to assess the vehicles, settle damages where appropriate and even front court hearings. 'I had my own caseload and was able to get involved in every stage of the case. It was terrific experience.'

Our interviewees were similarly positive about commercial litigation, a department that recently boosted its numbers by recruiting an ex-Clifford Chance litigator. The firm represents a company that insures universities, so there are 'lots of student claims for failure to teach and the odd defamation claim by a lecturer.' Such matters sit alongside insolvency and contractual disputes, sometimes for quite small sums, 'like a building firm chasing for money. My supervising partner even took on a small case specifically to give me the experience of running it. There's the chance to do some of the advocacy, which is

Chambers UK rankings

Banking & Finance • Clinical Negligence • Commodities • Construction • Corporate Finance • Debt Recovery • Dispute Resolution • Employment • Environment • Family/Matrimonial • Health & Safety • Healthcare • Insurance • Intellectual Property • Pensions • Personal Injury • Private Client • Professional Negligence • Real Estate • Real Estate Litigation • Shipping • Sports Law • Transport • Travel

terrifying.' On bigger cases, expect a fair amount of research, as well as going to court to sit behind a barrister and take notes.

The construction team covers contentious and non-contentious work, dealing with projects, securing collateral warranties and handling breach of contract issues. Again, trainees can have their own caseload. 'I was given files right from the start and would be in charge of an investigation. There was a lot of interaction with witnesses and it was pretty much up to me to find out what had happened.' The team was praised for showing consideration to trainees: 'They avoid bogging us down with repetitive tasks and ensure we have a varied workload.' Naturally all contentious seats involve bundling duties and one trainee ranted about the piles of photocopying required. 'If you're in a tribunal, you need eight or nine copies of everything, which I think is shocking. When are we going to progress to a CD and a whiteboard? It's like we're living in the Dark Ages.' Not so much a criticism of the firm as of the entire UK legal system then.

Cruisin' for a bruisin'

As you'd expect, Hill Dicks' pedigree in shipping law is impressive. The new City of Liverpool Cruise Terminal opened in September 2007 and still feeds instructions. In London the team worked on several high-profile cases such as the sinking of a passenger cruise ship off 'Santorini' in Greece and the grounding of a cargo ship off the coast of Chile, which was refloated after several weeks. With such plumb cases it's a shame that the current crop of London trainees found themselves a little out of their depth in shipping. 'It's an odd seat. Structurally no one person was responsible for me. I'd get ad hoc bits of work but it was quiet a lot of the time.' On enormous litigations the most a trainee can expect is research and document management, so they always like it when arbitrations come in. At least 'the department is laid back and friendly and no one works stupid hours.'

The London PI seat sounds more promising. The department assists shipowners and ports with claims that range from 'someone slipping on a cruise trip, to bigger things like exposure to asbestos or deafness claims.' Trainees say 'there are lots of little files to juggle and you see cases through from start to finish.' Adding glamour to the proceedings, the yacht team deals with sales and purchases, employment contracts for crew and charter agreements. 'I didn't meet any clients myself,' confessed one source, 'but we're talking about very rich people who want everything to be done immediately.'

According to one trainee who may or may not have been perusing the firm's marketing material before being interviewed, 'an overriding principle of the firm is to ensure trainees are not worked far beyond standard hours.' A different source, who had worked long hours without his team knowing, was able to confirm this claim. 'As soon as they found out my hours they started kicking me out at 6pm. They said I was here to learn and not to slog it out.' For others, juggling cases for different fee earners proved more of a challenge, but all agreed 'the onus is on trainees to alert their supervisor if there's a problem.'

Star power

Liverpool staff have relocated and by all accounts 'a transformation' has taken place. 'We used to inhabit four buildings of varying degrees of pleasantness, whereas now I'm in a lovely room with comfy chairs and a view over the Mersey, climate control and huge floor-to-ceiling windows.' Communal areas, a roof terrace and a subsidised restaurant complete the new look. Manchester, meanwhile, has undergone a revamp of a different kind. The building may be the same but 'there's an internal programme to get as many people actively involved in the firm's development as possible.' Rejuvenated by the arrival of former DLA partner and top corporate lawyer Darryl Cooke, 'the office feels extremely positive and wants everyone to know they can play a genuine part in where the firm's going.' To this end the firm has created various 'star teams' to improve both business and the working environment. The 'people team' ups morale with social events, 'bowls of fruit in the kitchen and a more flexible benefits package.' The 'corporate social responsibility team' works on the firm's green credentials and organises charity events such as 'Nintendo Wii competitions for WaterAid or a pub quiz where everyone competes at the same time across the different cities.'

These developments must be a welcome addition to a firm whose social life is admittedly 'pretty slow – people have their home lives and it's difficult with all the different offices.' When people do get together it's more often for 'video nights and walking trips' than heavy drinking. In London firm life is 'rather quiet beyond a few larger events.' Things are looking up: 'We've started to have informal drinks every fortnight so I think they are making more of an effort.'

And finally...

All the growth and change meant that in 2008 there were more NQ jobs offered than candidates to fill them. After considering their many options, 14 of the 17 qualifiers stayed. If you fancy joining a firm that is 'reinventing itself and is open to your initiative and drive,' then put it on your shortlist.

- **Research rarely reveals rapid rewards:** There isn't always a clear answer to the research you'll be asked to do. If there was an easy answer the partners would know it already.

Holman Fenwick Willan

The facts

Location: London

Number of UK partners/solicitors: 72/88

Total Number of Trainees: 30

Seats: 4x6 months

Alternative Seats: Overseas seats, secondments

Extras: Pro bono – Morden CAB

> The scope of HFW's international work is especially alluring to trainees with a taste for travel.

Celebrating its 125th birthday this year, 11-office HFW is one of the most respected shipping practices afloat today. With its sails filled with maritime expertise and litigation capability, this firm is also making waves in other practice areas.

Ship shape

We apologise for the string of poor puns and dodgy metaphors, but when shipping is the powerhouse of a firm we just can't help ourselves. HFW acts for some of the biggest charterers, insurers, banks and shipowners in the world, and with profits increasing year on year things are looking pretty shipshape for this old sea dog. Ships are still responsible for moving 90% of the world's traded goods and, no matter which seas they sail, ships encounter problems. If these strike at sea then this area of law is known as wet shipping. Such unforeseen disasters include oil spills (lately in China's Yangtze River), collisions, loss of cargo and modern day piracy. In one case a large Greek-owned bulker called 'Ocean Crown' grounded off the coast of Chile with about 50,000 tons of copper concentrate on board. HFW acts for all cargo interests in relation to the salvage in this high-value case.

Dry shipping, on the other hand, concerns cargo and contractual matters and is largely based on the principles of tort. This could be delays in delivery, stolen goods or the unsatisfactory condition of goods – either damaged at sea or simply not turning out to be exactly what they are meant to be. The firm has been behind some headline-grabbing news, for instance the salvage of 'MSC Napoli' following its grounding off the coast in Devon. You may remember the stories of BMW motorcycles being washed ashore and into the hands of scavengers.

The firm has also worked on the supermarkets faulty fuel scare and the insurance ramification of the Buncefield storage depot explosion and fire. Wet or dry, cases are frequently complex multiparty matters that span jurisdictions.

This past year has been a fantastic one for HFW. When Clifford Chance pulled out of shipping law its team effectively moved straight over to HFW. The main partner Mark Morrison brought seven solicitors with him and there have been other new arrivals, both solicitors and mariners. But what if you don't know a lanyard from a halyard or even your port from your starboard? No need to worry you won't be allowed on board. A number of the trainees we spoke to confessed to knowing nothing about shipping before joining, but have since discovered it to be a 'fascinating' area. They like the fact that 'it is tangible: you can visualise a ship hitting the rocks and the damage that is caused, rather than invisible corporate cases.' As one astute interviewee pointed out: 'It's not magic, you just need commercial acumen to solve disputes, be it for ships or not.' Although the 'maritime theme' does pervade most departments, 'shipping is not all Holmans does' and the firm is expanding in areas such as energy and aviation finance. *Chambers UK* hasn't missed this point and ranks HFW among the best in areas such as civil fraud, road transport and projects and energy.

Man overseas

For the record there are seats available in shipping litigation, commercial litigation, insurance litigation, shipping finance, trade and energy, EU, employment, property and corporate projects and finance. No seats are compulsory, and after the first seat trainees are asked for their preferences at each rotation and 'usually' get them. For added excitement, overseas postings are offered in Paris, Dubai and Greece. Sometimes specific trainees are asked if they would go to a particular office, otherwise it's a free-for-all. If time abroad doesn't suit your personal circumstances then 'you don't have to go,' but those of our interviewees who had been abroad spoke of 'really excellent experiences.'

Litigation generates the lion's share of the firm's revenue, and in the past trainees have generally done three contentious and one non-contentious seats. Nowadays 'it's not unusual for people to do two and two, and very occasionally it can be three [non-contentious] and one the other way.' This could be a result of the corporate and other transactional teams 'really growing and becoming a focus for the firm.' Shipping and transport litigation is said to be the 'flagship' of the firm ('don't tell the insurance guys') and trainees work on either the wet or dry side. Either way there's 'lots of paperwork, arbitrations and hearings.' The ever-present bundling duties can't be ignored as 'lots of the cases are huge and it has to get done.' Trainees do have a level of autonomy and run small cases by themselves; they also instruct and liaise with foreign lawyers much of the time.

The shipping finance team has continued to grow over the past year and offers a seat that is 'known to be hard.' The department advises on the buying, selling, building and disposal of ships, acting mainly for banks but also shipowners. The work is highly international. This department contains a luxury yacht team to cater for the growing demands of the super rich, and an aviation practice that got a boost with the arrival of specialist David Relf from Stephenson Harwood. Unlike the shipping department, which is 'probably the most popular and the biggest – it has such a great reputation you want to try it,' the smaller EU, property and employment teams seem to be less in demand. 'They are really interesting but there is not usually an NQ job on offer,' meaning trainees generally prefer to spend their time in areas they can look to for qualification.

Pieces of freight

The growing trade and energy group deals with a host of issues ranging from the transportation of commodities such as grain, beans and coal, to oil disputes. The department offers a contentious seat that exposes trainees to arbitrations or court litigation, even if their role is 'limit-

Chambers UK rankings

Asset Finance • Commodities • Corporate Finance •

Dispute Resolution • Fraud: Civil • Insurance • Projects,

Energy & Natural Resources • Restructuring/Insolvency

• Shipping • Transport • Travel

ed when the cases are large' and mainly requires them to ensure bundles are correct and look after witnesses. Nevertheless, sitting in on briefing meetings and heading back to chambers to analyse the day's proceedings ensures 'a really good opportunity to see how cases progress.' When not in hearings, trainees research for the team and have a go at drafting pleadings. There is also a trade and energy transactional seat where days are spent working on contracts, for example to enable someone to drill in the North Sea. Trainees find they are given plenty of opportunity to deal with clients on a daily basis.

The insurance/reinsurance seat exposes trainees to 'a whole raft of things' from drafting letters to counsel and instructing experts to occasionally jetting off to foreign parts to take witness statements. There is crossover with shipping but the seat also covers professional indemnity cases. Lastly, the commercial litigation seat steers clear of shipping matters (but not shipping clients) and involves things like international asset recovery, fraud and insolvency.

Across all seats, responsibility is there for the taking: 'Trainees are not just cannon fodder, they are a genuine part of the team.' When asked about the grunt work such as photocopying, our interviewees commented: 'If it needs doing it needs doing,' but it only becomes an issue when there's a huge case at a delicate stage of play. As for another dreaded chore – paginating – this is only a burden 'if you are working for one of the few partners who insists it is done by hand in the belief it looks better.' Most supervisors are said to be 'extremely approachable and helpful,' which rendered mutterings about 'one or two partners who have a reputation for being difficult and demanding the impossible' less of a concern. The trainees' recommendation is simple: 'Learn to adapt.' Another minor grumble related to appraisals (mid and end-of-seat): the reality is 'you have to push for them and some people have had trouble getting them.'

Clocking off

We have always painted HFW as rather traditional; trainees again agreed this was still the case, but insisted it is 'not stuffy.' To make the point our sources pointed out some recent developments that they believe make the firm more 'modern.' The firm's logo has been revamped and an '&' has been ditched from the name ('not a great change', our interviews acknowledged but a step in the right direction) and 'the website is so much better now. Before it was awful.' The firm is also in the process of moving to 'snazzy' new offices just around the corner, ending its 100-year association with Lloyd's Avenue. What is still a little old-school is the partnership make up, which is still predominantly white male. We're assured that this is due to the traditional nature of the shipping industry and were asked to consider the lower ranks of the firm, where there is greater diversity. Certainly here there is a 50/50 split of men and women, and several people with non-UK backgrounds. One source did point out a clear benefit of working in a traditional industry – 'the nature of shipping and insurance means that long lunches are not unusual, nor are drinks with clients.'

The scope of HFW's international work is especially alluring to trainees with a taste for travel. The graduate recruits who move to the UK for their training contracts (and often their legal education too) add to the enormous catalogue of languages spoken within the firm. There is also a 'general trend towards slightly older trainees' and 'personality is a big deal – shipping is a small world so you need to get on with people.' On the subject of personalities, every interviewee alluded to the presence of 'some real individuals' at the firm.

Traince socialise over drinks at the pub, dinners and lunches. Departmental events have lately included pub Olympics and a Lebanese-themed night. Firm-wide there is a monthly buffet lunch to encourage cross-departmental networking and Christmas and summer parties. There is also a fair amount of client entertaining to be done and trainees are included in this. Sometimes it's drinks in the City, at others a trip to the horses or golf. 'They don't hide us,' insisted one source; 'we are trusted.' On the sports front HFW has teams for rugby sevens, cricket and football. If there's nothing going on in your sport, 'the firm would definitely help and encourage you to set up a team.' Pretty reasonable hours of 9am to 6.30pm also mean it's perfectly possible to keep up with outside interests. Happy with the deal, in 2008 all 11 qualifiers stayed with the firm after a fittingly informal process of allocating jobs.

And finally...

With 'top-rate international work,' more characters than you can shake a yardarm at, and the possibility of working on international emergencies, you can see the appeal of Holman Fenwick Willan.

Howes Percival

The facts

Location: Leicester, Milton Keynes, Northampton, Norwich

Number of UK partners/solicitors: 32/76

Total number of trainees: 25

Seats: 4x6 months

Alternative seats: None

> Although HP likes to recruit people with links to its regions, it has no qualms about taking both youngsters fresh out of uni and older hands with another career behind them.

Just about sneaking into the list of the top 100 most profitable firms in the UK, Howes Percival offers a broad commercial training contract out of four offices.

How's Percival?

Howes Percival 'prides itself on being able to compete with the bigger firms,' and it manages this in more ways than one. The client list is filled with national names such as ATS Euromaster Limited; HBOS; HSBC; Kia Motors UK; Renault Trucks; Spar UK; RBS and Lloyds TSB. The quality of work is high – *Chambers UK* ranks the firm amongst the best in the South for property litigation and top in East Anglia for insolvency.

The firm has offices in Leicester, Milton Keynes, Northampton and Norwich, and on the face of it the training contract offered in each looks much the same. All four have seats in coco, commercial property and employment. Leicester, Norwich and MK offer commercial litigation as well, while Northampton has a private client seat instead. Many trainees choose to return to the department they wish to qualify in for their fourth and final seat. While Norwich trainees will stay in one place for the duration of their contract, those recruited to the offices in the M1 corridor can move around between them if they wish. Some do prefer just to stick to one location, although business needs sometimes dictate that travel may be required. In short, 'you will always be given a chance to state your preference and the firm will accommodate you as best they can.'

Though similar seats are on offer, trainees say the experience in each location is very different indeed. A lot of this is down to the partners who head up the individual offices: all have stamped their own personal style on the work-place. Each office also has its own client base and case-load, so 'they operate quite separately from each other.'

MKing its mark

Leicester, with its 'swanky' building and 'up-tempo' atmosphere, has the most corporate mindset. 'Rapid growth' over the last couple of years means it needs more space. Indeed, trainees briefly found themselves working on a landing before a welcome move back in with the other fee earners. The coco team, which covers corporate, commercial and banking matters, completed about 30 deals last year with a combined value of £250m, one of the largest being the sale of the CS2 Group to car hire company Helphire. Trainees get exposure to a range of work, including 'looking at terms and conditions for clients' on the commercial side and 'a lot of exposure to good drafting' of sale and purchase agreements on the corporate side. There is 'perhaps less banking stuff at the moment because of the state of the market.' The supervision is described as 'quite stringent – everything gets looked at and marked up and discussed.' In employment, meanwhile, respondent tribunal work is 'the bread and butter of the team.' Here trainees praised 'the perfect blend' of contentious and non-contentious experience. As well as taking witness statements and drafting tribunal forms, one trainee had to get into scrubs and go to hospital to watch a surgical procedure in order to be au fait with the complexities of a race discrimination claim. Employment is one of the busier Leicester departments and so trainees are expected to pull their weight. Said one: 'I was doing 8am until 7pm at times.'

Avant-garde concrete cows roaming the main shopping centre, an American-inspired grid road system and a football team poached from Wimbledon make Milton Keynes one of Britain's best-known and least understood towns. Its legal market is thriving, consistently taking work from nearby towns with more established markets, not least Northampton. Howes Percival is at the forefront of this development, and the atmosphere in its MK office is that of a 'modern, vibrant law firm with a lot of big personalities.' Trainees say of life here: 'You have to be willing to treat it as if you were working at a City firm,' perhaps because MK has become quite a competitive legal marketplace. Again, that means hours can be reasonably long, and even if nowhere near as bad as the worst excesses of the capital, some trainees did feel that 'sometimes when you've done your work, you don't feel you can go because someone more senior will make a comment.' Despite having said this, they also told us: 'You can walk into any partner's office to ask questions. It's very open in that way, and a genuinely nice place to work.'

We mentioned big characters earlier and it's clear that trainees were thinking of the MK litigation department specifically. 'They like the fight. They like it when it gets juicy and a bit uncomfortable,' said one source. While not everyone appreciates the 'bullish' nature and 'lack of social niceties' of this team, others enjoy 'being part of their gang.' There's no denying that 'they get the job done' and all acknowledge it's 'the best seat for exposure to great work and great clients.' The biggest case currently running is Fiona Trust v Privalov, a $540m Commercial Court dispute in which a shipping company claims two individuals are guilty of fraud. Howes Percival, acting for one of the defendants, is lining up opposite international shipping giant Ince & Co. MK's proximity to London means a lot of work comes from there, and trainees spend a lot of their time jumping on the train at the last minute. 'They sometimes treat it as a test. They say, 'You have 50 minutes to deliver this to the RCJ – see if you can do it.'' In common with the litigation team, the MK coco team has a large number of automotive clients: ATS Euromaster; Camden Motors; Colbourne Garages and Kia among them. The corporate team recently acted for HR Owen on the sale of the majority of its BMW and Mini dealerships in London to Marsh Wall. Another of their highlights was advising entrepreneur Ian Lenagan on his acquisition of both Wigan Warriors Rugby League Club and Oxford United FC.

Haunted Howes

Northampton was HP's original office, and compared to the others it has a reputation for being relaxed and easy-going. It usually appeals to trainees who prefer 'a more

Chambers UK rankings

Agriculture & Rural Affairs • Banking & Finance • Corporate Finance • Dispute Resolution • Employment • Intellectual Property • Licensing • Private Client • Real Estate • Real Estate Litigation • Restructuring/Insolvency

regional type of lifestyle.' Our interviewees did foresee 'the attitude of Leicester and Milton Keynes possibly rubbing off on Northampton in the future,' but for now viewed it as more settled than its counterparts. The office building is markedly different too: in keeping with the firm's long history, an enormous chandelier hangs above the boardroom table and rumours persist of an unusual added extra in the basement. 'The guy who does our stationery swears he saw a ghostly woman down there,' whispered a source. We're sorry to go all Scully on you, but we can't help but doubt this claim, especially since when asked what this apparition looked like, the best our informant could say was that she dressed in 'the usual ghost-like attire.'

The largest team within the office is commercial property. While the MK property department specialises in smaller landlord and tenant and refinancing cases, 'Northampton relies on a smaller core of larger clients' and is involved with development projects for housebuilders. Trainees act as 'the right hand to a partner' and can get involved with every part of a deal, taking the reins on the ancillary aspects like infrastructure agreements with the local utility providers. The coco team in Northampton is very small, with just one partner, but 'he can run multimillion-pound deals in his sleep.' The employment department, unlike in Leicester, is 'about 80% non-contentious. There are claims lodged but they tend to get settled early on.' This means trainees spend the bulk of their time on day-to-day company support work. A lot of research is necessary in this fast-moving area of law and our contacts had been heavily involved with preparing seminars on unfair dismissal and redundancy. 'Employment solicitors spend a lot of time in front of PowerPoint,' joked one.

Removed from the other HP offices, Norwich is left to do its own thing, recruiting and keeping its own trainees for the full two years. Commercial property and corporate are the two most important areas of practice here: in the past year the property team took 38 instructions on behalf of Ford Retail on the sale and acquisition of motor dealership sites across Britain, advised the Dean and Chapter of Norwich Cathedral on all its landlord and tenant matters, and acted for several major UK banks, including NatWest and Bank of Scotland. The corporate team's clients are mainly East Anglian, with a few national names thrown in. Trainees 'don't just do the little jobs,' but get heavily involved with business sales and acquisitions. The licensing team has also performed well in recent years and is top ranked in the region by *Chambers UK*.

This time it's Percival

HP isn't afraid to splash the cash when it comes to salary – while not quite at London levels, our interviewees admitted that 'sometimes we feel quite smug when talking to other trainees in the area about our pay.' Although HP likes to recruit people with links to its regions, it has no qualms about taking both youngsters fresh out of uni and older hands with another career behind them. Trainees say 'they want people who can be client-facing' so an 'outgoing and bubbly' personality is looked for.

When it comes to throwing a party 'you can guarantee HP will do it well.' The big bash of the year is the AGM, and full marks to the firm for making a traditionally dull event into one of the highlights of the social calendar. The last one was held at Sandringham, and our contacts remembered clay pigeon shooting, dragon boat racing, quad biking, a bucking bronco and a free bar among the attractions. Awards were made to the firm's most dedicated employees and the review of the year took the form of 'a presentation where the managing partners all dressed up and did it in a Starsky and Hutch style.' Good humour is

a feature of life at Howes Percival. Trainees told us: 'You have to be willing to take a bit of banter and gentle rib tickling – especially between first and second years. But we're not a bunch of jokers; we work hard.' The day to day social scene at HP is not the liveliest and we're told 'the people who work here like it that way.' A Leicester trainee did say: 'In all honesty there's not as good a social life as perhaps was suggested,' but most of our contacts felt that 'some firms overdo it a bit with the social scene. If people are going out then I'm happy to go out too, but if not, then I'm grateful to have the time to see my friends outside work.' Trainees do regularly go for lunch together; indeed in Northampton they are to be seen so often in the Baroque coffee bar that one of the waitresses sent them a goodbye card when she left.

In 2008 there were a total of eight qualifiers and five stayed on. Three took jobs in MK, one in Leicester and one in Northampton.

And finally...

If we had to create a cheesy PowerPoint presentation on this outfit, we'd entitle it 'Howes Percival: a firm of contrasts'. Choose it if you want an excellent broad commercial training.

Hugh James

The facts

Location: Cardiff, London

Number of UK partners/solicitors: 48/75

Total number of trainees: 17

Seats: 4x6 months

Alternative seats: None

> We just can't wait to hear what influence the Merthyr staff will have on the Cardiff Christmas party.

Top Welsh firm Hugh James has signalled its English ambitions by opening a London office. It's long been renowned for its claimant-led litigation practice and is a popular choice for trainees with diverse interests.

Huge aims

Hugh James has streamlined its business into three divisions: corporate and banking; claimant litigation; and property and construction. Having once been much better known as the champion of the little guy, it is now focusing on developing its commercial practice because, frankly, there's a good deal more money to be made here. Naturally this shift in emphasis has had an effect on the firm, gradually making it feel more corporate, but our interviewees weren't worried. 'You get the sense they'll bring you along with everything, rather than adopt an elitist, snobbish attitude of just trying to get the top dollar,' said one. Going forward you mustn't imagine that claimant litigation will be neglected; it's more a case of developing other areas to try and match the success of these contentious teams. 'Accepting that we have two personalities and trying to cater for two types of client independently' is the way forward, it seems.

Operations have expanded most noticeably in Cardiff where, having already filled floors four through six of its current office block, HJ has now occupied the third floor. 'We're on a mission to take over the whole building,' chuckled a source. A London office at Canary Wharf has popped up like a daffodil in spring and while this 'glamorous but very small' branch in the English capital is 'still in its infancy,' everyone is excited as 'it gives the firm a bit more prestige' and 'it's a good marketing tool.' Cynics that we are, we'll believe it when we see proof of one enthusiastic trainee's claims that this new addition

signals deeper ambitions for 'an international side to the firm.' For now, jet-setting is limited to a one-month secondment to a law firm in Finland. Currently available to qualified solicitors, trainees may soon be eligible to apply. From small, slightly frostbitten acorns do mighty oaks grow, right?

When behaviour is just not cricket

In the main Cardiff HQ the commercial seat options are proving popular with trainees, not least among them the recently introduced construction law seat. Working with this team provides 'a good balance of contentious and non-contentious experiences' and thus 'requires different skills, which keeps you on your toes.' The team is advising the Welsh Assembly on housing and community development projects, Glamorgan County Cricket Club on a stadium redevelopment in time for the Ashes 2009 and Dwr Cymru/Welsh Water on the implications of new construction health and safety regulations. Also popular is the employment seat: it's 'closely linked to the corporate and commercial departments,' so recruits get used to working with colleagues in these areas. Employment clients include Memory Lane Cakes, Cardiff City Council and Cardiff City Transport. Over in the large commercial property department, lawyers have acted for a consortium made up of Taylor Wimpey, Persimmon Homes and Barratt Homes on the £53m acquisition of Barry Waterfront and advised Cardiff Bus on a multimillion-pound exchange of property that will see its old Sloper

Road depot redeveloped for housing. The property litigation department, meanwhile, incorporates a special anti-social behaviour unit that represents local authorities and housing associations throughout Wales.

The claim game

The high-volume fast-track insurance litigation seat is an 'intense' and 'very target-driven' experience. Working for insurers, the aim of the game is to 'get rid of' an insurer's claims 'for the lowest amount possible.' What does that entail? 'Basically you're given a big caseload and the idea is you run these quite low-value cases through a case management system [called Streamline] and settle as many as you can.' Having 60 to 80 files is not unheard of for a trainee and the experience really hones your negotiating skills. Some may sniff at the seat, saying it doesn't offer much in the way of interest or variety, but it does give a good overview of the litigation process from beginning to end. As one source put it: 'There's no prestige attached to it, but there's a lot to be gained.'

Earning your stripes in fast-track insurance is good preparation for a claimant-led contentious seat. Most of this business used to be handled in the firm's Merthyr office, just up the A470 from Cardiff, although the Merthyr teams have been moving one by one to Cardiff. Various teams deal with a range of issues from clinical negligence and workplace injuries to nursing care costs. This last team seeks recompense from health authorities for the cost of care paid by elderly clients. There's usually not much court time, but if a case does reach that stage 'it goes to a big judicial review in London.' The clinical negligence team is well respected and here claims can result from anything from straightforward pressure sores to brain damage. With some settlements worth millions of pounds, trainees are more likely to merely assist senior fee earners. 'One day you could be working on a brain injury case and another just a fracture.' Trainees handle new inquiries, taking details of potential claims and attending weekly meetings to decide which new clients to take on. 'You get to see what to look for in a successful case,' explained one interviewee. Among recent successes was a £4m settlement on behalf of an infant client with cerebral palsy. Given the circumstances of some of the clients, trainees need to be comfortable 'dealing with people in emotional situations.'

One of the most interesting teams litigates over harmful products. This type of practice is usually referred to as product liability litigation, however 'the partner felt 'harmful products' was a name the public could relate to.' Its biggest case at the moment – a group claim by 650 people against GlaxoSmithKline over the anti-depressant drug Seroxat – has been the subject of no fewer than four *Panorama* documentaries. HJ has an excellent reputation in this field and is also involved in claims regarding

Vioxx, cataract lenses and lumbar discs. 'With a group action there's inevitably a lot of repetition in the work,' but there are few complaints about trainee tasks: typically they are kept busy taking witness statements and reviewing medical reports and records. A seat that's even more medical-based is 'neurolaw' (or catastrophic injury as it was previously known). This relatively small team handles some big claims for individuals who've suffered severe brain and spinal injuries. Trainees get their own files on which they draft documents and prepare for and attend hearings. The team's philosophy is not to tell patients 'you've just had this accident, let's see what we can get for you,' but rather to 'ensure a client's wellbeing.' After seeing how the lawyers look after clients' affairs and take care of everyday practical concerns, one interviewee told us: 'It completely opened my eyes.'

Diagnosis Merthyr

Seat rotation is anything but predictable: if a trainee wants more experience in a department it's possible to repeat or extend a seat. We've even heard of recruits finishing their contracts having sat with only two different teams. It's equally possible for a seat to be cut short if that's what suits the firm's needs. With the process of applying for post-qualification positions sorted out early (a list of available jobs is published before Christmas, with interviews held in January/February), a trainee's last seat is commonly taken in the department that has a job waiting for them.

It's no longer the case that all recruits should expect to take a seat in the Merthyr office because HJ has decided to close that branch down and move everyone lock, stock and barrel into Cardiff. Staff from Merthyr won't feel too out of place as the decor in both offices is the same – 'a lot of frosted glass and Murray Mints in all the rooms.' They'll also find the working day to be reasonable ('the one thing you'll never find is people trying to outdo each other in terms of hours'), although there tends to be less of a lunch-hour culture in Cardiff. Socialising will probably be a bit easier in Cardiff city centre, and we just can't wait to hear what influence the Merthyr staff will have on the Cardiff Christmas party. Merthyr's festive shindigs were always described to us as 'legendary' and usually involved partners dressing up and performing skits, karaoke and plenty of 'drunken dancing.'

Hugh are we?

Compared to many of the trainees we speak to up and down the country, we'd say all our HJ interviewees were extremely sociable and gregarious. These traits come in handy as the firm 'encourages you to network with peers, other firms and potential clients.' Many of those taken on as new trainees have worked as HJ paralegals or at the very least completed a vacation scheme. The majority have a pre-existing connection to Wales, often through Cardiff and Glamorgan Universities. Cardiff comes in for masses of praise: trainees like the fact that it's a buzzing city that's just a short drive from the countryside and the beach. As much as the city has to offer in the way of social life, the firm makes a pretty good effort too, perhaps responding to bygone criticisms that 'the social side of things needed improvement.' Now there's a trainee social committee that receives a budget for events like bowling and ice skating, and on Fridays at nearby bar Copa 'you can always go in and find some-body from the firm.' Involvement with the local branch of the Law Society's Junior Lawyers Division is high, and as we were conducting our interviews the HJ trainees were getting ready for Law Idol, a karaoke night for trainees across Cardiff. Those more comfortable chanting from the terraces than wailing into a microphone can play inter-firm football, and we have it on good authority that if you're in the office on a Friday night you can spy rugby matches at Cardiff Arms Park from the office windows. Apparently you can see almost the entire pitch.

And finally...

If you're a keeno for Cymru you can hardly do better than Hugh James. As it diversifies there's greater scope for involving yourself in commercial practice and it remains a cracking choice for claimant litigation. In 2008 seven out of nine people stayed with the firm after qualifying.

Hunton & Williams

The facts

Location: London

Number of UK partners/solicitors: 14/16

Total number of trainees: 5

Seats: 6x4 months

Alternative seats: None

Hunton's data protection practice is world renowned and described as 'fairly outstanding' to work in.

Gazing out over the City skyline from floors 18 and 19 of The Gherkin, Hunton & Williams' London office is still in its infancy, but thanks to its American connections it has expertise in two cutting-edge areas of law.

Small but perfectly formed

Founded in 1901, Virginian law firm Hunton & Williams has been expanding steadily ever since. It acquired branches along the East Coast before establishing an international foothold in the 1990s and finally making the leap into the Californian market in 2006. It now has 19 offices in six countries worldwide. A London office was set up in 1999, although it didn't start practising UK law until 2004. While staff numbers are still relatively small, this has proved no obstacle to H&W quickly building a number of formidable teams. In the States it is known for its outstanding energy work (with a focus on climate change), and it leads the field for data security and privacy law. The London office is Hunton's Mini-Me: much the same areas of expertise as in America, but a lot smaller. *Chambers UK* ranks it among the best in the UK for both data protection and energy projects. It also has a corporate finance team with a good reputation for AIM work.

Until recently London concentrated on these core areas, but in the last year it has upped its game and there is 'now a drive to become a full-service office.' A real estate practice was launched in July 2008 – a move welcomed by trainees, who see it not only as an important addition to their training contract, but also a common sense move, since 'most deals involve property work at some point and previously we had to outsource it all.' Trainees normally complete four seats of six months, although this is open to change. In addition to energy; corporate; and global technology, outsourcing and privacy, they can also visit

tax, banking and employment teams. The restructuring and insolvency team took a hit recently with the loss of a partner to Orrick. While this gap has been plugged with a lateral hire from Freshfields it's fair to say that, at the moment, litigation is not the firm's main focus. However, after pressure from the trainees H&W is taking steps to arrange a secondment to the litigation department of another law firm and the firm may in time grow its contentious arm.

A lot of hot air

The highly rated energy practice counts power companies and major financial institutions among its clients, with Nord/LB and Citi two of the most prominent. Also worthy of note: H&W was one of only two firms (the other being Norton Rose) to win a place on The Crown Estate's new energy panel. Trainees agreed that this is a difficult seat, as they deal with 'quite a discrete part of the law. There aren't many precedents, so everything you do is new.' The team is essentially divided into two. One half works on energy trading, a field that is becoming increasingly attractive for banks and hedge funds as they seek to find new and reliable areas of profit in the wake of the credit crunch. Hunton's role entails negotiating the terms of the trading contracts around a house position. These are 'short-term transactions that are useful for trainees to see all the way through.' Most of the actual negotiating is done over the telephone by more senior fee earners, but 'when there is less time pressure' trainees are encouraged to draft and send negotiation e-mails of their own. 'Dovetailing nicely' with the trading of gas and electricity is the projects half of the team, which specialises in getting renewable energy and climate change projects off the ground. These have included wind farms, carbon capture and wood waste gasification projects. H&W also advises several clients on their environmental schemes, particularly in relation to carbon emissions trading. 'There are schemes your average layperson wouldn't have heard of, and that means a lot of research is needed to get up to speed,' trainees said. There was praise, however, for the quality of teaching on offer. 'The energy team are quite aware that what they do is not mainstream for a student. The guy I sat with often took me to one side and explained stuff to me – that was invaluable.'

To protect and serve

H&W's data protection practice is 'world renowned' and described as 'fairly outstanding to work in.' GE, Estée Lauder, NBC Universal, Goldman Sachs, Macmillan Publishing and Morgan Stanley are among the major multinational corporations that have come to the London office for advice. It's an area of law that's expanding rapidly and is right in the public eye at the moment ever since high-profile data losses, such as the 25 million records mislaid by HM Revenue & Customs. 'When you think of data protection, you think of the 1998 Data Protection Act and nothing else,' said a trainee remembering their LPC revision notes, 'but it is more wide ranging than that.' In the past year the team has advised several clients during data breaches, but has also worked to ensure such breaches do not occur in the first place, undertaking projects that enable companies to transfer personal data internationally while still complying with EU data protection law. The differences between EU and US laws are causing problems for large corporations, and H&W also advises clients on this. A trainee's role can include everything from writing reports and client alerts, to research and 'drafting memorandums on data encryption or the powers of customs officials.'

The department known within the firm as 'global capital markets, mergers and acquisitions' (that's corporate to you) has a solid base of AIM clients. In the past year it has overseen the admission to AIM of Vietnam Infrastructure Limited (valued at $402m); Timan Oil & Gas (£123m); Renewable Power & Light (£60m); Range Resources Limited (£44m); DiamondTech (£22m); Bluewater Bio International (£3.7m) and Medusa Mining Limited (AU$11.1m). It also advised Island Gas on its £47m reverse takeover of KP Renewables, Strand Partners Limited on the reverse takeover and readmission to AIM of Platinum Diversified Mining, valued at $300m, and Central Rand Gold on its placing and dual listing on the Official List and Johannesburg Stock Exchange, valued at £308.2m. In short, very decent-sized

Chambers UK rankings

Climate Change • Corporate Finance • Data Protection • Information Technology • Outsourcing • Projects, Energy & Natural Resources

deals abound. Trainees do note that, in the current climate, 'we are seeing slightly less AIM work of late, but we are developing other areas.' The small size of H&W may well mean that it escapes the worst ravages of the credit crunch – it appears to have no dead weight to lose. Said one contact: 'We are certainly the only office I know in full recruitment mode, when others are desperately trying to find people to lay off.' The corporate team is praised as being non-hierarchical: 'We all sit round together and thrash things out.' There is a fair bit of drafting for trainees: 'I was trusted to do placing agreements and stuff a bit more complex than your average board minutes,' said one satisfied source. Due diligence 'plays its part,' and there's 'an awful lot of verification,' but our interviewees seemed to have avoided the worst grunt tasks and seemed satisfied that 'the thought process behind training is less 'the trainees are cheap, let them do the grunt work,' and more 'what work does he need to see to make him a better lawyer?''

Who wants to be a millionaire?

H&W is a classic American firm, but the London office isn't star-spangled to the hilt. Though trainees often work in conjunction with their colleagues in Brussels, they have less to do with the US branches, and there is no great interference from across the pond. The office is getting 'more American clients than a year ago,' however. 'I think what's happening is that as we move towards full service and generate far more income, America is sitting up and taking notice and giving their clients a nudge in our direction.' The staff are described as 'knowingly ambitious. Every one of the lawyers here is young enough to want to make their mark.' Most of the partners are 'around 40,' and most of the solicitors are in their 30s. 'They appreciate what it's like to be a trainee' and feedback is always forthcoming. 'For my last appraisal,' said one contact, 'my supervisor wrote ten sides of A4.' The reputation that US firms have for working obscene hours doesn't really hold weight here: our contacts agreed that 8.30am until 7pm was about the average. The firm pays mid-Atlantic-level salaries.

With just two H&W training contracts available per annum, we asked our sources what set them apart from the 300 or so other hopefuls who apply each year. After some modest 'gosh-I-don't-knowing' on their part, we found that first of all the university you went to doesn't mean too much. Our sources hailed from reputable institutions, but not the ones traditionally known for producing legions of City lawyers (you know where we're talking about). More important is 'ambition and entrepreneurialism' – those we spoke to had things on their CV which hinted at gumption and initiative. Trainees all concurred that the recruitment team are careful about picking people who will fit in with the ethos of the firm, and that 'the informal lunches [during the interview process] are quite important' for making a good impression. A written exercise and a presentation in front of the other candidates are also key elements to the assessment day. 'We had a week to prepare,' recalled one source; 'it's not just the way you present but also what you say that's important.' The topic last year was the old 'what would you do with a million pounds' question and needless to say, simply waxing lyrical about that 1961 Aston Martin DB4 in British racing green that you've always wanted won't cut the mustard. Trainees agree that confidence – but not arrogance – is the order of the day and that 'the main ethos is cohesiveness. We are still a small office and everybody supports each other.'

While one trainee joked several times about alcohol intake, we suspect that actually life at H&W doesn't revolve around booze. Office drinks take place on a quarterly basis and there were no tales of regular Friday night debauchery. 'I wouldn't say it's as wild as other firms, from what I've heard or read on the internet,' admitted another contact. Instead, 'everyone has fitness in common.' The firm is just about large enough to support a netball team, although for the moment there's no football or rugby team for the boys – they make do with cycling. Indeed, 'some of the solicitors have a penchant for turning up in lycra and wearing it for a disproportionate amount of time before they get changed in the morning.' Love of sport extends to spectating, and trainees recently enjoyed a day out at Ascot. No expense is spared for departmental retreats – the corporate team went to Miami last year, while Brussels is on the cards this time round. Networking is 'a big part' of the social scene and trainees can expect to get involved with all sorts of client events.

And finally...

Hunton & Williams would be a good choice for someone who is predisposed to its specialisms and thinking about staying with the firm for longer than a couple of years. In 2008 H&W's sole qualifier stayed on, going into the corporate department.

- **Shameless Plug:** To explore the individual strengths of American firms in more detail, search www.chambersandpartners.com/usa

IBB Solicitors

The facts

Location: Uxbridge, Chesham, Ingatestone

Number of UK partners/solicitors: 30/46

Total number of trainees: 12

Seats: 4x6 months

Alternative seats: Secondments

The Chesham office, home to a private client practice, is located in a stately country manor. 'It's like going to someone's house: the staff in reception treat you like one of their children, bringing in baked goods and making you hot drinks all the time.'

Located at the two westernmost stops on London Underground's Metropolitan Line, there's a definite doubleness to IBB. Quiet country manor or modern, swish digs? Private client instructions or high-flying commercial transactions? Trainees here get to try the lot.

Courting success

Where 'other firms have narrowed their scope to only concentrate on specific commercial areas, IBB wants to be the firm with breadth.' So say trainees when explaining the appeal of this suburban frontrunner. IBB has recently generated impressive growth and broke the £13m earnings mark for the first time in 2007. It's now aiming for the top 100. IBB's advancement can be credited to its commercial group, which has steadily extended its remit over the past year and a half. 'It's quite exciting being part of an expanding firm and it's a great time to join,' said one source. Trainees sampling commercial work find themselves at Capital Court in Uxbridge, one of the firm's four branches. The sleekest by far, its thoroughly modern look (plasma screens in reception, air conditioning) is indicative of a business with its eyes firmly on the prize. Here trainees can try their hand at property, litigation, finance and general commercial work for the firm's roster of financial institutions (among them RBS, NatWest and Svenska Handelsbanken, one of the largest banks in the Nordic countries), charities, property developers and corporates (some of them well-known plcs). Recently, for example, the commercial group advised RBS on Budgens Stores' franchising funding, a deal valued in excess of £15m. In complex commercial litigation in particular, the firm frequently finds itself coming up against City or large regional practices, a further indication of its prominence in this field and the calibre of work trainees will be contributing to.

Commercial leaps and bounds aside, private client work and criminal law are still 'the firm's bread and butter,' or at least a decent portion of the loaf. *Chambers UK* consistently gives IBB a first-tier ranking for crime and it's on the Legal Services Commission panel for serious fraud cases. Crime falls under the banner of the community legal services department, meaning the trainees assigned to the team will handle not only crime but also childcare issues and personal injury claims for mostly local clients. This department is situated in Lovell House in Uxbridge, an open-plan office that's 'quite basic really, which is suited to the work that goes on there.'

Crime is 'a big team composed of a lot of young solicitors.' Trainees report that they have a lot of responsibility in this seat, in part because 'partners spend a lot of their time in court.' Trainees take care of their own files, which revolve around 'basic crime' in the magistrates' and Crown Court. This doesn't mean you won't encounter some major cases though: in addition to general crime IBB has a highly regarded subgroup that specialises in matters involving major fraud investigations of companies and individuals. Called the business investigations and governance group – BIG to trainees – if you get this seat you'll encounter some of the largest fraud cases around. Recently this has included such exciting matters as Operation Lochgelly, a nine-handed allegation of conspiracy to defraud; arguably the largest credit card fraud in the UK, with the 'fraud spend' in the region of £35m.

Also it acted in Operation Holbein, an investigation into cartel activity by various pharmaceutical companies and price fixing in relation to the supply of drugs to the NHS. Trainees said: 'Crime seats are a lot of fun because you're dealing with people and human nature, and also because a lot of what you're working on gets publicised.' It's also 'quite exciting going to court and seeing the process through from start to finish.'

Park life

Home to a private client practice, the firm's Chesham office is an entirely different animal. It's located in 'a stately country manor' set in 'huge gardens' with 'a beautiful lake' filled with swans and geese. This setting is 'perfectly geared towards private clients' and the trainees seem well suited to it too. 'It's like going to someone's house: the staff in reception treat you like one of their children, bringing in baked goods and making you hot drinks all the time.' As well as winning the most-picturesque-setting prize, the Chesham office is also the one with the best history. It's the site of IBB's original home and trainees are convinced that Sir Arthur Conan Doyle was a one-time customer. The building is additionally said to have a resident ghost.

IBB's living clients in Chesham are mostly high net worth individuals in need of assistance with matters like trusts, estate planning and management, and high-stakes divorces. The group has also been acting for an increasing number of wealthy clients with overseas assets, which therefore entails advising on more complex issues. If you've already studied some law you'll know that these areas have 'highly technical aspects.' In estate management, for instance, 'you do a lot of drafting, which is really good for your basic skills and actually more interesting than you would think.' In the family law group there's quite a few administrative chores too, which some people find 'a bit tedious,' especially after doing seats in crime. Nevertheless the seat is 'great if you have an interest in the area as there are a number of high-profile cases.' Much more than just a walk in the park, a seat in Chesham provides trainees with the opportunity to sharpen critical skills by 'learning from specialists and through direct contact with clients.' There are more private client services in the conveyancing-heavy Ingatestone office in Essex, although trainees do not work in that branch.

Independent people

At this firm, none of the many and varied seats are compulsory, but 'the flipside is that there's sometimes space for just one trainee in each department at any given time,' which can lead to competition and the need to compromise. 'Everyone has done a seat they didn't want,' warns one trainee. Right now, corporate seats are often a source of tension, as trainees vie for a spot in one of the firm's

Chambers UK rankings

Banking & Finance • Charities • Crime • Dispute Resolution • Employment • Family/Matrimonial • Personal Injury • Private Client • Real Estate • Real Estate Litigation • Restructuring/Insolvency

most dynamic departments. 'Everybody's quite busy and buys into the ethos of pushing the firm to the next level,' said one corporate convert.

The trainees we spoke to told us they never felt overwhelmed by the responsibility they were given, as 'the level seems to go up as you move through your seats... which is how it should be.' When it comes to the typical grunt tasks that are 'part and parcel' of the trainee experience, our sources felt fairly treated. 'The thing is, especially in crime, you see senior partners doing their own photocopying and admin work; even the managing partner doesn't have his own secretary. The firm prizes self-sufficiency.' Overall trainees were thoroughly satisfied with the assignments they were given and spoke of plenty of interesting experiences. As one explained: 'This firm is not so big that they can afford to just keep you in the wings.' The ability to just get on with things might strike literary-leaning (and obscurity-prone) readers as a characteristic IBB trainees share with the protagonist of Halldór Laxness' Nobel Prize-winning novel *Independent People*. While a two-year training contract isn't quite as epic as Laxness' tale of life in turn-of-the-century rural Iceland, it does seem to be self-sufficient and strong candidates who choose to make something of themselves at IBB.

When prompted to pinpoint the type of person that ends up training here, most interviewees were at a loss, saying only that the group was 'very mixed.' We managed to tease out a few key traits though: most IBB trainees have had some prior 'life experiences' before getting a contract with the firm, partially because it doesn't fully fund LPC fees and paid work before joining is a necessity for many. To be fair IBB does provide some funding and is working towards upping this amount.

Gallows humour

As you may have guessed the atmosphere does vary from office to office and town to town. The Chesham branch is in 'a small town with not many shops.' While it's 'very friendly,' due to its remote location 'there isn't very much going on here; most people drive in so there's not really an opportunity to go out after work.' As one trainee aptly put it: 'Not everything social has to involve alcohol but it does help, doesn't it?' Making matters worse, 'there's usually only two trainees up there at a time.' The Queen's Head is by far the best pub in town ('but that's really it') and a recommended destination for Thai food at lunch. The good news is that 'especially in the summer' the gorgeous setting almost makes up for the lacking social scene. The feel of the offices in Uxbridge is 'completely different really.' There's 'a strong trainee community' there with 'office drinks every Friday' in Capital Court and generally a 'noisier, faster-paced' work environment in Lovell House. 'The crime team can be quite jokey and people are always relating stories of what's happened at court.' If you travel to Uxbridge from London it's usually a very decent commute 'because you're going the opposite way to all the other commuters and can always get a seat.'

Even in Uxbridge IBB trainees acknowledged that the social life 'can't really compare to being in the centre of London.' Nonetheless they spoke of 'a definite feeling of community.' Group social events are occasionally organised by departments or more often by 'trainees who take it upon themselves to send around an e-mail.' As for firm-wide events, there has recently been a barbecue, a summer ball and an outdoor theatre event that was also open to the public. When left to their own devices you'll find trainees in the Three Tuns, Uxbridge's cheapest pub. 'There's also a chance you might bump into a local criminal client.' Don't get the idea that the propensity for cheap beer is indicative of trainees' pay status; at IBB 'it's not City money but it's far from the minimum.' Trainees were appreciative of regular pay rises and felt that 'salaries are quite evenly distributed.' Generally 'the firm makes real efforts to listen to any complaints or suggestions you may have; they don't just bat you off as a trainee.'

In 2008 three of the five qualifiers stayed with the firm. Those that declined positions stated the location as a deciding factor so obviously this is something to take into careful consideration before deciding to train here.

And finally...

For those happy make the trek west, a training contract at IBB offers diverse experiences, lots of responsibility and good future prospects.

Ince & Co

The facts

Location: London

Number of UK partners/solicitors: 55/63

Total number of trainees: 24

Seats: 4x6 months

Alternative seats: Overseas seats

Extras: Language training

> Ince trainees must be confident and self-starting. Clones they are not: all the partners have their own oddities or outside interests, and trainees are the same.

Ince & Co has shipping and insurance litigation licked and is wetting its lips at the prospect of a dash more transactional work. This game 140-year-old also has a well-developed international network and an unusual non-rotational training contract.

Altogether now

Our nose for bull is as sensitive as a bespectacled schoolboy with a bad case of acne on his first day at a trendy new school. That said, even we have to allow that Ince's 'altogether different' slogan has a ring of truth. The firm eschews the departmental approach, instead encouraging its lawyers to develop broad practices. At the same time it centres its efforts on core business sectors. All in all it makes for an interesting life as an Ince lawyer. The lack of departments doesn't stop trainees switching supervisor every six months, but it does mean they aren't forced to abandon their caseload when they do, nor rely on a new supervisor for future work. In other words, from almost the first day 'you need to act not as a trainee but as a solicitor, building up relationships with partners and clients, building up your own practice.'

The first month is spent on courses designed to initiate the newbie into the more esoteric aspects of the firm's business. Shipping, for example, is a whole new world to most trainees. Once that initial period concludes it's a case of 'putting yourself out there to generate work,' whether by responding to e-mails or the more nerve-wracking tactic of approaching partners directly. 'The first few times you prepare a speech, spend ages building up your confidence, then go in and feel a bit silly afterwards.' Either way 'it's not virgin territory, everyone is expecting you to do it,' so for the majority it's an almost disconcertingly easy process. Initially the supervising partner's specialisms are likely to influence a trainee's work, but of course at Ince the expert in insurance litigation will probably have a sideline in something else…

Giving the green light

The benefits of the system become apparent when trainees develop their own interests or get involved in major cases. Said one: 'I've been working on a massive fraud case that won't go to trial until 2009. As a trainee you're at the bottom of the pile bundling, but over time because you stay on the case you get more understanding, more responsibility and more client contact.' By the same token, becoming a point of contact for a client means 'an awful lot of repeat work. I've done charter disputes and oil contamination cases for a petrochemicals multinational.'

Develop a preference for a particular sector and you've the freedom to seek out the people and work you want. 'To begin with you take what comes then decide whether that sort of work is to your taste.' The arrival of a new batch of first-years is a 'watershed' as 'they start to pick up the capacity e-mails and you start getting repeat work from partners and moving more into particular areas.' Trainees quickly learn that 'work comes from the relations you have with the people – you work with one partner and don't like her style or she yours, so you gravitate elsewhere. I'm nearly at the end of training and I work mostly with a team of five partners.'

Reputations stand or fall on the quality of a person's work. Bungle or delay something and 'work dries up from that partner.' The reverse is also true so care must be taken not to accept too much because 'in the end no one knows exactly what you're doing apart from you.' Mechanisms to monitor trainees' workloads do exist: supervisors and a 'resource committee' keep a general eye out for 'anyone doing 15-hour days' and they will 'pull you aside if you do four weekends in a row.' They also make sure 'work is spread evenly among the group.' A traffic light system allows trainees to code their capacity to take more work. In theory 'partners look at that before approaching you,' even so 'there are times when you are ridiculously busy,' not least because when working in an area that interests you the 'temptation is to take everything that comes.' Trainees generally leave the office by 7pm to 7.30pm unless things get hairy.

To cope with the demands Ince trainees must be 'confident' and 'self-starting.' On some occasions 'it's just you and the partner and they might ask what you think about a case. They're not being condescending, they're asking because you're the only other person who's read all the papers.' Ince finds the strong personalities it needs at a range of universities and takes on people with other career experiences. Clones they are not: 'All the partners have their own oddities or outside interests, and trainees are the same.' There are 'full-on people who you can guarantee will be at all the marketing events' and 'quieter ones who get on with their work in their own way.' Dispute resolution accounts for around 80% of revenue, and even bearing in mind a desire to increase its transactional income stream to 25%, Ince will always suit contentiously minded applicants.

Spills and thrills

Together, Ince's overseas offices generate some 25% of the firm's revenue. Consider where they are located – Hamburg, Le Havre, Paris, Piraeus, Hong Kong, China, Singapore and Dubai – and the importance of the shipping industry becomes apparent. The firm has assured itself a key role in international trade, as well as 'wet' (collisions, pirates, sinkings, spills) and 'dry' (contractual disputes, ship mortgages, charter parties, building contracts) shipping law.

Recent hires have expanded a practice that already enjoyed a near monopoly on major disasters at sea. Lawyers acted for crew, ship owners, managers and P&I clubs in a variety of matters relating to a huge crude oil spill in the Yellow Sea off South Korea, which occurred when a ship was struck by a giant crane barge. They also assisted in the case of a vessel that was engulfed by fire off the coast of Venice. In fact Ince's 24-hour emergency response service exists precisely to act quickly when disaster strikes. After years of self-restraint we finally

Chambers UK rankings

Asset Finance • Aviation • Commodities • Dispute Resolution • Insurance • Professional Negligence • Projects, Energy & Natural Resources • Shipping

clicked on the alluring big red emergency button on Ince's website. Thankfully no siren sounded, and pressing the big red button revealed nothing more than the response team's phone number.

Dry shipping cases mean 'analysing contractual disputes and charter parties' or 'starting proceedings and managing cases.' Recent highlights have included $15m Chinese proceedings for alleged damage to a soya bean cargo and a claim by the Greek owner of a Panamax bulk carrier against Norwegian charterers arising out of the loss of a propeller blade during voyage.

Insurance and reinsurance law is a big area for Ince. Lawyers recently acted for Standard Life on a multimillion-pound claim under its professional indemnity policy, advised underwriters following a fire at a major factory and shipyard underwriters following a construction delay resulting from Hurricane Katrina. Trainees can assist on such cases, as well as on non-contentious issues such as new policy products designed to provide credit risk mitigation.

Oil in a day's work

In the area of business and finance Ince has been 'recruiting left, right and centre,' including an 'excellent partner from Clifford Chance' who handles huge ship finance deals. Keeping lawyers busy there's been a $600m syndicated loan facility to finance the construction of two LNG regasification vessels, a $150m underwritten debt facility for Revus Energy and advice to Serco on the maritime aspects of the £1bn MoD Future Provision of Marine Services PFI project. Trainees who had taken on ship finance cases noticed that the lawyers working in this area 'feel more like a department' because 'transactional work is so different to most of what Ince does.' We also hear they are 'always desperate for trainees because they have so much work,' whereas most trainees 'have a predilection for litigation.' Our sources believed there is 'more than enough good non-contentious work' on offer at the firm, yet still say 'you wouldn't necessarily come here for a hard-core corporate experience.'

Ince has developed its energy and aviation abilities and in 2007 hired experienced aviation claims handler and qualified pilot Tim Scorer, whose CV includes involvement in the litigation over major air crashes such as Lockerbie. London lawyers represent a client in relation to the ADC Crash in Nigeria that killed 95, and have joined forces with their Paris colleagues to advise Heli Air Monaco and its insurers in relation to the loss of a helicopter operating between Nice and Monaco. While such disputes play to the firm's insurance and litigation strengths, a presence in this sector has led to greater demand for regulatory and commercial aviation advice. The same is true in relation to the energy sector, where Ince has relationships with companies like Daewoo, Vitol and US pipeline contractor Willbros Group. The lawyers advise on loss of life claims, kidnappings and ransoms, incidents of force majeure and general contract terminations relating to deterioration of the security situation in the oil-rich Niger Delta. They are also involved in the ongoing litigation bundle following the Buncefield oil depot explosion and a case involving an Uzbek well blow-out.

Keeping it Ince the family

Trainees' hours are determined by the needs of the clients and court deadlines; Ince doesn't impose billing targets, which is a huge relief all round. Similarly, no one need compete with their peers in the run up to qualification because no one has to pick a department. These factors must influence people's desire to stay with the firm, and in 2008 all nine of the qualifiers did so.

A move from 'scummy' offices to spacious new digs at St Katharine's Dock on the Thames has undoubtedly 'changed the dynamic of the firm.' As well as allowing staff numbers to grow, it's given the firm a boost in all kinds of ways and 'younger partners are implementing new ideas.' It hasn't depreciated 'a strong, positive link with the past' though. 'Maybe it's the nature of the work, but we're still quite old school and that's a good thing,' one source said, while another confessed to enjoying the 'slightly old-fashioned lunches where you sit down with beer and wine, maybe an external speaker, and discuss how things are.' The survival of this distinctive character must in part be due to the fact that 'so many of the partners trained at the firm and lots of the staff have been here for 30 years or more.' The annual May Ball brings all staff together and features a speech 'either by a fee earner or a long-standing support staff member.' Kudos to the senior partner for this year being 'the last to leave [local bar] The Vineyard afterwards.' This lot must certainly like socialising as there are drinks laid on for the entire firm every second Thursday of the month. In between times trainees often sample the bars around St Katharine's Dock, while those of a more musical disposition can join the Ince & Co choir.

And finally...

For top-class international shipping and insurance litigation and a bit more besides, Ince & Co is a unique choice. Definitely one for applicants with well-developed people skills.

Irwin Mitchell

The facts

Location: Birmingham, Glasgow, Leeds, London, Manchester, Newcastle, Sheffield

Number of UK partners/solicitors: 103/235

Total number of trainees: 46

Seats: Switching to 3x4 + 1x12 months

Alternative seats: None

Extras: Pro bono – RCJ CAB

It's all change with the IM training programme. Applicants will now be given the choice of a PI-based training or a business/private client programme.

A far cry from its humble beginnings in Sheffield, Irwin Mitchell is now the fourth largest firm in the UK by number of fee earners.

Every little case helps

Although it provides services from corporate and employment law to Court of Protection and family advice, IM's largest areas of activity are personal injury and the allied field of clinical negligence. One recent triumph was the successful representation of over 80 workers and local residents in claims for damages for physical and psychological injuries following an oil refinery explosion. Lawyers also assisted on the Armed Forces Compensation Scheme claim for Ben Parkinson, said by medics to be the most severely injured British serviceman to survive his wounds. The claim ignited a media campaign resulting in the MoD changing the rules to account for multiple-injury cases. The past year also saw the firm represent a client who received compensation after suffering retroperitoneal fibrosis from exposure to asbestos brake linings, in the first case of its kind. These examples barely scratch the surface of a vast and varied caseload, at the less noteworthy end of which are many thousands of low-value PI claims. Another area in which the firm relies on bulk instructions is residential conveyancing and remortgaging.

It's obvious that the firm is a goliath in these fields and equally clear it intends to keep it that way. In line with its image as the champion of the man on the street, IM has eyed the Legal Services Act with interest and been quick to launch new initiatives with the AA and RAC. In doing so it neatly managed both to play a role in giving people access to legal advice, and to align itself with two of the major brands that are seeking to break into the sector. In 2007, for example, the AA launched Home Buyer

Advice, a free legal service to its customers. IM will advise on the will-writing aspect. Marks & Spencer is another company that turns to IM to advise its staff – and when Barclays' business customers with premium accounts pick up the phone for legal assistance, who could that be on the end of the line? Such moves convey the firm's desire to stay ahead of the game and position itself well in the 'Tesco Law' era.

All change

It's all change with the IM training programme. Applicants will now be given the choice of opting for a PI-based training or a business/private client programme. This will help the firm produce sufficient NQs for its vast PI division, something it is struggling to do at the moment. Additionally, trainees will no longer move between offices – a practice the firm now recognises has not always been easy for some people. Interestingly, some of our sources showed surprisingly strong support for office-hopping: 'Not every office has every department; there's no corporate work in Birmingham, for example,' said one. The point to make here is that when you apply you'll need to be certain that the type of work is offered in the location you're going for. Sheffield, Leeds and London are strong bets for commercial seats.

When we spoke to trainees in 2008 all these changes were still in the planning stage and our sources were following the old regime of four seats of six months. Under the new regime they will take three four-month seats in the first year and a much longer single seat in a preferred area for the second year.

Until now PI seats were common first-year postings. Fans of the work described the experience as 'fantastic, absolutely fantastic,' and arguably if this is what you see yourself working on in the future there's no better place to train. PI is offered in each of the six main offices, some specialising in neuro-trauma, workplace accidents, industrial diseases, abuse claims and group actions. The latter team handled Cadbury's salmonella claims and the Vioxx drug litigation, and recently brought actions against the NHS in relation to contaminated blood products and the MoD on behalf of soldiers who fought in Iraq. Trainees tend to work for multiple fee earners: 'I was helping out with high-value cases, mostly concerning acute brain injuries,' remarked one source. After they've learnt the ropes, supervisors are happy for trainees to speak to clients, take witness statements and instruct barristers. 'They let you get involved in all areas of a case and you're encouraged to develop your own relationships with clients, which is rewarding.'

When industrial disease cases relate to long-historical events, securing evidence can be difficult. 'Then there's the fact that the clients aren't around for very long. Sometimes you phone up to speak to them and it's too late. On the other hand if you do manage to get results you know their families are going to be looked after and that's a good feeling.' Neuro-trauma cases can be worth a considerable amount of money so at times trainees may feel like 'a glorified secretary.' If you get a good supervisor though you can run small fast-track cases by yourself, 'and even on the bigger files I was given decent responsibility – ringing a client's accountant for example.'

Spanish hurl 'em

One of our sources declared love for the clinical negligence department: 'I was accompanying fee earners to client interviews, starting my own files from scratch, obtaining medical records, issuing claim forms and instructing medical experts. You get a great overview of how the whole process works.' Birth injury cases involve learning about gynaecology. 'It's an eye opener for us chaps,' confessed one trainee. 'I had no idea what went on until I read up on it all.' Cases can be sad and surprising: the firm is representing young clients whose mother died as a result of failure to diagnose a DVT pulmonary embolism following the birth of her youngest child, and another case was for a man who, as a result of surgical error, had both testicles removed instead of just the one. The subject matter might be tough but the team is 'incredibly supportive.'

These mammoth departments have spawned niche practices such as the Court of Protection group, which man-

Chambers UK rankings

Administrative & Public Law • Banking & Finance • Civil Liberties • Clinical Negligence • Corporate Finance • Crime • Debt Recovery • Dispute Resolution • Employment • Environment • Family/Matrimonial • Fraud: Criminal • Health & Safety • Intellectual Property • Personal Injury • Police Law • Private Client • Product Liability • Professional Discipline • Real Estate • Real Estate Litigation • Restructuring/Insolvency • Tax • Travel

ages the affairs of people lacking the capacity to do so themselves. 'It's a frenetic pace here; you're constantly doing lots of small things and responding to clients' demands to get things done yesterday. In fact sometimes it wasn't like being a lawyer at all – I was sorting out people's direct debits.' The seat can bring drama, such as the client who visited the office, picked up an award the firm had won and threatened to throw it at a trainee. Another specialist team deals with travel accidents. 'Mostly it's just broken limbs but you do have group actions where a thousand people get food poisoning. They can be quite high profile and also quite revolting.' Trainees don't visit the resorts themselves; instead they liaise with IM's offices in Madrid and Marbella or with other local lawyers.

Down to business

Over on the commercial side of the firm there are seats in litigation, employment and corporate. Trainees were quick to point out the quality of the work they saw. 'DLA, Eversheds and Pinsents are often on the other side of our deals so we are definitely up there.' In Yorkshire, lawyers advised the shareholders of a £100m engineering company in connection with a further investment by 3i. London litigators were instructed by a group of major DVD and CD producers and distributors, including Universal Music, Sony BMG and EMI, following the collapses of various retail chains including Music Zone Services, Fopp and Choices. Their remit was to recover goods supplied and multimillion-pound debts. Meanwhile, employment lawyers in Sheffield advised Age Concern on its challenge to the government's mandatory retirement age of 65. They were also instructed to act on a Court of Appeal age discrimination case.

Trainees perceived a different atmosphere in commercial teams – 'less of an IM ethos, with people more happy to do things their own way.' Bearing in mind the scale of the firm, the offices inevitably have different characters. 'Sheffield is more anonymous. It's a huge office spread over two separate sites so you can't pretend you're an individual here.' Smaller offices such as Manchester and Newcastle are 'more chilled out and chatty.' Although the firm tries to promote cohesion, some trainees reported: 'It doesn't really feel like it's one firm. Birmingham and Manchester, for example, don't look anything like each other.' Maybe identical colour schemes would help? 'We don't have one to be honest – everything's white.'

'Sheffield is so big you only really get to know people on your floor.' It's a good place for trainees though: 'There's about 20 of us so there's always something going on after work, maybe a night out at the dogs or just drinks.' Smaller branches are more intimate but less goes on after hours. 'It's up to the trainees to sort out things themselves and frankly it can be a bit subdued if there's only three of you.' The firm is big into charity events and 'there's an emphasis on getting involved in fundraising pub quizzes and the like.' IM practises what it preaches, recently offering its expertise to Pro Uno, a project set up by Sheffield Volunteering to provide a legal research facility for non-profit organisations in South Yorkshire.

From time to time the different departments gather their lawyers together from all offices on away days. 'It is more of a study day,' we learned from someone rather disappointed; 'there was no skiing or raft building.' Annual events such as the Christmas party are split between offices. 'The Christmas party is fantastic if you're based in Sheffield and a bit rubbish if you're anywhere else,' moaned one trainee. In Sheffield a local sports centre is 'completely transformed.' Last year 'there was a Motown theme with glitter balls everywhere. The food was fantastic and there was a free bar all night. And obviously the faint smell of chlorine…'

Open access

Without any bias towards redbrick unis and no minimum A-level grade requirements, the firm's training scheme is open to a variety of people including its own paralegals. 'You need different personalities to fill the different seats,' explained a trainee. 'We've got a qualified dentist and doctor in our year, and then people who are straight from uni.' IM is largely 'a non-intimidating place to work.' For one of our interviewees, the firm's openness at all levels was its best attribute: 'People are so approachable… though I'm not including my first seat in that!' Less said the better perhaps.

Under the current regime, the decision to stay post-qualification has usually come down to the simple question of whether the firm can offer what you want. For example, it's not so great if Birmingham is your ideal location but you want a corporate NQ job. The move to single-site training should alleviate this problem. In any event the numbers were pretty good in 2008, with 16 out of 21 qualifiers finding their spot.

And finally...

Irwin Mitchell's new style of single-site training will be a big change. So long as applicants are fully aware of what they're likely to get in each location, everyone should be a winner.

Jones Day

The facts

Location: London

Number of UK partners/solicitors: 51/120

Total number of trainees: 30

Seats: Non-rotational

Alternative Seats: None

Extras: Pro bono – eg Waterloo Legal Advice Centre, Caribbean death row appeals; LawWorks

> The system makes you feel you're running your own practice right from day one. There's no risk of getting stuck in an area you hate or of being transferred out of a fascinating piece of work just as it reaches conclusion.

Cleveland native Jones Day employs 2,300 lawyers in 29 worldwide offices and has one rather unusual method of training its London recruits. Allow us to enlighten you...

Cleveland hold 'em

Jones Day London was born in 2003 when Gouldens – a London 'golden circle' commercial firm with a reputation for refusing to follow the crowd – attracted the attention of US giant Jones Day. The big JD saw Gouldens had a strong hand and raised them an extensive international network, a formidable reputation for litigation and the allure of a famous name. The firms threw their chips in together later that year. The merger dust has long settled, but we mention it because the spirit of Gouldens lives on within the practice, not least through the non-rotational training system it bequeathed Jones Day London.

Seats are not taken within specific departments and nor do trainees move on after four or six months. Instead they are given an office and the responsibility to find work for themselves. True, each is also given a partner-mentor whose job it is to keep a general eye on progress, but aside from that it's up to trainees to find work in the departments of their choosing. While work can be sourced from any area, the main practices are corporate, banking, litigation and property, with employment, tax, IP and insolvency also available. At first 'the onus is on you to go out, walk the floors and introduce yourself.' This means 'a lot of door-knocking,' and while almost everybody is happy to sit down and have a brief chat with the newbies, 'if you're a shy guy it's not going to be a great place for you on your first day.' Things do get easier: recruits gradually get to know all the lawyers; busy partners who've given work to trainees will push more their way and may even introduce them to other partners. Nor is it all one-way traffic. Trainees described the systems as being 'a bit like a free-market economy' because partners always need trainees and 'they know that if they're not nice to you, you won't want to work for them.' Despite the ability to shape their contract, trainees are still trainees and we were warned: 'You shouldn't imagine you'll come here and never have to do due diligence.'

The people we spoke to were all enthusiastic about a system that 'makes you feel you're running your own practice right from day one.' There's no risk of getting stuck in an area you hate or of being transferred out of a fascinating piece of work just as it reaches conclusion. Trainees relish the opportunity to 'build up relationships of trust with partners,' and while 'it's probably a bit lonelier than [life at] some of the big firms,' the lack of constant supervision 'makes you learn.' Add a generous salary to this mix of responsibility and autonomy and it's not hard to agree with the source who hazarded that JD trainees might be 'a little bit spoiled.' However, one hard-bitten Jones Dayer assured us: 'I'd rather do this job for less money than be someone's little trainee for most of the day and surf the net for the rest.'

Another feature of the system is that instead of breeding a Machiavellian environment in which trainees try to nab spots on the best deals, harmony abounds. With NQ retention rates high, there's 'no sense you're fighting against each other for a job' and trainee interests are sufficiently diverse to ensure minimal competition. 'It's like being in the trenches,' said one source, reflecting (we presume) on an atmosphere of camaraderie rather than widespread foot rot and rat infestation. Trainees often pop down the corridors to each other's offices to share war stories. Ah yes, the offices. They're all 'huge' with large windows, several bookcases and three desks. Said one trainee, with just a shade of irony: 'I'd die with just one desk now.' An open-door policy means 'we don't all sit in our little pods and beaver away,' although really busy trainees are forgiven for occasionally shutting out the world.

In the Gould mould

Purely on the basis of atmosphere and attitude, 'Jones Day in London is Gouldens – it still is.' Sure, many back office chores are processed through Cleveland and UK partners get paid in dollars, but most are 'still home-grown from Gouldens.' A 200-strong complement of lawyers in the office also makes it one of the biggest in the JD network, which together allows trainees to feel London is much more than an adjunct of the US operation.

In terms of work, access to the JD international network and a subsequent capacity for multi-jurisdictional practice means the office regularly deals with sizeable instructions. An impressive client roster includes Procter & Gamble, Deutsche Bank and JPMorgan Chase, and the capital markets team last year advised Kazakhstan mining company Eurasian Natural Resources Corp on its £1.36bn London listing, one of the biggest flotations of 2007. It also worked on ENRC's approach for copper producer Kazakhmys, a tie-up which would create a £20bn mining giant. Other international work concluded through the London office included Madagascar Oil's $85m loan from Credit Suisse and a major New York-based fund's long-running dispute with the Republic of Nicaragua. The firm has inherited 'the medium-ticket work for which Gouldens used to be famous' and our colleagues at *Chambers UK* now rank the firm in the top bracket for mid-market corporate finance. Recent highlights included advice to JF Lehman on the $140m acquisition of BAE Systems' Inertial Products business, Linden Holdings' £244.5m acquisition by Galliford Try and Sibir Energy's $456m merger with Moscow Oil & Gas Company.

Meanwhile, the property department advises on many UK-based finance and development deals, such as Hercules Unit Trust's sale of 50% of Speke Unit Trust to Bank of Ireland for £209m and Goodman's £336m acquisition of the Rosemound Group, a deal which made it the second-largest industrial developer in the UK. Commercial litigation is another strength, both internationally and in London, where a strong historic client base includes Standard Bank, Arthur J Gallagher, RBS, Hanson, Waste Recycling Group, Camelot Group and property clients like British Land. All these turn to the

Chambers UK rankings

Banking Litigation · Corporate Finance · Dispute Resolution · Employment · Environment · Fraud: Civil · Intellectual Property · Outsourcing · Pensions · Planning · Private Equity · Real Estate · Real Estate Finance · Restructuring/Insolvency · Tax

firm for representation on major disputes, and instructions are also flying in from newer sources such as Digicel, Motorola and Occidental Petroleum. In the past year the team has acted in some major multi-jurisdictional oil and telecoms disputes.

On the Jones Day way

It's a lip-smacking selection of work and all of it is on offer to trainees. But while they can shape the direction and content of their contract, their freedom isn't absolute. A checklist is employed to ensure satisfaction of SRA requirements in the right practice areas and there are regular meetings with a training manager to double-check the checklist. Most trainees manage to tick everything off after 18 months, leaving them free to focus almost entirely on the work they prefer. Those uninspired by the firm's excellent contentious work can take a short litigation course instead. Beyond this the system privileges autonomy and 'if something's going wrong you generally have to shout.' The training manager 'can get you tugged off a deal or moved to something else if you're being swamped with work you don't want.' There may not be constant supervision so learning from mistakes is expected. 'It puts hair on your chest,' chuckled one presumably hirsute recruit.

Unquestionably the Jones Day way suits outgoing, confident and self-motivating people, and boy does the firm attract them. The allure of 'not having a supervisor looking over your shoulder,' the promise of greater profile than at other City firms and the ability to 'tailor your contract to do what you want' lures those who 'enjoy their freedom.' That said, our interviewees didn't feel they were all of a type and much credit is given to the recruitment team for 'very astutely' picking complementary individuals instead of 'the big characters I expected.' Despite a preponderance of Oxbridge graduates, the firm 'isn't an academic hothouse.' What it can be described as is 'maybe a bit more ballsy' than other firms. In future, trainees will all get the chance to become acquainted on a Jones Day-specific LPC course at BPP in London. The firm has recently signed an exclusive deal with the school.

If you're intrigued by the training, heed the warning that 'this system isn't for everybody: if you like to be led and aren't particularly self-confident in your ability you will struggle.' As a means of testing yourself our sources recommend attending the vac scheme. 'Only when I started as a trainee did I realise how realistic it is,' said one interviewee. Adding true verisimilitude, vac-schemers get their own office and must look for their own work.

Harrowing moments

Socially, staff are well served. Granted there 'isn't the drinking culture there once was,' but there are regular Friday outings to The Harrow, described variously as 'a horrible, horrible little pub,' and 'a dirty little pub.' Amazingly 'the whole firm goes there.' Frequent trainee socials and attendance at client events are contrasted by pro bono or charity initiatives, and let's not forget the annual all-expenses-paid trip to Washington, DC for September starters. This junket allows new trainees to meet all other new members of the firm's global family, attend seminars and get taken out to dinner a lot. If our sources are to be believed, the best bits are the hotel-room after-parties. Closer to home the 'institution' that is the trainee Christmas pantomime involves a performance at the Mermaid Theatre, with after-work rehearsals for six weeks beforehand. Second-year trainees write it, first-years get the major roles and whatever the ostensible plot (*Macbeth* last year) the name of the game is lampoonery. On the day of performance everybody gets time off and there's a party afterwards. Apparently partners 'get offended if they're not made fun of.'

With all this talk of leisure time, could it be that burning the midnight oil isn't as mandatory as legal lore would have it? Well, trainees do have targets but they're sufficiently low to be comfortably and regularly exceeded. Besides, as one source chuckled, 'no one tells you that you have to be there as you have your own office and no supervisor.' In quieter periods most trainees leave by around 6pm; when the workload increases the late nights become more regular and can stretch on until morning. Even though this lot 'like being worked hard,' some of our interviewees were still a little surprised by how much work they were expected to do. 'It's been fine,' one told us, 'but I wish I'd known what it would be like to do it consistently.' Consider this fair warning. Some 16 of the 19 2008 qualifiers decided the regime was for them and stayed on with the firm.

And finally...

To thrive during Jones Day's distinctive training requires confidence and an independent outlook. The vac scheme is a great litmus test, but you'll probably already have a hunch if this inimitable firm is for you.

- **Average trainee starting salary:** **£21,518.** You're best off if you're a male trainee starting in Central London, where the average was £29,495 as of 2007. But it's less lovely news for lasses in the land of leeks: females at Welsh firms pull in an average of £15,648 during their first two seats.

K&L Gates

The facts

Location: London

Number of UK partners/solicitors: 57/64

Total number of trainees: 16

Seats: 4x6 months

Alternative seats: Secondments

Extras: Pro bono – Battersea Legal Advice Centre, LawWorks; language training

> The office retains its traditional strengths of property and corporate finance, teams which both now have new American clients to play with.

'Hopefully people won't skip over this feature' said a K&L Gates trainee worried that his firm doesn't have instant name recognition. If you do, it's your loss: not only because it is particularly insightful and well written, but also because after a series of mergers and name changes K&L Gates is now starting to forge a new and unique personality.

What's in a name?

K&L Gates (or Kirkpatrick & Lockhart Preston Gates Ellis LLP to give it its full name) might not be a firm that's familiar to you, since in the past few years it's gone though a quick succession of name changes with the result that sometimes even the trainees seem confused about who they are working for. You may possibly have heard of the firm's past incarnation though. Until 2005, the London office was the well-respected if sleepy mid-sizer Nicholson Graham & Jones. Then, in an uncharacteristic display of dynamism, it joined forces with some ambitious Americans to become Kirkpatrick & Lockhart Nicholson Graham. Two years after that the firm merged again, this time with Bill Gates' dad's firm, Preston Gates & Ellis, to become the K&L it is today. All clear so far? The firm continues to grow, hoovering up smaller concerns in Asia and America, but from a British perspective it seems the immediate turmoil is over. While all these mergers are good for getting big US corporate clients through the doors in London, the downside is that the office has suffered 'something of an identity crisis.' Now that the dust is settling, the big question is: what sort of place has K&L Gates become?

That's the question we asked this year's trainees, coincidentally the last set to be recruited before the initial merger. Some of them even had their interviews on the day the change was announced. 'It still retains the personality of a mid-sized City firm,' they said, pointing out that nearly all of the Nicholson Graham & Jones partners had stayed on after the transition. So it hasn't become an American corporate machine? 'Not really. There's lots of talk about increasing billable hours, and we're all aware that influential decisions are being made elsewhere, but London is one of the firm's biggest offices. We were never going to get squashed.' There are no high-ranking Yanks prowling the corridors looking to fire the lowest earner, and the overall impression we get is that a lot of good old NGJ remains intact. 'It's more like we're a satellite of the Americans: we are pretty self-sufficient.' The office retains its traditional strengths of property and corporate finance, teams which both now have new American clients to play with, while the merger has also provided a boost to the IP department. In an attempt to encourage cross-border togetherness, at the beginning of their contract trainees fly out to one of the American offices to meet other new starters from around the world.

Wrestlemania

The HR team makes every attempt to ensure everyone gets the seats they want, but 'sometimes it's just a case of going where you are needed. If corporate and real estate need five people each, that's the way it is.' It's pretty much a cert that in the four-seat rotation trainees will spend time in both these departments. Even people who aren't particularly interested in the work find real estate a useful seat to do since 'the level of client contact is greater than in any other, and you feel like a real solicitor because you are running files.' The department has both contentious and transactional lawyers, and its clients include AOL, Lloyds TSB, Laing O'Rourke and Nationwide Building Society. Since the merger the lawyers have begun acting for US clients, recently advising one real estate investment trust on its first European acquisition, an £11.2m purchase in Coventry. Trainees get involved in the larger deals, and several seem to have got a lot out of one particular transaction – the sale of residential apartments in Henley. For one it was getting to go on a site visit that was exciting – 'it makes it seem more real' – while another enjoyed 'the big challenge' of getting the paperwork for all 15 apartments sorted in a short space of time.

Corporate is described as 'a fun place to work, upbeat with plenty of banter.' It's needed 'because people work so hard there.' Even so, the hours are reasonably okay, with ultra-late nights the exception rather than the rule. Trainees can normally expect to be out by around 7.30pm. There are several seats available within the department, in M&A, private equity, AIM, and the big growth area of financial services. Stateside K&L's FS practice is 'enormous and very highly rated. The partners over there are very knowledgeable and they can sometimes show you up on English law.' Not that it's a one-way relationship: 'There's a lot of American feeder work in corporate.' In the M&A seat, 'because the deals are quite large you'll never run your own,' so trainees beaver away behind the scenes, ensuring things run smoothly and 'knowing there's a greater purpose to what we're doing.' The work mostly involves drafting board minutes, having a stab at first drafts of documents, performing research tasks and, in FS, pulling together information for prospectuses. In the past year K&L Gates has been behind Sportech's purchase of Vernons football pools from Ladbrokes for £51m, and Halliburton's purchase of PSL Energy Services for $240m. It also advised Leed Petroleum, an American oil and gas exploration company, during its £50m fundraising and admission to AIM.

The dispute resolution department contains a number of specialist teams. Already popular, the IP group, which also includes technology and sports lawyers, is set to become even more desirable now it only takes one trainee at a time. The upside is that 'as the sole trainee you will get exposure to pretty much everything.' Among the clients are Orange, the British Film Institute, HBO, Sheffield Wednesday FC and Puma. Lawyers here represented World Wrestling Entertainment (formerly the World Wrestling Federation) in a protracted legal battle with the World Wide Fund for Nature over the use of the initials WWF. Trainees who'd done this seat found them-

Chambers UK rankings

Construction • Corporate Finance • Dispute Resolution • Environment • Information Technology • Intellectual Property • Licensing • Parliamentary & Public Affairs • Planning • Real Estate • Real Estate Finance • Real Estate Litigation • Sports Law • Telecommunications • Travel

selves with very respectable levels of responsibility, drafting licensing and sponsorship agreements and running a few small files of their own, mostly registering trade marks. Another leading case for the department was the CD Wow! litigation. Hearing people discussing it on the radio was a real highlight for one source.

Any questions?

The construction department is another prestigious group, and here the firm acts for Young & Co's Brewery, Scottish property developers Kilmartin, London Underground and Arena Leisure, which redeveloped Doncaster Racecourse. One trainee had seen part of a professional negligence claim brought by Costain and Skanska against a firm of engineers that has now gone bust. 'There was a hotel refurbishment that had been severely delayed. The contractors were being sued and they were suing the engineering firm in turn, claiming they'd botched drawings.' The hotel, FYI, is the Great Western Royal Hotel (now Hilton Paddington) and the refurbishment was worth £37m. There's ample non-contentious work too; for example, K&L is advising Laing O'Rourke on several PFI projects, including the construction of new hospitals in Middlesbrough and Stoke-on-Trent, and the 25-year $16bn MoD defence training review rationalisation programme. This construction practice has gone international and now London lawyers work in conjunction with American colleagues for the likes of Halliburton and KBR (both big players in the reconstruction of Iraq).

Other seats include real estate finance, insolvency, planning, environment, IP, pensions and employment; client secondments are available at Orange, CBS Outdoor and Warner Music, and we hear that overseas postings to the USA and Berlin are being considered. Everyone gets mid and end-of-seat reviews: 'Written forms give structure to the process. Some supervisors take it quite seriously; others will simply say they don't have any issues with your performance.' If there's something a trainee can't talk about in an appraisal, it might be appropriate to drop it in the managing partner's suggestions box, which exists to allow any member of staff to ask any question anonymously.

Making the office taste better

When asked how K&L Gates could improve, our contacts all agreed it could raise its profile here in the UK. 'People look at us blankly when we say we're from K&L Gates, then when you tell them we used to be Nicholson Graham & Jones, they go, 'Oh yeah, NGJ.'' Perhaps the new marketing campaign – complete with new buzz word 'velocity' – will do just that (who cares if some of our sources were baffled by the choice?). Trainees worry that the best applicants could pass the firm by, though we can't say if this is why the annual intake of trainees dropped from ten to eight recently. The sort of person who'd fit here is thought to be 'deep-down confident but not in your face. When you're at law school there's loads of arrogant people, especially among the guys,' recalled one source. Arrogance just isn't the style of this office: 'I don't think it has changed hugely since merging with the Americans,' said one source. 'It still retains the personality of the mid-sized City firm, even if increasingly the influential decisions are made elsewhere.'

The current group of trainees is close knit and tries to lunch together as often as possible. There's a fee earners-only lunchroom called The Lawyers Lounge, where they can get 'a good home-cooked meal for about £4,' yet trainees prefer Ampersand, the staff canteen that's open to everyone. Here they have no qualms about chatting openly about who wants to qualify where. The majority were lucky in 2008, when seven out of ten qualifiers took jobs with the firm.

Out of hours, Friday nights are regularly spent in The Vintry, and at seat changeover time departments have welcome and goodbye drinks. The firm recently paid for the football team to participate in the Legal and Financial Cup in Lisbon. 'In true English style, we went out in the semi on penalties!' Keen to meet colleagues from other K&L offices? Trainees spend a week in one of the American offices getting to know young associates from the USA, Asia and continental Europe. 'It was great. We got along well and had a laugh,' one source recalled. Trainees are encouraged to get involved with the Battersea Legal Advice Centre: 'It's something the firm is really pushing; internationally they take pro bono very seriously.' The centre helps individuals with an interesting mix of problems. Said one source: 'A lot of people come in with landlord troubles. I've had a couple of debt claims, a harassment claim and plenty of driving offences to deal with.'

K&L Gates is vacating its Cannon Street home in 2011 for a new office next to St Paul's Cathedral. The 'fantastic glass building' is being constructed on the site of Allen & Overy's old office at One New Change and will have space for twice as many lawyers. They won't need to worry about where to buy a sandwich lunch – the bottom floor will be occupied by Sainsbury's.

And finally...

Reassuringly, trainees tell us this is 'a place where you can be yourself.' Whether the London office will retain its 'quintessentially English' feel is anybody's guess, but for now we'd recommend it to those who want great work for big US clients without big US pressure.

Latham & Watkins

The facts

Locations: London

Number of UK partners/solicitors: 41/124 (UK + US)

Total Number of Trainees: 18

Seats: 4x6 months

Alternative seats: Overseas seats

> 'We have our own London client base which is really strong and clients are coming from Asia, the Middle East and Russia as well. America now values us more than ever.'

Latham & Watkins is a massive American firm with a London office that has become key to its worldwide business. Its relatively new training scheme began in 2006.

Big bucks

Latham is one of the biggest players in the big league. Since opening for business in Los Angeles in 1934, it has risen to the top of the pile and achieved the remarkable feat of becoming the first Californian firm to conquer both London and New York. Latham now has more than 2,100 lawyers in 27 offices worldwide, the newest of these being Dubai, Abu Dhabi and Doha. It became the first firm to announce annual revenues of over $2bn, and *Chambers UK, Chambers USA* and *Chambers Europe* all heap praise on its lawyers. Major clients include Credit Suisse, Barclays Capital, Goldman Sachs, Wells Fargo, ExxonMobil, Bechtel, drug company Boehringer Ingelheim, Ericsson, Yahoo!, Global Crossing and several sovereign states. Latham is the epitome of the full-service global law firm.

Since opening in 1996 as a finance boutique, the London office has grown to more than 160 lawyers offering a full range of commercial services. For years it stayed below the radar, happy to maintain relative anonymity while it built up its practice groups and clientele. Now the cat is out of the bag. 'I think London is valued ridiculously highly by the firm,' said one source. 'We have our own London client base which is really strong and clients are coming from Asia, the Middle East and Russia as well. America now values us more than ever.' London clients include Volvo, EMI, Goodyear, E.ON, Diageo, Tyco, Coral Eurobet and Alliance Boots.

The training programme is central to the strategy to make London Latham's second-largest office behind New York. The initial intake of two rookie lawyers was quickly quadrupled, and the firm now looks for between 15 and 20 recruits each year. Trainees complete four six-month seats, three of which must be finance, corporate and something contentious. The final seat can be taken in any area of practice. As the training programme matures, things are likely to change – in fact they have already. Overseas seats are now available in Brussels, Paris, Tokyo and Singapore. Postings to the USA and elsewhere should follow.

The F-word

In London, Latham has been best known for finance. It has a leading high-yield practice, it impresses on structured transactions involving bond financing and it works on a whole host of other specialist lending and capital markets transactions for a diverse clientele of lenders, borrowers, banks, hedge funds, private equity sponsors and corporate buyers. Lawyers advised Barclays on its $4.8bn loan to Thomson Corporation to buy Reuters Group, and acted for ABN AMRO, Credit Suisse and Dresdner Kleinwort, which were set to provide billions to Qatari Investment Authority (QIA)/Delta Two for the acquisition of Sainsbury's. Finance trainees mostly work for mid to senior-level associates, handling standard tasks such as drafting simple documents and board minutes, and acting as a point of contact for clients and other lawyers. It goes without saying that the credit crunch has impacted the department, with business in debt markets and securitisations slowing down. One trainee readily admitted to not getting as much exposure as might ordinarily be expected. 'There's no denying there's very little leveraged work right now, but there's certainly other smaller deals in the market – there's a lot of project finance work and we're taking on more work in other areas than maybe we could have done before.'

The 'exciting, fast-paced' corporate department is increasingly at the fore of the London operation. Last year it recruited several new lawyers and advised on more than 50 transactions worth over £140bn. Among these were Iberdrola's €17.2bn acquisition of ScottishPower and QIA's acquisition of strategic holdings in LSE and the Swedish stock exchange OMX. Trainees explained: 'We are staffed on a deal and then get to see it as it progresses.' And should they wish for more responsibility, all they have to do is ask. One even boasted: 'I was often doing work at junior associate level.'

At first glance it would appear that there's not a whole lot of scope to tailor your contract to your tastes. Not so, our sources promised. Greater flexibility comes of greater initiative, so if you request it 'the firm might be open to you doing a more niche area.' Obviously 'it's a corporate and finance firm so you'll have to work around those areas,' but under these practice umbrellas are a host of subdivisions. One of the corporate options is outsourcing and technology transactions, an area in which trainees experience 'so many different aspects of IP/IT and outsourcing that it's effectively like doing two seats.'

PIL popping

General litigation seats are always available and there are several other specialised contentious options. Since the credit crunch, the restructuring/insolvency team has been busy with structured investment vehicle (SIV) restructurings. If we explain that the classic method for buying up (potentially crappy) mortgage portfolios was to create an SIV, you can probably figure out why so many of them now need restructuring. The competition seat, meanwhile, typically involves 'trying to find answers that aren't in textbooks' and 'having to think in a different way.' The team advised adidas/Reebok on antitrust aspects of their joint venture, assisted Coca-Cola Enterprises on a wide range of antitrust compliance issues, and represented Singapore Airlines in a worldwide air cargo cartel investigation. The employment team puts trainees in contact with clients like Diageo, Alliance Boots, Nike and EMI, sometimes acting as the point of contact for lawyers in several jurisdictions. 'I did a lot of drafting service contracts and workplace handbooks. Quite a few resignation letters, albeit coming from our standard forms and tailor-

ing them to the situation. The rest was researching issues like redundancy and dismissal.' A spell with Latham's top-ranked public international law team has to be one of the most exciting seats on offer. Lawyers have been acting for a family bringing a suit against Romania under the European Convention of Human Rights over claims of harmful pollution, represented the Republic of Azerbaijan in an ICSID arbitration, and steered the Government of Barbados through maritime boundary negotiations. Trainees help by preparing for hearings, bundling documents, conducting research and contributing to business development activities.

Overpaid and over here

How does the Latham London experience sit with the usual stories about American law firms? Well it depends which ones you mean. The recruits we spoke to compared the Latham life favourably with English training schemes. 'Each deal is staffed quite thinly,' so trainees need to shoulder responsibility from the outset. 'In a British firm it's easy to know your place,' they told us. 'You can only do work that's deemed to be at your level, and you're never allowed to step beyond that. Here you'll be given as much as you can handle.' Furthermore, 'you're never made to feel like you're at the bottom of the pile,' for example, a first-come-first-served rule trumps seniority in the queue for photocopying or print jobs, and 'it doesn't say on our business cards whether you're a partner or a trainee.' Our sources rejected the idea that the working day is any longer than at top English firms: 'Whenever you're here at 4am, the lawyers on the other side are also there.' Said one source: 'It was a shock in the first couple of months, but you adapt quickly.' On average trainees estimated they worked until 6.30–7pm, 'although this is during the credit crunch so that's probably a little bit lower than a normal average of 8–8.30pm.' Trainees' billing targets are set at 1,200 hours per year. Partners understand these might not be met and there are no repercussions if they aren't.

The office conforms to some US norms. Its salaries are difficult to overlook – Latham tops the market with an astonishing £96,970 for new qualifiers. Then there's the stereotype about US firms being more involved in pro bono activities. In 2006 London lawyers each contributed an average of 33 hours free legal advice, among the beneficiaries were the Roundhouse Theatre, Green Space and Learning for Life. The fact that pro bono work counts towards billable targets is 'a good incentive.'

Trainees reject the idea that the London office is an American enclave. Some deals do originate Stateside, however large cross-border transactions are just as likely to span European and Asian jurisdictions. 'We act as a stepping-stone between Europe and the States,' explained one trainee, while another summed it up by saying: 'It all feels very global.' One drawback to the link with the USA is that 'Americans print on a different sized paper, so occasionally you'll find that half of your documents will be a different size.' There are also benefits (other than the stonking salary): 'In the sense that we have openness and teamwork, I think that makes us quite American. And although we don't have donuts, we do have a pizza lunch once a week... I definitely think this is an American work environment.'

California soul

Readers of the popular blawg *Above the Law* voted Latham the coolest firm in America, but how well does the West Coast mindset translate on this side of the Atlantic? Our interviewees thought Latham wasn't as 'unnecessarily aggressive' as some East Coast firms. Instead of macho individualism 'everything's run by committee, including bonuses – it's very transparent. The attitude filters down to how people approach their work, for example arrogance is not really appreciated. Everybody is felt to be on the same level and so there's no need for it.' Once a candidate has reached the interview stage it's 'more about them as a person' than what's on the CV. The interview process involves multiple meetings with potential team mates, some quite junior, so don't be surprised if the interview day goes on a bit. Successful applicants share a desire to take on responsibility and produce good results. 'You have to take a lot of satisfaction from your work, as you do a lot of it,' quipped one source. In 2008 one of the two qualifiers stayed with the firm.

In any smaller office 'you get to know people better.' Said one trainee: 'When I started I went to the IT department and everyone already knew my name. You feel you're part of something here, as opposed to just a number.' Socially there are monthly drinks, pizza lunches and breakfasts ('the only time everyone's guaranteed to be in at 9am') and a nice tradition for monthly tea parties to mark birthdays. Organising trainee drinks after work isn't easy because 'everyone's hours are so unpredictable' and 'as a group, we're split up with not many on each floor. We're good at meeting up in twos or threes but not as a group.'

If travel is your thing, you'll be pleased to learn that trainees attend annual departmental retreats and a summer associates' academy in the USA. 'When you're qualified there's an opportunity to spend a month or two in another office and there are also first, third and fifth-year associates' academies. The firm is very keen to have everybody know each other as much as possible.'

And finally...

Latham plans to 'grow its own' lawyers by providing trainees with the best work possible. From now on it will have many more new recruits to work with.

Lawrence Graham LLP

The facts

Location: London

Number of UK partners/solicitors: 81/113

Total number of trainees: 45

Seats: 4x6 months

Alternative seats: None

> The firm doesn't want people who need to be told something twice, it wants people who take the work seriously without being overly serious themselves.

London firm Lawrence Graham always played the mid-tier conservative role to perfection. Then it adopted a new abbreviated name, moved house, rubbed the sleep out of its eyes and fixed them on brave new corporate targets. Goodbye old Lawrence Graham, hello LG.

Different, just

Long known as a thoroughly decent sort of place with an admirable breadth of work and a hefty real estate practice, the old Lawrence Graham warmed the cockles but didn't set pulses racing. Then after a swift bout of self-refashioning it was out with the old and dull and in with the bold, new and bright. Then there's the trendily abbreviated LG name and the 'Lawyers: Just Different' strap line. Leaving aside the perplexing issue of what the slogan means, it does raise the rhetorical question – Does anyone really speak like that outside a Soho creative's office?

Trainees assure us the rebranding speaks volumes: 'Our look and feel has become more polished and focused,' said one, tying the change to a shift in practice emphasis. 'There are all these e-mails flying around about corporate instructions that are coming in, and you know that's where they want us to grow.' Another sleuth observed a subtler change: 'The firm used to refer to itself as property and commercial firm Lawrence Graham, now it's City firm LG.' We asked trainees to expand on the changes within the firm, and some admitted that despite increased emphasis on the 'very productive and profitable' corporate team, 'the firm knows that it has good private client and real estate teams and corporate growth is not going to be at the expense of other departments.' True, corporate does now bring in as much income as the property department, however 'you're not going to look at LG in ten years' time and see an entirely different place.'

Bolly good business

Breadth of practice will remain a defining feature of LG as there's no way it would allow its respected real estate practice to wither. At least no more than can be helped in the current economic climate: unfortunately the credit crunch bit into the department and this impacted on firm-wide financial results in 2008. Such is business life; undoubtedly the department will recover. Meanwhile, recent hires boosted the litigation team to allow it to take on more cases against financial institutions. Given the general reluctance of most City firms to bite the hands that feed them, this is a genius move. Indeed in several other ways LG is capable of weathering a downturn: its corporate tactic has been to develop its Asia-Pacific clientele, particularly via the AIM deals on which around half its corporate lawyers work. In 2007 they advised on 49 AIM transactions, raising over £1.8bn through such deals as Strand Partners' £48.7m dual flotation of Xcite Energy on both AIM and the Toronto Stock Exchange. Then there was The Indian Film Company's £55m flotation, LG's fifth AIM float of an Indian-focused corporate. The M&A lawyers have been busy too: Swordfish Investments used them on a £95m acquisition of Asquith Day Nurseries, and care service provider Careforce Group took their advice on the £22.2m recommended offer made by Mears Group. M&A advice is now given to India-based clients including Satyam Computer Services and Patni Computer Systems.

Just as significantly, LG's focus on Chinese business is beginning to bear fruit through recent instructions such as Xiamen Zijin Tongguan Investment Development Co's £94m recommended cash takeover offer for Monterrico Metals, the first-ever such offer for a UK-listed company by a Chinese company. To strengthen its reach even further, LG has launched a small Dubai office.

Making a splash

Undoubtedly LG is on the hunt for corporate-minded trainees. Those of our sources who'd already done seats in this department spoke excitedly about 'clients from India and the cut-and-thrust of deals for newly won clients.' They had encountered 'a mix of AIM deals on which you help draft ancillary documents, and the corporate bits of real estate deals where maybe you draft the sale documents.' There are 'the inevitable verification exercises to be done' and a few administrative chores; however, we heard genuine praise for the 'definite increase in the level of responsibility and quality of work as the seat progresses.' As in other departments, mid-seat appraisals are key to progression. Said one trainee: 'My supervisor told me at that stage that I'd done enough of the nuts-and-bolts elements of transactions and I needed to do more.' Another added: 'I wanted to make sure I was doing work reflective of what you'd get as a qualified solicitor and I didn't have to push for it to happen.'

The remaining business and finance division seats are banking, competition/EU, local government, IT and outsourcing, and commercial and technology. Otherwise known as comtec, this last seat involves working for the National Lottery and exposes the trainee to 'general commercial contracts, little corporate bits and pieces, website terms and conditions, direct selling and lots of IP.' The hire of a new partner into the team underlines wider ambitions of serving Indian technology clients. Some trainees work with the local government team on the regeneration of town centres. These lawyers are expert in a range of public procurement issues and the creation of leisure and heritage trusts for clients including several London Boroughs. One recent deal saw them advise Fusion Lifestyle on the PPP refurbishment of historic Brockwell Lido.

Precision bundling

The hours may be more regular in the real estate team but the work is no less demanding. Seats can be taken in construction, planning, environment or straight real estate, and in the latter trainees might sample 'site acquisition work for a property developer or a lot of landlord and tenant issues for institutions and funds.' With the right supervisor 'you get it all.' Among the clients are NFU Mutual, Zurich Assurance, Oxford City Council, British Telecom and Debenhams, and LG is making the most of

Chambers UK rankings

Advertising & Marketing • Charities • Construction • Corporate Finance • Dispute Resolution • Employment • Environment • Fraud: Civil • Insurance • Investment Funds • Licensing • Local Government • Media & Entertainment • Planning • Private Client • Public Procurement • Real Estate • Real Estate Finance • Real Estate Litigation • Restructuring/Insolvency • Social Housing • Tax

its reappointment to Sainsbury's legal panel. Client relationships come easily to these property lawyers: they have built on their appointment to Castlemore's panel and the company is now one of their biggest clients. Meanwhile last year's first-time instruction from £1bn private equity fund Lasalle UK Ventures has resulted in other deals. Running 'your own files under supervision' proves popular, but so too does the possibility of 'dealing with the same clients regularly so you build up a rapport and understand their business.'

Seats are also available in tax, private client and reinsurance, not forgetting occasional client secondments. The hot favourites are corporate, real estate and the smaller tax and private client teams, which 'are maybe not up there with Macfarlanes or Withers, but are very good.' The seat allocation process best suits those who make it clear what they want and, if that want is contentious in nature, there is plenty of choice, even if it's unlikely someone will get more than one contentious seat. The litigation seat options deal with reinsurance, property disputes, employment, construction claims and plain old commercial lit. On major, sometimes multi-jurisdictional disputes, trainees become adept at 'preparing all the court forms' and 'going through the court bundles page by page… the last thing you want is the judge asking why page 174 is upside down.' Such chores aren't all-consuming and trainees do learn that 'running smaller debt claims by yourself' brings greater satisfaction. Nevertheless it is worth taking a ringside seat on larger cases: recent highlights include Scottish & Newcastle's VAT & Duties Tribunal hearing, an application at the High Court to restrain Texas proceedings brought against Satyam, and the defence of Land Planning Group against a Financial Services Authority investigation into allegations regarding an illegal collective investment scheme.

Same as it ever was

LG has made efforts to improve its appraisal system and the handling of trainees' problems. Previously we heard the odd complaint about difficult partners and learned how trainees must be proactive in protecting their own interests. This year our interviewees told us: 'Generally supervisors are great, but the firm was made aware of a couple of people who weren't and they no longer have trainees. You'd be very unlucky now to find someone you couldn't get on with.' One explained: 'Forthright personalities are inevitable in a successful law firm, and here there are driven people, though I haven't come across anyone combative.' In fact, with a buddy system in place for first-years, and some departments featuring training partners as well as supervisors, it sounds as if there's ample opportunity to talk through any difficulties.

LG trainees still need to be self-sufficient. 'Of course frustrations crop up, but it's up to you to handle them and not take them personally.' Thankfully, in this relatively compact trainee group people band together and there is 'no aggressive competition between trainees... we all muck in and help each other out.' Recruits tend not to arrive with substantial previous experience, and they also share the characteristic of 'not being big-headed or boastful. There's no one here that makes you think, 'Oh, just shut up' when they're talking.' Going further: 'The firm doesn't want people who need to be told something twice, it wants people who take the work seriously without being overly serious themselves.' Mulling over whether the firm's change in identity might alter the typical LG trainee, they said: 'You used to look at Larry G and think it was a good bet for a decent, rounded London training that wasn't too hardcore. With the mix of work, that just won't change, so I think the same sort of people will continue to apply.' In 2008 17 of the 20 qualifiers pinned their hopes on LG's future prospects and accepted qualification jobs.

How green is my envy?

Have we mentioned LG's new building? In particular trainees waxed lyrical about 'the café with glass doors opening onto a sunken garden,' from which 'you can see Norton Rose people gazing out enviously.' Even 'the odd plastic sculpture' can't dampen the pleasures of 'sitting out there at lunchtime or chatting to a client at an event held in it.' Up on the lofty client floors there are pleasing views of London's landmarks. It's City life without the 'claustrophobia of being in the City.' Generally favourable hours of '9am-6.30-7pm, maybe a few weeks of later nights if you're busy in corporate or litigation,' mean 'we don't need doctors, dentists and hairdressers on-site like a magic circle firm.' They did need an on-site generator in Spring 2008 when a burst water main flooded the basement leaving partners to thank the weather gods they hadn't put any vital technical equipment down there.

In a balanced social life that doesn't involve 'all being out every night getting trolleyed,' there are still opportunities to sample the many nearby bars. When it comes to a big bash, the firm retains its old touch: the annual ball is a good source of amusing tales, and last year's Venetian-themed extravaganza at the Park Lane Hilton was no exception. 'The managing partner, partners and some trainees did an opera sing-a-long; some classic bits and some songs rewritten with LG lyrics.' Must have been a hoot.

And finally...

While LG isn't such a different beast these days it does now crave upward mobility. A rounded training and a decent life are what you get here, but moribund it ain't.

Lester Aldridge

The facts

Location: Bournemouth, Southampton, London

Number of UK partners/solicitors: 38/40

Total number of trainees: 13

Seats: 4x6 months

Alternative seats: Occasional secondments

In 2007 Stonewall named LA one of their diversity champions regarding LGBT staff.

Lester Aldridge is an established South Coast player with offices in Bournemouth, Hurn and Southampton. Not content with dominating its local market, the firm is now looking to its newer London office to take it forward.

London Bridge over troubled water

In 2004 LA opened outposts in London and Milton Keynes. This proved worthwhile in the capital but less so in MK where the firm subsequently scuttled its operation. In truth the past four years have not been plain sailing for LA. There was a minor ruckus after the head of banking and finance jumped ship, reports that Southampton would be the target of expansion proved premature and around a dozen redundancies were made following a restructuring on the advice of business consultants Hildebrandt. So what has been the effect of all this on trainees and where do they think the firm will go from here?

The answer to the first question seems to be: negligible. Regarding the redundancies, trainees say it is 'pretty much all water under the bridge.' As one pragmatic source put it, such changes 'always create a bit of friction at the time, but now people think it was the right thing to do.' Morale-wise, trainees saw few signs of the mood flagging, instead expressing the widespread hope that the redundancy programme was 'a one-off thing.' There was some suggestion that the Southampton office, having borne the brunt of the cuts, might have been harder hit, but 'with hindsight people have appreciated the reasons behind it.' As for the closure in Milton Keynes, this was never going to affect trainees as there had never been a seat there and it had always felt 'out of the way.' Most of the people we spoke to had barely even registered its passing.

The Bournemouth supremacy

The heart of the training programme lies in LA's South Coast homeland, so for the purposes of this report we'll concentrate on this part of the business. The firm's impressive roster of clients and wide-ranging activities are not lost on otherwise modest trainees. 'A lot of the local firms look at us with envy for the quality of clients we attract,' said one. To give you an idea, the firm's Christmas card list includes waste management company Biffa, Chelsea Football Club, Bournemouth Orchestras, Bournemouth Borough Council, the South West Redevelopment Agency, the National Care Association and Southern Cross Health Care, for whom it took a Human Rights Act case to the House of Lords.

Within the firm the Bournemouth office is undoubtedly the central hub, and it is where you'll find most trainees. While LA has been keen to stress the unity between its locations, some of the people we spoke to thought otherwise. In fact, said one, Bournemouth, Hurn and Southampton can feel like 'three different firms.' Each has a different character: Bournemouth is 'more old-school,' whereas Hurn is 'faster-paced' and trainees there are 'given more responsibility.' The Southampton office, meanwhile, is said to be younger in feel and possessed of 'the skills and potential to be bigger then Bournemouth.' London, although tipped for big things, has yet to capture the imagination of most trainees.

Perhaps it is LA's multifaceted character that makes the training contract quite so interesting. The firm is a good choice for someone who wants to 'experience a wide variety of law.' That isn't to say that LA is a jack of all trades. It's actually a grand master of some, as our colleagues at *Chambers UK* will testify. The firm achieves top-tier rankings in family law and debt recovery in the South of England, also performing very well in partnership law, private client, charities, construction and consumer finance. The commercial property department attracts clients such as Big Yellow Group, Grant Thornton and 3 UK to its Bournemouth and London offices. The development of this practice group was 'one of the main reasons the firm opened in London,' and it did so very cleverly by merging with a boutique property firm called Park Nelson. The offices in Bournemouth and Hurn meanwhile have an established reputation in consumer finance and act for prominent clients such as Volkswagen, Toyota and Xerox. Somewhat newer to the party is a specialist shipping law team in Southampton.

One area in which LA has a superb reputation is family. Here there are two partners and an associate, Natalie Gamble, who was named a Lawyer of the Week by *The Times* in January 2008. As a fertility law expert, she has advised many sperm donors and has also helped put the firm on the map with regard to same-sex couples. Such 'progressive' attitudes don't just benefit clients: in 2007 Stonewall named LA one of their diversity champions regarding gay, lesbian and bisexual staff.

Right time, wrong city

Trainees fit four seats into their two-year contracts. As we've already indicated, they have a 'fantastic' range of options. While there's some reassurance to be had from the fact that almost everyone starts out in either Bournemouth or Southampton, notifications as to which office they'll go to have often been given too late in the past, meaning that new joiners have 'rented accommodation in the wrong city.' The firm has assured us this problem has now been addressed; however it's clearly something to double check before you autograph a new tenancy agreement and plan your trip to IKEA. For second and subsequent seats trainee input is considerable, with the firm occasionally willing to create new seats to accommodate special interests. Favourites 'vary year by year' and 'none are really hotly contested.' Strictly speaking no seat is compulsory, though everyone must try something contentious and 'pretty much everybody does a property-based seat at some stage.' This is no bad thing as it's one of the most hands-on experiences. One person told us that by the second half of their commercial property seat 'I was operating as a fee earner in my own right.' Property trainees should definitely expect highs and lows – the highs being their contributions to multimillion-pound acquisitions and 'freebie residential work that's come in

Chambers UK rankings

Asset Finance • Banking Litigation • Charities • Construction • Debt Recovery • Dispute Resolution • Employment • Family/Matrimonial • Healthcare • Partnership • Planning • Real Estate • Real Estate Litigation • Retail

off the back of commercial work;' the lows being the wodge of post-completion form filling. The corporate seat in Bournemouth is more of a 'feast or famine' experience depending on how many deals are coming through the pipeline.

Those tempted by boat shows and an international clientele might consider the marine team. In fact the private client team is not a bad one for encounters with wealthy folk. There's some pretty intriguing stuff going on when it comes to contentious probate cases. Anyone after time in the capital can ask for a London seat. This posting (usually property or private client) has become regular and there are sometimes two trainees at a time in the City. The firm pays travel costs and gives London-based trainees a salary top up. Time and again we heard that no matter what the seat, trainees were happy with the levels of responsibility afforded to them.

Here come the girls

When trainees spoke about the differences between offices, they didn't want us to portray four locations operating in splendid isolation. There is interaction between them and 'you do know the main characters in all the offices.' Large gatherings such as the Christmas party – 'always a good laugh' – allow staff to let their hair down together and it's then that 'you see people's real personalities seeping out.' We've always admired the enthusiasm with which LA parties, and over the years we've heard about some ingenious costumes and themes, so we do wonder if a recent trend for 'more serious, posh do's' is in character. The last Christmas party had a relatively conventional Venetian masquerade theme, which disappointed some trainees but didn't deter some staff from dressing to the nines. Social events are frequent and 'non-hierarchical' (a phrase used by LA recruits rather often) and involve 'everyone from the partners down to the guys who deliver the post.' One source told us: 'We get e-mailed constantly about going out,' and this seems to be true in both Bournemouth and Southampton, where they 'tend to be into real ales.' Downes Wine Bar and The Cricketers are the respective venues for a Friday evening out, though Bournemouth trainees are quite likely to already have snuck in a cheeky early drink at the happy hour event on the seventh floor of the office.

As in so many firms these days, the trainee group is disproportionately female. The firm seems to have it quite bad though – since September 2005 only three males have joined the ranks. Other than the ability to carry a frock well, is there a typical LA recruit? Apparently not – 'there's a role for any kind of trainee.' Still, perhaps it's best if you're not 'too serious' or 'solitary.' As for any preference for taking on locals, one interviewee estimated that 'maybe two-thirds' of their intake grew up in the Bournemouth area, though other years seemed 'more mixed.' Of the people we spoke to, several had been won over after spending time at LA during their vacations before applying for a training contract.

This is a fairly relaxed firm and you 'shouldn't apply if you think law is all about working long hours and making loads of money.' It's only to be expected that trainees have some grumbles about money. In Bournemouth, for example, it's expensive to use the nearby multi-storey car park (£3.50) if you don't want to endure 'the nightmare of trying to get free parking' in the limited number of spaces available at the office. Salaries are a common concern, but such complaints are usually tempered by an acknowledgement that while 'more money would be great,' the trade-off of decent hours is worth it. There is 'certainly not a long hours culture… there's usually a mass exodus at 5.30pm.' And who wouldn't want to leave at a decent hour when 'you can head out the door and onto the beach.' Even in London the atmosphere is 'surprisingly relaxed' and 'they like to have their long extended lunches.' In case you were wondering, trainees posted to London do get a salary top-up for the duration of their stay.

And finally...

Loyalty among recruits is borne out by very decent NQ retention figures. In 2008, four of the seven qualifiers decided to become LA Lawyers. Our sources encouraged students to take a long-term view when considering the firm: despite its London ambitions they say that for now at least 'this is still a South Coast firm.'

- **Dig deep:** Find your inner Lois Lane and do some investigative work. Legal gossip websites aren't always reliable... but their forums are useful for picking up snippets of insider information.

Lewis Silkin LLP

The facts

Location: London, Oxford

Number of UK partners/solicitors: 45/76

Total number of trainees: 11

Seats: 6x4 months

Alternative seats: Secondments

Extras: Language training

> We aren't wacky but what we are is particularly unstuffy, straightforward and not prone to formality.

Lewis Silkin is a London firm with some terribly trendy practice specialisms, a downright sexy clientele and an ethos that can only be described as pleasantly fuzzy. What's not to like?

Scape the City

Put simply, not much. Glance at Lewis Silkin's website and you'll quickly get the flavour of this self-proclaimed 'rather more human' law firm. The orange branding, the quirky cartoons and the informal tone speak of a deliberate positioning at the less austere end of the City. Whether you find it a little fey or deeply pleasing is probably a good barometer of your suitability, but it certainly isn't try-hard. Trainees explain: 'Clients view us as quite an open-necked sort of firm, but in the end, at meetings, one lawyer isn't that different from another. We aren't wacky, but what we are is particularly unstuffy, straightforward and not prone to formality.' This outlook and identity closely relate to the sectors in which the firm excels and the expectations of the clients who instruct. So, to understand Lewis Silkin, get to grips with the areas – or in its own terms the 'scapes' – in which it works.

'Peoplescapes' encompasses the firm's stellar employment practice, an area that it has pioneered over the past 20 years. This giant among employment law teams represents employees and employers from around the UK and worldwide, and made headlines with its victory for Freshfields in the age discrimination claim brought by a former partner. It also defended the ICC on cricket umpire Darrell Hare's race discrimination claim. The client list reveals everything from financial institutions to supermarkets to ad agencies: the London Stock Exchange, Rio Tinto, Sainsbury's, Saatchi & Saatchi, Simon & Schuster, Xerox, Marks & Spencer and Gondola

Group (PizzaExpress, Ask, Zizzi). Membership of international employment law network ius laboris has given LS almost unparalleled international reach. The Viacom Group (MTV Networks Europe, Universal, Nickelodeon) is a happy customer, and via an innovative helpdesk covering 35 countries, LS now handles all MTV's employment work outside the USA. Immigration issues crop up for clients like Abercrombie and Fitch when staff move countries, and domestic instructions arrive from clients such as Oxford University Press, Pret a Manger and the Lawn Tennis Association. A trainee's lot in what is 'the most varied of seats' involves 'attending tribunals with counsel,' 'drafting basic pleadings' and 'many different research points.' Time here is never less than 'very interesting' because 'people bring you all kinds of problems.'

Mediascalps

If you noticed a media slant to those employment clients, that's because LS has long associations with the sector. It all started on the ski slopes on 28 January 1970, when former senior partner and advertising law guru Roger Alexander secured his first agency client. Some 40 years on, the 'mediascape' lawyers in the MBT (media, business and technology) team advise clients as diverse as Invesco, BNP Paribas, ABN AMRO, Barclays Global, Apple, Nokia and Trafficmaster on matters as varied as software licensing, advertising within computer games, and domain name and trade marks issues, not to mention major litigations like the lengthy dispute between

Hutchison 3G and O2 over alleged infringement of O2's bubble imagery. Because the department is essentially 'lots of sub-specialisms together, contentious and non-contentious,' trainees sample 'everything from hard IP to general commercial agreements.' A common trainee task would be preparing a first draft of a commercial contract for an advertising client or dealing with an Advertising Standards Authority complaint. These are 'great because you get to know an enormous amount about a client quickly, liaise with them, build an argument then present it to the ASA and await a decision.'

The 'landscapes' sector focus is the preserve of the commercial property, construction and social housing teams. Commercial property lawyers assisted computer games company Electronic Arts on the sale of its flagship Norman Foster-designed corporate headquarters, and auctioneers Bonhams on the property aspects of a substantial group restructuring. Primary industry giant Rio Tinto is another important client. Admittedly property trainees can feel 'a million miles away from the sexy media matters;' however they do get the 'classic property experience' of 'your own transactions – high-end residential conveynancing and smaller commercial lease negotiations.' These require 'many meetings' and 'non-stop days.' Some trainees work with the 'incredibly committed' social housing team, which is 'heavily shaped and defined by its registered social landlord and charity clients.' It is a leader in its field and represents organisations such as Notting Hill Housing Group, Peabody Trust and Salvation Army Housing, not to mention a swathe of smaller housing associations and local authorities. The firm is currently working on multiple matters relating to the regeneration of the Elephant & Castle in South London. No small beer, the regeneration covers 170 acres and will include 5,300 new and replacement homes, five new open spaces, two tram routes and loads of retail units. The dedication of lawyers to 'the social housing ethos' makes the seat 'a contrast to other areas of the firm,' even if 'the work is quite similar to commercial property.'

Ivy league

We're not sure in which scape to place them, but that's not going to stop us mentioning another couple of the firm's standout teams. The commercial litigators count EDF Energy and ad agency Abbott Mead Vickers as regular clients; they also assisted Mohamed Al Fayed to the bitter end on the inquest into the deaths of Princess Diana and his son Dodi. Various trainees spent time on that case, and other sizeable litigations, one recalling watching agog at 'some intense moments of drama in a High Court hearing.' At the other end of the spectrum, 'debt collection teaches you a lot about how a claim works from beginning to end,' and there are all the usual low-level tasks like 'bundling, research and liaising with counsels' clerks.'

Chambers UK rankings

Advertising & Marketing • Construction • Corporate Finance • Defamation/Reputation Management • Dispute Resolution • Employment • Immigration • Intellectual Property • Media & Entertainment • Partnership • Real Estate • Real Estate Litigation • Social Housing • Sports Law

The corporate department is 'far from run of the mill.' Trainees see small and mid-market M&A, plus AIM deals for 'PR companies, media companies, betting and gaming companies, publishers, you name it.' Described by one enthusiast as 'engrossing, focused and appealing,' the team recently assisted Swiss-listed banking group EFG International with its acquisition of UK-based Marble Bar Asset Management for around $517m. It was a case of 'all guns blazing' when we conducted interviews in spring 2008, although our sources wisely suggested 'it might quieten later in the year.'

The fact that 'advertising, marketing services and media clients have been the bread and butter for a long time' means that – with the exception of social housing and construction – no matter where they roam, trainees come into contact with 'top-level, well-known clients.' But sounding a note of caution, our interviewees pointed out 'you'd be naïve to imagine dining out at The Ivy every day; you still have the daily toil of an average trainee.' Not that this stops MBT from being as sought-after a seat as employment. If you arrive at the firm wanting to try both then do 'make it clear from the outset and be prepared to not get your third choice of seat as well.' This proviso aside, there are no compulsory seats, and with client secondments also on offer, there is plenty of opportunity to heed the advice of this wise young head: 'I came sure I wanted media law, but the experience of my contract has taken me into a different area entirely. I'd urge people to keep an open mind.'

Silkin threads

The firm's relatively long history is threaded with left-leaning tendencies dating back to the decidedly Labour Silkin family, who gave parliament a number of MPs and, via Mr Lewis Silkin himself, the country's town and country planning legislation. Even as recently as the 1990s a Labour MP was leading the firm. But what does that mean in 2009? The social housing team is a concrete legacy of that political commitment, but trainees reflected: 'We were given a presentation on the history and origins of the firm when we arrived, but I couldn't say it's defined my time here.' Although hard to pin down, we think the major bequest of that past is the tolerant and community-minded identity of a firm that offers a refreshing alternative to the profit-before-all-else norm. In this respect, growth is spoken of as 'something that happens organically,' there is a continuing commitment to lower-profit areas like social housing and '9am to 6pm, occasionally longer,' is an average day.

Trainees speak of 'a relaxed culture in which you work hard, but with maybe a bit more humour than at other firms.' This equitable life finds its expression in 'chinos, open-necked shirts and incredible informality' in the employment and MBT teams, where 'the dynamic between junior and senior staff is a lot like that in a start-up internet company.' There's a touch more starch in the litigation team: 'They wear ties, it's just the way litigators are.' Trainees praised the diversity of race, gender and sexual orientation at all levels, and they appreciate the opportunity to contribute to a firm-wide forum and a trainee-only forum. They have personal mid and end-of-seat feedback sessions and there are even follow-up meetings with the training principle 'to see if any issues have arisen.'

LS's trainees are 'not just 21-year-olds rolling off the production line' and a few arrive via previous careers, sometimes media-related. The 'eclectic group' is also full of 'very different in personalities, so you can't generalise a type.' Except perhaps to say, that people are typically 'balanced.' When it comes to retaining qualifiers there are unlikely to be jobs for all in the popular MBT and employment teams. Indeed, even if job availability and trainees' preferences match, the firm doesn't always choose its own, perhaps knowing that it can offer appealing NQ roles to escapees from bigger City firms. It's certainly an incentive to work hard during training, and possibly even 'have a couple of preferences for qualification.'

In 2008 four of the six qualifiers stayed with the firm and there were a total of nine positions on offer.

All hands to the pumpkin

Life in the 'very nice, spacious' Chancery Lane office is predictably convivial, though a little more so for some than others as 'some people are three to an office.' The lower-ground-floor canteen is a popular meeting place, however The Strand, Holborn and the West End are within easy striking distance. Friday nights 'tend to be spent with colleagues from your department,' rather than exclusively with other trainees. An ongoing series of firm-wide parties, hosted by each department in turn, always produce sizeable turnouts, perhaps because 'people like to see partners dressed up and making idiots out of themselves.' In the past year there was an Olympics-themed event with egg and spoon races, a Halloween party for which each department designed a pumpkin display and a Valentine's 'litigation love in' that saw the reception 'made over as a boudoir.' The latter included a 'blind date spoof involving people in the firm who are couples,' of which there are 'a significant number.' Great training and true love, who could ask for more?

And finally...

Lewis Silkin offers interesting work and clients and a training infused with the firm's distinctive ethos. This firm's senses of balance, perspective and humour add up to an appealing package.

- **Philately will get you everywhere:** Extracurricular activities on your CV prove you are more than just a mean lean legal machine.

Linklaters LLP

The facts

Location: London

Number of UK partners/solicitors: 210/700

Total number of trainees: 278

Seats: 4x6 months

Alternative seats: Overseas seats, secondments

Extras: Pro bono – Hackney Legal Connections, Mary Ward Legal Advice Centre, FRU, RCJ CAB, Disability Law Service, A4ID and others; language training

> In terms of training, Linklaters has thought of everything and there are all the resources you'd ever need.

Magic circle firm Linklaters has set its sights on world domination and isn't content unless it is setting the trends for its competitors to follow.

Mumbo jumbo

Linklaters positions itself on the cutting edge and takes it upon itself to 'influence and drive change.' This stance is evident in so much of what it does, from its willingness to risk lucrative relationships with top banking clients by litigating in the finance sector, to its participation in the new work-based learning pilot run by the Solicitors Regulatory Authority. If there's a new financing technique to be tried or a post-credit crunch precedent to be set, Links wants to lead the way. It's even got special jargon – 'super-jumbo' – to refer to financing deals worth over €5bn, an area in which the firm has done very well. By way of example, Linklaters was involved in the $40bn financing for mining company Rio Tinto's offer to purchase aluminium giant Alcan.

Across its 30 offices in 23 countries, Linklaters is 'in the news a lot, for all the right reasons.' Recently lawyers advised RBS on the OFT's test case over bank charges and the €71bn consortium takeover of ABN AMRO. They've also worked on the Eurotunnel restructuring and were instructed by Rio Tinto to help rebuff a takeover approach by Australian rival BHP Billiton. The leveraged buyout of Alliance Boots and the €13.5bn financing for Continental's bid for Siemens VDO have also kept the firm in the headlines. And let's not forget a fetching feature in the *Sunday Times' Magazine* profiling the highest-earning lawyers in the City, many of whom were Linklaters partners.

Clear blue water

From the first day, the firm drills its 'very ambitious' ethos into new recruits to instil a desire to 'create clear blue water between Linklaters and the competition.' Cheekier trainees play 'a bit of a game to see how many times you can work [the slogan] into conversation with a partner.' On a serious note, there is a legitimate concern that Linklaters is 'trying to grow at such a rate they're overworking people.' However, trainees who come here clearly do so with their eyes open, fully expecting long hours and lots of them. 'When I started I was star-struck by all the massive deals. Now I'm a little less star-struck and a little more tired,' admitted one. Exhaustion is made bearable by 'genuinely friendly' colleagues, and during manic periods of '80 hours a week,' 'it's a lot easier when you've got people you get on with.'

In its bid for world domination, Linklaters is presently focusing on Russia, Asia and the Middle East. In the global scrum, several European offices have been left behind: Cologne work was relocated to Düsseldorf and a raft of lawyers were lost in the process, and as of November 2008 Warsaw was the only Eastern European office left standing. These lost offices 'can't have been making enough money to justify keeping them,' one trainee speculated. To promote international cohesion, 'all junior lawyers from all of the international offices' converged on Silk Street this year for the first annual New Lawyers' Global Orientation Programme. Additionally a three-week London induction brings together newbies, already chummy from their Linklaters LPC at the College of Law, for the PSC, some diversity training and presentations on different practice areas.

Trainees spend three seats in the 'departments that bring in 80% of the revenue,' namely corporate, banking, capital markets, projects, derivatives, structured finance, asset finance, litigation and real estate. The fourth is chosen from an array of specialist areas, including tax, pensions, employment, competition and technology, media and telecoms. In corporate the hours are 'kind of brutal, but it's scary how quickly it becomes normal.' Some trainees perceived the department as 'hierarchical,' citing 'an unbridgeable gap between trainees and everybody else.' Others had 'a really good time' there, perhaps because 'after a while you just accept that you're on the bottom rung and the grunt work has to be done.' In addition to typical trainee tasks like due diligence, if there's an IPO or smaller deal on, trainees can find themselves 'running signings and closings.' Within one of the smaller teams that shelter under the corporate umbrella (eg restructuring/insolvency, private equity), trainees enjoy greater responsibility. In the 'growing' but still 'immature' private equity team, they speak to clients, negotiate appointment agreements and draft sale and purchase agreements. If corporate doesn't sound like your cup of tea, you might first want to question why you're attracted to Linklaters and then consider the wisdom of the trainee who 'went from saying, 'I'm never going to qualify here' to wanting to. You have to take a long-term view of what you'll be doing as an associate.'

People have a 'love-hate' relationship with banking seats because of their reputation for 'horrific' hours. 'You can have nothing to do, then suddenly get snowed under and not leave until 4am.' Banking trainees see investment-grade and leveraged deals, the former offering them more responsibility 'drafting facility agreements and amendments.' On the leveraged side the work is 'ridiculously complicated,' so they must content themselves with 'really mundane tasks like bibling,' as well as working on the conditions precedent. Some people positively thrive in this fast-paced environment, loving 'being involved in headline deals.'

Mañana

Although we did speak to some people who adored banking and nothing else, others were grateful for seats in smaller teams. 'Advisory seats are generally more relaxed than transactional seats,' for example real estate is 'almost like its own little firm,' with a markedly more mañana attitude. 'People aren't here all night every night. A lot of stuff can wait until tomorrow.' Here, and in seats like TMT and pensions, trainees are given 'really fantastic work at the level of junior associates.'

Chambers UK rankings

Asset Finance • Banking & Finance • Banking Litigation • Capital Markets • Climate Change • Competition/European Law • Construction • Corporate Finance • Data Protection • Dispute Resolution • Employee Share Schemes • Employment • Environment • Financial Services Regulation • Fraud: Civil • Information Technology • Insurance • Intellectual Property • Investment Funds • Life Sciences • Media & Entertainment • Outsourcing • Partnership • Pensions • Pensions Litigation • Planning • Private Equity • Professional Negligence • Projects, Energy & Natural Resources • Public Procurement • Real Estate • Real Estate Finance • Real Estate Litigation • Restructuring/Insolvency • Retail • Shipping • Tax • Telecommunications • Transport

Many people shun litigation seats in favour of a two-week course at the College of Law. For those who fancy some real contentious experience, the litigation department is a busy environment, currently with a number of matters arriving as a result of the fallout from the credit crunch. In addition to disputes arising from the failure of structured investment vehicles, trainees deal with employment, regulatory and oil and gas issues among other things. While the task of 'sifting through e-mails can be quite tedious,' the 'eureka moment when you come across something very important to the case' is 'fantastic.' Recent cases include Southern Water's investigation by Ofwat and representing PwC as liquidators of MG Rover. Linklaters' litigation team is well muscled, even if it doesn't pack the revenue-boosting punch of the biggest departments. At trainee level, this translates to great experience but slim chances for qualification.

Bye bye BlackBerry

The trainees we spoke to recited a litany of cancelled plans, weekends in the office and even 'losing the document I was working on at 2am and nearly killing myself.' Thankfully most felt more than adequately compensated for their sacrifices. Said one: 'I had to cancel plans but still thought it was good because I felt like I was contributing.' A few said they would welcome more appreciation: 'Everyone who comes here knows it's going to be tough at times, but you want a bit of compassion and that doesn't always happen.' Things may be looking up. According to our sources, 'there seems to have been a shift away from a very hard culture to a slightly more reasonable one.' Perhaps the recent policy of discouraging associates and partners from taking their BlackBerrys on holiday is a concrete example.

Arriving at One Silk Street for the first time can be daunting, and the feeling lingers for some trainees. 'I wander around the building feeling a bit lost. It's very quiet with everyone working away in their own little pod.' An extensive support network is in place to help trainees make the most of their experience, and in every seat there is a Group Trainee Solicitor Partner for guidance. Opinion was divided as to how well the system works: while some felt that 'if you have a problem you can speak to [the GTSP],' others said: 'Some GTSPs don't even seem to notice the trainees.' Like most things, the supervision is only as effective as the people involved. Perhaps understandably, 'if you sit with a managing associate or junior partner you get a lot from them,' whereas senior partners adopt a 'more laissez-faire' approach because 'they're very busy and have lots of other people to supervise.' In terms of training, Linklaters 'has thought of everything and there are all the resources you'd ever need.' As well as enthusing about the breadth of subjects covered, trainees appreciated the variety of ways in which training was presented, including breakfast and lunch sessions and hands-on activities as well as lectures.

Backroom deals

Client secondments are a golden opportunity to work 'nine to five instead of Linklaters hours.' Trainees say the in-house experience 'gives you a lot of confidence,' even if it's initially hard when 'someone rings you and wants an answer immediately.' Overseas seats are hugely popular. Experiences vary massively between offices: some reportedly saddle trainees with 'prolonged periods of unbusyness,' leading a few people to speculate that 'a lot of secondments seem to be more of a graduate recruitment tool than a business need.' By contrast, others bring more responsibility and 'bloody hard work.' Hong Kong, Tokyo and Dubai are 'massively oversubscribed,' in large part because the lifestyle is so good. Hong Kong trainees are proud that Linklaters has the biggest junk of all the law firm boats in the harbour and the 'luxury flats with swimming pools and maids' don't sound too shabby either. For a full list of international placements see page 670.

Some trainees found the process of allocating overseas seats 'quite political,' but agreed: 'You'll definitely get to go somewhere.' It is worth noting that other trainees were pleased as Punch with the allocation process. We sensed that much depends on timing and luck. In the same vein, a few people speculated about 'backroom deals' when it came to qualification and suggested that 'it's very important to chat to partners.' As Linklaters starts its qualification process later than some other firms, a few of our sources felt they'd been 'left hanging.' However, there is a sense that the firm 'wants to keep you on qualification' and year on year the majority do stay. In 2008 the figure was lower than is usual, with 112 of the 133 qualifiers

taking up positions. As in some other firms, posts were available in certain overseas locations this year.

Strategic thinking

For every trainee that moaned: 'With this job its impossible to have a night out,' others assured us: 'You can go out together, it's just a question of whether you want to.' Alas, two local boozers recently closed down and when we spoke to trainees, they hadn't yet settled on a suitable alternative. The nearby Rank & Tenter was dismissed as 'a bland City bar full of office workers,' while the 'small old-man's pub up Bunhill Row' was deemed 'nice but full of Slaughters people or postmen.' In the office 'the weekend starts at the drinks trolley,' which goes round most departments weekly or fortnightly. Apparently, litigation's trolley even comes with the occasional wine tasting notes. Every other year the firm splashes out on a trainee summer ball and there's a trainee social committee which 'has a tough time coming up with ideas to please everyone,' given that there are roughly 250 of them at any one time. Department dos are a reliable source of organised fun and every so often 'a big partner invites the whole department to their huge house. You get to go peek in all the rooms.' Who could resist? Finally, getting onto one of Linklaters' sports teams might see you jetting off to Milan, Stockholm or, if you're part of the well-funded cricket team, Hong Kong.

Whether it's being musical, sporty, multilingual or downright brilliant, among the trainees 'everyone has a number of strings to their bow.' The firm's new 'share the thinking' campaign is aimed at recruiting trainees who fancy working internationally and who actually read the *FT* even when they're not prepping for interviews. To that end, recruiters travel to top Indian and Australian universities and are looking at other common law countries. The aim is to recruit trainees with 'wider international backgrounds,' not just the candidates 'on the doorstep.' Given that sources told us: 'Having a lot of other nationalities makes it quite a nice, diverse group,' it's clear that Links' strategy is working well. Indeed the firm must be commended for its efforts to recruit from a wide range of sources here in the UK too: for the record, the Oxbridge contingent is now a much lower 30–40% of the group.

And finally...

Linklaters knows exactly what it wants from its business and its employees – a dedication to being the best. For those who love the buzz of working for the biggest clients on the biggest deals, across borders at all hours, choosing this firm is a perfect move.

Lovells LLP

The facts

Locations: London

Number of UK partners/solicitors: 144/413

Total Number of Trainees: 155

Seats: 4x6 months

Alternative seats: Overseas seats, secondments

Extras: Pro bono – eg Disability Living Allowance and Criminal Injuries Compensation hearings, National Centre for Domestic Violence, CABs; language training

> The people who find the qualification process easiest are those who view their training contract as a daily job interview and make the effort to step up and be counted.

In the theme park of training contracts, Lovells appeals to those who want to ride the rollercoaster of magic circle-calibre deals but haven't yet abandoned the desire to spin round in the teacups of more niche areas of law.

Can't buy me Lovells

Lovells is conducting a delicate balancing act: it wants to maintain its position at the top end of the silver circle while simultaneously repositioning itself as a mainstream corporate and finance firm. And all without undermining its other strong practice groups. Phew! Having aspired to magic circle status, a turbulent few years of partner departures and slightly disappointing financial results mean trainees see the firm as delicately poised between former identity and current ambition. 'Competing to get in [to the magic circle] is what's keeping the firm where it is. God knows what would happen if we stopped trying,' thought some, others concluding that Lovells is not quite 'hitting the big stakes' because of a reluctance to entirely abandon its 'friendly' reputation by completely 'beasting' its workforce. Being all things to all people clearly isn't easy, but revenue and profits improved on previous years. The firm ratcheted up the numbers in 2008, largely due to good performance from its international offices, whose billings now exceed London's – some 40% of total revenues now come from continental Europe alone.

Despite a slight wobble in the top echelons of the corporate and finance groups in recent years, Lovells' corporate department is pulling in some impressive instructions. New client Autogrill sought advice on a £545m deal that sees it gain exclusive rights to run 58 duty-free shops at Heathrow, Gatwick and Stansted, while lawyers advised Goldman Sachs on Australian mining company BHP Billiton's proposed takeover of rival Rio Tinto, which would have been one of the biggest City deals of the past year had it been accepted. Other big-name corporate clients include SABMiller, ING, Xerox, Ford, 3i and ITV. In this mammoth department, it is unsurprising that trainees end up with 'a lot of rubbish grunt work,' such as creating and manning data rooms, conducting due diligence and verification exercises. The simple fact is that major transactions require major input at the lowest level. Leaving at 8pm is deemed reasonable, but there are 'pretty horrific' days, nights and weekends when you're on a big transaction. One we heard about was 'so huge that a firm-wide e-mail was sent out asking people to come in over Easter weekend.'

Finance seats in the banking or capital markets groups can be daunting in prospect but provide a great opportunity to experience 'life at the coalface.' 'Busy departments are the best way to learn,' reflected one source. After the first few head-spinning weeks, 'you grow into the responsibility given to you' and typical trainee tasks involve research and drafting facility agreements using the established precedents. In project finance seats they help put together 'great big bits of kit for schools, hospitals, roads, you name it.' The team recently advised on the £445m PFI project for Peterborough hospitals.

Sub role

Lovells' dispute resolution lawyers are proving the received wisdom that litigators do well in a bear economy, when businesses scramble for every penny they can recover. They've advised Lloyds TSB in the very public litigation over bank charges and taken on some of the big banking fiascos that have already arisen from the credit crunch. Most notably they represented a group of Northern Rock shareholders in a judicial review application designed to secure more government compensation, and as this book went to print they had just landed a role acting for the Financial Services Authority on regulatory aspects of the shock bankruptcy filing of Lehman Brothers. In the area of product liability litigation – a really strong suit for Lovells – lawyers have worked on some fascinating matters, including assisting Merck on claims arising from the withdrawal of its Vioxx painkiller and the alleged links between its MMR vaccine and autism in children.

Lovells' global litigation head has reportedly announced his intention to throw weight behind the idea of sub-practices to provide more specialised services in this litigation-friendly economic climate. The fact that seats are available in investment banking and funds; manufacturing, commercial and product liability; corporate and banking litigation; international commercial litigation; contentious Chancery indemnity litigation; fraud/contentious insolvency; insurance/reinsurance litigation; projects, construction and engineering disputes; and real estate litigation should tell you the firm has no shortage of specialisms. A trainee's role in corporate and banking litigation, for example, can be 'a nightmare of photocopying and copy checking,' leaving some people feeling 'litigation is just grunt work because the cases are so huge.' The more astute take advantage of their exposure to massive cases by 'making an effort to understand the bigger issues, not just the day-to-day tasks.' Impress your supervisor with knowledge gleaned from actually reading the papers you're photocopying and you might get more interesting work, perhaps 'interviewing witnesses and drafting witness statements.' It is a fortunate trainee who stumbles upon a niche litigation seat. Real estate litigation, for example, offers a great deal more responsibility in a much smaller team. Trainees find it challenging working on 'up to 30 of your own files,' 'doing basic advocacy before a master' and even 'taking photos of offices to see if the tenants have breached their user covenants.' With levels of responsibility so varied between litigation teams, no wonder 'a lot of people are passionate about which litigation seat they do.'

Credit for time served

Lovells offers an array of specialist seats, but beware – getting your favourite seats can be complex. In their first months at the firm, trainees are asked to state their preferred seats for the entire two years. Employment and competition are beloved by many, but all must first serve time in at least one corporate or finance team and a litiga-

Chambers UK rankings

Administrative & Public Law • Advertising & Marketing • Asset Finance • Banking & Finance • Banking Litigation • Capital Markets • Climate Change • Competition/European Law • Construction • Corporate Finance • Data Protection • Dispute Resolution • Employee Share Schemes • Employment • Environment • Financial Services Regulation • Fraud: Civil • Information Technology • Insurance • Intellectual Property • Investment Funds • Life Sciences • Media & Entertainment • Outsourcing • Parliamentary & Public Affairs • Pensions • Pensions Litigation • Planning • Product Liability • Professional Negligence • Projects, Energy & Natural Resources • Public Procurement • Real Estate • Real Estate Finance • Real Estate Litigation • Restructuring/Insolvency • Retail • Tax • Telecommunications • Transport

tion team. If you are lucky enough to get your favourite, 'the unwritten rule is that if you get a supremely popular seat HR has a licence to give you two other rubbish seats.' To soften the disappointment, trainees who are allocated undesired seats in big departments can generally choose where to sit among the department's subgroups.

Real estate seats, whether in the mainstream department or the smaller planning team, offer a lot more responsibility and high-quality work. 'Busier during the day than other groups,' generally 'the hours in real estate are shorter and by 7.30pm the office is pretty empty.' The department is known for its big-ticket deals and is currently advising on the £2bn regeneration of 67 acres around King's Cross. John Lewis also recently employed Lovells to advise on the opening of stores in Sheffield, Leeds and Stratford in east London.

Now seems an excellent time to sample the delights of the IP department. The team is expanding, thanks to five lateral hires and more partner promotions this year than in corporate, and has been busy advising long-standing client Merck in relation to patents for its diabetes and osteoporosis drugs. On a tastier note, chocolate giant Mars sought advice on film tie-ins between *The Devil Wears Prada* and Galaxy and *Die Hard 4* and Snickers. Then, scattered about the building, are 'little pockets of teams' dealing with 'more cerebral' areas of law like pensions, tax, competition, employment and telecoms, media and technology. In addition to providing the chance to give the grey cells a proper workout, these involve sitting with smaller teams where 'you get to know everyone well.' Their popularity means that the key to securing a seat here is a mix of 'shouting about [what you want] to HR,' 'speaking to partners' and pure dumb luck.

A brighter shade of pale

The people who find the qualification process easiest are those who view their training contract as a 'daily job interview' and make the effort to 'step up and be counted.' It also helps if you're interested in a corporate or finance job rather than positions in 'heavily oversubscribed' departments like litigation, employment or planning. The firm employs a formal system of applications and interviews, and although the process can be 'stressful,' it is widely viewed as 'fairer than the informal little chats used by smaller firms.' Spare a thought for the qualifying trainees who went after a tax position this year. The selection process involved a two-hour interview including a 'really tough' scenario based on brand new legislation. In 2008, 56 out of 79 qualifiers stayed on. The firm attributed its slightly higher than average attrition rate to 'a bumpiness we couldn't smooth out in terms of where people applied.' Translation: there were plenty of jobs in corporate and finance but not enough in other areas to satisfy demand.

We hear that Lovells attempted to redress the balance of its Oxbridge-heavy recruitment by actively targeting other universities more. Maybe it just can't win because a few of our sources perceived 'positive discrimination against Oxbridge' had caused 'grumblings' among the ranks. And given that trainees also reckon 'about 65% of the current vac scheme students are Oxbridge,' the tide may have turned again. Whatever the truth, most interviewees believed 'it helps if you went to Oxbridge, but it's not the be-all and end-all.' The recruitment process features an assessment day involving a group negotiation of a business scenario, a critical thinking test and an interview. Our spies suggest that successful candidates left the assessment 'pale and shaking' rather than 'happy and relaxed.'

Tales from the crypt

Working at a top ten firm can be 'all-consuming' and it goes without saying the hours are beastly on occasion. Just as well then that within 'fantastic' Atlantic House there's a canteen, a GP, a chiropodist and a masseuse. There are even 'functional' sleeping pods for those who have to pull an all-nighter. More glamorous is the hidden door in the canteen that leads to Bacchus, the establishment next door. 'You swipe through an anonymous wooden door and the next thing you know you're in a wine bar, even though you've never left the building.'

Luckily for those who spend a large part of the day (and night) in the office, Lovells is a very sociable place. Outside the office, its lawyers get fresh air playing rugby, cricket, football and netball. There are parties galore, summer balls and winter fêtes, departmental Christmas jollies, team lunches over fish and chips, and even gatherings at partners' homes. Trainees appreciate the chance to 'meet people's families' and can't resist the chance to be nosey. 'All the partners have pools,' claimed one. Most of our interviewees made Lovells sound like one big, happy (if slightly overworked) family, complete with 'a few characters' but 'no one who you'd look at and think, 'My god I cannot stand you.'' Senior partner John Young is now very well known for his antics at a circus-themed summer party: not only was he 'suspended from the ceiling wearing silver Lycra,' but he also allowed the photographs to be widely circulated. The firm is generous with its social budget and this year the trainees' summer party was held in the crypt of a local church. Far from frightful, it was an 'absolutely beautiful' venue and a great party.

And finally...

The widely held perception of Lovells as 'less cut-throat than magic circle firms' is a big draw for prospective trainees, but training here is most certainly not an easy ride. Those who are prepared to be proactive and accept the occasional all-nighter will gain solid magic circle-esque training.

Lupton Fawcett

The facts

Location: Leeds

Number of UK partners/solicitors: 25/29

Total number of trainees: 6

Seats: 4x6 months

Alternative seats: Occasional secondments

Extras: Language training

> Lupton Fawcett should appeal to people who value work-life balance. Trainees say: 'We all work hard but equally know where to draw the line.'

Lupton Fawcett trainees introduce their employer as 'a traditional Yorkshire firm with strong roots.' If you want a rounded commercial training at a midsizer in Leeds, it could be just the ticket, especially if you need help getting through your five-a-day.

Panel beaters

Through a century of legal practice Lupton Fawcett has cemented itself in the Leeds mid-market and offers a full service to a core of owner-managed, Yorkshire-based businesses. One trainee kindly explained the firm's approach as follows: 'As we've expanded we've focused on the owners of businesses and strived to offer a fully integrated service to them. That means offering solutions on contract issues, property acquisitions, etc. We've got a strong IP team and an ancillary employment wing, so we can offer the whole package for the companies that come to us.' The firm has built a charities and social enterprises department and, in recognition of the importance of meeting business owners' personal legal needs, there's a private client team. The Lupton Fawcett personal injury department may be the longest serving member of the RAC panel, even so trainees suggest 'the focus on the firm's corporate and commercial side will become increasingly prevalent.'

This is a firm that knows the value of a sharp image and website. Here you will find something it calls 'the law of advantage,' which trainees tried to explain was all about 'adding value through a strong commercial approach and awareness.' We hear this from many firms, of course, but Lupton Fawcett trainees are convinced the claim has substance. Whatever the truth of the matter, there's no denying LF's solid client list. Although its bread and butter work comes from the owner-managed business market,

the client list is now studded with some big-name companies. It has done well to win smaller instructions from major plc and institutional clients and now sits on the legal panels of American Tobacco, National Tyco, Citi, AIB, RBS, Serco, TI Automotive, Federal Mogul and United Business Media. The firm gets involved in a number of marketing activities, one of them being Leeds Legal, a collective initiative to promote the city's law firms to national and international clients.

Another thing in its favour is the hire of partners from local rivals Gordons, DLA Piper and Cobbetts. Trainees say the introduction of new blood has sparked a positive mood, and to provide more space for its burgeoning ranks the firm recently renovated its offices and took extra floor space.

Raising agents

Trainees complete four seats chosen from a menu of six options – corporate, commercial property, commercial litigation, insolvency, IP and employment. There's nowt compulsory and second-years get first dibs, leaving first-years to tussle over what's left. One of the most popular seats is insolvency, an area in which the firm handles high-profile personal bankruptcies and small to medium-sized corporate insolvencies. 'They make you feel very much part of the team rather than just a trainee,' our sources confirmed. 'You're included and invited along to everything,' and that includes client lunches and socials.

In between wining and dining, our interviewees had handled their own receivership and administration files, and worked closely with clients to draft all necessary documents.

Integration can prove trickier in the corporate department, which is usually a second-year assignment. Some people feel the seat is 'very much limited to classic trainee tasks;' we're talking about 'dealing with Companies House, writing board minutes, appointing directors, proof-reading agreements, lots of due diligence, and printing and putting documents together.' The department mostly wins instructions from clients in the Leeds, Huddersfield and Sheffield areas. In 2007, for example, it represented the independent directors of ICM Computers throughout the company's £107.8m takeover by Phoenix IT. It also worked on an equity investment into cake manufacturer Mrs Beeton's Rediscovered. 'If the department is dead then there can be nothing to do, but when it's busy you work full throttle until 7pm or 8pm, and sometimes for as long as it takes. I never stayed past 11pm in that seat, but some trainees have stayed until 2am.'

A fairly large property department completes the transactional side of the firm. It is split into teams for property finance and commercial real estate. The finance side is populated with ex-Pinsent Masons partners and here trainees assist on larger deals, busying themselves with 'general title checks and drafting securities documents.' On the commercial property side they deal with landlord and tenant issues, enter into new lease negotiations for retail clients and help out on development deals. There's even some 'quite quirky work for a Church involving selling off burial sites.' One person who improves life for the trainees is the paralegal whose duties include post-completion registrations. Lupton Fawcett lawyers recently acted for the Environment Agency in the lease of premises for its new National Flood Defence Call Centre in Sheffield, for Leeds Grammar School on the funding of a £35m redevelopment of a school site and for Town Centre Securities in connection with lettings in the Merrion Centre in Leeds, including units for Sainsbury's, Costa, Birthdays, Trespass and 3UK. When several large deals come in at the same time the hours can be demanding; otherwise, across the transactional seats trainees can expect to leave the office by 6.30pm.

Pips 'n' dips

The broad commercial litigation seat is subject to 'wet and dry spells.' It handles property, contract and construction disputes and has 'a strong niche in contested probate and professional negligence claims.' The most common kind of property dispute requires an application for the forfeiture of a lease because its tenants have tried to wrig-

Chambers UK rankings

Banking & Finance • Corporate Finance • Dispute Resolution • Employment • Family/Matrimonial • Intellectual Property • Private Client • Real Estate • Restructuring/Insolvency

gle out of their obligations. On commercial contracts cases, trainees draft particulars of claim and instructions to counsel, also helping out on initial letters of advice. The department only admits one trainee per rotation, so this lucky character will have attention lavished on them by several people. The downside of this is 'less consistency,' the upside is 'variety in the types of work and research that come your way.'

The IP and commercial seat is relatively new but has already gone down a storm with trainees who admire the fact that the team represents a few major brands such as Textron, Jacuzzi and GMC, the Aussie power tool manufacturer. Because this is a small team, the lawyers are 'keen to get trainees involved' with commercial drafting, brand reviews, registering trade marks and trade mark infringement litigation. The employment seat is an eye-opener. 'I have been really involved in the run up to a few tribunals, liaising with the other side, bundling, drafting witness statements, speaking with clients and doing a lot of research,' revealed one source.

On the whole, the nature and volume of work suits trainees well. For a while, growth in the commercial teams meant 'people were crammed in together' and some trainees had to sit with the secretaries, quite far from their supervisors. Although far from ideal, supervisors were at least aware of the need to supply regular feedback. Ongoing refurbishments and the extension of the office should remedy these problems.

Trainees say Lupton Fawcett's website is indicative of a firm that 'prides itself on doing things slightly differently.' One of the best illustrations is its healthy lifestyle initiative. The programme revolves around bowls of fruit for staff, regular leaflets and advice on how to lead a healthy lifestyle and the odd group hike in the Dales or lunchtime trip to the swimming pool. 'Any campaign like that will have hits and misses,' one source conceded. 'I have received the odd flyer encouraging us to eat oranges and apples, which I thought was pretty useless, but there are other tangible benefits like heart screening and external activities like lunchtime walks.'

Lupton's got talent

On occasions the pint overpowers the banana. Take the annual dinner dance, at which last time two partners performed a Pet Shop Boys song, another paid tribute to the king of croon Engelbert Humperdinck and a third became an Elvis impersonator. Trainees like the fact that partners are prepared to risk making fools of themselves: 'It shows they're keen to get stuck in and have laugh.' The office has the advantage of being located on lively Greek Street, though trainees are certainly aware of the danger this poses. One admitted: 'We have a couple of bars below us that I've started to believe are almost part of the office.' This includes the firm's 'spiritual home' – All Bar One – where half the firm can be found on Friday nights. We think we may have discovered the inspiration for the firm's obsession with theatrical parties. 'A Japanese karaoke bar opened across the road and we went to opening night. Alcohol lowers your inhibitions so we were all singing.' The Greek Street location does have one disadvantage: if you have to work late in the run up to Christmas 'you can hear all the parties going on below.'

Trainees believe the firm is looking for 'outgoing' candidates with 'something beyond academics.' A connection of sorts to the region undoubtedly helps convince the firm of your suitability: 'There are a few Mancs knocking about, so not everyone is from Yorkshire, but it is a very Northern firm.' Happily, we can report that Lupton Fawcett should appeal to people who value work-life balance. Trainees say: 'We all work hard but equally know where to draw the line.'

Our sources understood why people would be attracted to the firm: 'Within the Leeds market it had a good reputation for traditional values and a good standing. It's generated a lot of growth over the previous five years and it's a good idea to go for a firm that is moving forward, going places.' This desire for change doesn't appear to detract from the fact that 'some of the directors here have been practising in Leeds for 25 years' or the value placed on 'a traditional and honest approach.' What you have is a firm that's been taking a pragmatic approach to its future. Said one source: 'In the post-Clementi era it's important that we've positioned ourselves as a purveyor of strong commercial advice and moved away from bog-standard volume work.' If this all sounds interesting in theory but hard to understand then Lupton Fawcett's approach to recruitment should help: 'You do a two-day sort of mini-training contract after a few rounds of interviews. It's four mini-seats with the emphasis being for applicants to get to know the firm and its work better. It goes beyond the hyperbolic recruitment pack stuff and you benefit a lot.'

In 2008 only two of the four qualifiers took permanent positions within the firm. 'The qualification process is bit hit and miss,' complained one source. 'It's haphazard and there could definitely be a better-structured process.'

And finally...

Any number of firms claim to champion the idea of a healthy work-life balance but few take it quite as seriously as Lupton Fawcett. If you're looking for a firm that 'sits nicely into Leeds market and is quite competitive but without big-firm pressures,' you could find a happy home here.

Mace & Jones

The facts

Location: Liverpool, Manchester, Knutsford

Number of UK partners/solicitors: 40/54

Total number of trainees: 11

Seats: 4x6 months

Alternative seats: Secondments

As a full-service firm, M&J offers trainees a wide choice of seats and experiences, from encounters with Joe Public in the Knutsford office to a busy and ambitious corporate team in Manchester.

The North West is a crowded legal market and, as one of its established names, Mace & Jones competes with the likes of DWF, Brabners Chaffe Street and Hill Dickinson, as well as national firms such as Pinsent Masons, DLA Piper and Addleshaw Goddard. So what does the firm offer trainees that others don't?

Art attack

Aside from the various activities depicted on the firm's captivatingly artistic website (jousting, playing on a seesaw, reaching for the stars and – in an undeniably surreal composition – winching two giant tightly clasped hands) solicitors at Mace & Jones have been nurturing a successful mid-tier practice, especially in the construction and employment law/partnership sectors. The employment department boasts a hefty band of private and public sector clients, including the Health and Safety Executive, for whom M&J recently won a mandate to handle tribunals, training and other human resources matters. Partnership law is one of the firm's best-known specialisms: *Chambers UK* puts M&J among the best in the country. Lawyers advise solicitors and accountants, GPs and dentists, often in relation to disputes and partner expulsions. The construction practice is also really successful: the team recently advised Balfour Beatty in a big-money arbitration over a marine structure and a national utilities company in relation to a £4.5m dispute involving the construction of a gas pipeline in southern England. On the development side, lawyers have been working on projects worth around £800m, including some of the region's most prestigious schemes at Central Spine, The Exchange, Greengate and Manchester City FC's old Maine Road ground.

'Major changes are now behind the firm,' say trainees conscious of M&J's desire to continue growing, 'particularly in commercial areas rather than in private client.' Indeed 'some departments have had to be rejigged in order to fit all the extra staff in.' Recent hires have bolstered the insolvency and property litigation teams in Manchester, and new managing partner Richard Corran looks set to keep up the pressure 'to keep pace with regional competitors.' Trainees have also picked up on Corran's determination to get all M&J offices singing from the same song sheet. Said one: 'An area that can be slightly improved is the communication and co-operation between the different offices. This has definitely been highlighted and is starting to happen now.'

Something for everyone

As a full-service firm, M&J offers trainees a wide choice of seats and experiences, from encounters with Joe Public in the Knutsford office to a 'busy and ambitious' corporate team in Manchester. The full list of seats is: coco (Man/Liv); commercial property (Man/Liv and Knutsford); employment (Man/Liv); dispute resolution (Man/Liv); construction (Man); family (Man) and a hybrid private client/family seat split between Liverpool and Knutsford. No one has a say as to where they take the first seat, however after that 'you do get a really good choice of all the departments, across all the offices.' An appointed trainee representative puts together 'a matrix of where everyone wants to go' and after everyone is content with the proposal it is sent for authorisation by the powers that be.

What each seat holds seems to depend on when you arrive. Those trainees who started their contracts in the property department found that 'it was initially quite heavy on post-completion tasks,' whereas those with more experience when they arrived in the department earned much more responsibility through negotiating and drafting small agreements, leases and licences, and being involved with 'massive development projects.' Even in these situations 'everything is very well supported and supervised, and the partners don't just leave you willy nilly with the file.' Among the most important deals handled in the past year are the £13m purchase of a boatyard for a residential development on the canal at Worsley, north of Manchester, and acting on behalf of the North West Development Agency with respect to the ongoing development of Daresbury Science Park. Other clients include NW Territorial Army and Cadets Association, Liverpool YMCA, developer Artisan and Umbro.

Litigation involves 'an excellent amount of client contact – including going out to take witness statements on your own.' It will also mean making your own applications in court, admittedly 'absolutely terrifying the first time you do it' but nothing to lose sleep over as 'your supervising partner will take you through stage by stage and the support is so good that by the time you actually get to court you know exactly what you have to do.' The Manchester-based litigation seat has the added appeal of being twinned with the construction department, so trainees are exposed to a substantial quota of their cases. In the employment team, public sector equal pay litigation is an important source of revenue. The firm has lately represented a group of NHS trusts and several local authorities on such claims. One of the firm's housing association clients last year embarked on a comprehensive reorganisation involving relocating staff and harmonising terms and conditions of employment, and an NHS trust sought advice on employment tribunal proceedings brought by a dismissed trainee doctor. Among the department's clients are Littlewoods Pools and Liverpool FC.

Straight family seats in Manchester and Liverpool are weighted towards ancillary relief and divorce cases, rather than children's work, although there was one recent case for a South African father who had not seen his children for three years due to an international abduction by their mother. Proceedings were issued in the UK after private detectives located the children. Most divorces are for comfortably-off individuals; some clients are worth millions and one pre-nuptial agreement was drawn up to protect a whopping £80m worth of assets. Trainees' day-to-

Chambers UK rankings

Banking & Finance • Construction • Corporate Finance • Dispute Resolution • Employment • Family/Matrimonial • Partnership • Real Estate

day experience of family law tends to be 'assisting on files rather than having overall responsibility for any,' but client contact is plentiful. One source told us of the excitement of working on 'a really high-value divorce, which involved leading counsel from London.' The hybrid seat in Knutsford gives a broader view of private client practice and 'more of a high street experience.' In Knutsford – once home to English novelist Elizabeth Gaskell and now one of Cheshire's many up-scale villages and towns – clients seek advice on wills and will disputes, family trusts, care home problems and mental incapacity.

In each department, mid-seat reviews are conducted by the supervising partner and the training partner. They are 'really just a chance to let the partners know if there is anything you would like to do that you haven't yet had a chance to try.' More formal end-of-seat appraisals are for dotting i's and crossing t's.

Commuters' fare

Trainees are encouraged to spend time in at least two of the three locations. Despite being aware of this policy from the off, some of our sources found the prospect of moving offices 'extremely daunting initially, mainly because of the costs and time associated with the travel.' They concede that 'everyone gets used to it and it does help you to see the firm as a cohesive whole, which is a key aim for the new managing partner.' The firm is 'getting better' at supporting people through the process of moving, as it 'makes sure it tells us in plenty of time – whereas in the past it was all quite last minute.' Nevertheless having to stump up the money for monthly train tickets weighs heavily on the pocket and many feel 'the firm could give us some sort of travel allowance when we have to work in a different location.' Indeed trainees questioned the level of their salaries, suggesting: 'We could be paid a bit more. For the size of firm this is, and the firms we compete with, they are perhaps lagging behind a bit.'

All three offices enjoy covetable centre-of-town locations. The Manchester branch is right off King Street and the Liverpool branch is on the waterfront opposite the Liver building, which makes it 'easy to pop out for lunch with friends.' Each has its own 'distinct character.'

Knutsford is arguably the most unique, as its clientele is 'much more likely to drop into the office from the street, rather than making an appointment.' While happy to sample the Knutsford experience, our sources were overwhelmingly fans of Manchester and Liverpool. As one put it: 'Most people prefer to be in the bigger cities as the offices and the social life are more vibrant.' Of the two, Manchester is 'slightly newer and more dynamic.' It is also open plan throughout, 'which makes it easier to ask people for help when you have a problem.' By comparison Liverpool is 'a bit more old school as the partners sit in their own offices.' This perception also impacts on the hours that the trainees work in each location. 'In Liverpool you can pretty much guarantee that you will be out of the door by 5.30/6.00 pm, in Manchester the workload seems more demanding and everyone stays a bit longer.'

The spice is not right

Moving from office to office does 'dampen the social life a bit as people often have a longish commute home to think about.' Trainees do try to organise events at which they can all meet. These are usually co-ordinated by the trainee representative (clearly an important figure) and the firm is generally happy to make a contribution to the cost. In our last edition we reported on a raucous Christmas party at which trainees and some of the partners dressed up as Spice Girls for a mock game show. Sadly (or not, depending on your view) there was no repeat at the last party. 'The firm has recently been getting professionals in rather than laughing at the expense of trainees.'

All our interviewees had a strong connection to the North West, and being rooted to the region certainly seems to be something that the firm looks for. 'It is proud of the fact that it is a North West firm and that it has a number of big regional clients… it looks for a similar attitude in its trainees.' Beyond this, our sources recognised 'there is definitely a type of person the firm goes for. The training partner refers to us as having the Mace & Jones personality.' And that is? 'Not someone who sits quietly behind the desk. They like people who are up for a bit of a laugh, who will work hard, but who are outgoing and you could sit in a pub and have a drink with,' explained one source. 'It is not just about academic brilliance' or going to a good university; the recruiters like people who've built up skills and knowledge in other careers or who have spent time paralegalling, especially 'if they have something they can bring to the firm and the work they will do later on.' One last point trainees wanted to make is that the recruiters are not simply interested in applicants' work experiences but also 'what goals they have achieved in their personal lives.' In 2008 four of the five qualifiers were offered jobs and three stayed on.

And finally...

For North West applicants who hanker after a broad-based training, decent hours and good client contact in a very pleasant mid-sized firm, Mace & Jones is an attractive option. Be sure how you feel about a potentially lengthy commute though.

Macfarlanes LLP

The facts

Location: London

Number of UK partners/solicitors: 75/155

Total number of trainees: 53

Seats: 4x6 months

Alternative seats: Secondments

Extras: Pro bono – Cambridge House, LawWorks, Bar Pro Bono Unit; language training

> Not only are the trainee retention rates consistently impressive but the firm engenders such loyalty that many stay on for their whole career.

While other law firms worry about brand image and market positioning, it's steady as she goes at Macfarlanes. This firm proves that quality never goes out of fashion.

You'll go Macfar

The Macfarlanes ethos can be summed up in one word, and if you haven't already guessed, it's quality. This idea is 'drilled into trainees from day one,' but it's not something they tend to boast about. A Macfarlanes lawyer is more likely to take pride in the fact that the firm is 'not too flashy and not too into its own corporate branding.' And yet you'll rarely meet a lawyer or a client who doesn't admire this firm for its work ethic, good conduct and excellent product. Chambers and Partners recognised this fact when it chose Macfarlanes to receive its award for Excellence in Client Service in 2008. We're sure they were congratulated many times over at the glitzy ceremony held in Barcelona, but we'd also like to add our own slap on the back from the *Student Guide* team. Clearly being way smaller than the magic circle firms proves no obstacle when it comes to keeping major clients happy. These include Allied Irish Banks, B&Q, DC Thomson (publishers of *The Beano*), ING, JD Wetherspoon, Pizza Hut, Royal Mail, Red Bull Racing, Reebok, Umbro and Virgin. Together with the others who instruct this polished firm, they helped Macfarlanes earn £110m last year.

Macfarlanes has a reputation as an old-fashioned kind of partnership that's loath to change anything that still works. That's perhaps a little unfair, as we have several updates to report this year. For starters, the firm recently moved into a shiny new office (although admittedly much of the workforce remains in 'shabby' ones). Lawyers have also been getting to grips with a new digital dictation system that is being trialled. And this year marks the end of an era as, following its conversion to LLP status, Macfarlanes now has a formal written partnership document, rather than relying on a gentleman's agreement as in the past. Trainees do know the firm is perceived as 'conservative with a small c,' but where that might be a weakness in other firms, at Macfarlanes it is viewed as a strength. 'We have a cohesive identity,' said one. 'We could have easily buggered off to Canary Wharf when we moved offices, like other firms have, but we don't want to be Clifford Chance, or something we're not.'

Number crunching

It's that gentlemanly, traditionalist, attitude that shapes the image of Macfarlanes as all pinstriped suits and old-school ties. Is this justified? Trainees say not: 'They just want the best people, whatever shape or size.' Time for some number crunching, then. Looking at the 54 trainees who were beavering away at the firm in 2008, 24 were Oxbridge-educated. Breaking this down even further, 67% of the second years were from Oxbridge, but only 27% of the first years were. When we conducted our interviews in May 2008, just under 15% of the partners were female; at trainee level the girls fared better, accounting for 42% of the group. At that time 98% of trainees were white. You can make what you will of these figures; our judgement, for what it's worth, is that while it has a bit to do yet, Macfarlanes is making a definite effort to widen access. To its credit it is now one of 13 City practices sponsoring the CSET summer scheme designed to encourage students from outside the top universities to consider law.

If you want to look at trainee personalities rather than backgrounds, a good place to start would be on the firm's website, where mini-biogs (and photos) of the entire group are provided. In terms of a common denominator, our contacts felt that 'an overarching attribute is the ability to take on, and relish, responsibility.' In some cases this starts even before the first day on the job. Recalling the vac scheme, one interviewee told us: 'I was sent off to the library to do some research for an afternoon. I came back, the partner cast an eye over my work and then rang the client. It was different from the other firm I went to, where I just got things to flick through between presentations.' Such early responsibility can be 'nerve-racking.' Trainees stress that 'you're not expected to know everything, but it is expected that you'll learn fast.'

That's the spirit

In a four-seat system, corporate and property are compulsory. After that, trainees are free to choose their seats, with many ending up in the litigation, debt finance and private client departments. Secondments to 3i are available, however anyone hoping for international travel should steer clear: Macfarlanes isn't that type of place. We're told that 'training is taken extremely seriously,' and the whole process is described as 'very structured, with a training programme for the whole six months set out when you arrive in a seat.' Since everyone shares an office with their supervisor, they are well looked after on a day-to-day basis, with supervision gradually decreasing as they find their feet.

Mergers and acquisitions is what it's all about in the corporate department. And in case you were in any doubt, corporate work is the beating heart of this firm. Last year's major coup was securing the custom of French spirit manufacturer Pernod Ricard for its £4.5bn buyout of Vin & Sprit from the Swedish government. Other recent deals include French transport company Norbert Dentressangle's £254m takeover of Christian Salvesen; and Heidelberg Cement's £8bn takeover of Hanson (the sand and gravel merchants, not the boy band). Trainees also find themselves in the thick of private equity deals. 'You get a lot on your plate quite quickly; I was on a pretty big private company takeover within a week of starting,' said one. Macfarlanes is renowned for having small teams on deals, which means trainees 'get the best work the firm can give you.' No one is 'hidden away;' instead they are 'constantly on the phone to clients,' helping run board meetings or spending time in clients' offices. Coupled with this is the more tedious document management and due diligence: looking after data rooms, proof-

Chambers UK rankings

Advertising & Marketing • Agriculture & Rural Affairs • Banking & Finance • Charities • Competition/European Law • Construction • Corporate Finance • Dispute Resolution • Employment • Environment • Financial Services Regulation • Franchising • Fraud: Civil • Intellectual Property • Investment Funds • Media & Entertainment • Pensions • Planning • Private Client • Private Equity • Real Estate • Real Estate Finance • Real Estate Litigation • Sports Law • Tax

ing documents and producing bibles. There's no escaping the hard slog of grunt tasks.

A property seat gives trainees the opportunity to get 'a mixture of work from the whole department.' One of our sources told us: 'My bread and butter was due diligence, looking at leases for large investors, or for companies that own lots of property.' The firm has been representing B&Q during a dispute with its landlord at a Bournemouth shopping centre over a defective car park, which meant the entire shopping centre was closed at short notice over the entire Christmas and New Year period. The problems are such that the car park will have to be demolished and rebuilt, and B&Q and other tenants in the centre are negotiating with the landlord over loss of earnings. There's some high-end conveyance work that trainees see through from start to finish, including the 'dreaded' scenario where 'you have to buy a house for a partner.' No pressure then. Also offered is the chance to take a seat in more specific areas within property. Until recently the planning team had been allowed to wither after the loss of a partner, but it's recently undergone a revival after, unusually for Macfarlanes, a couple of lateral hires. It's now an 'interesting, active area,' and one in which trainees can handle files of their own.

Virgin worth

The top-notch private client practice is an accident of history as much as anything else: Macfarlanes was originally founded as a private client firm and simply kept it up 'through the hard times and the good.' The long-standing nature of the practice means there are 'families we've advised for ever and ever,' although it has moved with the times and is a now a 'cutting-edge' outfit that attracts mega-rich non-doms in need of complicated tax advice and clever places to stash the cash. A constant stream of work trickles through from other departments. 'A lot of our corporate clients run their private lives like businesses,' said one trainee. 'We can offer the company director everything – give him pensions advice and write his will for him.' One client name that has somehow found its way into the public domain is Sir Richard Branson. Is he their major private client? As far as Macfarlanes is concerned, 'there is no concept of major clients.'

The successful litigation team does a good job of showing trainees how disputes progress. 'I sat in on most of the client calls, prepared file notes and e-mails to go out, and I was involved in a big debate at a case management conference,' said one. That wasn't all: 'I was involved in negotiations and prepared witness statements and applications to court.' About the only thing trainees rarely cover is advocacy, which is hardly surprising given the size and length of most disputes. Well-known clients include Anheuser-Busch, Barclays, Kentucky Fried Chicken, Umbro and Reebok.

Kings of the castle

If you are used to a collegiate system at university you'll recognise something similar at Macfarlanes. It certainly has an intimate atmosphere and 'once you've rotated through four seats you know practically everyone in the firm.' When it comes to social activities, employees prefer to be left to their own devices. Firm-wide drinks happen about once every six months and 'there's no three-line whip to attend.' Mostly trainees organise their own nights out, which inevitably start at The Castle, a pub described as 'infamous' by some and 'a sh*theap on the corner with a certain charm' by others. When the firm does organise something big, it really pushes the boat out. The summer ball every four years is spectacular – there was one imminent at the time we spoke to trainees, so you'll have to check back next year for the gossip. Keen sports people can sign up for football, netball and cricket, and many of the trainees are active in the group that organises fundraising events for charity.

Once it's got its hands on someone, Macfarlanes doesn't like to let go. Not only are the trainee retention rates consistently impressive – 24 out of 25 in 2008 – but the firm engenders such loyalty that many stay on for their whole career. 'I don't really like the idea of working somewhere else,' said one trainee, sounding queasy at the very thought of having to leave. Fortunately, that's not something to worry too much about, as the firm prefers to promote from within. Some trainees did sound a word of caution: 'They still have this model of earning your spurs; seven years and then they decide if they want to make you up or not,' said one. 'These days more people want to have a life as well as a career. If the firm simply promotes the associates who are most hungry, they run the risk of losing good people who want more of a balance.' That said, the hours are not unreasonable for the City, with 8.30am until 7pm about average.

And finally...

No nonsense, just excellence. Macfarlanes doesn't have to make a big fuss about being the best; it just is. A contract here offers everything a seriously bright trainee could wish for: a great selection of seats, a secure and welcoming environment, responsibility by the bucket load, and always that unwavering commitment to quality.

Manches LLP

The facts

Location: London, Oxford, Reading

Number of UK partners/solicitors: 58/75

Total number of trainees: 20

Seats: 4x6 months

Alternative seats: Occasional secondments

With a new office in Reading and well-respected commercial capability across a broad range of sectors, there's more to this grand old dame than meets the eye.

For a well-balanced mix of commercial and private client work in a comfortably traditional setting Manches is a good bet. Just watch out for some of its sharper, cutting-edge clients.

The ties that bind

Manches is a family firm in more ways than one. Since it was founded in the 1930s it has been home to three generations of Manches. Brother and sister Louis Manches and Jane Simpson, the founder's children, are currently the firm's London managing partner and chairwoman. A third generation Manches works in the litigation department. And yet the firm isn't afraid of changing when necessary: it completed a small merger in 2005 and lately made several senior lateral hires. With a new office in Reading and well-respected commercial capability across a broad range of sectors, there's more to this grand old dame than meets the eye.

First-year trainees are generally allocated family and real estate (encompassing commercial property, property litigation and construction), as these are the biggest departments. Second-years choose from commercial litigation, corporate, employment and IP/tech/media. Be aware that construction is only offered in London, and secondments to London Underground can be taken by both Oxford and London trainees.

The name Manches is synonymous with the crème de la crème of family law, and this department has yet again been ranked top by *Chambers UK*. Over the years the department has acted in some of the leading divorce cases, including that of Beverley Charman, who received a massive £48m divorce payout from her insurance magnate husband. Thus far it is the largest award in UK divorce history. Everyone from guru Jane Simpson to the humblest of new trainees is 'expected to cross every t and dot every i,' and the combination of 'frantic, deadline-conscious' colleagues and 'pressure' to maintain the department's reputation makes this team 'a very exacting place to work.' Trainees are generally given less responsibility than in other departments, although this at least allows you to 'absorb what's going on around you.' Not that 'spending a whole week doing 12 hours of photocopying every day' is what you'd call a valuable learning experience.

Lest you imagine family trainees chained to the copier, know that there's also plenty of 'preparing papers for counsel and drafting simple documents.' The seat teaches that the personal aspect to family law is just as important as the legal. 'When a client starts crying there's always a moment when you think, 'Do I keep taking an attendance note?'' Luckily, trainees can rely on the presence of a partner who is 'completely capable and used to seeing this sort of thing on a daily basis.' Proof that a fat bank balance is no protection from the stresses of divorce, trainees are sometimes required to be the reassuring voice on the phone: 'Family clients ring up a lot because it is so personal to them.'

Zeitgeist

Led by the indomitable Louis Manches, the property department represents an impressive list of retailers, banks, developers and investors, including French Connection, Gap, Jigsaw, Pizza Hut, Anglo Irish Private Equity, Merrill Lynch and Persimmon Homes. Last year the team advised long-standing client WHSmith on the franchise agreement to open Post Office outlets inside its shops. Taking a property seat early is perfect as it's 'good for learning the basics of how all the firm's systems operate.' Trainees are able to quickly take responsibility for files, even if some other aspects of their day-to-day work is repetitive. Although Mr M 'doesn't have much contact with trainees at work,' he is easy to find at client events and trainees are always eager to capitalise on the chance to 'have a beer with the boss.'

The other departments, although smaller, hold plenty to interest a new lawyer. The litigation team, led by trainees' favourite Clive Zeitman, has deftly stepped into a gap left in the market by the biggest law firms, which can't act in disputes against major banks because of conflicting interests. Manches' newly created banking litigation team has already advised on some impressive finance sector disputes, including BNP Paribas' multimillion-pound tussle with Lloyds TSB over the administrative receivership of Hibernia Foods. The team is also acting in a claim against two Iraqi ambassadors over their alleged breach of fiduciary duty to a business partner. One smitten trainee enthused: 'It's so exciting never quite knowing what's coming next and having to make tactical plans.'

Corporate trainees muck in on 'AIM listings, takeovers and smaller M&A.' For them it's 'the usual due diligence and disclosure, which is pretty basic and mechanical but means you can get stuck in.' Even in this seat, the hours are usually manageable: 'We don't have a Freshfields culture of working until 2am, but the week up to completion is always manic.' The team has attracted some interesting new clients, including Kurawood, which sells organically hardened softwood as an environmentally sustainable alternative to hardwood flooring. Manches is particularly adept at providing licensing advice to gaming clients like Goldbet Gaming, the company responsible for the most fruit machine/betting terminal arcades in Germany. It also advises Telegraph Media Group in relation to licence applications, compliance issues and the international dimensions of its Fantasy Football and Fantasy Cricket games.

Constant advances in digital media give trainees in the 'boys and their toys' technology, media and IP department the thrill of 'seeing the law develop as you look at it.' They get to work with impressive clients such as Endemol, Universal Pictures, Telegraph Media Group and Darryn Lyons' photographic agency Big Pictures. On offer is a variety of contentious and non-contentious IP work, including trade mark disputes, design rights issues and copyright advice. Typical tasks include 'writing memos to clients about podcasting or new European directives' and

Chambers UK rankings

Banking & Finance • Corporate Finance • Dispute Resolution • Education • Employment • Environment • Family/Matrimonial • Information Technology • Intellectual Property • Licensing • Media & Entertainment • Real Estate • Real Estate Litigation • Retail • Social Housing

conducting pre-litigation research into 'what people have got away with so far.' Trainees might even find themselves at a TV studio, adjudicating a game show like *Golden Balls*.

Social networking

Manches is 'still very old school at its heart,' say our sources; for example there's no dress-down policy and things feel quite hierarchical, particularly in family, where 'you have to be aware of what you're saying and who you're saying it to.' Some people expressed a slight disappointment over a perceived separateness between departments, however 'new blood is coming through' and there are rumours of a 'reshuffle' to make the departments more cohesive. It's important for trainees to get to know people in the different departments as this benefits them in their quest for a job on qualification. Said one source: 'It's not as if they say, 'Now is the time to start networking,' but if you don't talk to people behind the scenes you do struggle.' Of the 12 2008 qualifiers eight took jobs with the firm, half of them going into the family department and one qualifying in Oxford.

Manches' West End location is 'brilliant,' even if the offices are 'getting a bit crowded.' The firm occupies two and a half floors of an impressive eight-floor building on the Aldwych, surrounded by theatres, hotels and hordes of tourists and students from the nearby London School of Economics. Trainees join colleagues for 'informal drinks at least every Friday, if not other days of the week,' at local hangouts like Pagliacci's and Bierodrome. These are a 'great way of getting to know people in other departments,' which could come in handy at qualification time. If you're feeling especially ambitious, partners can sometimes be found sampling the vintages at Daly's Wine Bar. The firm organises the usual summer and Christmas parties, as well as the 'amazing' Manches Cup sailing regatta, which is one of the high points in the legal sporting calendar. 'It's ridiculous to see Manches' name on Linklaters' boat. It makes you proud.' Our interviewees kept the details of the 'wicked' assistants' ski trip to the French Alps under wraps, except to reveal that although aimed at trainees and assistants 'a few partners snuck along and hoped nobody would notice.'

Bande à part

The distance between the London and Oxford offices is 'not just geographical.' Each has its own client base, and at trainee level interaction is pretty much limited to the initial induction. The two or three trainees recruited to Oxford each year are generally allocated their first two seats. Second-years can then choose from corporate, litigation, property, employment and tech/IP seats. Secondments to tech/IP clients are sometimes also available.

The IP team in Oxford mostly works separately from London, and it deals with more patent and publishing work because of the nature of its Oxford clients. These include the JRR Tolkien Estate and Oxford University Publishing. The team is also big on biotech matters, an area best suited to those with a science degree as the many R&D clients 'want to talk to someone who can relate 100% to what they're saying.' A seat in the corporate department involves 'drafting ad infinitum and a lot of company secretarial work.' In the experience of one source at least, rather than champagne, completion meetings offered only the odd 'cup of tea and a biscuit' and corporate meetings can be 'a bit deathly.' Litigation and property seats went down well though, perhaps because trainees felt they had greater responsibility. Property incorporates commercial deals and projects, as well as the work of the highly rated social housing practice. The department is quite close and staff have been on punting trips together. Mostly the Oxford office's social life is fairly sedate, as 'a lot of people don't live in Oxford and there's only a rubbish Beefeater pub nearby.' Manches has done what most of the big Oxford firms have and located itself in 'a bland business park' on the ring road. Wisely the partners make the most of their proximity to the dreaming spires by holding the annual summer and Christmas parties in the grounds of an Oxford college.

Oxford trainees sometimes find the lack of structure to their training programme difficult. 'There is a certain vagueness to the whole thing,' said one, perhaps referring to the varying levels of supervision. With any luck an increased HR presence in the office should help. On the flip side, being part of such a small group means trainees are 'treated like proper fee earners.' For now, Reading is 'a convenient outpost,' mostly used by Oxford partners and assistants. If the work is there it will be grown, but don't hold your breath for a trainee vacancy any time soon.

There's more than one non-Brit among Manches' current trainee ranks, and almost all have 'done something else along the way' before starting, whether it be another career, further study or simply travelling. People arrive via good universities and seem to be the type who appreciate the importance of social graces. The best advice we heard from a trainee was to 'learn how to fix a photocopier and where to find food at two in the morning.' You may not want to brag about them on your application form, but such 'down-to-earth' skills will be much appreciated by your colleagues.

And finally...

A distinctive firm full of 'big characters,' Manches appeals to those who want to sidestep the hardcore City experience in order to try a more classic style of legal practice. If the statement that 'Manches will always be Manches' makes you sigh with relief not despair, this might be your firm.

Martineau

The facts

Location: Birmingham, London

Number of UK partners/solicitors: 48/100

Total number of trainees: 20

Seats: 6x4 months

Alternative seats: None

Extras: Pro bono – various projects

> Many trainees spend an additional four months in a favoured department, usually taking their final seat where they plan to qualify.

Quietly industrious Martineau has a lengthy pedigree: its roots go back to 1828. This caused one of our interviewees to fret that it had become 'the forgotten firm' of Britain's second city. With its broad practice and wealth of seat options it certainly shouldn't be.

Martin (no Johnson)

Martineau – until last summer Martineau Johnson – has 'a reputation any firm would be proud of.' It is known for its solid and reliable service in a host of practice areas. If that makes it sound like just another bog-standard commercial law firm, you must understand that the firm's main strengths are its niche areas. To be specific we're talking about Martineau's expertise in the education, private client, charity and energy sectors. So concerned is the firm to stress this last area, its website has a climate change portal complete with a brief history of the West Midlands' manufacturing industry and a rundown of the science behind global warming. As well as advising long-term client National Grid on services and gas metering issues, Martineau has accepted instructions on a range of green projects and initiatives from recycling to renewables. Energy clients are now responsible for around 10% of the firm's turnover.

Last year proved a good one for Martineau as profits shot up 48%. Signs point to steady improvement, 'if not taking-over-the-world type growth,' and according to the 2008 AGM, an increase in revenue from the IP and banking teams offset the effects of a 'fairly stagnant' property market. At the same 'really theatrical' meeting the firm revealed an immediate rebranding, something that came as 'a complete surprise to most people.' The meet-

ing was on a Friday. By the following Monday management had rolled out a new website, dropped its Johnson and subtly changed its logo to show three 'i's, which apparently stand for integrity, inspiration and innovation. We spoke to trainees in the days after the changes and reactions were mixed. Some were doubtful of how committed the firm would be to following through on its good intentions; others were upbeat, seeing it all as 'indicative of management trying to move forward, embrace change and engage employees a bit more.' Some had clearly been won over by new business cards, mugs and chocolates.

Martineau's plans for the future centre on growth and receiving new instruction across the entire range of its practice, although 'maybe not crusading like some other firms that are constantly merging.' Our sources thought management would 'stick to the tried-and-tested formula that's kept the firm going.' More ambitiously, Martineau is looking to recruit some lawyers into its small London office and is 'forging links with people internationally.' Managing partner Bill Barker has been elected to the chair of Multilaw, 'a worldwide network of Martineau's preferred law firms' and the senior partner 'spends a lot of time meeting delegates from places like China.' Asia is a particular target as the firm feels it can become 'a core part of team-based projects on a reasonably big scale in those markets.'

A scoop full

A pick and mix of seats is offered to trainees, who complete six four-month stints. Education is 'one of the main sectors' and these clients instruct several departments. Martineau focuses on the higher and further education markets and its clients include Oxbridge colleges, law schools, Warwick University and pretty much every other university in the West Midlands. The education team's range of work is immense: in the past year alone the lawyers handled mergers (eg between Aberystwyth University and the Institute of Grassland and Environmental Research), financing and refinancing deals, allegations of racial discrimination and harassment, and submissions to the Information Commissioner on behalf of a research university resisting requests from animal rights activists. No wonder *Chambers UK* ranks this as one of the best firms in the country for education clients. Our sources say the seat is 'largely research-based,' but also spoke of opportunities to practice drafting skills and meet clients or respond to their one-off queries.

The private capital and charities team is another strong group. The lawyers advise on tax planning, trusts, wills and probate for 'some incredible, extremely wealthy individuals.' This makes things all the more interesting when trainees are 'going to meetings on an almost daily basis.' Furthermore, 'without a doubt it's the nicest team in the firm.' When it comes to clients with charitable status, Martineau advises the likes of the Diocese of Birmingham, United Hospitals Birmingham and Christian Vision, a West Brom-based organisation that hopes to spread the word through radio stations around the world.

All trainees are required to complete a property seat. The department has been pretty busy and worked on £1.5bn worth of deals last year. As well as acting for banks like Lloyds TSB on property refinancings, the team helped Suffolk College on a major redevelopment of its Ipswich campus and Barnet College in relation to campuses across the London borough. Recruits told us: 'Property does lend itself quite well to having a decent amount of control over your own files, and there's more potential to get trainees involved.' Trainees still need to do 'some rubbish chasing' of paperwork, but these activities are countered by the opportunity to try their hand at drafting leases.

Martineau likes its trainees to do a corporate seat, and this can be satisfied by four months with the funds, M&A or banking teams. One source suggested that 'a better name for corporate finance would be the private equity team,' as this type of deal accounts for much of the group's activity. Martineau worked on 15 private equity transactions in 2007 with a combined value of £61m. The corporate

Chambers UK rankings

Agriculture & Rural Affairs • Banking & Finance • Charities • Competition/European Law • Construction • Corporate Finance • Debt Recovery • Dispute Resolution • Education • Employment • Information Technology • Intellectual Property • Pensions • Private Client • Private Equity • Real Estate • Real Estate Litigation • Restructuring/Insolvency

department as a whole advised on over £1.8bn worth of deals. Clients include PR company Freshwater UK, which instructed on a £10m IPO on AIM, and NASDAQ-listed telecoms provider CTI Group.

Nice one Heather

Trainees were generally satisfied with their seats, although some grumbled about getting 'a lot of the grunt work.' Said one: 'There's a reasonable opportunity for an enthusiastic person to get beyond that and get involved with more interesting and challenging and engaging things, but you'd have to put yourself out a bit.' A seat in banking, where the firm represents Lloyds TSB, AIB, RBS, Alliance & Leicester and Nationwide, is one 'without the stress of running your own files but with enough responsibility to keep you on your toes.' Universally popular with those who've done it is the banking litigation seat in Martineau's London office. In such a small office 'you're expected to pull your weight' and the hours can be longer than those in Birmingham. One of the real highlights is appearing before High Court masters in small chambers' hearings, and trainees particularly praised the 'absolutely brilliant' supervision from head of the London office Heather Leeson. 'She is so on the ball and she's willing to invest the time in you and sees your potential.' The other London seat is property-based, with some commercial work. Secondments come with a 'fantastic' rent-free flat just a short walk from Tower Bridge, travel expenses and a salary top-up. No wonder one source 'went to work every day with a big smile on my face.'

Aside from banking litigation there are other ways to get contentious experience. Property litigators handle a lot of landlord and tenant disputes (such as claims of security of tenure following threats of eviction) and a fair bit of work for education clients. There's very little court time or personal advocacy experience, but recruits get to sit in on mediations and hearings. The commercial litigators tackle breach of contract claims and insolvency matters for a clientele that includes npower, ArcelorMittal and the Solicitors Regulation Authority. Trainees are 'largely left to get on with' a portfolio of small claims. The reputation of the 'ever-so-popular' employment seat is 'improving by the year,' and we're reliably informed it 'feels like a good time to be moving into it.' There's a lot of crossover with the education team when advising on the implications of mergers or defending institutions against claims of unfair dismissal.

New thinking

A trainee's experience varies according to their supervisor. Despite the odd tale of individuals with 'explosive personalities,' the open-plan seating means you can always find work from people and, ultimately, 'you'll have a decent time in any seat.' Many trainees spend an additional four months in a favoured department, usually taking their final seat where they plan to qualify. The qualification process came in for some criticism this year, as trainees felt the requirement to submit a formal application, regardless of whether or not the position was contested, was 'over the top and unnecessary.' Several found the procedure stressful. Whether or not because of this, the retention rate in 2008 was down on previous years – only four stayed on out of nine.

Martineau has been making a real effort to improve internal communication. Trainees get appraisals halfway through and at the end of their seats, and there are associate-level mentors with 'an allowance to take you out for lunch a few times.' Clearly a popular system, 'there are more people volunteering to be mentors than there are trainees.' At trainee meetings concerns can be voiced and tips passed on about how to get the most out of seats, and the open-plan office means recruits regularly 'meet people to trust and confide in.'

Whatever Martineau looks for in its recruits, a connection to Birmingham isn't top of the list. Our interviewees had come from all over the country and told us: 'Once you fit the Martineau mould, you're in no matter where you're from.' Trainees describe themselves as ambitious and hard-working, but also 'willing to do things for other people' and definitely not 'snooty.' Most recruits have taken gap years or are a little bit older, and the firm 'doesn't just look for straight 'A's, but maybe someone who has different experiences or new ideas.'

Get me out of here

In a lot of ways, the firm is generous to its trainees and generally they 'never have to pay a penny for the LPC.' Unfortunately some sources felt their salaries could be higher, although when we spoke to HR about this they suggested any differential between Martineaus' and other Birmingham firms' was due to the timing of reviews. On the other hand, trainees' hours are very reasonable, allowing a work-life balance not achievable at some larger Birmingham firms. 'By 6pm on a lot of nights a large proportion of the desks are empty – they don't really seem to try to get a pound of flesh out of people.'

Trainees are 'usually out in force' at social events, perhaps because 'there are partners willing to put their arm around you and tell you you've done a good job and buy you a drink.' Breakfast events in the swanky client suite serve as an extra incentive to be on time, and earlier this year the social committee organised a well-attended pub quiz. The Christmas party – held in January – was at Villa Park last time, though 'thankfully it wasn't football-themed.' Martineau likes its trainees to involve themselves with the Birmingham Trainee Solicitors Society and pays for tickets to balls and other events. The BTSS also organises a lot of sport and Martineau recruits don't let the side down. Various efforts are being made to improve the firm's slightly staid image, and the partners are apparently leading the charge by getting involved in a host of charity events. According to our sources, a slave auction to raise money for the Burma Cyclone Appeal saw legs waxed and partners dressed in pinnies pushing the tea trolley. A round of 'I'm a Partner Get Me Out of Here' featured some of the bigwigs eating dried insects.

And finally...

'We've got so much to offer,' promised the trainee who'd feared that Martineau was being overlooked. The firm has a huge breadth of options for trainees and its integrity is a big pull. Birmingham bound but don't want to end up somewhere huge? Martineau definitely deserves consideration.

Maxwell Winward

The facts

Location: London

Number of UK partners/solicitors: 22/37

Total number of trainees: 7

Seats: 4x6 months

Alternative seats: Potentially secondments

> A trainee who doesn't need to be spoon-fed at every opportunity is going to do much better in an environment where you're not going to have someone patting you on the back every five minutes.

Created from the 2007 merger of Winward Fearon and Maxwell Batley, this small London firm is still in transition. Unsurprising, considering it has a new office, a new training structure and ambitious new plans for its future. All that said, Maxwell Winward is far from unsteady on its new legs.

Laying down a Winward anchor

The Maxwell-Winward marriage brought two complementary practices together. On one side stood 20-year-old Winward Fearon, a well-known and successful West End construction specialist; on the other Maxwell Batley, a 110-year-old City firm with a noteworthy reputation in real estate matters. The combined firm now works in five practice areas: real estate, construction, dispute resolution, corporate/commercial (including employment) and projects. Of those, real estate and construction are the most dominant departments. The former counts British Land, Hermes, Thames Water, Stadium Group (the developer of land at the former Arsenal FC ground), BP Pension Fund and HM Duchy of Lancaster among its clients, while the construction team represents the likes of Barratt Homes, Hochtief UK (one of the shortlisted bidders for the construction of the London 2012 Aquatic Centre), Kier Construction and UBS.

Said one trainee: 'We're not the kind of firm that has deals on the front page of the *FT* every day,' and yet Maxwell Winward does have grand ambitions. Tantalisingly hinted at in a desire to recruit trainees with the ability to speak Russian, Maxwell Winward's international aspirations have come to the fore. New partners have joined the firm – one with a great deal of Russian work – and it hopes to develop its relationships in the Middle East and Germany. In the past year even quite junior solicitors have visited Berlin, Egypt and Thailand.

Building up

The Maxwell Winward training contract is essentially a revamp of the old Winward Fearon scheme, as Maxwell Batley hadn't recruited trainees for years. A source admitted this 'was a worry for us when we merged,' as there was some concern that the Batley side would think trainees were 'just glorified photocopiers.' Luckily, such fears proved unfounded and in fact the training scheme has been given a shot in the arm since the merger, with the annual intake increasing to three or four. There are now four distinct seat options – real estate, construction, coco/projects and dispute resolution – each department hosting a new trainee every six months. One interviewee speculated that one of Maxwell Winward's ambitions was to offer 'a complete service to its clients' and this seat programme may reflect such an objective.

When Maxwell Winward was created, 'commercial property initially took over the ethos of the firm' as it was the biggest department. Already it seems like the construction practice is 'fighting back' and it can certainly claim to be the vanguard of the firm's plans for the future. In the construction seat, trainees are exposed to both contentious and non-contentious work and can expect 'quite a steep learning curve.' Although the partners are 'good at explaining the basics of how things work,' as a recruit much of the time you're 'pretty much left to your own devices.' Described as 'traditional trainee tasks,' photocopying and bundling duties are a reminder that it's a rare small firm that has a legion of paralegals and reprographics staff. Thankfully the trainee's remit also includes plenty of drafting of consultancy agreements, appointment documents, warranties and so forth. Client meetings are always an eye-opener, as is the trainee's introduction to the world of adjudications. 'The beauty of adjudication is that it's quite quick so you can really get involved with it.' And speaking of getting involved, the department encourages trainees to join and attend lectures given by the Society of Construction Law.

Shed loads of property

In real estate, as in all other departments, trainees sit with a supervising partner or senior solicitor. The team handles acquisitions and sales, property finance and development, joint ventures, landlord and tenant matters and portfolio management, and our parent publication *Chambers UK* is certainly impressed, placing the firm highly in its real estate rankings. On behalf of British Land, the lawyers sold Castle Vale Shopping Park in the West Midlands for £90m and re-jigged lease arrangements at the Orbital Shopping Park in Swindon to accommodate Comet, Homebase and Marks & Spencer. In the specialist area of property funds it has made a splash with its work for Hermes on the settling up of a £500m 'big shed' fund, and the lawyers were recently appointed to the panel of the Norwich Property Trust fund, the UK's first authorised property unit trust. Not wanting to leave the international business to construction lawyers, the real estate team has lately advised South African and Danish investors on £30m and £250m worth of deals respectively.

Following the merger, coco and projects have been combined into one seat. On the corporate side trainees can expect to get stuck into drafting, but whereas on property deals 'you'd use a precedent more,' in coco trainees often find themselves drafting 'bespoke agreements.' The seat will also expose trainees to employment law and some surety issues, such that they 'finish coco with a broad overview of commercial matters.' Among the deals handled were the merger of two fruit storage and packing businesses to create the largest such operation in Europe and the sale of London Children's Practice, an independent provider of specialist pre-school, day and residential schools for children and young people. The projects aspects of the seat encompass high performance bonds, PFI/PPP (including projects relating to tunnelling, motorways and bridges), and matters for clients in the energy sector.

The work of the dispute resolution group reflects Maxwell Winward's real estate leanings and covers landlord and tenant disputes, leasehold enfranchisement and professional negligence, as well as more mainstream commercial disputes. This seat can leave trainees with 'quite a lot of admin work,' especially in enfranchisement cases. Still,

Chambers UK rankings

Construction • Real Estate

one source revealed that over the course of a property dispute, they 'got to go to the trial basically on my own.'

Maxwell vineyard

We asked our interviewees if Maxwell Winward had established a new identity post-merger. 'We're still looking to really develop it,' thought one, recommending we wait and see. Some things haven't changed though: 'In the past,' said one recruit, 'Winward Fearon tended to take older trainees, people with a gap year, longer degrees.' The firm still looks for 'someone with more life experience than just having gone through university,' indicated another, although the firm itself suggested this was less important a feature now the firm was expanding. A trainee 'who doesn't need to be spoon-fed at every opportunity' is going to do much better in an environment where you're not going to have 'someone patting you on the back every five minutes.' Furthermore, Maxwell Winward trainees are often 'from good universities, but not so much the Oxbridge type,' which is 'generally true of the firm as a whole.'

Although trainees are 'made to feel very welcome' and monthly gatherings in the office have made things 'quite sociable,' the nights are 'not amazingly well attended.' A recent office move has meant that there's not yet a favourite local, but it shouldn't take long, as there are 'so many bloody pubs' around Ludgate Hill. Even so, 'there isn't a huge drinking culture at the firm.' Instead a social committee organises events such as bowling, karaoke, paintball and an annual golf day, 'which was good fun if you play golf.' The Christmas party was also praised highly. 'A lot of people made an effort,' despite the fact that the old Winward Fearon practice of theming the event was lost in the merger. Our thanks to the source who let slip that one of the partners owns an Australian vineyard, 'so he always brings a few bottles of his home brew and we all get royally drunk.' No drinking culture indeed.

Better suited

Certain small-firm benefits have survived the recent expansion. Work hours are one of these. The typical trainee day begins by around 9am and is usually finishes around 7pm, which might not impress those looking for their contracts outside London, but must look awfully tempting for someone considering the City. Generally, 'you're not asked to stay and work ridiculous hours,' but 'if you're more interested in a department you naturally take on more work.' There is no formal system of telling trainees which positions are opening up for qualifiers, but 'everyone talks to each other,' so word gets out anyway. Both of the 2008 qualifiers stayed with the firm. Of course there have been some teething problems following the merger, mostly to do with incorporating 'two different ways of doing things across all levels.' One source suggested the firm 'take the bull by the horns more and let everyone know which standards we're working to.'

On the whole, trainees seem to be reaping the rewards of the alliance. Electronic resources have been greatly improved – 'now we have an on-site IT department,' said one clearly relieved source. By far the most popular change has been the new office on Ludgate Hill. Not only is it 'probably a better location' than tourist-clogged Covent Garden, it's 'well fitted-out' and 'much swankier.' Open 24 hours a day with security, you no longer need to 'leave at 9pm and lock up after yourself.' The change is more than aesthetic, as the new location 'raises expectations' for trainees. 'The idea that you're in new premises affects the way you work,' said a recruit. 'I've worked later in this office.' Perhaps it has something to do with being 'surrounded by people in suits instead of tourists' when you exit the office.

And finally...

With the doubling of trainee intake and broadening of the scope of expertise, all agree that the birth of Maxwell Winward was a great idea. It's an ideal pick for driven, practical-minded people who are happy to get stuck in with real estate and construction clients in a smaller-firm environment.

MAYER · BROWN

1*

The day that you will count as a vital part of our firm.

When you are a trainee solicitor at Mayer Brown, you are more than just a number. We focus on giving you the one-on-one attention, support and opportunities you need to succeed in the legal world.

For more information on trainee solicitor opportunities at Mayer Brown visit: mayerbrown.com/london/careers/gradrecruit

Alternatively, get in touch with Maxine Goodlet, Graduate Recruitment Manager in London
E graduaterecruitment@mayerbrown.com

Mayer Brown LLP

The facts

Location: London

Number of UK partners/solicitors: 118/190

Total number of trainees: 62

Seats: 4x6 months

Alternative seats: Overseas seats, secondments

Extras: Pro bono – RCJ CAB, Toynbee Hall Legal Advice Centre, Islington Law Centre, Fulham Legal Advice Centre, Liberty, LawWorks and others; language training

There are around 25 different seats to choose from, which means something to suit most tastes, so long as they're commercial.

As one of the biggest firms worldwide, Chicago native Mayer Brown has 1,800 lawyers in the Americas, Europe and – after last year's merger with Hong Kong firm Johnson Stokes & Master – Asia. JSM added seven offices from mainland China to Bangkok, proving that expansion is the name of Mayer Brown's game.

London stirrings

MB London is the lovechild of UK all-rounder Rowe & Maw and Windy City playa Mayer Brown & Platt, which got it on in a 2002 merger. Yet, it is anything but an American brat: 'Before we merged this was an established English law firm with an English culture. A lot of people from the old Rowe & Maw are still here so the culture is still English.' Even if a sizeable London-based US contingent and opportunities to work Stateside mean life isn't entirely tea and tiffin, the survival of this character is in no small part due to the presence on the global management team of influential vice-chairman and Londoner, Paul Maher, who trainees described as 'impressive' and 'compelling.' It also seems likely that the rest of the firm has no desire to erode the strong sense of collegiality in a London office, whose partnership model and method of remunerating partners has been instructive.

Reflecting on a hefty partner cull in the USA in 2007, trainees suggested 'the firm is streamlining,' adding 'when you want to expand you don't always want to hang on to everything from the past.' As well as the 45 or so being pushed, others jumped, meaning around 100 people left the partnership that year, some apparently encouraged by the lawsuits Mayer Brown has been facing from some ex-clients in the USA. The most talked about case involves the collapse of commodities brokerage Refco, a

sorry tale that led to the indictment of Joe Collins, the former head of the firm's derivatives group. The UK arm's separate LLP structure means it is isolated from any ensuing fallout, so that London sources feel this is a great time for Mayer Brown. 'We opened up in Hong Kong and São Paolo, then we had the merger in Asia – it can't be long before we start going into India.' The prospect of sizeable expansion in London may have been dampened for the time being by the economic downturn, but the benefits of the merger are still coursing through its veins. Roused from the sleepy Rowe & Maw incarnation, impressive new clients and instructions have accompanied a metamorphosis into an international business, which can only be good news for future arrivals.

A finger in every pie

Corporate is compulsory for all trainees and the growing importance of the finance division also makes a seat there highly likely. Mayer Brown provides a classic corporate training, placing recruits within teams of qualified lawyers who work on a range of public and private transactions. 'Each trainee is allocated to a number of fee earners who are their first port of call for work,' so the different seniority and workloads of associates defines each trainee's experience. Recent impressive mandates include acting with Slaughter and May as co-counsel on Akzo

Nobel's £2.7bn sale of the ICI adhesives and electronics materials businesses, a multi-jurisdictional transaction involving Mayer Brown teams throughout the world. Lawyers also worked on the outsourcing of IBM's global proprietary telecoms network to AT&T, a deal spanning 40 countries that was worth an estimated $6bn, as well as steering Unilever through its sale of the Lipton Ice Tea business throughout Europe to Pepsi Lipton International. A 'brilliant team atmosphere – they won't leave trainees there doing work on their own,' means the department is popular. In general, hours are not terrible, although mammoth deals like Akzo Nobel can make for some 'relentless' periods. Late nights are at least made more bearable by free meals and taxis home.

In the finance department 'the intention is that everyone tries everything.' However, depending on the supervisor, some might see more capital markets deals, others more real estate finance, others insolvency, financial restructuring or financial dispute resolution. Being proactive about gaining new experiences is viewed favourably: 'They drilled it into us that they didn't want us to be specialist lawyers.' At a time when the financial markets are in flux, it's no bad thing to keep fingers in several pies. 'We're always trying to look at where the market is going,' explained a source, 'so now we're going to concentrate on building up in restructuring.' The department's clients include AIB, Citi, UBS and Santander, which it assisted on a recent £1.025bn financing.

Deals crossing multiple time zones can mean 'it would be easer to come into work at 11pm and stay until 7am,' but the department treats trainees well. After-work drinks are not uncommon, and an attitude amongst partners of 'not flying off the handle' but 'saying 'let's find the best way of dealing with this,"' definitely 'makes the atmosphere less intense.'

Get that passport!

Keeping their end up, in 2007 dispute resolution lawyers successfully defended BASF in relation to regulatory proceedings over vitamins cartels in the 1990s and EMI in its defence of a royalties claim by The Beatles. Clearly no stranger to hefty commercial disputes, the department can place high demands on trainees and so they often prefer working in the smaller contentious teams where the process of litigation is more apparent. That said, there is scope to learn: 'I did much more drafting in litigation than in corporate,' insisted one source; 'definitely real legal work but, yes, there was also a lot of bundling of documents and disclosure to do.' Predictable busy times and a workload that is easier to manage make for better hours here. Because it counts as a litigation seat while also offering non-contentious work, insurance and reinsurance is super-popular. The team's location in a satellite office on the 31st floor of the Gherkin is a factor in this popu-

Chambers UK rankings

Advertising & Marketing • Banking & Finance • Banking Litigation • Capital Markets • Competition/European Law • Construction • Corporate Finance • Dispute Resolution • Employee Share Schemes • Employment • Environment • Information Technology • Insurance • Intellectual Property • Investment Funds • Media & Entertainment • Outsourcing • Pensions • Pensions Litigation • Professional Negligence • Projects, Energy & Natural Resources • Real Estate • Real Estate Finance • Real Estate Litigation • Restructuring/Insolvency • Tax • Telecommunications

larity. Back in the main Pilgrim Street HQ, a somewhat formal atmosphere pervades: 'You know who the partners are and you think carefully about going into their offices,' whispered one source.

Enjoying the technically challenging 'pure law with your statute books' of tax apparently means 'you have to be a bit geeky.' Games of corridor football and cricket offer light relief. In employment, 'only one of the 14 assistants is male,' and the group is said to 'embrace trainees.' By contrast, real estate can be 'a shock to the system' because 'it's a very traditional department where you're aware of the pecking order.' One source told us: 'Real estate has had a bad press among the trainees and we've had girls crying in the loos at times.' Why? 'Some of the partners are demanding and hard to work for.' Apparently the experience 'separates the good trainees from the really good.' The seat certainly has its fans, especially those who enjoy independence in their work. As well as 'adminny post-completion stuff' on transactions like Canary Wharf Group's joint venture to redevelop offices at Drapers Gardens in the City, trainees run their own files and can be the main contact for those clients.

There are around 25 different seats to choose from, which means something to suit most tastes, so long as they're commercial. Beyond the seats we've mentioned there's pensions, financial services, property litigation, construction and engineering, IP, EU/competition or environmental law, and many trainees go on client secondments for three or six months. There's big news this year in relation to overseas seats, as several more have come on stream. Whereas only not so long ago the only option was Brussels, there's now the possibility of Paris, Hong Kong, São Paolo, Chicago or New York as well.

Deal junkies

Successfully qualify at Mayer Brown and you'll sample the annual three-day October trip to Chicago, bringing together new lawyers from across the firm in glorious contact-developing harmony. It also hammers home, if training hasn't done so, the realities of working in an international organisation. This is a key attraction for sources who chose Mayer Brown because they wanted 'a City training' without the mammoth scale of trainee life at the magic circle or bigger US firms. Said one: 'I don't think it is quite as intense here as at most American firms.'

It's been a busy old time for Mayer Brown in London. In corporate and finance the hours can be 'hit and miss – when there's no work to be done you're out the door between 6pm and 7pm,' otherwise it can be much, much later. Remembering an especially busy phase, one trainee told us: 'At the time I couldn't see myself staying in this career as the hours were too long, then you realise you just have to suck it up.' For self-confessed 'deal junkies' when thoughts of 'holy shit what am I doing in this career?' subside, they find they 'miss the buzz' of the transactional teams and eventually return to qualify into the corporate or finance departments. In 2008, a very healthy 26 of the 29 qualifiers stayed with the firm, 13 of them going into these departments.

Kaplan in hand

Mayer Brown types need to be 'enthusiastic and energetic, with the willingness to be lighthearted at times,' but also 'prepared to work hard as part of a team,' because 'those who do well try to fit in and don't hide away in their offices.' The firm is refreshingly non-traditional in recruiting, with around a third of trainees from non-Russell group universities and plenty of second careerers.

A relatively casual attitude to dress either pleases or irritates, and apart from a small number of 'uppity' lawyers, the vast majority of staff are helpful and approachable. Future trainees all study for the LPC together at Nottingham Law School's London operation, the new Kaplan Law School.

The firm's social scene is good, with the office hosting quarterly drinks evenings and frequent departmental events. Groups of trainees often go out to local bars together and have even been known to jet off on city breaks, while the six-monthly arrival of 'new kids' means trainee socials abound. The approach to playing sports is 'whatever your ability, just turn up,' and there's scope for joining partners in matches against clients. Every year the corporate department challenges the rest of the firm to a footie game.

Leaving the St Paul's area will be wrench, but a new home at 201 Bishopsgate is almost ready and a move to the financial heart of the City makes sense for those who perceive it as 'symbolic of the firm's ambition and the direction it wants to go in.'

And finally...

The downturn in the financial markets might have put a check on growth, but Mayer Brown is in a good place to fulfil its potential. It already offers the same pay as the magic circle, but still manages to retain aspects of its smaller firm persona, not least the ability for a trainee to be 'more of a face.' Just make sure you share its transactional mindset.

- **Vacation vacation vacation:**
Firms just want to know that you care. If you have your heart set on a firm, get on its vac scheme; they're an increasingly important a way to show an outfit you're serious about them.

McDermott Will & Emery

The facts

Location: London

Number of UK partners/solicitors: 32/52

Total number of trainees: 7

Seats: 4x6 months

Alternative seats: Brussels, secondments

Extras: Pro bono – LawWorks, Amnesty International, A4ID, Lawyers Without Borders, Public Interest Law Institute

> Unlike some of its more streamlined American stablemates in London, McDermotts' broad range of seats means it's a more viable option for people who haven't yet made up their minds about the field into which they want to qualify.

Happily defying the stereotype that American firms in London are only interested in colossal transactions, Chicago native McDermott Will & Emery combines its own financial nous with an atypically broad range of practices and some cutting edge-niche work.

Emery broad

Founded in Chicago in 1934, MWE began life as a small tax practice and has now grown into a full-service outfit spanning 15 offices across America and Europe. It has mushroomed in the last two decades – the firm had 150 lawyers on its 50th anniversary and over 1,100 on the eve of its 75th. In London, for the last ten years the firm's strengths have been its employment and IP practices (unusual enough for a US firm), however the number of lawyers working in other areas mean it's never going to be a place with just two strings to its bow. The last couple of years have seen some vertiginous ups and downs in the London partnership: additions to the restructuring, projects and employment groups were offset by the loss of its IP chief, and after MWE lost its head of corporate, it wasted no time in swiping Lovells'. With energy partner Doron Ezickson taking over as office head from employment practitioner David Dalgarno, the firm doesn't look like sitting still any time soon.

The new head of office and an expected change in style makes this 'quite an exciting period.' A Paris office may be on the cards and higher visibility is planned for the London office, which is to be the firm's 'stepping-stone' into Europe. Reflecting on recent departures, however, one recruit sounded a note of caution: 'There's a reluctance to grow too much and take people on for the sake of saying how many associates we've got,' and there's no sense MWE will do anything to jeopardise an environ-

ment where trainees are 'not just one of many, but a person, a colleague.' Indeed, our interviewees couldn't speak highly enough about the training they receive. They sit with associates or partners, who act as a first point of contact, and work flows in 'from every direction.' Recruits do 'nothing even vaguely administrative or secretarial,' and more than one told us they'd been treated like an associate. In small departments where 'everyone knows you by name,' trainees are most definitely 'a part of the team.'

Unlike some of its more streamlined American stablemates in London, McDermott's broad range of seats means it's a more viable option for people who haven't yet made up their minds about the field into which they want to qualify. Trainees can dip their toes into employment, IP/IT, tax, international dispute resolution, structured finance and securitisation, corporate, banking finance (which also includes project finance and energy), pensions and competition. We also heard of trainees being seconded to Brussels and Bank of New York (albeit in London).

More than meets the eye

McDermott's employment team is well renowned – *Chambers UK* ranks it among the best in Britain. Accordingly, it represents some big names such as Nike Europe, Expedia, Coors Brewers, Balfour Beatty and BAE Systems. The sensitive nature of the cases means details have to be kept confidential, but we can tell you the firm acts on multimillion-pound multi-jurisdictional projects and last year won six cases which went to full hearing, including the highest value claim in the Employment Tribunals. Our interviewees reported being 'involved in the substance of stuff' and performing 'roles beyond those of normal trainees.' Much of their time is spent keeping on top of large sets of court bundles, liaising with counsel and drafting contracts, letters and staff handbooks. MWE's broad IP practice, meanwhile, offers trainees a mix of contentious and non-contentious experience, often on the UK aspects of very large global cases. Particularly noteworthy in litigation, the team last year successfully represented SanDisk in a major patent and antitrust case, and CibaVision/Novartis in relation to a patent covering extended wear contact lenses. It also obtained an interim injunction for Nike against a sportsman in breach of a sponsorship agreement and advised Facebook (US) and Bebo (UK) on monetising their social networks.

In 2007 the tax group increased its revenues by over 30%. It advised Lloyds TSB on the tax aspects of the securitisation of a $6bn portfolio of small and medium-sized enterprises, but the group isn't reliant on its transactional expertise. It carries out a lot of tax-led consultancy work on issues such as debt restructurings, funds structuring, and risk evaluation. Invariably trainees won't know the necessary black letter law, so they conduct a lot of research for partners: 'They'll ask you a question and tell you to write a memo on it, so you have to come to a conclusion rather than just copy and paste.'

Entrepreneurial spirit

Dispute resolution is a small department (even by McDermott's standards) headed by the 'extremely approachable' Juliet Blanch, whom *Chambers UK* ranks as one of the best arbitrators working in London. Trainees found they were 'effectively spending 12 hours a day with the client,' attending tribunals and acting as support for the partner during hearings. Typically 'she'll request a document and you go get it.' The client base is quite varied, though particular attention should be paid to the number of instructions the team receives from clients in the energy sector. Structured finance and securitisation may be rude words in the legal market right now, but our interviewees had nothing but praise for the 'very rewarding' seat in this area. It's a photocopying-free zone, as trainees help with initial drafts, get 'involved in internal discussions about the structure of deals' and gain 'a hell of a lot of client contact.' The corporate team predominantly acts on M&A mandates for companies like Nippon Oil and Acolyte Biomedica, and takes an even balance of domestic and overseas-referred work. There's been a bit of flux in the last year. Morale was low after department head William Charnley jumped ship for Mayer Brown, but it was bolstered again with the hire of Hugh Nineham from

Chambers UK rankings

Capital Markets • Competition/European Law • Dispute Resolution • Employment • Intellectual Property • Projects, Energy & Natural Resources • Sports Law • Tax

Lovells. One trainee had a typically pragmatic take on the whole affair: 'Seeing a partner leave isn't a nice thing, but it forces you to be a bit more proactive and get out there. It's the best possible training you can have – it's real life, you're not hidden away from it... Seeing new people come through is equally as interesting and challenging. I think that's why [MWE] attracts a certain kind of entrepreneurial person.'

'Entrepreneurial' is a word that came up repeatedly in our interviews and really seems to be a key tenet of the McDermott character. Our sources saw the choice as simple: 'You either want to shy away and be a quiet trainee or see what it's really about.' Here, 'you have to be a person that tries to make things happen and seek openings.' 'If you really want to make an impression,' confided one, 'McDermott is a good choice.' So does this pioneering spirit mean recruits are left to fend for themselves? Not at all. 'When I first started here,' elaborated one, 'I was eased into it, but if you're capable enough you're given responsibility within a couple of weeks. That's not a scary thing as you're always supervised.' New starters get 'really helpful' integration buddies when they join, and with 'very little sense of hierarchy' in the office, a trainee 'definitely wouldn't feel afraid to step into a partner's office or have lunch with one.' Just make sure you time any big photocopying jobs before the secretaries leave at 5.30pm. The only area in which MWE fell down in our interviewees' eyes was its lack of a formal training structure. With very few lectures on the specifics of practice areas, one commented: 'I feel I'm missing out on some valuable training,' although this is mitigated by supervisors who take the time to explain things to you.

Trainees' work hours vary, with contentious seats providing a more relaxed pace than the transactional practices, which tend to run hot and cold. One source told us that during an especially busy period, 'I think worked every weekend for two months, and though I was usually out of the office by 9pm, I often worked until midnight or 1am.' While in some seats 'you can only do so much before your head explodes,' do tread lightly if you want to knock off at a sane hour when it's really hopping: 'They'd say okay and wouldn't force you to stay, but you may be written out of the deal.' Following a straightforward application process, both qualifiers stayed on this year.

Unpindownable

It's difficult to say what kind of person MWE looks for, given the ostensibly few similarities between current recruits. Some arrived straight after law school while others had 'diametrically different careers before ending up here.' The firm is 'broad minded' about university backgrounds, but academics are important in the sense that a high 2:1 or first is expected and a written test means 'the interview process is more challenging than at other places.' In a small office, personality is obviously important, and we've also learned that the mood among trainees is 'non-competitive' with 'no mini-partners coming in wearing red braces and pinstriped suits.'

All our interviewees had deliberately looked for American firms when applying for training contracts. Explained one: 'They seem to be more meritocratic, less bureaucratic – an atmosphere percolates over from the USA – it's about getting the thing done rather than filling in forms.' Also appealing were the smaller trainee intake and the quality of clients that comes from being part of a large international network. 'There's, what, five trainees here? An English firm with five trainees certainly wouldn't be working on huge deals.' How American does MWE London feel? With most work sourced from the UK, it apparently has the air of an English office, and yet there are still a few telltale signs. The firm makes a real effort to push pro bono work, and the first week of induction for new trainees is usually held at the Chicago HQ, where they have lectures and talks from the partners by day and 'free jollies' by night. One frustrated trainee felt the need to fight against the stereotype of American firms in London: 'People have these ideas from god knows where that US law firms are full of Gordon Geckos wearing two-tone shirts and yelling at each other, but everyone's very friendly here.' Others point out that 'a lot of the American firms are Wall Street corporate powerhouses... but you can't easily pin down McDermott.' True enough, MWE does appear intent on ploughing its own furrow.

A formerly limited social calendar has seen some big improvements in the past year. As well as trips to the pub with partners on Fridays, there's an annual summer barbecue at Corney & Barrow in Exchange Square and a Christmas party, usually held at the Guoman Tower Hotel near Tower Bridge. Quiz nights, curry evenings and the odd racing night fill out the schedule, but if you've got a hankering for more, trainees are given a budget to go out once every couple of weeks. We heard whispers of secret plans afoot to celebrate the firm's 75th birthday, but alas no one was spilling any details.

And finally...

We advise you to keep a watchful eye on partner comings-and-goings, but this is a good fit for someone who wants to be as much a part of the team as a trainee.

McGrigors LLP

The facts

Location: London, Manchester, Scotland, Belfast

Number of UK partners/solicitors: 81/261

Total number of trainees: 24

Seats: 4x6 months

Alternative seats: Scotland, Falklands, secondments

Extras: Pro bono – legal advice clinic in Hackney through LawWorks

Client secondments add another dimension to the seat menu and trainees are encouraged to visit Glasgow, Edinburgh or Aberdeen for a seat.

For over two centuries McGrigors' Scottish roots have allowed it to stand tall north of the border. Now, with an office in England, it's looking to be recognised as a national player.

Kwick off the mark

The firm's move south in 2002 came about following the dramatic collapse of Texan power and communications company Enron. When the worldwide accountancy firm Arthur Andersen became a casualty of Enron's bankruptcy, the legal profession looked long and hard at its relationship with accountants, and those few UK law firms that had flirted with providing joint legal/accountancy services were suddenly forced to reconsider. Accountancy behemoth KPMG wasted no time in dropping its London legal arm KLegal.

McGrigors swooped in and invited KLegal's partners and staff to become the firm's English flag bearers. It was a smooth move that provided the Scottish firm with a readymade office in London and good referral relationships with KPMG. To this day, strong links to the accountancy firm are visible across all departments, but particularly in tax litigation, corporate and employment. Add in work from blue-chip clients such as BP, RBS, O2 and Royal Mail and you can see why McGrigors has been able to establish itself in London mid-market. Its award-winning tax litigation team is pure dynamite and is consequently top rated in our parent publication *Chambers UK*. Partners have arrived from DLA Piper and Berwin Leighton Paisner to boost banking and finance capabilities and, in a move bordering on audacious, the firm has formed a 17-lawyer dedicated capital markets team, spread across its London, Edinburgh and Glasgow offices.

As if that wasn't exciting enough, at the end of 2007 McGrigors decided to open an office in Manchester. It now has a presence in Edinburgh, Glasgow, Aberdeen, Belfast, Manchester and London – that sounds pretty national to us. The Manchester offering will focus on construction, real estate funding, project finance and employment matters; the first full-time lawyer to be installed there was projects partner Nick Ogden, formerly of Addleshaw Goddard. For now, at least, McGrigors is keen to grow on its own, and rumours of it merging with Eversheds have been scotched (if you'll excuse the pun). Trainees assure us that McGrigors 'wants to develop as its own firm and nobody else's.'

It's shoe time

In the four-seat training scheme, everyone must spend six months in either banking or corporate and six in a contentious area such as construction, tax litigation, employment or commercial litigation. Trainees are asked to state their top three choices before each seat and to justify their decisions. 'If you really want a seat you can write an essay explaining why you should get it,' explained one source, although we're not sure it will always work in your favour. Although trainees aren't 'entirely sure how the seat allocations are worked out,' most reported satisfactory outcomes to their bids for placements. Certain seats are harder to get than others. 'Employment has been heavily oversubscribed recently,' noted one source, 'and banking and corporate are always really popular.'

Corporate seats are hectic but worthwhile as 'you get great exposure to a variety of work' on M&A and AIM deals. Lately, the office worked on a spate of AIM transactions including the listings of UK pharmaceutical company Neuropharm and Valiant Petroleum. These two transactions were shortly followed by instructions to float an Indian oil and gas company, the firm's first deal from India. Occasionally the hours are tough ('I finished at 6am and was back in the office for 9.30am that same day… I almost cried'), however the department is a welcoming one, having 'parted company with 'one partner who was mean.' The banking department benefits from 'an impressive client base including RBS, so there's a steady flow of work. Trainees start out with discrete tasks such as registering mortgages and other securities, progress through to managing the long lists of conditions precedent before deal completions, and constantly liaise with colleagues in the real estate and construction departments to get documents in order. 'It's a fantastic place to see how all the departments interrelate.' Client contact is good in both corporate and banking, and those who had already sat in contentious seats noted the difference in attitude: 'In transactional seats they're far happier to let trainees e-mail and speak to clients directly.'

Like banking, the well-respected real estate department permits trainees to be a first point of contact for clients and always has plenty of smaller, trainee-sized pieces of work. 'It's the second-largest team in this office' and 'the variety of work is great, it definitely makes the day go quickly.' Although technically within the technology and commercial department, there is a dedicated O2 team, and if you're an O2 trainee you'll be handling leases and licences for mast sites. Meanwhile, well-heeled readers will be pleased to learn the department recently advised Jimmy Choo on the relocation of its headquarters from Chelsea to Kensington. Most interviewees spoke of 'a high degree of autonomy over files.' These can include residential purchases, which are great at teaching the basics of property practice and client-handling skills. Smart trainees don't show too great an aptitude for mundane tasks because 'if you're seen as being good at corresponding with the Land Registry, for instance, the work will just pile up.' Should a trainee get bogged down, it's up to them to speak up and make sure they are getting the variety they need. 'People do try [to remedy a situation] as soon as you bring it up, so it's definitely worth voicing your concerns.'

Toptastic tax

Despite being the jewel in the London crown, McGrigors' tax litigation team is said to be 'not trainee-friendly.' Some sources were also of the impression that 'unless you're really interested in tax, it's too niche to be of value.' To an extent even some people who'd sat in the department agree: 'Because it's such specific and techni-

cal law, it can be difficult for trainees to get stuck in, and there's more admin than elsewhere.' On the other hand, there's the chance to get some excellent court experience: 'I was involved in a huge tribunal case and was in charge of six-volume bundles, which was pretty major. I would sit through the tribunal, watching them turn the pages of my bundle and praying all the pages were in the right order.' Trainees are encouraged to attend client meetings and business development events in this department, so it's by no means a drudge seat. Indeed, we can only hope the team manages to build as good a reputation among its own trainees as it has with the rest of the profession – it's right up there with the best in the UK.

Of the other contentious seat options, construction litigation involves 'all kinds of proceedings – adjudication, mediation and litigation, and there are some international aspects to the work too.' The small department can be 'absolutely manic, but they're bringing more solicitors in and trying to recruit. If you have to work late, it's impossible to resent it because the team is so lovely.' The commercial disputes seat includes property litigation, insolvency and simple debt disputes, so trainees can manage some of their own files.

March of the penguins

Client secondments add another dimension to the seat menu and trainees are encouraged to visit Glasgow, Edinburgh or Aberdeen for a seat. Someone with commitments down south won't be dragged north of the border against their will, but do make your situation clear from the outset. Those who make the trip 'absolutely love it. You get a really good range of work and I think the responsibility is probably higher. There are more smaller cases that trainees can get stuck into.' McGrigors has no problem filling its Falkland Islands seat either, although our sources were rather mystified by this. 'I'm surprised it's always filled,' mused one, 'but those who've been say it's fantastic. I suppose they join the TA there and go off shooting things or dancing with penguins or whatever it is they do.' The deal is a sweet one: 'The firm pays for flights and gives you a couple of weeks to sightsee afterwards. The work sounds great, and obviously you're earning your London salary out there.' We hear quite a few trainees have expressed an interest in the affiliated Azerbaijan office, although it's not yet an option.

In most seats it's likely you'll work for numerous people and your supervisor won't know exactly what's on your plate. We hear that 'certain supervisors are better than others,' so trainees advocate being vocal: 'If you're feeling overloaded, put your hand up and speak out. And if there's something you're particularly interested in, let everyone know.' It sounds easy enough, particularly in an environment described as lacking in arrogance and with 'no pretentiousness.'

Opinion was divided over the extent to which the London office is influenced by its tartan-wearing big brothers in Glasgow and Edinburgh. 'I think we're pretty independent, and if we were to stand alone it would be fine,' said one. Others disagreed: 'We are making a concerted effort to be seen as a national firm, but Scotland is clearly still the bigger part of McGrigors. It doesn't define the London office, but then the head of HR is in Glasgow. It's little things like that which remind you where the firm's heart is.' Certain departments have closer links than others. Banking, for instance, has a Scottish flavour thanks to major Scottish banking clients, whereas tax litigation and corporate are 'thoroughly London-centred.'

These trainees have 'a good dose of common sense' and note 'the firm seems to be very good about hiring experienced people who are doing this as a second career. We've got an accountant, an insurer and an HR person on board at the moment.' The fresh graduates in the group recommend the vac scheme as 'a great way to get in. They like recruiting people that way and I'd say a majority of new-bies start from there.' Socially, 'there are always drinks on a Thursday or Friday and lots of sports.' Office-wide events celebrate Britain's high days and holidays – St George's and St Patrick's days, Burns Night and Halloween. Burns Night means ceremonial toasts and a ceilidh. Hopefully recent belt-tightening (free lunches were scrapped) won't dampen the party spirit.

A small number of staff in the London property department were made redundant in the wake of the credit crunch in 2008, and only nine out of the 15 qualifying trainees secured positions. 'It was a bit of a shock when they sent round the jobs list. There was only one in corporate and about nine people wanted it.' The corporate vacancies were increased to three, but some of our sources still felt McGrigors had been 'more ruthless than other firms.' It's worth noting that trainees who went to Scotland for corporate seats wondered if this had put them at a disadvantage. 'They tell you it doesn't matter, but if the partners have to choose between someone they know first hand and someone they don't... of course it makes a difference.' We checked with the firm and it assured us it didn't.

And finally...

McGrigors has a lot going for it. Trainees like the 'sense of community' and say 'you're always encouraged to get involved.' Combine this with the plan to improve visibility across the UK and McGrigors is one to consider.

Michelmores

The facts

Location: Exeter, Sidmouth, London

Number of UK partners/solicitors: 38/72

Total number of trainees: 9

Seats: 4x6 months

Alternative seats: None

> With so much change, we wondered if the firm had lost some of its charm. Trainees assure us there's nothing to worry about.

After more than a century of peaceful existence on Exeter's Cathedral Green, Michelmores has undergone a transformation. Its lawyers have doubled in number over the past four years and now rock up to work in a large purpose-built office on a business park. In the words of its trainees, Michelmores has become 'a commercial go-getter.'

Everyone welcome

'I think they're really going for it,' reported one interviewee of the firm's bid for legal stardom in the West Country and beyond. 'Our new office has just been extended because we've outgrown it already, and they're constantly looking to recruit new staff.' A London office, established in 2005, is also going great guns. Unlike some other firms in the South West, Michelmores' plans don't involve mergers; the firm instead favours the organic approach to growth – if you overlook a spot of poaching from rivals that is. Recent additions include Andrew Tobey as head of employment from Bond Pearce, Shivaji Shiva a charity law guru from Russell-Cooke and technology specialist Rehman Noormohamed from Eversheds. Recent client wins include Stroud and Swindon Building Society, the Healthcare Purchasing Consortium and London Procurement Programme Legal Panel (which represents around 130 NHS bodies in London and the West Midlands), Tenovus (the cancer charity) and UWS Ventures (the venturing arm of Swansea University). The firm is also proud of its appointment to the government's Catalist panel, which is a fruitful source of instructions.

With so much change, we wondered if the firm was in danger of losing some of its charm. Trainees assure us there's nothing to worry about. 'It's true it's not a high street firm anymore,' said one, 'but it's still a welcoming, nurturing place, just one that happens to have commercial aspirations.' Another agreed: 'Even with all the new recruits, the aim is to bring in people who fit in with the firm's mentality. Partners are entirely amiable and everyone wants to keep it that way.' Trainees are a similarly friendly bunch, although apart from that they prove difficult to categorise. 'Some are straight through from uni, others are in their thirties, and a few have foreign nationality.' The firm is now much less insistent on recruits having links to the area. Said one trainee: 'My year mostly had connections, but future intakes aren't particularly based here, and some have never been to Devon until the interview.' The crucial thing is that you can demonstrate your intention to stay in the region long term.

You name it, they've got it

The four-seat training contract covers property, litigation, corporate/commercial and private client. Within these departments, there is plenty of variety. Property, for example, includes property litigation and projects, as well as work for developers and public sector clients. The litigation experiences range from medical negligence and family law to construction and IP cases. Those in search of geographical variety can spend six months in the London office, although the private client-orientated

Sidmouth office doesn't take trainees at all. The seat allocation process sounds fair and 'if people want specific seats they have a reasonable chance of getting them.' Anyone unsure of where they want to end up can accept potluck as there are no 'horror seats.'

Commercial property is the biggest department in the firm, so it attracts a fair amount of interest. The team advises numerous government departments, including the Ministry of Justice and HM Prison Service. It recently acted for the Ministry of Justice in a deal with Kier Group to deliver the refurbishment of the new UK Supreme Court, which includes the renovation of the Middlesex Guildhall in Parliament Square. It also acted for the MoD's Defence Estates in the disposal of Chelsea Barracks, valued at a cool £959m. Other prominent clients include The Bank of England, NatWest and The National Trust. It's an impressive client list and trainees can expect 'a lot of very good work.' Research tasks on bigger projects are balanced with 'small files you can run on your own; you get heaps of client contact and can take charge of negotiation elements as well.' We heard glowing reports about the supervision here, and the public sector supervisor was particularly praised for 'really getting trainees involved. Even if you aren't contributing that much, she makes you feel like you are, which is a great ego boost for a first-seater.' The department is a 'positive place to work, studious but welcoming.' Hours are reasonable, although many trainees are happy to stay longer 'to get good work and get it done well.' For others leaving at 5.30pm, 'people aren't checking what time your jacket has disappeared.'

A seat in the 'high-flying' projects department involves 'lots of responsibility, but in a nurturing way.' Trainees draw up schedules of outstanding issues, explain procurement documents to clients and help produce tenders. The seat requires 'spending quite a lot of time in London: we had client meetings there, negotiations and the odd judicial review.' Michelmores is advising HM Treasury and HMRC in respect of their flagship PFI for headquarters in Whitehall. This requires the lawyers to advise on a parallel transaction to incorporate additional service provisions, finance issues, particularly relating to the bond financing, and further documentation governing the impact of changes in working practices. There are many other great projects we could tell you about, were they not confidential.

For better and for worse

In the litigation department, if you show you're capable you will get your own caseload. 'I've got a contentious probate matter which I'm running,' said one source, 'and some smaller commercial claims as well.' Trainees pick up work from a variety of fee earners, meaning subject matter can range from general debt claims and partner-

Chambers UK rankings

Agriculture & Rural Affairs • Banking & Finance • Clinical Negligence • Construction • Corporate Finance • Dispute Resolution • Employment • Family/Matrimonial • Planning • Private Client • Real Estate • Real Estate Litigation • Restructuring/Insolvency

ship disputes to involvency, IP and international litigation. 'Interacting with so many different partners means you learn about different working styles.' Thanks to the credit crunch, the department has been 'intensively busy,' so trainees get 'all the responsibility you can handle.' Timid readers should be aware that 'it's a tough-love kind of department with a fairly macho, 'get on with it' attitude. You have to assert yourself more here than elsewhere, show you want the work and speak out if you have too much on your plate.' It is possible to do advocacy when it's appropriate, and while there is the inevitable bundling, 'disclosures here don't last months, it's more likely to be half a day here or there.'

A private client seat can focus on either conveyancing or general wills, tax and trusts, where trainees can have a stab at coming up with creative tax solutions for high net worth clients. Like litigation, this department seems to take more of a back seat when it comes to keeping an eye on trainees' workloads. 'I had a supervisor,' said one, 'but they didn't really do a lot of supervising. It felt like I was being drip-fed work at times.' Across the board, trainees noted: 'There are better and worse supervisors,' but appreciated the firm was trying to improve consistency. For now, it's probably still worth keeping in mind that 'some people will really guide you through everything and others will expect a bit more initiative.' As for our private client source: 'If I could do it again, I would be more proactive about getting work and being enthusiastic.'

A seat in the London office is 'a fantastic experience because you get to work directly with the partners.' The firm sorts you out with a flat, an Oyster card for the Tube and train tickets back to Exeter once in a while, which sounds like a good deal to us. If, however, you've just bought a house or there's some other reason why six months in the capital would be problematic, 'nobody is forced to go.' While there doesn't seem to be much general crossover between the two offices, the Exeter commercial property team is closely tied to the London group, and 'there are some insolvency specialists in the London office who get involved with stuff down in Exeter.' Looking at the big picture, one trainee noted:

'You are increasingly aware of the London office and the vibe of the firm is changing from the South West to more of a national feel.'

I bet your dad's a thief...

Seeking to promote its changing reputation, Michelmores has put its marketing drive into fifth gear and 'is really keen for all trainees to get involved. There's a huge marketing surge going on across all the departments – lunches, seminars, wine tastings, sporting events, you name it.' Some sources reported a bit of pressure to attend such events, saying: 'You certainly aren't doing yourself any favours if you don't go.' We also heard mutterings that 'you can feel a bit like cheap labour, handing out drinks, etc.' However, most interviewees enjoyed the experience of getting out there and mingling with clients. 'Part of being a solicitor is learning how to market yourself, after all.' Sure, corporate bigwigs can be intimidating if they brush you aside, but in the words of one stoic chap: 'It's much worse being turned down by a woman than a client.'

Time-keeping stats proved another bone of contention among our interviewees. 'I don't like it,' said one. 'All the trainees' hours are recorded on the intranet where everyone can see them, and it does make me feel like I need to put in face time.' For others, it isn't such a big deal, although perhaps that's because they impose even stricter measures on themselves: 'The targets aren't onerous. I choose to work really long hours anyway. When I qualify I want to cruise through the transition, so I'm preparing myself for life as a solicitor.' A wise move given that all four of the 2008 qualifiers stayed on with the firm.

Thankfully, even the most dedicated of trainees have to leave the office at some point, and when they do there are plenty of extra-curricular activities to keep them occupied, particularly on the sporting field. 'I played tennis last night and there's also squash, cricket and football. I must admit, quite a lot of the sport is male-orientated,' reported one trainee. 'There was netball but it was mostly guys playing that as well...' While we hope this changes sharpish, there is at least a gym in the office and the firm gets a personal trainer to come out on Mondays and Thursdays. 'He does classes and fitness assessments and takes people out running at lunch.' When it comes to Friday night, the firm's location at the edge of the city hampers the fun somewhat: 'After-work drinking doesn't happen so much because we all drive home.' Monthly firm-wide drinks similarly 'take a lot more effort than they used to.' Still, there are department away days, involving surfing, blokarting or other 'silly activities in a country park,' and we quite fancied the annual treasure hunt. 'You rove Exeter trying to find clues and end up in the pub afterwards.' What's the prize? 'I don't know! Alas, we've never won...'

And finally...

Despite Michelmores' determination to become a bigger, gutsier player in commercial law, trainees attest to its warm and pleasant culture. Its current size is perfect for good all-round training. 'In terms of experience, you get it all, from blue-chip fancy deals to little straightforward claims.'

Mills & Reeve LLP

The facts

Location: Birmingham, Cambridge, Norwich, London, Leeds, Manchester

Number of UK partners/solicitors: 90/330

Total number of trainees: 46

Seats: 6x4 months

Alternative seats: Occasional secondments

Extras: Pro bono – Free Legal Advice Group, ProHelp, Business in the Community

> Fortunately grand ambitions and growth have not resulted in swelling egos.

Blink and you'll miss Mills & Reeve as it whooshes both up the league tables and up the country. This old firm is on the move and breaking new ground.

Empire building

From its early beginnings in Norwich, M&R ventured to Cambridge in 1987 and became a dominant presence in East Anglia. A relatively small London office was added, focusing on insurance clients, and then came the galloping Birmingham office, which turns ten this year. In February 2008, M&R's latest move was to launch not one but two new offices in Leeds and Manchester. Planting a flag in the North came about relatively easily after the firm adopted Addleshaw Goddard's disowned North West family practice, and in doing so it signalled its desire to be known as nothing less than a national firm. Having shown itself capable of steady double-digit financial growth, M&R now aims to double its revenue in the next five years.

To do this it has identified several areas for growth. As the arrival of Addleshaws' family team suggests, private client services are one area of focus, as are real estate and public sector healthcare law. And just in case that's not enough, the firm wants to tap into the international scene, particularly China. It has established alliances with several Chinese firms, and has already won its first instruction to assist a Chinese herbal remedy producer tie up with a UK university.

Fortunately, grand ambitions and growth have not resulted in swelling egos. Trainees tell us the firm is 'very proud of its Mills & Reeve culture, and is doing its best to preserve it as we expand. Partners don't want us to become some kind of billing machine.' So what exactly is that culture? 'Having spent time in London firms, the difference is stark,' said one source. 'People here are friendly, supportive and most importantly we have lives outside of work. You don't feel like you have to give up your life to get somewhere here. If you try to stay late as a trainee, partners will send you home.' This attitude spans the offices, even if each branch is distinctive in other ways. Open-plan Birmingham, for example, feels 'younger and people are very excitable. With all the lateral hires from other firms, there's a mishmash of culture.' In Norwich and Cambridge, 'people have been working with each other for ages, and it's more structured and academic.'

The firm presently recruits for Birmingham, Cambridge and Norwich and is keen to accommodate trainees who wish to sample more than one office, either to experience a specialist seat not available in their home office or to simply try out a new city. Some trainees enjoy the change so much they end up qualifying in a different office to where they began. In all offices the training contract consists of six seats of four months, with the option to repeat a favoured seat. The vast list of options ranges from the more general (corporate, real estate, family and commercial disputes) to the more specialised (education, technology, planning and environment, regulatory defence and tax).

Healthy growth

Birmingham's healthcare focus spans litigation, general commercial advice, employment, construction and real estate. It serves clients such as Nottingham Healthcare Trust and the NHS Blood and Transplant authority, and was recently reappointed in a joint tender exercise run by Dudley and Wolverhampton City PCTs and West Midlands Ambulance Service. Imperial College London sought advice on the establishment of the UK's first Academic Health Science Centre – a high-profile Blair initiative bringing together academia and the NHS. The office is additionally home to a large private client group as well as experts in construction law. Trainees were unanimous in their assessment of construction: 'It's a tough area of law and a demanding team with very high standards.' Looking back, however, our sources were impressed: 'At the time I was with a tough supervisor, but now I can see he wanted me to be the best that I could be. The partners are perfectionist – every little bit of grammar has to be right. At the time you feel like throwing them out the window, but in hindsight I see I'm technically so much stronger now.' The team runs mock trials and adjudications for clients, using actors as witnesses. 'For a trainee it's great as you get a real feel for the process.'

The employment group is another common stop for trainees. 'You get involved in a variety of work, from tribunals to drafting and analysing contracts.' The team is split into subgroups, one focusing on NHS clients and one on local government. 'The NHS work was fascinating,' recalled one source. 'You have to remember that it's all public money, so when you're defending a claim you feel you're a guardian of public funds. It makes you fight that little bit more.' Adding to the group's charm are 'amazing supervisors and relaxed hours.'

Seats of learning

Despite fierce competition from Birmingham, the Cambridge office remains the largest, for now at least. It is weighted towards corporate/commercial work and is well known for its IP and technology expertise. The IP team receives work from around the country: new private sector clients include innovative hi-tech companies such as Pelikon and GeoAcoustics, and the team continues to act for the UK's top university R&D departments, among them Cambridge University, Imperial College and Nottingham University. Real estate and real estate litigation are also common destinations for trainees. It's best to take a proactive approach in real estate though, as some feel 'it's not the most nurturing place – I was kind of left to my own devices.' As one source explained: 'It's a very busy team and it can be difficult to get supervision when your partner is buried in work.' Some people lamented the mundane nature of certain tasks, while others got 'enough exposure to feel important, but not so much that you don't know what you're doing.' Take the seat towards the end of your contract and you'll 'run files and grant short-term leases and licences. We do lots of work for educational institutions, where the files aren't too big and there's client contact on the phone.'

Chambers UK rankings

Agriculture & Rural Affairs • Banking & Finance • Charities • Clinical Negligence • Construction • Corporate Finance • Dispute Resolution • Education • Employment • Environment • Family/Matrimonial • Healthcare • Information Technology • Insurance • Intellectual Property • Licensing • Local Government • Pensions • Planning • Private Client • Professional Discipline • Professional Negligence • Projects, Energy & Natural Resources • Public Procurement • Real Estate • Real Estate Litigation • Restructuring/Insolvency • Tax

The specialist education team has around 90 higher education institutions on its books and our trainees encountered cases ranging from freedom of information requests to students complaining about their degree classification. The team's connections benefit other departments too: the construction group, for example, is assisting University Campus Suffolk on its new £100m campus in Ipswich and West Thames Further Education College on its £45m refurbishment of its Isleworth campus. Take a private client seat and you'll get work that is 'hands-on and relatable – the subject matter is complex so it never gets boring and there is a lot of client interaction.' The team 'understands that you are a trainee and that you're there to learn.'

Moving on

When the local corporate team from Eversheds joined M&R's plush Norwich office in 2005, it boosted the commercial side, such that it's now a match for the established agricultural and private client teams. Our sources enjoyed their time in corporate, saying: 'It's a fairly big team for Norwich, but the people are supportive. I was thrown in at the deep end because it was incredibly busy, but I was never pressured to stay late.' Indeed, the entire Norwich office has staunch views on hours and 'partners go out of their way to make sure you're not overdoing it.' The corporate team handles all the usual M&A and deal financing and has scored major new client wins recently, including Oasis Healthcare, which is acquiring 36 dental practices. It also advised SPC Group on the disposal of scrap metal recycler Easco to a subsidiary of the giant French-listed company SITA. 'Norwich is less public sector-oriented than the other offices and so there's more pure corporate work.' Trainees' duties include the usual document management and assistance with due diligence. 'By the end I was completely managing due diligence, to the point where I was getting phone calls out of the office asking me questions,' said one satisfied source. That might not sound ideal, but for our trainee 'it proved that I had real responsibility and made me feel highly important.'

Leeds and Manchester currently each have space for one family trainee. 'It doesn't necessarily feel like Mills & Reeve just yet, but it'll get there,' a source confirmed. The team handles some significant cases, so 'there are exciting trials with QCs down in London – you find yourself travelling quite often.' The Cambridge family team is also popular: 'I had a lot of responsibility – I was drafting consent orders, speaking to clients on the phone and attending court frequently.' Across the firm, the practice group is 'hot on the marketing front' and made headlines when it launched a website giving helpful hints as to what to take with you when you first visit your solicitor, and even advice on how to tell your partner it's over.

Trainees say they are happy with the seats they're given, although 'it can get pretty late before we find out what we're doing – sometimes you only get a week's notice.' When we raised the point, HR advised us this would only really happen in in relation to the May seat change due to the need to accommodate those approaching qualification. Trainees say that when seat changes involve moving cities the short notice can be problematic, even if you get a day off work to organise yourself. Our sources were diplomatic on this subject, which left us thinking they must be a relatively laid-back bunch. 'We're confident and approachable people,' one added. 'Work is not the be all and end all, everyone has outside interests and enjoys the social side of things.' Trips to the pub, sports and charity events abound after hours – or at least they do if you're in Cambridge or Birmingham. 'There's a pub next door to the Cambridge office called The Flying Pig – we're familiar faces there,' said one source. 'I play cricket, rounders and football,' chimed in another, 'and there are always environmental activities where you go round digging holes and planting seeds.' The Birmingham Trainee Solicitors Society keeps people busy salsa dancing and wine tasting. We'd say the Brummies consider themselves the epitome of sophistication: 'We're more cosmopolitan than the other offices. It's bars rather than pubs here!' Norwich comes third in the fun stakes. Said one Norfolk-based trainee: 'Most people do their own thing here, to be honest.'

Summer and Christmas parties unite the offices: 'This year we're heading to London for a trip on the Eye and a fancy-dress boat cruise. I think the theme is the Roaring Twenties. Or is it the Forties? It's whichever decade was roaring…' Training courses also bring people together, but aside from this 'the offices do operate reasonably separately.'

And finally...

An impressive selection of seats and locations with tonnes of extra-curricular activities and enough free time to get involved, its no surprise trainees consider Mills & Reeve to be a hidden gem. The more you find out about it, the more impressive it is. In 2008 19 of the 23 qualifiers stayed on with the firm.

Morrison & Foerster (UK) LLP

The facts

Location: London

Number of UK partners/solicitors: 17/27 + 9 US

Total number of trainees: 6

Seats: 4x6 months

Alternative seats: Secondments

Extras: Language training

> Even though much of the bio-science venture capital work comes from the West Coast, most business is UK-sourced.

It's hard not to like a firm that refers to itself as MoFo. The acronym has been toned down in official marketing, but that's not going to stop us from using it. It calls to mind an organisation that doesn't take itself too seriously, even though an annual income of $894m suggests it could.

What the Fo?

San Francisco's Morrison & Foerster grew up at the same time as the city's cable car system and Victorian architecture. It stayed a local shop for local clients until 1974, when it opened in LA. The following three decades saw the firm mushroom, and it now has 17 offices, ten in the USA, five in Asia and one each in London and Brussels. It is celebrated in the States for a warmth and congeniality that befits its West Coast origins. People say it's less 'uptight' than East Coast counterparts. That's not to say its East Coast presence is underpowered – MoFo's New York office has its fair share of billion-dollar deals. And the firm competes with the best in Asia, having been one of the first international firms to break into Japan, and then China.

Though full-service, MoFo is best known for its work in litigation, IP and life sciences. In patent litigation, for example, it secured a defence verdict for EchoStar Communications in an infringement suit that implicated virtually the entire cable and satellite television industry, and its attorneys have written some of the most significant patents in the biotechnology sector, including Cetus/Chiron's patent for a hepatitis C vaccine.

Following its opening in 1980, the London office pottered for a while and then grew in earnest post-millennium. Here, MoFo's practice profile is like a three-legged stool resting on a trio of transactional practice groups: the technology transactions group (TTG), the corporate group and the financial transactions group (FTG). Orbiting these primary groups are smaller teams of capital markets, tax, employment and litigation lawyers. Most work is locally sourced, with the remainder coming via North America and Asia, and true to MoFo form the client base is loaded with technology and life sciences businesses. According to *Chambers UK* the firm has made real headway in capital markets, corporate, venture capital, outsourcing, IT and life sciences, achieving good rankings in all these areas. And the view from the inside? 'We fairly regularly get senior partners from Tokyo or the USA coming over and talking about firm strategy and how London can be involved. I think London has a good level of visibility throughout the firm and I think the firm holds London in fairly high regard.'

Scientific Americans

The life sciences team is responsible for some of the office's biggest instructions, such as an $825m licensing deal for drug researcher Renovo and a $273m alliance between GW Pharmaceutical and Otsuka Pharmaceutical that gives Otsuka a licence to develop and market a groovy cannabis-derived pain-relieving mouth spray. In case you were wondering, this is no biotech boutique: African Lakes, one of Africa's oldest companies, used the lawyers when it sold Africa Online to Telkom, and

Avocent called for help on its $475m acquisition of a multinational software company.

Now three years old, the London training programme came through infancy with virtually no tears. In that time the office has grown substantially through lateral hires, so its CityPoint accommodation at Moorgate is getting crowded. The firm hopes to take more space from Simmons, which occupies much of the building and controls the air conditioning. The plan is to expand by servicing US and Asian companies as they move into Europe and by capturing more domestic business in the IP, life sciences, telecoms and clean technology sectors.

TTG, FTG, CMG, AOK

Trainees complete seats in the technology transactions group (TTG), corporate and either litigation or employment (litigation is more common). Their fourth seat can be taken in tax, the capital markets group (CMG) or the financial transactions group (FTG). There are no overseas seats yet, though we did hear about discussions with the Hong Kong office.

TTG (by far the biggest department) is divided into two halves – outsourcing and life sciences/technology. Lawyers handle outsourcing projects for clients such as Lloyds TSB, Royal & SunAlliance and HMRC, to which they have given advice on the extension and restructuring of its IT outsourcing contract to meet the Chancellor's requirement to reduce annual IT spending by £100m. We wonder who's teaching them how not to lose confidential disks in the post. Other technology deals have included a €350m IT agreement between Amadeus IT and Cathay Pacific Airways, and the National Policing Improvement Agency project to enable police officers to use radios on the London Underground, the significance of which became apparent on the day of the 7/7 attacks.

The corporate team's clear emphasis on science, technology and clean technology clients is reflected in deals such as Avocent Corporation's $475m acquisition of a software company, and energy company KP Renewables' £50m reverse takeover of Island Gas and subsequent readmission to AIM. Corporate trainees love the exposure they get as part of a small team and say they are regularly taken to meetings and 'put in a position straight away where we are a main point of contact with the company.' Their work comes from several fee earners and no one worries about being stuck on verification for months. The seat leaves people 'very happy, although very busy.' Said one source: 'I really had a sense for whole transactions. I may not have been involved in each issue, but I knew about them.' FTG, meanwhile, maintains a broad practice, while CMG, the newest addition to the seat roster, was strengthened last year by the arrival of two Freshfields partners.

Chambers UK rankings

Corporate Finance • Data Protection • Information Technology • Life Sciences • Outsourcing • Private Equity

Our sources admitted the seat went 'a bit quieter' because of the credit crunch. At least this will allow newbies the time to 'do a lot more background learning.'

Litigation has been a small and 'very independent' department. In 2008 managing partner Julian Thurston declared MoFo's intention to build up the practice through the hire of three partners from Irwin Mitchell specialising in fraud, competition, financial disputes, insolvency and asset tracing. Given the shift in the economy, these were smart hires. Litigation seats provide 'a balance between the academic and the practical,' and for one source it was a time to 'quickly start picking up good habits.'

Nice guys do finish first

Despite its small size, the London office 'doesn't have the feel of a satellite of the US mothership.' Even though much of the bioscience venture capital work comes from the West Coast, overall most business is UK-sourced, not least because lateral hires brought domestic clients with them. Said one trainee: 'I don't know what an American office feels like, but this feels very much like an English office. The flipside is that all the systems and processes are top-notch as MoFo is so big in the States.' The hours are deemed 'reasonable,' which usually means quitting at 7.30pm (slightly later in corporate). Working past 11pm or at weekends isn't regular, though as one source pointed out: 'It's the law, so sometimes clients call you at 5.30pm, and sometimes California wakes up and calls you.' People take off as early as they can when things aren't busy, and 'the firm is very much of the opinion that trainees are trainees; they're not going to squeeze you until your eyes pop out.' Trainee salaries match top UK firms; NQ wage slips slightly exceed them. Knowing how hard friends at some of the top-paying US firms work, our sources believe MoFo offers the better deal.

Two evaluations are scheduled for every seat, and a previously underused mentoring programme is now more formalised. However the scheme evolves in future, 'the firm wants to make sure we participate in developing it' and is 'open to criticism.' This is typical of MoFo's 'collaborative' environment, in which 'sink or swim' is an alien concept. Yet this is no cotton wool and hugs kind of place: 'It's up to you what experience you get' and 'there's not a lot of hand-holding.' In London 'the firm doesn't have the level of resources that giant firms have;' instead the focus is on self-reliance and taking advantage of close contact with partners and senior solicitors. 'The partners' offices are just opposite ours so if you have a question it's no problem to go in. And if they go for a drink, they ask if you want to come. It works very well.'

MoFo USA is praised for its open culture and commitment to diversity. It recruits and promotes a healthy number of women and has a number of openly gay partners. In London the majority of lawyers are English and 'there's a good balance of minorities across the firm and quite a large number of black people, which is not true of every firm. They've also got a women's committee, which has started to organise marketing events more targeted for women.' A flat rather than hierarchical structure ensures the lines of communication stay open.

As for the trainees, the firm hasn't quite got a 'specific mould.' Good academics are a must, as are a sense of curiosity and independence, however 'if they've got two candidates, one from Oxbridge and one from another less good uni, but he's a really proactive person who can relate to people, that would count more. They look really for a person who can integrate well, take on responsibility and move fast.' We believe applicants with scientific degrees would get a lot out of this firm. The firm hired its very first qualifying trainee in 2007, and in 2008 one out of two stayed. 'When you qualify you get to go to San Francisco for a week to see the main office,' said one source. Another looked forward to the process itself: 'I won't feel I'm competing with other trainees in the year and I won't have to fill in any forms or mark second-choice preferences. Because of the nature of the office I'll be able to knock on the door of any department head and have a chat.'

Nights out around CityPoint usually end up in Corney & Barrow or 'the awful Rack & Tenter,' and we also heard about trips to 'various nightclubs with partners.' The firm lays on wine and cheese every Friday after work and a cooked lunch on the first day of the month. 'It's good food... today it's Moroccan. We don't have a canteen, but there are two kitchens with big bowls of fruit and biscuits, which is a problem as you tend to take them.' Prizes dished out at last year's Christmas party included flights to New York, and there's an annual ski trip, last time to Morzine in France. Alas we've no gossip to report as 'what goes on on tour stays on tour.' Making no secret of its American sensibilities, MoFo designates the Fourth of July a 'Community Day' and invites staff to spend it volunteering.

And finally...

Still flying well under the radar for most students, Morrison & Foerster hasn't yet blazed a trail on the recruitment circuit. Don't worry about that: if you're attracted to its client sectors or its style of working then try and get onto its vac scheme.

Morgan Cole

The facts

Location: Cardiff, Swansea, Reading, Oxford, Bristol

Number of UK partners/solicitors: 52/140

Total number of trainees: 20

Seats: 4x6 months

Alternative seats: None

The English and Welsh offices recruit their own groups of trainees: applicants plump for one or the other side of the firm and are committed to it for the duration of the contract.

Medium-sized Morgan Cole is a major presence in the Thames Valley and one of the top players in the less-crowded Welsh market. A gulf between the training schemes in England and Wales means it's crucial to pick the right side.

M4gan Cole

This firm came into being through a merger in 1998 between South Wales outfit Morgan Bruce and Thames Valley operator Cole & Cole. After a rocky patch involving partner exits and low profits, the firm has managed to get itself back on course. It now has offices in Reading, Oxford, Bristol, Swansea and Cardiff, which you could say makes it king of the M4 Corridor. Well, almost. Unfortunately, at the London end of the motorway the firm had to close its branch in the capital and more recently it also shut its specialist insurance office in Croydon after it lost its place on AXA Insurance's legal panel. Some of the Croydon lawyers relocated to Morgan Cole's Reading office, which did retain AXA as a client.

Until recently, revenues had remained fairly static over the past few years. This year things looked up and in 2007/08 income reached £32.1m, an increase of nearly 10% on the previous year. In that same period equity partners' profits also jumped by nearly a quarter to £241,000. To get into some of the specifics, insurance and healthcare clients account for 25% of income, and they supply more than bread-and-butter work. For example, the firm recently won a place on the first ever panel for the Human Fertilisation & Embryology Authority. Shrugging off the loss of its employment law practice head to Eversheds in Cardiff, Morgan Cole has just been appointed as an employment adviser on the biggest public sector combined legal instructor in Welsh history. The parties involved include the Welsh Assembly, the Countryside Council for Wales and the Arts Council of Wales.

Meanwhile, the newly opened and already 'very profitable' Bristol office is going from strength to strength. Having started out with just a small corporate team, it is now 'expanding rapidly' and includes a specialist insurance team. Our sources were all rather proud of Bristol's success and happy that it conveniently 'fills in the gap between Cardiff and Reading.' Said one trainee: 'It's been a real asset in terms of having another presence in the M4 Corridor.' For now Bristol is not a trainee destination.

Heads or Wales?

The English and Welsh offices recruit their own groups of trainees: applicants plump for one or the other side of the firm and are committed to it for the duration of the contract. It's not yet clear quite where Bristol sits in Morgan Cole's bipartite structure and – if and when trainees arrive there – it'll be interesting to see to which side of Offa's Dyke the Bristol recruits will face. Perhaps in time this new office will be the thing that breeds cross-office trainee links, but for now a fortnight spent together in an Oxford college for PSC training is about as full-on as it gets. Aside from an annual away day and the occasional trainee-organised outing, geography is an ever-present social hindrance.

Work-related communication is more common and has markedly increased on previous years, even for trainees. If a department like corporate is swamped in one location, lawyers from elsewhere who have more capacity can be summoned to plug the gap. So, English trainees 'could quite often be doing work for the Welsh office' and Welsh trainees habitually find themselves popping to Reading for completions or to meet clients. As each office specialises in different areas there's a limit to inter-office co-operation, but the barrier can now be said to be a permeable one.

In each location, the seat allocation system allows trainees to name up to three preferences for their next seat and one they definitely wouldn't want to do. Secondments with clients are intermittently available, most likely through the commercial department and the English offices. In the past these have included ESAB, a large engineering company.

Leave your cenadwri after the tone

On the Welsh side of the firm, most trainees grew up in the region or came to Cardiff to attend university and/or law school. There's no doubt as to people's patriotism: some staff choose to record their voicemail greetings in English and Welsh. While the majority of trainees live in or around Cardiff, all should expect to spend at least one seat in Swansea. Trainees sometimes indicate a preference not to go there, but often the decision is out of their hands and 'people just do it when they're told to.' An allowance for the rail fare or petrol is available.

The broad choice of seats in Cardiff includes EPB (employment, pensions and benefits), construction, corporate, banking, health, commercial property, insolvency, and finally DMG (litigation), which is a major strength of the firm in Wales. Clients include the Royal Mint, the Commercial Directorate of the Department of Health and the National Assembly for Wales, which has turned to the firm for advice in procurement disputes and claims against pharmaceutical companies and medical equipment manufacturers. Litigators are also busy with matters arising from the ongoing judicial review of the multibillion-pound development of a liquefied natural gas terminal at Milford Haven. Sources told us the DMG seat involves 'a heavy workload from the off,' but 'you're able to bat questions back and forth with the top dogs.' Depending on whether you're in Cardiff or Swansea, the work can range from general commercial litigation to debt recovery.

In relation to corporate deals Morgan Cole is certainly a dominant force in Wales, and this ensures it consistently wins high-quality instructions from clients such as the Welsh Assembly, HSBC, Bank of Scotland and Cardiff University. In short: 'If you want to do big deals in

Chambers UK rankings

Banking & Finance • Construction • Corporate Finance • Debt Recovery • Dispute Resolution • Education • Employment • Family/Matrimonial • Health & Safety • Healthcare • Immigration • Information Technology • Insurance • Intellectual Property • Licensing • Media & Entertainment • Pensions • Personal Injury • Private Client • Professional Discipline • Professional Negligence • Real Estate • Real Estate Litigation • Social Housing

Wales,' the only other credible choices are Eversheds or Geldards. A reputation for public company transactions has seen Morgan Cole assist Tinopolis on the hostile takeover of The Television Corporation and its subsequent AIM re-admission, as well as HSBC on funding for AIM-listed Finsbury Foods' £10m acquisition of various other food producers. Deals handled in 2007 ranged in value from £1m to £100m, several of them for leading workplace services provider PHS.

Right in the city centre, the Cardiff office is 'a mix of old school and new,' of open-plan and individual offices. Friday nights out at the Fat Cat bar will introduce you to 'lawyers from throughout the firm.' Some 40 miles away, the 'lovely' Swansea office overlooks the marina and has 'a very small, close-knit environment.' This office offers seats in DMG and commercial property. As well as commercial property, Morgan Cole is experienced at advising on social housing and represents a number of regional housing associations.

Valley rally

In the Thames Valley, most trainees are based in Reading and take one of their seats in Oxford; a few people do things the other way round. In all cases, travel allowances are available when commuting becomes necessary. Reading offers seats in corporate, EPB and insurance, while Oxford lets trainees try their hand at commercial property, commercial IP, DMG and private client.

Reading's biggest department by far is insurance. It counts Thames Water, Norwich Union and AXA among its clients and took on over 4,000 new instructions last year, a figure boosted by winning the contract for AXA third-party recoveries work. It's 'a really good general litigation seat,' involving property, employer's liability and personal injury claims – all defendant-led, high-volume work. One consistently popular seat is employment, which offers some 'really quite juicy' matters involving 'people saying inappropriate things in e-mails' and the thrills of representing Thames Valley Police in tribunals. Oxford is the place to try private client and family practice, a good area for court experience. The family team specialises in higher value divorces and acts for a number of City bigwigs. One of the lawyers is an expert in farming and cross-jurisdictional cases, particularly those with parallel proceedings in the USA and Australia.

Like most of Oxford's larger law firms, Morgan Cole's office is located out on the ring road near Botley and is described as 'quiet,' maybe even 'academic.' Truthfully, Morgan Cole's Thames Valley heart is in Reading, where staff are split between two offices. There is said to be 'a buzz' about the Reading offices; they are decidedly 'more corporate' than the one in Oxford and benefit from city-centre locations. Apex Plaza's palm-decorated atrium gives it a touch of 'glamour,' while Kennet House (home to most of the insurance team) is friendly but can seem 'dingy' by comparison. Socially there are fairly regular nights out including a monthly curry night. The Oxford office is trying to pick up the pace, though 'you have to make much more of an effort' to go out for a drink.

Yin, yang, flip, flop

We're told that Welsh recruits have tended to be a bit younger, while over in the Thames Valley a greater number of older recruits bring experience from previous careers. Whether this will continue we can't say, but all seem drawn to the prospect of decent work for regional business. Across the various offices, shared values of openness and teamwork mean 'there isn't a culture of them and us.' A dress-down Friday policy across the firm allows 'pretty much anything except trainers and flip-flops, which they don't like for health and safety reasons.'

Even then, 'suits aren't compulsory' during the rest of the week. On arrival, new recruits are assigned a mentor, and while most prefer to deal directly with supervisors who are 'more familiar with your situation,' the presence of mentors at appraisals is useful because they build up 'an overview of your time at the firm.'

Morgan Cole trainees are a sporty lot: they play netball, football, rugby, golf and softball and 'quite a few people run marathons.' Work hours are typical for a regional firm, which means 'there aren't too many late nights,' and 6pm is a standard time to clock off. We did hear a few complaints that salaries were low compared to some other firms in the regions, even so, most of our sources pragmatically accepted that these are 'going in the right direction.'

We were told by one interviewee that the firm wasn't 'training us to leave and go somewhere else.' Indeed it wasn't: in 2008 11 of the 12 qualifiers stayed on. The firm has the final say as to which office they qualify into, though almost all stay in the half of the firm in which they started.

And finally...

At Morgan Cole there are two sides to the coin. Whichever you call, you can expect sound training and good work for regional clients.

A light bulb, an apple and a lump of coal.

At Nabarro, you'll be involved in the real business of business. This commitment to detail is what our clients have come to expect. And it means life is never monotonous.

For a little clarity on our unique process of training in commercial law visit our microsite at www.nabarro.com/graduates

NABARRO
CLARITY MATTERS

Nabarro LLP

The facts

Location: London, Sheffield

Number of UK partners/solicitors: 129/294

Total number of trainees: 70

Seats: 6x4 months

Alternative seats: Brussels, secondments

Extras: Pro bono – LawWorks; language training

> Nabarro has a calm character compared to most firms of its size, and people tend not to push and bark their way to the top.

For years a reliable if low-key mid-market firm, Nabarro is 'sticking its head above the parapet' with a bold new image.

Image is everything

In 2007, realising that it was perceived as 'solid and dependable' but little more, Nabarro Nathanson went in for a facelift. The name was nip-tucked to simply Nabarro and in came a brand new logo that looked like an optical illusion, along with the dynamic slogan 'Clarity Matters' – a promise that the firm would never baffle its clients with legal gobbledegook. The rebrand was so smoothly done, with all the old stationery in the offices replaced overnight, that many from both inside and outside the firm were cynical, suspecting that new Nabarro was simply mutton dressed as lamb. Two years down the line and the trainees have been converted: 'The initial reaction to the logo was 'oh no, what have we done' but it's worked – people now see Nabarro as a totally different sort of firm,' said one. Everyone is still sticking to the new principles. 'There's a new initiative every few months to remind us that it's not marketing spin,' said a trainee, drawing attention to clear-English training, talks from the firm's branding agency, and a YouTube ad starring comedians John Bird and John Fortune that promotes the ethos of the firm. Search for the 'Ungobbledegooked' clips if you want to watch.

Property has always been Nabarro's strongest area: its clients include six of the ten largest British property companies (Land Securities, British Land, Liberty International, Hammerson, SEGRO and Quintain). It has also advised Apple, JPMorgan, Krispy Kreme, Gap, Merrill Lynch, Planet Hollywood, Bank of Scotland and the UNITE Group. While property remains a central practice area (and one every trainee must do a seat in),

Nabarro is keen to enhance its position elsewhere, particularly in corporate. Trainees point out that this part of the business brings in 'an equal amount of income to the property department,' so they must now take a corporate-based seat as well. And due to the current economic climate several other departments, notably insolvency, are 'going absolutely mad' with work.

A six-seat system means most trainees can sample several types of practice before settling down in the one they hope to qualify into. They are usually supervised by a fee earner with at least five years' experience, with a supervising partner keeping an eye on them from above. The two years begins with a fortnight of initiation, at which all trainees are present, before they go their separate ways, most to the London headquarters, some to the Sheffield office. The two groups keep contact throughout the traineeship, each paying visits to the other's patch for training exercises.

Real deals

Despite those assurances that Nabarro isn't just about property (or real estate as everyone in the firm is now being told to call it), the fact remains that with over 150 members, the department is hugely important to the firm's success. Sales and acquisitions of shopping centres have always been a big part of the business, and Nabarro recently advised Land Securities, Europe's biggest property company, on the £253m sale of Whitefriars Shopping Centre in Canterbury and the £105m sale of a 50% stake in an Oxford Street retail block. It also acted for Apollo

Real Estate on a £442m deal for Telford Shopping Centre. Don't be under any illusion that it's all about shopping: there really isn't any kind of property work that Nabarro can't handle.

Such is the importance of the department that around ten trainees work there at any one time. Their experiences vary, with some claiming that 'every day is very hectic,' with 9am until 7pm or 8pm days not uncommon, while others found it 'not massively busy.' That's the nature of transactional seats though. The word 'juggling' is a good way to describe the main activity of a property – sorry real estate – trainee: it's all about keeping scores of different files up in the air and moving smoothly. They assist on larger transactions by putting sales packs together or creating bibles of key documents, while also managing their own smaller deals, usually as part of the asset management programme of a big client. It's a great way to learn how to draft and review leases, negotiate terms and complete transactions.

Nabarro also has a superb property litigation team, ranked among the best in London by *Chambers UK*. It's not the most popular seat with trainees though, as it has a reputation for 'long hours and tough work.' We hear the problem of some partners 'dumping laborious tasks on trainees' has been addressed, so presumably that just leaves long hours and tough work. The team acts mainly for landlords attempting to police (or ditch) troublesome tenants.

Coal seller

Up in Sheffield, the health claims team harks back to the office's previous incarnation as the in-house legal team of the old nationalised mining industry, British Coal. Trainees who try this seat spend four months representing the Department for Business, Enterprise & Regulatory Reform (formerly the Department of Trade & Industry) in respect to compensation claims made by miners for injuries suffered at work: vibration white finger, miner's knee and chronic obstructive pulmonary disease. A scheme to allow group litigation closed in 2005, but the 'hundreds of thousands of claims' that were made before the cut-off date means the team will be busy for a while yet. Trainees can expect 'lots of court time' and plenty of hands-on experience with their own caseload.

Corporate is the area that Nabarro is most keen to grow into, and trainees say that there's 'strong evidence now that we're really pushing forward.' The seat is described as 'very commercial' in nature as 'it's important to be able to see the bigger picture and understand what your client wants.' The team advises on mergers and acquisitions, with the London team recently acting for Sondex Plc on a £289m takeover by GE Energy Services. The Sheffield office meanwhile has worked for UK Coal, advising on the disposal of Maltby Colliery. Big deals involve moun-

Chambers UK rankings

Banking & Finance • Competition/European Law • Construction • Corporate Finance • Dispute Resolution • Education • Employment • Environment • Health & Safety • Information Technology • Intellectual Property • Investment Funds • Local Government • Partnership • Pensions • Pensions Litigation • Personal Injury • Planning • Private Equity • Professional Discipline • Projects, Energy & Natural Resources • Public Procurement • Real Estate • Real Estate Finance • Real Estate Litigation • Restructuring/Insolvency • Retail • Tax

tains of documents so trainees need to spend time verifying information for potential investors and keeping track of all the components of a transaction. Across Nabarro, but particularly in corporate, trainees are encouraged to network. There are regular client lunches and nights out and some trainees have been known to give presentations at client seminars.

As well as looking after major clients of their own, Nabarro's banking lawyers have an important role as 'a support team for the corporate and property practices. In any corporate deals that need funding we'll act for the borrowers, or on property deals we'll assist clients who want to borrow money, say to buy a big office block.' The team has big banks on its books, and up in Sheffield the lawyers act for UK Coal Refinancing. Trainees get 'a pretty good level of responsibility,' drafting security documents and attending to the conditions precedent on which deals rest.

Cheap flights and bluebirds

The commercial litigation team has high-profile clients: for example, a new partner brought Ryanair with him when he arrived from an American firm. Football fans will know that surprise FA Cup finalists Cardiff City have been in a spot of financial bother. Swiss investment bank Langston was demanding immediate repayment of a £24m loan, an action that threatened the club's existence. Nabarro successfully argued that repayment was not due until 2016. Cases mostly settle out of court, as Nabarro (like most firms) is keen on alternative methods of dispute resolution, such as arbitration and mediation. In this seat, trainees may get to try advocacy. 'There is a court rota, and if the clerk who normally appears is unavailable, one of the trainees takes his place.' The employment seat leans towards the contentious, mostly defending employers against unfair dismissal and discrimination claims. Trainees get to attend tribunal and liaise with clients, preparing their witness statements and 'steadying their nerves' on the day of the hearing. Nabarro recently advised Oxford University on its employment of several research teams funded by Cancer Research UK and the Medical Research Council, defended HSBC against a claim for unfair dismissal and sex discrimination by a female financial consultant, and helped Pfizer on a major restructuring which involved the closure of its UK manufacturing plants and several hundred redundancies.

There are several secondments to be had at clients like RAB Capital and Oxford University. Another distant seat is to be found at the firm's office in Brussels. Heavily research-based, this seat puts the trainee in a team that supports all the others by answering any queries on EU law. Since this particular area of law changes so often, the trainee must produce a newsletter every fortnight with updates, which they then distribute both within the firm and to clients. There's no need to worry about feeling lonesome tonight – or any night – in the city of beer and bureaucrats: new arrivals are added to an e-mail list of all the English law firm trainees and meet up with them to party.

Vac attack

Back in Britain, 'there's no Friday night drinking culture' either in London or Sheffield. According to our sources the social scene is 'not too full-on, everyone recognises we've got our own friends outside of work.' End-of-month 'wind-down drinks' are usually well attended, and many people enjoy playing sport together. The football team narrowly escaped relegation from the top tier of the London Legal League last season. The corporate team recently went on a team-bonding weekend in Swanage, while the tax team ran a rather cryptic pub quiz: 'You should have heard the questions. They were very intellectual.' Our favourite activity has to be the *Hell's Kitchen* initiative that ran on Wednesday evenings. A handful of staff and partners took six weeks of cookery lessons and then served up a meal for 50 people, donating the profits to charity. Knowing the firm of old, we doubt whether there was anything like the heat and stress that you'd find in one of Chef Ramsay's kitchens. Nabarro has a calm character compared to most other firms of its size, and people tend not to push and bark their way to the top. Certainly trainees receive a gentle introduction to the firm and buddy events are organised to allow future recruits to meet the people they will work with.

Last year we mentioned that the best way to get noticed by Nabarro is to win a place on its vacation scheme, as it is now the method used to recruit 'nearly all' trainees. This year we heard that applications for the scheme rose from 500 to 940. Coincidence? We'd love to think not, but the firm has been pretty active itself in wooing students at law fairs and the like. Those who do nab a traineeship at Nabarro tend to stay with the firm: in 2008 29 of the 31 qualifiers took jobs, nine going into the property department and ten into corporate and banking.

And finally...

Nabarro attracts students wishing to avoid the excesses of City law, and those who come here tend not to be disappointed. If you hate property law then think twice; otherwise this is a smart choice for a sustainable career in a respected and successful mid-sizer.

Needham & James

The facts

Location: Stratford-upon-Avon, Birmingham, Shipston-on-Stour, Moreton-in-Marsh

Number of UK partners/solicitors: 28/19

Total number of trainees: 6

Seats: 4x6 months

Alternative seats: None

> Our contacts spoke of their peers in the most glowing terms, and it's clear that lasting friendships have been forged.

With offices in Birmingham, Stratford-upon-Avon and two Cotswold villages, Needham & James manages to be a regional commercial player and a high street practice all rolled into one.

City slickers or hicks from the sticks?

Needham & James has graced the West Midlands with its presence since 1956. The N&J website claims the firm was one of the first in Europe to embrace computer technology and trainees say: 'Apparently Mr James was Mr IT in Birmingham back in the day.' The founding partner is still involved as a consultant, but any techie tendencies the firm might once have had don't show in its current practice profile. N&J provides an all-round service, covering corporate, banking, commercial, property, dispute resolution, employment, family, social housing, private client and motoring offences. It also has a notable agriculture team, and is on the panel of firms that advise members of the National Farmers' Union.

The firm has recently splashed out on new offices in all four of its locations, and each one has a very different atmosphere. In Stratford, 'N&J is probably the dominant firm;' by contrast, in Birmingham, despite a prestigious address at One Colmore Row, it's a small fish in a big pond. The difference is reflected in the working practices of the offices. 'In Stratford it's a lot louder walking round. In Birmingham, since competition for work is a lot greater, the environment is more heads-down. You work when you work and you play when you play.' There's no rule that says trainees have to spend time in both Stratford and Brum, but most split their four seats between the two. Likewise, there's nothing to stop them going out to the Cotswolds, where N&J has outposts in the evocatively named rural towns of Shipston-on-Stour and Moreton-in-Marsh. These are mostly dedicated to private clients but also have successful commercial property practices. Actually we've no knowledge of any trainee taking a full seat in either; they do however visit them at least once – 'in your first few days you get taken over for afternoon tea.'

Powered up

In size and quality of work, the commercial property team leads the way. 'The firm prides itself on that, particularly in Stratford,' and in recent years several trainees have chosen to qualify into this field at the end of their contract. The surfeit of junior lawyers has caused the difficulty level of trainee work to drop slightly, though they still get to run their own files, which are sometimes quite high in value. N&J has several blue-chip companies among its property clients, particularly in the utilities sector, meaning that the 'backbone' of the team's work is for National Grid, E.ON and Cable & Wireless. The seat is described as 'varied and busy. You could be doing a lease for a jewellery shop in Stratford one day and then a multimillion-pound deal the next.' Sorting out rights of way for companies provides a lot of work for trainees; the firm also represents a number of major housing associations – Mercia Homes, Severn Vale, Heart of England, Gloucestershire Housing Association – and recently beat several London firms to win a £300m contract for a social housing project for Merton Borough Council.

The corporate seat is called 'M&A' in Birmingham and 'coco' in Stratford. 'Basically they are the same department,' and some trainees spend three months in each. Birmingham first, then. 'I spent the majority of my time on the big stuff,' recalled one source. One of the firm's biggest deals was the sale of a horticultural business to a US firm. The document management falls to trainees, of course, but they also attend every meeting and take on small discrete tasks like preparing shareholder agreements and 'drafting board minutes and Companies House forms.' 'My normal working hours are 8.30am to 6pm,' explained one corporate trainee. 'One day a week it might be a 7pm or 8pm finish. You don't get 2am completions here.' It should also be noted that although trainees record their time to get used to the process, 'we don't have individual targets, which means it is possible to pause for a second and have a chat.'

'If you want an extra nought on the end of the transaction then Birmingham is the place, but if you're not hung up on the size of the deal, the work quality in Stratford is just the same.' Stratford offers an 'out-and-about seat,' where trainees get to meet clients, work on employee incentive or share schemes, do some company secretarial work and tinker with partnership agreements. There's 'a lot of drafting to do, plus due diligence, dealing with enquiries and visiting clients outside the office.' Supervised by Marcus Everett, a partner who is 'everything you imagine and hope a supervisor would be like,' trainees are challenged here. Said one: 'I was implementing a share scheme, which was rock-hard to do. I knew there was no way I was going to get it all right, but my supervisor was happy to spend three hours going through it afterwards.' The team acts for local business and farming clients as well as a few larger companies such as US energy giant ConocoPhillips. It has also landed a role on the advisory panel for easyJet.

Employment is another area where the supervision is praised, and since it's also the department of training partner Andrew Owen, 'lots of feedback' is assured. The team advises both claimants and respondents on contentious and non-contentious issues. Most trainees favour the contentious aspect. 'You get more out of it,' they said. 'It's less rigid, and the approach is very much your own.' 'Companies expect a partner to lead the case,' but when working for claimants trainees can get 'hands-on' experience. 'In discrimination claims there's always a raft of issues and it's a question of picking out the most pertinent ones.' For example, on one sex discrimination case the point that carried most weight was the fact that the employee had worked far more hours than she was paid for, rather than the instances of bullying and harassment. In another matter, one of the firm's social housing clients was implementing a change in the terms and conditions for staff they had inherited from another authority. 'They were moving from the public to the private sector. The

Chambers UK rankings

Agriculture & Rural Affairs • Real Estate

unions were getting involved and the workers were going on strike. We managed to pick a fault in their balloting procedure and derailed their strike action.' Once again, prestigious clients prove the firm is punching above its weight: one notable patron is Marylebone Cricket Club.

Anyone hoping for litigation or private client work won't be disappointed: N&J offers these too. Birmingham's litigation team revolves around financial disputes such as insolvency, while in Stratford they do more general commercial work and 'a little PI.' Contentious probate can be difficult: 'Your key witness is dead so you are up against the wall from the start. It's very much a fact-finding mission.' The trainees also run all the debt recovery files. Other seats are available in banking, matrimonial and social housing.

Girls on top

Anyone reading between the lines of this feature might have picked up on the fact that trainees prefer working in Stratford to Birmingham. One trainee put it bluntly: 'We are treated differently in Stratford. There is a grown-up approach; everyone is on a par. In Birmingham the partners like to keep people in their place.' Others feel this assessment is too harsh, telling us: 'It's just one department in Birmingham.' We'll let you find out which one for yourself, but we did get the impression that the trainees found an undercurrent of office politics somewhat tiresome.

Happily, it doesn't affect relations between trainees. All our contacts spoke of their peers in the most glowing terms, and it's clear that lasting friendships have been forged. There isn't a Needham & James type at the moment, but there soon will be. The trainees in the next two intakes are all female. This is a coincidence rather than a conscious policy decision, but needless to say, 'the boys are all very excited.' Actually there's big news regarding the next two intakes. Due to the downturn in the economy, N&J has deferred its 2008 starters until 2009, with the subsequent year's newbies waiting until 2010. The firm hopes this will ensure everyone gets to experience the full range of seats and that everything will be back to normal by 2010.

The play's the thing

Stratford-upon-Avon is, of course, home to one of the greatest playwrights England has ever known. No, not

William Shakespeare, but the young Needhamite who penned the firm's last Christmas revue. It's the task of the trainees to write and perform this seasonal sketch, which this year was based on Dickens' *A Christmas Carol*. Set in the 'completely fictional, yet strangely familiar-sounding' firm of Jeedham & Names, it featured a poor trainee worked to half to death by a cruel, Scrooge-like master. Obviously, any similarity to persons living or dead was entirely coincidental. 'We were nervous in case we were all going to lose our jobs,' confided one participant, 'but it went down a treat.' Having sneaked a peek at the script, we can confirm that the Bard himself would have been proud – as anyone familiar with *Henry VI, part 2* will know, he could write a pretty mean lawyer joke himself.

All the hopping between offices makes regular nights out as a group difficult. Stratford trainees are also hampered by the fact that most of them drive to the office. 'There's lots of banter, but after work people tend to go home.' Fortunately Stratford is a great place to take a relaxing lunch break, if you can negotiate your way past the swans that patrol the town: 'They chase me!' one trainee whimpered. The Pen & Parchment gives a 10% food discount to N&J employees, a benefit they take full advantage of.

The evening scene is more active in Birmingham, but there's never a set destination. 'We just work out where the partners are going and either follow them or not, depending on what we want to talk about.'

All four qualifiers were offered jobs with N&J in 2008, but only one stayed on. The firm left it quite late to make offers and trainees found other positions while it was procrastinating. Although 'genuinely sad to be leaving,' all three were picked up by top-notch Birmingham firms – proof that in the West Midlands 'having trained at Needham & James carries a certain cachet.'

And finally...

Trainees view Needham & James as a Stratford player with a presence in Birmingham, not the other way around. Choose it with this in mind, and you will benefit from 'a good, varied training that's very client-facing.'

- **It's never too late:** Good news for mature applicants. They are more than welcome in most firms: plenty of our interviewees this year didn't commence their training contracts until they were in their thirties.

Putting you in the picture

Can you see yourself as part of Norton Rose Group? Do you want to be part of the bigger picture? Before you decide anything, you need to do your research.

Our clients are among the world's top corporate bodies and financial institutions and our job is to provide them with world-class legal advice. We are looking for people who we can train to do that.

We need individuals who show ambition and determination and who want an international career. We already have over 2000 people worldwide, including more than 1000 lawyers. The work is hard, but it's fascinating. It's the toughest intellectual challenge you could hope for.

If you can picture yourself as part of that mix, we'd li to hear from you.

Norton Rose Group is a leading international legal practice, offering a full business law service from of across Europe, the Middle Eastand Asia. We are str in corporate finance; financial institutions; energy a infrastructure; transport; and technology. The Grou comprises Norton Rose LLP and its affiliates.

To find out more, go to our website for graduates or contact our graduate recruitment team on +44 (0)20 7444 2113.

www.nortonrose.com/graduates

NORTON ROS

Norton Rose LLP

The facts

Location: London

Number of UK partners/solicitors: 137/356

Total number of trainees: 114

Seats: 6x4 months

Alternative seats: Overseas seats, secondments

Extras: Pro bono – FRU, Tower Hamlets and Tooting Law Centres; language training

> In case we haven't made it clear enough, it bears repeating that finance and corporate deals are what the firm is all about.

One of the City's oldest and best-known players, Norton Rose is in a really positive phase after moving into impressive new digs at the Norman Foster-designed More London development on the South Bank of the Thames.

Following the money

The firm's new office offers a spectacular panorama of London and a spy's-eye view of the adjacent City Hall. 'I used to see Ken in the gym,' said one of our contacts, 'but Boris is keeping a low profile.' The move has boosted morale across the board and trainees have a spring in their step, sensing a bright future despite the credit crunch. Global revenue was up 27% in 2008, and further international offices have been opened in Tokyo, Riyadh and Abu Dhabi, bringing the tally to 23.

While the firm has many respected departments, it is in finance and corporate matters where it really shines. No less than ten individual members of the stellar asset finance team are ranked by *Chambers UK*, which rates the department as one of the very best in the UK. The corporate finance squad is equally highly ranked for its AIM work, and one trainee noted 'a concerted effort to have Norton Rose instructed by as many AIM businesses as possible in the hope that they will grow into blue-chip companies.' The firm has a handful of key clients from the FTSE 100 as well, and major deals from the past year have included China Development Bank's acquisition of a £1.5bn stake in Barclays and HSBC's acquisition of a majority stake in Korea Bank, a $6.3bn deal.

NR has been in the Middle East for longer than most, and so has a head start as other firms scramble for a piece of this lucrative market. 'We've been quite a trailblazer in the Middle East and we have built up good relationships

there. Our loyalty will be rewarded,' one trainee said, perhaps anticipating the importance of established relationships with Middle and Far-Eastern sovereign wealth funds in the tough few years ahead.

Only here for the beer

In case we haven't made it clear enough, it bears repeating that finance and corporate deals are what the firm is all about. Since trainees will probably visit at least two of the nine finance teams in the six-seat contract, it's fair to say that if you don't have at least some interest in these areas then NR isn't for you. However, that six-seat training scheme is 'a huge draw for those wanting choice and variety in their training.' It can lead to some oddities, though, especially since trainees aren't just asked to give their top two or three preferences for their next seat. No, they rank the seats they want in order of preference from 1 to 24 and hope for the best. It may be 'an imperfect science,' but it seems to work most of the time.

Every trainee spends time in one of the corporate finance seats – M&A, AIM and private equity. There is no shortage of big deals; lately NR advised the likes of easyJet on its £103.5m acquisition of GB Airways, Franco-Spanish tobacco company Altadis on an offer by Imperial Tobacco, and Katanga Mining on a $3.3bn merger. 'I'd heard a big deal was brewing and I wanted in on it,' said one interviewee, explaining why they were so keen to do the seat. Brewing turned out to be the operative word: the firm was acting for Carlsberg in a £10.2bn joint venture with Heineken for the takeover of Scottish & Newcastle. 'I sat in the same room as a partner, so I was privy to pretty much everything, it was very interesting tactically,' said our contact. Perhaps surprisingly, 'the hours weren't so bad... except for the last few weeks.' Another trainee started the seat at the time another big deal was going through: 'They said to us, 'We need you to look after the verification, deal with it please,' so I was in at the deep end.' Information verification was something most of our sources had done at some point, along with vast amounts of proof-reading, running data rooms, researching ('conflicts of UK and foreign law'), going to meetings and preparing first drafts of various documents. Perhaps inspired by the Magna Carta (or perhaps not), some departments have a 'team charter,' guaranteeing trainees the right to habeas corpus, trial by a jury of their peers, and not to be given proof-reading without getting something more interesting to balance it out.

It can be a 'dog-eat-dog' world in transactional departments, and naturally that isn't for everyone. Litigation seats cater for 'the thinkers rather than the do-ers.' 'It's real law, the intellectual side of it,' a trainee explained. The contentious teams – including shipping, real estate, pensions, construction, fraud and professional negligence – represent clients in some of the most interesting topical cases around. Indeed, 'one of the joys of the litigation seat is not knowing what will land on your desk next.' How about investigations into allegations of corruption in the UN oil-for-food programme for Iraq, or representing the Italian state in the murky Berlusconi/Mills criminal proceedings? The Italians, you may remember, allege that Prime Minister Silvio Berlusconi paid David Mills (husband of our then culture secretary Tessa Jowell) some £344,000 to help him pervert the course of justice. The firm is also advising P&O Ferries in the criminal trial of an officer of the watch who is being prosecuted for the manslaughter of three yachtsmen by gross negligence. The litigation trainee's role is 'more research-based. It's down to you to get it right: nobody checks up on what you've come up with.' Just as some people can't abide corporate, others don't take to litigation: 'It just seems to drag on, I prefer faster moving deals,' said one trainee, adding: 'I was checking bundles to make sure the print was straight; they could have got a student in for that.' Other London departments that trainees can visit are competition and EC; tax; property, planning and environment; incentives and pensions; and corporate finance, media and technology.

Travel is a big bonus. 'Everyone should do time abroad,' one of our sources enthused, and most of the people we spoke to had followed that advice. Athens, Paris, Moscow, Rome, Dubai, Bahrain, Singapore, Hong Kong and Beijing are just some of the locations on offer, and

Chambers UK rankings

Administrative & Public Law • Asset Finance • Aviation • Banking & Finance • Banking Litigation • Capital Markets • Climate Change • Commodities • Competition/European Law • Construction • Corporate Finance • Dispute Resolution • Employee Share Schemes • Employment • Environment • Financial Services Regulation • Fraud: Civil • Information Technology • Insurance • Investment Funds • Outsourcing • Pensions • Professional Discipline • Professional Negligence • Projects, Energy & Natural Resources • Public Procurement • Real Estate • Real Estate Finance • Restructuring/Insolvency • Shipping • Tax • Transport • Travel

everyone comes back with tales to tell. Our favourite was about the chef in one of the foreign offices who 'would whip us with a tea towel if we didn't eat all his food.' Apart from the obvious attraction of seeing new and exotic locations, many trainees claim the work in foreign seats is 'so much better' than in London. There are 'inevitably a lot more client-facing duties... you could spend a year in banking and not meet a client, but abroad I was giving advice and going to signing meetings.' The workload depends partly on the state of the office at the time and partly on local culture. A Singapore secondment is 'extremely hard work in a very busy office. You are expected to take things on and run with them,' while Paris 'has a completely different pace of life, especially in the summer.' Some trainees wangle a second overseas seat; others opt for a client secondment to the likes of AIG, ExxonMobil and Nestlé.

English rose

Last year a marketing campaign featuring trainees fooling around on vintage scooters was an apt metaphor for the firm. NR is not a noisy, aggressive Harley Davidson, it's a fun, classic, internationally known model. We thought it such a good analogy we were going to use it again this year, until someone compared the firm to a woman – not a high-maintenance supermodel, but a stylish yet approachable woman like, say, Myleene Klass. In a roundabout and hopefully non-sexist way, we're trying to say that NR will never be viewed in the same category as a magic circle firm, but it has a good-looking clientele and an unblemished reputation for its work and its culture. As for Myleene's less-impressive Hear'Say phase, well, NR too has had its underperforming years, but this past year hasn't been one of them.

This is a nice firm with a nice culture. That doesn't mean it's an easy life here – indeed certain partners are known for dumping 'quite obscene' amounts of work on trainees – it's just that the firm has a good understanding of what makes a workplace pleasant. Our sources liked the fact that 'when we've been working extra-long hours the firm will recognise it; we'll get days off in lieu or at the very least not be expected in first thing next morning.' Another thing the firm is good at is helping trainees find a team to fit into long term. The six-seat system allows them to sample a few, to repeat a seat and to work in areas closely related to a favourite seat. Being allocated a partner-level mentor is also really useful in terms of guidance into the complex world of grown-up lawyering.

Having already introduced an alternative career path for those not hoping to become partners, NR has now devised a new pay structure based on performance rather than years of experience. Most trainees approve because 'it stops people getting complacent, which can happen in a place where you're getting paid sixty-something grand as soon as you qualify.' Alas, we wouldn't know…

A sporting chance

NR loves sport. Sky Sports is a fixture in the canteen, and rugby and cricket players in particular can expect indulgent smiles from partners if they need to knock off early for a match. For those trainees who think that bowling a maiden over has something to do with impressing the ladies, other provisions have been made. The office has a music room, replete with baby grand piano, and NR provides subsidised private lessons for staff. Recently, the adjoining park was cordoned off for a family day: though many of our interviewees were mysteriously absent that day, one who was present observed small children covered in face paint 'running around saying 'Mummy, Mummy, is this your desk?' It was very sweet.'

NR trainees are 'normal people you'd be friends with outside of work.' Apparently it's about half and half between outgoing types and the quieter, more academic folk, and we're assured there's 'no weird little geeky chap in the corner' that you might have come across at law school. There are too many of them to regularly socialise together, however you'll see groups dotted around the canteen complaining about the price of salad, and many have adopted The Bridge on Tooley Street as the official NR pub. They do all get together for the annual trainee party, which one of our sources described as 'great fun – it was sad knowing that it would be my last one…' Once qualified, trainees are no longer eligible to attend, but at least they can still hang out with most of their friends: 42 of the 48 2008 qualifiers stayed on. By the way, some advice for those trainees looking to qualify into their first-choice team: 'Don't rely on HR, take the bull by the horns and find yourself a patron within the firm.'

And finally...

Many students hope for a successful career in City law, while still worrying about the City's cut-throat nature and back-breaking demands. Norton Rose's timeless appeal could well be down to the fact that it displays many of the best attributes of City law and few of the worst.

- **Resist the urge to become an expert on daytime TV:** Watching Judge Judy does not count as research.

Olswang

The facts

Location: London, Reading

Number of UK partners/solicitors: 102/216

Total number of trainees: 48

Seats: 4x6 months

Alternative seats: Brussels, secondments

Extras: Pro bono – LawWorks, ProHelp; language training

> The 'Swang is undoubtedly refocusing its energies, but we doubt it will change its character.

Known for its media law savvy, Olswang has successfully diversified its practice and made significant strides in the property and corporate spheres. Now it just has to wait for everyone else to cotton on.

Making your mind up

Back in 1981, the year Olswang was founded, Thatcher was in power, Robert Murdoch purchased *The Times* and *The Sunday Times* for a tiddly £12m, Bucks Fizz won the Eurovision Song Contest and Paris Hilton entered the world a tiny bundle of innocent joy. Our theme here, readers, is that times have changed and so has Olswang. Yes, the client roster still sparkles with technology and media clients (eBay, FilmFour, MTV, Guardian Newspapers), but there is now much, much more to Olswang. In the past five years it has swallowed up a series of specialist property practices, adding substantial real estate capabilities, while senior partner Mark Devereux says corporate has been the firm's largest group for more than ten years. Yet Olswang has struggled to shake off its TMT image. In 2007 it even went as far as to launch a six-month marketing campaign to emphasise its breadth and to distance itself from its boutique roots.

In one sense Olswang makes things difficult for itself: it just won't stop scoring high-profile entertainment and defamation victories that keep it in the headlines. Lawyers recently defended *Jerry Springer: The Opera* in the High Court against accusations of blasphemy, arguing that such a prosecution would contravene the right to free speech. It also triumphed over the Ministry of Justice to secure a High Court ruling for three national newspapers to give the public and the media automatic access to court documents in judicial review cases. That case was brought after the press was initially refused access to court files during the judicial review of the Serious Fraud Office's decision to abandon its investigation into secret payments made by BAE Systems to a member of the Saudi royal family. Elsewhere the firm picked up a new client, Arts Alliance Media, advising it on five deals concerning the rollout of digital cinema for Twentieth Century Fox, Universal Pictures, Paramount, Sony and Walt Disney across Europe.

Would-be trainees take note: future growth in Olswang's business lies elsewhere. In 2007 it appointed Brian McDonnell from Berwin Leighton Paisner to launch its financial services practice and poached tax man Gerald Montagu from Sidley Austin. Internal promotions also reveal the firm's corporate focus, as the department took the lion's share of the latest round of partner promotions. If you're thinking about working for Olswang, base your decision on what it is now rather than what it once was.

Pizza the action

All trainees spend a seat in the corporate department, whether it's private equity/mainstream corporate or tax. 'It wasn't my cup of tea but we have to do one,' was the typical resigned response from our sources. One trainee didn't shy away from saying: 'I pretty much hated it.' These would be the folk who signed up for non-stop media mania. 'They tell us we'll have to do a corporate seat at some point, but most people hope that day will never come.' Those with a better understanding of the firm make the most of the corporate experience. 'The tax team is great,' enthused one trainee; 'there's a lot of research and it can be a bit dry, but the hours are good and your work does go straight into advice and notes for the client, so you do feel it's worthwhile.'

Corporate seats at least land you with work for media clients from time to time. 'I was dealing with telecoms clients and rights management companies. At the end of the day it is the same kind of work though.' We say, why complain when the work's this good: the team recently advised long-standing client Richard Caring, owner of swanky restaurant The Ivy, on the acquisitions of a majority share in private leisure chain Soho House and the sale of the Strada pizza chain. It also acted for communications company Photon Group on a string of acquisitions, the most recent being the purchase of an independent communications planning agency – the intriguingly titled Naked Communications.

Finance is an exciting place to be right now. 'This team didn't exist 18 months ago, it was part of corporate, so it's new and growing fast. It's nice to be part of a group that's so positive about its future.' The department is busy, which means 'trainees get loads of responsibility. They pretty much treat you like a junior lawyer. I've been speaking to clients, drafting ancillary documents and dealing with the other side,' reported a satisfied source. Inevitably it can feel a bit admin-heavy at times, as there are conditions precedent to check, board minutes to draft and people to chase for documents. The hours go up and down like a yoyo: 'When you're not on a deal you're encouraged to leave at 5.30pm. When there's work to be done you can often be there until 9pm or even midnight.' And if, in corporate, you find yourself in the middle of a private equity deal 'it's intense. You may find yourself leaving the office at 10am the next day.'

Property seats allow trainees to take more control of their lives. 'I loved it. The amount of responsibility there is over and above what you'd get elsewhere. You run your own files and have day-to-day conduct of matters.' The department has a landlord-heavy clientele, although there are a couple of big tenant clients, including TKMaxx. 'There's a lot of licensing work as well as corporate support, and towards the end of the seat you can take control of lease negotiations.' A 'relaxed team' and steady work hours make this arguably 'the most fun department in the firm.' Real estate litigation also has much to recommend it: 'You get an overview of how it all works, and the team for one trial was just me and a partner – I felt like an associate.' Other contentious seats include commercial litigation and employment, both of which involve 'some pretty decent High Court litigation.' The employment experience slightly underwhelmed one source: 'There wasn't as much drafting as I would have liked… and you can only do so much because there's so much law to learn.' Having

Chambers UK rankings

Administrative & Public Law • Advertising & Marketing • Banking & Finance • Construction • Corporate Finance • Data Protection • Defamation/Reputation Management • Dispute Resolution • Employee Share Schemes • Employment • Information Technology • Intellectual Property • Licensing • Life Sciences • Media & Entertainment • Outsourcing • Planning • Private Equity • Real Estate • Real Estate Finance • Real Estate Litigation • Restructuring/Insolvency • Retail • Sports Law • Tax • Telecommunications

said that, they admitted: 'As a trainee your exposure across the whole department is good.'

Cannes we go?

The commercial group includes an IP team, a media, communications and telecoms (MCT) team and a competition and regulatory team. MCT lawyers cover Internet, e-commerce and data protection issues, as well as broadcasting, TV, film, publishing and advertising matters. Trainees here can delve into all areas, but film finance is a common source of work. 'There is a debate about whether it's just banking under another name,' confessed one interviewee, 'but for me it really does make a difference that it's about film. It's simply more interesting.' Just as well, as negotiations between financiers and film studios can be 'pretty brutal. There can be huge rushes and I did a few 20-hour days.' On big projects, trainees compose acknowledgement letters and work on sections of documentation. On smaller TV deals 'there's more room to manoeuvre and you can do some of the negotiating.' The team also covers production work, essentially cast, crew and directors' agreements. 'You get to meet producers but you're not hobnobbing with people your mum has heard of.' The group is proud of the films they work on: 'We're all passionate about the end product and there's a real buzz about what you're creating.' And further up the ladder there is glamour – 'The team does go to the Cannes Film Festival every year.'

A few trainees are able to gain useful in-house experience through client secondments, some of them with internet and media companies. Despite a strategic alliance with US firm Greenberg Traurig, stateside seats have yet to appear, but there is a Brussels posting for competition work.

MCT, IP and media litigation seats are 'hotly contested,' even though 'the firm is making a conscious effort not to attract a whole group of media junkies.' Trainees say that while there is still 'a discrepancy between where the firm is going and what current trainees have come here to do,' the message is getting through. 'I wouldn't be surprised if people coming in the next two years are less media-oriented,' said one, although trainees who attend university law fairs 'still feel they spend the whole day saying, 'We're not a boutique anymore!'' Rumours that the firm may set trainees up with not one but two corporate seats each might hammer the message home.

Pasha's fake tashes

The 'Swang is undoubtedly refocusing its energies, but we doubt it will change its character. 'It's not stuffy or based on tradition. There are a lot of young people, and partners aren't upper-class, stuffed-shirted sorts.' 'I can only think of two people I even slightly dislike,' imparted one source generously. Among the trainees there's 'quite a mix of personalities; however, we're all outgoing and have something to say for ourselves.' In the past the firm has attracted people with media backgrounds (including a DJ who was 'a significant player on the hard house scene'). Increasingly it is trying to bring in people who are 'more amenable to the direction of the firm. They tend to be younger and don't have the media background.' In 2008 18 of the 23 qualifiers stayed with the firm.

There's a vibrant social scene. 'Many trainees have lunch together in the upstairs café, and there are Friday pub trips and dinners out.' The size of the trainee group is 'just right – you know who everyone is and there are always enough people who are up for doing something.' The IP department has monthly drinks 'religiously,' while the corporate group 'goes out and gets smashed on a huge social budget. Each party is bigger than the last.' Olswang's Christmas do is 'not your typical black-tie event:' this year it hired club Pasha and went for a superheroes theme. The desire to dress up was far from universal, so we salute the person who suggested having a room full of costumes and face paint at the venue. 'By the end of the night everyone was into it. One of the heads of department was Zorro, complete with an eyeliner moustache.' The biggest social perks are all-expenses-paid departmental weekends away. Budapest, Barcelona and Bruges have all been destinations of choice, 'although the banking team went to Bath this year because they're worried about their carbon footprint.' Eco-consciousness is already evident in the office, where there are areas on each floor with bins for wet waste, dry waste and confidential waste. 'Not having bins in our rooms is good for the environment but a right pain in the butt if you're busy.'

And finally...

While some current trainees have been left 'wishing they'd known the direction Olswang was heading,' future recruits will have no excuses. If you are interested in media law but equally happy to have 'your fair share of late nights and corporate work,' Olswang is ideal.

Orrick, Herrington & Sutcliffe

The facts

Location: London

Number of UK partners/solicitors: 19/33

Total Number of Trainees: 18

Seats: 4x6 months

Alternative seats: Overseas seats

Extras: Pro bono – eg microfinance work

Orrick's international character is reflected in its London trainee group, with recruits from America, Sweden, Italy, Russia, Ukraine, Kazakhstan and a few Brits.

Reminding us that Orrick, Herrington & Sutcliffe's ten-year anniversary in London was approaching, trainees told us: 'The firm has made great progress but there's more to do.'

Meteorrick

Orrick began in the San Francisco of 1863, at a time when the city was flourishing after the California Gold Rush. The firm's website tells the story that John R. Jarboe, one of the original founders, was admitted to the Bar after inviting his examiners for drinks in a nearby saloon. Crafty, yes, but it shows a cordiality that survives today, if our sources are to be believed. 'They're San Francisco, not New York,' said one, talking about more than just geography.

The firm now has offices as far afield as Shanghai and Taipei, as well as considerable swathes of the United States and Europe within its grasp. It all adds up to 21 offices, more than 1,000 lawyers and a devilishly handsome global turnover of $772m, an even higher figure than the preceding year's $666m. Orrick's international expansion has come about through a series of chesslike moves, the most significant of which for the London office took place in 2005 when Orrick scooped up the London partners, staff and trainees of Coudert Brothers, a now-defunct international firm. The following year it was out courting Dewey Ballantine in a very public way. Despite that romance fizzling, the plan for London hasn't changed: the UK capital is still at the forefront of the firm's European operations and there are designs to 'double or maybe triple in size.' There have been important lateral hires and plenty of talk of further mergers. Providing concrete evidence of the desire for growth, Orrick has taken another floor in

its Tower 42 office in the City. Incidentally, the building provides great views of the capital, though 'as it's really high up it takes quite a while to get down.' That's 'a killer' during fire drills, but 'they normally give you ample warning and then you can schedule a doctor's appointment over it.'

The finance countdown

With finance at the heart of London business, virtually all trainees will take a turn within the department. Last year it worked on CDOs for clients such as Goldman Sachs and Citi and closed a high-profile transaction for Deutsche Bank involving the establishment of Europe's first credit derivative product company. It also assisted CompuCredit in purchasing approximately $970m-worth of Monument Credit Card receivables from Barclaycard for approximately $770m. You'd have to have been on the moon, or at least stranded in Timbuktu, to not know about sub-prime problems and the credit crunch. Orrick's finance practice, along with many others, was hit by these problems so it's worth asking one simple question. If securitisation and structured finance have been mainstay activities, how will the firm cope with the loss of business? The answer: 'There's a lot of emphasis on innovation and coming out as stronger firm. My finance seat was right in the middle of everything crashing but we were busy as could be. They think, 'Let's see if we can use what we've done here to solve problems in the future.' We're not just doing plain, mass-produced CDOs, we're doing the weird stuff and cutting-edge stuff.' One source described it as finance with flavour because there's 'nothing plain vanilla about the deals.'

In theory seats are supposed to be split into 'a structured half and a projects half, though there's no sharp delineation.' Trainees who'd worked in the department told us they'd been 'left to get on with things,' albeit under supervision, and one source found themselves 'dealing with bank directors on a daily basis.' They sensed that 'supervisors there are more prepared to delegate complex tasks that stretch and challenge your ability.' Another agreed: 'You are not cannon fodder or just there to do the dirty work. Your opinion is very much asked for, and sometimes you're put on the spot. You have to say what you think but know you're not going to get laughed out of the room.' Being taken out to dinner by the partner every now and then to say thanks is a really nice touch.

Finance-minded trainees can pitch for overseas seats in Orrick's Hong Kong office, where the firm takes good care of its own, arranging airport pick-ups and providing accommodation. There's even an increased living allowance, which 'softens the blow of eating out a lot.' The city has a large ex-pat trainee community so there's plenty of scope for socialising. Just remember, 'they're looking for ambassadors from the London office to send on these secondments!'

Action figures

With various areas of finance slowing down this may be a perfect time for the firm to expand some of its other practices in London. Particular attention has already been paid to the corporate team. Trainees say it has 'doubled in size' in the last year or two and warned us to 'watch this space.' Luring partner Hilary Winter away from Jones Day is a source of great pride: she's 'fantastic, incredible' and 'galvanising the department.' The team has lately advised on the sale of a 50% interest in the Earls Court and Olympia entertainment venues to Liberty International plc and was part of a global deal to achieve the combination of three companies that between them manufacture and distribute *Star Wars*, Disney, Marvel, *Doctor Who* and *Harry Potter* collectibles. Another recent hire was restructuring partner Mark Fennessy from Hunton & Williams.

To clock up necessary contentious hours you can try commercial litigation or international arbitration. These lawyers have represented Vivendi in various multi-jurisdictional litigations and arbitrations concerning disputes with Deutsche Telekom and Elektrim over the control of a leading Polish mobile telecommunications company worth in excess of $5bn. In the UK High Court they also represented UPEK in dispute with IDEX over alleged infringement and invalidity of four fingerprint recognition patents.

Chambers UK rankings

Capital Markets • Corporate Finance • Investment Funds • Social Housing

Orrick's property team has recently expanded and of all the seats on offer it has the most exclusively UK-based caseload. Its key client is Capital Shopping Centres and there's a well-regarded social housing division that pulls out all the stops for long-standing client Notting Hill Housing Group and other registered social landlords. Trainees get into lease negotiations, drafting licences and preparing certificates of title. 'There's quite a well-structured system for delegating work to trainees: you have either one or two direct supervisors, generally including a partner. You usually only work for those people.' The two other seat options – competition law and employment – are both popular.

Our sources told us the way American firms in London are usually portrayed is 'absurd,' and the 'myths' definitely don't apply to Orrick. The working day can easily elongate in finance and corporate seats, but 'if a trainee is efficient and good at communicating they can have a good work-life balance – I'm generally out of the office by eight in the evening.' Because the trainee intake is smaller than at the big-name English firms, trainees believe they receive 'a substantial amount of responsibility' and rarely end up with basic administrative tasks. The fact that you 'have to step up to the plate a little bit more' means that 'if you're not a person who wants to fade into the background this could be the right fit for you.' Trainees are rewarded for their labours with a Mid Atlantic-level salary that is 'not as high as Latham but higher than the magic circle. It's a very attractive deal.'

The London office is 'very much part of the larger international Orrick.' All the resources of the American operation are at a trainee's disposal, and when working with a US-based team 'it's absolutely acceptable to scan things and e-mail them to New York, picking up where they left off the next day.' In fact London IT problems and document production issues can all be handled by an operations centre based in the USA. Things like this mean 'you do feel very much that you're part of a US firm.' London knows how to stand its ground: 'The firm recognises that London is equal to, if not surpassing, NYC as a global financial centre and we're getting extra resources as a result. A lot of the work that comes here originates here, but a lot comes from New York and one trainee has been working closely with our Paris office. We're very much in touch with what's going on with each of the offices.'

Award winners

Orrick's international character is reflected in its London trainee group, which presently includes recruits from America, Sweden, Italy, Russia, Ukraine and Kazakhstan, as well as a few Brits. As if that didn't make them a diverse enough bunch, between them they also cover a relatively large age range. Logically this isn't necessarily the best firm for those following 'the usual student career path into law;' for example, one interviewee told us Orrick tends to take on candidates who are 'quite mature in outlook' and have 'something a bit standout on their CV.' Previous recruits have worked in the music industry, as a chef and as a ski instructor. We also learned that while 'academic ability is important,' recruiters are 'open-minded when it comes to CVs, so a 2:2 wouldn't necessarily be a bar to someone coming in.' One thing that is vital is 'passion – they're good at spotting people who aren't all that interested but have decided to pursue City law anyway.'

'I enjoy coming to work here,' said one trainee, 'you know everyone's name and say hello when you pass people in the hall. I don't want to paint the firm as being too warm and fuzzy as we do serious work, but we get on well with each other.' Nevertheless, trainees still can't put together a sports team. 'The problem is we're so diverse it's hard to find a sport we can all play or want to play.' Socialising as a group can also be a challenge when there's a difference in ages. There are monthly drinks evenings and a swinging Christmas party, which last year was themed around 1930s movies. Trainees get a budget for their own events, including a second Christmas party held at favourite restaurant Rocket.

Perhaps inspired by the diligence of colleagues in America, Orrick London takes pro bono commitments seriously and a dedicated council sends e-mails about new projects. Alongside microfinance for third world nations and work for a Czech environmental institution, the firm is open to new suggestions. Fee earners have annual pro bono targets, and if a supervisor has something on their plate they will 'give tasks on it like any other piece of work.'

And finally...

For finance law and cross-border work Orrick is well worth a look. The trainees of 2008 were confident Orrick would emerge from the credit crunch stronger than it went into it by broadening its London practice. Helping it along the way will be five of the batch of eight 2008 qualifiers.

Osborne Clarke

The facts

Location: Bristol, London, Reading

Number of UK partners/solicitors: 113/217

Total number of trainees: 40

Seats: 4x6 months

Alternative seats: Overseas seats, secondments

Extras: Pro bono – various projects

By the early noughties OC had built up a large portfolio of technology-based clients. After the dot.com bubble burst a change in focus was needed, despite many of those clients staying loyal to the firm.

Spread across the south of England, OC has its headquarters in the firm's spiritual home of Bristol, a reasonably large London office and a third branch in Reading. It's also developed a network of overseas offices and affiliated law firms, most of these in Western European countries.

Cool for cats

Every year students mull over Osborne Clarke's big cat logo and wonder what breed it is. One informant was initially coy, making a vague attempt to imply that trainees are only told the nature of the beast after being sworn to secrecy in a lengthy initiation ceremony, but after gentle coaxing, they spilled the beans: 'Okay, it's a puma.' On the downside this means that we can't use our lame tiger gag – Osborne Clarke, they're grrrrrrrreat! – but at least it does allow us to assess whether the firm lives up to the puma's reputation as a 'powerful and stealthy' operator. As far as power is concerned, OC has corporate finance muscle to compete with many of the best mid-sized UK law firms, and is pumping iron to build up its property biceps. As for stealthy: well, we don't think so. By its own admission, the firm 'isn't hugely aggressive in its work practices,' and is known in Bristol as the laid-back, trendy counterpart to the supposedly more formal Burges Salmon, so we can't really envisage the partners scheming away on some hidden agenda.

In keeping with OC's 'one firm, three offices' mantra, in the past trainees weren't recruited to one particular site – meaning a fair amount of office-hopping went on over the course of four seats. This became a logistical nightmare and the trainees weren't too happy about being constantly uprooted either. Consequently, all future trainees will be recruited for individual offices, although those who would like to do six months or more in one of the other locations will still be given the opportunity. This is important, because London, Bristol and Reading all offer different seats. London offers corporate, general commercial, commercial litigation, banking, insolvency, property, planning and employment. Bristol offers corporate, commercial litigation, banking, private client, tax, incentives, property, pensions and construction. Reading offers corporate, banking, property, commercial litigation, general commercial and employment. OC also has three foreign offices, in Cologne, Munich and Silicon Valley, California. Secondments are available to Germany; the small Californian team doesn't host trainees at the moment.

Naked ambition

By the early noughties OC had built up a large portfolio of technology-based clients. After the dot.com bubble burst a change in focus was needed, despite many of those clients staying loyal to the firm. Giant companies like Microsoft, 3i, Motorola and Vodafone are all still on the books and OC remains well known for its technology sector expertise. The success of the firm's shift towards corporate work is highlighted by a wealth of new AIM clients: exactly the sort of high-quality, mid-market work OC was looking for. The corporate finance team was involved in transactions with a total value in excess of £800m last year. It advised the shareholders of Cowlin Group on its sale to Balfour Beatty, Tribal Group on the

£77m sale of Mercury Health to Care UK, and Novera Energy on its admission to AIM. Corporate is the only seat that is compulsory for trainees (though trainees in London should probably expect to do property as well). The seat brings all the standard tasks; some with decent level of responsibility, others purely document management exercises. 'There's a lot of drafting of ancillary documents, due diligence and verification, plus good client contact,' confirmed one source.

OC also offers secondments to some of its major finance clients. A trainee who spent six months at RAB Capital praised the 'fantastic experience; they throw you straight in and expect an extremely high quality of work. It's very high-pressure, but it gave me exposure to things you never see in a law firm. I was dealing directly with the CEO and senior fund managers every single day.' Backing up corporate, but also 'consistently pulling in a good quality of work' for itself, is the banking department. The firm acts for RBS, Barclays, Lloyds TSB, HSBC and Bank of Ireland. Again, the seat can at times feel 'admin-based,' but trainees do get responsibility on the day-to-day management of smaller files, and get to draft things like whitewash resolutions (don't worry, it's an official term under the Companies Act). Also, we never thought we'd have cause to write this of a law firm, but trainees doing a banking seat in Bristol can expect hardcore nudity. 'The City Inn hotel is right opposite us. I don't think the people inside realise we can see right through their tinted windows…'

The incentives seat straddles both tax and employment law. One trainee gave a succinct example of the type of work it entails. 'A university spin-off company starts up, say in the biosciences sector. It has employees with scientific know-how, but the company won't make profit for a few years. It wants to keep its skilled employees but can't pay them loads yet, so it gives them share options to take every year. That's where we come in.' Of course share schemes aren't limited to start-up companies; in this field OC acts for the likes of The Carphone Warehouse, Mulberry, Motorola and, increasingly, US companies wanting to recruit staff to their UK concerns. The seat involves a lot of drafting – 'ancillary documents, submissions to the Revenue, share scheme rules; they are good at letting you have first go at things, and later on letting you run with your own drafting ideas.'

There are a selection of contentious seats to choose from, including general commercial, construction, insolvency, employment and IP litigation. The construction litigation team works for both contractors and employers, often in matters concerning delays on site. These can become rather technical so 'you suddenly have to become an expert in quite detailed stuff.' The IP team acts for the three major Avon universities, Bath, Bristol and UWE, along with the likes of Honda, Arriva, the Met Office and

Chambers UK rankings

Advertising & Marketing • Agriculture & Rural Affairs • Banking & Finance • Banking Litigation • Charities • Competition/European Law • Construction • Corporate Finance • Data Protection • Dispute Resolution • Employee Share Schemes • Employment • Environment • Health & Safety • Healthcare • Information Technology • Intellectual Property • Investment Funds • Media & Entertainment • Outsourcing • Partnership • Pensions • Planning • Private Client • Private Equity • Projects, Energy & Natural Resources • Public Procurement • Real Estate • Real Estate Litigation • Restructuring/Insolvency • Retail • Sports Law • Tax • Telecommunications • Transport

Fat Face. Outside of a couple of big cases, it's not hugely busy at the moment, and so trainees may get sent over to commercial litigation to get more experience. Here (in the Bristol seat at least) 'the supervisors have an awful lot of time for you and they are perfectly willing to spend half an hour going over an individual document.'

The final major area is property. This department has just wrapped up 'the biggest deal the firm has ever done,' advising on the £308m purchase of a retirement homes management business for one of its trophy clients, the Consensus Business Group. That's saying something, as already this year the team has been involved with two other massive deals: letting the 60 retail outlets, including the champagne bar at the brand new Eurostar terminal at St Pancras, and acting for the company regenerating 17 acres of Swindon town centre in the 'New Swindon' development. Naturally, projects of this size can lead to a lot of spreadsheet work and bundling for trainees, so it's good to hear that the firm makes up for it with more varied and complex tasks on smaller deals. 'You are given as much as you can take, and can go off on your own and run your own files,' confirmed a satisfied customer. At times the hours can be long: one source had worked 'three weekends in a row, sitting and looking through boxes of documents.' Corporate can mean longer hours too: 'I was lucky,' said one trainee; 'the latest I worked was about 1am and on average until about 8pm.'

West is best?

Curious about OC's 'one firm' ethos, we asked how unified the three offices felt. The consensus was that there is cohesiveness and contact between them, but that 'each one has its own individual personality.' For example, 'for every corporate deal that goes through in London or Reading there will be tax implications, so there will be constant videoconferencing with the tax team in Bristol.' By contrast, 'commercial London, commercial Bristol and commercial Thames Valley are in effect three completely different departments with different clients.' The set-up in all the OC offices is the same: open-plan and 'non-hierarchical – everyone from top to bottom has the same-quality computer, the same amount of desk space, same everything. Coming into the firm, you wouldn't know who was important and who wasn't.' The structure of training is also the same: trainees are allocated a supervisor, but in each department work within teams of four to eight fee earners, usually getting work from all of them at some point.

We did detect some rivalry between the offices. 'All the Bristol trainees want to come here, whether for a seat or to qualify,' said a London trainee. A second was proud of the fact that 'in London a lot of people have come from magic circle firms, especially in corporate.' A third went so far as to say: 'I think the partners have to accept that London is where the firm's future lies.' The Bristolians beg to differ. 'Over in London they see Bristol as chinoland, and then they come to do a seat here and really enjoy it,' said one. 'I don't think the London trainees are as close as in Bristol or Reading,' added a second. 'There's no real communal area for London trainees to hang out in. Bristol's more relaxed… and Reading's a small office so everyone knows each other.' For its part, the ten-year-old Reading office seems happy to get on with business. 'There are only 50 or 60 people, so everybody knows everybody. The commercial department gets really good work from the biotech sector and the private equity team is at least as strong as London. We're doing lots of work for London clients and the likes of 3i.' We'll give the final say to a trainee who had spent time in both London and Bristol: 'London is good for bringing work in, but it's more prone to losing its identity because of the liquidity of the market there. Osborne Clarke has real name recognition within the South West.'

Is there a classic OC trainee? Maybe. Many of them are a few years out of uni, with a bit of life experience under their belt. The firm has no problem with taking on trainees old enough to have both children and mortgages, or those whose education or route to the law has been unconventional. 'Relationships between people are civilised and grown up' and communication from the top is deemed pretty good. Every week managing partner Simon Beswick sends out an e-mail and every year he gives a state of the nation talk. Beyond this, trainees in Bristol like to distinguish themselves from their counterparts over at Burges Salmon, seeing themselves and their firm as less old-school than their Bristol rival. Elsewhere there's a sense of some similarity with Olswang, which also works out of London and Reading.

The social life in Bristol is marginally better than in London. The ever-disreputable Lizard Lounge and The Apple, a floating cider bar, are currently popular for Friday nights in Bristol, while The Lord Raglan is still the venue of choice in London. Some of the trainees did recently go on a camping trip, and our straw poll suggests most were intending to make an effort for the fancy dress firm-wide summer party. An 'auction of promises' for charity also raised a good crowd, resulting in 'a bidding war for a cheesecake.' On the sporting front several staff participate in charity runs, including the Bristol Half Marathon. We also heard about 'lots of very keen cyclists.' As for mental exercise, there's a French club for anyone keen to brush up on half-forgotten language skills.

After mediocre retention rates in the past two years, it looks like the big cat is back on form, as 12 out of 15 qualifiers were hired in 2008. 'My NQ position was signed, sealed and delivered in April. It makes an enormous difference because you can get on and do your fourth seat without having to worry,' said one contact.

And finally...

People used to come to Osborne Clarke for its TMT and commercial teams, and maybe they still do; however, the message from current trainees is clear: 'We're definitely not a technology firm any more.'

Palmers Solicitors

The facts

Location: Basildon, Thurrock, South Woodham Ferrers

Number of UK partners/solicitors: 10/19

Total number of trainees: 6

Seats: 4x6 months

Alternative seats: None

> Looking for people who will stay with the firm long-term has resulted in consistently good retention rates.

One of the largest firms in Essex to offer a commercial/private client mix, Palmers Solicitors celebrated its 25th birthday in 2008. It marked the occasion with a rebrand, and of course the obligatory big cake with the firm's new logo on it.

Basildon's best

Palmers has three offices strung out like beads along a 20-mile stretch of the A13, the major road for commuters travelling from southern Essex into London. Chief among the offices is Basildon, which has six of the firm's ten partners and most of its trainees. The other two, in Thurrock and South Woodham Ferrers, are much smaller operations but cover a surprising number of practice areas all the same. All three offices do residential and commercial property; corporate finance; coco; family and a little IP work. In addition, Thurrock has capability to do litigation, and South Woodham Ferrers has a partner for wills, trusts and probate. Basildon has the widest mix, also doing litigation; wills, trusts and probate; employment; licensing; road traffic offences and crime.

While most of these departments have been open to trainees at one time or another, some of them are very small – litigation in Thurrock consists of just one partner, for instance. It follows then that due to logistics and business needs, a full choice of all departments at every seat rotation is unlikely. Nevertheless, Palmers encourages trainees to express their preferences, and this is a good place for a broad training contract. Small teams can also lead to huge amounts of responsibility, even in the first seat. 'I like that, but I think some other trainees get a little freaked out by it,' said one interviewee. If that's the case, no one admitted it – all our contacts seemingly living up to the request on the firm's website for trainees

who enjoy responsibility. One prime example of why they need to enjoy it is the so-called 'trainee clinic'. If a potential new client stops by or telephones with an enquiry and the reception staff are unsure who should deal with it, the trainees take over and are then responsible for dealing with the enquiry or pointing the person in the right direction.

Bread and battering

Nowhere is this responsibility more apparent than in the litigation seat, where trainees said that they get 'pretty much free rein' from their principal to run files by themselves. The seat brings 'quite an even split between commercial and private clients,' primarily from the local area. Landlord and tenant cases involving chasing rent arrears or tenants who refuse to leave the property make up a large proportion of the work. There are also plenty of land disputes: 'We have an ongoing High Court case where there's a guy trying to get an injunction against our client, who has been parking cars and horses on what he says is his property.' Another trainee chuckled when remembering 'a boundary dispute over a piece of land that's about the size of a baguette. There have been fisticuffs.' Opportunities for advocacy arise on occasion and trainees are encouraged to go to court when they do. It's the level of personal contact in litigation that is most highly praised, with 'a lot of liaising with clients and barristers.' There is also a one-man crime department in Basildon.

While the partner doesn't often take a trainee, when he does they can get involved with a whole world of hurt, working on cases that range from GBH, domestic violence and sexual assault right down to motoring offences, with lots of court time a given.

As in litigation, the property team is split between commercial work for local businesses and residential work for the denizens of deepest Essex. Trainees describe it as 'one of those seats where something can happen that completely changes your day.' An ability to cope with pressure is a useful skill to have here, and 'you really learn to prioritise.' It's a great seat too for developing drafting and negotiation skills. Property is quite often combined with another seat, so trainees often find their six months flavoured with a dollop of corporate and commercial work. Coco brings a diet of business acquisitions and disposals, franchise deals, joint ventures and licensing agreements. The firm profits from its location: it has 'some big clients in London' to add to the many 'massive industrial firms' that populate Essex and the new businesses that are springing up due to the regeneration of the Thames Gateway. 'Though you are often trawling through lease agreements, there are still negotiations involved and chances to come up with innovative solutions,' one trainee said. Client contact increases as the seat goes on. Though the convenience of e-mail has put paid to most face-to-face contact, phone calls are still considered 'a nice touch' when dealing with clients.

A family affair

You may be starting to notice a common theme that runs though every department. Family, an ever-changing concoction of divorce, cohabitation, financial agreements, childcare arrangements and injunctions in cases of domestic violence, is no different. 'They are really good with giving me lots of responsibility, I think that's where we have the edge over what the bigger firms do.' Palmers trainees certainly won't see too much of the low-level tasks like bundling and pagination: 'I was getting to go to court quite a lot,' a family trainee told us, 'and the level of client contact was really good. I have taken witness statements and instructed counsel.' Of course, 'everything is still overseen,' though supervision is different from seat to seat. 'You learn how your principal works. I tend to have a chat with mine every morning.'

Trainees enjoy employment law for the human aspect. 'All the claimant cases we do are really interesting because everyone has a different story.' One that finished recently involved a man claiming for constructive dismissal. He worked for a family business but his father had already left and his brother had gone off to set up a rival company, leaving the man working for his uncles. 'Most cases settle but in this case no one wanted to admit that they were wrong. It went to hearing and he turned down

their offers. It was a bit worrying.' Fortunately, in the end, Palmers' client was awarded more than he had originally been offered. Another case involved an employer that had a man off work on statutory sick pay due to an injury, 'but they had seen him out and about and wanted to know if they could terminate his contract.' The firm offers non-contentious employment advice as well, and trainees often find themselves drafting employment contracts and company handbooks.

For the long haul

Our sources spoke with one voice on the subject of their work and training, but when it came to life in the office, their opinions started to differ. Some described 'an open-door kind of environment' in which 'everyone's on an equal level.' Others claimed that 'partners here are very old-school' and that the firm is 'still very hierarchical.' What to believe? Our hunch is that it's somewhere between the two. We got the impression that Palmers offers a nice working environment where everyone is willing to help trainees (even bringing one a cup of coffee halfway through our interview) but that – aforementioned big cake and new logo not withstanding – Palmers remains quite traditional in many ways. In particular, our contacts couldn't tell us much about future plans for the firm, as partner-level meetings remain 'hush-hush.' A lack of communication is a bone of contention for some: 'With the economy as it is, you look to your leaders to reassure you... certainly the admin staff can get a little worried.' Even the harshest critics acknowledged that Palmers is deliberately 'trying to inject a bit more youth' into its set-up. The firm also makes it very clear in its grad recruitment literature that it's not interested in a two-year fling with a trainee who'll then go and shack up with some floozy of a City firm. Looking for people who will stay with the firm long-term has resulted in consistently good retention rates. In 2008 both of the two qualifiers stayed on, one going into wills, trusts and probate in South Woodham Ferrers, the other into the property team at Basildon. It's the second year running that retention has been 100%.

We noticed a slight Essex twang in the voices of several of our interviewees, and most had some kind of link to the region. Not many lived close to the office though, preferring to commute from distance. This isn't surprising, as the level of excitement on offer in the district can best be summed up by a typical headline from the *Basildon Echo:* 'Pensioner wants action on rest room idea.' Fortunately the bright lights of London are only a short train journey away. The geographical spread of trainees does make socialising difficult, and besides, 'everyone here is very settled – it's that sort of suburban lifestyle where people have fiancées and husbands to go home to.' Fittingly, the hours are a respectable 9am to 5.30pm. What's idyllic for some is anathema to others and we suggest that party animals look elsewhere. Not that we're suggesting that life at the firm is a two-year graveyard shift – quiz nights are a popular pastime – and Palmers people are not totally averse to getting down and boogying on occasion. What began as an occasional event called Girls Night Out has been expanded to include everyone in the firm and is now called… well, still Girls Night Out, actually. It normally takes the form of drinks, dinner and a spot of dancing. Partners have also been known to let their hair down at the Christmas party, which usually takes a fancy dress theme and this year saw half the cast of *Star Wars* in attendance.

And finally...

Sometimes it's hard to sum up a firm in a few pithy words, but not with Palmers. Responsibility; a broad range of work; commitment to keeping trainees on; Essex. If these four key themes appeal, this is the firm for you.

- **In 2007 the number of ethnic minority solicitors in England and Wales hit 10,000 for the first time. The total number of solicitors declaring membership of a minority group rose to 10,306 to be precise – out of 108,407 practising in total.**

Penningtons

The facts

Location: Basingstoke, Godalming, London

Number of UK partners/solicitors: 55/78

Total number of trainees: 22

Seats: 4x6 months

Alternative seats: None

> This part of Surrey is crammed with wealthy people needing legal advice, so private client is a must-do seat.

The 200-year-old South of England firm Penningtons is now applying a one-firm philosophy to its three-office business. It offers a healthy balance of commercial and private client work in each location.

No country for town ten

With offices in Surrey and Hampshire as well as the capital, is this a London firm with Home Counties offices or vice versa? 'When I joined I thought of it as a South of England firm, but also a City firm at the same time,' mused one source; 'now I realise it is not London-led… the current managing partner is in London, but that could change next time.' Emphasising the decentralised approach, the graduate recruitment team operates out of the Godalming office and the trainee group is spread across the three offices – London has around ten, Godalming seven and Basingstoke five. The only discernible difference between the three groups of trainees is that the London recruits are confirmed City dwellers, while the others have more of an interest in county living and country pursuits. When choosing which office you'd like to be your home for training, pick wisely because it is nigh on impossible to switch locations for a seat, and although each has the same main departments – property, dispute resolution, corporate and private client – they also have distinct specialist areas of practice. We'll outline these in more detail on the following tour of the offices.

Coup, er, gosh!

Since moving into swish new accommodation in 2007, London staff have been working open-plan. Echoing the comments of trainees across the offices, one source explained: 'Everyone is relaxed, no one is notoriously traditional or hard. I don't think they attract people who

are that way… it does not help you be a better lawyer or firm to have shouting or books being thrown.' They also stressed the variety of work on offer, not only in the mix of commercial and non-commercial options but also within each seat. 'You are not pitched into one thing that you will repeat a thousand times, you get involved across the spectrum.'

Taking three trainees at any one time, commercial property is an important area for London and has recently been augmented by a small banking team. Trainee work includes 'all the typical tasks such as helping to draft leases and licences to assign, dealing with rent reviews, liaising with managing agents, etc.' Typically taken in the first year, it's 'a very busy first seat and a case of quickly being responsible for a lot of things.' Immigration is also an option and the team has worked on some unusual cases, such as the asylum claim made by *Big Brother 6* contestant Makosi Musambasi from Zimbabwe. Some lucky trainees might even get to work with the partner specialising in electoral issues for the Conservative Party. And if you thought UK politics were intriguing, then how about cleaning up after a coup? The dispute resolution team is involved with civil law suits that followed the attempt by a group of mercenaries to overthrow the government of Equatorial Guinea in 2004. Penningtons has been in the media spotlight for its dealings with this client, not only because the case reached the House of Lords, but also because of criticisms of its decision to represent a state accused of human rights breaches. Naturally most of the dispute resolution team's work is entirely uncontroversial – a broad portfolio includes employment law, property litigation and professional regulatory issues for numerous health sector and other professional regulators. 'I went to court quite a lot during my seat,' said one trainee with pride; 'and to the Solicitors Disciplinary Tribunal and conferences with counsel.'

Unlike most City firms, Penningtons does not make a corporate stint compulsory. Some people prefer the broader commercial seat, which also covers IP. Most trainees do take a private client seat, replete with 'hands-on experience, meetings with clients and taking the lead on drafting wills.' On the tax side 'you pick up quite a bit through research.' Far from being six months of drinking tea with old ladies, the experience exposes trainees to 'international clients and non-doms.'

The type of work and the type of people in London leads to 'pretty good hours;' starting around 9am and leaving at about 6.30pm and 'very rarely past 7pm.' Sometimes 'a partner or associate will say, 'Come for a drink,'' in which case who knows when you might be home.' The trainees we spoke to felt 'happy with the salary; it's less than the magic circle, but I think I am better paid per hour.' Almost without exception 'the people that applied here didn't apply to the bigger firms, and certainly for me that wasn't something I had my heart set on.' The social highlights are an annual dinner dance in January and 'very competitive' pub quizzes.

Godalmit!

Featuring in the Jude Law-Cameron Diaz romcom, *The Holiday*, as little more than a twee village, Godalming in fact has a fine industrial heritage: first quarrying, then cloth making and finally the early motor industry. It now plays host to a top public school (Charterhouse) and pandas (WWF has its HQ here), and is set to become one of the first town centres in the country with public wireless access. Many lawyers in the office are 'ex-London' looking for good-quality work away from the rat race. 'There's one partner who came from Withers because she wants more time to exercise her horse.' It sounds like there's plenty of time to do it. Said one trainee: 'I was here at 7pm one night and was told, 'What are you doing? Go home!''

This part of Surrey is crammed with wealthy people needing legal advice, so private client is a must-do seat. 'The clients tend to have well over a million in assets – I am becoming blasé about organising cheques for trustafarians,' one source joked. On the trusts side 'there are plenty of international private clients – the Russians are moving in to Surrey.' Also on offer are personal injury/clinical negligence and a specialist travel litigation seat assisting unfortunate holidaymakers. 'In the autumn

Chambers UK rankings

Clinical Negligence • Corporate Finance • Dispute Resolution • Immigration • Parliamentary & Public Affairs • Personal Injury • Private Client • Professional Discipline • Real Estate • Social Housing • Travel

it's summer holiday accidents – Mediterranean hotels with wet marble floors, nasty falls, steps without banisters – then in the winter it's skiing accidents. You get a few food poisoning cases but they are hard to prove.' As well as attending inquests alone, confident trainees can run their own files and take client meetings. Everyone should experience the property department and there's also a small corporate team that acts 'mostly for family businesses and partnerships.'

As in all three offices, a sports and social committee livens up the after-hours scene, last year with a black-tie Christmas party and a summer party at Godalming's Inn on the Lake. Impromptu evenings out usually mean The Lounge. 'Mostly people only go for one drink as they don't want the hassle of leaving their car here.' Car parking is free and if you drive from Guildford the roads aren't too bad. Commute by train from South London and you can score a double seat most mornings, although your salary will be lower (presently by about £4,000 for a first-year trainee) than London peers. The office plays host to the annual Penningtons rounders tournament and has teams for football and badminton. The only downside to working in Godalming is that staff are split between two premises, meaning a move is on the cards 'if we find the right building.'

Good Lords!

Basingstoke features 'a lot of ex-City people' and is emphatically 'not a country bumpkin practice.' The corporate team 'is growing and growing and we get some really good-quality clients that distinguish us from other firms locally… having a City base helps.' In the last year corporate bods have acted on M&A transactions with a total value of £50m, including the sale of Autointermediate's aerospace events business to Reed Exhibitions. The private client team's secret weapon is that 'we get referrals from City firms and do some great contentious probate cases,' including representing the Conservative Party Association in resisting a widely publicised claim involving a will contested over the alleged mental incapacity of the deceased. Other Basingstoke seat options are property, employment and PI/clin neg, but it's those contentious opportunities that trainees in London and Godalming envy.

Alas, Basingstoke is neither the prettiest nor most exciting town and 'a lot of people commute from London.' This can dampen the after-work social scene, but thanks to the local sports and social committee, staff can participate in mixed netball, golf days and ice skating. Not to be outdone, the marketing department has organised a day at Lord's with the firm's adopted cricketer, Paul Collingwood.

All change

In the words of trainees, the firm seems to have 'trundled along without much happening' since the late 1980s. 'When I started there was a sense that it had lost direction,' admitted one. That changed after a strategic review in 2007, when Penningtons resolved to improve its inter-office relationships and created three pan-office divisions – business services, commercial property and private individuals. Each department is running 'road shows to present what they do to each other' and sources had attended presentations on the two international networks to which Penningtons belongs – Multilaw and the European Law Group. Sadly, these don't mean trainee seats abroad, but 'if you speak another language you can get more involved with foreign clients and work.' A review of the firm's bonus scheme and time-recording system has seen teams 'more focused on figures and time-recording than before,' and we heard 'things are going forward pretty well, soon we'll have a new website, new computers and a new intranet.' Trainee links between the offices are fostered by a monthly seminar, usually held in London.

If it's bringing positive change, the review is also perceived to have prompted the partners at Penningtons' old Newbury office to vote to leave the firm and plough their own furrow. They broke away at the start of 2008 to join South East rival Thomas Eggar, but the loss didn't overly concern our interviewees. 'Out of the four offices they were always a bit of a separate entity,' said one, another agreeing: 'As a firm we feel lighter on our feet now...'

With Penningtons being a partner-heavy firm, trainees receive close attention from the most senior figures as well as assistants and HR staff. New arrivals get a mentor in the year above, and for impartial advice are assigned a principal, with whom they might 'have lunch regularly' or just 'a chat every now and then.' Appraisals are three-monthly and the small size of the trainee population seems to limit problems in realising seat preferences. Each intake of trainees nominates one of their number to represent them at staff meetings: 'We asked for qualification job offers to come out earlier and this year they did.' In all, seven of the ten qualifiers stayed on in 2008.

And finally...

This is an interesting and respected firm with a renewed sense of purpose. Each Penningtons location offers experience rich in private client and commercial work, making it perfect for anyone seeking a City or Home Counties training without a heavy corporate emphasis.

- **Think ahead:** 'You can read an article in the *Times Law Reports* the day before you go for interview and think you've got a feel for the topic, but it's probably just the latest update in an ongoing story. If you have been reading the same publication for two or three months beforehand, you will be much more sound on the way it has developed.'

When we say law
we mean business

Pinsent Masons LLP is a law firm with a bold vision – we work in partnership with our clients delivering real value and expertise in their industry sectors.

- Top 15 UK law firm
- Top 100 international law firm
- An industry recognised sector-focused business model
- High quality work with a prestigious portfolio of UK and international clients
- A strong commitment to team work and early responsibility
- A supportive culture driven by an inspiring set of values embodying respect and co-operation, ambition and excellence, and openness and approachability

For further information and to apply please visit

www.pinsentmasons.com/graduate

London   Birmingham   Bristol   Edinburgh   Glasgow   Leeds   Manchester   Beijing   Brussels   Dubai   Hong Kong   Shanghai

Pinsent Masons

The facts

Location: Birmingham, Bristol, Leeds, London, Manchester, Scotland

Number of UK partners/solicitors: 300/700

Total number of Trainees: 132

Seats: 4x6 months

Alternative seats: Overseas seats, secondments

Extras: Pro bono – eg Birmingham Employment Rights Advice Line; language training

Pinsent Masons is a very managed environment where trainees have appraisals every month and must keep a detailed diary.

Pinsent Masons was forged in the crucible of the 2004 merger between prestigious national firm Pinsents and world-renowned construction and engineering specialist Masons.

Playing with the FTSE

The rationale for the merger was to provide a broader range of services to Masons' contractor-led construction clientele, while providing a whole new client base for Pinsents to get its teeth into. Some four years on and it looks as if the deal was a good one for both parties. Certain practice groups have visibly flourished since the merger, not least projects/construction and technology/outsourcing. And there's a great portfolio of clients including Carillion, HSBC, John Lewis, Marks & Spencer, BT, Newcastle United, Manchester United, Diageo, ScottishPower and Severn Trent. The firm represents 53 companies listed on AIM and Chambers and Partners' annual FTSE survey showed that in 2007 it advised 15 FTSE 100 companies – the same number as Clifford Chance. One recruit told us proudly: 'You constantly find yourself working on things you see in the *FT*.'

Working out of seven UK cities, Pinsent Masons is a big firm. Beyond the UK it is a member of the Pinsent Mason Luther Group, a network of independent European firms with 36 offices. It has its own foreign offices in Brussels, Shanghai, Beijing, Hong Kong and Dubai and there is a further alliance with a Singaporean law firm. Holding all its offices together, even just the ones in the UK, requires 'a lot of effort and money.' Initiatives like the Values Programme and UK-wide training events are at the forefront of the campaign. Said one trainee: 'I can't tell who's an old Pinsents partner or a Masons partner. We're all pulling the same oar.' Both at home and abroad we're told

the aim is to be bigger and better, something hinted at by a series of raids on other firms and organisations. DLA Piper, Eversheds, Addleshaw Goddard and even the dear old BBC have all given up key lawyers.

UK trainees usually stay in a single office but may be sent to another for a seat. Each takes four six-month seats. On offer are banking and finance, competition, corporate, employment, pensions, property litigation, restructuring, planning and environment, tax, UK construction and engineering (UK C&E), projects and international construction (PIC), dispute resolution and litigation (DRL), and outsourcing, technology and commercial (OTC). Incidentally, 'you get used to acronyms being thrown around.' There are popular client secondments to blue-chip companies, a six-month seat in Dubai and sometimes a three-month seat with German allied firm Luther. While specific offices do have particular strengths, departments will usually provide similar experiences across the offices. In the following tour of the firm, where we mention a seat, readers should assume our comments apply to all offices where the seat is offered.

Brum notes

Most seat options are available in Birmingham, which hosts around 20% of the annual intake of trainees. We heard a good deal about OTC, which trainees said is 'commercial with an IP flavour.' They spoke of tasks ranging from drafting conditions of sale and purchase to reviewing the terms and conditions on promotional materials and scratch cards. In planning and environment seats they learn how to make planning applications, negotiate with local authorities and deal with compulsory purchase orders, all of which require 'direct contact with clients.' With instructions relating to the redesign of town centres and airport planning applications, it's a good seat for those 'interested to see that initial phase of a project before it develops.' No office is wholly devoted to local work, so while the Birmingham planning team did advise Advantage West Midlands and Wolverhampton City Council last year, it also counts among its clients the Olympic Delivery Authority and the developers of the first prototype eco-town in the UK at Northstowe in Cambridgeshire.

At last the Birmingham office building has had a well-deserved makeover so the interior, at least, is now 'really spacious' with 'lots of life.' This branch is said to be one of the most socially minded in the firm. Trainees get involved in sports events with other firms and go for regular evenings out at bars like Old Joint Stock and SubLounge. The 'infamous' office Christmas party is always themed and usually involves some inter-departmental competition. Last year's Top of the Pops-theme prompted some staff dress as Christmas number ones.

B is for bang, R is for road rage

As the second-smallest office, Manchester has a compact trainee group of around ten. Trainees can choose from UK C&E, OTC, property, corporate, pensions, banking, employment, DRL and restructuring. A seat in UK C&E is very likely as the Manchester construction team is central to the success of the office. Recruits are sometimes in awe of the lawyers and their work for some of the largest construction companies in the country – we're talking Balfour Beatty, Carillion, Alfred McAlpine, Bovis Lend Lease, Wilmott Dixon and Laing. The team gives advice on projects such as Drax Power's £100m-plus Turbine Modernisation investment, and weighs in when clients are in dispute. One recent case concerned the sculpture on the main approach to the City of Manchester Stadium. A number of defects have become apparent in 'B of the Bang', which was commissioned by Manchester City Council to commemorate the 2002 Commonwealth Games. Because of the size and duration of deals and cases, trainees can end up shouldering 'more menial tasks' than in other seats. However, those who show initiative say there is potential for more responsibility and client contact. One exhilarated source even described their time in the seat as 'a bit hair-raising.'

According to our sources Manchester is 'generally more relaxed' than other locations and there's 'a buzzing trainee scene' in the city. The end of every month is marked with drinks and buffet food, and for those who just can't wait

Chambers UK rankings

Administrative & Public Law • Banking & Finance • Competition/European Law • Construction • Corporate Finance • Data Protection • Dispute Resolution • Education • Employee Share Schemes • Employment • Environment • Health & Safety • Healthcare • Information Technology • Insurance • Intellectual Property • Local Government • Media & Entertainment • Outsourcing • Pensions • Pensions Litigation • Planning • Private Client • Private Equity • Product Liability • Professional Negligence • Projects, Energy & Natural Resources • Public Procurement • Real Estate • Real Estate Litigation • Restructuring/Insolvency • Retail • Social Housing • Tax • Telecommunications • Transport

there are staff drinks every Friday at 5pm. In summer there's a barbecue and at Christmas the office has its own black-tie party. To ease a squeeze in Manchester, a move to larger accommodation is being mulled over.

Leeds, as the larger of the two Northern offices, hosts around 25 trainees. The property department is the big gun here, and as property typically involves 'getting to grips with the basics of everything' and 'managing little files,' it's a seat that many trainees are happy to start off with. There can be some administrative grind, but after paying their dues trainees are rewarded with more challenging tasks. In the past year the team advised, among others, IKEA, DEFRA and Leeds City Council, which needed help with two major developments worth over £1bn. Lime Property Fund also turns to the firm, most recently in relation to the second phase of the Wales Millennium Centre, Cardiff Bay, which includes a 350-seater auditorium that's been earmarked by BBC Wales as the new home for the BBC National Orchestra and Chorus of Wales.

If you want to find a Leeds trainee on a Friday night then head for Greek Street where they'll be propping up one of the many bars. Throughout the year there's plenty going on socially: the last Christmas party was held at the majestic Harewood House and go-karting has been all the rage. 'One of the trainees got blocked by one of the cars and turned to say something nasty, but it was a partner.'

From top to toe

Pinsent Masons has a Scottish training programme in its Glasgow and Edinburgh offices from which trainees will occasionally venture south of the border for individual seats. At the other end of the UK is a tiny, 'close-knit' office in Bristol, offering experiences in projects and construction to trainees visiting from other offices. Those who make the trip here soon learn that work isn't limited to the South West; indeed one of the Bristol construction team's top cases last year was for major international construction company Laing, which was in dispute with Haden Young over the Gateshead Music Centre and Coventry Stadium.

London has the biggest trainee group and hosts up to 50 people at a time. Presently split over two sites with a 15-minute walk between them, the aim is to find a single office that is large enough to appease all those who say 'it would be much better if we were all under one roof.' London offers the widest range of seats, with corporate being the obvious standout choice. In 2007 the team advised on over 220 transactions with a combined value of almost £19bn, a hefty chunk of which was the £906m sale of a long-standing client, oilfield services group Abbot, to First Reserve. The department is always busy, which means trainees are too. 'Preparing documents and bibles is very much the day-to-day work,' but often senior associates and partners will pass down more challenging tasks. Although the customary Pinsent Masons training philosophy applies – giving recruits more responsibility as they prove their ability – the size and nature of the corporate practice means that you'll usually have 'a much smaller role within a much bigger transaction.'

The social scene in London conforms to City standards, with both offices coming together for drinks events and a big Christmas blow-out, last year at the Natural History Museum. Tennis, football and squash are on the agenda but in particular 'everyone's pretty keen on rugby.' Pinsent Masons, it seems, is 'a very rugby firm.'

Gone starfishin'

The people we interviewed saw Pinsent Masons as 'one big firm.' Claimed one: 'We all know each other, trainees especially.' Another added: 'You are constantly working with people from different departments in dif-

ferent offices.' The entire intake spends its first week together in London, and a few weeks later they're all bussed to Bedfordshire for more training. There is a presumption that trainees will remain in their home offices, though some will move in order to try a seat that's only available elsewhere. They find they have constant contact with HR. Pinsent Masons is a very managed environment, where trainees (at least theoretically) have appraisals every month and must keep a detailed diary. This approach influences the qualification process too: everyone submits a CV and attends interviews. Most qualifiers seem not to mind jumping through these hoops and 57 out of 64 stayed on with the firm in 2008.

We heard few moans about hours. Most people said that, the odd week of late nights aside, they tended to finish by 6.30pm or 7pm. Coupled with this are competitive salaries and a bonus scheme for trainees that rewards the hardest workers with up to £5,000 on qualification. Looking beyond billing, the firm shows admirable commitment to corporate social responsibility activities through its Starfish programme. With the firm's encouragement, recruits can volunteer for activities such as hosting costumed Christmas parties for disadvantaged families, building adventure playgrounds and running orienteering courses for children. Gay and lesbian readers especially will be interested to know that Stonewall named Pinsent Masons the most gay-friendly firm in the UK.

And finally...

In Birmingham, Leeds and Manchester, PM is one of the biggest and most reputable firms on the block, whereas in London it must compete with scores of others for the attention of talented students. Should it attract yours, you'll have to work hard to gain entry, but our sources say the effort will most definitely be worth it.

Prettys

The facts

Location: Ipswich, Chelmsford

Number of UK partners/solicitors: 18/23

Total number of trainees: 12

Seats: 4x6 months

Alternative seats: None

Extras: Pro bono – CAB, LawWorks, Will Aid

> The training experience is deemed less stressful than it might be in a major city, but this should not be assumed to be at the cost of quality. Prettys, say our sources, is 'a wolf in sheep's clothing.'

Recent centenarian Prettys is one of Suffolk's best-known characters due to its well-regarded mix of commercial and private client services. Wanting to become even prettier, it's treated itself to a facelift and headed into Essex.

See another site

Prettys recently underwent a rebrand with a view to projecting 'a funkier image.' Although the process was still unfinished at the time we rang trainees this year, we were told to expect new header paper, a new logo, a redesigned website and a new slogan – 'See another side'. The changes aren't merely cosmetic, we learned. In the past few years Prettys 'has gone through a real period of change.' Specifically, trainees sense that its new outlook is 'much more commercial and corporate driven' and these practice groups are expanding. Although trainees are thus far exempt, the firm is 'hotter' on fee earners fulfilling their billable-hours targets than it used to be and the marketing department now has a full team, where before it was 'one woman and her secretary.' The new gung-ho attitude seems to have filtered down to the recruits too, most of whom are 'quite commercially focused.'

One of the biggest changes was the opening of a Chelmsford office in 2007 to focus on commercial clients. The firm has thrown its weight behind the venture and there are already lawyers specialising in employment, corporate and property law. The driver is Prettys' desire for 'growth, growth, growth!' Said one trainee: 'Whereas before we were just a regional firm in a town many people hadn't heard of, we now have our foot in the door of another busy town.' The firm's goals aren't officially London-centred, but more than one of our sources expressed a hope that they might become so. The

Chelmsford office itself has met with immediate success and already outgrown its first premises. The fact that the latest, open-plan office feels 'fresher' and 'really, really swanky' has made trainees realise that the main Ipswich offices 'really, really aren't.'

Sitting pretty

Recruits typically do four seats of six months, the first of which is allocated without their input. As the contract progresses, trainees indicate their preferences during their mid-seat reviews. While there are no compulsory seats, the firm tries to allocate first-years a mix of contentious and non-contentious work, so giving second-years more control over where they sit. There's space for trainees in virtually every department, and the once irregular family law seat is now almost always offered. Actually there's just one caveat – the French property team only suits someone qui parle bien le français. Chelmsford opens its doors to trainees too, with those who make the trip having any additional travel expenses taken care of.

Virtually everyone we spoke to named commercial litigation and employment as the most popular seats. The 'big and established' comlit team keeps trainees 'busy all the time' on everything from humble photocopying to more challenging drafting exercises. Always educational for a young lawyer, there was recently 'a professional negligence file against a firm of local solicitors.' The employment seat is split between Ipswich and Chelmsford. Mainly working for big employers including Air New Zealand, Care UK and Fred Olsen, trainees find they need to conduct a lot of research to keep up with the rapid changes in the law and write articles for newsletters. Understandably tribunals are the most exciting aspect of the work, and these can cover anything from unfair dismissal to discrimination.

Plenty of people want to try a corporate seat because of the scope for 'really good drafting experience' as well as more workaday company secretarial tasks. Prettys recently assisted a Norwegian client with its acquisition of a Norfolk-based marine technology company and worked on the disposal of a national container haulage business for £27.5m. Taking advantage of its location near to the ports of Felixstowe, Ipswich and Harwich, Prettys has a team that is well versed in all aspects of 'dry' shipping matters. Far from dry in every other respect, time spent with the shipping team can be an eye-opener. While many tasks are 'the general things that come with a litigation seat,' including whole-day mediations and arbitrations, the work stands out as some of the more exciting available at Prettys. It may not be Captain Jack Sparrow fighting giant squid, but in the past year the firm has acted in the arbitration of a dispute over the legal definition of delivery and defended a claim brought for the loss of a cargo of human plasma. The one criticism often made of a shipping seat is that it is 'not a particularly busy seat' that can leave you 'thumb-twiddling.' Then again, this was also said to be true of seats in other departments where the work comes in 'peaks and troughs.'

Private thoughts

Trainees are understandably glad of the 'sheer volume of client contact' they receive over the course of their contracts. One source assured us that Prettys wasn't 'scared to put their trainees in front of clients,' and nowhere is this more evident than on the private client side of the firm. The estates and financial services seat is the 'most structured and the most client-facing,' although ironically its probate aspect – seen as 'quite dull' and yet also 'complicated' – makes it less popular. The family seat is rated as 'amazing,' however. There are no Legal Aid cases and, as with the estates and financial services seat, the clients generally have a few bob in the bank.

'Quite a few trainees still filter through here interested in private client and family,' and Prettys isn't going to abandon them. Because of its reputation in the area, the firm will 'always have a private client base' and the French property team has grown steadily for years. Because we sensed a greater interest in commercial practice yet were keen not to be swept too far by the tide of pro-commercial comments, we checked in with the firm on this subject. For the record the firm says that its private client business

Chambers UK rankings

Corporate Finance • Debt Recovery • Employment •

Family/Matrimonial • Real Estate • Restructuring/

Insolvency • Shipping • Transport

is as important as ever. This should provide reassurance for all applicants interested in this type of practice.

An Ipswich you can't scratch

An uncharitable soul – or an interviewer playing devil's advocate – might suggest that for good commercial experiences there are better places to go than Ipswich. Each time we asked the question we received the same answer – Prettys' clients are from all over the country (and indeed the world), so 'it's not so relevant where we're based.' Naturally we then asked why someone might want to live in Ipswich and learned that East Suffolk is 'one of the nicer parts of the country' and has 'beautiful' scenery. Ipswich itself is apparently a 'touchy-feely' kinda place with 'a very good high street' and a newly developed waterfront where many trainees end up living. 'People who aren't attracted to living in big sprawling cities will like it.' Granted, one also mentioned that Ipswich was 'a little behind' and bemoaned the closure of the town centre's bars and pubs on Sundays, but they were sure 'it'll be a real great place to be in five or ten years' time.' We should probably mention that a lot of Prettys recruits have a local connection, having either grown up or attended university in the East of England.

Howl at the moon

What you find at Prettys are people who 'want to work in the regions and have made an active choice to do just that.' They talk about having made a lifestyle choice and finding a firm with 'a better attitude to work.' Most trainees leave the office by 5.30pm and 'there's none of that taking an extra jacket and leaving it on the chair kind of thing.' In short, people are 'not expected to work long hours as we're not paid to work long hours.' When it comes to salaries these are described as 'enough to get by on' and Ipswich isn't judged to be an especially expensive place to live. In all, the training experience is deemed 'less stressful' than it might be in a major city but this should not be assumed to be at the cost of quality. Prettys, say our sources, is a 'wolf in sheep's clothing.'

Prettys has a noteworthy gender imbalance. Most of its trainees are female, with 'one token boy' in 2008. The opposite is true of its partners. One source told us that as far as they knew 'it's been like this for years,' though there are hopes of it changing, particularly with regard to partners. 'Socialising can be a bit weird,' joked one trainee. Generally 'Prettys isn't that hot on organising social events,' although the partners took the whole firm out to a country house in Lowestoft for the centenary celebrations and they stump up for departmental Christmas lunches each year. Trainees are quite capable of making their own fun with others in the local chapter of the Junior Lawyers Division and last year four of them were on its committee. The regeneration of the Ipswich docks means the bar and pub scene is 'certainly on the up.' For now favourite haunts include Morgans and Tonic. If partners happen to be there too – 'Ipswich isn't huge so you usually end up in the same place' – it seems they're not averse to buying the drinks, and if trainees are kept late at a work function the firm will put them into taxis. In fact during the spate of killings in the town in 2007 partners showed great concern and 'offered to pay for taxis to train stations during the whole chilling thing.' The gruesome events hadn't affected the trainees we spoke to too much, beyond the sentiment offered by one, whose interview was interrupted by the noise of news helicopters covering the end of the trial. It was, they said, 'unusual to have Ipswich as the centre of attention.'

Previously lacking a defined process for qualifiers, Prettys used to rely on 'just a wink and a nod' to indicate which jobs would be available. After formalising everything in 2008 three out of five people stayed on, going into the shipping, employment and probate departments.

And finally...

Fighting quite an old-school reputation, Prettys has more to offer than one might assume for a firm tucked into the eastern corner of England. And then there's the push into Essex to consider. Students already convinced of the merits of a Suffolk lifestyle should need little persuasion.

- **In English, please?** Capital whats? Wet and dry shipping? Derivatives? Our Practice Area pages explain the mysteries of specific sectors of law, describe what lawyers actually do within them and tell you which firms covered in the True Picture section handle such work.

Well Connected

At Reed Smith you'll feel part of the wider wor

That might be because our 23 offices, located over 3 continents, handle so much international work, or because our departments are structured across our offices so that you are regularly in touch with colleagues and clients in different countries. It could even be because all our trainee solicitors have the option to take international or client secondments.

But we think you'll feel connected mostly because we'll encourage you to get involved from the outset. You'll get access to real work, opportunities to take part in community projects or pro bono work and you'll still have a work/life balance that allows you to get out and do your own thing.

WINNER
LEGAL
BUSINESS
AWARDS
2008
CSR FIRM OF THE YEAR

ReedSmith

The business of relationships.

www.reedsmith.com

NEW YOR
LONDON
HONG KO
CHICAGO
WASHING
BEIJING
PARIS
LOS ANG
SAN FRAM
PHILADEL
PITTSBUF
OAKLAND
MUNICH
ABU DHA
PRINCETC
N. VIRGIN
WILMING
BIRMINGH
DUBAI
CENTURY
RICHMON
GREECE

Reed Smith LLP

The facts

Location: London, Birmingham

Number of UK partners/solicitors: 111/143

Total number of trainees: 59

Seats: 4x6 months

Alternative seats: Overseas seats, secondments

Extras: Pro bono – Advocates 4 International Development, Liberty, Fairbridge; language training

> A real plus of working at Reed Smith is that if someone finds out you have a particular skill they will take advantage of it.

When Pittsburgh giant Reed Smith got hitched to Richards Butler, the feisty UK mid-sizer with an international outlook, it looked like a partnership of equals on this side of the Atlantic. It even went for a double-barrelled name in London – Reed Smith Richards Butler. The Brit firm's moniker has been dropped and the firm is now simply Reed Smith...

History lesson

Here's a brief synopsis of how this 1500-lawyer firm came to be in the UK. Reed Smith first gained a foothold here by taking up with London-Coventry concern Warner Cranston in 2001. Initially known as Reed Smith Warner Cranston, the Americans dumped the British name shortly after the honeymoon. The Warner team took this with good grace and carried on as they had always done. It was a cool little London and Midlands firm that was great at employment law, corporate and real estate. The UK team totalled only 50 or so fee earners, so hooking up with Reed Smith was a big deal.

Richards Butler was an established full-service London mid-market player with a formidable reputation in shipping and media finance in particular. It was known among trainees for its relaxed nature, niche practice areas and fashionable client secondments. The firm's overseas offices – heavily shipping-focused – were hugely important bringing in around half of its revenue. In 2007 Reed Smith and Richards Butler joined forces, and here we are a year later finding out how it's all gone.

Opinions on the union are divided. No one denies the Americans' influence has been good for business – the firm overshot its UK financial targets last year. Most also agree that RS and RB are a good cultural match: 'I had

this fear that working with Americans would be awful, but we've picked nice ones,' said one source. Merging, trainees conclude, was a good move for the firm, and London is now the largest office in the international network of 24 in eight countries. And yet minor niggles suggest it hasn't all been plain sailing. 'It's a real annoyance that everything needs to go through the States, so if you have a computer problem you have to call some guy in LA, who'll refer you straight back to the floor upstairs. And we get ridiculous firm-wide e-mails from US lawyers on a daily basis saying, 'Pardon the interruption, but does anyone know a district court judge in Florida?'' We also heard whispers that streamlining the name hasn't pleased everyone. 'I know the shipping guys were up in arms when they saw the name dropped with no consultation,' said one trainee. 'Richards Butler had such a strong standing there and now they're on the phone having to explain who they are to clients.'

Putting corporate on the map

In London there's an abundance of departments for trainees to try out. In the UK, Reed Smith was essentially a straightforward corporate specialist, while Richards Butler was something of a jack of all trades. Their union provided 'a choice of seats that has almost been a burden.' Said one trainee: 'I was hired to Reed Smith, where trainees always used to do two seats in corporate, one in litigation and then real estate or employment. Now it's a really difficult decision. You think, well, my heart likes the sound of the trendy seats, but my head says I should probably do something with better employment prospects.' Needless to say, those recruited by RB had a different view of things: 'The main drive of the merger was to ramp up corporate and none of us joined Richards Butler to do that.'

The corporate team has been bolstered, 'and the plan is to expand to be a real alternative to the magic circle.' Star clients now include prestigious media names such as the BBC, ITV, Channel 4, MTV and The Rank Group, as well the likes of Tate & Lyle, Merrill Lynch, Eurostar and GNER. Reed Smith works for Microsoft on a regular basis, and trainees recently grafted hard on its takeover of Multi Media Mapping, creators of the Multimap internet application. The department also won a role advising AOL on the UK aspects of its buyout of social networking site Bebo. Despite not being the most popular department among trainees, corporate has a reputation for giving good responsibility. 'There were a lot of disclosure letters and ancillary documents to draft; I gained loads of experience,' said one. Another told us: 'I sat with a supervisor who involved me in everything. I was always in the negotiations and conference calls, and had the side documents to deal with myself.' Rather than being tied to one supervisor, corporate trainees are now a pooled resource and, as such, find work all over the department. The hours are good for the City – even in corporate – with relatively few all-nighters and even 8.30pm finishes described as pretty late.

All at sea

The 'sizeable' real estate department is strong in the hotel and leisure industry, where it represented Showcase Cinemas on the pre-letting of a chain of new Cinema de Lux venues, and it is advising on the £400m disposal of Battersea Power Station. Another client is UAE Developments, a company that is building an Entertainment City leisure district in Qatar and a new hotel resort in Muscat. 'I know for a fact they are trying to grow the real estate finance team,' said one trainee. He wasn't divulging any great secret; the firm raided DLA Piper for partners a couple of years back and made further progress in 2008, winning places on the panels of Lloyds TSB, Alliance & Leicester and Anglo Irish Bank to go alongside a long-standing relationship with Barclays. 'I was given 50 files and told to go away and deal with them, and that's how I like to work,' said one trainee on the subject of supervision. 'You do get that autonomy at Reed Smith. There was supervision when I asked for it but essentially I was left to my own devices.' Within the department the type of work trainees do can be very different. 'I was dealing with the Land Registry on a daily

Chambers UK rankings

Asset Finance • Banking Litigation • Commodities • Competition/European Law • Corporate Finance • Defamation/Reputation Management • Dispute Resolution • Employment • Fraud: Civil • Insurance • Intellectual Property • Life Sciences • Media & Entertainment • Pensions • Product Liability • Professional Negligence • Real Estate • Real Estate Litigation • Shipping

basis,' said one contact, 'but towards the end of my seat another property trainee came and asked me how to do it. I was like, 'What do you do all day?'' The answer could well have been liaising with landlords and tenants, drafting licences to assign and simple leases.

Shipping law can seem incomprehensible to those who aren't in the know. 'I found the first three weeks like learning a new language: you find yourself speaking it before long, although I'm still using the word boat rather than ship,' confessed one landlubber. Seats are available in the dry, wet, and Admiralty shipping teams. Dry shipping is basically disputes where no physical accidents are involved. This is perhaps the most 'old-school blazers and braces' team, which means there's 'not a lot of office banter' and the supervision 'could be better,' however the work is acknowledged as 'fantastic.' It's an academic, research-based subject requiring 'creative thinking to find answers to problems that have never come up before, and then lot of drafting those solutions into useful advice for the client.' Wet shipping lawyers cover accidents at sea: oil spills, groundings and the like. Reed Smith runs a 24-hour service so as to always be on call when disaster strikes and the team is used by Svitzer, one of the world's largest salvage companies. Finally, the Admiralty team's focus on The Law of the Sea requires knowledge of international treaties. 'About a third of my time was spent doing research. Another third was court work – bundling, filing forms and preparing witness statements – and the rest was spent dealing with miscellaneous people in the industry,' said a trainee who'd worked here.

Getting away with any old junk

The niche areas for which Richards Butler were justly famed are still very much alive and kicking under the new regime, and the mouth-watering media secondments are enough to make trainees elsewhere green with envy. Competition for postings to the BBC and MTV is fierce and equally popular are overseas placements to locations such as Piraeus, San Francisco, Abu Dhabi and Dubai. The 'flagship secondment' is to the Hong Kong office, which due to legal reasons is the only place in the world where the Richards Butler name survives. 'The work there was great, but they also tell you to make the most of being in Hong Kong and when you have friends or family visiting they encourage you to take the office junk out for a sail around the bay.' The office is split about 50/50 between local lawyers and expatriates. A real plus of working at Reed Smith is that 'if someone finds out you have a particular skill they will take advantage of it,' and in addition to foreign seats, trainees with language skills may be sent off to other parts of the world as and when the need arises.

In 2007 Reed Smith moved its Coventry office to a business park near Solihull, just off the M42, 'where you can see sheep and cows from the window.' The two trainees recruited to the 50-person Solihull branch every year have virtually no choice of seats: employment, coco, litigation and property are the only ones available. This may sound a duff deal compared to the London offering, however we doubt there's another training contract in the vicinity with such a large and well-resourced international firm. DLA in central Brum would compare favourably, but then not everyone wants to work in a huge office as one of a large cohort of trainees. The clients Midlands trainees have access to include Akzo Nobel, Countryside Properties, Sara Lee Corporation and Warwick District Council.

Finding a niche

Richards Butler was always a good-natured place. 'It was the only law firm I interviewed at where people managed to crack a joke,' said one contact. Accordingly, it liked to hire 'confident, laid-back' and 'resourceful' types. On the other hand, the Reed Smith of old preferred those who, 'while all perfectly nice, are perhaps more academic and serious-minded.' It seems RB's sense of humour endures: 'We watched our 'core values' video last week – everyone was in hysterics,' giggled a trainee who couldn't tell us exactly why. You probably had to be there. The social scene is lively: 'Just last night

we had a fantastic party with the vac scheme guys. [Grad recruitment head] Mark Matthews was moon-walking at one point.' Final-seaters mentioned a trip out to Paris to visit a mate on secondment – '12 of us were sleeping on their kitchen floor, it was great!' There are football, cricket and softball teams, and regular drinks, parties and client events to get involved with. As the Solihull crew drive to work, it's more a case of lunches out than boozy post-work shenanigans.

'I don't regret a single day of my contract,' said one trainee, 'but it's just not the firm I joined.' Others shared this sentiment, a few expressing disappointment that 'the first thing that comes up in any conversation now is, 'Is there the budget? Will Pittsburgh approve?'' There's a feeling that the US HQ doesn't always understand certain aspects of UK law firms, including (and here our contact adopted a John Wayne accent) 'who the hell these trainee people are and what it is they do.' The main problem this year was the 'horribly mishandled' qualification process in which positions were available for qualifiers but several of them were abroad and 'a lot of the niche jobs were missing. There were loads of corporate vacancies, including four in the Middle East. People were thinking, 'Errrm… where have all the niche departments gone?'' As a result only 19 of the 28 qualifiers stayed.

And finally...

Every single one of our contacts was positive about the seats, secondments, atmosphere, hours and work on offer at Reed Smith. This is a firm with a bright future; it just needs to recruit more corporate-minded trainees than the ones RB took on before the merger.

Reynolds Porter Chamberlain LLP

The facts

Location: London, Tiverton

Number of UK partners/solicitors: 64/200

Total number of trainees: 33

Seats: 4x6 months

Alternative seats: Secondments

Client Associated Newspapers provides access to juicy defamation and libel claims. In the past year it has crossed swords with HRH the Prince of Wales, celebrity chef Marco Pierre White and queen WAG Colleen McLoughlin.

There was a time when you simply wouldn't dream about applying to this mid-sized City outfit unless you were committed to hardcore insurance litigation. A fresh new image and a decision to beef up its transactional offering now allows for a much more rounded training.

Eyes on the pies

When many of the firm's current trainees applied to RPC they did so in order to sink their teeth into juicy, high-end litigation for the firm's insurance clients. However, the market was already moving on and the insurance industry was beginning to plod more slowly than before. RPC realised it had posted consecutive years of static profits and saw that it was time for a change. Cue the beginning of a new era at the firm, one in which RPC has set its sights on a bigger piece of the corporate pie. Summing up this story, one trainee told us: 'When I was being groomed for the firm it was about 70% insurance and litigation work, but these days they are certainly more eager to push for half and half insurance and commercial work.'

The shift has been accompanied by a wider desire to modernise the firm and sharpen its image. This is epitomised by its 2006 move to the super-swanky Tower Bridge House, an attendant clean-desk policy and abolition of dress-down Fridays. Overall trainees were upbeat about the changes, with one proud to tell us: 'It's a very impressive building, so it's nice to tell people you work here.' Another trainee, while casting an eye over St Katharine's Dock and 'the playthings of the rich and famous bobbing about on the Thames,' was equally effusive in his praise for the direction in which the firm is heading. 'It's a good business model as it means we are covered during down times but equally can benefit when everyone in the City is happy.' The fact that trainees are sharing the firm's new vision of the future is in itself a positive sign and a clear endorsement of the inclusive, open working environment that the firm has created in its new office.

Insuring success

Commercial posturing aside, insurance work still accounts for 60% of the firm's turnover, and with many of the industry's heavy-hitters on its books, including the likes of ACE Group, Allianz and Swiss Re, RPC is not going to release its grasp on this market. Most trainees can still expect to do two of their four seats on this type of work, although given the range of matters undertaken this was not seen by our interviewees as restrictive, with many thoroughly confused by the sheer number of seats on offer. This fact is not helped by regular reshuffles and rebranding of departments, although one helpful source, finger firmly on the pulse, explained the full insurance menu as follows: 'They currently offer seats in the professional risk, medical negligence, defendant PI, construction, reinsurance, financial institutions and property risk departments.' The one constant across these seats is that RPC is always the defence side, handling claims passed on by its 'high-profile insurer and reinsurer clients.'

One of the cornerstones of the firm's insurance reputation is its defence of professional liability claims. This work featured prominently in the experiences of our sample trainees, who had largely experienced it from either a financial services stance – 'a lot of work defending the Big Four accountancy firms' – or solicitors' liability, but the firm also works extensively in relation to negligence by actuaries and other pension professionals, construction professionals, financial advisers, insurance brokers, professional trustees, surveyors and barristers. The area offers 'factually interesting cases' and a popular mix of 'big-case work, sitting on the bottom rung' and smaller files to run under supervision. When working on big cases, typical tasks are 'research, admin and document management,' as well as 'handling discrete tasks such as disclosure.' On their own files trainees are able to 'speak with clients, insurers and the other side, as primary contact.' The most memorable experience for one person was 'making a guy bankrupt.'

Many of the insurance disputes on which the firm is instructed require assistance from foreign lawyers, so RPC makes good use of its membership of the TerraLex network of overseas law firms. Recent cases have concerned a €60m claim arising from a fire at an oil refinery in Sicily, widespread losses from an oil spill in Colombia in 1998 and a $180m Nick Leeson-style fraud on a Cayman Islands investment fund. One of the most interesting UK-based cases is the liability dispute brought against Bedfordshire Police Authority under the Riot (Damages) Act 1886 following the riot and resulting fire that destroyed the Yarl's Wood immigration detention centre in 2002. This important case could go all the way to the House of Lords.

In all insurance seats trainees seemed thoroughly impressed by the level of client contact. This includes 'monthly client seminars where you're encouraged to come along and mingle.' The culmination of the insurance social calendar is an annual quiz between partners and clients, at which trainees are integrally involved, from 'going around taking in answers and helping clients if there are issues,' to 'making full use of the free bar.' Overall, time spent socially with clients is 'quite light-hearted – as you would expect from the insurance market – and thoroughly good fun.' These evening duties aside, the hours in insurance seats are 'a quite reasonable 9.30am to 6.30pm most days.'

A tissue, a tissue

The respectful hours and steady pace of the insurance group is not everyone's idea of fun, so those seeking a more adrenalin-fuelled existence get their fix in the firm's growing corporate team. 'Some impressive partners have been attracted from A&O, Jones Day and Addleshaws,' explained one trainee; 'some of these guys are real go-getters who are looking to bring in top work.' Among the firm's recent deals are corporate sales and purchases for Swedish paper experts SCA, most notably its acquisition of Procter & Gamble's European tissue business in 2007.

Chambers UK rankings

Advertising & Marketing • Clinical Negligence • Construction • Corporate Finance • Defamation/Reputation Management • Dispute Resolution • Education • Employment • Family/Matrimonial • Insurance • Intellectual Property • Media & Entertainment • Partnership • Personal Injury • Product Liability • Professional Negligence • Tax

While the nuances of tissue branding may not inspire at first glance, at a whopping £350m this transaction is a good measure of the firm's growing mid-market capabilities. A more regular diet of work for trainees includes support on 'small to medium-sized AIM listings and M&A work for large limited companies and small plcs.' There is also 'company secretarial work for your own small clients.' Perhaps caught up in the buzz of the department, trainees assured us that hours are 'not preposterous,' backing it up with the slightly ominous but philosophical reasoning that 'the low of a long week of midnight finishes always ends with the high of a completion.'

The other main transactional seat is similarly prone to peaks and troughs. 'In real estate there were some extreme highs and lows when I was there,' said one interviewee. 'You get so much responsibility and there's a real sense of achievement when you complete something, but it can be stressful on a day-to-day basis.' Trainees handle their own small files, largely relating to leasehold property, and on these they must become 'the driving force.' The partners have been good at winning over clients from other departments; their list includes Daily Mail Group, Electrolux plc, HMV/Waterstone's Group, KLM and the Royal Embassy of Saudi Arabia.

Trainee in High Court jury scandal

RPC has one other major drawcard for those intent on bagging a sexy training contract – we're talking about its highly regarded media law group. Its appeal is easy to understand, with flagship client Associated Newspapers (publishers of the *Daily Mail*, *Mail on Sunday*, *Metro* and *Evening Standard*) providing access to some juicy defamation and libel claims. In the past year alone it has crossed swords in courts up to the House of Lords with HRH the Prince of Wales, celebrity chef Marco Pierre White, queen WAG Colleen McLoughlin and ex-Chief Executive of BP, Lord Browne. Despite the attendant glamour, trainees were of the opinion that 'in reality the seat probably isn't as sexy as people think, as you won't be rubbing shoulders with the rich and famous on a daily basis.' They did give the quality of work on offer a big thumbs-up, with one thoroughly satisfied source explaining his joy at completing a six-month stint that included 'a High Court trial in front of a jury lasting two weeks, and a small claim that I managed myself and achieved a settlement on.' The main problem with this popular department is the frustration involved in trying to secure a seat within it. Other sought-after opportunities for adventurous trainees include client secondments to the likes of Carillion, BDO Stoy Hayward and Sportsworld. There are usually three trainees out with a client at any one time and 'the legal teams seem very happy to have you. They are usually quite small so you get tons of responsibility.'

Decision possible?

If you are still able to get your hands on a copy, check out RPC's tongue-in-cheek 'Decision Impossible' trainee brochure from 2007. This natty publication charts the rise and fall of two trainees, one of whom takes his time to research what is on offer and chooses the bright lights of RPC, while his unfortunate friend joins a Law Factory inhabited by Fat Cat Partners and The Clones. If you read this and are still not convinced that RPC is what you're looking for, the vac scheme also comes recommended and is responsible for snaring many of the current trainees. 'They really made efforts to make you feel like a part of everything; even though you are only there for two weeks you get real work and immediately feel part of the team.' This inclusive approach continues into the training contract and is exemplified by the new open-plan office. 'For trainees it makes people seem accessible and approachable. There's no hovering and wondering whether to knock on a partner's door. It's also nice to not have that physical hierarchy.' Or as one chirpy interviewee put it: 'You can chat away to partners all day, every day and you learn not to see them as intimidating.' This communication also has the practical benefit of 'helping to ensure you always have the right amount of work and that you are getting on okay with it.'

'People here are hard-working but not obsessed with their work,' one trainee declared. The current batch are indeed a far cry from The Clones and include a few people with life experiences under their belt. After work they can get involved with the usual departmental, sporting, trainee and firm-wide socials, although the firm should not be viewed as capable of providing a brand new social life. Trainees say they are able to maintain their individuality at RPC and perhaps this is why so many of them choose to stay after qualification. Matching previous years' healthy results, in 2008 12 of the 13 qualifiers elected to make their tenure in Tower Bridge House a permanent thing.

And finally...

RPC represents a great opportunity for anyone who wants to get their fix of big cases while also testing the waters of mid-level transactional practice. Top tip: ask to see the office sheep if you're invited for an interview. No, we're not winding you up.

Salans

> People don't like it if you just say yes and agree; they like you to make your own views known. If you disagree with something a senior partner has said, they respect you more if you come out and say it.

For a firm stretching from New York to China by way of Azerbaijan, Salans is still relatively anonymous here in the UK. With its canny focus on emerging markets, we suspect it won't be too long before its name is on everyone's lips.

Back to Baku

Established as a Franco-American venture in 1978, what started as Salans Hertzfeld & Heilbronn embarked on its sustained period of growth way back in 1997 when it absorbed a niche London finance firm and then operations in France and New York. Ever since, it's been acquiring offices across Europe and Asia, most recently opening in Frankfurt, and with further offices planned for Hong Kong and Beijing. More than 700 lawyers now work in 18 offices, including such diverse locations as Shanghai, Kyiv, Istanbul, Barcelona, Budapest, St Petersburg, Moscow, Baku (Azerbaijan) and Almaty (Kazakhstan – leave the Borat jokes at the door, people). You may have noticed a lot of Eastern and Central European names in that list: Salans focuses on economies that are expanding as Western markets feel the pinch. Arguably, Salans' prestige increases the further east you go, and it competes with the likes of White & Case in Central Europe. As one interviewees reflected: 'It's great to be in the same league as a firm like that.'

We reckon Salans is a dark horse. Its trainees point out that it's 'quite a young firm' with a lot of associates in their mid-to-late twenties and early thirties and 'partners at their apex.' The firm's continual expansion and healthy turnover – up 65% since 2005, with last year seeing revenues rising by a third – suggest the strategy of focusing on emerging markets is working. It's certainly in a stronger position than many of its London competitors during the credit crunch. 'Because the firm is decidedly

global... we can afford to expand,' boasted a recruit. Merger talks with Kirkpatrick & Lockhart to bolster the firm's US presence failed in 2006, but with Salans' past history of mergers, we wonder how long it will be before another potential partner steps up.

Salans y!

Contrary to what you may read on popular online encyclopaedias, Salans doesn't have an official headquarters. When questioned where the balance of power lay, the answers from our interviewees were as varied as the firm's addresses. London and Moscow (eclipsing the 'pretty small' New York office) are at the front of the global charge, and their respective activities are often intertwined, but the consensus was that Paris is numéro un. At least, 'at times it feels like certain people in the French office have a slightly haughty approach and think everyone is subservient to them.' Another source put it more diplomatically: 'The balance of power lies somewhere in the middle of the Channel. The Paris office wants to drag it their way and the London office wants to drag it our way every now and again.' Certainly Salans has made a bigger impression on the City of Lights than on the crowded London market. 'When I speak to French people they recognise the name,' said one recruit. 'In London we're not quite there yet.'

Almost all London work has a cross-border element, and while banking and corporate get the lion's share, 'the firm as a whole is very internationally focused' and even the conference rooms are named after cities in which it has offices. Last year the Central African Mining and Exploration Company instructed Salans on a £125m acquisition of a 20% stake in Katanga, and the firm advised on a joint venture between GazpromBankInvest and TriGranit to develop Russian real estate. Actually a lot of work comes to the UK via Moscow, such as Salans' assistance to Deutsche Bank on loan agreements for hotel and other real estate financings in the Russian capital, the showcase being the $600m five-star Four Seasons Moskva Hotel on Red Square. Moscow is the only office to offer trainees a short, predominantly corporate-based secondment. It's only three months long, which requires some juggling of seats when the trainee returns. Despite the international nature of the firm, and the occasional business trip to Eastern Europe, opportunities for travel are generally minimal until after qualification.

Continent please, Carol

Seats are available in corporate, banking, insolvency, employment, litigation, property and (new this year) shipping litigation. Trainees invariably try either corporate or banking, the areas in which the firm's primary focus lies. 'The English work isn't huge, but you get enormous deals out of Moscow worth billions.' For example, Italian energy giant Enel's joint venture with Eni to acquire $5.83bn of gas assets formerly owned by controversially bankrupted petroleum colossus YUKOS. With as many partners in the corporate team as associates, 'you tend to get good experience and scope to do first drafts.' Of course, 'there's always a risk you could get stuck on an enormous deal that takes over half your seat, but they're good at ensuring you get a broad range of work.' Corporate also offers business trips, with some recruits (albeit often acting as 'glorified couriers') jetting off to Eastern Europe and North America.

The banking seat mixes 'classic finance' with real estate finance, asset finance and consumer credit work. The latter sees trainees reviewing and advising on consumer credit adverts. Not those irritating daytime telly ones starring minor personalities, it's 'mostly print ones. I think you'd go stir-crazy if you were forced to watch Carol Vorderman talking about loans for too long.' A recent foray into 'e-money' has the firm doing the regulatory work associated with Oyster and other pre-paid cards. Straight banking offers the most international experience, and last year the team assisted the European Bank for Reconstruction and Development on lending throughout Eastern and Central Europe, as well as the funders of a €62.5m loan to the second-largest Ukrainian motor vehicle manufacturer. The pace of an insolvency seat 'depends on the time of year and how the economy is going.' Hint: troubled times mean busier insolvency lawyers. Through the banking team, the firm also offers a six-month sec-

Chambers UK rankings

Asset Finance • Corporate Finance • Debt Recovery •

Dispute Resolution • Employment • Financial Services

Regulation • Real Estate • Restructuring/Insolvency

ondment to a major client, which is advisable if you plan to qualify into a finance-related field. The down side is its location out in Essex: the long commute means 'it can be quite lonely there.'

No weak links

Interviewees raved about the employment seat. 'We mainly act for employers,' explained one; 'occasionally employees, if they earn enough.' One such employee was quiztress Anne Robinson, who needed extricating from her previous agent's terms ahead of a new £10m deal with the BBC. Recruits get to draft defences, letters of advice, service agreements and possibly even witness statements. 'I felt less like a trainee and more like a proper fee earner,' beamed one. The litigation team handles everything from international arbitrations to smaller matters like a woman suing over the loss of her sunglasses. It's 'a real mixed bag.' Trainees attend conferences with barristers and try their hand at drafting, as well as preparing 'the inevitable trial bundles.' International arbitration is a growth area, with three partners, a consultant and four assistants hired this year. So is a firm that focuses most effort on its corporate and banking practices a good fit for contentious-minded students? 'Even though it wouldn't strike you as a litigation type of firm,' a source assured us, 'there's more than enough interesting work out there.'

Overall 'Salans is the kind of place where you get on best if you get yourself involved.' Departments differ greatly – some provide 'the security blanket you need to do the best work you can,' 'some are more of the 'throw them in and let them struggle' school,' while others 'make you feel quite lost and overwhelmed and wish you had someone to comfort you.' All respond well to recruits showing initiative in forming relationships around the team to seek a broad range of work. Last year we noted that rapid expansion and an emphasis on self-reliance meant formal structures and communications left something to be desired, but Salans has caught on and is polishing up its act. This year it tapped a former Freshfields HR manager to be its new global head of human resources.

Mid-seat appraisals were also introduced, even if some teams still need to be prodded. Provisions for formal training have improved too: there's a general induction covering IT and anti-money laundering, as well as regular departmental training and in-depth sessions on legal writing and communication. Ultimately, 'the formal structure is there, but as a trainee you sometimes have to make sure you get the benefits.' Work hours are good for an international firm: most trainees are regularly out the door between 6pm and 7pm, and 'only very rarely do you get really late nights.'

Globe trotters

So what does Salans look for? Naturally an international mindset is key, and having a little international experience yourself won't hurt. Foreign languages are useful rather than crucial. Salans has 'so much contact with overseas offices you couldn't be expected to speak them all, and they mostly speak English to you.' Few trainees come to the firm straight after uni and law school: in fact many didn't study undergraduate law. 'Almost everyone has something quirky about them,' reflecting a 'broader and more mature approach' to recruitment. As for common personality traits, 'people aren't afraid to be forcible when they need to be.' No one at the firm is 'easy to push around' and 'wallflowers wouldn't do well.' As one recruit elaborated: 'People don't like it if you just say yes and agree; they like you to make your own views known. If you disagree with something a senior partner has said, they respect you more if you come out and say it.'

Socialising is mostly of the impromptu and departmental variety, and while 'on the whole it's not the most outwardly sociable of firms... if you want to go to the pub you can always find someone to go with.' Favourites include Cos Bar and Shaw's The Booksellers. Recent intakes have organised a few events that include trainees-to-be, who previously complained that 'you literally don't know anyone at the firm until you walk in the door.' Sports-wise, a group of guys play football against client teams and the Bromley office, and every year the firm enters people into the 5 km City Race. Salans' big blowout is its Christmas party, which was held at the Selsdon Park Hotel in Croydon last year. Not the most glamorous of backdrops, to be sure, but it was a nice gesture to the Bromley office and the firm paid for transport home or a room for the night. Unfortunately it was held on a Thursday night, so everyone 'stayed up late and in the morning had to make their way to work.' Back in central London, the office's location near the Millennium Bridge is perfect for jaunts to art galleries or the Globe Theatre, although one interviewee sheepishly admitted: 'We've had lunches at the Tate, but I've never actually seen anything there.' Salans might have to find extra space soon – 'we don't really fit anymore.'

During the informal qualification process trainees discuss their desired department with the training partner, who squares it with the relevant people. This year all three qualifiers got jobs in their first-choice teams.

And finally...

Its relatively low UK profile and offices in places you need a map to find make this a real dark horse, but a good bet for someone interested in cross-border corporate and finance deals.

Shadbolt LLP

The facts

Location: London, Reigate

Number of UK partners/solicitors: 24/25

Total number of trainees: 8

Seats: 4x6 months

Alternative seats: Overseas seats, secondments

> Essentially construction law is made up of your old law school friends, contract and tort, dressed up in bricks and mortar.

Young in years but long on experience, Shadbolt is as indispensable to the construction and engineering sector as high-rise cranes and liquid concrete injectors.

Building fairy tales

Like the porkicide-minded villain of a certain children's cautionary tale, Shadbolt came out of nowwhere to scare the wits out of its opposition and gather together some of the best construction practitioners in the country. However, this bad-ass wolf of a specialist firm is all about putting houses up, not blowing them down. It was formed as recently as 1991, when Dick Shadbolt (previously a construction law supremo at what is now CMS Cameron McKenna) hung up his commuting spurs and moved his practice to the Surrey countryside. He soon acquired an office space in Reigate and the touchpaper was lit on Shadbolt's phenomenal ascent. Mr S moved into a consultancy role back in 2006, around the time another young Shadbolt joined as a trainee. After 15 years of hard graft, he left his successor Liz Jenkins in control of a firm with 50 lawyers in Reigate and London, a dinky but growing Paris office and associated outposts in Greece, Romania and Tanzania. Now, as in 1991, the majority of clients come from the construction industry, including some of the biggest contractors in the business like Costain, Amey, Carillion and Galliford Try. Then there's a whole raft of subcontractors (builders, equipment providers, mechanical and electrical engineers, etc) and various public and private sector organisations for whom buildings and projects are constructed.

As many a fairytale character will testify, a rapid rise can lead to a swift fall. If Shadbolt didn't exactly fall down the chimney last year, a drop in revenue of around 10% certainly put a check on its momentum. The decrease was attributed to the conclusion of major litigation for clients Citibank and Degrémont and does highlight the firm's reliance upon contentious construction matters. Aware of this, Shadbolt has built up its PFI and projects practice, handling defence, healthcare and education sector matters across the UK. What's more, in early 2008 the firm launched a non-exclusive alliance with Belfast firm C&H Jefferson, hoping to cash in on the boom in PFI and PPP in Northern Ireland. Will this gradual shift change the identity of the firm? Talking to trainees, we heard differing opinions. 'There's more and more work on the projects side and we're getting instructions at the main contractor level,' said one. Another considered 'the two largest departments – disputes and projects – are heavily weighted towards construction and even the current PFI focus could change if the climate changes. We're not going to stop being defined by construction expertise.'

On the roads again

You won't be surprised to hear that the training contract is 'geared around construction,' with trainees spending one or more seats dealing with this kind of work. The departments on offer are projects (including non-contentious construction), real estate, corporate and commercial (including employment), and disputes (including construction and engineering disputes). It is 'unusual not to spend a seat in London' and there does seem to be a 'fluidity of movement at all levels' between the offices.

Client secondments, a disputes/arbitration seat for French-speaking trainees in Paris or even a 'corporate-style' placement in Dar Es Salaam offer other destinations to consider.

Contentious construction in the Reigate office is almost a dead cert and introduces trainees to a variety of domestic and international instructions. A trainee could encounter anything from 'a UK contractor doing luxury home renovation with a dispute as to payment' to 'cutting-edge High Court cases.' For the former they might 'help to initiate proceedings to get the money back' and on the latter there is 'a lot of bundling and admin for trainees,' as well as 'research on out-of-the-ordinary matters.' Occasionally a trainee might win the responsibility lottery: 'I got to draft instructions to counsel and witness statements for a big dispute,' beamed one. The fact that the firm continues to take instructions from 'down-to-earth, sometimes in-your-face' subcontractors means that trainees have the opportunity to 'run matters under supervision.' The benefit of handling these smaller cases is that 'you do manage to see progress... and you do get an overview of the litigation process.'

Shadbolt's growing international expertise also exposes trainees to adjudications and arbitrations in emerging markets; indeed the level of activity in Eastern Europe encouraged the formation of an alliance with Romanian law firm Oana Irina Firca. Shadbolt's existing links to Greece and Africa have seen the firm acting, for example, for an international contractor in dispute with an East African government concerning a multimillion-dollar roads contract. No matter the provenance, construction cases usually involve masses of often highly complex evidence and our interviewees were unequivocal that 'you have to work hard to get to grips with it all.' However, the contentious team also deals with some general commercial litigation, so 'you can end up handling broader stuff, say a freezing injunction on aircraft in a trusts dispute.'

The 'increasingly projects-dominated' non-contentious side of construction law can mean assisting on anything from 'street lighting to hospitals to schools issues' and the team has started working on Olympics instructions. Initially, trainees will stick to 'bog-standard' documentation, but 'because you're in small teams, by the end of the seat you can be dealing directly with the clients and banks.' It's small wonder that these non-contentious construction seats are sought after. Commercial property also had favourable reviews: 'You run files totally under your own steam, negotiate things, do all the correspondence and client calls, so if you cock up you have to put your hand up – the responsibility is just great!' Just like general commercial and employment departments, the team does a lot of support work for the construction lawyers. Another 'hugely popular' way to spend a seat is to go on

Chambers UK rankings

Construction • Corporate Finance • Dispute Resolution •

Employment • Information Technology • Intellectual

Property • Projects, Energy & Natural Resources •

Real Estate

secondment to a major client. These postings bring experience of 'anything from PI claims, to construction disputes to general litigation' and 'a lot of freedom and responsibility.'

Constructive comments

Essentially construction law is made up of your old law school friends, contract and tort, dressed up in bricks and mortar. While the odd trainee may arrive possessing 'some experience of the sector,' it's 'far from a prerequisite to be up-to-the-minute informed about construction law.' Seminars and training sessions soon provide the necessary grounding, and some trainees pursue a construction law qualification at night school. The need to 'get up to speed quickly' is just one of the demands of a Shadbolt training. A 'partner-heavy structure' and 'few paralegals' means on the one hand an abundance of 'bundling and grunt work,' but on the other 'a lot of decent drafting and research.' Trainees are assigned to a partner in each seat and 'it's made clear that it's not your responsibility to get work, it comes to you.' On the up side, close interaction with partners means 'a reasonable amount of supervision' and 'you're trusted with responsibility.' Working at close quarters with lawyers at or near the top of their field makes for an exhilarating experience that is as inspiring as it is demanding. A cheery self-sufficiency was evident among our interviewees, who were 'mostly a little older.' 'We're not conventional City types,' one source emphasised; 'we've a variety of experiences and the firm seems to value your present abilities more than how many A-levels you've got.' This is a training for grown-ups, rather than a gentle induction into the legal profession. While the hours can be long (because 'all-nighters do happen'), trainees appreciate that 'partners will call it a day if the work isn't urgent and they're whacked.' An average day is 9.30am until 7pm.

Who's Surrey now?

'The atmosphere is that of a fairly small-firm,' trainees explained; 'you get to know most people across the two offices within a year.' However 'the dynamism and the excellence of our work mean it isn't a desperately friendly place. You feel there could be some work done to make you feel valued... that side hasn't quite caught up yet.' This isn't to say that Shadbolt is overtly unfriendly; it's perhaps more an indication of how focused people are on the work. There are formal social events and 'the Paris, Tanzania and Romanian lawyers make an effort to come over.' What's more, some UK partners 'are good at arranging drinks for after work.' Brush down those networking skills because 'the firm's size means there's a lot of scope for going to client social events as a trainee.'

In past years we've heard a great deal about the London/Reigate divide and the question of whether the firm should develop and present itself as a London or Surrey firm. This year trainees played down the issue, telling us 'there isn't a bias to either Surrey or London. We were a Surrey-based firm, but they've recruited more and more people who wanted to be in London and so now there's a lot of hot-desking between the two.' The Reigate HQ is 'the larger of the offices and it's structured around small rooms of two or three people' with 'a slightly older population... people tend to have families and live a drive away.' As a consequence 'the social life is a wee bit dismal, it basically doesn't exist except for the organised summer and Christmas parties.' Most trainees are based here at any one time, albeit working 'different hours in different departments.' Those in litigious seats will make the short train journey to London 'a couple of times a month.' Up in the capital, around 40 staff are based in an open-plan office 'located near St Paul's, with views of the cathedral on one side and the river on the other.' 'More laid back' in atmosphere, the prevalence of bars, restaurants and various London attractions definitely appeal to younger staff: 'trainees and associates are often out for drinks together on a Friday.' However, with some recent qualifiers opting for the rural delights of Reigate, the divide in preference isn't strictly along age lines. Whether a committed City or country dweller, the annual summer and Christmas parties see everyone 'crammed into some hotel, last year in Croydon,' with 'future trainees invited as well.' In 2008 three out of four qualifiers stayed on with the firm in the disputes and projects departments, with all three opting for London as their base office.

And finally...

When applying here you need to be very clear about the firm's raison d'être. If you're sure you want to focus on the construction sector then you're in for a treat as you'll be able to spend two years working alongside some of the best practitioners in the field.

Sheridans

The facts

Location: London

Number of UK partners/solicitors: 21/18

Total number of trainees: 2

Seats: 4x6 months

Alternative seats: None

Extras: Pro bono – various projects, including music industry trusts

> It's no hardship to entertain clients or market for new business. Trainees often accompany partners or other fee earners and are also likely to be sent out on their own to represent the firm.

This small media and entertainment firm has advised some of the biggest names in music, film, television and theatre for over 50 years. For a training contract that offers glitz and the glam as well as a grounding in company/commercial law, litigation, employment and property, Sheridans could be just the ticket.

Stage, screen, script

Sheridans' client list could easily fill a whole season's worth of episodes of *The Culture Show*. In fact we apologise now if the rest of this reads as if we're name-dropping. In film, Sheridans' expertise has impacted on *Amazing Grace* and Mike Leigh's most recent film *Happy Go Lucky*. In TV, the firm undertakes work for production companies such as RDF (producers of *Wife Swap* and *Faking It*) and Shed Media (*Footballers Wives* and *Bad Girls*), as well as for broadcasters Channel 4 and the BBC. Keeping theatregoers happy, the lawyers advised Sir Andrew Lloyd Webber and Littlestar Services on *Mamma Mia!* shows globally, and all aspects of the music used in the feature film starring Meryl Streep and Pierce Brosnan. Lastly, let's not forget the musicians who have benefited from their services – Sir Paul McCartney, Pink Floyd, Van Morrison, The Propellerheads and CSS to name just a few.

Just how much exposure will trainees get to such clients? Lots from the reports we heard. Sheridans' trainees take seats from the following options: music, theatre and media; film and television; property; company commercial; employment and litigation. Where you sit is 'very much open for discussion and they take your views into account.' A seat can also be a hybrid; with your time split between two departments simultaneously. This arrange-

ment usually comes into play with the smaller departments, and in the past has been seen with litigation, employment and property. Of course it does mean 'you're on the go the whole time.' Thus far trainees haven't always followed a standard four-by-six-month seat structure, however the firm does intend for this to become the norm. The best advice is for people to remember that 'trainees do need to be flexible and help where they are needed. We are small, so seats may be extended or shortened to meet the needs of the firm.'

Let me... entertain you

At the heart of the firm is the music, theatre and media department and quite naturally it's 'the seat everyone tends to do and wants to do.' Trainees may be given their own caseload or help partners on larger, more complex transactional matters by drafting, negotiating or perhaps doing research. To this day the team follows the beliefs of its founder Bernard Sheridan, who passed away last year: it acts primarily for artists rather than record labels. Already regarded as one of the best in the UK, the music practice was further bolstered in 2006 with the arrival of James Sully from Harbottle & Lewis and it now sits firmly in the top spot, according to *Chambers UK*. Sully brought a number of band managers with him, including those representing Franz Ferdinand and Kaiser Chiefs.

The firm supports emerging artists and partner Stephen Kempner is 'regularly to be found in a meeting room with the latest NME magazine.' Trainees are regularly out and about at gigs checking out talent and trying to establish future clients; in fact one trainee joked that 'music lawyers are the new A&R people.' The music team covers a broad spectrum of issues, from band member agreements and copyright issues to royalty audits and distribution contracts. Through it all trainees gain ample commercial experience.

The scope of the film and TV department's work is equally extensive, covering all aspects of development, financing, production and distribution of films and television programmes. This includes working on format licences, cast and crew agreements and talent deals for producers, broadcasters, financiers and lending institutions. The Osborne family has relied on the lawyers for numerous projects, as has Kylie Minogue, who consulted them over her cameo role in *Doctor Who*. As one trainee put it: 'They really let you get involved with interesting stuff across the board.'

Behind the scenes

If you are chomping at the bit to become the next top media lawyer, we must ask you to slow down and read on because there's more to this firm than the world of entertainment. The property, employment, litigation and corporate/commercial departments are all very decent practices in their own right. These growing areas do not stand separately from the media and entertainment practices, and trainees stress that 'departments work together on deals; there's a lot of crossover.' For example, when the firm advises on tours, such as Kylie's Showgirl extravaganza, this involves not only the music department but usually the employment and corporate/commercial teams, both of which are key to sorting out contracts with tour managers and crew and protecting IP rights. Property department trainees are exposed to a wider variety of clients and touch on commercial and residential matters, sometimes 'liaising with foreign lawyers, undertaking property searches and ensuring everything is running smoothly.' Additionally there is a certain amount of lease drafting and assignments of leases.

In the litigation seat there's scope for newbies to hone their advocacy skills. Cases feed through from the rest of the firm and cover management, publishing and recording disputes, infringements of IP rights and the occasional defamation matter. There is also a fair bit of commercial litigation (banking, insolvency, corporate) and some landlord and tenant disputes. In employment you could be advising well-paid executives on their exit from production companies and broadcasters, or perhaps advising on contracts for their new positions. Corporate clients also seek assistance with compromise agreements for the peo-

Chambers UK rankings

Media & Entertainment

ple they let go and disciplinary policies to keep them out of employment tribunals. This seat is known for the high level of client contact. Time in corporate/commercial is overseen by new head of department Rex Nwakodo, who we heard described as 'a really good source to learn from.' Our sources had been kept busy on 'usual trainee stuff' on company sales – due diligence and board meetings, etc – but apparently the partners will give more responsibility when they feel someone is ready for it.

Within each seat, work tends to come from a number of sources, and there's direct contact with partners and 'a good level of supervision, so you don't feel as though you are unsupported.' The appraisal system is fluid: trainees receive ongoing feedback on their work, followed by a formal end-of-seat appraisal – basically 'you get told how you're doing as you go, which is good for gauging where you are at.' In-house training sessions are usually held on Thursday mornings and cover things such as 'band member agreements, artist agreements and any new things that have come up in the law.' Said one source: 'I couldn't fault the training.' Perhaps this is why the last two trainees to qualify both stayed with the firm, going into the litigation and music, theatre and media teams.

Play your cards right

Sheridans trainees are academically strong and believe themselves to have an 'analytical approach' and a 'work ethos that is heads down.' Unsurprisingly all our sources had an interest in the media. Trainees have to be prepared to help out where needed, as this firm takes 'an all hands on deck approach.' As expected, 'some people are really quite trendy,' though not to the extent that it interferes with a good sense of camaraderie. The offices are open plan, with all staff sitting together on the same floor. The firm is described as 'young and ambitious' with a 'professional but relaxed atmosphere.' During work hours, 'everyone gets down to it' because people tend to have things they want to do afterwards. The typical day runs from 9am until 6.30pm. Said one source: 'If I am there past 7.30pm questions are raised.'

The social scene is 'informal.' Sunny afternoons might prompt an e-mail calling for after-work drinks at one of the many local pubs. The Christmas and summer parties are big events, and the last summer party saw the firm taken to Leicester Square's Empire Casino to learn blackjack and gambling tricks. Whatever the venue, 'parties continue well into the night.' Staff must have been very good last year as we heard Father Christmas delivered them all a Wii console and games pack.

It sounds like it's no hardship to entertain clients or market for new business. From watching bands, going to drinks receptions or helping at a firm-hosted event in the 'wonderful gallery space on the seventh floor of our building,' trainees often accompany partners or other fee earners and are also likely to be sent out on their own to represent the firm. The space upstairs has held numerous events and meetings, such as last year's 50-50 event held in conjunction with Getty Images to celebrate 50 years of famous directors and 50 years since the firm's establishment. The firm has no intention of standing still during its second 50 years, and trainees say the partners are 'always trying to improve and are looking out for opportunities.'

We got an inside scoop that Sheridans is pushing itself as a legal fashionista, an area in which it already boasts a well-known designer or two as clients.

And finally...

Applicants are drawn primarily to Sheridans' media and entertainment teams, however trainees strongly suggest that you look at the firm for all the work that it does. Only one place is up for grabs, so make your application really stand out. And remember not to look like you're starstruck.

Shoosmiths

The facts

Location: Birmingham, Basingstoke, Milton Keynes, Northampton, Nottingham, Reading, Solent, London

Number of UK partners/solicitors: 113/237

Total number of trainees: 36

Seats: 4x6 months

Alternative seats: Secondments

Extras: Pro bono – Business in the Community

> Open-plan workspaces encourage everyone to engage with colleagues, and partners seem more than willing to get involved with juniors, even opening their homes for the occasional dinner or barbecue.

Strolling comfortably past the line that divides regional firms from national ones, Shoosmiths has eight offices, all of which take trainees except its tiny new London branch.

Becoming city slick

Once best known for high-volume bulk conveyancing and personal injury ('areas out of which you can only get a certain amount of profit these days'), Shoosmiths' commercial practice has blossomed. Clients such as Thomas Cook, Volkswagen and British Waterways use one or several of its offices, confident that the Shoosmiths network can satisfy their diverse legal needs. The firm has set its sights higher and grown in confidence since 2001, when its new commercial appetite was revealed and it opened in the super-competitive Birmingham market. And now the organisation that was once happy to stick to out-of-town business parks in the provinces has done the unthinkable – it has opened up in the capital. Though its volume business had to make redundancies because of reduced mortgage lending activity, at the big picture level the firm has achieved much lately and recorded its first annual revenue above the £100m mark.

Trainees were generally positive about the 'ambitious' direction the firm is taking, though a few were wary of what the strategy might herald. 'You can only grow so much without losing a bit of your identity,' worried one. Others noted that the firm needs to build a strong cohesive identity: 'It feels very much like you're part of one trainee group in one office.' Said one: 'As it grows, Shoosmiths needs to address how it approaches being a national firm.' All trainees spend their first week together on an induction course, and there are cross-office departmental training weekends throughout the year. Otherwise they serve out their entire contract in their home office, unless a business case is made for doing a seat in another office. The Northampton and Milton Keynes offices are considered one for the purposes of training.

Waine's world

Back in 1845 Mr William Shoosmith started the business in Northampton, and the town is still home to the firm's largest office out on the A45 at The Lakes business park. Most first-year Northampton/MK trainees start here, where they can try seats in finance litigation and recovery (aka lender services); health and safety; private client; personal injury; insurance litigation; asset finance and debt recovery. Prodigious expansion of the lender services division – nicknamed 'Waine's World' for its team leader, Waine Mannix – meant that several other commercial divisions migrated along the M1 to the growing MK office. Lender services is by far the largest team in Northampton: its 222 case handlers and 17 qualified solicitors work for banks and companies like Coca-Cola and Toyota. In this 'very, very busy department' you might even get 'packed off to court on your first day,' and the recent jitters in the economy mean there's a trainee in court 'almost every day' for charging orders and repossessions. Dealing with debtors can be 'daunting,' and 'you can get emotionally attached at times, but once you detach yourself it gets easier.' Another common seat option is with the health and safety team, which assists companies that have fallen foul of workplace safety regs and need advice on 'criminal aspects' such as corporate manslaughter. Trainees undertake research, attend 'countless hearings' and gain oodles of client contact.

While the journey between MK and Northampton can take 40 minutes, apparently it can be shaved to 25 by using back roads. As well as needing extra space for Waine's World in Northampton, Shoosmiths decided its commercial teams would fare better in MK, now Europe's fastest-growing city. It's not the only firm to take this view: several others have decamped there to at the expense of Northampton. By comparison with the young and buzzy atmosphere at The Lakes, we hear that the MK office feels more like 'a traditional law firm.' Trainees have access to a commercial property team, commercial litigation, property litigation, corporate banking, plus commercial, IP, pensions and employment teams. MK is one of only two offices where IP seats are offered, and here its fêted lawyers advise Dr Martens, Jimmy Choo, Nike and other non-shoe related brands. Sadly the seat is not always available at every rotation. Property litigation will 'knock off any rough edges you had from law school,' and liaising with British Waterways patrol officers you may hear hair-raising stories from the canal network.

The MK branch is due to move to 'swanky new offices' by March 2010. Socially, there's a preference for trips to quirky pubs in outlying villages and visits to London. Northampton's business park location means 'lunch is difficult unless you eat junk food or drive into town.' Driving to work can hamper the social scene, still Northampton has an infamously good Christmas party and trainees make the effort to go for regular pub lunches and occasionally venture to Birmingham.

It's a bling thing

The Birmingham office used to share Northampton and MK's trainees. It has now blossomed and made many lateral hires across all departments, for example a 31-strong social housing team from Cobbetts. Dedicated Brum trainees choose from seats in property, construction, planning, corporate/commercial (sometimes split into two seats), commercial litigation, property litigation, lender services, personal injury and employment. The property group 'dwarfs most of the other teams' and, although not always the most popular with trainees, it gets some great work. Lawyers acted in the development of Essex County Cricket Club, advised on a £160m redevelopment of Birmingham's Jewellery Quarter and was appointed to the legal panel for motorway services operator Moto. The corporate team 'has a bit of the x-factor about it,' while commercial seats provide 'a steady stream of all the things you want as a trainee.' Its city centre office is 'bursting at the seams' following the Cobbetts invasion and feels like 'quite a party office.' As well as oodles of

Chambers UK rankings

Asset Finance • Banking & Finance • Competition/European Law • Construction • Corporate Finance • Debt Recovery • Dispute Resolution • Employment • Health & Safety • Information Technology • Intellectual Property • Licensing • Pensions • Personal Injury • Planning • Product Liability • Real Estate • Real Estate Litigation • Restructuring/Insolvency • Retail • Shipping • Social Housing

bars, clubs and restaurants on its doorstep, its reputation for 'fantastic' Christmas celebrations is impressive. At a footballers' wives-themed bash staff went for it with David Beckham-style sarongs and wag-tastic frocks.

Having also outgrown its surroundings, the Nottingham office has found a new home in Waterfront Plaza, 'probably one of the best buildings in the city.' Three of the ten lawyers made up as partners in 2008 came from this office, which is a reflection of how well it is doing. Trainees have a narrower range of options than their counterparts: they can sample commercial property, coco, employment and property litigation. Commercial property is Nottingham's strongest team; its lawyers advised IKEA on the opening of new stores in Coventry and Belfast, and helped Alliance Boots restructure its property portfolio. In this 'really busy' seat, all the drafting and post-completion duties can keep a trainee working straight through lunch at times. After work Nottingham staff 'socialise together as an office.' If you attend Nottingham Law School you might already know some of the trainees – they take part in a mentoring scheme for GDL students.

From the valley to the sea

In Reading's Apex Plaza, Shoosmiths' Thames Valley office offers the usual seat choices, plus debt recovery and IP. Employment is a popular area, despite being 'a technical seat' with 'a steep learning curve.' The team is used to its cases attracting press attention. Recently lawyers successfully represented Hitachi Data Systems in the largest gender reassignment unfair dismissal case ever to be heard in the UK. The work may be top-notch but trainees did have a bit of a moan about their salaries, complaining that they are relatively low for the region. We checked, and while they are indeed lower than some of the most successful commercial firms in the M4 corridor, they compared well to smaller firms. Trainees certainly make the most of what they earn and find excuses for 'occasional epic nights out.'

Those training in Basingstoke visit Reading to fulfil their non-contentious seat requirement. Back in their home office the main focus is personal injury and there's a small employment team. The PI crew work for insurance companies like the AA and RBS; it's primarily low-value road traffic claims, but there's also a serious injury unit that deals with more complex and lucrative cases. Trainees take new files 'from around the time of the accident' and 'run the whole process from start to finish,' gathering details of the accident from the client, assessing the claim, arranging medical appointments and, if the case reaches court, instructing counsel. While we were assured Basingstoke doesn't feel as 'left out of the network' today as it has previously, it still acquires its trainees from within by promoting from the large pool of case handlers.

Down on the south coast at Fareham is the expanding Solent office. Generally attracting trainees with ties to the area, this branch offers seats in corporate, commercial property, commercial litigation, commercial and employment. There's also an intermittent seat in marine law. The ace up Solent's sleeve is corporate, which counts aerospace company Cobham, BAE Systems and Toys 'R' Us among its clients. Last year lawyers worked on more than 60 deals with a substantial combined value. They're an active bunch down there – we heard tales of charity runs and cycle rides, and a few people from Solent entered the Reading Half Marathon with others from the firm. 'Shoosmiths hired out a suite at the Madejski Stadium. You could go back up after the marathon and watch everyone else come in, assuming you weren't the last.' Events organised by the social committee are well attended and games of football and golf are often thrown together.

That voodoo that shoo do so well

Recruits speak highly of a training scheme that strikes the right balance between responsibility and guidance. Open plan workspaces encourage everyone to engage with colleagues, and partners seem more than willing to get involved with juniors, even opening their homes for the occasional dinner or barbecue. Above all, say trainees, 'they're a nice bunch of people, and if you're a trainee, people being nice to you is a huge thing.' FYI: any Shoosmiths trainee can ask to be considered for a client secondment. 'Seen as gold dust,' there are regular placements with VW and sporadic invitations to other companies.

One Shoobie told us this might not be a firm to come to if you're looking for 'something too high pressured,' so don't sign up if you want an intense City experience, not least because the new London office doesn't take trainees. People value their free time and Shoosmiths can legitimately claim to be a lifestyle choice; indeed many of its senior staff quite deliberately escaped Big City law. As for which office you should choose, some people opt for their home region but just as many base their decision on the practice areas offered and the lifestyle they want. Describing themselves as 'easygoing' people with 'good chat and good banter,' Shoobies say they are intelligent but not 'overly back-room clever.' Importantly, 'there are no odd characters.'

Shoosmiths has a reasonable record for retaining qualifying trainees. It also operates a (widely unpopular) penalty system, whereby 'it pays for the LPC, but if you don't take a position they offer you or you leave before two years after qualification you have to pay it back – and they do enforce that.' Apparently 'it's a good faith issue.' In 2008 ten of 13 qualifiers stayed on at the firm.

And finally...

Shoosmiths' training experience should be materially similar wherever you go – good clients, responsibility and, Basingstoke aside, a commercial focus. Add in the promise of an employer that recognises the importance of lifestyle issues as well as profitability and this firm is going to appeal.

Sidley Austin

If you come to Sidley Austin, the implication is you want to do finance.

'Sidley Austin doesn't do quirks,' said one interviewee from the no-nonsense American finance specialist, and we can believe it. Sidley has an excellent standing in areas like structured finance and securitisation, and it didn't get there by being kooky.

Austin's powers

Sidley & Austin, which in 2001 merged with high-financiers Brown & Wood to form the present firm, originated in Chicago in 1866. Today it has over 1,800 lawyers in 16 offices worldwide. Interestingly, years ago one of its summer associates was a young Barack Obama, who eventually married his assigned mentor. Its London office opened in 1974, expanding to include an English law practice 20 years later. Now London is the firm's largest office in Europe and home to over 130 lawyers, the majority of whom are UK-qualified. Sidley's prime area of focus, its international finance group (IFG), has received recognition as one of the largest in the City and is often second only to certain magic circle firms in the size and number of its instructions. For example, only Clifford Chance and Allen & Overy are ranked higher for securitisations by *Chambers UK*.

The London office's revenues increased by 12.4% in 2007, boosted by instructions such as Barclays Capital's €866m commercial mortgage-backed security transaction of Juno (Eclipse 2007 – 2), involving Barclays Bank buying credit protection regarding 17 loans secured by real estate assets in Belgium, France, Germany, Italy, Monaco and Sweden. Other clients include virtually all the big banks and lenders, such as Citi, Morgan Stanley, Merrill Lynch, UBS and Société Générale. IFG makes up around half of the London office, and according to one trainee it governs the style of the office: 'You have the

same culture you'd have in a bank. Your readers can make what they want of that.' While a seat in the department isn't officially compulsory, it is effectively so. 'If you come to Sidley Austin, the implication is you want to do finance,' warned a source.

RMBS RIP?

A trainee in IFG will sit in one of several areas – general banking, derivatives, regulatory, RMBS and CMBS (Residential and Commercial Mortgage-Backed Securitisation respectively). With such a wide array of work on offer, the tasks given to recruits can vary accordingly. There can be a lot of 'bog-standard trainee stuff' like proof-reading – especially when the department is quieter, as it has been recently. 'Partners need work, so what came down to trainees wasn't very highbrow... Everyone was very apologetic there wasn't more to give you.' The possibility of better work is there, however. RMBS for trainees spells a document-heavy seat incorporating companies, drafting services agreements, liaising with the FSA, organising board minutes and experiencing a lot of client contact, while general banking provides less drafting but the opportunity to be taken along to meetings and 'a lot of post-completion stuff.' One trainee put it like this: 'Your training contract is always spent in one of two positions: one where you have no responsibility and are just doing chores that have to be done; and one where what you're doing might have important consequences.'

Last year Sidley trainees told us they'd wanted more for-malised training to help them get to grips with the complex processes most recruits enter IFG knowing nothing about. The firm seems to have heard their concerns, because provisions for training have 'greatly improved.' There are now regular fortnightly talks written by associates and 'pitched at the right level' to supplement the learning 'you pick up as you go along.'

At the time of writing, with the credit crisis still going full-bore, Sidley's core practice of securitisation and structured finance was feeling the pinch along with the rest of the market. With those areas of law attracting much of the blame for the economic turmoil, trainees told us it was 'interesting to see just how important the work you were doing was, and how pivotal it was in the finance industry.' Unfortunately so. As for the firm's own prognosis, our interviewees had an array of opinions, although they admitted they weren't always kept in the loop when it came to future plans. One recruit responded bluntly: 'Everything revolves around finance, so if finance is dead, everything is dead.' Others were more confident that Sidley will 'ride out the storm.' While they acknowledged the finance department had been quieter since August 2007, they thought 'it may be turning the corner.' Teams of experienced lawyers mean there are always 'guys in finance coming up with more weird and wonderful ways of making money for guys in banks.' The frequency of large deals has decreased, but smaller matters still come through and that's 'quite good for trainees.' Most importantly, emphasis is being shifted to other departments like corporate, and the firm is working to diversify its London practice.

A Sidley medley

With Sidley working to expand its other practice areas, this may be a good time for trainees to sample some of the other seats on offer. The corporate department is essentially split into capital markets (debt) and M&A, but there's also a small IP practice and a funds team bolstered by recent partner hires from SJ Berwin and Covington & Burling. Highlights for the team last year were First Data Corporation's €120m acquisition of a 51% shareholding in Allied Irish Banks' UK and Ireland merchant acquiring business, and acting as counsel on over $9bn of extendible notes issued in the US capital markets by Spanish financial institutions. Clients include GlaxoSmithKline, HBOS and Goldfish Bank. We're told a seat in corporate 'pushes you out of your comfort zone.'

The tax team only takes one trainee at a time but 'wants to see a lot more trainees,' so it's solved the problem by switching to three-month seats. The 'pure research' work is 'a challenge,' and we were pleasantly surprised to hear the team described as 'very girly – it's all girls apart from the partners and one associate.' Property has underpinned

Chambers UK rankings

Capital Markets • Investment Funds • Real Estate Finance • Restructuring/Insolvency • Tax

a lot of Sidley's securitisation work, so while trainees in the real estate seat will see some commercial lease instructions, most of their time will be spent working in conjunction with the finance practice. 'I don't think they'd bill themselves as a support department, but I think that's what they are in spirit,' said one recruit. To ensure they experience the very basics of conveyancing at least once, 'they give trainees the odd residential property deal if it's being done as a favour to a client.'

The litigation seat offers a 'refreshing exposure to different kinds of work' as the team handles all contentious elements of the work of the transactional teams, plus some standalone instructions. This seat and the 'research-heavy' competition law posting are trainees' only chance for contentious experience, so Sidley sends most trainees on a multi-weekend course at Kaplan Law School. There were few fans of the course among our sources. The remaining seat options are non-contentious insurance, regulatory and insolvency. Wherever you are, say trainees, 'if you're proactive they respond very well to it,' so sticking your neck out might land you more interesting work.

No comment

For what it's worth, we thought morale generally seemed low, even if it was hard to pinpoint exactly why, and the use of 'no comment' answers didn't help matters. There was some frustration with the fact that 'no matter what they tell you, your experience as a trainee will always depend on who you sit with,' as some supervisors prove less willing than others to match a trainee's growing capability with greater responsibility. There were also a few gripes about the long hours. 'When all your mates are out on the Friday night and you know you're going to be in the office until God knows when, it's not the best,' confessed one trainee. An early finish is around 7pm, and recruits considered themselves 'lucky' if they'd 'only done a handful of 2am or 3ams.' Making it all a bit more bearable is the evening chef in the canteen, who cooks what hungry late-nighters want until around 9.30pm: 'You ask for something off the menu and it's there in five minutes.'

Long hours are common to US firms in London, and there were a few other transatlantic habits drawing our interviewees' ire. For example, 'pretty much from the first week you realise everything comes from Chicago.' Client files 'have to be given the go-ahead from up above' before they can be set up, and timesheets are monitored by the Chicago office, through which all manner of day-to-day processes must run. Even so, recruits don't believe there's a particularly American atmosphere in London. There are a few US-qualified lawyers (especially in capital markets) 'but it's not in your face or anything.' 'A lot of work comes in via the US offices – it's always gratefully received, as we've got to get paid – but we largely generate our own,' said one trainee. 'You don't get the feeling you're the puppet of American parents.'

Questions about provisions for pastoral care got a mixed reaction from our interviewees, ranging from 'no comment' to laughter at the idea of a mentoring programme, which most indicated would be unnecessary. 'It depends on your relationship with your supervisor,' offered one. 'They're your first port of call. Otherwise, I suppose you could go to HR.' Hot cross buns on Good Friday and cupcakes on the Fourth of July help keep recruits happy. Most of our interviewees expressed a modest satisfaction with their traineeship. Said one: 'I don't think I've had amazing days. Obviously there are stressful days, but no particular low points. I've had a really smooth contract.'

Cowboy diplomacy

Our sources weren't sure it was possible to pinpoint a 'standard Sidley type' as people come from a cross-section of undergraduate disciplines and a number of top universities. Obviously background knowledge of finance is an asset, but it's not a prerequisite. 'Everyone's fairly normal here,' concluded one trainee.

We heard rapturous praise for the 'fabulous' black-tie Christmas party and six-course meal at Claridges, and the annual summer party at Merchant Taylor's Hall, this last time with a *Wild, Wild West* theme. Just how wild was it? 'West of Ealing, maybe,' one trainee scoffed, perhaps not entirely won over by the bucking bronco and line dancing. 'It was like *Brokeback Mountain* in there,' averred an attendee, eventually clarifying that they were referring to

'men with neckerchiefs and hats.' What with barbecues on the roof terrace, Halloween parties, pub quizzes, touch rugby, sponsored runs and football matches, 'there's always something going on.' The one thing Sidley lacks is a regular drinks night for trainees. Some interviewees lamented the oversight; others pointed out that after working long hours 'it's a relief you don't get dragged to the pub.' Though 'not the kind of firm to all go out on Friday nights,' recruits will occasionally organise impromptu outings to a local watering hole. 'We like to talk about what's going on in the office and sometimes you don't want people to overhear.'

In 2008 five of the eight qualifiers took jobs at Sidley. Trainees did mention the credit crunch in this context and more than one qualifier ended up in a department in which they'd not done a seat. Said one: 'A year ago they should have reviewed what to do with the trainees and encouraged us to do seats in other areas.' For some the process had obviously concentrated the mind and they advise you to 'analyse what you want out of a training contract' before making applications. For example, 'if you have a dream of moving to Devon one day and practising in a little office it's pointless doing securitisation' and 'once you've spent two years in London doing finance it's really difficult to convince people you're not after a career in finance.'

And finally...

Sidley's predominance in the very area at the heart of the liquidity crisis begs the question of how well it is faring post-crunch. *Chambers UK* believe its securitisation lawyers to be the best in the game, so the banks will likely want to instruct these clever folk on whatever new types of deal emerge.

Simmons & Simmons

The facts

Location: London

Number of UK partners/solicitors: 118/222

Total number of trainees: 100

Seats: 4x6 months

Alternative seats: Overseas seats, secondments

Extras: Pro bono – Battersea Legal Advice Centre; language training

> Simmons' international network is a draw, especially for those with language skills, but you can also experience worldwide thrills from the safety of London.

One of the City's most established and multifaceted firms, Simmons & Simmons opened its latest office in autumn 2007 in Moscow. Employing around 2,000 people across 14 European, three Asian and three Middle Eastern offices, about half of its £250m-plus revenue is generated outside the UK.

Keeping it international

Now in a positive phase after lean times, Simmons has shaped a clearer identity for itself through tireless work on international business and four core client sectors – financial institutions, energy and infrastructure, life sciences and technology. Healthier financials have resulted and the banking department has certainly been pulling its weight, scooping impressive mandates including advice to HSBC on the financing of E.ON's cash offer for Endesa in 2007. At €42.32bn it was the world's largest syndicated loan. Strong relationships with numerous banks include those with Standard Bank, BNP Paribas, Credit Suisse and Commerzbank. In the world of hedge funds and private capital, Simmons lawyers have excelled, creating a strong structured finance brand through the activities of the capital markets department.

Given the financial sector's current doom and gloom, Simmons' diverse skills and experience are vital. Growing the international corporate practice – with a particular focus on high-value M&A instructions – is a key goal and recent major successes have included advice to Telefónica on its £2bn sale of UK police communication network Airwave, and to RP Capital on the £3.3bn merger of Katanga Mining and Nikanor (creating Africa's largest copper producer and the world's largest cobalt producer). Meanwhile the life sciences sector has

turned up interesting deals, such as helping Dutch outfit Cryo-save, Europe's largest stem cell storage company, on its AIM admission.

Then there's a dispute resolution department that has been in on some of 2008's most important trials, including client Shell's attempt to recover substantial losses from Total, the owner of the Buncefield oil storage depot that exploded in 2005. Simmons lawyers are also representing Barclays in the dust-up between the Office of Fair Trading, six banks and a building society regarding the legality of overdraft charges made to the likes of you and us. And this is not to forget a swathe of specialist practices like the information, communications and technology group or the employment and IP teams, each of which is ranked extremely highly by our colleagues at *Chambers UK*.

Crunch time

Diversity of practice means plenty of choice for trainees. Seats can be taken in four categories: financial markets, corporate, contentious and a miscellaneous fourth area covering anything left over. In general, one seat must be taken from each of the first three categories and a final choice is made from any area. Gone, it seems, are the days when the firm's highly successful niche areas drew in too many people for the number of seats and NQ jobs on offer. Plenty of room in corporate and finance accommodates a trainee group increasingly in tune with the firm's direction. 'People now apply here knowing that Simmons is growing in these areas,' a source assured us, so it's the kick-ass hedge funds practice or an overseas posting that are prized now.

Simmons' 'big push' in corporate means trainees experience a 'very busy' and 'very sociable' six months. One source praised the great atmosphere in a team where 'when I was working late, the senior people were too.' Seemingly free from overbearing egos, the partners are said to have 'charisma and ambition – they want to get the deal done the best possible way. And they want you to do well too.' Of course, 'trainees always want more responsibility,' but with 'no paralegals in corporate' the big deals mean document management and bibling. However, 'I was able to get involved in drafting and setting up companies,' said one source who'd also enjoyed plenty of client contact.

Capital markets is just one seat option in the financial markets department, offering highly complex but nevertheless rewarding work. 'You have a go at drafting something using a precedent and then give it to a partner to look at,' we heard. Simmons' focus on 'a specific type of capital markets work which is very, very structured – CDOs and swaps,' means that as the credit crunch has crunched the department 'has got quieter.' However, there's been a 'consistent stream of work on restructuring products.' The other seat choices here are banking, asset finance and financial services (including hedge funds).

Content providers

Many who want 'finance, finance, finance,' wouldn't mind replacing the compulsory contentious seat with a two-week litigation course were it available. As it isn't, the shared experience of commercial litigation seats is the combination of 'donkey work' bundling with more engaging times interviewing witnesses and drafting their statements. The department takes on cases for big pharmaceutical companies, financial institutions and all manner of corporate clients, so a lucky few trainees will get to watch a High Court trial. Trainees observed that 'our white collar crime team is growing and gaining in prominence' and there are also teams working in insurance, professional negligence and construction litigation.

The IP seat may not be high on most people's agenda, but there's 'interesting work' on patent litigations for the likes of Nokia Siemens Networks and Virgin Media, or big pharma companies such as GlaxoSmithKline and sanofi aventis. 'At a trainee level there is more grunt work than in other seats,' recalled one source, but 'you may get to see a hearing.' The world-beating employment law team

Chambers UK rankings

Administrative & Public Law • Asset Finance • Banking & Finance • Banking Litigation • Capital Markets • Commodities • Competition/European Law • Construction • Corporate Finance • Dispute Resolution • Employee Share Schemes • Employment • Environment • Financial Services Regulation • Fraud: Civil • Health & Safety • Information Technology • Insurance • Intellectual Property • Investment Funds • Life Sciences • Outsourcing • Pensions • Product Liability • Professional Negligence • Projects, Energy & Natural Resources • Real Estate • Real Estate Finance • Real Estate Litigation • Restructuring/Insolvency • Retail • Tax • Telecommunications • Transport

handles the sort of claims that go all the way to the front pages of the newspapers. 'Many of our employment clients are in the financial services sector, so as long as you are interested in corporate and financial services as well, then Simmons is a great place for employment law.'

Other seat options include real estate and projects, where the team is aligning itself with the firm's sector focus on energy and infrastructure. This department always takes a handful of trainees and offers a blend of UK and international experiences. In March 2008 the firm brought a £13bn project to a close for the MoD, which will see the RAF's air-to-air-refuelling fleet replaced by 2011. Simmons' outsourcing department, meanwhile, is going great guns, recently edging out other major law firms to become the preferred adviser for £1bn-a-year outsourcing giant Sitel.

In the bank

Simmons' international network is a draw, especially for those with language skills, but you can also experience worldwide thrills from the safety of London. 'In capital markets I dealt with people internationally on a daily basis,' one trainee confirmed. The list of potential locations for a six-month stint abroad now includes Tokyo, Hong Kong, Amsterdam, Paris, Dubai, Abu Dhabi, Moscow and Lisbon, and language classes are on offer in anything from French to Mandarin. UK-based client secondments are readily available, usually to investment banks such as UBS.

An individual's seat combinations, and the personalities of the supervisors and teams with whom they work, produce unique pictures of life pre-qualification. The variables are the hours, the amount of responsibility given, the volume and quality of client contact and the extent to which trainees receive useful feedback through mid and end-of-seat appraisals. 'That's a minor gripe I have,' one source said. 'The appraisal process is not what it is touted to be. I'm still waiting to have my last end-of-seat appraisal.' In case they need extra guidance, a partner-level mentor is on hand for the duration of the contract. Everyone agrees that the organised training is vital, with seat-specific and general sessions aplenty.

Larkin' about

Opting for Simmons means you are likely to be 'genuinely interested in City law – people do have a passion for Simmons,' but don't want 'such a hot-house environment as the magic circle.' Trainees drew a clear line between the firm and the magic circle: 'We don't do the absolute mega corporate deals, and as a trainee that's better because you're one or two people down the chain not four.' Of course no one complains that trainee and NQ salaries are the same, as are sums paid for law school sponsorship.

Our interviewees were a decent lot who enjoyed 'the big positive' of 'good relationships with senior staff, particularly partners.' Consequently they felt Simmons' reputation as a nice place to work is justified, although one wit added: 'It is a nice place to work hard.' Certainly staff satisfaction surveys, quarterly news-update e-mails, on-screen interviews with the managing partner and regular departmental progress meetings keep everyone in the loop.

Pre-crunch, when the cost of borrowing vast amounts of money was cheaper than a second-hand Craig David CD on eBay, trainees often worked until 'silly o'clock in the morning' in finance and sillier o'clock in corporate, so the 'owl and lark leave' programme was introduced to make antisocial hours more bearable. Once they've worked ten extra hours per month, every three subsequent hours worked after 9pm or before 7am give staff an hour of personal time. Even better, owl and lark leave can be banked up to gain valuable days off. In truth, hours are 'not something that people obsess over' and grumbles only arise when a slow day is followed by a '7pm request to wait for a document.'

Getting on famously

Simmons' famous assessment day and infamous document exercise are an acid test. 'If you're put off at that stage well, fine, you wouldn't have been right for the work we do here.' Apparently everyone finds it tough, so just relax – 'scan read the document and do what you can in the time allotted. When you are discussing it don't be afraid of having a stab at something or simply saying where you can't give an answer.' Being 'similar to Oxbridge interviews' makes the process familiar to many assessment-day attendees, as Simmons recruits much of its intake from top unis and Oxbridge.

At the start of the training contract there's a strong 'herding instinct' to go out to the pub with the rest of your intake. This is replaced by departmental jollies – drinks, bowling, go-karting – and eventually 'you end up with friends in several departments.' Visiting the subsidised canteen at lunchtime or the nearby Corney & Barrow wine bar in the evening are perfect ways to maintain friendships, and every second year Simmons puts on a big summer party for staff. Those with a taste for fine art, or at least art, are well served. Simmons has amassed a large 'interesting' collection, including a picture of a naked man running, Damien Hirst blobs, Tracey Emin sketches and a piece described as 'a black, swirly mess.'

Post-qualification prospects are particularly good in corporate and financial markets departments, sometimes disappointing those with less mainstream interests. On the basis that bigger is better some head off to magic circle or US firms, but loyal sources tell us: 'Simmons has worked really hard to prove that this is not necessarily the case.' In 2008 33 out of 42 qualifiers stayed on with the firm.

And finally...

Simmons seeks hard-working, academically successful individuals with a clear interest in working on big international deals for big international clients. This is a great place to find out what makes the City tick.

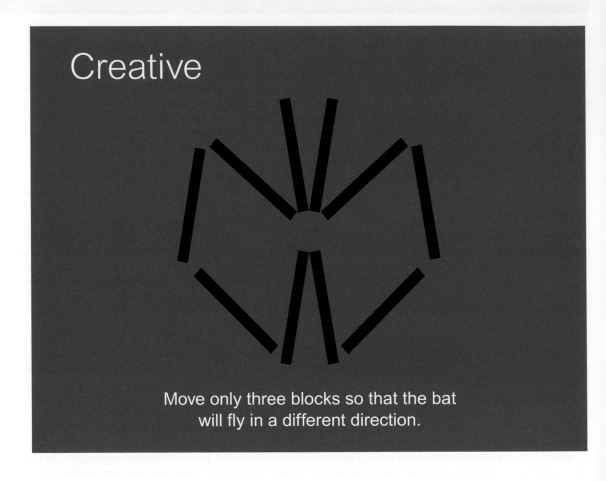

Creative

Move only three blocks so that the bat
will fly in a different direction.

Interested in a career in law?

For open days, Easter/summer vacation schemes
and training contracts please apply on-line at
www.sjberwin.com/gradrecruit

For enquiries contact:
E graduate.recruitment@sjberwin.com
T Graduate Recruitment Helpdesk 020 7111 2268

www.sjberwin.com

sj**berwin**

SJ Berwin LLP

The facts

Location: London

Number of UK partners/solicitors: 108/264

Total number of trainees: 98

Seats: 4x6 months

Alternative seats: Overseas seats, secondments

Extras: Pro bono – Toynbee Hall Law Centre; language training

> The firm wants to identify those things that make SJ Berwin unique and enshrine them as it carries on growing. As one trainee put it: 'I came here on a vac scheme and loved it right away. You could say I was Berwinised.'

Born about the same time as many of its current trainees, top-15 outfit SJ Berwin has an insatiable appetite for hard graft that propels it onwards and upwards.

Berwinisation

It was Stanley J Berwin who gave this lean, mean, deal-concluding machine its distinctive ethos when he founded the firm back in the cash-flush, me-centric eighties, and his legacy continues today, long after Thatcherism, aerobics, power dressing and even Stanley himself have become the stuff of history. The buoyant economy of recent years has seen the firm produce consistently good financials, and even with the credit crunch its 2007/08 income broke the £200m barrier. One senses that SJB's hard-nosed approach will allow it to weather any storm relatively unscathed because, whether you call it 'aggressive' or 'entrepreneurial,' SJB has always known 'exactly what kind of place it is and what it wants.' It has a dynamism that is deeply appealing to ambitious students surveying a London legal market in which 'lots of the firms seem stagnant by comparison.'

Yet, as Stanley Berwin's long shadow recedes, we wonder whether there are signs of change on the horizon. People got hot under the collar back in 2007 when a new system offered a whopping 75% bonus for lawyers billing 2,500 or more hours per year, however more recently the firm's new Associates' Forum proposed the introduction of alternative career paths and flexible working. Trainees admitted: 'As we get bigger the dynamic has to change; we have to be more organised and there can't be such an ad hoc, entrepreneurial approach to work.' The old values are unlikely to disappear entirely however, as 'there are still people who worked under Stanley who are determined to

keep the punchy, dynamic air he gave the firm, even if he was apparently a bit of a tyrant sometimes.' By way of compromise 'the firm wants to identify those things that make SJ Berwin unique' and 'enshrine them as we carry on growing.' As one trainee put it: 'I came here on a vac scheme and loved it right away. You could say I was Berwinised, and we just couldn't lose that character.'

I bill therefore I am

The firm runs a transaction-heavy training scheme in which a full year must be spent in corporate seats, and if you're anything like the ambitious lot we interviewed, you'll relish this prospect. Work within the corporate group includes M&A, equity capital markets, private equity, venture capital and investment funds. Finance seats are also deemed to come under the corporate umbrella for training scheme purposes. Thanks to the firm's strong network of offices in Berlin, Frankfurt, Madrid, Milan, Munich, Paris and Turin, in the past year, trainees were able to get up close and personal to Guernsey-based private equity fund Princess Private Equity, which was one of the first investment companies to list under new rules on the Frankfurt Stock Exchange, and to long-term client Universal Music Group, which had to dispose of its 19 and Zomba labels in order to purchase BMG Music Publishing. 'Towards the end of my seat I was doing research and preparing notes for clients,' said one source who'd 'struck gold with my supervisor, she was great at giving work and understanding my level of experience.' By contrast, another trainee's experience was that 'you work incredibly hard and long and partners can sometimes forget that you don't know what they know.' Such moments can lead to 'sitting in the toilet at 2am going, 'What am I doing with my life?'' although hardy Berwinites soon 'just get over it.'

The value of working on mighty transactions is that 'you're assigned a job and people leave you to it.' And when we say mighty, we really do mean mighty. Vector Hospitality, a newly created hotel group, used the firm for its proposed £2.64bn IPO on the London Stock Exchange, Matrix European Real Estate Investment Trust instructed on a £170.78m LSE placing and old friend Lion Capital stopped by regarding the proposed £260m flotation of the Wagamama chain. The firm has another shining star in Team C, a fund formation practice which is only rivalled for pre-eminence by Clifford Chance and seems to have weathered the loss of three key partners in 2007. Advising on fund-raisings totalling £44bn across Europe, the firm has expanded its already stellar client list. Team C lawyers recently established Scandinavian funds for Industri Kapital and Segulah, with values of £1.16bn and £375m respectively. Sitting here at a busy time can leave trainees feeling pretty pleased with their achievements. 'You look at your utilisation at the end of a week and it's way over 100%.'

Time to breathe?

Quite how much any chill in the economy will affect these departments remains to be seen, but as one interviewee noted: 'Last summer we were operating at absolutely full tilt.' Current conditions haven't lessened the firm's desire to 'grow the finance side to match corporate,' and trainees pointed to 'lateral hires, partners made up and double the number of trainees in the department.' Finance seats are popular, even though 'the hours can be dreadful' and they can tick off one of a trainee's two required corporate stints. What floats boats here is 'the round tour of all the major disciplines – acquisition finance, structured finance, the lot,' and 'because the structure of most deals is similar you can get your head around them and be useful almost straight away.' Being exposed to '20 different transactions' in the course of a single seat makes for 'fantastic work on the project management side' and plenty of other good experiences.

As you'll have already gathered 'SJB just does not do nine to five' in its transactional departments. News flash: 'In niche seats it's no different.' With only two seats out of four not taken in corporate or finance, the best advice is to 'make it clear right at the beginning if you really want a certain seat, and then keep asking.' And remember, once in your preferred department you'll need to work your socks off to impress prospective post-qualification bosses. Financial services and tax no longer count as corpo-

Chambers UK rankings

Banking & Finance • Banking Litigation • Competition/European Law • Construction • Corporate Finance • Dispute Resolution • Employment • Environment • Financial Services Regulation • Fraud: Criminal • Information Technology • Intellectual Property • Investment Funds • Life Sciences • Media & Entertainment • Outsourcing • Parliamentary & Public Affairs • Planning • Private Equity • Real Estate • Real Estate Finance • Real Estate Litigation • Restructuring/Insolvency • Retail • Tax • Telecommunications

rate seats for the purposes of rotation, the latter being popular for 'regular hours but hard work of a different kind.' This seat 'teaches you to think intensely and very carefully about applying the law and what you write.' Other options include real estate, media and communications, commerce and technology, construction, employment, EU/competition, financial services, IP, planning and environment, reconstruction and insolvency.

In the weighty real estate department you'll get 'as much work as you prove you can handle.' Contributing around a fifth of the firm's income, it is 'one of the reasons we're well equipped to weather a downturn,' trainees claimed. 'Property clients aren't as dependent as finance clients on having to borrow, and they are reacting quickly to take advantage of the sale of distressed assets to make a quick buck.' The excellence of the team's work can't be underestimated: it advised RBS on the sale of 25 Canada Square, Canary Wharf for £1bn, acted on two of the three largest ever single property acquisitions in the UK and helped Evans Randall on the €1.5bn structured syndicated acquisition of various properties. Lawyers also advised on a €264m purchase by Deutsche Telekom in Munich and assisted regular client British Land on its £1.017bn purchase of Sheffield's Meadowhall Shopping Centre. Trainee life here is 'very different – you're encouraged to take on your own files and manage matters,' meaning 'your work is more structured and predictable, so you can work late on a Monday to leave early on a Tuesday.' Of course, being drafted in on one of those huge property deals can blow such carefully laid plans out of the water.

Let them eat cake

Some trainees dislike contentious work and for them the option of attending a brief College of Law litigation course and assisting on the firm's pro bono programme is perfect. Others have the time of their lives in commercial litigation seats. Said one: 'I went overseas alone to do some diligence for clients, plus I got to work on the *OK!-Hello!*-Michael Douglas case in the House of Lords.'

With so many big-money clients on the books it's no surprise that SJB is pulled in on big-money litigation, such as helping investment boutique LV Finance settle a $2bn dispute over a 25% stake it held in a Russian telecoms company. Litigators have also been working on a £350m early credit crunch dispute involving eight major banks.

Completing the seat menu are secondments to the firm's European offices, for which language skills are necessary, but even if your Spanglish is no better than your Franglais you can still get away on a client secondment. 'De Beers is always popular' and there's even a placement in Westminster with corporate partner and Conservative MP Jonathan Djanogly.

Al fresco working

Stanley Berwin was renowned for his open-minded recruitment, so it's only right this approach continues. The name of your university might not get you a job but your personality as sure as heck might. 'This isn't a place for feeble minds or shrinking violets,' we heard. 'The firm doesn't want people who shout the loudest, but it does want people who fit its self-improving drive.' As one source put it: 'There are a lot of hungry types here, who like the sense of identity and purpose that maybe doesn't exist in the magic circle.' Embracing this ethos undoubtedly means 'being here until 11pm or midnight' for prolonged periods and 'proving you are up to the job.'

Three-monthly appraisals help keep things in check, and 'seniors look out for you, so you know the difference between working hard and getting swamped.' At times the enthusiasm of some trainees can be a problem though: 'You watch some people volunteer for so much in an effort to please that they can't handle it all.' But if there's privation and hard work, the 'flipside is great work.' Said one source: 'On one deal I was working opposite a magic circle firm and a friend from law school was a trainee for them. At the completion meeting I was dealing with the qualified solicitors and discussing the documents on the table; my friend's job was checking that the documents had been signed. That's when it hit me that I'd made the right choice.' Perhaps such experiences are what prompt statements like 'I can see myself here in 20 years.'

In 2008 36 of the 42 qualifying trainees accepted NQ positions, distributing themselves right across the firm. Something that may help sway the decision to stay is the offer of eight weeks off during the first six months after qualification.

Having toured SJB's office at Southwark Bridge, we can attest to its wow factor and confirm that the facilities cater for almost every need a young lawyer could have. It has an enormous roof terrace, replete with 'grass and WiFi so you can go up there with your laptop and work in summer' and there are regular free lunches in firm restaurant Stanleys. Monthly drinks and regular socials are enjoyed by many, but the staple of the social life is The Banker, a nearby pub where 'every Friday a group of trainees, associates, sometimes even partners go for drinks.' Trainees use a generous budget to arrange a couple of events a year and the Christmas party is always a good laugh. Last time 'the partners were e-mailed to ask that no one work late on the day and they were understanding about the hangovers the day after.'

And finally...

'Working hard is what City law is all about,' say our sources. For anyone looking to make this their maxim, SJ Berwin can offer an exhilarating and exhausting two years.

Skadden, Arps, Slate, Meagher & Flom (UK)

The facts

Location: London

Number of UK partners/solicitors: 27/38 (+54 US/other qualified)

Total number of trainees: 9

Seats: 4x6 months

Alternative seats: Overseas seats, secondments

Extras: Pro bono – LawWorks

> Skadden tends to attract people who have no middle gears, and that completely includes the social side of things.

Skadden, Arps, Slate, Meagher & Flom's global reach is almost as long as its name. The New York-based juggernaut employs over 2,000 people and works from 24 locations around the world, Shanghai and São Paulo, Brazil being the latest additions. Its London office is getting into the swing of a training programme begun just three years ago.

Flom Russia with love

Skadden's success was largely built on the back of its M&A expertise, which still accounts for some of its biggest deals. Last year lawyers represented News Corporation in its $5.6bn takeover of Dow Jones, and Yahoo! in both its $160m acquisition of Maven Networks and its rejection of a $44.6bn hostile takeover bid by Microsoft. In other established practice areas – corporate restructuring, banking and litigation – the firm works for some of the world's biggest companies, and in 2008 Skadden became one of the first three firms to achieve annual global revenues of over $2bn. A reputation as a hard-headed, take-no-prisoners firm is the enduring legacy of Mr Joe Flom, the firm's first associate (hired in 1948 at an annual salary of $3,600) and its only surviving name partner. In 1999 Flom was named as one of the Lawyers of the Century by *The American Lawyer* magazine.

In years gone by you might have said that Skadden's UK arm was merely an adjunct of the New York headquarters. This is no longer the case for what is now 'the nerve centre for the firm's European operations' and 'a link to Asia.' Skadden's forte in London is cross-border M&A; indeed we hear there is 'hardly any UK-only work at all.' Some of its most celebrated achievements have been in the steel industry, where it helped Arcelor fend off an unsolicited $22.8bn takeover bid by Mittal, before subsequently assisting the company in its $33.8bn merger with the Indian steel giant. Lawyers also helped Nasdaq when it bought into, and out of, the London Stock Exchange. Some London office clients do come from the States, but our sources estimated that 'about 85%' of work comes from Europe. Trainees liaise with and travel to clients and offices around the world and this can bring unique challenges, as 'things don't always go the way you want them to when you're dealing with 18 different jurisdictions and lawyers who are not always fluent in English.'

It's difficult to predict the direction that Skadden will take in London, as it grows 'reactively,' opportunistically exploiting new openings in the market. 'It's a tracker,' declared one recruit; 'it really does follow the market.' One example would be the growth in Russian business. Various Russian companies have listed on UK exchanges and Russian deals are frequently conducted under English law. Another example would be the creation of a class action litigation team in readiness for an anticipated rise in such proceedings in the UK.

Pure capitalism

First-year trainees take seats in corporate and litigation. The second year brings greater choice – capital markets, tax, banking, corporate restructuring, energy and project finance or an overseas secondment. At the beginning of the contract 'partners understand you're not going to be able to go in all guns blazing,' then more testing tasks quickly become available to those with the aptitude for them. Of all the seats corporate is 'slightly more fast-paced' and sure to 'kick-start your adrenalin.' Trainees stress that when you're working in a smaller office you get 'a high level of exposure' as there's 'not much of a buffer zone within the junior levels.' The teams working on deals are usually more compact than those on the other side of the table, so trainees tend to shoulder more responsibility than their opposite numbers. 'If partners see you're being wasted doing due diligence lists they'll let you do more challenging work,' said one. There's certainly a lot of drafting on offer, and towards the signing of a major deal trainees are the main contact for all the overseas lawyers.

Corporate-type experiences can be gained in other seats too – after all big transactions are the stock in trade here. For a change, however, you can try out contentious work. As well as the commercial litigation team, Skadden has arbitration lawyers who conduct their own advocacy without recourse to outside barristers. Rather impressively, the head of the team recently became one of the few solicitors to be appointed as Queen's Counsel. *Chambers UK* ranks Skadden in its second-highest tier for international arbitration, which is impressive for a relative newcomer to the UK. Trainees have a largely research-based role on disputes between sovereign states, banks and multinational companies. Many of the cases relate to oil or telecommunications and span Russia, the former Soviet Union, Europe and Africa.

It's possible for trainees to go the whole hog and work overseas in either Moscow or Hong Kong. They don't need to speak Russian or Chinese, although the firm is thinking about introducing lessons. In each location there will be an airport pick-up, impressive accommodation and a salary uplift. During a six-month Hong Kong secondment trainees see a mixture of corporate, capital markets, banking and Chinese IPO deals, predominantly for Hong Kong-based clients investing in China, or vice-versa. The Moscow secondment – only three months long – introduces them to a 'fascinating' business environment that is 'very direct and competitive – basically pure capitalism.' With fewer precedents to rely on, trainees 'get down and dirty with the drafting.' They don't typically get too involved with due diligence, as almost all company information will be written in Russian. Though 'at times the seat can be a rough ride,' it is 'great fun.'

The BlackBerry way

The annual new associates' retreat in New York is a chance to meet recent arrivals to the other worldwide offices. Not that the London office is a Little Britain – 'there are plenty of Americans here, as well as an equal number of English and people from all over the world.' As training contracts are unheard of in the USA, London trainees are 'treated just like junior associates.' The UK programme is still relatively new, so the structure is still pretty fluid and 'it's up to you to tell them what you expect.' The firm appears keen to hear trainees' suggestions, either through chats with supervisors, appraisals with the training principal or via the associates' forum. For example, after raising the matter trainees now get Amex cards. As the scheme expands – and it is doing so rapidly – we envisage things will become more structured.

US firms are commonly perceived to be cut-throat places where people work excessively long hours in return for exorbitant salaries. There's no denying you can find things at Skadden to support this idea, after all this was the firm where, in the 1960s, New York associates used to give a Beast of Burden award to their hardest-working colleague in honour of a partner who is said to have literally worked himself to death. As for the big bucks, well, Skadden salaries are at the top of the scale in the UK – newly qualifieds get a phenomenal £94,000 per year. Our sources felt their salaries were well earned and 'a nice recognition of the intense focus' they must place on their careers. Yet they deny that the salary is what drew them to the firm. Said one: 'I could go to other professions for more money if that was my main concern.' They also emphatically reject the 'myth' that lawyers at American firms in London work longer hours than their peers in the magic circle, telling us the schedule is 'not as horrific as everyone makes out.' 'When you're not so busy, or the market isn't as vibrant,' explained a source, 'people won't look over your shoulder if you leave early.' For the record, the office doesn't keep New York hours, so trainees sometimes take transatlantic calls at home. Blackberrys are a blessing in this respect, although some readers find chilling the thought of being permanently attached to technology that 'allows you to deliver a degree of service while getting on with your life.' It didn't scare off the qualifying trainees of 2008: three out of four remained with the firm.

Think you're hard enough?

If not driven by money, what does motivate Skadden trainees? Those who flourish view the times of intense and sustained effort as highlights rather than drawbacks. 'It's brain work, it's balls work,' enthused one source, while another spoke of 'a proper pressure-cooker environment.' It's all about rising to challenges in the knowledge that 'not everybody could do this.' Be warned: the job 'has such a buzz it can take you quite a long way from the real world.' Academic ability is extremely important and Skadden 'fishes in the same pond as the magic circle firms.' The key difference is that it takes 'the slightly brasher applicants' – confidence and independence are absolutely vital. As one interviewee frankly and generously elaborated for us: 'If you have the intellectual ability and capacity to be great lawyer but need pastoral care along the way, the magic circle would be better for you – Skadden wouldn't benefit you at all.'

'Work hard, play hard' was a cliché we heard a lot during our interviews. 'Skadden tends to attract people who have no middle gears, and that completely includes the social side of things.' Once a year at the so-called retreat (last venue, the Four Seasons in Hertfordshire) trainees can 'let their hair down' with associates and partners. They're also invited on the annual ski trip, and as the managing partner is a director of Chelsea FC, there are sometimes seats for matches at Stamford Bridge. In a nod to its American heritage Skadden plays in a softball league against other law firms and has a big Fourth of July party.

The firm's accommodation is on the 20th to the 24th floors of a building at Canary Wharf. Despite the area being somewhat 'soulless,' there's 'everything you need down at the bottom of the lift.' The dress code is 'smart casual but very much on the casual side,' and there's a well-observed dress-down Friday. Basically 'as long as you haven't got a client in the room and you're not wearing a swimsuit you're fine.'

And finally...

This is a place for driven people who consider themselves the cream of the crop. One interviewee called it the Marmite of firms – if you're right for it, you'll love it, possibly too much. If you don't, you'll absolutely hate it.

- **Can't find the firm you were looking for?** We insist that every firm we cover in the True Picture provides us with a full list of trainees to choose from in order to ensure total fairness and anonymity in our interviews. If they don't agree, they don't go in.

Slaughter and May

The facts

Location: London

Number of UK partners/solicitors: 118/382

Total number of trainees: 166

Seats: 4x6 months

Alternative seats: Overseas seats

Extras: Pro bono – RCJ CAB, FRU, Islington and Battersea Law Centres, LawWorks; language training

> To find Slaughters' true personality you need to examine how the concepts of individualism and common endeavour work in harmony. There's a freedom to be yourself, but a cultural expectation that you don't speak off the cuff.

Slaughter and May is an exceptionally successful UK law firm. A member of the elite magic circle, this corporate king does business on its own terms.

The M&A team

When it comes to the biggest, most complex domestic and cross-border M&A transactions, 'often without any precedent,' Slaughters' corporate lawyers cannot be bettered. In the last year they parachuted in to advise The Bank of England on its credit crunch-palliating £50bn liquidity programme, assisted on the £11bn takeover of Alliance Boots, helped Corus on its £6.7bn takeover by Tata Steel, aided HM Treasury on Northern Rock problems and smoothed Taylor Woodrow's merger with George Wimpey to create a £5bn UK housebuilding group. The newly formed Taylor Wimpey also joined the FTSE 100 with Slaughters as its adviser, adding one more name to the mind-boggling array of major UK plc, FTSE 100 and 250 companies that rely on the firm. Also advising overseas investors into the UK, recent work includes Banco Santander's consortium acquisition of ABN AMRO for €79bn and Akzo Nobel's recommended £8bn cash offer for ICI.

Slaughters' prowess extends well beyond M&A: real estate bods are advising Lend Lease on the development of the London Olympic Village, and the tax team helped Marks & Spencer on a pension fund involving its retail stores. Competition lawyers appealed to the ECJ on behalf of Sony BMG, following a decision to annul the European Commission's merger clearance decision, and they represented British Airways in passenger fuel surcharges class actions.

With friends like these

So far, so same old magic circle, we hear you say. And yes it's true that mega-deals involving ludicrous sums are commonplace among the elite law firms. What differentiates Slaughters is a generalist approach that keeps four corporate and three finance groups ploughing wide furrows. 'Even at partner level people regularly take on work they don't know so much about and have to learn quickly.' Another defining feature is the firm's reliance on a carefully cultivated network of 'best friend' firms, each one a top player in its own jurisdiction. With only three of its own overseas offices (Paris, Hong Kong and Brussels), Slaughters prefers to leave costly empire building to rivals.

Some legal pundits speak of over-reliance on UK plc clients and predict that the absence of an international footprint will be the firm's undoing. Yet without the financial drain of an overseas network, Slaughters routinely reports eye-watering profits. Arguably its best friend network and generalist philosophy will serve it very well in a leaner economy. 'The corporate groups are still very busy here,' a source explained; 'you look at the big, highly specific teams dedicated to, say leveraged buyouts, at other firms and you wonder, 'What the hell work can they be doing?' It would take the sky falling in for any of our departments to find themselves without work.' In short, people are confident that the simple tactic of 'being the best at what we do' will ensure a healthy future.

Broad beings

Slaughters' approach has a couple of immediate implications for trainees. The first involves working alongside 'scarily bright people who can be quite daunting.' As one trainee reflected: 'At partner and senior associate level the quality is unrivalled.' Secondly, the generalist approach is not to everyone's taste. Sit with the 'nominally debt capital markets-focused team' and you might experience 'everything from financing work to bond issues to plain vanilla loan agreements.' If you prefer 'to be regularly confronted with similar deals and develop a sophisticated understanding of a particular area' then this system is not for you. Most think it 'makes life a great deal more interesting' and 'gives a broader understanding.'

Everyone spends at least six months in one of the groups named after the corporate partners who lead them. The average seat encompasses 'general corporate, Blue Book takeovers and private acquisitions,' even if board minutes, notes and research are the stock in trade for trainees. Returning to a corporate team or 'proving you're capable of handling responsibility,' results in more interesting work. The trainee who spoke of 'seeing a whole transaction though and doing some drafting' was by no means an exception. Then again, even admin tasks can be instructive: 'In my first seat I liaised with lawyers in ten jurisdictions on a deal – it was great for developing professional communication skills.' Some lucky so-and-sos get to assist on sports transactions for the likes of Arsenal, Tottenham Hotspur and the England & Wales Cricket Board.

Other seats can be chosen from finance, financial regulation, environment, IP, TMT, competition, tax, pensions/employment, real estate and dispute resolution. Tax is a three-month posting, the last three in that list can be three or six months long, everywhere else requires six months' attendance. Prior to joining, recruits are asked to indicate their preferences for the full two years and then HR is 'as flexible as they can be' in accommodating requests for change.

Have briefs will travel

Described as 'fairly humane' in atmosphere, trainees find the work in finance teams 'more complex' and team-based. One finance fiend remembered 'the occasion when I saw a transaction through from start to finish, from the preparatory work to the last-minute drafting and all-night negotiation, followed by very tired celebratory drinks.' Naturally there are similarities with corporate seats – the most notable being how busy things get.

Real estate seats bring opportunities to draft leases, licences and rent deposits, plus 'a lot of responsibility on smaller transactions.' In the 'cerebral' tax seat the complexity of work means 'drafting is very much in the hands

Chambers UK rankings

Administrative & Public Law • Asset Finance • Banking & Finance • Banking Litigation • Capital Markets • Competition/European Law • Construction • Corporate Finance • Data Protection • Dispute Resolution • Employee Share Schemes • Employment • Environment • Financial Services Regulation • Fraud: Civil • Information Technology • Insurance • Intellectual Property • Investment Funds • Life Sciences • Media & Entertainment • Outsourcing • Partnership • Pensions • Pensions Litigation • Planning • Private Equity • Professional Negligence • Projects, Energy & Natural Resources • Real Estate • Restructuring/Insolvency • Retail • Sports Law • Tax • Telecommunications

of associates and partners,' leaving trainees to research and reporting assignments. As for grunt work, it's barely there. The same isn't true in a competition seat, where the 'odd bit of pre-deal market analysis or state aid work' take a definite back seat to providing corporate support that 'doesn't guarantee the best experience.'

Many nominally 'contentious' options in fact offer predominantly transactional support or advisory experiences. That said, the small IP team offers some 'drafting for trade mark and patent assignments' and the 'challenging' employment and pensions seat may involve attendance at a tribunal. Everyone agrees: 'If you're set on seeing the inside of a courtroom, you're best off in dispute resolution.' The seat is 'more procedural and document-based than the rest of the training contract,' and trainees can expect a fair amount of document management and disclosure exercises.

Completing the picture are overseas secondments to Slaughters' offices and those of best-friend firms. Paris seats are finance-heavy, Brussels predictably means EU/competition, Hong Kong is transactional, and then there are ad hoc opportunities from Auckland to Stockholm. At each rotation around 20 people pack up their smalls to nip off elsewhere. Accommodation and a living allowance smooth the transition.

Ice, ice, maybe

Despite 'very good facilities across eight identical floors,' the design of the London HQ at Bunhill Row is relatively austere. This could be seen as epitomising Slaughters' cool demeanour; indeed all our sources were aware that their employer has a reputation that verges on the frosty. Some thought it derived from the 'distinctly traditional

English element,' others insist it arises from a misreading of the signs. Let's look at the facts: on the one hand Slaughters is filled with 'the type of people who prefer to have their own door that can be shut from time to time' and it is definitely not a place for whooping or backslapping. On the other, 'we call each other by first names' and there's a 'joint determination to be up to date and at the forefront of what we do.' To find Slaughters' true personality you need to examine how the concepts of individualism and common endeavour work in harmony. 'There's a freedom to be yourself, whatever that is, but a cultural expectation that you don't speak off the cuff and you come to a job with detailed preparation.' Put another way: 'The personality that coheres despite the variety of individuals' is one of 'considered intellectual excellence.' Expect the unexpected too: new senior partner Chris Saul is an 'exuberant' character who's always first on the dance floor at big parties. To celebrate his appointment a funfair was brought to Bunhill Fields, which appropriately is associated with English Nonconformism.

Trainees are aware of the firm's hierarchy and their place within it. Working with such 'universally fantastic' yet 'diverse' lawyers inevitably means 'some you might not get on with because your styles or personalities don't match.' The partners set the tone in the relationship and 'the way they interact with you is up to them.' 'Some you see at social events and get on with famously; others you might be warned about and they'll turn out to be perfectly pleasant.' Things don't always go swimmingly and more than one of our sources had felt 'like I was written off early on in a seat and wasn't given responsibility, and I don't think I could have done anything to change it.' A true Slaughters type has the composure and self-confidence to not be disturbed by such an experience. And anyway, 'for every 'reputation' partner there are at least two who are entirely approachable.' Even with the warmest supervisor 'you quickly learn it's never sensible to ask which printer to use – their minds are on higher things.'

Hour of need

Depending on the supervisor, feedback can mean 'red pen all over each piece of work' or 'nothing until the end-of-seat appraisal when comments come as a surprise.' Without billable targets hanging over them, fee earners aren't focused mind, body and soul on the number of hours spent in the office. Working days can be either 'dreadful' or 'more easygoing,' depending on client demands alone. In corporate 'you're much less in control of your time. As soon as possible means yesterday, soon means today, and fairly soon means the end of the week.' Several sources had 'worked until midnight five days a week for a while,' others had done some weekends; all recognised that 'qualifying into corporate means deciding to put everything else on hold.' Elsewhere, even in finance seats, 'unless there's a rush you can generally arrange your work so as to be free on a specific night.' Average days finish anywhere between 5.30pm on a quiet day in IP and 7.30pm in corporate or property. Late finishes bring the small consolation of a free canteen meal.

There's no question that 'as a brand on the CV, Slaughters is great, and the formal training can't be knocked.' Given prevailing economic conditions, it's perhaps unsurprising that 'people harbour ambitions of staying for three or four years after qualification, not just two or looking elsewhere immediately.' Only a few people make partner (it's the same in the other magic circle firms), but at least in 2008 the female trainees could take heart from the fact that three of the four partner promotions were women. Slaughters usually retains the majority of its qualifiers and did so again in 2008, when a typically high 78 out of 85 took NQ jobs.

No nonsense

Slaughters has had something of a reputation for employing 'middle-class Oxbridge graduates.' Said one source: 'On my vac scheme there were 31 people and only one was from another university.' As the firm's website statistics now confirm, efforts to increase diversity are bearing fruit, with the trainee population 47% female and 18% non-white at May 2008, not to mention women making up 18% of the partnership. Oxbridge still dominates, though sources pointed out: 'There are trainees from places which wouldn't have been associated with the firm in the past.' The no-frills selection process – a two-partner, 40-minute interview – appeals to the no-nonsense, self-assured types who thrive at the firm.

The trainee social committee has a small budget to arrange events and the firm-wide Christmas party pitches all staff together, partners sitting next to secretaries. While it's 'noticeable that some associates do nothing but work, all the partners seem to have major outside interests,' whether it's 'international cricket and horse racing festivals' or 'attending the sorts of gigs that you'd think they wouldn't be seen dead at.' There's a 'serious' football team, rugby, hockey and cricket teams and an 'ad hoc choir that performs carols every Christmas.' Sadly the jazz group split because of 'musical differences.'

And finally...

Slaughter and May won't deviate from the business methods and personality traits that define it, and this can only be good news for the coolly detached, smart and sensible graduates who each year are drawn to its cordial formality.

Got that Speechlys something?

Here at Speechly Bircham, we're as interested in your personal qualities as we are in your qualifications. We're looking for graduates who share our passion for the law and who relish the idea of building relationships with colleagues and clients alike. In return we're offering an environment where you'll be encouraged to make your own mark and you'll be rewarded for the difference you make.

Think you've got that Speechlys something?
Find out more at speechlys.com/trainingcontracts

SpeechlyBircham

Speechly Bircham LLP

The facts

Location: London

Number of UK partners/solicitors: 67/109

Total number of trainees: 18

Seats: 4x6 months

Alternative seats: Occasional secondments

> Many choose the firm because they want to experience both private client and commercial law; certainly they get a fair picture of what trainee life will be like after attending the three-week vacation scheme.

This mid-sized City firm has strengths in property, construction, corporate and employment, as well as a flagship private client practice. With optimism in the air, profits good, and an ever-growing client base, Speechly Bircham appears to have had its foot firmly on the accelerator.

Looking good...

In November 2006 Speechlys completed its long-awaited conversion to an LLP, in 2007 it underwent a rebrand and this year it uprooted and moved to fancy new offices. A steady stream of new partners has joined a range of departments, and the number of trainees has jumped from six per year in 2006 to ten per year in 2008. 'There is rather a different feel here now compared to how it was three years ago,' mused one source; 'it is growing and expanding and there's lots of energy.' Clearly buzzing on this vibe, trainees told us the firm is 'likely to grow further, but not in such a dramatic way as over the last few years.' After all this modernisation and change, we wondered if Speechlys still held its traditional views on client service. Absolutely, say trainees: 'We are still traditional' and 'clients can still pick up the phone and speak to a partner.'

With all its departments undertaking solid work for respectable clients, Speechlys is the kind of place where 'you get out what you put in.' Managing partner Michael Lingens talks to staff twice a year about the firm's future plans and has a column in a monthly staff newsletter that also offers updates on each department. This means trainees feel involved in the firm's strategy and are aware of team successes. They might well have noted how well the family and IP/technology/commercial groups have been doing this year, something our colleagues at *Chambers UK* certainly picked up on.

Waxing work

A Speechlys training is a straightforward four-by-six-month affair, with HR trying to accommodate everyone's preferences as best they can. The second and third seats are viewed as the all-important ones and trainees usually get their first or second choices for these. 'We generally try to sort it out amongst us and reach a compromise, so you feel like you have lots of input rather than decisions being made from on high.' Seats are available in all the core departments, and as one astute trainee pointed out, 'the expansion means that there are new areas offering seats and more seats available in existing areas, so there is a better chance of getting what you want.'

Private client is a hot favourite year on year. Its clientele ranges from high net worth individuals from the waxed-jacket-and-wellies brigade to entrepreneurs and media types, even a few 'Mr and Mrs Bloggs off the street.' The team also caters to overseas clients and has created regional focus groups to offer tailored advice covering India, the USA, France, Italy, Scandinavia and Latin America. In the past, private client trainees additionally experienced family and contentious trusts work. As the firm has grown, so have these areas, and this year they have taken a trainee between them to help cope with the increasing volume of work.

Flatly speaking

The property department regularly handles deals for clients RBS and property companies Derwent and Howard de Walden Estates, plus one-off matters for the likes of Henderson Global Investors, which recently relocated its head office to British Land's new City development at 201 Bishopsgate. Other clients include The Bank of England, Lord Lloyd-Webber and The Royal College of General Practitioners. Trainees familiarise themselves with leases and licences, manage online data rooms and prepare documentation for completions, including getting them all properly executed in time for the big event. According to our interviewees, 'the more you prove you can do the more you get.'

The property litigation team deals with smaller 'enfranchisement matters and recovery of rents,' plus larger claims that can end up in major litigation or mediation. One recent case for Howard de Walden Estates, relating to the collective enfranchisement of a large block of flats, went all the way to the Court of Appeal. Property lit can be a great introduction to litigation, as trainees can often take a file from start to finish. This might not include doing their own advocacy, however it is sometimes necessary for trainees to appear before a master in the High Court or a district judge in a county court. Also worth a mention, as it shares a floor with property, is the small but 'very friendly' construction department, where 'the characters make the days go quickly.' Our sources reported working on both contentious and non-contentious matters for several large corporate clients, including The P&O Estates, Derwent and Lloyds TSB. On smaller disputes trainees are able to liaise directly with clients and counsel.

Fast cars, designer labels

In corporate trainees have to 'work as part of a team, which other departments don't expect as much.' The lower end of the mid-market is the firm's natural territory and it undertakes a decent amount of AIM work. Trainees say they work on 'fairly standard stuff' – drafting board minutes, researching points of law for fee earners, writing articles on behalf of partners and attending meetings. The department also encompasses a 'partner-heavy' financial services team, which advises finance houses and traders on Financial Service Authority regulations. Corporate also currently has a trainee on secondment two days a week to a telecoms client.

The recently established IP, technology and commercial team sits under the corporate umbrella and trainees are lining up to work there. One recent case involved defending designer shoe label GINA, whose brand was under attack from high street company Moda in Pelle, which was selling copycat versions of its shoes. Another client, Elle Macpherson, seeks advice on all aspects of her brand

and business interests, including her multimillion-pound Revlon deal. She came to the firm after her regular lawyer Alex Carter Silk moved to Speechlys from Manches. In this seat, trainees attend meetings, take witness statements, make trade mark applications and prepare bundles of documents for court. IP is not the only glitzy team; there's also a group of lawyers working for sports industry clients. Most notably, strength and expertise is pulled from the family and employment teams, which act for a few famous names. The commercial dispute resolution team, meanwhile, boasts one of the leading motor sport lawyers in the country, whose clients include the owner of the F1 Circuit in Bahrain, veteran motor sports legend John Surtees OBE and Hines International Racing.

Cloakroom not dagger

Trainees usually receive work from across their department, a system that works well in the open-plan environment. Supervisors sit close by and can be easily pinned down – metaphorically, of course. There are two formal appraisals per seat for which the whole department is encouraged to provide feedback. Supervisors were said to be 'supportive' and 'encouraging,' and our sources agreed they were 'genuinely interested in you and your development.' We did hear a few complaints about inconsistent departmental training: for example 'property has a fantastic introductory training session;' while areas such as financial services saw trainees 'lost at the beginning, so a front-end training session would have really helped.' However, there is excellent training in networking, which is just as well, as trainees are regularly required to get involved with clients. Departments host events such as Grand National-themed drinks parties, wine tastings and race days at Brands Hatch. Client events are a good way to get to know people better. Trainees help out at seminars and parties: 'sorting out name badges and coats' may not be the most taxing of jobs but it is a good icebreaker and 'you're always invited in for the food and drink.'

Spaced out

Situated in the heart of legal London, close to Chancery Lane and the Royal Courts of Justice, Speechlys' new offices are appealing, 'light and airy.' The firm now operates a clear desk policy and is striving for 100% recycling credentials. The new open-plan layout goes down well with some people ('there is more opportunity to bump into people while making a coffee' and 'you chat to and get noticed by partners and equity partners more now') but not with others ('it can be rather quiet, if you are talking about the weekend you think everyone can hear. Also the secretaries are much quieter than before as they are sat amongst the partners now'). It is early days, so no doubt it will take a little while for everyone to get used to the place.

There's no questioning the popularity of the new 6@6 staff cafe, but if you miss out on the lunchtime gossip just head for the pub on a Friday evening, when it is 'not just trainees who go out.' Trainees do socialise together on occasion, even if 'not as regularly after the start of the training contract.' The sports and social committee was rightfully praised for its efforts. It has organised trips to Paris, a family day out to the *Star Wars* exhibition and is always responsible for the Christmas and summer parties. Teams for football, hockey, cricket and netball are 'an excellent way to get to know people in other departments,' as is a reading group that meets over a meal each month.

The length of the average working day is a big plus. At just 9am till 6.30pm it's very good by City standards. 'There is no culture of just sticking around to look good,' trainees said, emphasising that late nights are 'really not the norm.' Said one: 'I was quite clear that I didn't want to go to a magic circle firm as I wanted a life, and it's definitely true when they say you have a work-life balance here.' Another agreed: 'I've been busy all the time, but it's been a good balance – it's not been high pressure, but it has been challenging enough.' These trainees are characteristically down to earth and pragmatic – sensible you could say. 'We're all quite friendly and wouldn't walk over each other to get ahead in the game.' In some ways Speechlys is a master of understatement. It's not that this doesn't have its appeal, but some trainees worry that 'the firm doesn't raise its profile as much as it could… if you look at the calibre of work we should have a bigger reputation.' Many choose the firm simply because they want to experience both private client and commercial law; certainly they get a fair picture of what trainee life will be like after attending the three-week vacation scheme. These days most trainees secure their contract this way.

And finally...

As one trainee put it: 'Speechly Bircham is not the sort of firm where you will get lost in the cracks.' Perhaps proving this point, five of the six 2008 qualifiers took jobs with the firm, four going into commercial areas and one into private client.

Stephens Scown

The facts

Location: Exeter, St Austell, Truro

Number of UK partners/solicitors: 35/43

Total number of trainees: 9

Seats: 3x8 months

Alternative seats: None

> Stephens Scown is the law firm behind many of the deals on the BBC's *Dragons' Den*. Dragon Deborah Meaden is native to the region and has been a client for many years.

The first thing you need to learn about Cornwall and Devon all-rounder Stephens Scown is how to pronounce its name.

Cream teas and scowns

This firm's moniker is something that even its own employees have had trouble with in the past. Many of them had always called it Stephens & Scown (to rhyme with *crown*) when in fact the original Mr Scown who founded the firm in 1936 always pronounced it to rhyme with *moan*. In a recent revamp, as well as dropping the 'and' from its name, the firm has sought to end the confusion once and for all by making it clear that the correct pronunciation of Stephens Scown sounds like 'Stephens Scone.' Unless you pronounce *scone* to rhyme with *gone*, that is. In which case it doesn't. Anyway, since trainees 'get clients ringing up saying, 'well, I've called it Stephens and Scown for fifteen years and I'm not changing now,'' it's probably a doomed enterprise, but try and get it right in your interview all the same.

However you say it, Stephens Scown operates out of three offices on the peninsula, in Exeter, St Austell and Truro. Since the former is over 75 miles from the other two, there's no great contact between the Cornwall offices and the one in Devon. When we rang, Exeter had eight trainees, the St Austell branch had two and Truro was hosting just the one.

An unusual rotation system sees trainees do three seats, spending eight months in each (although there some flexibility). Even if one trainee admitted: 'You don't get to experience all the departments, so choosing my last seat was where I really had trouble,' in general our contacts were happy with the system. 'I prefer it,' said one; 'six months is quite a short stint to get your head round any

one department.' On the subject of choosing seats, Stephens Scown trainees were some of the most relaxed we've ever come across. 'The first you get no choice in,' they said, 'and then at appraisal time you get the opportunity to suggest where you would like to be next.' Few seemed anxious to seize this chance. 'I didn't really mind where I went, so I didn't express a preference,' said a number of sources. In Exeter, seats are traditionally available in commercial property (including planning), family, civil litigation and corporate/commerce, while the private client department is just starting to open up to trainees. The St Austell and Truro branches offer much the same areas, while doing a good deal more private client and residential property work than Exeter and quite a lot of criminal litigation.

Here be dragons

Stephens Scown's four main departments are pretty much the same size, and we're told there's a 'friendly rivalry' between them as to which is the best. Naturally, we took it upon ourselves to be the judge. In terms of prestigious clients, the corporate team wins hands down. You might be surprised to learn that Stephens Scown is the law firm behind many of the deals on the BBC's *Dragons' Den*. Dragon Deborah Meaden is native to the region and has been a client for many years. The firm was behind the sale of her Weststar Holidays business for £30m in 2005. Twelve of the deals made on the show last year came Stephens Scown's way. These include the only product that all the Dragons invested in: a wheelie water filter that purifies as it moves and could save many lives in developing countries. Since they are deals with 'a strong formulaic aspect to them,' trainees can often lead these files. The rest of the work comprises sales and purchases of local companies and businesses, with schools and hotels among the subjects of recent transactions. On the client roster are many of the South West's biggest companies, notably the St Austell Brewery and Trago Mills. There are supporting employment and insolvency teams, but trainees are mainly involved with the 'pure corporate' side of things. 'You do quite a lot of drafting and due diligence work,' as well as bits and pieces of bundling, on which 'trainees and paralegals are treated just the same.' Although 8.30am to 6pm (with a full hour for lunch) is about standard across the firm, 'when it all kicks off' corporate trainees might stay as late as 9pm.

It might not come out on top when it comes to fee earning, but as far as quality is concerned, the family team is a winner: *Chambers UK* ranks it in the top tier in the South West. 'I love dealing with people,' said one fan of the family seat. 'What I really wanted to do was help people, and in family I love helping them deal with real problems.' There's a high level of client contact in the department, and the firm works for a lot of high net worth individuals, particularly those from a farming background. This can bring its own complications, not only because 'big money brings a broader range of assets,' but also because since farms tend to be passed down through generations, the spouse who has married into the family often finds it difficult to get a good settlement. Family is one department where the eight-month seat really bears dividends, as 'you are more likely to be involved with cases from start to finish.' Even so, 'some are not fortunate enough to go to a final hearing, whereas others will get to see the full shebang.' Trainees are mainly involved with division of matrimonial assets. Some of our contacts had done a little childcare work, but admit 'a bit more experience on that side would really give the seat an extra dimension.'

The property team just about sneaks top spot when it comes to size, lately bringing in about a third of the firm's work. Minerals are big business in the South West, and Stephens Scown has carved itself a niche as a specialist in the mineral extraction game, winning a couple of big industry clients. One is Imerys, the world's largest producer of china clay and a major employer in the region. 'These large companies own awfully large chunks of land' and the task selling off little bits of it at a time is a staple of the department. Many trainees spend time with the partner in charge of development, helping out on his larger cases, buying up sites for clients and selling off the plots after they have been developed. There's a little bit of residential work in Exeter, but 'St Austell and Truro do the bulk of the resi,' which up to now has often been 'buy-to-let for high net worth individuals who have dealt with

Chambers UK rankings

Agriculture & Rural Affairs • Banking & Finance • Corporate Finance • Debt Recovery • Dispute Resolution • Employment • Environment • Family/Matrimonial • Personal Injury • Planning • Private Client • Projects, Energy & Natural Resources • Real Estate

the firm for a long time.' Though there's 'not so much on the client side of things,' property has the bonus of being 'less stressful, with none of the strict deadlines and tactics' that are a feature of contentious departments.

For sheer variety of work, litigation takes the crown. The expanding team contains financial services, immigration, construction, property and IP specialists, who last year issued several claims for breach of copyright against companies in the Far East. Mineral clients provide instructions too. 'I was running the disclosure and doing the witness statements for a £5m contract dispute between a mineral company and a large chemical provider,' said one trainee. 'I was involved in a dispute concerning the amount of royalties to be paid on the lease of a waste disposal site,' added another. We suggested that to be a waste litigator you need a mind like a suer, but it didn't get a laugh for some reason. There's also 'contentious probate, contractual disputes, boundary arguments – the lot.' Very few cases go to trial because of the cost consequences, but trainees do manage to rack up court time: 'I have done my own injunctions, I've sat behind counsel and I went to the court to appeal a debt matter,' said one contact.

Olympic spirit

Trainees joked that Stephens Scown remains 'a local firm for local people,' and while the firm has no deliberate policy of recruiting from the region, most of the current trainees have South West links. The regional commitment is reflected in the firm's expansion policy. Offices in Dorset and Somerset are on the partners' minds for the future, but opening up any further away from the firm's traditional heartland is a definite no-no. If you think that sounds unambitious, remember that the four counties the firm is thinking about cover 6,600 sq m, over 13% of the total area of England. That's a big stretch of land, and anyone who doubts the potential of the peninsula should look at Stephens Scown's recent financial performance. 'When I arrived in 2007 the turnover was £11m and the aim was to double it by 2012,' one trainee said. The firm could well meet that target as turnover had already hit £16m by 2008.

The two Cornish offices currently only have three trainees between them, so naturally the social scene is limited. This doesn't bother the current intake, who hang out with some of the NQs and, being locals, have their own friends outside of work anyway. Exeter is livelier and trainees can often be spotted at Rendezvous Wine Bar, a stone's throw from the firm's Southernhay West office. One female source revealed that a ladies' marketing group (beauty evenings and so forth) is proving a little controversial: 'Some of the men think that means they should have a men's marketing group, but they all go out and play golf anyway.' Stephens Scown trainees are the driving force behind the local Young Professionals group and organise four or five events a year. When we rang them they were gearing up for 'an alternative Olympics' in the local park, featuring events such as tug of war, egg and spoon and sack races, welly wanging and 'that one where you stand in a line and put a ball over your head and then through your legs.' Alas, the Scowners were umpiring rather than competing, but at least they got the chance to pile into the barbecue afterwards. Other Young Professionals events have included a ghost walk and an Easter egg hunt. Within the firm, bowling is currently in vogue. 'There are one or two quite competitive people – not the trainees though!'

And finally...

Sometimes what you're looking for can be right on your doorstep. Candidates who are searching for good work but dont want to give up the surfboard should check out this firm. The region's salaries aren't spectacular but the firms retention rates are excellent: all five 2008 qualifiers stayed.

- **Nobody's perfect:** Whether you're at a firm where trainees get bawled out for putting too much sugar in the partners' tea, or one where your supervisor has a halo and sings duets with bluebirds every morning, remember that they were all trainees once and probably made the same mistakes you are now making. Don't beat yourself up about errors – learn from them.

Adventures in business.
Careers in law.

How would you like to cut your teeth guiding
a major Singapore property and development company
through a £300 million reverse takeover bid?
Or working on the launch of a renewable energy fund
on London's Alternative Investment Market? Or advising
a middle-eastern airline startup on its fleet financing
requirements under Shari'a law?

A lot of firms talk about early responsibility. We can point
to just what that means – day-to-day, working closely with
international clients across a full spectrum of sectors and
services. Solving their real-life business problems out in the
real commercial world is what we do. And from day one,
it's what you'll be doing too.

- 14 training contracts starting 2011
- Vacation Schemes: Winter, Easter and Summer
- Open Days: March and April

For further information and details on how to apply,
please visit our website.

London - Guangzhou - Hong Kong - Paris - Piraeus - Shanghai - Singapore

shlegal.com/graduate

sh
STEPHENSON HARWOOD

Stephenson Harwood

The facts

Location: London

Number of UK partners/solicitors: 70/101

Total number of trainees: 31

Seats: 4x6 months

Alternative seats: Overseas seats, secondments

Extras: Pro bono – RCJ CAB, Camden Community Law Centre; language training

> Trainees suggest this is a good time to join Stephenson Harwood because the firm is on the way up.

A long-time leader in shipping and finance, this mid-sized City firm's wide circle of expertise extends to AIM listings, commercial litigation, general transport and aviation.

Ships, planes and automobiles

Founded in 1875, international firm Stephenson Harwood has had its ups and downs but seems to have found its feet. Trainees all agreed that although the firm excels in the world of shipping it's not accurate to describe it as a shipping firm. After all, its other strong suits are numerous and spotlight stealing in their own right. The commercial litigation department handles consistently good work, corporate, real estate and financial services are also standout practices, and the firm is known as one of the best for AIM listings. Even the transportation lawyers no longer deal solely with ships, since the team branched into general transport and aviation. All trainees complete one seat in either litigation or finance. Beyond that 'there's quite a big choice,' although some seats are often more popular than others, not least the coveted seats in SH's overseas offices and the ones in 'hotly contested' smaller departments like employment. 'Over your four seats you should be able to do what you want, although possibly not in the order you want,' trainees confirmed.

Those who sampled commercial litigation described it as 'a really buzzy department where you are busy all the time, but not oppressively so.' This comes as no surprise given the firm's outstanding reputation in the area; *Chambers UK* gives the firm a top-tier ranking for its work in mid-market dispute resolution. In this seat you will receive 'a very broad range of litigation experience,' doing work for financial institutions and banks but also clients as diverse and recognisable as JD Wetherspoon

and Daewoo Electronics. The work is heavy hitting; recently the group represented IXIS Corporate & Investment Bank on claims against WestLB, CIBC World Markets and Terra Firma Capital Markets for losses and damages arising out of a £750m securitisation transaction involving the Boxclever Group. There's a chance to work on shipping litigation too, which trainees assured us 'isn't too technical so you'll feel comfortable even if you don't have a huge interest in shipping.' Some of the shipping team's cases don't even relate to matters maritime: you may remember when thousands of cars in the UK broke down last year as a result of purchasing contaminated unleaded petrol from well-known supermarkets. Vopak Terminal London and its insurers sought advice from SH when it was alleged that the contaminated petrol had been stored in Vopak's facility in Essex. Potential claims are estimated to be worth approximately $100m.

Cruise control

The real estate department offers 'a good work-life balance,' and sources tell us it's 'a good one to get first.' One interviewee added that 'there are a lot of young associates there who can remember what it is like being a trainee, so they're very approachable.' Trainees take on leasehold management, real estate finance and environmental matters, reinforcing the idea that 'you can really shape the seat as you want.' Real estate is also one of the seats with the most responsibility, including lots of interaction with clients. 'It was a bit hard being dropped in at the deep end,' one admitted, 'but there was always someone to ask for help and you're never forced to make big decisions on your own.'

Personal responsibility comes thick and fast in the finance department, where many trainees find themselves drafting documents and 'basically running files.' These include matters for some of the biggest names in the sector. Transportation is the finance team's greatest strength, with an emphasis on shipping and, increasingly, aviation and rail. The team recently advised HSBC in relation to the £212m financing of five cruise ships for the Fred Olsen Group. 'You'll get a lot of transactional experience acting for banks and ship owners,' confirmed a satisfied source. SH is making headway too in the burgeoning area of Islamic finance, and to help build this practice it has an association with Kuwait and Bahrain-based law firm Al Sarraf & Al Ruwayeh. SH lawyers act for governments, state banks and royal families as well as companies and businessmen, and they have been involved in some high-profile deals. Lawyers have also worked with UK and international banks to develop Shari'a-compliant products and deals for the UK market.

Waterloo Sunset

It's hard to beat the location of the firm's London office, just opposite the steps of St Paul's Cathedral. It has accessibility to the heart of London, 'but it doesn't feel like it's deep in the City, where you're constantly surrounded by suits.' The roof terrace is everyone's favourite: 'When the weather's nice you can get away from your desk at lunchtime without going too far,' and it's frequently the venue for barbecues and client parties. It goes without saying that 'the views are amazing, especially when there's a royal function at the cathedral.' The office interior, though 'fairly standard and maybe looking a little worn around the edges,' does have some key innovations. The floor plan is composed of glass-walled offices hugging the sides of the building, with secretaries and support staff at desks in the middle. 'It's a good compromise between an open-plan office and an office full of shut doors,' and all the glass means 'the light really shines through.'

The firm has five offices in Asia and Europe, two of which currently welcome trainees from London. Seats in Singapore and Hong Kong are always incredibly popular choices, but don't let the competition put you off. At any one time there are four trainees abroad, so your chances of going are good. The Singapore office is located on the 49th floor of the OUB centre, 'a wicked address' in one of Singapore's tallest buildings. Doing a seat in Singapore gives you 'a great opportunity to travel,' and the high prices of rent in the city – comparable to London – make the rent-free apartment during your time there a major perk. Located in the Bank of China Tower, one of the most

recognisable and, again, tallest buildings in the city, the firm's Hong Kong office is also in 'a very modern, plush building with a terrific view.' It's just ten minutes away from Wan Chai, 'a bustling, cool area' known as a foreign and Chinese cultural hub. 'There's a big ex-pat lifestyle' in Hong Kong which trainees fit right into: 'You really feel in the centre of things.' Their accommodation is 'well positioned but small, as is to be expected in the city,' and just a 15-minute walk from the office. There has also been talk of Paris seats becoming available in the near future, so fingers crossed!

Gadhia-n angel

Trainees suggest this is a good time to join Stephenson Harwood because 'the firm is on the way up, going in the right direction and growing by the year.' This wasn't the case a few years ago. After merging with shipping specialist Sinclair Roche & Temperley, it found itself in a state of flux, suffering numerous partner and staff losses and a general identity crisis. This all changed when managing partner Sunil Gadhia took control. 'He has really turned the firm around; no one could have done more.' Far from some mysterious force, many trainees get the chance to work directly with Gadhia in the commercial litigation department. The 'oh my God factor' soon evaporates as 'he really puts you at ease. He doesn't act superior or anything and is actually really approachable and great at giving constructive feedback.' Trainees speculate that his 'amazing way with people and obvious intelligence' are the keys to his success. 'You feel very safe with him behind the wheel.'

Gadhia's open manner is no anomaly. One trainee assured us: 'There is no hierarchy here,' and while clearly an impossibility – this is a law firm after all – there is a general culture of mutual respect at the firm. 'Everyone shows gratitude to people for what they do, and everyone is approachable.' SH is known for taking on people who are a bit older, including candidates who've taken time off to travel before their training contract or for whom law is a second career. 'They like people with experiences of life other than just academia, people who have done something a bit different.' Trainees believe that SH's size allows their learning experience to be personalised and say: 'Everyone knows you're here to learn, not to be a dogsbody.' A fairly substantial increase in pay over a year ago has left trainees feeling more appreciated and they tell us: 'It's very competitive and since our workload and hours are nicer than in magic circle firms, we may even be making more money comparatively.'

And how do you become a part of the family? 'There's definitely not one type of person the firm looks for,' speculated trainees, 'it's more of an attitude... a quiet confidence, if you will: the ability to hold your own but not be arrogant.' The once floundering firm seems to be building its identity in the same way, with the phrase 'quiet confidence' popping up more than once in talks with trainees. 'The brand identity of the firm is still less than what it should be, but it's steadily improving and the firm is coming into its own.' One word of warning: because of the firm's relatively small size for a City firm, qualifying trainees don't always have the pick of the litter. For example, due to the current state of the market, the property group didn't recruit in 2008. For some trainees it was a disappointment that 'the process doesn't really give you the opportunity to qualify into every department.' In 2008 seven of the nine qualifiers stayed with the firm.

Cheeky one?

'You won't find many people who are pure academics with no social skills' at this firm, making for 'an excellent social life.' After-work drinks are a mainstay, with trainees usually ending up in Shaw's Booksellers, the Cockpit or the Rising Sun, above which is popular lunch spot the Malai Thai restaurant. The office doesn't have a canteen, but this is never a problem as 'there are so many choices around the office,' including Paternoster Square 'if you want something a bit more up market.'

Firm-organised events are always good fun. Junior associates often act as informal social secretaries, organising bowling, team quizzes, barbecues, tapas outings and karaoke. Karaoke has proved 'really popular – some people can actually sing quite well!' Trainees are also frequently invited to client events, which is 'great because it's an informal atmosphere but you get to network as well.' At SH, 'trainees are encouraged to do everything that associates and partners do.' What's more, the firm has plenty of sports teams if you're that way inclined, including cricket, tennis, golf, football, netball, hockey, rugby, softball and sailing. For those who favour more highbrow activities, the firm has access to concessions to more than 200 galleries and museums, privilege seats for concerts at the Royal Albert Hall and, fittingly, free entry to St Paul's Cathedral.

And finally...

This firm offers a friendly atmosphere and a good compromise between hours and salary. Say trainees: 'It's a mutual relationship at Stephenson Harwood: if you're willing to work hard and are a sociable person it's rewarded in pretty much every way.'

Stevens & Bolton

The facts

Location: Guildford

Number of UK partners/solicitors: 30/62

Total number of trainees: 8

Seats: 4x6 months

Alternative seats: None

> Not even the influx of ex-City lawyers has eroded the friendly atmosphere here.

Stevens & Bolton prides itself on getting London-quality work even though it's based in Surrey. Quite a few regional firms make such a claim, so read on if you want to put this Guildford player to the test.

Up, up and away

The last couple of years have been storming ones for S&B. In 2006/07 partner profits surpassed £300,000 for the first time and then grew last year to £360,000 as the firm reaped the benefits of several years of growth, hard work and determined optimism. 'We want the best lawyers, big client names and more of a national reputation,' one trainee summed up the plan. And it's exactly what S&B has been getting. Partners, associates and consultants from the likes of Allen & Overy, Herbert Smith and Lovells have been tripping over themselves to join the ranks, which already feature an ex-Simmons & Simmons corporate head in the form of Ken Woffenden, employment expert Stephanie Dale formerly of Denton Wilde Sapte and David Wilkinson, a one-time Bristows lawyer who has been upping the ante on the IP side. There's no sign of abatement: in the past year construction partner Matthew Needham-Laing signed up from London construction boutique Fenwick Elliot. If you want to see for yourself, take a look at the jobs featured on S&B's website. 'They're always looking for new people to join, there's been constant recruitment, particularly in the corporate department,' which in the last year alone saw three senior assistants promoted to partner and three new recruits at assistant level.

In large part, the success of the firm lies with the corporate group, which last year handled a string of deals totalling more than £750m. Notable new clients include international food services outsourcing company Bunzl,

Kuoni Travel and Connells, the estate agency arm of Skipton Building Society. The team has handled a number of transactions for Rentokil Initial, including its acquisition of Lancaster Office Cleaning Group. It also advised German-listed client Bilfinger Berger Industrial Services on its acquisition of O'Hare Engineering, a major engineering group based in Manchester. Other departments have benefited from this corporate boom: the employment team, for example, advised Rentokil and other corporate clients on employment aspects of acquisitions, as well as assisting Amazon in relation to restructuring and resulting redundancies and a FTSE 250 client on claims of unfair dismissal and sex discrimination from a former senior executive.

Coco for breakfast

S&B's training contract consists of four six-month seats. A stint in coco is almost inevitable, given that this department is the lifeblood of the firm, while contentious requirements can be fulfilled with dispute resolution, family or employment. Our sources confirmed that if you express an interest in a certain department, 'the firm is great at opening doors for you. You get a chance to discuss your interests before you start, with a phone call about where you'd like to go.' Tax and trusts for private clients and real estate complete the balance sheet.

Coco is a common starter seat, as it makes for a good introduction. 'It's the hub of the firm and there's a buzz about the place. It's a good way to make contacts, as people are always passing by.' Although we heard it's 'the most hard-core department' in terms of workload and what is expected of a trainee, our interviewees were pleasantly surprised by how 'the team is great at getting you involved in big deals and they make an effort to tell you why you're doing what you're doing. There are a lot of former trainees in the department so they know what it's like.' The fact that two trainees are placed there at any one time also takes a bit of the pressure off. Tasks include buying shelf companies for clients, co-ordinating due diligence, producing draft reports and eventually acting as a day-to-day contact for clients. 'There are also the more mundane tasks,' sighed one source, 'more so in this department because it's the busiest. The days I spent in the data room were not a highlight.' Nevertheless trainees are more than compensated with plenty of quality work and 'you share a secretary with other fee earners, so there's less admin than you might expect. You're certainly not standing by a photocopier for two years here.' The hours are entirely reasonable – we hear most workdays run from 8.30am to 6.30pm.

Bringing home the bacon

Across on the other side of the River Wey the dispute resolution folk share a second office with the new IP group. 'It's an amazing building with a lot of space and a great library, but it does feel a bit separate, and it's open plan unlike the main building, so it's a different style of working too.' Although trainees agreed it would be better to have everyone under one roof, relocation plans are hampered by the limited selection of suitable premises in the area, 'and there's no way the firm is leaving Guildford.' The blues quickly disappear, however, when the 'big clients and cases' are mentioned. In the past year, for example, the litigators represented Brown's Hotel in its £6m claim against a contractor and its insurers for damages arising out of defective work on the hotel's refurbishment. 'You get to go to meetings with clients, draft witness statements and go to court hearings. A couple of the lawyers have Higher Rights of Audience so it's great going to watch them in action.' Trainees try advocacy for themselves on smaller cases, 'debt recovery or unsatisfactory quality of goods, that kind of thing. The first time you're told what to say word for word, the second time it's more up to you, and within no time you're surprisingly confident.' Although IP hasn't yet taken on a trainee, it's possible for litigation seat trainees to sample some of the team's work. This is good news, as the IP group attracts some cracking instructions. It advises BSkyB on a wide range of trade mark and domain name disputes, and represented leading auction house Christie's in a High Court action relating to copyright in the works of Francis Bacon.

Real estate is another big department, and while some label it 'the unpopular one,' others find much to like. 'I

Chambers UK rankings

Banking & Finance • Corporate Finance • Debt Recovery • Dispute Resolution • Employment • Environment • Information Technology • Intellectual Property • Partnership • Pensions • Private Client • Real Estate • Restructuring/Insolvency

couldn't precisely recall the ins and outs of property law when I started that seat,' admitted one trainee, 'but everyone is very patient, they give you time to read up on things and are happy to go at whatever pace you're comfortable with.' That doesn't mean you won't be pushed a little, but 'I don't think there's a lawyer here who I wouldn't be able to go up to and say, 'I don't have a clue about how to go about this.'' Although there are plenty of residential conveyancing matters, trainees focus on the commercial files, dealing with pure real estate deals and corporate support issues.

The employment team is much smaller 'and you're given a lot more responsibility because of it. It's wonderful actually,' gushed one interviewee. 'The team is very inclusive and down to earth.' Right from the start trainees are on the phone to clients and counsel, 'and I went to a tribunal very early on too, which was highly entertaining.' By the end of the seat you'll be running your own files and negotiating compromise agreements. Ample client time even stretches to hosting your own meetings on occasion. 'They want you to get hands-on practical experience rather than just reading about it. There's a real emphasis on giving trainees proper work.' The family team is similarly smaller, and we hear it also offers trainees a rewarding six months.

Ascot...or not

It's clear trainees rate the quality of their training highly. 'They are always giving you work to turn you into a good lawyer,' remarked one. In fact it sounds like the S&B staff are an all-round lovely bunch. 'Before I started I had this idea that you didn't speak to partners,' admitted one source. 'When you get here you realise they have time for anyone.' Not even the influx of ex-City lawyers has eroded the friendly atmosphere. 'They wouldn't take on a bull-dog type lawyer, no matter what sort of work they'd bring in.' Staff at all levels can have a say, be this in firm-wide meetings or via the anonymous suggestion box.

When it's time to qualify 'the firm is very conscious of how stressful it is and start talking to us really early on about where we'd like to be. They want to keep us.' This statement was borne out by the fact that two of the three qualifiers took jobs with the firm in 2008. Asked what sort of people the firm prefers to recruit, trainees were noncommittal. 'It may sound silly, but everyone here is just normal. They're all the sort of people you want to go to the pub with, although don't get me wrong, we work hard too.' A link to the area exists in most cases, whether they've lived locally or attended the College of Law's Guildford branch.

The firm's social life has 'peaks and troughs. It can be great but there are quieter periods too' because, as one source acknowledged, 'lots of people have come here because they value their home time.' However, free drinks on the last Thursday of the month 'are a starting point for bigger and better things afterwards,' and with an hour and a quarter for lunch, there are plenty of meals out. All are encouraged to participate in monthly sporting events and summer barbecues, and come Christmas, 'there's a sit-down meal in a gorgeous location.' Such as? 'Well... I can't remember the name of the hotel. It might have been near Ascot... but then again it might not. It was very nice wherever it was.' Thank goodness the firm organised taxis to take people home.

And finally...

The Guildford setting, proximity to London, generous trainee salaries and top-notch partners make this firm a big hit with its trainees. Don't be fooled however: 'Just because we advertise a work-life balance, it doesnt mean you can get away with being lazy.'

Taylor Wessing LLP

The facts

Location: London, Cambridge

Number of UK partners/solicitors: 103/173

Total number of trainees: 48

Seats: 4x6 months

Alternative seats: Occasional overseas seats, secondments

Extras: Pro bono – Blackfriars Settlement (inc. Older People's Service); language training

> TW's corporate department pulls in clients from all over the globe, and thanks to the firm's European network it has the capability to handle cross-border transactions from the Continent.

Taylor Wessing used to be known as an intellectual property firm. It's still strong there, but the corporate side of the business now leads the way and IP is an increasingly niche department (albeit a large and powerful one) in a much broader commercial spectrum.

Taylor made

The product of a merger between London's Taylor Joynson Garrett and German firm Wessing some six years ago, TW has recorded fairly consistent profits over the last couple of years, hitting £97.5m in 2007/08, an 11% increase in turnover on the previous year. No doubt this is due to the fees that the burgeoning corporate department can pull in: it is particularly strong in the mid-market, where it represents AIM-listed clients including Synergy Healthcare and Blueheath Holdings. TW is still quite the whizz in IP and is ranked among London's finest for patent litigation by *Chambers UK*. Some trainees do choose the firm for this reason, but many confess to having no interest in IP whatsoever, and say they chose it for its broad range of work and respectable hours. Indeed, many of our contacts said they had a sibling or boyfriend/girlfriend at one of the biggest City firms, and this may have been an influence when they were 'making a conscious decision to shun the magic circle.'

Whether the choice has paid off is open to debate. It seemed to us that despite the credit crunch, the Taylor Wessing trainees were as busy as ever. Given its core status, it should come as no surprise that a seat in corporate is compulsory for trainees, and they admitted that in this department, 'at times,' the hours can match those of the magic circle ('though not the US firms, thankfully – they work obscenely hard'). Even if cancelling appointments with friends for the occasional all-nighter can't be ruled out, 'there's no staying-on culture' during the less busy periods. Incidentally, TW was actually in merger talks with US firm Nixon Peabody in 2008, though things subsequently turned ugly when the Americans lured twelve of TW's French partners away following the breakdown of negotiations.

After corporate, a trainee's remaining three seats are up for grabs. The firm tries hard to make the allocation process 'stress free,' and most of our contacts had got exactly what they wanted. 'If there's any you particularly don't want, you can always go and have a quiet word with HR,' advised one contact. IP and employment are the most consistently popular; real estate; construction; commercial disputes; insolvency; pensions and private client are also available. The four corporate seats on offer are projects and finance; corporate tax; financial services and general corporate.

Promising the world

TW's corporate department pulls in clients from all over the globe, and thanks to the firm's European network it has the capability to handle cross-border transactions from the Continent. 'I find I am picking up the phone and talking to lawyers from everywhere,' a trainee told us. Hochtief, a major airport management company, used the department during a €1.9bn acquisition of a majority shareholding in Budapest Airport, as did the French materials business Compagnie de Saint-Gobain for its €2.125bn purchase of Maxit Group from HeidelbergCement. The team's customer base isn't confined to Europe: quite a few instructions come from American technology companies, and lawyers recently advised a superwealthy Middle Eastern family on its £20m acquisition of the Astoria hotel in Brussels. Other clients include chains Kew Green Hotels and European Hotels Corporation, private equity organisations Ion Equity, BP Marsh and Rutland Partners, along with Brentford FC, Webroot Software and Visa. While trainees do their fair share of due diligence and data rooming on the biggest deals, for smaller clients they can run matters more independently. 'I was drafting 30 or 40 transaction documents by myself,' said one contact; others spoke of drafting minutes, resolutions, and company articles, setting up LLPs, attending 'lots of meetings' and being sent off to other countries to work on deals there. Foreign trips happen from time to time, and go some way to making up for the fact that TW doesn't do overseas seats. What it does offer are highly popular secondments to Google and British Airways. Only a couple of trainees get to go each year, 'but they inevitably come back raving about it.'

Taylor Wessing's construction team received the seal of approval from *Chambers UK* and was also commended by our trainee sources. 'I found it so much more varied than I thought it was going to be,' said one. 'They were good at getting me to do different things, even if it wasn't the most convenient thing for the department,' added another. The seat was also praised for being 'well balanced in terms of time management. You just have to do all the boring jobs, but on the other hand you would be drafting instructions to counsel and parts of the defence, and on the smaller matters you will be running the file and giving the clients advice.' The commercial disputes team has an equally good reputation. 'People have a bit of a laugh, and I dibbed and dabbed into lots of cases,' recalled one source. The workload ranges from finance and insurance cases to contract law and partnership disputes. 'I got my teeth into a case where the minority shareholders were feeling unfairly treated by the majority shareholders,' said one contact. Some trainees have a stab at advocacy, and although nervous beforehand, the verdict is that 'it's good to get used to the conventions of how to address people…' even if one trainee 'felt like Gollum having to call people maaaaster.'

Calm down dear, it's only a logo

IP may no longer be so central to the business, but it's by no means a fading star. This side of the firm is divided into three teams – hard IP (patent matters), soft IP (copyright and trade marks) and IT and telecoms. A long list of big name clients includes Abbott Laboratories; Amgen; Burberry; BMG Music Publishing; Cambridge Biotechnology; Canon; The Discovery Channel; Ecolab;

Chambers UK rankings

Advertising & Marketing • Agriculture & Rural Affairs • Banking & Finance • Climate Change • Construction • Corporate Finance • Data Protection • Defamation/Reputation Management • Dispute Resolution • Employment • Environment • Financial Services Regulation • Franchising • Fraud: Civil • Immigration • Information Technology • Insurance • Intellectual Property • Life Sciences • Media & Entertainment • Outsourcing • Pensions • Pensions Litigation • Planning • Private Client • Private Equity • Product Liability • Real Estate • Real Estate Finance • Real Estate Litigation • Restructuring/Insolvency • Tax • Telecommunications

Google; Fox; Fujitsu Corporation; Hasbro; Hewlett-Packard; Innate Pharma; Macmillan Publishers; MGM Networks; National Geographic; Oxford BioMedica and UCB Celltech. Many of these clients are advised in conjunction with the firm's German offices.

In each trainee intake there are usually a handful of people with a science background that makes them ideally suited to the hard IP seat, where they can get a taste of 'the leading pharmaceutical actions in which the firm is heavily involved.' In one such case – Monsanto v Cargill – a patent relating to genetically modified crops was deemed to have not been infringed by Cargill's importation of soymeal into the UK. In the case of Mayne Pharma v Sanofi and Debiopharm the team obtained a declaration of non-infringement and pursued revocation proceedings concerning ten patents relating to oxaliplatin, a platinum-based drug used in the treatment of colon cancer. The firm has also been acting for W.L. Gore, the company behind the waterproof/breathable fabric Gore-Tex, against a company that has registered a similar patent for a material in their footwear. 'Perhaps my expectations were too high,' said one of our contacts, 'but I didn't quite get to use my scientific background specifically.' This may have been because there were a couple of big trials going on at the time and so bundling and court visits were two major aspects of the seat. We were assured that other trainees had been able to make more use of their science heads.

Non-scientists fight it out for the soft IP seat. The firm has advised the likes of Christian Dior and ITV on non-contentious matters, while on the contentious side they recently represented esure in a long-running dispute over a logo. The company applied to register a trade mark for a computer-mouse-on-wheels logo in 2004, which was opposed by Direct Line on the basis of its earlier telephone-on-wheels logo. Direct Line subsequently launched its own mouse-on-wheels logo, and the matter has since gone to a Trade Marks Registry hearing, a High Court appeal and a contested Court of Appeal hearing. Defamation is another hot area and the firm has worked for the likes of Associated Newspapers, Al-Jazeera and David Mellor on such matters. Trainees praised the quality of experiences offered by this team. Again the seat is research-heavy, with all the additional litigation tasks you might expect, such as drafting witness statements and attending court.

Why so modest?

We found TW to be an exceptionally modest firm, perhaps too much so. The trainees described it as an exceedingly 'down-to-earth' place to be, and when asked how they thought outsiders saw the firm, they answered, 'I think we're perceived to be quite bland.' When we mentioned in passing the name of another international midsizer we thought was roughly comparable, we got the response: 'Really? I'd be quite flattered to be compared with them.' If it wasn't for the fact that TW is doing very nicely as it is, thank you, we'd suggest a radical marketing campaign to boost its profile. As it is, the firm is neither stuffy ('although one or two partners would aspire to stuffiness') nor quite as trendy as some of its achingly hip counterparts. Instead, a 'comfortable' atmosphere permeates the place. There's a feeling among trainees that the imminent move to fresh premises off Fleet Street might herald the start of a new era. Construction is coming on apace and the partners are keen to make sure everybody is consulted on all aspects of the new office. 'They got the secretaries testing the chairs and we are currently trialling the coffee machines,' a trainee revealed. A committee is deciding on the interior décor and 'the reception is being designed so there will be an amazing art wall with a constantly changing exhibition.' A competition has been launched to name the ninth-floor restaurant, though our contacts seemed resigned to the fact that the kitchen staff will be moving along with the rest of the office (the fare currently on offer is described as 'appalling').

There's nothing bland about the TW trainees themselves, who identify 'a lot of laughter' as a feature of their social group. Come Friday, 'a hardcore eight or nine in each year' can be seen at the firm's local haunts – The Witness Box and The Evangelist. Said one: 'I was away last weekend and came back on Monday to find 45 e-mails about Friday night in my inbox.' They like their sports too: there are teams for football, hockey, cricket and touch rugby, and there's a league-winning netball team. Trainees have also been on a Go Ape mid-air assault course experience and trips to the dogs and The Comedy Store. The one date to keep clear is the annual quiz night – the winning team gets a full day off work. Hurrah! And the firm doesn't stint when it comes to Christmas fun: 'I went to the trainee party, my departmental party, my team's party and the corporate party,' chuckled one contact. A dislike of arrogance was prevalent among our interviewees. Although most went to leading universities: 'I wouldn't say there's any ridiculous people here. At law school there was a gang of posh girls, all living in the West End – you know the type. I don't know where they went, but they're not here, thank God!'

And finally...

In 2008 17 out of 23 qualifiers stayed with Taylor Wessing. IP is often oversubscribed but nevertheless recruited four NQs this year. A host of other strong departments make this firm worth considering for anyone interested in a non-pretentious London outfit with all-round capabilities.

Teacher Stern LLP

The facts

Location: London

Number of UK partners/solicitors: 22/22

Total number of trainees: 7

Seats: 4x6 months

Alternative seats: None

Extras: Pro Bono – Toynbee Hall Legal Advice Centre

> Still the largest team in the firm, TS's real estate lawyers handled so many deals in 2007 that their deal-o-meter melted after it had clocked up £1bn worth of transactions.

Teacher Stern marked the year of its 41st birthday with a full rebrand, a conversion to LLP status, an office spruce-up, a new website and a party at the Royal Academy. Times they are a changin' at this once property-centric London firm.

New thinking

Strictly speaking we should say Teacher Stern Selby did all that, because a key part of rebranding involved dropping the Selby. Another element was the adoption of a new website complete with key slogans such as 'Lawyers with intelligent foresight'. This did make us wonder what constitutes stupid foresight but, hey, we're nitpickers. Trainees say the rebrand was designed 'to market ourselves more... we've been seen as a low-key firm, even though our deals are substantial and we've a strong client base.' In this respect they're not wrong: TS has some impressive corporate, sports, media and defamation lawyers, and its property team has long been the engine room of the firm. The challenge now is to 'highlight our skills and what we've got to offer, trying to rely less on existing clients or referrals and open ourselves out to the market and a younger, more modern clientele.'

Given his reputation for unorthodoxy, we can only conclude that the installation of Graham Shear as managing partner is as much a part of the firm's makeover as anything else. This – dare we use the cliché – maverick lawyer has gained a high profile in defamation and sports law, where his willingness to use an unconventional approach seems to takes its cue more from the philosophies of celebrity publicists like Max Clifford than standard legal texts. Daniel Craig, Jude Law, Matthew Perry and a whole host of footballers, agents and football clubs have turned to him for assistance, and he's lately been representing long-term client Ashley Cole via a crafty no-win, no-fee arrangement in a case concerning a kiss-and-tell feature in *The Sun*. Clearly, Shear is a man who likes to be in – and be seen to be in – the thick of it. The case hinges on UK interpretations of the European Convention on Human Rights, so if the TS team is successful, the case may well be instrumental in knocking kiss-and-tells on the head for good. If Teacher Stern's new identity has a media-savvy feel, it's probably something to do with Shear. Trainees believe that 'day to day he sums up what the firm wants to be: younger, more connected with the media and more commercial.'

The heat is on

TS doesn't recruit many trainees, but it has treats in store for its chosen few. All visit the property, litigation and coco departments before being allowed 'input' into the decision as to where they will spend their final months. The system isn't as restrictive as it might sound. The aim has always been to keep trainees' experiences fairly broad and to get them working for people across their team, not just a single supervisor. The firm also listens to trainees' preferences as to who they sit with in a department, a policy that comes into its own in relation to litigation, where TS handles exceptionally interesting cases in the fields of sports law, media law, defamation/reputation management and education-related litigation.

Still the largest team in the firm, TS's real estate lawyers handled so many deals in 2007 that their deal-o-meter melted after it had clocked up £1bn worth of transactions. The firm is proud that the last few years have brought increasingly larger and more complex deals, such as the restructuring and further lending for a £218m leisure site in Sheffield, a £207m investment acquisition of City offices, an £80m Manchester shopping centre purchase and a £73m investment acquisition of a Midlands storage and distribution depot. While such transactions might not be accessible to all trainees, those who'd been exposed to them praised the partners for being 'accessible with their advice and supervision' and willing to 'delegate a lot of responsibility.' In this department, everyone is likely to experience 'the management of large shopping centres or commercial developments.' This means 'drafting leases, licences and surrenders, and the odd sale and purchase.' Our sources enjoyed their relative independence in this department and noted the usefulness of a certain amount of residential conveyancing.

While happy to acknowledge the strong links between the property finance team and the finance aspects of the corporate team's work, trainees suggest 'coco is definitely growing as a standalone practice and its commercial, media, IP and IT instructions are all increasing.' The team has been busy for sports clients: it worked on the AIM listing of Watford FC, advised prospective purchasers of West Ham, assisted on Alfonso Alves' move from SC Heerenveen to Middlesbrough FC and smoothed Javier Mascherano's transfer to Liverpool FC. It's also worth pointing out that Graham Shear was instrumental in setting up the Football Agents Association and the team has advised both domestic and overseas licensed agents on a successful challenge of the English FA's attempts to introduce wide-reaching new regulations governing their activities. As for media clients, Hollywood TV Limited used the firm on its proposed disposal of the television channel Pitchgaming 2, while newspaper owner Northern & Shell sought copyright licensing advice following joint venture agreements in Australia and New Zealand.

A seat with the coco team means anything from property-flavoured transactional work, to IP, employment and commercial or regulatory sports law (especially if it's transfer window time). The common denominator is 'very friendly people who want to help you get involved.' Quite clearly there's never going to be magic circle-sized deals, but some work will have international aspects and there are plenty of 'start-ups and joint ventures for entrepreneurial clients.' Happily, this 'makes client contact more likely and more interesting.' And we're told you should never underestimate the glamour of 'meeting the sports and media clients.'

Chambers UK rankings

Defamation/Reputation Management • Sports Law

Jack'll fix it for you

The litigation seat offers equally broad experience. Time spent in property litigation now has an added dash of 'secured lending recovery work, acting for lenders involved in debt portfolios,' which is 'a new area for the firm.' This equates to 'real responsibility because you're communicating directly with lenders, working with receivers and drafting documentation.' There's also a plethora of other tasks on other types of case, such as attending court to observe and take notes, drafting particulars of claim and statutory declarations for insolvency matters, and even potential involvement in IP litigation for clients like Portuguese clothing brands owner Calzeus. Because 'Graham Shear has his own trainee,' there's little contentious sports or celebrity defamation work on offer in a mainstream litigation seat. If you want some of that action you'd better start crossing your fingers now. Those who do manage to sit with him could end up working for Hollywood celebs and sports stars including Rio Ferdinand, Kieran Dyer, Ledley King, John Hartson, Carl Cort, Titus Bramble and Dwain Chambers.

One lucky trainee is assigned to Jack Rabinowicz, who excels in the fields of medical and educational negligence. Assist him on an education case, perhaps involving a child or adult claiming wrongful exclusion from the education system, and you'll witness 'emotional real-life stories relating to autism and special needs' and 'a compassionate, listening and understanding Jack.' The 'total flip side of the coin' is assisting him on 'large commodities litigation matters,' where he exhibits a different commercial persona. 'He's so quick and concise, extremely bright and thinks ahead of everyone at light speed,' gasped one trainee. 'It's brilliant to watch him in action.'

As this overview of the seats suggests, despite its new ambitions Teacher Stern is still a smaller firm offering the attractive prospect of 'broad commercial law experience and a personal feel' for those who decidedly 'don't want the magic circle life.' If these are the benefits of a compact London firm, the compromise that most trainees are more than happy to make is a 'less developed HR function, procedures and policies.' When it comes to feedback, for example, because 'you tend to work for most fee earners in a team, if you get something wrong they tell you,' meaning 'you figure out for yourself how you're doing.' However, showing that the 'systems are catching up with the scale of the firm,' there are now monthly meetings for all trainees with two partners and a departmental mentor system is more or less in place. Formal training tends to take second place to 'applying knowledge and carrying forward the learning process yourself,' although there are 'general talks about due diligence, research, disclosure, transactions and systems' at the start of each seat.

Finding the perfect fit

The process of NQ recruitment continues to be an area where trainees would appreciate 'more formal processes and more communication between decision makers and us.' The retention rate for qualifiers has varied between 16% and 100% over the past six years, so it's understandable why the prospect of not finding out whether you've a job until late in the summer creates unease. In the event three out of four qualifiers stayed with the firm in 2008.

Trainees reckon they've spotted a pattern as to who makes the grade, first as new recruits and then as NQs. 'Seeing the people who didn't get a place after the vac scheme, I'd say you can't be cocky or overconfident,' said one, while another suggested: 'You've got to be headstrong, responsible, a real hard worker and bright, but more than anything it's really important to get on with people and show you can establish a rapport with them.' This, they ascribe to the fact that 'the firm is smaller, so you're more noticeable and personality fit is a massive feature.' Yes, a solid redbrick or even top-ten university background will help, but the most important thing is whether or not your personality fits.

TS has given its Bedford Row premises a makeover: 'The client floor is now light, airy and clean – quite different really,' and, floor by floor, 'nice carpets and glass-sided offices' appeared over the summer of 2008. Another change in recent times is the ebbing of a well-defined Jewish side to the firm's personality. TS has been a multicultural place for yonks, but last year Jewish holidays were made normal working days that could be taken off using the enhanced personal holiday entitlement. This year some of our interviewees weren't even aware of the firm's cultural heritage before joining. 'I worked it out when I got here,' said one, 'but so many people are not Jewish that it clearly doesn't affect your treatment or ability to succeed.'

Teacher Stern's identity has more to do with the fact that 'it's not massive, so you do know everyone and automatically notice a new face.' Firm-wide drinks are held in the boardroom on the last Friday of every month and regular trips to local pubs The Enterprise and The Old Nick create plenty of opportunities to bring new arrivals into the fold, while an increasingly active social committee takes up any slack. The pièce de social résistance is a highly popular office party in December.

And finally...

Teacher Stern's smart new attitude can only enhance its appeal to students, so we'd advise getting on the vac scheme. Do remember, though, that the most eye-catching work is not necessarily the most accessible to trainees.

Thomson, Snell & Passmore

The facts

Location: Tunbridge Wells, Thames Gateway

Number of UK partners/solicitors: 38/31

Total number of trainees: 10

Seats: 4x6 months

Alternative seats: None

Extras: Pro bono – CAB

> Recently an office was opened in Greenhithe to take advantage of the ongoing regeneration of the Thames Gateway and the opening of nearby Ebbsfleet International on the Eurostar line.

Its Kent roots traceable to 1570, Thomson, Snell & Passmore well deserves the title Most Durable Law Firm, apparently bestowed on it by the *Guinness Book of Records*. Sheer longevity isn't the only ace up its Elizabethan sleeves, as it combines a strong private client tradition with a thriving commercial practice.

438 years young

Many firms have potted histories on their websites, but TS-P's is the lengthiest we've ever seen. The firm goes back well over four centuries to when one Nicholas Hooper, a curate of Tonbridge Parish Church, set about drawing up wills, charters and indentures. Apparently in 1604 both Christopher Marlowe's *Dr Faustus* and John Hooper's indenture in respect of 30 acres of Tonbridge were completed – we're sure they were both equally celebrated.

TS-P has never stopped working for the well-to-do of Tunbridge Wells and its private client team brings in just under a quarter of the firm's income. Even commercially minded trainees told us they'd done seats with the team because they 'didn't want to miss out on a big part of the firm's business.' But while TS-P's centuries-old heritage is occasionally traded upon – after all, 'it sets it apart from newer, wacky firms' – its recruits say it isn't entirely representative of the firm today. 'We're proud of how long we've lasted,' sighed one, 'but it's not like we get 1570 tattooed on our foreheads.' They tell us that everyone from the 'young, thrusting' senior partner to those who've been with TS-P for a long time is 'quite modern in their outlook' and the firm is 'really pushing to become slicker.'

There's been a conscious effort to raise the profile of commercial departments and the new senior partner is a former head of coco. Recently an office was opened in Greenhithe to take advantage of the ongoing regeneration of the Thames Gateway and the opening of nearby Ebbsfleet International on the Eurostar line. By virtue of it being only 12 minutes by train from Central London and easily accessible from the Continent, the second office is designed 'to bring new and innovative areas of work to the firm.' Surpassing expectations, the venture has already 'paid dividends.' A number of teams, including dispute resolution, coco, commercial property and employment now maintain a permanent presence there, and most of the construction team is now based out of the TG office. Clients here include Britannia Refined Metals, a subsidiary of MIM Holdings, one of the world's largest mining and minerals groups, and Ring Containers, the UK subsidiary of Ring Container Technology, a US-based packaging manufacturer. Other notable names are Royal British Legion Industries, State Bank of India and English Wines Group.

Coupled with TS-P's private client strengths and solid reputation in clinical negligence, it's fair to say the firm has a rather successful 'dual personality.' One trainee explained the conundrum: 'It's a very split marketing approach, as you don't want to go too corporate and scare off private clients, and your personal injury and clinical negligence clients aren't attracted by the same things big corporate players are.' Ultimately there's no room for sentimentality with 'Tesco law on the horizon' and large corporations looking to take over private client process work and 'bash it out factory-style.' TS-P plans to protect itself by securing instructions at the quality end of the market and making itself 'as profitable as possible.'

Wills and grace

TS-P demonstrated its commitment to private client practice by hiring several new lawyers last year. The department is split into teams for wills, probate, tax and trusts, and Court of Protection advice ('acting on behalf of people who can't look after themselves, for example those with mental illness'). Private client trainees do 'a bit of everything,' though it pays to show initiative and ask for new types of work. 'Drafting wills is always going to be a big part of the seat,' and strangely they come in waves, so 'sometimes there are 300 on your desk, other times you don't see any for days.' Differing individual circumstances mean wills rarely stick to the standard precedent, and this is what trainees like about the work. Moreover, 'you're doing something that can make a real difference in the clients' lives and take pressure off them at a time when they really need that.' Clients are generally wealthy and may even be descended from families who've used the firm for generations. The same clients pop up in the residential conveyancing seat, where trainees start with small tasks and eventually run their own files, dealing with 'pretty much every aspect of the transaction.' Unsurprisingly, 'the more expensive the property, the more interesting the work.'

Instructions for the personal injury and clinical negligence teams (united for purposes of training) come from across the country. 'For a small regional firm, we're up against some big players.' The PI lawyers handle everything from slips and trips to road traffic accidents and catastrophic injuries, while the clin neg team is skilled in childhood brain injuries. In the past year it has finalised several cerebral palsy settlements for around £5m and took a role in the £3m compensation awarded to 360 veterans of Cold War experiments at the Porton Down military research facility. Trainees prepare witness statements, attend conferences with barristers and conduct complex quantum and causation research. Speaking about their contact with clients, our interviewees told us 'It's a huge privilege to play such a role in their lives. There are some very personal moments they share with you, and it's incredibly rewarding.'

These and other departments fill a number of small buildings clustered together in the centre of Tunbridge Wells, but as 'medical files take up so much space,' staff find the

Chambers UK rankings

Charities • Clinical Negligence • Corporate Finance • Dispute Resolution • Employment • Family/Matrimonial • Personal Injury • Private Client • Real Estate • Real Estate Litigation

offices cramped. 'It's not battery hens or anything,' however the firm is looking for bigger premises.

No stalling

The commercial property department handles 'everything from developments to leasehold and general commercial deals.' One trainee was let loose on their own caseload of 'about 20 files, working directly with developers.' Last year was a busy one for the coco team, which received around 300 instructions, approximately a third of them from new clients. Highlights included advising the shareholders of London branding consultancy Karakter on the £2m sale of the company, and Koelliker UK's purchase of UK car distributor SsangYong's assets. Trainees' work runs the gamut from data protection and copyright law to M&A, from monitoring clients' websites, drafting contracts and even 'being let loose to set up a company.' Best of all, completion meetings are 'quite exciting, and you get a bit of champagne!' It's a hectic seat, but 'your workload is heavily monitored, so you don't feel too pressured.' Our interviewees took issue with the criticisms we reported last year that coco trainees weren't given enough responsibility. They insisted they have 'a sizeable input into drafting key legal documents' and are 'involved at a much more engaging level' than they imagine a trainee at a City firm would be.

You may have noticed how varied the training is here, and the dispute resolution seat doesn't buck the trend. Our interviewees had seen land and boundary issues, as well as health and safety cases and instructions relating to the new points-based immigration system. 'The advocacy is really character-building. Sometimes you're facing some grumpy guy who's shouting, and you just have to try to disarm him with a smile.' In the Thames Gateway office, the seat feels 'closer to an NQ position,' with trainees getting more client contact and running their own files. It is preferable for trainees to already have some experience in a department before they go to TG, so it's a good choice for people who want extra time in an area marked out for qualification. Dispute resolution now accounts for the majority of lawyers in the office, although all commercial departments have lawyers who spend either all or part of their week in

Greenhithe. Apparently 'the girls love going up there' because it's just around the corner from Bluewater.

Seat allocation is decided before trainees begin their contracts and after seeking their preferences. 'There's always the problem of not being sure what you want to do,' but given that there's scope to change or even repeat seats, it's not an insurmountable difficulty. Discussions about qualification start at the beginning of the second year, allowing trainees to either 'set their stall out' or defer a decision until they hit the final seat. In 2008 all four qualifiers found positions with their first-choice department.

Kent buy me love

TS-P has 'a close-knit community feel,' so people get to know one another quickly. This evidently means partners as well, as our interviewees reminisced about 'the relief on your first day when you meet your supervisor, the person you're going to share a room with for six months, and they're a perfectly normal person.' Hours are good. 'As long as you get all your work done,' you can stroll out of the office door at 5.30pm and the lunch break is 'a popular hour and a quarter,' just 'long enough to go home in winter or to the park in summer.'

Our questions about the typical TS-P trainee prompted a few thoughtful answers. 'You see other firms around the South and think they definitely go for a certain type,' pondered one. 'I wonder what they think of us?' Probably 'quietly intelligent,' 'sociable' and 'quite self-effacing,' if our sources have it right. 'We all grew up in the area, so we're minded more towards work-life balance than work-hard, play-hard.' Recruits were divided as to whether TS-P showed a bias toward local applicants, but they agreed its first concern is for applicants to be committed to the firm and not just 'trying to get a contract to go to London later.'

Pubs and restaurants abound in Tunbridge Wells, and while there isn't 'a raving nightlife, it can keep you entertained if your friends come down for a visit.' London is just a short train ride away, though trainees generally fail to make it further than The Barn, just down the road from the office. 'We live there when we're not at work,' confessed a fan. Quarterly firm drinks in the Pitcher & Piano attract 'the usual regulars,' while last year's Christmas party had a masquerade ball theme. After snooping around for costumed hanky-panky, we were assured 'it's not really a firm for anonymous indiscretions.' Outings to the West End and Thorpe Park, and a day trip to France fill out the social calendar.

Thanks to a few trainees and postroom boys the 'historically awful at football' TS-P has managed to gain bragging rights by beating local rivals Cripps Harries Hall a few times. This sporting triumph clearly affected them all deeply, because this year's summer party took a school sports day theme. Unsurprisingly, for a 'family-oriented' firm, 'a lot of people have kids here,' and they were all invited. One trainee didn't rate their chances much: 'I'll have to get blue-tack for the egg and spoon or I might just watch the little people race instead.'

And finally...

While this wouldn't be the best place if you're after a fast pace and massive international deals, it's ideal for those who prefer a quieter life and closer involvement with clients.

- **Shameless Plug:** The entire contents of our *Chambers UK* directory can be read and fully searched online for free at www.chambersandpartners.com. The fruits of thousands of interviews with lawyers and clients, searching the rankings and editorial will tell you who is top in which practice areas and what work specific firms have been up to. It makes for perfect interview crib notes.

Thring Townsend Lee & Pembertons

The facts

Location: Swindon, Bath, Bristol, London, Marlborough, Chippenham, Cirencester

Number of UK partners/solicitors: 55/65

Total number of trainees: 14

Seats: 4x6 months

Alternative seats: Secondments

Those who thrive here take on responsibility with obvious enthusiasm and adapt to the multi-office training without complaining.

This fast-growing and broad-based South West firm always comes up trumps: each year the *Student Guide* gets to report on another merger. This year it added a niche private client operation in Wiltshire and South Gloucestershire.

Getting on the Monopoly board

TTLP has undergone dramatic change since most of the current trainees fired off their applications. Back then it was plain old Thring Townsend with offices in Swindon, Bath and Newbury (now gone), and it had a good handle on commercial, agricultural and private client business in that part of the world. In 2005, the firm took over Laytons' Bristol office, and then in 2007 hooked up with 200-year-old Westminster firm Lee & Pembertons, which had a superb roster of agricultural and private clients. 'The London office complements us very well in terms of contacts, skills and structure. We get a lot of referrals and it's great having a London base for meetings,' trainees explained. Now ensconced in 'absolutely amazing' new premises, the London branch adds prestige, and the address – One Pall Mall East – looks impressive on the firm's notepaper.

Most recently there was the merger with venerable old firm Wood Awdry & Ford of Marlborough, Chippenham and Cirencester. Its senior partner William Wyldbore-Smith is a Deputy Lieutenant of Wiltshire and once held the position of president of the Gloucestershire and Wiltshire Law Society. Wood Awdry's pedigree and location now provides TTLP with access to even more wealthy Wiltshire and Cotswold folk.

These unions have pushed TTLP's annual turnover to more than £20m and allowed it to move into the lists of the top 100 firms in the UK, something which had taken

certain of our sources by surprise. 'I was a bit worried about the mergers,' said one; 'when I first came here it was so nice and friendly, and I didn't want that to change.' Thankfully, the head honchos share this view and organised workshops and coaching to help preserve the firm's core values. Trainees say the firm's attitudes are becoming 'increasingly commercial,' yet still feel staff welfare is a priority. To win over hearts and minds, 'the managing partner has been going around the offices telling us the latest happenings and giving people the chance to ask anonymous questions about anything that's bothering them.' As for the future, no one knows if there will be further mergers, although there's little doubt TTLP wants to continue building its core private client, agricultural and commercial practices. Say trainees: 'It has a strong vision, and it's exciting to be part of that.'

Free range, well fed

As yet, the old Wood Awdry offices haven't hosted TTLP trainees, meaning that Swindon, Bath, Bristol and London are regarded as the training centres. Admittedly, none of the West of England trainees has yet opted to travel to London for a seat, but the firm is keen for this to change 'so the offices can cross over and mingle a bit more.' In theory no one has any objections, though one source cautioned that 'the firm would have to sort out an accommodation allowance.' For now most trainees swap between Swindon, Bristol and Bath, and fortunately the commutes aren't too arduous. While the majority spend the bulk of their time in the Swindon office, trainees like the fact that they're expected to move around. 'You get to know other fee earners and can raise your profile. The partners move around too, so it's very much part of firm life.'

The large, open-plan Swindon branch is 'a fun, social place' just a ten-minute drive from town. 'There's a café on site so absolutely everybody eats together and mixes. It's extremely inclusive and it would be a bit strange to go and eat sandwiches at your desk by yourself.' The Bath operation is smaller but 'also lovely,' and it too has an all-important café. Both offer free (full English) breakfasts for early risers, as well as subsidised lunches and dinners. 'We're very well fed,' commented one trainee cheerfully; 'it's quite easy to get fat here.' The Bristol city centre office comes across as 'a little older,' both in terms of its building and staff.

Raising the stakes

Because TTLP has one of the largest commercial real estate teams in southern England, property and property litigation seats are a common feature of the training contract. The firm represents a broad spectrum of clients and its top deals last year included a warehouse/office acquisition for packaging and office products manufacturer DS Smith Group, as well as several matters for Gaming International relating to greyhound stadia. The London office tends to deal with clients at the higher end of the market. 'Recently I've worked on some £5m transactions,' confirmed one source. Property litigation trainees frequently field general enquiries from people coming in off the street, and while this may present challenges, 'you learn things fast when you have to answer random queries.' It's a busy seat with disclosure lists and claim forms to draft, barristers to liaise with and court hearings to watch. 'My supervisor was excellent,' commented one interviewee, who'd spent time with this 'very supportive group.'

Family law is described as 'absolutely brilliant, a dream seat,' not least because you gain confidence and feel a part of the team straight away. Once familiar with files, trainees are able to run things solo: 'I did a hearing on a child matter once. I had to arrange counsel, a court time, the witness statements and everything. It was scary at the time but afterwards I thought, 'Well done me!'' The firm no longer handles legal aid cases, instead focusing on divorces and financial relief for clients with assets. The Swindon and Bath teams work closely, requiring trainees to travel between the offices to help different fee earners. 'It's great but can be emotionally draining,' admitted one. 'I had a client who would ring up every day for a half-hour chat, just to get things off her chest. You definitely learn how to put up a professional barrier.'

Chambers UK rankings

Agriculture & Rural Affairs • Construction • Corporate Finance • Dispute Resolution • Employment • Environment • Intellectual Property • Personal Injury • Private Client • Real Estate • Real Estate Litigation • Restructuring/Insolvency

TTLP's personal injury department is ranked in the top tier for its region in *Chambers UK*. The lawyers deal with complex, high-value claims and can offer fantastic court experience. They specialise in industrial diseases and serious injuries, recently securing a £5.1m settlement for a young man who suffered a serious brain injury. His previous solicitors had advised his family to expect a settlement offer between £300,000 and £1m. Trainees can opt for either claimant or defendant experience; if they choose the latter they deal with insurance and pharmaceutical companies. Although most cases tend to be 'too big for us to run ourselves,' trainees are encouraged to have a go at most things, especially drafting. 'I met a lot of clients and went to the Royal Courts of Justice,' confirmed one. The bundling and photocopying can pile up at times, so it's good to hear there is an all-hands-to-the-pump attitude in the department.

Don't forget your wellies

The large agriculture team benefited greatly from the merger TT/L&P merger. Primarily located in Bath and London, its lawyers specialise in actions against DEFRA, access to land cases, subsidy law, prosecutions by the Environment Agency, rights of way issues and complex farm transactions. 'You have one sort of client, but a myriad of matters that can come up,' we learned. The clients are farm businesses and landed estates, and the firm is on the NFU legal panel for 11 counties. 'I met a lot of clients and went out to their farms – they're a nice bunch,' said one fan of the seat.

In the corporate/commercial group trainees are either rushed off their feet or asking for more work. 'When I first started they had about three completions, so my first month was hectic,' reported one. It's not all transactional work here; sometimes clients just need help drafting their own business terms and conditions. That's just fine with trainees who say: 'It's great to be able to dabble in both corporate and commercial, you get twice as much experience.' No prizes for guessing the working day can be longer than elsewhere, however 'the good thing about Thring is that it's not a firm to work you into the ground.

You get a great [work-life] balance and that's as important to the firm as it is to you.'

Overall, our sources had plenty of praise for the firm's approach to training: 'They see us as a real future resource rather than people who might be leaving after two years.' Supervisors are good at 'giving you the exact amount of responsibility you can handle at the time,' and 'most will drop everything if you're struggling.' In 2008 seven of the nine qualifiers stayed on.

Pastymania

The fact that this report on TTLP was ever finished is a miracle. While diligently crawling over the firm's website we discovered a link to a frighteningly addictive stress-busting, pastry-based game called Pasty Panic. Two days later our high score was stuck at 291, a paltry result compared to the all-time record of 529. Desperate to know the identity of the pasty masters we interrogated a few people. 'I don't play it,' said one interviewee innocently, before pointing the finger at the corporate team. 'I reckon they sit there playing it at ten o'clock at night while pretending to work.'

TTLP trainees are amiable sorts. 'You do have to be friendly, hard-working and outgoing to get along here,' concluded one. Another agreed, saying: 'It's more about personality than anything academic – there are no bookish types.' Those who thrive take on responsibility with obvious enthusiasm and adapt to the multi-office training without complaining. As for where they come from: 'Most people have been at uni in the West, at places like Bristol, Cardiff and Swansea, but there's a couple from Durham too, so some have completely relocated to the area.'

Because the social committee is packed full of trainees and legal executives, the events they organise appeal to the younger crowd. 'There are monthly drinks in all the offices, theatre trips, picnics, bowling evenings, barbecues, and we've just got permission to close the office one day for Pimm's in the sun.' Department meals and family-oriented events ensure no one is excluded from the fun. If sports are your thing there's tag rugby, football and golf. 'We tried to get a netball team together but we were all hopeless so that didn't go very far.'

As the largest office, Swindon was singled out as the social hub; London, on the other hand, sometimes feels somewhat out of the loop. Still, we hear things are better than they were pre-merger. 'Back then there would be about two drinks evenings a year,' recalled one source. 'It's more partner-heavy up here so people have different priorities,' another explained. An influx of younger staff has changed things, and the London trainees try to get to as many of the other offices' jollies as possible. We hear the last TTLP Christmas party was a 'grand, noisy affair,' thanks to the efforts of professional party planners and subsidised hotel rooms 'to stumble into afterwards.'

And finally...

TTLP offers quality training, open communication and genuine work-life balance. In return, it expects to see dedication and enthusiasm, so 'if you want a firm where you can hide behind 50 other trainees and go unnoticed, don't bother applying.'

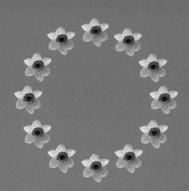

A top 100 law firm, with some 650 people across Bristol, London and Piraeus, Greece, including 72 Partners. One of the fastest growing firms in the country and, in the eyes of many, the one to watch. Impressive, we think you'll agree. As is TLT's commitment to nurturing talented people.

OUR WORK

A full-service UK law firm, we provide industry focused multi-discipline integrated solutions, with particular strengths in the financial services and leisure sectors. Other key markets include retail, the built environment, technology and media.

VACATION PLACEMENT SCHEMES

At Easter and during July or August, we run a number of one week placements, open to second year law students, final year non-law students, graduates and mature students. What will you get out of it? Live case work and first-hand experience for starters.

TRAINING CONTRACTS

We take on 20 trainees each year across March and September. As well as continuous support and regular partner contact, you'll have a designated Trainee Supervisor. Challenging? You wouldn't have it any other way.

HOW TO APPLY

You'll find more information and an online application
www.TLTcareers.com/trainee

It's time to grow, come and put down roots with TLT.

TLT LLP

The facts

Location: Bristol, London

Number of UK partners/solicitors: 70/87

Total number of trainees: 21

Seats: 4x6 months

Alternative seats: Secondments

Extras: Pro bono – competition law advice scheme

TLT hasn't been shy about sharing its ambitions with the world: 'Top 50 law firm by 2008' has been the battle cry for the last few years.

The young gun of the Bristol legal scene, TLT was created in 2000 through the merger of Trumps and Lawrence Tuckets. Since then its rise to prominence has been spectacular.

Pester power

TLT hasn't been shy about sharing its ambitions with the world: 'Top 50 law firm by 2008' has been the battle cry for the last few years. Cometh the hour, has it managed to achieve this lofty goal? Trainees think so; 'and I certainly see the drive for a continued push on to top 30,' added one. That's big talk from a regional firm, especially one that is still only the third largest in Bristol, but TLT has the stats to prove that this is no idle boast. Since 2002 turnover is up nearly 300% to £38m and the firm has merged twice more, both times with small London boutiques, to acquire a presence in the capital. Staff numbers have increased by 40% in the last year alone, bringing the tally to over 700. Quality hasn't been compromised: *Chambers UK* ranks TLT top in the South West for licensing, family, debt recovery and insolvency, and as one of the three best firms outside London for banking litigation. On its books are the likes of Alfred McAlpine, Barclays, British Waterways Board, HBOS, Lloyds TSB, Merlin Entertainments, Orange and Somerfield; indeed, the firm has an impressive 25 FTSE-listed companies as clients. The architect of all this is David Pester, whose face stares wistfully off into the middle distance on the TLT homepage. Pester has been rewarded for his efforts with the crown of Managing Partner of the Year at an awards ceremony run by *Legal Week*.

Of course, it's a rare firm that's immune from the current economic gloom and trainees freely admit that at the most recent AGM 'positive messages were slightly tempered this year because of the dreaded credit crunch.' TLT also let several fee earners go in 2008, mainly from the licensing team, though as trainees explained, 'a huge amount of the work on the 24-hour drinking laws that we did for Punch Taverns is now coming to its natural end.'

TLT's chief practice areas are corporate, property, and banking and lender services, and it's recommended that all trainees experience life in at least one of these departments. The other seats available are a broad mix – employment, insolvency, construction, social housing. Planning, asset finance and general commercial. Family, the sole private client seat, is a slight oddity given TLT's size and strong commercial focus. It consistently attracts trainees who want to try high-calibre family law with a larger firm, but opportunities to qualify into this department crop up only infrequently.

Cracking firm, Gromit

TLT believes in giving trainees responsibility right from the start, and nowhere is this more apparent than in banking and financial services litigation. 'I was off to court on my own within a month,' said a trainee who'd done their first seat there. 'It quickly becomes second nature when you've been doing two or three hearings a week for a while.' There's no sink-or-swim culture, however: in this department 'the first couple of weeks are amazing for training – I had several private tutorials with solicitors.' Trainees mainly work on value negligence files. This is where a bank has repossessed a home, sold it at a loss and ends up pursuing the professional who overvalued the property in the first place. Anglo Irish Bank, Bank of Ireland, Barclays, RBS, Stroud & Swindon Building Society and a host of others all use the team. The work involves drafting letters of claim, instructing expert witnesses and day-to-day contact with the client. Some people found the tasks 'a bit repetitive,' saying it's 'not terribly complex,' but everyone acknowledged that co-ordinating up to 40 different claims at once is certainly good for developing organisational skills.

Property is regarded as a particularly useful seat to do for two reasons. Firstly, it complements other areas of law very well, so even those who have no interest in qualifying as property lawyers can benefit from it. Secondly, time here is well spent in terms of networking – 'If you miss out property you won't meet about 25% of the firm.' The 'huge' department, TLT's largest, takes several trainees at a time. Landlord and tenant files are a staple and 'you get client contact and your own files from the start, so it really helps build your confidence.' Trainees have also been involved in the sale and leaseback of many Somerfield stores. Another local client is Aardman Animations, which the property and construction teams acted for in the acquisition of new headquarters after its old building was gutted by fire in 2005. The general commercial seat is a broad mix of competition, IT and non-contentious IP work, and here the firm also acts for Aardman, protecting characters like Wallace and Gromit against trade mark infringements.

'What I really enjoyed about corporate,' said one source, 'was getting to work closely with other teams, like employment and property. It's a great introduction to the firm.' As a central part of the business, liaising with other teams is part and parcel of life in corporate. There is less client contact here than in some other seats, 'but my supervisor explained on my first day not to worry about that because the work is more partner-centric.' On the subject of supervision, our interviewees 'couldn't fault' the firm in terms of the 'opportunity to ask questions and just have a crack at something without worrying that they will rip it to shreds.' One told us: 'I have feedback after every piece of work.' Corporate has a client base that includes small Bristol businesses, national companies (especially 'younger and riskier' AIM-listers), and international corporations. Major transactions of the last year have included advising the majority shareholders of Williams Medical Supplies on the sale of their £40m business to a management buyout team and acting for Mitsubishi on an investment in a European retail business. Many of our contacts had the good fortune to arrive in a corporate seat just as a new deal was starting, and for most of them working on one main transaction took up the majority of their time, 'with a few company secretarial bits on the side.'

Chambers UK rankings

Banking & Finance • Banking Litigation • Competition/European Law • Construction • Corporate Finance • Debt Recovery • Dispute Resolution • Employment • Family/Matrimonial • Franchising • Intellectual Property • Licensing • Partnership • Pensions • Planning • Projects, Energy & Natural Resources • Real Estate • Real Estate Litigation • Restructuring/Insolvency • Social Housing

Trainees are often put in charge of due diligence – collating all the relevant information, looking for risk areas and drafting the disclosure documents. There's also what's described at TLT as 'the washing up' – sorting out bibles and so forth after the deal has closed.

Parfit gentil knights

While TLT is already well established in Bristol, its London office is starting to gain momentum. It merged in 2005 with Lawrence Jones and then again in 2007 with a firm in the very same building on the South Bank. Constant & Constant, a commercial practice with strength in shipping law, also brought an office in Piraeus to the table. The two firms were 'a good match' for TLT's style, and though 'there's lots of tweaking to be done,' they have blended well into the organisation. Trainees are keen to play up their own part in this. Some of the Bristolians have gone to do six-month secondments in London, while the last handful of trainees recruited by Constant & Constant have travelled in the opposite direction to get a taster of life in the West Country. Both sets are convinced that their occasional six-month stints in the other office have been instrumental in promoting cross-firm unity. London will recruit a full complement of trainees from September 2009, so opportunities for crossover may be slightly reduced in the future. The main difference between the two locations is that Bristol is open plan, while the South Bank office is not. TLT is very keen on 'approachability' at work. According to one trainee, working at the Bristol office is 'a little bit like the knights of the round table – no matter what your role at the firm, it's easy to wander up to people and ask questions.' We suppose David Pester must be King Arthur, but can't help but wonder who occupies the Siege Perilous, the round table's legendary seat of death? The lease of the London office expires in two years' time, and the suspicion is that there will be a move to a building more suited to TLT's chivalric philosophy.

A firm with strong Bristol roots, TLT inevitably draws comparisons with the city's other major names. Trainees cited a 'youthful, commercial, pragmatic' approach to work, and an 'entrepreneurial' spirit that 'sets the firm apart from Osborne Clarke and Burges Salmon.' When asked for examples of this dynamism, they told us: 'We spot gaps and opportunities in the market. We do mortgage enforcement and lender sales work that some law firms might turn their nose up at, but banks need that work done – and that usually leads to more work from them down the line.'

The firm also attracts a different kind of person to Burges Salmon and OC: 'there's no-one from Oxbridge,' for a start. When applying for training contracts, many had deliberately targeted the smaller Bristol concerns, although all were glad to be part of TLT's current growth spurt. Around 'two thirds to three quarters have a distinct and obvious connection to the region.' For many, this is a university background: the firm garners much interest from UWE, Bristol, Exeter, Cardiff, Southampton and Reading. However, it is less averse to recruiting talent from outside the area than many other regional practices, and some trainees come from further afield.

The annual firm-wide party is the chief event in the social calendar. This was formerly held at Christmas, but TLT is now 'too big' for everyone to be packed into one indoor venue, so it now takes place after the AGM in the summer and is hosted by Bristol Zoo (of which TLT is a sponsor).

Each of our contacts remembered something different about the event – human table football, a bucking bronco and a free bar were among the attractions. Trainees are grateful that they no longer have to put on their traditional Christmas performance for the amusement of the partners and staff, but they do still have their own celebratory meal in December. At other times, Toto's Wine Bar is the place to be seen. The sporting side is well catered for, with cricket, football, hockey, netball and softball teams all performing respectably in their leagues. The social life is 'not forced,' however 'a lot rests on the third and fourth-seaters grabbing new trainees by the scruff of the neck and marching them down to the pub.'

And finally...

One interviewee described TLT as a 'hungry' firm, and we think that sums it up very well. You can sense that underneath the firm's friendly nature lies a certain steel – the ambitious streak that has seen it balloon in size and yet still have an appetite for more. In 2008, eight of the 11 qualifiers stayed on.

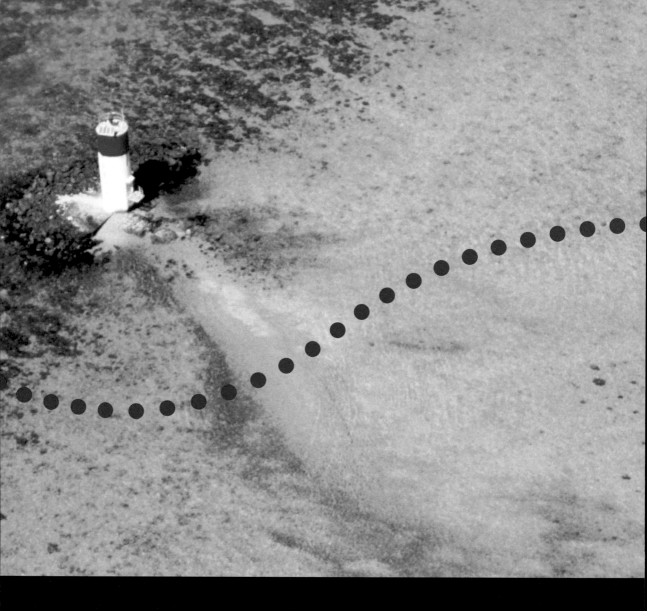

The adventure you're looking for, the guidance you need

It starts the moment you do – work of the highest quality with the support and guidance of some of the best people in the business. At Travers Smith, we are big enough to offer the most exciting opportunities but small enough for each individual to count. Choose a more inspiring path.

Please visit **www.traverssmith.com** or contact Germaine VanGeyzel, Graduate Recruitment Manager: **graduate.recruitment@traverssmith.com** Travers Smith LLP, 10 Snow Hill, London, EC1A 2AL, 020 7295 3000

Travers Smith

The facts

Location: London

Number of UK partners/solicitors: 65/187

Total number of trainees: 41

Seats: 4x6 months

Alternative seats: Paris, occasional secondments

Extras: Pro bono – Paddington Law Centre, City Law School Advice Centre, Caribbean death row appeals; language training

> By keeping a watchful eye on the quality of its lawyers, Travers has maintained a reputation as one of the most trusted advisers around.

Travers Smith subscribes to the 'if it ain't broke don't fix it' school of thought. And why not? Its classic formula of stability, quality and professionalism is a winner.

City smitten

This firm has been a City institution for centuries. Way back in 1801, one of the partners drafted the constitution for the first Stock Exchange and it's never looked back since. 'In terms of strategy,' said one source, 'I think we're going to keep doing what we're doing, there are no radical changes planned. We've got a good section of the market and a good selection of clients.' These clients include private equity houses, companies such as Collins Stewart, Trainline Group, Associated British Foods and BAE Systems, financial institutions including Abbey National, RBS, Macquarie Bank and NatWest, and British institutions like Transport for London and the John Lewis Partnership.

It's no accident that Travers hasn't grown into one of the giants of the City; the firm has no appetite for mergers at home or empire building abroad. By keeping a watchful eye on the quality of its lawyers it has maintained a reputation as one of the most trusted advisers around. And by staying relatively small it appeals to those students keen to steer clear of the magic circle. 'I prefer smaller, more intimate environments,' said one trainee. 'To be honest you get access to great work at all of the top firms, but whether you really get to be a part of it all you can't tell until you get there.'

All hands to the trump

The training scheme follows a four-seat model and requires six-month stints in corporate, either litigation or employment, either banking or real estate and then something else chosen by the trainee. New recruits are invited to consider their preferences before starting, safe in the knowledge that they can speak up if they have a change of heart.

In each department, trainees share a room with an assistant and a partner, a popular set-up because 'you've always got someone to ask questions.' Roommates are 'not only exceptional at their jobs but fantastic teachers.' One interviewee puzzled: 'I don't understand why other firms don't do the same. You're hearing how partners deal with clients or difficult calls, and as a trainee you're getting work directly from them.' Another agreed the approach was unbeatable: 'When you qualify you feel you've been trained well. That's Travers' trump card.'

Obviously trainees' lives vary according to the lawyers with whom they're billeted: 'If you get a quiet partner who tends to be more serious, you get a different experience of a department than if you're in a lively, entertaining room.' Not that this need be problematic. Partners are generally 'incredibly approachable' and 'the assistant is definitely not a buffer.' Trainees say partners 'genuinely care about us as individuals.'

Cereal deal closer

Corporate is Travers' core practice. In 2007 the department completed more than 70 deals with an aggregate value of £20bn. These included the acquisitions of Aston Villa, Derby and West Ham football clubs, with this last club then also instructing it on the tricky signings of Argentine players Carlos Tévez and Javier Mascherano. If you've a company to float on the LSE's Official List or you're pitching for the higher end of AIM there's a good chance you'll choose Travers. It's also known for its excellent private equity practice, as evidenced by instruction from Langholm Capital when it offloaded Dorset Cereals to Wellness Foods. If you prefer sandwiches to muesli then the estimated £350m private equity buyout of Pret a Manger would have got you salivating. 'People are often surprised by how strong the department is. The firm is small but the work we get is…wow! On the other side it's always the magic circle or some firm with a bigger team.' The department is ostensibly split into private equity and corporate finance, but apparently the line is 'a little blurred.' Admittedly a trainee's role can become 'admin-heavy,' so it's a good job there is regular client contact and the buzz of seeing your transactions in the business press.

If becoming a corporate lawyer is your priority then choosing banking rather than real estate makes sense, whereas the advantage of a real estate seat is the 'immediate contact with clients' and 'loads of your own files to run.' As an added bonus, it has 'a very good social side.' Among recent deals are the redevelopment of the Swiss Centre at London's Leicester Square, a major hotel development at Liverpool's Kings Waterfront and Diageo's £47m disposal of the Guinness brewery site at Park Royal in London.

The contentious requirement can be fulfilled by general litigation or employment law. The litigators take on some major cases, not least in banking, where they have done well on the high-profile NatWest v Rabobank litigation. The best moment for one litigation trainee was drafting instructions to counsel on a complicated point and then watching him use the briefing in a client conference. Employment trainees do everything from 'taking witness statements from head honchos who've flown in from New York' to 'advising on immigration issues concerning foreign students.' The team's clients include AIG, Channel 5 and Pinewood Shepperton Studios. One trainee described the experience as 'everything I'd hoped for and more.'

The remaining seat options are tax, financial services, pensions, competition, commercial or a visit to Travers' sole overseas office in Paris. Tax is 'good for working in a small team that has a real impact on deal structures.' There's masses of black letter law and tricky tax points to keep boffins happy, though they might also enjoy financial services, which 'probably involves more research than any other area.' Paris-bound trainees are given a

Chambers UK rankings

Banking & Finance • Banking Litigation • Corporate Finance • Dispute Resolution • Employee Share Schemes • Employment • Environment • Financial Services Regulation • Fraud: Civil • Information Technology • Investment Funds • Media & Entertainment • Pensions • Planning • Private Equity • Real Estate • Real Estate Finance • Restructuring/Insolvency • Retail • Tax

sixth-floor apartment close to the small office and about two minutes from the Champs-Élysées. The breadth of advice required by clients means 'you find yourself doing stuff you wouldn't get in London.'

As a leading City firm, the demands on staff are reflected in the hours they work. 'There are times when I think I'm worth every penny,' joked one source. Leaving at 7pm or 8pm is the norm for trainees, and while in some seats the hours might be 'more reasonable,' there's never much downtime. Team spirit keeps people going during late nights in the office: 'It makes a massive difference when you're working late for the third or fourth night in a row and you can still have a laugh.'

Clubbing together

The fact that the original Mr Travers Smith was a port and cigars man still influences the firm's reputation today. Rightly or wrongly, outsiders regard it as a gentlemanly, clubby kind of place. 'We're seen as being quite conservative with a small c,' accepted one source. 'I think it's true in that there are values running through the firm, like courtesy, but that can be misread and comes across like we're too traditional, which isn't the case.' Loyalty and collegiality are key characteristics of the trainees: 'My friends mock me, saying I've got Travers Smith tattooed on my bum,' said one. Everyone we spoke to was eager to stress how well their group got on, though one added: 'I don't want to say everyone's friendly as that makes us sound like a bunch of wetties.' Here, outgoing doesn't tend to mean loud or brash, but people do have 'backbone.' A Travers lawyer isn't the kind to 'brag about what they've done in the pub,' which if true is a shame for the two associates who climbed Everest and raised £25,000 for charity. This is not a firm for boat-rocking radicals or below-the-radar cruisers: 'Travers suits people who care about their work and set high standards for themselves.'

When you look at the demographics of the firm it appears male-dominated at all levels. At the time of going to press there were only eight female partners out of 67, corporate having appointed its first, a specialist in private equity. Among the qualified solicitors men heavily outnumber women, and until very recently even the trainee group was light on women. A few trainees acknowledged the bare facts, but were still unconvinced it was material to the firm's atmosphere. Most hadn't noticed any gender imbalance and couldn't explain why there should be one, other than 'maybe people just stopped and had babies.' Travers took steps to address the subject by introducing a diversity panel and it now has an alternative to partnership in the form of an 'of counsel' career path, which 'a fair few women have taken on.'

Another issue is the relatively narrow band of universities from which Travers has traditionally recruited. There have always been a high number of Oxbridge, Durham, Bristol types, although, again, a number of our sources said they'd not particularly noticed this. After giving it some thought, one told us: 'In one way the facts speak for themselves, but I know and completely believe that they don't just want people from those universities. They do want a certain type of person: they go for people they think will fit in here and they'll get on with. For example, pretty much all the Durham people at Travers are from the Hill colleges [supposedly less pretentious and posh than the older Bailey colleges]... they're taking the more normal people from the good universities. I think when people are applying all they should consider is whether they have good A levels and are going to get a 2:1. Any decent university and their application will be taken seriously.' The majority view from our sources was that personality would win over a college scarf, and the plain fact is that Travers attends law fairs at 24 universities.

Full herbal jacket

The firm's devotion to local pub The Bishop's Finger is quite remarkable. There's 'not so much a well-beaten track over there as a massive groove in the pavement.'

New trainees should have no fear of bumping into seniors – 'because there's not this hierarchical atmosphere you can be happily chatting away to partners.' If you're looking for characters then sidle up to managing partner Chris Carroll when he's at the bar, he's 'absolutely hysterical.' Aside from the pub, 'the firm's good at sticking its hands in its pockets' for social events. 'My word, it's decadent,' rhapsodised one interviewee about the 'epic' black-tie Christmas party. Every Easter a drinks party is held for trainees and future new starters, and there are regular departmental drinks. Travers loves its sports too, most notably hockey, rugby and football, and trainees recently organised a squash ladder for the whole firm. When we learned that some staff were tackling the New York and Paris marathons, we began to understand why someone had said: 'People in the firm are quite fit.' The most casual get-togethers take place over lunch in the staff canteen, run by a chef who pushes the boat out – 'Our jacket potatoes with beans have herbs in them,' chuckled a source.

Ultimately, trainees' loyalty to Travers Smith shows itself in consistently high retention statistics. In 2008 15 of the 18 qualifiers stayed on.

And finally...

Speak to a trainee here and they will single out two positives above all others – the quality of the work and the quality of the relationships they have with those who train them. Nothing broken to fix.

Trethowans

The facts

Location: Southampton, Salisbury

Number of UK partners/solicitors: 25/23

Total number of trainees: 8

Seats: 4x6 months

Alternative seats: None

If you're super organised and have an idea of where you'd like to qualify right from the start, the firm tries to make sure all your seats complement that area.

With over 130 years of history behind it, this Hampshire and Wiltshire firm has had plenty of time to build up a solid reputation in the private client sphere and extend its reach into the commercial side of things.

Sure bet

In the heart of rural southern England, Trethowans first set up shop in charming Salisbury, just a stone's throw (if you can throw a stone ten miles) from Stonehenge. After a century's work assisting the good folk of Salisbury with their legal requirements, the firm decided to venture further afield and enter the Southampton market by way of a small merger. Having successfully secured a staple diet of private client work, this Southampton addition was intended to give the firm a piece of commercial action. And it appears to have worked. The firm's licensing team has developed a stellar reputation advising on liquor licensing for major restaurant chains such as Pizza Hut and Nando's, as well as pub chains, supermarkets and holiday parks. Ladbrokes turns to the firm for betting and gaming advice (presumably of the legal sort, rather than which horse is a sure thing). The commercial property practice has evolved plenty, this year benefiting from the lateral hire of a partner from regional heavyweight Clarke Wilmott.

On the private client side, Trethowans is known for its clinical negligence and personal injury expertise, and this year the clin neg group secured a top ranking in our parent publication *Chambers UK* for the first time. The team is handling ongoing cases worth £50-60m, including several catastrophic cerebral palsy cases, a claim concerning a below-the-knee amputation and case for a national hockey player who suffered pain in his calf after exercis-

ing and was recommended for corrective surgery. The Salisbury personal injury group is located within two miles of the specialist Duke of Cornwall Spinal Injuries Unit, so it's only to be expected that it handles a lot of spinal injury claims. One case featured an unfortunate chap who fell out of a grounded helicopter while at work, and in another a farm worker was unhinging barn doors when they collapsed onto him, knocking him backwards into a cattle feeder.

Less unfortunate farmers go to the firm's landed estates team for advice on day-to-day commercial issues or the sale or purchase of land. Collectively, the firm's landowner and tenant clients farm over 35,000 acres, although banks and pension trustees also feature on the client roster of this team. The partner in charge is fully immersed in country life: he breeds Shetland ponies, is a Trustee of The Royal Agricultural Society of England, the Chief Horse Steward at the Royal Show and a Liveryman and Court Assistant of the Worshipful Company of Farriers. As well as advising on the ownership and sale of agricultural land and beautiful country houses, the lawyers have lately helped a client buy a multimillion-pound 1,200-acre sporting estate and drafted a lease for an offshore wind farm.

Tailor made

Trethowans recruits have it pretty good when it comes to choosing seats, as there's so much scope for building a bespoke training contract. Currently there are seats in corporate/commercial, commercial litigation, commercial and residential property, employment, licensing, personal injury and clinical negligence, family and private client. Occasionally a landed estates seat also crops up. If you're super organised and have an idea of where you'd like to qualify right from the start, the firm tries to make sure all your seats complement that area. Second-years understandably get priority, but even newbies' desires can be accommodated. 'I really felt they listened to me and tailored my seats around my interests,' confirmed one source. It's made clear at the outset that a training contract here will involve stints in both the Southampton and Salisbury offices, but this doesn't usually cause any problems. 'A lot of the trainees live somewhere in-between, so it's a short commute whichever office you're in.' Besides, sampling both offices is 'a good way to get your face seen throughout the firm.'

Those with an interest in property start off in residential conveyancing and progress to a commercial seat after learning the ropes. 'Residential property makes a good first seat,' we hear. 'It offers client contact and by the end of it you reach the stage where you can manage your own files and hold client meetings yourself.' After six months of buying, selling and remortgaging houses, trainees are well equipped to play a part in more complex commercial transactions. 'As well as doing some things on your own – I handled a few auction purchases – you do a lot of corporate support on bigger projects.' Trainees comment favourably on the levels of responsibility offered in this seat and tell us: 'You're expected to draft everything from the word go.' Lest that sound a little scary, sources were quick to explain that 'the first couple of things you take your time on, but by the end you'll be drafting your own leases and contracts, no problem.' One source typified the feeling of property trainees, saying: 'I really feel I'll be prepared by the time I qualify.'

Hire homes, Tonto away!

Commercial litigation involves 'a varied workload and interesting subject matter – you get a really broad base.' Photocopying and bundling is kept to a minimum. 'I think I've done one court bundle the entire time I've been here,' reported one interviewee. 'The vast majority of it is all thinking work – drafting witness statements and claims, going to court.' There doesn't seem to be much opportunity to do any advocacy as a trainee, but then 'all the chambers applications we do are quite procedural – anything interesting is passed onto counsel so you don't miss out on much.'

The personal injury seat goes down well, in large part thanks to the people on the team. 'My supervisor spends up to two hours a day going through things with me and gets me involved in a lot of client events,' said one fan.

Chambers UK rankings

Agriculture & Rural Affairs • Clinical Negligence •

Debt Recovery • Employment • Licensing •

Personal Injury • Real Estate

Such events range from business breakfasts to the opening of a local brain injury hospital. The department concentrates on higher value claims. 'We do deal with RTAs but that's more the paralegals' area. As a trainee the sort of work you're doing is quite specialist; you might be calculating schedules of losses or doing research.' As the seat progresses, files are handed over to trainees allowing their responsibilities to expand to include 'going off with clients on your own and collecting witness statements.' The potentially upsetting subject matter is more than offset by the reward of 'knowing that you're helping people.'

The private client team also makes an effort with its trainees; 'they get you involved from the start, going to meetings and doing real work.' It's a friendly department with regular hours and clients ranging from 'the little old ladies to really rich folk, which makes the work that much more interesting.' One of the team's most satisfying achievements must have been obtaining a rebate of six years' worth of care home fees (£180,000) for an individual who had previously been denied continuing care funding by their Primary Care Trust. Some clients, it seems, have the most interesting lives, like the couple who sold their recording studio and sound system business and used the sale proceeds to buy a portfolio of rental properties to support them for a year while on a charitable expedition to ride on horseback through the USA.

Moving stories

Trainees seem happy with the support on offer. 'Supervisors go at the pace you want and you can ask as many questions as you need to. There's no stuffy hierarchy here either, we're all involved and on the same level.' Partners also 'put in a big effort because the firm wants to keep you – it has an eye on the future.' Indeed interviewees described the firm as forward-thinking in other ways too. 'It has a good marketing side, which is important for finding new clients and keeping old ones.' And then there is the new Salisbury office. We'd been told the move was imminent for a while and now the firm has finally relocated. With free parking, shuttle buses to the city and 'sandwich men going round at lunchtime,' there's a lot to like about the new digs. 'It definitely suits the image of the firm – the building is brand new and open plan. I'll miss being in the city centre but it's time for us to move on.'

There are no hard and fast rules when it comes to recruitment. 'In the second year, none of the trainees did a law degree, they all converted. In the first year, we're all about 23 and have come straight from law school. There's no pattern to it.' What does seem to matter is that you're a team player who gets on with people and works hard. It wouldn't hurt to have sporting interests either, because staff play football, touch rugby, netball and cricket, as well as participating in charity runs and swimming. 'They definitely like you to get involved, though there isn't any pressure. Some people are more competitive than others... I prefer to play for a laugh,' explained one interviewee. Off the sports field, trainees are given an allowance every quarter to organise drinks or a dinner. 'We do something different each time and we alternate between Salisbury and Southampton. It's nice because we don't see each other as a whole group that often.' Between the two offices, trainees did notice a slight difference in after-hours activity. 'Salisbury is more of a country place, people finish at 5pm and then trot off home. Southampton has more after-work drinks.' Everyone is consulted about firm-wide socials, and this year staff chose a theatre trip to see *Chitty Chitty Bang Bang*. We hear the managing partner dressed up as Santa Claus last year 'and went round giving everyone presents. I think he was embarrassed, but it gave us all a laugh.' Such nice little touches are visible throughout the year: ice creams are distributed around the office in summer and one internal newsletter was accompanied by a KitKat 'and a note telling you to have a break.'

And finally...

Trainees at Trethowans feel the firm makes them a high priority. Its smaller size allows them to 'personally tailor' the two years and they say it's a good place to strike a balance between working on complex issues and going home at a decent hour. It's little wonder all three 2008 qualifiers stayed on.

- **Have faith:** 'Failing to get a training contract at the end of university is not the end of the world,' says one current trainee; 'even though you feel bad because all your friends have got theirs. Get some paralegal experience – a firm will be more likely to take you on.'

th trowers & hamlins

www.trowers.com

For further information about our graduate process please contact the graduate recruitment team on tel +44 (0)20 7423 8312 or hking@trowers.com

Trowers & Hamlins is an equal opportunities employer

Trowers & Hamlins

The facts

Location: London, Manchester, Exeter

Number of UK partners/solicitors: 82/164

Total number of trainees: 40

Seats: 4x6 months

Alternative seats: Overseas seats

Recent instructions include advice to the Knowledge Economic City Development Company on a deal to develop the network infrastructure for a new $8bn city in Saudi Arabia.

Bipartite of name and nature, Trowers & Hamlins has a flair for the apparently unrelated fields of UK social housing and Middle Eastern business. However, a steadily growing general commercial practice encompassing commercial real estate, banking, corporate and public sector teams shows the firm is far from bipolar and has instead capitalised on these dual strengths to generate significant oomph in the London mid-market.

Nude? Nose? Nerd?

Trowers is really on a roll. Revenue has flown up by around 84% in the past five years, with profits soaring 124% to £559,000 per equity partner in the same period. True, the firm retains a commitment to lower-margin areas like social housing (which brings in 13% of its income), but at the same time corporate, banking and commercial property teams each increased their revenues by 40% last year. It all gives weight to trainees' assertions that 'we're not just about social housing and the Middle East – the rest of the firm is going really well, with ambitious plans and goals for lots of the teams.' Nevertheless, we couldn't talk finances without a nod to that high-performing Middle East operation, which last year brought in a whopping 19% of income off the back of a slew of telecoms, infrastructure and projects deals. Income is expected to grow further, with recent instructions including advice to the Knowledge Economic City Development Company on a deal to develop the network infrastructure for a new $8bn city in Saudi Arabia.

If our sources were excited by the 'tangible growth' they'd witnessed, they were also quick to point out that 'Trowers is ambitious but sensible, it doesn't want to grow too fast or overreach itself.' This is, after all, a firm that has enjoyed prominent listings in the *Sunday Times*' 'Best Companies To Work For' surveys, and cut-throat commercialism wouldn't quite square with its character or trainees' expectations of 'City work combined with a more humane atmosphere.' Sources make a lot of the 'low turnover of staff – lots of people have been here for decades,' but whatever the reason – and whisper it quietly – the best way to describe the place is apparently by using 'a four letter word that begins with n.' We're stumped. Anyway, this atmosphere combined with the 'eclectic mix of seats on offer' explains Trowers' appeal to students. Although the idea of working on big-bucks public sector work had 'aroused the curiosity' of some trainees, and we heard of others with Arabic language skills, several sources insisted: 'You definitely don't need to be fascinated by a specific facet of the firm's business. Most people come here for the broader picture and don't have a clear idea about the area they want to work in.' Nor is location an issue. The majority of staff and trainees are based in the London office, with smaller UK outposts in Manchester and Exeter taking a couple of their own trainees each, plus overseas offices in Abu Dhabi, Bahrain, Cairo, Dubai and Oman.

Precedent setters

A property seat – whether commercial or social housing – is a given. In the former, trainees run 'a portfolio of smaller cases,' relishing the 'frequent contact with clients' and times when they are drafted in to assist on larger matters such Morley Fund Management's recent £101m purchase of the London office building 27 Knightsbridge. The department also works closely with the corporate team on major deals, so they get a peek at that side of the business as well. Life isn't generally too different for a trainee in the social housing department. Here they can bask in the glow of the firm's peerless reputation in the field. Let's not underplay this point: Trowers *is* social housing law, having been at the forefront of the sector for decades. Its lawyers are responsible for many of the structures, contracts and leases that are now standard. National and local governments, housing associations by the bucketload and many a regulatory body seek its advice. Proving that it's still the King Kong of the sector, Trowers this year scooped instruction from the London Borough of Lewisham on a £250m South London PFI project to refurbish and maintain 1,900 homes. The deal was significant because it was the first PFI project completed entirely under the government's housing procurement pack model guidance. Naturally Trowers was there to set the precedents.

If the idea of working with the aim of providing affordable housing for all strikes you as a little touchy-feely, it's worth reflecting on a few points. Firstly, the sector is partly defined by the passion of those who work within it, and that is no bad thing. Secondly, even as we approach a potential property slump, the issue of affordable housing is a perennial political hot potato. Thirdly, as the example above illustrates, the complexity and commerciality of such projects are no less demanding than corporate transactions. As well as working on 'discrete tasks on the large projects,' trainees take on many of their own files.

Social housing offers 'a steep learning curve,' as does the large projects and construction team, where trainees encounter both commercial clients and local authorities. Trowers is a pacesetter in construction law, having introduced the project partnering contracts (PPCs) concept and recently won instructions from regular client the London Borough of Newham on its joint venture with developers Countryside Properties and the William Sutton Housing Association for a major £125m redevelopment in Canning Town, itself only one part of the wide Thames Gateway scheme. Another flagship matter is Birmingham City Council's £10bn 'Masterplan' project for its city centre. Drafting contracts, phone contact with clients and attending meetings characterise the work here, as does a certain initial impenetrability of the subject matter. The specifics of the sector can make the first month 'quite daunting,' but trainees report that 'you're trained

very well – a professional support lawyer gives intensive training and everyone contributes an hour of their expertise. It helps to translate the construction lingo.'

Almos intelligible

Working in the public sector commercial and the public sector housing teams means getting to grips with 'a continually evolving area of law' and any number of acronyms. Dealing with ALMOS (Arms Length Management Organisations which manage local authorities' housing stock), handling corporate matters for IPSs (Industrial and Provident Societies, which are a sort of charity) and plenty of work on PPPs (Public Private Partnerships) are all par for the course. Once fully genned-up, trainees 'provide support in meetings' and 'do drafting where possible.' Said one: 'I drafted a development agreement for a Building Schools for the Future project and took a supporting role on a multimillion-pound strategic services partnering agreement for a regional City Council.'

Over in the corporate department the boost from Middle East deals is plainly evident. Trainees also get involved with purely domestic matters, including advice to GI Partners on the £571m acquisition of 290 pubs from Punch Taverns, and Adeem Investment's £250m purchase of Grosvenor House Apartments. As for contentious experience, this component of the training contract can be fulfilled by a short course or a seat in property lit or construction lit. 'I've been in court eight times, pursuing tenants for rent and service charge arrears and on possession proceedings,' enthused one fan. 'Testing my advocacy skills in the real world has been great.' Other seats on offer include employment, housing projects, banking and finance, tax, trusts and pensions or a sojourn in Exeter. Free accommodation sweetens that deal, as does lashings of client contact. Further north, the Manchester office's two trainees can plot a course through commercial litigation, projects and construction, housing and commercial property teams.

In the Middle East, Trowers' long-standing presence is giving it an edge as other UK firms rush to take advantage of the current wave of development in the region. A new tie-up in Saudi Arabia is seen to complement the firm's energy and power sector expertise, while recent instructions highlight its broader abilities. Trowers advised the Asia Cell consortium on its $1.25bn Iraqi telecoms licence and Qatar Telecom on its participation in that consortium. Anyone who wants a Middle East posting can be fairly sure of getting one, complete with expat perks – car, accommodation and one return flight home. Expect 'corporate and commercial work, some litigation, maybe some banking.' English may be the language used in business, however those with language skills loved 'using Arabic in a legal context, it was hugely enriching.' Actually, anyone can enjoy 'learning about a completely different legal system' and the 'culturally beautiful surroundings, as well as great beaches and mountains within easy reach.' Experience shows that a '26°C winter' trip is more pleasant than going in summer, when the mercury can top 45°C.

Warm glow inside

Trowers' London office might be aglow with industry, but this has never been a firm associated with white-hot burning ambition. 'The aim here is to be professional, successful, better than the others, but not at the cost of everything else.' In a firm where senior partner Jonathan Adlington regularly entertains groups of staff for lunch to discuss any ideas or problems they have, trainees happily expound upon a ethos that means 'you work hard and are respected for it, but you're not given a sense that you're under pressure or on your own. You have the freedom to be your own person, not fit some ideal.' In this atmosphere 'it's possible to build relationships with partners' and 'people might approach your supervisor with bits of extra work, so that interesting projects are accessible.' Keeping things ticking over, 'generally well-managed' quarterly appraisals see comments gathered from around the trainees' current department. There's also 'a good deal

of training,' be it departmental or Monday lunchtime trainee sessions, when 'Exeter and Manchester are videoed in so we can all see each other eat in three different locations.'

'Bizarre,' 'unique' and 'ugly' are all adjectives used to describe the firm's triangular, pinkish premises. Apparently the 'swivelling front door always causes problems, sending people flying or trapping them.' There's a glimmer of hope: the firm's growth could mean an office move in the not-too-distant future, but for now the 'mainly two-to-an-office' layout is snug rather than overcrowded. The social life centres on a summer party of some note, with Christmas celebrations in-department and 'a load of trainee-specific or trainee-organised events.' Happy memories of a summer's evening spent chasing a baseball in Regent's Park weren't clouded by the fact that 'all the pitchers' gloves were left-handed but no one playing was.' More spontaneous socialising occurs in local drinking holes like The Minories.

All up, trainees paint a very positive picture and even those we spoke to who had not secured a qualification job at Trowers had words of praise for the rigorous and timely process of applying for one. In 2008 13 of the 18 qualifiers stayed on.

And finally...

If you are passionate about social housing or the Middle East, Trowers & Hamlins is absolutely the firm to go for. It also works well for would-be trainees eyeing a decent City training with a more user-friendly, mid-sized touch.

Veale Wasbrough Lawyers

The facts

Location: Bristol

Number of UK partners/solicitors: 37/61

Total number of trainees: 16

Seats: 4x6 months

Alternative seats: None

Extras: Pro bono – Bristol Law Centre, BRAVE Enterprise

> The emphasis on a people culture ensures there's laughter in the office and you can always have a good old chat with a partner.

Bristol firm Veale Wasbrough combines top public sector work with successful private sector commercial practice. In particular, it is nationally renowned for its advice to the education sector.

Reveal Wasbrough

It was the education practice that turned the heads of some of our VW interviewees when they were applying for training contracts. The firm counts no fewer than 700 independent or maintained schools, nurseries, academies, further education colleges and universities as clients, so there's a chance your old alma mater has put in a call or two to VW over the years. The team suffered a blow when its leader Robert 'Mr Schools' Boyd passed away last year, though it has pulled together under the stewardship of new team head Barney Northover. A hefty presence in the classroom isn't the only reason for public law aficionados to rejoice. VW is on the government's Catalist legal panel, works for the MoD and the Highways Agency, and last year advised local authorities on town centre regenerations across the South and Wales. Just in case public sector clients don't wow you, we'll reveal some of VW's private sector clients. How about PwC, Quintain Estates & Development, Airbus, Crest Nicholson, Dreams plc, HSBC and Allied Irish Banks?

VW recently opened a meeting facility in London for the benefit of its clients in the capital, though our interviewees couldn't say for certain if it ever intends to build a permanent presence in the Big Smoke. A more definite sign of immediate growth is an increase in the annual trainee intake from seven to ten in 2008.

Teachers' pets

Quiet at the back! The lesson has started and today we're learning more about VW's sizeable education department, because apparently it is 'a privilege' to work there. The sheer number of institutions it represents is hugely impressive; 'I was really surprised by how many independent schools actually exist,' admitted one source. As the department's remit is so extensive, trainees are assigned to one of several smaller teams. The corporate team handles school mergers and acquisitions (just who do you think educates those cut-throat City types?), one of the most notable being the merger of Malvern College's preparatory school with The Downs School, valued at £11m. The role of the fee recoveries lawyers is to send out threatening letters to parents, while the employment team guides institutions through sticky situations involving staff. They also end up with random questions, such as the feasibility of keeping animals in classrooms. The pastoral team is responsible for drafting parent contracts (governing the relationship between a private school and the parents of little Johnny/Chardonnay) plus child protection and special needs issues. Basically, the team takes care of external issues and 'everything to do with the relationships within a school – the school and children, children and staff – all the touchy-feely stuff.' Every now and then 'you'll get a sudden fax or phone call and a litigation matter will come through. Quite often it will be a parental complaint or a child being dismissed by a school, perhaps a parent claiming the child has a disability and has been discriminated against.' One of the perks of the seat is visiting independent schools, some of which require 'driving for hours through beautiful countryside.'

VW is much more than its education team. 'We're a full-service commercial firm that happens to have a well-regarded education department,' insisted one source. This is quite true, however the education clients are hugely important to other departments. The property team, for example, represents major property developer Quintain on a multimillion-pound programme of site acquisitions for the development of student accommodation. It has already embarked on projects in Bristol, Sheffield, Salford, Leeds, Birmingham, Oxford and Kingston upon Thames. The property seat exposes trainees to other public and private sector clients – local authorities, the MoD, PwC, all of which 'demand an incredibly high standard' of service. Trainees draft leases and licences, and 'partners are quite happy to let you have the responsibility of sending things out in your own name.'

The construction team also advises Quintain on the student accommodation programme and has lately pursued a £313,000 claim against Somerset County Council's former architect over design defects and breach of planning conditions. Construction matters range from small contractual disputes (where 'the client will say we might not get the money, but throw a couple of grand at it and write a few nasty letters') to large projects ('some of the work was on such a scale that I couldn't get involved.') On major matters, trainees simply gain 'a snapshot of the overall picture,' and focus instead on tasks like drafting warranties for architects and members of design teams.

Claimant personal injury seats are taken with Augustines Injury Law, a separate division of VW situated just a hop, skip and an accident claim away from the main office. In 2007 Augustines recovered more than £8m on some 2,600 claims. 'People don't tend to choose the seat, but I don't know why,' said one source; 'I've told everyone how much I enjoyed it… It's not always standard road accident cases.' On more interesting and complicated stress claims 'you get to read through claimants' medical records… and just be generally nosey.' The seat suits people with well-developed interpersonal skills, as 'one minute you'll be speaking with everyday people, then the next you'll be communicating with solicitors on the other side.' Taking witness statements, liaising with employers and drawing up schedules of loss are all in a day's work, however it's the client contact that wins trainees over. 'Everything you do is checked before it is sent out, but when you're speaking on the phone you have to think on your feet.'

In the projects seat, a trainee becomes absorbed by one or two larger matters, perhaps a strategic partnering arrange-

Chambers UK rankings

Banking & Finance • Charities • Construction • Corporate Finance • Debt Recovery • Dispute Resolution • Education • Employment • Partnership • Personal Injury • Private Client • Real Estate • Real Estate Litigation • Restructuring/Insolvency

ment between a private company and a public body. 'I wasn't negotiating myself, but I did witness the negotiating. I was there as minute-taker for most of the meetings and I did get involved in some drafting. There's quite a lot of admin – updating definition schedules, checking consistency throughout documents and things like that.' The Somerset ISiS project (value up to £500m) sees three public authorities enter into a joint venture with IBM, while two Welsh local authorities in Blaenau Gwent and Torfaen jointly instructed VW to advise on an integrated waste management project.

The other available seats are commercial, commercial litigation, corporate, employment, private client and, potentially, tax, estates and IP. Trainees say: 'The focus is on giving people a training rather than just satisfying the demands of where paper needs to be pushed.' People's views differed about the level of responsibility given to trainees. One first-year remembered 'asking my supervisor to not be frightened of pressurising me, and he said they weren't there to pressure trainees. They want to ease us into the work.' Another interviewee told us: 'If you're comfortable ploughing ahead they'll not hold you back.' In general there was effusive praise for partners, who 'really focus on training rather than just using you as an extra resource.'

Best westerners

VW has a reputation as a friendly, welcoming employer and many people apply to the firm on the basis of personal recommendations from lecturers and are then charmed during the recruitment process. The emphasis on 'a people culture' ensures 'there's laughter in the office' and you can always have 'a good old chat with a partner.' When it comes to vac schemers, our sources revealed that 'HR listen very carefully to who we think would make a good trainee,' so remember to flash a winning smile.

Trainees judge themselves to be 'a mixed bag' of 'bookwormy, sporty and all kinds of people.' They believe VW looks for hard-working all-rounders with transferable inter-personal skills. What links them is team spirit ('it's cheesy but our motto is 'Working together to succeed"), a degree of humility ('people here aren't bullshitters, if you'll pardon the phrase') and a desire to have the time for a full life outside work. Cardiff and Bristol Universities are common recruiting grounds; in fact one source wanted VW to forge even closer links with good universities because 'you need to employ Category A. If you employ Category B, you'll get C, and then you'll eventually end up with a load of Zs.' Most people either grew up or studied in the region. It's 'not necessarily because the firm is looking for that, but more that people from the West look at Veale Wasbrough.' And if at first you don't succeed, there may be an alternative route in: 'If you were offered a legal assistant position you'd be silly not to take it, as some people don't sit as a legal assistant too long before getting a contract.'

Chargeable hours are monitored but never revealed to the trainees themselves. This is not a hard-slog kind of place: 'You're never given work at 5pm and told it needs to be in at 9am. You're given work at 10am and told to get it out that day.' Clocking off at 5pm is common. Actually 7.30pm was the latest any of our sources had stayed at work. Said one: 'I get everything I could hope for, but I don't have to spend every hour God made in the office.' Regional salaries could be seen as a potential downside, even so our sources were confident that £22,000 (rising to £24,000 in the second year and £38,000 on qualification) was enough to live comfortably in Bristol. They certainly compare very favourably with firms outside the city.

Take me to the river

Several of the current trainees commute to VW's city centre office from Bath or Cardiff, so they don't always attend all the social events. Since a couple of younger partners took it upon themselves to develop the Friday night drinks scene there are regular trips to The River, down on the waterfront. 'As soon as you go out, it's not partners and staff, but mates having a pint together.' Teams organise events, for example the education group's recent karaoke night. A social committee plans firm-wide events, including bowling, an Oktoberfest party in the office café and the annual summer party, last time at the Pump Room in Bath. Mixed football, netball and softball teams play against other firms and clients. One source advised caution when tackling clients: 'I'm afraid of fouling one by mistake.' Trainees may also be invited onto the golf course so, again, take care not to swing a club at an important client or make a hole-in-one while they're stuck in the rough. As for other perks, how about one of life's simpler pleasures: during our interviews, we heard the cry of seagulls from the other end of the phone. 'It is amusing being in a meeting and having seagulls doing funny things outside the window,' chuckled one birdwatcher.

Keeping up its consistently good retention record, VW offered jobs to all seven 2008 qualifiers. Six accepted, the seventh reluctantly moving on to find a firm with a bigger tax practice.

And finally...

Veale Wasbrough may be one of Bristol's mid-sized players but when it comes to its clientele and the quality of its work there's nothing middle of the road about it.

Vinson & Elkins

The facts

Location: London

Number of UK partners/solicitors: 7/13 + 3 US

Total number of trainees: 8

Seats: No formalised rotation

Alternative seats: Overseas seats

Extras: Pro bono – eg LawWorks; language training

> Texan firms have a slightly different mentality – they're a bit more relaxed, and a back-slapping camaraderie makes you feel like you're part of the team very early on.

Texan Vinson & Elkins is a dynamo when it comes to energy law and its London office makes full use of the firm's extensive international network. We wonder if y'all can resist its Southern charm.

Texas tea

Vinson & Elkins was founded in Houston in 1917 and first made its name in the boomin' trade for bubblin' crude. Oil, that is. Black gold. Texas Tea. The firm's website has a section detailing the endearingly awkward conversation between Misters Vinson and Elkins when they decided to go into business together ('How would you like to come to Houston?' 'That is the ambition of my life, make me a proposition'). V&E still prides itself on its sense of congeniality, even if it is more than 700 lawyers strong and operating out of 13 offices worldwide. The London office opened in 1971 and became one of the first American legal outposts in the UK. It's not grown hugely over the past 37 years and still has fewer than 25 solicitors – quite small for an office that acts as a hub for Asian and European work.

V&E places its greatest emphasis on energy matters, and clients from that sector provide the vast majority of its instructions in London. Energy clients are 'more cutting edge' than most, especially those in the extra-sharp renewables sector. While other areas slow down, this is an interesting period for the industry as oil prices continue to rise and interest in sustainable energy grows. 'Friends of mine around the City concentrating on funds aren't getting any work,' explained one recruit, 'but energy is booming.'

V&E's comprehensive energy practice in London has expertise in oil and gas; this is complemented by strength in electricity, nuclear, and of course renewables. Project finance and M&A form the bulk of instructions, and one especially proud trainee boasted that the firm is 'responsible for many of the biggest private equity deals on the planet.' Last year lawyers dealt with a virtual Who's Who of industry names, representing Devon Energy in a multibillion-dollar disposal of upstream oil and gas assets across Africa, and Gate LNG on the €800m development of the first LNG receiving facility in the Netherlands. Shoring up its green credentials was an instruction for the development and financing of an integrated carbon capture and hydrogen power plant, with an estimated capital cost of $2.2bn. V&E also represented Hg Capital in relation to renewable power project investments. Other clients include BG Group and Gazprom.

With the collapse of major client Enron hitting the firm hard a few years ago, London has tried to broaden its practice outside its traditional energy projects base. For example, instructions in capital markets and M&A transactions have risen, and the litigation department is 'going from strength to strength.' The firm acts on 'pioneering' deals in Islamic finance, advising on the first sukuk from Swiss renewable energy company EnergyMixx. It also represented BSEC and Merrill Lynch on the structuring and formation of a $180m sukuk – the first Shari'a-compliant gas-backed securitisation. A growing focus on the Middle East was further highlighted last year when V&E opened an Abu Dhabi office.

V&E can work it out

The training structure at V&E is non-rotational, so we asked our interviewees just how (and how well) it works. Essentially, trainees sit with a partner or senior associate for six months and get most of their work from them. They also make themselves available to lawyers across the office. The system provides both 'a ready source of work and the potential to exercise choice in the type of work you get.' Trainees say: 'If there's something you definitely want to do you can easily say so and people try to accommodate you as much as they can.' It means that 'you might not know from one day to the next what you'll be involved in,' but by moving to a different partner's office every six months the contract does have some degree of shape.

Our interviewees were impressed by the system. Most of all they raved about their ability to 'stay on a deal from beginning to end,' even having involvement after moving to another office or going away on secondment. Said one: 'If I'd just done a seat in M&A I would only have seen half of what I've done.' Trainees are kept busy with the usual tasks – drafting articles of association, putting together conditions precedent documents, etc – but have a surprising level of contact with clients, 'speaking to them on the phone, e-mailing them, attending client meetings and being present at negotiations.'

With a small trainee intake a lot of responsibility is divided among few people, so naturally we heard all the talk about steep learning curves and deep ends. However, this is not an eat-what-you-kill environment and young lawyers are well looked after. Supervisors take care to know exactly how much work their charges have on and how much more they can take. Likewise, if stalking the corridors looking for work doesn't come naturally, you won't be left idling. As well as a supervisor, recruits are allocated a mentor whose job it is to monitor their training diary.

Work hours are 'very up and down,' with slower and medium-paced periods book-ended by times when 'everything is manic for two weeks and very exciting.' Our interviewees took the heavy workload in their stride. Said one: 'I haven't had to do too many all-nighters, and the majority of days you're home by 8pm or 9pm. On most days you'll bill nine or ten hours.' Towards the end of a deal considerably less time is spent at home, 'but no one's going to tell you off for having an hour-and-a-half lunch break when it's quiet.'

Have passport, will travel

As most of V&E's work is international, the London lawyers engage often with their counterparts in other countries and jet around a fair bit. What gave us pause for

Chambers UK rankings

Projects, Energy & Natural Resources

thought were the opportunities trainees have to accompany them on these business trips. One trainee painted an exciting picture: 'I woke up one morning and checked my answerphone to find a message saying you're going to Budapest tonight.' We also heard tales of travel to Holland, Singapore, Hong Kong and Oman. Obviously these trips are only made if a trainee's presence is genuinely required – 'they won't just send you for a jolly.'

Overseas seats are a relatively new addition to this relatively new training programme and so far six-month secondments have been offered to Moscow and Dubai. Anyone interested in time abroad needs to put themselves forward, make a well-reasoned case for going and then be persistent. The firm sorts out airport pick-up and accommodation, and both cities have established social networks of English trainees. In 'obscenely expensive' Moscow, salary top-ups and gym membership are just two of the perks on offer. The work in Russia is mostly a mix of energy projects and M&A, for which recruits do a lot of drafting and research and wind up with masses of client contact.

In Dubai the client base includes 'a number of sovereign wealth funds and private Middle Eastern banking firms that you generally wouldn't have too much access to in the UK.' Some argue that the Dubai office is 'more willing to give trainees a free hand' than in the other offices. Even if true, neither Dubai or Moscow secondees are left unsupervised and all have mentors to fulfil the same role as those left behind in Blighty. Apparently the partners are really pleased with how the secondment programme is working out and they plan to extend it to other offices, in particular Hong Kong and Abu Dhabi. At V&E English-qualified lawyers are 'popping up all over the globe,' so in the future overseas seats 'will form an integral part of the training process.'

Join the family

We wondered just how Americanised V&E London feels. In the opinion of trainees, 'there isn't an in-your-face American culture, but we're fully aware it's an American firm.' You may be aware of the stereotypes that have attached to American firms – how their lawyers are overworked and overpaid and the environments are cut-throat. One of them at least has a ring of truth. Trainee salaries are extremely generous and newly qualified lawyers earn £80,000. As for the safety of your neck area, it's worth remembering this is no New York-based taskmaster.

'Texan firms have a slightly different mentality – they're a bit more relaxed,' explained one source. 'You have to work hard, but they try to make sure your work-life balance isn't disrupted too much,' and a back-slapping camaraderie makes you 'feel like you're part of the team very early on.'

We also heard it described as 'a family-oriented firm,' and one interviewee revealed that whenever they met someone from the Houston HQ, 'one of the first questions they ask is if you're married.'

Socially, V&E is 'great.' The Rack & Tenter bar below the CityPoint office isn't a favourite 'though it tends to be where we end up.' At Christmas there's always a swanky party and an annual ski trip saw people venture to Davos in Switzerland last season. Naturally there's a Fourth of July party, and come here and you'll never again forget 2 March, which is Texas Independence Day. To celebrate the firm usually hires the Texas Embassy Cantina for a hoe down and horseshoe throwing.

The self-proclaimed 'outgoing, bright and fun' trainees who spoke to us agreed the firm doesn't deliberately seek out a particular type of applicant. They did, however, give us a few handy pointers. Things that will 'give you a boost' include experience in other jobs, time spent travelling, working or studying abroad and speaking a second language. One helpful soul revealed that 'as this is an energy firm, if you have a scientific background it's helpful,' while another stated the more obvious: 'The firm likes someone who's an all-rounder but has achieved consistently highly in every aspect, whether it be academic, sporting or whatever else.' Our top tip is to make sure you at least look into what's going on in the energy sector before firing off an application form. And should you make it to the interview stage, you'll need to do considerably more than review your spiralling gas and electricity bills.

And finally...

V&E's informal qualification process fits the firm's character. Trainees are made aware of whether they'll be taken on about six months beforehand. There's a strong investment in trainees these days. In 2008 both of the qualifiers took up permanent positions.

- **Want to work for Chambers and Partners?** Our research and editorial team is about 80 strong and works on a range of legal guides. If you have good interviewing and writing skills, why not take a look at our website and find out more about us and what we do? Some of our researchers are with us while waiting for a training contract to start. We're especially interested in people who speak a foreign language.

Walker Morris

The facts

Location: Leeds

Number of UK partners/solicitors: 51/125

Total number of trainees: 37

Seats: 6x4 months

Alternative seats: Occasional secondments

'We believe in steady, gradual improvement. We're a very stable firm that's always done well and will continue to in the future.'

'Outside London, Leeds is the next best place for legal services,' chirped one Walker Morris trainee. While Manchester and Birmingham lawyers might have something to say about this, there is no denying that Leeds is 'a developing legal market and great place to be.' And there can be no meaningful discussion about Leeds without talking about Walker Morris.

Home grown

The Leeds commercial scene is dominated by the ominously named Big Six law firms. Walker Morris is a fully paid-up member of this elite group, although it sets itself apart from its peers by being the only pure Yorkshire thoroughbred within the ranks. The other five (Addleshaw Goddard, DLA Piper, Eversheds, Hammonds and Pinsent Masons) are multi-site national firms. WM, by contrast, stubbornly refuses to follow the trend to set up offices in other cities, preferring organic growth within Yorkshire's cold damp soil. It's an approach that's worked for rhubarb for many years and it is clearly working for WM. Just ask its equity partners, who in 2007 earned an average of £672,000, smashing their local rivals for six.

Loyalty to Leeds doesn't stop the firm winning big-ticket transactions. Recently it helped Land Securities form a joint venture for the proposed £650m Trinity Leeds project, a one-million sq ft shopping centre, set to include an iconic glass roof designed by the late Catalan architect Enric Miralles (who also designed the new Scottish Parliament building). Proving how 'deeply rooted' the firm is up North (again, like rhubarb) it also acts for many key local authorities, working on things like £235m regeneration projects for Hull and Liverpool City Councils. Lawyers have advised on some massive waste disposal PFI projects, the latest being for Barnsley,

Doncaster and Rotherham Waste Partnership, which was hot on the heels of a landmark £2bn PFI to help Lancashire County Council dispose of its rubbish in an environmentally friendly fashion.

Speaking to trainees we soon learned not to view the firm as an entirely Northern phenomenon: 'We work with clients on a national and international basis. Something like 80% of our work comes from outside Yorkshire,' one source insisted. Others went on to point out the lower costs but equivalent 'exceptionally high standard of work' the firm offers in comparison to its London rivals, which has allowed it to lure 'some famous and very big client names.' Nowhere is this truer than in real estate, where the client roster could happily fill any high street in the UK – Debenhams, LK Bennett, Monsoon, Footlocker, RBS, Starbucks and Netto are all there. We're told to expect more of the same from the firm: 'We're not about to do anything too dramatic – it's not the Walker Morris style. We believe in steady, gradual improvement. We're a very stable firm that's always done well and will continue to in the future.'

Dunkirk spirit

Trainees are unambiguous in their views on the advantage of working in a one-city firm: 'The one-site approach means all the good work is done here,' beamed one, another adding: 'You get a really strong sense of being a part of something.' But the prize for most enthusiastic comments goes to the trainee who reeled off this list of benefits: 'You're frequently able to experience proximity to people who are leaders in the field. Whether you're sharing a room, floor or are even across the road from them you are never that far away, and even subconsciously you pick stuff up. It's also a great opportunity to get yourself known round the firm.' On this last point, the six-seat rotation is a big help, and it led one trainee to claim: 'I've now been here two years and at least 50% of the partners know me by name.' Return visits to favourite departments are another advantage.

First-year trainees are assigned seats and can expect to be placed in each of the firm's core areas – property, corporate and litigation. Second-years are then rewarded for their earlier obedience by being granted carte blanche to choose whatever seats they wish. Despite a good range of options, conflicts inevitably emerge, and when they do, the firm steps back and allows trainees to resolve things. 'Pistols at dawn and arm-wrestling' aren't required.

Property is described as 'very much the driving force of the firm and our biggest department.' A seat here brings work for big-name retailers and developers. How much you enjoy the seat can depend on the luck of the draw, because although most people have 'hands-on' experiences, including site visits, client meetings and document drafting, a few who'd been involved in the very largest of transactions were a little disappointed to have had their four months consumed by document juggling and isolated tasks. Whatever their lot, in this extremely busy department trainees are expected to muck in and join the 8.30am club for their four months. This was not enough to stop five candidates vying for the three NQ jobs offered in 2008, a pretty solid endorsement of the department's popularity.

In stark comparison to the consistent hours in property, corporate brings the ups and downs that are to be expected in any large commercial firm. One trainee spoke of 'absolutely mental' hours, while another found themselves twiddling their thumbs during a summer lull and bolting for home or the pub at 5.30pm. Unsurprisingly, those who'd experienced tougher schedules felt they'd gained more from the seat and (albeit in hindsight) sung the group's praises. 'I had an epic three-week period of working stupid hours. It sounds horrendous, but there was a Dunkirk spirit about the whole thing, with our little band of merry men up against an army of London lawyers. It was one of the best periods of my training contract.' The corporate clients are generally 'mid-range national companies or big local firms,' frequently with 'an entrepreneurial streak.' Isolated tasks and 'unglamorous grunt work' are

Chambers UK rankings

Banking & Finance • Banking Litigation • Construction • Corporate Finance • Debt Recovery • Dispute Resolution • Employment • Environment • Intellectual Property • Licensing • Local Government • Pensions • Planning • Real Estate • Real Estate Litigation • Restructuring/Insolvency • Retail • Sports Law • Tax

par for the course in this fast-paced department, but for most this did not dampen their enthusiasm for the intrinsic thrills of corporate deals.

Stodge

For their contentious seat, a first-year could be placed in one of several teams, although commercial dispute resolution is quite likely. Even though the firm handles big cases, trainees were keener to speak about being let loose on 'little claims worth £10,000 or less.' A similar pattern emerged in relation to the property litigation seat, although banking litigation sounds like it's hands-on experiences all the way. 'I was running 40-50 small debt recovery files, which was terrifying,' said a former banking litigation trainee. Across these seats, court hopping in Leeds, Manchester and Derby County Courts and even the Royal Courts of Justice are likely.

Many second-year trainees sample the firm's celebrated insolvency group, which has gone from strength to strength, bagging some cracking instructions such as the rescue of Homeform Group, the UK's leading provider of all things fully-fitted for the kitchen, bathroom or bedroom, through a pre-packaged administration that saved around 170 stores and 2,000 jobs. It also acts for deep-pocketed lenders such as RBS and Lloyds TSB, and has been building a strong name for itself in football finance and administrations after representing KPMG as administrators of Leeds United during the club's fall from grace. Other trainees were lured into the projects seat by the firm's reputation for waste management PFIs. Here the time scales are 'so massive compared to corporate' that there is plenty of time to catch up on lost tea breaks. The employment group exposes them to contentious and non-contentious work and is known for being a 'more laid back' assignment. Tax is the other main area of work our sources had sampled, and they recommended it as a good way of complementing corporate experiences.

Across all these seats trainees were impressed with the faith the firm showed in their abilities. There have been times when I've felt a bit panicky and out of my comfort zone but I'd rather do that than just admin,' one explained. When the job does become demanding, a helping hand is never far away as they usually share an office with their supervisor. 'Recognition is what you want as a trainee, and they are not frightened to give you that here.' The only slight murmurs of discontent from our sources related to the 'shabby and tired' premises that the firm occupies in Kings Court. Despite overspill into the adjacent Bank House, WM's continuing growth even led to the canteen being converted to office space. One source was extremely vocal about the injustice of being denied their daily fix of 'bland canteen stodge.' Another stated plainly: 'We really need to find newer-looking offices, as we're not competing with the other big firms in Leeds in terms of aesthetics.'

Sleeves up, tie down

The fact that 'an unusually high number of the partners here trained at Walker Morris' was not lost on trainees, and judging by recent NQ retention rates the firm does equally well in inspiring loyalty at the junior end. In 2007 it was one of the few firm's nationwide to boast a 100% retention rate, and although it was unable to match that in 2008's cooler market, keeping eight of its 11 qualifiers was not to be sniffed at. We sense the firm is good at picking new recruits who fit well with the character and ethos of the firm. Many of our sources spoke of the 'big personalities' they had worked with, and judging by our random sample of interviewees, the same description can be applied to several trainees. They also described themselves as an 'enthusiastic and motivated' bunch, telling us: 'Everyone comes here to work hard and go far.'

It takes more than a willingness to roll one's sleeves up and 'get stuck in.' Trainees believe the firm favours candidates who 'have a bit of joie de vivre,' so it's a good job there's plenty of scope for loosening the tie at the end of a hard day's work. Certain departments – especially corporate and insolvency – are renowned for frequent client socials, and periodically there are departmental away days to places such as Whitby, Dublin and Alton Towers. Well attended firm-wide drinks occur monthly at Indie Joze ('an excuse to wang a load of cash behind the bar and get bashed up'), and more active types can forge stronger bonds on the sports field through one of the netball, cricket or football teams. A generous social budget has funded some interesting trainee nights out, including a superheroes and villains fancy dress night ('a lot of body paint and random outfits') and a more civilised wine-and-cheese-tasting event at which the wine went down much better than the cheese. Add to this active membership of the Leeds Junior Lawyers Division and plenty of ad-hoc lunches, dinners and post-work drinks, and you'll see why no one complains of boredom.

And finally...

'If you want to be in this part of England and are looking for a firm with a great reputation, variety of departments, first-class training and somewhere where can be yourself, this is it.' By reduction, shy and retiring types, or those unconvinced by the charms of Leeds, might be better off looking elsewhere.

Only those who stand out from the crowd need apply

Described as "progressive… exudes ambition and confidence"*, Ward Hadaway offers graduates an ideal opportunity to develop an outstanding legal career.

If you are a high achieving student looking to give your career a head start, then look no further.

For details on our training contracts contact the Graduate Recruitment Team on 0191 204 4000 or email recruitment@wardhadaway.com

*Source: Chambers Student Guide 2008

INVESTOR IN PEOPLE

Ward Hadaway is an equal opportunities employer

wardhadaway
lawfirm

Ward Hadaway

The facts

Location: Newcastle, Leeds

Number of UK partners/solicitors: 62/86

Total number of trainees: 22

Seats: 4x6 months

Alternative seats: Secondments

Ward Hadaway has a string of high-performance teams including a dispute resolution department that litigates the pants off almost every other firm in the region.

Ward Hadaway is the Lewis Hamilton of the Newcastle legal scene. It's an attractive and successful young firm that has gone far, and fast.

An eye on pole position

Ward Hadaway is the bright young thing of Newcastle's thriving legal market. Founded in 1988, it lost no time in giving other, longer-established law firms a run for their money and embarked on an aggressive expansion plan. One firm that must be all too aware of its ambitions is Eversheds – Ward Hadaway has poached four of its partners in the past three years, most recently top corporate finance man Mike Spetch. Eversheds has also just lost a couple of long-standing clients to the firm, in a move that we imagine might have left its senior partner grinding his teeth and shaking his fist in the manner of a thwarted cartoon villain. There is also an ongoing rivalry with Dickinson Dees, the region's biggest player, based a stone's throw from Ward Hadaway's Quayside offices. We've heard some of the amusingly insulting nicknames the two firms have for each other, but it's clear there's a healthy mutual respect underneath.

Not that Ward Hadaway needs other firms to define it. It has a string of high-performance teams, including one of the largest property departments in the North, a dispute resolution department that litigates the pants off almost every other firm in the region, a top-ranked employment squad and a forceful corporate team. More about trainees' experiences in these areas later.

The NHS is an important source of work and Ward Hadaway has a coveted position on the NHS Litigation Authority legal panel, a line-up of 11 law firms that defend the service against clinical negligence actions. As one partner told our colleagues on *Chambers UK*: 'You're

not a player in the market unless you're on it.' Sticking close to the NHS in other areas of business too, the firm represents a swathe of primary care trusts, among them Barnsley, Cumbria, Darlington, Doncaster, Gateshead, Middlesbrough, Newcastle, North Tyneside, Redcar & Cleveland, Rotherham and Sheffield. Sign on the dotted line with Ward Hadaway, pick the right seats and you'll have the NHS coming out of your ears.

Slog on the Tyne

What Ward Hadaway offers trainees is the chance to experience both mainstream commercial practice plus more niche areas such as agriculture, construction, environment, health and safety, pensions and tax. There are even seats in family law and crime for those wanting to represent individuals rather than companies or public sector bodies.

Let's look first at property. To give you an idea of how well it's been doing, the department has doubled its income in the past five years and represents clients such as Aldi, Durham County Council, Gala Coral (the bingo people), The National Trust, Northern Rock, Northumbrian Water, the North East Ambulance Service, Sage, Sunderland City Council and Wilkinson Sword, plus several banks and major residential house builders. This last group of clients have used the firm when buying up greenfield and brownfield sites for residential development. Unfortunately, the slump in the property market recently led to quite a few redundancies from this part of the firm. Non-residential deals, meanwhile, have included Nexus's £22m revamp of the Haymarket metro station and Rotherham PCT's PFI development of a new joint service centre, which includes leisure, health care facilities and office accommodation. By the end of a seat, trainees could be dealing with as many as 60 or 70 smaller files of their own. If that sounds daunting, be assured they don't all need attention at the same time and not everything is complex, 'so it's mostly a question of good file management.'

The property litigation team deals primarily with landlord and tenant disputes, as well as a few squabbles over boundaries and that sort of thing. Taking instructions and giving straightforward advice are fairly common tasks; there are also trial bundles to prepare, though if you're lucky you might witness a trial or even venture into small-scale advocacy yourself. 'Commercial litigation is a very hot seat at the moment, it's considered sexy,' said one source tantalisingly. In one of its most interesting and ground-breaking cases this year, Ward Hadaway acted for the unfortunate Graham Calvert, a Wearside man who lost £2.1m through gambling and sued William Hill, claiming that the bookmaker was negligent in allowing him to continue to place bets after he had asked them not to accept any more from him. The firm also acted for an individual bringing a claim against his former employer for failure to pay his pension entitlement on retirement. Among its corporate clients in this field are Persimmon Homes and Imperial Pharmaceuticals.

Did someone mention bundling? There's some of that in all contentious seats, and its transactional equivalents are due diligence, bibling and proof-reading. 'Seven thrilling hours on the phone to someone in Manchester, saying, 'Page one looks like this, page two looks like this,'' recalled one source wearily. At least such grunt tasks are only thrust upon them when absolutely necessary, thanks to a healthy number of support staff. 'It was two months before I worked out how to use the photocopier,' said one trainee, while another looked on the bright side by claiming 'bibling is an excellent way of understanding how a transaction works.'

Drug deals

There are several different teams within the firm's company and commercial department. Some trainees find themselves in a split-seat arrangement dividing their time between two supervisors, depending on their own interests or the firm's needs at the time. The corporate finance team deals with company start-ups, sales and acquisitions, for example the sale of Henderson Pharmacies to Alliance Boots. Trainee tasks include drafting disclosure letters, helping with completions and, whether by phone, e-mail or in person, plenty of liaising with clients. The public sector team deals with PFI projects and advises NHS trusts on purchasing agreements. There's a very

Chambers UK rankings

Agriculture & Rural Affairs • Banking & Finance • Clinical Negligence • Competition/European Law • Construction • Corporate Finance • Debt Recovery • Dispute Resolution • Employment • Family/Matrimonial • Healthcare • Intellectual Property • Planning • Private Client • Professional Discipline • Real Estate • Real Estate Litigation • Restructuring/Insolvency

strong team ethos in this area, and trainees 'really feel crucial to the deals. You get more responsibility than normal and a lot more client contact.'

Take a clin neg seat and you'll be exposed to 'quite meaty bits of work.' The senior partner is an expert in the fields of paediatrics and mental health law, and Ward Hadaway has handled a number of high-value cerebral palsy cases. Trainees take a supporting role on the big cases, initially 'looking at the risk to the trust and the potential value of any claim before preparing an initial report.' They move on to 'dealing with counsel to arrange meetings, preparing witness statements and drafting proceedings,' all the while keeping their fingers crossed for the chance to watch a trial. The most complex cases can last years so no trainee will see the entire process in a six-month seat. Lower-value cases provide scope for more autonomy and 'that's brilliant because although your supervisor signs everything off, you try to settle the cases and decide what to do on your own.'

Across the seats the complexity of work is 'matched to the individual's abilities and confidence.' As for the volume of it, well, this varies hugely, from sitting staring into the middle distance to the occasional 23-hour day. It all averages out: as one source put it: 'No one objects if you leave at 5pm some days, because they all know there are other days when that's not going to be possible.' Generally 8.30am until 6pm is the norm.

Ward award

The common consensus was that there is a Ward Hadaway 'type', even if people find it hard to express what exactly everyone has in common. Our most forthright contact confidently declared that the firm looks for 'outgoing people who aren't afraid to put themselves forward;' others were more circumspect, which perhaps proved their point. They see themselves as less formal than Eversheds and Dickinson Dees trainees and view their firm as 'more flexible and dynamic' than each of those others. Ward Hadaway recruits heavily from the universities in Durham and Newcastle, and many of the trainees completed their LPC at Northumbria University. Graduates of other universities are welcomed, although everyone we spoke to had at least some Northern credentials. In an admirable display of forethought, future trainees are invited to Christmas parties, something which helps them settle in more easily come the start of their contracts.

Speaking of the Christmas party, Ward Hadaway sponsors the Newcastle Falcons rugby club and often enjoys corporate hospitality at its ground. This year the firm broke with tradition and instead held its annual festive bash at what one trainee described as 'a museum-y thing, I think it was something to do with science… sorry, I was quite drunk.' Fortunately, someone else was able to confirm that the venue was Newcastle's Discovery Museum. The Employee of the Year award was presented at the event. Other dates in the social calendar are the summer barbecue, quizzes, football, netball and touch rugby matches and nights at the dogs. Work permitting, trainees meet for lunch most days ('it's just the right-sized group to be really sociable') and on Friday evenings the staff of the Pitcher & Piano are swamped by an invasion from the firm.

The marauding hordes don't have to go far as the firm occupies two buildings on the Quayside (plus a third office for its PI team). The main building has fantastic views over the Tyne and is almost parallel with the Baltic.

A new office in Leeds opened in summer 2008 and, if successful, further expansion seems probable, with Manchester likely to be the next location. Trainees reckon the firm will do things at 'a steady pace' to avoid what they see as 'Watson Burton's mistake' of expanding too far too soon. 'We've already grown beyond belief in the past ten years,' our sources told us, now fully expecting the firm to keep its Geordie soul and stay 'passionately regional.' Though one interviewee predicted: 'I can't see the firm going further south than Leeds,' it is likely that the training scheme will include seats, or even whole contracts, away from Newcastle by 2011. Hopefully, the firm's superb record on retention will continue: in 2008 all ten qualifiers were offered and accepted positions.

And finally...

If ever a law firm exuded confidence, it's this one. Ward Hadaway is now in its 20th year but shows no sign of getting over its adolescent growth spurt. Look it up if you've a yen for life in the North East and an eye for a firm that's still going places.

Warner Goodman LLP

The facts

Location: Fareham, Southampton, Portsmouth

Number of UK partners/solicitors: 15/32

Total number of trainees: 7

Seats: 3 or 4 (flexible)

Alternative seats: None

Many staff junior and senior are graduates of Southampton University, and the firm maintains links with the institution through open days, etc.

Warner Goodman is one of Hampshire's largest and oldest law firms. It has over 200 staff and can trace its roots back to 1852. The firm converted to LLP status in 2007 in response to the changing legal marketplace. Other developments are afoot: it recently disposed of its crime practice and is now driving forward its separately branded commercial law business, WG Commercial.

Uncontroversial commercial

Warner Goodman used to have two smaller offices in Waterlooville and Park Gate, but now operates entirely from its three main offices in Fareham, Southampton and Portsmouth. Southampton is the largest office and 'has everything except financial services and wills and probate.' In other words there are lawyers working in company-commercial, family, personal injury, employment, residential conveyancing, financial services, commercial litigation and commercial property. The Fareham office is home to the IT and accounts departments, the managing partners and several fee earning teams in different practices. Portsmouth is another multidisciplinary office and offers the strongest evidence of the drive to grow WG Commercial. In summer 2008 the firm opened a coco department in Portsmouth, and an employment team will follow later in the year. Initially it is envisaged that some of the Southampton employment lawyers will move across to get the practice up and running.

The firm didn't want us to name any of its clients or recent deals or cases; suffice to say it represents businesses in the so-called Solent corridor, as well as a broad spread of individuals – some wealthy, others classic high-street clients. 'It's important for a regional firm to have a commercial as well as private client practice; commercial is where the future lies,' one trainee told us in no uncer-

tain terms. Warner Goodman is 'definitely going in the commercial direction,' commented another. WG Commercial, although 'fully integrated into the rest of the firm,' has been separately branded in order to 'put it out to the market' and make the expansion plans obvious. Trainees say the division is now 'well known locally.'

All but one of the trainees were based in Southampton when we interviewed at the firm. The other was working in Portsmouth; no one was taking a seat in Fareham. The commercial seats have been particularly popular with trainees recently, and this is unsurprising since 'that's where the firm is expanding and that's where the jobs are likely to be.' We mustn't talk up the commercial side too much because the lion's share of the firm's revenue still comes from private clients. Between a quarter and a third of its business is in conveyancing; personal injury accounts for another big chunk, and family, wills, trusts and probate bring in another hefty slice of income. Since last year's edition of this guide, the criminal department has been dispatched lock stock and barrel to another local firm 'because it wasn't very profitable any more.' Presumably the decision to abandon crime had nothing to do with the jailing a couple of years ago of a former partner for perverting the course of justice and, in the words of the judge, '[breaking] every rule in the book.' One trainee quipped that since the criminal department moved on 'we've had fewer people stealing hot chocolate.' None of our sources were bothered by the loss of the department and told us the current batch weren't interested in this area of law anyway.

We must also point out that between ten and 15 redundancies were made from a residential conveyancing team of between 80 and 90 people. Blame was put squarely at the feet of the downturn in the residential property market and certainly Warner Goodman is not the only firm to have been forced to swing the axe. While there has been talk of redundancies elsewhere in the firm, these are 'not expected to be significant.'

Off the leash

In truth, trainees were keener to explain the ins and outs of their contracts. 'The flexibility of the seat allocation really appealed,' one told us, echoing the sentiments of others. 'I have friends in other firms who have been told their seat allocation for the whole of the next two years... what happens if you change your mind or find you hate a particular seat? Warner Goodman assured me at the outset that they're open to accommodating trainees as far as possible, and they've been true to their word.' Trainees gave several examples of the firm's flexibility on this matter – one moved seats simply because they didn't like the one they were in; someone had rejigged the structure and length of their training contract to take into account prior legal work experience; and another had returned to the department they planned to qualify into rather than go through the 'distraction' of a seat in a completely different practice.

Of course, where there is give there is usually take, and if a department can't offer enough work 'they'll move you.' In this sense, 'you lose certainty' about when exactly you will be changing seats, and the trainee group won't necessarily move together at the same time. The seat programme is 'not as structured as it could be,' our sources eventually concluded, though on balance they believed the benefits of flexibility 'far outweighs the downside.' Seat moves take place after discussions with the managing partner, who is also the firm's training partner. 'More time could be spent planning them,' one or two people suggested. There is also a feeling that supervisors in each seat don't spend quite enough time preparing feedback on trainees' performance, so the managing partner doesn't necessarily get the full picture of their capabilities. However, we hear that 'the firm is aware of this and they are sorting it out.'

The employment seat revolves around tribunals for, say, unfair dismissal and discrimination claims. Trainees inevitably get stuck preparing bundles for hearings, but they also enjoy client interaction. In commercial property trainees get to grips with 'plot sales, new leases for new-

Chambers UK rankings

Employment

build properties, lease extensions, basic sales and purchases, landlord and tenant matters and mortgages.' Recently lawyers acted on the sale of two pubs. Sensibly, 'trainees do residential work for commercial clients too, rather than farm this out to the conveyancing department.' It sounds as if the lawyers are working hard to keep clients sweet though: the team bussed some them to the Hawk Conservancy Trust in Andover to fly birds of prey for the day.

In commercial litigation 'things get passed down.' An e-mail may go out containing a new enquiry and 'if one of you wants to phone up and find out about it, off you go.' Cases include negligence claims and contract and boundary disputes. 'There's not a great deal of admin' and trainees get to try advocacy when they have built up enough confidence. 'It's down to you, they don't hold you back.'

Public service

'Most trainees have done family and PI, but they aren't necessarily the favourites.' There can be compromise, so the firm might say 'if you do family then we'll guarantee your preferred seat next time...' In residential conveyancing there are walk-ins from the street and referrals from estate agents. London Road, where Warner Goodman is based, is a street full of estate agents. There are perks dealing with members of the public, if they're happy with your work. One trainee revealed that as well as receiving thank you cards and letters from happy clients, 'some clients can be particularly generous... though obviously there are rules.'

WG's culture is 'open and trainees have no qualms about approaching partners;' indeed 'it's not uncommon to see a partner photocopying.' Feedback on training was good, and if you want training on something that isn't catered for then you just need to ask. Trainees 'are encouraged to do marketing and, for example, recently had a training session on networking.' An external consultant gave a presentation and then led role-play situations. When the employment department hosted an event for 70 clients and contacts at the Rose Bowl cricket ground, trainees played a full part.

Oh when the Saints...

Many staff – junior and senior – are graduates of Southampton University, and the firm maintains links with the institution through open days, etc. A large proportion of the staff comes from the Hampshire region. Some told us they 'regularly bump into old university friends' who work for different firms in the area. On qualification in 2008, three out of five people stayed on.

The dress code is a fairly standard 'suit and tie' for the boys and 'smart trousers or skirt for the girls.' In Southampton there are monthly charity dress down-days for which people pay a pound and take it in turns to nominate a charity. Trainees praise the work-life balance; on the downside the pay is the 'minimum recommended level for the area,' but you 'don't have to work 7am till 9pm.' The working day lasts from 9am to 5.15pm. Lunch is an hour and a quarter to give people time to walk into the town's main shopping area. People 'rarely stay late' and one trainee told us that when they were still in the office at 5.30pm one evening a senior colleague exclaimed: 'Haven't you got a home to go to?'

Sports fans can watch fantastic football at St Mary's, home of the mighty Saints, and incredible cricket at the Rose Bowl, both within spitting distance of the office. The New Forest, Isle of Wight, Bournemouth, cathedral cities Winchester and Salisbury, and Dorset are all on the doorstep. London is only an hour and a half from Portsmouth and Southampton by train. Previously trainees were spread around all the offices, but as most are now based in Southampton they have the opportunity to socialise together more. They have their own entertainment budget of about £1,000 to spend how they like and

'once it's gone, it's gone.' Southampton staff hang out in the bars of Bedford Place and London Road and in Chambers, a bar and pizza place next to the office where every lunchtime you can get a large pizza and a drink for little over a fiver. The trainees also get involved in the local branch of the Junior Lawyers Division, which organises various social events. There's no longer a firm-wide Christmas party – individual offices do their own thing – but there is a spring bash for everyone, which this year took place in the historic dockyards in Portsmouth. The firm paid for everyone's taxis home afterwards. It also organised a day at the Goodwood races, again open to all.

Playing sport isn't currently high up the list of extra-curricular activities, though there's nothing stopping trainees organising teams if they want to. At the time of writing there was talk of a cricket team being set up by one or two enthusiastic willow-wielders. There's also an annual football tournament when Team Warner Goodman takes on its clients and contacts.

And finally...

Warner Goodman has a genuine mix of high-street private clients and an expanding commercial practice. If you want a balanced South Coast lifestyle, it's one to consider.

Watson Burton

The facts

Location: Newcastle, Leeds, London

Number of UK partners/solicitors: 42/147

Total number of trainees: 20

Seats: 4x6 months

Alternative seats: Occasional secondments

Trainees say the firm values the concepts of openness, honesty and fairness.

Over 150 years old, top Toon firm Watson Burton bounded into the 21st century as fearlessly and tirelessly as Alan Shearer in front of goal. The firm's rapid expansion and modernisation would doubtless bring a smile to the face of its great Victorian founder, Robert Spence Watson, whose other glorious achievements included helping to create Newcastle University.

Gherkin around

WB enjoyed tremendous growth in the early Noughties under ex-senior partner Andrew Hoyle. On his watch, the PI, construction and engineering, corporate and private client departments bulged; profits soared by over 20% year on year; a spanking new open-plan Newcastle office replaced the old 'compartmentalised' rabbit warren; and new offices in Leeds and London burst on the scene. Since Hoyle's sudden departure in 2006, WB has continued to progress, albeit taking things at a much steadier pace. According to our sources, 'the firm has stabilised in Leeds and London and is now looking to push forward.' So far this has meant a merger with Trevor Robinson & Co, bringing significant technology expertise and new clients including Panasonic and software company SAP. The resulting technology practice is based in London in the landmark Gherkin building. It's worth asking what opportunities the merger might throw up in London in the future, as some trainees speculate that 'in two or three years there'll be opportunities for us down there' – maybe even a seat or two. However, given the loss of revenue following the end of the miners' compensation scheme, and given WB's exposure to the construction and real estate downturn, one wonders how quickly it will really want to expand in the capital.

Most trainees work in Newcastle, doing four six-month seats. The first three are compulsory – litigation (either construction or commercial), property and corporate – and then trainees get to choose their final seat from the firm's many sub-departments, including three different types of employment, various additional litigation options (including insurance, fraud and regulatory), corporate teams (such as business recovery, commercial business services), technology, family and PI.

The firm's senior partner, Rob Langley, is head of the construction and engineering team, so it's no surprise this core department continues to receive a lot of attention. *Chambers UK* ranks the team top in the North East; meanwhile the London office was founded by two construction partners concentrating on non-contentious instructions for developers and funders. Trainees going into construction litigation seats 'work to tight deadlines as part of a team of three or four on quite heavy litigation.' You don't get your own files because of the size of the cases, and inevitably the work involves some paper shuffling and bundling. Thankfully more rewarding tasks such as drafting witness statements are also par for the course and there are court and client visits with the partners to liven up the day. One source 'enjoyed working as part of the team' and didn't mind the occasional long hours. We heard about another trainee who was able to go on secondment to a construction client for three months. Among the clients are Bank of Scotland, South East England Development Agency, Sunderland City Council, Channel Islands Electricity Grid, Persimmon, Taylor Woodrow Developments, Zurich and Durham University.

At the coalface

By contrast, the commercial property training is 'completely different because a file is typically handled by one fee earner' and even trainees get their own small files. This seat is much more 'office-based, but there's very little grunt work,' and there's also 'tons of client contact' (whereas in construction litigation 'partners have the client contact'). Property can be 'misunderstood' and 'daunting' at first 'because it is hard to get to grips with and the hours are long – 9am to 6pm on average but sometimes until 7pm or 8pm.' However 'people revel in the responsibility.' Clients include Newcastle Building Society, the Co-op, Bellway Group, Silverlink Property Developments and the University of Sunderland. The total value of transactions handled by the department has shot up in recent years and pushed £2bn last year.

Watson Burton has one of the strongest commercial litigation practices in the North East and handles many large-scale cases, some in the areas of commercial fraud, dispute resolution and regulatory matters. A seat here may involve a stint working on professional indemnity disputes, where 'there's a lot of tax-related work because one partner is a chartered accountant.' According to our sources, the work is 'difficult and takes a couple of months to get used to' and involves 'a lot of research.' If you love football, you'll have loved the case of McGill v Gavin McCann involving a football agent pursuing a Bolton Wanderers player for a six-figure sum after an alleged breach of contract. Working in an entirely different area, partner Mark Heath acts for a substantial portfolio of NHS bodies in relation to healthcare fraud. Indeed if you make it to an interview or vac scheme at the firm, you're likely to meet him.

In employment – where again WB is one of the top firms in the North East – trainees gain contentious tribunal experience, assist on corporate support and learn how to give standalone advice. There's plenty of 'drafting contracts, writing submissions for tribunals, client meetings with partners, background research and checking figures.' The department's head, Dr John McMullen, is also part-time professor of labour law at Leeds University. The team recently helped the British Association of Colliery Management win a large-volume redundancy case when 350 miners were laid off. Other clients include Northern Foods, the NHS, Berwick Council and several other local authorities.

Chambers UK rankings

Banking & Finance • Charities • Construction • Corporate Finance • Debt Recovery • Dispute Resolution • Employment • Environment • Family/Matrimonial • Intellectual Property • Planning • Professional Negligence • Real Estate • Real Estate Litigation • Restructuring/Insolvency

In 2007 the Newcastle corporate department completed almost 60 deals worth over £490m. The Leeds office, which only opened in 2005, racked up 30 deal tombstones that year. Corporate trainees become involved in 'whole transactions – major projects, due diligence work, reviewing documents, writing board minutes and so on.' They told us they felt they were given more than enough responsibility. Indeed feedback across all seats was positive: 'They check up on you but let you get on with things.' A diverse corporate clientele includes National Co-operative Chemists, CWS Retail, Lloyds TSB Commercial Finance, American Golf Discount Centre and Surrey County Cricket Club.

Toon Army v Leeds

Historically, WB's personal injury practice has been known for its claims on behalf of miners and other industrial workers afflicted with work-induced ailments such as lung damage and vibration white finger. Indeed it's no secret that the firm made a considerable amount of money from this type of work, and also that it became embroiled in the widespread furore over the conduct of numerous solicitors' firms involved in the government's miners' compensation scheme. Although there are still a few miners' claims outstanding 'which have run for years and years,' this type of work is now in decline, so if your heart's set on PI you should definitely ask the firm about likely training opportunities in this field. For now it is not looking for people to qualify here.

Because the Leeds office is newer and smaller, with around 40 staff to Newcastle's 200-plus, the range of seats there is more limited. One Newcastle trainee viewed the Leeds office as simply an extension of the Toon HQ, with no discernible cultural differences. By contrast, Leeds sources told us: 'This office is different to Newcastle. It has the backing of a medium-sized firm, but is a small and friendly office with partners closely seated next to trainees. Leeds colleagues socialise as an office; in Newcastle there's not as much interaction between different floors.' Also, in Leeds 'work is delegated directly by partners, not junior solicitors.' Leeds trainees join their Newcastle counterparts for their PSC sessions at

Northumbria University, but it seems Newcastle trainees rarely have cause to venture to the other offices. Some occasionally accompany a partner to London for client or marketing meetings. Officially, interaction is encouraged and, for example, the firm once 'paid for three Newcastle trainees to spend time in Leeds.' Leeds is 'not looking to hugely expand' right now, although the ratio of partners and associates to junior solicitors makes it 'top-heavy,' leading sources to observe that WB is particularly 'keen to push trainees through its second office.'

The good news is that 'HR are quite trainee-focused right now.' The appraisal process has been updated from September 2008, such that line managers attend appraisal meetings along with HR and training partner Gillian Hall. This allows for 'more in-depth questioning.' Formal training sessions 'vary from department to department.' Employment, for example, uses 'lots of external speakers at seminars, brings in barristers to speak, etc.' Recently, cross-departmental sessions have entertained the troops; for example 'the property department talking to the rest of the firm' about their recent deals. HR has undertaken a firm-wide 'performance project' to improve internal communications and 'try to bring everyone together more.' It seems to be working as our sources claimed: 'Communication is improving.' Sounds ideal for a firm that trainees say values the concepts of openness, honesty and fairness.

Climbing to the top

The majority of trainees come from or went to university in the North. The current group is a mix of 'a couple of Oxbridge grads and, basically, Geordie lads,' according to one Geordie lad. The consensus is that WB hires 'down-to-earth people who aren't aloof, people who will get on with clients.' This skill comes into its own at marketing events, when trainees help meet and greet clients. Several of our sources remarked on how WB 'is not purely focused on academic achievement,' though it has to be said that most 'tend to come from redbrick universities.' Some insisted:

'It's very much about outside interests and personality,' telling us: 'The firm tries to recruit a balanced mix and looks for evidence of extra-curricular activities, whether charity work or sport.' A few of the current batch worked as paralegals with the firm before being awarded training contracts. 'Failing to get a training contract at the end of university is not the end of the world,' advised one source, 'even though you feel bad because all your friends have got theirs. Get some paralegal experience – a firm will be more likely to take you on.'

'There is work-life balance here: no one expects you to stay until 7pm or 8pm each night,' our interviewees confirmed. In Newcastle the firm sponsors summer and winter football leagues involving local businesses, among them rival law firms. WB's own team, which includes a couple of the more energetic partners, won a trophy earlier this year for coming 'top of the bottom half of the league.' There are also teams for netball, cricket and softball, and a group of sure-footed staff hiked up Helvellyn in the Lake District recently. The trainees have their own social committee to organise things like quiz nights and camping weekends. Meanwhile, future trainees can periodically expect an invitation to meet people over pizza and a glass of wine. The managing partner hosts drinks for all staff on the first Friday of every month, but to the chagrin of some, the firm-wide Christmas party was scrapped last year and staff were given a cash bonus instead.

And finally...

Tough economic conditions may have slowed ambitious expansion for now, but opportunities for trainees abound. In 2008 seven of the eight qualifiers stayed with the firm. If you're looking for a down-to-earth regional player with national aspirations, it's well worth looking up Mr Watson.

London • New York • Paris • Hamburg • Munich • Rome • Milan • Athens • Piraeus • Singapore • Bangkok

Begin a new journey

Many City firms have a string of offices outside the UK. The chances are, as a trainee, you won't be the one to go and work there.

Here at Watson, Farley & Williams we believe in letting you find out how an international firm works by seeing for yourself.

This means that during your training period with us in London, you'll be offered a four month seat in one of our overseas offices.

We look for people who get a buzz out of being part of the commercial world and a valuable member of busy teams pecialising in Corporate, Finance, Litigation and Tax.

For more information on vacation placements in 2009 and/or training contracts to commence in 2011, please visit our website at **www.wfw.com** or email us at **graduates@wfw.com**

Watson, Farley & Williams

www.wfw.com

Watson, Farley & Williams

The facts

Location: London

Number of UK partners/solicitors: 43/65

Total number of trainees: 26

Seats: 6x4 months

Alternative seats: Overseas seats

Extras: Pro bono – eg Toynbee Hall Legal Advice Centre; language training

> A seat in Singapore or Bangkok can make you feel like you've won the lottery.

Watson, Farley & Williams' modest size in London belies its global reach. If asked to sum it up, many people would refer to it as an asset finance specialist that's especially good at shipping finance. That's only half the story.

Wind farm wonders

In 2007 the firm celebrated the 25th anniversary of its founding by three former Norton Rose partners. Two were shipping finance lawyers and the other an aviation specialist, so it's no surprise the firm's reputation lies primarily in asset and shipping finance. Bear in mind too that Martin Watson (the first W) was elected president of the UK Chamber of Shipping in spring 2008, and the firm's clients include lenders Citi and RBS, energy shipping company Teekay, and cruise lines Royal Caribbean International and Carnival.

Essentially WFW has an 'anchor in shipping' while being keen to build up other areas. It's a sensible strategy in light of comments about the London shipping finance market having 'reached a plateau' and looking 'gloomy.' WFW's energy practice is now centre stage in the firm's vision of the future. As well as doing impressive work in relation to oil and gas, much of it LNG, the firm has come over all green thanks to the efforts of a successful renewable energy team. The lawyers handle financing projects in biomass, waste energy and landfill gas, and there's a clear focus on wind farms, mostly because 'they're the furthest down the line in terms of being commercially viable.' Last year they advised Millenium Wind Energy, Investec and BNP Paribas, among others, on wind farms in Scotland, Greece and Germany. They were also instructed by Dexia Bank Belgium and Dexia Crédit Local on the €190m financing of Belgium's first wind farm, a deal that won it Europe-wide plaudits. So important has renewable energy become that WFW recently reorganised its finance division to better serve its various client sectors. Shipping finance has become a distinct division, and the non-shipping finance practice now includes much of the energy and projects work that was previously handled by the corporate practice.

As if to emphasise the importance of the energy sector, in 2007 WFW was in merger talks with New York-based projects bigwigs Chadbourne & Parke. Since they foundered in the November, it looks as if the firm has not closed its mind to other opportunities. In 2008 it opened offices in Munich and Milan through small mergers.

Six-shooters

WFW trainees take six seats. This can have its drawbacks, for example, 'when you're really getting into the swing of things after three months and you know you're moving on in a couple of weeks.' There are major pluses too, such as 'learning more about areas we might want to qualify into.' The firm requires everyone to sample the finance, corporate and litigation departments, plus one seat from tax, property, employment or EU/competition. Then there's a guarantee of four months in an overseas office and the remaining choice is left up to the trainee. It's quite common to opt for a second stint in finance or whatever department the trainee plans on qualifying into. Our interviewees had no complaints about seat allocation, telling us: 'Nine times out of ten people get what they ask for, with maybe the exception being overseas seats.'

Let's examine the shipping finance seat, where trainees work under the guidance of senior associates. The firm handles big deals; indeed, in 2007 it worked on the biggest in the industry – Nordea Bank Norge and DnB NOR's $1.6bn financing of crude oil tanker operator Euronav. This busy seat can be rewarding: 'I learnt a hell of a lot there,' declared one source. The department manages to blend the mundane and the glamorous. On the one hand there are administrative aspects such as managing all the post-completion documentation on a deal; on the other trainees have plenty of contact with clients and banks. 'You get to know clients well,' explained one interviewee, 'we're always off at meetings or visiting embassies.' We even heard about trainees attending celebratory meals with bankers at Michelin-starred restaurants.

One of our interviewees joked that it was 'blasphemy' to want to do something other than shipping finance at WFW, however there are several other directions a trainee can go in. The corporate department, for example, accounted for around 30% of the firm's revenue prior to donating much of its energy and projects functions to the finance group. As well as working for transport and energy clients, the department represents a number of companies involved in gold, diamond and other types of mining. A seat with the oil and gas team is a really good choice. Trainees get stuck into due diligence, shareholder agreements and plenty of minute-taking at meetings. 'With the price of oil as it is at the moment, and that introducing political factors, it's quite an interesting area.' The projects team covers construction and property aspects, while also incorporating finance elements on renewable energy deals, 'for the most part wind farms.'

The litigation department has lost a few partners and associates, leaving one trainee to claim hopefully: 'I think they're in the process of becoming a phoenix to rise out of the ashes again.' A worsening economy favours litigation, so the reduced team could be kept busy with international arbitrations over wind farms and dry shipping disputes, as well as domestic property and banking claims. A seat in EU/competition can fulfil the requirement to sample contentious law as it involves regulatory issues as well as merger clearance. To do well here you need to 'take a step back and look at how each bit of the market functions,' a process that gives a 'basic understanding' of different industries. 'Marine transport is quite big here, but equally you might be looking at hotel-booking systems or needle production.'

More Bangkok for your buck

Most recruits request to go overseas for either their second or third seat, which fits nicely with the desire to

Chambers UK rankings

Asset Finance • Corporate Finance • Employment • Projects, Energy & Natural Resources • Shipping

'focus the second year on London.' The Bangkok seat is primarily a litigation gig, while Singapore trainees cover corporate and finance, often being delegated smaller transactions to run themselves. The shipping finance experience is similar to that in London, except you're 'closer to clients and the shipyards, and you can sometimes see the vessels floating past outside.' Long hours are par for the course. Said one source: 'If I was ever out by seven-thirty, it was normally am not pm.' Trainees heading to Asia are well looked after with a salary top-up. Incoming and outgoing Singapore trainees overlap for a few days, so the previous seat occupant meets the new one at the airport, takes them to their new two-bedroomed, ninth-floor apartment and introduces them to the office. The apartment building has its own sauna, pool, gym, hairdresser and shops, so in theory you'd never need to leave. Spare time is spent within the city's large trainee network and the 'crazy' ex-pat lifestyle can get expensive, especially if you take advantage of weekend travel opportunities by jetting off to Cambodia, Vietnam, Borneo, Malaysia, Indonesia and any number of astonishingly gorgeous islands. A seat in Singapore or Bangkok can make you 'feel like you've won the lottery.'

One-on-one Greek and French classes help prepare for the European options. They're not essential for getting by in the office, but why turn down the chance to learn business French or 'basic survival Greek for reading road signs?' The Paris office is reputed to have 'a calmer pace' than any of the others. Here, finance transactions dominate, though if you speak enough French you'll have the chance to work in other departments. Living in Le Marais you'll get to visit all the tourist attractions and eat your way through restaurant guides. Again, there's a sizeable network of UK trainees. In Piraeus, the port city near Athens, the trainee has a large flat just ten minutes' walk from the office. A close-knit community of English trainees make nights out and road trips pretty enjoyable, although with summer temperatures hovering around 40°C, it's not exactly sightseeing weather. As Piraeus is the centre of the Greek shipping industry, the seat focuses exclusively on shipping finance. Our sources concluded that the deals done in the UK office are longer and more complicated, whereas in Greece trainees might handle eight or nine in a week. Nearby Athens 'fits well around a late-working lifestyle. In England if you work until 9pm, there goes your evening. Here you wouldn't be seen dead in a restaurant before 10pm.'

Michelin men

Though not unheard of, all-nighters are rare back in London. Trainees aren't expected to stay late very often, however it's important to 'realise this is how law firms work and you will have strict deadlines.' Comparing their lot to their peers at bigger firms ('where you could be replaced by a monkey if you had to be') they enjoy feeling they're 'actively participating' in matters. If problems arise, there are people to talk to and we're told the chino-wearing WFW partners are 'all very approachable.' One interviewee generously expanded on this point: 'It doesn't matter if you get something wrong at first, but you need to do it and ask what you've done wrong rather than asking questions at every juncture. Unless you can take the plunge and just do things, whether they're wrong or right, I'm not sure how long you'd last.'

Someone who gets nothing but praise from recruits is WFW chef and 'brilliant French guy' Philippe, who creates the canapés for firm parties and oversees the subsidised canteen, where you get 'a huge plate of excellent food' for £2.50. Even though that's cheaper than going out for a sandwich, 'you'd get very fat if you ate there every day.' Away from the canteen, the rest of the office is in the process of being refurbished to update the conference rooms ('all wood panelling and terrible artwork') and shore up the firm's green credentials with more energy-efficient features. Drinks evenings, the firm Christmas party, wine-tastings and discount theatre tickets are some of the highlights organised by the social committee, and nights out will usually end up in the nearby All Bar One or other 'bars filled with City-types drinking expensive beer.'

Last year we heard a few grumblings that WFW's qualification process wasn't as smooth as it could have been. This year's interviewees insisted we'd been given an 'incorrect' impression. They assured us the firm is 'honest' about what jobs will become available, including any overseas opportunities. Would-be qualifiers can state up to two preferences and are interviewed by partners for each. Simple, unless you've applied for litigation, in which case you also have to pass 'quite a difficult technical test.' In 2008 nine of the 11 qualifiers stayed on at the firm.

And finally...

Shipping finance may still be a cornerstone of the practice, but Watson Farley & Williams offers a good deal besides. The firm is generating heat in the field of renewable energy and should appeal to anyone keen on spending time abroad.

Wedlake Bell

The facts

Location: London

Number of UK partners/solicitors: 40/55

Total number of trainees: 14

Seats: 4x6 months

Alternative seats: Secondments

Extras: Pro bono – Mary Ward Centre

> Pulling booze, fast car and fashion companies is a fine achievement for an organisation at the grand old age of 228.

Providing 'character from the outside and a nice modern interior,' Wedlake Bell's Georgian Bedford Row office reflects the firm itself. This mid-market London player combines a seasoned private client team with a rounded commercial offering.

Bigger, brighter, better?

This top-100 player has a refreshingly personal approach to business. Its commercial arm works for massive clients such as Tesco, as well as sexy ones like Diageo, BMW and Lacoste. Pulling booze, fast car and fashion companies is a fine achievement for an organisation at the grand old age of 228, especially when you consider there's a gazillion firms in the Square Mile chasing anything in a corporate skirt. Such glamorous elements are only half the story though, and WB keeps things nice and balanced. A period of expansion has meant growth in all its key areas of practice, the private client team being no exception.

Having grown at a rate of knots, WB now appears to be at something of a crossroads, prompting much speculation amongst trainees as to its future aspirations. 'We're expanding but we are not trying to be a Linklaters,' said one, adding: 'I think we would like to become a top-50 firm in a few years.' Other interviewees confimed this optimistic projection, and some even ventured to suggest a merger might be on the cards in order to achieve such a goal. Outwardly, the new management has been more reserved in its statements about targets, singling out corporate for significant growth but careful to emphasise the importance of other departments. Given recent partner-level departures from the corporate team, and predictions of general malaise in the corporate world, this is unsurprising. Nevertheless, the fresh management structure,

with new managing partner and newly created Chief Executive role, is itself a clear sign of ambition in a firm that trainees believe is 'looking for a bigger, brighter, better future.'

Proper yo

Trainees here are asked to provide HR with a list of their seat preferences in the summer before their training starts. This allows the firm to map out the whole two years in advance for each new starter. Most trainees appreciate the 'direction' that this gives to their training and the avoidance of 'end-of-seat worries about what is coming next.' At the same time they accept that 'it can make it more difficult to change focus if your preferences change during your contract,' although we did catch wind of trainees 'getting together to swap and change seats.'

While many trainees claimed to have been lured by WB's reputation for private client or even IP law, they quickly learned that you'll be 'hard pushed' to avoid a property seat as 'it's where the firm generates a lot of its fees.' The department has an impressive roster of retail and real estate fund clients, and the past year alone saw the addition of brewer Fuller Smith & Turner (with its portfolio of 360 pubs and six hotels) and Residential Land Limited (with a portfolio and trading company valued at £224m). With this in mind it's easy to see why a trainee's visit to the department is action-packed. Options include commercial or residential property and construction, where the firm recently advised Yotel, a venture by Yo! Sushi founder and ardent supporter of the sideburn Simon Woodroffe, on the construction and procurement of the UK's first micro-hotel in Gatwick Airport. On such matters trainees cannot expect a frontline role, but they can anticipate 'a whole filing cabinet of files for which they are the primary contact.' While 'you have to get up to speed fast,' it's definitely worth it. 'It's what being a lawyer is all about, having a client call you directly to let you know what they want.'

Unsurprisingly the transactional property groups also feed a very healthy property litigation practice: 'We act for funds with hundreds of millions of pounds and properties all over the UK, so they get into quite a few scrapes.' Step forward property litigators. These guys are also used to mop up property-related disputes coming from the private client department. Trainees therefore spoke of switching hats between 'dealing with high-up people in chunky commercial companies' and 'comforting a wealthy old lady being bothered by children.' The seat can be a baptism of fire, with one poor trainee 'up in front of a master in the third week of my training contract.' Such an experience can 'set you up for the rest of your training in terms of confidence and ability to conduct yourself.' Having so many files to run across the property seats also 'hones the organisational skills so that in other seats you have super organised files.'

FTSE fetish

Many trainees are keen to sample WB's corporate department, which is currently 'settling down and moving forward' after the loss of two key partners in 2007. New managing partner Philip Matthews has called for a doubling of the department's ranks, however even this would not be enough to make it a place for anyone with a serious FTSE lust, as 'most of the clients just aren't that big.' Instead trainees receive a diet of 'AIM listings for mid-sized clients' and small-end, mid-level M&A. One of the firm's greatest achievements in 2007, for example, was the £26.9m sale of property agency Edwin Hill to Canadian company Altus Group. On such sales trainees reported duties ranging from verification to 'plenty of document drafting.'

Commercial litigation experiences are twinned with work from the ever-popular IP department, resulting in a mixed seat with 'general commercial cases as well as a lot of brand protection work for clients like BMW that have people trying to rip off their wheels or set up websites using their name.' The good news is that 'as a trainee you get small-value claims of up to £10k, where you liaise with counsel and draft all of the witness statements, etc,' as well as the opportunity to take more of a background

role on the multimillion-pound cases. The non-contentious IP/commercial seat is a winner, and our sources confirmed that it lives up to the hype: 'I was handling brand work for some pretty cool clients, so you can walk down the street and see what you are working on.' Other tangible benefits include 'working with some really brainy people that you can't help but be inspired by and learn from.' An alternative to this seat is a secondment to drinks company Diageo, helping them manage their hefty portfolio of beverage brands and sponsorships. The seat brings 'a great insight into the commercial side of things, as opposed to just the legal.' It also has the bonus of a heavily subsidised on-site bar, although our source regretted to inform us during an 11am interview from a quiet corner in said bar that 'they are big on responsible drinking, so it might be a bit early to start.'

Wedding bells

WB has strong appeal for those with a taste for the traditional. Its private client team has 'been around since the firm was founded,' and far from sacrificing it to the commercial sword, the firm has worked hard to keep things buzzing. 'There's a quite decent old-school client base and also some new-money characters.' A second office in Guernsey brings in offshore instructions 'and there are clients who are domiciled in various different jurisdictions.' Described as an 'academic,' 'completely varied' and 'hands-on' seat, trainees 'attend meetings with clients to discuss amending their wills and then draft the will and codicils,' 'locate missing beneficiaries on probate matters' and even sort out rogue utility bills for disgruntled clients. In short you should be prepared to 'just pick up and run with whatever is thrown at you, even if you don't know anything about the subject.'

Other seat options include the 'extremely busy' employment group or the more sedate 'out the door by 5.30pm every day' pensions team. Whatever the seat, trainees are likely to share a two-person office with their supervisor in the firm's 'bright and airy' headquarters. Between monthly meetings with supervisors, more formal end-of-seat reviews and meetings with the training principal and HR, there are plenty of opportunities to receive and give feedback. Not that anyone has anything very bad to say: our sources were far keener to sing WB's praises for letting them loose on clients, some of whom kept in touch (and in one case even sent pictures of a daughter's wedding) well after the trainee had moved seats.

Caught on camera

WB can confidently encourage its trainees to schmooze clients, as it clearly places great weight on such skills when selecting them. Most participate in the three-week vacation scheme, which is effectively an extended interview 'to see if you will fit in with the character of the firm.' WB has 'a tendency to recruit people with some life experience behind them,' suggesting that this might be because 'they bring something extra to the table when dealing with clients.' Typically the majority are non-law graduates and, interestingly, the current crop of trainees is also overwhelmingly female (five out of the seven in each year), which 'certainly keeps you on your toes,' according to one cheeky male trainee.

By recruiting sociable types, the firm has nurtured 'a very human place to work.' 'It's small, so after a while you get to know everyone from secretaries to guys in the general office to the senior partner. It makes a big difference to my day to be able to speak to someone in the lift.' An intranet message board also means that 'if someone is getting married or having a baby it's the first thing you see when you turn your computer on in the morning.' The intranet can be the downfall of a trainee, as incriminating pictures are posted after social events. Luckily, at the last black-tie Christmas party the show was stolen by a group of shoeless partners throwing shapes and 'attempting to breakdance.' There's further

scope for embarrassment at quarterly drinks, where you can either slope off after the managing partner's business update or 'hang around with the boozers.' Those doing the latter soon learn not to take their eyes off the waiters, whose guile in refilling a wine glass has claimed many a victim. On a normal Friday, trainees can be found in 'any of the haunts familiar to BPP students,' or maybe one of Holborn's swanky wine bars (if a partner is in tow to pick up the bill).

The lively social scene probably flourishes due to the 'generally reasonable hours' expected of trainees. Horror stories are few and far between. Without hours to moan about, the main reservations voiced by our sources concerned the qualification process, with many finding the wait until May for the process to start to be unnecessarily long and stressful. In the end, seven of the eight qualifiers took jobs at the firm, hoping to one day become 'one of the whole tranche of partners who trained here.'

And finally...

While overall very satisfied, trainees did add a note of caution as to the difficulty the firm is likely to face in 'retaining its character and friendly atmosphere as it seeks further growth.' Having made a name for marrying tradition and modernity over the last 228 years, we think it might just be alright.

Weil, Gotshal & Manges

The facts

Location: London

Number of UK partners/solicitors: 24/75

Total number of trainees: 23

Seats: 4x6 months

Alternative Seats: Overseas seats

Extras: Pro bono – LawWorks, Bar Pro Bono Unit, Battersea Law Centre; language training

> WGM has publicly stated its ambition to be the best private equity practice in the market, and it's getting closer to that goal.

Weil, Gotshal & Manges dares prospective applicants to do something that scares them. If you're frightened of working for a US firm with a global reputation for restructuring and insolvency, and a London office specialising in private equity corporate finance, then you've got Weilophobia.

Rhymes with Ganges

With a New York pedigree stretching back to 1931 and the Great Depression, WGM now employs over 1,300 lawyers across 20 offices on three continents. Its newest location opened in Beijing, just in time to catch the Olympics. The London office, launched in 1996, doesn't share the same focus on business and financial restructuring (BFR) that made the firm's name and saw it act on such high-profile restructurings as Enron and Parmalat. It was founded to service New York private equity client Hicks Muse Tate & Furst (now HM Capital) when it launched in Europe. Private equity has been London's meat and potatoes ever since, while London itself has become 'the hub of the European practice' and is now the firm's second-largest office. There is huge scope for cross-border work, as 'everything, almost without exception, has an international element.' Recent highlights include advising on a $2.9bn offer for Australia's fourth-largest media company APN News & Media, and the colossal £3.2bn take private of EMI.

In an ambitious lateral hiring strategy, a particularly notable coup was the poaching of Lovells' star head of private equity Marco Compagnoni and his team. They brought with them a huge book of valuable clients including HG Capital, Barclays and 3i and transformed WGM's private equity practice into one generating most of its work from London. Initially the new team tended to work and socialise amongst themselves – 'even now people will refer to the Lovells lot' – but the move was undoubtedly great for the firm, and one eager trainee told us: 'Working with Marco has been a highlight.'

WGM has publicly stated its ambition to be the best private equity practice in the market, and it's getting closer to that goal. *Chambers UK* this year ranked it in the second tier nationally, with only behemoth Clifford Chance above it. Other departments are also slated to grow, and with current economic conditions making BFR all the more relevant, one recruit unhesitatingly said: 'If I were interested in that area I'd definitely look at Weil.'

Equity party

Along with a finance seat, corporate finance – more specifically, private equity – is compulsory for trainees. Last year lawyers acted on the £360m sale of Fat Face by Advent International, and the acquisition of juice producer Nidan Soki by remnant of HM Capital, Lion Capital. Lion also instructed the firm in its £303m acquisition of the maker of Russia's biggest vodka brand. For trainees 'there's not much to learn as it's mostly transaction management and not that much law.' They begin with low-level due diligence and document review, with a view to ultimately managing the process. Drafting opportunities come thick and fast with deal closings, and some may even run a small deal. On occasion they will accompany a partner overseas: 'It's not easy going abroad, but if you can grab a few hours after the meeting it's nice.'

Tax is a small support department where 'it's nice to be able to think again' after so much heavy lifting in corporate. Trainees typically liaise with foreign counsel and HMRC, get involved with tax planning and help set up acquisition structures. Six months in banking and finance 'has become unpopular as it's seen as the seat where you work the hardest.' The hours fluctuate wildly, with quiet periods when trainees 'wander in at 10am and leave at 5pm' following periods of 'continually working until 2am or 3am every night for two weeks and working weekends.' Exacerbating this, but providing excitement, is the international nature of the work, which saw one of our sources 'up early talking to Singapore then up late talking to San Francisco.'

Capital markets seats give trainees a lot of responsibility. Sources talked of high-yield debt offerings for hedge funds and putting together first drafts of prospectuses for companies listing on AIM. While this seat involves plenty of corporate support chores, the same cannot be said of the 'very standalone' securitisation team. Here 'you need to have an uncluttered brain' to cope with the complex documentation. Minimal bibling and grunt tasks give way to 'big chunks of work over and above what you imagine yourself doing.' A seat in the signature restructuring practice is 'law-heavy, so if that's your thing and you like intricate detail it's a good one.' The presence of complicated structured finance vehicles requires 'a lot of training to get on top of the terminology,' and recruits start slowly until they show an aptitude for the work. 'It's a very inclusive team,' said one, 'so it's quite rare that an important call goes on without you being asked to join.'

Litigation promises 'intellectual research work' alongside 'enormous disclosure projects' within a supportive team, if not a lot of court time or client contact. If this doesn't ring your bell, there's a two-week opt-out course that is taken by roughly a third of the trainees. In fact, several of our interviewees pined for more theoretical training to supplement what they learn on the job. Induction sessions at the beginning of each seat and updates along the way had left them hungry for more.

Where there's a Weil...

The opacity of various decision-making processes niggles some people. For example, the procedure for qualification is very informal, not involving much beyond a trainee talking to the head of their intended department. It's all over within a few weeks and then everybody goes out for champagne. Except, 'it's important to have a partner shouting your case.' Similarly, seat allocation is 'opaque at best.' Trainees are more likely to get preferred seats as

they approach qualification, but again it sounds like the deciding factor may be a partner in your corner. 'You need to make sure you're on people's radar' and swallow your pride about asking for a good word in the right ear.

For those who sprechen le lingo there are spots in Frankfurt and Paris. More common are postings to the USA – Silicon Valley is usually an IP seat while New York-bound trainees have more choice. 'There were some people I'd worked with before,' trilled someone back from the Big Apple, 'and it was so nice to meet them face to face.' WGM really lets trainees 'live the dream' by sorting out an 'amazing' Midtown apartment and bunging in a cost-of-living allowance. It's worth noting that WGM also sends vac schemers to NY.

...there's a way

When one source told us 'you can't stay in your comfort zone,' they were, knowingly or otherwise, referencing WGM's recent recruitment brochure. Words like 'Intense' and 'Challenging' accompany drawings of dark rooms and candles burning at both ends. The firm likes to tell students how many applications it receives for each vac scheme place because 'anyone who's intimidated should be weeded out straight away.' It's a bold approach, yet our interviewees acknowledged that it is largely reflective. This is a tough contract and 'you do feel chucked in at the deep end,' nonetheless the firm could perhaps do more to publicise its genuinely supportive atmosphere. In 2008 a healthy seven out of eight qualifiers stayed with the firm – a big improvement on past years' figures.

WGM has a specific idea of who it's looking for, not that it's anything you can necessarily express in a CV. 'If you take one criterion – background – it's incredibly diverse. We're not all cloned, London-born blah, blah, blah.' There's a spread of redbrick and ancient universities, though one recruit told us they'd noticed 'a push towards Oxbridge.' It's more that trainees must be 'willing to muck in and give things a go.' Importantly 'they need to be realistic about what they want out of a training contract.' WGM looks for 'someone who wants the job and knows what it entails' – hard work. 'There really is no place to hide at all and all your work will be challenging. You can't share the blame if it goes wrong – you'll be accountable for it.' Commitment is key because 'if you want to get your pay cheque and leave as soon as possible you'll have a really hard two years.'

Aside from appraisals every three months and an elective mentor scheme, 'there aren't many official channels in place.' Recruits certainly aren't afraid to ask for help but usually prefer to solve problems themselves. 'No one's going to get annoyed if you're asking silly questions, but as a trainee you're better off trying to figure things out yourself.' Maybe this makes the firm sound scarier than it actually is. In fact, we got the impression that once they get over the initial challenge of adjusting to office life, trainees feel included. The 'higher-ups' seem to know and care what their subordinates are doing, and far from having a competitive or strained atmosphere, 'by your second seat you know everyone in the firm – it means you have personal relationships everywhere.'

There's no escaping the fact you'll be catching a few night buses home. Some late nights might have more to do with trainees' team spirit: 'There's obviously the odd night when people are snowed under and it's only polite to help. Either you both leave at midnight or one person works through the night.' There are compensations. Last year NQ salaries jumped to a whopping £90,000, a rate that places them on par with or slightly above their New York counterparts depending on the exchange rate. In 2008 a package of flexible benefits came in that allows staff to buy (and sell) holiday days. By now you'll appreciate that WGM trainees' 'night buses' are metered and take them straight to their front doors.

Re: treats

The last summer party was a Pimm's-and-champagne reception at trendy Smiths of Smithfield, and there's a biannual European retreat. Last year's was in Lisbon, where 'the workload was kept to a minimum to leave more time for drinking and dancing.' If a group of lawyers head out on a Friday night they use 'a shotgun approach' to choose one of the many bars around Moorgate, or they head over to Coq d'Argent if they're feeling especially flush. Post-work socialising isn't regular, as long hours leave people eager to spend time with other friends and family. It may also be the result of 'not a whole lot of mingling' between departments, or even their respective floors. Within departments there are great events, such as a tax team retreat to Paris (first-class on Eurostar, swanky hotel) or a barbecue for corporate lawyers at the managing partner's house.

WGM London is 'definitely English' in character, with 'American attitudes to some things.' Dedication to diversity can be seen in the Women@Weil programme, which is open to all but focuses on women's issues. Furthermore, the firm places a huge emphasis on pro bono work. Every lawyer is expected to do 50 hours per year, which can come from volunteering at, say, Battersea Law Centre, mentoring GCSE students at a Bermondsey school or assisting charitable clients such as Oxfam or NSPCC. WGM was one of the founding members of Advocates for International Development (A4ID).

And finally...

We'll take a frank tone to conclude because we know WGM can handle it. This is a tough contract, but with its attentive atmosphere and opportunities for trainees to have close involvement on huge deals, it offers a heck of a lot for the right applicant.

Make the right choice
www.whitecase.com/trainee

WHITE & CASE

White & Case

The facts

Location: London

Number of UK partners/solicitors: 72/277

Total number of trainees: 55

Seats: 4x6 months

Alternative seats: Overseas seats

Extras: Pro bono – RCJ CAB, LawWorks, Social Enterprise for London, Bar Pro Bono Unit; language training

> W&C was one of the first American law firms in the UK. After several years of rapid growth it now has almost 380 lawyers from 18 different countries working in our capital.

Finance giant White & Case goes toe-to-toe with some of the UK's biggest practices, but don't go thinking it's just any old Yankee interloper. Trainees insist this is 'a global firm, not an American firm.'

On the case

Founded in New York in 1901, the firm quickly parlayed a friendship with JPMorgan's influential financier Henry P. Davison into a successful banking and finance practice. Entering Paris in 1926, it became a vanguard of international law and, never one to shirk a challenge, it charged into Eastern Europe as early as 1989. The firm developed an enviable 'sovereign practice', helping former communist countries with privatisations, and nations like Indonesia in rescheduling billions of dollars of debt. Now W&C has over 2,300 lawyers in over 25 countries and its focus on emerging markets continues, most recently through new offices in Bucharest and Abu Dhabi.

Here since 1971, W&C was one of the first American law firms in the UK. After several years of rapid growth it now has almost 380 lawyers from 18 different countries working in our capital, and its multi-jurisdictional expertise lands it a role on truly gigantic transactions. Consider, for example, the $21.3bn Qatargas series – the largest ever energy project financing. This and other instructions for clients like BNP Paribas, Citi, ArcelorMittal, Deutsche Bank, Rio Tinto, EDF, ExxonMobil and ConocoPhillips allowed London revenues to rise by 37% in 2007 – almost the exact level of growth recorded for each of the past five years.

The success story momentarily soured earlier in 2008, when Mike Goetz (co-head of the London office) and Maurice Allen (heavyweight co-head of global banking) jumped ship to Freshfields, precipitating doom-laden predictions in industry journals. We were surprised by how willingly trainees discussed the matter. 'It's not an elephant in the room – everyone's very open about it,' they said. No one pretended it was a good thing, and there was initial uncertainty for those wanting to qualify into banking, but the general view was that 'by the time Mike and Maurice left, London was in such a strong position it hasn't really had that negative an impact. No associates or partners followed them and everything's back to normal.' Important clients have stayed, and Goetz and Allen have even set up a referral relationship between Freshfields and W&C.

In the bag

'W&C is a finance firm first and foremost,' so if you're not interested in this, look elsewhere. The finance practice is split in two: on one side the energy, infrastructure, projects and asset finance (EIPAF) group; on the other, banking and capital markets, which also includes structured finance. Last year EIPAF advised Spanish Egyptian Gas Company on the refinancing of the $1.02bn Damietta LNG plant in Egypt, advised in connection with the $3.2bn financing of a hydropower plant and aluminium smelter in Siberia, and tackled everything from mining, nuclear decommissioning and gas pipelines to new schools and MoD projects. The firm proudly claims its projects transform economies and countries, but with transactions going on for years, trainees might only see small bits of them, so their work 'isn't particularly sophisticated.' Being taken along to meetings is a welcome relief from ever-present proof-reading and conditions precedent checklists.

The banking and capital markets department is 'like the younger brother to the flagship project finance practice.' In 2007 it handled top-dollar instructions from the arrangers in a $1.7bn acquisition of luggage supremo Samsonite, and represented Cinven and Goldman Sachs on the €1bn refinancing, restructuring and recapitalisation of Nordic distribution business Ahlsell. As well as getting stuck into drafting, trainees are 'on the phone a lot, which makes it a little bit more interesting than just staring at a computer screen.' Charged with making sure everything runs smoothly as completions approach, recruits liaise with other legal teams and overseas counsel. Meanwhile, aircraft finance dominates the asset finance seat, where trainees work on jet purchases for Thomas Cook, Aeroflot and Société Générale. Getting a seat in perpetually busy capital markets is 'lucky or unlucky, depending on how you look at it.' Sources recalled being 'annihilated for a three or four-month spell,' doing a mix of mundane and progressively more creative tasks like proof-reading, drafting prospectuses, liaising with the FSA and running conference calls. This seat involves some foreign travel, with trainees jetting off to Central Asia and Africa. Somewhat more subdued since the credit crunch is structured finance, but even when the team was really hopping it was 'good at giving trainees responsibility.'

Other seat options include corporate, litigation, employment, construction, IP and real estate. Corporate is 'a fun group' with lots of Aussies and Kiwis providing 'a great camaraderie.' That might make it sound relaxed, but this year 'the hours have been crazy! What credit crunch?' Instructions from ABN AMRO, Ford, BAA, Rolls-Royce, Shell and Novartis have kept the team busy. Sources had worked on numerous public takeovers and private acquisitions, including KKR's $1.3bn purchase of a Turkish freight company and other deals in Russia, Israel and Nigeria. Litigation seats are in high demand since W&C has started to pay greater attention to this area. It has captured Lovells partner Phillip Capper in its effort to bring arbitration in London up to the standard of its global practice, and in March it successfully fought the extradition of former Morgan Crucible chief exec Ian Norris to America on price fixing charges. This House of Lords victory received massive press attention as it questioned key aspects of the UK-US extradition treaty. Trainees' testimonials about the seat ran the gamut from 'horrific' to 'fantastic,' with complaints over the amount of 'monotonous' bundling balanced by letter drafting and the chance to go to court. Trainees can also gain contentious experience through seats in construction, employment or IP.

Chambers UK rankings

Asset Finance • Banking & Finance • Banking Litigation • Capital Markets • Construction • Corporate Finance • Data Protection • Dispute Resolution • Employee Share Schemes • Employment • Financial Services Regulation • Information Technology • Intellectual Property • Investment Funds • Projects, Energy & Natural Resources • Real Estate • Real Estate Finance • Restructuring/Insolvency • Telecommunications • Transport

Monkey business

W&C guarantees everyone six months – usually their fourth seat – in New York or almost any of its locations in Europe and Asia. In fact, there are invariably more options than trainees to fill them. Even far-flung Kazakh hotspot Almaty is on the cards, where 'you can live like a king… but there's no one to do it with.' W&C has an excellent reputation in Central and Eastern Europe, and a seat in Prague sees recruits living the high life, taking part in border-hopping disclosure exercises and being wined and dined in castles. Tokyo may be the land of conveyor-belt sushi, but there are no hasty meals at your desk – 'Everyone goes out for an hour for lunch no matter how busy they are.' A somewhat split culture sees recruits leave work earlier than their Japanese counterparts, but after all 'you're out here as much for the cultural experience as the job.' That experience involves weekend travel and bar hopping in trendy Roppongi, where the firm has a small flat for secondees.

The Big Apple is one of the newest additions to the roster and offers a lot of associate-level finance work and some dabbling in New York law. A salary top-up and rent-free apartment in Hell's Kitchen (trust us, it's nicer than it sounds) seals the 'cushy deal.' As one of the more unusual destinations, Johannesburg is really popular. This small but busy office takes on masses of project finance work, especially in mining and metals. Trainees must quickly grasp South African law, documents are often difficult to access, rolling power cuts regularly caused 'chaos' and 'baboons raid your fridge,' but 'you learn to be patient – it's amazing how tolerant you become after a few weeks.' A top tip from one of our sources: 'You apply for your overseas seat within the first two weeks of arriving, so it's good to have thought about it beforehand.'

W&C has delivered on a promise to provide more formal training. Not everyone we surveyed thought it necessary ('I prefer learning by doing rather than being taught in a classroom,' one swaggered), but now there are inductions to new seats and ongoing training in each. Weekly reports to the training partners and HR, and monthly meetings in some of the bigger teams, mean workloads are monitored so as not to be too repetitive or overwhelming. Our fears that previously high levels of attention to recruits might be diluted by the rapid expansion of the training programme (there were 16 trainees in 2001 and 52 in 2008) were somewhat allayed by sources who told us the number of HR personnel looking after them had risen accordingly, and 'the firm is doing all it can to ensure growth isn't detrimental to the training.'

A kind of magic

W&C asks long hours of its lawyers and not even an economic slowdown has put paid to that. A few sources spoke of solid weeks of staying until 2am or even 3am, but one interviewee assured us they worked 'no harder than trainees at 'other' magic circle firms.' This Freudian slip perhaps says a lot about the standard against which W&C trainees match themselves. The atmosphere varies greatly depending on the department you're in. EIPAF, for example, is said to be most hierarchical. Or maybe that should be least non-hierarchical – the office has a relaxed dress code and a culture that usually means 'you can talk to a partner like you'd talk to a trainee.' What's more, 'it's no problem having a beer with a partner.' Our interviewees told us the firm has an open and honest culture, and this was borne out by recruits' frank answers to our questions about those partner departures. As one summed up: 'At other firms trainees might be prepped on what to tell you. There's nothing of that at all here. They're not worried about the opinion we'll give.'

Confidence is common among trainees, who have come from 'every nook and cranny of the planet.' As one put it: 'If I bumped into a couple of W&C people in a bar, I'd be surprised if they were both English.' There are a fair few Oxbridge scarves in the crowd, but all the top universities get a look in. In an environment where 'meritocracy is the key,' diversity isn't just a buzzword. 'People are quite comfortable being gay' here, and the firm flies people to other offices to participate in diversity weeks. However, one interviewee did worry that in certain departments' long hours made juggling work and a family difficult.

Socially we hear that going to the pub with smaller teams can feel a bit 'like hanging out with your uncles,' however larger groups live a bit larger. Departments have ski trips, and if you organise your seat choices well you could end up going on more than one. The summer and Christmas parties are always fun, and trainees can sign up for yoga or salsa classes. The White & Case World Cup brings five-a-side teams from most of the global offices – it's football for the guys and volleyball for the girls. The Prague team consistently owns all comers: 'We're not sure how much work they do in Prague. Maybe it's all just training.' Pro bono is 'a big deal' and staff have given advice at the Royal Courts of Justice CAB, helped set up a London branch for an AIDS awareness charity and even received awards for their work with human rights groups. You may notice at law fairs that W&C pledges money to charity instead of giving away free goodies.

And finally...

Anyone with a strong interest in finance, a desire for major international work and a passport itching to be stamped will thrive at W&C. In 2008 21 out of its 25 qualifiers stayed on.

Wiggin LLP

The facts

Locations: Cheltenham, London

Number of UK partners/solicitors: 16/22

Total Number of Trainees: 8

Seats: 4x6 months

Alternative seats: Occasional secondments

> Wiggin's success so far suggests the wisdom of its founders' idea of the happy medium – a London-quality outfit in a relaxed regional setting, it transcends geography and is a London firm outside of London.

Do you love film and TV? Do you wonder whether it's possible to combine your passion with the law? You can, and Wiggin is the place to do it – its client list reads like Steven Spielberg's Rolodex. Calm yourself for a minute: this media law specialist only offers a few contracts each year, so get in line.

Boutique call

Judging by its slick website, being at the cutting edge of media practice isn't enough for Wiggin, it also needs clients to perceive it as being at the most honed point of that cutting edge. Buzzwords like 'web 2.0', 'new media' and…er…'cutting edge' abound on a site festooned with the firm's multicoloured, asymmetric branding, randomly ticking counters and a flashy corporate video. Delicate and cloistered legal-geeks that we are at the *Student Guide*, the thumping techno soundtrack and flashing slogans in the video soon had our pulses racing, and with even the telephone hold music achingly avant-garde, we soon needed a long lie-down in a darkened room. As a true boutique firm, Wiggin has no such sensitivities. It lives, breathes and believes all things media. It has teams of lawyers specialising in film, sport, broadcast, technology, music, gaming and publishing. Heck, fashion is rumoured to be the next frontier. In the past year the lawyers have worked for Virgin Media on all aspects of the launch of the Setanta Sports News channel, helped Manchester United acquire ITV's one-third stake in Manchester United TV, defended *FHM* in libel claims brought by Frank Warren and Ricky Hatton, and secured one of the highest-ever copyright damages awards for the British Phonographic Industry (BPI) in its £41m victory against CD WOW! It was also appointed a preferred adviser on Man U's first-ever legal panel. And it doesn't stop there – Wiggin works for Al Jazeera, Granada International, Channel 4, Channel Five, Twentieth Century Fox, EMI, Warner Bros., New Line, Paramount, FilmFour, MySpace, Playboy, Virgin Media, BT, Macmillan, *Heat* magazine, *Condé Nast*…

The rights stuff

The good news is that Wiggin's four-seat rotation is permeated with media work. Indeed, every team apart from the small music group takes its own trainees, so 'there's no desperate competition to get a specific seat.' And with Wiggin being a 'partner-heavy' operation, there's plenty of direct exposure to whatever the chief Wiggsters are working on. In the field of electronic and online gambling, BT asked the firm to look at the competitions/gambling portal on its 'BT Vision' ADSL platform and ITV asked for advice on its deal with PartyGaming for the use of ITV services and content. Meanwhile, the broadcast media team covers TV, radio and 'all the new online stuff,' perhaps advising clients like Emap or UKTV on negotiations with Sky for digital carriage of their channels' portfolios. This kind of work shows trainees that 'you really having to know the business of your clients.' Growing on the back of the broadcast team and via a prominent hire from Olswang, sports law has increased in importance for Wiggin. It now receives instructions from the likes of Setanta, the ICC, and the less well-known Passion TV concerning pan-African distribution of 2008 Beijing Olympics audiovisual rights. Exciting times are to be had in the film team, where the two partners have first-hand experience as studio executives. Between them, they handle both the financing and production of films. 'You see the guys representing the producer and the moneymen,' trainees enthused. Our sources had also been involved in drafting agreements for writers, director, actors, crew, and pretty much anyone else who might be involved in making a movie. The finance side is more transactional, so there's the odd midnight deal closing and 'conference calls about how to tie down the rights to a film.' Clients include all the major studios and a fair few independent production companies. *Night at the Museum 2* and the *Wolverine* prequel are just a couple of the features on which the team has worked recently.

Wiggin's contentious practice is largely split between publishing and music. Last year lawyers defended *Look* magazine from privacy claims made by Geri Halliwell and Ashley and Cheryl Cole, and they successfully overturned a libel conviction against Orion Books and the author of police tell-all *Bent Coppers*. In relation to music, the firm acted in several illegal downloading cases for the UK record industry, including UK proceedings against Russian website AllofMP3. And then there was the defence of Turf TV, which had become embroiled in a major dispute with the bookmaking industry concerning competition law issues surrounding the licensing of audio-visual and data rights to British racing. That case led to 'some bleak times' for trainees. Over the course of three months every available body in the office was called in to help complete a mammoth disclosure exercise numbering up to a million documents. Trainees say it was 'an astounding example of everyone pulling together.'

Another pure media seat option is a secondment to the BPI in London. Here, trainees answer questions from every section of the organisation, while working with ISPs to stop illegal downloading. The seat is made all the more exciting by perks such as free tickets to the Brit Awards or their classical counterparts and a generous budget for London accommodation. One trainee recently spent three months at BPI's international sister organisation, the IFPI, and this may be repeated in the future. Back in Cheltenham, corporate and property seats are probably the least popular options, but even these 'support departments' work almost exclusively for the firm's media clients. The client might be selling one arm of its business, refinancing music catalogues, acquiring a trendy new Soho office or needing landlord and tenant advice. Corporate in particular is 'a good first seat,' as it involves plenty of research tasks and provides client contact. There's also some involvement with more adminny chores, such as running bankruptcy checks and document bibling ('the bane of every trainee's life'), but trainees know that they are 'a valuable member of the team and people do need our help.'

Chambers UK rankings

Defamation/Reputation Management • Intellectual Property • Licensing • Media & Entertainment • Sports Law

All our interviewees raved about the exposure and responsibility they'd had; however, the job can be tough and 'just because you're in the Cotswolds it doesn't mean you escape long hours.' The working days can take it out of you, particularly when a journey to London is required. Everyone agrees: 'This is not a place for the faint-hearted.'

Walloping good fun

So let's talk about the elephant in the room. Cheltenham seems an odd place for a media boutique, right? 'Major Hollywood studios probably haven't heard of it,' deadpanned one source. Maybe not, but there are no plans to grow too much bigger or shift permanent legal staff to London. Wiggin's success so far suggests the wisdom of its founders' idea of 'the happy medium' – a London-quality outfit in a relaxed regional setting. Our sources say Wiggin transcends geography and is 'a London firm outside of London.' It has achieved this partly through its hot-desking office in the capital that is used as temporary base for fee earners. A 'slightly more garish' version of the Cheltenham HQ, the decor in the London pad is judged to perfection: widescreen televisions, Nintendo Wii and bowls of sweeties smack of an ad agency. The office has even been used as a film location. When going to London, trainees hop on the train or cadge a lift in one of the firm's chauffeured cars. Longer trips mean the ordeal of staying in glitzy hotels.

Once back in beautiful Cheltenham, the benefits of Cotswold life are obvious. You can walk to work from a house you can afford, and long hours become more bearable when 'you know you don't have far to go home.' The 'gorgeous' office is in 'a really nice Regency-style building' with a few surprises on the inside. The fuchsia pink, lime green, orange-yellow, purple and grey website colour scheme 'is unfortunately reflected on the walls and floors.' Apparently, each team was allowed to choose its own colour scheme, and while most opted for subtlety, the litigators didn't. 'It's extremely bright there,' said one dazed recruit. It must be hard for people to dress to match the office decor. Everyone is 'suited and booted for meetings,' but otherwise 'there's no code whatsoever.' Even when in the London office trainees can get away with kicking off their shoes.

London will always trump the Cotswolds for nightlife, but Cheltenham has its moments. The town is famous for its literature and jazz festivals, and there are always things going on at the theatre, ballet and, of course, the racecourse. Bar-wise, the Hotel du Vin makes a mean mojito cocktail. Most of the firm's organised events are guaranteed to be well lubricated. 'I had all these grand visions of outdoor exercise,' sighed one recruit, 'but it turns out all I do is eat cake and drink alcohol.' We're really not suggesting that staff and partners are overly fond of pop, but it's interesting that trainees received a bottle of champagne on their first day, crates of wine each at Christmas and a few bottles of the firm's 2007 Christmas card substitute – Wiggin Wallop beer. Calories gained can be worked off by joining the Wiggin football team, which must be half decent because two associates were recently chosen to play for the London Lawyers team in the Lawyers World Cup.

Bigwiggs

As befits its meeja identity and sociable nature, Wiggin likes its trainees to be outgoing, 'not someone who's going to be a spud in the corner.' Some of our sources had been taken out for a drink by partners after their training contract interview: 'They wanted to see what you were like inside and outside the office.' It goes without saying that evidence of genuine enthusiasm for media work will distinguish you from the crowd of applicants. Some trainees will have worked in, say, publishing or the music industry before applying to Wiggin, but don't worry too much if all you have on your CV is some relevant summer work experience or student journalism.

In this partner-heavy firm, where the big-Wiggs are generally preoccupied with top-level work, trainees need to be independent-minded. Seat allocation is also best navigated by those who reiterate their preferences as they go along, and don't be too surprised if appraisals don't always happen when they're supposed to. Some sources told us they found it 'refreshing' not being endlessly looked after; others clearly would have preferred more formal feedback than the 'trickle-down' they'd received. This said, no one is left in the dark about how they're doing: informal feedback is always available and partners are approachable. So much so that trainees will wax lyrical for hours about individual partners.

The 'frightening' qualification process did cause a few grumbles. While the failure to retain any trainees in 2007 was described as a one-off, it was playing on trainees' minds when we interviewed them. There was better news in 2008: two of the three qualifiers accepted jobs with the firm.

And finally...

Anyone seriously interested in media law should apply here. We had a tip-off that partners appreciate applicants who show a little initiative in their applications, yet we'd advise you to interpret this with care. As media lawyers these recruiters will have seen more gimmicks than most.

Wilsons

The facts

Location: Salisbury

Number of UK partners/solicitors: 30/37

Total number of trainees: 10

Seats: 4x6 months

Alternative seats: Occasional secondments

The firm worked on the establishment and registration of new charity Help for Heroes, which supports wounded servicemen and women.

This Salisbury firm has been around for more than 275 years, but it wasn't until the mid-1970s that its star began to ascend beyond Wiltshire.

Wiltshire gem

In the 1990s, as big City firms ditched their private client departments in favour of commercial practice, Wilsons took up the slack, hiring lawyers from the best London firms – most notably the team of McKenna & Co (now CMS Cameron McKenna). Accompanied by a substantial increase in individual wealth in the UK, this decision has paid dividends: its turnover has doubled over the past six years, hitting the £13m mark. Not only is Wilsons ranked in the top band of *Chambers UK* for its tax, trusts and probate advice, the firm is a whiz at family law, agricultural affairs and charity law, where its team is one of the biggest in the country. With litigation, these areas make up a substantial portion of the firm's business, commercial property, corporate and employment filling in the gaps.

An old firm doesn't have to be old-fashioned, say trainees, who describe Wilsons as 'exciting and expanding.' True, the dress code might be formal and things might get a little 'stuffy and public school-esque' in the private client department, but 'on the whole it's incredibly forward-thinking, and they're great at training you and keeping you up-to-date. I'd say 95% of the partners are helpful and approachable.' Not one to rest on its laurels, Wilsons has clients from 45 countries and sends staff to Hong Kong twice a year to promote business. Something like 10% of its revenue is due to international activities, with demand for offshore tax and trust advice for overseas clients particularly high. Pretty impressive for a Salisbury firm.

And speaking of Salisbury, trainees just love their location, telling us the firm is unlikely to change its hometown. Maybe so, but that's not to say another office isn't on the cards. Indeed, Wilsons has already indicated that a London branch would be a 'natural progression,' and its current recruitment drive is taking place with this possibility in mind.

All squashed up

Just as last year, the trainees we interviewed at Wilsons were happy to report that 'nearly all of us have got all the seats we wanted.' Where sacrifices have to be made, people can be brought around to the firm's thinking: 'I was told I had to drop one of my choices and wasn't happy about it. In hindsight, it was justified because now all of my seats complement the area I want to qualify into.' Unless economic conditions dictate otherwise, trainees also benefit from knowing exactly which seats they'll cover from day one. 'The whole two years are mapped out before you start,' explained one source, adding: 'It's great to have that certainty.' The firm encourages as many people as possible to try the property and charities law departments and the main private client seat is justifiably popular.

Seen as something of a poor relation by some trainees, the probate seat is not the main prize. Not that time spent there is wasted: the focus is on wealthier clients whose assets exceed the £300,000 taxable threshold and it's actually a good choice for charity-minded folk, as they learn 'there's a lot of administration of estates for charities so it ties in nicely.' Total independence isn't possible in probate; the rewards come instead from good client contact, with 'lots of meetings with other solicitors and clients, from little old ladies with wills to wealthy individuals with massive estates.' The job entails trawling through old files, tying up loose ends, selling off shares and that kind of thing. The more glamorous side of the private client department has two sub groups – 'the off-shore/new wealth is on one side, the landed estates/old money on the other.' Trainees can dabble in both. Said one: 'There were a couple of matters I managed myself, but trusts can be complex, so often you can't take charge of anything as a trainee.' Towards the end of a seat here, some people might be lucky enough to see clients on their own: 'Just for simple things like will drafting, helping them to understand documents or taking instructions.' 'I went to a gentleman's house to witness the signing of his will,' added one source. Clients are for the most part entirely courteous to rookie lawyers – clearly times have changed since managing partner Jonathan Stephens was a trainee. In a recent interview he recounted his worst experience as the time he went with a partner to an old lady's house to witness her will. The partner enjoyed a glass of champagne, while he, at 22 years old, was offered orange squash.

Where there's muck there's brass

The property department features its own landed estates team. 'I ran a few files,' recalled a source; 'there was a purchase of unregistered woodland, which was a bit unusual, a statutory declaration for a restriction to be noted at the Land Registry, and some dabbling in residential stuff.' Such dabbling is pretty useful as residential property experiences provide an important foundation for more complex files. The firm works on numerous agricultural matters, whether it's the sale of farms or leases of farmland. You'd better dig out those festival wellies because trainees can expect to tramp around a fair few fields and farmyards. As well as sizing up the boundaries, 'if it's a huge piece of land, you have to get an idea of where the pipelines lie.' Churches are another interesting area of work. 'They're registering a lot of land, so I'm going through old deeds. There are sometimes unusual cases, such as registering land which wasn't there until the sea moved further out.'

The litigation department offers an equally engaging experience and covers a variety of disputes. There's a contentious trust and probate team and a property/commercial litigation group. 'They're very good at taking you along to meetings,' remarked one interviewee, 'and sometimes you're the point of contact for the client.' Typical tasks include researching obscure points, drafting simple documents and liaising with barristers. 'One of the highlights is the week-long secondment to barristers chambers

Chambers UK rankings

Agriculture & Rural Affairs • Charities • Corporate Finance • Dispute Resolution • Employment • Family/Matrimonial • Private Client • Real Estate

in London. I was in the High Court every day, which was simply excellent. It's good for developing relationships with barristers too, and they're lovely – they really look after you while you're there.'

The firm's renowned charities practice has recently become a victim of its own success. In 2008, head of the group Alison McKenna was appointed as president of the recently formed Charity Tribunal, which will provide an independent route of appeal for charities. Still, we have no doubts the team will continue to thrive. It recently won the mandate to set up Butterfly World, a £25m butterfly dome near St Albans, and also worked on the establishment and registration of new charity Help for Heroes, which supports wounded servicemen and women. Trainees split their time between setting up and managing charities and sampling contentious matters. The contentious lawyers represent prestigious charities such as Cancer Research UK, RSPCA, RNLI and Guide Dogs for the Blind, helping them resolve disputes over wills and legacies. 'The seat can be really interesting. On the contentious side there's a bit of bundling, but when there's a trial on it means you really know the case after all the preparation, so you can follow it through point by point.'

Gaining experience of commercial law wasn't a priority for the trainees we spoke to, and it's understandable given Wilsons' prowess in the areas we've already outlined. However, the firm does offer employment and corporate/commercial seats where you can encounter 'a completely different sort of client,' and our interviewees acknowledged that the commercial group provides 'great training' and does good-quality work. The business clients attracted to the firm include Turftrax, which provides horseracing data to the betting and television industries, bookshop chain Blackwell, Plum Baby organic baby foods and up-market estate agency Savills.

Being Jeremy Clarkson

Across the departments, the hours are said to be 'excellent,' even if you can be 'horrendously busy' at times. 'They don't want to overburden you with work,' explained one trainee. 'And the supervisors are quite good at keeping an eye on your workload. They take an interest without being completely overbearing.'

Wilsons has four offices, one of which is 'modern, new and airy,' while the other three are 'more typically officey.' No guesses as to which building the client rooms are in. While working in one building would be preferable – 'it can be irritating if you need something from another building' – so often the only way to achieve this is decamping to a business park. Trainees balk at this idea, telling us they'd miss the city centre. 'It's such a pretty place, and we're just down the street from Debenhams if you fancy some lunchtime shopping.' At least all four offices are within easy walking distance of each other.

A busy social life gets staff together for quizzes, wine tastings, go-karting and the odd fancy dress party. 'They have stuff going on all the time. There's netball and cricket in the summer, and we sponsor the Salisbury Playhouse so we get free tickets.' Last year Wilsons' Christmas ball was held at the National Motor Museum at Beaulieu, which proved popular with the boys. 'There were cars everywhere; we had champagne in the museum and then a lovely meal.' The one thing our interviewees thought could improve their social life is a few trainee-only events funded by the firm. 'But we go for lunch and drinks anyway, it's quite easy to meet up.'

In 2008 the trainees were mostly younger graduates, but 'one of us has been a secretary here for years and next year there will be some people in their thirties joining.' A link to the area is likely to help your application, if only because the firm looks for candidates who are interested in the long haul. It's clearly not a deal breaker though as 'there's a girl with a very broad Yorkshire accent in our year.' We also learned that bagging a 2:1 was not always essential, although the firm has now made this a requirement. 'I know they've changed the system of interviewing trainees,' remarked a source. 'It used to be an interview in the same year that you started your contract, but now they're doing it two years in advance and they're setting exams.' Before you start panicking, we checked with HR and it's a straightforward assessment day.

Wilsons is a member of a training network called Law South and this allows trainees to acquaint themselves with their peers at other reputable firms. It also provides an opportunity to see where Wilsons comes up trumps. And where does it? 'Well, the salary may not be as good as elsewhere, but I think we get quite a lot of responsibility here, and the hours are great.' It's a package that appealed to two of the four 2008 qualifiers: they took jobs in the private client and litigation departments.

And finally...

We'll let one of the trainees have the final word: 'This firm has a great reputation and the quality of work you get, particularly in the private client area, doesn't get much better than this. A barrister from Switzerland randomly rang me up one day with a question about a trust worth £50m.'

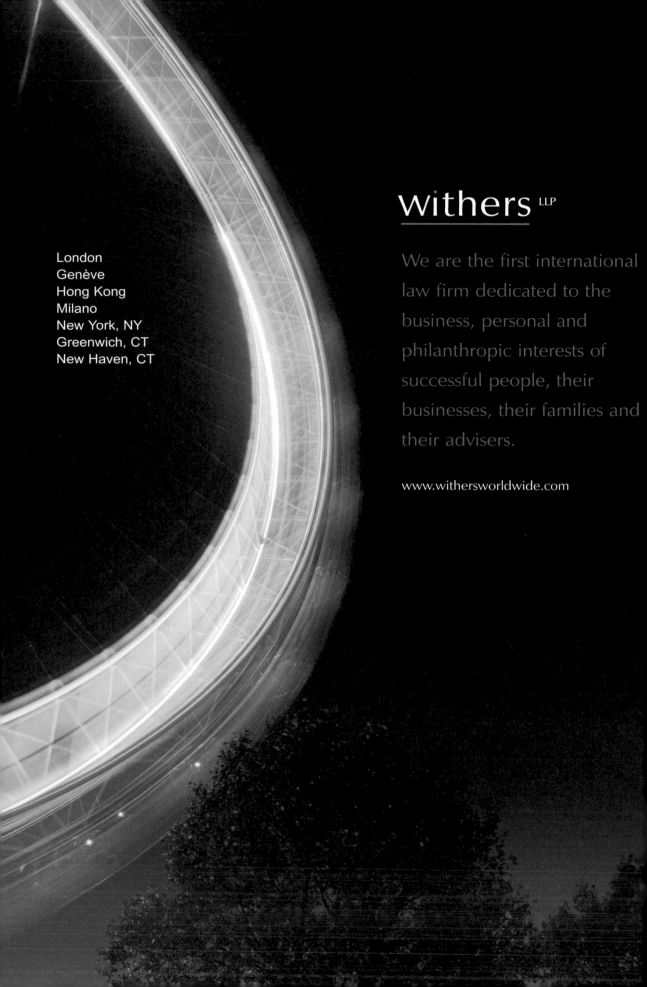

Withers LLP

The facts

Location: London

Number of UK partners/solicitors: 65/112

Total number of trainees: 32

Seats: 4x6 months

Alternative seats: Overseas seats, secondments

Extras: Pro bono – CAB at the Principal Registry, Own-It IP advice service; language training

Withers reportedly acts for 15% of the *Sunday Times Rich List*, and thanks to their deep pockets trainees get involved in some juicy and rather hush-hush work.

Withers is a thoroughbred among law firms. Although known for its top-notch private client practice, you shouldn't assume that means fusty offices, blue-blooded clients and doddery partners. Al contrario, while its core practices are as firmly set in stone as the office's Georgian façade, its steel-and-glass office interior is almost as slick as its award-winning website.

Whither Withers?

Commercial practice group leader and Milan managing partner Anthony Indaimo has recently been appointed as Withers' new chairman, to succeed Diana Parker, the 'fabulous' doyenne of family law who acted for Mrs Miller in the ground-breaking divorce case Miller v Miller. So does Indaimo's appointment, together with a 'shiny-gloss' rebrand, signal a fundamental shift towards commercial work and away from the firm's traditional strengths? As one astute trainee observed: 'It could suggest the firm is moving in a more corporate direction, but I don't see that happening in practice. Private client is still nearly half the firm.' All our sources agreed on this point: Withers may well have undergone a 'catchy and cool revamp' which 'sells well,' but the firm is likely to stay much the same no matter how many new commercial clients are attracted to do business here. And besides, the type of commercial organisations that come Withers' way tend to be fashionable and fun – we're talking Renault Formula One, UK Film Council, Moschino, Matthew Williamson and Soho House.

One of Withers' key selling points is its spread of offices around Europe and America's centres of wealth. At the beginning of 2008 a Hong Kong office was launched, adding the firm's first Asian base to a list that already included Geneva, Milan, New York, New Haven and Greenwich, Connecticut. The firm seems intent on pursuing further expansion wherever it perceives a profitable gap in the private client market. We even heard rumblings of 'two or three more places they may go to in future.'

More Dragons' Den than Brideshead Revisited

No seat is compulsory, but because of the sheer size of the department 'you will probably do a seat in wealth planning.' The middle classes might be feeling the squeeze, yet there is no sign of a credit crunch among Withers' 'mega-rich' clientele. Just how rich are they? According to one trainee, a client with only £4–5m to throw around is practically a pauper, or at least the sort of person whose business would be handled by a trainee. It follows, you'd think, that for considerably wealthier foreign clients £30K is a small price to pay for freedom from being taxed on their worldwide income. Yet Withers, along with rivals Macfarlanes and Charles Russell, recently lobbied against the government's proposed non-dom tax reforms. It's the principle of the thing.

Domestic and international wealth planning for trust companies, private and investment banks and the super-rich remains central to Withers' success, and year on year the firm is top-rated by *Chambers UK* in this field. Its client base is changing: 'The focus has moved on from the old-school, green wellies type of client to the new-money entrepreneur who has made a lot and wants to make more.' Withers reportedly acts for 15% of the *Sunday Times Rich List,* and thanks to their deep pockets trainees get involved in some juicy and rather hush-hush work. 'I helped on a huge piece of tax planning for some overseas-based clients who wanted to put about half a billion dollars into trust to protect it from political unrest,' revealed one. More often clients are motivated by the simple desire to keep their money from the taxman.

The private client group encompasses three subsections – international wealth planning, FAB and FITT. FAB stands for 'family and business' but apparently almost picked up an even odder name. 'For a long time it was going to be called family planning. They got quite far into the process before they realised that wasn't a good idea.' The FITT (funds, investments, tax and trusts) team is a recent invention, launched last year following the arrival of a new partner. Reflecting the link between the two, FITT's work covers private client and corporate matters. 'Being the FAB trainee doesn't sound quite as sexy as being the FITT trainee,' suggested one source, however FAB's landed clients have their own appeal. Many 'have been with the firm for centuries' and own 'vast swathes of countryside and several villages.'

Breaking up is hard to do

In almost all private client seats 'you must get to grips with the Yellow Book,' a delightfully dense compendium of tax legislation. It takes much longer than six months to build up sufficient technical knowledge, nevertheless trainees have a go at drafting 'letters and explanatory memos to clients, trying to put a fantastically complicated answer into easily understandable language.' Don't be put off by the complexity of tax and trusts law: 'You pick up little snippets along the way and eventually you see how it all comes together.' Weekly training sessions run by partners and assistants are a great help. However, just before we went to press it was announced that four Withers partners were jumping ship to join Forsters' private client team, following in the footsteps of two other private client partners in 2007. When we last checked, the two firms had locked horns over the matter.

Many would-be family lawyers dream of working at Withers. Read any text on matrimonial finance and you'll see Withers' cases – Miller, Charman, Crossley, et al. This is the place where wealthy ex-wives are made. As a novice in such an eminent team, it's a thrilling experience the first time you find yourself 'striding through the High Court' or 'watching a partner negotiate a good deal, so the client can still put his children through private school.' In this 'fast and busy' environment, trainees tend to be given less responsibility than in other seats, so they 'spend a lot

Chambers UK rankings

Agriculture & Rural Affairs • Charities • Employment • Family/Matrimonial • Fraud: Civil • Intellectual Property • Private Client • Professional Negligence

of time putting together bundles of documents and attendance notes from all the exciting meetings you get to go to.' One explained that 'people are paying an awful lot of money for what is essentially divorce and tax advice, so the firm needs to justify the hourly rates by providing an absolutely top level of service. Trainees make mistakes.'

Given Withers' reputation in the field, the view is that 'it would be stupid not to do a seat in family,' and quite naturally 'there is always more than one person who turns up wanting to do it, firing on all cylinders and desperate to make a good impression.' What they soon learn is that only a few NQ jobs become available in the department (only one in each of the past three years) and some family-hungry qualifiers find themselves without a job. Withers hopes to solve this problem by hiring trainees 'who are interested in more than just family or private client.' It may be difficult to break the cycle because, as one typical source put it: 'Why would you come to Withers if you weren't interested in private client?' Perhaps disproving the point, in 2008, 11 out of 13 qualifiers were offered jobs and accepted them.

Get fitt

On the corporate side of the FITT team trainees find themselves 'working one minute for a banking partner on some £50m security deal, then drafting board minutes and agreements for a share buy-back.' Withers provides standalone corporate and financial advice to 'small to medium-value entrepreneurs,' often referred from the wealth planning side of the business. The exchange between corporate and private client lawyers is made all the easier by their proximity, so 'if you've got a daft question on funds, rather than ploughing through research you can just pop over and ask.' In the highest (read most expensive) echelons, corporate and private client work begin to look quite similar – 'in both departments you're just moving £150m of assets about.' One trainee exemplified a typical client as a millionaire hedge fund manager who comes to Withers to set up a family trust and leaves with 'a tax-efficient corporate structure for his latest investment fund.'

As a private client seat has its commercial elements, so too does a charities seat. The team 'acts for huge money-making machines,' providing 'the same commercial advice, just tinged with charities legislation.' Commercial litigation could involve anything from media and art disputes to complex fraud cases or professional negligence claims, where trainees might help defend barristers and discover 'it's good fun to be a lawyer's lawyer.' The employment team represents both employers and employees. Until she reportedly decided that the firm's fees were a bit too rich for her blood, Gillian Switalski, former legal head of F&C Asset Management, instructed the department in her multimillion-pound sex discrimination, harassment and victimisation claim. In this smaller team trainees can sink their teeth into 'drafting briefs to counsel and witness statements and generally doing what qualified solicitors do.' The IP department was 'a particularly pleasant surprise' for one source who hadn't even realised it existed. The team has now been transformed into a multidisciplinary amalgam of straight IP, IP-related commercial litigators and corporate lawyers, charmingly if rather inexplicably called Sparkle. Clearly the marketing gurus couldn't come up with a suitable acronym.

Speaking in tongues

Parla italiano, parlez vous français or sprechen Sie Deutsche? If so, you'll fit right in. Almost all trainees have some linguistic capability, no surprise given Withers' large international client base. One trainee hinted it wouldn't go down well if in a meeting with French clients the trainee's attendance note simply read: 'There has been some discussion in French.' Italian speakers are especially sought after because of the buzzing Milan office. Before you brag about your italiano on your application form, make sure your Gucci shades are packed, as 'if you speak Italian you will be sent to Milan.' Get your English up to scratch too – the recruitment process includes a test of your ability to translate verbose phrases into plain English, as well as a presentation on one of five set topics. Those who make it through are described as 'quite scarily bright and very focused.' The Oxbridge contingent is always present, even if its size varies with each intake. And confidence is a necessary characteristic, as people are often left to 'just get on with it.' Ambition is a recurring theme too: 'The partners look like they've got it all. It makes you aspire to become one of them one day.'

After hours, trainees seem to be as comfortable shooting in wax jackets as they are sharing drinks over 'highly acrimonious games of Connect Four and Guess Who' or duking it out at a pub quiz organised by the social committee. Our sources actually admitted that Withers is 'a bit on the quiet side socially because we don't have a jolly corporate budget to take clients out boozing.' At least individual departments are good for the occasional cocktail. After a rather disappointing office-bound fête a few years ago, Withers 'is getting good at the Christmas party.' Last year it splashed out on festivities at the top of Tower Bridge and 'everyone made an effort to look a bit glam.' Apparently 'after a few drinks, with everyone dancing, the bridge starts to sway...'

And finally...

Like its trouser-shaped London office, Withers straddles private client and commercial work. It is rooted in its esteemed past but focusing hard on a more commercial future. If you fancy striking a similar pose, then start practising your presentation skills.

Wragge & Co LLP

The facts

Location: Birmingham, London

Number of UK partners/solicitors: 112/330

Total number of trainees: 63

Seats: 4x6 months

Alternative seats: Secondments

Extras: Pro bono – College of Law and other advice schemes; language training

> Wragges is known for its emphasis on the individual. There is an element of unconventionality and people are not straightlaced.

Wragge & Co has all the ingredients for a great training contract. It has a stellar client list, including many FTSE 100 and FTSE 250 companies, lets trainees get stuck into meaty work and is renowned for its team ethos.

Message in a bottle

Wragge has built itself a fine reputation both within and beyond its original hometown Birmingham. The firm is highly regarded in many fields, as evidenced by the top-level rankings it achieves in *Chambers UK*. It's a powerhouse in all the mainstream commercial areas – real estate, corporate finance, dispute resolution – and excels in a variety of specialist areas – tax, employment, pensions, intellectual property, information technology projects and outsourcing, to name just a few. Wragge's client list is a testament to its achievements: British Airways, Heinz Europe, Pirelli UK, E.ON, AstraZeneca, The Wellcome Trust, 3i, Cadbury Schweppes and Marks & Spencer are all fans. The HQ in Birmingham is much bigger than the second office in the capital, and each now recruits its own trainees, 25 in Brum and five in the capital. Unsurprisingly, London 'has more of a relaxed, small-firm atmosphere, where everyone knows your name.' Birmingham is both the seat of power and the firm's spiritual home. Presently split over three buildings in Brum, in 2011 everyone will move into a newly built office at Two Snowhill.

A major plc famously said of this firm: 'If you could bottle the atmosphere in your offices and sell it, you'd make a fortune.' Wragge also gets the nod of approval from the *Financial Times* and *Sunday Times,* appearing in both the 50 Best Large Workplaces in Europe and 100 Best Companies to Work For in the UK surveys. What exactly makes Wragge so different? Open-plan offices and glass walls contribute to the 'non-hierarchical and happily busy' atmosphere. Workstations are the same throughout the office, 'so at first you can't tell who is a partner and who is a secretary.' Partners are described as 'approachable and willing to come out drinking on a Friday night,' while senior partner Quentin Poole is 'happy to do his fair share of the tea round… although perhaps not quite in the waiter style shown by the recruitment brochure.' Trainees are given ample opportunity to voice their opinions, from a monthly intranet chat room hosted by Poole and managing partner Ian Metcalfe, to the People First Committee – a forum for everyone from secretary to partner. There is also a Bright Ideas Page on the intranet, with the added incentive of a bottle of bubbly if your idea is used. The firm earned green credentials as winner of the 2008 Lafarge Eco-Efficiency Award and commits much to the pro bono cause – in 2007 staff spent 7,000 hours on such activities. Unquestionably Wragge considers the interests of its staff and endeavours to give this aspect of its business high priority.

A-list clientele

As well as the obligatory contentious seat, trainees must do a stint in real estate and a corporate seat (which can be 'pretty much anything that isn't property'). In the mainstream corporate/M&A department they can expect to be involved in massive transactions. Last year there was a trio of cross-border deals worth £1.03bn for leading European developer of distribution centers Parkridge, and the team represented Lloyds TSB Development Capital on its £40m investment in property consultancy GVA Grimley. It also advised the management of The AA on its £6.15bn merger with Saga. Other clients include Northgate Information Systems, Barratt Homes and Dyson. Private equity is a key element of the practice and we did note that some sources spoke regretfully of their lack of experience with public company work. No one had any problems with the level of responsibility they'd been given: trainees are able to take rewarding roles on deals, with plenty of client contact and drafting assignments to accompany more adminny tasks. And trainees' names are included when deals are announced, leading some of our sources to cite this recognition as a real high point of their time at the firm.

For a fast-paced six months try one of the two commercial development and investment teams within the property department. This group is composed of 'incredibly driven people working for big, big names.' Here, 'you can get involved almost straight away;' trainees are given their own files and there is plenty of over-the-phone client contact. The other team consists of 'more typically Wragges people – extremely friendly and never an angry word.' Much of the work centres on large shopping developments, and again trainees can get stuck in, making site visits, handling queries and running lease assignments. In London, lawyers have been helping client Development Securities on its acquisition of a 1.5-acre site in Hammersmith town centre from London Underground. The office-led, mixed-use scheme will have an estimated end value of around £250m. The Birmingham lawyers have a hand in numerous city centre projects, including Argent Group's purchase of a former catering academy at Brindleyplace and ROC International Towers' plan to build a skyscraper and theme park in the sky at Eastside.

The litigation team handles all manner of disputes from bog-standard contractual spats, to banking and insurance claims and political dingdongs. The Liberal Democrats turned to Wragge when it had the Electoral Commission on its back following £2.4m of donations from fraudster Michael Brown. In another case, lawyers represented insurers in connection with a £150m claim arising out of a leak at the Thorp reprocessing facility at Sellafield. Other clients include Scottish and Newcastle, QinetiQ, Goodyear Dunlop Tyres UK, government department BERR and Birds Eye.

Public displays of affection

Away from the main departments, choice seats include the highly successful IP team and employment/pensions, both of which are oversubscribed. For the latter, trainees seem to prefer the London group for its 'extremely driven vibe – you get the impression they are pioneers paving the way and it's exciting to be part of that.' Secondments

Chambers UK rankings

Administrative & Public Law • Advertising & Marketing • Aviation • Banking & Finance • Banking Litigation • Competition/European Law • Construction • Corporate Finance • Debt Recovery • Dispute Resolution • Employment • Environment • Healthcare • Information Technology • Insurance • Intellectual Property • Life Sciences • Local Government • Outsourcing • Pensions • Pensions Litigation • Planning • Product Liability • Projects, Energy & Natural Resources • Public Procurement • Real Estate • Real Estate Litigation • Restructuring/Insolvency • Retail • Tax • Telecommunications • Transport

to household-name clients are also on offer and trainees seem to enjoy the opportunity to 'be in the arms of the client, yet still attached to Wragge.' For now there are no overseas seats, although the firm has recently opened a Hong Kong office.

Supervision ranges from 'hands-off to hand-holding, relaxed to rigorous' and all stages in between. Trainees agree that 'despite being busy, people here have always got time to talk something through.' For a firm of this size and with the calibre of clients it serves, we are delighted to report 'fantastic hours, with very few obscenely late nights.' In fact, some trainees pass their whole contract without a single all-nighter and 'leaving at 5.31pm is fine as long as you've done your work.' Designed to aid work-life balance, Wragge recently launched a flexible working policy. Staff only need informal permission from their immediate line manager and are not required to give reasons for keeping flexible hours. In June 2008, 28% of associates and 5% of equity partners were working flexible hours.

Trainees are allocated a buddy in the year above them, and each person has a principal for impartial advice and out-of-office drinks. Appraisals are scheduled every three months, both part way through and at the end of each seat. When it comes to training, internal, external, online and video-linked sessions abound.

Capital connections

One criticism from some Brum trainees related to the number of seats they could take in London. Usually it is just the one, though clearly a few people had hoped for more. One spoke of 'cut-throat competition' for time in the capital. Arguably anyone wanting to spend so much of their training in London should now be looking at one of the five London contracts, although Brum trainees will still be able to ask for London seats and London trainees will be able to request time in the Midlands 'mothership.' Current trainees are interested to see how the new two-site recruitment will fit with Wragge's single-team ethos. 'It's a sensible move, but I don't think the two concepts gel,' said one. 'They'll have to be careful how they market this to fit with the single-team brand.'

Opportunities to socialise are in hearty supply in Birmingham. Trainees go to departmental drinks and then head on to the Old Joint Stock or the less sophisticated Walkabout on Broad Street. There is also 'a large platter' of sporting activities to choose from, including football, cricket, netball, Ultimate Frisbee and pub Olympics. With fewer trainees in London, outings tend to be team or office-wide. In each location 'Wragge really makes an effort to ensure trainees get to know each other,' and this includes being invited to the Christmas party before you even start your contract. Be sure to accept – the party is a corker and includes all sorts of amusements, including an indoor helter-skelter. The annual trainee away day is another great bonding opportunity: at the last one they rejuvenated a school allotment in the morning and went off-road karting in the afternoon. A decision to team up with the College of Law in Birmingham to provide a compulsory, bespoke LPC now means that new trainees will all know each other when they start their contracts.

Ballbreakers or Hansel & Gretel?

'We don't like to follow conventions… we prefer to challenge them…' Thus reads Wragge's recruitment material. The 'Go break the law!' red button on its website challenges the reader to step well away from 'Law Bore & Partners – doing things like everyone else since 1960.' It's a clever recruitment campaign designed to draw like-minded spirits into this firm of tough non-conformists. Perhaps it is also an effort to counterbalance the firm's

sweeter side, which has been amply demonstrated by staff handing out gingerbread men and women at graduate recruitment fairs. This year we understand the gingerbread figures will be inedible USB sticks. One trainee was quick to debunk the fluffy image: 'People think of us as a soft firm, but it's not a soft option, you have to work hard. It's not quite as cuddly as it's made out to be – you need more than just enthusiasm and they don't suffer fools gladly.'

Wragges is known for its emphasis on the individual. Some trainees told us: 'There is an element of unconventionality and people are not straightlaced.' Others noted a cultural shift in the type of trainees recruited, with people 'getting geekier and more academic, more likely to have a First from Cambridge than to be a Sheffield rugby player.' Some things haven't changed: if you're 'hard-working, sociable and well-rounded' then it's likely you'll fit into the Wragge mould. Our sources advise those who reach interview to 'just be yourself, and if you fit the culture it will shine through.' Some of our interviewees worried that the atmosphere is changing as the firm grows. If you want to make up your own mind, a vacation scheme (in either Birmingham or London) is a great way to get a feel for the place. Even assessment days should give a good picture of what it must be like to be part of the Wragge team.

And finally...

Wragge's trainees invariably fall for the firm's charms and it consistently keeps between 85 and 95% of them on qualification. Some stay even if they don't get their first-choice department and location. Typically, 'once you're here you really click with the firm and don't want to leave.' In 2008 26 out of 28 people took up NQ positions.

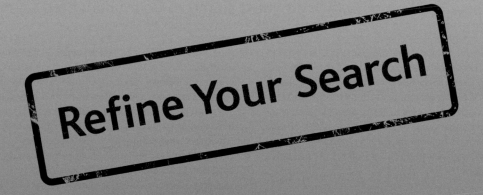
Refine Your Search

Refine your search

We know just how disorienting, disheartening and crazily time consuming it can be to get lost in acres and acres of recruitment material from law firms telling you how they are the best thing since sliced bread. We're sure they are, but how can you tell which are most suited to your undoubted talents?

Snap yourself out of that haze and glance at our crystal clear comparison tables which show you the facts you really want to know, in an instant. Which firms are flashing the cash? Which have mothballs in their wallets? Who will post you to sunnier climes for a working holiday... ahem, overseas placement? What other carrots are firms prepared to dangle in front of you to secure your signature? Who will pay you to go to law school? And finally, how do you apply?

This section is divided into three easy-to-use reference tables which enable you to narrow down your longlist of target firms. They show at a glance the application and selection procedures of each firm, the number of rival applicants you're likely to compete against for that coveted place, the salaries and benefits on offer, and the locations of overseas seats among those firms that offer them.

- The application and selection methods table on the following page allows you to compare in seconds how each law firm requires you to apply – whether by a letter crafted in your best handwriting, posted CV or online. It shows you what minimum degree is required and how many interviews and/or assessment days you face. Finally, and equally crucially, it gives the number of training contracts available alongside how many applications each firm receives.

- Our table of salaries and law school sponsorships on page 660 reveals the current salaries on offer for first and second-year trainees at each firm plus the salary for newly qualified solicitors. It also gives details of sponsorship and awards available to help you pay for law school, along with information about other benefits once you join the firm, like gym membership, health insurance and financial bonuses.

- The final table on page 670 lists the locations of overseas seats, so if your main criteria for choosing your shortlist of firms are whether they offer secondments in Abu Dhabi, Kiev, the Falkland Islands or Muscat then we'll show you which firms to apply to before you can say: 'Money, tickets, passport!'

Applications and Selection

Firm name	Method of Application	Selection Process	Degree Class	Number of Contracts	Number of Applications
Addleshaw Goddard	See website	Interview + assessment centre	2:1	45-50	1,500
Allen & Overy	Online	Interview	2:1	120	2,500
Anthony Collins	See website	Interview + assessment centre	2:1 preferred	6	700
Arnold & Porter	Online	Interviews	2:1	2	700
asb law	Application form	Interview + assessment centre	2:1	5	500
Ashurst	Online	2 interviews	2:1	55	2,500
Baker & McKenzie	Online	Oral presentation + interview	2:1	38	2,000
Barlow Lyde & Gilbert	Online	Interview day	Not known	20	2,000
Bates Wells & Braithwaite	Online	Interviews	2:1	5	750+
Beachcroft	Online	Assessment centre	2:1 preferred	30	Not known
Beale & Company	CV & Covering letter	Interview + assessment	2:1	Not known	Not known
Berwin Leighton Paisner	Online	Assessment day + interview	2:1	40	1,500
Bevan Brittan	Online	Not known	Not known	Not known	Not known
Bingham McCutchen	Online	Interviews	High 2:1	2	Not known
Bircham Dyson Bell	See website	2 interviews, presentation + assessment	2:1 preferred	10	650
Bird & Bird	Online	Assessment day	2:1	17	900
Blake Lapthorn	Online	Interviews & assessment day	2:1	17	400+
Bond Pearce	Online	Assessment day	2:1	15-20	Not known
Boodle Hatfield	Online	Interviews + assessment	2:1	6	Not known
B P Collins	Handwritten letter & CV	Interview + selection day	2:1	Not known	Not known
BPE Solicitors	Application Form	Assessment day	2:1	6	100
Brabners Chaffe Street	Online	Interview + assessment day	2:1 or postgrad	10	Not known
Bristows	Application form	2 interviews	2:1 preferred	Up to 10	3,500
Browne Jacobson	Online or CV & covering letter	Telephone interview + assessment centre + interview	2:1	10	700
Burges Salmon	Application form	Not known	2:1	25	1,500
Campbell Hooper	Online	Assessments + 2 Interviews	2:1	5	150
Capsticks	Application form CV & letter	Interview	2:1	5	200
Charles Russell	Online	Assessment day	2:1	21	1,500
Clarion Solicitors	Application form	Not known	2:1	4	Not known
Clarke Willmott	Online	Assessment centre	2:1 preferred	10	500
Cleary Gottlieb Steen & Hamilton	CV & covering letter	Usually via vac scheme	High 2:1	10-12	Not known
Clifford Chance	Online	Assessment day	2:1	130	3,500
Clyde & Co	Online	Interview + assessments	2:1	24	1,200+
CMS Cameron McKenna	Online	Interview + assessment centre	2:1	60	1,500
Cobbetts	Online	Assessment day	2:1	25 approx.	1,500
Coffin Mew	See website	Interview	2:1 (usually)	5-6	400+
Collyer Bristow	Online	Interviews	2:1	Not known	Not known

Applications and Selection

Firm name	Method of Application	Selection Process	Degree Class	Number of Contracts	Number of Applications
Covington & Burling	Online	2 interviews	2:1	6	Not known
Cripps Harries Hall	Application form	Interview	2:1	8	Up to 750
Davenport Lyons	Online	Interviews	2:1	8	800
Davies Arnold Cooper	Application form	Not known	2:1 (usually)	7	Not known
Dechert	Online	Interviews + assessments	2:1	10-15	1,000
Denton Wilde Sapte	Application form	2 interviews + assessments	2:1	35	1,500
Dewey & LeBoeuf	Online	2 interviews + assessments	2:1	15	900
Dickinson Dees	Online	Interview + assessments	2:1	Up to 21	800
DLA Piper	Online	2 interviews + assessments	2:1	100	2,400
DMH Stallard	Online	Assessment days	2:1	10	525
Dorsey & Whitney	CV & Letter	Not known	2:1	4	Not known
Dundas & Wilson	Online	Assessment day	2:1 preferred	12 (London)	300
DWF	Online	2 interviews	2:1	18	800
Edwards Angell Palmer & Dodge	Online	Interview & assessments	2:1	Up to 8	500
Eversheds	Online	Assessment day	2:1	80	4,000
Farrer & Co	Online	Interviews	2:1	10	800
Field Fisher Waterhouse	Online	Assessment Centre	2:1	20	800
Finers Stephens Innocent	CV & covering letter	2 interviews	2:1	6	800
Foot Anstey	Online	Assessment day	2:1 preferred	15	Not known
Forbes	Handwritten letter & CV	Interview	2:1	4	350+
Ford & Warren	Handwritten letter & CV	Interviews + exercise	Not known	4	500
Forsters	Online	2 interviews	2:1	6	Not known
Freeth Cartwright	Online	Interview + selection day	Not known	Not known	Not known
Freshfields Bruckhaus Deringer	Online	2 interviews + written test	2:1	100	2,000
Geldards	Online	Assessment days	2:1 preferred	8	500
Gordons	Online	Interviews + assessment	2:1	8	300
Government Legal Service	Online	Online test + assessment day	2:1	22-30	500+
Halliwells	Online	Group exercise, presentation + interview	2:1	37	1,500
Hammonds	Online	Assessment + interview	2:1	40	1,300

Applications and Selection

Firm name	Method of Application	Selection Process	Degree Class	Number of Contracts	Number of Applications
Harbottle & Lewis	CV & letter	Interview	2:1	5	800
Hay & Kilner	Online	Interviews + Assessments	2:1	4	200
HBJ Gateley Wareing	See website	Not known	2:1	Not known	Not known
Henmans	Application form	Assessment day	Not known	3	300
Herbert Smith	Online	Case study + interview	2:1	Up to 105	2,000
Hewitsons	Application form	Interview	2:1	10	850
Higgs & Sons	Online or letter & CV	Interview	2:1 usually preferred	5	250+
Hill Dickinson	Online	Assessment day	Not known	Not known	Not known
Holman Fenwick & Willan	Online	2 interviews + written exercise	2:1	12-14	1,000
Howes Percival	Online	Assessment centre	2:1	5	300
Hugh James	Online	Interview & presentation	Usually 2:1	8	500
Hunton & Williams	CV & handwritten letter + app form	Interview + assessment day	2:1	2-3	300
IBB Solicitors	Online	Interview + assessment day	2:1	6	500
Ince & Co	Online	2 interviews + written test	2:1	15	1,000
Irwin Mitchell	Online	Assessment centre + interview	None	20-25	1,500
Jones Day	CV & letter online	2 interviews	2:1	15-20	2,000
Kirkland & Ellis	CV & letter	Interview	Not known	Not known	Not known
K&L Gates	Online	Assessment day	2:1	Up to 15	1,000
Latham & Watkins	Online	3 interviews	2:1	15-20	Not known
Lawrence Graham	Application form	Interview	2:1	20-25	800
Laytons	Application form	2 interviews	1 or 2:1 preferred	8	2,000
Lester Aldridge	Letter, CV & application form	Interview & assessment	2:1	10	300
Lewis Silkin	Online	Assessment day	2:1	5	500
Linklaters	Application form	2 interviews + assessments	2:1	130	3,500
Lovells	Online	Assessment day	2:1	90	2,500
Lupton Fawcett	Online	Interview + assessment day	2:1 preferred	2-3	300
Mace & Jones	Online	Interview	2:1	5-6	300
Macfarlanes	Online	Assessment day	2:1	30	800
Maclay Murray & Spens	Application form	2 interviews + assessments	2:1	30 London/Scotland	150 (London)
Manches	Online	2 interviews	2:1	10	900
Martineau	Online	Half-day assessment centre	2:1	10-12	500

Applications and Selection

Firm name	Method of Application	Selection Process	Degree Class	Number of Contracts	Number of Applications
Maxwell Winward	CV & covering letter	2 interviews	2:1	4	800
Mayer Brown	Online	Interview + assessments	2:1	35-40	1,000+
McDermott, Will & Emery	Online	Interview + assessment day	Not known	Not known	Not known
McGrigors	Online	Half-day assessment centre	2:1	12-15 (London)	Not known
Michelmores	Online	Interview + assessment	Usually 2:1	10	200
Mills & Reeve	Online	Assessment day	2:1	23	650
Mishcon de Reya	Online	Not known	2:1	12-15	1,000+
Morgan Cole	Online	Assessment centre	2:1 preferred	Not known	Not known
Morrison & Foerster	See website	Interviews	2:1	3	500
Mundays	Online	Assessment centre + interview	2:1	3	150
Nabarro	Online	Assessment day	2:1	35	1,600
Needham & James	Online	Assessment day	2:1	5	Not known
Norton Rose	Online	Interview + group exercise	2:1	55	2,500+
Olswang	Online	Interview + assessments	2:1	24	2,000
O'Melveny & Myers	Online	Interview	Not known	Not known	Not known
Orrick, Herrington & Sutcliffe	Online	2 interviews	2:1	10	Not known
Osborne Clarke	Online	Assessment day	2:1	20	1,000
Pannone	Online	2 interviews	2:1	14	1,200
Paul Hastings	Online	Interview	2:1	4-5	Not known
Payne Hicks Beach	Letter & CV	Interview	2:1	3	1,000
Penningtons Solicitors	Online	Not known	2:1	11	1,000
Pinsent Masons	Online	Assessment day	2:1	55	2,000+
Prettys	Letter & CV	Not known	2:1 preferred	5-6	Not known
PricewaterhouseCoopers Legal	Online	Not known	2:1	8	Not known
Pritchard Englefield	Application form	Interview	Generally 2:1	3	300-400
Reed Smith	Online	Interview + assessment	2:1	32	1,500
Reynolds Porter Chamberlain	Online	Assessment day	2.1	15	900
Salans	Letter & CV	Interviews + workshop	2:1	3-4	300-400
Shadbolt	Online	Interview + assessment	Usually 2:1	4	100
Shearman & Sterling	Online	Interview + assessment centre	2:1	15	Not known

Applications and Selection

Firm name	Method of Application	Selection Process	Degree Class	Number of Contracts	Number of Applications
Sheridans	CV & letter	2 interviews	2:1	1	Not known
Shoosmiths	Online	Full-day assessment centre	2:1	20	800
Sidley Austin	Application form	Interview(s)	2:1	15	500
Simmons & Simmons	Online	Assessment day	2:1	50	2,000
SJ Berwin	Online	2 interviews	2:1	50	2,000
Skadden	Online	Interview + exercise	2:1	10-12	700
Slaughter and May	Online	Interview	2:1	95 approx.	2,000+
Speechly Bircham	Application form	Interview + assessment	2:1	10	654
Stephens Scown	CV & application form	Interview + assessment	2:1	Not known	Not known
Stephenson Harwood	Online	Assessment centre	2:1	12	Not known
Stevens & Bolton	Online	2 interviews + assessments	2:1	4	60
Taylor Wessing	Online	Assessment centre	2:1	24	1,200
Teacher Stern	Online	2 interviews	2:1 (not absolute)	3	500
Thomas Eggar	Online	Assessment centre + interview	2:1	11	Not known
Thomson Snell & Passmore	Online	Assessment interview	2:1	5	500
Thring Townsend Lee & Pembertons	Application form & CV	2 interviews	2:1 preferred	9	300
TLT Solicitors	Online	Assessment centre	2:1	Up to 20	700+
Travers Smith	CV & covering letter	2 interviews	2:1	25	2,000
Trethowans	Letter & application form	Interview + assessment day	2:1	3-4	100+
Trowers & Hamlins	Online	Interviews + assessments	2:1	22	1,600
Veale Wasbrough	Application form	Interview	2:1 preferred	8-10	Not known
Vinson & Elkins	Application form	Interview	2:1	3	400
Walker Morris	Online	Interviews	2:1	20	Approx 800
Ward Hadaway	Application form	Assessment centre + interview	2:1	12	400+
Warner Goodman	Online	Interview	Not known	Not known	Not known
Watson Burton	Application form	Not known	2:1	6	500+
Watson, Farley & Williams	Online	Assessment centre + interview	2:1	12-14	1,000
Wedlake Bell	Application form	2 interviews	2:1	7	Not known
Weightmans	Online	Not known	Not known	Up to 14	Not known
Weil, Gotshal & Manges	Online	Not known	2:1	14	Not known

Applications and Selection

Firm name	Method of Application	Selection Process	Degree Class	Number of Contracts	Number of Applications
White & Case	Online	Interview	2:1	35-40	1,600
Wiggin	Online	2-day selection	2:1	4	500
Wilsons Solicitors	Online or CV	Interview + assessment day	2:1	4	Not known
Winkworth Sherwood	Online	2 interviews	2:1	4	50
Withers	Application form	2 interviews + exercises	2:1	16	700
Wollastons	CV & online application form	3-stage interview	2:1	3	500
Wragge & Co	Online	Telephone discussion + assessment day	Not known	30	1,000

- **Training contracts offered in 2007:** 6,012. Of those 6,012 training contracts, 47.4% were based in London.

Salaries and Benefits

Firm name	1st Year Salary	2nd year salary	sponsorship/ awards	Other Benefits	Qualification Salary
Addleshaw Goddard	£24,750 (Manch/Leeds) £36,000 (London)	£27,500 (Manch/Leeds) £39,500 (London)	GDL & LPC: fees + £7,000 (London) or £4,500 (elsewhere)	Corporate gym m'ship, STL, subsd restaurant, pension, pte healthcare	£40,000 (Manch/Leeds) £64,000 (London)
Allen & Overy	£38,000	£42,200	LPC: fees + £7,000 GDL: fees + £6,000 (London), £5,000 (elsewhere)	Pte healthcare, PMI, STL, subsd restaurant, gym m'ship, in-house medical facilities	£65,000
Anthony Collins	£20,000	£22,000	Not known	Not known	£34,500
Arnold & Porter	US Firm Market Rate	US Firm Market Rate	GDL & LPC: fees & £7,250	Health incentive bonus, Childcare vouchers, life ass, STL, Private Health Insurance	£70,000
asb law	£22,000	Not known	LPC: interest-free loan	Not known	Not known
Ashurst	£37,000	£41,000	GDL & LPC: fees + £7,500, £500 for first-class degree or LPC distinction, language bursaries	PHI, pension, life ass, STL, gym m'ship	£65,000
Baker & McKenzie	£37,000 + £3,000 'joining bonus'	£40,000	GDL & LPC: fees + maintenance	PHI, life ins, PMI, pension, subsd gym m'ship, STL, subsd restaurant	£64,000
Barlow Lyde & Gilbert	£36,000	£39,000	GDL & LPC: fees + maintenance	Not known	£61,000
Bates Wells & Braithwaite	£30,000	£32,500	LPC: fees + interest paid on student loans during training contract	STL, subsd gym, subsd restaurant, pension, 1 month unpaid leave on qual	£45,000
Beachcroft	£34,000 (London) £26,000 (Regions)	£37,000 (London) £29,000 (Regions)	GDL & LPC: fees + £5,000	Flexible scheme inc holiday, pension, pte healthcare, EAP	Not known
Beale & Co	£28,000 (London) £23,800 (Regions)	£30,000 (London) £25,500 (Regions)	Not known	STL, work attendance bonus	Competitive
Berwin Leighton Paisner	£37,000	£40,000	GDL & LPC: fees + £7,200	Not known	£65,000
Bevan Brittan	Not known	Not known	GDL & LPC: fees + bursary	Not known	Not known
Bingham McCutchen	£40,000	£45,000	GDL & LPC: fees + £8,000	PHI, travel ins, disability ins, STL, life ass, subsd gym	£94,120
Bircham Dyson Bell	£31,000	£32,000	GDL & LPC: fees	Pte healthcare, life ass, STL, PHI, pension, subsd gym	£51,000
Bird & Bird	£37,000	£40,000	GDL & LPC: fees + £5,500	BUPA, STL, subsd sports club m'ship, life cover, PHI, pension, childcare and eyecare vouchers	£60,000
Blake Lapthorn	£28,000 (London) £21,000 (Regions)	£31,000 (London) £22,500 (Regions)	LPC: fees + maintenance	Pte healthcare, life ass, pension, childcare vouchers	£48,000 (London) £35,000 (Regions)
Bond Pearce	£24,000	£25,000	GDL & LPC: fees + £6,000	PHI, BUPA, life ass	Not known

Notes: PHI = Permanent Health Insurance; STL = Season Ticket Loan; PMI = Private Medical Insurance; EAP = Employee Assistance Programme

Salaries and Benefits

Firm name	1st Year Salary	2nd year salary	sponsorship/ awards	Other Benefits	Qualification Salary
Boodle Hatfield	£32,000	£34,500	GDL & LPC: fees + maintenance	Pte healthcare, life ass, STL, pension, PHI, PMI, conveyancing grant	£52,000
BP Collins	£22,000	£23,000	Not known	Not known	Not known
BPE Solicitors	£20,000 (first seat) £20,500 (second seat)	£21,000 (third seat) £21,500 (fourth seat)	PSC sponsorship	Pension, subsd gym, death-in-service cover, long-term illness cover, sabb scheme	Market rate
Brabners Chaffe Street	£21,000	Not known	LPC: assistance available	Not known	Not known
Bristows	£33,000	£36,000	GDL & LPC: fees + £7,000	Pension, life ass & health ins	£53,500
Browne Jacobson	£24,500	£27,000	GDL & LPC: fees + £5,000	Life ass, PMI, pension	Market rate
Burges Salmon	£30,000	£31,000	GDL & LPC: fees + £7,000	Bonus, pension, pte healthcare, mobile phone, laptop, gym m'ship, Xmas gift, life ass	Under review
Campbell Hooper	£30,500	£33,500	GDL & LPC: fees + £5,000	Pension, PMI, life ass, STL, childcare vouchers	£51,000
Capsticks	£28,000	£29,000	GDL & LPC: financial support	Bonus, pension, PHI, PMI, death-in-service-cover, STL, childcare vouchers	£45,000
Charles Russell	£32,500	£36,000	GDL & LPC: fees + £6,000 (London) £4,500 (Guildford & Cambridge) £3,500 (Cheltenham)	BUPA, PHI, life ass, pension, STL	£58-60,000
Clarion Solicitors	Competitive	Competitive	Not known	Not known	Competitive
Clarke Willmott	£24,000	£25,500	GDL & LPC: fees	Life ass, pension, gym m'ship, bonus, STL, eyecare & childcare vouchers	£36,500-£39,000 (dependant on location)
Cleary Gottlieb Steen & Hamilton	£40,000	£45,000	GDL & LPC: fees + £8,000	Pension, PHI, disability ins, gym m'ship, BUPA, life ins, childcare vouchers, EAP subsd restaurant	£92,000
Clifford Chance	£37,400	£42,200	GDL & LPC: fees + maintenance	Subsd restaurant, fitness centre, pension, up to 6 weeks' leave on qual	£66,600
Clyde & Co	£35,000	£38,000	GDL & LPC: fees + £7,000 (Lon/Guild) £6,000 (elsewhere)	Interest-free loan on joining, pension, life ass, PMI, subsd gym m'ship, STL	£64,000
CMS Cameron McKenna	£37,500	£41,500	GDL & LPC: fees + up to £7,500	Bonus, gym m'ship, life ass, pension, pte healthcare, STL, care line, subs'd rest, buy-holiday scheme	£66,000

Notes: PHI = Permanent Health Insurance; STL = Season Ticket Loan; PMI = Private Medical Insurance; EAP = Employee Assistance Programme

Overseas seats: Who goes where?

Location	Firm
Abu Dhabi	Allen & Overy, Clyde & Co, Denton Wilde Sapte, DLA Piper, Norton Rose, Reed Smith, Simmons & Simmons, Trowers & Hamlins, White & Case
Almaty	White & Case
Amsterdam	Allen & Overy, Clifford Chance, Freshfields Bruckhaus Deringer, Linklaters, Norton Rose, Simmons & Simmons, Slaughter and May
Athens	Norton Rose
Auckland/NZ	Herbert Smith, Slaughter and May
Bahrain	Charles Russell, Norton Rose, Trowers & Hamlins
Bangkok	Allen & Overy, Watson Farley & Williams
Barcelona	Freshfields Bruckhaus Deringer
Beijing	Allen & Overy, Freshfields Bruckhaus Deringer, Linklaters, Norton Rose
Berlin	Freshfields Bruckhaus Deringer, Hammonds
Bratislava	Linklaters
Brussels	Allen & Overy, Arnold & Porter, Ashurst, Baker & McKenzie, Berwin Leighton Paisner, Cleary Gotlieb Steen & Hamilton, Clifford Chance, Dechert, Dickinson Dees, Freshfields Bruckhaus Deringer, Hammonds, Herbert Smith, Latham & Watkins, Linklaters, Lovells, Mayer Brown, McDermott Will & Emery, Nabarro, Norton Rose, Olswang, SJ Berwin, Slaughter and May, White & Case
Bucharest	Allen & Overy, CMS Cameron McKenna, Linklaters
Budapest	Allen & Overy, CMS Cameron McKenna, Linklaters
California	Dechert
Chicago	Baker & McKenzie, Mayer Brown
Cologne	Freshfields Bruckhaus Deringer, Osborne Clarke
Copenhagen	Slaughter and May
Dubai	Allen & Overy, Ashurst, Clifford Chance, Clyde & Co, Denton Wilde Sapte, Dewey & LeBoeuf, DLA Piper, Freshfields Bruckhaus Deringer, Herbert Smith, Holman Fenwick & Willan, Linklaters, Lovells, Norton Rose, Pinsent Masons, Reed Smith, Simmons & Simmons, Trowers & Hamlins, Vinson & Elkins
Düsseldorf	Bird & Bird, Freshfields Bruckhaus Deringer, Slaughter and May
Falkland Islands	McGrigors
Frankfurt	Ashurst, Bird & Bird, Clifford Chance, Freshfields Bruckhaus Deringer, Lovells, Norton Rose, SJ Berwin, Slaughter and May, Weil Gotshal & Manges, White & Case
Geneva	Withers
Helsinki	Slaughter and May
Hong Kong	Allen & Overy, Baker & McKenzie, Barlow Lyde & Gilbert, Bingham McCutchen, Cleary Gotlieb Steen & Hamilton, Clifford Chance, Clyde & Co, DLA Piper, Freshfields Bruckhaus Deringer, Hammonds, Herbert Smith, Linklaters, Lovells, Mayer Brown, Norton Rose, Orrick, Reed Smith, Simmons & Simmons, Skadden, Slaughter and May, Stephenson Harwood, White & Case
Johannesburg	White & Case
Kiev	CMS Cameron McKenna
Luxembourg	Slaughter and May
Madrid	Allen & Overy, Ashurst, Bird & Bird, Clifford Chance, Freshfields Bruckhaus Deringer, Hammonds, Latham & Watkins, Linklaters, SJ Berwin, Slaughter and May
Melbourne	Baker & McKenzie

Overseas seats: Who goes where?

Location	Firm
Milan	Allen & Overy, Ashurst, Clifford Chance, Freshfields Bruckhaus Deringer, Linklaters, Norton Rose, SJ Berwin, Slaughter and May, Withers
Moscow	Allen & Overy, Baker & McKenzie, Cleary Gotlieb Steen & Hamilton, Clifford Chance, CMS Cameron McKenna, Denton Wilde Sapte, Dewey & LeBoeuf, DLA Piper, Freshfields Bruckhaus Deringer, Herbert Smith, Latham & Watkins, Linklaters, Lovells, Norton Rose, Salans, Skadden, Vinson & Elkins, White & Case
Munich	Bird & Bird, Clifford Chance, Dechert, Norton Rose, Osborne Clarke, SJ Berwin, Slaughter and May
Muscat	Denton Wilde Sapte
New York	Allen & Overy, Cleary Gotlieb Steen & Hamilton, Clifford Chance, Dechert, Edwards Angell Palmer & Dodge, Freshfields Bruckhaus Deringer, Linklaters, Mayer Brown, Slaughter and May, Weil Gotshal & Manges, White & Case
Oman	Trowers & Hamlins
Oslo	Slaughter and May
Paris	Allen & Overy, Ashurst, Cleary Gotlieb Steen & Hamilton, Clifford Chance, Dewey & LeBoeuf, Eversheds, Freshfields Bruckhaus Deringer, Hammonds, Herbert Smith, Holman Fenwick & Willan, Latham & Watkins, Linklaters, Lovells, Mayer Brown, Norton Rose, Shadbolt & Co, Simmons & Simmons, SJ Berwin, Slaughter and May, Travers Smith, Watson Farley & Williams, Weil Gotshal & Manges, White & Case
Philadelphia	Dechert
Piraeus	Clyde & Co, Hill Dickinson, Holman Fenwick & Willan, Reed Smith, Watson Farley & Williams
Prague	Allen & Overy, Clifford Chance, CMS Cameron McKenna, Linklaters, Norton Rose, Slaughter and May, White & Case
Qatar	Eversheds
Riyadh	Freshfields Bruckhaus Deringer, White & Case
São Paulo	Clifford Chance, Linklaters, Mayer Brown
San Francisco	Reed Smith
Shanghai	Allen & Overy, Clifford Chance, Eversheds, Freshfields Bruckhaus Deringer, Linklaters
Silicon Valley	Weil Gotshal & Manges
Singapore	Allen & Overy, Ashurst, Barlow Lyde & Gilbert, Clifford Chance, DLA Piper, Herbert Smith, Latham & Watkins, Lovells, Norton Rose, Stephenson Harwood, Watson Farley & Williams, White & Case
Sofia	CMS Cameron McKenna
Stockholm	Bird & Bird, Slaughter and May
Sydney	Baker & McKenzie, Slaughter and May
Tokyo	Allen & Overy, Ashurst, Clifford Chance, DLA Piper, Freshfields Bruckhaus Deringer, Herbert Smith, Latham & Watkins, Linklaters, Lovells, Simmons & Simmons, Slaughter and May, White & Case
Vienna	CMS Cameron McKenna (client secondment), Freshfields Bruckhaus Deringer
Warsaw	Allen & Overy, Clifford Chance, CMS Cameron McKenna, Linklaters
Washington	Baker & McKenzie, Dechert, Freshfields Bruckhaus Deringer

A-Z of Solicitors

Addleshaw Goddard

150 Aldersgate Street, London, EC1A 4EJ
Sovereign House, PO Box 8, Sovereign Street, Leeds LS1 1HQ
100 Barbirolli Square, Manchester, M2 3AB
Website: www.addleshawgoddard.com/graduates
Tel: (020) 7606 8855 / (0161) 934 6000
Fax: (020) 7606 4390 / (0161) 934 6060

Firm profile

As a major force on the legal landscape, Addleshaw Goddard offers extensive and exciting opportunities to all its trainees across the entire spectrum of commercial law, from employment and banking to real estate, corporate finance, intellectual property, employment, PFI and litigation. Ranked 15th largest law firm in the UK with a fee income in 2007/08 of over £195 million, Addleshaw Goddard is listed in both The Sunday Times and The Times as one of the 'Top 100 Best Companies to Work For' and 'Top 100 Graduate Employers' and, as a trainee with this firm, you'll be a key member of the team from day one. Whether based in the London, Leeds or Manchester office (or out on secondment), you'll work closely with blue-chip clients within a supportive yet challenging environment, and be part of a structured training programme designed to ensure your success – now and in the future.

Main areas of work

The firm has four main business divisions: Finance and Projects, Contentious and Commercial, Corporate and Real Estate. Within these divisions as well as the main practice areas it also has specialist areas such as sport, intellectual property, employment and private client services such as trusts and tax.

Trainee profile

Graduates who are capable of achieving a 2:1 and can demonstrate commercial awareness, motivation and enthusiasm. Applications from law and non-law graduates are welcomed, as are applications from students who may be considering a change of direction. We also have a diversity access programme for applicants on GDL or LPC with less conventional academic backgrounds. Further details can be found on our website.

Training environment

During each six-month seat, there will be regular two-way performance reviews with the supervising partner or solicitor. Trainees have the opportunity to spend a seat in one of the firm's other offices and there are a number of secondments to clients available. Seated with a qualified solicitor or partner and working as part of a team, enables trainees to develop the professional skills necessary to deal with the demanding and challenging work the firm carries out for its clients. Practical training is complemented by high-quality training courses provided by both the in-house team and external training providers.

Sponsorship & benefits

GDL and LPC fees are paid, plus a maintenance grant of £7,000 (London) or £4,500 (elsewhere in the UK). Benefits include corporate gym membership, season ticket loan, subsidised restaurant, pension and private healthcare.

Vacation placements

Places for 2009 – 90; Duration – 1, 2 or 3 weeks (over Easter and the summer); location – all offices; Apply by 31 January 2009.

Partners 178
Associates 500+
Trainees 91

Contact
The Graduate Recruitment Team
grad@addleshawgoddard.com

Selection procedure
Interview, assessment centre

Closing date for 2011
31 July 2009

Application
Training contracts p.a. 45-50
Applications p.a. 1,500
% interviewed 10%
Required degree grade 2:1

Training
Salary
1st year
London £36,000
Leeds/Manchester £24,750
2nd year
London £39,500
Leeds/Manchester £27,500
Holiday entitlement
25 days
% of trainees with
a non-law degree p.a. 45%

Post-qualification
Salary
London £64,000
Leeds/Manchester £40,000
% of trainees offered job
on qualification (2006) 80%

Other offices
London, Leeds, Manchester

Allen & Overy LLP

One Bishops Square, London E1 6AD
Tel: (020) 3088 0000 Fax: (020) 3088 0088
Email: graduate.recruitment@allenovery.com
Website: www.allenovery.com/careeruk

Firm profile

Allen & Overy LLP is an international legal practice with approximately 5,000 people working across 29 major centres worldwide. The firm's client list includes many of the world's top businesses, financial institutions, governments and private individuals.

Main areas of work

Banking, corporate, international capital markets, dispute resolution, tax, employment and employee benefits, real estate and private client. Allen & Overy Partners frequently lead the field in their particular areas of law and the practice can claim both an enviable reputation amongst clients and unrivalled success in major deals.

Trainee profile

You will need to demonstrate a genuine enthusiasm for a legal career and Allen & Overy. The firm looks for a strong, consistent academic performance and you should have achieved or be predicted at least a 2:1 degree (or equivalent). At Allen & Overy you will be working in a team where you will use your initiative and manage your own time and workload, so evidence of teamwork, leadership and problem solving skills are also looked for.

Training environment

Allen & Overy offers a training contract characterised by flexibility and choice. The seat structure ensures that you get to see as many parts of the firm as possible and that your learning is hands-on, guided by an experienced associate or Partner. Your choice of a priority seat is guaranteed when you begin your training contract. Given the strength of the firm's International Finance Practice, trainees are required to spend a minimum of 12 months in at least two of the core departments of banking, corporate and international capital markets. The firm now offers its trainees the option of completing a litigation course. This means that trainees will no longer need to spend time in the firm's dispute resolution or employment departments to gain their contentious experience if they are sure their interests lie elsewhere. There are also opportunities for trainees to undertake an international or client secondment during their final year of training.

Vacation placements

Allen & Overy offers approximately 100 vacation placements across the year. The winter placement is for finalists and graduates who should apply from 1 October to 31 October 2008. The spring and summer placements are for penultimate year undergraduates, who should apply from 1 October 2008 to 16 January 2009. Remuneration: £250.00 per week.

Benefits

Private healthcare, private medical insurance, in-house medical facilities, interest-free season ticket loan, free in-house gym, subsidised staff restaurants, multi-faith prayer rooms and music rooms.

Sponsorship & awards

GDL and LPC course fees are paid in full along with contributions towards your maintenance costs. For the Allen & Overy LPC in London, a £7,000 maintenance grant is provided. For the GDL, £6,000 is provided in London and £5,000 elsewhere. Financial incentives are also offered to future trainees achieving a first class undergraduate degree or a distinction in the LPC.

Partners 474*
Associates 1882*
London Trainees 240
*Denotes world-wide number

Contact
Graduate Recruitment

Method of application
Online application form

Selection procedure
Interview

Closing date for 2011
Non Law candidates
16th Jan 2009
Law candidates
31st July 2009

Application
Training contracts p.a. 120
Applications p.a. 2,500
% interviewed p.a. 15%
Required degree grade 2:1
(or equivalent)

Training
Salary
1st year (2008) £38,000
2nd year (2008) £42,200
Holiday entitlement 25 days
% of trainees with a
non-law degree p.a. 45%
% of trainees with a
law degree p.a. 55%
No. of seats available
in international offices
38 seats twice a year and
11 client secondments

Post-qualification
Salary (2008) £65,000
% of trainees offered job
on qualification 90%
% of partners who joined as
trainees over 50%

International offices
Abu Dhabi, Amsterdam, Antwerp, Bangkok, Beijing, Brussels, Bratislava, Budapest, Bucharest (associated office), Dubai, Dusseldorf, Frankfurt, Hamburg, Hong Kong, London, Luxembourg, Madrid, Mannheim, Milan, Moscow, New York, Paris, Prague, Riyadh (associated office), Rome, Shanghai, Singapore, Tokyo, Warsaw

Anthony Collins Solicitors LLP

134 Edmund Street, Birmingham, B3 2ES
Tel: (0121) 200 3242   Fax: (0121) 212 7442
Website: www.anthonycollins.com

Firm profile

Anthony Collins Solicitors is a full service commercial and private client law firm advising businesses, not-for-profit organisations, local authorities, public sector bodies and individuals throughout the UK.

The firm has adopted seven themes which represent the outworking of its mission and the focus for delivering its service: adult health and social care, children and young people, entertainment and leisure, enterprise, housing, transforming communities and faith communities.

Trainee profile

Academically the firm asks that you have, or are on course for, at least a 2:1 degree and a minimum of 320 UCAS points and that you have the potential to successfully complete the legal practice course.

Further, the firm seeks applicants who combine a strong academic record with innovative thinking, not to mention a compassionate and caring approach to clients and an appreciation of their needs and concerns.

Training environment

Your training contract will last for a period of two years, during which time you would spend six months in four seats, in both contentious and non contentious areas of the practice.

During each seat of your training contract you will be appointed a supervisor who will provide you with regular feedback and you will also receive formal feedback through an appraisal system that takes place in the middle and at the end of each seat. Additionally, regular formal and informal (review) meetings with your supervisor and appraiser also ensures that you are able to discuss and raise any concerns or feedback that you may have.

Further, as part of your training contract with Anthony Collins Solicitors, you will attend the Professional Skills Course (PSC), which covers the compulsory subjects of finance and business skills, client care and professional standards, and advocacy and communication skills in addition to your own chosen electives.

Partners 21
Assistant solicitors 71
Total trainees 17

Contact
Laura Hinson (HR Officer)
(0121) 214 3533
laura.hinson@anthonycollins.com

Selection procedure
Graduate testing session - half a day, structured interview - two hours, assessment centre - one day (all of the above take place in the firm's offices)

Closing date
The firm invites applications two years in advance of your preferred intake date and run up to two recruitment processes each year; whilst there is no formal deadline for applications, it is preferable that they are received by July 31 of each year i.e. for September 2010 applications, applications to be received by 31 July 2009

Application
Training contracts p.a. 6 (on average)
Applications p.a. 700
% interviewed 10%
Required degree grade 2:1 preferred

Training
Salary
1st year £20,000
2nd year £22,000
Holiday entitlement 23 days

Post-qualification
Salary
£34,500
% of trainees offered job on qualification (2007-08) 90%

Anthony Collins
solicitors

Arnold & Porter (UK) LLP

Tower 42, 25 Old Broad Street, London, EC2N 1HQ
Tel: (020) 7786 6100   Fax: (020) 7786 6299
Email: graduates@aporter.com
Website: www.arnoldporter.com

Firm profile

Arnold & Porter is a US-based firm with a deserved reputation for its quality of service and expertise in handling the most complex legal and business problems requiring innovative and practical solutions. The firm's global reach, experience, and deep knowledge allows it to work across geographic, cultural, technological, and ideological borders, serving clients whose business needs require US, EU, or cross-border regulatory, litigation, and transactional services.

Main areas of work

The London office is home to the firm's European regulatory, life sciences, IP, competition, corporate, employment and telecoms practices. The UK Legal 500 recently ranked its London office as recommended in administrative and public policy, EU competition, IP, M&A, pharmaceuticals and biotechnology, product liability, publishing, rail, telecommunications, and venture capital.

Trainee profile

The firm looks for talented law and non-law graduates from all backgrounds who share the firm's commitment to excellence, and want to be part of the continued growth of its London office. Candidates need to demonstrate a consistently high academic background; the firm looks for well-rounded individuals who can demonstrate their participation in a range of extra curricular activities and achievements.

Training environment

Four six-month seats: Pharmaceuticals, IP, corporate and securities and commercial. The firm encourages individuals to work across specialisms, and emphasises teamwork, so trainees may find that whilst they are working in one group, they undertake work in a variety of different areas throughout the firm. Trainees will be expected to work on several matters at once, and assume responsibility at an early stage. Trainees may also have an opportunity to work in the firm's Brussels office and where the occasion permits, to work on projects in one of the firm's US offices.

An important aspect of the firm's culture is its commitment to pro bono. Trainees and all lawyers at the firm are encouraged to take part and devote 15% of their time to it, which helps young lawyers develop client managements skills from an early stage.

Vacation schemes

The firm takes up to eight summer vacation students each year. Whether you are a law or non-law student, the firm will introduce you to life in a busy city law firm, spending two weeks working on a variety of projects and workshops with partners and associates throughout the London office. Apply via the firm's website by 28 February 2009.

Benefits

Health incentive bonus, luncheon vouchers, Christmas bonus, child care vouchers, private health insurance, life assurance, season ticket loan.

Sponsorship & awards

CPE/LPC: fees paid; £7,250 pa maintenance.

Partners 16
Assistant Solicitors 20
Total Trainees 0

Contact
Graduate Recruitment

Method of application
Apply via website

Selection procedure
Interview with partners and associates

Closing date for 2011
31 July 2009

Application
Training contracts p.a. 2
Applications p.a 700
% interviewed 2%
Required degree grade 2:1

Training salary
1st year TBC (US firm market rate)
2nd year TBC (US firm market rate)
Holiday entitlement 25 days

Post-qualification
Salary £70,000
% of trainees offered job on qualification 100%

Overseas, regional offices
London, Washington DC, New York, Los Angeles, Denver, Northern Virginia, San Francisco, Brussels

ARNOLD & PORTER (UK) LLP

asb law

Innovis House, 108 High Street, Crawley, West Sussex RH10 1AS
Tel: (01293) 861218 Fax: (01293) 861250
Email: donna.flack@asb-law.com   Website: www.asb-law.com

Firm profile

A rising-50 firm, asb law has clear strategic plans and both the capacity and determination to earn the place as the leading full service firm in the South East. From regional centres in Crawley and Maidstone the firm offers unrivalled coverage throughout the South east.

This is a vibrant partnership intent on capitalising on its position within some of the most dynamic development areas in the country, the Gatwick Diamond, Thames Gateway and Ashford.

The firm's diverse client range includes businesses, financial institutions and public sector bodies of all shapes and sizes. The firm also has significant private client capability with full service offerings for mid- and high net worth individuals from the Family and Tax, Trusts and Probate Teams.

The firm's prestigious clients and the range of services it provides demonstrate effectively that it is more than possible to enjoy a challenging and rewarding career without the grind of a daily commute to the City.

Main areas of work

Principal areas of work include corporate finance, commercial (contracts), employment, recovery and insolvency, commercial litigation, commercial property and defendant. The firm has clients across many industry sectors and has developed particular expertise in a number including banking, travel, aviation, technology and property litigation.

The Private Client Sector Teams are amongst the largest in the region and include members of STEP, Resolution and the Law Society Children Panel. The firm also has Partners qualified in collaborative law

Trainee profile

As you would expect, the firm is looking for strong intellectual ability. That ability must combine with drive, initiative, a clear client focus and a commercial approach. You should also be articulate and have demonstrable interpersonal skills. You should relish the prospect of early responsibility and contact with clients in a supportive environment.

Training environment

The firm's two year programme divides into four six-month seats tailored to your strengths and particular interests. Training is structured to empower you to learn, take responsibility and interact with clients from an early stage. The seats can be either centre, so a degree of flexibility is required. The firm is proud of its history of retaining its trainees on qualification, and on the number who go on to become associates and Partners themselves.

When and how to apply

Applications can be downloaded from www.asb-law.com and must be submitted online.

Sponsorship and benefits

An interest-free loan is available for the LPC which is repayable over the period of the training contract.

Partners 37
Vacancies 5
Total Trainees 10
Total Staff 260

Contact
Donna Flack
Tel: (01293) 861218

Method of application
Application form downloaded
from firm's website

Selection procedure
1 interview and an assessment
centre

Closing date for 2011
31 July 2009

Application
Training contracts p.a. 5
Applications p.a 500
% interviewed 5%
Required degree grade 2:1

Training salary
£22,000 (2008)

Offices
Crawley, Maidstone

Ashurst LLP

Broadwalk House, 5 Appold St, London EC2A 2HA
Tel: (020) 7638 1111 Fax: (020) 7638 1112
Email: gradrec@ashurst.com
Website: www.ashurst.com

Firm profile

Ashurst LLP is a leading international law firm advising corporates and financial institutions, with core businesses in mergers and acquisitions, corporate and structured finance. The firm's strong and growing presence around the world is built on extensive experience in working with clients on the complex international legal and regulatory issues relating to cross-border transactions.

Main areas of work

Corporate; employment, incentives and pensions; energy, transport and infrastructure; EU and competition; international finance; litigation; real estate; tax; and technology and commercial.

Trainee profile

To become an Ashurst trainee you will need to show common sense and good judgement. The firm needs to know that you can handle responsibility because you will be involved in some of the highest quality international work on offer anywhere. The transactions and cases you will be involved in will be intellectually demanding, so Ashurst looks for high academic achievers who are able to think laterally. But it's not just academic results that matter. Ashurst wants people who have a range of interests outside of their studies. And they want outgoing people with a sense of humour who know how to laugh at themselves.

Training environment

Your training contract will consist of four seats. For each, you will sit with a partner or senior solicitor who will be the main source of your work and your principal supervisor during that seat. Seats are generally for six months. Anything less than that will not give you sufficient depth of experience for the responsibility Ashurst expects you to take on. The firm asks trainees to spend a seat in the Corporate Department and one seat in the International Finance Department. Trainees spend their two remaining seats in the firm's other practice areas.

Benefits

Private health insurance, pension, life assurance, interest-free season ticket loan, gym membership and 25 days holiday per year during training. Other benefits can be found on the 'benefits and salaries' section of the firm's website.

Vacation placements

Places for 2009: A two-week Easter placement scheme primarily aimed at final-year non-law undergraduates and all graduates. Two three-week summer placement schemes primarily aimed at penultimate-year law undergraduates. Remuneration £275 p.w. Closing date 31 January 2009.

Sponsorship & awards

GDL and LPC funding plus maintenance allowances of £7,500 per annum. LPC distinction and first class degree awards of £500. Language tuition bursaries.

Partners 217
Assistant Solicitors 785
Total Trainees 100

Contact
Stephen Trowbridge
Graduate Recruitment and
Development Manager

Method of application
Online

Selection procedure
Interview with Graduate
Recruitment and Development
Manager followed by interview
with two Partners

Closing date for 2011
31 July 2009

Application
Training contracts p.a. 55
Applications p.a. 2,500
% interviewed p.a. 10%
Required degree grade 2:1

Training
Salary (2008)
First year
£37,000
Second year
£41,000
Holiday entitlement 25 days
% of trainees with a non-law
degree 58%
Number of seats abroad
available p.a. 11

Post-qualification
Salary (2008) £65,000
% of trainees offered job
on qualification (2008) 93%

Overseas offices
Abu Dhabi, Brussels, Dubai,
Frankfurt, Madrid, Milan,
Munich, New Delhi, New York,
Paris, Singapore, Stockholm,
Tokyo

Baker & McKenzie LLP

100 New Bridge Street, London EC4V 6JA
Tel: (020) 7919 1000 Fax: (020) 7919 1999
Email: london.graduate.recruit@bakernet.com
Website: www.mutliplyingyourpotential.co.uk

Firm profile

Baker & McKenzie LLP is a leading global law firm based in 70 locations across 38 countries. With a presence in virtually every important financial and commercial centre in the world, the firm's strategy is to provide the best combination of local legal and commercial knowledge, international expertise and resources.

Main areas of work

Corporate; dispute resolution; banking; EU, competition and trade; employment; intellectual property; information technology and commercial; pensions; tax; projects; property; structured capital markets. In addition the firm has cross-departmental practice groups, such as media and communications, insurance and reinsurance, business recovery and environmental law.

Trainee profile

The firm is looking for trainee solicitors who are stimulated by intellectual challenge and want to be 'the best' at what they do. Effective communication together with the ability to be creative and practical problem solvers, team players and a sense of humour are qualities which will help them stand out from the crowd.

Training environment

Four six-month seats which include a corporate and a contentious seat, usually within the firm's highly regarded dispute resolution department. There is also the possibility of a secondment abroad or to a client. During each seat you will have a meeting to discuss individual seat preferences. In addition, you will receive formal and informal reviews to discuss your progress. Your training contract commences with a highly interactive and practical induction programme which focuses on key skills including practical problem solving, interviewing, presenting and the application of information technology. The firm's training programme includes important components on management and other business skills, as well as seminars and workshops on key legal topics for each practice area. There is a Trainee Solicitor Liaison Committee which acts as a forum for any new ideas or raises issues which may occur during your training contract. Trainees are actively encouraged to participate in a variety of pro bono issues and, outside office hours, there is a varied sporting and social life.

Benefits

Permanent health insurance, life insurance, private medical insurance, group personal pension, subsidised gym membership, season ticket loan, subsidised staff restaurant.

Vacation placements

London Summer Placement - Places for 2009: 30; Duration: 3 weeks; Remuneration (2008): £270 p.w.; Closing date: 31 January 2009.

International Summer Placement - Places for 2009: 3-5; Duration: 8-12 weeks divided between London and an overseas office; Remuneration (2008): £270 p.w.; Closing date: 31 January 2009.

Partners 84
Assistant Solicitors 209
Total Trainees 77

Contact
Justine Beedle

Method of application
Online application form

Selection procedure
Candidates to give a
short oral presentation based
on the facts of a typical client
problem, interview with two
partners, meeting with an
associate

Closing date for 2011
Non-law 18 Feb 2009
Law 31 July 2009

Application
Training contracts p.a. 38
Applications p.a. 2,000
% interviewed p.a. 10%
Required degree grade 2:1

Training
Salary
1st year (2008) £37,500 +
£3,000 'joining bonus'
2nd year (2008) £40,000
Holiday entitlement 25 days
% of trainees with a
non-law degree p.a.
Approx 50%
No. of seats available
abroad p.a. Variable
post-qualification
Salary (2008) £64,000
% of trainees offered job
on qualification (2008) 83%

Barlow Lyde & Gilbert LLP

Beaufort House, 15 St Botolph Street, London EC3A 7NJ
Tel: (020) 7247 2277 Fax: (020) 7643 8500
Email: grad.recruit@blg.co.uk   Website: www.blg.co.uk

Firm profile

Barlow Lyde & Gilbert LLP is a leading international legal practice with more than 80 partners and over 300 lawyers. The firm has offices in London, Oxford, Hong Kong, Shanghai and Singapore. The firm provides an extensive range of legal services to clients from many industries across the world, and is renowned for its litigation and insurance expertise. Its Dispute Resolution Practice is one of the UK's largest and highest rated. The firm's experience is wide-ranging, from complex boardroom or IT disputes to professional negligence actions and major reinsurance arbitrations. The firm scooped "Litigation Team of the Year" at the Legal Week Awards in 2005, and again at both The Lawyer Awards and the Legal Business Awards in 2006. Its top-ranked insurance and reinsurance practice is one of the largest in the world, providing services of unparalleled breadth across the sector. The firm was ranked 'best in Europe' in the Reactions 2007 annual legal survey of over 100 in-house counsel, top executives and claim handlers at insurers, reinsurers and brokers. The firm's lawyers are also leaders in the international transport and trade sectors. The firm has significant experience representing and advising some of the world's major players in the aerospace and marine, energy and trade fields, including airlines, ship owners, charterers, manufacturers, airports, insurers, regulatory agencies and international trade associations. The firm's highly regarded Non-Contentious Department handles the full spectrum of corporate, financial, commercial, I.T, outsourcing, employment and pensions work for public and private companies from a wide range of sectors as well as financial institutions.

Trainee profile

The firm recruits 20 trainees a year. It looks for intelligent and motivated graduates with good academic qualifications and excellent communication skills. Trainees must be able to work independently or in a team, and are expected to display common sense and initiative. An appreciation of the client's commercial interests is essential.

Training environment

During your training contract you will have six-month seats in four different practice areas. The firm always tries to accommodate a trainee's preference for a particular type of work. There are opportunities to spend time in its other offices, on secondment with clients or on exchange programmes with overseas law firms. A capable trainee will deal regularly with clients from an early stage in his or her training, subject to supervision. All trainees are expected to undertake and assist in practice development and client care. Successful candidates will enjoy a wide variety of social and sporting events at Barlow Lyde & Gilbert LLP, ensuring that trainees have the chance to meet and stay in contact with employees from across the firm.

Work placement scheme

An increasing number of trainees come to the firm through vacation schemes. Whether you are a law or non-law student we will introduce you to life in a City law firm. You can even choose which department you want to spend time in. The closing date for applications is 30 January 2009. The firm also runs open days and drop-in days throughout the year. Full details are available from the website www.blg.co.uk.

Whether you wish to apply for an interview day or a vacation scheme, please apply via our website at www.blg.co.uk. The closing date for the interview days is 31 August 2009.

Sponsorship & awards

A maintenance grant is provided and law school fees are paid in full.

Partners 88
Vacancies 20
Trainees 41
Total staff 716

Contact
Caroline Walsh
Head of Graduate Recruitment
& Trainee Development

Method of application
Online application form

Selection procedure
Interview day

Closing date for 2011
31 August 2009

Application
Training contracts p.a.
20
Applications p.a. 2,000
% interviewed p.a. 10%

Training
Salary
1st year £36,000
2nd year £39,000
Holiday entitlement
5 weeks
post-qualification
Salary £61,000
Trainees offered job
on qualification (2008)
17 out of 19

Offices
London, Oxford, Hong Kong,
Shanghai, Singapore

BARLOW LYDE & GILBERT

Bates Wells & Braithwaite London LLP

2-6 Cannon Street, London EC4M 6YH
Tel: (020) 7551 7777 Fax: (020) 7551 7800
Email: trainee@bwbllp.com
Website: www.bwbllp.com

Firm profile

Bates Wells and Braithwaite is a commercial law firm servicing a wide range of commercial statutory, charity and social enterprises. The firm is expanding, progressive and is doing high quality work for clients and providing high quality training for those who work with the firm.

Whilst the firm is ranked joint first in three areas of law by the Legal 500 and ranked by them or Chambers in 15 other areas of law, the firm also believes in its staff enjoying a good work/life balance and living a life outside as well as inside the office.

Main areas of work

The firm is well known for its work for a wide range and variety of clients given its size. This includes working with the charities and social enterprise sector, commercial organisations and individuals. The firm also has particular expertise in the arts and media, sports and immigration arenas together with strong departments dealing with employment, property and dispute resolution.

Trainee profile

The firm is looking for trainees with not only a sound academic background and the ability to communicate clearly and effectively, but most importantly it is looking for trainees who positively want to join a firm such as Bates Wells & Braithwaite.

Training environment

In the first year there are two six month seats, whilst in the second year there are three four month seats which, between them, cover a wide range of the work with which the firm is involved. From time to time the firm arranges secondments to clients on an ad hoc basis.

The firm runs a programme of internal seminars specifically addressed to trainees and operates a mentoring system, all designed to ensure that the trainees enjoy their time with the firm and to maximise the opportunities that are available for them during their training contract and beyond.

Benefits

Interest-free loan for season ticket travel, subsidised use of gym and squash court, subsidised restaurant, one month's unpaid leave on qualification and the firm's pension scheme with match funding provided.

Vacation placements

Places for 2009: 12 people for a duration of one week each. Closing date: 19th February 2009.

Sponsorship & awards

LPC course fees paid and interest paid on student loans during the training contract.

Partners 26
Assistant Solicitors 56
Trainees 9

Graduate recruitment contact
Peter Bennett (020) 7551 7777

Method of application
Online via website

Selection procedure
Interviews

Closing date for 2011
July 2009 - see website

Application
Training contracts per annum 5
Applications p.a. 750+
% interviewed p.a. 5% Required
degree 2:1

Training
Salary
1st year, £30,000
2nd year, £32,500
Holiday entitlement
5 weeks
Post-qualification
Salary £45,000
% of trainees offered job
on qualification (last 3 years)
100%

Beachcroft LLP

100 Fetter Lane, London EC4A 1BN
Tel: (020) 7242 1011 Fax: (020) 7831 6630
Email: trainee@beachcroft.co.uk
Website: www.bemore.beachcroft.co.uk

Firm profile

Beachcroft LLP is one of the largest commercial law firms in the UK, with a turnover of over £112 million. An enviable client base and over 1,400 people working out of eight offices means they can provide truly exceptional career opportunities, whatever your aspirations.

Their national teams allow clients to benefit from some of the best specialists in the UK with expert local knowledge and a consistent commercial view wherever they are. For their fee earners and support staff it's a chance to work alongside nationally respected lawyers as part of progressive multi-disciplinary teams.

Main areas of work

The firm operates through specialist practice area teams to deliver an integrated service to clients in six main industry groups: Financial Institutions (including the insurance industry), Health & Public Sector, Real Estate, Technology & Telecommunications, Industrial Manufacturing & Transportation and Consumer Goods & Services. Key clients include Guy's and St Thomas's NHS Foundation Trust, Balfour Beatty, Westfield Shoppingtowns, Zurich, Allianz Insurance, BAE Systems, L'Oreal, Unilever, Waitrose, Freescale Semiconductor and Getronics. The firm is helping them get more from their businesses, and they can help you get more from your career.

Trainee profile

The firm looks for outgoing, commercially minded people preferably with a 2:1 honours degree in any subject. You will need to be an excellent team player and possess a mind capable of analysing, interpreting and applying complex points of law.

Training environment

Training takes place over a two year period in London, Bristol, Manchester or Leeds, during which time you'll pursue a demanding study programme, whilst occupying four six-month seats in some of the key areas of commercial law. Responsibility will come early and the firm provides the supervision and support to enable you to develop and grow.

Benefits

The firm operates a flexible benefits package where you can personalise your rewards – 'buying' or 'selling' options such as pension entitlement and private health care. Additional benefits include well woman/man checks, free eye test, employment assistance programme, discounted insurance and many other fringe benefits.

Vacation placements

Beachcroft runs a paid placement scheme for law and non-law students each summer.
Please visit www.bemore.beachcroft.co.uk for further details.

Partners 140
Assistant Solicitors 297
Total Trainees 68

Contact
Carrie Daniels
Graduate Recruitment Officer
Email:
trainee@beachcroft.co.uk

Method of application
Apply online at
www.bemore.beachcroft.co.uk

Selection procedure
Assessment centre

Closing date
1 August each year

Application
Training contracts per annum
30
Required degree 2:1 preferred

Training
Salary
1st year, regions
£26,000 p.a.
2nd year, regions
£29,000 p.a.
1st year, London
£34,000 p.a.
2nd year, London
£37,000 p.a.
Holiday entitlement - 25 days
% of trainees with a
non-law degree p.a. - 45%
Beachcroft provides payment
for GDL, LPC and £5,000
bursary.

Offices
Birmingham, Bristol, Brussels,
Leeds, London, Manchester,
Winchester

Beale and Company Solicitors LLP

Garrick House, 27-32 King Street, Covent Garden, London, WC2E 8JB
Tel: (020) 7240 3474   Fax: (020) 7240 9111
Email: h.kapadia@beale-law.com
Website: www.beale-law.com

Partners 13	
Assistant Solicitors 25	
Trainees 8	
Contact	
Mrs Heidi Kapadia	
Method of application	
CV and covering letter	
Selection procedure	
Interview and assessment	
Closing date for 2009/2010	
Not applicable	
Training	
Salary	
1st year, £28,000 (London)	
1st year, £23,800 (Regions)	
2nd year, £30,000 (London)	
2nd year, £25,500 (Regions)	

Firm profile

Beale and Company is a specialist niche practice based in the West End, Bristol and Dublin. With the firm ranked as a leading practice for Technology and Construction Professional Negligence and Construction in London; and for Professional Negligence generally in the Regions, it provides the perfect opportunity for trainees to explore their legal capabilities in a range of challenging areas. It combines the cut and thrust of a practice focussed on providing the best service to clients who are nationally and internationally recognised leaders in their fields with the community and balance that the ethos of a smaller firm embodies. With an active participation in a European Network of law firms, and a regular overseas dimension to the matters handled, trainees are able to experience a diversity of legal issues.

Main areas of work

The firm specialises in: construction, professional negligence; dispute resolution; insurance; IT; corporate and commercial; employment; health and safety; and property (domestic and commercial) together with some private client work.

Trainee profile

The firm is looking for candidates with a strong academic background (having obtained or being predicted a 2:1 honours degree in any subject), and a real interest in pursuing a career in the law. Trainees need to be commercial, motivated and analytical. A candidate should have the ability to work both as a team player and the initiative to be involved in matter strategy and management from an early stage so as to achieve the most from the training experience.

Training environment

The two year training contract will include six month seats in the key areas of the practice, two of which will be within the Dispute Resolution Department. There may be opportunities to spend time in a different office within the firm, or to go on secondment to clients. Trainees also enjoy a number of social and sporting activities throughout the year, both internally and within the local business community.

Benefits

The firm's benefits include: holiday entitlement; interest free loan for a season ticket for travel; discretionary annual bonus; work attendance bonus; and a very competitive salary.

Berwin Leighton Paisner

Adelaide House, London Bridge, London EC4R 9HA
Tel: (020) 7760 1000 Fax: (020) 7760 1111
Email: traineerecruit@blplaw.com   Website: www.blplaw.com

Firm profile

Berwin Leighton Paisner LLP is a premier, full service City law firm, with particular strengths in real estate, corporate tax, finance and a strong litigation and dispute resolution capability. The firm has an open and friendly culture, combined with a strong commitment to career development and internal communication means that it has become a magnet for quality staff.

Main areas of work

The full range of real estate work including investment, development, planning, construction, property finance, litigation and funds. Traditional corporate finance areas of M&A, equity capital markets and investment funds, as well as outsourcing, EU, competition, IT, telecoms and employment. An active Banking and Capital Markets Team with a growing securitisation capability, a Project Finance Team that is expanding internationally, and an Asset Finance Team. Strong and growing Corporate Tax Team, intellectual property, commercial litigation, and reinsurance and insurance. The firm is widely recognised for its expertise in a number of industry sectors, including real estate, hotels, leisure and gaming, defence, energy, utilities and retail.

LPC+

The firm runs the UK's first tailor-made LPC Course, called the LPC+. All trainees study at the College of Law, where tutors are joined by BLP lawyers and trainers who help to deliver some of the sessions, using BLP precedents and documents, discussing how theory is applied to real cases and transactions.

Trainee profile

The firm is looking for intelligent, energetic, positive and hard-working team players who have an interest in business and gain a sense of achievement from finding solutions.

Training environment

BLP is an exciting, ambitious, dynamic and entrepreneurial firm. Yet when recruiting trainees, the focus is on quality rather than quantity. As a result, trainees are rewarded with a high degree of responsibility and involvement underpinned by an exceptional standard of training and support. BLP has always prided itself on providing the right environment for people to grow. Employees believe that BLP is a genuinely innovative and friendly firm with a refreshing lack of hierarchy, the open-door policy is something that trainees value tremendously. An induction covers the practical aspects of working in a law firm, from billing to client care. There are technical education programmes for each department, with weekly skills sessions and seminars for trainees as well as Professional Skills Courses.

Vacation placements

Places for 2009: Assessment centres held during December, January and February at the firm's London office, applications accepted online before 31 January 2009 (at www.blplaw.com). Easter vacation scheme, one week, aimed at final year law students and those at a later stage of legal education/employment. Summer vacation scheme, two weeks, aimed at those in their penultimate year and above (law and non-law).

Sponsorship

CPE/GDL and LPC+ fees paid and £7,200 maintenance p.a.

Partners 180
Assistant Solicitors 318
Total Trainees 80

Contact
Debbiella Gould

Method of application
Firm application form online

Selection procedure
Assessment day & partner interview

closing date for 2011
31 July 2009

Application
Training contracts p.a. 40
Applications p.a. 1,500
% interviewed p.a. 5%
Required degree grade 2:1

Training
Salary
1st year (2008)
£37,000
2nd year (2008)
£40,000
Holiday entitlement 25 days
% of trainees with a
non-law degree p.a. 46%
No. of seats available
abroad p.a. 1

Post-qualification
Salary (2006) £65,000
% of trainees offered job
on qualification (2008) 86%
% of assistants who joined
as trainees (2005) 47%
% of partners who joined
as trainees (2005) 30%

Offices
London, Brussels, Paris,
Singapore, best friend networks
in 65 countries

Bevan Brittan

Kings Orchard, 1 Queen Street, Bristol, BS2 0HQ
Tel: (0870) 194 3050 Fax: (0870) 194 8954
Email: hr.training@bevanbrittan.com
Website: www.bevanbrittan.com

Partners 59	
Total Trainees 33	
Contact	
HR and Training	
(0870) 194 3050	
Method of application	
Online application	
Closing date for 2011	
31 July 2009	
Post-qualification	
% of trainees offered job	
on qualification (2007) 75%	
Other offices	
Birmingham, Bristol, London	

Firm profile

Bevan Brittan has firmly established itself as a truly national law firm and continues to attract high profile national and international clients and challenging, groundbreaking work. The firm is nationally recognised for its expertise in providing legal advice to clients in both the public and private sectors and is notable for being one of the very few practices whose work is equally strong in both sectors.

Main areas of work

The firm is structured around four primary areas of the UK economy: built environment, health, government and education, and commerce, industry and services. The firm operates in cross departmental teams across these markets, harnessing the full range of skills and experience needed to provide top quality legal advice in the context of specialist knowledge of both the sector concerned and the client's business. Areas of work covered include banking, corporate, commercial, commercial litigation, projects, employment, medical law and personal injury, property, planning and construction.

Trainee profile

Bevan Brittan recognises that the firm's success depends upon a team of lawyers dedicated to service excellence. Its success is maintained by attracting and retaining enthusiastic, bright people with sound common sense, plenty of energy and the ability to work and communicate well with others.

Training environment

During each six-month seat, the core of your training will be practical work experience in conjunction with an extensive educational programme. Together the training is aimed at developing attitudes, skills and legal and commercial knowledge essential for your career success. You are encouraged to take on as much work and responsibility as you are able to handle, which will be reviewed on a regular basis with your supervising Partner. The firm is friendly and supportive with an open-door policy along with a range of social, sporting and cultural activities.

Vacation placements

Places available for 2009: 40 across the three offices. Closing date: 31st March 2009.

sponsorship & awards

Bursary and funding for GDL and LPC.

Bingham McCutchen (London) LLP

41 Lothbury, London, EC2R 7HF
Tel: (020) 7661 5300 Fax: (020) 7661 5400
Email: graduaterecruitment@bingham.com   Website: www.bingham.com

Firm profile

With nearly 1,000 lawyers in 13 offices spanning the United States, the United Kingdom and Asia, Bingham focuses on serving clients in complex financial transactions, high-stakes litigation and a full range of sophisticated corporate and technology matters.

Bingham's London team of 40 high-flying finance, litigation and corporate lawyers is dedicated to providing a seamless and responsive service to international financial institution clients. The firm's London office capabilities have been carefully shaped to meet the complex needs of a demanding client segment. Through practical experience and in-depth study of the legal and business issues facing these clients, the firm's London lawyers provide counsel in an intelligent, savvy, forceful and focused way. Members of Bingham's London office have represented institutions and funds in precedent-setting workouts and restructurings in the UK and across Europe, including Concordia Bus, Damovo Group, Focus DIY, Gate Gourmet, IWP International, Jarvis, J R Crompton, LeisureLink Holdings, Luxfer Holdings, Marconi, Northern Rock, Parmalat, Queens Moat Houses, Schefenacker, Schieder Möbel, Sea Containers, TH Global and TMD Friction. The financial restructuring practice in London is closely integrated with the firm's restructuring and insolvency practice in the United States, Tokyo and Hong Kong, leading The International Who's Who of Business Lawyers to name Bingham as 'Global Insolvency and Restructuring Law Firm of the Year' in 2006 and 2007. London lawyers also have extensive experience in the areas of finance, corporate, litigation and financial services regulatory.

Main areas of work

Bingham's London office capabilities include financial restructuring, finance, corporate, litigation and financial services regulatory.

Trainee profile

The firm is looking for top quality candidates who can demonstrate an exceptional academic record combined with evidence of extra-curricular achievement. Prospective trainees will show initiative, be solution driven and seek to be part of a challenging yet friendly environment.

Training environment

The firm currently recruits two trainee solicitors a year. The training contract consists of four six-month seats, rotating between the office's primary practice areas: financial restructuring, finance, corporate, litigation and financial services regulatory. Trainees also have the opportunity to spend one of their second year seats in the firm's Hong Kong office. The intimate nature of the London office means that you will benefit from a bespoke training programme with a high level of Partner involvement. With the firm's small team approach, you will assume responsibilities from day one.

Benefits

The firm offers an extensive compensation programme for trainees. As well as a highly competitive salary, the firm offers private health insurance, travel insurance, long term disability insurance, season ticket loan, life assurance, subsidised gym membership, discretionary bonus and critical illness cover.

Sponsorship & awards

LPC fees and maintenance grant of £8,000 per annum. PgDL fees and maintenance grant of £8,000 per annum.

Assistant solicitors 25
Total Trainees 4

Contact
Vicky Anderson, Human Resources Officer.
(020) 7661 5300

Method of application
Online application via firm website at www.bingham.com or via CV Mail

Selection procedure
Currently face to face interviews

Closing date for 2011
31 July 2009

Application
Training contracts p.a. up to 2
Required degree grade:
High 2:1 from a leading university and excellent A-levels

Training
Salary
1st year £40,000
2nd year £45,000
Holiday entitlement
25 days

Post-qualification
Salary (2007) £94,120
% of trainees offered job on qualification (2006) 100%

Overseas offices
Boston, Hartford, Hong Kong, Los Angeles, New York, Orange County, San Francisco, Santa Monica, Silicon Valley, Tokyo, Walnut Creek, Washington

Bircham Dyson Bell LLP

50 Broadway, London SW1H 0BL
Tel: (020) 7227 7000 Fax: (020) 7222 3480

Firm profile

Bircham Dyson Bell is one of the UK's most progressive law firms. Over the past five years, the firm's approach and track record has enabled it to double its turnover, and to attract and retain some of the brightest people in the profession. This is achieved through the breadth and variety of work that the firm does, with all departments acting on some of the most high profile cases in their field.

Main areas of work

Located in central London, the firm is recognised as having leading departments in the parliamentary, planning, public law, charity and private client fields. The firm also has strong corporate commercial, real estate and litigation teams.

Trainee profile

Applications are welcome from both law and non-law students who can demonstrate a consistently high academic record. The firm is looking for creative thinkers with a confident and practical outlook who will thrive in a friendly, hard-working environment. Many of the firm's current trainees have diverse interests outside law.

Training environment

The firm's training is designed to produce its future partners. To achieve this they aim to provide a balance of both formal and practical training and will give early responsibility to those who show promise. The two-year training contract consists of four six-month seats during which you will work alongside partners and other senior lawyers, some of whom are leaders in their field. As the firm practises in a wide variety of legal disciplines, trainees benefit from a diverse experience. Trainees undergo specific technical training in each seat in addition to the mandatory Professional Skills Course (PSC). Great emphasis is also placed on soft skills training and development so when you qualify you have the breadth of skills required to be an excellent solicitor.

Benefits

Bonus scheme, group health care, life assurance, pension scheme, on site subsidised café, season ticket loan and corporate rate gym membership

---

Partners 51
Fee Earners 122
Total Trainees 17

Contact
Graduate Recruitment Team
(020) 7227 7000

Method of application
Please visit the careers section of the firm's website, www.bdb-law.co.uk and go to the graduate area

Selection procedure
Two interviews with members of the Graduate Recruitment Team, comprising a number of partners, associates and HR. In addition you will be required to complete a verbal reasoning test, in-tray exercise and presentation

Closing date for 2011
31 July 2009 for autumn 2011

Application
Training contracts p.a. 10
Applications p.a. 650
% interviewed p.a. 8%
Required degree grade:
2:1 or above degree preferred

Training
Salary
1st year (1 October 2008)
£31,000
2nd year (2008) £32,000
Holiday entitlement
25 days

Post-qualification
Salary £51,000
% of trainees offered job on qualification (2006) 85%

Bird & Bird

15 Fetter Lane, London EC4A 1JP
Tel: (020) 7415 6000 Fax: (020) 7415 6111
Website: www.twobirds.com

Firm profile

Bird & Bird is a sector focused, full service international law firm. The firm has 187 Partners and over 1,200 staff across offices in Beijing, Brussels, Dusseldorf, Frankfurt, The Hague, Helsinki Hong Kong, London, Lyon, Madrid, Milan, Munich, Paris, Rome and Stockholm. The firm is proud of its friendly, stimulating environment where individuals are able to develop first class legal, business and interpersonal skills. The firm's international reach and focus on sectors will enable you to work across borders and for a variety of companies, many of which operate at the cutting edge of the industries in which they operate. The firm has a leading reputation in many of the sectors on which it focuses: aviation and aerospace, communications, electronics, energy and utilities, financial services, information technology, life sciences, media and sport. From each of its offices, the firm provides a full range of legal services including:

Main areas of work

Commercial, corporate, corporate restructuring and insolvency, dispute resolution, employment, EU and competition law, finance, intellectual property, outsourcing, public procurement, real estate, regulatory and administrative, tax.

Trainee profile

The firm recognises that its lawyers are its most important asset and that is why the firm recruits strong graduates capable of developing expert legal skills and commercial acumen. A certain level of intelligence and common sense is a prerequisite. The firm looks for well rounded candidates with excellent A-levels and a strong 2:1.

The firm's trainee solicitors are outgoing, articulate team-players, willing to work hard when called upon and genuinely interested in progressing their careers. The firm aims to recruit people who will stay with the firm and therefore seek candidates who have a long-term interest in Bird & Bird and the sectors and areas of legal practice it focuses on.

Training environment

The firm's trainees take on responsibility from day one and enjoy varied and challenging work for industry-shaping clients. If you become a trainee with us, you will be given the chance to excel.

We run a business skills development programme to provide you with the basic building blocks for your future development within the business of law. The firm is still personal enough for its trainees to make their mark in the firm's friendly, stimulating work place.

Trainees will spend six months in three of the firm's practice areas. Trainees will then have a choice of spending their last six months in the area in which they would like to qualify.

Trainees are encouraged to join the number of sports teams at the firm and to attend various social events.

Benefits

BUPA, season ticket loan, subsidised sports club membership, life cover, PHI, pension, childcare and eyecare vouchers.

vacation placements

Places for 2009: 20; Duration: 2 x 3 weeks; Remuneration: £275 p.w; Closing Date: 31 January 2009.

Sponsorship & awards

LPC and PgDL fees paid and a yearly maintenance grant of £5,500.

Partners 187*
Assistant Solicitors 410*
Total Trainees 33 in London
*denotes worldwide figures

Contact
Lynne Walters, Graduate &
Trainee Manager
lynne.walters@twobirds.com

Method of application
Online application form via the firm website.

Selection procedure
Insight and selection days in February 2009 for Summer placements and August 2009 for Training Contracts.

Closing date for 2011
31 July 2009 for law and non-law students.

Application
Training contracts p.a. 17
Applications p.a. 900
% interviewed p.a. 10%
Required degree grade 2:1

Training
Salary
1st year (2008) £37,000
2nd year (2008) £40,000
Holiday entitlement
25 days
% of trainees with a non-law degree p.a. Varies

Post-qualification
Salary (2008) £60,000
% of trainees offered job on qualification (2008) 80%

Overseas offices
Beijing, Brussels, Dusseldorf, Frankfurt, The Hague, Helsinki, Hong Kong, London, Lyon, Madrid, Milan, Munich, Paris, Rome and Stockholm

Blake Lapthorn

New Kings Court, Tollgate, Chandler's Ford, East Leigh, Hampshire, SO53 3LG
Tel: (02380) 908090 Fax: (02380) 908092,
Email: graduateinfo@bllaw.co.uk
Website: www.bllaw.co.uk

Firm profile

Blake Lapthorn is one of the largest regional law firms in the UK, with offices in London, Hampshire and Oxford. Their clients include a wide range of UK and multinational companies, from well-known retailers, banks, local authorities and property developers to major charities. They also act for private clients offering specialist services such as French property, tax planning and clinical negligence. Although a large practice they have retained a sense of community. The firm values diversity, which adds breadth to its expertise. Their professionals have very different backgrounds and skills, many having worked in city firms and in-house. Their advice is practical, providing clients with tailored solutions. They encourage innovation and imagination in order to enhance their client services.

Main areas of work

The core practice areas are corporate and commercial, real estate, litigation and dispute resolution, and private client.

Trainee profile

Fitting in at Blake Lapthorn is about ability, enthusiasm and contribution. In order to maintain their standards of excellence, they need high-calibre people. To be successful you need to demonstrate significant personal achievement and strong interpersonal skills as well as an excellent academic record.

Training environment

Training is carefully structured and designed to provide variety, responsibility and intellectual challenge. You will have a series of six-month placements in a range of departments. Working with a partner or senior solicitor, you will be exposed to a wide range of clients and work, in private and commercial practice areas. During each placement your supervisor will involve you directly in work so you learn from hands-on experience, as well as observation and instruction. The greater competence you demonstrate, the more responsibility you will be given.

Benefits

Private healthcare, life assurance, contributory pension scheme, childcare vouchers and 'You at Work' flexible benefits.

Sponsorship & awards

LPC fees and maintenance grant.

Partners 107
Assistant Solicitors 263
Total Trainees 34

Contact
Mrs Lynn Ford

Method of application
Online application form with link from website.

Selection procedure
Interviews and Assessment Day

Closing date for 2011
12 July 2009

Application
Training contracts p.a. 17
Applications p.a. 400+
% interviewed p.a. 25%
Required degree grade 2:1

Training
Salary
1st year (2007)
Region £21,000
London £28,000
2nd year (2007)
Region £22,500
London £31,000
Holiday entitlement
26 days

Post-qualification
Salary (2007)
Region £35,000
London £48,000
% of trainees offered job on qualification (2007) 88%
% of trainees offered job on qualification (2008) 79%

Offices
Southampton, Portsmouth, Oxford, London and Winchester

Bond Pearce LLP

3 Temple Quay, Temple Back East, Bristol, BS1 6DZ
Tel: 0845 415 0000   Fax: 0845 415 6900
Email: sam.lee@bondpearce.com
Website: www.bondpearce.com

Firm profile

With aspirations to become a top five national business law firm in the next three years this is an exciting time to be thinking about joining Bond Pearce. The firm's recent growth has been based on forging strong client relationships, providing effective business solutions and recruiting high calibre people across the firm. The firm has recently been named by Chambers Guide to the UK Legal Profession 2007 as a "regional leader and highly credible national force".

Outstanding client service is something the firm is passionate about, as it helps to build and reinforce relationships, improve the timeliness of advice and encourage teamwork. The result: commercial legal advice that is proactive rather than simply reactive. According to the most recent Chambers FTSE survey the firm is ranked as the joint-leading choice, regionally, for FTSE 100 clients.

Main areas of work

The firm's particular strengths lie in its sector expertise and much of its work lies at the cutting edge of developments in key sectors such as energy, retail, financial services, real estate and the public sector.

Trainee profile

The firm is looking for individuals who are capable of combining great legal knowledge with a sound commercial focus; people who are driven, creative and have a genuine enthusiasm for both the law and the firm's business and individuals with a natural ability in dealing with people.

Training environment

You couldn't ask for a better start to your legal career. The firm offer's a first class training and development programme ensuring that you qualify with the best possible legal, business and personal skills. The firm has worked hard to create a culture that encourages, inspires and challenges. The firm's Graduate Team, consisting of partners, associates and HR provide all the support and encouragement that you need to see you through your two years with the firm. Structured over four seats the firm offers a good range of practice areas for you to train and qualify into.

Vacation placements

Two weeks in June/July.

Sponsorship & awards

Full GDL and LPC £6,000 maintenance grant for both.

Trainees 33
Partners 76
Lawyers 350
Total staff 650

Contact
Samantha Lee
Sam.lee@bondpearce.com
0845 415 6521

Method of application
Electronic application form

Selection procedure
Assessment days

Closing date
31 July 2009

Application
Training contracts p.a. 15-20
Required degree grade 2:1

Training
Salary
1st year £24,000
2nd year £25,000
Holiday entitlement
25 days

Offices
Bristol, Plymouth, Southampton, London, Aberdeen

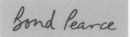

Boodle Hatfield

89 New Bond Street, London, W1S 1DA
Tel: (020) 7629 7411 Fax: (020) 7629 2621
Email: traineesolicitors@boodlehatfield.com
Website: www.boodlehatfield.com

Firm profile

Boodle Hatfield is a highly successful medium-sized firm which has been providing bespoke legal services for more than 275 years. They still act for some of their very first clients and are proud to do so. The firm has grown into a substantial practice, serving the full spectrum of commercial and private clients, both domestically and internationally.

Main areas of work

The ethos of facilitating private capital activity and private businesses underpins the work of the whole firm. The interplay of skills between four major areas – private client and tax, property, corporate and litigation – makes Boodle Hatfield particularly well placed to serve these individuals and businesses.

Trainee profile

The qualities the firm looks for in its trainees are commitment, flexibility and the ability to work as part of a team. Students with 2.1 or above and high A levels should apply.

Training environment

Trainees spend six months in up to four of the firm's main areas: Property, Corporate, Private Client & Tax, and Litigation. Boodle Hatfield is well known for the high quality of its training. All trainees are involved in client work from the start and are encouraged to handle their own files personally as soon as they are able to do so, with the appropriate supervision. The firm's trainees therefore have a greater degree of client contact than in many firms with the result that they should be able to take on more responsibility at an early stage. Trainees are given formal appraisals every three months which are designed as a two-way process and give trainees the chance to discuss their progress and to indicate where more can be done to help in their ongoing training and development.

Benefits

Private healthcare, life assurance, season ticket loan, pension scheme, private health insurance, conveyancing grant, permanent health insurance, employee assistance line, childcare vouchers, cycle to work scheme, give as you earn scheme.

Vacation placements

Two week placement between June and September, for which 10 students are accepted each year. Applicants should apply via the application form on the website at www.boodlehatfield.com.

Sponsorship & awards

LPC and GDL plus maintenance grant.

Partners 30
Assistant Solicitors 37
Total Trainees 12

Contact
Justine Fowler
(020) 7079 8200

Method of application
Online application

Selection procedure
Interviews with the Training Principal, a Partner and the HR Director plus an ability test in verbal reasoning

Closing date for 2011
See website

Application
Training contracts p.a. 6
Required degree grade 2:1

Training
Salary
1st year £32,000
2nd year £34,500
Holiday entitlement
25 days

Post-qualification
Salary £52,000

Regional offices
Oxford

B P Collins

Collins House, 32-38 Station Road, Gerrards Cross SL9 8EL
Tel: (01753) 889995 Fax: (01753) 889851
Email: jacqui.symons@bpcollins.co.uk
Website: www.bpcollins.co.uk

Firm profile

B P Collins was established in 1966, and has expanded significantly to become one of the largest and best known legal practices at the London end of the M4/M40 corridors. At its main office in Gerrards Cross, the emphasis is on commercial work, including corporate/commercial work of all types, commercial conveyancing and general commercial litigation. Alongside this there is a highly respected private client department specialising in tax planning, trusts, charities, wills and probates, and an equally successful family law team.

Main areas of work

Corporate/commercial, employment, IT/IP, civil and commercial litigation, commercial conveyancing, property development, private client and family law.

Trainee profile

Most of the partners and other fee-earners have worked in London at one time or another but, tired of commuting, have opted to work in more congenial surroundings and enjoy a higher quality lifestyle. Gerrards Cross is not only a very pleasant town with a large number of high net worth private clients but it is also a convenient location for serving the extremely active business community at the eastern end of the Thames Valley including West London, Heathrow, Uxbridge, Slough and Windsor. The firm therefore looks for trainees who are likely to respond to this challenging environment.

Training environment

The firm aims to have eight trainee solicitors at different stages of their training contracts at all times. Trainees serve five months in four separate departments of their choice. The final four months is spent in the department in which the trainee intends specialising. The firm has a training partner with overall responsibility for all trainees and each department has its own training principal who is responsible for day to day supervision. There are regular meetings between the training principal and the trainee to monitor progress and a review meeting with the training partner midway and at the end of each departmental seat. The firm also involves its trainees in social and marketing events including football and cricket matches, and other sporting and non-sporting activities.

Partners 20
Assistant Solicitors 32
Total Trainees 8

Contact
HR Manager Mrs Jacqui Symons

Method of application
Handwritten covering letter & CV
selection procedure
Screening interview & assessment day

Closing date for 2010
31 May 2009

Application
Required degree grade 2:1, A & B 'A' level grades.

Training
Salary
1st year £22,000
2nd year £23,000

BPE Solicitors

St James' House, St James' Square, Cheltenham GL50 3PR
Tel: (01242) 224433   Fax: (01242) 574285
Email: bpe@bpe.co.uk
Website: www.bpe.co.uk

Firm profile

BPE thrives on being different to many other law firms.

It is prepared to pioneer new approaches to provide a better service for its clients. And invests time and resources in new teams where it sees potential for growth. The firm's partners do not hide behind closed doors but instead work alongside their assistants and trainees so you have an opportunity to learn from their experience every step of the way.

With a presence in Birmingham and Cheltenham you can enjoy the challenge of working in two different legal marketplaces.

Main areas of work

BPE offers a full range of services including: Corporate, commercial property, commercial, employment, dispute resolution, construction and engineering, credit and asset finance, insolvency, private client and personal injury. Clients range from blue-chip multi-nationals, property developers and entrepreneurs to charities and local authorities.

Trainee profile

BPE looks for high-calibre, commercially astute individuals with character. The firm's 'work hard, play hard' ethos makes it an ideal workplace for dedicated and driven lawyers-to-be who are keen to socialise with colleagues outside of the office. Applications from law and non-law graduates are welcome provided you have a 2:1 degree.

Training environment

BPE adopt a flexible approach to your training. If you suspect commercial property may be your eventual specialisation or you have a passion for corporate work the firm will try to accommodate you.

Trainees at the firm are required to spend a six month seat in each of the following disciplines and are encouraged to spend their last six-month seat in the team of their choice: Corporate; commercial property; dispute resolution. Although your training will be hands-on, the firm offers a comprehensive trainee induction programme to help you understand the firm's style of working, its culture, policies and procedures.

Benefits

A contributory pension scheme, 25 days holiday, discounted gym membership, income protection to cover long-term illness, death in service benefits and a sabbatical scheme.

Sponsorship & awards

BPE supports trainees in attending the Professional Skills Course (PSC).

Partners 24
Assistant Solicitors 28
Total Trainees 8

Contact
Amanda Coleman
(01242) 248231

Method of application
Application form, available on website

Selection procedure
Shortlisted applicants are invited to attend an open day in September each year. A final shortlist of applicants is invited to attend an assessment day which includes formal interview, case studies and a numerical and verbal reasoning test.

Closing date for 2011
31st July 2009

Application
Training contracts p.a. 6
Applications p.a. 100
% interviewed p.a. 25%
Required degree grade 2:1

Training
Salary
1st year £20,000 (then an additional £500 on completion of each seat)
Holiday entitlement
25 days

Post-qualification
Salary Market rate
% of trainees offered job on qualification 80%

Regional offices
Birmingham, London (Please note training contracts are only available at the Cheltenham and Birmingham offices)

Brabners Chaffe Street LLP

Horton House, Exchange Flags, Liverpool L2 3YL
Tel: (0151) 600 3000 Fax: (0151) 227 3185
55 King Street, Manchester M2 4LQ Tel: (0161) 236 5800 Fax: (0161) 228 6862
7-8 Chapel Street, Preston PR1 8AN Tel: (01772) 823921 Fax: (01772) 201918
Email: trainees@brabnerscs.com
Website: www.brabnerschaffestreet.com

Firm profile

One of the top North West commercial firms, Brabners Chaffe Street LLP, in Liverpool, Manchester and Preston, has the experience, talent and prestige of a firm that has a 200-plus-year history. Brabners Chaffe Street LLP is a dynamic, client-led specialist in the provision of excellent legal services to clients ranging from large plcs to private individuals.

Main areas of work

The LLP carries out a wide range of specialist legal services and Brabners Chaffe Street's client base includes plcs, public sector bodies, banks and other commercial, corporate and professional businesses. The LLP's client focused departments include banking, corporate, commercial (including sports law), employment, litigation (including media and sports law), property (including housing association and construction) and private client.

Trainee profile

Graduates and those undertaking CPE or LPC, who can demonstrate intelligence, intuition, humour, approachability and commitment.

Training environment

The LLP is one of the few law firms that holds Investor in People status and has a comprehensive training and development programme. It is listed in the Sunday Times Best 100 Employers to work for in 2006, 2007 and 2008. Trainees are given a high degree of responsibility and are an integral part of the culture of the firm. Each trainee will have partner-level supervision. Personal development appraisals are conducted at three and six-monthly intervals to ensure that trainee progress is valuable and informed. The training programme is overseen by the firm's Director of Training and Development, Dr Tony Harvey, and each centre has a designated Trainee Partner. It is not all hard work and the firm has an excellent social programme.

Sponsorship & awards

Assistance with LPC funding is available.

Partners 58
Associates 24
Assistant Solicitors 39
Fee Earners 28
Total Trainees 18

Contact
Liverpool office:
Dr Tony Harvey
Director of Training and Risk Management

Method of application
Online

Selection procedure
Interview & assessment day

Closing date for 2011
Apply by 6th July 2009 for training contracts commencing in September 2011 and for the summer vacation scheme 2009

Application
Training contracts p.a. 10
Required degree grade
2:1 or post-graduate degree

Training
Salary
Not less than £21,000
Holiday entitlement 25 days

Offices
Liverpool, Manchester, Preston

Bristows

100 Victoria Embankment, London EC4Y 0DH
Tel: (020) 7400 8000 Fax: (020) 7400 8050
Email: info@bristows.com
Website: www.bristows.com

Firm profile

Bristows specialises in providing legal services to businesses with interests in technology or intellectual property. The firm acts for some of the largest companies in the world and helps protect some of the most famous brands. Its work reaches beyond intellectual property law to corporate and commercial law, property, tax, employment

law and litigation.

Main areas of work

Intellectual property, IT, bio/pharma, corporate, competition, commercial litigation, mediation, ADR, publishing and media, employment, real estate and tax.

Trainee profile

Bristows is looking for applicants with outstanding intellects, with strong analytical skills and engaging personalities. It is also looking for people who will contribute to the

ethos of the firm. Bristows is a very friendly firm and believes that you get the best from

people if they are in a happy and supportive working environment.

Training environment

The firm's training programme gives you the knowledge and skills to build on the extensive hands-on experience you will gain in each of its main departments. You will be working closely with Partners, which will accelerate your training. Part of this training may also involve a secondment to one of a number of leading clients. With the international spread of its clients, the probability of overseas travel is high, especially upon qualification.

Benefits

Excellent career prospects, a competitive package, firm pension scheme, life assurance
and health insurance.

Placement schemes

Schemes are run for one week during Easter break and two weeks during the Summer break. Remuneration: £250 p.w.; Closing Date: Easter/Summer – 28 February 2009/ Christmas 20 November 09.

Sponsorship & awards

CPE/LPC fees plus £7,000 maintenance grant for each.

Partners 27
Assistant Solicitors 48
Total Trainees 14

Contact
Trainee Recruitment & Training Officer

Method of application
Application form

Selection procedure
2 individual interviews

Closing date for 2011
31 January 2009 for February interviews,
31 July 2009 for
August interviews

Application
Training contracts p.a.
Up to 10
Applications p.a. 3,500
% interviewed p.a. 6%
Required degree grade
2:1 (preferred)

Training
Salary
1st year (2008) £33,000
2nd year (2008) £36,000
Holiday entitlement
4 weeks
% of trainees with
a non-law degree p.a. 86%

Post-qualification
Salary (2008) £53,500
% of trainees offered job
on qualification (2008) 100%
% of assistants (as at 5/6/06)
who joined as trainees 46%
% of partners (as at 01/08/07)
who joined as trainees 33%

Browne Jacobson

Nottingham, Birmingham, London
Tel: (0115) 976 6000 Fax: (0115) 947 5246
Email: traineeapplications@brownejacobson.com
Website: www.brownejacobson.com/trainees.aspx

Firm profile

Browne Jacobson is one of the largest full service commercial law firms in the Midlands with regional and national reach through its offices in Nottingham, Birmingham and London. The firm is also one of the fastest growing law firms in the UK, having trebled in size over the last nine years - this has been organic and not by way of mergers which has maintained a strong culture. The firm is currently out-performing its rivals in delivering consistent growth.

With over 500 people, Browne Jacobson is large enough to attract some of the best talent in the country, but small enough to foster a supportive and flexible working environment. The firm's people are the key to its success and it has a track record of attracting and retaining outstanding people. This was recognised by the Lawyer HR Awards 2008 when the firm picked up the Graduate Recruitment Campaign of the Year Award.

Browne Jacobson focuses on long-term relationships that are friendly, flexible and straightforward, both with its people and its clients. The firm's modern, progressive working environment and its friendly and open culture mean that its people enjoy working here so they stay. This allows good working relationships to develop and provides consistency for clients. It's a simple tactic yet one that works; a large proportion of the firm's client base has been with the firm for a number of years.

Main areas of work

The firm has a long established and nationwide reputation in all areas of its commercial, public sector and insurance practices and is recognised as regional heavyweight for corporate, property, public enquiry, litigation and professional risk work.

Trainee profile

Brown Jacobson is looking for talented law and non-law graduates who can bring with them enthusiasm, commitment, client focus and a flexible and friendly attitude.

Training environment

Trainees start with a comprehensive induction programme, a fast track professional skills course and then go onto a trainee development programme. Trainees will spend four periods of six months in some of the principle areas of the firm, gaining an overview of the practice. Trainees get great training, a friendly and supportive working environment, and real career opportunities. They are also given quality work and exposure to clients from early on, but are supported in achieving results and recognised for their contribution.

Sponsorship & awards

LPC/PGDL tuition fees paid, plus maintenance grant for LPC/PGDL of £5,000.

Benefits

Life assurance, private health insurance, corporate discounts, and after the first year, the option to join the firm's pension and private medical insurance schemes.

Partners 56
Associates 55
Assistant Solicitors 71
Total Trainees 22
Total Staff 502

Contact
Philippa Shorthouse, HR Advisor

Method of application
Apply online at www.brownejacobson.com/trainees.aspx or by CV and covering letter

Selection procedure
Telephone interview, assessment centre and partner interview

Closing date
31 July, two years before the training contract is due to commence

Application
Training contracts p.a. 10
Applications p.a. 700
% interviewed p.a. 8%
Required degree grade 2:1

Training
Salary
1st year (2008) £24,500
2nd year (2008) £27,000
Holiday entitlement 25 days
% of trainees with a non-law degree p.a. 40%

Post-qualification
Salary Market Rate
Holiday entitlement 25 days
% of trainees offered a job on qualification (2007) 66.6%

brownejacobson

Burges Salmon

Narrow Quay House, Narrow Quay, Bristol BS1 4AH
Tel: (0117) 902 2766 Fax: (0117) 902 4400
Email: katy.edge@burges-salmon.com
Website: www.burges-salmon.com

Firm profile

Burges Salmon is proof that law doesn't have to mean London.

Based in Bristol, the firm's turnover has more than tripled in recent years as it continues to win prestigious clients out of the hands of City rivals. Clients such as Orange, the Ministry of Defence and Virgin Mobile rely on its legal expertise and in doing so have helped cement the firm's reputation for creative, lateral thinking. Burges Salmon's primary asset is its people. Trainees benefit from supervision by lawyers who are leaders in their field with a formidable depth of experience. All this against the backdrop of Bristol: a city with a quality of life you would be hard pressed to find anywhere else in the UK.

Main areas of work

Burges Salmon provides national and international clients such as The Crown Estate, Reuters and Chanel with a full commercial service through six main departments: corporate and financial institutions; commercial; property; tax and trusts; commercial disputes and construction; and agriculture, property litigation and environment.

Trainee profile

Burges Salmon lawyers are hard working, motivated individuals with a strong academic background and enthusiasm for a career in law. Candidates must be commercially aware and possess excellent communication skills.

Training environment

Trainees play a vital role in shaping the future of the firm and Burges Salmon invests a great deal of time and resource into training and development. Training is personalised to suit each individual, and the six seat structure allows the opportunity to experience a wider range of practice areas before making a decision on qualification. This dedication to trainees is demonstrated by a high retention rate, which is well above the industry average.

Vacation placements

Burges Salmon runs two open days in February and offers 40 two-week vacation placements during the summer. Individuals visit two departments of their choice supervised by a Partner or senior solicitor, and attend court visits and client meetings. Current trainees run skills training sessions, sports and social events. Remuneration: £250 per week.

Sponsorship and awards

The firm pays GDL and LPC fees at the institution of your choice. Maintenance grants of £7,000 are paid to LPC students, and £14,000 to students studying for both the GDL and LPC (£7,000 p.a.).

Benefits

Annually reviewed competitive salary, 24 days paid annual leave, bonus scheme, pension scheme, private health care membership, life assurance, mobile phone, laptop, Christmas gift, corporate gym membership, sports and social club.

Partners 72
Assistant Solicitors 279 Total
Trainees 43

Contact
Katy Edge, Recruitment
Manager

Method of application
Employer's application form
available on website

Selection procedure
Penultimate year law students,
final year
non-law students, recent
graduates and those
considering a change of career
are considered for open days,
vacation placements and/or
training contracts.

Closing date for 2011
31 July 2009

Application
Training contracts p.a.
25
Applications p.a. 1,500
% interviewed p.a. 10%
Required degree grade 2:1

Training
Salary
1st year (2008) £30,000
2nd year (2008) £31,000
Holiday entitlement 24 days
% of trainees with
a non-law degree p.a. 50%

Post-qualification
Salary (2008) £TBC
% of trainees offered job
on qualification (2008) 94%
% of assistants who joined as
trainees (2008) 50%
% of partners who joined as
trainees (2008) 30%

Campbell Hooper Solicitors LLP

35 Old Queen Street, London, SW1H 9JD
Tel: (020) 7222 9070   Fax: (020) 7222 5591
Website: campbellhooper.com
Email: hr@campbellhooper.com

Firm profile

Campbell Hooper is a leading London law firm based in the heart of Westminster. Providing comprehensive commercial and private client services, Campbell Hooper serves clients' interests through an integrated approach. This incorporates the firm's expertise in a number of market sectors, the sharing of key information across relevant practice areas, and a profound knowledge about each client's business, history and specific needs.

Main areas of work

Construction, corporate and commercial, employment, litigation, media, private client and family, real estate, tax.

Trainee profile

The firm sees trainees playing a central part in its continuing development. Being a trainee is a fantastic opportunity and the firm looks for people who want to make the most of it. The firm wants you to feel confident to ask valuable questions and to contribute ideas. The firm looks for trainees that are committed to undertaking that role, willing to play their part and are excited by the opportunities working at Campbell Hooper can offer.

Training environment

As a trainee you will develop your commercial acumen and legal flair through exposure in four of the firm's practice areas. Trainees are actively involved in business development, marketing and client-facing activities, and a variety of training and development activities as well as providing some basic administrative support to partners and fee earners.

The firm sees supervision as being continuous, facilitated through direction and support from a Partner or solicitor, and structured mid and end-of-seat reviews. Additionally, trainees receive mentoring from the firm's dedicated Trainee Principal who conducts regular trainee surgeries which provides an opportunity for review and reflection.

Benefits

Starting salary of £30,500 (2008); 25 days holiday; Contributory pension plan; Private medical insurance; Private health insurance; Life assurance; Season ticket loan; Staff introduction scheme; Employee assistance programme; Childcare vouchers; Maintenance grant of £5,000 for each year of study; LPC/GDL/CPE sponsorship.

Partners 24
Assistant Solicitors 52
Total Trainees 10

Contact
Grant Robinson

Method of application
Online at
www.campbellhooper.com

Selection procedure
Verbal reasoning
psychometrics, 2 interviews

Closing date for 2011
30 June 2009

Application
Training contracts p.a. 5
Applications p.a. 150
% interviewed p.a. 20%
Required degree grade 2:1

Training
Salary
1st year (2007) £30,500
2nd year (2007) £33,500
Holiday entitlement 25 days

Post-qualification
Salary (2007) £51,000
% of trainees offered job
on qualification (2008) 100%

Overseas offices
None (London only)

Capsticks

77-83 Upper Richmond Road, London SW15 2TT
Tel: (020) 8780 2211   Fax: (020) 8780 4811
Email: career@capsticks.co.uk
Website: www.capsticks.com

Firm profile

Capsticks is the leading provider of legal services to the healthcare sector. The firm has over 100 fee earners and has ambitious plans for further growth, both in its core market and by promoting its broader capability and expanding private sector client base.

Main areas of work

The firm acts for a wide range of healthcare clients, including NHS Trusts and Health Authorities, the NHSLA, regulatory bodies, charities and independent healthcare providers. The firm's main practice areas are clinical law, corporate/commercial, dispute resolution, employment and property.

Trainee profile

The firm is committed to recruiting the best people to maintain its market leading position. The firm recruits five trainee solicitors each year and welcomes applications from candidates who are either on course for or have achieved at least a 2.1 (or equivalent) in their undergraduate degree. The firm expects candidates to be committed to a career in healthcare law and to be able to demonstrate they are highly driven, but well rounded, team players, with good problem solving and communication skills.

Training environment

The firm's broad range of practice areas and healthcare clients enables it to give its trainees an opportunity to experience a wide variety of legal work. Trainees are therefore able to acquire an in-depth knowledge of both healthcare law and the healthcare industry, in addition to developing the skills that any good lawyer needs.

The training contract is designed to give trainees maximum exposure to the work of the firm and trainees undertake seats in all of the firm's practice areas, including clinical law, corporate commercial, dispute resolution, employment and property.

Benefits

Bonus scheme, 25 days holiday, pension contribution, permanent health insurance, private medical insurance, death in service benefit, childcare voucher scheme and season ticket loan.

Vacation placements

The firm's vacation scheme runs from the end of June through to the middle of August and placements last for two weeks each. In order to be eligible for the 2009 vacation scheme you should be looking to secure a training contract with the firm in September 2011. The firm welcomes applications for a place on its 2009 vacation scheme between 17 November 2008 and 28 February 2009. Further details are available from the website.

The firm encourages all prospective trainee solicitors to participate in the vacation scheme as this is their primary means for selecting future trainee solicitors.

Sponsorship & awards

The firm offers its future trainees financial support for both the Graduate Diploma in Law and the Legal Practice Course.

Partners 30
Assistant Solicitors 60
Total Trainees 10
Other Fee-earners 20

Contact
HR department,
career@capsticks.co.uk

Method of application
Application form, CV and covering letter

Selection procedure
Interview with Partner and Director of HR

Closing date for 2011
31 August 2009

Application
Training contracts p.a. 5
Applications p.a. 200
% interviewed p.a. 7%
Required degree grade
2:1 or above

Training
Salary
1st year £28,000
2nd year £29,000
Holiday entitlement
25 days p.a.
% of trainees with a
non-law degree p.a. 50%

Post-qualification
Salary (2008)
£45,000
% of trainees offered job
on qualification (2008) 100%

Charles Russell LLP

8–10 New Fetter Lane, London EC4A 1RS
Tel: (020) 7203 5000 Fax: (020) 7203 5307
Website: www.charlesrussell.co.uk

Firm profile

Charles Russell LLP is a leading legal practice, providing a full range of services to UK and international businesses, governments, not-for-profit bodies, and individuals. It has eight offices: two in London, Cheltenham, Guildford, Cambridge, Oxford, Geneva and Bahrain. The practice is known for its client care, high quality, expertise and friendly approach. The strategy is simple – to help clients achieve their goals through excellent service. Many lawyers are ranked as leaders in their field. Experienced in carrying out cross-border corporate and commercial work, the practice also provides clients with access to 150 recommended law firms across the world as part of the two major legal networks, ALFA International and the Association of European Lawyers. The practice's lawyers and staff are highly motivated and talented people and many are ranked as leaders in their fields. The practice's commitment to training and development and strong team spirit is a key ingredient to being known as a friendly practice to work with and work at.

Main areas of work

75% of the Practice's work is commercial. Principal areas of work include corporate/commercial, litigation and dispute resolution, intellectual property, employment and pensions, real estate, technology, media, communications and sport, charities, private client and family.

Trainee profile

Trainees should be balanced, rounded achievers with an excellent academic background and outside interests.

Training environment

The practice recruits a small number of trainees for its size each year. This allows trainees to undergo the best possible training. Trainees spend six months in four of the following training seats – corporate/commercial, employment/pensions, family, litigation and dispute resolution, private client and real estate. Secondments to clients are also often available. Wherever possible the practice will accommodate individual preferences. You will be seated with a partner/senior solicitor. Regular appraisals are held to discuss progress and direction. Trainees are encouraged to attend extensive in-house training. The PSC is taught both internally and externally. Trainees are encouraged to take on as much responsibility as possible. A social committee organises a range of activities from quiz nights through to sporting events.

Benefits

BUPA; PHI; Life Assurance; pension; season ticket loan; 25 days holiday plus additional day for house moves.

Sponsorship & awards

The practice pays for course fees whilst you are at law school and also offers a grant per academic year of £6,000 to London trainees, £4,500 to Guildford and Cambridge trainees, £3,500 to Cheltenham trainees.

Partners 104
Other fee-earners 233
Total trainees 39
Total staff 681

Contact
graduaterecruitment@
charlesrussell.co.uk

Method of application
Online application via the website

Selection procedure
Assessment days to include an interview & other exercises designed to assess identified performance criteria

Closing date for 2011
31st July 2009

Application
Training contracts for 2011: 21
Applications p.a.
Approx 1,500
% interviewed p.a. 7%
Preferred degree grade 2:1

Training
Salary (London)
1st year (2007) £32,500
2nd year (2007) £36,000
Holiday entitlement
25 days + additional day for house moves

Post-qualification
Salary (2008) £58-60,000

Regional offices
Also offers training contracts in its Cheltenham (2 places) Guildford (4 places) offices and Cambridge (1 place).

Clarion Solicitors LLP

Britannia Chambers, 4 Oxford Place, Leeds, LS1 3AX
Tel: (0113) 246 0622 Fax: (0113) 246 7488
Email: l.jackson@clarionsolicitors.com

Partners 14
Associate solicitors 35
Trainees 10
Contact
Linda Jackson
Method of application
Application form, available on website
closing date for 2011
27 February 2009
Application
Training contracts p.a.: 4
Preferred degree grade 2:1
Training
Salary
Highly competitive
Post-qualification
Salary (2008)
Highly competitive
% of Partners (as at 01/04/08) who joined as trainees 40%

Firm profile

Clarion Solicitors LLP is a major presence in Leeds, handling legal services for a growing number of leading businesses and individuals both locally and nationwide. The firm believes that legal services can and should offer genuine benefits and add real value to the lives of the businesses and individuals who use them. To accomplish that, it draws on all the intellectual capability and ability to innovate all its people, as well as on their human values of humour, communication and engagement with the community. Clarion Solicitors LLP approach rests on an unwavering commitment to the traditions of integrity and professionalism, and also on a clear vision that more can be delivered to clients: greater clarity and innovation in thought and expression, more and better communication at all levels of the firm's activities, enhanced transparency in the processes through which the firm guides its clients, and a commitment and energy which focus clients' needs and intentions into a clear call to action.

Main areas of work

Clarion Solicitors LLP divides its people into ten departments as follows: corporate and commercial; employment; intellectual property; property, dispute resolution, private client, family, corporate recovery, business crime and regulatory, and law costs drafting. The firm therefore handles a complete range of services to businesses and individuals, and offers a range of possible career paths for its trainees.

Trainee profile

The firm believes that to be involved in Clarion Solicitors LLP is to be at the heart of one of the most exciting projects the legal profession can offer. The firm is looking for trainee solicitors who will share that belief and the values the firm stands for, and who will work with it over the long term to realise the immense potential of the firm.

Training environment

At Clarion Solicitors LLP trainees are considered to be part of the team from the very outset. Each of the firm's departments (excluding law costs drafting) offers the opportunity to the firm's trainees to spend one of their four six month seats as part of the department. The training given is hands-on, and driven by an ethos of openness, innovation, ambition and intellectual enquiry. The firm believes Clarion Solicitors LLP offers a magnificent opportunity to trainee solicitors in a friendly, team-based environment.

Summer placement scheme

Clarion Solicitors LLP's summer placement scheme is used to assess candidates applying for training contracts. Candidates have the opportunity to spend the week in one of its departments. On the final day of the placement they take part in assessments in the morning followed by an interview with members of the graduate recruitment panel in the afternoon. In 2009 the firm will be offering a total of 24 one-week placements. Full details of the dates of the placements are available from our website. Applications must be received by 27 February 2009. All applications must take place via the firm's website at www.clarionsolicitors.com.

Clarke Willmott

138 Edmund Street, Birmingham, B3 2E5
Tel: (0845) 209 1729   Fax: (0845) 209 2516
Email: heather.cooper@clarkewillmott.com
Website: www.futurepilots.co.uk

Firm profile

Clarke Willmott is a UK law firm with a national reputation in key commercial and private client services. With 84 Partners and over 620 people in total, the firm operates from five locations: Bristol, Birmingham, Taunton, Southampton and London (serviced office).

The firm's lawyers are, first and foremost, business advisers whose objectives are to help clients achieve their goals and to enhance the value of their opportunities. The firm takes a straightforward, proactive approach, and has helped enterprises of all sizes and at all stages of the business lifecycle navigate a range of complex legal issues with positive results.

Main areas of work

Services include corporate, commercial, real estate and construction, business recovery, dispute resolution, employment, health and safety, intellectual property, property and private capital as well as a range of services to private clients. The firm has specialist industry expertise in real estate (development, investment, residential and urban regeneration), banking & financial services, sport, agriculture, leisure, renewable energy and food & drink.

Trainee profile

The firm recruits commercially aware trainees who can demonstrate a clear commitment to a career in law. Clarke Willmott looks for trainees who have a confident, energetic approach and who have the ability to work and communicate well with others. Applications are welcomed from both law and non-law graduates, with ideally a 2:1 degree.

Training environment

Trainees complete four six-month seats, providing a wide range of practical experience and skills in contentious and non-contentious work. Individual preference is sought and will be balanced with the firm's needs. Trainees work closely with partners and solicitors in a supportive team structure, and have regular reviews to ensure they are reaching their potential. Training in both legal and non-legal areas is provided to meet the needs of the individual trainee and the PSC is undertaken in-house.

Sponsorship & benefits

Life assurance, group personal pension, gym membership, performance related bonus, funding for the GDL and LPC, occupational sick pay, season ticket loans, eyecare vouchers, childcare vouchers.

Partners 86
Solicitors 145
Trainees 24

Contact
Heather Cooper, Graduate
Recruitment Manager

Method of application
Online application form

Selection procedure
Assessment centre
closing date for 2011
31 July 2009 (interviews
September 2009)

Application
Training contracts p.a.: 10
Applications p.a. c. 500
% interviewed p.a. 15%
Preferred degree grade 2:1

Training
Salary
1st year (2008) £24,000
2nd year (2008) £25,500
Holiday entitlement
25 days

Post-qualification
Salary (2008) £36,500-
£39,000 (dependant on
location)
% of trainees offered job
on qualification (2008) 63%

Regional offices
Birmingham, Bristol,
Southampton, Taunton, London

Cleary Gottlieb Steen & Hamilton LLP

City Place House, 55 Basinghall Street, London, EC2V 5EH
Tel: (020) 7614 2200 Fax: (020) 7600 1698
Email: longraduaterecruit@cgsh.com
Website: www.cgsh.com/careers/london

Firm profile

Cleary Gottlieb is one of the leading international law firms, with 12 closely integrated offices located in major financial and political centres around the world. For more than 60 years, the firm has been pre-eminent in shaping the globalisation of the legal profession. Its worldwide practice has a proven track record for innovation and providing advice of the highest quality to meet the domestic and international needs of its clients.

Main areas of work

Core practice groups in London are mergers and acquisitions, private equity, financing, and debt and equity capital markets (IPOs), plus additional self-standing practices in dispute resolution, competition, tax, financial regulation, intellectual property and information technology.

Trainee profile

Cleary looks for candidates who are enthusiastic about the practice of law in a challenging and dynamic international setting. Whilst academic excellence is a pre-requisite, the firm places particular emphasis on recruiting candidates that they and their clients will enjoy working with. A sense of humour is as important as the ability to think critically and creatively about cutting-edge legal issues.

Training environment

By limiting its graduate intake to just 10-12 trainees a year, Cleary is able to offer bespoke training that is individually tailored to the interests, experience and aptitudes of the individuals that join it. The firm does not believe that the transition from trainee solicitor to associate occurs overnight on qualification, but rather that the transition should be a smooth and gradual one. It therefore encourages its trainee solicitors to accept increased responsibility as soon as they are ready to do so. With appropriate levels of supervision, trainees operate as lawyers of the firm from the day that they join.

Benefits

Virgin Active gym membership, employer pension contributions, private healthcare cover (personal and family), life insurance of twice annual salary, long-term disability insurance, childcare vouchers, employee assistance programme and subsidised staff restaurant.

Vacation schemes

The firm's London office offers 35 vacation places each year (five at Christmas, ten at Easter and ten in each of two summer schemes). The firm actively encourages all candidates that are seriously considering applying for a trainee solicitor position with it to undertake a vacation placement with the firm. Applications for Christmas vacation placements should be received by November 15. The deadline for Easter and Summer vacation scheme applications is January 28.

Sponsorship & awards

Cleary funds the LPC for all future trainee solicitors. For non-law graduates, the firm also funds the GDL. A maintenance grant of £8,000 is paid for each year of professional study.

Trainees 15
Partners 196
(16 in London)
Total Staff 2500
(200 in London)

Contact
Shaun Goodman
Graduate Recruitment Partner

Method of application
Cover letter and CV

Selection procedure
Future trainees are primarily selected from among those having completed a vacation scheme with the firm

Closing date for 2011
July 31 2009

Application
Training contracts p.a. 10-12
Required degree grade
High 2:1

Training
Salary
1st year £40,000
2nd year £45,000

Post-qualification
Salary £92,000

Overseas offices
New York, Washington DC, Paris, Brussels, Moscow, Frankfurt, Cologne, Rome, Milan, Hong Kong and Beijing

Clifford Chance

10 Upper Bank Street, Canary Wharf, London, E14 5JJ
Tel: (020) 7006 3003 Fax: (020) 7006 5555
Email: Recruitment.London@CliffordChance.com
Website: www.cliffordchance.com/gradsuk

Firm profile

Clifford Chance is a leading international law firm delivering innovative and practical legal solutions to corporate, institutional and government clients globally.

Trainee profile

Clifford Chance are looking for your potential to become a first-class business lawyer. Communication, analytical and team-working skills all have a role to play.

Training environment

Each seat will bring you into contact with new clients and colleagues, and you can expect to work on a variety of deals and projects, large and small.

Benefits

As well as a competitive salary, you'll enjoy: a subsidised restaurant; free use of fitness centre, swimming pool, squash courts and wellness centre; the option of up to six weeks' leave on qualification and a pension.

Vacation placements

The firm runs two-day winter workshops, based in the London office, and longer schemes during the spring and summer. A number of international placements will also be available during the summer. Selected candidates will have the opportunity to spend two weeks in London, followed by two weeks in one of the firm's European offices.

Sponsorship & awards

Fees for GDL and LPC covered. Maintenance is also provided, please refer to website for details.

*Who's Who Legal Awards 2007. Employer of Choice for Law 2008, The Times Graduate Recruitment Awards.

London office
Partners 219
Lawyers 777
Trainees 260

Contact
Recruitment London (020) 7006 3003

Method of application
Online at www.cliffordchance.com/gradsuk

Selection procedure
Verbal reasoning test, group exercise, case study, competency-based interview

Application
Training contracts p.a. 130
Applications p.a. 3,500
% interviewed p.a. 25%
Required degree grade 2:1

Training
Salary
1st year £37,400
2nd year £42,200
Holiday entitlement 25 days
% of trainees with a non-law degree p.a. 40%
No. of seats available abroad p.a. 108 (54 in each six month seat)

Post-qualification
Salary £66,600
% of trainees offered job on qualification (2007) 95%

Overseas offices
Abu Dhabi, Amsterdam, Bangkok, Barcelona, Beijing, Brussels, Bucharest, Budapest, Dubai, Düsseldorf, Frankfurt, Hong Kong, London, Luxembourg, Madrid, Milan, Moscow, Munich, New York, Paris, Prague, Riyadh (co-operative office), Rome, São Paulo, Shanghai, Singapore, Tokyo, Warsaw, Washington DC

Clyde & Co

51 Eastcheap, London EC3M 1JP
Tel: (020) 7623 1244 Fax: (020) 7623 5427
Email: theanswers@clydeco.com   Website: www.clydeco.com/graduate

Firm profile

With roots in international trade, Clyde & Co LLP's main objective is to help clients do business in over 120 countries around the globe. The firm values entrepreneurialism, commercial problem solving, excellence and the freedom to be an individual. Clients value the firm's hand on innovative approach. The firm's lawyers know the industries, the clients, and most importantly understand the commercial realities of business. Availability and responsiveness are key in the firm's core industries and these characteristics have become part of the mindset of a Clyde & Co lawyer.

The firm has expanded rapidly in recent years and is a dominant player in the insurance, reinsurance, international litigation, shipping, aviation, transport, international trade and energy, and commodities sectors. Clyde & Co has one of the largest Litigation Practices in the UK.

Main areas of work

Aviation and Aerospace, Corporate/Commercial, Dispute Resolution, EC/Competition, Energy, Trade and Commodities, Insurance and Re-insurance, Real Estate Shipping, Transport and Logistics.

trainee profile

The firm is looking for graduates with excellent academic records, outgoing personalities and keen interests. Trainees need to have the social skills that will enable them to communicate effectively and build relationships with clients and colleagues. The ability to analyse problems, apply common sense and provide solutions to situations are all qualities the firm seeks. Ultimately Clyde & Co recruits to retain and they are seeking candidates who will remain with the firm beyond qualification.

Training environment

You will gain early responsibility and be supported through close personal supervision and day-to-day coaching complemented by a wide range of training courses. You will undertake four six-month seats in London and Guildford, which will cover both transactional and contentious work. You may also choose to be seconded to one of the firm's overseas offices or have the opportunity for a client secondment.

Benefits

An optional £1,000 interest free loan on joining, pension, life assurance, private medical insurance, subsidised gym membership, interest-free season ticket loan and coffee shop.

Legal work experience

The firm runs two-week summer vacation schemes for 20 students. The dates for the 2009 schemes are 22 June to 3 July and 21 July to 31 July. Applications are made online and the closing date is 31 January 2009. For more details please visit the website at www.clydeco.com/graduate.

Sponsorship & awards

GDL and LPC fees paid plus a maintenance grant of £7,000 in London/Guildford and £6,000 elsewhere.

Partners 140
Assistant Solicitors 270
Trainees 48

Contact
Kate Wild
Trainee Solicitor Recruitment
Manager

Method of application
Online via website
www.clydco.com/graduate

Selection procedure
Assessment session with
Graduate Recruitment followed
by interview with 2 partners
closing date for 2011
31 July 2009

Application
Training contracts p.a. 24
Applications p.a. 1,200 +
% interviewed p.a. 10%
Required degree grade 2:1

Training
Salary
1st year (2008) £35,000
2nd year (2008) £38,000
(Reviewed annually)
Holiday entitlement 25 days
% of trainees with
a non-law degree p.a. 60%

Post-qualification
Salary (2008) £64,000

Overseas offices
Abu Dhabi, Caracas, Doha,
Dubai, Hong Kong, San
Francisco, Moscow, Nantes,
New York, Paris, Piraeus, Rio de
Janeiro, Shanghai, Singapore,
and associate offices in
Belgrade and St Petersburg

CMS Cameron McKenna LLP

Mitre House, 160 Aldersgate Street, London EC1A 4DD
Tel: (0845) 300 0491 Fax: (020) 7367 2000
Email: gradrec@cms.cmck.com   Website: www.law-now.com

Firm profile

CMS is the leading European organisation of law and tax firms with more offices across Europe than any other firm. CMS brings together nine unique firms including CMS Cameron McKenna, which operates in the UK and across Central and Eastern Europe. The firm advises on a wide range of transactions and issues, and has developed many long-term relationships throughout the business world, meaning that the firm's clients benefit from working with teams that really understand their issues and concerns.

Main areas of work

The firm's clients benefit from an extensive range of tailored services, delivered through offices in the UK, Central Europe, North America and Asia. The firm's services include banking and international finance, corporate, real estate, commercial, energy projects and constructions, insurance and re-insurance.

Trainee profile

The firm looks for high achieving team players with good communication, analytical and organisational skills. You will need to show initative and be able to accept personal responsibility, not only for your own work, but also for your career development. You will need to be resilient and focused on achieving results.

Training environment

The firm is highly supportive and puts no limits on a trainee's progress. It offers four six-months seats over a period of two years. You will be awarded a priority seat when you start your training contract and will undertake a compulsory seat in these areas: corporate or banking, and a contentious seat. To develop you and your legal skills even further, you can expect to be seconded to a client or spend time in one of their international offices. In each seat you will be allocated high quality work on substantial transactions for a range of government and blue-chip clients. The three compulsory modules of the Professional Skills Course will be completed on a fast track basis during the trainee induction. This enables trainees to be effective and participate on a practical level as soon as possible. The Professional Skills Course is complimented by a comprehensive in-house training programme that continues up to qualification and beyond.

Vacation placements

Places for 2008/2009: 60: Easter, Christmas and summer. Duration: 2 weeks. Remuneration: £250pw. Closing date for Christmas scheme: 14 November 2008; Easter and summer: 13 February 2009.

Benefits

Annual bonus, gym membership/subsidy, life assurance, pensions scheme with firm contributions, private healthcare, season ticket loan, confidential care line, subsidised restaurant and 25 days holiday with options to buy a further five days.

Sponsorship & awards

GDL and LPC sponsorship is provided. From September 2007 you will be required to undertake your LPC at BPP Law School London where the firm will pay your fees and provide a maintenance grant of up to £7,500. Further details will be supplied on offer of a training contract.

Partners 131
Assistant Solicitors 603
Total Trainees 120

Contact
Graduate Recruitment Team
(0845) 300 0491

Method of application
Online application form
www.cmstalklaw.com

Selection procedure
Online application form and psychometric test, Interview and presentation, analysis exercise, group exercise, partner interview

Closing date
31 July 2009

Application
Training contracts p.a. 60
Applications p.a. 1,500
% interviewed p.a. 35%
Required degree grade 2:1

Training
Salary
1st year (2008) £37,500
2nd year (2008) £41,500
Holiday entitlement
25 days + option of flexible holidays
% of trainees with a non-law degree p.a. 50%
No. of seats available abroad p.a. Currently 12

Post-qualification
Salary (2008) £66,000
% of trainees offered job on qualification (2007) 96%

Cobbetts LLP

58 Mosley Street, Manchester M2 3H2
Tel: (0845) 165 5045
Email: gr8training@cobbetts.com
Website: www.cobbetts.com/graduate

Firm profile

Cobbetts is a top 50 law firm with offices in the UK's most exciting commercial centres, Birmingham, Leeds, London and Manchester.

The firm continues to place high-quality and long-term relationship building with clients at the forefront of its strategy for success. This leads to a requirement for talented individuals with first-class legal expertise and the people skills to really deliver value to both the firm and its clients.

The firm's varied client base gives its trainees the opportunity to get involved in the legal work of PLCs, mid-sized corporates, financial institutions, public sector and not for profit clients. Working in a firm with a reputation for quality work and innovation, and surrounded by business focused, forward thinking individuals, trainees have the perfect opportunity to make their mark in a growing and successful legal business.

The firm employs around 750 people (including approximately 50 trainee solicitors) across the four offices. Currently, half of all training contracts are offered in the Manchester office with the remaining spread between Birmingham, Leeds and London.

Main areas of work

Cobbetts operates through a number of flexible service teams based on work type and managed across five areas of practice: banking, dispute resolution, corporate (including business restructuring, technology media trade and infrastructure and private capital), employment and real estate. Cobbetts' legal expertise spans many industry sectors, especially banking and finance, leisure, retail, IT, media and regeneration.

Trainee profile

The firm looks for high academic achievers who show potential to offer something above and beyond the undertaking of legal work. Individuals must demonstrate the confidence and commitment to thrive in a strong client centred commercial environment and have a desire for responsibility early in their training.

The firm welcomes applications from students of any discipline who are in the penultimate or final year of study and from those who have already graduated.

Training environment

Trainee solicitors are supervised by partners and solicitors who have the expertise to turn trainees into confident and capable newly qualified solicitors. Trainees are currently supervised through four six-month seats. Depending on business needs, opportunities may also arise for a trainee to spend time on secondment at client or partner organisations.

Trainees are also developed through activities with students who have been offered a contract with the firm and through the firm's structured CSR initiatives.

Trainees are supported with development during their contract via practice area induction workshops and the PSC. In addition, once trainees qualify, they will undergo the Cobbetts NQ programme and gain the benefit of a structured legal training programme in their first two years of qualification.

Benefits

Opportunity to join BUPA scheme after four months, gym membership, social club, pension scheme, travel loan, death in service, counselling service.

Sponsorship & awards

GDL and LPC fees paid. Maintenance grant of £5000 during LPC year.

Partners 99
Other fee earners 256
Total Trainees 45

Contact
Laura Williams
(0845) 165 5011

Method of application
Online

Selection procedure
Assessment days

Closing date for 2011
31 July 2009

Application
Training contracts p.a. Approx 25
Applications p.a. approx.1,500
% interviewed p.a. approx 10%
Required degree grade 2:1

Training
Salary for each year of training
1st year   £25,000
2nd year   £27,000
(both reviewed annually)
Holiday entitlement
Starting at 23 days

Post-qualification
Salary NQ £37,000
Reviewed annually

% of trainees offered job on qualification 78%

Other offices
Birmingham, Leeds, London

Coffin Mew LLP

Fareham Point, Wickham Road, Fareham PO16 7AU
Tel: (01329) 825617 Fax: (01329) 825619
Email: sarajlloyd@coffinmew.co.uk
Website: www.coffinmew.co.uk

Firm profile

Coffin Mew LLP offers an exceptional training opportunity. The firm is rapidly expanding to become one of the larger southern regional firms with major offices located in the cities of Portsmouth and Southampton and just off the M27 Motorway at Fareham. The firm is in the enviable position of operating a balanced practice offering top quality commercial and private client services in approximately equal volume and is particularly noted for a number of niche practices with national reputations.

Main areas of work

The firm is structured through nine core departments: corporate and corporate finance, commercial services, employment, commercial litigation, property litigation, personal injury, property; family and childcare and trust/ probate. Niche practices (in which training is available) include intellectual property; insolvency; finance and business regulation; social housing; and medical negligence.

Trainee profile

The firm encourages applications from candidates with very good academic ability who seek a broad based training contract in a highly progressive and demanding but friendly and pleasant environment.

Training environment

The training contract is usually divided into six seats of four months each which will include a Property Department, a Litigation Department and a Commercial Department. The remainder of the training contract will be allocated after discussion with the trainee concerned. The firm aims to ensure that the trainee spends the final period of his or her training contract in the department in which he or she hopes to work after qualification.

Sponsorship & awards

LPC funding available by discussion with candidates.

Vacation placements

Open Week in July each year; applications for the 2009 Open Week may be made to the Practice Manager with accompanying CV between 1 November 2008 and 31 March 2009.

Partners 23
Associates 20
Assistant solicitors 28
Total trainees 16

Contact
Mrs Sara Lloyd
Practice Manager

Method of application
Please see firm's website

Selection procedure
Interview

Closing date for July 2011
31 July 2009 (not before
January 1 2009)

Application
Training contracts p.a. 5/6
Applications p.a. 400+
% interviewed p.a. 5%
Required degree grade
2:1 (save in exceptional
circumstances)

Training
Salary
1st year
Competitive market rate
2nd year
Competitive market rate
Holiday entitlement currently
20 days
% of trainees with a
non-law degree p.a. 42%

Post-qualification
Salary Competitive market rate
% of trainees offered job
on qualification (2008) 100%
% of assistants who joined
as trainees 25%
% of partners who joined
as trainees 20%

Collyer Bristow LLP

4 Bedford Row, London, WC1R 4DF
Tel: (020) 7242 7363 Fax: (020) 7405 0555
Email: recruitment@collyerbristow.com
Website: www.collyerbristow.com

Firm profile

London and Geneva based, the firm celebrates the breadth and diversity of its client base which includes multinationals, public and private companies, businesses and partnerships, public sector organisations and a substantial private client practice. Many of the firm's lawyers have trained and qualified with the firm and share their diverse experiences, outlooks and expertise with the firm's clients. The firm is famous for its ground-breaking in-house art gallery and is passionate in its support for the contemporary arts.

Main areas of work

The firm advises a diverse range of businesses and individuals on challenges of all shapes, sizes and complexity and offers top quality legal advice in private client, family, property, company commercial and dispute resolution.

Trainee profile

The firm is looking for self-starting graduates with a 2.1 degree. The firm also positively encourages those embarking on their second career. Common sense and an ability to understand the client's business are essential attributes.

Training environment

You will spend six months in four of the firm's five key practice areas working with a range of people from senior Partners to more recently qualified solicitors. The firm has a mentoring, training and appraisal programme which nurtures the development of your technical expertise and client advisory skills. You will be encouraged at an early stage to take responsibility for your own files and to participate in managing the client's work.

Benefits

25 days holiday, pension, private medical insurance, life assurance and season ticket loan.

Sponsorship & awards

Full LPC funding and maintenance grant of £4,000.

Partners 32
Trainees 7
Total Staff 147

Contact
Terry Collins
Graduate co-ordinator

Method of application
Online application form

Selection procedure
Interviews

Closing date for July 2010
To be confirmed, please look at website

Training
Salary
1st year (2007) £27,500
2nd year (2007) £31,000
(Both reviewed annually)

Covington & Burling LLP

265 Strand, London WC2R 1BH
Tel: (020) 7067 2000 Fax: (020) 7067 2222
Email: graduate@cov.com
Website: www.cov.com

Firm profile

Covington & Burling LLP is a leading US law firm, founded in Washington, with offices in London, New York, San Francisco, Brussels and Beijing. The London office was established in 1988 and has continued to grow progressively since then.

Main areas of work

In London, the main areas of work are corporate & commercial, employment, insurance, tax, life sciences, dispute resolution, IP/IT, and competition. The firm is known worldwide for its remarkable understanding of regulatory issues as well as its depth and expertise in areas including IT, e-commerce and life sciences. In such work, the firm represents many blue-chip clients including Microsoft, Pfizer, Qualcomm, Bacardi, Krispy Kreme, Business Software Alliance and Armani.

Trainee profile

The firm is looking for outstanding students who demonstrate genuine commitment to the legal profession and who have not only excellent academic ability, but also imagination, and the necessary practical and social skills required to respond to the evolving needs of its clients. In return, the firm can offer innovative and fascinating work in a stimulating and supportive environment.

Training environment

The firm offers a unique and personal training programme to suit the individual needs of each trainee. Following a comprehensive introduction, trainees will spend six months in each of corporate and dispute resolution departments. The third and fourth seats will be spent in two of the life sciences, employment, IP/IT or tax practice areas. The firm encourages trainees to take early responsibility in order to get the most out of their training period and trainees will receive regular feedback to enhance their development.

Benefits

Pension, income protection, private health cover, life assurance and season ticket loan.

vacation placements

24 places during summer vacation. Closing date for applications 28 February 2009.

Sponsorship & awards

GDL and LPC fees paid. Maintenance grant of £8,000 per annum.

Partners: 190
Associate Lawyers & Other
Fee-earners: 516
Total Trainees London:

2009	11
2010	12
2011	12

Contact
Graduate Recruitment Manager
(020) 7067 2098
graduate@cov.com

Method of application
Online Application Form
See website www.cov.com
selection procedure
1st & 2nd interview

Closing date for 2011
31 July 2009

Application
Training contracts p.a. 6
Required degree grade 2:1

Training
Salary:
1st year   £40,000
2nd year   £44,000
(subject to review)
Holiday entitlement 25 days

Overseas offices
Beijing, Brussels, New York, San Francisco, Washington

COVINGTON
COVINGTON & BURLING LLP

Cripps Harries Hall LLP

Wallside House, 12 Mount Ephraim Road, Tunbridge Wells TN1 1EG
Tel: (01892) 506006 Fax: (01892) 506360
Email: graduates@crippslaw.com
Website: www.crippslaw.com

Firm profile

A leading regional law firm and one of the largest in the South East, the firm is recognised as being amongst the most progressive and innovative regional practices.

The firm's organisation into client-focused, industry sector groups promotes a strong ethos of client service and ensures the firm's solicitors are not only excellent legal practitioners but also experts in specialist business sectors. The firm is regarded by many businesses, institutions and wealthy individuals as the natural first choice among regional law firms. Although long-established, the firm's profile is young, professional, forward-thinking, friendly and informal.

The firm achieved the Lexcel quality mark in January 1999, the first 'Top 100' firm to do so.

Main areas of work

Commercial 18%, dispute resolution 18%, private client 26%, property 38%.

Trainee profile

Individuals who are confident and capable, with lively but well organised minds and a genuine interest in delivering client solutions through effective and pragmatic use of the law; keen to make a meaningful contribution both during their contract and long term career with the firm.

Training environment

The firm offers a comprehensive induction course, a well structured training programme, frequent one to one reviews, regular in-house courses and seminars, good levels of support and real responsibility.

The training programme is broader than most other firms and typically includes six seats in both commercial and private client areas. Trainees usually share a room with a partner or an associate and gain varied and challenging first hand experience.

Sponsorship awards

Discretionary LPC funding: Fees – 50% interest free loan, 50% bursary.

Partners 40
Assistant Solicitors 54
Total Trainees 15

Contact
Jim Fennell
Head of HR & Development

Method of application
Application form available on website

Selection process
One interview with Managing Partner and Head of Human Resources

Closing date for 2011
31 July 2009

Application
Training contracts p.a. 8
Applications p.a. Up to 750
% interviewed p.a. 6%
Required degree grade 2:1

Training
Salary
1st year (2008) £21,500
2nd year (2008) £23,500
Holiday entitlement 25 days
% of trainees with a non-law degree p.a. 37%

Post-qualification
Salary (2008) £37,000
% of trainees offered job on qualification (2008) 100%
% of assistants/associates (as at 1/5/08) who joined as trainees 50%
% of partners (as at 1/5/08) who joined as trainees 22%

CRIPPS HARRIES HALL LLP

Davenport Lyons

30 Old Burlington Street, London W1S 3NL
Tel: (020) 7468 2600 Fax: (020) 7437 8216
Email: mmardner@davenportlyons.com
Website: www.davenportlyons.com

Firm profile

Davenport Lyons is a leading corporate and rights law firm offering a full service to clients in a range of market sectors including media, entertainment, property, retail, leisure, sport and banking. With a 38 Partner strong practice, over 60 fee earners and supporting operational function, they are a commercially focused law firm based in the luxurious surroundings of Mayfair. Coupled with the firm's desire to retain its warm and friendly environment, Davenport Lyons is the ideal place to start your career as a successful solicitor.

Main areas of work

The firm provides a full range of services through its five departments: corporate, contentious rights and dispute resolution, property, employment and private client. Areas of expertise include: corporate, commercial, corporate tax, film and TV, music, defamation, contentious and non-contentious IP/IT, commercial dispute resolution, insolvency, liquor and entertainment licensing, property, property dispute resolution, tax and trusts, matrimonial and employment.

Trainee profile

Davenport Lyons is looking for candidates with excellent academic qualifications (2:1 and above, good A level results) and interesting backgrounds, who are practical and can demonstrate good business acumen. Candidates should have a breadth of interests and foreign language skills are an advantage. In short, the firm is looking for well-rounded individuals.

Training environment

The training programme consists of four six-month seats. During each seat trainees receive mid and end of seat reviews, and each seat has a dedicated trainee supervisor. Davenport Lyons has an on-going in-house training and lectures programme. They pride themselves on offering interesting, hands-on training with trainees being encouraged to develop their own client relationships and to handle their own files under appropriate supervision, therefore being treated as junior fee earners. The firm aims to make its training contracts informative, educational, practical, supportive and, let us not forget, as enjoyable as possible.

Benefits

Season ticket loan; client introduction bonus; contribution to gym membership; discretionary bonus; 23 days holiday; life assurance; Employee Support Programme; pension scheme and private health.

Vacation placements

A limited number of places are available on the Summer Vacation Scheme which runs during July and August. Remuneration is £200 per week. Closing date for applications 31 January 2009.

Sponsorship & awards

The firm does not offer financial assistance.

Partners 44
Assistant Solicitors 36
Total Staff 209
Total Trainees 16

Contact
Marcia Mardner
Head of HR
Michael Hatchwell
Training Partner

Method of application
Online

Selection procedure
Interviews
closing date for 2011
30 July 2009

Application
Training contracts p.a. 8
Applications p.a. 800
% interviewed p.a. 8.6%
Required degree grade 2:1

Training
Salary
1st Year trainee
£33,000 - £33,666
2nd Year trainee
£34,332 - £35,000
Holiday entitlement 23 days
% of trainees with a
non-law degree p.a. 70%

Post-qualification
% of trainees offered job
on qualification
(2006) 71%

Davies Arnold Cooper LLP

6–8 Bouverie Street, London EC4Y 8DD
Tel: (020) 7936 2222 Fax: (020) 7936 2020
Email: daclon@dac.co.uk
Website: www.recruit.dac.co.uk

Partners 67
Total Fee-earners 175
Total Trainees 17
Total Staff 332

Firm profile

Davies Arnold Cooper LLP is an international law firm particularly known for its dispute resolution and real estate expertise. It advises in relation to specialist areas of law, including insurance, real estate, construction, employment and product liability, and has a leading Hispanic practice. The firm has offices in London, Manchester, St Albans, Madrid and Mexico City.

Main areas of work

Dispute resolution: 60%; real estate: 40%.

Trainee profile

If you secure a training contract with Davies Arnold Cooper you will most probably have a first class or a 2:1 degree, either in law or in another academic subject, as well as good A level grades. You will definitely be a self-starter with plenty of energy and common sense. What you've done with your life so far counts for much more than where you went to school/university. The firm has a number of dual-qualified lawyers whose previous professions were medicine, accountancy, public service or the armed forces. They recognise that for you, a law career is a bigger decision than someone just leaving university, especially when it means starting training on a lower salary.

Training programme & environment

The firm encourages you to take on responsibility as soon as you join and will give you as much as you can handle, although you will always be supervised and never left alone to struggle. You will experience both contentious and non-contentious work and because the firm only takes on up to ten trainees every year, the chances are you will be able to select your preferred seats. There are seven training contract positions available for September 2011. Applications should be made using the firm's application form which is available on request or from the website.

Benefits

Current first year salary is £29,000 with 25 days holiday, private medical insurance and season ticket loan.

Sponsorship & awards

CPE and LPC fees paid plus maintenance grants.

Dechert LLP

160 Queen Victoria Street, London EC4V 4QQ
Tel: (020) 7184 7000 Fax: (020) 7184 7001
Email: application@dechert.com   Website: www.dechert.com

Firm profile

Dechert LLP is a dynamic international law firm, with 2,000 people across the USA, Europe and Asia. London is the third largest office, after Philadelphia and New York. The London office has particular strengths in investment funds, corporate and securities including private equity, and finance and real estate; and smaller teams in employment, IP, litigation and tax.

Trainee profile

Dechert looks for enthusiasm, intelligence, an ability to find practical solutions, and for powers of expression and persuasion. Graduates from any discipline are welcome to apply.

Training environment

The highly personalised six seat rotation system allows trainees to structure their training contract to their interests and aspirations, and allows ample opportunity for secondments to Brussels, Munich, Hong Kong or the USA as well as to clients. A training contract with Dechert is international from day one, starting with a trip to Philadelphia to take part in the firm-wide induction programme. Your seat plan and professional development are guided by both the firm's Director of Training and by your dedicated trainee partner, who meet with you regularly. Your trainee partner is allocated to you when you start your training contract and acts as a sounding board and a source of support until you qualify.

Vacation placements

Work placement programmes at Easter, and in the summer. The firm's work placement programmes are aimed at penultimate year law students. The closing date for applications is 28 February 2009.

Sponsorship & awards

The firm pays LPC fees plus £10,000 sponsorship.

Trainee comments

1. My training contract commenced with a week in Philadelphia and was rounded off with a six week secondment to the Washington DC office. Spending time in another Dechert office was a great way to get a feel for the firm's international dimension, and it also helped me to understand how my chosen practice group operates in the US. Dechert's six seat programme has given me the flexibility to tailor my training contract to really focus on the areas that I find most interesting. In each of my seats, I have been able to engage in challenging and exciting work which, together with the legal and practical training that is available at Dechert, has helped me to develop the necessary knowledge and skills that will be required of me upon qualification.

Angela Coote, Warwick, Law, qualified into Financial Services

2. Dechert's six seat rotation was perfect for me as it provided a lot of flexibility but I soon realised that Corporate was where my interest lay. So I spent half of my training contract in the Corporate department, including a seat on secondment to the Corporate team in New York. I have appreciated many of the benefits of working for an international law firm – not least the very generous salary on offer! In particular, I appreciated the international aspect which allowed me to gain real exposure to international deals, such as the time when I was responsible for liaising with counsel in 12 jurisdictions including the US, Korea and Brazil on a refinancing deal. Dechert offered as much responsibility as I could handle, but I never once felt overwhelmed as this was coupled closely with attentive supervision, a closely tailored training program, words of occasional wisdom from my mentor and a genuinely supportive working environment.

Jessica O'Gorman, Bristol, Law, qualified into Corporate and Securities

---

Partners 37*
Assistant Solicitors 79*
Total Trainees 25*
*denotes London figure

Contact
Graduate Recruitment Manager

Method of application
Online

Selection procedure
An assessment morning or afternoon which includes interviews with partners, associates and recruiters, and written tests

Closing date for 2011
31 July 2009

Application
Training contracts p.a.
10-15
Applications p.a. Approx 1,000
% interviewed p.a. Approx 12%
Required degree grade 2:1 (or capability of attaining a 2:1)

Training
Salary
1st year £38,000
2nd year £43,000
Holiday entitlement 20 days
% of trainees with a non-law degree p.a. Varies
No. of seats available abroad p.a. three in Brussels and others in the US

Post-qualification
Salary c.£65,000 to £73,000 (depending on practice area)
% of trainees offered job on qualification 80%

Overseas offices
Austin, Beijing, Boston, Brussels, Charlotte, Hartford, Hong Kong, Luxembourg, Munich, Newport Beach, New York, Palo Alto, Paris, Philadelphia, Princeton, San Francisco, Washington

Denton Wilde Sapte

One Fleet Place, London EC4M 7WS
Tel: (020) 7242 1212 Fax: (020) 7320 6555
Email: kate.raggett@dentonwildesapte.com
Website: www.dentonwildesapte.com

Firm profile

Denton Wilde Sapte is an international law firm with a network of offices and associate offices spanning the UK, Europe, Middle East, CIS and Africa.

Main areas of work

The firm provides a full range of commercial legal services in the following areas: banking and finance; corporate; dispute resolution; employment and pensions; energy infrastructure and project finance; EU and competition; real estate and planning; tax; technology, media and telecommunications.

Trainee profile

The firm looks for candidates who are team players with a strong academic and extra curricular record of achievement.

Training environment

As a trainee you will undertake four six-month seats. Which includes a contentious seat, a banking section. You will also have the opportunity to work in one of the firm's international offices or with one of the firm's clients.

You will be given as much responsibility as you can handle, and will be working with the law, with your team and with clients in real business situations.

The firm works hard to maintain a friendly and open environment where ideas are shaped and people work together to achieve goals.

Given the diversity of the firm's business, it looks for people with wide-ranging skills, aptitudes and personalities. You will need drive and ambition, with the potential to contribute to the growing success of the firm.

Benefits

Flexible benefit scheme including promote health insurance and sports club membership allowance. Season ticket loan.

Vacation placements

Open days during December 2008 and summer schemes during July 2009. Closing date for applications for open days is 21st November 2008 and for summer schemes 6 February 2009.

Sponsorship & awards

GDL and LPC tuition fees covered plus £6,000 maintenance grant for each year of study, £7,000 if studying in London.

Partners 180
Fee-earners 600
Total Trainees 75

Contact
Kate Raggett

Method of application
Application form

Selection procedure
First interview; selection test; second interviews and case study

Closing date for 2011
31 July 2009

Application
Training contracts p.a. 35
Applications p.a. 1,500
% interviewed p.a. 15%
Required degree grade 2:1

Training
Salary
1st year £37,000
2nd year £40,000
Holiday entitlement 24 days
% of trainees with a
non-law degree p.a. 40%
No. of seats available
abroad p.a. Currently 8

Post-qualification
Salary (2007) £64,000
% of trainees offered job
on qualification (2008) 85%

Dewey & LeBoeuf

No 1 Minister Court, Mincing Lane, London, EC3R 7YL
Tel: (020) 7459 5000   Fax: (020) 7444 7379
Email: londongraduate@dl.com   Website: www.dl.com

Firm profile

Dewey & LeBoeuf is a full-service international law firm advising a wide range of clients throughout the United States, Europe, Russia/ the CIS, the Middle East, Asia and Africa.

With more than 1,400 lawyers in virtually all major financial and commercial centers, the firm represents multinational corporations, financial institutions, government agencies and state-owned entities in their most complex legal matters.

The London office of Dewey & LeBoeuf is the firm's largest international office with 49 partners and over 130 legal staff. The majority of the firm's London based partners and associates are English qualified solicitors, and the London office is the natural centre of some of the firm's most interesting and diverse work.

Main areas of work

Banking, mergers and acquisitions, corporate finance, project finance, dispute resolution, arbitration, intellectual property and information technology, EU/ competition, tax, real estate, environmental and employment. The firm also possesses leading industry experience in sectors including insurance, energy and utilities, environment and banking.

Trainee profile

Dewey & LeBoeuf is looking for dynamic, internationally minded, versatile individuals who demonstrate commercial awareness and a genuine enthusiasm for the law. The firm wants people who are dedicated to delivering excellent advice and client service. Language skills are desirable but not required.

Training environment

The firm emphasises learning through one-on-one interaction with its partners and experienced associates. Trainees are encouraged to see and experience as much of the practice as possible and you can expect to be exposed to high quality work with early responsibility. Trainees typically undertake four six-month seats within different practice areas. Six month client secondments, as well as secondments to the firm's International offices in Paris, Moscow and Dubai are also available.

The firm's training programme is comprehensive, and in addition to the professional skills course, covers an induction programme and attendance at internal and external courses. Trainees will also participate in regular training sessions run through its own internal 'Dewey & LeBoeuf University' (DLU), which offers regular seminars on law and practice. Progress and training needs are formally reviewed every three months.

Benefits

The firm offers 25 days holiday per annum, private medical insurance, permanent health insurance, life assurance, employee assistance programme, private GP services, Ride2Work scheme, worldwide travel insurance, season ticket loan, childcare vouchers, and preferential rates for dental care and for gym membership.

Vacation placements

The firm offers one-week spring vacation and two-week summer vacation schemes for penultimate year law undergraduates and graduates of all disciplines. Places for 2009: 20; Remuneration: £400 per week; closing date 31 January 2009. Apply online at www.dl.com .

Sponsorship & awards

Full payment of GDL/LPC fees and maintenance grant of £8,500 provided per annum.

Partners 49
Other lawyers 130
Total Trainees 27

Contact
Louise Boyle, Graduate Recruitment & Diversity Co-ordinator

Method of application
Apply online www.dl.com

Selection procedure
Verbal and numerical testing, two interviews with the firm's partners, associates and graduate recruitment team

Closing date for 2011
31 July 2009

Application
Training contracts p.a. 15
Applications p.a. 900
% interviewed p.a. 6%
Required grades AAB at A-level and 2:1 degree or equivalent

Training
Salary
1st year (2008) £40,000
2nd year (2008) £45,000

Post-qualification
Salary (2008) £80,000
% of trainees offered job on qualification (2008) 100%

Offices
Albany, Almaty, Beijing, Boston, Brussels, Charlotte, Chicago, Dubai, Frankfurt, Hong Kong, Houston, Johannesburg, London, Los Angeles, Milan, Moscow, New York, Paris, Riyadh, Rome, San Francisco, Silicon Valley, Warsaw, Washington DC

Dickinson Dees LLP

St. Ann's Wharf, 112 Quayside, Newcastle upon Tyne NE1 3DX
Tel: (0191) 279 9046 Fax: (0191) 279 9716
Email: graduate.recruitment@dickinson-dees.com
Website: www.trainingcontract.com

Firm profile

Dickinson Dees enjoys an excellent reputation as one of the country's leading commercial law firms. Based in Newcastle upon Tyne, Tees Valley and York the firm prides itself on the breadth of experience and expertise which enables it to offer services of the highest standards to clients. Whilst many of the firm's clients are based in the North, Dickinson Dees works on a national basis for national and internationally based businesses and organisations.

Main areas of work

The firm has over 850 employees and is organised into four key departments (Company Commercial, Commercial Property, Litigation and Private Client) with 38 cross departmental units advising on specific areas.

Trainee profile

The firm is looking for intellectually able, motivated and enthusiastic graduates from any discipline with good communication skills. Successful applicants will understand the need to provide practical, commercial advice to clients. They will share the firm's commitment to self-development and teamwork and its desire to provide clients with services which match their highest expectations.

Training environment

Trainees are relatively few for the size of the practice and the environment is supportive and friendly. You are fully integrated into the firm and involved in all aspects of firm business. The training contract consists of four seats -one in each of the Commercial Property, Company Commercial and Litigation departments. You may be able to specialise for the fourth seat. Trainees sit with their supervisors and appraisals are carried out every three months. The firm has its own Training Department as well as a supportive Graduate Recruitment team. There are induction courses on each move of department with opportunities for trainees to get involved in the firm's training programme. The firm offers a tailored in-house Professional Skills Course which is run in conjunction with the College of Law.

Work placements

Places for 2009: 40; Duration: 1 week; Remuneration: £200 p.w. The firm's work placement weeks are part of the recruitment process and all applicants should apply online at www.trainingcontract.com. Apply by 31 January 2009 for Easter and Summer placements.

Sponsorship & awards

GDL/LPC fees paid and maintenance grant offered.

Partners 76
Total Staff 850
Total Trainees 38

Contact
Sally Brewis, Graduate
Recruitment Adviser

Method of application
Apply online at
www.trainingcontract.com

Selection procedure
Aptitude and ability tests,
negotiation exercise,
personality questionnaire,
interview
closing date for 2011
31 July 2009

Application
Training contracts p.a.
up to 15 (Newcastle)
up to 3 (Tees Valley)
up to 3 (York)
Applications p.a. 800
% interviewed p.a. 10%
Required degree grade 2:1 in
any subject

Training
Salary
1st year (2008) £20,500
2nd year (2008) £21,500
Holiday entitlement 25 days
% of trainees with
a non-law degree p.a. 40%
No. of seats available abroad
p.a. 3
(3-month secondments)

Post-qualification
Salary (2007) £36,000
% of trainees offered job
on qualification (2008) 92%
% of partners (as at 01/08/08)
who joined as trainees 35%

Other offices
Tees Valley, York, London
Brussels (associated office)

DICKINSON DEES

DLA Piper UK LLP

Victoria Square House, Victoria Square, Birmingham B2 4DL
Tel: (020) 7796 6677 Fax: (0121) 262 5793
Email: recruitment.graduate@dlapiper.com
Website: www.dlapiper.com

Firm profile

DLA Piper are one of the world's largest full service commercial law firms. They now have more than 8,000 employees working from over 60 offices across Europe, Asia, the Middle East and the US. Their current vision is to be the leading global business law firm. Clients include some of the world's leading businesses, governments, banks and financial institutions. This impressive client base coupled with an emphasis on providing high quality service and teamwork, offers a challenging fast-paced working environment.

DLA Piper offers its trainees the opportunity to apply for international secondments to their Abu Dhabi, Dubai, Hong Kong, Moscow, Singapore and Tokyo offices, as well as a number of client secondments.

In 2008 DLA Piper won the prestigious National Graduate Recruitment Awards' 'Diversity Recruitment Award' proving their commitment to recruiting people from a wide variety of backgrounds and ages. This progressive approach to recruitment creates a mix of talents that contributes to their success.

DLA Piper is committed to making sure you feel part of the firm once you accept a training contract with them. Future trainees have access to their website 'Inside DLA Piper' where they can, amongst other things, contact one another via chat forums, and keep up to date with what is going on in the firm wherever they are in the world.

Main areas of work

Corporate; employment, pensions and benefits; finance and projects; litigation and regulatory; real estate; and technology, media and commercial.

Trainee profile

The firm is looking for individuals from either a law or non-law background who have a minimum of 3 Bs at A Level (or equivalent) and expect, or have achieved a 2.1 degree classification - however, a strong academic background alone is no longer sufficient. DLA Piper looks for highly motivated and energetic team players with sound commercial awareness, outstanding communication and organisational skills. As well as this, in line with the firm's main focus of work, a keen interest in the corporate world is essential - as is an appetite for life!

Training environment

Following a comprehensive residential induction, trainees complete four six month seats during the course of their training contract. If you want responsibility, they will give you as much as you can handle and your progress will be monitored through regular reviews and feedback. The compulsory Professional Skills Course is run in-house and is tailored to meet the needs of the firm's trainees. This combined with on-the-job experience, provides trainees with an excellent grounding on which to build their professional careers.

Summer placements

DLA Piper runs two week summer placement schemes across all of its UK offices. The scheme aims to give a thorough insight into life at the firm. There will be approximately 200 places available for 2009. The closing date is 31 January 2009.

Sponsorship & awards

Payment of LPC and GDL fees plus maintenance grant in both years of up to £7,000.

Partners 1300
Fee-earners 2200
Total Trainees 181

Contact
Sally Carthy, Head of Graduate Recruitment

Method of application
Online application form

Selection procedure
First interview, second interview, assessment afternoon

Closing date for 2011
31 July 2009

Application
Training contracts p.a. 100
Applications p.a. 2,400
% interviewed p.a. 20%
Required degree grade 2:1

Training
Salary (2008)
1st year (London) £37,000
2nd year (London) £41,000
1st year (Regions) £26,000
2nd year (Regions) £29,000
1st year (Scotland) £23,000
2nd year (Scotland) £26,000
% of trainees with a non-law degree p.a. 40%

Post-qualification
Salary (2008)
£64,000 (London)
£41,000 (English Regional offices)
£36,000 (Scotland)

UK offices
Birmingham, Edinburgh, Glasgow, Leeds, Liverpool, London, Manchester, Sheffield

Overseas offices
Austria, Belgium, Bosnia-Herzegovina, Bulgaria, China, Croatia, Czech Republic, France, Georgia, Germany, Hong Kong, Hungary, Italy, Japan, Netherlands, Norway, Poland, Russia, Singapore, Slovak Republic, Spain, Thailand, Ukraine, UAE, USA.

DMH Stallard

100 Queens Road, Brighton BN1 3YB
Tel: (01273) 744270 Fax: (01273) 744290
Email: recruitment@dmhstalard.com
Website: www.dmhstallard.com

Firm profile

DMH Stallard is an approachable and innovative firm with an open culture which encourages personal development and provides its personnel with a high level of support in order to achieve this. The firm offers expertise and service comparable to City firms to a range of commercial organisations, non-profit institutions and individual clients. By focusing on the client's needs DMH Stallard provides practical and creative solutions. DMH Stallard operates from offices in Brighton, Gatwick and London.

Main areas of work

Corporate; real estate; construction; planning and environmental; employment, intellectual property/IT; real estate asset management; dispute resolution; personal injury; private client; real estate dispute resolution.

Trainee profile

The firm welcomes applications from motivated graduates from all backgrounds and age groups. Enthusiasm and commercial awareness are as prized as academic ability, and good communication skills are a must. Ideal applicants are those with the potential to become effective managers or strong marketeers, as well as technical experts

Training environment

Usually four six month seats taken from the following areas: employment, intellectual property/IT, corporate, planning and environmental, real estate, dispute resolution, real estate dispute resolution, personal injury, real estate asset management, construction, technology and media, and private client. Trainees are closely supervised by the partner to whom they are attached but have every opportunity to work as part of a team and deal directly with clients.

Vacation placements

Places for Summer 2009: Limited number of unpaid places; Duration: 1 week; Closing Date: 31 January 2009.

Sponsorship & awards

50% loan and 50% funded, conditional on remaining with the firm. Bonus payments for those who have previously funded their own LPC.

Partners 54
Assistant Solicitors 43
Total Trainees 19

Contact
Jessica Leigh-Davis

Method of application
Online application form

Selection procedure
First and second stage assessment days including interviews

Closing date for 2011
31 July 2009

Application
Training contracts p.a. 10
Applications p.a. 525
% interviewed p.a. 7.6%
Preferred degree grade 2:1

Training
Salary
1st year (2007)
£22,000 (Brighton & Gatwick)
£27,000 (London)
2nd year (2007)
£24,000 (Brighton & Gatwick)
£29,000 (London)
Holiday entitlement 25 days

Dorsey & Whitney

21 Wilson Street, London EC2M 2TD
Tel: (020) 7588 0800 Fax: (020) 7588 0555
Website: www.dorsey.com

Firm profile

Dorsey & Whitney is amongst the largest law firms in the world with more than 18 offices situated across three continents. The firm has over 650 lawyers worldwide. The London office of Dorsey & Whitney has over 50 fee earners. It continues to build on its traditional strengths in corporate law, litigation, real estate and intellectual property work through its wide range of practice groups.

Main areas of work

The London office offers the full range of legal services including corporate finance, cross-border M&A, commercial litigation, tax, employment, real estate, intellectual property and private equity.

Trainee profile

Dorsey & Whitney is looking for 'self-starters', capable of meeting the intellectual and business challenges of a successful multi-national practice. Candidates should be committed team players who enjoy rewarding client work. An honours degree at 2:1 level or above and some relevant work experience is also required.

Training environment

The training contract is split into four individual 'seats' of six months each. Each trainee will be required to complete litigation and corporate seats. Secondments to major clients are available. All trainees are supplied with the encouragement and support necessary to maximise their potential. Through the mentoring, professional development and evaluation programmes, the firm strives to develop and retain the highest calibre lawyers.

Benefits

Non-contributory pension schemes; health insurance and life insurance.

Partners 10
Total Fee Earners 55
Total Trainees 8

Contact
Andrew Rimmington, Partner
(020) 7588 0800

Method of application
Application by letter with a current curriculum vitae addressed to Andrew Rimmington.

Closing date for 2011
31 July 2009

Application
Training contracts p.a. 4
(currently under review)

Training
Salary
1st year (2008) £35,000
2nd year (2008) £40,000 (plus £7,000 payment towards LPC cost)
Holiday entitlement 25 days plus public holidays

Post-qualification
Salary (2008) £65,000+ automatic bonus of up to £30,000 depending on number of billable hours
Dorsey & Whitney aims to offer a qualified position to all candidates who have shown the appropriate level of performance during training, subject to the needs of the firm

Dundas & Wilson LLP

Northwest Wing, Bush House, Aldwych, London, WC2B 4EZ
Tel: (020) 7240 2401 Fax: (020) 7240 2448
Email: lorraine.bale@dundas-wilson.com

Firm profile

Dundas & Wilson is a leading UK commercial law firm with offices in London, Edinburgh and Glasgow. The firm services a wide range of prestigious clients, including major companies and public sector organisations, throughout the UK and abroad.

Main areas of work

Lawyers are grouped into key areas of expertise including banking and finance, construction and engineering, corporate, corporate recovery, dispute resolution, environment, employment, EU and competition, IP / IT, outsourcing, pensions, planning and transport, projects, property, property finance, public law and Tax.

Trainee profile

D&W are looking for applicants with enthusiasm, commitment, adaptability, strong written and oral communication skills, excellent interpersonal skills, commercial awareness and an aptitude for problem solving and analysis.

Training environment

The two year traineeship is split into four six-month seats. The firm aims to accommodate trainees' preferences when allocating seats as the firm wants to encourage trainees to take an active part in managing their career development.

During the traineeship trainees receive on-the-job training, two day seat training at the beginning of each seat, training in core skills such as drafting and effective legal writing and regular seminars. Trainees receive a formal performance review every three months and are allocated a mentor for each seat.

The firm's open plan environment means that trainees sit amongst assistants, associates, senior associates and Partners – this provides daily opportunities to observe how lawyers communicate both with clients and each other. This type of learning is invaluable and great preparation for life as a fully fledged lawyer.

Benefits

Life assurance, permanent health insurance, group personal pension, season ticket loan, holiday purchase scheme.

Vacation scheme

Dundas & Wilson offers four-week summer placements. To apply, please visit the website and complete the online application form. The closing date is 30 January 2009.

Sponsorship & awards

GDL/CPE and LPC fees paid plus maintenance grant.

Partners 86
Lawyers 300
Trainees 64

Contact
Lorraine Bale

Method of application
Online application

Selection procedure
Assessment day comprising interview, group exercise, occupational personality questionnaire and aptitude tests

Closing date for 2011
31 July 2009

Application
Training contracts p.a. 35 (12 in London)
Applications p.a. 300
% interviewed p.a. 15%
Required degree grade 2:1 preferred

Training
Salary
1st year (Scotland) £19,000
(England) £30,000
2nd year (Scotland) £22,000
(England) £33,500
Holiday entitlement 25 days with ability to purchase an addtional 5 days

Offices
London, Edinburgh, Glasgow

DWF LLP

Bridgewater Place, Water Lane, Leeds, LS11 5DY
5 St Paul's Square, Old Hall Street, Liverpool, L3 9AE
5-10 Bury Street, London, EC3A 5AT
Centurion House, 129 Deansgate, Manchester, M3 3AA
6 Winckley Square, Preston, PR1 3JJ
Tel: (0161) 603 5000   Fax: (0161) 603 5050

Firm profile

DWF LLP is a leading, full service law firm. The Firm provides a full range of legal services to businesses and private clients across the UK.

The Firm employs over 930 people, including 129 Partners and with over 500 fee earners, DWF is ranked as the largest in the North West by number of fee earners by independent legal directory Legal 500.

The Firm is able to serve clients on a national basis from offices in Leeds, Liverpool, London, Manchester and Preston and internationally through its relationships with law firms around the world. The business continues to expand through a combination of organic growth, lateral hires and other consolidation activity.

The Firm prides itself on providing outstanding client service that combines excellent commercial advice with an approachable style.

Main areas of work

DWF provides a full range of legal services: banking and finance, business recovery, corporate, insurance, litigation, employment, pensions, private client and real estate. A full list of these services can be found on the Firm's website at www.dwf.co.uk.

DWF also provides legal services across a range of different industries and sectors, and has developed particular expertise in a number of specific areas. To enable clients to benefit from this expertise, the Firm has developed a series of sector-focused teams: automotive, education, food, legal expenses, public sector, police law, resourcing and retail and leisure.

Trainee profile

DWF's future depends on recruiting and retaining the right people. DWF only recruit people of the highest quality and are always on the look out for ambitious and driven professionals who are able to add value to their developing team. DWF wants its trainee solicitors to play a part in building on its success. The Firm is looking for trainees who enjoy working as part of a busy team, respond positively to a challenge and have what it takes to deliver results for clients. The firm is looking for its Partners of the future and in recent years virtually all of its qualifying trainees have been offered jobs. DWF is an equal opportunities employer and is committed to diversity in all aspects.

Training environment

DWF provides a well structured training programme for all new trainee solicitors which combines the day to day practical experience of working with a Partner, associate or senior solicitor, backed by a comprehensive in-house lecture and workshop programme and the PSC course. You will very quickly become a vital member of the team, being delegated the appropriate level of responsibility from an early stage in your training.

Full supervision is provided and it is the Firm's policy for each trainee to sit with a Partner or associate, whilst working for a legal team as a whole. The two year training contract is divided into "seats"; four seats of four months' duration followed by eight months in their chosen area, enabling a detailed period of pre-qualification experience.

Trainees will work in the Firm's main departments (banking and finance, business recovery, corporate, insurance, litigation, people, private client and real estate) which gives opportunities to look at specialist areas of work within each department.

Partners 129
Assistant Solicitors 367
Total Trainees 35

Contact
Vicky Macmillan
Recruitment Co-ordinator

Method of application
Online application

Selection procedure
2 stage interview/selection process

Closing date for 2010/2011
24 July 2009

Application
Training contracts p.a. 18
Applications p.a. c. 800
% interviewed p.a. 20%
Required degree grade 2:1

Training
Salary
1st year (2008) £24,500
Holiday entitlement
25 days p.a. minimum +
option to buy & sell holidays

Post-qualification
% of trainees offered job
on qualification (2007) 100%

Benefits
Flexible benefits scheme
including insurance, life
assurance, pension and other
benefits

Vacation placements
50 places offered p.a.
Paid summer vacation
placements lasting 1 week
One week in Easter

Sponsorship & awards
LPC funding for tuition fees

Edwards Angell Palmer & Dodge UK LLP

One Fetter Lane, London, EC4A 1JB
Tel: 020 7583 4055
Fax: 020 7353 7377
Email: traineerecruitment@eapdlaw.com
Website: www.eapdlaw.com

Firm profile

Following the merger with internationally recognised UK law firm Kendall Freeman, EAPD now combines the expertise of over 600 lawyers in 30 practice groups, across the US and UK offering a full array of legal services to clients worldwide.

Main areas of work

In London, the firm's main practice areas are litigation, regulatory and transactional, insolvency and restructuring and intellectual property. Within these areas the firm has many specialisms including insurance, employment, public international law, asset recovery and life sciences.

Trainee profile

The firm seeks engaging and motivated individuals from law or non-law backgrounds with initiative, good commercial sense and who want to make their mark. The firm's trainees work hard and are rewarded with early responsibility and influence over the matters they work on. You will also have lots of client interaction so excellent people skills are vital. An excellent academic background will give you the analytical skills and rigorous approach needed to provide focussed and effective commercial advice to clients. The firm also looks for those who want to get involved in the life of the firm as a whole, socially through contribution to the various committees or pro bono activities. The firm recognises the importance of your life outside work and actively encourages you to keep a good balance.

Training environment

The firm believes you learn best by doing, getting involved in real work from the start and because of its size in London, it can offer excellent training with high-quality work in a more personal environment. The firm gives trainees the chance to meet clients, be responsible for their own work and join in marketing and client development activities. Trainees spend six months in four of the firm's major practice areas. Frequent workshops on the firm's tailored training programme help develop the technical skills and knowledge needed in those areas. Regular structured feedback, reviews and constructive advice enable you to fulfil your true potential. A multi-level support network including buddies, partner mentors and the Trainee Recruitment Team, ensures you have the correct level of guidance and support is never overstretched. Any suggestions or concerns can be voiced at a trainee solicitors' committee, which meets quarterly.

The firm won the LawCareers.Net 2004 award for best training at a medium-sized City law firm and was nominated again in 2008. The firm received the award for the best work placement scheme in 2008. The firm is also a frequent category winner in the Lex 100 surveys.

Benefits

Bupa, STL, subsidised gym membership, bonus scheme, pension scheme, life assurance

Vacation placements

The firm offers a structured two-week placement for up to 10 students in July of each year.

Summer placements: up to ten p.a. Open days: three, accommodating up to 100 students. Closing date for summer placements: 27 February 2009. Closing date for open days: 15 May 2009

Sponsorship & awards

CPE/GDL and LPC funding, plus a maintenance grant of £7,000 (London) / £6,500 (outside London).

Partners 21
Assistant Solicitors 17
Total Trainees 15

Contact
Sarah Warnes 020 7556 4414

Method of application
Online applications only
www.eapdlaw.com/careers

Selection procedure
Assessment morning plus one interview with two partners

Closing date for 2011
31 July 2009

Application
Training contracts p.a. up to 8
Applications p.a. 500
% interviewed p.a. 10%
Required degree grade 2:1

Training
Salary
1st year £36,000
2nd year £39,000
Holiday entitlement 25 days

Post-qualification
Salary £61,000

Offices
London, New York, Boston, Hartford, Providence, Stamford, Washington, West Palm Beach, Wilmington, Madison

Eversheds

1 Wood Street, London, EC2V 7WS
Tel: (0845) 497 9797 Fax: (0845) 497 4919
Email: gradrec@eversheds.com
Website: www.eversheds.com/graduaterecruitment

Firm profile

Eversheds LLP is the largest full service international law firms in the world with over 4,000 people and 38 offices in major cities across the UK, Europe and Asia. The firm works for some of the world's most prestigious organisations in both the public and private sector, offering them a compelling mixture of straightforward advice, clear direction, predictable costs and outstanding service.

It's a winning combination that has meant the firm is now expanding quicker than any of the firm's closest competitors. The firm acts for 111 Listed companies including 43 FTSE 250 companies, 30 of the 37 British based Fortune 500 companies and now has one of the fastest growing corporate teams in the City.

The firm has recently laid out a strategic plan that will see the firm build on these achievements and grow over the next few years. The firm is looking for highly ambitious and focused trainees to help it achieve its goals.

Main areas of work

Core work: company commercial, litigation and dispute management, real estate, human resources (employment and pensions) and legal systems group.

Trainee profile

Eversheds people are valued for their drive and legal expertise but also for their business advice too.The firm develops the same qualities in its trainees. As a trainee you'll be given as much responsibility as you can handle and will benefit from the firm's hands-on philosophy. The firm takes learning and development very seriously and will help you build the career you want.

Training environment

The firm offers a full well-rounded training programme with the opportunity to focus your technical skills in each of the various practice groups as you rotate through four six-month seats. You will also take part in a full programme of personal and commercial development skills training, including finance and business, communication, presenting, business writing, client care, professional standards and advocacy.

Vacation placements

Places for Summer 2009: 100. Duration: two weeks. Remuneration: London £240, regions £175. The following offices run a one-week Easter vacation scheme: Birmingham, Cambridge, Cardiff, Leeds, Manchester and Nottingham (London's Easter scheme is two weeks). Closing Date: 31 January 2009.

Sponsorship & awards

GDL and LPC fees and maintenance grants in accordance with the terms of the firm's offer.

Partners 400+
Assistant Solicitors 2,000+
Total Trainees 180+

Contact
gradrec@eversheds.com

Method of application
Apply online at
www.eversheds.com/graduater
ecruitment

Selection procedure
Selection days include group
and individual exercises,
presentations and interview
closing date for 2011
31 July 2009

Application
Training contracts p.a. 80
Applications p.a. 4,000
% interviewed p.a. 20%
Required degree grade 2:1

Training
Salary
1st year London (2007)
£35,000
2nd year London (2007)
£37,000
Holiday entitlement 25 days
% of trainees with
a non-law degree p.a. 45%
No. of seats available
abroad p.a. Up to 12

Post-qualification
Salary London (2007) £62,000
% of trainees offered job
on qualification (2005) 82%

Offices
Barcelona*, Birmingham,
Brussels, Budapest*,
Cambridge, Cardiff,
Copenhagen, Doha** Ipswich,
Kuala Lumpur*, Leeds, London,
Madrid*, Manchester, Milan*,
Munich*, Newcastle, Norwich,
Nottingham, Paris, Rome*,
Shanghai*, Singapore*, Sofia*,
Stockholm*, Valladolid*,
Vienna*, Warsaw*, Wroclaw*
* Associated office
** In co-operation

Farrer & Co LLP

66 Lincoln's Inn Fields, London WC2A 3LH
Tel: (020) 7242 2022 Fax: (020) 7242 9899
Email: training@farrer.co.uk
Website: www.farrer.co.uk

Firm profile

Farrer & Co is a mid-sized London law firm. The firm provides specialist advice to a large number of prominent private, institutional and commercial clients. Farrer & Co has built a successful law firm based on the goodwill of close client relationships, outstanding expertise in niche sectors and a careful attention to personal service and quality.

Main areas of work

The firm's breadth of expertise is reflected by the fact that it has an outstanding reputation in fields as diverse as matrimonial law, offshore tax planning, employment, heritage work, charity law, defamation and sports law.

Trainee profile

Trainees are expected to be highly motivated individuals with keen intellects and interesting and engaging personalities. Those applicants who appear to break the mould – as shown by their initiative for organisation, leadership, exploration, or enterprise – are far more likely to get an interview than the erudite, but otherwise unimpressive, student.

Training environment

The training programme involves each trainee in the widest range of cases, clients and issues possible in a single law firm, taking full advantage of the wide range of practice areas at Farrer & Co by offering six seats, rather than the more usual four. This provides a broad foundation of knowledge and experience and the opportunity to make an informed choice about the area of law in which to specialise. A high degree of involvement is encouraged under the direct supervision of solicitors and partners. Trainees attend an induction programme and regular internal lectures. The training partner reviews trainees' progress at the end of each seat and extensive feedback is given. The firm has a very friendly atmosphere and regular sporting and social events.

Benefits

Health and life insurance, subsidised gym membership, season ticket loan.

vacation placements

Places for 2009: 30; Duration: 2 weeks at Easter, two schemes for 2 weeks in summer; Remuneration: £250 p.w.; Closing Date: 31 January 2009.

Sponsorship & awards

CPE Funding: Fees paid plus £6,000 maintenance. LPC Funding: Fees paid plus £6,000 maintenance.

Partners 67
Assistant Solicitors 63
Total Trainees 20

Contact
Trainee Recruitment
Manager

Method of application
Online via the firm's website

Selection procedure
Interviews with Trainee
Recruitment Partner and
partners

Closing date for 2011
31 July 2009

Application
Training contracts p.a.10
Applications p.a. 800
% interviewed p.a. 5%
Required degree grade 2:1

Training
Salary
1st year (sept 2008) £32,000
2nd year (sept 2008) £34,500
Holiday entitlement 25 days
% of trainees with non-law
degrees p.a. 40-60%

Post-qualification
Salary (2008) £51,000
trainees offered job
on qualification (2008) 88%
% of partners (as at July 08)
who joined as trainees 57%

Field Fisher Waterhouse LLP

35 Vine Street, London EC3N 2AA
Tel: (020) 7861 4000 Fax: (020) 7488 0084
Email: graduaterecruitment@ffw.com   Website: www.ffw.com/careers

Partners 122
Assistant Solicitors 235
Vacancies 20
Total Trainees 40

Contact
Lucie Rees
Graduate Recruitment

Method of application
Apply online via the firm
website, www.ffw.com/careers

Selection procedure
Assessment Centre

Closing date for 2011
31 July 2009

Application
Training contracts p.a. 20
Applications p.a. 800
Required degree grade 2:1

Training
Salary
1st year £35,000
2nd year £38,500
Holiday entitlement
25 days

Post-qualification
Salary (2008) £62,000
% of trainees offered job
on qualification (2008) 89%

Offices
London, Brussels, Hamburg and
Paris

Firm profile

Field Fisher Waterhouse LLP (FFW) is a mid-sized City law firm that provides a broad range of legal services to an impressive list of clients that range from small unlisted UK companies to multinationals and foreign corporations. The firm prides itself on offering creative solutions and practical advice for clients in an ever-changing commercial world. Europe is its domestic market. It has offices in Brussels, Hamburg, Paris and London and an exclusive relationship with leading firms in Spain and Italy. The firm also has long standing affiliations with firms in the Czech Republic, Hungary and Poland.

Main areas of work

Throughout their training contract trainees have the opportunity to work within IP & technology, corporate and commercial, banking and finance, regulatory and real estate. They also offer trainee seats in a wide range of other areas including public sector, litigation, employment, aviation, and personal injury and medical negligence.

Trainee profile

The firm is looking to recruit trainees from both law and non-law backgrounds who have a strong academic background, excellent communication skills, enthusiasm and the ability to work as part of a team.

Training environment

FFW offers a six seat training contract and their range of practice areas enable them to offer outstanding opportunities for training. Trainees are treated as a valued part of the team and are encouraged to assume early responsibility. Practical training is complemented by a comprehensive programme of in-house seminars, workshops and external courses, accompanied by regular feedback and a formal assessment at the end of each seat. The firm invests highly in the development and training of all its trainees and provides good quality work within a friendly, relaxed and supportive working environment. You will also have additional support from your fellow trainees, a buddy and a mentor who is a senior solicitor.

Sponsorship & benefits

Sponsorship and a GDL (£5,500) and LPC (£6,000) maintenance grant are paid. Other benefits include: 25 days' holiday, life assurance, season ticket loan, medical insurance, GP service, and pension in addition to having two squash courts in the firm's offices.

Vacation placements & open days

Increasingly, trainees have come to the firm through the summer vacation scheme, which provides a useful way of getting an insider's view of FFW. The firm runs schemes at Easter and during July where you have the opportunity to spend a week in two different departments and take part in a variety of work and social activities.

The firm also runs open days during the spring that give you the opportunity to find out more about them.

Deadline for 2009 Vacation Schemes and Open Days: 31 January 2009.

Deadline for 2010 Training Contracts: 31 July 2009.

Finers Stephens Innocent

179 Great Portland St, London W1W 5LS
Tel: (020) 7323 4000 Fax: (020) 7580 7069
Email: gradrecruitment@fsilaw.com
Website: www.fsilaw.com

Firm profile

Finers Stephens Innocent is an expanding practice in Central London, providing a range of high quality legal services to corporate, commercial and private clients. The firm's philosophy includes close partner involvement and a cost-effective approach in all client matters. They have a working style which is unstuffy and informal, but still aspires to the highest quality of output, while offering a sensible work-life balance. The firm is a member of the Meritas international network of law firms.

Main areas of work

Commercial property, company commercial, employment, private client, family, media, defamation. See the website for further details.

Trainee profile

The firm requires academic excellence in all applicants. It also looks for maturity, personality, a broad range of interests, initiative, strong communication skills, and the ability to write clear English, and to think like a lawyer. The firm has for several years given equal consideration to applicants whether applying straight from university or having followed another career previously. Trainees get early responsibility, client contact and close involvement in transactions and litigation matters.

Training environment

Between offering you a training contract and the time you start, the firm aims to keep regularly in touch with you, including offering you some work experience with them. When you start they provide a careful induction programme, after which you complete four six-month seats in different departments, sharing a room with either a Partner or Senior Assistant. The firm has three Training Partners who keep a close eye on the welfare and progress of trainees. There are regular group meetings with trainees, and an appraisal process which enables you to know how you are progressing, as well as giving you a chance to provide feedback on your training. The firm runs a variety of in-house training courses for trainees.

Benefits

25 days holiday; pension; private medical insurance; life insurance; long-term disability insurance; season ticket loan, EAP scheme.

Sponsorship & awards

LPC and CPE course fees.

Partners 37
Assistant Solicitors 36
Total Trainees 12

Contact
Personnel Department

Method of application
CV & covering letter

Selection procedure
2 interviews with the Training Partners

Closing date for 2011
30 June 2009

Application
Training contracts p.a. 6
Applications p.a. 800
% interviewed p.a. 3%
Required degree grade 2:1

Training
Salary
1st year £30,000
2nd year £32,000
Holiday entitlement 25 days
% of trainees with a non-law degree p.a. 0-50%

Post-qualification
Salary £47,000
% of trainees offered job on qualification (2008) 60%

Foot Anstey

21 Derry's Cross, Plymouth PL1 2SW
Tel: (01752) 675000 Fax: (01752) 675500
Email: training@foot-ansteys.co.uk   Website: www.foot-ansteys.co.uk

Firm profile

Foot Anstey is primarily focused on the south west although the quality of its service attracts clients from outside the region for whom it acts nationally. The firm has doubled in size in the past five years and has a turnover of £20m. With new offices already in Exeter and Taunton, a further brand new harbour front office will open in Plymouth in Spring 2009 with another planned for its Truro base later in the year. Foot Anstey is both IIP and Lexcel accredited and holds a Legal Services Commission Specialist Quality Mark. The firm is proud to have been the national winner of The Law Society's "Excellence in Practice Standards" Award.

Main areas of work

As a full service law firm, Foot Anstey delivers the spectrum of services associated with a major regional law firm. Main areas of work include: commercial property, property and construction litigation, company and commercial, dispute resolution, banking, employment, insolvency, clinical negligence, criminal advocates, family and childcare, private client and residential property. The firm has an extensive range of clients from commercial, public and private sectors, acting for numerous local, regional and national companies and high net worth individuals.

Trainee profile

The firm welcomes applications from all law and non-law graduates who have a strong academic background, excellent communication skills and the ability to work as part of a team. Trainees are welcomed into a friendly and supportive environment where they will find the quality and variety of work both challenging and rewarding.

Training environment

Foot Anstey's wide range of legal services enables it to offer trainees experience in a wide range of disciplines throughout its four offices. Trainees undertake four seats of six months. Whenever possible (with the exception of the first seat) trainees are able to select their seats. Individual monthly meetings are held with supervisors and appraisals are conducted halfway through each seat. Regular communication between the trainees and supervisors ensures an open and friendly environment.

Benefits

Include contributory pension, 25 days' holiday.

Vacation placements

The deadline for the 2009 summer placement scheme is 31 March 2009.

Sponsorship & awards

£9,600 grant towards LPC and living expenses.

Vacancies 15
Trainees 16
Partners 47
Total Staff 397

Contact
Louise Widley
(01752) 675069

Method of application
Apply online at
www.foot-ansteys.co.uk

Selection procedure
Assessment day
application
Training contracts p.a. 15
Required degree grade
2:1 (preferred)

Closing date for 2011
31 July 2009

Training
Salary
1st year (2008) £19,500
2nd year (2008) £21,000
Holiday entitlement 25 days

Post-qualification
Salary (2008) £31,500-
£36,000
% of trainees offered job on
qualification (2008) 100%
% of assistant solicitors who
joined as trainees
(as at 30/04/08) 29%
% of partners who joined as
trainees (as at 30/04/08) 17%

Offices
Plymouth, Exeter, Taunton &
Truro

Forbes

73 Northgate, Blackburn BB2 1AA
Tel: (01254) 580000 Fax: (01254) 222216
Email: graduate.recruitment@forbessolicitors.co.uk

Firm profile

Forbes is one of the largest practices in the north with 31 partners and over 350 members of staff based in nine offices across the north of England. The firm has a broad based practice dealing with both commercial and private client work and can therefore provide a varied and exciting training contract. The firm is however especially noted for excellence in its company/commercial; civil litigation; defendant insurer; crime; family and employment departments. It has a number of Higher Court Advocates and the firm holds many Legal Service Commission Franchises. Underlying the practice is a strong commitment to quality, training and career development – a commitment underlined by the fact that Forbes was one of the first firms to be recognised as an Investor in People and its ISO 9001 accreditation. For applicants looking for a 'city' practice without the associated hassles of working in a city then Forbes could be it. The firm can offer the best of both worlds – a large firm with extensive resources and support combined with a commitment to quality, people and the personal touch.

Main areas of work

Company/commercial, civil litigation, defendant insurer, crime, family and employment services.

Trainee profile

Forbes looks for high-calibre recruits with strong North West connections and good academic records, who are also keen team players. Candidates should have a total commitment to client service and identify with the firm's philosophy of providing practical straightforward legal advice.

Training environment

A tailored training programme involves six months in four of the following: crime, civil litigation, defendant insurer in Leeds or Blackburn, matrimonial, and non-contentious/company commercial.

Partners 31
Assistant Solicitors 53
Total Trainees 15+

Contact
Graduate Recruitment Manager

Method of application
Handwritten letter and CV

Selection procedure
Interview with partners

Closing date for 2011
31 July 2009
If no invite to interview is received by 31/08/09 applicants to assume they have been unsuccesful.

Application
Training contracts p.a. 4
Applications p.a. 350 plus
% interviewed p.a. Varies
Required degree grade 2:1

Training
Salary
1st year At least Law Society minimum
2nd year (2008) £18,820
Holiday entitlement
20 days p.a.

Post-qualification
Salary
Highly competitive
% of trainees offered job on qualification (2008) 9/10

Ford & Warren

Westgate Point, Westgate, Leeds, LS1 2AX
Tel: (0113) 243 6601 Fax: (0113) 242 0905
Email: Lee.Lewis@forwarn.com
Website: www.forwarn.com

Partners 21
Assistant Solicitors 70
Total Trainees 6

Contact
Lee Lewis

Method of application
Handwritten letter and CV or email

Selection procedure
Interviews and exercise

Closing date for 2011
31 August 2009

Application
Training contracts p.a. 4
Applications p.a. 500
No minimum degree grade

Firm profile

Ford & Warren is one of the largest single office commercial law firms in the region. With roots in Leeds stretching back almost 200 years, the firm has achieved its present size entirely by generic growth without mergers or acquisitions. The cost effective and quality services have enabled the firm to achieve a national reputation in key industry sectors and specialised areas of work. Areas of particular specialisation include: employment and industrial relations, road and rail transportation, licensed and leisure industry, commercial litigation and finance. Ford & Warren has a significant presences in the public sector, particularly in health, education and local authority.

Main areas of work

Employment and industrial relations; road and rail transportation; corporate; insurance and personal injury; commercial property/real estate; public sector; tax and inheritance; matrimonial. The Dispute Resolution/Commercial Litigation Department has five sections: commercial dispute resolution, property litigation, finance litigation, insolvency and debt recovery.

Trainee profile

The firm is looking for hard working, self-reliant and enthusiastic individuals who will make a contribution to the firm from the outset. Applicants must have a strong academic background, a genuine enthusiasm for the law and the social abilities required to work effectively with colleagues and clients. The majority of lawyers practising at the firm joined as trainees.

Training environment

The firm offers seats in employment, commercial litigtion, corporate, insurance and personal injury, commercial property and private client. Usually, trainees will undertake four seats of six months, although split seats may sometimes be available. The firm has a comprehensive in-house training programme for all lawyers and the PSC is also provided internally.

Selection procedure

First interviews for 2011 will take place in late 2009 with a Partner and Associate of the firm. Successful candidates are invited to a second assessment interview involving at least one member of the managing board.

Forsters LLP

31, Hill Street, London W1J 5LS
Tel: (020) 7863 8333 Fax: (020) 7863 8444
Email: gradrecruitment@forsters.co.uk
Website: www.forsters.co.uk

Partners 33	
Assistant Solicitors 60	
Total Trainees 13	
Contact	
Amy Sweetland	
Method of application	
Online application form	
Selection procedure	
First and second interview with	
2 Graduate Recruitment	
Partners	
Closing date for 2011	
31 July 2009	
Application	
Training contracts p.a. 6	
Required degree grade 2:1	
Required UCAS points 320	
Training	
Salary	
1st year (2008) £31,500	
2nd year (2008) £33,500	
Holiday entitlement 24 days	
Post-qualification	
Salary (2008) £52,000	

Firm profile

Forsters is a successful firm committed to being the best at what it does. Based in Mayfair in London's West End, Forsters was founded in 1998. Now with over 100 fee-earners, it is recognised as being a progressive law firm which is highly regarded for its property and private client work as well as having thriving commercial, litigation and family law practices. The working atmosphere of the firm is friendly and informal, yet highly professional. A social committee organises a range of activities from quiz nights to sporting events.

Main areas of work

The firm has a strong reputation for all aspects of commercial and residential property work. The groups handle investment funding; development; planning; construction; landlord and tenant; property taxation and residential investment and development. Forsters is also recognised as one of the leading proponents of private client work in London with a client base comprising a broad range of individuals and trusts in the UK and elsewhere. The firm's commercial practice specialises in acquisitions and financing for technology, communication and media companies whilst its litigation group conducts commercial litigation and arbitration and advises on a broad spectrum of matters.

Trainee profile

Successful candidates will have a strong academic background and either have attained or be expected to achieve a good second class degree. The firm considers that factors alongside academic achievements are also important. The firm is looking for individuals who give a real indication of being interested in a career in law and who the firm feels would readily accept and work well in its team environment.

Training environment

The first year of training is split into three seats of four months usually in three of the following departments: commercial property, private client, company commercial or litigation. In the second year the four month pattern still applies, but the firm discusses with you whether you have developed an area of particular interest and tries to accommodate this. The training is very 'hands on' as you share an office with a partner or assistant who will give you real responsibility alongside supervision. At the mid-term and end of each seat your progress and performance will be reviewed by way of an appraisal with a partner from the relevant department.

Sponsorship & benefits

24 days holiday p.a., season ticket loan, permanent health insurance, life insurance, subsidised gym membership, contributory pension scheme, employee assistance programme, private healthcare (after six months), active social programme. Sponsorship: Payment of LPC and GDL fees, plus a maintenance grant of £5,000 per year of study is offered to future trainees who have yet to complete these courses.

Vacation placements

Opportunities available in 2009: Forsters offers a one-week Easter vacation scheme and 2 two-week Summer vacation schemes. Remuneration is £250 per week. Closing date is 15 February 2009.

Freeth Cartwright LLP

Cumberland Court, 80 Mount Street, Nottingham NG1 6HH
Tel: (0115) 901 5504 Fax: (0115) 859 9603
Email: carole.wigley@freethcartwright.co.uk
Website: www.freethcartwright.co.uk

Firm profile

Tracing its origins back to 1805, Freeth Cartwright LLP became Nottingham's largest firm in 1994 with successful offices now established in Birmingham, Derby, Leicester and Manchester. Whilst Freeth Cartwright LLP is a heavyweight commercial firm, serving a wide variety of corporate and institutional clients, there is also a commitment to a range of legal services, which includes a substantial private client element. This enables it to give a breadth of experience in training which is not always available in firms of a similar size.

Freeth Cartwright is extremely pleased to have been awarded The Sunday Times 100 Best Companies to Work for 2008 status and is also winner of LawCareers.Net Training & Recruitment 2008 award for the 'Best Trainer' category for National/ Large Regional Firms.

Main areas of work

Real estate and construction, commercial services, private client and personal litigation.

Trainee profile

Freeth Cartwright LLP looks for people to bring their own perspective and individuality to the firm. The firm needs people who can cope with the intellectual demands of life as a lawyer and who possess the wider personal skills which are needed in its diverse practice.

Training environment

Freeth Cartwright LLP is committed to providing comprehensive training for all its staff. The firm's training programme is based on in-house training covering technical matters and personal skills, supplemented with external courses where appropriate. The firm endeavours to give the best possible experience during the training period, as it believes that informal training on-the-job is the most effective means of encouraging the skills required in a qualified solicitor. One of the firm's senior partners takes responsibility for all its trainees and their personal development, overseeing their progress through the firm and discussing performance based on feedback. Normally, the training contract will consist of four six month seats in different departments, most of which are available in the firm's Nottingham offices, although it is possible for trainees to spend at least one seat in another location.

Members 79
Assistant Solicitors 89
Total Trainees 15

Contact
Carole Wigley, Senior HR Manager

Method of application
Online application form

Selection procedure
Interview & selection day closing date for 2011
30 June 2009

Training
Starting salary (2008) £22,000

Offices
Nottingham, Birmingham, Derby, Leicester and Manchester

Freeth
Cartwright
LLP

Freshfields Bruckhaus Deringer

Freshfields Bruckhaus Deringer LLP
65 Fleet Street, London EC4Y 1HS
Tel: (020) 7936 4000 Fax: (020) 7832 7001
Email: uktrainees@freshfields.com
Website: www.freshfields.com/uktrainees

Firm profile

Freshfields Bruckhaus Deringer is a leading international firm with a network of 28 offices in 16 countries. The firm provides first-rate legal services to corporations, financial institutions and governments around the world.

Main areas of work

Corporate; mergers and acquisitions; banking; dispute resolution; joint ventures; employment, pensions and benefits; asset finance; real estate; tax; capital markets; intellectual property and information technology; project finance; private finance initiative; securities; antitrust, competition and trade; communications and media; construction and engineering; energy; environment, planning and regulatory; financial services; restructuring and insolvency; insurance; investment funds; public international law; arbitration.

Trainee profile

The firm is looking for candidates with proven academic ability, an excellent command of spoken and written English, high levels of drive and determination, good team working skills and excellent organisational ability.

Training environment

The firm's trainees receive a thorough professional training in a very broad range of practice areas, an excellent personal development programme and the chance to work in one of the firm's international offices or on secondment with a client. You'll be working with and learning from one of the most talented peer groups in the legal world, and will get the blend of support and freedom you need to evolve your career.

Benefits

The firm offers a flexible benefits package which includes: life assurance; permanent health insurance; group personal pension; interest-free loan for a season travel ticket; private medical insurance; subsidised gym membership and an interest-free loan when you start.

Vacation placements

Places for 2009: 80; Duration: 3 weeks; Remuneration: £825 (net); Closing Date: 16 January 2009 but apply as early as possible after 17 November 2008 as there may not be places left by the deadline.

Sponsorship & awards

GDL and LPC fees paid plus maintenance grant of £7,250 for those studying the LPC and £6,250 for those studying the GDL.

Partners 463
Assistant Solicitors 1,754
Total Trainees 199
(London based)

Contact
uktrainees@freshfields.com

Method of application
Online application form

Selection procedure
2 interviews and written test

Closing date for 2011
31 July 2009

Application
Training contracts p.a. 100
Applications p.a. c.2,000
% interviewed p.a. c.12%
Required degree grade 2:1

Training
Salary
1st year £39,000
2nd year £44,000
Holiday entitlement 25 days
% of trainees with a
non-law degree p.a. c.40%
No. of seats available
abroad p.a. c.86

Post-qualification
Salary £66,000
% of trainees offered job
on qualification c.95%

Overseas offices
Abu Dhabi, Amsterdam, Bahrain, Barcelona, Beijing, Berlin, Bratislava, Brussels, Cologne, Dubai, Düsseldorf, Frankfurt, Hamburg, Hanoi, Ho Chi Minh City, Hong Kong, Madrid, Milan, Moscow, Munich, New York, Paris, Rome, Shanghai, Tokyo, Vienna, Washington DC

Geldards LLP

Dumfries House, Dumfries Place, Cardiff, CF10 3ZF
Tel: (02920) 3914951
Website: www.geldards.com

Firm profile

Geldards LLP is a top 100 regionally based commercial practice. It serves its clients from offices located in Cardiff, Derby and Nottingham, drawing business from all parts of the United Kingdom. Geldards' approach to life is collegiate and supportive. The firm has succeeded in establishing long-term relationships with its clients and staff and has an enviable reputation in developing its people. A number of the firm's partners were previously trainees with the firm.

Main areas of work

Within the firm are some of the strongest core practices in the regions, with particular emphasis on corporate finance, property and dispute resolution.

Over recent years there has also been rapid growth within the firm of what might once have been considered niche areas; such as commercial law, planning and environmental law, energy law, rail and transport law, construction contracts and building arbitration, employment law, restructuring and insolvency, trusts and tax. The firm offers candidates an opportunity of seats in all of these areas.

Trainee profile

Like everyone else, Geldards LLP is looking for candidates with a strong academic background who display evidence of being motivated and hard working. Beyond that, it is looking for individuals with a sense of humour, a degree of self-confidence and the ability to work in a team environment. The firm often finds that successful candidates can demonstrate an involvement in extra curricula activities, which indicates that they will be like minded individuals to Geldards' employees.

Training environment

Training is divided into six four-month seats in the firm's main practice areas. Trainees are allocated to a particular team and are supervised by the lead partner or senior solicitors within the team. Trainees are formally reviewed at the end of each seat but informal feedback is given throughout a seat. An open-door policy applies and trainees are regarded very much as an integral part of the team. Formal training will be a combination of external course and internal seminars.

Benefits

Salary of no less than £21,000; 3x annual salary life assurance; 25 days annual leave; Non-contributory pension; Matched pension contributions.

Sponsorship & awards

Full sponsorships for LPC; Maintenance grant of £4,500 for LPC; Contribution towards GDL / CPE.

Partners 54
Assistant Solicitors -
Total Trainees 16

Contact
Beverley Greeves, (02920) 391 495

Method of application
Apply online
www.geldards.com

Selection procedure
Assessment days

Closing date for 2011
Summer Placement - 1st March 2009
Training Contracts - 31st July 2009

Application
Training contracts p.a. 8
Applications p.a. 500
% interviewed p.a. 20%
Required degree grade 2:1 (ideally)

Training
Salary
No less than £21,000

Post-qualification
Salary £35,000 (min)
% of trainees offered job on qualification (2008) 87.5%

Regional offices
Cardiff, Derby, Nottingham

Gordons LLP

Riverside West, Whitehall Road, Leeds, LS1 4AW
Tel: (0113) 227 0100 Fax: (0113) 227 0113
14 Piccadilly, Bradford, BD1 3 LX
Tel: (01274) 202202 Fax: (01274) 202100
Email: karen.mills@gordonsllp.com
Website: www.gordonsllp.com

Firm profile

Gordons is one of the largest law firms based entirely in Yorkshire, with offices in Leeds and Bradford. The firm provides commercial and personal legal services to a wide range of businesses and individuals across the region and beyond, from the individual entrepreneur and small family business to the large PLC, and the firm's private client service is equally as comprehensive. The firm's approach is that of a straight-talking, hard-working, ambitious law firm that puts its clients' success before its own.

Main areas of work

Commercial property; planning and environmental; construction; corporate; banking; insolvency; commercial litigation; intellectual property; employment; personal injury; personal law; family law and residential property.

Trainee profile

The firm is looking for trainees who are eager to learn, have good interpersonal skills, can relate well to clients and who welcome responsibility at an early stage. Initiative, commercial awareness, IT skills and a friendly and professional manner are all essential qualities along with ambition to succeed. The firm sees its trainees as its partners of tomorrow!

Training environment

The firm's trainees spend a minimum of six months in at least three of the following departments: company/ commercial; commercial property, litigation, private client. During the second year of the training contract trainees may state their preference for a particular department and the firm will try to accommodate the request where possible. The firm's trainees work closely with a partner or senior solicitor in each seat and get 'hands on' training with plenty of client contact. They are actively encouraged to get involved with marketing, networking, training, and other events hosted by the firm and/ or clients, and the firm itself has regular social activities on offer, both formal and informal. The environment is supportive and friendly with an open door policy across the firm, and the trainees have regular meetings with their supervisors to ensure their progress. The firm aims to offer its trainees positions within the firm on qualification wherever possible.

Benefits

Group personal pension; life assurance of three x salary death in service benefit; interest-free season ticket loan; childcare vouchers scheme; 24 days holiday per year plus statutory holidays, weekly yoga sessions.

Sponsorship & awards

The firm contributes £5,000 towards LPC course fees.

Partners 39
Assistant Solicitors 65
Total Trainees 16

Contact
Karen Mills, HR Manager Philip Paget, Training Principal

Method of application
Online application via website www.gordonsllp.com

Selection procedure
One stage interview process, including practical exercise and opportunity to meet current trainees

Closing date for 2011
1st August 2009

Application
Training contracts p.a. 8 (recently increased)
Applications p.a. 300
% interviewed p.a. 10%
Required degree grade 2:1

Training
Salary
1st year £21,500
2nd year £24,000
Holiday entitlement 24 days and statutory
% of trainees with a non-law degree p.a. 50%

Post-qualification
Salary £37,500 p.a.
% of trainees offered job on qualification 100%

Government Legal Service

GLS Recruitment Team, Chancery House, 53-64 Chancery Lane, London WC2A 1QS
Tel: (020) 7649 6023
Email: glstrainees@tmpw.co.uk
Website: www.gls.gov.uk

Firm profile

The Government Legal Service (GLS) is the collective term for the 1900 lawyers working in the legal teams of approximately 30 of the largest government departments and agencies. GLS lawyers have one client, the government of the day, which requires advice and support across the entire spectrum of its activities.

Main areas of work

There are many parallels between the GLS' work and that found in private practice. The government employs staff, purchases goods and services, buys and sells land and enters into contracts. GLS lawyers advise and represent the client on a huge range of issues which are often high profile and politically sensitive.

In addition to interpreting existing laws, GLS lawyers also have the opportunity to make new legislation. GLS lawyers are part of the teams that breathe life into the policies pledged by governments. They advise ministers and policy officials on what can (and can't) be done under existing legislation. If new legislation is required, GLS lawyers will help to draft and take it through Parliament in the form of a Bill. They will work closely with policy officials and Ministers and even support Ministers in Parliamentary debates. This type of work is unique to the GLS.

Trainee profile

To join the GLS as trainee solicitor or pupil barrister, you'll need at least a 2:1 degree (which need not be in law). You must also provide evidence of strong analytical ability, excellent communication and interpersonal skills and motivation for working in public service.

Training environment

The GLS provides a unique and varied training environment for trainees and pupils. Generally, trainee solicitors work in four different areas of practice over a two-year period in the government Department to which they are assigned. Pupil barristers divide their year's pupillage between their Department and chambers. The GLS prides itself on involving trainees and pupils in the full range of casework conducted by their Department. This frequently includes high profile matters and will be under the supervision of senior colleagues.

Benefits

These include professional development opportunities, excellent pension scheme, civilised working hours, generous holiday entitlement and subsidised restaurant facilities.

Vacation placements

Summer 2009 vacation placement scheme; approx 60 places. Duration: 2-3 weeks. Closing date: end of January 2009. Remuneration: £200-£250 pw.

Sponsorship & awards

LPC and BVC fees as well as other compulsory Professional Skills Course fees. Funding may be available for the GDL. The GLS also provides a grant of around £5-7,000 for the vocational year.

Total Trainees around 50

Contact
glstrainees@tmpw.co.uk or visit www.gls.gov.uk

Method of application
Online application form and verbal reasoning test

Selection procedure
Half day at assessment centre involving a group discussion exercise, a written exercise and an interview

Closing date for 2011
31 July 2009

Application
Training contracts p.a. 22-30
Applications p.a. 500+
% interviewed p.a. 10%
Required degree grade (need not be in law) 2:1

Training
Salary begins at over £22,600 in London and varies acording to Government Department. It is lower outside London.

Holiday entitlement 25 days on entry

Post-qualification
Salary varies according to Government Department; the vacancies section of the GLS website will give a flavour of what to expect.
% of trainees accepting job on qualification (2007) at least 87%

Halliwells

3 Hardman Square, Spinningfields, Manchester, M3 3EB
Tel: (0844) 875 8000 Fax: (0844) 875 8001
Email: ekaterina.clarke@halliwells.com

Firm profile

Halliwells is one of the largest independent commercial law firms in the North West and specialises in providing a full range of legal services to the business community. With clients on a local, national and international level, Halliwells has high aspirations far beyond its regional boundaries. The firm has grown rapidly in recent years and embraces an internal culture of commitment, enthusiasm and reward.

Main areas of work

Corporate (Corporate, Banking and Pensions), Corporate Recovery, Real Estate (Property, Planning and Licensing), Business Services (Employment and Intellectual Property), Dispute Resolution (Commercial Litigation, Insurance Liability, Regulatory and Construction), Private Client (Family and Trusts & Estates).

Trainee profile

Candidates need to show a good academic ability but do not need to have studied law at university. Candidates should exhibit the characteristics necessary to thrive in a busy commercial environment and the ability to fit into a hardworking team. In particular, the firm is looking for candidates who will continue to develop with the firm after their initial training.

Training environment

Each trainee will have five seats in at least four separate departments. These will usually include commercial litigation, corporate and commercial property. Individual requests from trainees for experience in a particular department will be accommodated wherever possible. Requests for inter-office and client secondments are also encouraged.

The trainee will work within one of the department's teams and be encouraged to assist other team members to help broaden their experience. Specific training appropriate to each department will be given and trainees are strongly encouraged to attend the firm's regular in-house seminars on legal and related topics.

A supervisor will be assigned to each trainee to support their development throughout the seat.

Benefits

25 days annual leave, season ticket loan, subsidised gym membership, life assurance.

Work placements

75 summer placements will be available during summer 2009. The firm operates three schemes at all its four offices, each lasts for two weeks. Schemes commence last week in June. Remuneration is £210 per week. Closing date for applications is 28 February 2009.

Sponsorship & awards

The firm pays GDL fees and LPC fees plus a £6,500 maintenance grant for each course.

Partners 154
Assistant Solicitors 417
Total Trainees 76

Contact
Ekaterina Clarke
(Graduate Recruitment Manager)
ekaterina.clarke@halliwells.com

Method of application
Online application only

Selection procedure
Group exercise, presentation and interview

Closing date for 2011
31 July 2009

Application
Training contracts p.a.
Manchester - 20
London - 7
Liverpool - 5
Sheffield - 5
Applications p.a. 1,500
% interviewed p.a. 9%
Required degree grade 2:1

Training
Salary
1st year (2008) £24,000
(London) £32,500
2nd year (2008) £25,000
(London) £33,500

Post-qualification
Salary (2008) £39,000
(London) £62,000
% of trainees offered job on qualification (2008) 75%

Hammonds LLP

Rutland House, 148 Edmund Street, Birmingham B3 2JR
7 Devonshire Square, Cutlers Gardens, London EC2M 4YH2 Park Lane, Leeds LS3 1ES
Trinity Court, 16 John Dalton Street, Manchester M6O 8HS
Tel: (0800) 163 498 Fax: (0870) 839 3666
Email: traineerecruitment@hammonds.com
Website: www.hammonds.com/trainees

Firm profile

Hammonds is one of Europe's largest corporate law firms and a member of the Global 100. In the UK alone, the firm advises over 200 London Stock Exchange quoted companies and 30 FTSE 100 companies. The firm has offices in London, Birmingham, Leeds, Manchester, Brussels, Paris, Berlin, Munich, Rome, Milan, Madrid, Turin, Beijing and Hong Kong. The firm has 1,400 staff, including 208 Partners, 550 solicitors and 80 trainees. The firm is regarded as innovative, opportunistic and highly successful in the markets in which it operates.

Main areas of work

Corporate; commercial dispute resolution; construction, engineering and projects; employment; EU and competition; finance law (including banking); intellectual property and commercial; media/IT; pensions; property; sports law; tax.

Trainee profile

Hammonds seeks applications from all disciplines for vacation work and training contracts. Consideration given to four elements in trainee selection: strong academic performance (2:1 degree classification), evidence of work experience in the legal sector, excellent communication skills and significant achievement in non-academic pursuits.

Training environment

40 trainee solicitors recruited each year. Trainees undertake six four-month seats during their training contract. Trainees have input in choice of seats and are encouraged to undertake a broad selection of seats to benefit their knowledge on qualification. Trainees benefit from two-tier supervision and challenging work. The firm provides a comprehensive induction programme including on-going departmental training, seminars and workshops throughout the training contract. Trainees undertake formal appraisal meetings with their supervisors during each seat. Hammonds' trainees benefit from exposure to clients, cross-border work and opportunity for seats on secondment. Trainees are involved in all aspects of professional life.

Benefits

Pension, life assurance, subsidised gym membership, interest free season ticket loan and a flexible benefits package.

Vacation placements

Places for 2009: 64 Summer Scheme; Duration: 2 weeks; Remuneration: £230 p.w. (London), £180 p.w. (Leeds, Manchester, Birmingham); Closing Date: 31 January 2009.

Sponsorship & awards

PgDL and LPC fees paid and maintenance grant provided. Maintenance grant presently:
GDL: London, £6,000; Regional, £4,500.
LPC: London, £7,000; Regional, £5,000.

Partners 208
Assistant Solicitors 550
Total Trainees 80

Contact
Graduate Recruitment Team

Method of application
Online application form

Selection procedure
Assessment and interview

Closing date for 2011
31 July 2009

Application
Training contracts p.a. 40
Applications p.a. 1,300
% interviewed p.a. 10%
Required degree grade 2:1

Training
Salary
1st year (2008)
£25,000 regional
£35,000 London
2nd year (2008)
£27,000 regional
£38,000 London
Holiday entitlement 25 days
% of trainees with a non-law
degree p.a. 40%
No. of seats available abroad
p.a. 15

Post-qualification
Salary (2008)
London £62,000
Other £40,000
% of trainees accepting job on
qualification (2006) 84%

Overseas offices
Brussels,Beijing, Paris, Berlin,
Munich, Rome, Milan, Turin,
Hong Kong, Madrid

Harbottle & Lewis LLP

Hanover House, 14 Hanover Square, London W1S 1HP
Tel: (020) 7667 5000 Fax: (020) 7667 5100
Email: kathy.beilby@harbottle.com
Website: www.harbottle.com

Firm profile

Harbottle & Lewis LLP is a London based commercial law firm providing specialist advice primarily to the media, entertainment and communications industries.

Main areas of work

Main areas of work encompasses all areas of media and entertainment including film, television, broadcasting, sport, music, publishing, computer games, advertising, fashion and theatre and the firm remains unique in having expertise right across these sectors. Much of the firm's work involves the technology, new media and telecoms industries and the firm has done ground-breaking work in connection with the digital exploitation of content and e-commerce generally. The firm's expertise in other areas such as aviation and charities is also widely recognised.

Trainee profile

Trainees will have demonstrated the high academic abilities, commercial awareness, and initiative necessary to become part of a team advising clients in dynamic and demanding industries.

Training environment

The two year training contract is divided into four six-month seats where trainees will be given experience in a variety of legal skills including company commercial, litigation, intellectual property and real property, working within teams focused on the firm's core industries. The firm has a policy of accepting a small number of trainees to ensure they are given relevant and challenging work and are exposed to and have responsibility for a full range of legal tasks. The firm has its own lecture and seminar programme in both legal topics and industry know-how. An open door policy and a pragmatic entrepreneurial approach to legal practice provides a stimulating working environment.

Benefits

Lunch provided; season ticket loans.

Sponsorship & awards

LPC fees paid and interest-free loans towards maintenance.

Partners 26
Assistant Solicitors 45
Total Trainees 10

Contact
Kathy Beilby

Method of application
CV & letter by post or email

Selection procedure
Interview

Closing date for 2011
31 July 2009

Application
Training contracts p.a. 5
Applications p.a. 800
% interviewed p.a. 10%
Required degree grade 2:1

Training
Salary
1st year £28,000 (2008)
2nd year £29,000 (2008)
Holiday entitlement
in the first year 23 days
in the second year 26 days
% of trainees with
a non-law degree p.a. 40%

Post-qualification
Salary (2007) £47-50k

Hay & Kilner

Merchant House, 30 Cloth Market, Newcastle upon Tyne, NE1 1EE
Tel: (0191) 232 8345   Fax: (0191) 261 7704
Email: ros.sparrow@hay-kilner.co.uk
Website: www.hay-kilner.co.uk

Firm profile

The firm's offices are in the centre of Newcastle, a thriving and exciting city with easy access to Northumberland, Durham, the Lake District and Scotland.

Established in 1946, Hay & Kilner has grown to become one of the larger firms in Newcastle with 21 partners and 170 staff. The firm provides a broad range of specialist services to both corporate and private clients. Dynamic and commercial in outlook, the firm aims to provide effective and practical advice to its clients in a professional and friendly manner. The firm is committed to quality. It is ISO9001 and Lexcel accredited and a Legal Aid franchise holder.

Main areas of work

The firm's main office is divided into three practice areas: commercial, litigation, and private client. The firm also has a branch office in Wallsend and a volume recoveries and re-mortgage operation, which trades as Wallers and acts for a number of financial institutions.

Trainee profile

The firm is looking for motivated, commercially aware and outgoing individuals. Its minimum entry requirement is a 2:1 degree (or an expectation of one). The firm welcomes applications from non-law graduates and the firm values outside interests and experience.

Training environment

The training contract is divided into four six-month seats, generally including time in each of the three main practice areas. You will be responsible for files and you will have client contact, and carry out advocacy, where appropriate. The firm's ethos is a supportive one and you will work closely with your supervisor and with other qualified fee earners. Along with a small number of other local commercial law firms, the firm has designed a commercial professional skills course for its trainees at the University of Northumbria.

Sponsorship & awards

The firm makes a contribution towards the cost of the LPC (subject to certain terms).

Partners 21
Trainees 6
Total Staff 170

Contact
Ros Sparrow

Method of application
Apply online www.hay-kilner.co.uk

Selection procedure
interviews & assessments

Closing date for 2009
Summer vacation placements;
28 February 2009

Closing date for September 2011
Training contracts 31 July 2009

Applications
Training contracts p.a. 4
Applications p.a. 200
% interviewed p.a. 15%

Training
Salary under review
Holiday entitlement 25 days

HBJ Gateley Wareing LLP

One Eleven, Edmund Street, Birmingham B3 2HJ
Tel: (0121) 234 0069   Fax: (0121) 234 0079
Email: graduaterecruitment.england@hbj-gw.com
Website: www.hbjgateleywareing.com

Firm profile

A 102 partner, UK commercial based practice with an excellent reputation for general commercial work and particular expertise in corporate, plc, commercial, employment, property, construction, insolvency, commercial dispute resolution, banking, tax and shipping.

The firm also offers individual clients a complete private client service including FSA-approved financial advice. The firm is expanding (608 employees) and offers a highly practical, commercial and fast-paced environment. HBJ Gatcley Wareing has built an outstanding reputation across the UK for its practical approach, sound advice and professional commitment to its clients. The firm is a full range, multi-disciplinary legal business with expertise in many areas.

HBJ Gateley Wareing has an enviable reputation as a friendly and sociable place to work. The firm is committed to equality and diversity across the firm.

Trainee profile

To apply for a placement in England: applications are invited from second year law students and final year non-law students and graduates. Applicants should have (or be heading for) a minimum 2.1 degree, and should have at least three Bs (or equivalent) at A-level. Individuals should be hardworking team players capable of using initiative and demonstrating commercial awareness.

Training environment

Four six-month seats with ongoing supervision and appraisals every three months. PSC taken internally. In-house courses on skills such as time management, negotiation, IT, drafting, business skills, marketing, presenting and writing in plain English.

Benefits

Current trainee offered as a 'buddy' – a point of contact within the firm, library available, invitation to summer party prior to joining.

Vacation placements

Two-week placement over the summer. Deadline for next year's vacation placement scheme is 11 February 2009 and the closing date for 2011 training contracts is 31 July 2009. Apply online at www.hbjgateleywareing.com.

Sponsorship & awards

CPE/LPC and a LPC maintenance grant of £5,000.

Partners 102 (firmwide)
Vacancies 12 (England)
Total Trainees 22 (Midlands)
TotalStaff 608 (firmwide)

Contact
Julie Joyce Graduate
Recruitment

Closing date for 2011
Training contracts:
31 July 2009
Vacation placements:
11 February 2009

Training
Salary
1st year £24,000
2nd year £25,000

Post-qualification
Salary £38,000

Offices
Birmingham, Edinburgh, Glasgow, Leicester, London, Nottingham and Dubai.

Henmans LLP

5000 Oxford Business Park South, Oxford OX4 2BH
Tel: (01865) 780000   Fax: (01865) 778682
Email: welcome@henmansllp.co.uk
Website: www.henmansllp.co.uk

Firm profile

Henmans LLP is the premier firm in Oxford, with several practice areas ranked as the leading experts in the Thames Valley by commentators. The firm has a national reputation in its specialist areas, handling commercial and personal matters for a wide range of clients both nationally and internationally. The firm also acts for a large number of third sector organisations and insurers.

More than half of the firm's senior lawyers are acknowledged as experts within their fields, so clients are confident of receiving the most authoritative advice available. It is the firm's belief that the best advisers are those who thoroughly understand your concerns, so the firm works hard to ensure that it has a detailed appreciation of your business or personal questions, and can offer the best possible advice.

Main areas of work

The firm's core service of litigation is nationally recognized for its high quality. The firm also has an excellent reputation for its personal injury, clinical negligence, property, private client and charity work. The breakdown of work is as follows: Professional negligence and commercial litigation: 24%; personal injury: 27%; property: 17%; private client (including family) /charities /trusts: 25%; corporate/employment: 10%.

Trainee profile

Commercial awareness, sound academic accomplishment, intellectual capability, IT literacy, able to work as part of a team, good communication skills.

Training environment

Trainees are an important part of its future. The firm is committed to providing a high standard of training throughout the contract. Trainees are introduced to the firm with a detailed induction and overview of its client base. A trainee manual is provided to familiarise the trainee with each department's procedures. Experience is likely to be within the PI, property, professional negligence/ commercial litigation, corporate/ employment and private client departments. The firm provides an ongoing programme of in-house education and regular appraisals within its supportive friendly environment. The firm values commitment and enthusiasm both professionally and socially as an integral part of its culture and trainees are encouraged to join in social activities and become involved with the life of the firm.

Partners 24
Other Solicitors &
Fee-earners 51
Total Trainees 6

Contact
Viv J Matthews (Mrs)
MA CH FCIPD
Head of HR

Method of application
Application form on website

Selection procedure
The interview process comprises an assessment day with Head of HR and partners, including an interview, presentation, verbal reasoning test, drafting and team exercise

Closing date for 2011
31 July 2009

Application
Training contracts p.a. 3
Applications p.a. 300

Training
Salary
1st year (2008/9) £22,000
2nd year (2008/9) £24,000
Holiday entitlement 23 days +
2 firm days at Christmas.
BUPA, pension, EAP scheme, free car parking, subsidised cafe, corporate massage, circuit training
% of trainees with a
non-law degree p.a. 40%

Post-qualification
Salary (2004) £32,000-33,000
% of assistants who joined as trainees 28%
% of partners who joined as trainees 15%

Herbert Smith LLP

Exchange House, Primrose Street, London EC2A 2HS
Tel: (020) 7374 8000 Fax: (020) 7374 0888
Email: graduate.recruitment@herbertsmith.com
Website: www.herbertsmithgraduates.com

Firm profile

Herbert Smith LLP is an international legal practice with 1,200 lawyers across Asia, Europe and the Middle East. In addition, its alliance with Gleiss Lutz and Stibbe, as well as a network of relationship firms across the rest of the world, enables Herbert Smith to provide a seamless, first class cross-border service.

Herbert Smith's blue-chip client base includes FTSE 100 and Fortune 500 companies, major investment banks and governments. Its strengths span the width of commercial law and its reputation for innovative legal work crosses most sectors of industry and commerce.

Main areas of work

Corporate (including international mergers and acquisitions); finance and banking (including capital markets); international dispute resolution; energy; projects and project finance; EU and competition; real estate; tax; employment and trusts; construction and engineering; insurance; investment funds; IP; US securities, IT & communications.

Trainee profile

As well as a strong academic record, trainees at Herbert Smith thrive on a good measure of common sense and the presence of mind to find their feet and make their own way in a large firm.

Training environment

The training process at Herbert Smith is carefully balanced between contentious and non-contentious work; early responsibility and close support. Great emphasis is placed on professional and personal development, with the firm running a mentoring scheme as well as its own legal development programme.

Herbert Smith also has a strong reputation for the training it provides its trainees. As a trainee at Herbert Smith you will rotate around four seats of six months each, which can include a seat in a specialist area such as IP, tax, trusts, EU/ competition, employment, pensions and incentives or the firm's advocacy unit. Alternatively you can apply to go on secondment to a client or to one of the firm's international offices.

Sponsorship & benefits

CPE/GDL and LPC fees are paid plus up to £7,000 maintenance grant p.a. Benefits include profit related bonus scheme, permanent health insurance, private medical insurance, season ticket loan, life assurance, subsidised gym membership, group personal accident insurance, matched contributory pension scheme and interest free loan.

Vacation placements

Places for 2008/09: 130. Winter 2008 (non-law students only), Spring and Summer 2009 (law and non-law students). Closing Dates: 10 November 2008 for Winter scheme; 31 January 2009 for Spring and Summer schemes. Opportunities in some of the firm's European offices.

Partners 237*
Fee-earners 742*
Total Trainees 203*
*denotes worldwide figures

Contact
Graduate Recruitment Team

Method of application
Online application form

Selection procedure
Case study and interview

Closing date for
Sept 2011/Mar 2012
31 July 2009

Application
Training contracts p.a. up to 105
Applications p.a. circa 2,000
% interviewed p.a. 30%
Required degree grade 2:1

Training
Salary
1st year £37,500
2nd year £42,500
Holiday entitlement
25 days, rising to 27 on qualification
ratio of law to non-law graduates is broadly equal

Post-qualification
Salary (2008) £64,000
% of trainees offered job on qualification (2008) 99%
(based on no. of jobs offered)

Overseas offices
Abu Dhabi, Bangkok, Beijing, Brussels, Dubai, Hong Kong, Moscow, Paris, Shanghai, Singapore, Tokyo
associated offices
Amsterdam, Berlin, Frankfurt, Jakarta, Munich, New York, Prague, Saudi Arabia, Stuttgart, Warsaw

Herbert Smith

Hewitsons LLP

42 Newmarket Road, Cambridge CB5 8EP
Tel: (01604) 233233 Fax: (01223) 316511
Email: mail@hewitsons.com (for all offices)
Website: www.hewitsons.com (for all offices)

Firm profile

Established in 1865, the firm handles mostly company and commercial work, but has a growing body of public sector clients. The firm has four offices: Cambridge, Northampton, Saffron Walden and Milton Keynes.

Main areas of work

Three sections: corporate technology, property and private client.

Trainee profile

The firm is interested in applications from candidates who have achieved a high degree of success in academic studies and who are bright, personable and able to take the initiative.

Training environment

The firm offers four six-month seats.

Benefits

The PSC is provided during the first year of the training contract. This is coupled with an extensive programme of Trainee Solicitor Seminars provided by specialist in-house lawyers.

Vacation placements

Places for 2009: A few placements are available, application is by way of letter and CV to Caroline Lewis; Duration: 1 week.

Sponsorship & awards

Funding for the CPE and/or LPC is not provided.

Partners 46
Assistant Solicitors 45
Total Trainees 15

Contact
Caroline Lewis
7 Spencer Parade Northampton
NN1 5AB

Method of application
Firm's application form

Selection procedure
Interview

Closing date for 2011
End of August 2009

Application
Training contracts p.a. 10
Applications p.a. 850
% interviewed p.a. 10%
Required degree grade
2:1 min

Training
Salary
1st year £23,500
2nd year £25,000
Holiday entitlement 22 days
% of trainees with a
 non-law degree p.a. 50%

Post-qualification
Salary £38,000
% of trainees offered job
on qualification (2008) 83%

Higgs & Sons

134 High Street, Brierley Hill DY5 3BG
Tel: (01384) 342100   Fax: (01384) 342000
Email: graduaterecruitment@higgsandsons.co.uk
Website: www.higgsandsons.co.uk

Firm profile

Founded in 1875, Higgs & Sons is now one of the largest and most respected law firms in the West Midlands, operating out of three offices in Brierley Hill, Stourbridge and Kingswinford and employing over 170 staff. The firm is well recognised in the Legal 500 and Chambers Guide to the Legal Profession.

Higgs & Sons is different from the typical law firm. The firm successfully combines traditional values with an innovative approach to legal problems which has helped to attract an impressive client base whilst also staying true to the local community. Clients and staff alike are attracted to Higgs' ability to offer an all round service in a number of areas. The firm is proud to provide a supportive and friendly working environment within which both colleagues and clients can thrive. The opportunity for career progression is also clear as more than half of the firm's partners trained with the firm.

Main areas of work

For the business client: corporate and commercial, insolvency, employment law, commercial litigation and commercial property.

For the private client: wills, probate, trusts and tax, employment law, personal injury, ULR and clinical negligence, conveyancing, dispute resolution, matrimonial/ family, private criminal and motoring offences.

Trainee profile

Applications are welcome from law and non law students who can demonstrate consistently high academic records, a broad range of interpersonal skills and extra curricular activities and interests. The firm would like to hear about what you have done to develop your wider skills and awareness. It is looking for people who want to get involved and participate fully in the business.

Candidates will preferably have a 2:1 class degree but graduates with a 2:2 class will be considered.

Training environment

A training contract at Higgs is different from those offered by other firms. There is the unique opportunity to undertake six four month seats in a variety of departments, including a double seat in the department in to which you wish to qualify as you approach the end of your training contract. Throughout the training contract you will receive a mix of contentious and non-contentious work and an open door policy means that there is always someone on hand to answer questions and supervise your work. Regular appraisals take place at the end of each seat and a designated Partner oversees you throughout the duration of your training contract, acting as a mentor. Participation in BTSS events and an active Higgs social environment ensures the work life balance.

Benefits

Private medical insurance, contributory pension, life assurance, 25 days holiday and BTSS Membership.

Sponsorship

Professional Skills Course.

Partners 29
Fee Earners 38
Total Trainees 9

Contact
Margaret Dalton

Method of application
Online application form or letter and CV

Selection procedure
Interview with trainee committee

Closing date for 2011
18th August 2009

Application
Training contracts p.a. 5
Applications p.a. 250 plus
% interviewed p.a. varies
Required degree grade preferably 2:1, will consider 2:2

Training
Salary reviewed annually
1st year £21,500
2nd year £24,000
Holiday entitlement
25 days p.a.

Post-qualification
Salary £32,000
% of trainees offered job on qualification 100%

Hill Dickinson

No. 1 Street, Paul's Square, Liverpool, L3 9SJ
Tel: (0151) 600 8000
Email: emma.mcavinchey@hilldickinson.com
Website: www.hilldickinson.com

Firm profile

Hill Dickinson LLP is one of the UK's leading independent law firms and is a national top 40 practice with offices in Liverpool, London, Manchester, Chester and Piraeus. Following the merger with Hill Taylor Dickinson in November 2006 and an aggressive programme of lateral hiring in the last year, the firm now has 152 Partners and a total staff complement of more than 1000.

Main areas of work

Hill Dickinson is a major force in insurance and is well respected in the company and commercial arena. The firm's marine expertise is internationally renowned and is one of the largest marine practices in the UK following a merger with Hill Taylor Dickinson on 1st November 2006. The firm has a highly reputable Commercial Litigation Practice, an award winning Property Practice and is widely regarded as a leader in the fields of employment, intellectual property, NHS clinical/health related litigation and private client.

Trainee profile

Commercial awareness and academic ability are the key factors, together with a desire to succeed. Trainees are viewed as the partners of the future and the firm is looking for personable individuals with whom it wants to work.

Training environment

Trainees spend periods of six months in four different practice groups. Trainees are encouraged to accept responsibility and are expected to act with initiative. The firm has an active social committee and a larger than usual selection of competitive sporting teams.

Vacation placements

Two one week schemes. 24 places available for 2009. Apply online by 31 March 2009.

Partners 152
Assistant Solicitors 143
Associates 42
Total Trainees 32

Contact
Emma McAvinchey

Method of application
Online application form

Selection procedure
Assessment day

Closing date for 2011
31st July 2009

Training
Salary
1st year (2008) £24,000
2nd year (2008) £26,000
1st year (London) £32,000
2nd year (London) £34,000
Sponsorship: LPC
Holiday entitlement
25 days

Post-qualification
% of trainees offered job
on qualification 94%

Offices
Liverpool, Manchester, London, Chester, Piraeus, Greece

Holman Fenwick Willan

Friary Court, 65 Crutched Friars, London, EC3N 2AE
Tel: (020) 7488 2300 Fax: (020) 7481 0316
Email: grad.recruitment@hfw.com

Firm profile

Holman Fenwick Willan is an international law firm and one of the world's leading specialists in maritime transportation, insurance, reinsurance, energy and trade. The firm is a leader in the field of commercial litigation and arbitration and also offers comprehensive commercial advice. Founded in 1883, the firm is one of the largest operating in its chosen fields with a team of over 200 lawyers worldwide, and a reputation for excellence and innovation.

Main areas of work

The firm's range of services include marine, admiralty and crisis management, insurance and reinsurance, commercial litigation and arbitration, international trade and commodities, energy, corporate and financial.

Trainee profile

Applications are invited from commercially minded undergraduates and graduates of all disciplines with good A levels and who have, or expect to receive, a 2:1 degree. Good foreign languages or a scientific or maritime background are an advantage.

Training environment

During your training period the firm will ensure that you gain valuable experience in a wide range of areas. It also organises formal training supplemented by a programme of in-house seminars and ship visits in addition to the PSC. Your training development as an effective lawyer will be managed by the HR and Training Partner, Ottilie Sefton, who will ensure that your training is both successful and enjoyable.

Benefits

Private medical insurance, permanent health and accident insurance, subsidised gym membership, season ticket loan.

Vacation placements

Places for 2009: Dates: 22 June- 3 July; 13 July- 24 July; Remuneration: £250 p.w.; Applications accepted 1 Dec. 2008 - 14 Feb. 2009.

Sponsorship & awards

GDL Funding: Fees paid plus £6,000 maintenance; LPC Funding: Fees paid plus £7,000 maintenance.

Partners 100+
Other Solicitors & Fee-earners 140+
Total Trainees 28

Contact
Marina Farthouat

Method of application
Online application form

Selection procedure
2 interviews & written exercise

Closing date for 2011
31 July 2009

Application
Training contracts p.a. 12-14
Applications p.a. 1,000
% interviewed p.a. 5%
Required degree grade 2:1

Training
Salary (Sept 2008)
1st year £32,000
2nd year £34,000
Holiday entitlement 25 days
% of trainees with
a non-law degree p.a. 50%

Post-qualification
Salary £60,000 (Sept 2008)
% of trainees offered job
on qualification
(Sept 2008) 100%

Overseas offices
Brussels, Hong Kong, Paris, Piraeus, Rouen, Shanghai, Singapore, Dubai, Melbourne

Howes Percival LLP

Oxford House, Cliftonville, Northampton NN1 5PN
Tel: (01604) 230400 Fax: (01604) 620956
Email: katy.pattle@howespercival.com
Website: www.howespercival.com

Firm profile

Howes Percival LLP is a leading commercial law firm with offices in Leicester, Milton Keynes, Northampton and Norwich. Last year the firm won the Leicestershire Law Society Firm of the year award and in 2006 the firm won the UK Regional Firm of the Year at the Legal Business Awards. The firm's working environment is progressive and highly professional and its corporate structure means that fee-earners are rewarded on merit and can progress to associate or partner status quickly. The type and high value of the work that the firm does places it in a position whereby it is recognised as being a regional firm by location only. The firm has the expertise, resources and Partner reputation that match a city firm.

Main areas of work

The practice is departmentalised and the breakdown of its work is as follows: corporate 30%; commercial property 25%; commercial litigation 20%; insolvency 10%; employment 10%; private client 5%.

Trainee profile

The firm is looking for five well-educated, focused, enthusiastic, commercially aware graduates with a minimum 2:1 degree in any discipline. Howes Percival LLP welcomes confident communicators with strong interpersonal skills who share the firm's desire to be the best.

Training environment

Trainees complete four six-month seats, each one in a different department. Trainees joining the Norwich office will remain at Norwich for the duration of their training contract. Within the East Midlands region, there is the opportunity to gain experience in each of the three East Midlands offices. Trainees report direct to a partner, and after three months and again towards the end of each seat they will be formally assessed by the partner training them. Trainees will be given every assistance by the fee-earners in their department to develop quickly and will be given responsibility as soon as they are ready.

Benefits

Contributory pension scheme. Private health insurance. LPC/GDL funding, maintenance grant.

Vacation placements

Vacation placements are available in June, July and August. Please apply via the online application form found on the trainee page of the firm's website. The closing date is 30 April 2009.

Partners 34
Solicitors 124
Total Trainees 20

Contact
Miss Katy Pattle
HR Officer

Method of application
Online application form

Selection procedure
Assessment centres

Closing date for 2011
31 July 2009

Application
Training contracts p.a. 5
Applications p.a. 300
% interviewed p.a. 10%
Required degree grade 2:1

Training
Salary
1st year £24,500
2nd year £26,500
Holiday entitlement
25 days p.a.

Post-qualification
% of trainees offered job
on qualification (2008) 76%
% of assistants who joined
as trainees 62%
% of Partners who joined as
trainees 15%

Hugh James

Hodge House, 114-116 St Mary Street, Cardiff, CF10 1DY
Tel: (029) 2039 1009 Fax: (029) 20388 222
Email: diane.brooks@hughjames.com
Website: www.hughjames.com

Firm profile

Hugh James is a dynamic, expanding leading regional practice. The Firm services clients both in the UK and internationally. Hugh James prides itself on its friendly atmosphere, which extends to both the staff and clients, and the firm's professionalism. The firm aims to find the best and most practical solution to clients' legal matters.

Main areas of work

The firm's three divisions: corporate and banking, property and Litigation, cover a diverse spectrum of legal work for a broad range of clients including major corporations, government bodies, charities and individuals.

Trainee profile

The firm see its trainees as the future of the Firm and has a very high retention rate on qualification. Apart from an excellent academic record, the firm looks for highly motivated individuals with common sense, good communication and social skills, commercial awareness and a good sense of humour!

Training environment

Trainees undertake four seats of six months each to ensure they get as broad a range of experiences of different aspects of the law as possible. The firm's trainees are treated as individuals. They form an integral part of whatever team they work in. They will have a great deal of responsibility and will be a useful and respected team member. They are not faceless photocopiers!

The training contract is very structured and Hugh James' trainees are given support and guidance throughout. Each trainee is allocated a supervisor in each seat. A formal appraisal is undertaken at the end of each six month period with a 'mid seat' appraisal every three months to make sure everything is running smoothly.

The first few weeks can be daunting and so we operate an induction programme. All new recruits are allocated a 'buddy' (one of the second year trainees), someone to call on for informal advice and support.

Ongoing education is provided through attendance at the Professional Skills Course and participation in the firm's in-house training programme.

Benefits

Pension opportunities, 25 days holiday.

Vacation placements

Places for summer 2009. Duration: two weeks; Closing Date:31st March 2009; Interviews April 2009.

Sponsorship & awards

LPC course fees paid.

Partners 47
Assistant Solicitors 160
Total Trainees 17

Contact
Diane Brooks
029 2039 1009

Method of application
Online application form

Selection procedure
interview and oral presentation

Closing date for 2011
31 July 2009

Application
Training contracts p.a. 8
Applications p.a. 500
% interviewed p.a. 10%
Required degree grade 2.1
(occasional exceptions)

Training
Salary
1st year £18,539
2nd year £19,677
Holiday entitlement
25 days p.a.

Post-qualification
% of trainees offered job
on qualification (2008) 86%
Salary £35,000 (Sept 2008)

Overseas offices
Cardiff, Methyr Tydfil, London

Hunton & Williams

30 St Mary Axe, London, EC3A 8EP
Tel: (020) 7220 5700 Fax: (020) 7220 5772
Email: LO_LegalRecruiting@hunton.com
Website: www.hunton.com

Firm profile

Founded in 1901, Hunton & Williams is an international law firm with more than 1,000 lawyers serving clients from 19 offices around the world. The firm provides its clients with advice covering virtually every discipline of the law. The firm currently has 14 offices in the United States, two in Europe and three in Asia and can respond knowledgeably, effectively and quickly, whether the issue is international, national, regional or local.

The London office was established in 1999 and has recently moved to Lord Norman Foster's iconic landmark in the heart of the city. The office is expanding with plans to double in size.

Main areas of work

In London the firm's major practice areas include: banking and finance; capital markets; corporate restructuring and insolvency; data protection; energy; environmental; employment; mergers and acquisitions; outsourcing; project finance; regulatory and technology. The office offers legal services under both English and US law and regularly advises on both UK and cross border transactions.

Trainee profile

Both law and non-law graduates who achieve a minimum 2:1 degree result will be considered. Applicants must demonstrate business acumen and the desire to succeed in a fast pace commercial environment.

Training environment

Relevant training is provided within the firm's main practice areas and regular appraisals are carried out during the course of each six month seat.

Trainees are highly integrated in office life and, in addition to transactional work, encouraged to be involved in business development and pro bono activities. Trainees are exposed to cutting edge legal work and given significant client contact and responsibility at an early stage.

Vacation placements

Please see the firm's website for information.

Benefits

Private Medical Insurance, Life Assurance, Permanent Health Insurance scheme, Pension and Occupational Health Service.

Sponsorship & awards

LPC and GDL are funded.

Partners 14
Associates 18
Total Trainees 5

Contact
Ms Joanne Mencarini,
Human Resources Manager

Method of application
Applications must include; a CV, hand written covering letter and the firm's application form. More information can be found on the website

Selection procedure
1st stage - interviews
2nd stage - assessment days

Closing date for 2011
31 July 2009

Application
Training contracts p.a. 2-3
Applications p.a. 300
% interviewed p.a. 10%
Required degree grade 2:1 (minimum)

Training
Salary
1st year £37,500
2nd year £40,000
Holiday entitlement
25 days p.a.

Post-qualification
% of trainees offered job on qualification up to 100%

Offices
Altanta, Austin, Bangkok, Beijing, Brussels, Charlotte, Dallas, Houston, London, Los Angeles, McLean, Miami, New York, Norfolk, Raleigh, Richmond, San Francisco, Singapore, Washington

IBB Solicitors

30 Capital Court, Windsor Street, Uxbridge, Middlesex, UB8 1AB
Tel: (08456) 381381 Fax: (01895) 381341
Email: Robert.Bushnell@ibblaw.co.uk
Website: www.ibblaw.co.uk

Firm profile

IBB Solicitors is recognised as a regional heavyweight and West London's leading law firm. IBB has four main practice areas: real estate; private client; commercial services; community legal services. The firm's teams are recognised in both Chambers and the Legal 500.

IBB has grown 20.9% since 2005 with revenues in 2008 of £13.9million. IBB has 30 Partners and 17 senior solicitors. Each year IBB recruits six trainees. Over the last four years 19 of those trainees have remained with the firm. IBB's strategy is to break into the top 100 law firms in England and Wales by the end of the current five year plan by growing the business organically.

Main areas of work

The firm's Real Estate Group is composed of individual teams specialising in: commercial development; property finance; investment; property management; real estate dispute resolution; construction; residential development. Clients include: financial institutions, investors and major commercial and residential developers (both local and national). Head of Practice, David Silva and Partner, Susan Mawson are ranked as leaders in Legal 500 and Chambers. Six other real estate lawyers are ranked as leaders in the Legal 500.

The firm's Commercial Services Group is composed of teams specialising in: corporate and commercial; commercial litigation; employment; charities. Clients include: charities, SMEs, UK subsidiaries of large multinationals, PLCs, AIM listed companies, large privately owned companies, private practices, Trade Unions and individuals. Four of the firm's Commercial Services Partners are ranked as leaders in Chambers.

The firm's Private Client Group offers a range of services including: residential property; new homes development; divorce and ancillary relief; wills, trusts, probate; tax and financial planning. The firm's clients include: high net worth individuals, charitable organisations, community bodies and the young and vulnerable.

The firm's Community Legal Services Group includes: general crime; serious crime and fraud; childcare; personal injury. The firm's clients include: the young and vulnerable, publicly funded individuals, community bodies and charitable organisations.

The Childcare Team is one of the largest in the country and the firm's specialist Criminal Defence Team is regarded as one of the best in London. The firm is on the serious fraud and VHCC panels. The firm has a well established Personal Injury Team that is recognised as specialists in head and spinal injury claims, often pursuing complex and high value cases.

Trainee profile

The firm looks for a track record of academic achievement, a commitment to working for a leading regional firm – and specifically in West London. The firm looks for individuals who can think on their feet and show how they will make a difference. You must be capable of taking on added client-facing responsibility far more quickly than your city contemporaries.

Training environment

Training with IBB offers the opportunity to complete four six-month seats in the firm's four practice groups. The firm operates a "pathways" programme allowing trainees input to the seats that they will undertake and is taking part in the work based learning pilot. You will be given early responsibility, gain experience of dealing with clients and supporting solicitors and partners on complex matters.

Benefits

25 days holiday, life assurance, stakeholder pension, private medical insurance.

Partners 30
Assistant Solicitors 46
Total Trainees 12

Contact
Rob Bushnell
Robert.Bushnell@ibblaw.co.uk
(01895) 207989

Method of application
Online – www.ibblaw.co.uk

Selection procedure
IBB creates a long list of applications and interviews about 60 people; from those, they shortlist 12 people who are invited to a full day assessment centre.

Closing date for 2011
31 July 2009

Application
Training contracts p.a. 6
Applications p.a. 500
% interviewed p.a. 15%
Required degree grade 2:1

Training
Salary for each year of training:
1st year £23,000
2nd year £25,000
Holiday entitlement: 25 days p.a.

Ince & Co

International House, 1 St Katharine's Way, London E1W 1AY
Email: recruitment@incelaw.com

Firm profile

From its origins in maritime law, the firm's practice today encompasses all aspects of the work areas listed below. Ince & Co is frequently at the forefront of developments in contract and tort law.

Main areas of work

Aviation, business and finance, commercial disputes, energy, insurance and reinsurance, shipping and trade.

Trainee profile

Hardworking, competitive individuals with initiative who relish challenge and responsibility within a team environment. Academic achievements, positions of responsibility, sport and travel are all taken into account.

Training environment

Trainees sit with four different partners for six months at a time throughout their training. Under close supervision, they are encouraged from an early stage to meet and visit clients, interview witnesses, liaise with counsel, deal with technical experts and handle opposing lawyers. They will quickly build up a portfolio of cases from a number of partners involved in a cross-section of the firm's practice and will see their cases through from start to finish. They will also attend in-house and external lectures, conferences and seminars on practical and legal topics.

Benefits

STL, corporate health cover, PHI, contributory pension scheme. Well Man/Well Woman health checks, subsidised gym membership.

Vacation placements

Places for 2009: 15; Duration: 2 weeks; Remuneration: £250 p.w.; Closing Date: 31 January 2009.

Sponsorship & awards

LPC/CPE fees, £6,000 grant for study in London & Guildford, £5,500 grant for study elsewhere.

Partners 85*
Senior Associates 22*
Solicitors 95*
Total Trainees 33*
* denotes worldwide figures

Contact
Claire Kendall

Method of application
online at www.incelaw.com

Selection procedure
Interview with HR professional
& interview with 2 partners
from Recruitment Committee
& a written test

Closing date for 2011
31 July 2009

Application
Training contracts p.a. 15
Applications p.a. 1,000
% interviewed p.a. 10%
Required degree grade 2:1

Training
Salary
1st year £36,000
2nd year £39,000
Holiday entitlement 25 days
% of trainees with a
non-law degree p.a. 55%

Post-qualification
Salary £64,000
% of trainees offered job
on qualification (2008)
100%. All accepted!
% of partners (as at 2008)
who joined as trainees Approx
70%

Overseas offices
Dubai, Hamburg, Hong Kong,
Le Havre, Paris, Piraeus,
Shanghai, Singapore

Irwin Mitchell

Riverside East, 2 Millsands, Sheffield S3 8DT
Tel: (0870) 1500 100 Fax: (0870) 197 3549
Email: graduaterecruitment@irwinmitchell.com
Website: www.irwinmitchell.com

Firm profile

Founded in 1912, the firm has grown from strength to strength and today employ more than 2300 people through its office network of major cities within the UK and its two offices in Spain.

Irwin Mitchell Solicitors has grown both organically and through a number of strategic mergers with firms and organisations in tune with the firm's values and culture.

The firm is the largest full service law firm within the UK with its services divided into two main categories; legal services for individuals and those for businesses, institutions and organisations.

As well as being recognised as the leading national personal injury firm in the UK, the firm has also developed a reputation for the delivery of strong commercial services that add real value to businesses, institutions and organisations. Over the last five years the firm as enjoyed substantial growth as its business strategies have reaped rewards.

Main areas of work

Corporate services and private client 30%; insurance 39%; personal injury 31%.

Trainee profile

The firm is looking for ambitious and well-motivated individuals who have a real commitment to the law and who can demonstrate a positive approach to work-life balance. Irwin Mitchell recruits law and non-law graduates and views social ability as important as academic achievement. Irwin Mitchell believes trainees are an investment for the future and endeavours to retain trainees upon qualification. In addition to the firm's training contract vacancies it also runs a work placement scheme giving potential training contract candidates a chance to experience what it is like to be a solicitor within the firm.

Training environment

From 2009 the firm's training contracts will be streamed so that as a trainee you would either undertake a training contract based within the firm's Personal Injury Practice Area, (where you can gain experience in personal injury, clinical negligence, court of protection and personal injury defence) or you would undertake a training contract based within the firm's business and private client practice area (where dependant on office location you could gain experience in departments such as insolvency, commercial litigation, corporate, public law and family). Trainees spend the first year of their training contract undertaking three seats of four months in duration. Having experienced three different areas of law, trainees are then likely to know where they wish to qualify so during the second year trainees undertake a twelve month seat, in the area which they and the firm wish them to qualify into. The firm offers a structured induction programme to trainees joining the practice.

Benefits

Healthcare scheme, contributory pension scheme, subsidised gym membership, away day and Christmas party.

Sponsorship & awards

Payment of PGDL and LPC fees plus a £4,500 maintenance grant.

Partners 137
Assistant Solicitors 210
Total Trainees 42

Contact
Alex Burgess,
Graduate Recruitment Assistant
graduaterecruitment@irwinmit chell.com

Method of application
Please visit the firm's website www.irwinmitchell.com and complete the online application

Selection procedure
Assessment centre & interview

Closing date for 2011
31 July 2009

Application
Training contracts p.a. 20-25
Applications p.a. 1,500
% interviewed p.a. 30%
Required degree grade: The firm does not require a specific degree grade
Salary
1st year £22,000
2nd year £24,150
(outside London)
reviewed annually in September
Holiday entitlement
24.5 days
post-qualification
% of trainees offered job on qualification 82%
Overseas/Regional Offices
Birmingham, Leeds, London, Manchester, Newcastle, Sheffield, Marbella & Madrid, Glasgow

Jones Day

21 Tudor Street, London, EC4Y 0DJ
Tel: (020) 7039 5959 Fax: (020) 7039 5999
Email: recruit.london@jonesday.com
Website: www.jonesdaylondon.com

Firm profile

Jones Day operates as one firm worldwide with 2,200 lawyers in 30 offices. Jones Day in London is a key part of this international partnership and has around 200 lawyers, including around 50 partners and 40 trainees. This means that the firm can offer its lawyers a perfect combination - the intimacy and atmosphere of a medium sized City firm with access to both UK and multinational clients.

Main areas of work

Principal areas of practice at Jones Day include: corporate finance and M&A transactions; investment funds, private equity and corporate tax planning, banking, capital markets and structured finance, business restructuring, litigation, intellectual property tax and real estate. The London office also has teams of lawyers who are experienced in such areas as competition/antitrust, environmental and employment and pensions law.

Trainee profile

The firm looks for candidates with either a law or non-law degree who have strong intellectual and analytical ability and good communication skills and who can demonstrate resourcefulness, drive, dedication and the ability to engage with clients and colleagues.

Training environment

The firm operates a unique, non-rotational system of training and trainees receive work simultaneously from all departments in the firm. The training is designed to provide freedom, flexibility and responsibility from the start. Trainees are encouraged to assume their own workload, which allows early responsibility, a faster development of potential and the opportunity to compare and contrast the different disciplines alongside one another. Work will vary from small cases which the trainee may handle alone (under the supervision of a senior lawyer) to larger matters where they will assist a partner or an associate solicitor. The firm runs a structured training programme with a regular schedule of seminars to support the thorough practical training and regular feedback that trainees receive from the associates and partners they work with.

Vacation placements

Places for 2008/09: Winter (non-law): 20 places; closing date 31 October. Spring 2009 (non-law): 20 places; closing date 31 January. Summer 2009 (law): 40; closing date 31 January. Placements last for two weeks with an allowance of £400 per week. Students get to see how the firm's non-rotational training system works in practice by taking on real work from a variety of practice areas. They also get to meet a range of lawyers at various social events.

Benefits

Private healthcare, season ticket loan, subsidised sports club membership, group life cover, salary sacrifice schemes and access to stakeholder pension.

Sponsorship & awards

GDL/PgDL and LPC fees paid and £8,000 maintenance p.a.

Partners approx 50
Assistant Solicitors 90
Total Trainees 40

Contact
Jacqui Megson
Graduate Recruitment Manager

Method of application
CV and letter online at
www.jonesdaylondon.com

Selection procedure
2 interviews with partners
closing date for 2011
31 August 2009 - please apply
by end of July to ensure an
early interview slot

Application
Training contracts p.a. 15-20
Applications p.a. 2,000
% interviewed p.a. 12%
Required degree grade 2:1

Training
Salary
1st year (2008) £39,000
2nd year (2008) £45,000
Holiday entitlement
5 weeks

Post-qualification
Salary (2008) £70,000
% of trainees offered job on
qualification (2008) 90%

Overseas offices
Continental Europe, Asia, North
America

K&L Gates LLP

110 Cannon Street, London, EC4N 6AR
Tel: (020) 7648 9000 Fax: (020) 7648 9001
Email: traineerecruitment@klgates.com
Website: www.klgates.com/europe_recruitment/graduate/

Firm profile

K&L Gates comprises 1,700 lawyers in 28 offices located in North America, Europe and Asia, and represents capitals markets participants, entrepreneurs, growth and middle market companies, leading FORTUNE 100 and FTSE 100 global corporations and public sector entities. Whilst the firm's international practice requires lawyers with diverse backgrounds and skills, the firm comes together in its shared values of investment and growth, both for the firm and the individual. The firm is committed to professional development and provides a cutting edge training programme.

Main areas of work

K&L Gates is active in the areas of investment management and related funds work, mergers and acquisitions, private equity, real estate, intellectual property, digital media and sport, travel and leisure, construction, insurance litigation, securities enforcement, environmental matters, litigation and other forms of dispute resolution.

Trainee profile

The firm welcomes applications from both law and non-law students. Law students should generally be in their penultimate year of study and non-law students should be in their final year of study. The firm also welcomes applications from relevant postgraduates or others who have satisfied the 'academic stage of training' as required by the Law Society. You should be highly motivated, intellectually curious, with an interest in commercial law and be looking for comprehensive training.

Training environment

The firm ensures each trainee is given exceptional opportunities to learn, experience and develop so that they can achieve their maximum potential. Trainees spend six month seats in four of the following areas: corporate, dispute resolution and litigation, intellectual property, construction, tax, real estate, employment, pensions and environment. Each trainee sits with a supervisor and is allocated an individual mentor to ensure all round supervision and training. The firm has a thorough induction scheme which includes attendance at the firm's First Year Academy in Washington, and has won awards for its career development programme. High importance is placed on the acquisition of business and professional skills, with considerable emphasis on client contact and early responsibility. The training programme consists of weekly legal education seminars, workshops and a full programme of skills electives. Language training is also available. Pro bono and corporate social responsibility activities are also encouraged.

Benefits

25 days holiday per annum, subsidised gym membership, season ticket loan, private health insurance, bonus scheme, life assurance, medicentre membership and pension.

Legal work placements

The firm's formal legal work placement scheme is open to penultimate year law students, final year non-law students, other relevant post graduates or others who have satisfied the 'academic stage of training' as required by the law society.

Sponsorship

GDL funding: fees paid plus £5,000 maintenance grant. LPC funding: fees paid plus £7,000 maintenance grant.

Partners 57
Trainees 18
Total Staff 290

Contact
Hayley Atherton

Method of application
Online at www.klgates.com/europe_recruitment/graduate/ or request a paper application

Selection procedure
Full assessment day

Closing date for 2011
31 July 2009

Application
Training contracts p.a. up to 15
Applications p.a. 1,000
% interviewed p.a. 10%
Required degree grade 2:1

Training
Salary
1st year (2008) 35,000
2nd year (2008) 38,000
% of trainees with a non-law degree p.a. Varies

Post-qualification
Salary (2007) £62,000
% of trainees offered job on qualification (2007) 80%

Overseas offices
Anchorage, Austin, Beijing, Berlin, Boston, Charlotte, Dallas, Fort Worth, Harrisburg, Hong Kong, Los Angeles, Miami, Newark, New York, Orange County, Palo Alto, Paris, Pittsburgh, Portland, Raleigh, Research Triangle Park, San Fransisco, Seattle, Shanghai, Spokane/ Coeur D'Alene, Taipei, Washington

K&L|GATES

Kirkland & Ellis International LLP

30 St Mary Axe, London, EC3A 8AF
Tel: (020) 7469 2000 Fax: (020) 7469 2001
Website: www.kirkland.com

Firm profile

Kirkland & Ellis International LLP is a 1,400-attorney law firm representing global clients in offices around the world.

For nearly 100 years, major national and international clients have called upon Kirkland & Ellis to provide superior legal advice and client services. The firm's London office has been the hub of European operations since 1994. Here, approximately 80 lawyers offer detailed expertise to a wide range of UK and international clients.

Main areas of work

The firm handles complex corporate, restructuring, tax, intellectual property, litigation and counselling matters. Kirkland & Ellis operates as a strategic network, committing the full resources of an international firm to any matter in any territory as appropriate.

Trainee profile

Your academic record will be excellent, probably culminating in an expected or achieved 2.1. You will have the initiative, the drive and the work ethic to thrive in the firm's meritocratic culture and arrive with an understanding of the work undertaken in the firm's London office.

Training environment

As one of a select number of trainees, you will be given early responsibility to work on complex multi jurisdictional matters.

The principal focus of your training will be on corporate law with a specialism in private equity. You will complete four, six month seats and obtain training in areas such as banking, arbitration, IP, restructuring and tax. In addition there will be an opportunity to undertake an overseas secondment to enable you to experience the international resources and capabilities of Kirkland & Ellis.

Your on the job training will be actively supported by an extensive education programme, carefully tailored to meet your needs.

Benefits

Private medical insurance, travel insurance, life insurance, employee assistance plan, corporate gym membership.

Vacation placements

Places for 2009: up to 20. Duration: 2 weeks. Remuneration: £300 per week. Closing date for applications: 31/01/09.

Sponsorship & awards

GDL and LPC course fees and a maintenance grant of £7,500 p.a.

Partners 611*
Assistant solicitors 1509*
* (firm-wide, as of May 31 2008)

Contact
Kate Osborne

Method of application
CV and covering letter to include a full % breakdown of degree results per subject

Selection procedure
Interview

Closing date for 2011
31 July 2009

Training
Salary
1st year (2008) £40,000
2nd year (2008) £43,000
Holiday entitlement
25 days

Post-qualification
(currently no data)

Overseas/ regional offices
Chicago, Hong Kong, Los Angeles, Munich, New York, San Francisco, Washington D.C.

KIRKLAND & ELLIS
INTERNATIONAL LLP

Latham & Watkins

99 Bishopsgate, London, EC2M 3XF
Tel: (020) 7710 1000 Fax: (020) 7374 4460
Email: london.trainees@lw.com
Website: www.lw.com

Firm profile

Latham & Watkins has more than 2,100 lawyers in 26 offices across Europe, America and Asia and the London office advises on some of the most significant and groundbreaking cross-border transactions in Europe. The firm believes that its non-hierarchical management style and 'one firm' culture makes Latham & Watkins unique.

Main areas of work

Corporate, finance, litigation, employment and tax.

Trainee profile

Candidates with a strong academic background, excellent communication skills and a consistent record of personal and/or professional achievement will be rewarded with first class training. The firm is dedicated to diversity and equal opportunity and values originality and creative thinking.

Training environment

Latham & Watkins can provide a very different training experience to that offered by the rest of the elite law firms. Each trainee receives bespoke supervision and outstanding support while being encouraged to recognise that they have their own part to play in the growth and success of the firm. Each trainee also has meaningful responsibility from the outset and significant legal experience on qualification. Trainees may also be given the opportunity to spend one of their four six-month seats in one of the firm's overseas offices.

Benefits

Healthcare and dental scheme, pension scheme and life assurance.

Sponsorship & awards

All GDL and LPC costs are paid and trainees receive a maintenance grant of £8,000 per year whilst studying.

Vacation placements

The firm has a one-week Easter vacation scheme and a two-week summer scheme. Students are paid £300 per week. The deadline for Easter scheme applications is 31st December and the deadline for Summer scheme applications is 31st January.

Partners 41
Assistant solicitors 124
Trainees 18

Contact
Alex Glaysher

Method of application
Online application form at
www.lw.com

Selection procedure
3 x 30 minute interviews with
a partner and an associate

Closing date for 2011
31 July 2009

Application
Training contracts p.a. 15-20
Required degree grade: 2:1

Training
Salary
1st year (2008) £41,000
2nd year (2008) £44,000

Post-qualification
Salary: £96,970

Overseas/regional offices
Barcelona, Brussels, Chicago, Dubai, Frankfurt, Hamburg, Hong Kong, London, Los Angeles, Madrid, Milan, Moscow, Munich, New Jersey, New York, Northern Virginia, Orange County, Paris, San Diego, San Francisco, Shanghai, Silicon Valley, Singapore, Tokyo, Washington DC.

Laytons

Carmelite, 50 Victoria Embankment, Blackfriars, London EC4Y 0LS
Tel: (020) 7842 8000   Fax: (020) 7842 8080
Email: london@laytons.com
Website: www.laytons.com

Firm profile

Laytons is a commercial law firm whose primary focus is on developing dynamic business. The firm's offices in Guildford, London and Manchester provide excellent service to its commercial and private clients who are located throughout the UK. The firm's approach to legal issues is practical, creative and energetic. The firm believes in long-term relationships, they are 'client lawyers' rather than 'transaction lawyers'. The key to its client relations is having a thorough understanding of businesses, their needs and objectives. Working together as one team, the firm is supportive and plays to each others strengths.

Main areas of work

Corporate and commercial, commercial property (including land development and construction), dispute resolution, debt recovery, insolvency, employment, intellectual property, technology and media, private client and trusts.

Trainee profile

Successful candidates will be well-rounded individuals, commercially aware with sound academic background and enthusiastic and committed team members.

Training environment

Trainees are placed in four six-month seats, providing them with an overview of the firm's business, and identifying their particular strengths. All trainees have contact with clients from an early stage, are given challenging work, working on a variety of matters with partners and assistant solicitors. Trainees will soon be responsible for their own files and are encouraged to participate in business development and marketing activities. The firm works in an informal but professional atmosphere and its philosophy is to invest in people who will develop and become part of its long-term success.

Vacation placements

Places for summer 2009: 6. Duration: 1 week. Closing Date: 31 March 2009.

Sponsorship & awards

LPC and CPE funding: consideration given.

Partners 34
Assistant Solicitors 36
Total Trainees 13

Contact
Stephen Cates &
Lisa McLean (London)
Christine Barker (Manchester)

Method of application
Application form (on website)

Selection procedure
Usually 2 interviews

Closing date for 2011
31 August 2009 (although posts are filled as soon as suitable candidates are identified)

Application
Training contracts p.a. 8
Applications p.a. 2,000
% interviewed p.a. 5%
Required degree grade
1 or 2:1 preferred

Training
Salary
1st year (2007) Market rate
2nd year (2007) Market rate
Holiday entitlement
23 days per year

Post-qualification
Salary (2007) Market rate
% of trainees offered job on qualification (2007) 83%
% of assistants (as at 1/9/07) who joined as trainees 45%
% of partners (as at 1/9/07) who joined as trainees 40%

Regional offices
Training contracts are offered in each of Laytons' offices. Apply directly to desired office. See website for further details: www.laytons.com

Lester Aldridge

Russell House, Oxford Road, Bournemouth BH8 8EX
Tel: (01202) 786161 Fax: (01202) 786110
Email: juliet.artal@LA-law.com
Website: www.lesteraldridge.com

Firm profile

Lester Aldridge LLP is a dynamic business providing both commercial and private client services. The firm has highly successful niche markets, including asset finance, marine, retail and care sector.

A key regional player, the firm has an impressive client repertoire supported by the recruitment of outstanding staff.

Lester Aldridge's positioning on the South Coast offers a positive working environment and a great work life balance, whilst providing opportunities to work with first class lawyers, impressive clients, and opportunity for City experience via LA's London office.

Main areas of work

Corporate, banking and finance 32%; litigation 30%; private client 21%; commercial property 12%; investments 5%.

Trainee profile

Candidates should have a consistently strong academic record, be commercially aware and possess a broad range of interpersonal skills. Applicants should be highly motivated and have a desire to succeed working with teams to advise clients in dynamic and demanding industries.

Training environment

Training contract consists of four six-month seats across the firm (preferences will be accommodated where possible). Direct client involvement is encouraged and each trainee is assigned a mentor to provide guidance and encouragement. Appraisals are carried out with team leaders at the end of each seat, as are regular group meetings with the Managing Partner, to ensure that trainees gain a range of work and experience.

Benefits

Life assurance, pension schemes, flexible benefits. Travel season ticket loan.

Vacation placements

Places for 2009: 8; Duration: 2 weeks; Remuneration: £125 p.w.; Closing Date: 31 March 2009.

Sponsorship & awards

LPC.

Partners 38
Total Trainees 14
Total Staff 289

Contact
Juliet Artal

Method of application
Letter, CV & completed application form

Selection procedure
Interview by a panel of partners as part of assessment and development day

Closing date for 2011
31 July 2009

Application
Training contracts p.a. 10
Applications p.a. 300
% interviewed p.a. 5%
Required degree grade 2:1

Training
Salary
Starting: £17,250 at present, increasing by £500 after each seat
Holiday entitlement 22 days
% of trainees with
a non-law degree p.a. 20%

Post-qualification
Salary (2008) £33,000
% of trainees offered job on qualification (2008) 66%
% of assistants (2008) who joined as trainees 36%
% of partners (2008) who joined as trainees 25%

Offices
Bournemouth (2), Southampton & London

Lewis Silkin LLP

5 Chancery Lane, Clifford's Inn, London EC4A 1BL
Tel: (020) 7074 8000 Fax: (020) 7864 1200
Email: train@lewissilkin.com
Website: www.lewissilkin.com

Firm profile

Lewis Silkin is a commercial firm with 45 partners. What distinguishes them is a matter of personality. For lawyers, they are notably informal, unstuffy…well, human really. They are 'people people'; as committed and professional as any good law firm, but perhaps more adept at the inter-personal skills that make relationships work and go on working. They place a high priority on the excellent technical ability and commercial thinking of their lawyers and also on their relationships with clients. Clients find them refreshingly easy to deal with. The firm has a friendly, lively style with a commitment to continuous improvement.

Main areas of work

The firm has a wide range of corporate clients and provides services through five departments: corporate, employment and incentives, litigation, property, housing and construction, and media, brands and technology. The major work areas are commercial litigation and dispute resolution; corporate services, which includes company commercial and corporate finance; defamation; employment; marketing services, embracing advertising and marketing law; property, construction, technology and communications, including IT, media and telecommunications. They are UK leaders in employment law and have a strong reputation within social housing and the media and advertising sectors.

Trainee profile

They are looking for trainees with keen minds and personalities, who will fit into a professional but informal team.

Training environment

The firm provides a comprehensive induction and training programme, with practical hands-on experience from day one. You will sit with either a partner or senior associate giving you access to day-to-day supervision and guidance. The training contract consists of six four-month seats, working in the firm's five departments.

Benefits

These include individual and firm bonus schemes, life assurance, critical illness cover, health insurance, season ticket loan, group pension plan and subsidised gym membership.

Vacation placements

There are three two-week work experience schemes which take place during June and July, giving 12 participants the opportunity to gain first hand experience of life at Lewis Silkin. Applications should be made via the firm's website between November 2008 and the end of January 2009.

Open days

Three open days will be held during spring 2009 to give participants an overview of the firm, its main areas of work and a chance to meet trainees and partners.

Applications should be made between November 2008 and the end of January 2009.

Sponsorship & awards

Funding for GDL and LPC fees is provided plus a £5,000 maintenanceg grant for each.

Partners 45
Assistant Solicitors 75
Total Trainees 11

Contact
Andrea Williams
HR Manager

Method of application
Online application form

Selection procedure
Assessment day, including an interview with 2 partners, an analytical exercise, and psychometric test

Closing date for 2011
31 July 2009

Application
Training contracts p.a. 5
Applications p.a. 500
Required degree grade 2:1

Training
Salary
1st year £32,000
2nd year £34,000
Holiday entitlement 25 days

Post-qualification
Salary (2008) £50,000

Lawrence Graham LLP

4 More London Riverside, London, SE1 2AU
Tel: (020) 7379 0000 Fax: (020) 7379 6854
Email: graduate@lg-legal.com
Website: http://graduates.lg-legal.com

Firm profile

LG is a London-based firm delivering a full range of commercial and legal solutions worldwide. Driven by its corporate and real estate practices, the key sectors in which the firm operates are financial services, real estate, insurance, hospitality & leisure, banking, IT, natural resources and the public sector. The firm has strong relationships with law firms around the world, particularly in the US and Asia, as well as a Monaco and Dubai office.

Main areas of work

The firm's four core departments are: business & finance (including corporate/M&A, banking & finance, IT & outsourcing, investment funds, employment, insurance, pensions, EU/competition, housing & local government); real estate (commercial property, planning, construction, environment & health & safety, real estate litigation and finance); dispute resolution (commercial litigation, corporate recovery, insurance & reinsurance disputes, shipping, contentious trusts & estates, corporate investigations); and tax & private capital. Work is often international in its scope.

Trainee profile

The firm is looking for individuals from a variety of backgrounds with refined communication skills who can demonstrate a commitment to a career in the commercial application of law. A strong academic track record with a minimum of 320 UCAS tariff points and a 2:1 degree is a basic requirement. Also required is a good record of achievement in other areas - indicative of the ability to succeed in a demanding career - and evidence of team working skills and the ability to handle responsibility.

Training environment

Under partner supervision trainees will be given early responsibility. Training is structured to facilitate the ability to manage one's own files and interact with clients. In addition to the Professional Skills Course, there are departmental training and induction sessions. Training consists of four six-month seats: a real estate, business & finance and a contentious seat are compulsory. The other seat can be either in tax & private capital or a second in business & finance or real estate.

Benefits

Season ticket loan, life assurance.

Vacation placements

Places for 2009: 32; Duration: 2 weeks during Easter break and 3 x 2 weeks between
June and July; Remuneration: £250 p.w; Closing Date: 31 January 2009.

Sponsorship & awards

GDL Funding: Course fees and maintenance grant. £6k outside London, £6.5k in London.
LPC Funding: Course fees and maintenance grant. £6k outside London, £6.5k in London.

Partners 85
Assistant Solicitors 117
Total Trainees 40

Contact
Vicki Baldwin Graduate
Recruitment Officer

Method of application
Firm's application form.
For law after 2nd-year results
For non-law after final results

Selection procedure
Interview

Closing date for 2011
31 July 2009

Application
Training contracts 20-25
Applications p.a. 800
Required degree grade 2:1

Training
Salary
1st year (2008) £36,000
2nd year (2008) £40,000
% of trainees with a
non-law degree p.a. 40%

Post-qualification
Salary (2008) £62,000
% of trainees offered job
on qualification (2008) 85%

Linklaters LLP

One Silk Street, London EC2Y 8HQ
Tel: (020) 7456 2000 Fax: (020) 7456 2222
Email: graduate.recruitment@linklaters.com
Website: www.linklaters.com/careers/ukgrads

Firm profile

Linklaters LLP is the global law firm that advises the world's leading companies, financial institutions and governments on their most challenging transactions and assignments. This is an ambitious and innovative firm: the drive to create something new in professional services also shapes a very special offer to graduates.

Main areas of work

While many law firms have strengths in particular areas, Linklaters is strong across the full range of commercial, corporate and financial law; this makes the firm an especially stimulating place to train as a business lawyer.

Trainee profile

Linklaters people come from many different backgrounds and cultures; by working together to achieve great things for clients, they are encouraged to achieve their own ambitions and potential. Training with Linklaters means working alongside some of the world's best lawyers on some of the world's most challenging deals. The firm expects a lot of its trainees, but the rewards – personal and professional as well as financial – are very high indeed.

Training environment

The firm recruits graduates from both law and non-law disciplines. Non-law graduates spend a conversion year at law school taking the Graduate Diploma in Law (GDL). All trainees have to complete the Legal Practice Course (LPC) before starting their training contracts. The firm meets the costs of both the GDL and LPC. The training contract is built around four six-month seats or placements in a range of practice areas. This develops well-rounded lawyers, but it also helps trainees plan their careers after qualifying.

Sponsorship & benefits

GDL and LPC fees are paid in full, plus a maintenance grant. Life assurance, private medical insurance (PPP), permanent health insurance (PHI), pensions, corporate health club membership & in-house gym, in-house dental service, medical services (including flu jabs, eye & eyesight tests), wedding cheques, subsidised staff restaurant, maternity & paternity arrangements (enhanced), interest-free season ticket loan, adoptive leave, group personal accident & holiday travel insurance, performance-related bonus, profit-related bonus scheme, concierge service.

Vacation placements

Linklaters offers a two-week Christmas Vacation Scheme for 30 final year non-law students, and three Summer Vacation Schemes (choice of either two or four weeks) for 80 penultimate year law students.

Partners 500+
Associates 1,500+
Trainees 250+*
*(London)

Contact
Charlotte Hart

Method of application
Application form
(available online)

Selection procedure
Critical reasoning test, 2 interviews plus commercial case study (same day).

Application
Training contracts p.a. 130
Applications p.a. 3,500
Required degree grade 2:1

Training
Salary
1st year (2007) £36,000
Holiday entitlement 25 days
% of trainees with a
non-law degree p.a. 40%

Post-qualification
Salary £64,000 + discretionary performance-related bonus

Offices
Amsterdam, Antwerp, Bangkok, Beijing, Berlin, Bratislava, Brussels, Bucharest, Budapest, Cologne, Dubai, Frankfurt, Hong Kong, Lisbon, London, Luxembourg, Madrid, Milan, Moscow, Munich, New York, Paris, Prague, Rome, São Paulo, Shanghai, Singapore, Stockholm, Tokyo, Warsaw

Lovells

Lovells LLP, Atlantic House, Holborn Viaduct, London EC1A 2FG
Tel: (020) 7296 2000 Fax: (020) 7296 2001
Email: recruit@lovells.com
Website: www.lovells.com/graduates

Firm profile

Lovells is an international legal practice comprising Lovells LLP and its affiliated businesses with offices in the major financial and commercial centres across Europe, Asia, the Middle East and the United States.

Main areas of work

The practice's international strength across a wide range of areas gives it an exceptional reputation. The practice's core areas are corporate, dispute resolution, finance and commerce with specialist groups including real estate, intellectual property, employment, EU/Competition, insurance and tax.

Trainee profile

The practice is looking for people whose combination of academic excellence and specialist knowledge will develop Lovells' business and take it forward. As well as demonstrating strong academic and intellectual ability, candidates should have strong communication and interpersonal skills, a professional, commercial attitude, and be happy working in a team yet capable of, and used to, independent action. Above all, candidates should have a single-minded ambition to succeed in a top legal practice.

Training environment

Lovells treats continuous training and development as a priority for both trainee solicitors and qualified lawyers, as clients expect informed, effective legal and business advice from all Lovells lawyers. As a trainee solicitor at Lovells you will participate in an extensive training programme, which covers legal, business and technology skills. The practice is committed to providing you with the highest possible standard of training, so that you will develop into an accomplished legal and business adviser.

Trainees spend six months in four different practice areas to gain as much experience as possible. All trainees must spend six months in a corporate or finance group, and six months gaining contentious experience in the practice's dispute resolution group. In the second year of training, there is the option to spend a seat on secondment either to one of the practice's international offices or the in-house legal team of one of the firm's major clients.

Throughout your training contract, Lovells will work closely with you to advise and provide feedback on your progress. This involves formal and informal assessments as well as advice on practice areas, secondments and qualification. Trainees are offered as much responsibility as they can handle as well as regular reviews, six-monthly appraisals and support when they need it.

Partners 355
Assistant Solicitors 1609
Total Trainees 155

Contact
recruit@lovells.com

Method of application
Online application form

Selection procedure
Assessment day: critical thinking test, group exercise, interview

Closing date for 2011
31 July 2009

Application
Training contracts p.a. 90
Applications p.a. 2,500
% interviewed p.a. 20%
Required degree grade 2:1

Training
Salary
1st year (2008) £37,000
2nd year (2008) £42,000
Holiday entitlement 25 days
% of trainees with a
non-law degree p.a. 40%
No. of seats available
abroad p.a. 25

Post-qualification
Salary (2008) £65,000

International offices
Alicante, Amsterdam, Beijing, Brussels, Budapest, Chicago, Dubai, Düsseldorf, Frankfurt, Hamburg, Ho Chi Minh City, Hong Kong, London, Madrid, Milan, Moscow, Munich, New York, Paris, Prague, Rome, Singapore, Shanghai, Tokyo, Warsaw, Zagreb

Lovells continued

Future trainee solicitor benefits

All trainees receive a £1,000 bonus and £1,000 advance in salary on joining the firm. The practice also offers £500 for a First Class degree result, £500 for getting the top overall marks within the Lovells LPC cohort, an interest-free season ticket loan (for London Underground and overground services) during the LPC year, Lovells discount card offering discounts at retailers local to the practice, and access to an extranet site specifically for future trainee solicitors.

Trainee solicitor benefits

PPP medical insurance, life assurance, PHI, season ticket loan, in-house gym, subsidised staff restaurant, access to dentist, doctor and physiotherapist, discounts at local retailers.

Vacation placements

The practice offers 90 vacation placements each year at Christmas, Easter and during the summer. Christmas 8-19 December 2008; Easter 23 March - 3 April 2009; First Summer 22 June - 10 July 2009; Second Summer 20 July - 7 August 2009. Applications for all schemes open on 1st October 2008. The closing date for Christmas is 11 November 2008. For Easter and the summer programmes, please apply by 31 January 2009. Remuneration: £300 per week.

Sponsorship & awards

GDL and LPC course fees are paid, and a maintenance grant is also provided of £8,000 for all students reading the LPC and GDL in London and £7,000 for students reading the GDL elsewhere.

Additional information

All second year trainees have the opportunity to apply to spend six months abroad. This is not compulsory and if you want to remain in London you can do so. The practice currently sends trainees to Brussels, Frankfurt, Moscow, Hong Kong, Dubai, Paris, Singapore and Tokyo. Currently about 12 trainees will go to the international offices and about 12 will go on client secondments at each seat change.

Future & current trainee comments

'When it came to choosing where to apply for a training contract, my first criterion was simple – I was only interested in applying to the very top firms. This goes well beyond the fact that Lovells is one of the largest firms in the city, though. What I was most interested in was that Lovells offers, first, an almost unrivalled breadth of practice, which means that during my first two years at the firm I will have ample opportunity to find the area into which I want to qualify. More important, though, is a client-list of the calibre that Lovells boasts which tells you that the quality of work here is amongst the highest in the city. You can't fail to be impressed – and tempted – by the prospect of working with high profile clients.' Nick Root [1st seat trainee]

'I chose Lovells for the reputation of the people as well as for the quality of work/client I knew I would experience. I have found partners to be approachable and helpful, and experienced a high level of client contact (I have enjoyed various client entertainment evenings) and a great team atmosphere. Adjusting to working life has been a bit of a challenge but I have made great new friends and am very happy with the level of training I have received. I have worked a lot of long hours but the support of the team has made it a lot easier. My knowledge and confidence has increased way beyond expectation in a very short time.' Una Ferris [4th seat trainee]

Lupton Fawcett LLP

Yorkshire House, East Parade, Leeds LS1 5BD
Tel: (0113) 280 2000 Fax: (0113) 245 6782
Email: hr@luptonfawcett.com
Website: www.luptonfawcett.com

Firm profile

Lupton Fawcett is a well-established yet dynamic and integrated practice. The firm offers a full range of legal services to both commercial and private clients alike on a quality-driven and client-led basis with the emphasis on providing first-class cost effective and practical solutions which exceed the clients' expectations. The firm was one of the first in Leeds to hold both Investors in People and the Law Society's Lexcel quality standard.

Lupton Fawcett is the trading name of Lupton Fawcett LLP, a limited liability partnership, registered in England and Wales, with partnership number OC316270. The registered office is at the above address, where a list of Members' names is open to inspection. Regulated by the Law Society. Authorised and Regulated by the Financial Services Authority.

Main areas of work

The commercial division offers the chance to gain experience in corporate, commercial property, employment, intellectual property, insolvency and commercial and chancery litigation. On the private client side, opportunities are available in financial services, trusts and probate, family and residential conveyancing. Further specialist areas of the firm include employment, licensing and advocacy, IT and e-commerce, sports law, debt recovery, insurance litigation and specialist personal injury.

Trainee profile

Although strong academic achievements are required, the firm places a high value on previous experience and interests which have developed commercial awareness, maturity and character. Trainees will also be able to demonstrate enthusiasm, confidence, good interpersonal and team skills, humour, initiative, commitment and common sense.

Training environment

Training at Lupton Fawcett is normally split into four six-month seats. Trainees office share with the director or associate with whom they are working and are an integral part of the team, assuming a high degree of responsibility. Appraisals following each seat take place to ensure that progress is monitored effectively. A full in-house training programme enables continual development as well as from training gained from excellent hands-on experience. Trainees will have the chance to meet clients and be responsible for their own work, as well as being involved in and actively encouraged to join in marketing and practice development initiatives. There is a full social programme in which the trainees are encouraged to participate as well as sporting events organised by the office and an excellent informal social culture.

Benefits

Health insurance, season ticket loans. All trainees are eligible to recieve a payment of £10,000 towards costs of CPE/GAL/LPC with the remainder to be used as a living allowance. Terms and Conditions apply.

Directors 28
Assistant Solicitors 17
Associate Solicitors 15
Total Trainees 4

Contact
HR Department
(0113) 280 2251

Method of application
Online at
www.luptonfawcett.com

Selection procedure
Interviews & assessment days
closing date for 2011
31 July 2009

Application
Training contracts p.a. 2-3
Applications p.a. 300
% Interviewed p.a. 10
Required degree grade 2:1
preferred

Training
Salary
Competitive with similar
size/type firms
Holiday entitlement
23 days

Post-qualification
Salary
Competitive with similar
size/type firms
% of trainees offered job on
qualification (2005-06) 99%

Mace & Jones

19 Water Street, Liverpool L2 0RP
Tel: (0151) 236 8989 Fax: (0151) 227 5010
Email: duncan.mcallister@maceandjones.co.uk
Pall Mall Court, 61-67 King Street, Manchester, M2 4PD
Tel: (0161) 214 0500 Fax: (0161) 832 8610   Website: www.maceandjones.co.uk

Firm profile

Mace & Jones is a leading regional practice in the North West with a national as well as a regional reputation for its commercial expertise, especially in employment, dispute resolution/insolvency, corporate and real estate. It also has one of the best Private Client Teams in the region. The firm's clients range from national and multinational companies and public sector bodies to owner managed businesses and private individuals, reflecting the broad nature of the work undertaken. Sound practical advice is given always on a value-for-money basis.

Main areas of work

Dispute resolution/insolvency 16 percent; real estate 29 percent; corporate 20 percent; employment 16 percent; personal injury/private client/family 19 percent.

Trainee profile

Ability, motivation and the determination to succeed are prerequisites. The trainee profile demonstrates the firm's commitment to appointing trainees from a wide range of backgrounds and experiences.

Training environment

Trainees complete an induction course to familiarise themselves with the work carried out by the firm's main departments, administration and professional conduct. Training consists of four six-month seats in the following departments: corporate, employment, dispute resolution/construction, real estate, family law and private client law. Strenuous efforts are made to ensure that trainees are able to select a training seat of their choice. Trainees are actively encouraged to participate in every aspect of the firm's activities and regularly act as mentors for undergraduates. The PSC is taught externally.

Partners 40
Assistant Solicitors 55
Total Trainees 11

Contact
Duncan McAllister
Liverpool Office

Method of application
Online

Selection procedure
Interview with partners and HR

Closing date for 2010
31 July 2009

Application
Training contracts p.a. 5/6
Applications p.a. 300
% interviewed p.a. 10%
Required degree grade 2:1

Training
Salary
1st year (2008) competitive
2nd year (2008) competitive
Holiday entitlement 20 days
% of trainees with a
non-law degree p.a. 40%

Post-qualification
Salary Negotiable
% of trainees offered job
on qualification (2008) 100%
% of assistants (as at 1/7/08)
who joined as trainees 25%
% of partners (as at 1/7/08)
who joined as trainees 25%

Macfarlanes LLP

20 Cursitor Street, London, EC4A 1LT
Tel: (020) 7831 9222 Fax: (020) 7831 9607
Email: gradrec@macfarlanes.com
Website: www.macfarlanes.com

Firm profile

Macfarlanes is a leading law firm in the City of London with a strong international outlook. The firm's success is founded on first-class lawyers, hard work and excellent training at all levels. Much of their work is international, acting in complex cross-border transactions and international disputes. This work is driven by the firm's excellent relationships with leading independent law firms outside the UK.

Main areas of work

The firm has a large corporate, real estate and litigation department and, unusually for a City firm, a significant private client department. They serve a broad range of clients in the UK and overseas, from multinationals, quoted companies and banks to private individuals.

Trainee profile

Trainees need to be highly motivated, high-achieving graduates from any discipline with (or expecting) a strong 2:1 degree or higher, who are looking for top quality work and training in a cohesive firm where everyone's contribution counts and can be seen to count. Macfarlanes needs people who can rise to a challenge and who will relish the opportunities and responsibilities that will be given to them.

Training environment

Anyone joining Macfarlanes cannot expect to lose themselves in the crowd. Because they recruit fewer trainees, each individual is expected to play their part. There are other benefits attached to working in a firm of this size: it helps retain an informal working atmosphere – people quickly get to know one another and are on first name terms across the board. There is the sense of community that comes from working closely together in smaller teams. Everyone at Macfarlanes has a vested interest in getting the best out of each other, including their trainees.

Benefits

A comprehensive benefits package is provided.

Vacation placements

Places for 2009: 75; Duration: 2 weeks; Remuneration: £250 p.w.; Closing Date: 28 February 2009.

Sponsorship & awards

CPE/GDL and LPC fees paid in full and a £7,000 maintenance allowance. Prizes for those gaining distinction or commendation on the LPC.

Partners 75
Assistant Solicitors 158
Total Trainees 54

Contact
Vicki Dimmick

Method of application
Online via website

Selection procedure
Assessment day

Closing date for 2011
31 July 2009

Application
Training contracts p.a. 30
Applications p.a. 800
% interviewed p.a. 20%
Required degree grade 2:1

Training
Salary
1st year £37,000
2nd year £41,500
Holiday entitlement 25 days, rising to 26 on qualification
% of trainees with a non-law degree p.a. 64%

Post-qualification
Salary (2008) £65,000
% of trainees offered job on qualification (2008) 96%
% of partners (as at 1/9/08) who joined as trainees 55%

Maclay Murray & Spens LLP

151 St Vincent Street, Glasgow G2 5NJ
Tel: (0141) 248 5011
Website: www.mms.co.uk

Firm profile

Maclay Murray & Spens is a full service, independent, commercial legal firm offering legal solutions and advice to clients throughout the UK and beyond. The firm has offices in Aberdeen, Glasgow, Edinburgh, London and Brussels and the firm's objective is to provide a consistently excellent quality of service across the firm's entire service range and from every UK office.

Main areas of work

Banking and finance, capital projects, commercial dispute resolution, construction and engineering, corporate, employment pensions and benefits, EU, competition and regulatory , IP and technology, oil and gas, planning and environmental, private client, property, public sector and tax.

Trainee profile

Applicants should have a strong academic background (minimum 2:1 degree) as well as demonstrate a number of key skills including an inquiring mind and a keenness to learn, commitment, professionalism, determination to see a job through, first class communication skills, the ability to get on with colleagues and clients at all levels, an ability to operate under pressure in a team environment, as well as a sense of humour. The firm welcomes non-law graduates.

Training environment

MMS will provide you with a very broad range of practice experience, including legal writing, drafting, research work, and an element of client contact. This is one of the firm's strengths as a business and a long standing attraction for candidates.

By working as a team member on more complex transactions, you are given the opportunity to gain experience over a broad range of work. You will also be encouraged to meet and work alongside clients from different backgrounds and diverse areas of industry and commerce.

Benefits

At MMS trainees are paid competitive salaries as well as provided with an attractive benefits package. All of the firm's employees receive a combination of fixed and variable holidays totalling 34 days each year. The firm also offers a contributory pension scheme, death in service benefit worth four times your annual salary, support with conveyancing fees, enhanced maternity and paternity pay, income protection insurance and discounted access to medical and dental plans.

MMS also believes that the benefits provided should be more than just monetary. As such, the firm encourages departments, teams and offices to meet on an informal basis.

Sponsorship & awards

From 2009, successful trainees will be supported with the cost of their Diploma of Legal Practice in Scotland and their Legal Practice Certificate in London.

In Scotland, trainees that do not receive a funded place on the Diploma will be able to apply for up to £3,000 towards the cost of the course. In London, MMS will contribute up to £10,000 towards the cost of the Legal Practice Certificate. These payments will be made when you start your training contract with the firm.

Partners 77
Assistant Solicitors 171
Total Trainees 65

Contact
trainee.recruitment@mms.co.uk

Method of application
Application forms only, accessed at
www.mms.co.uk/traineeship

Selection procedure
Following an initial interview a number of candidates will be invited to attend a second interview with 2 Partners, where they will also complete a roleplay and research exercise. Offers will be made to the successful candidates very soon after the second interview

Closing date for 2010
London traineeship Monday 3 August 2009
Scottish traineeship Monday 12 October 2009

Application
Training contracts p.a. 30
Applications p.a.
Scotland 300
London 150
Required degree grade 2:1

Training
Salary (2008)
(Scotland) 1st year £18,000
(London) 1st year £34,000
Holiday entitlement All of our employees receive a combination of fixed and variable holidays totalling 34 days per year.
post-qualification
Salary (2008)
(Scotland) £34,000
(London) £58,000

Overseas/regional offices
Aberdeen, Edinburgh, Glasgow, London and Brussels

Manches

Aldwych House, 81 Aldwych, London WC2B 4RP
Tel: (020) 7404 4433 Fax: (020) 7430 1133
Email: sheona.boldero@manches.com
Website: www.manches.com

Firm profile

Manches is a full-service commercial firm based in London and the Thames Valley with strengths across a range of services and industry sectors. Their current strategy will see a greater concentration and focus on the firm's core industry sectors, while continuing to be market leaders in family law. The firm offers 10 trainee places each September.

Main areas of work

Industry Sectors: Real estate, International wealth protection, retail business, commercial technology.

Legal Groups: Commercial property, commercial litigation, corporate finance, construction, family, trusts & estates, employment, intellectual property, information technology, biotechnology (Oxford and Reading offices only), and environment & planning.

Trainee profile

Manches aims to recruit a broad cross-section of candidates with different ranges of experiences and backgrounds. However, all candidates should demonstrate consistently good academic records, together with cheerful enthusiasm, high levels of commitment, an appreciation of commercial issues, the ability to think for themselves and have warm and approachable social skills. A sense of humour is an asset!

Training environment

The firm gives high-quality individual training. Trainees generally sit in four different seats for six months at a time. The firm's comprehensive induction week, followed by its practically based "learning by doing" training programme enables them to take responsibility from an early stage, ensuring that they become confident and competent solicitors at the point of qualification. Trainees have the opportunity to actively participate in departmental meetings, presentations, client seminars and briefings and they receive regular appraisals on their progress.

Benefits

Season ticket loan, BUPA after six months, permanent health insurance, life insurance, pension after six months.

Vacation placements

Places for 2009: 24 approx.; Duration: 1 week; Closing Date: 15th February 2009; Remuneration: £200 (under review).

Sponsorship & awards

GDL and LPC fees are paid in full together with an annual maintenance allowance (currently £5,000 p.a.).

Partners 59
Assistant Solicitors 65
Total Trainees 20

Contact
Sheona Boldero
sheona.boldero@manches.com

Method of application
Online application form

Selection procedure
1st interview with HR, 2nd
Interview with 2 partners.

Closing date for 2011
31 July 2009

Application
Training contracts p.a. 10
Applications p.a. 900
% interviewed p.a. 5%
Required degree grade 2:1 min

Training
Salary
1st year (2008)
London £30,000
2nd year (2008)
London £33,000
Holiday entitlement 24 days

Post-qualification
Salary
London £52,000
% of trainees offered job
on qualification (2008) 90%

Martineau

No 1 Colmore Square, Birmingham B4 6AA
35 New Bridge Street, London, EC4V 6BW
Tel: (0870) 763 2000 Fax: (0870) 763 2001
Email: jennifer.seymour@martineau-uk.com
Website: www.martineau-uk.com

Firm profile

Martineau is a dynamic and passionate law firm that combines a commercial and vibrant atmosphere with a personal and caring attitude.

Brand values are based on the three 'i's - integrity, innovation and inspiration. They reflect the working cutlure where they are inspired to deliver innovative solutions to clients, ensuring to exceed their needs, wants and expectations.

Providing national and international advice to its clients, the firm is recognised as market leader in many of its areas of practice and is well known for providing high level expertise.

Martineau look for enthusiastic and committed graduates with good degrees, not necessarily in law, to contribute to its successful practice.

State of the art premises in the heart of Birmingham city centre, coupled with its expanding London office, provide trainees with an ideal base to gain experience in a variety of core and niche practice areas.

As a founder member of Multilaw, an international network of law firms, opportunities also stretch far beyond the UK.

Martineau are also a member of State Law Resources which is a network of independent law firms with a focus on energy and climate across 43 State and Canada.

The firm's commitment to client care and quality is endorsed by the ISO 9001 standard.

Main areas of work

Commercial 27%; corporate 23%; commercial disputes management 22%; property 17%; private client 11%.

Trainee profile

Trainees are vital to Martineau future and no effort is spared to give the best possible experience and support to them, whilst treating them as individuals. There is a very high retention rate at the end of training contracts, when trainees are generally offered roles in their preferred departments and specialisms.

Training environment

Martineau aim is to work in partnership with trainees, providing them with mentoring, supervision, support and an exposure to the key areas of the firm's practice. Trainees are actively encouraged to be an integral part of the team delivering legal solutions to its clients whilst benefiting from quality work, flexible seat rotation in a small and friendly team environment. Trainees gain experience in three main areas, corporate, commercial disputes, commercial property and they are then given the opportunity to experience commercial work in areas of their chosen specialism. There are opportunities for Birmingham-based trainees to be exposed to the London scene.

Trainees benefit from a bespoke career development and training programme which is tailored to their personal needs; it covers not only legal technical matters, but also a business and commercial approach which has never been more central to successful professional careers.

In giving training and offering experience that matches the best city firms Martineau offers a rare opportunity for trainees to lay great foundations for their legal career in a fast moving, ever changing but caring environment.

Partners 48
Assistant Solicitors 100
Total Trainees 21

Contact
Jennifer Seymour

Method of application
Online application form
www.martineau-uk.com

Selection procedure
Assessment centre - half day
closing date for 2011
31 July 2009

Application
Training contracts p.a. 10-12
Applications p.a. 500
% interviewed p.a. 10%
Required degree grade 2:1

Training
Salary
1st year (2007) c. £21,000
2nd year (2007) c. £22,500
Holiday entitlement 25 days
% of trainees with a
non-law degree (2005) 40%

Post-qualification
Salary (2008) £38,000
% of trainees offered job
on qualification (2007) 77%
% of assistants (as at 1/9/07)
who joined as trainees 49%
% of partners (as at 1/9/07)
who joined as trainees 42%

Maxwell Winward LLP

100 Ludgate Hill, London EC4M 7RE
Tel: (020) 7651 0000   Fax: (020) 7651 4800
Email: recruitment@maxwellwinward.com
Website: www.maxwellwinward.com

Firm profile

Maxwell Winward, created when leading property firm Maxwell Batley and built environment specialist Winward Fearon merged on 1 April 2007, specialises in a number of key areas which have been strengthened considerably by the merger. The firm is experiencing a period of unprecedented dynamism and growth, whilst remaining a compelling alternative to larger firms in its specialist fields of practice. The firm has a modern focus and a friendly, unstuffy cthos where trainees are treated as future solicitors of the business. Trainees are encouraged to interact with everyone in the firm as one of the team to develop the abilities they will need on qualification and into the future.

Main areas of work

The firm specialises in Real Estate, Construction (both contentious and non-contentious), Corporate, Company/Commercial, Employment, Projects and Dispute Resolution. As well as acting for several high-profile blue-chip clients, the firm also acts for a number of smaller commercial clients and some high net worth individuals.

Trainee profile

Successful candidates will have at least a 2:1 in any discipline. It is important that candidates are willing to learn and have enthusiasm, common sense and commercial awareness as well as a genuine interest in the firm's specialist areas.

Training environment

The varied nature of the firm's work means that trainees are given a range of experience from all of the different practice areas. The training contract is split into four six-month seats in each of the different practice areas. Whilst trainees are closely supervised, the firm is keen to ensure that they are given valuable practical experience, as much client contact as possible and the responsibility to gradually gain the confidence to tackle matters with little supervision.

The firm arranges internal seminars for trainees in order to give them formal training to complement the day to day experience that comes with assisting on 'real-life' matters.

Benefits

20 days holiday, Season ticket loan, Private health insurance.

Sponsorship & awards

Contribution towards fees and maintenance for GDL and LPC.

Partners 22
Assistant Solicitors 38
Total Trainees 7

Contact
The Practice Manager

Method of application
CV and covering letter

Selection procedure
Two interviews
closing date for 2009, 2010
and 2011
01 July 2009

Application
Training contracts p.a. 4
Applications p.a. 800
% interviewed p.a. 6%
Required degree grade 2:1

Training
Salary
1st year (2007) £29,000
2nd year (2007) £31,500
Holiday entitlement 20 days

Post-qualification
Salary (2007) £48,000
% of trainees offered job
on qualification (2008) 100%

Mayer Brown[1]

11 Pilgrim Street, London EC4V 6RW
Tel: (020) 7248 4282 Fax: (020) 7782 8790
Email: graduaterecruitment@mayerbrown.com
Website: www.mayerbrown.com/london

Firm profile

Mayer Brown is a leading international law firm with 21 offices in key financial centres across the Americas, Europe and Asia. It has approximately 1,000 lawyers in the Americas, 500 in Europe and 300 in Asia. This unrivalled on-the-ground presence ensures its clients have complete access to local expertise on an international basis. With more than 300 lawyers spread across the heart of the City, the firm provides a full service presence working together with its US, European, and Asian counterparts to provide clients with complete representation on local and multi-jurisdictional matters alike.

Main areas of work

The firm's lawyers practise in a wide range of areas including corporate, finance, litigation and dispute resolution, real estate, insurance and reinsurance, pensions and employment, competition and trade, tax, intellectual property and information technology. The firm understands the challenges faced by businesses and tailors its advice accordingly to help each client achieve its goals. Clients include many of the FTSE and Fortune 500 companies from the worlds of banking, insurance, communications, industrials, energy, construction, professional services, media, pharmaceuticals, chemicals and mining.

Trainee profile

The firm is interested in motivated students with a good academic record and a strong commitment to law. Commercial awareness gained through legal or business work experience is an advantage. Applications are welcomed from both law and non-law students.

Training environment

Mayer Brown advises some of the world's most sophisticated and complex businesses and institutions. You will have the opportunity to work alongside some award-winning teams and individuals with the advantage of being able to choose from 25 different seats. For a large international firm, the London office remains a tightly knit team harbouring an open and inclusive culture. You will nevertheless be given significant opportunities to assist on matters which may be multi-disciplinary, cross-border, complex and high-profile in nature. The firm has an extensive support network in place throughout the training contract in the form of senior-level support and continuous appraisals. The firm currently offers five overseas secondments to Brussels, Chicago, Hong Kong, New York, Paris and São Paolo. If you don't want to stray too far, a wealth of in-house experience is also available via client secondments within the UK.

Benefits

Benefits include 25 days holiday per annum, an interest free season ticket loan, subsidised sports club membership and membership of private health scheme.

Work experience programmes

Places for 2009: 36. Duration: two weeks at Easter and three weeks in the summer. Experience in two of the principle work groups plus a programme of seminars, visits and social events.

Sponsorship & awards

The firm will cover the cost of the GDL and LPC fees and provide a maintenance grant of £7,000.

[1] *Mayer Brown is a global legal services organisation comprising legal practices that are separate entities ("Mayer Brown Practices"). The Mayer Brown Practices are: Mayer Brown LLP, a limited liability partnership established in the United States; Mayer Brown International LLP, a limited liability partnership incorporated in England and Wales; and JSM, a Hong Kong partnership, and its associated entities in Asia. The Mayer Brown Practices are known as Mayer Brown JSM in Asia.'*

Partners 125
Assistant Solicitors 229
Total Trainees 61

Contact
Gemma Baker, Graduate
Recruitment Manager

Method of application
Online application form

Selection procedure
One stage assessment process including an interview, a written exercise, a group exercise and an online verbal reasoning test
closing date for
Sept 2011/March 2012
31 July 2009

Application
Training contracts p.a. approx 35-40
Applications p.a. 1,000+
% interviewed p.a. 10-15%
Required degree grade 2:1

Training
1st year £37,500
2nd year £40,000
Holiday entitlement 25 days
% of trainees with a
non-law degree p.a. 50%
No. of seats available
abroad p.a. 12

Post-qualification
Salary (2008) £65,000
% of trainees offered job
on qualification (2008) 89% %
of partners who joined as
trainees 35%

Overseas offices
Bangkok, Beijing, Berlin, Brussels, Charlotte, Chicago, Cologne, Frankfurt, Guangzhou, Hanoi, Ho Chi Minh City, Hong Kong, Houston, London, Los Angeles, New York, Palo Alto, Paris, Sao Paulo, Shanghai, Washington DC.

McDermott Will & Emery UK LLP

7 Bishopsgate, London EC2N 3AR
Tel: (020) 7577 6900 Fax: (020) 7577 6950
Website: www.mwe.com/london
Email: graduate.recruitment@europe.mwe.com

Firm profile

McDermott Will & Emery UK LLP is a leading international law firm with offices in Boston, Brussels, Chicago, Düsseldorf, London, Houston, Los Angeles, Miami, Munich, New York, Orange County, Rome, San Diego, Silicon Valley and Washington DC. The firm's client base includes some of the world's leading financial institutions, largest corporations, mid-cap businesses, and individuals. The firm represents more than 75 of the companies in the Fortune 100 in addition to clients in the FTSE 100 and FTSE 250. Rated as one of the leading firms in The American Lawyer's Top 100, by a number of indicators, including gross revenues and profits per Partner.

London Office: The London office was founded in 1998. It is already recognised as being in the top 10 of the 100 US law firms operating in London by the legal media. The firm has 80 lawyers at present in London, almost all of whom are English-qualified. The firm provides business oriented legal advice to multinational and national corporates, financial institutions, investment banks and private clients. Most of the firm's partners were head of practice at their former firms and are recognised as leaders in their respective fields by the most respected professional directories and market commentators.

Main areas of work

Banking and finance; securitisation and structured finance, corporate, including international corporate finance and M&A; private equity, EU competition; employment, energy, IP, IT and e-business; litigation and arbitration; pensions and incentives; taxation; telecoms and US securities. London is the hub for the firm's European expansions and the firm coordinates legal advise from here for all multinational clients across Europe and elsewhere.

Trainee profile

The firm is looking for the brightest, best and most entrepreneurial trainees. You will need to convince the firm that you have made a deliberate choice.

Training environment

The primary focus is to provide a practical foundation for your career with the firm. You will experience four seats over the two-year period and the deliberately small number of trainees means that the firm is able to provide a degree of flexibility in tailoring seats to the individual. Trainees get regular support and feedback.

Benefits

Private medical and dental insurance, life assurance, permanent health insurance, season ticket loan, subsidised gym membership, employee assistance programme, 25 days holiday.

Sponsorship & awards

GDL and LPC funding and maintenance grant.

Partners 625 (worldwide)
32 (London)
Associate Lawyers &
Other Fee-earners
540(worldwide)
52 (London)
Total Trainees 3 in 2007
4 in 2008

Contact
Áine Wood

Method of application
Apply online at www.mwe.com

Selection procedure
Assessment day, written test
and one interview with
Partners

Closing date for 2011
31 July 2009

Training
Salary
1st year (2008) £39,000
2nd year (2008) £43,000

Post-qualification
Salary (2008) £75,000

McGrigors LLP

5 Old Bailey, London, EC4M 7BA
Tel: (020) 7054 2500
Email: graduate.recruitment@mcgrigors.com
Website: www.mcgrigors.com

Firm profile

McGrigors is a law firm based across the UK with 81 partners and 397 lawyers in total. As the only law firm in the UK that practices in all three jurisdictions, McGrigors has the strength and depth to commit to multiple, large, complex and high-value transactions simultaneously, and has earned an enviable reputation for providing excellent technical legal services, whilst retaining a friendly feel. The firm has a blue-chip client list which includes KPMG, Royal Bank of Scotland, BP, O2 and Royal Mail.

Main areas of work

Practice areas include banking and finance, commercial litigation, competition, construction procurement, contentious construction, corporate, dispute resolution, employment, energy, health & safety, human rights, intellectual property & commercial, planning & environment, projects/PPP, project finance, public law, public policy, real estate, tax litigation, and telecoms. McGrigors has a particular focus on a number of key industry sectors including energy & utilities, house builders, regeneration, financial services, infrastructure & public sector.

Trainee profile

The firm takes on people, regardless of background, who have drive, ability, and confidence. Trainees need to prove that they are interested in business, not simply black letter law, as the firm prides itself on providing commercial solutions to clients. In addition, its trainees are highly visible in the firm and are expected to get actively involved, whether in business or social events.

Training environment

The firm's training is based upon a standard rotation of six-month seats in four main practice areas. To widen trainees' experience and enable them to see a broader range of legal work, the firm encourages trainees to spend a seat in one of the other offices, and there are also opportunities for a secondment to a client. The firm was recently nominated as Best Trainer amongst Large City Firms in the lawcareers.net awards and their last Law Society Monitoring Visit concluded that training of trainee solicitors at McGrigors was 'excellent and of a very high standard'.

Benefits

The firm offers private medical cover, income protection, life assurance, pension, 35 days holidays including bank holidays, season ticket loan, and plenty of social events throughout the year.

Sponsorship & awards

CPE and LPC fees are paid plus maintenance of £6,000 for each year in England.

Partners 81*
Assistant Solicitors 241*
Total Trainees 67*
*denotes firm wide

Contact
Margaret-Ann Roy

Method of application
Online application

Selection procedure
Half day assessment including interview, presentation and aptitude tests
closing date
31 Jan 2009 for summer scheme
31 July 2009 for 2010 training contracts

Application
No. of training contracts p.a.
12-15 in London
15-20 in Scotland
1 in Belfast
% interviewed - 15%
Required degree grade realistic estimate of 2.1 or higher

Training
Salary
London 1st year £32,000
         2nd year £37,000
Scotland 1st year £18,000
         2nd year £21,000
Holiday 35 days including bank holidays

Post-qualification
Salary
London £62,000
Scotland £35,000
% offered job 85%

Overseas/regional offices
London, Edinburgh, Glasgow, Aberdeen, Manchester, Belfast (Baku, Azerbaijan and a satellite office in the Falkland Islands)

Michelmores LLP

Woodwater House, Pynes Hill, Exeter, EX2 5WR
Tel: (01392) 688 688   Fax: (01392) 360 563   Email: enquiries@michelmores.com
Clarges House, 6-12 Clarges Street, London, W1J 8DH
Tel: (020) 7242 5905 Fax: (020) 7242 2058

Firm profile

Michelmores is a dynamic Exeter and London based full service law firm providing first class service to a wide range of local, national and international clients including several central government departments. The firm has an established track record of attracting quality recruits at every level and the firm's trainee solicitor retention rate is excellent. Combining state of the art technology in a new purpose built building with a management style which promotes the highest professional standards and an informal atmosphere, the firm has created a great place to work capable of attracting the very best lawyers. The partnership has retained a collegiate style which helps to foster a happy law firm renowned for the enthusiasm of its lawyers from Senior Partner down to first year trainee. The firm has just been included in The Lawyer 'Rising 50' list of law firms nationally seen as rising stars

Main areas of work

The firm enjoys a high reputation for its work in the fields of company commercial, dispute resolution and commercial property while the firm's Private Client Department (including the firm's Family Team) continues to thrive. The firm also has specialist teams in areas such as Projects/PFI, Technology and Intellectual Property, Construction and Medical Negligence.

Trainee profile

The firm welcomes applications from both law and non-law graduates. The firm is looking for trainees with a strong academic background who are team players who genuinely want to share in the firm's success and help it to continue to grow and improve. Common sense and strong inter personal skills are prerequisites.

Training environment

As a Michelmores' trainee you will usually spend 6 months in each of the firm's main departments (company commercial, litigation, commercial property and private client). You will work closely with your supervisor in each department and will be pleasantly surprised at the level of client exposure, responsibility and involvement that is afforded to you. The firm's trainees are given both the opportunity to handle work themselves while under supervision and to work as part of a team. The quality of the firm's training is high. You will be expected to attend relevant training sessions within the firm on areas such as marketing and IT skills and time management and will also be encouraged to attend conferences, seminars and marketing events. The firm offers the opportunity of spending part of your training contract in the London office.

Sponsorship & benefits

Optional private healthcare, permanent health insurance, payment of LPC fees, subsidised staff restaurant, subsidised gym with fitness assessments and personal training, free parking. Prize for first class degrees and distinction in LPC.

Vacation placements

The firm runs an annual vacation scheme in the early part of July for one week. Application forms are available on the website. Completed forms should arrive by 28 February 2009.

Partners 39
Total Staff (inc. Partners) 320
Assistant solicitors 76

Contact
Kim Tomlinson
(kjt@michelmores.com)

Method of application
Online application form

Selection procedure
interview and written assessment

Closing date for 2011
1 July 2009

Application
Training contracts p.a.10
Applications p.a. 200
% interviewed - 15%
Required degree grade 2:1 (occasional exceptions)

Training
Salary
1st year (2008) £20,000
2nd year (2008)£21,000
Holiday entitlement
28 days p.a.
% of trainees with a non-law degree 10%
number of seats available abroad 0 (although occasional foreign secondments available)

Post-qualification
Salary (2008) £34,000
% offered job 100%

Mills & Reeve

112 Hills Road, Cambridge CB2 1PH
Tel: (01223) 222336 Fax: (01223) 355848
Email: graduate.recruitment@mills-reeve.com   Web: www.mills-reeve.com/graduates

Firm profile

Mills & Reeve act for commercial organisations; ranging from PLCs to multinationals to start-ups, as well as more than 70 universities and colleges, more than 100 healthcare trusts and NHS bodies, and over 65 local government institutions. The firm also has a national centre of excellence in private client services.

Mills & Reeve has offices in Birmingham, Cambridge, Leeds, London, Manchester and Norwich.

For the fifth year running Mills & Reeve has been listed in the Sunday Times Top 100 Best Companies to Work For, which recognises that the firm puts people at the centre of its business.

Main areas of work

A full-service law firm. Core sectors are: corporate and commercial, banking and finance, technology, insurance, real estate, healthcare, education and private client.

Trainee profile

The firm welcomes applications from both law and non-law disciplines. Candidates should already have or expect a 2.1 degree or equivalent. Trainee solicitors should display energy, maturity, initiative, enthusiasm for their career, a professional approach to work and be ready to accept early responsibility.

Training environment

Trainees complete six four-month seats and are recruited to the Birmingham, Cambridge and Norwich offices. Trainees can temporarily move to another office, to complete a seat not practised in their base office. The firm will support the move with an accommodation allowance.

Trainees work alongside a partner or senior solicitor. Regular feedback is given to aid development. Performance is assessed by a formal review at the end of each seat.

The firm encourages early responsibility. Training is supported by a full induction, in-house training programme developed by the firm's team of professional support lawyers and the professional skills course (PSC).

Job opportunities on qualification are good and a high proportion of trainees remain with the firm.

Benefits

Life assurance, a contributory pension scheme, 25 days holiday, bonus scheme, sports and social club, subsidised staff restaurants and catering facilities, season ticket loan, discounted rate for private medical insurance, corporate gym membership. The firm runs a flexible benefits scheme.

Vacation placements

Applications for two week placements during the summer must be received by 31 January 2009.

sponsorship & awards

The firm pays the full costs of the CPE/GDL and LPC fees and a maintenance grant during the GDL and LPC.

Partners 90
Assistant Solicitors 330
Total Trainees 45

Contact
Fiona Medlock

Method of application
Online

Selection procedure
Normally one day assessment centre

Closing date for 2011
31 July 2009 for training contracts
31st January 2009 for work placements

Application
Training contracts p.a.23
Applications p.a. Approx 650
% interviewed p.a. 10%
Required degree grade 2:1

Training
Salary
1st year £24,000
2nd year £25,000
Holiday entitlement
25 days p.a.
% of trainees with a non-law degree 40%

Post-qualification
% of trainees offered job on qualification (2008) 87%

Mishcon de Reya

Summit House, 12 Red Lion Square, London WC1R 4QD
Tel: (020) 7440 7000 Fax: (020) 7430 0691
Email: recruitment@mishcon.com
Website: www.mishcon.com

Firm profile

Mishcon de Reya is a mid-sized central London law firm offering a diverse range of legal services for businesses and individuals. The firm's foundation is a dynamic range of corporate clients that seek effective advice through close collaboration. Through expertise and entrepreneurial spirit the firm delivers legal and commercial solutions to businesses of all sizes.

Main areas of work

Mishcon de Reya's expertise falls into four main areas: corporate, litigation, real estate and family. The firm also has a number of specialist groups including banking & debt finance, betting & gaming, IP, insolvency, fraud, corporate tax, employment, financial services, immigration, IT, media & public advocacy and personal tax, trusts and probate.

Trainee profile

Applications are welcome from penultimate-year law students, final year non-law students and other graduates wishing to commence a training contract in two years' time. The firm wants people who can meet the highest intellectual and business standards, while maintaining outside interests. Candidates should therefore be enterprising, enthusiastic and committed, and see themselves as future Partners.

Training environment

Trainees have the opportunity to experience four different seats of six months each. All trainees get exposure to at least three of the four core departments and are also able to gain experience in specialist groups during their time with the firm. Trainees share a room with a Partner or assistant solicitor. Because of the relatively few training contracts offered, trainees can expect to be exposed to high quality work with early responsibility. In order to support this, the firm has a wide-ranging training programme and provides extensive internal training in addition to the Professional Skills Course. Quarterly appraisals and monitoring in each seat ensures trainees gain a range of work and experience.

Benefits

Medical and travel insurance, EAP, subsidised gym membership, season ticket loan, group income protection, life assurance and pension, in-house doctor.

Vacation placements

Places for 2009: 15; Duration: 2 weeks; Expenses: £250 p.w.; Closing Date: 31st January 2009.

Sponsorship & awards

CPE and LPC funding with annual allowance.

Partners 54
Assistant Solicitors 92
Total Trainees 25

Contact
Charlotte Pogson, HR Officer,
Graduate Recruitment

Method of application
Online application form

Closing date for 2011
31 July 2009

Application
Training contracts p.a. 12-15
Applications p.a. 1,000+
% interviewed p.a. 5%
Required degree grade 2:1

Training
Salary
1st year £32,000
2nd year £34,000
Holiday entitlement
25 days p.a.
Occasional secondments
available

Morgan Cole

Bradley Court, Park Place, Cardiff, CF10 3DP
Tel: (029) 20385385 Fax: (029) 20385300
Email: recruitment@morgan-cole.com Website: www.morgan-cole.com

Firm profile

Morgan Cole is one of the leading regional commercial law practices in the country, providing a comprehensive service to both individual and corporate clients in both the public and private sectors. The firm has a reputation for excellence and therefore attracts the highest quality of staff from all fields. The firm's areas of work consists of seven practice areas: insurance, health and regulatory; dispute management; commercial; corporate; private client; employment and banking. Within these practice areas the firm's work includes: acquisitions and disposals; technology; insolvency; intellectual property; joint ventures; management buy-outs and buy-ins; partnerships; PFI; commercial property; construction; personal injury; professional indemnity; commercial litigation and alternative dispute resolution.

Trainee profile

Successful candidates should be commercially aware, self motivated individuals with drive and initiative who are able to apply a logical and common-sense approach to solving client problems. The firm is seeking applications from graduates/undergraduates in both law and non-law subjects, preferably with at least a 2:1 degree. Practical and social skills are as important as your qualifications.

Training environment

Trainees spend six months in four different practice areas, and since each practice area handles a wide variety of work within its constituent teams, there is no danger of over specialisation. Training includes client contact and there is always a possibility of a secondment to a major blue-chip client! You must show initiative and take responsibility, but the firm will not leave you stranded. You will be assigned a seat supervisor (a partner or senior solicitor) to advise and guide you. You will have a mentor for support to act as a sounding board.

Vacation scheme

A vacation scheme is held in the Oxford, Reading, Cardiff and Swansea offices between June and July. The application deadline date is 30 April annually.

Sponsorship & awards

£5,000 maintenance grant per course and payment of course fees.

Partners 50
Lawyers 220
Total Trainees 21

Trainee Places for 2008:
Cardiff/Swansea 6
Oxford/Reading 6
Total 12

Contact
Guy Constant, Training Principal
Suzanne Norman, Recruitment Manager

Method of application
Apply online at www.morgan-cole.com/careers or www.apply4law/morgancole.com

Selection procedure
Assessment Centre

Closing date for 2011
31 July 2009

Application
Required degree grade
Preferably 2:1

Training
Salary
1st & 2nd year
The firm pays competitive salaries which are reviewed annually in line with market trends
1st year £18,500 (Wales)
1st year £21,000 (Thames Valley)
2nd year £20,500 (Wales)
2nd year £23,000 (Thames Valley)

Other offices
Cardiff, Bristol, Oxford, Reading, Swansea

Morrison & Foerster

CityPoint, One Ropemaker Street, London, EC2Y 9AW
Tel: (020) 7920 4000 Fax: (020) 7496 8500
Email: LNAttyRecruit@mofo.com   Website: www.mofo.com

Firm profile

Morrison & Foerster is an international firm with over 1,000 lawyers across offices in the U.S., Europe and Asia. Founded in 1883, the firm remains dedicated to providing clients, which include some of the largest financial institutions, highly capitalised companies, and technology and life science companies, with legendary service. The firm's attorneys share high standards, a commitment to excellence and a passion for helping clients succeed. The firm is also recognised for its longstanding commitment to pro bono work.

Main areas of work

The firm as a whole covers antitrust, bankruptcy and restructuring, capital markets, communications and media, corporate, energy, entertainment, environmental, financial services, financial transactions, government contracts, intellectual property, investment management, land use and natural resources, life sciences, litigation, outsourcing, privacy, project finance and development, real estate, tax and technology transactions. The London office specialises in capital markets, corporate, financial transactions, employment, life sciences, litigation, outsourcing, tax and technology transactions.

Trainee profile

Morrison & Foerster takes pride in promoting a diverse workplace. The firm is looking for individuals with academic and other achievements that evidence their talent, motivation, energy and creativity. As a trainee, you will receive work assignments suitable for a first or second year associate, and the support and training to excel in your work. The firm welcomes applications from all degree backgrounds.

Training environment

The training contract comprises four six-month seats. All trainees take seats in Technology Transactions and Corporate, plus a contentious seat in either litigation or employment law. The fourth seat is either Tax, Capital Markets or Financial Transactions. While the firm believes that direct participation and hands-on training provide the most rewarding opportunity, practical experience will be supported by both a mentor and a comprehensive training programme throughout your training contract. You will work directly with associates and Partners; playing an active part in each matter to which you are assigned.

Benefits

Life assurance; health, dental and long-term disability insurance; group personal pension; season ticket loans.

Vacation placements

Places for Summer 2009-10; Duration: 2 weeks; Remuneration: Travel and subsistence allowance.

Sponsorship & awards

100% CPE, GDL & LPC paid plus £8,000 maintenance p.a.

Partners 19
Associates 30
Total Trainees 5

Contact
Margaret Mannell (020) 7920 4000

Method of application
Please see our website
http://www.mofo.com/career/index.html

Selection procedure
Interviews

Closing date for 2010
Suitable applicants are considered throughout the year

Application
Training contracts p.a. 3
Applications p.a. 500
% interviewed p.a. 10%
Required degree grade 2:1

Training
Salary
1st year £36,000
2nd year £42,500
Holiday entitlement
25 days p.a.

Post-qualification
Salary
£70,000 (2008)
% of trainees offered job on qualification 100%

Overseas offices
Beijing, Brussels, Denver, Hong Kong, Los Angeles, New York, Northern Virginia, Palo Alto, Sacramento, San Diego, San Francisco, Shanghai, Singapore, Tokyo, Walnut Creek, Washington D.C.

Mundays LLP

cedar House, 78 Portsmouth Road, Cobham, Surrey, KT11 1AN
Tel: (01932) 590500   Fax: (01932) 590220
Email: hr@mundays.co.uk
Website: www.mundays.co.uk

Firm profile

Mundays is one of Surrey's leading law practices, operating from modern offices in Cobham, with easy access to London and the M25. The practice has grown significantly over the past 10 years and continues to expand. Many of the firm's lawyers have worked in the City but have chosen to relocate to a practice where the firm aims to offer a service as good as (if not better than) competitors in London at more economic rates, while enabling its lawyers to achieve a better work/life balance. The firm offers its diverse range of clients (both corporate and private) comprehensive, responsive and commercial advice, with separate departments working closely together as appropriate.

Main areas of work

The firm is divided into five principal departments: property, corporate/commercial, dispute resolution, private wealth and family. Within these departments we have specialisms in banking, employment, construction, insolvency and intellectual property.

Trainee profile

Candidates will need to demonstrate their confidence, ability to communicate and personability. They are also required to have (or expect to receive) at least a 2.1 degree (applications from law and non-law graduates are welcome) and 3 A levels (AAB or better). We are looking for well-rounded individuals who are keen to develop their career with us as trainees and beyond.

Training environment

At Mundays there is a relaxed, informal working style; Fee-earners have a willingness to share their knowledge and experience in the belief that, with hard work, trainees of today are potentially the firm's partners of the future.

Trainees typically spend periods of six months in each of the corporate/commercial, property and dispute resolution departments; where they spend the fourth period will depend on whether they wish to gain experience of another specialist area. Trainees are encouraged to take on responsibility from the beginning of their training through direct experience of dealing with matters and working alongside fee-earners. Progress is closely monitored and training given to reflect the needs of individual trainees.

Benefits

25 Days annual holiday; Option to buy and sell up to five days per holiday year; Death in Service Scheme at 3x Salary on joining; Pension Scheme at three, four or five percent matching after successful completion of three month probation; Private Healthcare Scheme – eligible to join after successful completion of three month probation; Childcare Voucher Scheme; Cycle to Work Scheme.

Vacation placements

Not offered at this time.

Sponsorship & awards

Mundays will make a contribution of £7,500 towards the cost of the LPC and will offer a maintenance grant of £4000.00 paid at month 2 and month 7 of LPC.

Partners 25
Fee earners 56
Total Trainees 5

Contact
HR Manager

Method of application
Online

Selection procedure
1 day Assessment Centre, 1 day individual interviews and legal scenario

Closing date for 2011
31st August 2009

Application
Training contracts p.a. 3
Applications p.a. 150
% assessed and interviewed p.a. 13%
Required degree grade 2:1

Overseas/ regional offices
Cobham office (Surrey)

Nabarro LLP

Lacon House, Theobald's Road, London WC1X 8RW
Tel: (020) 7524 6000 Fax: (020) 7524 6524
Email: graduateinfo@nabarro.com
Website: www.nabarro.com

Firm profile

Nabarro is a major UK law firm renowned for its positive, practical approach. The firm operates across a number of industry sectors and legal disciplines and aims to deliver the highest quality legal advice as clearly and concisely as possible.

Main areas of work

Corporate and commercial law, real estate, TMT, IP/IT, projects, PPP, PFI, pensions and employment, dispute resolution, construction and engineering, planning and environmental law, banking and finance, restructuring and insolvency, tax.

Trainee profile

The firm is committed to making the most of diverse skills, expertise, experience, attitudes and backgrounds. Accordingly, there is no typical Nabarro trainee. You will need a strong academic record and, in keeping with clients' needs, the firm also wants you to demonstrate a flexibility of thinking and a flair for creative problem solving that will allow you to provide its clients with the best advice and assistance. A positive attitude and proactive approach, strong interpersonal skills, team working and entrepreneurial skills, drive and enthusiasm are also required.

Training environment

Trainees undertake six four-month seats to ensure maximum exposure to the firm's core practice areas, as well as the opportunity to spend time in more specialist seats or possibly in Brussels or on secondment to a client. Your development and future seats are discussed with you half way through each seat.

Benefits

Private medical insurance, 26 days holiday, pension, season ticket loan, subsidised restaurant, subsidised gym membership. Trainee salaries are reviewed annually.

Vacation placements

Places for 2009: 65; duration: 3 weeks between mid June and mid August. Closing date: 8 February 2009

Sponsorship & awards

Full fees paid for the GDL and LPC plus a maintenance grant: LPC London and Guildford: £7000, regions £6000. GDL London and Guildford £6000, regions £5000. The firm pays full fees retrospectively if you have completed your GDL/LPC.

Partners 129
Assistant Solicitors 423
Total Trainees 70

Contact
Jane Drew

Method of application
Online only

Selection procedure
Assessment Day (including interview)

Closing date for 2011
31 July 2009

Application
Training contracts p.a. 35
Applications p.a. 1,600
Required degree grade 2:1

Training
Salary
1st year (2008)
London £37,000
Sheffield £25,000
2nd year (2008)
London £40,000
Sheffield £28,000
Holiday entitlement 26 days

Post-qualification
Salary (2008)
London £64,000
Sheffield £41,000
(reviewed annually)

Overseas offices
Brussels. In Europe the firm has an alliance with GSK Stockmann & Kollegen in Germany, August & Debouzy in France, Rodés & Sala abogados in Spain and Nunziante Magrone in Italy.

Needham & James LLP

Needham & James House, Bridgeway, Stratford-upon-Avon, Warwickshire, CV37 6YY
Tel: (0845) 630 8833   Fax: (0845) 630 8844
Website: www.needhamandjames.com

Firm profile

Needham & James is a well established, well respected and progressive Midlands based legal practice.

Main areas of work

Agriculture, banking, commercial property, corporate, corporate crime, dispute resolution, employment, family, leisure, licensing, notary, planning, residential property, road traffic offences, social housing, wills & probate .

Trainee profile

The firm is looking for high calibre trainees who share its vision and dedication to its clients. The firm wants people with an enthusiastic, 'can do' approach, keen to experience a wide range of work. Potential trainees will also have to demonstrate a high level of academic achievement, an analytical and enquiring mind and a sensitively to clients' needs. Good interpersonal skills are a must. Candidates should normally have, or expect, at least a 2.1 honours degree (in any subject), and a minimum of 260 UCAS points from their best three A level results, excluding General Studies. Candidates with lesser qualification who have achieved distinction in another field will always be considered. The firm is committed to recruiting the highest quality trainees, irrespective of background.

Training environment

The firm's trainees take on significant personal responsibility at an early stage, and make an important contribution to client matters very quickly. All trainees are supervised by experienced lawyers who are themselves trained in trainee management. The firm strives to work in genuine partnership with its trainees and to assist them to develop their full potential.

A typical two-year training contact comprises four seats, each of six months' duration, with trainees visiting three or four teams during the contract. Trainees' preferences regarding the choice of seat are taken into account wherever possible, subject to the requirements of the business. Trainees are allocated a supervising partner or senior solicitor in each seat and exposed to a wide variety of work and clients. There is an informal appraisal after three months and a more formal written appraisal at the end of each six month period. The firm has a dedicated training partner who overseas the supervision and management of trainees.

Benefits

Life assurance, pension scheme, corporate rates and discounts from many local businesses.

Sponsorship & awards

The firm will pay 50% of your LPC fees.

Partners 28
Assistant Solicitors 9
Total Trainees 10

Contact
Andrew Owen, Trainee Recruitment Partner (0845) 630 8833)

Method of application
Online application form

Selection procedure
Assessment Day

Closing date for 2011
31 July 2009

Application
Training contracts p.a. 5
Applications p.a.
% interviewed p.a. 10%
Required degree grade 2:1

Training
Salary
1st year (2011) £24,000
Holiday entitlement 24 days

Post-qualification
% of trainees offered job on qualification 100%

Norton Rose

3 More London Riverside, London, SE1 2AQ
Tel: (020) 7283 6000 Fax: (020) 7283 6500
Email: grad.recruitment@nortonrose.com
Website: www.nortonrose.com/graduate

Firm profile

Norton Rose LLP is a constituent part of Norton Rose Group, a leading international legal practice offering a full business law services from offices across Europe, the Middle East and Asia. Knowing how Clients' businesses work and understanding what drives their industries is fundamental to the firm. Norton Rose lawyers share industry knowledge and sector expertise across borders, enabling the firm to support clients anywhere in the world. The firm is strong in corporate finance, financial institutions, energy and infrastructure, transport and technology. Norton Rose Group comprises Norton Rose LLP and its affiliates and has over 1000 lawyers operating from offices in Amsterdam, Athens, Bahrain, Bangkok, Beijing, Brussels, Dubai, Frankfurt, Hong Kong, Jakarta*, London, Milan, Moscow, Munich, Paris, Piraeus, Prague, Rome, Shanghai, Singapore and Warsaw.

Main areas of work

Corporate finance; banking; dispute resolution; property, planning and environmen- tal; taxation; competition and regulatory; employment, pensions and incentives; intellectual property and technology.

Trainee profile

Successful candidates will be commercially aware, focused, ambitious and team-orien-

tated. High intellect and international awareness are a priority,and language skills are appreciated

Training environment

Norton Rose LLP operates an innovative six-seat system. The first four seats (16 months) include one seat in each of the practice's core departments – corporate finance, banking and dispute resolution – plus an optional seat in one of the firm's other, non-core departments – employment, pensions and incentives, tax, competition and EC, intellectual property and technology, or property, planning and environmental. The remaining eight months can be spent in the department in which you wish to qualify, or you can visit a different practice area for four months to help you to decide, and spend the last four months in your qualification seat. Alternatively, from your third seat onwards, you can elect to spend four months in one of the practice's international offices or apply for a client secondment. The practice's flexible seat system makes the transition from trainee to qualified solicitor as smooth as possible. The system has won the practice's trainees'approval, and from their point of view, develops associates with the adaptability and expertise the firm needs for its future.

Benefits

Life assurance (21+), private health insurance (optional), season ticket loan, sub-sidised gym membership.

Placement programmes

Places for 2008: 20 winter. Places for 2009: 40 summer and 20 winter; Duration: summer: Four weeks, winter: Two weeks; Remuneration: £250 p.w.; Closing

Date: 31 October 2008 for Christmas 2008, 31 January 2009 for summer and 31 Octo-

ber 2009 for Christmas 2009. Approximately six open days per year are also held.

Partners 248*
Assistant Solicitors 689*
Total Trainees 102
*denotes worldwide figures

Contact
Karen Potts

Method of application
Online only

Selection procedure
Interview and group exercise

Closing date for 2011/12
31 July 2009

Application
Training contracts p.a. 55
Applications p.a. 2,500+   %
interviewed p.a. 9% Required
degree grade 2:1

Training
Salary
1st year £35,700
2nd year £40,200
Holiday entitlement 25days %
of trainees with a non-law
degree p.a. 40% No. of seats
available abroad p.a. 22 (per
seat move)

Overseas offices
Amsterdam, Athens, Bahrain, Bangkok, Beijing, Brussels, Dubai, Frankfurt, Greece, Hong Kong, Jakarta,* London, Milan, Moscow, Munich, Paris Piraeus, Prague, Riyadh,* Rome, Shanghai, Singapore, Warsaw
*Associated office

Olswang

90 High Holborn, London WC1V 6XX
Tel: (020) 7067 3000 Fax: (020) 7067 3999
Email: traineesolicitor@olswang.com
Website: www.olswang.com/traineesolicitor

Firm profile

Olswang is a leading law firm renowned for its ground-breaking work in the technology, media, communications and real estate industries. Founded in 1981, the firm has grown to a staff of more than 650, including over 100 partners and four European offices. In 2007 the firm extended its international capability by opening an office in Berlin that focuses on the real estate and finance industries. Olswang also has an established alliance with US law firm Greenberg Traurig LLP, as well as providing its services in over 80 countries through a network of like-minded leading law firms. For the past four years Olswang has been ranked among the top 100 UK employers in The Sunday Times' 100 Best Companies to Work For.

The firm continues to be acknowledged as a leading practice in many of its core areas. Olswang has been voted M&A Law Firm of the Year 2008 (M&A Awards), Corporate Team of the Year - Mid Markets 2008 (The Lawyer Awards) and TMT Team of the Year 2008 (Legal Business Awards).

Main areas of work

Advertising; banking; bio-sciences; commercial litigation; corporate and commercial; media litigation; e-commerce; employment; EU and competition; film finance and production; information technology; insolvency; intellectual property; music; private equity; real estate; sponsorship; sport; tax; telecommunications; TV/broadcasting.

Trainee profile

Being a trainee at Olswang is both demanding and rewarding. The firm is interested in hearing from individuals with a 2:1 degree and above or equivalent, exceptional drive and relevant commercial experience. In addition, it is absolutely critical that trainees fit well into the Olswang environment which is challenging, busy, individualistic, meritocratic and fun.

Training environment

Olswang wants to help trainees match their expectations and needs with those of the firm. Training consists of four six-month seats in the corporate, commercial, litigation, finance or real estate groups. You will be assigned a mentor, usually a partner, to assist and advise you throughout your training contract. In-house lectures supplement general training and three-monthly appraisals assess development.

Benefits

Immediately: life cover, medical cover, dental scheme, subsidised gym membership, subsidised staff restaurant, season ticket loan. After six months: pension contributions. After 12 months: PHI.

Vacation placements

Places for 2009: June & July; Duration: 2 weeks; Remuneration: £275 p.w.; 17 students per scheme; Closing Date: 31 January 2009.

Sponsorship & awards

LPC and GDL fees paid in full. Maintenance grant of £7,000 (inside London), £6,500 (outside).

Partners 102
Fee-earners 216
Total Trainees 54

Contact
Sarmin Ghosh
Trainee solicitor recruitment officer

Method of application
Online

Selection procedure
Commercial case study, interview, psychometric test and written exercises

Closing date for 2011
31 July 2009

Application
Training contracts p.a. 24
Applications p.a. 2,000
% interviewed p.a. 4%
Required degree grade 2:1

Training
Salary
1st year (2007) £35,000
2nd year (2007) £39,000
Holiday entitlement 25 days
% of trainees with a non-law degree p.a. 50%

Post-qualification
Salary (2007) £63,500

Overseas offices
Brussels, Berlin

O'Melveny & Myers LLP

Warwick Court, 5 Paternoster Square, London, EC4M 7DX
Tel: (020) 7088 0000 Fax: (020) 7088 0001
Email: graduate-recruitment@omm.com   Website: www.omm.com

Firm profile

A top 20 global law firm staffed by over 1,000 lawyers in 13 offices, O'Melveny's clients include many of the world's largest financial institutions, leading private equity houses, investment banks and corporates. The London office is known for its entrepreneurial leadership and its commitment to excellence which underpin its approach to recruitment. The expertise of the team can also draw on the extensive reservoir of know-how and experience within the firm's offices around the world.

Main areas of work

The London office was effectively re-launched in 2004 and offers a full service transactions practice with a focus on private equity fund formation and deals and supported by leading tax, acquisition finance, regulatory, competition/ anti-trusts, real estate and IP lawyers. In July 2007 it also established an adversarial and arbitration capacity with the hiring of a leading team from Watson, Farley & Williams. Virtually all of our lawyers in London are UK qualified with most having joined from Magic Circle and other leading UK and international law firms.

Trainee profile

The London office is seeking to recruit four to six high calibre graduates for training contracts each year. Successful candidates must be ambitious, have proven academic ability, high levels of drive and determination, good team working skills and sound commercial awareness. The office has a strong entrepreneurial and collegiate style and to date, virtually all of our trainees have remained with the firm on qualification.

Training environment

The firm aims to take into account individual preferences when tailoring the training programme subject to the trainee completing the core competencies and subject to the demands of the business. Trainees will usually complete seats with partners or senior lawyers in each of our corporate, finance and funds formation practices and will also be able to obtain contentious experience in our litigation/arbitration practice and possibly in our competition/anti-trust practice (based partly in London and partly in our Brussels office). There will also be opportunities to work with our tax, IP and real estate practitioners. The firm has also initiated trainee secondments to its Hong Kong and Brussels offices. The firm encourages trainees to be proactive and take responsibility at an early stage. As a firm, O'Melveny & Myers places great importance on training for its lawyers at all levels which it views as key to the firm's ability to offer high quality legal services to its clients and so trainees will participate in the legal and non-legal skills training programme established by the London office. The Professional Skills Course is run by an external provider. Progress of each trainee is monitored with mid and end of seat reviews and feedback is given throughout each seat.

Vacation schemes

The office does run a series of vacation schemes, currently for 2 weeks at a time between June and September. For applications for 2009 Summer vacation schemes, please apply by 1 February 2009. The application process for places on vacation schemes is managed alongside the application procedure for training contracts.

Benefits

5% non contributory pension, travel insurance, private medical insurance, subsidised gym membership, death in service benefit four x annual salary, holiday entitlement 25 days, Permanent Health insurance.

Sponsorship & awards

GDL/LPC tuition fees incurred post recruitment plus a maintenance grant during the GDL/LPC course (currently £7,000 per annum).

Partners 9
Other fee-earners 40+
Trainees 9

Contact
Jan Birtwell, Graduate Recruitment Partner

Method of application
www.cvmailuk.com

Selection procedure
Interview process
closing date for 2011
31 July 2009

Training
Salary
1st year (2008): £39,000
2nd year (2008): £42,500
These are current rates which are reviewed annually

Post-qualification
Market rate

Overseas offices/ regional offices
Beijing, Brussels, Century City, Hong Kong, Los Angeles, Newport Beach, New York, San Francisco, Shanghai, Silicon Valley, Tokyo and Washington D.C.

Orrick, Herrington & Sutcliffe

Tower 42, Level 35, 25 Old Broad Street, London EC2N 1HQ
Tel: (020) 7562 5000 Fax: (020) 7628 0078
Email: recruitlondon@orrick.com
Website: www.orrick.com/london/gradrecruitment

Firm profile

Orrick is a leading international law firm with more than 1,000 lawyers in 18 offices located throughout Asia, Europe and North America. Orrick has earned a global reputation advising both established and emerging companies, banks and international financial institutions. Much of Orrick's client work involves cross-border transactions which have increased substantially in recent years with the development of the firm's network of global offices.

Main areas of work

Acquisition finance, arbitration and litigation, banking, capital markets, trade and asset finance, competition and European Union law, corporate and corporate finance, employment, energy and project finance, global bankruptcy and debt restructuring, international dispute resolution, private investment funds, real estate, structured finance and securitisation, tax.

Trainee profile

If you set your standards high, have a strong work ethic and are a bright, talented graduate of any discipline, you will be guaranteed broad-based experience. Applicants should have at least three A level passes at grades A and B and a 2.1 degree.

Training environment

Orrick is a firm for academically outstanding graduates. The firm values team players and reward collaboration over competition. It aims to give individuals the opportunity to flourish in a lively and supportive work environment and encourages interaction among lawyers across international offices at every level of experience within the firm. It supports learning through a steadfast focus on training and a mentoring programme that will provide you with the right foundation for building your legal career and for working with clients. Trainees work closely with fee earners and gain practical experience in research, drafting, procedural and client-related skills. There are regular training sessions and they draw on a range of speakers including in-house experts, clients and specialist professionals in their fields to provide an extensive and varied programme. The two-year training programme comprises four six-month seats with the opportunity to sit a seat in their Hong Kong office. Trainees undertake the Professional Skills Course during their induction programme.

Benefits

Pension, health insurance, subsidised gym membership, season ticket loan, private medical insurance, dental care and childcare voucher scheme.

Sponsorship & awards

GDL and LPC: fees paid plus £7,000 maintenance.

Open days

Orrick hold several open days each year. Applicants get to spend the day in Orrick's London office and these are a great way to see the office of a US law firm in action. See website for dates and details on how to apply.

Partners 20 (London)
Associates 40 (London)
Total Trainees 18

Contact
Simon Cockshutt

Method of application
Online at
www.orrick.com/london/gradrecruitment

Selection procedure
2 interviews with partners

Closing date for 2011
31 July 2009

Application
Training contracts p.a. 10
Required degree grade 2:1

Training
Salary
1st year (2008): £38,000
2nd year (2008): £42,500
Holiday entitlement 25 days
% of trainees retained on qualification (2008) 80%

Overseas offices
Beijing, Hong Kong, Los Angeles, Milan, Moscow, New York, Orange County, Pacific Northwest, Paris, Rome, Sacramento, San Francisco, Shanghai, Silicon Valley, Taipei, Tokyo and Washington DC.

Osborne Clarke

2 Temple Back East, Temple Quay, Bristol BS1 6EG
Tel: (0117) 917 3484
Email: graduate.recruitment@osborneclarke.com
Website:www.osborneclarke.com

Firm profile

Osborne Clarke is one of Europe's most respected and dynamic law firms. The firm's success is the result of delivering excellent business-focused legal advice in an energetic, straightforward and efficient way.

Osborne Clarke advises market leading and high performing organisations on their UK and international legal needs from its City, national and European offices and the Osborne Clarke Alliance.

The firm's main areas of expertise include corporate, finance and property transactions and the full spectrum of business law services, including commercial contracts, employment, pensions, outsourcing and dispute resolution.

Main areas of work

Banking, corporate, employment, pension & incentives, litigation/dispute resolution, property, commercial and tax.

Trainee profile

If you are a highly driven individual with good analytical, communication and organisational skills the firm would like to hear from you. Commercial acumen and the ability to build relationships with clients and colleagues are essential and foreign language skills are an advantage. Ideally, candidates should have grades A - B at A Level or equivalent, as well as a minimum 2:1 degree grade in any discipline. Applications are welcomed from candidates seeking a career change who can demonstrate strong commercial skills.

Training environment

The focus at Osborne Clarke is on developing a high performance culture and the firm's aim is to develop trainees into legal business advisers. The Osborne Clarke trainee development programme offers legal, management and business skills training to develop the professional skills needed to progress as a lawyer in the firm.

The training contract is made up of four seats, each lasting six months in four different practice areas. Three of these seats are usually corporate, property and litigation. Trainees work closely with their training supervisors and fee earners in the department and can expect a high level of responsibility and client contact at an early stage in their training contract. Regular reviews and coaching sessions are held to ensure that trainees are reaching their potential. There are also opportunities for trainees to spend a seat in one of the firm's other offices, including Germany, or on a client secondment.

Benefits

25 days holiday entitlement, life assurance, private medical insurance, permanent health insurance, employer's pension contributions, profit share scheme, interest free season ticket loan, gym discount.

Vacation schemes

Places for 2009 – 20 placements in Bristol, London and Reading during April, June and July.

Sponsorship & awards

The firm provides full funding for GDL and LPC tuition fees plus a maintenance grant for sponsored candidates.

Partners 113
Lawyers 251
Trainees 40

Contact
Zoe Hancock, Trainee
Recruitment Officer

Method of application
Online application form

Selection procedure
Assessment centre comprises of group exercises, psychometric test, partner interview

Closing date for 2011
31 July 2009

Application
Training contracts p.a. 20
Applications p.a. 1,000
% interviewed p.a. 12%
Required degree grade: 2:1, any discipline

Training
1st year £30,000-£34,000
2nd year £31,000-£35,000
Holiday entitlement 25 days
% of trainees with a non-law degree p.a. 43%

Post-qualification
£41,000-£63,000

Offices
Bristol, Cologne, London, Munich, Silicon Valley, Thames Valley

Pannone LLP

123 Deansgate, Manchester M3 2BU
Tel: (0161) 909 3000 Fax: (0161) 909 4444
Email: graduaterecruitment@pannone.co.uk
Website: www.pannone.com

Firm profile

A high-profile Manchester firm continuing to undergo rapid growth. The firm prides itself on offering a full range of legal services to a diverse client base which is split almost equally between personal and commercial clients. The firm was the first to be awarded the quality standard ISO 9001 and is a founder member of Pannone Law Group – Europe's first integrated international law group. Pannone was voted 5th in the 'Sunday Times' 100 Best Companies to Work For in 2008 and is the highest placed law firm in the survey.

Main areas of work

Commercial litigation 16%; personal injury 25%; corporate 13%; commercial property 8%; family 8%; clinical negligence 6%; private client 5%; employment 5%; construction 3%; regulatory 6%; residential property 5%.

Trainee profile

Selection criteria include a high level of academic achievement, teamwork, organisation and communication skills, a wide range of interests and a connection with the North West.

Training environment

An induction course helps trainees adjust to working life, and covers the firm's quality procedures and good practice. Regular trainee seminars cover the work of other departments within the firm, legal developments and practice. Additional departmental training sessions focus in more detail on legal and procedural matters in that department. Four seats of six months are spent in various departments and trainees' progress is monitored regularly. Trainees have easy access to support and guidance on any matters of concern. Work is tackled with gusto here, but so are the many social gatherings that take place.

Vacation placements

Places for 2009: 112; Duration: 1 week; Remuneration: None; Closing Date: Easter 20th February 2009, Summer 10 July 2009. Recruitment for training contracts is primarily through vacation placements.

Sponsorship & awards

Full grant for LPC plus fees at The College of Law, Manchester.

Partners 110
Assistant Solicitors 106
Total Trainees 37

Contact
Amy Bell

Method of application
Online only

Selection procedure
Individual interview, second interview comprises a tour of the firm & informal lunch

Closing date for 2011
31st July 2009

Application
Training contracts p.a. 14
Applications p.a. 1,200
% interviewed p.a. 10%
Required degree grade 2:1

Training
Salary
1st year (2008) £23,000
2nd year (2008) £26,000
Holiday entitlement 23 days
% of trainees with a non-law degree p.a. 25%

Post-qualification
Salary (2008) £34,000
% of trainees offered job on qualification (2006) 92%
% of assistants who joined as trainees 27%
% of partners who joined as trainees 21%

Paul, Hastings, Janofsky & Walker (Europe) LLP

10 Bishops Square, 8th Floor, London, E1 6EG
Tel: (020) 3023 5100 Fax: (020) 3023 5109
Email: melaniedamecourt@paulhastings.com
Website: www.paulhastings.com

Firm profile

With 1,200 attorneys serving clients from 18 worldwide offices, Paul Hastings provides a full range of services to clients around the globe. The firm has established long standing partnerships with many of the world's top financial institutions, Fortune 500 companies and other leading corporations. Paul Hastings represents and advises clients across a full range of practices, industries and regions.

Main areas of work

Paul Hastings' principle practice areas in London are corporate, employment, finance, litigation, real estate and tax.

Trainee profile

The firm seeks individuals with a wide variety of skills who combine intellectual ability with enthusiasm, creativity and a demonstrable ability to thrive in a challenging environment. The firm expects candidates to have a high level of achievement both at A level (or equivalent) and degree level. This would typically mean an upper second or first class degree and a majority of A grades at A level. The firm recruits both law and non-law graduates.

Training environment

Paul Hastings will provide you with a first class training and development programme, combining on-the-job training and professional courses. The firm will monitor your progress on a formal and informal basis to ensure you receive ongoing training and have the opportunity to give feedback on the programme itself and on those areas that are most important to you.

Trainees spend six months in four of the following practice areas: Corporate, employment, finance, litigation, project finance, real estate and tax.

Benefits

Private healthcare, life assurance, pension scheme, season ticket loan, on-site gym.

Sponsorship & awards

Paul Hastings offers sponsorship and maintenance grants.

Vacation placements

Places for 2009: 7; Duration: 2 weeks; Remuneration: £500 per week; Closing date: 28th February 2009.

Partners 13	
Assistant Solicitors 22	
Total Trainees 7	
Contact	
Graduate Recruitment	
Method of application	
online application form available on website	
Selection procedure	
Interview	
Closing date for 2011	
31 July 2009	
Application	
Training contracts p.a. 4-5	
Required degree grade 2:1	
Training	
Salary	
1st year (2008) £40,000	
2nd year (2008) £45,000	
Holiday entitlement	
25 days	
Post-qualification	
Salary (2008) £90,000	

Overseas/regional offices
Atlanta, Beijing, Brussels, Chicago, Frankfurt, Hong Kong, London, Los Angeles, Milan, New York, Orange County, Palo Alto, Paris, San Diego, San Francisco, Shanghai, Tokyo, Washington DC

Paul Hastings

Payne Hicks Beach

10 New Square, Lincoln's Inn, London WC2A 3QG
Tel: (020) 7465 4300 Fax: (020) 7465 4400
Email: lstoten@phb.co.uk
Website: www.phb.co.uk

Firm profile

Payne Hicks Beach is a medium-sized firm based in Lincoln's Inn. The firm acts for both private clients and businesses. It is highly rated for private client and matrimonial advice and also specialises in commercial litigation, property and corporate and commercial work.

Main areas of work

Private client 41%; matrimonial 22%; property 17%; commercial litigation 13%; corporate and commercial 7%.

Trainee profile

The firm looks for law and non-law graduates with a good academic record, an ability to solve practical problems, enthusiasm and an ability to work hard and deal appropriately with their colleagues and the firm's clients.

Training environment

Following an initial induction course, trainees usually spend six months in four of the firm's departments. Working with a partner, they are involved in the day to day activities of the department, including attending conferences with clients, counsel and other professional advisers. Assessment is continuous and trainees will be given responsibility as they demonstrate ability and aptitude. To complement the PSC, the firm runs a formal training system for trainees and requires them to attend lectures and seminars on various topics.

Benefits

Season travel ticket loan, life assurance 4 x salary, permanent health insurance, contribution to personal pension plan.

Sponsorship & awards

Fees for the GDL and LPC are paid. Maintenance grant of £4,500 pa.

Partners 29
Assistant Solicitors 28
Total Trainees 5

Contact
Miss Louise Stoten

Method of application
Letter & CV

Selection procedure
Interview
closing date for 2011
1 August 2009

Application
Training contracts p.a. 3
Applications p.a. 1,000
% interviewed p.a. 3%
Required degree grade 2:1

Training
Salary
1st year (2008) £30,000
2nd year (2008) £32,000
Holiday entitlement
4 weeks
% of trainees with a
non-law degree p.a. 50%

Penningtons Solicitors LLP

Abacus House, 33 Gutter Lane, London, EC2V 8 AR
Tel: (020) 7457 3000 Fax: (020) 7457 3240
Website: www.penningtons.co.uk

Firm profile

Penningtons Solicitors LLP is a thriving, modern law firm with a 200-year history and a deep commitment to top quality, partner-led services. Today, the firm is based in London and the South East with offices in London, Basingstoke and Godalming.

Main areas of work

In the business sphere, Penningtons advise on matters relating to all aspects of commercial property, intellectual property, management buy-outs and buy-ins, mergers, acquisitions and joint ventures, as well as dispute resolution. Advice is also given on information technology, business recovery, commercial contracts, agricultural and environmental law, and company secretarial services are offered. The firm helps individuals with advice on property, tax and estate planning, general financial management, the administration of wills and trusts, charities, personal injury, clinical negligence and immigration. Clients often ask Penningtons to advise on both their private and commercial affairs.

Trainee profile

Penningtons seeks high calibre candidates with enthusiasm and resilience. A high standard of academic achievement is expected: three or more good A level passes and preferably a 2:1 or better at degree level, whether you are reading law or another discipline.

Training environment

You will be given a thorough grounding in the law, spending time in three or four of the firm's divisions; commercial property, business services and private individuals. The firm ensures a varied training is given, avoiding too specialised an approach before qualification. Nonetheless, the experience gained in each department gives you a solid foundation, equipping you to embark on your chosen specialisation at the end of your training contract with the firm. Penningtons knows its trainee solicitors are happiest and most successful when busy with good quality work. The firm believes in introducing trainees to challenging cases. The value of giving its trainees responsibility, and allowing direct contact with clients is recognised. However, experienced solicitors are always ready to give support when needed.

Benefits

Life assurance, critical illness cover, pension, private medical insurance, 23 days holiday, interest free season ticket loan, sports and social events.

Vacation placements

The firm offers both summer vacation placements and information days. Applications are accepted from 1 December 2008 to 31 March 2009.

Sponsorship & awards

Full fees and maintenance for the LPC plus a maintenance grant of £4,500.

Partners 55
Assistant Solicitors 110
Total Trainees 22
* denotes worldwide figures

Contact
Tamsin Kennie

Method of application
Online via firm's website

Closing date for 2011
31 July 2009

Application
Training contracts p.a. 11
Applications p.a. 1,000
% interviewed p.a. 5%
Required degree grade 2:1

Training
Salary
1st year (2007)
£30,000 (London)
2nd year (2007)
£32,000 (London)
Holiday entitlement 23 days

Pinsent Masons LLP

CityPoint, One Ropemaker Street, London, EC2Y 9AH
Email: gradrecruiting@pinsentmasons.com
Website: www.pinsentmasons.com/graduate

Firm profile

Pinsent Masons is a top 15 UK law firm that is committed to sector-focused growth through its core sectors approach. This approach aligns the firm to specific business sectors to achieve market-leading positions. As a result, the firm has developed a successful and innovative approach to building strong, broad and deep corporate relationships. Client service is at the core of the firm and it works with a substantial range of FTSE 100 and FTSE 250, Fortune 500 and AIM quoted organisations as well as a variety of public sector clients.

Main areas of work

Banking & finance, corporate, dispute resolution & litigation, employment, insurance & reinsurance, international construction & energy, outsourcing, technology and commercial, pensions, projects, property, tax and UK construction & engineering.

Trainee profile

The firm welcomes applications from both law and non-law graduates with a good honours degree. In addition to a strong academic background, the firm is looking for people who can combine a sharp mind with commercial acumen and strong people skills to work in partnership with its clients' businesses.

Training environment

Trainees sit in four seats of six months across the practices, and are supervised by partners or associates. There are also opportunities for trainees to be seconded to clients. The firm offers a supportive team culture with early responsibility and contact with clients is encouraged.

In addition to the training required by the Law Societies, the firm offers a broad-ranging and custom-made training programme designed to deliver superb technical and management skills that link with the needs of the business. This is the first stage in the firm's focused development programme that supports individuals on the route to partnership.

The firm has an open-door policy and informal atmosphere with a positive focus on work-life balance.

Summer vacation placements

Places for 2009: 150; Duration: 2 weeks; Closing Date: 31 January 2009.

Sponsorship & awards

In England, a full sponsorship is offered for the CPE and LPC fees, as well as a maintenance grant. In Scotland, financial assistance is offered for Diploma fees, together with a maintenance grant.

Partners 290+
Lawyers 1,000
Total Trainees 135

Contact
Spencer Hibbert

Method of application
Online application form
www.pinsentmasons.com/graduate

Selection procedure
Assessment day including interview

Closing date for 2011
31 July 2009 (English offices) and 21 October 2009 (Scottish offices)

Application
Training contracts p.a. 55
Applications p.a. 2,000+
Required degree grade 2:1

Training
Salary
1st year (2008)
£36,000 (London)
2nd year (2008)
£39,000 (London)
Holiday entitlement 25 days

Post-qualification
Salary (2007) £63,000 (London)

UK offices
London, Birmingham, Bristol, Edinburgh, Glasgow, Leeds, Manchester

Prettys

Elm House, 25 Elm Street, Ipswich IP1 2AD
Tel: (01473) 232121 Fax: (01473) 230002
Email: agage@prettys.co.uk
Website: www.prettys.co.uk

Firm profile

Prettys is one of the largest and most successful legal practices in East Anglia. The firm is at the heart of the East Anglian business community, with the expanding hi-tech corridor between Ipswich and Cambridge to the west, Felixstowe to the east and the City of London 60 minutes away to the south. The firm also has an office in Chelmsford which has expanded rapidly since it was established in 2007. It provides an even closer link to London. The firm's lawyers are approachable and pragmatic. It provides expert advice to national and regional businesses.

Main areas of work

Prettys' broad-based practice allows it to offer a full-service to all its clients. Business law services: company, commercial, shipping, transport, construction, intellectual property, information technology, property, property litigation, employment, commercial litigation, insurance, professional indemnity, health and safety and executive immigration. Personal law services: French property, financial services, estates, agriculture, conveyancing and family.

Trainee profile

Prettys' trainees are the future of the firm. Applicants should be able to demonstrate a desire to pursue a career in East Anglia. Trainees are given considerable responsibility early on and the firm is therefore looking for candidates who are well motivated, enthusiastic and have a good common sense approach. Good IT skills are essential.

Training environment

A two-week induction programme will introduce you to the firm. You will receive continuous supervision and three-monthly reviews. Training is in four six-month seats. Trainees work closely with a partner, meeting clients and becoming involved in all aspects of the department's work. Frequent training seminars are provided in-house. The Law Society's Monitoring of Training Officer visited the firm and concluded "Prettys offers a very strong commitment to training within a supportive environment."

Additional information

One day placements are available (apply to Angela Gage).

Directors 1
Partners 17
Total Trainees 12

Contact
Angela Gage
Human Resources Manager

Method of application
Application letter & CV

Closing date for 2011
14 August 2009

Application
Training contracts p.a. 5/6
Required degree grade
2:1 preferred in law or other
relevant subject. Good A Levels

Training
Salary
Above Law Society guidelines

Holiday entitlement 25 days

Post-qualification
% of trainees offered job
on qualification (2008) 100%

PricewaterhouseCoopers Legal LLP

1 Embankment Place, London, WC2N 6DX
Tel: (020) 7212 1616 Fax: (020) 7212 1570
Website: www.pwclegal.co.uk

Vacancies 8 Trainees 16 Partners 18 Total staff 153
Method of application Complete the online application form from the website www.pwclegal.co.uk
Closing date for 2011 Trainees: July 31 2009 Summer vacation scheme 2009: March 31 2009 Winter vacation scheme: 30 October 2009
Application Required academic grade 280 UCAS points or equivalent 2:1 degree or equivalent
Training Salary London 1st year (2008) £30,000 2nd year (2008) £35,000

Firm profile

PricewaterhouseCoopers Legal LLP (formerly Landwell) is a member of the PricewaterhouseCoopers international network of firms. It has a unique positioning in the UK market place as the only law firm able to provide a seamless multi-disciplinary approach by working alongside experts in tax, human resource services, corporate finance, investment funds and financial services regulation in PricewaterhouseCoopers ("PwC").

PwC Legal prides itself in providing creative solutions and responding quickly and efficiently to clients' needs, whether it be general legal advice or complex legal and commercial expertise from a combination of multi-disciplinary experts within PwC Legal and PwC. Depending on the transaction type, the firm's lawyers work either on a domestic standalone basis or as part of a wider team of lawyers from the international network. As part of the network, PwC Legal has access to 1,300 business lawyers in over 63 countries and immigration expertise in over 90 countries.

The firm's services include corporate restructuring, mergers and acquisitions, intellectual property, information technology, immigration, pensions, employment, financial services, banking, commercial contracts, real estate and litigation.

Clients include local, national and multinational companies; partnerships and LLPs; governments and financial institutions. The firm recognises that today's lawyers must adapt to the changing needs of clients and offer more than just legal services. The firm's strategy reflects a commitment to make the firm distinctive by offering a superior client experience and developing qualities in their people that generate consistent and genuine engagement with clients and colleagues.

Trainee profile

The firm recruits trainees with a strong academic record and a variety of skills and experiences, demonstrating a genuine interest in business law. The firm recruits two years in advance and therefore focuses on penultimate year law students and final year non-law students.

Training environment

The firm delivers a formal induction programme to introduce trainees to the firm, teamed with monthly know-how sessions, business skills training and coaching. Trainees receive continuous supervision and three-monthly reviews over four (six-month) seats. Training is focused on quality experiences and exposure, encouraging trainees to be involved with matters as a key member of a project team.

Vacation schemes

The firm runs paid summer and winter vacation programmes for two weeks in June/July and January each year.

Sponsorship & awards

Trainee lawyers joining the firm are eligible to apply for a scholarship award to assist with the costs of the Graduate Diploma in Law Course and the Legal Practice Course. If successful, trainees will receive the total cost of the tuition and examination fees and also a significant contribution towards living expenses. More details can be found on the firm's website.

Pritchard Englefield

14 New St, London EC2M 4HE
Tel: (020) 7972 9720 Fax: (020) 7972 9722
Email: po@pe-legal.com
Website: www.pe-legal.com

Firm profile

A niche City firm practising a mix of general commercial and non-commercial law with many German and French clients. Despite its strong commercial departments, the firm still undertakes family and private client work and is renowned for its ever-present international flavour.

Main areas of work

All main areas of commercial practice including litigation, commercial/corporate/ banking (UK, German and French), IP/IT, property and employment, also estate and trusts (UK and off-shore), pensions, charities, personal injury and family.

Trainee profile

High academic achievers with fluent German and/or French.

Training environment

An induction course acquaints trainees with the computer network, online library and finance & administrative procedures and there is a formal in-house training programme during the first week. Four six-month seats make up most of your training. You can usually choose some departments, and you could spend two six-month periods in the same seat. Over two years, you learn advocacy, negotiating, drafting and interviewing, attend court, use your language skills every day and meet clients from day one. Occasional talks and seminars explain the work of the firm, and you can air concerns over bi-monthly lunches with the partners comprising the Trainee Panel. PSC is taken externally over two years. The Social Committee of the firm organises regular drinks parties, French film evenings, quiz nights and of course a Christmas party.

Benefits

Some subsidised training, monthly luncheon vouchers, and eligibility for membership of the firm's private medical insurance scheme as well as an interest free loan for an annual season ticket.

Sponsorship & awards

Full funding for LPC fees.

Partners 21
Assistant Solicitors 13
Other Fee Earners 7
Total Trainees 6

Contact
Graduate Recruitment

Method of application
Standard application form available from Graduate Recruitment or online

Selection procedure
1 interview only in September

Closing date for 2011
31 July 2009

Application
Training contracts p.a. 3
Applications p.a. 300–400
% interviewed p.a. 10%
Required degree grade
Generally 2:1

Training
Salary
1st year (2007) £22,250
Subject to 6 month review
Holiday entitlement 25 days
% of trainees with a non-law degree p.a. Approx 50%

Post-qualification
Salary (2007)
Approx £42,000
% of trainees offered job on qualification (2002) 75%
% of assistants (as at 1/9/03) who joined as trainees 50%
% of Partners (as at 1/9/03) who joined as trainees 40%

Reed Smith

Beaufort House, 15 St. Botolph Street, London, EC3A 7EE
Tel: (020) 7247 6555 Fax: (020) 7247 5091
Email: graduate.recruitment@reedsmith.com
Website: www.reedsmith.com

Firm profile

Key to Reed Smith success is its ability to build lasting relationships: with clients and with each other. United through a culture defined by commitment to professional development, team-work, diversity, pro bono and community support, the firm has grown to become one of the 15 largest law firms in the world. Its 23 offices span three continents and include almost 700 people in London and Birmingham (that's around 20% of its global presence). While the offices benefit from an international framework, but each one retains key elements of the local business culture.

Main areas of work

The firm is particularly well known for its work advising leading companies in the areas of financial services, life sciences, shipping, energy, trade and commodities, advertising, technology and media. It provides a wide range of commercial legal services for all these clients, including a full spectrum of corporate, commercial and financial services, dispute resolution, real estate and employment. Much of the work is multi-jurisdictional.

Trainee profile

The firm is looking for individuals with the drive and potential to become world-class business lawyers. They want 'players' rather than 'onlookers' with strong intellect, initiative, the ability to thrive in a challenging profession and the personal qualities to build strong relationships with colleagues and clients.

Training environment

On offer is a four-seat programme in which trainees are able to exercise much influence over the choice and timings of seats. There are many opportunities for secondments to clients and the firm's overseas offices. Trainees also benefit from being able to take a wide range of courses in its award-winning corporate university, developed in partnership with the highly rated Wharton School of the University of Pennsylvania. There are 30 vacancies for training contracts commencing in August 2011 and February 2012.

Benefits

Performance related bonus, pension, life insurance, private health insurance, interest-free season ticket loan, subsidised staff restaurant, staff conveyancing allowance.

Vacation placements

The firm offers up to 25 places each year to applicants who will, on arrival, have completed at least two years of undergraduate study. Placements are available in both the London and Birmingham offices.

Sponsorship & awards

GDL Funding: Fees paid plus £6,000 maintenance. LPC Funding: Fees paid plus £7,000 maintenance

---

Partners 111*
Fee-earners 147*
Total Trainees 61
* denotes UK figures

Contact
Mark Matthews

Method of application
Online application form

Selection procedure
Selection exercise, interview, verbal reasoning assessment

Closing date for 2011/12
31 July 2009

Application
Training contracts p.a. 32
Applications p.a. 1500
% interviewed p.a. 7%
Required degree grade 2:1

Training
Salary
1st year (2009) £37,000
2nd year (2009) £40,000
Holiday entitlement 25 days
% of trainees with a
non-law degree p.a. 35%
No. of seats available
abroad p.a. 10

Post-qualification
Salary (2008)
£64,000 plus bonus
% of assistants who
joined as trainees 59%
% of partners who
joined as trainees 45%

Overseas offices
New York, London, Hong Kong, Chicago, Washington DC, Beijing, Paris, Los Angeles, San Francisco, Philadelphia, Pittsburg, Oakland, Munich, Abu Dhabi, Princeton, N. Virginia, Wilmington, Birmingham, Dubai, Century City, Piraeus, Richmond

Reynolds Porter Chamberlain LLP

Tower Bridge House, St Katharine's Way, London, E1W 1AA
Tel: (020) 3060 6000 Fax: (020) 3070 7000
Email: training@rpc.co.uk
Website: www.rpc.co.uk/training

Firm profile

Reynolds Porter Chamberlain LLP is a leading London-based practice with over 250 lawyers. Based in the City, the firm works in an open, collaborative environment designed to bring out the best in its people and to ensure that the service it offers to clients is second-to-none. The firm is particularly well known as one of the top insurance and litigation firms in the country, with renowned professional indemnity and medical malpractice departments. But its range of activities does not stop there. The firm has a highly-rated corporate group which handles the full spectrum of corporate and commercial work for national and multinational companies across several industries, and is particularly well regarded for its media and technology related work.

On the subject of media, the firm has one of the country's largest and leading defamation teams whose clients include multinational newspaper groups, broadcasters and publishers.

The firm also has a substantial dispute resolution group, with significant practices in IT, IP, employment and insolvency. The firm's construction group deals with building disputes and environmental claims, along with building and engineering, major projects and PFI work. The real estate group handles all aspects of commercial real estate work.

Trainee profile

The firm appoints 15 trainees each year from a law or non-law background. Although proven academic ability is important (the firm requires a 2.1 degree or above) the firm also values energy, enthusiasm, business sense, commitment and the ability to communicate and relate well to others. Recruitment usually takes place in the September, two years before commencement of the training contract. Short-listed candidates will be invited to one of the assessment days during which they will have the opportunity to meet the firm's existing trainees and partners.

Training environment

As a trainee you will receive first-rate training in a supportive working environment. You will work closely with a Partner and will be given real responsibility as soon as you are ready to handle it. At least six months will be spent in four areas of the practice and the firm encourages it's trainees to express preferences for the areas in which they would like to train. This will provide a thorough grounding and the chance to develop confidence as you see matters to their conclusion. In addition to the Professional Skills Course the firm provides a complementary programme of in-house training. When you qualify, you will have the choice to remain with the firm and they will endeavour to place you in the area of law that suits you best.

Benefits

The firm feels it is important to offer its employees a creative and competitive benefits package with choice and flexibility. The full range of benefits can be viewed via the firm's website.

Vacation placements

The firm also runs Easter and Summer vacation schemes each year to enable prospective trainees to spend time with them, getting a feel for their work and atmosphere.
Places for Easter 2009: 12; Duration: 1 week; Remuneration: £275 p/w.; Closing date: 30 January 2009.
Places for Summer 2009: 24; Duration: 2 weeks; Remuneration: £275 p/w.; Closing date: 30 January 2009.

Sponsorship & awards

Bursaries are available for the GDL, if applicable, and the LPC. Bursaries comprise course and examination fees and a maintenance grant of up to £6,500.

Partners 60
Assistant Solicitors 200
Total Trainees 30

Contact
Trainee Recruitment Team

Method of application
Online application system

Selection procedure
Assessment days held in September

Closing date for 2011
31/07/09

Application
Training contracts p.a. 15
Applications p.a. 900
% interviewed p.a. 6%
Required degree grade 2:1

Training
Salary
1st year (2008) £33,000
2nd year (2008) £37,000
Holiday entitlement 20 days
% of trainees with a non-law degree p.a. Approx 25%

Post-qualification
Salary (2008) £58,000
% of trainees offered job on qualification (2007) 90%
% of assistants (as at 1/9/06) who joined as trainees 20%
% of partners (as at 1/9/06) who joined as trainees 30%

Salans

Millennium Bridge House, 2 Lambeth Hill, London EC4V 4AJ
Tel: (020) 7429 6000 Fax: (020) 7429 6001
Email: london@salans.com

Firm profile

Salans has an open and friendly culture with an informal, but hardworking environment. It is a multinational law firm with full-service offices in the City of London, Paris and New York, together with further offices in Almaty, Baku, Berlin*, Beijing**, Bratislava, Bucharest, Budapest, Hong Kong**, Istanbul, Kyiv, Madrid, Moscow, Prague, Shanghai, St Petersburg and Warsaw. The firm also has operations Doha, Qatar and the French Pacific. Building on the success of the firm's emerging markets practices and with a long established presence in Shanghai, The firm currently has over 600 fee-earners, including 178 Partners worldwide, with 30 partners residing in the London office. Its lawyers strongly believe in assisting individuals and groups unable to access legal services, through a positive commitment to pro bono work. In 2007 and 2008 Salans were finalists at the Lawyer Awards for 'International Law Firm of the Year'.

Main areas of work

London Office: Banking and finance; corporate and commercial litigation; employment; real estate; insolvency and corporate recovery; information technology and communications; betting and gaming; shipping and arbitration.

Trainee profile

You will have high academic qualifications, including good A-Level (or equivalent) results, and the ability to approach complex problems in a practical and commercial way. The firm is looking for highly motivated, creative and enthusiastic team players. It looks to recruit trainees who make a difference, want early responsibility and contribute to the ever-changing legal world. Relevant work experience demonstrating a desire to pursue a career in law will be viewed positively, and language and computer skills are also valued.

Benefits

Private healthcare, pension, life assurance, critical illness cover, season ticket loan.

Sponsorship & awards

LPC tuition fees paid.

Partners 178
(Worldwide)
Assistant Solicitors
(Worldwide) 400+
Total Trainees
(London) 10

Contact
Keely Smith
HR Manager

Method of application
Letter & CV

Selection procedure
Interview programme and
selection workshop

Closing date for 2011
31 July 2009

Application
Training contracts p.a. 3-4
Applications p.a. 350-400
% interviewed p.a. 8%
Required degree grade 2:1

Training
Salary
1st year (2008) £33,000
2nd year (2008) £35,000
Holiday entitlement 25 days
% of trainees with a
non-law degree p.a. Variable
No. of seats available
abroad p.a. One (occasional)

Post-qualification
Salary (2009) TBA
% of trainees offered job
on qualification (2008) 75%

Overseas offices
Almaty, Baku, Berlin*, Beijing**,
Bratislava, Bucharest, Budapest,
Frankfurt, Hong Kong**,
Istanbul, Kyiv, Madrid, Moscow,
New York, Paris, Prague,
Shanghai, St Petersburg and
Warsaw
*Salans LLP
**Subject to regulatory
approval

Shadbolt LLP

Chatham Court, Lesbourne Road, Reigate RH2 7LD
Tel: (0845) 4371000 Fax: (0845) 4371001
Email: recruitment@shadboltlaw.com
Website: www.shadboltlaw.com

Firm profile

Shadbolt LLP is an award-winning, dynamic, progressive firm committed to high quality work and excellence both in the UK and internationally. The atmosphere at the firm is friendly, relaxed and informal and there are various social and sporting activities for staff. The firm comprises a lively and enterprising team with a fresh and open approach to work. The firm's qualified staff have a high level of experience and industry knowledge and some are widely regarded as leading practitioners in their field.

Main areas of work

The firm is well known for its strengths in major projects, construction and engineering and dispute resolution and litigation with established expansion into corporate and commercial, employment, commercial property and IT and e-commerce. The firm provides prompt personal service and its client list includes some of the world's best known names in the construction and engineering industries.

Trainee profile

Applicants must demonstrate that they are self-starters with a strong academic background and outside interests. Leadership, ambition, initiative, enthusiasm and good interpersonal skills are essential, as is the ability to play an active role in the future of the firm. Linguists are particularly welcome, as are those with supporting professional qualifications. The firm welcomes non-law graduates.

Training

Four six month seats from construction and commercial litigation, arbitration and dispute resolution, major projects and construction, employment, corporate and commercial and commercial property. Where possible individual preference is noted. Work has an international bias. There are opportunities for secondment to major clients and work in the overseas offices. Trainees are treated as valued members of the firm, expected to take early responsibility and encouraged to participate in all the firm's activities, including practice development. The firm is accredited by the law society as a provider of training and runs frequent in-house lectures. The PSC is taught externally.

Sponsorship & benefits

Optional private healthcare, permanent health insurance, group life assurance, paid study leave, season ticket loan, discretionary annual bonus of up to 5% of salary, paid professional memberships and subscriptions, full refund of LPC upon commencement of training contract.

Vacation placements

Places for 2009: 6; Duration: 2 weeks; Remuneration: £200 p.w.; Closing Date: 28 February 2009; Interviews: March 2009. Please submit the online form no earlier than January 2009.

Partners 24
Snr Assoc/Assoc 25
Total Trainees 8
Total Staff 111

Contact
Andrea Pickett

Method of application
Online application form

Selection procedure
Interview (1) written
assessment & group exercise

Closing date for 2011
31 July 2009 (interviews
September 2009)

Application
Training contracts p.a. 4
Applications p.a. 100
% interviewed p.a. 20%
Required degree grade 2:1
(occasional exceptions)

Training
Salary
1st year (2008) £31,000
2nd year (2008) £35,000
Holiday entitlement
20 days rising to 25 on
qualification, with opportunity
to 'buy' an additional 5 days
holiday p.a.
% of trainees with a
non-law degree p.a. 50%
No. of seats available
abroad p.a. 1

Post-qualification
Salary (2008) £52,000
% of trainees offered job
on qualification (2008) 100%
% of Snr Assoc/ Assoc (2008)
who joined as trainees 50%
% of partners (2008)
who joined as trainees 0%

Other offices
Reigate, City of London, Paris,
Associated offices:
Bucharest, Dar es Salaam

SHADBOLT/LAW

Shearman & Sterling LLP

Broadgate West, 9 Appold Street, London EC2A 2AP
Tel: (020) 7655 5000 Fax: (020) 7655 5500

Firm profile

Shearman & Sterling LLP is one of New York's oldest legal partnerships, which has transformed from a New York-based firm focused on banking into a diversified global institution. Recognised throughout the world, the firm's reputation, skills and expertise are second to none in its field. The London office, established in 1972, has become a leading practice covering all aspects of English and European corporate and finance law. The firm employs over 200 English and US trained legal staff in London and has more than 1,000 lawyers in 19 offices worldwide.

Main areas of work

Banking, leveraged finance and structured finance. Project finance. M&A. Global capital markets. International arbitration and litigation. Tax. EU and competition. Financial institutions advisory & asset management (legal and regulatory advice to financial instititions and infrastructure providers, both in a retail and wholesale context, and both online and off-line). Executive compensation & employee benefits (sophisticated advice on the design and implementation of compensation and benefits arrangements). Intellectual property. Real estate.

Trainee profile

The firm's successful future development calls for people who will relish the hard work and intellectual challenge of today's commercial world. You will be a self-starter, keen to assume professional responsibility early in your career and determined to become a first-class lawyer in a first-class firm. The firm's two year training programme will equip you with all the skills needed to become a successful commercial lawyer. You will spend six months in each of four practice areas, with an opportunity to spend six months in Abu Dhabi, New York, Hong Kong or Singapore. You will be treated as an integral part of the London team from the outset. The firm will expect you to contribute creatively to all the transactions you are involved in. The firm has an informal yet professional atmosphere. Your enthusiasm, intellect and energy will be more important than what you wear to work. The firm will provide you with a mentor, arrange personal and professional development courses and give you early responsibility.

Sponsorship & awards

Sponsorship for the CPE/ PgDL and LPC courses, together with a maintenance grant of £7,000.

Partners 25
Assistant Solicitors 105
Total Trainees 31

Contact
Rebecca Leitch
Tel: (020) 7655 5088

Method of application
Online at www.shearman.com

Selection procedure
Assessment centre and interview

Closing date for 2011
31 July 2009

Application
Training contracts p.a. 15
Required degree grade 2:1, 340 UCAS points

Training
Salary
1st year (2008) £39,000
2nd year (2008) £41,500
Holiday entitlement
24 days p.a.
% of trainees with non-law degree p.a. 40%
No of seats available abroad 5

Post-qualification
Salary (2008) £80,000
% of trainees offered job on qualification (2008) 57%

Overseas offices
Abu Dhabi, Bejing, Brussels, Düsseldorf, Frankfurt, Hong Kong, Menlo Park, Munich, New York, Paris, Rome, San Francisco, Sao Paulo, Shanghai, Singapore, Tokyo, Toronto, Washington DC

Sheridans

Whittington House, Alfred Place, London, WC1E 7EA
Tel: (020) 7079 0100   Fax: (020) 7079 0200
Email: info@sheridans.co.uk
Website: www.sheridans.co.uk

Firm profile

Sheridans is a full-service law firm with an established reputation for its work in the creative industries. Representing many internationally recognised names in music, film, TV and theatre, it also has a thriving commercial practice offering corporate, private client, dispute resolution, property and employment services.

Main areas of work

ENTERTAINMENT & MEDIA: The music department advises recording artists and recording and management companies on contract negotiation, popular and classical music publishing, merchandising and sponsorship. The film and TV department advises broadcasters, TV and feature film production companies, distribution and sales agents, financiers and talent. Other specialist areas include the theatre, sport, book and magazine publishing, trademarks and domain names, computer games, online and digital media.

DISPUTE RESOLUTION: The firm provides advice and representation in relation to disputes arising in the media and entertainment industries. The disputes typically range from privacy and defamation claims against the national press to rights disputes.

CORPORATE/ COMMERCIAL: The firm advises on commercial contracts, mergers, acquisitions and disposals, management buy-outs and buy-ins, corporate finance, joint ventures, corporate reorganisations, company formations and insolvency.

PROPERTY: Services include the sale and purchase of commercial property, involving investment, leasehold and planning matters, secured lending, building and development schemes and property financing, as well as domestic conveyancing for high net worth individuals.

EMPLOYMENT: The employment practice handles contentious and non-contentious matters, representing both employers and employees, including senior executives.

Trainee profile

Excellent academic background (2.1 and above, good A levels), commercial awareness, great interpersonal skills and an ability to think strategically. Trainees should have an enthusiasm for and a demonstrable commitment to the firm's areas of practice.

Training

The training contract is divided into four six month seats, although trainees are expected to be flexible and assist any department as required. Trainees are given a challenging range of work and exposure to a significant level of responsibility.

Partners 21
Consultants 3
Assistant solicitors 15
Total trainees 2

Contact
Claire Lewis (Training Principal)

Method of application
CV and covering letter, by email to training@sheridans.co.uk (see website)

Selection procedure
2 stage interview process

Closing date for 2011
31 July 2009

Application
Training contracts p.a. 1
Required degree grade 2:1

Training
Salary
1st year competitive with similar firms
2nd year competitive with similar firms
Holiday entitlement
20 days

Post-qualification
Salary Competitive with similar firms
% of trainees offered job on qualification (in last two years) 100%

Shoosmiths

The Lakes, Northampton NN4 7SH
Tel: (0870) 086 3223 Fax: (0870) 086 3001
Email: join.us@shoosmiths.co.uk
Website: www.shoosmiths.co.uk

Firm profile

Shoosmiths is one of the UK's fastest-growing national law firms with offices across the midlands and south of England. The firm is a progressive, forward-thinking law firm with a real spirit of enterprise. The firm really values its people by giving them the freedom, recognition and support to succeed.

Main areas of work

The firm is a full service law firm with numerous practice areas including commercial property, corporate, commercial and dispute resolution.

Trainee profile

You'll be open-minded, flexible, and will be looking to work in a non-hierarchical, open plan environment. You'll also value a life outside of the office. Workwise, you'll care about the quality of service you give to clients (both internal and external) and you'll want to make a real and direct contribution to the firm's success.

Training environment

Trainees are given real work from day one. Experience is built around a practical workload, complemented by technical and business skills training. Over the two years, trainees complete four six-month placements around the firm.

The firm only places one or two trainees in each department which means that you'll be listened to and valued, and will get a good level of access to your supervising Partner and colleagues.

Benefits

Flexible holidays, pension (after three months' service), life assurance, various staff discounts, Christmas bonus.

Vacation placements

The firm offers two-week placements during June and July. Please apply online via the website. The closing date for summer placements will be 5pm, 30 January 2009.

Sponsorship & awards

GDL & LPC funding; the firm pays fees plus a maintenance grant.

Partners 113
Total staff 1500
Total Trainees 36

Contact
Sally Stagles

Method of application
Online application form

Selection procedure
Full day assessment centre

Closing date for 2011
31 July 2009

Application
Training contracts p.a. 20
Applications p.a. 800
% interviewed p.a. 10%
Required degree grade 2:1

Training
Salary
from £24,000
Holiday entitlement
23 days + option to flex

Post-qualification
Salary £38,000

Offices
Northampton, Nottingham, Solent, Thames Valley, Milton Keynes, Basingstoke (not available to trainees), Birmingham

Sidley Austin LLP

Woolgate Exchange, 25 Basinghall Street, London EC2V 5HA
Tel: (020) 7360 3600 Fax: (020) 7626 7937
Email: ukrecruitment@sidley.com
Website: www.sidley.com

Firm profile

Sidley Austin LLP is one of the world's largest full-service law firms. With more than 1,700 lawyers practising on four continents (North America, Europe, Australasia and Asia), the firm provides a broad range of integrated services to meet the needs of its clients across a multitude of industries.

Main areas of work

Corporate and securities, capital markets, corporate reorganisation and bankruptcy, employment, financial services regulation, insurance, IP/IT, real estate, real estate finance, securitisation, structured finance, and tax.

Trainee profile

Sidley Austin LLP look for focused, intelligent and enthusiastic individuals with personality and humour who have a real interest in practising law in the commercial world. Trainees should have a consistently strong academic record and a 2:1 degree (not necessarily in law).

Training environment

The firm is not a typical City firm and it is not a 'legal factory' so there is no risk of being just a number. Everyone is encouraged to be proactive and to create their own niche when they are ready to do so. Trainees spend time in the firm's main groups. In each group trainees will sit with a partner or senior associate to ensure individual training based on 'hands on' experience. You will be encouraged to take responsibility where appropriate. Regular meetings with your supervisor ensure both the quality and quantity of your experience. In addition, there is a structured timetable of training on a cross-section of subjects and an annual training weekend.

Benefits

Private health insurance, life assurance, contribution to gym membership, interest-free season ticket loan, income protection scheme, pension and subsidised restaurant.

Sponsorship & awards

Tuition fees for the GDL/CPE and the LPC Maintenance grant of £7,000 p.a.

Partners 41
Assistant Solicitors 78
Total Trainees 14

Contact
Lucy Slater,
HR Administrator

Method of application
Application form

Selection procedure
Interview(s)

Closing date for 2011
31 July 2009

Application
Training contracts p.a. 15
Applications p.a. 500
% interviewed p.a. 15
Required degree grade 2:1

Training
Salary
1st year (2007) £38,000
2nd year (2007) £42,000
Holiday entitlement 25 days
% of trainees with a
non-law degree p.a. 50%

Overseas offices
Beijing, Brussels, Chicago, Dallas, Frankfurt, Geneva, Hong Kong, London, Los Angeles, New York, San Francisco, Shanghai, Singapore, Sydney, Tokyo, Washington DC

Simmons & Simmons

CityPoint, One Ropemaker Street, London EC2Y 9SS
Tel: (020) 7628 2020 Fax: (020) 7628 2070
Email: recruitment@simmons-simmons.com
Website: www.simmons-simmons.com/traineelawyers

Firm profile

Dynamic and innovative, Simmons & Simmons has a reputation for offering a superior legal service, wherever and whenever it is required. The firm's high quality advice and the positive working atmosphere in its international network of 20 offices has won admiration and praise from both the legal community and business clients.

Main areas of work

Simmons & Simmons offers its clients a full range of legal services across numerous industry sectors. The firm has a particular focus on the world's fastest growing sectors, namely: energy and infrastructure; financial institutions; life sciences; and TMT. Simmons & Simmons provides a wide choice of service areas in which its lawyers can specialise. These include corporate and commercial; information, communications and technology; dispute resolution; employment and benefits; EU, competition and regulatory; financial markets; IP; projects; real estate; taxation and pensions.

Trainee profile

Simmons & Simmons is interested to find out about your academic successes but will also explore your ability to form excellent interpersonal relations and work within a team environment, as well as your levels of motivation, drive and ambition.

Show evidence of a rich 'life experience' as well as examples of your intellectual capabilities and you will be provided with everything you need to become a successful member of the firm.

Training environment

The training programme at Simmons & Simmons is constantly evolving to build the skills you will need to be successful in the fast moving world of international business. The firm provides experience in a range of areas of law and a balanced approach to gaining the knowledge, expertise and abilities you will need to qualify in the practice area of your choice.

Vacation placements

The firm's summer internship scheme is one of its primary means of selecting candidates for a career at Simmons & Simmons. Your placement will enable you to gain first-hand experience of a busy and dynamic international law firm, as well as gain exposure to everything from the firm's service areas to the kinds of deals and transactions the firm works on.

Undergraduates usually apply for internships in their penultimate year. However, the firm is also happy to offer internships to final year students, graduates, mature and international students and those changing career.

Simmons & Simmons also run winter insight workshops aimed specifically at final and penultimate year non-law students, and a series of open days (available to first year students) thoughout the year.

Sponsorship & awards

The firm will cover your full tuition fees at law school and offer a maintenance allowance of up to £7,500.

Partners 238
Assistant Solicitors 599
Total Trainees 144

Contact
Anna King Graduate
Recruitment Officer

Method of application
Online application, at
www.simmons-
simmons.com/traineelawyers
Applications should be made
from 01 November, 2008

Selection procedure
Assessment day

Closing date for 2011
31 July 2009

Application
Training contracts p.a. 50
Applications p.a. 2,000
% interviewed p.a. 15%
Required degree grade 2:1

Training
Salary
£36,000, 1st and 2nd seat
£40,000, 3rd and 4th seat
Holiday entitlement 25 days
% of trainees with a
non-law degree p.a. 50%
No. of seats available
abroad p.a. varies

Post-qualification
Salary (2008) £64,000
% of trainees offered job
on qualification (2008) 83%

Overseas offices
Abu Dhabi, Amsterdam,
Brussels, Dubai, Düsseldorf,
Frankfurt, Hong Kong, Lisbon,
London, Madeira, Madrid,
Milan, Moscow, Padua, Paris,
Qatar, Rome, Rotterdam,
Shanghai, Tokyo.

SJ Berwin LLP

10 Queen Street Place, London, EC4R 1BE
Tel: (020) 7111 2268   Fax: (020) 7111 2000
Email: graduate.recruitment@sjberwin.com
Website: www.sjberwin.com/gradrecruit

Firm profile

SJ Berwin LLP is a pan-European firm and was formed 26 years ago. The firm was founded with the objective of providing outstanding legal advice in a dynamic and different environment. The firm's growth has been fast and furious and in less than 20 years we achieved Top 20 City Firm status. Much of the firm's work is international and clients range from major multinational business corporations and financial institutions to high net-worth individuals. As a result the firm has established a strong reputation in corporate finance.

Main areas of work

SJ Berwin's clients are sophisticated buyers of legal services, principally entrepreneurial companies and financial institutions, whom the firm advises on a comprehensive range of services including: corporate/M&A, commercial, communications, media and technology, energy and natural resources, employment and pensions, EU and competition, finance, financial markets, intellectual property, investment funds, litigation and dispute resolution, pharmaceutical and life sciences, private equity, real estate, reconstruction and insolvency, retail and tax.

Trainee profile

The firm wants ambitious, commercially minded individuals who seek a high level of involvement from day one. Candidates must have a strong academic record, be on track for, or have achieved, a 2:1 or equivalent in their undergraduate degree, and have demonstrated strong team and leadership potential.

Training environment

The two-year training contract is divided into four six-month seats. Trainees will spend two seats (which may include a seat abroad) within the following areas: finance, mergers and aquisitions, equity capital markets, private equity, venture capital and investment funds. Trainees are given early responsibility and are supported throughout the training contract.

How to apply

The firm welcomes applications from all disciplines and all universities. Applications must be made using the firm's online form available at www.sjberwin.com/gradrecruit. The same form can be used to indicate your interest in an open day, a vacation scheme and/or a training contract.

Benefits

25 days holiday, private healthcare, gym membership/subsidy, life assurance, pension scheme, season ticket loan, free lunch.

Partners 170
Assistant Solicitors 400
Total Trainees 98

Contact
Graduate Recruitment Team

Method of application
Online application form

Selection procedure
2 interviews
closing date for 2011
31 July 2009
Easter & summer vacation
schemes 31 January 2009

Application
Training contracts p.a. 50
Applications p.a. 2,000
10% interviewed p.a.
Required degree grade 2:1

Training
Salary
£36,000, 1st year
£40,000, 2nd year
Holiday entitlement 25 days
% of trainees with a
non-law degree p.a. 50%

Post-qualification
Salary (2009) £65,000
% of trainees offered job
on qualification (2008) 89%

Overseas offices
Brussels, Frankfurt, Madrid,
Berlin, Paris, Munich, Milan,
Turin.

Skadden Arps, Slate, Meagher & Flom (UK) LLP

40 Bank Street, Canary Wharf, London E14 5DS
Tel: (020) 7519 7000 Fax: (020) 7519 7070
Email: graduate@skadden.com   Website: www.skadden.com

Firm profile

Skadden is one of the leading law firms in the world with approximately 2,000 lawyers in 24 offices across the globe. Clients include corporate, industrial, financial institutions and government entities. The London office is the gateway to the firm's European practice where they have some 250 lawyers dedicated to top-end, cross-border corporate transactions and international arbitration and litigation. The firm has handled matters in nearly every country in the greater European region, and in Africa and the Middle East. The firm is consistently ranked as a leader in all disciplines and amongst a whole host of accolades, the firm was recently voted 'Global Corporate Law Firm of the Year' (Chambers and Partners), 'Best US Law Firm in London' (Legal Business) and 'Best Trainer' in the US law firm in London category (Law Careers. Net Training and Recruitment Awards) for the second year running.

Main areas of work

Lawyers across the European network focus primarily on corporate transactions, including domestic and cross-border mergers and acquisitions, private equity, capital markets, leveraged finance and banking, tax, corporate restructuring and energy and projects. The firm also advise in international arbitration and litigation and regulatory matters.

Trainee profile

The firm seeks to recruit a small number of high-calibre graduates from any discipline to join their highly successful London office as trainee solicitors. The firm is looking for candidates who combine intellectual ability with enthusiasm, creativity and a demonstrable ability to rise to a challenge and to work with others towards a common goal.

Training environment

The firm can offer you the chance to develop your career in a uniquely rewarding and professional environment. You will join a close-knit but diverse team in which you will be given ample opportunity to work on complex matters, almost all with an international aspect, whilst benefiting from highly personalised training and supervision in an informal and friendly environment. The first year of your training contract will be divided into two six month seats where you will gain experience in corporate transactions and international litigation and arbitration. In the second year of your training contract, you will have the opportunity to discuss with the firm your preferences for your remaining two seats. The firm also offers the opportunity for second year trainees to be seconded to our Hong Kong or Moscow office for a six month seat.

Benefits

Life insurance, private health insurance, private medical insurance, travel insurance, joining fee paid at Canary Wharf gym, subsidised restaurant, employee assistance programme and technology allowance.

Work placements

Skadden offers the opportunity for penultimate year law and non-law students to experience the culture and working environment of the firm through two week work placements. Placements are paid and take place during Easter and over the course of the summer. The deadline for applications is 12 January 2009 for placements in 2009.

Sponsorship & awards

The firm pays for GDL and LPC course fees and provides a £8,000 grant for each year of these courses.

Partners 27*
Assistant Solicitors 120*
Trainees 9*
*London office

Contact
Kate Harman
Graduate Recruitment
Specialist

Method of application
Online application

Selection procedure
A selection event comprising of an interview and a short exercise

Closing date for 2011
31 July 2009

Application
Training contracts p.a. 10-12
Applications p.a. 700
% interviewed p.a. 8%
Required degree grade 2:1

Training
Salary
1st year £40,000
2nd year £43,000
Holiday entitlement 25 days
% of trainees with a non-law degree p.a. 50%

Overseas offices
Beijing, Boston, Brussels, Chicago, Frankfurt, Hong Kong, Houston, London, Los Angeles, Moscow, Munich, New York, Palo Alto, Paris, San Francisco, São Paulo, Shanghai, Singapore, Sydney, Tokyo, Toronto, Vienna, Washington DC, Wilmington.

Slaughter and May

One Bunhill Row, London EC1Y 8YY
Tel: (020) 7600 1200 Fax: (020) 7090 5000
Email: trainee.recruit@slaughterandmay.com (enquiries only)
Website: www.slaughterandmay.com

Firm profile

One of the most prestigious law firms in the world, Slaughter and May enjoys a reputation for quality and expertise. The corporate, commercial and financing practice is particularly strong and lawyers are known for their business acumen and technical excellence. As well as its London, Paris, Brussels and Hong Kong offices, in order that the firm provides the best advice and service across the world, it nurtures long-standing relationships with the leading independent law firms in other jurisdictions.

Main areas of work

Corporate, commercial and financing; tax; competition; financial regulation; dispute resolution; technology, media and telecommunications; intellectual property; commercial real estate; environment; pensions and employment.

Trainee profile

The work is demanding and the firm looks for intellectual agility and the ability to work with people from different countries and walks of life. Common sense, the ability to communicate clearly and the willingness to accept responsibility are all essential. The firm expects to provide training in everything except the fundamental principles of law, so does not expect applicants to know much of commercial life. Trainees are expected to remain with the firm on qualification.

Training environment

Four or five seats of three or six months duration. Two seats will be in the field of corporate, commercial and financing law with an option to choose a posting overseas (either to one of the firm's offices or to a "best friend" firm), or competition or financial regulation. One seat in either dispute resolution, intellectual property, tax or pensions and employment is part of the programme and a commercial real estate seat is also possible. In each seat a partner is responsible for monitoring your progress and reviewing your work. There is an extensive training programme which includes the PSC. There are also discussion groups covering general and specialised legal topics.

Benefits

BUPA, STL, pension scheme, subsidised membership of health club, 24 hour accident cover.

Work experience:

One or two week work experience schemes are available at Easter, Christmas and during the summer period for those considering a career in law. Please visit the website for full details.

Sponsorship & awards

GDL and LPC fees and maintenance grants are paid.

Partners 132
Associates 428
Total Trainees 172

Contact
Charlotte Houghton

Method of application
Online (via website)

Selection procedure
Interview

Application
Training contracts p.a. Approx 95
Applications p.a. 2,000 approx
% interviewed p.a. 25% approx
Required degree grade Good 2:1 ability

Training
Salary (May 2008)
1st year £38,000
2nd year £43,000
Holiday entitlement
25 days p.a.
% of trainees with a
non-law degree Approx 50%
No. of seats available
abroad p.a. Approx 30-40

Post-qualification
Salary (May 2008) £65,000
% of trainees offered job
on qualification (2008) 93%

Overseas offices
Paris, Brussels and Hong Kong, plus "Best Friend" firms in all the major jurisdictions.

Speechly Bircham LLP

6 New Street Square, London, EC4A 3LX
Tel: (020) 7427 6400 Fax: (020) 7427 4456
Website: www.speechlys.com

Partners 67
Assistant Solicitors 121
Total Trainees 18

Contact
Helen Wiggs
Human Resources Manager

Method of application
Application form (available online)

Selection procedure
Interview and psychometric testing

Closing date for 2011
31 July 2009

Application
Training contracts p.a. 10
Applications p.a. 654
% interviewed p.a. 18%
Required degree grade 2:1

Training
Salary
1st year
£32,000-33,000
2nd year
£34,000-£35,000
Holiday entitlement 23 days

Post-qualification
Salary (2008) £58,000
Holiday entitlement 25 days

Firm profile

Speechly Bircham is a City law firm that provides a distinctive blend of advisory, transactional and disputes services in its six core areas of practice: construction, corporate, employment, IP, technology and commercial, private client and real estate. With over 200 lawyers, the firm acts for UK and international listed companies, banks and financial institutions, privately owned companies as well as high net worth individuals, families and trusts.

The firm's several discrete practice groups have an acknowledged reputation and performance which are competitive with those of larger firms. The structure of the firm and its ability to provide partner time and attention make it a good alternative to large City firms for many clients. The legal affairs of each client are managed by a single Partner, responsible for ensuring that the service is delivered quickly and cost effectively.

Much of the firm's work has an international dimension, whether for UK clients doing business overseas, supervising and co-ordinating the work of foreign law firms, or advising overseas clients with business and financial interests in the UK.

Main areas of work

Speechly Bircham's principal practice areas are: banking and finance, charities, commercial litigation, construction and engineering, corporate, corporate tax, employment, family, financial services, IP, technology and commercial, pensions, private client, private equity, property litigation and real estate.

Trainee profile

Both law and non-law graduates who are capable of achieving a 2:1 degree. The firm seeks intellectual individuals who enjoy a collaborative working environment where they can make an impact.

Training environment

Speechly Bircham's trainees are regarded as a highly valued part of the team and play an integral role to the future development of the firm. Emphasis is given to early responsibility and supervised client contact providing trainees with a practical learning environment. Training contracts are divided into four six-month seats.

Benefits

Season ticket loan; private medical insurance; life assurance; stakeholder pension scheme, 23 days holiday rising to 25 days on qualification.

Vacation placements

Places for 2009: 20. The firm's summer placement scheme for students gives them the chance to experience a City legal practice. In a three-week placement, students will undertake real fee-earning work, which is likely to include research, drafting letters, attending clients meetings and going to court. As part of the end of scheme assessment process, students will be asked to research and present on a current topical issue and to sit a psychometric test. Duration: 3 weeks; Remuneration: £275 p.w; Closing Date: 13 February 2009.

Sponsorship & awards

GDL and LPC fees paid in full together with a maintenance grant.

Stephens Scown

Curzon House, Southernhay West, Exeter, EX1 1RS
Tel: (01392) 210700 Fax: (01392) 274010
Email: personnel@stephens-scown.co.uk
Website: www.stephens-scown.co.uk

Firm profile

Founded in 1935, Stephens Scown today is one of the leading specialist lawyers operating in the mining and mineral extraction industry in the UK and is also a leader in many other specialisms. The firm continues to climb the annual top 150 League of West Country businesses and is quoted as being 'one of the most active corporate firms in the region' in the Western Morning News Deals Review. The firm's heart is in Devon and Cornwall with significant involvement in the local community, but expansion into Dorset and Somerset are on the cards.

Main areas of work

Corporate: strengths include public funding, mineral extraction issues, insolvency, employment and corporate restructuring. The team has had its brush with celebrity this year, advising on deals coming from the BBC's Dragons' Den programme.
Property: strong Commercial and Residential Property Teams which are supported by separate specialists in planning and environment.
Litigation and Dispute Resolution: broad range of contractual and property litigation, professional negligence, financial services, education law and intellectual property issues.
Family: the firm has a busy and successful team with an enviable reputation, especially in high-net-worth divorce and related financial topics.
Private Client: the firm provides a full range of services to clients, including personal injury, residential property, remortgage, tax, trust and probate advice.

Trainee profile

The firm welcomes applications from candidates who have achieved - or are on a course for at least a 2:1 (or equivalent) degree, ideally with some practical experience and who are enthusiastic, ambitious and committed. Candidates are chosen on the basis that they are the future of the firm and that is why the retention rate post qualification is virtually 100%.

Training environment

The firm's inclusive team structure means that, as a valued team member, you will work alongside an experienced fee earner who will provide support through mentoring, monitoring and delegation of work. Through the firm's key practice areas you will have the opportunity to gain broad experience and to enhance and expose your skills to a variety of different work. The firm will consult with you throughout your training to ensure the programme is tailored to your needs and those of the business. Your hands-on experience will be complemented by formal personal development and business learning. It is not just about becoming a great lawyer. You also have to be commercially minded to progress within the firm and provide clients with business and commercially-focused advice. The firm's unique Marketing Group for trainees will give you the opportunity to be actively involved in marketing and business development activities from the word go, whilst strengthening business relationships with other professionals in the region.

Benefits

Stephens Scown has ambitious plans to be one of the largest firms in the South West. The firm offers a competitive trainee salary and benefits package. The location of its offices in Exeter, Truro and St Austell means it is close to some of the area's most beautiful countryside and beaches, with its regional city positions offering a wide choice of social, sporting and leisure activities. As a trainee with Stephens Scown, therefore, you can enjoy the prospect of a rewarding career and an uncompromised lifestyle.

Sponsorship & awards

From 2009 the firm is offering financial support to trainees for the LPC.

Partners 35
Associates 9
Total Trainees 9
Contact personnel@stephens-scown.co.uk
Method of application CV and application form
Selection procedure interview and worked based assessment
Application Required degree grade 2:1
Training Salary (September 2008) 1st year £19,500 2nd year £20,500 Holiday entitlement 23 days (and public holidays)
Post-qualification % of trainees offered job on qualification (2008) 100%

Stephenson Harwood

One St Paul's Churchyard, London EC4M 8SH
Tel: (020) 7809 2812 Fax: (020) 7003 8263
Email: graduate.recruitment@shlegal.com
Website: www.shlegal.com/graduate

Firm profile

Established in the City of London in 1828, Stephenson Harwood was the overall winner at the 2006 Association of Graduate Recruiters Awards, an independent national voice for all employers involved in graduate recruitment. The firm was praised for its entire campaign as well as being singled out for the prize for best literature. Stephenson Harwood has developed into a large international practice, with a commercial focus and a wide client base.

Main areas of work

Corporate (including corporate finance, funds, corporate tax, business technology); employment, pensions and banking and finance; dry and wet shipping litigation; commercial litigation; and real estate.

Trainee profile

The firm looks for high calibre graduates with excellent academic records, business awareness and excellent communication skills.

Training environment

As the graduate intake is relatively small, the firm gives trainees individual attention, coaching and monitoring. Your structured and challenging programme involves four six month seats in areas of the firm covering contentious and non-contentious areas, across any department within the firm's practice groups. These seats include 'on the job' training and you will share an office with a partner or senior associate. In-house lectures complement your training and there is continuous review of your career development. You will have the opportunity to spend six months abroad and have free language tuition where appropriate. You will be given your own caseload and as much responsibility as you can shoulder. The firm plays a range of team sports, offers subsidised membership of a City health club (or a health club of your choice) and has privileged seats for concerts at the Royal Albert Hall and access to private views at the Tate Gallery.

Benefits

Subsidised membership of health clubs, private health insurance, BUPA membership, season ticket loan and 25 days paid holiday per year.

Vacation placements

Places for 2008: 40; Duration: 1-2 weeks; Remuneration: £260 p.w.; Closing Date: 12th November for Christmas and for Easter, and 15th February 2009 for Summer.

Sponsorship & awards

Fees paid for CPE and LPC and maintenance awards (if still studying).

Partners 84*
Assistant Solicitors 156*
Total Trainees 31
* denotes world-wide figures

Contact
Ushma Patel (Graduate Recruitment)

Method of application
Online application form only

Selection procedure
assessment centre
closing date for
Sept/March 2010/2011
31st July 2009

Application
Training contracts p.a. 12
% interviewed p.a. 40%
Required degree grade 2:1

Training
Salary
1st year (2007) £35,000
2nd year (2007) £40,000
Holiday entitlement 25 days
% of trainees with a
non-law degree p.a. 50%
No. of seats available
abroad p.a. 8

Post-qualification
Salary (2007) £63,500
% of trainees offered job
on qualification (2008) 89%

Overseas offices
Paris, Piraeus, Singapore, Guangzhou, Hong Kong, Shanghai

Associated offices
Greece, South Africa, Kuwait, Croatia, France, Bucharest

Stevens & Bolton LLP

The Billings, Guildford, Surrey GU1 4YD
Tel: (01483) 302264 Fax: (01483) 302254
Email: gradrec@stevens-bolton.co.uk
Website: www.stevens-bolton.co.uk

Firm profile

Stevens & Bolton LLP is a major force in the south east region and the firm's reputation is growing nationally. The firm's vision is to be the South's top independent law firm – and a great place to work. In 2008 the firm was named Corporate Law Firm of the Year at the Insider Dealmakers South East awards for the second year running.

Clients include mid-tier businesses (whether quoted or owner managed), household name PLCs and other major international groups and high net worth private clients. Bunzl plc, Hanson Limited, Philips Electronics, Rentokil Initial plc and SABMiller plc are examples of well known companies and brands that entrust their legal work to us.

The firm is a full service law firm and particular features of its approach to client service include the responsiveness of lawyers and strength in depth in all key areas; an emphasis on sound, practical advice aimed at achieving clients' commercial objectives; open, collaborative and friendly relationships with clients and a constructive approach with other advisers; a continuing investment in know how, training and technology to enhance the value of the firm's services. Increasingly the firm's work involves an international element and the firm has established relationships with overseas firms in key jurisdictions.

The firm has a number of active groups so that everyone is able to contribute ideas in areas such as marketing, profile raising, 'greening the office' and corporate and social responsibility.

Main areas of work

Corporate and commercial, real estate, dispute resolution, employment pensions and immigration, tax & trust, private client and family.

Trainee profile

The firm would like to hear from you if you have (or expect) a 2:1 or first class degree. Just as important is the kind of person you are. Tell us about your motivations, achievements, interests and hobbies – what gets you out of bed in the morning? Initiative is a quality that the firm looks for too, so think about situations you have been in where your involvement has made a real difference.

Training environment

Usually you will sit with a Partner who will act as your supervisor and you will get real responsibility early on. You will see first hand that the quality of the service the firm provides is on a par with national and City firms. Your training with the firm will see you working for six months at a time in four different areas of the firm. One seat will be corporate and commercial plus three others from real estate, dispute resolution, employment pensions and immigration, tax and trust and family. The majority of the firm's trainees go on and qualify into their chosen areas of work in the firm.

Benefits

Private medical insurance, life assurance, pension, rail or car park season ticket loan, permanent health insurance and 25 days holiday.

Sponsorship & awards

Providing no local authority grant is available, full fees for the GDL and LPC plus a £4,000 maintenance grant for each course.

Vacation placements

The firm runs a placement scheme, each summer. Please see the firm's website for further details.

Partners 30	
Associates 45	
Total Trainees 8	
Contact	
Julie Bounden	
(01483) 302264	
Method of application	
Online application form	
available from website	
Selection procedure	
Two interviews & other	
processes	
Closing date for 2011	
30 September 2009	
Application	
Training contracts p.a. 4	
Applications p.a. 60	
% interviewed 13%	
Required degree grade 2:1	
Training	
Salary	
1st year (2008) £25,500	
2nd year (2008) £27,500	
Holiday entitlement 25 days	
Post-qualification	
Salary (2008) £43,500	
Overseas/regional offices	
Guildford only	

Taylor Wessing LLP

Current: Carmelite, 50 Victoria Embankment, Blackfriars London EC4Y 0DX
Tel: (020) 7300 7000   Fax: (020) 7300 7100
Website: www.taylorwessing.com

November 2008: 5 New Street Square, London, EC4 3TW

Firm profile

Taylor Wessing offers a full service to its clients providing a powerful source of legal support for commercial organisations doing business in Europe and the emerging markets in Asia and the Middle East. The firm's clients include large and medium size, private and public companies, financial institutions, professional service firms, public sector bodies and wealthy individuals. The firm offers industry-focused advice by grouping together lawyers from different legal areas with in-depth sector experience. The firm's core industries include banking, construction, engineering, fashion, finance, healthcare, infrastructure, leisure, life sciences, media and entertainment, information technology and telecommunications and projects.

Taylor Wessing is based primarily in the three largest economies in Europe, and has offices in other countries, including China where the firm's Shanghai office serves a thriving Chinese market and its Beijing office, which opens in September 2008, as well as Dubai, which opened at the start of 2008. Clients also have the added benefit of the firm's wide network of partner law firms. In Germany, it is one of the leading law firms, with a team of more than 300 lawyers.

Main areas of work

The firm's core services underpin the main areas of business activity including: corporate transactions and restructuring, finance, tax, property and construction, intellectual property, commercial contracts, employment and employee benefits, dispute resolution and private client advice.

Trainee profile

High intellectual ability is paramount - the firm seeks a minimum of ABB grades at A level and a 2.1 degree in any discipline. It looks for team players with the potential to build relationships with clients and who have a desire to take on responsibility and make a real impact on the firm's business. Excellent communication skills, energy, ambition, an open mind and a willingness to learn are also key attributes along with the ability to demonstrate a commitment to a career in law.

Training environment

As part of your training programme, you will spend six months in four different practice groups, including a contentious seat and another in the firm's corporate area. There are also secondment opportunities to other offices or one of the clients. All our trainees work closely with a number of partners and associates in the practice groups so you will be directly involved in high quality work from the outset. Throughout your training contract you will have ongoing discussions about your interests and how they fit in with the growth and needs of the firm. There is support every step of the way, with regular feedback and appraisals in the middle and at the end of each seat.

Not forgetting the essential Professional Skills Course, which is run in-house, along with other training courses as necessary during the two years.

Benefits

Private medical care, permanent health insurance, life assurance, season ticket loan, pension scheme and employee assistance programme.

Vacation placements

Places for 2009: 40; Duration: 2 weeks; Remuneration: £275 per week; Closing date: 31 January 2009.

Sponsorship & awards

GDL and LPC fees sponsored. A Maintenance grant of £7,000 per annum is provided.

Partners 285
Fee-earners 395
Trainees 48 (UK)

Contact
Graduate Recruitment
Department

Method of application
Online application form

Selection procedure
Assessment Centre to include interview with a partner and a member of human resources, group exercise and psychometric test

Closing date for 2011
31 July 2009

Application
Training contracts p.a. 24
Applications p.a. 1,200
% interviewed p.a. 10%
Required degree grade 2:1

Training
Salary
1st year £35,000
2nd year £39,000
Holiday entitlement 25 days
% of trainees with a non-law degree p.a. 40%

Post-qualification
Salary £63,500
% of trainees offered jobs on qualification (2008) 96%

Overseas offices
Beijing, Berlin, Brussels, Dubai Dusseldorf, Frankfurt, Hamburg, Munich, Paris and representative offices in Alicante and Shanghai.

Teacher Stern LLP

37-41 Bedford Row, London WC1R 4JH
Tel: (020) 7242 3191 Fax: (020) 7197 8010
Email: r.raphael@teacherstern.com
Website: www.teacherstern.com

Firm profile

A central London-based general commercial firm, with clientele and caseload normally attributable to larger firms. It has a wide range of contacts overseas.

Main areas of work

Commercial litigation 25%; commercial property 41%; company and commercial 23%; secured lending 9%; private client 2%.

Trainee profile

Emphasis falls equally on academic excellence and personality. The firm looks for flexible and motivated individuals, who have outside interests and who have demonstrated responsibility in the past.

Training environment

Eight months in three departments (corporate commercial, litigation and property). Most trainees are assigned to actively assist a partner who monitors and supports them. Trainees are fully involved in departmental work and encouraged to take early responsibility. Trainees are expected to attend in-house seminars and lectures for continuing education. The atmosphere is relaxed and informal.

Vacation placements

Places for 2009: Approximately 25 places to those that have applied for training contracts.

Sponsorship & awards

Considered.

Partners 21
Assistant Solicitors 20
Total Trainees 7

Contact
Russell Raphael

Method of application
Online application

Selection procedure
2 interviews

Closing date for 2011
31 July 2009

Application
Training contracts p.a. 3
Applications p.a. 500
% interviewed p.a. 5%
Required degree grade
2:1 (not absolute)

Training
Salary
1st year (2011) £32,000
Holiday entitlement
25 days
% of trainees with a
non-law degree p.a. 50%

Post-qualification
Salary (2008) £50,000
% of trainees offered job
on qualification (2008) 75%
% of assistants (who joined as
trainees 45%
% of partners who joined as
trainees 50%

Thomas Eggar

The Corn Exchange, Baffins Lane, Chichester PO19 1GE
Tel: (01243) 813156
Email: mick.cassell@thomaseggar.com
Website: www.thomaseggar.com

Firm profile

Thomas Eggar is one of the top 100 law firms in the UK. Based in the South East, it is one of the country's leading regional law firms with a staff of over 600. The firm offers both private client and commercial services to a diverse range of clients, locally, nationally and internationally. It also offers financial services through Thesis, the firm's investment management arm, which is the largest solicitor-based investment unit in the UK.

Main areas of work

Apart from its strength in the private client sector, the firm handles property, commercial and litigation matters; among its major clients are banks, building societies and other financial institutions, railway and track operators and construction companies, football clubs and sports personalities.

Trainee profile

The firm seeks very able trainees who exhibit good business acumen, with a 2.1 degree in any discipline. Applications can be made up to 1 August 2009 for training contracts to commence in September 2011. Applications should be online. You should give details of your attachment to the South East region in your online application. The online application is www.apply4law.com/thomaseggar.

Training environment

Trainees would normally have four seats covering commercial property, commercial, litigation and private client. In order to give good exposure to various specialisations, some of the seats are likely to be in different offices.

Vacation placements

There is a limited summer placement scheme in July and August each year: this runs for five days and can be within any one of our locations. Applications should be made online. Please give details of your accommodation plans in your application. Travel expenses are paid.

Sponsorship & awards

LPC 50% grant, 50% loan.

Vacancies 11
Partners 68
Trainees 22
Total Staff 600

Contact
Mick Cassell

Method of application
On-line
www.apply4law.com/thomaseggar

Selection procedure
CV, assessment centre and interview

Closing date for 2011
1 August 2009

Training
The firm aims to pay the going rate for a South Eastern regional firm. A London weighting is paid to those who undertake seats in the London office.
Required degree grade
2:1 (any discipline)

Other offices
Chichester, Gatwick, London, Worthing, Newbury, Southampton

Thomson Snell & Passmore

3 Lonsdale Gardens, Tunbridge Wells, Kent TN1 1NX
Tel: (01892) 510000 Fax: (01892) 549884
Email: solicitors@ts-p.co.uk
Website: www.ts-p.co.uk

Firm profile

Thomson Snell & Passmore continues to be regarded as one of the premier law firms in the South East. The firm has a reputation for quality and a commitment to deliver precise and clear advice which is recognised and respected both by its clients and professional contacts. It has held the Lexcel quality mark since January 1999. The firm is vibrant and progressive and enjoys an extremely friendly atmosphere. Its offices are located in the centre of Tunbridge Wells and attract clients locally, nationally and internationally.

Main areas of work

Corporate and commercial 10%; employment 5%; dispute resolution 11%; commercial property 11%; residential property 9%; private client 27%; clinical negligence/ personal injury 18%; family 8%.

Trainee profile

Thomson Snell & Passmore regards its trainees from the outset as future assistants, associates and partners. The firm is looking for people not only with strong intellectual ability, but enthusiasm, drive, initiative, strong interpersonal and team-working skills.

Training environment

The firm's induction course will help you to adjust to working life. As a founder member of Law South your training is provided in-house with trainees from other Law South member firms. Your two-year training contract is divided into four periods of six months each. You will receive a thorough grounding and responsibility with early client exposure. You will be monitored regularly, receive advice and assistance throughout and appraisals every three months. The Training Partner will co-ordinate your continuing education in the law, procedure, commerce, marketing, IT and presentation skills. Trainees enjoy an active social life which is encouraged and supported.

Sponsorship & awards

Grant and interest free loan available for LPC.

Partners 38
Solicitors 46
Total Trainees 10

Contact
Human Resources Manager
Tel: (01892) 510000

Method of application
On-line application form
available from website

Selection procedure
Assessment interview

Closing date for 2011
31 July 2009

Application
Training contracts p.a. 5
Applications p.a.
Approximately 500
% interviewed p.a. 5%
Required degree grade
2:1 (any discipline)

Training
Competitive regional salary
Holiday entitlement 25 days

Post-qualification
% of trainees offered job
on qualification 100%

Overseas/regional offices
Network of independent law
firms throughout Europe and
founding member of Law
South

Thring Townsend Lee & Pembertons

6 Drakes Meadow, Penny Lane, Swindon, SN3 3LL
Tel: (01793) 410 800 Fax: (01793) 539 040
Email: solicitors@ttuk.com   Website: www.ttuk.com

Firm profile

With offices across the South West and London, employing nearly 400 staff, Thring Townsend Lee & Pembertons has built a sustainable, growing and successful law business by balancing its commercial and private practices with a strong sector speciality in agriculture. The firm has an impressive national and international client base.

The commitment from the management of the firm to employees, their career development and non-legal skills training has led to an open and friendly culture and a vibrant work ethic.

Main areas of work

Agriculture: believed to be the largest stand-alone, specialist Agriculture Team in the country as well as legal panel solicitors for the NFU in the South East. Commercial property: one of the largest teams in Southern England with an excellent reputation for specialist areas of work. Corporate and Commercial: acting for a wide variety of clients including many national and international household names. Litigation: a substantial practice with specialists in commercial litigation and claimant professional negligence work. The Insolvency and Corporate Recovery Department is one of the largest in the region and is attracting diverse and complex quality work. Personal Injury: a niche practice specialising in catastrophic brain and spinal injuries and industrial disease claims. Family: one of the largest family teams in the region with specialist expertise in collaborative law, civil partnerships and divorce for farmers and business owners. Wills and Probate, Tax and Trusts: specialising in sophisticated capital tax planning, private family trusts, heritage property, business assets and landed estates. Private Property: advising individuals and companies including investment landlords and clients who are resident abroad.

Trainee profile

The firm wants confident, well-rounded individuals who are pro-active, dedicated and commercially aware. The firm expects a minimum 2:1 degree and strong A-levels but we are open to applicants with a 2:2 degree who perhaps have something else to offer.

Training environment

A dynamic learning environment with an equal mix of structure and flexibility to cater for individual needs and career goals.

A structured two-year training contract split into four six-month seats. Trainees gain experience within at least three different practice areas including contentious and non-contentious.

In addition, the firm offers: dedicated partner supervisor; mid-seat and end-seat appraisal feedback; client management skills development; training courses; social events; competitive salary and benefits package.

Benefits

Three extra concessionary days holiday. Private medical insurance. Private healthcare. Subsidised restaurants. Life Assurance. Paid professional memberships and subscriptions.

Sponsorship & awards

Not currently offered.

Partners 55
Assistant Solicitors 65
Total Trainees 15

Contact
Pat Mapstone (01793) 412 502

Method of application
application form and CV

Selection procedure
1st and 2nd stage interviews, 2nd comprising an interview with Partner and senior solicitor

Closing date for 2011
31 July 2009

Application
Training contracts p.a. 9
Applications p.a. 300
% interviewed p.a. 10%
Required degree grade
2:1 preferred

Training
Salary: £22,000 (1st year)
        £24,000 (2nd year)
Holiday entitlement
25 days

Post-qualification
Salary (2008) £34,000
% of trainees offered job
on qualification 80%

Overseas/regional offices
Bath, Bristol, Cirencester,
London, Marlborough, Swindon

TLT Solicitors

One Redcliff St, Bristol BS1 6TP
Tel: (0117) 917 7777 Fax: (0117) 917 7649
Email: bee.yazdani@TLTsolicitors.com   Website: www.TLTsolicitors.com

Firm profile

TLT is built around the needs of its clients and is described by industry commentators as 'the firm to watch'. TLT remains one of the fastest-growing law firms in the UK and on 1 June 2007 London-based commercial law firm Constant & Constant joined TLT, representing the latest move in the firm's 12-month investment strategy. Turnover has risen threefold since 2002. Headcount has increased to 650. Growth for the firm provides the resources to be able to support its clients.

A high percentage of the firm's lawyers are identified as true experts in their respective fields and behind their legal advice is an insight and understanding of the commercial challenges clients face. The firm encourages and supports involvement in the wider community, which includes 'pro bono' legal advice to a variety of charities and TLT staff volunteering.

Main areas of work

TLT is an award winning, full-service, UK law firm. It concentrates on providing industry focused multi-discipline integrated solutions. The firm's leading strengths are in the financial services and leisure sectors. Other chosen markets include retail, the built environment and technology and media. Constant & Constant is the maritime division of TLT. TLT's core legal specialisms are real estate, banking and finance, commercial, corporate, employment, dispute resolution and litigation. Client services are provided through dedicated, cross-firm specialist teams including banking and asset finance, construction, debt recovery (on behalf of lenders), environmental, insolvency and turnaround, IT and IP, total reward, property development, leisure, licensing, regulatory, retail, maritime and international trade, social housing and tax.

Trainee profile

TLT looks for talented people with a strong academic background together with the commitment and drive to succeed.

Training environment

TLT's commitment to excellence will ensure that trainees benefit from a well developed and challenging training programme. Training is delivered through four seats of six months duration, chosen in consultation with the trainee. In each seat the trainee will sit with a lawyer although their work will be drawn from all members of the team in order to gain the widest possible experience. Regular monitoring and development planning ensures that trainees get the most out of their training and helps them to identify their long term career path from the varied specialisms on offer.

Benefits

Pension, private medical insurance, life assurance and subsidised sports/health club membership, 25 days holiday entitlement, flexible benefits launching on 1st September 2008.

Vacation placements

40 paid placements available, each lasting one week. One week at Easter and three over Summer. Apply online by 31 January each year.

Sponsorship & awards

CPE and LPC fees plus maintenance grant.

Partners 72
Fee earners 300
Total Trainees 20

Contact
Human Resources

Method of application
online application form via
www.TLTcareers.com/trainee

Selection interview
Assessment Centre
closing date for training
contracts
31 July each year

Application
Training contracts p.a. up to 20
Applications p.a. 700+
% interviewed p.a. 12%
Required degree grade
2:1 or above
non-law degree p.a. 17%

Training
Salary: £27,000 (1st year)
        £28,000 (2nd year)
Holiday entitlement 25 days

Post-qualification
Market rate

Offices
Bristol, London, Piraeus

Travers Smith LLP

10 Snow Hill, London EC1A 2AL
Tel: (020) 7295 3000 Fax: (020) 7295 3500
Email: graduate.recruitment@traverssmith.com
Website: www.traverssmith.com

Firm profile

A leading City firm with a major Corporate and Commercial Practice. Although less than a quarter of the size of the dozen largest firms, they handle the highest quality work, much of which has an international dimension.

Main areas of work

Corporate law (including takeovers and mergers, financial services and regulatory laws), commercial law (which includes commercial contracts, IT and intellectual property), litigation, corporate recovery/insolvency, tax, employment, EU/competition, pensions, banking and real estate. The firm also offers a range of pro bono opportunities within individual departments and on a firm wide basis. The firm also carries out commercial work for a number of UK charities.

Trainee profile

The firm looks for people who combine academic excellence with common sense; who are articulate, who think on their feet, who are determined and self motivated and who take their work but not themselves seriously. Applications are welcome from law and non-law graduates.

Training environment

Travers Smith has earned a phenomenal reputation in relation to its size. The work they undertake is exciting, intellectually demanding and top quality involving blue-chip clients and big numbers. This means that their trainees gain great experience right from the outset.

The firm has a comprehensive training programme which ensures that trainees experience a broad range of work. All trainee solicitors sit in rooms with partners and assistants, receive an individual and extensive training from experienced lawyers and enjoy client contact and the responsibility that goes with it from the beginning of their training contract.

Benefits

Private health insurance, permanent health insurance, life assurance, corporate health club membership, subsidised bistro, season ticket loan.

Vacation placements

Summer 2009: 3 schemes with 15 places on each; Duration: two weeks; Remuneration: £250; Closing Date: 31 January 2009. The firm also offers a two week Christmas scheme for 15 students.

Sponsorship & awards

GDL and LPC paid in full plus maintenance of £7,000 per annum to those in London and £6,500 per annum to those outside of London.

Partners 66
Assistant Solicitors 187
Total Trainees 41

Contact
Germaine VanGeyzel

Method of application
CV and covering letter online
or by post

Selection procedure
Interviews (2 stage process)

Closing date for 2011
31 July 2009

Application
Training contracts p.a. 25
Applications p.a. 2,000
% interviewed p.a. 15%
Required degree grade 2:1

Training
Salary
1st year (2008) £36,000
2nd year (2008) £40,000
Holiday entitlement 25 days

Post-qualification
Salary (2008) £64,000
% of trainees offered job
on qualification (2008) 90%

Trethowans

The Director General's House, 15 Rockstone Place, Southampton, SO15 2EP
Tel: 023 8032 1000   Fax: 023 8032 1001
Email: kate.lemont@trethowans.com   Web: www.trethowans.com

Firm profile

Trethowans is a major law firm in the South, advising business and individual clients and has over 150 people, including 25 partners and 76 lawyers across offices in Salisbury and Southampton. The firm represents international and national household brand names, owner-managed businesses, entrepreneurs and major regional employers across the UK. The firm's teams work for clients in a variety of market sectors including charities, construction, distribution, education, engineering, finance, insurance, IT, leisure, manufacturing, motor, NHS, pensions, property development, professionals, retail and transport. Service excellence is a priority - clients value the firm's ability to deliver top-quality, expert advice, on time, in a very personable manner and at a competitive price. May 2008 saw the move to purpose-built premises in Salisbury with continued strong growth in Southampton.

Main areas of work

The firm's business lawyers, who specialise in different areas of the law, work together to regularly advise international and national household brand names, owner-managed, entrepreneurial and major regional employers across the UK, Hampshire and Wiltshire. Four of the firm's six teams that advise business clients are rated in the two independent guides to the legal profession, Chambers Guide to the Legal Profession and Legal 500. Legal advice to businesses include: corporate, commercial, commercial property, commercial litigation, employment and licensing.

For individuals who require help for personal matters, the firm's teams of expert lawyers deliver advice in a down-to-earth and approachable manner. It is here that the 'Trethowans' personality is particularly beneficial so that individual clients can meet the 'real person' behind the lawyer. Four of the firm's five teams that advise individual clients are also rated in Chambers Guide to the Legal Profession and Legal 500. Legal advice to individuals include: personal injury, private client (Wills, trusts and tax), landed estates, family and residential property.

Trainee profile

Trainees should possess sound academic abilities and be able to demonstrate commercial acumen. Flexibility, ambition and enthusiasm are valued. Candidates should be good communicators and adopt a problem solving approach to client work.

Training environment

Trainee solicitors normally undertake four separate specialist seats, each lasting six months. The firm offers a flexible approach in deciding trainees' seats to suit individual needs, while providing a broad training programme in accordance with the Law Society's guidelines. Trainees have their own desks and work closely with the supervising fee-earner/Partner to whom they are responsible. They are considered an integral part of each team and become closely involved in the department's work to obtain first-hand legal experience. Each trainee is appraised every six months by their supervisor and the Training Partner. This enables the trainee scheme to be continually evaluated and also ensures that the highest possible standards are maintained. Prospects for trainees are excellent, most trainees are offered a post as an assistant solicitor at the end of their training contract.

Benefits

Incremental holiday entitlement up to 28 days, contributory pension scheme, death in service benefit, PHI scheme, performance-related bonus scheme, car parking, new staff recruitment bonus, childcare voucher scheme.

Sponsorship and awards

Course fees paid for LPC

Partners 25	
Assistant Solicitors 24	
Total Trainees 7	

Contact
Kate Lemont
023 8082 0503

Method of application
Applications by application form (available online) and covering letter

Selection procedure
Two stage process; interview and assessment day

Closing date for 2011
31 July 2009

Application
Training contracts p.a. 3-4
Applications p.a. 100+
% interviewed p.a. 20%
Required degree grade
2:1

Training
Salary: in excess of Law Society minimum
Holiday entitlement 23 days

Post-qualification
Market rate
% of trainees offered position on qualification 85%

Regional offices
Salisbury, Southampton

TRETHOWANS

Trowers & Hamlins

Sceptre Court, 40 Tower Hill, London EC3N 4DX
Tel: (020) 7423 8000 Fax: (020) 7423 8001
Email: hking@trowers.com   Website: www.trowers.com

Firm profile

Awarded the prestigious title of Law firm of the Year at the 2007 Lawyer awards was a fantastic achievement for Trowers & Hamlins. However, proving that it is possible to combine great business acumen with a social conscience the firm also placed third in the Pro Bono Firm of the Year category and was named winner in the Economic Regeneration category of the Dragon Awards 2007 in recognition of the work undertaken within the local area. Combine this with achieving 52nd place in the 2008 Sunday Times Best Companies report and you will see a firm committed to giving excellent service, supporting the local community and providing a supportive environment with an emphasis on organic growth and developmental opportunities.

Main areas of work

The training contract is split into four six month seats. Offering secondment opportunities in the Middle East, Manchester and Exeter alongside seats in departments ranging from Social Housing to Corporate to Litigation, it is not surprising that trainees gain a varied and interesting experience. Trainees are paired with either a senior solicitor or Partner acting as their supervisor to ensure that a suitable level of supervision is provided. Assessment takes place constantly with trainees completing both a mid seat and end of seat appraisal, providing the opportunity to gain feedback and continuously progress.

Responsibility is given from a very early stage with trainees in some departments running files on their own on joining the department. Trainees are encouraged to take as autonomous a role as is possible safe in the knowledge that there is a structured support system in place to provide assistance should they require it .

Training forms an integral part of the training contract with trainee solicitors receiving departmental training every week as part of the Monday Lunchtime Training Programme. In addition to this, further training is provided covering vital skills such as presentation technique and negotiation practice.

All trainees are assigned a mentor from the commencement of their training contracts to provide impartial work and career advice. In addition to this the Trainee Solicitors' Committee comprising the Training Principal, Partners, HR and two trainee representatives meet bi-monthly to discuss trainee issues and providing the trainees with a forum to voice their thoughts.

Trainee profile

The firm recruits twenty-two trainees each year split equally into September and March intakes. The firm is of course looking for an excellent academic record but in addition to this recognises that there are supplementary skills required and actively seek out candidates with exceptional commercial awareness, outstanding communication skills and a genuine passion for the law. Trainee solicitors are all individuals and the firm is genuinely committed to maintaining a diverse workforce as evidenced in its recent 13th place positioning in the recent league table of diversity conducted by the Law Society on behalf of the Black Solicitors' Network and the Commission for Racial Equality.

Vacation placements

Application is via an online application which can be found at www.trowers.com. The deadline for vacation placement applications is 1 March and for training contracts commencing in September 2010 and March 2011 applications should be submitted by 1 August.

Partners 106
Assistant Solicitors 179
Total Trainees 39

Contact
Hannah King, Graduate
Recruitment Officer

Method of application
Online application form

Selection procedure
Assessment centre, interviews, psychometric tests & practical test

Closing date for 2011
1 August 2009

Application
Training contracts p.a. 22
Applications p.a. 1,600
% interviewed p.a. 4%
Required degree grade 2:1 or higher

Training
Salary (subject to review)
1st year £35,000
2nd year £38,000
Holiday entitlement 25 days
% of trainees with a
non-law degree p.a. 50%
No. of seats available
abroad p.a. 12

Post-qualification
Salary (2007) £60,000
% of trainees offered job
on qualification (2007) 80%

Offices
London, Exeter, Manchester, Abu Dhabi, Dubai, Oman, Bahrain and Cairo

Veale Wasbrough Lawyers

Orchard Court, Orchard Lane, Bristol, BS1 5WS
Tel: (0117) 925 2020   Fax: (0117) 925 2025
Email: aparfitt@vwl.co.uk
Website: www.vwl.co.uk

Firm profile

Veale Wasbrough is a regional firm with a national presence. The firm's staff of over 260 operate from offices in the heart of Bristol – a vibrant and growing business community. The firm's goal is to help its clients succeed, through high standards, technical expertise, a creative approach and its commitment to its people. Veale Wasbrough is proud to be accredited as a top 100 firm to work for by the Managing Partners Forum, the firm is also Investors in People and Lexcel accredited.

Main areas of work

The firm provides full commercial law services and specialises in five key client sectors: public sector, education and charities, real estate, healthcare and regional corporates. The firm also has two distinctly branded divisions, Augustines Injury Law and Convey Direct.

Trainee profile

The firm recruits 8-10 trainees annually. It is looking for graduates that will become dynamic lawyers, who will make the most of the training opportunities and positively contribute to the future of the firm. Applicants should have proven academic ability, be good team players, with strong communication skills and commercial awareness.

training environment

The firm offers its trainees early responsibility. It provides four seats of six months in a variety of departments, including Augustines injury law, commercial, commercial litigation, corporate, education, employment, private client, projects and real estate. Trainees therefore benefit from experience in a wide range of practice areas. Many of the firm's present Partners and senior lawyers trained with the firm and are now widely respected experts in their chosen field of specialism.

Sponsorship and awards

Successful candidates may be eligible for sponsorship for the Diploma in Law and/or Legal Practice Course, consisting of a grant for LPC fees and an interest-free loan.

Work experience/ schemes

The firm's summer vacation scheme offers a week's work experience, providing an insight into the day to day workings of a large firm of commercial lawyers as students spend time in different legal teams.

Partners 37
Assistant Solicitors 61
Total Trainees 17

Contact
Angela Parfitt, Recruitment Manager

Method of application
Application form on website

Selection procedure
Interview

Closing date for 2011
31 July 2009

Application
Training contracts p.a. 8-10
% interviewed (2008) 15%
Required degree grade
Preferably 2.1

Training
1st year £23,000
2nd year £25,000
Holiday entitlement 25 days plus bank holidays

Post-qualification
Salary £38,000
% of trainees offered job on qualification (2008) 100%

Vinson & Elkins

CityPoint, 33rd Floor, One Ropemaker Street, London, EC2Y 9UE
Tel: (020) 7065 6000   Fax: (020) 7065 6001

Firm profile

Vinson & Elkins is one of the largest international law firms and has been repeatedly ranked as the world's leading energy law firm. Founded in Houston in 1917 (and with an office in London for over 30 years), Vinson & Elkins currently has over 750 lawyers with offices in Abu Dhabi, Austin, Beijing, Dallas, Dubai, Hong Kong, Houston, London, Moscow, New York, Shanghai, Tokyo, Washington, D.C.

Main areas of work

Cross-border M&A, private equity, corporate finance and securities advice (including London Main Market and AIM listings and international equity and debt capital markets), banking and finance, international energy transactions, project development and finance transactions, litigation and arbitration.

Trainee profile

The firm is looking for ambitious individuals with strong academic results and sound commercial awareness. The ability to think laterally and creatively is essential, as is a need for common-sense and a willingness to take the initiative.

Training environment

The firm currently offers three training contracts commencing each September. These are not run on a rigid seat system, but instead a trainee will gain wide experience in many different areas, working with a wide variety of associates and partners from across the firm.

Whilst the trainees are based in London, the firm is currently regularly seconding its trainees to other offices (particularly its offices in Dubai and Moscow).

Benefits

Private medical and dental, pension, season ticket loan, life assurance.

Vacation placements

Vinson & Elkins views vacation placements as a key part of its recruitment process. For summer 2009 apply by 28 February 2009, by way of application form. Please visit the website www.velaw.com to obtain vacation placement application forms.

Sponsorship & awards

The firm pays all LPC course fees and a discretionary stipend (of up to £7,500) to assist with the LPC year.

Partners 8
Assistant Solicitors 14
Total Trainees 7

Contact
Mark Beeley (020) 7065 6046

Method of application
Application form

Selection procedure
Interview

Closing date for 2011
31 August 2009

Application
Training contracts p.a. 3
Applications p.a. 400
% interviewed p.a. 10%
Required degree grade 2:1

Training
Salary
1st year £40,000
2nd year £42,000
Holiday entitlement 25 days
% of trainees with a
non-law degree p.a. 40%
No. of seats available
abroad p.a. 4

Post-qualification
Salary £80,000
% of trainees offered job
on qualification 95%

Overseas, Regional offices
Abu Dhabi, Austin, Beijing,
Dallas, Dubai, Hong Kong,
Houston, London, Moscow,
New York, Shanghai, Tokyo and
Washington D.C.

Walker Morris

Kings Court, 12 King Street, Leeds LS1 2HL
Tel: (0113) 283 2500 Fax: (0113) 245 9412
Email: hellograduates@walkermorris.co.uk
Website: www.walkermorris.co.uk

Firm profile

Based in Leeds, Walker Morris is one of the largest commercial law firms in the North, with over 580 people, providing a full range of legal services to commercial and private clients both nationally and internationally.

Main areas of work

CDR, commercial, commercial property, construction, corporate, employment, finance, intellectual property, insolvency, liquor licensing and gaming, PFI/ public sector, planning and environmental, regulatory, sports, tax.

Trainee profile

Bright, articulate, highly motivated individuals who will thrive on early responsibility in a demanding yet friendly environment.

Training environment

Trainees commence with an induction programme, before spending four months in each main department (commercial property, corporate and commercial litigation). Trainees can choose in which departments they wish to spend their second year. Formal training will include lectures, interactive workshops, seminars and e-learning. The PSC covers the compulsory elements and the electives consist of a variety of specially tailored skills programmes. Individual IT training is provided. Opportunities can also arise for secondments to some of the firm's major clients. Emphasis is placed on teamwork, inside and outside the office. The firm's social and sporting activities are an important part of its culture and are organised by a committee drawn from all levels of the firm. A trainee solicitors' committee represents the trainees in the firm but also organises events and liaises with the Leeds Trainee Solicitors Group.

Vacation placements

Places for 2009: 48 over 3 weeks; Duration: 1 week; Remuneration: £250 p.w.; Closing Date: 31 January 2009.

Sponsorship & awards

LPC & PGDL fees plus maintenance of £5,000.

Partners 51
Assistant Solicitors 130
Total Trainees 38

Contact
Neil Lupton

Method of application
Online application form

Selection procedure
Telephone & face-to-face interviews

Closing date for 2011
31 July 2009

Application
Training contracts p.a. 20
Applications p.a.
Approx. 800
% interviewed p.a.
Telephone 16%
Face to face 8%
Required degree grade 2:1

Training
Salary
1st year (2008) £26,000
2nd year (2008) £28,000
Holiday entitlement 24 days
% of trainees with a
non-law degree p.a.
30% on average

Post-qualification
Salary (2008) £40,000
% of trainees offered job
on qualification (2008) 75%
% of assistants (as at 1/7/08)
who joined as trainees 60%
% of partners (as at 1/7/08)
who joined as trainees 50%

Ward Hadaway

Sandgate House, 102 Quayside, Newcastle upon Tyne NE1 3DX
Tel: (0191) 204 4000 Fax: (0191) 204 4098
Email: recruitment@wardhadaway.com
Website: www.wardhadaway.com

Firm profile

Ward Hadaway is one of the most progressive law firms in the North East and is firmly established as one of the region's heavyweights. The firm attracts some of the most ambitious businesses in the region and its client base includes a large number of plcs, new start-ups and well established private companies.

As a business founded and located in the North East, the firm has grown rapidly, investing heavily in developing its existing people, and recruiting further outstanding individuals from inside and outside of the region. The firm is listed in the top 100 UK law firms.

Main areas of work

The firm is divided into five main departments; litigation, property, corporate, commercial and private client, with a number of cross departmental teams. The firm is commercially based, satisfying the needs of the business community in both business and private life. Clients vary from international plc's to local, private clients. The firm is on a number of panels including; the Arts Council, NHS (four panels), English Heritage, Department of Education and the General Teaching Council.

Trainee profile

The usual academic and professional qualifications are sought. Sound commercial and business awareness are essential as is the need to demonstrate strong communication skills, enthusiasm and flexibility. Candidates will be able to demonstrate excellent interpersonal and analytical skills.

Training environment

The training contract is structured around four seats, each of six months duration. At regular intervals, and each time you are due to change seat, you will have the opportunity to discuss the experience you would like to gain during your training contract. The firm will give high priority to your preferences. You will sit with a Partner or Associate which will enable you to learn how to deal with different situations. Your practical experience will also be complemented by an extensive programme of seminars and lectures. All trainees are allocated a 'buddy', usually a second year trainee or newly qualified solicitor, who can provide as much practical advice and guidance as possible during your training. The firm has an active social committee and offers a full range of sporting and social events.

Benefits

25 days holiday (27 after five years service), death in service insurance, contributory pension, flexible holiday scheme.

Vacation placements

Vacation placements run spring/summer between April and July and are of 1 week's duration. Applications should be received by 28 February 2009.

Sponsorship & awards

CPE GDL and LPC fees paid and maintenance grants in accordance with the terms of the firm's offer.

Partners 57
Total Trainees 21

Contact
Graduate recruitment team

Method of application
firm's application form

Selection procedure
Assessment Centre and interview

Closing date for 2011
31 July 2009

Application
Training contracts p.a. 12
Applications p.a. 400+
% interviewed p.a. 10%
Required degree grade 2:1

Training
Salary
1st year (2008)
£20,500
2nd year (2008) £21,500
Holiday entitlement 25 days
% of trainees with a
non-law degree p.a. Varies

Post-qualification
Salary (2008)
£37,500

Warner Goodman LLP

Portland Chambers, 66 West Street, Fareham, Hampshire, PO16 0JR
Tel: (01329) 288 121 Fax: (01329) 822 714
8/9 College Place, London Road, Southampton, SO15 2FF
Coleman House, 2-4 Landport Terrace, Portsmouth, PO1 2RG
Email: enquiries@warnergoodman.co.uk   Website: www.warnergoodman.co.uk

Firm profile

Warner Goodman LLP is highly regarded in Hampshire as one of the county's most forward thinking and dynamic firms. The firm values its people highly and invests a lot of time in developing and nurturing their many talents. Work-life balance is respected and a flexible approach for those with caring responsibilities helps the firm retain many high performing fee earners. The firm takes particular pride in delivering professional client friendly services across its six legal disciplines. Advances in e-conveyancing, HIPs and paperless transactions are all exemplified at Warner Goodman.

Main areas of work

Conveyancing, Private Client, Personal Injury, Clinical Negligence, Family, Financial Services and WG Commercial which handles all aspects of Employment, Company Commercial, Commercial Litigation, Commercial Property, Landlord and Tenant and Licensing.

Trainee profile

The firm seeks to recruit talented and bright law graduates with a flair for communication and a common sense approach to business. They value an approachable, down to earth attitude. This way they can continue their track record in first-rate client service and can continue to put their clients first. Although law graduates are preferred, the firm's primary focus is on character and intellectual strength, and outstanding graduates of other disciplines are always considered.

Sponsorship & awards

Please see our website.

Partners 15
Total Trainees 3 per year

Contact
Pamela Praine

Method of application
online

Selection procedure
Interview

Closing date for 2011
31 July 2009

Application
Online application form.

Training
Training is provided across the firms three main offices, and covers each of the practice groups. Input from trainees is sought as to their preferred choice of seat

Post-qualification
Continuing Professional Development is promoted throughout the firm. Departmental meetings are regularly held where team members provide updates on their specialist practice areas

Regional offices
Fareham, Southampton, Portsmouth

Watson Burton LLP

1 St James' Gate, Newcastle upon Tyne NE99 1YQ
Tel: (0191) 244 4444 Fax: (0191) 244 4500
Email: enquiries@watsonburton.com
Website: www.watsonburton.com

Firm profile

Watson Burton LLP is one of the top law firms in the North of England with almost 200 years' experience and a well earned reputation for helping its clients succeed. Over the last few years, the firm has grown rapidly, opening an office in Leeds in 2005 and in London in 2006.
During the last 12 months Watson Burton LLP's higher national profile has facilitated the strategic recruitment of new Partners and associates, bringing greater depth to key areas of the firm and attracting major new clients including several plcs.
For the firm's trainees, this represents an exciting time to join the firm, providing you with an opportunity to work across the full range of legal services for a leading law firm that is going places and also has a strong commitment to corporate social responsibility.

Main areas of work

Watson Burton LLP's business is mainly commercial and they have particular strengths in business advice, property services, construction, employment, dispute resolution, debt recovery, professions and insurance, technology, IP and media, corporate finance, education and wealth protection.

Trainee profile

The firm seeks to recruit talented and bright law graduates with a flair for communication and a common sense approach to business. They value an approachable, down to earth attitude. This way they can continue their track record in first-rate client service and can continue to put their clients first. Although law graduates are preferred, the firm's primary focus is on character and intellectual strength, and outstanding graduates of other disciplines are always considered. They have positions in both the Newcastle and Leeds offices and recruit separately to appoint trainees into these positions.

Training environment

The firm provides top-class training from modern office environments in both Leeds and Newcastle. They have the best technology and the right resources to provide a thorough and comprehensive introduction to the law. And they have a vast team of experienced lawyers who you can call on for assistance and guidance where needed. Watson Burton LLP's training programme includes both in-house and external seminars. Trainees are encouraged to assist in the firm's marketing from day one. Alongside careful and regular supervision, they offer trainees a high level of responsibility at an early stage.

Sponsorship & benefits

The firm provides ample study leave, offers paid professional memberships and subscriptions, and give full payment for LPC fees.

Partners 42
Assistant Solicitors 68
Total Trainees 20

Contact
Human Resources
(0191) 244 4444
human.resources@watsonburton.com

Method of application
Application forms are available on the website at www.watsonburton.com Email a completed application to human.resources@watsonburton.com or submit online

Closing date for 2011
31 July 2009

Application
Training contracts p.a. 6
Applications p.a. 500+
% interviewed p.a. 10%
Required degree grade 2:1

Training
Salary
£20,000 rising by £1,500 each completed seat rotation.

Post-qualification
Salary
Not less than £37,000
% of trainees offered job on qualification (2008) 90%

Regional offices
Newcastle, Leeds and London

Watson, Farley & Williams LLP

15 Appold Street, London EC2A 2HB
Tel: (020) 7814 8000 Fax: (020) 7814 8017
Email: graduates@wfw.com
Website: www.wfw.com

Firm profile

Established in 1982, Watson, Farley & Williams has its strengths in corporate, banking and asset finance, particularly ship and aircraft finance. The firm aims to provide a superior service in specialist areas and to build long-lasting relationships with its clients.

Main areas of work

Shipping; ship finance; aviation; banking; asset finance; corporate; litigation; e-commerce; intellectual property; EU/Competition; taxation; property; insolvency; telecoms; project finance.

Trainee profile

Outgoing graduates who exhibit enthusiasm, ambition, self-assurance, initiative and intellectual flair.

Training environment

Trainees are introduced to the firm with a comprehensive induction course covering legal topics and practical instruction. The firm, aiming to provide trainees with a solid commercial grounding. There is also the opportunity to spend time abroad, working on cross-border transactions. Operating in an informal and friendly atmosphere, trainees will receive support whenever necessary. You will be encouraged to take on early responsibility and play an active role alongside a partner at each stage of your training. The practice encourages continuous learning for all employees and works closely with a number of law lecturers, producing a widely-read 'digest' of legal developments, to which trainees are encouraged to contribute. All modules of the PSC are held in-house. The firm has its own sports teams and organises a variety of social functions.

Benefits

Life assurance, PHI, Norwich Union, STL, pension, subsidised gym membership, Employee Assistance Programme.

Vacation placements

Places for 2009: 40; Duration: 2 weeks; Remuneration: £250 p.w.; Closing Date: 22nd February 2009.

Sponsorship & awards

CPE and LPC fees paid and £6,500 maintenance p.a. (£5,500 outside London).

Partners 76
Total fee-earners 220
Total Trainees 26

Contact
Graduate Recruitment Manager

Method of application
Online application

Selection procedure
Assessment centre & Interview

Closing date for 2011
31 July 2009

Application
Training contracts p.a. 12-14
Applications p.a. 1,000
% interviewed p.a. 20-30%
Required degree grade
Minimum 2:1 & 300 UCAS
points or above

Training
Salary
1st year (2007) £34,000
2nd year (2007) £38,000
Holiday entitlement 25 days
% of trainees with a
non-law degree p.a. 50%
No. of seats available
abroad p.a. 14

Post-qualification
Salary (2008)
Not less than £62,500 at the
time of writing
% of trainees offered job
on qualification (2008) 80%
% of assistants (as at 1/9/04)
who joined as trainees 60%
% of partners (as at 1/9/04)
who joined as trainees 4%

Overseas offices
New York, Paris, Hamburg,
Munich, Rome, Milan, Miens,
Piraeus, Singapore, Bangkok

Wedlake Bell

52 Bedford Row, London, WC1R 4LR
Tel: (020) 7395 3000 Fax: (020) 7395 3100
Email: recruitment@wedlakebell.com
Website: www.wedlakebell.com

Firm profile

Wedlake Bell is a medium-sized law firm providing legal advice to businesses and high net worth individuals from around the world. The firm's services are based on a high degree of partner involvement, extensive business and commercial experience and strong technical expertise. The firm has approximately 100 lawyers in central London and Guernsey, and affiliations with law firms throughout Europe and in the United States.

Main areas of work

For the firm's business clients: banking & asset finance; corporate; corporate tax; business recoveries; commercial; intellectual property; information technology; media; commercial property; construction; residential property.

For private individuals: tax, trusts and wealth protection; offshore services; residential property.

Trainee profile

In addition to academic excellence, Wedlake Bell looks for commercial aptitude, flexibility, enthusiasm, a personable nature, confidence, mental agility and computer literacy in its candidates. Languages are not crucial.

Training environment

Trainees have four seats of six months across the following areas: corporate, corporate tax, business recoveries, banking, construction, media and IP/IT, employment, pensions, litigation, property and private client. As a trainee the firm encourages you to have direct contact and involvement with clients from an early stage. Trainees will work within highly specialised teams and have a high degree of responsibility. Trainees will be closely supervised by a partner or senior solicitor and become involved in high quality and varied work. The firm is committed to the training and career development of its lawyers and many of its trainees continue their careers with the firm, often through to partnership. Wedlake Bell has an informal, creative and co-operative culture with a balanced approach to life.

Sponsorship & benefits

LPC fees paid and £4,000 maintenance grant where local authority grant not available. During training contract: pension, travel loans, subsidised gym membership, health insurance and life assurance.

Vacation placements

Places for 2009: 8; Duration: 3 weeks in July; Remuneration: £200 p.w.; Closing Date: End of February, 2009.

Partners 41
Assistant Solicitors 62
Total Trainees 14

Contact
Natalie King

Method of application
Application form

Selection procedure
Two interviews

Closing date for 2011
End of July 2009

Application
Training contracts p.a. 7
Required degree grade 2:1

Training
Salary
1st year (2008) £29,000
2nd year (2008) £31,000
Holiday entitlement
1st year 23 days
2nd year 24 days
% of trainees with a
non-law degree p.a. 50%

Overseas offices
Guernsey

Weightmans LLP

India Buildings, Water Street, Liverpool L2 0GA
Tel: (0151) 227 2601 Fax: (0151) 227 3223
Email: careers@weightmans.com
Website: www.weightmans.com

Partners (over) 100
Trainees p.a. up to 14
Total staff (over) 800
Method of application
online: www.weightmans.com
Closing date for 2011
19 July 2009
Other offices
Birmingham, Leicester, London, Manchester

Firm profile

Weightmans is a top 60 national law firm with offices in Birmingham, Leicester, Liverpool, London and Manchester.

With over 800 people in dedicated teams, including over 100 partners, the firm's aim is to be both the law firm and employer of choice.

The firm offers a comprehensive range of legal services to commercial, insurance and public sector clients, including insurance litigation, healthcare, professional indemnity, commercial property, commercial dispute resolution and employment.

Trainee profile

Weightmans looks to recruit up to 14 trainee solicitors each year. When considering training contract applications, the firm looks for applicants from diverse backgrounds who can demonstrate an ability to achieve results. Above all, the firm values well-motivated candidates with a practical and pragmatic approach who can make a positive impact on a team.

Training environment

Weightmans offers trainees real legal experience during the training contract, including attendance at court and client meetings. Challenged from the outset, trainees have the opportunity to demonstrate their talents across a range of seats. They follow a focused training plan which will enable them to develop business as well as legal skills.

The quality of the firm's training is an important commercial investment, its retention rate is high and it wants today's trainees to remain at Weightmans and be leaders in the future.

Application details

Apply before 19 July 2009. Their application form is available online at www.weightmans.com

Benefits

Weightmans pay a starting salary well above the minimum recommended by the Law Society and this is reviewed every year to ensure that it is competitive. The firm also offers an excellent benefits package which includes flexi-time, pension, health cover, life assurance and 25 days holiday.

From the moment you accept a training contract with Weightmans, the firm pledge support to you, paying all course fees for the LPC and the GDL.

Weil, Gotshal & Manges

One South Place, London EC2M 2WG
Tel: (020) 7903 1074 Fax: (020) 7903 0990
Email: graduate.recruitment@weil.com
Website: www.weil.com

Firm profile

Weil Gotshal & Manges is a leader in the marketplace for sophisticated, international legal services. With more than 1,300 lawyers across the US, Europe and Asia, the firm serves many of the most successful companies in the world in their high-stakes matters and transactions.

Main areas of work

Established in 1996, the London office now has over 110 lawyers. It has grown rapidly to become the second largest of the firm's 20 offices – it is the hub of the firm's European practice. Key areas are private equity, M&A, business finance and restructuring, capital markets, securitisation, banking and finance, dispute resolution and tax. The firm's expertise covers most industries including real estate, manufacturing, financial services, energy, telecommunications, pharmaceuticals, retailing and technology. Due to the international nature of the business, the firm's lawyers are experienced in working closely with their colleagues from other offices – this ensures a co-ordinated approach to providing effective legal solutions efficiently.

Vacation placements

Places for 2009 Easter & Summer: 20 places. Closing date for applications by online application form: 31 January 2009.

In addition five vacation students will have the opportunity of spending three weeks in the firm's New York office.

Partners 24
Assistant Solicitors 64
Total Trainees 22

Contact
Jillian Singh

Method of application
online application form

Closing date for 2011
31 July 2009

Application
Training contracts p.a. 14
Required degree grade 2:1

Training
Salary
1st year (2008) £41,000
Holiday entitlement 23 days

Overseas offices
Austin, Beijing, Boston, Budapest, Dallas, Frankfurt, Hong Kong, Houston, Miami, Munich, New York, Paris, Prague, Providence, Silicon Valley, Singapore, Shanghai, Warsaw, Washington DC, Wilmington

White & Case LLP

5 Old Broad Street, London EC2N 1DW
Tel: (020) 7532 1000 Fax: (020) 7532 1001
Email: trainee@whitecase.com
Website: www.whitecase.com/trainee

Firm profile

White & Case LLP is a global law firm with more than 2,300 lawyers worldwide. The firm has a network of 37 offices, providing the full range of legal services of the highest quality in virtually every major commercial centre and emerging market. They work with international businesses, financial institutions and governments worldwide on corporate and financial transactions and dispute resolution proceedings. Their clients range from some of the world's longest established and most respected names to many start-up visionaries. The firm's lawyers work on a variety of sophisticated, high-value transactions, many of which feature in the legal press worldwide as the firm's clients achieve firsts in privatisation, cross-border business deals, or major development projects.

Main areas of work

Banking and capital markets; construction and engineering; corporate (including M&A and private equity); dispute resolution (including arbitration & mediation); employment & benefits; energy, infrastructure, project & asset finance; IP, PPP/PFI; real estate; tax; and telecommunications.

Trainee profile

Trainees should be ambitious, creative and work well in teams. They should have an understanding of international commercial issues and have a desire to be involved in high profile, cross-border legal matters.

Training environment

Trainees undertake four seats, each of six months in duration. The firm guarantees that one of these seats can be spent overseas. Regardless of where they work, trainees get a high level of partner and senior associate contact from day one, ensuring they receive high quality, stimulating and rewarding work. Trainees are encouraged to take early responsibility and there is a strong emphasis on practical hands-on training, together with plenty of support and feedback.The firm recruits and develops trainee solicitors with the aim of retaining them on qualification.

Benefits

The firm operates a flexible benefits scheme, through which you can select the benefits you wish to receive. Currently, the benefits include private medial insurance, dental insurance, life assurance, pension, critical illness insurance, travel insurance, retail vouchers, gym membership, season ticket loan and green bikes.

Vacation placements

Places for 2009: 20-25 one-week Easter placements and 40-50 two-week Summer placements available. Remuneration: £350 per week; Closing Date: 31 January 2009.

Sponsorship & awards

GDL and LPC fees paid and £7,500 maintenance p.a. Prizes for commendation and distinction for LPC.

Partners 72
Assistant Solicitors 263
Total Trainees 51

Contact
Ms Emma Fernandes

Method of application
Online application via firm website

Selection procedure
Interview
closing date for 2011
31 July 2009

Application
Training contracts p.a.35-40
Applications p.a. 1,600
Required degree grade 2:1

Training
Salary
£41,000, rising by £1,000 every 6 months
Holiday entitlement 25 days
All trainees are guaranteed to spend a seat overseas

Post-qualification
Salary £78,000

Overseas offices
Abu Dhabi, Almaty, Ankara, Bangkok, Beijing, Berlin, Bratislava, Brussels, Bucharest, Budapest, Dresden, Düsseldorf, Frankfurt, Hamburg, Helsinki, Hong Kong, Istanbul, Johannesburg, London, Los Angeles, Mexico City, Miami, Milan, Moscow, Munich, New York, Palo Alto, Paris, Prague, Riyadh, São Paulo, Singapore, Shanghai, Stockholm, Tokyo, Warsaw, Washington DC

Wiggin LLP

10th Floor, The Met Building, 22 Percy Street, London, W1T 2BU
Tel: (020) 7612 9612   Fax (012) 4222 422395
The Promenade, Cheltenham GL50 1WG
Tel: (01242) 224114   Fax: (01242) 224223
Email: law@wiggin.co.uk   Website: www.wiggin.co.uk

Firm profile

Wiggin are experts in the constantly evolving field of media law. They focus exclusively on media with particular emphasis on film, music, sport, gaming, technology, broadcast and publishing. They are recognised for the uncompromising excellence of their work and an unrelenting determination to deliver the best possible results for their media clients. They have an international reputation for their innovative approach, fresh thinking and cutting edge experience in media law; a sector that is changing with mesmerizing speed. The firm offers a highly personalised relationship, working in partnership with its clients to address the complex legal challenges that the fast evolving media industry presents. They have the knowledge and experience, as well as the commitment and confidence, to deliver straightforward and genuine advice motivated only by the need to achieve the best possible outcome for clients. Based primarily out of their Cheltenham office, and also in London, and with blue-chip clients based all over the World (primarily London and the west coast of America) the firm goes to where clients need them to be.

Main areas of work

Commercial 50%, Corporate 18%, Litigation 28%, Property 4%.

Trainee profile

If you want to experience high profile media issues in a forward thinking environment then contact Wiggin. They're looking for you if you can demonstrate a passion for media and the law, strong academic ability and a commitment to success... One word of warning though, their seats are not for the faint hearted! They need trainees that relish hard work and a challenge. They'll be at the law fairs so come and see what they are all about.

Training environment

Training is split into four seats and these will be allocated from company/commercial, commercial media (2 seats), media litigation, employment, film and property. Although based at the Cheltenham office, you will be meeting clients in London and could end up on a six-month secondment there with the British Phonographic Industry (the record industries trade association).

They don't want you to do the photocopying. Their trainees are encouraged to take an active role in transactions, assume responsibility and deal directly with clients. In-house seminars are held regularly and training reviews are held every three months. You'll get an experience just like your friends in the City but within the exciting and niche area of media law and within a firm small enough to recognise the importance of a personal approach.

Benefits

Life assurance, private health cover, pension scheme, permanent health insurance, gym membership at corporate rates.

Sponsorship & awards

PgDL and LPC fees and £3,500 maintenance p.a.

Partners 16
Assistant Solicitors 21
Total Trainees 8

Contact
Office Manager

Method of application
Online application only –
www.wiggin.co.uk

Selection procedure
Two-day selection

Closing date for 2011
31 July 2009

Application
Training contracts p.a. 4
Applications p.a. 500
% interviewed p.a. 8%
Required degree grade 2:1

Training
Salary
1st year (2008) £26,500
2nd year (2008) £31,500
Holiday entitlement 20 days +
one day per annum up to max
25 days
% of trainees with a
non-law degree p.a. 50%

Post-qualification
Salary (2008) £50,000
% of trainees offered job
on qualification (2008) 67%
% of assistants (as at 2008)
who joined as trainees 20%
% of partners (as at 2008)
who joined as trainees 19%

Wilsons Solicitors LLP

Steynings House, Summerlock Approach, Salisbury, Wiltshire, SP2 7RJ
Tel: (01722) 412 412 Fax: (01722) 427 610
Email: jo.ratcliffe@wilsonslaw.com
Website: www.wilsonslaw.com

Firm profile

Wilsons is ranked as one of the leading private client law firms in the country and now has the largest team of private client lawyers outside London, eleven of whom are considered to be 'leaders in their fields'.

Clients include wealthy individuals, entrepreneurs, companies, landed estates, trust companies and charities and many have an international dimension to their interests. The work the firm does for clients is best described as 'quirky' because of the particular issues they face.

Main areas of work

Private client business is the firm's largest single area of work and it permeates the other areas of the firm, which include Charity, Family, Tax and Trusts, Probate, Agriculture, Property, Company Commercial, Employment and Litigation Teams.

Trainee profile

Clients expect quality in the advice given and the service received and that is why the firm aims to employ the highest quality people. The firm places considerable emphasis on teamwork. An open approach to management means information is available across the firm and a flat structure means plenty of potential for positions of responsibility.

Training environment

Despite the firm's national and international client base it is situated 90 miles outside London in Salisbury. Many of the firm's lawyers come from London firms and many of the clients continue to be London-based. This ensures an exceptional quality of work within a beautiful location. If quality of life is crucial to you, the firm would like to meet you.

A two-year training contract enables trainees to sample four disciplines in six-month seats from different areas.

Benefits

Pension (2% in first year, 3% in second year), life assurance (2 x salary), choice of optional benefits and private medical insurance.

Work experience placements

1 week available in July at the firms offices in Salisbury.

Sponsorship & awards

On joining the firm as a trainee the firm can offer you an interest free loan of up to £4,500 for the Legal Practice Course. The firm is committed to your training contract and would hope to retain you once you qualify. If you stay with Wilsons for two years after qualifying the loan will be written off.

Partners 30
Trainees 8
Total Staff 160

Contact
Mrs J Ratcliffe
jo.ratcliffe@wilsonslaw.com

Method of application
Application via website or CV

Selection procedure
interview and assessment day

Closing dates for 2009-2011
training scheme:
31 July 2009 for training
contract to commence in
September 2011

Application
Training contracts p.a. 4
Required degree grade 2:1
Salary
market rate
Holiday entitlement 22 days

Office
Salisbury

Winckworth Sherwood

35 Great Peter Street, London, SW1P 3LR
Tel: (020) 7593 5000   Fax: (020) 7593 5099
Email: hr@wslaw.co.uk
Website: www.wslaw.co.uk

Firm profile

Winckworth Sherwood is a highly individual law firm where its diversity is its strength. The firm firmly believes that technical excellence and high quality client service can be delivered in harmony with a healthy work-life balance.

The firm provides a wide range of services to its clients and much of its work is highly innovative. The firm's lawyers include highly rated specialists in their fields, many with deep personal investment in the firm's client sectors. This gives trainees a broad exposure to the law as well as a deeper understanding of the sectors which the firm supports. The firm is over 200 years old and its success is largely due to the awareness of the importance of flexibility and the ability to adapt to a changing world. The firm believes business sector knowledge is as valuable as legal expertise. The firm has offices in central London, Oxford and Chelmsford. The firm's trainee programme is based in its central London offices.

Main areas of work

Company and commercial, social housing, real estate, housing finance, planning, environmental, employment, construction, licensing, litigation and dispute resolution, commercial property, ecclesiastical, education, charity law, parliamentary, public law and private client.

Trainee profile

The firm requires a strong academic record both at school and university, but it also looks for attributes which demonstrate the potential for making a positive contribution to the firm. It is important to be able to empathise with clients whilst at the same time keeping a clear business head; the firm looks for evidence of these qualities at the outset.

The firm is also interested in indications of high achievement in non-academic pursuits.

The firm is a highly individual firm and it wants independent, intelligent and personable trainees – not a type. The firm wants people who, after training, can provide a client with new ideas, bring a fresh approach and help them achieve desired results in a changing legal environment. These qualities help the firm to develop and its trainees are the future of the firm.

Training environment

As a Winckworth Sherwood trainee you will rotate through four departments in six month placements or 'seats.' The purpose of each seat is to give you a solid grounding in that area of the law. The firm encourages substantial client contact from the start and you will be involved in all phases of a matter. Trainees are not expected to bill heavily, but will need to learn the principles of time recording and develop good professional habits.

As a trainee you will usually sit with a Partner or senior solicitor and may be given the opportunity to manage your own files, subject to suitable supervision. Each trainee has a bespoke training diary which is reviewed on a regular basis. At the end of each seat the Training Partner, with the assistance of the relevant head of department, will review your progress.

The firm has a well developed in-house continuing education programme which draws upon the expertise of partners, qualified staff and guest professionals, in which trainees are encouraged to participate.

Benefits

Private health insurance, season ticket loan, life insurance, permanent health insurance. The holiday allocation is 24 days plus public holidays and one extra day at Christmas.

Sponsorship & awards

Under certain conditions the firm also provides financial assistance to trainees attending the Legal Practice Course (LPC) or studying for a Graduate Diploma in Law (GDL).

Partners 29
Assistant Solicitors 101
Total Trainees 8

Contact
Hugh MacDougald, Training Partner (020) 7593 5000
Heather Cornish (HR) (020) 7593 5077

Method of application
Online application form on website www.wiggin.co.uk

Selection procedure
Two interviews

Closing date for 2011
30 September 2009

Application
Training contracts p.a. 4
Applications p.a. 50
% interviewed p.a. 80%
Required degree grade 2:1

Training
Salary
1st year (2008) £27,000
2nd year (2008) £31,000
Holiday entitlement 24 days + one day at Christmas

Withers LLP

16 Old Bailey, London EC4M 7EG
Tel: (020) 7597 6000 Fax: (020) 7329 2534
Email: jaya.louvre@withersworldwide.com
Website: www.withersworldwide.com

Firm profile

Withers LLP is the first international law firm dedicated to the business, personal and philanthropic interests of successful people, their families, their businesses and their advisers.

The firm's mission is to offer a truly integrated legal service to people with sophisticated global wealth, management and business needs.

Main areas of work

The wealth of today's private client has increased in multiples and many are institutions in their own right. The firm has been able to respond to these changing legal needs and offers integrated solutions to the international legal and tax needs of its clients. The firm has unparalleled expertise in commercial and tax law, trusts, estate planning, litigation, charities, employment, family law and other legal issues facing high net worth individuals.

Withers' reputation in commercial law along with its status as the largest Private Client Team in Europe and leading Family Team sets it apart from other City firms.

International exposure at Withers does not mean working in one of the firm's foreign offices, (although trainees can do seats abroad). Much of the work undertaken in London crosses numerous jurisdictions. Currently the firm acts for around a quarter of The Sunday Times Rich List and a significant number of the US 'Forbes' and Asian 'Hurun' Rich Lists.

Trainee profile

Each year the firm looks for a diverse mix of trainees who are excited by the prospect of working with leaders in their field. Trainees must have an excellent academic background and great attention to detail. Team players with leadership potential are of interest to the firm, as is an international outlook and foreign language skills.

Training environment

Trainees spend six months in four different departments. Working in a team with a partner and an assistant solicitor provides autonomy, responsibility and fast development. Buddy and mentor systems as well as on the job training ensure trainees are fully supported from the outset.

Application

Apply online by 31 July 2009 to begin training in August 2011. Interviews usually take place between April and September.

Vacation scheme

The firm runs two week long placements at Easter and over the summer in London and during the Summer in Milan. Apply online by 31 January 2009 for places in 2009. Interviews take place between February and April.

Sponsorship

Fees plus £5 000 maintenance for both the PgDL or CPE and/or LPC are paid.

Partners 107
Total Staff 600
Trainees 32

Contact
Jaya Louvre
Recruitment Manager

Method of application
Application form (available online)

Selection procedure
2 interviews incl. written exercise and presentation

Closing dates for 2011
training scheme:
31 July 2009
2009 vacation placements:
31 January 2009

Application
Training contracts p.a. 16
Applications p.a. 700
% interviewed p.a. 10%
Required grades 2:1, AAB at A-Level

Training
Salary
1st year (2008) £33,000
2nd year (2008) £35,000
Holiday entitlement 23 days
% of trainees with a
non-law degree p.a. 50%

Post-qualification
Salary (2008) £58,000

Offices
London, Milan, Geneva, New York, New Haven, (Connecticut), Greenwich (USA), Hong Kong

837

Wollastons

Brierly Place, New London Road, Chelmsford, Essex CM2 0AP
Tel: (01245) 211211 Fax: (01245) 354764
Email: graduate.recruitment@wollastons.co.uk
Website: www.wollastons.co.uk

Firm profile

Wollastons is a dynamic, regional law firm, widely recognised as the leading, commercial practice in Essex. Wollastons has a strong reputation as a forward-thinking and energetic organisation, offering high levels of service to both businesses and private clients. The firm's first-class resources, including sophisticated IT, and the lively atmosphere attracts high calibre lawyers, keen to work in a modern, professional environment. The Investors in People and Best Companies accreditation demonstrates a strong commitment to staff development and training at all levels.

Main areas of work

Main practice areas include corporate and commercial; commercial property; commercial disputes; employment; planning and property disputes; private client and family.

Trainee profile

Applications are welcomed from able and ambitious graduates with 300 UCAS points (gained in 3 subjects, excluding general studies) and a 2:1 degree. Candidates should have a commercial outlook, be confident, outgoing and able to demonstrate a wide range of interests.

Training environment

Trainees have four six-month seats. These will normally include: company and commercial; commercial disputes; commercial property and employment. Trainees sit with a partner or a senior solicitor and form an integral part of the team. Trainees are fully involved in a wide range of interesting work and, although work is closely supervised, trainees are encouraged to take responsibility from an early stage. The firm is very friendly and informal and trainees receive a great deal of individual attention and support. Progress is kept under constant review with mid-seat and end of seat appraisals.

Benefits

Private medical cover, 25 days holiday, Christmas bonus, Subsidised gym membership, on site subsidised staff restaurant

Work experience placements

The firm offers unpaid work experience placements covering a number of practice areas. Work experience candidates are given the opportunity to work alongside experienced fee earners and partners and gain a real insight into how a law firm works. Please apply online at www.wollastons.co.uk.

Sponsorship & awards

LPC fees paid.

Partners 9
Fee-earners 43
Total Trainees 5 (3 p.a.)

Contact
Jo Goode, Graduate
Recruitment Manager
(01245) 211253

Method of application
CV and online application
form, see website for details

Selection procedure
3 stage interview process

Closing dates
31 October 2009 (for 2010)
31 October 2010 (for 2011)

Application
Training contracts p.a. 3
Applications p.a. Approx 500
Interviewed p.a. Approx 50
Required degree grade 2:1

Training
Salary
1st year £24,000
2nd year £25,000 (for 2009)

INVESTOR IN PEOPLE

best company
2008

Wragge & Co LLP

55 Colmore Row, Birmingham B3 2AS
Tel: Freephone (0800) 096 9610
Email: gradmail@wragge.com
Website: www.wragge.com/graduate

Firm profile

Wragge & Co is a major UK law firm providing a full service to some of the world's largest and most successful organisations, including 27 FTSE 100 and 22 FTSE 250 companies. It is the only law firm in both the Financial Times 50 Best Workplaces in the UK and the Sunday Times 100 Best Companies to Work For. Working from London or Birmingham on high profile national and international instructions, you will be part of a team passionate about providing the very best client service.

Wragge & Co is a relationship firm, taking time to form lasting relationships with clients to ensure understanding of what makes their businesses tick. Relationships and excellent client service are two of the firms driving forces. To make sure it gets both right, you may find yourself on secondment, experiencing life and work as a client. Relationships within the firm are just as important. The firm is a single team, working together to support colleagues and clients alike. The firm values minimum hierarchy so it is open plan. Everyone has the same space. In fact, being open and honest is one of the firm's most precious values.

Main areas of work

The firm has nationally recognised teams in specialist areas including employment, banking, antitrust, outsourcing, private finance initiatives and regeneration. This year Wragge & Co was named European Pensions Law Firm of the year at the European Pensions Awards.

The firm's core areas of legal advice include corporate finance, dispute resolution, finance and projects, human resources, real estate and technology and commerce. The quality of work is reflected in the firm's client list which includes British Airways, Ministry of Defence, Astrazeneca and E.ON UK.

Trainee profile

The firm is looking for graduates with some legal or commercial work experience gained either via a holiday job or a previous career. You should be practical, with a common sense and problem solving approach to work, and be able to show adaptability, enthusiasm and ambition.

Vacation placements

Easter and summer vacation placements are run at Wragge & Co. As part of our scheme you will get the opportunity to experience different areas of the firm, attend client meetings and get involved in real files. You can apply online at www.wragge.com/graduate.

Training contracts

The firm is currently recruiting for 30 training contracts to commence in September 2011/March 2012. You can apply online at www.wragge.com/graduate. The closing date is 31 July 2009. If you are a non-law student, please return your form as soon as possible, as the firm will be running assessment days over the forthcoming year.

Partners 112
Qualified Solicitors (excluding partners) 330
Total Trainees 60

Contact
Joanne Dowsett or Michelle Byron
Graduate Recruitment Advisor

Method of application
Applications are made online at www.wragge.com/graduate

Selection procedure
Telephone discussion & assessment day

Closing date
Sept 2011/March 2012: 31 July 2009. If you are a non-law student, please complete your application form as soon as possible, as the firm will be running assessment days over the forthcoming year

Application
Training contracts p.a. 30
Applications p.a. 1,000
% interviewed p.a. 25%

Training
Salary Birmingham (Sept 2008)
1st year £25,750
2nd year £28,750
Holiday entitlement 25 days
% of trainees with a non-law degree p.a. Varies

Post-qualification
Salary (2008)
Birmingham £41,000
London £63,000
% of trainees offered job on qualification
(Sept 2008) 89%

Wragge&Co

- **Think all law firms are the same?** They're not. Take Clyde and Ince. What's that you say? Two similar mid-sized shipping firms? Nothing to distinguish one from the other? Think again. Even two firms as alike in dignity as these are a whole world apart in the way they do things.

Fortunately one tool exists to sort the wheat from the chaff, the cat's whiskers from the dog's dinners and the Holly Willoughbys from the hopeless wannabes.

Turn back to page 134
for The True Picture

The Bar

Barcode

Don't let the often curious terms used at the Bar confuse or intimidate you!

Barrister – a member of the Bar of England and Wales

Bench – the judiciary

Bencher – a senior member of an Inn of Court. Usually silks and judges, known as masters of the bench

Brief – the documents setting out case instructions

BVC – the Bar Vocational Course. Currently, its successful completion entitles you to call yourself a barrister in non-legal situations (ie dinner parties), but does not of itself give you rights of audience. Moves are afoot to require part of pupillage to have been completed before the title is conferred

BVC Online – the application system through which applications to Bar school must be made

Cab-rank rule – self-employed barristers cannot refuse instructions if they have the time and experience to undertake the case. You cannot refuse to represent someone because you find their opinions or actions objectionable

Call – the ceremony whereby you become a barrister

Chambers – a group of barristers in independent practice who have joined together to share the costs of practising. Chambers is also the name used for a judge's private office

Circuit – The courts of England and Wales are divided into six circuits: North Eastern, Northern, Midland & Oxford, South Eastern, Western, and Wales & Chester circuits

Clerk – administrator/manager in chambers who organises work for barristers and payment of fees, etc

Counsel – a barrister

Cracked-trial – a case that is concluded without a trial. This will be because the defendant offers an acceptable plea or the prosecution offers no evidence. Cracked and ineffective trials (where there is a lack of court time or the defendant or a witness does not attend) frustrate the bench and are considered a waste of money

Devilling – (paid) work done by a junior member of chambers for a more senior member

Employed bar – some barristers do not engage in private practice at chambers, but are employed full time by a company or public body

First and second six – pupillages are divided into two six-month periods. Most chambers now only offer 12-month pupillages, however it is still possible to undertake the two sixes at different sets

Inns of Court – ancient institutions that alone have the power to 'make' barristers. There was a time when there was a proliferation of them but now there are only four: Gray's Inn, Inner Temple, Lincoln's Inn and Middle Temple. Read more about the Inns on page 847

Junior – a barrister not yet appointed silk. Note: older juniors are known as senior juniors

Junior brief – a case on which a junior is led by a senior. Such cases are too much work for one barrister alone and may involve a lot of research or run for a long time. Ordinarily, junior counsel will not conduct advocacy

Keeping term – eating the dinners in hall required to be eligible for call to the Bar

Mini-pupillage – a short period of work experience spent in chambers

OLPAS – the Online Pupillage Application System

Pupillage – the year of training undertaken after Bar school and before tenancy

Pupilmaster – a senior barrister with whom a pupil sits and who teaches the pupil. The Bar Council is encouraging the term pupil supervisor

QC – one of Her Majesty's Counsel, formerly appointed by the Lord Chancellor. The system fell into abeyance in 2004 and has now been revived with a new, more open appointments system

Set – as in a 'set of chambers'

Silk – a QC, so named because of their silk robes

Supervisor – the new name for a pupilmaster

Tenant/tenancy – permission from chambers to join their set and work with them. A 'squatter' is someone who is permitted to use chambers' premises, but is not actually a member of the set. A 'door tenant' is someone who is affiliated with the set, but does not conduct business from chambers' premises

A career at the Bar

Being a barrister is, to quote one sage QC, 'quite simply, the best job in the world.' True, the Bar is a highly competitive world in which the hours can be punishing and the work arduous, but the equation of excitement, advocacy, extraordinary experiences, a sense of personal fulfilment and kudos are unique.

Nice work if you can get it

Small wonder then, that becoming a barrister is so deeply competitive. The statistics are sobering: the number of candidates taking the BVC rose from 1,406 in 2003/04 to 1,932 in 2006/07, while the total number of first-six pupillages fell from 518 in 2003/04 to 417 in 2007/08. Hoping to address this over-subscription by raising admission standards for the BVC, the Bar Council has proposed various changes, including an entrance examination which may affect applicants in a few years' time. However, the hard fact is that about one in four who commence the BVC gain pupillage and even fewer gain tenancy. These odds might and probably should discourage the casual applicant, but the average would-be barrister is made of stern stuff and usually has a deep-seated commitment to this branch of the profession.

Will you make it?

So, we've established your vocational drive, but what else helps you make the grade? This is a hard one. Meet enough pupils and barristers and you can see what makes someone successful. The fact that you're gobby/argumentative/confident doesn't mean you'll make it, nor is success guaranteed by ten A*s at A-level and an ability to complete *The Times* crossword in three minutes. Somewhere between the two is probably accurate, but ask a chambers recruiter to define the qualities they look for and they will speak in fairly general terms (academic credentials, people skills, analytical skills, commitment, passion, an ability to express ideas) with the vague caveat that 'you know a good one when you see one'. Perhaps it's best to say that those who thrive at the Bar are people who offer the right traits for their chosen area of practice. Crime is all about guts, personality and advocacy ability, and being to-the-point, down to earth and able to assimilate and recall facts easily is more important than genius. Commercial practice is a more sophisticated game. Brains, commercial acumen and an easy manner with business clients are a must in construction, commercial or Chancery work, while specialisms like tax attract true brainboxes. Advocacy is still important in these areas, however deriving pleasure from crafting a masterpiece of written advice or delivering a phenomenally complex legal argument succinctly is even more so.

By reading the **Chambers Reports** and **Practice Areas at the Bar** you will understand more about the skills required in the Bar's various specialist practices.

Is the cost of training prohibitive?

In a word, yes. The GDL conversion course is quite expensive, the BVC is painfully expensive, and many criminal or general common law sets are happy to pay their pupils The Bar Council bare minimum award of £833.33 per month. Some commercial sets make large pupillage awards available, ensuring that they are in line with the salaries of trainee solicitors at big City solicitors' firms; they will even advance funds for the BVC year, but unless you've a source of cash, getting to tenancy is a pricey business most commonly funded through bank loans. Read the **Funding** section on page 80 for more ideas. Of all the potential sponsors out there, the four Inns of Court have the deepest pockets and they make nearly £4m available each year to students.

Huge debts aren't so much of a problem if you'll soon be earning a fat income, but the common perception that all barristers are loaded isn't quite right. Those determined to serve their community will find publicly funded civil, family and criminal work in the midst of a rationalisation by the Legal Services Commission (LSC) that is particularly affecting the availability of work at the junior end. Taking some cues from Lord Carter of Coles' 2006 overarching review/shake-up of the provision of publicly funded legal services – and often doing its own thing as well – the LSC's changes, funding cuts and focus on solicitors tendering for contracts as a means of ensuring value for money is causing disquiet at the Bar. Smaller sets are already feeling the pinch. Despite this gloomy description, is it worth remembering that big sets continue to thrive, and each of those fields continue to attract privately paying clients. By contrast, there's no question that the Commercial Bar pays very well. Comm Bar stars can earn as much as £2m or more per year, while pupils who make it to tenancy in good-quality sets can outstrip solicitor colleagues within a couple of years. To give some substance to this comparison, baby juniors in commercial sets can earn from £45,000-£100,000 in their first year alone, while their Criminal Bar contemporaries will be aiming for something like £20,000-£40,000.

Do remember that within each practice at the Bar there are a few Premier League sets and many others in lower divisions: the difference in earnings between the top and the bottom is substantial.

Mini-pupillages

If you're still at university there's plenty you can do to prepare yourself for a shot at the Bar. If there is anything a little outré about your CV – you're mature or you have poor A-levels, for instance – getting a First is a really good idea. Applicants with 2:1s are two a penny and a 2:2 will scupper your chances unless you can evidence some pretty remarkable mitigating circumstances or other qualities. In general, chambers are much more interested in your undergraduate performance than what you can muster up on the GDL or BVC, but there's never any harm in getting the best grades at every stage. As for post-graduate degrees – a master's from a very good university, either in the UK or abroad – it must be your choice whether to take one or not. All we can say is that many of the Bar's most successful candidates have such a qualification, though by no means all of them. A master's degree is not a silver bullet.

The best way to demonstrate commitment to the Bar is to undertake mini-pupillages – that's barristerspeak for work experience. Whether assessed or unassessed, minis all involve observing barristers in chambers and probably also in court, although the degree of involvement varies hugely from one set to another. A good mini will see you sit in on a pre-trial conference (with the client's permission) and be included in discussions about the law. Don't become fixed on the idea of spending a whole week in chambers, as you may find it easier, more economical and just as beneficial to get a couple of days here and there. Assessed minis are the same, with an added element of paperwork or grading through oral discussion. A typical scenario will see mini-pupils given a set of papers to analyse before producing a piece of written work, which may then be discussed with a supervisor. Some sets only conduct assessed minis or make them a formal part of the recruitment process, but the average outfit recognises that would-be pupils can't go everywhere. On our travels around the Bar this year we met many pupils who hadn't done a mini at their own set.

A mini-pupillage is an important point of contact with a set, an opportunity to show your mettle and create a good impression for a later application. It's also CV and interview fodder: take notes, don't be afraid to ask ques-

tions at appropriate moments and be sure to reflect on what was good and bad about your experiences. Recruiters tell us that candidates who simply list or describe legal work experience fall down in comparison with those who can articulate what they've learned from shadowing practitioners.

Not all sets offer mini-pupillages, and some will only take students in the final year of academic legal studies (be it degree or GDL), so start off by checking their websites carefully for how and when to apply. In general you should aim for as many as it takes you to decide which areas of practice interest you. Gaining pupillage may be a strictly fair process these days, but personal contacts can still help in obtaining a mini. Apply to an Inn of Court to be assigned a sponsor or if you've started dining at your Inn then start schmoozing.

How to stand out from the crowd

The Bar Council prescribes that BVC students must undertake a certain amount of pro bono work. To ensure that you do land something that interests you and adds real weight to a pupillage application form, it is a good idea to investigate the options as soon as possible.

You should also heed the advice of the QC who said: 'Do everything you can.' Get involved with every debating and mooting opportunity that crops up, enter mock trial competitions at law school and keep an eye out for essay competitions. The scholarships offered by the Inns are not just a way of funding your education – don't underestimate the capacity of a prize or award to mark you out from other well-qualified candidates.

OLPAS: getting a foot in the door

The Online Pupillage Application System has operated since 2001. It is not compulsory for chambers to participate, but every pupillage provider is required by the Bar Council to advertise its vacancies on the OLPAS website www.pupillages.com. The info is also produced in the *Pupillages and Awards Handbook*, published to coincide with the opening of the online system and the National Pupillage Fair held in March in London. OLPAS has two 'seasons' – summer and autumn. The closing date for summer season applications is 1 May, allowing three months for interviews, with offers made after 31 July. The autumn season opens at the end of August and closes on 29 September, with just a month for interviews and offers being made after 31 October. A set of chambers may participate in one or other season.

Students may apply through OLPAS during as many seasons as they like, but are limited to 12 sets in each. Most LLB candidates make applications during their final year at uni, although some of the top commercial sets encourage students to apply in their penultimate year in an attempt to snap up the best candidates. Twelve-month pupillages are the most convenient and common option, although it is not unheard of for pupils to end up doing a 'first six' in one set and a 'second six' in another. The beauty of OLPAS is that all correspondence regarding interviews, offers and rejections is sent via e-mail.

Think carefully when choosing where to apply. If you know you're top dollar and that's what you're after then off you go. If you're not sure of your calibre then take a look at the CVs of a set's latest recruits. This will give you some indication of the kind of person it wants. If you didn't go to one of 'those two' universities, why apply exclusively to sets whose members are all dyed-in-the-wool Oxbridge types? Also, you must appear consistent. Chambers won't see which other sets you are applying to but because of the way the OLPAS form is designed, they will see the list of your preferred practice areas.

OLPAS is not the only fruit

A good number of sets recruit pupils outside the OLPAS machinery because they don't like its format or timetable and feel their interests will be better served by other means. Some chambers choose not to participate because their special interest in aspects of an applicant's background cannot be adequately satisfied by reading a completed OLPAS form.

The application method at each non-OLPAS set will be different; however, all must still advertise vacancies on www.pupillages.com. Research things well in advance to make sure you don't miss any deadlines. As one successful applicant counselled: 'Applying to non-OLPAS sets requires a great deal of motivation. There are a lot of them out there and many of them are very good. They should be taken very seriously.' Some sets choose to mirror the OLPAS timetable in their own application procedures, but many don't and this can bring its own problems. One pupil cautioned: 'The exploding offer phenomenon is a real difficulty. Shortly before my first OLPAS interview I was made a very attractive offer from a non-OLPAS set that I just couldn't pass up. While they were a great set, it did stop me from trying my hand elsewhere.'

Interviews: expect the Spanish inquisition

So you've got an interview – well done. Dress neatly and discreetly with hair tidy, teeth flossed, tie sober, jacket done up. Most chambers will be grading you on standard criteria that include everything from intellect to personality and many publish these guidelines online.

As a rough guide, you can expect your first interview to involve a discussion of the hottest topics in your prospective practice area and some gentle investigation into you and your application form. This stage will generally be reasonably painless and you'll face a panel that wants you to stand out. Naturally you should read *The Times Law Supplement* every Thursday (you can get it e-mailed), keep your subscription to *Counsel* up to date and maybe even set the Bar Council's website as your homepage. Preparation for your interviews should consist of more than boning-up on the law; it's important to be clued-up on current affairs too. Finally, think about what isn't on your CV and how you can account for disappointing grades or anything that is missing.

For second interviews expect a larger panel made up of a broader cross-section of people from chambers. While the format of the interviews may vary between sets, the panel will always want to assess the depth of your legal knowledge, your advocacy potential and your strength of character. Weaknesses on your CV will be sniffed out and pursued with tenacity. Don't let them push you around; if you can support your position then stick to it. Resolve is just as necessary for a career at the Bar as receptivity; they want to know that you can fight your corner. Observed one recruiter: 'It is amazing how many people can't stand up for themselves, which is all you want to see.'

Criminal and mixed sets will commonly give you an advocacy exercise, such as a bail application or a plea in mitigation (their basic structures will fit on a post-it, so why not note them down and keep with you at all times). Most, if not all, sets will pose a legal problem of some sort, with the amount of preparation time you are given ranging from ten minutes to a week. If you know that this is going to happen then do take an appropriate practitioner's text unless you know that one will be made available to you. That said, chambers generally aren't looking for faultless knowledge of substantive law, but are trying to get an insight into how your mind works. As one seasoned interviewer explained: 'We are more interested in seeing how a candidate approaches a problem than whether or not they get the right answer.'

A second interview is also often the time when an ethics question may raise its head. You can prepare by reading the Bar's Code of Conduct, which is available on the Bar Council's website. It's a real page turner.

Of course, to all rules there are exceptions, but these days sets are pretty good about detailing their procedures online, so with the right research you shouldn't be in for any shocks.

Try, try and try again

What if you still don't have pupillage by the time you have finished the BVC? Rather than seeing an enforced year out as a grim prospect, view it as a time to improve your CV and become more marketable. If you are interested in a specialist area of practice consider a master's degree. If the thought of another year in education brings you out in a cold sweat then seek out some useful practical experience. The most obvious answer is to apply for paralegalling and outdoor clerking jobs at solicitors' firms. The work you do as a paralegal should teach you how cases actually work and how solicitors – your future clients – work. As an outdoor clerk you will be in court all the time taking notes. This will give you insight into the procedures and politics of trials. The year might also be spent with an organisation that works in an area related to your legal interest. We have interviewed several lawyers who secured pupillages following a period with a charity or not-for-profit organisation.

Pupillage

If you do gain a pupillage, congratulations! Now the hard work really starts. How the year is divided varies from set to set, but no matter how many pupil supervisors are allotted, the broad division is between the first, non-practising six months and the second, when pupils are permitted to be on their feet in court. During the first six, pupils are tethered to their supervisor, shadowing them at court, conferences and in chambers. They will also likely draft pleadings, advices, skeletons or do research for matters that the supervisor is working on. The nature of the second six will depend on the specific area of practice. At a busy criminal set it can mean court every day, and many civil or commercial sets specialising in areas like employment, PI, construction or insurance will send their pupils out up to three times a week. Some big commercial or Chancery sets actively prefer to keep pupils in chambers throughout the year, either for the purposes of assessment or because of the nature of the work means pupils are too inexperienced to take it.

Tenanceasy?

Tenancy is the prize at the end of the year-long interview that is pupillage. Effectively, an offer of tenancy is an invitation from a set to take a space in their chambers as a self-employed practitioner, sharing the services of the clerking and administrative team. How many tenants a set takes on post-pupillage is usually as dependent on the amount of space and work available in chambers as on the quality of the candidates. If you are curious about a set's growth, check to see how many new tenants have joined in recent years by viewing the list of members on its website and compare that against the number of pupillages offered in the same period.

Usually tenancies are awarded after a vote of all members of chambers, after recommendations from a tenancy committee, clerks and possibly also instructing solicitors. Decisions are commonly made in the July of the pupillage year, allowing unsuccessful pupils time to cast around for other tenancy offers or a 'third six' elsewhere. There is evidence to suggest that civil and commercial sets have higher pupil-to-tenant conversion rates than criminal sets. Certainly, it is quite usual for a 12-month criminal pupillage to be followed by a third or subsequent six somewhere other than a pupil's first set. However, plenty of commercial pupils do also find themselves looking for a third six. The general rule is that if a third six is not successful, it is time to look outside the Bar, with it common for pupils to move to a solicitors' firm, either as an advocate or with a view to qualifying as a solicitor.

And finally...

Few readers will have changed their minds about a career at the Bar after reading these pages. If there's one thing wannabe-barristers have in common it is a firm belief that they are one of the lucky ones who will succeed.

our top five tips

- Keep it personal: Anchor your spiel in your own experiences and your application will be more persuasive. For example, only list FRU if you've actually signed out a case.
- Keep it pithy: As Shakespeare once said, brevity is the soul of wit. It should also be the spirit of an OLPAS form. For each section you can write no more than 150 words. Keep it concise and this will be plenty.
- Avoid being trite: Why do you want to be a barrister? Why are you interested in a set? You will be asked to explain yourself, so think what the obvious answer is and then write something more meaningful.
- Write proper: The profession is based upon exact and careful use of the English language, so be eloquent, direct and accurate. One common mistake to remember: 'practice' is the noun; 'practise' is the verb.
- Don't make silly mistakes: Your mantra should be: 'Save, print, check. Save, print, check.' With some sets getting 500 applications, they are itching for a reason to put yours in the bin. Don't give them this one.

The Inns of Court

The four ancient Inns of Court bear a striking resemblance to Oxbridge colleges (chapel, hall, library, etc) and were originally places of residence and learning for young barristers. The Inns still perform some important functions: they alone have the power to 'call' a person to the Bar and before you can be called you must 'keep term' by attending 'dinners' or other 'qualifying sessions' organised by the Inns.

Students must join one of the Inns by the June before they start their BVC, but our advice is to investigate what they have to offer much earlier than this as the Inns have millions of pounds to award in annual scholarships to GDL and BVC students as well as to pupils. Take care not to miss the deadlines for applying as these fall earlier than you'd imagine: commonly in the calendar year before the start of the course to which the award relates. You don't have to be a member of an Inn to apply for one; the trick is to make applications and then join the Inn where you've been successful. You must join an Inn if you're going to take its money and having picked one of the four, that's it – you can't then switch. There's a competitive selection process for scholarships, so expect an interview. The panel will look at the usual criteria: academics, commitment to a career at the Bar, etc. With some awards, but certainly not all, the Inn will consider your financial circumstances.

The Inns reserve funds to help students from the regional BVC institutions meet their costs when visiting the Inn, and for students of any BVC provider to help pay for qualifying sessions. There are additional funds for certain international internships. For specific details of the amounts on offer, start by checking the Inns' websites and ask them if they publish any other related material.

The Inns can be a great source of general help and advice to a prospective barrister. If you want to go and visit them just ring to arrange a tour. All have mentoring schemes that will match student members with a practitioner in their chosen field, and they also run marshalling schemes so students can spend a week sitting alongside a judge, observing court proceedings and discussing the case at the end of the day. For pupils there are advocacy workshops and seminars at Cumberland Lodge in the heart of Great Windsor Park. All four Inns offer mooting, whether it be at internal, inter-Inn or national competition level, and the Inns' various students' associations all have active social calendars.

	99-00	00-01	01-02	02-03	03-04	04-05	05-06	06-07	07-08
BVC applicants	2,370	2,252	2,119	2,067	2,570	2,883	3,211	3,227	2,550 (1st round only)
BVC enrolments	1,490	1,407	1,386	1,332	1,406	1,697	1,745	1,932	n/a
Students passing the BVC	1,201	1,081	1,188	1,121	1,251	1,425	1,515	1,425	n/a
First-six pupils	681	695	812	586	518	571	515	527	417 (1)
Second-six pupils	704	700	724	702	557	598	127	563	521 (1)
Pupils awarded tenancy	511	535	541	698	601	544	531	499	268 (2)

Certain figures were unavailable from the Bar Council at the time of going to press.

(1). Figures from period 1st October 2007-16th June 2008

(2). Figures from period 1st October 2007-17th December 2007

	Lincoln's Inn	Inner Temple	Middle Temple	Gray's Inn
Contact	Tel: 020 7405 1393 www.lincolnsinn.org.uk	Tel: 020 7797 8250 www.innertemple.org.uk	Tel: 020 7427 4800 www.middletemple.org.uk	Tel: 020 7458 7800 www.graysinn.info
Architecture	Everything from the Mediaeval Old Hall to the neo-Classical Stone Buildings to the Victorian gothic Great Hall. Survived the Blitz largely unscathed.	12th-century Temple Church stands opposite the modern Hall built after the original was destroyed in WWII; otherwise the Inn largely resembles a car park.	Splendid Elizabethan Hall tucked down an intricate maze of alleys and narrow streets.	Suffered serious war damage and is largely a 1950s red-brick creation, albeit with its ancient Hall and Chapel intact.
Gardens	Small and shaded; always open.	Stretching down to the Thames. Croquet may be played.	Small but handy for the Bar.	Famous walks good for nearby City Law School students.
Style	Friendly, international and large.	Sociable, progressive, switched on and hard-working.	Musical, arty and very sociable. Christmas revels are notorious.	Intimate, traditional and formal.
Gastronomy	Lunch served every day.	Lunch served every day, suits must be worn.	Decent and varied lunch served every day, smart attire required.	Lunch served every day.
Accommodation	For scholars, in the Inn.	Not for students.	For scholars, in the Inn and in Clapham.	Not for students.
Bar	Briefs – fairly dismal and quiet. Open for lunches and snacks during the day.	The Pegasus Bar has terraced open-air area. Good for people watching but not a place to go incognito.	Modern bar conveniently located beneath the library and opens onto the lawns. Good for intimate chats in winter.	Functional bar.
Old Members	John Donne Lord Hailsham LC Lord Denning MR	Bram Stoker Judge Jeffreys of the 'Bloody Assizes' M K Gandhi	Sir Walter Raleigh William Blackstone Charles Dickens	Sir Francis Bacon Lord Birkenhead LC
Points of Interest	Together with the Royal Navy, Lincoln's Inn takes the Loyal Toast seated. Fifteen Prime Ministers, from Pitt to Blair, have been members.	Temple Church includes part of Knights Templar's round church, which was modelled on the Church of St. Sepulchre in Jerusalem. Chaucer claimed as an old member.	Shakespeare's Twelfth Night first performed here in 1602. 2008 marks the 400th anniversary of the Temple's Charter which granted the freehold of the land to Inner and Middle Temple.	Shakespeare's Comedy of Errors first performed here. Been law teaching on the site of Gray's Inn since the reign of Edward III.
Scholarship Interview Process	Applicants are selected for 20-minute interview but there is only one round. Merit and academic excellence prioritised.	20-minute interview. GDL scholars normally expect automatic funding for BVC, but can apply for higher award. Merit and academic excellence prioritised.	Every applicant will be interviewed. Reputation for giving weight to need as well as merit.	Must have an upper second-class degree to be eligible for BVC scholarship.
Scholarship Money:	Recently refocused funds onto GDL and BVC students. Entrance awards. GDL: up to 32 grants of £7,000. BVC: up to 70 grants of up to £15,000 (some for Inn accom) and up to 40 grants of £3,000.	Entrance awards. GDL: five major scholarships and awards totaling £125,000. BVC: five major grants and awards totaling £712,500.	Entrance awards. GDL: around 20 scholarships of up to £10,000. BVC: around 150 scholarships of up to £18,000. Subsidised accom awards.	Entrance awards. GDL: awards totaling £130,000. BVC: awards totaling £700,000.

Practice areas at the Bar

We've summarised the main areas of practice at the Bar to help you work out which ones you want to try. Read in conjunction with the Chambers Reports, they should help solidify your initial ideas.

The Chancery Bar

In a nutshell

The Chancery Bar is tricky to define. The High Court has three divisions: Family, Queen's Bench (QBD) and Chancery, with cases allocated to the most appropriate division based on their subject matter. What makes a case suitable for the Chancery Division? Historically it has heard cases with an emphasis on legal principles, foremost among them the concept of equity. Put another way, Chancery work is epitomised by legal reasoning. Cases are generally categorised as either 'traditional' Chancery (trusts, probate, real property, charities, mortgages) or 'commercial' Chancery (company law, shareholder cases, partnership, banking, pensions, financial services, insolvency, professional negligence, tax, media, IP). Most Chancery sets undertake both types of work, albeit with varying emphases. The distinction between Chancery practice and the work of the Commercial Bar (historically dealt with in the QBD) is less apparent now – barristers at commercial sets can frequently be found on Chancery cases and vice versa, though some areas, such as tax and IP, beg specialisation.

The realities of the job

- This is an area for those who love to grapple with the most complex aspects of the law. It's all about the application of long-standing principles to modern situations.
- Barristers must practical in the legal solutions they offer to clients. Complex and puzzling cases take significant unravelling and the legal arguments/principles must be explained coherently to the solicitor and the lay client. Suave and sophisticated presentation when before a judge is also vital.
- Advocacy is important, but the majority of time is spent in chambers perusing papers, considering arguments, drafting pleadings, skeletons and advices, or conducting settlement negotiations.
- Some instructions fly into chambers, need immediate attention and then disappear just as quickly. Others can rumble on for years.
- Variety is a key attraction. Traditional work can involve human interest, for example wills and inheritance cause all sorts of ructions among families. Commercial Chancery practitioners deal with the blood-on-the-boardroom-table disputes or bust-ups between co-writers of million-selling songs.
- Schedules aren't set by last-minute briefs for next-day court appearances, so barristers need self-discipline and good time-management skills.
- The early years of practice feature low-value cases like straightforward possession proceedings in the county court, winding-up applications in the Companies Court and appearances before the bankruptcy registrars. More prominent sets will involve babies as second or third junior on larger, more complex cases.

Current issues

- The Chancery Bar attracts plenty of high-value, complex domestic cases, as well as offshore and cross-border instructions. Russian and Eastern European business affairs are taking up a sizeable amount of court time in the commercial arena, and massive off-shore business and private client trusts in the Cayman Islands, the British Virgin Islands, Bermuda and the Channel Islands are increasingly turning to barristers in the field.
- The scope of the Chancery Division means that practitioners get involved in the most enormous commercial and public law matters.

Some tips

- An excellent academic record is essential. Most pupils in leading sets have a First-class degree. You should enjoy the analytical process involved in constructing arguments and evaluating the answers to problems. If you're not a natural essay writer, you're unlikely to be a natural-born Chancery practitioner.
- Don't wander into this area by accident. Are you interested in equity, trusts, company law, insolvency or tax?
- Though not an accurate portrayal of modern practice, Dickens' novel *Bleak House* is the ultimate Chancery saga. Give it a whirl, or rent the DVD.

Read our Chambers Reports on...

3 Verulam Buildings • 3-4 South Square • 4 Stone Buildings • Maitland Chambers • Serle Court • Wilberforce Chambers • XXIV Old Buildings

The Commercial Bar

In a nutshell

The Commercial Bar handles a variety of business disputes. In its purest definition a commercial case is one heard by the Commercial Court or a county court business court. A broader and more realistic definition includes matters dealt with by both the Queen's Bench and Chancery Divisions of the High Court, and the Technology and Construction Court (TCC). The Commercial Bar deals with disputes in all manner of industries from construction, shipping and insurance to banking, entertainment and manufacturing. Almost all disputes are contract and/or tort claims, and the Commercial Bar remains rooted in common law. That said, domestic and European legislation is increasingly important and commercial barristers' incomes now reflect the popularity of the English courts with overseas litigants. Cross-border issues including competition law, international public and trade law and conflicts of law are all growing in prominence. Alternative methods of dispute resolution – usually arbitration or mediation – are also popular because of the increased likelihood of preserving commercial relationships that would otherwise be destroyed by the litigation process.

The realities of the job

- Barristers steer solicitors and lay clients through the litigation process and advise on strategy, for example how a client can position themselves through witness statements, pleadings and pre-trial 'interlocutory' skirmishes.
- Advocacy is key, but as much of it is paper-based written skills are just as important as oral skills.
- Commercial cases can be very fact-heavy and the evidence for a winning argument can be buried in a room full of papers. Barristers have to work closely with instructing solicitors to manage documentation.
- Not all commercial pupils will take on their own caseload in the second six. At first, new juniors commonly handle small cases including common law matters like personal injury, employment cases, possession proceedings and winding-up or bankruptcy applications.
- New juniors gain exposure to larger cases by assisting seniors. As a 'second junior' they carry out research and assist the 'first junior' and the QC leading the case. They use the opportunity to pick up tips on cross-examining witnesses and how best to present arguments.
- In time, a junior's caseload increases in value and complexity. Most commercial barristers specialise by building up expertise on cases within a particular industry sector – eg shipping, insurance, entertainment or banking.
- Developing a practice means working long hours, often under pressure. Your service standards must be impeccable and your style user-friendly, no matter how late or disorganised the solicitor's instruction. In a good set you can make an exceedingly good living.

Current issues

- After a quiet start to 2007 the litigation market picked up considerably and is now thriving. Non-doms and Russian oligarchs feature heavily and there has also been plenty of juicy litigation coming in from elsewhere. Among the biggest cases of 2008 were the collapse of The Accident Group, fallout from the explosion at the Buncefield oil depot and the bank charges litigation, which looks at the legality of financial penalties for customers with unauthorised overdrafts. The credit crunch is now fueling litigation and pundits expect to see more disputes across the board, most especially in relation to insurance and professional negligence.
- The trend for increased mediation and arbitration continues. One effect of this increase in ADR is that only the big, multi-issue cases get to court, as there are so many other opportunities for dealing with smaller, less complex cases before the courtroom doors open.
- Following criticisms of the conduct of the BCCI case, a Long Trials Report has been commissioned to examine the proper orchestration of major litigation. Its recommendations continue to excite debate at the Bar.

Some tips

- Competition for pupillage at the Commercial Bar is fierce. A First-class degree is commonplace and you'll need impressive references.
- Don't underestimate the value of non-legal work experience; commercial exposure of any kind is going to help you understand the client's perspective and motivations.
- Bear a set's specialities in mind when deciding where to accept pupillage.

Read our Chambers Reports on...

2 Temple Gardens • 3 Verulam Buildings • 3-4 South Square • 39 Essex Street • 4 Stone Buildings • 7 King's Bench Walk • Atkin Chambers • Blackstone Chambers • Crown Office Chambers • Four New Square • Henderson Chambers • Keating Chambers • Littleton Chambers • Maitland Chambers • One Essex Court • Serle Court • Wilberforce Chambers • XXIV Old Buildings

The Common Law Bar

In a nutshell

English common law derives from the precedents set by judicial decisions rather than the contents of statutes. Most common law cases turn on principles of tort and contract and are dealt with in the Queen's Bench Division (QBD) of the High Court and the county courts. At the edges, common law practice blurs into both Chancery and commercial practice, yet the work undertaken in common law sets is broader still, and one of the most appealing things about a career at one of these sets is the variety of instructions available. Employment and personal injury are the bread and butter at the junior end, and such matters are interspersed with licensing, clinical negligence, landlord and tenant, winding-up and bankruptcy applications, as well as small commercial and contractual disputes. Some sets will even extend their remit to inquests and criminal cases.

The realities of the job

- Barristers tend to engage with a full range of cases throughout their careers, but there is an opportunity to begin to specialise between five and ten years' call.
- Advocacy is plentiful. Juniors can expect to be in court three days per week and second-six pupils often have their own cases. Small beginnings such as 'noting briefs' (where you attend court simply in order to report back on the proceedings) and masters' and district judges' appointments lead to lower-value 'fast-track' personal injury trials then longer, higher-value, 'multi-track' trials and employment tribunals.
- Outside court, the job involves research, an assessment of the merits of a case and meetings with solicitors and lay clients. The barrister will also be asked to draft statements of claim, defences and opinions.
- Dealing with the volume and variety of cases requires a good grasp of the law and the procedural rules of the court, as well as an easy facility for assimilating the facts of each case.
- Interpersonal skills are important. A client who has never been to court before will be very nervous and needs to put at ease.
- At the junior end, work comes in at short notice, so having to digest a file of documents quickly is commonplace.
- Acting as a junior on more complex cases allows a younger barrister to observe senior lawyers in court.

Current issues

- The trend for mediation and arbitration of disputes, and the trend for solicitors to undertake more advocacy themselves, have to some extent reduced work at the junior end. However, while solicitor advocates frequently take on directions hearings, they are still rarely seen at trial.
- Conditional fee agreements – especially for PI claims – have definitely affected remuneration. Ongoing changes to the public funding of legal services are also having an impact: see our feature on page 18.

Some tips

- Though there are a lot of common law sets, pupillages and tenancies don't grow on trees. You'll have to impress to get a foot in the door and then make your mark to secure your next set of instructions.
- If you want to specialise, thoroughly research the sets you apply to.

Read our Chambers Reports on...

2 Temple Gardens • 39 Essex Street • Cloisters • Crown Office Chambers • Old Square Chambers • Henderson Chambers

The Criminal Bar

In a nutshell

Barristers are instructed by solicitors to provide advocacy or advice for individuals being prosecuted in cases brought before the criminal courts. Lesser offences like driving charges, possession of drugs or benefit fraud are listed in the magistrates' courts, where solicitor advocates are increasingly active. More serious charges such as fraud, supplying drugs or murder go to the Crown Courts, which are essentially still the domain of barristers. In extension, complex cases may go all the way to the Court of Appeal and the House of Lords. See the diagram of the Criminal Courts of England & Wales on page 102. The average criminal set's caseload incorporates everything from theft, fraud, drugs and driving offences to assaults of varying degrees of severity and murder. Many top-end chambers are also leveraging their forensic analysis and advocacy skills to move into regulatory, VAT tribunal and professional discipline work. A summary of the expanding opportunities at the Crown Prosecution Service is given on page 23.

The realities of the job

- Criminal barristers need a sense of theatre and dramatic timing, but good oratory skills are only half the story. Tactical sense and time management are important.
- The barrister must also be able to inspire confidence in clients from any kind of background.
- Some clients can be tricky, unpleasant or scary. Some will have pretty unfortunate lives, be addicted to alcohol or drugs, have poor home lives or little education.
- Barristers often handle several cases a day, maybe at different courts. Some will be poorly prepared by instructing solicitors. It is common to take on cases at short notice and to have to cope with missing defendants and witnesses. Stamina and adaptability are a must.
- Sustained success rests on effective case preparation and an awareness of evolving law and sentencing policies.
- Pupils cut their teeth on motoring offences, committals and directions hearings in the mags' courts. By the end of pupillage they will be instructed in their own right and not infrequently make it into the Crown Court.
- Juniors quickly see the full gamut of cases. Trials start small and then move onto ABH, robbery and possession of drugs with intent to supply. Impressing an instructing solicitor could lead to a role as a junior on a major Crown Court trial.
- Pupils and juniors rely on the relationships that seniors and managers have built with instructing solicitors.

Current issues

- Until recently, being on the CPS list meant barristers could prosecute as well as defend. On cost-saving grounds the Crown Prosecution Service has now decided to bring a significant proportion of advocacy in-house by encouraging its own lawyers to develop the required skills. The CPS wants many of its lawyers to develop to become Senior Crown Advocates and handle contested trials in the Crown Court. Quite where an equlibrium between the Bar and CPS prosecutors is reached remains to be seen, but the move has already reduced the amount of work at the junior end. The financial security (albeit not vast riches) offered at the CPS may help it entice barristers from private practice.
- Legal aid cutbacks and the Legal Services Commission's implementation of legal aid reform following on from the Carter review are also hitting the number of criminal instructions and their remuneration. The system of fixed fees for work under the Graduated Fee Scheme is irritating many practitioners and the requirements of the Unified Contract (Crime) are forcing many solicitors out of the area, which in turn is affecting barristers' workloads. Read our feature on page 18 for more information. Of course, if you're willing to accept the likelihood of more limited financial rewards, the legal aid Criminal Bar should still prove irresistible, and our research suggests top sets will ride out the changes with ease.
- Private paying criminal practice is as healthy as ever.

Some tips

- Mini-pupillages and plenty of mooting/debating are required before you can look like a serious applicant.
- Some top sets will want to see your OLPAS practice area choices restricted to crime and crime/mixed civil.
- The Criminal Bar tends to provide more pupillages than other areas, but these don't always translate into tenancies. Third and fourth sixes are not uncommon, so be prepared for this possibility.
- There are many ways of getting exposure to the criminal justice system. See page 32 for tips.

Read our Chambers Reports on...

2 Bedford Row • 2 Hare Court

The Employment Bar

In a nutshell

The Employment Bar deals with any and every sort of claim arising from the relations or breakdown of relations between employees and employers. Disputes are generally resolved at or before reaching an Employment Tribunal, which deals with cases relating to redundancy; unfair dismissal; discrimination on the grounds of gender, sexual orientation, race, religion or age; workplace harassment; contract claims and whistle-blowing. Appeals are heard at an Employment Appeal Tribunal (EAT) and high-value claims and applications for injunctions to prevent the breach of restrictive covenants or use of trade secrets are usually dealt with in the county courts or the High Court. Accessibility is a key aim of the employment tribunal system. Legal representation is not required and only rarely will there be a costs penalty for the unsuccessful party. Such is the emphasis on user-friendliness that employment claims can even be issued online. Applicants making claims will often represent themselves, meaning a barrister acting for a respondent company faces a lay opponent. Nonetheless, many cases are so complex, or worth so much money, that both parties seek specialist legal representation from solicitors and barristers.

The realities of the job

- Most advocacy takes place in employment tribunals or the Employment Appeals Tribunal, where the atmosphere and proceedings are deliberately less formal. Hearings are conducted with everyone sitting down and barristers do not wear wigs.
- Tribunals follow the basic pattern of examination in chief, cross-examination and closing submissions; however barristers have to modify their style, especially when appearing against someone who is unrepresented.
- A corporate respondent might consider a QC well worth the money, while the applicant's pocket may only stretch to a junior. Solicitor advocates feature prominently in this area of practice.
- Employment specialists need great people skills. Clients frequently become emotional or stressed, and the trend for respondent companies to name an individual (say a manager) as co-respondent means there may be several individuals in the room with complex personal, emotional and professional issues at stake.
- Few juniors limit themselves solely to employment practice; most also undertake civil or commercial cases, some criminal matters. Similarly, few juniors act only for

applicants or only for respondents. Seniors' fees mean they act largely for respondents or well-paid execs.
- UK Employment legislation mirrors EU law and changes with great rapidity. Cases are regularly stayed while others with similar points are heard on appeal.

Current issues

- High-value claims by employees in the banking sector continue to make headlines.
- Layoffs and bonus disputes resulting from the current economic downturn are likely to lead to an increase in the number of employment claims.
- Equal pay cases are currently very important and providing the Bar with a lot of work. Group actions such as Degnan & Others v Redcar & Cleveland Borough Council at the Court of Appeal are setting precedents for sizeable awards and cases are spreading across the UK regions.
- The Work and Families Bill covering new rights to maternity and paternity leave for parents, and the relationship between employer and parent during a period of childcare leave has also generated work. The Bill includes a new right to request flexible working.
- The advent of Employment Equality (Age) Regulations means age discrimination cases are coming to the fore and various aspects of the law will be tested in the near future.

Some tips

- Get involved with the work of the Free Representation Unit (see www.freerepresentationunit.org.uk). FRU employment law opportunities are varied and no application for pupillage will look complete without some involvement of this kind.
- Practically any kind of temporary or part-time job will give you first-hand experience of being an employee. Not to be underestimated, especially when you consider that as a barrister you will be self-employed.
- High-profile cases are regularly reported in the press, so there's no excuse for not keeping abreast of the area.

Read our Chambers Reports on...

Blackstone Chambers • Cloisters • Littleton Chambers • Old Square Chambers

The Family Bar

In a nutshell

Family law barristers deal with the array of cases arising from marital, civil-union or cohabitation breakdown and related issues concerning children. Simple cases are heard in the county courts, while complex or high-value cases are listed in the Family Division of the High Court. Emphasising the importance of this area, UK Government stats reveal that 53% of the couples divorcing in 2004 had at least one child aged under 16, and together their divorces affected nearly 150,000 children, some 64% of them under the age of 11. Consequently, a huge amount of court time is allotted to divorce, separation, adoption, child residence and contact orders, financial provision and domestic violence.

The realities of the job

- Financial cases and public and private law children's work each offer their own unique challenges.
- Emotional resilience is required, as is a capacity for empathy, as the work involves asking clients for intimate details of their private life and breaking devastating news to the emotionally fragile. Private law children's cases can sometimes involve serious allegations between parents and require the input of child psychologists. The public law counterpart (care proceedings between local authorities and parents) invariably includes detailed and potentially testing medical evidence.
- For many clients, involvement with the courts is out of the ordinary and they will rely heavily on their counsel to guide them through the process. The law can never fix emotional problems relating to marital breakdown or child issues, but it can palliate a situation.
- The job calls for communication, tact and maturity. Cases have a significant impact on the lives they involve, so finding the most appropriate course of action for each client is important. The best advocates are those who can differentiate between a case and client requiring a bullish approach and those crying out for settlement and concessions to be made.
- Where possible, mediation is used to resolve disputes in a more efficient and less unsettling fashion, requiring a different approach to litigation.
- Teamwork is crucial. As the barrister is the link between the client, the judge, solicitors and social workers, it is important to win the trust and confidence of all parties.
- The legislation affecting this area is comprehensive, and there's a large body of case law. Keeping abreast of developments is necessary because the job is more

about negotiating general principles than adhering strictly to precedents.
- Finance-oriented barristers need an understanding of pensions and shares and a good grounding in the basics of trusts and property.
- The early years of practice involve a lot of private law children work (disputes between parents), small financial cases and injunctions in situations of domestic violence.

Current issues

- A few years ago barristers believed that mediation and an increase in solicitor advocates threatened a downturn in work for juniors. Yet, with the exception of children's cases, in which solicitors have always been encouraged to do their own advocacy, the volume of instructions appear to have continued largely unabated… as has the incidence of divorce in the UK. The financial crisis has caused a surge in the number of people seeking advice on divorce.
- Big divorces are big news. The wealth and assets involved in cases such as McCartney v Mills far outstrip the reasonable needs of the parties, but precedents for huge payouts have been established and such cases draw significant attention, with the media often being used strategically.
- Cases involving the division of assets/child law issues following the breakdown of a civil partnership are beginning to appear.
- Ongoing reform of the legal aid system and substantial proposed cuts to the amounts budgeted for publicly funded family work are hitting the Family Bar hard. Read our feature on page 18 for more details.

Some tips

- The Family Bar is quite small and competition for pupillage is intense. Think about how you can evidence your interest in family law. See our Pro Bono and Volunteering section on page 32.
- Younger pupils might find it daunting to advise on mortgages, marriages and children when they've never experienced any of these things personally. Arguably those embarking on a second career, or who have delayed a year or two and acquired other life experiences, may have an advantage.
- Check the work orientation of a set before applying for pupillage, particularly if you don't want to narrow your options too early. For example, some sets specialise only in the financial aspects of divorce.

Public Law at the Bar

In a nutshell

Centred on the Administrative Court, public law cases range from pro bono or legal aid matters for individuals to instructions from government or magic circle firms regarding commercial judicial review. Human rights cases usually relate in some way to the UK's ratification of the European Convention on Human Rights (the Convention) through the Human Rights Act 1998 (HRA). These crop up in criminal and civil contexts, often through the medium of judicial review, a key tool in questioning the decisions of public bodies. Cases concerning community care issues and the provision of social services by local authorities feature heavily, and judicial reviews of immigration decisions make up a chunk of the Administrative Court's case list. Then there are contentious matters such as right-to-life or right to NHS treatment cases. Where an event is deemed to be of great public importance, inquiries are commissioned by the government and then operate independently. The Bloody Sunday Inquiry and the Hutton Inquiry into the death of Dr David Kelly are illustrative. Planning inquiries feature regularly in a public law set's caseload, dealing with anything from an airport expansion to construction of a wind farm. Most public law barristers and sets also work in other areas: some are crime specialists; others have commercial caseloads. Criminal barristers will often handle issues relating to prisoners or breaches of procedure by police, and commercial barristers might handle judicial reviews of DTI decisions. A barrister with a local authority clientele will cover planning, housing or environmental matters, education, health and children. Even those who do not profess a specialism in public law may also undertake judicial review work.

The realities of the job

- The Administrative Court is inundated, so an efficient style of advocacy is vital. That means cutting to the chase and delivering the pertinent information, case law or statutory regulations.
- Public law is a discursive area of practice in which complex arguments are more common than precise answers.
- The combination of real-world facts, rarefied legal principle and complex, emotive cases demands practicality, common sense and legal intellect.
- Barristers who work on planning inquiries may have to spend periods of time away from home.
- Junior barristers hone advocacy skills early. The preliminary 'permissions' stage of judicial review provides excellent opportunities in the form of short 30-minute hearings. However, reviews tend not to involve juries, witnesses or cross-examination.

Current issues

- The Freedom of Information Act has heightened the ability of pressure groups, individuals and the media to scrutinise the actions of public bodies.
- Ongoing changes to legal aid funding will affect public law cases and the livelihoods of barristers acting for legally aided clients. See our feature on page 18.
- Immigration law changes constantly, recently in relation to rules and regulations affecting the Highly Skilled Migrant programme and applications for leave to remain or settle in the UK. A new points-based immigration system is effective from late 2008.
- The interface between terrorism and public law, and between public law and the HRA and the Convention, has become even more acute, as evidenced by the furore surrounding the Counter-Terrorism Bill and its 42-day detention clause.
- There are an increasing number of coroners' inquests, with prison and military deaths dominating the field.
- Proposed changes to planning legislation – including the removal of the public inquiry stage in certain high-value developments – have caused controversy.

Some tips

- Getting a public law pupillage is phenomenally competitive. Not only are the highest academic standards required, many pupils also arrive with significant hands-on experience in the charities, lobbying or local authority sectors, or related further academic study.
- Public international law appeals to many students but there are few early openings. Traditionally, PIL has been the preserve of academics; the leading names are predominantly sitting or ex-professors at top universities and Foreign Office veterans, with the occasional pure but very experienced barrister thrown in.
- If administrative and constitutional law subjects were not your favourites, rethink your decision.
- Interesting opportunities are available within the Government Legal Service. See pages 351 and 874.
- A healthy interest in current affairs and knowledge of the latest cases in the news is vital.

Read our Chambers Reports on...

Blackstone Chambers • 39 Essex Street • 4-5 Gray's Inn Square

Shipping and international trade at the Bar

In a nutshell

This is such a well-defined specialism at the Commercial Bar it requires its own summary. Shipping and trade work mostly centres upon contract and tort; indeed English case law is awash with examples from the world of shipping. Barristers handle disputes arising from or concerning the carriage of goods or people by sea, air and land, plus all aspects of the financing, construction, use, insurance and decommissioning of the vessels, planes, trains and other vehicles that carry them. There is often a complex international element to such cases, drawing in multiple parties – for example a wrecked vessel might be Greek-owned, Pakistani-crewed, Russian-captained, last serviced in Singapore, carrying forestry products from Indonesia to Denmark, insured in London and chartered by a French company – but English courts are very often the preferred forum for the resolution of such matters, not least because of the worldwide significance of the London insurance market. Trade disputes are often resolved through arbitration conducted in various locations, Paris and London being among the most important. 'Wet' cases deal with problems at sea, while 'dry' cases relate to disputes in port or concerns over the manufacture and financing of vessels. The Bar also has a number of aviation, road haulage and rail specialists, and the sets that dominate these areas also tend to be able to offer commodities trading experts.

The realities of the job

- Cases are fact-heavy and paper-heavy. To develop the best arguments for a case, barristers need an organised mind and a willingness to immerse themselves in the documentary evidence. This can be time-consuming and exhausting.
- There are opportunities for international travel.
- Cases can run on for years and involve large teams of lawyers, both solicitors and barristers. Young barristers work their way up from second or third junior to leader over a number of years. New juniors do get to run their own smaller cases, eg charter party and bills of lading disputes.
- The world of shipping and trade has its own language and customs.
- Solicitor clients will usually work at one of the established shipping firms, but lay clients will be a mixed bag of financiers, shipowners, operators, traders and charterers, P&I clubs, salvors and underwriters.

Current issues

- There is a general downturn in cargo claims due to the increased safety of ships and the success of various conventions such as the International Safety Management Code.
- P&I clubs in particular continue to be increasingly watchful of costs. This has sparked the recent development of instructing barristers directly, cutting out the solicitor middleman.
- Clients are further trying to save money by embracing mediation, although gloomier economic conditions always see a rise in cases going to court.

Some tips

- The leading sets are easy to identify. A mini-pupillage with one or more of them will greatly enhance your understanding and chances.
- Despite the prominence of English law, the work calls for an international perspective and an appreciation of international laws. This can be developed within a first or master's degree and on the BVC.

Read our Chambers Reports on...

Quadrant Chambers • 7 King's Bench Walk

- **Make full use of sets' websites:**
  Take note of the identity of any clients mentioned and check which recent cases a set is most proud of. These things will help you at interview. If you get wind of who will be on the interview panel do your homework on them before you submit yourself to a grilling.

Chambers Reports: introduction

Making an informed choice about where to apply for pupillage isn't easy. Having established the practice area in which you want to specialise, you then need to select your dozen OLPAS sets and consider how many other non-OLPAS choices to make. How do you know where you'll fit in and whether a set will be interested in you?

These days the majority of chambers' websites deliver all the pertinent information – not just about their size, nature of work and location, but also about pupillage and mini-pupillage. Many even carry their full pupillage policy documentation online. However, internet surfing will only take you so far and there is no substitute for seeing inside a set on a mini-pupillage. Because it is impossible to do minis at every set, we've done some of the hard work for you.

Since the summer of 2003 we have been calling in on chambers, taking time to speak with pupils, juniors, QCs, clerks and chief execs. The task is a big one so we visit chambers every second year, reprinting the existing Chambers Report on them in the intervening year. This year's roll call of 26 sets includes 12 new features and 14 features reprinted from our 2008 edition. We have tried to visit as many different types of set as possible to give a good flavour for the range of potential areas of practice out there. Our tour took us from the grandeur of the Chancery Bar to the more modest surroundings of sets conducting a significant amount of publicly funded work. There should be something to suit all tastes, be they commercial, common law, criminal, IP, tax, or otherwise.

The sets covered this year are all in London, where the majority of chambers (and pupillages) are based, but in your wider research remember that there are some excellent chambers in Leeds, Liverpool, Manchester, Birmingham and Bristol. The wild card in the pack is the Government Legal Service, which although not a set operating out of chambers, still offers what we regard as a cracking pupillage. What we have deliberately avoided is poor-quality sets and we make no excuses for our deci-sion to review only top sets. Bear in mind, however, that our selected sets are not the only ones in the Premier League in each practice area. Given the time we would visit many others.

Whichever chambers you do choose, be reassured that the prime aim of recruiters is to find talented applicants and then to persuade them to accept an offer. They do not expect ready-formed barristers to turn up at their door for interview, and gladly make allowances for candidates' lack of knowledge or experience on specific subjects. Much has been said and written about how awful pupillage interviews can be, and how pupillage itself amounts to little more than a year of pain and humiliation. From what we can tell, in an increasingly modern, business-oriented profession that is taking greater notice of what constitutes good HR practice, this is not the norm. Sure, interviews can be challenging, but they are for the most part designed to get the best out of candidates. As for pupillage, it is in the best interests of any set that it should provide a useful and rewarding experience for pupils.

The itinerary for our visits included conversations with members of the pupillage committee, pupilmasters or supervisors, the senior clerk, junior tenants and, most crucially, current pupils. The aim was not merely to get the low-down on pupillage at each set but also to learn something about each chambers' life and to pick up tips for applicants. To this end we drank endless cups of tea, self-lessly munched our way through kilos of biscuits and took numerous guided tours, checking out artwork and libraries along the way. If we've communicated the qualities that make each set unique then we've done our job and it's over to you to make your choices.

Set	Location	Head of Chambers	QCs/Juniors
Atkin Chambers	London	Nicholas Dennys QC	14/24
2 Bedford Row	London	William Clegg QC	17/47
Blackstone Chambers	London	Mill QC/Beazley QC	31/42
Cloisters	London	Robin Allen	5/44
Crown Office Chambers	London	Antony Edwards-Stuart QC	14/68
One Essex Court	London	Lord Grabiner QC	22/45
39 Essex Street	London	Davies QC/Wilmot-Smith QC	24/53
Government Legal Service	London	N/a	500
4-5 Gray's Inn Square	London	Appleby QC/Straker QC	11/35
2 Hare Court	London	David Waters QC	15/39
Henderson Chambers	London	Charles Gibson QC	10/32
Keating Chambers	London	John Marrin QC	18/33
7 King's Bench Walk	London	Gavin Kealey QC	18/27
Littleton Chambers	London	Clarke QC/Freedman QC	12/39
Maitland Chambers	London	Michael Driscoll QC	16/47
Four New Square	London	Roger Stewart QC	14/49
XXIV Old Buildings	London	Mann QC/Steinfeld QC	8/27
Old Square Chambers	London	John Hendy QC	10/57
Pump Court Tax Chambers	London	Andrew Thornhill QC	10/19
Quadrant Chambers	London	Persey QC/Rainey QC	10/34
Serle Court	London	Alan Boyle QC	13/34
3/4 South Square	London	Michael Crystal QC	18/26
4 Stone Buildings	London	George Bompas QC	6/22
2 Temple Gardens	London	Benjamin Browne	8/48
3 Verulam Buildings	London	Symons QC/Jarvis QC	16/41
Wilberforce Chambers	London	Jules Sher QC	21/29

Atkin Chambers

The facts

Location: Gray's Inn, London
Number of QCs/Juniors: 14/24 (8 women)
Applications: 200
Olpas: Summer season
Pupils per year: 3
Seats: 2x3 months + 1x6 months
Pupillage award: £47,500 (can advance £15,000 for BVC)

If you think direct experience of the construction industry or specialist academic knowledge is a prerequisite for an Atkin pupillage then you're mistaken.

Tucked between the Inns of Court School of Law and BPP, Atkin Chambers is a stalwart of the Construction Bar. It's also home to a good proportion of the best practitioners in the field.

Building a premier league set

But things weren't always so: 'Chambers grew out of an administrative law set. In 1959 Ian Duncan Wallis helped edit *Hudson's* (a leading text on building contracts), and he and his generation of members turned chambers into a well-known set for construction.' These days, all members take instructions from, or relating to, the construction or engineering sector. A few have other related specialisms, for example IT or energy. Over the years Atkin barristers have played their part in many of the big clashes in the Technology and Construction Court (TCC), and even the House of Lords. When it comes to international practice, some members have deliberately edged into overseas cases, notably in Asia and the Middle East.

Rather than a burning passion for construction law, it is Atkin's quality reputation and high earning potential that usually attracts pupils. As one explained: 'On a day-long visit here they gave me a set of papers, and speaking to people it became clear that the work is simply contract and tort in a construction context.' As a premier league set, Atkin unsurprisingly receives many applications. Some 15 candidates face a single, 'not unfriendly' interview with a panel of six barristers. A legal question is posed ten minutes before interview and there's also a discussion on a topic with a moral or ethical angle. The panel appreciates that 'no one has studied construction law,' so what they want to see is a good grasp of contract and tort. Many successful candidates have Firsts; being 'articulate and sensible' are the most crucial attributes.

A flood of work

Each pupil sits with the same pupilmasters, who 'take training very seriously.' Apparently 'there's no intellectual let-up.' The first three months are spent shadowing the PM as they write opinions, draft pleadings and represent clients in trials and interlocutory applications, arbitrations, mediations and adjudications, all the while observing how they negotiate with other counsel and deal with questions of ethics. In the second three months there's more emphasis on pupils producing work, either for the PM or other members. A mixture of 'current work and papers from the previous year' makes for 'a good learning process.'

The subject matter is 'not all bricks and mortar, sewers and drains;' the pupils we spoke to had experienced 'a worldwide Mareva injunction to freeze bond monies on a project in India,' a claim 'concerning a flooding in a hotel at Heathrow' and 'Tube safety questions,' not to mention issues affecting 'rail networks and power stations...' In terms of the technical aspects of claims, whether it's understanding experts and 'using them to your advantage,' or talking to a PM and trawling the internet to but-

Chambers UK rankings

Construction • Energy & Natural Resources • Information Technology • Professional Negligence

tress a 'no-knowledge standpoint,' pupils must be constantly prepared to display 'logical, reasoned analysis.' The scale of many cases requires large teams of barristers, solicitors, technical experts/quantity surveyors working together, and there will often be mind-boggling quantities of documentary evidence. With all this, there is some risk of pupils becoming 'document fags,' and for those in the earlier part of their careers it means taking a junior or second junior role on large cases for some while. That said,

> **Members edit the following leading texts: Hudson on Building Contracts, The Building Law Reports and The Construction Law Review. Atkin is one of only two sets to hold the Queen's Award for Enterprise: International Trade.**

'the clerks ensure juniors have experience of small trials and hearings too.'

The List, The Test and The Decision

After six months the pupillage committee takes written soundings on a pupil's progress and provides an assessment. It's rare for the break opportunity to be exercised at this stage. Pupils may then accept small-end instruction of their own, though in truth their second six will be a more chambers-based experience than in many sets. Over five weeks, pupils must complete set pieces for each of five members on 'The List'. Then there's 'The Test', which is based around a fictional set of papers and culminates in advocacy. Another testing aspect is a series of three formal advocacy exercises. Even if 'the feedback is good' it can be 'difficult to shake the sense of being assessed.' This sense is heightened during the 'stressful period' of The List; pupils continue to handle their regular workload, meaning weekend graft is practically essential. Despite the stresses, pupils wouldn't have it otherwise: 'It relieves a lot of pressure and politics.'

Other than in List weeks, there is no real reason for pupils to stay late. It's a different story after pupillage: Chambers' reputation ensures a steady flow of great work. Barristers 'never have worry about where the next case is coming from,' however it requires them to work 'very, very hard.' To demonstrate their suitability, sources suggest pupils 'work their socks off.' The all-member tenancy decision is made in July. Usually a single pupil is taken

on, though Atkin insists there's room for anyone who meets the required standard and in 2008 two out of three pupils were granted tenancy.

The thorough and 'meritocratic' assessment regime makes meeting members at afternoon tea less trying. 'Actually it can be fun if you get some of the characters down for tea; it's not often that people talk about work.' The junior end is reasonably Oxbridge-dominated and around 40% are women. Said one female source of potential difficulties with construction clients: 'It's more a case of you being young than being female.' Atkin is a 'very professional' and 'reasonably quiet, pretty relaxed' place. 'Every member has their own room' and 'everyone has a vote.' That said, most members seem to be 'busy concentrating on their practices.' So who really runs chambers? 'Augusto, our housekeeper – we could not function without him.'

Separated at birth?

Atkin's great rival is Keating Chambers, so we wondered what differentiates them. In short, chambers believes that less is more. 'We are more homogeneous, smaller. We have not gone down the expansionist route through external recruitment. That's been a conscious decision,' members explained. A 'more collegiate, less corporate' place, no one we spoke to at Atkin was sure there's truth to the perception that their set is more academic and reserved than Keating. However, they did stress that Atkin's clients are more often the employer in a building dispute, while Keating frequently represents the contractors. The director of a large multinational can require a different style of service than a director of a building company.

Baby juniors are in court 'at least every month,' which may not sound like much, but when construction claims go all the way to court they can be there for a while. Moreover, more than in almost any other sector, construction cases often settle by way of an alternative to court litigation, so 'right from the junior end you will be exposed to arbitrations, mediations and adjudication.'

> ## And finally
>
> An Atkin mini-pupillage will give good insight into construction law. Remember that generations of pupils have chosen this chambers for its premier status, not its specialisation. As one canny pupil put it: 'The work is as lucrative as at the top general commercial sets and similarly international.'

2 Bedford Row

The facts

Location: Bedford Row, London
Number of QCs/Juniors: 17/47 (15 women)
Applications: up to 500
Olpas: Summer season
Pupils per year: 4
Seats: 2x6 months (2 supervisors in tandem per six)
Pupillage award: £10,000 plus earnings and travel expenses

Gritty and workaholic, 2 Bedford Row is one of the Criminal Bar's brightest stars, with a caseload that's equal parts crime, fraud and regulatory.

In 25 years 2 Bedford Row has shot to prominence in relation to crime and fraud cases. Some of the highlights include representing Soho nail bomber David Copeland, Chillingden murderer Michael Stone and Tony Martin, who shot a burglar in his own home, not to mention involvement on the Herald of Free Enterprise prosecution.

Criminally intent

In part, the set's drive can be credited to legendary founder William Clegg QC, who in recent years successfully defended a British paratrooper accused of murdering an Iraqi teenager and helped Barry George secure his acquittal. Between them, members have also appeared for the defence in the 7/7 Conspiracy Trial, the Jubilee Line fraud and the QPR blackmail trial, as well as for a defendant in the Cheney Pension fraud, in which over £2.8m was stolen. Numerous sportspeople, including Joey Barton when he faced assault charges over a training ground fracas, have used the set and it also has a 'nice sideline acting in road traffic cases for high-profile media types.' Crime sells papers and so you've probably heard of the trials of hammer killer Levi Bellfield, Mark Dixie, who murdered Croydon model Sally Ann Bowman, and the case of the Polish nursing assistant killed in crossfire between two drug gangs. As the senior clerk was happy to reflect: 'If you can think of a recent high-profile case, we will probably have been on it' and not necessarily for the defence. Chambers is equally skilful in prosecutions and public inquiries, having acted in the Harold Shipman, Victoria Climbie and Stephen Lawrence inquiries.

Proud of the 'brand recognition' chambers has earned, members are united behind and invested in 'a corporate identity,' rather than simply engrossed in their own careers. As such, they were in a good position to 'anticipate some ten years ago the challenges facing the Criminal Bar' and respond by expanding into the regulatory work that now makes up a substantial part of the caseload. Not only is this one of the only criminal sets in the country with a national reputation for health and safety cases, tenants often work for HMRC, the General Medical Council, the General Optical Council and sports regulatory bodies like The FA. They also defend clients right across the regulatory spectrum, not least in relation to football, an arena in which the set is instructed by seven Premiership clubs. Chambers' prescient diversification has put it a step ahead of most crime sets, and a willingness to 'take cues from the way the Commercial Bar has had success' looks likely to keep it there. Sending juniors on secondment to solicitors, regulatory bodies and HMRC 'generates work and good relations.'

Chambers UK rankings

Crime • Fraud: Criminal • Health & Safety

Parkinson's law

Pupillage is characterised by 'general crime, serious fraud, some exposure to regulatory work' and a distinctive system of supervision. During each six pupils are assigned two supervisors, one junior, one more senior, ensuring experience of 'the full range of work from the smallest to largest cases' and 'two different sets of opinions and advice.' Pupils like it because 'if your senior supervisor

> Arguably, the set's ongoing and increasingly diverse success has just as much to do with the phenomenal 'appetite for hard work' of a group of barristers who are, in the words of pupils, 'roundly brilliant but very normal people.'

gets stuck on a long trial, you can hop out and go see a two-to-three day-er.' Initially, pupillage is characterised by 'watching and learning: you're in a cocoon and see the more serious cases, how your practice might be in ten years.' It can be high-profile stuff. A source remembered: 'One of my contemporaries helped on the Barry George appeal and I drafted a House of Lords petition.'

Come the second six, 'pupils work like absolute stink.' One enthused: 'I can count on the fingers of one hand the days I've stayed in chambers.' Trips to watch third-sixers in magistrates' courts prepare them for the first 'knee-trembling' appearance, as do 'short secondments to the solicitors who brief second-six pupils you start to forge relationships and learn what they want.' After the first day defending a client, 'you're never, ever as well prepared again, although later you realise you could have prepared in four hours what took you 12.' Thereafter the pace is ferocious and pupils 'earn very well,' but supervisors remember that they are still in training. 'We try to provide a support network so there is always someone to speak to, whatever the time,' one explained. 'The professional and ethics problems you face in those first months are probably more testing than at any subsequent point.' When a 'client's wife passes a twist of drugs in front of you' or a 'client changes what they are saying and the solicitor isn't there,' it's definitely good to have back-up on the phone.

The set 'takes the training aspect of pupillage very seriously' and supervisors 'expect pupils to ask for help,' often inviting them up from the basement library where pupils tend to congregate, to work in their rooms. Said one: 'We want to make sure they're doing alright in work,

socially in chambers, and in their own lives.' Pupils use supervisors as their 'first port of call for questions, feedback and advice. In-house advocacy training during the second six is 'assessed with the aim of improving performance not marking pupils.' Early sessions take the form of a bail application or plea in mitigation, and these culminate in 'a full-blown, day-long trial with actors playing witnesses in a mock courtroom.' Describing it as 'terrifying but brilliant,' pupils are observed by up to seven members of chambers and the actors 'really get into role as difficult witnesses, so the artificiality soon evaporates.' Whatever the result, there's plenty of feedback.

Winning ways

The tenancy decision is made in September after a formal interview process that includes an advocacy exercise. References from solicitors help back up a pupil's credentials, as they face a panel of objective juniors and seniors. Pupils are very aware that 'you've got to be outstanding and meet the criteria' because generally speaking only one person will gain tenancy, although this is not set in stone. 'Having the 2 Bedford Row brand on your CV is a major advantage' for those who do need to look elsewhere. 'After being here you'll feel confident that your future at the Bar is assured. Whenever you tell people where you're from, they always look at you with more respect.'

'Everyone here has something extra to offer, a bit of personality about them,' probably because '70% of your time is spent with lay clients and if you can't be normal you won't get the work from solicitors.' Chambers isn't fixated on academics in its quest to find 'evidence of a strong human touch' and excellence in advocacy. As well as straight law graduates, tenants include an ex-police officer, a former tabloid journo and a one-time banker. 'People with 2:2s are considered, if seen in the right context,' backing up pupils' claims that 'they will give anyone a chance to shine at interview.' Around 90 applicants are invited to a short meet-and-greet with one or two legal questions gently thrown in. A lucky 18 make get a more rigorous grilling at a second interview.

> ### And finally...
>
> The pace of life may be exacting here, but in what is 'a close unit, especially at the junior end,' pupils can also rely on 'a friendly experience' and 'a great social muddle,' whether it's a supervisor inviting them home for dinner with the family or 'someone encouraging you out for a glass of wine.'

Blackstone Chambers

The facts

Location: Temple, London

Number of QCs/Juniors: 31/42 (18 women)

Applications: 200

Olpas: Summer season

Pupils per year: 4-5

Seats: 4x3 months

Pupillage award: £42,500 (can advance £10,000 for BVC)

> **There's a great deal of substance to its style.**

Many sets claim to be forward-thinking but Blackstone is the original Bar innovator. Its trés chic premises at Blackstone House are just the outer trappings of a genuinely steely drive to be a modern organisation in a sometimes archaic profession.

Question everything

Enjoying a top-drawer reputation for public law, employment and civil liberties issues, as well as being highly respected for its commercial law capabilities, Blackstone barristers have worked on some of the highest-profile, precedent-setting cases of recent years. Members have represented a Guantanamo Bay detainee in the judicial review of his refusal of British identity, assisted a cancer patient in obtaining the drug Herceptin from the NHS and secured a ruling that the SFO's decision to drop a corruption investigation into a BAE Systems' arms deal with Saudi Arabia was unlawful. They represented F&C Asset Management in its defence of a multimillion-pound sexual harassment claim made by City worker Gillian Switalski, and former shareholders of Northern Rock in their request for a judicial review of the government's decision to nationalise the beleaguered bank.

Blackstone has 'a programme of building slowly but surely, only looking for stars when we recruit.' Nevertheless there has been an expansion in focus. EU/competition and regulatory advice is 'very much a growth area for the future of the Commercial Bar,' and the presence of five Blackstone barristers in Optigen v HMCE (a major ECJ carousel fraud case with EU-wide ramifications) highlights the set's ability to move with the times and find synergies between its competition, public and regulatory strengths. Chambers is also keen to expand its public international practice, with long-running involvement for Serbia & Montenegro against Bosnia & Herzegovina in the case at the ICJ the perfect calling card. Strength in media, sports and environmental law continues to develop: cases include representing Ashley Cole's agent in disciplinary proceedings brought by The FA and advice to the adjudicator appointed by the ICC regarding ball-tampering charges against Pakistan captain Inzamam-ul-Haq.

Thoroughbreds

Even securing an interview, let alone a pupillage, is tough. The set looks for 'an ability to write in an elegant and concise way' and 'some first-class marks in a 2:1, if not a First,' plus' clear enthusiasm for the Bar via mini-pupillages or similar.' That said, recruiters appreciate that 'two potentially great pupils may be utterly different in terms of personality and strengths.' A 'very thorough' first-round interview is essentially a light grilling on a subject

Chambers UK rankings

Administrative & Public Law • Civil Liberties • Commercial (Dispute Resolution) • Competition/European Law • Employment • Environment • Financial Services Regulation • Fraud: Civil • Immigration • Insurance • Media & Entertainment • Professional Discipline • Public International Law • Public Procurement • Sports Law • Telecommunications

selected by the candidate from a topical list. If they impress by demonstrating 'an ability to assimilate information and put together an argument,' they may be offered a week-long (potentially part-funded) mini-pupillage. At that stage, 'shadowing a barrister and completing a set piece of written work' gives chambers a better idea of candidates' 'real potential and skills.' Around 15 people attend a second interview designed to assess 'their fit with Blackstone' as much as anything else. Candidates are usually asked to talk about their time in chambers.

> Michael Fordham QC represented Royal Mail in its attempt to resist a judicial review request brought by a disabled woman who objected to Post Office closures following a decision to exempt it from disability equality laws.

Pupillage is 'characterised by a focus on learning.' After a week of induction, there is a three-month 'settling-in period' during which pupils 'acclimatise to the practice of law' and work on 'the basics of producing pleadings and structuring arguments.' One of the aims at this point is to ensure pupils are 'happy in chambers and engaged in a pleasant environment.' Life isn't all easy: in addition to working on a supervisor's caseload and attending court, pupils spend two days each month on a blind-marked written assessment. In total, seven assessments, together with copies of 'full formal feedback in written form' for each seat, plus pupil supervisor reports are integral to the tenancy decision. 'The feedback varies according to the style of the supervisor, but it's always with the tone 'you deserve to be here, but here are areas you've fallen below the highest standards'.'

Pupils rotate between the same supervisors. 'The best pupils are helpful and you'll incorporate some of their thoughts, which makes for a collaborative process,' reflected one supervisor. For their part, pupils tell us: 'What's amazing about barristers here is their ability to deal with cases of 20 files, yet summarise the essence incredibly succinctly.' Sitting with a commercially focused supervisor might mean 'helping a sports personality appeal a ban.' Time with a public law practitioner can entail 'lots of immigration,' perhaps 'helping to sue a Russian oligarch by proving he's domiciled in England.' Employment brings 'plenty of discrimination cases and tribunals.' Daily life may be 'front-page work, glamorous and important,' but pupils must be prepared to accept they will 'not always agree morally' with those they're working for.

Late developers

There is 'a conscious decision not to send pupils out to court alone,' so second-sixers continue to work for supervisors and beat their advocacy skills into shape via seven in-house sessions, two of which are videoed. Being taped as you cross-examine 'ham-acting witnesses from chambers' sounds dreadful to us, but chambers pays for drinks after each outing and apparently 'it's useful to see how you appear and what your faults might be.' Said one source: 'There's such a steep learning curve that within weeks you're aware that what you did a fortnight ago could be much better, not least because people are prepared to spend time with you going through your work.'

It's 'the overall story' that counts in the tenancy decision. 'Some people will become great advocates, others will become creative lawyers shaping the law, while others will excel at processing information and presenting a case there's no chambers type.' For those who gain tenancy the support continues by way of an interest-free loan of up to £30,000 for the first 15 months and a three-month training period to 'shadow juniors at county courts and tribunals.' Blackstone feels this is necessary because 'tenants come out of the traps rapidly in terms of volume of instructions' and, with such a range of work, it tends to be 'two years before you sit down with the clerks and decide where you want to specialise.' In 2008 three of the four pupils were granted tenancy.

Blackstone has a 'gregarious' atmosphere and, for the benefit of pupils, effort is made to 'create a relatively relaxed environment during what is a naturally stressful period.' Although a dress-down code does not apply to pupils because 'they have to be in meetings at a moment's notice,' hours 'between 8.30ish and 6.30ish' are reasonable compensation. Pupils attend the Christmas party and other socials, including drinks parties on the roof terrace and Friday night outings. 'Champagne – there seems to be a lot of drinking champagne,' mused one pupil.

And finally...

'The cross-section of work on offer lends itself to diversity' and 'the set is as good as its word in being open-minded as regards to who and what you are, and where you come from.' While this is a laudable sentiment, few members have a CV that mentions neither Oxford nor Cambridge University. Wherever you're applying from, remember that for Blackstone the overriding criterion is excellence.

Cloisters

The facts

Location: Temple, London

Number of QCs/Juniors: 5/44 (17 women)

Applications: 400+

Olpas: Summer season

Pupils per year: 2-4

Seats: 4x3 months

Money: £30,000 (can advance £5,000 for BVC)

> Each barrister does at least five days of pro bono work per year, either at legal advice centres or for clients who just miss out on legal aid.

At 54 years of age Cloisters is a modern, innovative set that, like Madonna, has remained up to date through constant reinvention. It was originally a criminal set that practised a little bit of civil law and then quite a bit more. To avoid a tug of war, members parted company, the criminal practitioners departing mostly for Charter and Tooks Chambers. What remained was the complex but cohesive unit specialising in professional negligence, personal injury and employment law.

Stand-up chameleons

Chambers' work often sets precedent, especially in the field of employment law. Members appeared in three of the four employment cases to reach the House of Lords in 2006, including the age discrimination case Rutherford v Secretary of State. Other big cases include Serco v Redfearn (race discrimination), Hendricks v Commissioner of Police (race and sex) and Wilson v South Cumbria Acute NHS Trust (the biggest ever equal pay case). Cloisters' personal injury practitioners are known for their expertise in occupational stress and bullying at work, and frequent crossover between discrimination and stress claims means cases go through both the employment tribunal and civil courts. As such, barristers must be adaptable – standing before a High Court judge is quite different to addressing an employment tribunal, where 'you dress less formally, you express yourself and put your questions differently, you don't stand up and you frequently find yourself dealing with litigants in person.'

Two good illustrations of Cloisters' PI work are a claim against the MoD relating to injuries sustained on a training exercise and a successful 1.5m claim made by an employee who was attacked by an inmate at a young offenders institution. Clinical negligence claims, commonly against the NHS, can be heart-wrenching and complicated. Catastrophic brain injuries, for example, can be worth over £5m. One pupil assisted his supervisor on 'a very complex quantum case involving figures of seven to eight million,' following a baby's oxygen starvation during birth. As these examples demonstrate, Cloisters' work comprises 'a massive amount of human interest on cutting-edge legal issues.' Members are also instructed in public law cases, touching on education, immigration, social security and mental health, and they advise the Commission for Equality and Human Rights.

Don't get left behind

The set conducts a healthy mix of claimant and defendant work: 'It would be naïve to take the view that it's always

Chambers UK rankings

Clinical Negligence • Employment

the employee being treated terribly.' Despite this overwhelming pragmatism, Cloisters has its roots in the radical left. It was set up by a group of conscientious objectors (several of them members of the Communist Party) back in the 1950s, and there is still 'a liberal ethos' in chambers. While the ideal of 'championing the rights of the individual against the evil, all-pervasive State' has, 'in reality, gone,' chambers clings to its egalitarian ideals, treating pupils like 'any other member of chambers.' Champagne socialists they definitely are not; indeed, senior clerk Glenn Hudson spoke disparagingly of the hypocrisy of certain sets that, having 'cornered an area of the market where they make money out of the least fortunate in life,' are still 'evangelical' about doing it.

A word of advice for applicants: the paper filter is 'the hardest stage,' so improve your chances by being succinct and avoiding 'unnecessary verbiage.' If you have underachieved in any particular area, explain the reasons why. Get to a second interview and you'll have a week to prepare a tort or contract-based legal problem. As well as displaying academic excellence, prospective pupils must show exceptional advocacy skills, the ability to deal with difficult clients and sufficient relevant experience to show well-founded reasons for wanting to do the job. The perfect way to do this is through FRU, as 'it gives you experience you won't get any other way.' A turn-off would be 'people who know all the answers but deliver them in a dull way.' Unless they're in court, the barristers go about their day-to-day business in casual dress, so don't turn up for interview expecting everybody to be in a flash Savile Row suit. All of this will become apparent should you get one of the set's 12 one-week internships.

EAT my words

The first six can feel like 'drowning under paper' as you read through complex medical reports and prepare to accompany supervisors to court. It's 'an intense period' and you'll spend a lot of time 'working at a desk in the library under a lot of time pressure.' While one supervisor's practice could be 80% PI and clin neg, another's might focus on international employment, for example 'a contract given to someone in London, who lives in Italy, but mostly works in Africa.' As well as raising jurisdictional questions, this could mean working unusual hours and taking part in teleconferences. First-six pupils learn how to draft grounds and notices of appeal, plus skeleton arguments for employment tribunals and EAT hearings. They also help to produce presentations on changes to

employment law. They also see some general commercial cases, drafting particulars of claim, attending conferences and taking part in mediations. 'You're much more of an observer than an active participant the client has come to get advice from a barrister, and that's not you!' At least there's the satisfaction of knowing that 'if your paperwork is good enough, it will be adopted.'

Second-sixers are given a free rein to take on their own cases and carry out advocacy in the county courts and employment tribunals. 'The transition is swift; you'll just get a call from the clerks on your first day saying, 'There's a hearing in the High Court, can you go?'' It goes without saying that the answer is 'yes'. Pupils continue to work for a supervisor during the second six, and as if that weren't enough, they are additionally expected to juggle work for other members and complete a series of rigorous assessments. These consist of a drafting exercise, a research exercise, advocacy and a formal interview. Assessments count a great deal in the September tenancy decision – up to 95% – and some of our sources felt disappointment that after a full year, supervisors' feedback only counts for 5%. In theory, as many pupils as reach the required standard will be offered tenancy. One per year is the norm, though the sole pupil did not stay on in 2008.

Second-six pupils find this period 'liberating.' Said one: 'If you don't find the first six a bit frustrating, you shouldn't have come to the Bar.' There's a real drive and enthusiasm about these pupils; they share a genuine interest in their work and seem to have endless reserves of energy. Equally thriving is the social life outside chambersthere are always lunches and impromptu parties to attend. 'You'll see us in Gaucho's a lot every time someone joins, leaves, has a baby or gets pregnant, it's a great excuse to crack open the champagne.'

And finally...

'Friendly, fun and adolescent' were just some of the adjectives used to describe the place, and maybe you'll pick up on this feeling when you visit. Amusingly, we noticed that some of the art hanging in the conference rooms was titled 'Inner Turmoil' and 'Mixed Emotions'. Hardly reflective...

Crown Office Chambers

The facts

Location: Temple, London
Number of QCs/Juniors: 14/68 (13 women)
Applications: 130
Not in Olpas
Pupils per year: Up to 3
Seats: 2x3 + 1x6 months
Money: £42,500 (can advance £15,000 for BVC)

> One senior clerk focuses on marketing. As well as relationships with firms such as Halliwells, CMS Cameron McKenna, Pinsent Masons, Lovells and Beachcroft, this willingness to spread the word has helped secure a foothold in the regions.

Created by the merger of two top-drawer insurance sets back in 2000, Crown Office Chambers is by some margin the largest common law set in the capital. Its strong backbone of insurance-based litigation expertise crosses several practice areas.

When the drugs don't work

Given that COC has enjoyed some great years in terms of billing, there seems little reason to deviate from its strategy of 'consolidating and developing of core strengths.' This isn't to say the set is averse to change. While construction, insurance, product liability, professional negligence and personal injury are at its heart, it continues to make strides in the education arena. Chambers has also raised its profile in health and safety law, 'aiming for the defence of regulatory prosecutions market.' Elsewhere, the overall balance between defendant and claimant insurance instructions – traditionally weighted towards the former – has edged to 'roughly 60/40' of late. Representing the human guinea pigs in the disastrous Northwick Park Hospital Parexel TGN 1412 drug trial is a case in point. That said, the defence of major class actions continues apace, with members involved in the 2007 Pleural Plaques case (one of 'the biggest disease suits of the last ten years') and advising Merck on litigation relating to its withdrawn drug Vioxx. The set has also been involved 'in all the Ladbroke Grove train crash claims for AIG and Thames Trains.'

Gaining one of the three pupillages offered each year is fairly tricky. The first hurdle is the substantial application form. You'll find a copy online and chambers takes its contents 'very seriously. It's hard to demonstrate good interpersonal skills on a written form, but it's very easy to show yourself badly.' Twenty or so make it to the first-stage interview and a mere 10 or so to the second. Candidates face ethics questions and off-the-wall posers to get them thinking on their feet. One of our recent favourites was 'Explain an iPod to a Martian.' The point is not to catch people out, but to assess 'applicants' oral skills and ability to present and analyse facts in different ways. We're looking for potential that we can exploit during pupillage.' Pupils agree that COC is 'as interested in your personality as your academic ability' – you might, for instance, be asked 'to justify why one charitable project should receive a grant over another, then have to argue the opposing case.' Privileging a balance of the oral and the academic is important here because 'the early years are centred around advocacy – in common law you have to think on your feet and have the adaptability to make persuasive arguments for positions that may not be particularly attractive.' We'd advise brushing up on these skills if offered an interview.

Chambers UK rankings

Clinical Negligence • Construction • Health & Safety • Personal Injury • Product Liability • Professional Negligence

A game of two halves

One of the set's main aims is 'to ensure that pupillage is a training period, not a year-long, nightmarish interview.' Listening to supervisors talk about 'the satisfaction of charting improvement' and their attempts 'to make pupils feel like part of the team,' it seems that reality matches the pitch. For their part, recruits told us: 'You always know what's expected of you.' Each sits with the same four

> The set operates out of several premises in the Temple, and while this distribution is not ideal, it feels the merger worked well. 'We've ironed out any cultural differences and there are no 'back in the day' issues.'

supervisors throughout the year, with the aim of maximising exposure to different areas of practice and facilitating consistent assessment.

Last year's supervisors offered pupils the experience of practice in 'clinical negligence, construction, PI/commercial and straight PI,' and no matter where you begin 'there tends to be a complete amnesty on mistakes for the first few weeks.' Pupils get to grips by 'working on smaller defendant PI or clin neg cases for a local authority or hospital trust' or handling 'discrete points of research relating to specialist construction proceedings.' In the second six the pattern of life continues in a similar fashion, with the working day lasting from 'around 8.30am to 6-6.30pm' and including weekly court visits with your supervisor. In each seat, pupils must complete 'two fixed, written tasks that are set and marked by a specialist in the practice area.' Together with the supervisor's report, these form the basis of an 'end-of-seat letter, which outlines points for you to consider.' After Christmas, a 'half-time chat' with the head of the pupillage committee is designed to keep pupils on track. At more or less the same time the 'serious' advocacy course begins, involving 'four different exercises in front of a panel of 'judges' played by members of chambers.' Supervisors emphasise that they are 'looking for a general upward trajectory during the year rather than landmarks in development. You know, people often do badly in their first advocacy test, or maybe they mess up a written assessment – our system is designed to not give mistakes such as these disproportionate weight.' This is noted by pupils, who appreciate chambers' clear assessments and open lines of communication.

Good relations

The early years of common law practice involve a broad spread of work: 'It's five to seven years before you begin to specialise,' not least because 'you think you know what area you're interested in but then opportunity takes you somewhere else entirely.' The second six is just the beginning of this process; there's 'an enormous amount of work for pupils' and little reason or opportunity to specialise. As well as working for their supervisors, pupils will be in court two or three times a week making small applications, appearing at CMCs or in small claims arbitrations. Although most of the pupils' proceedings are within reach of the M25, juniors can expect to clock up the miles on countrywide expeditions.

The July tenancy decision is 'taken very seriously' and the process is under constant review. Essentially the pupillage committee considers written and advocacy assessments, supervisors' reports and comments from other members. The system wins the support of pupils, who are confident that they are 'judged on merit, not what some crusty old member thinks of the one piece of work you did for him.' In 2008, one of the two pupils was successful.

From among the juniors, pupils are assigned 'aunts and uncles' of whom they may ask 'the stupid questions you don't want to put to anyone else.' Their other job is to take pupils out for drinks. Continuing with the social theme, there are weekly gatherings in chambers, which 'everyone attends.' As well as using these as an opportunity to get used to the recent introduction of the use of first names 'for everyone from clerks to senior members' pupils can sample 'a bottle or two opened by a wine-mad QC.' An annual Christmas party is also on the cards, as are other regular drinks and events with clients. Importantly, 'the fair structure of assessment means that all of us pupils get on with each other – we go for lunch, dinner and drinks together.' Recent intakes have been Oxbridge-heavy, but 'it doesn't feel like there's a set type of candidate or fixed criteria for entrance.'

And finally...

'Whatever happens come July, I'll be happy to have been a pupil here,' said one source, reflecting the views of others we spoke to and endorsing the set's attempts to create a welcoming and learning-focused atmosphere.

One Essex Court

The facts

Location: Temple, London
Number of QCs/Juniors: 22/45 (10 women)
Applications: 185
Olpas: Summer season
Pupils per year: 4-5
Seats: 2x3 + 1x6 months
Pupillage award: £45,000 + earnings (can advance £15,000 for BVC)

> 'We're not a set that's been providing judges to the Chancery Division for the last hundred years, and we're not the slightest bit concerned who your parents are or where you went to school.'

One of the magic circle commercial sets, One Essex Court prides itself on having generalist practitioners. As a result, its specialism could be described as 'providing high-quality advice on highly complex problems at the highest level.'

Monsieur, with these cases you're really spoiling us

In the course of a week, one member's highly busy schedule included working on a commercial property case in Derbyshire, an aluminium fraud in Tajikistan, a contractual dispute involving gas pipelines between Singapore and Indonesia, advising the government of a country we are unable to name on arms procurement, and acting for Ferrero in a case about Turkish hazelnuts. No wonder pupils speak enthusiastically about witnessing 'all sorts of crazy stuff all over the world' – and in outer space, as the 'freezing injunction in relation to a satellite' demonstrates.

OEC claims to be 'the most relaxed and informal' of the magic circle commercial sets 'by a considerable margin.' It was founded in 1966 by four barristers, along with legendary 'fifth man,' senior clerk Reg Murrell. They came from a set in Mitre Court where the dictatorial head of chambers was apparently making life extremely difficult. OEC is still viewed by some as a Johnny-come-lately at the Commercial Bar, but members are proud of the set's history and keen to continue its ethos of open access. 'We're about as meritocratic as you can be,' said one. The management style is open: every committee has clerks on it, and while pupils spoke of hearing 'appalling stories about other sets' where there might be 'an officer and NCO sort of relationship between pupils and supervi-

sors,' here barristers, pupils and clerks are all on first-name terms.

Head of chambers Lord Grabiner QC is 'a committed and powerful figurehead who believes in his clients' cases,' but also 'not a snob – he doesn't use long Latinate terms.' This down-to-earth style runs throughout chambers: 'You're providing a solution that is practical and user-friendly, not writing a legal essay,' explained one barrister. Another commented: 'I run my meetings as conferences in the true sense. I don't sit there and pontificate from on high, we operate very much as a team.' The dress code is relaxed: 'I would generally wear jeans and a T-shirt to work,' said one barrister. For pupils, this would be a mistake, as there is supposedly 'an elderly member of chambers who would be offended to see a pupil not dressed in a suit, but we haven't identified who it is yet!' Pupils keep up a fierce pace from around 9am until 7pm: 'You do put

Chambers UK rankings

Arbitration (International) • Banking & Finance • Commercial (Dispute Resolution) • Company • Energy & Natural Resources • Fraud: Criminal • Insurance • Intellectual Property • Professional Negligence

pressure on yourself... you don't want to disappoint your supervisor.'

Heavyweight champions

A pie chart of chambers' work would have to be cut differently from year to year, as these commercial barristers turn their hand to insolvency at one moment, mergers and acquisitions the next and a contractual bust-up after that everything depends on the economy. You'll need intellectual curiosity to enjoy solving complex legal problems and, at the least, 'not be repelled by the commercial world.' OEC recruiters believe there's no blueprint for a successful barrister. 'Some pupils come out of the egg with the confidence of Muhammad Ali;' others are 'very diffident.' They therefore ask 'what value chambers can add' and 'what latent potential is there for us to build on?'

Being a 'practical thinker' is just as important as a stunning academic background. 'Once they get to interview, it's astonishing the number of people with the most glittering academic records who just bomb, and those without who absolutely cane it.' If you don't have superb grades, you're going to have to make one hell of a case. 'If you've got a First from any university, we'll interview you, but if you haven't, there has to be another string to your bow, and having won a gold medal at the Chelsea Flower Show won't help you.' As an example, one successful applicant who had a 2:1 had been a former president of the Oxford Union. Finally, chambers looks for 'people we can enjoy spending time with if there's a spark about them that's a great asset to the set.'

Northern Rock 'n' roll

Pupillage is 'an amazing learning curve; you start off as a very naïve BVC student who's done a few pleadings and suddenly you're into incredibly exhilarating, complex stuff, assisting on huge, sprawling cases.' One pupil attended a three-day trial in her first three months. The preparation took several weeks, but then watching QCs Ian Glick and Laurie Rabinowitz argue it out in the House of Lords, with five law lords questioning them, was described as 'the best tutorial ever.' There will be a great deal of interpretation of contracts (a Bulgarian bank's shareholders' agreement, a contract for supply of gas or a telecommunications company in Nigeria) and the rest of time will be spent researching legal points, drafting advices and skeleton arguments, occasionally pleadings. In some cases, a pupil's work will be used. 'They always say thank you so much, but it actually feels like an amazing privilege when you've contributed, even in some small way.'

Advocacy is central to this pupillage: after seven or eight court visits in the first six, second six-pupils are on their feet for small county court claims, mainly possession hearings and road traffic accidents. Though 'you might have a hearing only once a week, you'll spend hours and hours preparing for it.' OEC believes that advocacy on your own cases is the best way of preparing for tenancy, when life will constantly throw curve balls and it's important to know how to deal with them. Supervisors 'very much take into account that people are still developing in the first three months of pupillage,' so it's generally the second and third seats that are 'taken more seriously.' Every three months, supervisor write reports and other members add their views. A formal review at the six-month stage inevitably means bad news for some people. 'If someone clearly isn't going to get tenancy, it's only fair to let them know.' Those who do not make the cut receive help with finding a third six, however four out of the five pupils gained tenancy in 2008.

Pupils are invited to all the social events and their name goes on the website. 'You even have a little CV on there, so it really feels as though they're holding you out as one of their people.' And when pupillage finishes, 'it's more than relief, it's euphoria.' As one person commented: 'One of the reasons pupillage gets such a bad press is that what comes after it is so amazing.' How could it not be? Think of a major case and the chances are someone from the set is involved with it – Hurricane Katrina claims, the Buncefield oil depot explosion, Northern Rock fallout, Virgin Media's squabble with Sky and the list goes on.

And finally...

One Essex Court is a thriving and supportive place to complete pupillage. As one pupil told us: 'I just look around me at the barristers here and think, 'I'd love to be like you.' Working with them is such a buzz.'

39 Essex Street

The facts

Location: Temple, London
Number of QCs/Juniors: 24/53 (19 women)
Applications: 300+
Olpas: Summer season
Pupils per year: Up to 3
Seats: 4 before July
Pupillage award: £40,000 (can advance £8,000 for BVC)

Anyone who fancies proving their mettle at 39 Essex Street is advised to get a place on a mini-pupillage. While not mandatory for pupillage applicants, perform well and you can expect it to count in your favour.

Bright, bustling and businesslike, 39 Essex Street is master of its many trades and possessed of an apparently inexhaustible desire for self-improvement.

Still room at the Inn

In the last seven years, 39 Essex Street has mushroomed from 30 to nearly 80 barristers, making it one of the larger London sets. Its broad coverage allows it to adopt a contemporary strategy of not only pursuing its core areas but also 'providing connections between them with the aim of being a one-stop shop for clients.' As it fills its airy premises on the western fringe of the Temple, it has already 'secured accommodation needs for the next ten years.' Said chambers director Michael Meeson with an acquisitive glint in his eye: 'We're ever-willing to take on new barristers if there's a business need.'

Many sets advertise broad coverage, few back up the claim as substantially as this one. It has two or more barristers ranked in 16 areas of practice in the latest edition of *Chambers UK*. The 'four genuine trunks of strength' are common law, environmental and planning, commercial/construction law and public law, and 39 also thrives on the areas of crossover. Construction 'isn't just construction, it brings in environment, planning, regulatory, even nuclear work in extension,' while 'serving the health industry isn't only clin neg or PI, it's professional negligence and commercial work for the NHS or private providers.' Multinational conglomerates like Esso and BP instruct members, as do some 85 local authorities.

Away from commercial and common law practice, chambers takes on some eye-catching human rights, immigration, administrative law and local government instructions and costs litigation. And its commitment to pro bono work is evident in links to the Environmental Law

Foundation, FRU and Liberty. Certainly the widow of a British serviceman killed in combat was grateful for help at the coroner's inquest that established his death was the result of US friendly fire.

Inspire, aspire, perspire

Some 30 support staff ensure chambers is 'run like an effective business.' It also means 'the pastoral aspects and structure of pupillage are not left to chance.' Indeed, pupils praised an 'entirely transparent, well thought-out process' that starts with their being given a detailed pupillage handbook. They sit with four supervisors in the first nine months, typically two each from the fields of public and private law. As a result they are exposed to anything from 'enormous VAT disputes' to 'redrafting statutes on education matters,' from common law work where 'you get to grips with the White Book' to 'construction disputes and immigration cases.' Our sources laughed at the absurdity of a pupil 'drafting a letter starting Dear Secretary of State,' but were clearly inspired by the prospect of doing so at some later stage. 'What's great

Chambers UK rankings

Administrative & Public Law • Civil Liberties • Clinical Negligence • Construction • Costs Litigation • Environment • Immigration • Local Government • Personal Injury • Product Liability • Professional Discipline • Professional Negligence • Tax

about chambers is that wherever tenancy takes you, the future horizons are broad. In none of its areas is chambers half-hearted, and you look up the food chain in any of them and see barristers doing interesting, sexy work.'

First-six supervisors take care that their charges handle pleadings and skeleton arguments, rather than running around as a gopher, researching minor points. Their policing role continues into the second six when everything

> **Pupils are invited to social events, whether it's the Christmas party for members' children (dressing as an Elf may be required) or the summer garden party, this year an elegant Bollywood affair.**

still has to be 'sanctioned by the supervisor.' Second-sixers go to court a couple of times a week on 'RTAs and credit hire cases,' with juniors providing support when needed. Pupils love the wealth of advocacy opportunities because it's all about 'developing witness-handling skills, making your mistakes and learning case strategy in a relatively safe environment.' So much so in fact, that we even heard one source utter the words: 'I really like going to Slough County Court.' Beyond the commonplace, 'more interesting things pop up.' One interviewee recalled 'going to the Privy Council, which meant asking a kindly silk where I had to sit.'

No competition

Predictably, feedback is detailed. As well as responses to each piece of work, pupils receive a formal appraisal and written report at the end of each seat, which 'flag problems as you go, so you're not storing up nasty surprises for just before the tenancy decision.' Unusually, the report also deals with the question of how well pupils have maintained their extra-curricular commitments. The reports are central to the tenancy decision, as are up to four written assessments set by a shadow pupillage committee and completed in the second six. Recalling these, a junior told us: 'They take a lot of hard work – around a week each. One of them was the most difficult legal problem I've ever faced.' The final hurdle is a tough assessed advocacy session in which pupils demonstrate witness-handling and technical skills to the watching panel while 'supervisors

play witnesses with aplomb.' Pupils say they're entirely satisfied that 'if you meet the objective criteria, you'll be taken on. We're not explicitly or quietly in competition with each other.' Perhaps proving this, in 2006 all three contenders gained tenancy, in 2007 two of the three did so and in 2008 the single pupil was not successful.

At the pupillage application stage around 30 people attend a first interview. 'You get a case an hour beforehand and are grilled for 20 minutes by a panel of five to assess your legal reasoning.' The 12 who are summoned back to the second round face a milder 'more traditional, general CV chat.' Even a brief glances at tenants' CVs reveals that 39 Essex is genuinely open to people of 'all backgrounds, types and skills.' A number arrived from other careers and our sources told us that 'brains in a vat just don't cut it here,' because 'trawling though paperwork is only half the job; our areas demand broader skills.'

Taking the biscuit

Work-life balance at chambers isn't so much a vague aim as a rigorously policed policy. Supervisors 'aggressively enforce 9am-to-6pm hours' for pupils and encourage a 'full hour for lunch.' Someone who initially doubted the curfew recalled: 'It was 6.04pm on the first day I tried to stay and my supervisor ejected me.' The set's concern to show pastoral care is also evident in the willingness of juniors to 'make an effort to look after the pupils.' It might mean 'post-work drinks together,' a friendly chat at the fortnightly lunch or simply patient forbearance as 'you call up for the nth time saying, 'Aarrgh, I've got this tomorrow, how do I do it?" There's also a confidential mentoring system, which sees a senior appointed as an additional point of contact for pupils in need of advice, and often this relationship generates work once tenancy is assured. This is a reasonably casual set on the inside: some of the members we met during our visit wore T-shirts and jeans, and they cheerfully dug into a pile of biscuits as we chatted to them about the set's 'positive atmosphere.' While munching away, one reflected: 'If I get a complicated, esoteric instruction I have no hesitation in asking anyone about it and I mean anyone.'

> ## And finally...
>
> Breadth of excellence and opportunity define a 39 Essex Street pupillage; go to any length to get one.

Government Legal Service

The facts

Location: London, Manchester
Number of Barristers: c.500 (c.270 women)
Applications: 200+
Not in Olpas
Pupils per year: Potentially 15-20
Seats: 2x6 or 3x4 months
Pupillage award: £22,640-£24,900+ BVC fees and £5,000-7,000 bursary

Unlike the independent Bar, where pupils must convince those training them of their ability to earn money, 'at the GLS they start from the premise you've got to do something wrong not to be employed on qualification.'

The 500 or so barristers at the GLS have a single client – the government. They advise on the implementation of policy and the implications of European and domestic legislation. The lawyers also provide advocacy in litigation, judicial reviews and other inquiries and tribunals.

Brothers and sisters in law

Over 30 government departments employ lawyers, so the subject matter is enormous in scope. Some of the issues our sources had encountered were the freezing of terrorists' assets, supporting a lasting peace in Northern Ireland, advising teams on emergency protocols to deal with animal disease, the implementation of the Gambling Act and prosecuting fraud cases. We could go on all day listing the different topics and areas of law; instead we'll point you www.gls.gov.uk for detailed info about the available work and which departments offer pupillages.

Applicants are considered alongside those looking to become solicitors with the GLS and some 15-20 of the training places available can potentially be filled by pupils. It is possible to apply to the GLS without committing to either the barrister or solicitor route, as everyone is viewed as a 'trainee'. In some departments 'barristers do much the same job as solicitors,' and one of our interviewees confessed they had 'a solicitor hat and a barrister hat.' For further details on the ins and outs of the application process, read the feature on training as a solicitor with the GLS on page 351.

Once assigned to a department, trainees complete two seats of six months or three of four months. All work comes from designated supervisor, with whom trainees chat about their progress on a weekly basis. 'There's a good deal of autonomy,' said one source, explaining that while trainees might show complex pieces of work to their supervisors they are 'able to get on with things and liaise with clients directly to a certain extent.' One seat is usually spent in a prestigious set of chambers working with barristers in private practice. With the work of barristers and solicitors overlapping in the civil service, it's a chance to see the 'more fast-moving' lifestyle of the independent Bar and 'sit on the other side of the professional fence.' Our sources said they were treated just like other pupils in chambers and observed 'some superb advocacy.' Secondments to the Crown Prosecution Service are available in some instances.

The thinker

In certain departments the trainee's work will be predominantly advisory and 'you usually have policy considerations to take into account.' Recent trainees have advised on the insolvencies of football clubs and the emotive collapse of the Swindon-based Farepak Christmas Club, which lost the hard-earned savings of customers in 2006. Others liaised with counsel to draft Acts of Parliament and pondered the implications of European directives. 'In legal terms,' explained one academically minded interviewee, 'I'm the one who sits and thinks about thorny issues.' Contentious work might typically include writing defences, drafting witness statements and orders, instructing investigating officers and advocates on commercial litigation, perhaps against or initiated by the Ministry of

Defence, or criminal prosecutions under the Insolvency Act, where much turns on the question of intention to defraud' – §a woolly, difficult area.'

It's worth pointing out that opportunities for trainees to conduct advocacy are rare, and 'if you want to go to court all the time you probably won't be interested in the GLS.' The size of legal teams and the even smaller number of barristers mean that 'anything outside the M25 goes to agents.'

> GLS lawyers take a holistic view of the law. In private practice its all about specialisation. The government absolutely doesn't want that kind of lawyer and you're expected to be a good generalist.

Trainees will generally see more of the magistrates' courts than the Crown Court, where government lawyers usually instruct private practice barristers. Our sources didn't feel too hard done by, as there's plenty of scope to develop drafting, interviewing and conferencing skills.

A job for a life

Aside from the quality and broad scope of work, there are other benefits to training with the GLS. Normal work hours 'really are nine to five,' and 'while they expect you to work hard during the day it's not something that becomes all-encompassing.' Flexible working is encouraged and everyone has a 30-day holiday allowance. Remember, barristers and pupils in private practice do not get paid holidays. The GLS pays BVC fees and awards a maintenance grant. It sometimes pays for the GDL year too. There's the security that comes from being an employed barrister without the worry of where the next instruction and pay cheque will come from, and then at the end of your career there's 'a very good pension.'

There are downsides, of course, one of them being a relatively low salary. Some of our GLS sources thought that attempts to run the service more like a business, and yet not make salaries competitive with those in private practice, smacked of 'the civil service wanting to have its cake and eat it.' One dedicated public servant had clearly done the maths: 'At the junior level, once you add in pensions and holidays, in terms of financial security you're on par with the civil Bar for a few years. After that they may go miles in front, but they have to sell themselves.'

Recently it was decided that the period of post-qualification supervision for barristers should be extended by 12 months and eventually everyone will spend two years after qualifying as 'legal officers' on a salary below that of a Grade 7 government lawyer. Some trainees have been left ruing their prospective loss of earnings, but others welcome what is essentially another year of training. The GLS told us the new standardised structure puts trainee barristers and solicitors on more of an equal footing, given the difference in the time it takes to qualify.

So exactly who shuns the long-term financial benefits and freedom of self-employment at the independent Bar? Many have already worked in the private sector, either in law or another career, and most have an interest in politics, even if personal convictions must be kept at arm's length. 'If you don't want to do something because it conflicts with your politics you can protest, but then you might have to resign if you still won't do what is asked.' The GLS is 'a natural choice' for someone with a strong interest in pubic and administrative law, but it also attracts people 'who don't have an incredibly specific idea of what they want to do.' Government lawyers are never in the same place for too long: typically they stay in a department for three years before moving on to another and this produces genuinely capable all-rounders.

> ## And finally...
>
> With trainees dispersed across the civil service, the Legal Trainee Network makes an admirable effort to get everyone socialising. There's no reason for pupillage to be the lonely and stressful experience it can sometimes turn into at the independent Bar.

4-5 Gray's Inn Square

The facts

Location: Gray's Inn, London

Number of QCs/Juniors: 11/35 (8 women)

Applications: 200+

Olpas: Summer season

Pupils per year: Up to 3

Seats: 4 in first 9 months

Pupillage award: £36,500 (can advance sum for BVC)

> **4-5 Gray's Inn Square combines planning expertise with significant ability in the many facets of public law, judicial review and local government work. It also has an ever-expanding commercial practice.**

After seven members departed to Matrix Chambers in 2000, this set considered, then dismissed, a merger with Monckton Chambers, subsequently losing a further eight barristers. It could simply have faded; instead it drew breath and went to work with a vengeance. Today it is a picture of health.

Inquiring minds

Nearly half of the membership is involved with public law and planning inquiries, High Court applications for judicial review and complex planning and environmental advice to developers, local authorities and objectors. For some this might be a major wind farm inquiry in Northumbria or preparing for a prospective major judicial review concerning National Air Traffic Control's proposed restacking of UK commercial airline flights. If you don't fancy a fleet of Boeing 767s flying over your house all of a sudden, you equally might dislike a high-rise building going up next door. Members have been drafted into the forthcoming planning inquiry concerning two new Blackfriars Road skyscrapers by the London Borough of Southwark, while others are assisting Coventry airport realise its expansion plans. The volume of instructions for big developers is slowing as the credit crunch bites deeper, however when the property market is busy, so too are the planning barristers.

You can't underplay the effect that economic and political factors have on planning work; indeed, so much of chambers' public law practice is at 'the intersection of policy, politics and law.' Basically, if it involves public bodies, 4-5 will get involved, be it judicial review, employment, social security or mental health tribunals, education, environment or European law. Some 300 local authorities regularly turn to the set across the full spectrum of their legal needs. Chambers has recently been advising around 30 of them on the government's eco-towns plans and many others on proposed changes to the unitary status of local authorities.

Some members have sports law expertise, which led to involvement in a challenge to the ICC's decision to alter the result of the controversial England v Pakistan 2006 Oval Test. Meanwhile strength in media/defamation issues meant JK Rowling turned to chambers over a press intrusion matter. In addition members handle commercial judicial reviews, multi-jurisdictional banking cases and international trade and insurance cases.

Smart choices

Proud of its knack for identifying talented applicants, the set recruits with the 'strong presumption that pupils are good enough to be tenants.' It's no empty boast: only one person hasn't made tenancy in the six years since the set reduced its annual pupil intake to three at most. Both of the pupils of 2008 were successful. The set takes an exacting approach to interviewing candidates, aiming to uncover 'fine analytical skills to go to the heart of a mat-

Chambers UK rankings

Administrative & Public Law • Education • Environment • Local Government • Planning • Professional Discipline

ter and present in a clear structured framework,' as well as 'excellent advocacy skills, the ability to be calm, confident and persuasive.' Around 40 applicants are called to a first-round interview of 'a little discussion about the CV to set people at ease, but mostly questions to probe reasoning.' The best prospects come back for a second-round day of advocacy, which current pupils remembered as 'the most fulfilling, most completely testing interview' of any in their experience. Applicants are given a bundle of doc-

> **Over 500 people apply for a mini-pupillage here every year, so check the set's website for details as early as possible.**

uments from which they must write submissions. Oral advocacy is before a panel of up to seven members; non-law grads needn't worry too much, as the test is one of 'raw ability to reason and present.' It's undoubtedly a 'nerve-racking' process, but at the end 'you feel like you've had a good chance to show your stuff.'

Pupils sit with up to four supervisors in the nine months before the tenancy decision is made, with these regular switches designed to ensure breadth of experience, not to mention 'exposure to widely different personalities.' 'The first period is very protected: you're allowed lots of time to do work and told to go home early.' There's a clear 'sense of progression, so that you start taking on bigger pieces like whole opinions or skeleton arguments for a supervisor. There's also devilling for other members and you have your own workload as well.' The public side might mean 'going to the European Court of Human Rights on a DNA retention case;' commercial work might equate to 'a heavyweight dispute involving a Kurdistan telecoms company;' while planning encompasses large and small-scale inquiries, 'perhaps where your supervisor is grilling an expert witness put up to defend an indefensible case by a local authority.' As an indication of the scope of experiences on offer, one pupil recounted being involved with 'public law-based tribunals, an extradition case, a big compulsory purchase order, mental health reviews and social security tribunals.'

On the road

Second-six pupils won't be on their feet much unless they take on pro bono instructions. The latter half of pupillage is still designed as a learning experience, learning for example that 'commercial work gives you lots of time to

work out a tactical move to wrongfoot the opposition,' while public sector work 'is very fast-moving and requires a specific skill set to deal with the many people involved in making decisions.' Regular court visits and trips to inquiries keep things exciting. It might be 'Northumbria one week, Southampton the next,' in which case 'you're likely to have lunch, dinner and maybe even breakfast with your supervisor.' This routine also gives an incredible insight into 'the sorts of travel and work pressures of practice proper.' Pupils may also take a short secondment to a law firm or local authority client.

Pupils are continually informed about their progress as supervisors offer comments 'on a piece-by-piece basis,' although as time goes by 'if nothing's said it means [your work] is good.' Whenever pupils do anything for other members 'they fill in a feedback form with a public and private section. You see the public bit' while the private comments form part of the feedback supervisors provide at three-monthly appraisals and are also taken into consideration at the tenancy decision. Similarly important are three assessed advocacy days that are 'very much like the second-round interview.' Of course the stakes are higher and the complexity greater. The subjects chosen are deliberately those with which pupils are likely to be unfamiliar, but there's feedback after each day and 'so far as possible, the same people are on the assessing panel, which is good for seeing your development or regression.'

It's small wonder that pupils feel 'well supported' and entirely clear about where they stand, despite the 'occasional inevitable moments of pupil paranoia.' This set thrives on a 'tough, hard-working culture' but is nevertheless 'very human there's no dreadful pressure cooker atmosphere.' Clerks, juniors and even seniors can be relied on to make pupils feel comfortable, particularly at an initial welcome dinner, but also at weekly lunches or occasional drinks. In the summer – weather permitting – chambers lunch takes the form of a picnic in Gray's Inn Gardens. Other notable features of the social calendar are a formal dinner in May and the Christmas party.

> ## And finally...
>
> More so than many sets, 4-5 Gray's Inn Square is deeply committed to its pupils. Successfully negotiate the testing interview process and you'll have every opportunity to embark upon a rewarding practice in planning, commercial and public law.

2 Hare Court

The facts

Location: Middle Temple, London

Number of QCs/Juniors: 15/39 (14 women)

Applications: 300+

Olpas: Summer season

Pupils per year: 2

Seats: 3x4 months

Pupillage award: Min. £24,000

If you want to be one of the 45 or so applicants invited to a shortish first-round interview, take recruiters' advice and use the Olpas form to 'show analysis of your experiences of mini pupillage or court visits,' don't just list them.

Once upon a time – about seven years ago – 2HC was primarily all about prosecution. The apparent ease with which it has made high-profile defence work an equal part of its caseload says everything about this set's smooth brilliance.

Crime bosses and canoeists

Members have recently prosecuted Barry George in the Jill Dando murder retrial, represented criminal mastermind Terry Adams (even the Krays called him Sir, apparently) in trial and confiscation proceedings, prosecuted the Suffolk strangler, successfully defended Sean Hoey, the accused in the Omagh bombing case, and acted for Kent Pharmaceuticals in a fraud case that is the SFA's largest ever investigation to date. Then there's the juniors involved in the 21/7 terrorist trial and the Darwin 'forgetful canoeist' case, not to mention head of chambers David Waters' starring role in the criminal prosecution of terrorism defendants including Omar Khyam.

Seeing itself as 'a progressive set in an increasingly competitive market,' and faced with the uncertainties common to the Criminal Bar, 2HC isn't resting on its laurels. It has moved into areas that suit its skills, and so barristers now regularly prosecute at professional disciplinary tribunals for the General Medical Council and on regulatory matters for organisations like The FA. VAT tribunal work for HMRC is also emerging as a strength. Additionally, individuals shine in licensing and environmental law. It's unlikely that crime will cease to be the mainstay, it's just that the set understands the value of developing these other public law abilities.

Several hundred applicants duke it out for the two pupillages available each year. Candidates face 'questions about a topic they should know about, perhaps a dissertation or specialism, whether law-based or not,' as well as probing on 'general legal topics.' The 12 who make it to the second round have 30 minutes to prepare for an advocacy exercise, 'such as an opening for a prosecution.' The main point is to demonstrate an 'ability to stand up and tell a story' rather than a grasp of legal proprieties. Pupils who'd navigated the process reflected on how '[the set] seemed most interested in your broader skills and experience' and felt interviews were 'tailored to you, not some pro forma list of questions.' Perhaps this it is because the set is seeking out 'rounded individuals with the capacity to deal one day with an erudite statutory construction in the Court of Appeal, the next day with a difficult client in a magistrates' court.' Looking at the backgrounds of 2HC tenants, there's no obvious formula for who makes it in. We'd add that the two pupils we met could not have been more different.

Seriously good

Gaining tenancy almost certainly involves a third six, meaning new pupils have senior pupils from whom to

Chambers UK rankings

Crime • Fraud: Criminal • Professional Discipline

take cues. During the long haul, 2HC invests a lot of time and effort in its pupils. As the senior clerk observed: 'We could take on solicitors' magistrates' court lists to secure their Crown Court stuff, but we don't like to treat our pupils that way; we prefer to see them in court on more serious cases' then 'back in chambers learning social and networking skills, being comfortable with more senior members.' Raising the pupillage award to £24,000, is one way the set has chosen to support pupils, and a new sys-

> **Murder, terrorism, international drug trafficking, fraud, corruption, sexual offences and corporate manslaughter are all in a day's work at 2 Hare Court. If you're serious about crime, few places will appeal more.**

tem of three supervisors in the first year is also designed to 'help them meet more people, get more work, and not face the prospect of a new supervisor and getting on their feet at the same time.' Similarly, the head of the pupillage committee is working hard to ensure 'supervisors and members of chambers don't overload pupils, because realistically they will never say no to work.'

The first six involves close observation of both supervisors, learning the ins and outs of court procedures and client-handling skills. Observing certainly isn't boring; indeed the delight on the faces of our interviewees was infectious. 'It's brilliant stuff: we were straight in at the Old Bailey on one murder trial after another. Murders, terrorism, you name it… it's what you've been training for and it's all within touching distance.' Back in chambers there are fortnightly advocacy exercises, 'when you get feedback there and then' and at the end of each seat supervisors will give an appraisal of your performance while in their charge. In the future this process may be handed over to, or supplemented by discussions with, the head of the pupillage committee.

At the end of the first six, a week is spent trailing senior pupils in the magistrates' courts, 'learning the things you'd forgotten and the things you didn't even know you needed to know.' Emphasising the importance of advocacy in the second six, a mock trial scheme helps prepare pupils, but it's practically the real thing. Staged in the evening at the Old Bailey, a couple of resident judges preside, 'the staff stay on wearing their full regalia' and 'members of chambers play witnesses,' (in)advertently revealing that they are 'all complete hams.' There's also a

secondment to the CPS, where pupils 'see the ropes and the sorts of pressures prosecutors are under.'

Daly life

Life thereafter is all about court – 'the full gamut of magistrates' court appearances, sentences, pleadings and summary trials,' plus 'maybe a little Crown Court stuff.' Fielding offers of work for other members, while managing their own practice and impressing a supervisor, the pressure mounts. It's here that supervisors do a good job of 'helping you keep track of what you've done and what you can take on.' Whether it's taking pleasure in 'getting an acquittal and the clients being grateful' or even 'losing, but taking satisfaction in performing professionally as a minister of justice,' pupils had no qualms about working as hard as possible to extract the most from their experiences. The set does look out for them by offering travel expenses for travel outside the M25, 'not charging them clerks' fees or rent during second or third six,' and perhaps equally importantly 'being just as busy collecting pupils' fees as tenants' fees.' For those kept on, the third six bring more of the same with a gradual increase in Crown Court work, conducting mentions, plea and directions hearings, sentences, applications to dismiss and legal arguments. Eighteen months is a long time to be a pupil and requires a combination of determination and grace under pressure: those who make the grade do so after the committee has considered feedback from instructing solicitors and judges, and assessed their performance in court and written work. Three new tenancies were awarded in 2008; one pupil did not get an offer.

You might think an 18-month-long interview would hamper a pupil's ability to socialise; our sources said otherwise. 'Daly's is the place for a lot of drinks,' they explained, taking pleasure in the fact that 'if there's a party or an event we'll be invited.' Given the Criminal Bar's stereotypical reputation for basing social life on alcohol, it was good to hear one add: 'I don't drink heavily and I've never felt out of place.' Relations between juniors and pupils are good and 'people will always pop by the pupils' room to have a chat.'

And finally...

'There's a self-confidence in the place that's justified because of the phenomenal quality of work,' one source suggested, another remarking on the set's 'flexibility – there are a lot of individual personalities contained in the joint effort and there's freedom to be yourself.'

Henderson Chambers

The facts

Location: Temple, London
Number of QCs/Juniors: 10/32 (5 women)
Applications: 200+
Olpas: Summer season
Pupils per year: Up to 3
Seats: 2x6 months (may change to 2x3 + 1x6)
Pupillage award: £35,000 + earnings
(can advance sum for BVC)

> Outwardly, Henderson appears to be the very essence of the traditional Bar. Inside, the plasma TV in reception suggests otherwise. Heck, head of chambers Charles Gibson even has an electric drum kit in his room.

Impressive common law set Henderson Chambers has a stellar reputation for health and safety and product liability cases, and is advancing rapidly in fields such as IT, local government and public law, real estate, environment, European law and professional discipline. If breadth of practice and advocacy aplenty appeal, read on.

On the right track

The contemporary, 'family and community-minded' world of Henderson Chambers is the product of some 70 years of gradually evolving practice in common law areas. The set now considers itself 'a specialist, but with a wider range of specialisms than other places.' By 'noting where our strengths are and focusing on them,' the set has ensured its members gain high-quality instructions in public inquiries, HSE defence, local authority prosecutions and industrial disease litigation. Of late these have included a criminal investigation arising from the Buncefield oil depot explosion and an HSE prosecution against British Waterways following a double canalside fatality. Well-developed links with rail companies and regulators mean that if you can name a recent rail accident inquiry or corporate manslaughter case, Henderson has probably been involved, from the Potters Bar inquest to the Lambrigg and Ufton Nervet rail disasters. Members have also been involved in some of the biggest product liability group actionsthe MMR/MR vaccine and Seroxat antidepressant claims, not to mention litigation over food dye Sudan Red 1 and last year's petrol contamination issues. It is additionally taking on claimant insurance matters.

Such matters may be chambers' most obvious strengths, but it has others, and if breadth of specialisation has become important, so too has 'cross-fertilisation' between practice areas. By way of example, 'only last year we got our largest ever environment case because the health and safety team at Eversheds referred us to their environment colleagues.' Another notable case saw barristers acting for a major oil company defending claims brought by Colombian residents alleging that an oil pipe caused nuisance and environmental damage. As well as a healthy stream of solicitors and local authority clients, Henderson is also taking direct instructions from big corporates like BT, Thallis and Network Rail. Keeping watch over it all, turbo-charged, entrepreneurial head clerk John White is keen for 'all our practices to develop relations in the communities around their specialisms, whether it's sponsoring an event or running seminars for associations of practitioners.'

Do something that scares you

For juniors, this approach sees them 'spending time with local authorities to understand their work.' They also gain

Chambers UK rankings

Health & Safety • Information Technology • Product Liability • Professional Discipline • Public Procurement • Real Estate Litigation

personal benefit from the increasing variety of instructions that come from investigating the crossover between areas. The emphasis on becoming a rounded practitioner is quite evident and specialisation is 'actively discouraged before five or six years' [call].' The court-heavy caseload means 'you're constantly challenged to get your head around new areas' and sometimes 'you find papers on your desk for something you know nothing about, say an employment tribunal.' As you might imagine, this is 'sometimes scary' in the early years.

A straightforward, if equally varied, pupillage does its best to provide as 'friendly and neutral' a year as possible. Pupils have one supervisor during each six, quarterly appraisals, two or three assessed advocacy exercises in the year ('something like a plea in mitigation and we perform against each other') and the certain knowledge that each piece of work completed for other members of chambers will be scrupulously assessed. It's also the case that supervisors 'protect their charges' for the first quarter before releasing them to work for others. Initially, working closely for supervisors might mean anything from health and safety prosecutions, employment and property litigation, product liability claims, consumer credit issues or large property damage and insurance coverage disputes. When pupils later work under their own steam, they can rely on the 'close relationships' established during this earlier period; 'your supervisor helps and advises I know it sounds trite but they're almost like a friend.' As a result, 'the sense of being assessed fades a bit.'

Brussels sprouts

Early in the new year, all pupils spend four weeks in Brussels sampling European law from inside a firm of solicitors. This is thanks to a relationship with two associated members who work within US legal giant McDermott Will & Emery/Stanbrook LLP. A month away from the hurly-burly of chambers, a 'fantastic social scene' and 'exposure to the priorities of clients,' means pupils tend to return 'relaxed, improved and more rounded.' The final month of the first six is then spent 'going to proceedings with juniors to explore the courts, meet ushers and get their feet under the table.' The second six then becomes an advocacy-fest. Said a barrister on the pupillage committee: 'We tell the clerks that a person's career in chambers starts at the beginning of the second six, because if we take them on we want them to hit the ground running with their own clients.' Pupils gobble up full helpings of 'possession hearings, RTAs, PI cases and property hearings,' and attend court up to four times a week. Commonly they will additionally work on big cases for their supervisors.

The July tenancy decision is made at 'a long and agonising meeting' that considers supervisor-penned overviews, feedback from any relevant members of chambers and – to a lesser extent – comments from instructing solicitors. 'We don't tend to consider the state of the market, just whether that person will be an asset and generate work,' a source explained. One of the two pupils is usually successful and third-sixers arriving from elsewhere also have a decent chance. In 2008 one out of two was offered tenancy, along with one third-sixer.

TGI Friday

Henderson sees itself as a set of 'normal people' with a distinctive 'family atmosphere.' Certainly we picked up on a fresh and informal mood the day we visited. 'At five o'clock on a Friday it's impossible to do work; Lauren from reception insists you come for drinks and everyone starts to relax for the weekend.' The annual Christmas party is a popular event and tenants explained: 'We're particularly good at celebrating notable events like a clerk's 40th birthday.'

The communal vibe extends to the recruitment process. It's not that the two required interviews aren't rigorous: a 15-minute first round and a 30-minute second round with a panel of senior members both involve 'in-depth discussion' of set questions and require candidates to 'respond fluently and eloquently, not crumple under pressure.' The recruiters told us there's also 'an imperceptible quality that you recognise when it's in front of you, some combination of courage, nerves under stress and a well-rounded personality.' The breadth of chambers' work means 'we'd be vaguely suspicious of anyone who claims too great a love of a specific area without previous experience to back it up,' so be reasonable and reasoned in any application. Academics aren't the be-all and end-all here because this set sees the Bar as 'a practical profession where you become expert in something via a case not simply for the love of it.'

And finally...

Henderson offers a commercially minded common law pupillage that presses the fast forward button on court experience and turns out down-to-earth advocates with broad experience. Highly recommended.

Keating Chambers

The facts

Location: Temple, London
Number of QCs/Juniors: 18/33 (12 women)
Applications: 100+
Olpas: Summer season
Pupils per year: 2-4
Seats: 4x3 months
Pupillage award: £42,500 (can advance £15,000 for BVC)

Sector bible *Keating on Building Contracts* was first authored by Donald Keating QC. Now in its eigth edition, it is still written by members of chambers.

Keating is a heavyweight at the Construction Bar. Its 48 experts take on the biggest domestic and international construction disputes and demonstrate flair in energy, professional negligence and procurement law.

Oil in a day's work

Keating began to specialise in construction in the early 1980s and quickly rose to the top. It now fields barristers in infrastructure projects in the Middle East, transport cases in the Far East and power station disputes in South Africa. Members have recently acted on both sides at the Court of Appeal in Multiplex v Cleveland Bridge (a major Wembley Stadium dispute) and represented Aldi as it brought actions against professionals engaged by its contractor. Given that construction law is 'at the sharp edge of the evolution of contracts and tort law,' it's no surprise to find chambers' stamp on crucial cases, such as one for Rolls-Royce that has recently provided guidance on the interpretation of joint names insurance and rights of subrogation. The construction sector leads the way in negligence law too: recently members acted in the Channel Tunnel Rail Link case Costain Ltd v Bechtel.

Clients in energy-producing regions have cottoned onto the set's skills and members are increasingly occupied with foreign business such as a case over a petrochemical plant in the Slovakia and a $200m dispute arising out of a Middle East oil and gas project. Closer to home, E.ON has a massive claim relating to contracts for the reprocessing of nuclear waste at Sellafield. What's more, while chambers' procurement expertise originally developed out of its construction and engineering PFI and projects work, members are now popping up on major cases in other areas, like the MoD's dispute concerning food supplies for British armed forces worldwide.

Straight to the pint

If Keating's apparently specialist work puts you off, take a moment. Only a handful of its practitioners come from a technical background, and chambers merely expects pupillage applicants to have 'done something which demonstrates commercial interest' rather than display a love of construction law. It's common for people to come to the set via a simple desire for a 'general commercial pupillage,' only later discovering that construction law is 'basically contract and tort with great clients.' Representing contractors, suppliers and 'the stereotypical hairy-arsed builder' brings all sorts of human and legal challenges. 'On a long case you get up close and personal, you basically live with these guys and you have to be able to get on with them,' explained a seasoned senior who suggested 'rolling up your sleeves and going for a drink goes a long way.' Junior sources relished the 'robust, straightforward nature' of clients and the fact 'getting the dispute sorted for them often means something like the ability to pay the school fees.' Managing expectations and communicating effectively are essential skills.

Chambers UK rankings

Construction • Energy & Natural Resources • Professional Negligence

The clients' distinctive real-world approach is at the heart of construction law's technical and academic appeal. Often this means 'you're untangling a massive, tangled ball of wool involving architects, builders, surveyors, employers, contractors and subcontractors' to determine the extent of a client's involvement, liability or grounds for claim. This requires a head for detail and the ability to process ring binder upon ring binder of information while looking for the salient points. In extension, getting to

> 'You're taking apart the academic law of contracts to find solutions in cases where agreements were formed in unusual ways – contracts of immense value sometimes arranged on the basis of a phone call.'

grips with the technical aspects of cases is an ongoing process; 'you need to find out how things work, so you understand how they've gone wrong.' The importance of this part of the job is most apparent when you're cross-examining expert witnesses.

Around 35 applicants are invited to the first round for general questions and a topical discussion (recently wearing veils in court and the 42-day detention ruling). The 14 who make the second round are grilled for half an hour: 'Ten minutes of Olpas chat, ten on a mainstream contractual case they've been given beforehand and a ten-minute presentation on a topic of their choice.' You'll find the set's detailed recruitment criteria online.

Advocating change

Moving pupils between four supervisors over the 12 months is 'less about different types of work as about exposure to different personalities.' Working closely with supervisors in the first six, pupils draft statements of case, particulars of claim, defences and replies, perhaps writing an opinion on a contractor's liability in a project, and definitely paying close attention as supervisors take matters to court or arbitration. While pupils do some work for other members, 'they're not expected to get around to everyone.'

In the second six there's masses of court action, often on unrelated subjects seven RTAs provide crucial advocacy experience. Sometimes a 'six or seven-day construction defence case' will pop up and on these a pupil can be a

useful contributor. The emphasis on advocacy in pupillage reflects the cross-examination and court-heavy life of a fully fledged construction barrister. Beyond court visits, Keating arranges three 'assessed (although they don't feel it)' advocacy exercises at which 'seniors pretend to be judges.' Additional non-assessed advocacy training is planned for 2008/09. Feedback from the exercises contributes to the July tenancy decision, along with reports from supervisors and other members. In 2008, a formal feedback session given 'roughly half way though' was designed to be 'late enough to be informative, but early enough to give pupils a chance to change.' Pupils found it a 'two-way process – you get to say what you need to as well.' Together with support they'd received from supervisors, it led our interviewees to say: 'The best thing about pupillage here is you feel that you've been given a clear shot to display your skills and become integrated.' The set is proud of its record in not only helping people get positions (at the Bar or with solicitors' firms), but also in maintaining good relations with ex-pupils. In 2006 three of four gained tenancy, in 2007 neither of the two pupils did, and in 2008 one out of three was successful.

Making your marquee

Within chambers we detected a warm, unfussy ethos. 'We were integrated socially from the first day. We had a buddy assigned and a group of juniors took us out for drinks,' said one source. As pupillage progresses, juniors continue to 'provide advice down the pub; they'll say, 'Do x, work for y, avoid z for this." They also get across the message that 'it's in our best interests for pupils to get on.' The group we met described themselves as 'very tight-knit,' not just 'meeting to polish off the chambers lunch scraps on a Thursday,' but also enjoying meals at each other's houses. They were clear that 'it's the institution that has allowed this relaxation to exist.'

Chambers' annual garden party is a red-letter day in the construction world. That's not to say hard work isn't on the cards: 9am-6pm may be the standard pupil day, but there are plenty of times when 'working later, or on the occasional weekend,' is required. Still, gain tenancy and within a couple of years barristers can expect to earn as much as their contemporaries at the major commercial and Chancery sets.

And finally

A specialism is one of the most valuable things a barrister can possess. At Keating that's exactly what you'll gain.

7 King's Bench Walk

The facts

Location: Temple, London

Number of QCs/Juniors: 18/27 (10 women)

Applications: 150

Olpas: Spring season

Pupils per year: Up to 4, usually 2-3

Seats: 4 in first 9 months

Pupillage award: £43,000 (can advance sum for BVC)

Legal history has played out in and around 7 King's Bench Walk. In 1820, resident Serjeant Wilde defended Queen Caroline's life and honour. In the 1850s, legal notables Lord Halsbury and Sir Harry Bodkin Poland occupied rooms.

Pre-eminent for insurance and reinsurance work and renowned for its shipping expertise, 7KBW is a compact commercial set cut on classical lines.

Lordy!

The modern 7KBW has a proud lineage that goes some way to explain an outside perception that the set is 'starchy and traditional.' Since its foundation in 1967, this set has produced a string of prominent judges, including the likes of Lords Denning, Mance, Goff, Brandon and Hobhouse. Insiders regard the set's stiff reputation with bemusement: 'We're not less approachable than some of the 'modern' commercial sets in their new buildings.' The senior clerks, whose joint experience in chambers totals some 40 years, are also quick to chip in that 7KBW's atmosphere has 'changed beyond all recognition in the last 15 years; we're much friendlier and less stuffy.' Leaving traditionally exacting standards and a commitment to excellence aside, our sources say: 'What really distinguishes us is our size and the fact that we all practise in the same areas.' The view is that these factors combine to create a 'tight-knit and collegiate group.'

The work of the set centres on two areas that are the bedrock of the Commercial Bar – shipping and insurance disputes. Members are well known for Commercial and Admiralty Court shipping cases (whether they relate to finance, shipbuilding, the sale and purchase of vessels, or transactional disputes arising from the day-to-day trading of vessels around the world) and the set leapt to prominence in the insurance world via its involvement in the 1990s in the enormous Lloyd's litigation. Looking more broadly at the set's commercial litigation pedigree, you'll find the Barings litigation, arbitrations relating to the Enron and WorldCom corporate collapses, and findings of fraud against KPMG in relation to its US tax avoidance advice.

It's easy to see how 7KBW has developed a reputation worldwide, and this is demonstrated by its involvement in high-end arbitration, such as that for a Middle Eastern government in a major ICC arbitration involving a billion-dollar oil production sharing agreement. General commercial cases in banking and professional negligence also figure prominently, and showing it has an eye for a business opportunity, the set has leveraged its insurance expertise to generate aviation sector instructions. Some members have additionally developed expertise in sports law, recently representing the Rugby Football Union in a dispute with the Premiership clubs, and Formula 1's British American Racing in the 2007 kerfuffle over Jenson Button's service.

Watch and learn

7KBW barristers have a reputation for brilliant technical application of the law. Juniors and pupils gushed about the experience of 'observing brilliant advocates in action' and 'learning so much about different ways of managing work and approaches.' The abundance of 'young, ambitious QCs' also means 'this is a great place to be a junior because of the enhanced levels of work' that trickle down. Needless to say the earning potential for members is vast.

Chambers UK rankings

Arbitration (International) • Commercial (Dispute Resolution) • Insurance • Professional Negligence • Shipping

So what of the small matter of getting a pupillage? Around 24 applicants are invited to a single-round interview, at which they are grilled on a skeleton argument they have prepared in advance. It is based on a 'pre-supplied, self-contained case that doesn't require in-depth legal knowledge' and conducted 'more like a Q&A than a formal advocacy exercise.' This part of the interview assesses 'how well candidates put themselves across on two pages and how well they get to grips with a problem.'

> 7 King's Bench Walk 'continues to distance itself from the pack' when it comes to handling insurance cases. Peers, solicitors and clients all agree 'it is extraordinarily difficult to deny their hegemony in this field.' *Chambers UK 2009*

You shouldn't be too surprised to hear that, as in many other top sets, 'often non-law graduates do better than those with law degrees, perhaps because they can take a step back.' Chambers tells us that 'the stereotype of the bookish student who's not worldly is not what we want;' however, looking at the CVs of baby juniors it's more than apparent that successful candidates invariably have a flawless academic record and attended an Oxbridge college. We asked some of them what they find so appealing about their work and their answers invariably turned on the intellectual challenges contained within. As one put it: 'There's a lot of law to get your teeth into; it's problem-based work involving pithy questions and seeking out holes in the law.'

Pupils each sit with four supervisors between October and July. The first stint is for three months and regarded as 'a time to make mistakes and learn.' Greater importance is placed on a pupil's 'performance trajectory' over the period than on individual pieces of work. Pupils then spend shorter periods with successive supervisors in a jam-packed six months in which they 'see a cross-section of chambers' specialisms and all facets of cases from advisory to advocacy to settling.' The expectation is that after the initial three months, pupils will do their utmost to impress supervisors and other members on each piece of work they receive, so it's understandable that they feel some pressure. Typically their work encompasses everything from discrete research assignments to wading through reams of paper to draft pleadings for a QC. At this set 'paper-based advocacy is just as important as court style,' so don't expect to be out and about on your own. This hadn't put off the pupils we spoke to, who were glad to 'have a good long period where you're learning and applying yourself, taking cues from seniors' before venturing into court themselves. Second-sixers don't normally appear in court alone until after the tenancy decision is taken.

Everyone's a winner

There's no question that 7KBW's exacting standards make for a demanding pupillage year, but chambers is keen 'not to do anything to add to the pressure,' and as such 'we don't compare them directly or encourage competition, or have things like advocacy exercises.' Pupils all work for 'the same four to five senior members, probably QCs,' to ensure fair assessment, and they benefit from regular feedback. In 2008 two of the three pupils were offered tenancy. Those who don't succeed soon get snapped up by other good sets looking for third-sixers. Those who do stay are fed a rich diet of their own lower-value cases – 'things like advice for P&I clubs and county court trials' or a position as a second or third junior on 'larger shipping, professional negligence and insurance cases.' Sometimes they are sent on short secondments to City law firms.

Chambers' focus, and the fact members frequently work together in teams, mean that juniors feel quite comfortable 'popping into anyone's room anytime for help.' Particularly among 'those under ten years' call' there is a ready exchange of 'invitations to weddings, birthdays and housewarmings.' The official social calendar is left in the capable hands of the senior clerks, who take steps to 'help reduce any pressure on pupils by encouraging them to come to functions, buying them drinks and making them feel welcome.' For the time being, formal gatherings for afternoon tea have fallen out of fashion at 7KBW, though evidently the demand for cakes most afternoons has not!

And finally...

There's something of an air of scholarly detachment here at 7KBW, but that doesn't mean this isn't also a commercially savvy operation. It's one of the very best for commercial litigation, so you'll have to be better than brilliant to get in.

Littleton Chambers

The facts

Location: Inner Temple, London
Number of QCs/ Juniors: 12/39 (9 women)
Applications: 120+
Olpas: Summer season
Pupils per year: 2
Seats: 3x4 months
Pupillage award: £40,000 (can draw down sum for BVC)

> In 2008 both pupils gained tenancy, as did all three contenders last year and both from the year before that.

Employment, commercial litigation and professional negligence specialist Littleton Chambers is not unique in its desire to be an efficient, modern business, but the strength of its determination is distinctive.

Because they're worth it

Back in the early 90s, Littleton was one of the first sets to appoint a CEO from outside the profession, and in 2007 the retiring incumbent was replaced by Gerard Hickie, formerly of L'Oreal, possessed of an MBA, an engineering background and exactly the sort of dispassionate take on the provision of legal services that chambers felt it needed. Littering conversation with terms that might give some old-school clerks a nasty turn, he told us: 'I want to increase the value of the business for shareholders, by which I mean barristers,' and 'we want to build market share.' Hickie's commercial acumen is clearly taking Littleton places. The last 18 months have brought a new IT system, three new clerks and a revamped marketing effort, including a new identity and website. The aim is 'to grow by 20-25% in the medium term.'

Littleton already has well-regarded core expertise in employment and commercial litigation, and this is backed up by expertise in sports law, professional negligence and arbitration/mediation. In 2008 members won a groundbreaking Court of Appeal case involving trade unions unlawfully discriminating against female members and provided counsel in relation to Dwain Chambers' challenge to his ban under British Olympic Association rules. However, perceiving 'the set was in some ways a sleeping giant,' management's aim is now to 'maintain our pre-eminence in employment and reputation for punching above our weight in commercial litigation,' while expanding to roughly 60 barristers.

The human side of the law

The pupillage recruitment process is more than a little concerned with finding candidates with the right people skills as well as intellectual abilities. Around 20% of applicants are invited to a first interview that assesses 'basic advocacy skills and the ability to summarise facts and make judgments' in a 'testing but not overly bullish' way. Great academics and pronounced intellect certainly help, but for the dozen or so who reach the second round (an assessed mini-pupillage), it's just as important to show an assured bedside manner. The candidates are set a written assessment – 'there's plenty of time to go to the library' – which is discussed at the end of the week with a barrister. A further one or two rounds of interviews face the seven or so who make it beyond mini-pupillage.

Pupillage itself is 'very much about commercial litigation and employment,' with pupils shuttling around three supervisors for four months each. 'I had one [specialist] from each area and a mixed practitioner,' a pupil recalled. The two core areas appeal for different reasons. Of commercial litigation, one barrister told us: 'It is less statute driven and there's more fundamental law. You're dealing with business people who are detached from the issues.'

Chambers UK rankings

Employment • Professional Negligence

By comparison, employment law centres on people and workplaces, so it's all about personal relationships breaking down. 'There are more human emotions: often it's people who loathe their boss or the company saying, 'You didn't promote me because I'm black or a woman.'' And employers are just as prone to emotional responses: 'Often the boss will in turn loathe being accused of being racist, sexist or discriminatory.' In short, employment practice is 'a complex interrelation of personal and professional legal issues; it's very exciting.'

Regardless of their area, supervisors tend to be good at 'giving pupils experience of work within their reach.' Our sources had found 'the first few months were more relaxed; you work 8.30am until 6pm' and 'your work is closely assessed, much more so than later in the year.' Rather than taking on their supervisor's work in parallel, pupils cut their teeth on 'a series of set tasks – things like advices and pleadings – from a collection that members contribute to when they have an appropriate case.' After four months of 'going to court and EAT tribunals with juniors, you get to know the work you'll be doing come the second six.'

The set 'regards advocacy experience as very important,' so second-six pupils are off to court once or twice a week, handling 'winding-up petitions in the Companies Court, paperwork for solicitors and small employment cases.' Littleton's reach means regular trips to Stratford and Croydon are on the cards, with occasional jaunts out to 'Reading, Bury St Edmunds and places like that.' Said one source: 'You learn first and foremost how long it takes to prepare for even the smallest case at this stage.' By its nature, employment law is more conducive to early advocacy experience than commercial litigation, but as a junior it's possible to get substantial commercial instructions. For example, one baby junior we spoke to was looking forward to 'a professional negligence construction case that's slated for a 20-day trial.'

Blah, blah, blah

The set's aim is 'to be constructive in feedback and to sort out problems.' Said one pupil: 'I was frankly amazed at how seriously they take it. I thought it would be, 'Well done, blah, blah, blah' but my supervisor had taken detailed notes on what I'd done and talked me through them.' At the end of each seat detailed feedback is given at a meeting attended by 'your old supervisor, your new supervisor, the CEO and the head of the pupillage committee.' Small wonder, pupils told us: 'These meetings are invaluable; they takes the terror out of the process but you also feel you're getting advice for your career, not just pupillage.' As well as the appraisals, there are four 'increasingly difficult' assessed advocacy exercises over the year. Pupils duke it out over an 'anonymised real case: you get bundles and instructions and advocate in front of a member who is sitting as a judge.' While 'competition kicks in,' it's still 'very pleasant natured' and there's oral feedback afterwards. A written report then goes to the tenancy committee, along with feedback from instructing solicitors and the results of three written assessments, set from January onwards. These are 'scrutinised by an independent member of chambers' who makes a report. The last weeks before the tenancy decision will also see 'court work scaled back' and pupils' supervisors 'push you to get exposure to more members of chambers,' so as to make the bid for tenancy more complete. Both of the 2008 pupils were successful.

Littleton resides in Kings Bench Walk in impressive premises that manage to combine the traditional architecture of the Inn with a 1990s extension at the rear. Definitely 'not a ripped denim sort of place,' members are well dressed. 'We work incredibly hard,' said one, 'but the culture is a mutually supportive one.' Littleton tenants are 'very familiar faces' in the nearby Pegasus Bar, and in the summer they can often be found entertaining clients on one of chambers' three roof terraces. Juniors and clerks' nights out, and even the occasional organised juniors' event, also keep things interesting. Pupils naturally find it hard to forget their status in chambers, but when they join in the post-work drinks 'it's like going out with your friends.'

And finally...

Pupils and members told us they were proud of the 'openness, approachability and sense of humour' they feel characterise the set. In part it reflects Littleton's 'collegiate cultural values,' but equally it is indicative of the heavy employment law caseload.

Maitland Chambers

The facts

Location: Lincoln's Inn, London
Number of QCs/Juniors: 16/47 (11 women)
Applications: 180
Not in Olpas
Pupils per year: 3
Seats: 1x3 months + 6-week seats
Pupillage award: £40,000 (can advance £10,000 for BVC)

> **Maitland has become synonymous with great brains, as evinced by the now familiar term of disparagement employed when describing another set: 'They're good but not a Maitland.'**

If Maitland has a big ego, it is at least justified. *Chambers UK* ranks it top for commercial Chancery, a position it has become well used to since forming through the merger of 13 Old Square and 7 Stone Buildings in 2001. Another merger came in 2004, when Maitland was joined by the members of 9 Old Square.

Club class fights

Combining a healthy mix of specialists and generalists, the set is sometimes compared to a solicitors' firm for its staffing and size. As well as Chancery cases, members are proficient in areas as diverse as IP, company law, agriculture, property and entertainment law. Instructions come from around the world, and there are particularly strong links with the offshore tax havens in the Caribbean, the Channel Islands and the Isle of Man. The nature of much of the set's offshore work means that members are also regularly instructed to attend the Privy Council. More general commercial work has its base in Hong Kong, whilst many US entities are represented in broad commercial litigation, 'not on US soil, but up in the multi-jurisdictional ether.' One highlight was Donegal International Ltd v Zambia & Another, a case involving a US vulture fund that bought cheap distressed debt in Zambia and forced a claim through the UK courts for more than ten times the purchase price. Although the fund achieved a favourable monetary judgment, Maitland won a 'moral victory' for its Zambian client.

Other examples include a multiparty dispute about online music downloads involving iTunes, Yahoo!, AOL and the British Phonographic Industry; a case in which JD Wetherspoon alleges its former property finder defrauded the company over a period of years; and The Crown's case against the two principal directors of collapsed claims management company Claims Direct. In one case the son of the late founder of Annabel's nightclub is disputing a will which all but cut him out of his father's £100m fortune.

Crunchy

Pupillage is a serious affair. Supervisors take a 'regulatory role' to protect charges from ambush by multiple members and ensure they receive a broad mix of quality work which will help 'tool them up for practice.' The first three months are spent 'getting embarrassing mistakes out of the way,' and then after Christmas a pupil's performance really counts. At this stage pupils change supervisors roughly every six weeks, which suits them fine because 'having to meet everyone and remember their names in the first week would be horrific.' They described cham-

Chambers UK rankings

Agriculture & Rural Affairs • Chancery • Charities • Commercial (Dispute Resolution) • Company • Fraud: Civil • Partnership • Professional Negligence • Real Estate Litigation • Restructuring/Insolvency

bers' work as 'crunchy,' a term translated as meaning 'mentally demanding' and 'involving a lot of mulling things over.' Given the crunchiness of it all, even with the civilised hours of 9am to 6pm during pupillage, it was understandable that pupils spoke of getting that Friday feeling as the week drew to a close. The first supervisor takes a less influential role in the tenancy decision, while supervisors from January to June have to ensure that everything on the pupillage checklist gets ticked off. In

Chambers and Partners Chancery Set of the Year and Real Estate Set of the Year 2008

May/June, written reports are gathered by the pupillage committee (Pupco) and a recommendation for tenancy is then made to the entire membership. Pupils describe the process as 'fair' and feel they are 'treated with respect and professionalism.' 'It's not a culture of aggressive assessment,' said one, 'but you're told when you get it wrong.'

Court time is an important part of pupillage, and supervisors insist that pupils take an active role, even if there is no prospect of them getting on their feet. 'They read through all the papers beforehand, decide what they would do if they were the advocate and then have a lengthy discussion with their supervisor.' With all the time this takes, 'it can be quite onerous being a supervisor' and we got the impression that not everyone was chomping at the bit to become one. There are five advocacy training exercises, the principal purpose of which is to 'get a feel for doing your own submissions before you have to do it for a paying client.' Said a source: 'You need to know what those nerves are going to feel like and you need to experience what it feels like to have some cranky judge turn your skeleton argument upside down.' Pupils divide the rest of their time between drafting, reading paperwork and legal research. At least the range of legal disciplines covered is wide – company law, insolvency, civil fraud, personal bankruptcy, partnership, professional negligence, property, probate, landlord and tenant and general commercial cases. 'One of the most difficult tasks is learning what all the books and authorities are.'

Thankfully 'your work is always taken seriously as a valid educational exercise, even if it isn't being used.'

Ice, ice, baby

The advantage of commercial Chancery, as opposed to straight commercial practice, is that 'you get a lot of your own cases and trials.' A baby junior's practice is generally split 50/50 between their own cases and being led. 'A full three-day trial over who owns some parking spaces may not be glamorous, but it is incredibly useful experience when you're the one heading up the litigation team.' Work varies between 'contractual spats over the delivery of widgets' and application-based insolvency work to cases where 'the precedents are fairly balanced and it hasn't yet been canvassed in the courts so you know the decision is likely to end up in a textbook.' In these cases, juniors will 'turn up at small application hearings,' while a QC will be called in to do the cross-examination, a fine art where 'asking the wrong question could get you in a lot of trouble.' As complexity and value bear no direct relation to one another, 'sometimes a thin set of papers with only five sheets will turn into a legal nightmare with some incredibly tricky arguments and questions over the choice of law.' Even work at the junior end can throw up meaty issues, however the time you dedicate to a problem is ultimately 'a question of costs' – something ardent perfectionists could find frustrating.

Maitland is big enough that members can opt in and opt out of social activities. Many drop in for afternoon tea on their way back from court; others prefer the weekly pub trips organised by the social committee (Pubco), which are far more relaxed affairs. The social side of pupillage provides 'a less artificial experience you get the chance to see people as they really are.' For the rest of the time: 'It can feel a bit like being at the bottom of a pond looking up at the world above the surface, it's all a blur.' If so, then gaining tenancy feels like 'breaking through the surface and seeing things clearly.'

And finally...

Maitland isn't known for attracting the most colourful characters: a top-notch brain and common sense are far more important. If you're anything less than a perfectionist you'd be happier elsewhere. As a pupil put it, the culture is 'a thinking one as opposed to the hours culture down in the Temple.'

FOUR NEW SQUARE

"The definitive professional negligence set," .... "the brand
name and the market-leading barristers to go with it."

(Chambers and partners 2008)

"Based in Lincoln's Inn, chambers combines a commitment to achieving and
maintaining high standards of advocacy and advice for all clients with the ve
highest standards of client service. This is reflected in the large awards and
guaranteed earnings offered to it's pupils, from whom its junior tenants are
regularly recruited."

(Legal 500 2008)

For full details of Chambers' work, individual members' practice profiles and clerking arrangements please visit www.4newsquare.com or contact Lizzy Wiseman on 020 7822 2000 or l.wiseman@4newsquare.com

4 New Square, Lincoln's Inn London WC2A 3RJ
Telephone: 020 7822 2000 Facsimile: 020 7822 2001
Email:barristers@4newsquare.com
DX: 1041 London, Chancery Lane

Four New Square

The facts

Location: Lincoln's Inn, London
Number of QCs/ Juniors: 14/49 (17 women)
Applications: 200
Olpas: Summer season
Pupils per year: Up to 4
Seats: 2x3 +1x6 months
Pupillage award: £37,500 + earnings
(can advance up to £12,500 for BVC)

Funky. Fresh. Voraciously ambitious. Can we really be describing a set of chambers? Professional negligence star Four New Square is all these things and more.

Step from the traditional environs of Lincoln's Inn into Four New Square's trendy reception area and several hundred years disappear in an instant. Huge modern canvases adorn the walls, there are acres of hip stretch-rawhide panelling and a computer for client use resembling a sci-fi film prop.

Style and substance

Such is the evident up-to-the-minute sensibility of this chambers you could almost be in a Soho creative agency. The set aims 'to project a modern image' and sees itself 'more like a firm of solicitors in our focus on providing a client-oriented service.' The emphasis on self-presentation doesn't mean Four New Square lacks substance: workaholic tendencies and undisguised ambition ensure that the glitz of the caseload perfectly complements the glamour of the decor. Eye-catching professional negligence instructions flood in from most major (and minor) litigation firms and insurers, occupying almost every member. The massive Accident Group litigation, a multiparty action involving solicitors' negligence, is one case on the go at present, and the members represent a multitude of accountants facing litigation over the film finance advice they gave clients. There's also continued involvement in Wembley stadium disputes, which 'endlessly rumble on,' while on the product liability side, 4NS barristers represent the government on a nuclear test veterans case. Chambers also generates broader commercial work, with members taking an increasing number of commercial, Chancery and insurance cases.

If professional negligence sounds like a narrow field, fear not. Although 'general principles of contract and tort underlie all the work,' there is 'so much variety because each profession is entirely different.' Considering that instructions span sectors as diverse as construction, medicine, insurance, reinsurance, law, accountancy, surveying and tax (not to mention the variety within those categories, say the difference between family lawyers and criminal lawyers), it isn't surprising that 'quickly assimilating information about different professions' is a both a major challenge and a source of job satisfaction. 'The other day I had to write an advice on a vet's case,' a pupil told us, 'and I certainly didn't know much about veterinary practice beforehand.' Possessing the skills to deal as easily with a rough-and-ready construction professional as a phenomenally qualified accountant is crucial.

Smile if you wanna go further

Mini-pupils will be given a good steer as to their future chances. They'll either be offered 'a bye through the first-round interview,' told 'to apply but expect a first-round interview' or recommended not to apply. A mini is no prerequisite for an application, which at every stage sees candidates assessed according to four main criteria: 'intellectual ability, most prominently displayed via a consistent academic record; potential as an advocate; commitment/motivation; and personal qualities – leadership, self-

Chambers UK rankings

Construction • Financial Services Regulation • Product Liability • Professional Negligence

reliance and the like.' It's worth noting that academic results carry '1.5 times the weight of other criteria.'

Around 70 attend a general first-round interview, up to 28 of which will proceed to the second round to face 'probing but not confrontational or contrived' questioning on *'moral, ethical or legal issues.'* Applications from construction professionals are not uncommon, but the most important fit is 'with the way in which we work – our

> An unassessed mini-pupillage will be helpful, but anyone seriously interested in 4NS should apply before the end of February for one of the paid, assessed minis. There are 12 week-long openings paying £500.

client focus and aim to provide brilliant service.' As such, 'proactive, optimistic, positive' applicants with 'good people skills and uplifting personalities' are favoured, so practising a genuine smile could be a good idea.

4NS fair ground

If the application process is scrupulously fair, pupillage itself is relentlessly so. The year is split into two three-month seats and one of six-months, with supervisors chosen from the 'ten to 14 years' call mark because that gives exposure to advanced work while not being too removed from junior practice.' These moves give broad experience of 'our core areas of professional negligence and general commercial work,' as well as 'exposure to more specialist areas, be it Chancery, insurance or construction.' The first six is about 'shadowing your supervisor, doing what they do in parallel then comparing it together.' Time after conferences or court visits is spent 'discussing matters so your advocacy skills are tested.' This 'ongoing process of appraisal,' is backed up by a three-monthly appraisal system that sees 'pupils assess themselves, then discuss it with their supervisor.' Supervisors then report to the pupillage committee and its head Ben Hubble goes back to the pupil wioth more feedback. Small wonder that pupils feel 'at every stage you know what you need to do to improve and how you're performing.' They also praise the 'teaching mentality' in chambers.

The second six continues to feature work set by supervisors, and pupils also handle small commercial debt claims, possession hearings, RTAs, simple fast-track trials and employment tribunals. Mortgage work often involves the challenge of 'litigants in person,' while RTAs are

'good for witness-handling skills.' There's also likely to be a first taste of professional negligence instructions: 'It tends to be writing advices on cases where maybe the insurer wants a cheaper fee for the pre-court work.'

If you think the assessment sounds full-on, you haven't heard the half of it. At around the five-month mark, pupils complete three written tasks set one a month by an in-chambers panel. Non-assessed advocacy training is followed up by an assessed moot that takes place either in chambers or an RCJ courtroom before Mr Justice Rupert Jackson, a former silk at the set and now a Court of Appeal judge. This year the audience was restricted to the pupillage committee and supervisors, but was 'still enough to be pretty scary.' Feedback from all these means of assessment is then considered by the committee that makes the tenancy decision. Chambers is hungry to recruit members, but not to the extent of compromising standards. In recent years, all, none or a couple of pupils have been offered tenancy. Two of the four made the grade in 2008 and, depending on the year, third-six applications may or may not fall on fertile ground.

The 4NS work ethic means pupils should expect to put in prodigious effort, despite days being 'fixed around ten hours, including a lunch hour.' In general, 4NS has a laudable policy of 'fully supporting members lifestyle choices, whether it's women having children, men wanting to spend more time with their kids or people simply anting a more flexible existence.' It's not all work though. A warm welcome helps initiate new arrivals so that 'within three to four weeks you get to know or have spoken to 90% of chambers.' Junior tenants are also on hand to provide after-work drinks and advice in what genuinely does seem to be a collegiate organisation. Pupils are welcome at all social events, whether it's watching one of the set's horses – Blunham Hill or Joe Twist – or knocking back the Pimm's at the summer barbecue or cultivating clients. When we visited, sore heads were being nursed after a party for 750 clients in Old Billingsgate. For senior clerk Lizzie Wiseman such events are useful 'because we recognise that people often instruct for reasons they don't consciously think about – personal relationships and emotional connections.' For one source the pleasure was in the novel experience of 'feeling like solicitors might actually want to talk to me.' You have to suspect that here, the feeling is a common one.

> ## And finally...
>
> Robust, modern and client-focused, Four New Square is a great bet for anyone with the requisite social skills. Get your head around professional negligence and try for an assessed mini.

- **Gauge your appeal:** Look at the list of members, and in particular the biographies of the set's cadre of junior tenants. This can reveal much about what appeals to chambers' recruiters, particularly in relation to academic and other achievements. You will also be able to see the areas in which baby juniors gain experience.

XXIV Old Buildings

The facts

Location: Lincoln's Inn, London

Number of QCs/Juniors: 8/27 (9 women)

Applications: 250+

Not in Olpas

Pupils per year: 2

Seats: 4x3 months

Pupillage award: £40,000 (can advance sum for the BVC)

'Not big but very successful,' XXIV Old Buildings offers a commercial/ Chancery pupillage with a rather international twist.

Characterised by broad traditional and commercial Chancery expertise, as well as significant international capacity, XXIV Old Buildings handles everything from commercial litigation, aviation and insolvency to pensions, partnerships and professional negligence.

Coups, fraud and yoghurt

XXIV Old Buildings has existed in its current form for 30 years, but with a Geneva annexe and an enviable caseload, it epitomises the modern Bar. Members have access to unique work, such as defending alleged coup plotter Simon Mann against charges brought by the government of Equatorial Guinea and the Iran v Bakarat case concerning artefacts smuggled from the ancient site of Jiroft, both of which approached the issue of whether sovereign states can bring cases under the British legal system. They also represented BMW in arbitration concerning alleged fuel temperature irregularities during the final 2007 Formula One race that could have changed the winner of the drivers' title. Meanwhile, an instruction from the Chinese joint venture partner of food giant Danone involving fallout from their £2.2bn partnership is putting barristers to work in five jurisdictions, including the British Virgin Islands and Samoa.

Economic conditions have brought 'an increase in fraud work and hedge funds litigation,' with a pronounced 'downward trend for settling, because companies don't have the capital to cover losses.' At the same time, a marked increase in 'arbitrations coming in from China, Kazakhstan, Russia, Gibraltar and the BVI' – not to mention Swiss solicitors via Geneva – has necessitated 'adjusting our model to market more internationally as well as domestically.' The decision to take on a Jersey-qualified lawyer and a QC with a '100% international practice' typi-

fies chambers' careful strategic growth. Aviation and travel expertise was seeded by new joiners several years ago, expanding the set's transport law abilities, so that 'we even took on some submarine work recently.' Offshore trusts know-how has prospered via a similar tack.

Complementary skills are what make this business work. Joint head of chambers Alan Steinfeld, for example, is ranked by *Chambers UK* in eight areas of practice, making him one of the most multi-talented members of today's Bar. Eager to showcase the cross-disciplinary talent available, one source gave us the example of 'a client who came to us with a case involving a BVI airline in difficulties, requiring BVI, aviation and insolvency expertise. They could get everything they needed from us.' Juniors can expect their early years to involve 'experience across the full range of our practice.'

Ain't no mountain high enough

Whether for commercial or private clients, Chancery work appeals because it is intellectually demanding and

Chambers UK rankings

Aviation • Chancery • Company • Partnership • Pensions • Professional Negligence • Restructuring/Insolvency academically rigorous. 'Once you get into it at the coal-face it is about people and emotion, the breakdown of relationships to do with fraud, lying, scams.' What's more, the prevalence of overseas instructions gives a XXIV pupillage a distinctly international flavour, requiring 'fluency in the idea of different jurisdictions and conflicts of laws, because even though work isn't all directly international, indirect offshore elements crop up.'

> Chambers has opted out of Olpas, so direct applications should be made by 16th March for pupillages commencing in October of the following year. XXIV's full pupillage and recruitment policy is on its website.

Roughly 40 people get a first-round interview involving discussion of a set problem ('equally accessible for law and non-law grads') given 15 minutes beforehand. A select eight make it though to the second round, where an 'entirely different panel including at least one silk' poses questions and tests advocacy potential. Candidates are given the scenario half an hour in advance, and be warned, it's usually 'a hopeless argument.' Only two pupillages are offered each year, and whether it's a feature of the high-calibre applicants chambers receives or it reflects the demands of the set's work, many seem to possess industry or commercial law experience. Recruiters stressed: 'As a chambers we're anxious not to be sexist or ageist,' but certainly in attitude and demeanour,'maturity is a key factor.' This is not infrequently displayed by candidates arriving via the 'conventional law degree and straight through' route, but chambers has also recruited 'former solicitors, an army officer and a pop video producer' in recent years. 'We're looking for something that makes the person stand out, whether it's climbing in the Himalayas or a previous career.'

Read my body language
Pupils rotate around four supervisors, so as to experience 'as wide a range of work as possible.' Said one pupil: 'I had two traditional Chancery masters and two more commercial ones.' Discouraging 'any direct competition,' chambers puts emphasis on learning, so pupils only take on their own court work after gaining tenancy. The first three months is 'a time when we expect and see a lot of mistakes.' Working in the shadow of supervisors, pupils handle the first drafts of pleadings, witness statements

and research, as well as watching closely at court and in client conferences. Supervisors generally 'explain your mistakes or offer comments,' although some can leave you 'trying to glean from the smallest evidence how you're doing the raising of an eyebrow, the inhalation of breath' Consequently, end-of-seat reviews can 'sometimes throw up the odd surprise,' but chats with the pupillage secretary help to keep everyone on track and pupils are encouraged to gain exposure to other members of chambers. Very occasionally someone will depart after six months; assuming they do stay, pupils' lives continue much the same until the June tenancy decision. The last few years have seen formal assessments dropped in favour of close consideration of supervisor reports and feedback. In an effort to ensure an even more level field of assessment, pupils also shared several supervisors in common last year. Usually only one pupil is kept on, but the set is adamant that 'if there is the work and they both achieve the required standard, no matter whether they are at different stages of development, two will stay.' Although in 2006 and 2008 only one made the grade, both pupils gained tenancy in 2007.

When they spoke to us about their involvement in the 'once in a lifetime' Mann and Equatorial Guinea case, one pupil's eyes lit up. There's huge scope for genuinely interesting cases here, even if new tenants cut their advocacy teeth on quite small cases, 'from pleas in mitigation in a magistrates' court to County Court applications.' Knowing that sooner or later a skeleton argument for a House of Lords appeal will land on their desk doubtless makes them more than willing to graft on small-end cases. Despite the prevalence of international work, travel isn't a pronounced feature of the early years, although there will be 'at least one secondment to a firm of solicitors.'

There's no afternoon tea ritual, although a monthly lunch provides some social cohesion and helps foster the 'collegiate atmosphere,' something that's important given so many members travel for their work. A posse of juniors organise the occasional jolly and keep pupils' chins up.

And finally...
In a set where there are 'few internal politics,' gaining tenancy also means dissolving the 'essential social distance there is between pupils and members – you're treated as an intellectual equal even as a pupil.'

Old Square Chambers

The facts

Location: Bedford Row, London and Bristol
Number of QCs/Juniors: 10/57 (22 women)
Applications: 300+
Olpas: Summer season
Pupils per year: 2
Seats: 4x3 months
Pupillage award: £22,000 + earnings
(can advance sum for BVC)

> Arriving at Old Square Chambers on a boiling summer's day, we were greeted by a cheery barrister in T-shirt and sandals. His attire spoke simply of the set's distaste for tradition.

Old and square by name but not nature, this set is very much of the here and now.

United we stand

For decades it has been known as a claimant PI and employment law hothouse, and perceived as 'a left-wing sort of place' because of its extensive union connections. Yet 'in the last 15 years chambers has diversified so that there's now a 50-50 balance of claimant and respondent work.' Trade union links still account for much of the caseload: recently members acted for the British Air Line Pilots Association against BA and for UNITE member Mrs Grundy in Court of Appeal equal pay disputes. Head of chambers John Hendy QC is standing counsel to nearly ten unions. Nevertheless, some eight members are on the Treasury's list of juniors and instructions pour in from employers like BT, Ford and Land Rover.

Now occupying tasteful premises at Bedford Row, the large London contingent has plenty of space for 'strategic growth,' both in its core specialisms and its developing areas of public inquiries, environmental law, clinical negligence, product liability and health and safety. The 14-barrister Bristol arm is growing too and 'may need a new base in a few years.' A surge in disciplinary cases 'as major organisations align their protocols' has seen the set pull in work from the General Medical Council and the General Dental Council among others; meanwhile there are 'thousands of equal pay disputes across the health sector and far beyond.' Health and safety-based corporate manslaughter instructions and environmental litigation pop up 'as and when,' and product liability cases are pretty common. On the cards is a six-month trial for the (epilepsy drug) Sabril Group Litigation, in which members will represent claimants. There are regular instruc-

tions from the Prison Officers Association on death or injury in custody inquiries, and chambers has been involved in almost every major rail crash inquiry of recent times. The Potters Bar inquiry is presently on hold due to investigations into the 2007 Grayrigg derailment in Cumbria, but the set is 'quite likely to be involved on that too in due course.'

Making a difference

Old Square ditched chambers tea, formal modes of address and other formalities years ago, but despite its progressive outlook it nevertheless values the 'independence of individuals' rather than subscribing fervently to the concept of corporate identity. There is a slick website and careful marketing to manage the set's public face; behind it the barristers view themselves as 'independent, very hard-working and mutually respectful,' co-existing in an 'atmosphere underpinned by an egalitarian attitude.' If you see yourself fitting into this collective-style environment, you'll be pleased to hear that the set has just recast its interview process as a two-stage affair, with the aim of 'giving a broader range of people a chance to impress us in person.' Previously only 20 applicants would be interviewed. Last time 40 attended a first-round

Chambers UK rankings

Employment • Environment • Health & Safety • Personal Injury

involving 'five minutes of CV chat, five to ten on a supplied statutory interpretation issue and some probing
questioning.' Around five make the 45-minute second
round to face 'a problem-based legal scenario with a lot
of detail to pick up on.' Candidates are asked to treat the
panel of three 'as if we're the clients,' and will then be
tested with 'an ethical question arising from the problem.'
Requiring the sort of basic contractual knowledge that
any law student will possess, the two per year who are
offered pupillage are likely to demonstrate 'clear, client-
friendly thinking.'

The importance placed upon these qualities reflects the
need for employment and PI barristers to 'understand the
client's perspective.' These areas often involve dealing
with individuals in stressful situations, so people skills are
as important as keeping up with constantly changing law.
Said a new tenant: 'What's great is that you're constantly
taking real situations, often involving dramatic events,
and applying legal principles to try and find a solution.'
Another barrister spoke of the pleasure in 'making a difference to claimants and to businesses.' Given this emphasis on well-developed people skills, its not surprising that
a number of pupils have already had careers, be they 'former solicitors, accountants, trade union workers or
builders.'

Stress relief

The pupillage has been revamped such that formal assessment is ongoing rather than saved up until one 'fearful
session' at the end of the year. 'We thought, why not
acknowledge that it is a stressful year and make it more
transparent?' Pupils are tested in advocacy and written
exercises by a three-person panel at the end of each seat
taken before the July tenancy decision. 'In the first three
[months] they try to give you a supervisor who is sympathetic, to help you settle in and get involved in chambers,'
a pupil explained, adding: 'The first assessment is also
more relaxed.' At the end-of-seat appraisals 'you hear
about the positives and negatives in your performance.'
During the second period it is expected that you'll take on
work for other members, each piece producing 'feedback
that goes to the pupil and to the tenancy committee.
There's a one-to-five grading, one being adequate and
five outstanding.' Recruiters are adamant: 'We don't
expect fives from day one;' pupils tell us: 'You feel they
want to see your trajectory of improvement over the year.'

Supervisors are chosen to reflect 'a spread of personalities
and chambers' work.' Employment and PI are the heart of
pupillage: research assignments and notes for clients or
conferences are regular tasks, and pupils will learn to draft

skeleton arguments and other court documents. In the PI
arena, our sources had valued 'learning to draft quickly
and succinctly in a way that just isn't taught at law school.'
Once into the second six, pupils are in court up to 'a maximum of three times a week, otherwise they can't keep up
with other work.' It's a steady diet of RTAs and infant
approval hearings. The former are 'great for getting your
cross-examination skills up to speed, the Highway Code is
pretty much your precedent book, and establishing what's
happened from different sources is very important.'
Smaller 'two to three-day employment cases' can also feature, requiring the pupil to make speeches to the district
judges. Throughout this period supervisors can be relied
upon to 'keep an eye out and help you keep juggling all the
balls,' while other members 'take a real interest in what
and how you're doing.' Helpfully, juniors give pupils their
phone numbers, so 'there's a stupid-question hotline to get
answers to the things you almost dare not ask.'

Social enterprise

Old Square barristers travel a fair bit. In part this reflects
the nature of the work, but also the set's strong connection
with the Western Circuit. It is possible for pupils to spend
all or part of their year in Bristol, if they so wish, and certainly all must spend one week there. 'The pace of life is
very different,' observed one, adding: 'That's not to say
that they don't work hard.'

There's no doubt about who's got the best deal in chambers' new London home – 'the clerks' room has amazing
facilities, with a break-out room and espresso makers.'
Senior clerk Will Meade even gets to watch over his team
from a 'Starship Enterprise-style control room.' Given
that chambers tea definitely 'falls into the too-stuffy-for-
this-set' category, get-togethers take the form of monthly
drinks. Beyond this, pupils are welcome at chambers'
Christmas and summer parties, as well as any client
events. Supervisors regularly take them out to lunch and
there are always a few people drinking in The Enterprise
on a Thursday or Friday night. In 2008 both pupils gained
tenancy and apparently there was a lot of congratulatory
hugging in the pub that night.

And finally...

Old Square is a poised and purposeful set
that offers a kicking PI and employment-
focused pupillage.

Pump Court Tax Chambers

The facts

Location: Bedford Row, London
Number of QCs/ Juniors: 10/19 (5 women)
Applications: 70+
Not in Olpas
Pupils per year: 2-3
Seats: Sit with 3 core supervisors
Pupillage award: £40,000
(can advance up to £8,000 for BVC)

Pump Court Tax Chambers is purely, simply and entirely about tax law. This compact, traditional but refreshingly frill-free set is an undisputed star across the length and breadth of a highly lucrative discipline.

After 50 years of practice Pump Court has earned the right to feel it is the litigation tax set of choice. It's also an advisory hothouse, with members offering expertise in every facet of tax law. And we do mean every facet...

Pumped up

The scope of work at this set is broad indeed. There's personal tax planning for individuals, trusts or estates, and employee remuneration cases on share options or pension schemes. Then there's the UK and international tax aspects of corporate M&A, demergers, transfer pricing and structured finance. By contrast, indirect tax work includes VAT, landfill tax and stamp duties on property transactions, not to forget professional negligence disputes involving tax advice. A steady stream of instructions flows in from UK and foreign governments, Big Four accountants and City law firms. When we visited, chambers was about to provide counsel on both sides of a House of Lords transfer pricing dispute involving a major multinational pharmaceutical company. Other highlights included representing HMRC in a case concerning a Vodafone subsidiary and Weight Watchers in a VAT dispute. One tenant we spoke to had even dealt with 'a case considering whether the sums strippers pay to the clubs they work in should be VAT taxed.'

Tax cases can involve public and European law, even drawing in human rights points. For example, 'the client who paid peanuts for a consignment of cigarettes he believed were duty-paid and has been slapped with a £13m duty bill by the Revenue... it's developed into a human rights case.' What's more, while advisory work is a key aspect of practice, the tough stance adopted by HMRC means 'there's less of a settlement culture than at the Commercial Bar.'

Chambers receives only 70 applications a year and is eager to dispel the 'cloistered academic' perception of tax practitioners. 'There's no one here with two heads,' one laughed: 'No one wears fob watches, smokes a pipe or wears tweed. Like most of the Commercial Bar we're very aware of being seen to be commercial and modern.' To counter students' misconceptions, chambers offers numerous unassessed mini-pupillages, as well as paid, assessed minis. Participants sit with a silk and will write an opinion. They'll also quickly realise that 'the people are undoubtedly very, very clever.' This need not mean geeky – the members we met were some of the most interesting, articulate and socially switched-on barristers we encountered in our tour of the Inns. However, tax law demands 'rarefied, involved and complex analysis of law,' suiting people with 'a taste for approaching practice from an academic angle.' There's also the exhilarating pressure of being instructed by 'phenomenally qualified' tax experts 'who know their stuff inside out, so if they're asking you for a judgement call, it can be very challenging.' So, if 'thinking about rules and principles' is more to your taste than 'going through a room full of Linklaters' files

Chambers UK rankings

Tax

to find the one operative provision of the one operative contract,' apply here.

The devil's in the detail

Unsurprisingly, recruitment focuses on intellectual rigour, self-discipline and concentration: 'We want stellar individuals... a top First could exhibit this, but it's no requirement.' The interview process aims to spot 'those who rea-

Chambers and Partners Tax Set of the Year 2008

son clearly, can express themselves and be precise about the small points that make all the difference.' Around 20 applicants make the first round, which is 'a mix of CV-based interview, assessing competencies and discussion of a legal problem given an hour beforehand.' Last year eight made it to the second stage – a written assessment. Previous knowledge of tax is not required, and although some commercial orientation can be an advantage, the three pupils who started in 2008 were all straight-through law graduates.

Some pupils come for a full year, and first, second and third sixes are also offered. One tenant we interviewed had arrived via a commercial pupillage for a third six; another had done a three-month stint after several years' practice as a commercial barrister. However long the training, there's an 'initial period with one pupilmaster to protect them and help them find their feet,' followed by rapidly accelerating work for other members, so that 'towards the end you're spitting pieces out.' Working with up to five supervisors during the year ensures 'exposure to a broad range of work, whether it's VAT, corporate or personal tax,' while 'spending weeks with silks, writing an opinion for them and going to court' offers even more exacting challenges. One pupil who had seen private client income and inheritance issues with one supervisor had also enjoyed 'VAT disputes for Oxfam and a Whitechapel art gallery' with another. Supervisor swapping is made manageable by the paper-light nature of many tax cases: 'Pieces of work are discrete, you can often read all the papers in time for a conference or to write a note, which makes pupillage more close to practice.'

Pumped for information

Pupils meet with the head of the pupillage committee after six months to gain a sense of their prospects. Assuming all is well, they complete a series of assessments. In each of the past few years, one or two pupils have been taken on as tenants, and two made the grade in 2008. Chambers recognises 'pupils can't be the finished article' and instead looks for those with potential. Even during the first couple of years of tenancy, 'you are protected from full exposure to the outside world because the work is so complex and, on the advisory side, the liability can be so great.' Initially new tenants devil for other members, then take on instructions from 'walk-in clients' – 'maybe a company director who got the boot and wants help with his payoff.'

'About twice the size of other tax sets,' Pump Court boosted its revenue by 28% last year. Prompted by 'an absolute abundance of work,' it is in the midst of 'a period of strategic growth' and is spreading into the building next door. Describing the place as a relaxed one where 'there's no strict pecking order,' juniors are proud of a 'switched-on younger end,' but also glad of the experience of seniors. At 11am each day, members gather for morning coffee and 'social chit-chat or collaborative discussion of members' legal problems.' It's 'a great opportunity to say, 'How on earth do I do this?' and have someone else chime in, 'That's new, do x, y and z.'' Given that tax law is 'an ever-changing field,' members admit they'd 'be crazy not to tap each other's expertise,' but the habit emphasises chambers' collegiate feel. Pupils may feel the need to be quieter during morning coffee, but whether it's venturing from their own room to listen in on a supervisor's phone calls or 'knocking on a senior's door to ask for advice,' they told us: 'People are very generous with their time.'

And finally...

Bizarrely, Pump Court Tax Chambers is a well-kept secret among students. If you're after a top commercial pupillage, getting in touch with your inner tax lawyer could open up a whole new world of opportunity.

Quadrant Chambers

The facts

Location: Fleet Street, London

Number of QCs/Juniors: 10/34 (6 women)

Applications: 110

Not in Olpas

Pupils per year: Up to 3

Seats: 2x3 months + 1x6 months

Pupillage award: £40,000 (can advance sum for BVC)

Quadrant's three-day mini-pupillages are offered at three specific times of the year, each with its own application deadline. See the set's website for details.

Highly successful aviation, shipping and commercial set Quadrant Chambers has its sights set on strategic reinvention.

Zen quadrantism

The glossy splendour of Quadrant's stunning Fleet Street premises – actually four buildings combined into one through architectural sleight of hand – may not apparently speak of ascetic introspection, but chambers is currently all about 'reaching a higher state of excellence.' There's been no attempt to discover collective inner tranquillity in Temple Gardens, instead chambers has brought in management consultants 'to reassess what we do and don't do well' and purge inefficiencies bequeathed by the past. 'We have the modern buildings, the up-to-date IT system and attitude, but the historical clerks-and-barristers staffing structure,' a senior told us from the comfort of the lotus position. 'So we're bringing in a CEO and an HR person.' Integral to the plan to 'apply business logic' is 'the major principle that we need to focus on sharing our skills and pulling together as a brand.' This means 'consolidating our position as a leading shipping, aviation, commercial and arbitration set.' It also means drawing out the 'strong work members are doing' in insurance and reinsurance, energy, banking and finance and international trade and highlighting that to potential new clients.

As it stands, there's little wrong with Quadrant's caseload. Commercial shipping matters abound, with recent prominent cases including a House of Lords judgement on The Achilleas (concerning late redelivery of a chartered ship and consequent loss of profits) that is now the leading case on remoteness of damage. Meanwhile, most members of chambers acted for cargo interests in claims arising out of the wreck of MSC Napoli off the Cornish coast. Aviation is equally strong, whether it's general carriage issues and tour operator disputes, or even liability arising from air crashes or deep vein thrombosis. Advising on the various aviation law and regulatory aspects of Easyjet's takeover of GB Airways, highlights the set's breadth of expertise in the sector. The number of good general commercial instructions is also growing, some in the banking sector, others relating to sports and media. A member recently represented Iain Dowie at the High Court over his employment contract with Crystal Palace FC. Last but not least we should emphasise the set's arbitration experience, not least in relation to insurance, reinsurance and aviation.

Thumbing the breadths

In recent years pupillage has been 'revamped and revitalised,' as a result of 'a sea change in attitudes towards pupils.' Said one senior: 'We've now got a panel of people who are really committed to making the effort.' Emphasising the extra effort, the set has recently introduced open days for groups of university students and reinstated three-day unassessed mini-pupillages. Neither is compulsory for applicants, but both provide an insight into the appeal of a pupillage covering 'everything from international trade and carriage of goods to insurance and aviation.' The rule of thumb is that 'if you're basically interest-

Chambers UK rankings

Aviation • Shipping • Travel

ed in anything that involves a contract,' then Quadrant's general commercial training will be entirely to your taste.

Around 110 people each year make a tilt at the set. The mountain of CVs ('name, gender and age blacked out') are thumbed through and marked according to strict criteria, after which 30 people are sent a written assessment to complete and return within five days. Probably 'something like a simple construction case,' the emphasis is on 'showing clarity of thought and expression, whether the candidate is a law or non-law graduate.' Around 16 will subsequently be invited to a 'tough' 45-minute interview to be 'quizzed on the written assessment' and 'discuss a case given out just before interview.' They also face 'an ethical question judging instincts and sensibilities' and are asked to discuss a topical issue, last year whether there should have been an inquest into Princess Diana's death. The style isn't confrontational, it's instead aimed at 'getting past comprehensive preparation to catch people on the topics they haven't discussed with their tutors, mums and partners.' Recruiters insist they aim to 'identify who will be a good lawyer in two years, not who is perfect now.' Having dropped out of Olpas 'to make decisions earlier and before people have to pay Bar School fees,' Quadrant clearly has an eye for swooping on the best talent, but it's equally happy to take no one if its standards aren't met.

Ship shape

The pupillage experience involves two supervisors in the first six and a single one in the second, when you'll also do work for other members. This arrangement exposes pupils to chambers' main areas of practice. Aviation might involve 'particulars of claim and small discrete tasks,' but also the challenge of 'going back to basics to learn about an interesting and exciting area.' For one pupil it taught 'so much about being persuasive in written form.' Shipping means charter parties, bills of lading and cargo damage, with our sources gaining from shadowing at conferences and salvage arbitrations. Pupils spending time with supervisors specialising in general commercial litigation might initially research points of law, but in time progress to full sets of papers with a view to presenting advice or drafting claims or defences.

Indicative of the set's desire to improve pupillage, a new system is being introduced whereby one barrister will act as a shadow supervisor for all pupils, setting them exercises throughout the year to provide consistency of assessment. For what it's worth, pupils praised the existing structure (written reports and appraisals from supervisors at the end of each seat), saying: 'You know what you have to work on at each stage.' Several sources spoke of the 'huge emphasis put on feedback throughout the year, from supervisors and other members' and a defined feeling of being 'let off the leash as time goes by.' A baby-junior remembered: 'I worked 9am–6pm hours to begin with, but towards the end your supervisor does turn the pressure up a bit. I think they want to see if you will work an evening or a weekend if you need to.'

Paid or court work is delayed until after the July tenancy decision. Initial advocacy experience is gained via assessed exercises of sufficient toughness that 'tears are sometimes shed.' Attended by members of the pupillage committee and any else who fancies it, these mock cases are presided over by some 'forensically terrifying' seniors. The assessments are the final piece of a rigorously structured process leading to a decision that 'doesn't leave it to the chance whim of some senior you've never met.' In 2008 both pupils were offered tenancy, meaning only one of six in the last five years has had to look elsewhere. New tenants share a room with a 'godparent' for six months, after which they graduate to their own space.

Lost

On our exhaustive tour of Quadrant's beautiful but piecemeal premises, we quickly became disoriented. Multiple lifts cope with floors at different levels; a junior's eyrie is known as The Frathouse; a conference room resembles a gentleman's club; and there's more plate glass than you could spend an afternoon throwing stones at. Beautiful, yes, confusing, certainly. We wondered if the spacious environs might dissipate social cohesion, but sources enthused about the 'great atmosphere,' all-inclusive chambers lunches 'whenever there's a good reason' and gatherings in nearby Daly's Wine Bar most Fridays.

And finally...

In this pragmatic and commercial set, kicking back isn't a number-one priority, however we did sense a pleasantly informal vibe from its members and staff. 'I came prepared to dislike things in case I didn't get taken on,' a junior remembered, 'but I've never had a member be anything other than entirely friendly, lovely and down-to-earth.'

Serle Court

The facts

Location: Lincoln's Inn, London
Number of QCs/Juniors: 13/34 (7 women)
Applications: 110+
Not in Olpas
Pupils per year: 2
Seats: 4x3 months
Pupillage award: £45,000 (can advance £15,000 for BVC)

> Since 2000, Serle has gone from strength to strength in over a dozen practice areas ranging from the mainstream (shipping, insurance, property, partnership law) to the specialist (sports law, charities, Arabic law).

Serle Court formed through the merger of the Chancery set at 13 Old Square and the commercial set at 1 Hare Court. Forget the fusty, ivory towers image traditionally associated with Chancery practice: this set is modern and innovative.

Exodus to the bench

High-profile cases such as NatWest v Rabobank, BCCI and the recent bank charges litigation illustrate how well Serle barristers are regarded in the finance sector; in partnership law, members played a notable role in developing the use of LLPs by professional services firms and other businesses; and in trusts matters members are regularly instructed in offshore jurisdictions. One QC was brought into the appeal of the Charman v Charman divorce judgment in respect of over £70m of assets held in a Bermuda trust. Commercial litigation and mediation continue to be growing areas (one member has just launched the first licensed barristers' chambers in Qatar), and in entertainment law, members successfully defended the Marley family against a claim by the former bassist of The Wailers, and acted in claims regarding the copyright of songs on Madonna's *Ray of Light* album and a record contract dispute involving The Bees.

With magic circle firms regularly instructing on behalf of blue-chip companies, it's no surprise that the list of Serle Court members, past and present, is pretty impressive. Sir Michael Briggs, recently appointed as a High Court judge, is just one of many senior members who have gone to the Bench, so it's a good job chambers has a healthy roster of juniors. Lately two senior judges – Mr Justice Lightman and Lord Justice Parker – crossed the other way to join Serle Court's cadre of mediators and arbitra-tors. The set is administered by chief executive Nicola Sawford and senior clerk Steve Whitaker, who insist that having a loyal and committed staff has cemented the set's success. 'After a merger you need people to buy in 100%, and that's exactly what happened here.'

Commercial Chancery is an intellectually demanding area of the Bar, and one that is hard to rival for factual complexity. Nevertheless, pupils described Serle Court as a set that 'allows you to be you,' and insisted: 'As long as you have the base ability, they appreciate that it manifests itself in different ways, allowing you to develop into the barrister you're meant to be.' While personalities vary, a stunning academic record is the norm, as is a long attention span, an excellent eye for detail and a capacity for hard graft. The biggest part of the job is providing written advice and drafting services, and when advocacy crops up 'you have ample preparation and know the facts backwards.'

Chambers UK rankings

Banking & Finance • Chancery • Commercial (Dispute Resolution) • Company • Financial Services Regulation • Fraud: Civil • Partnership • Professional Negligence • Real Estate Litigation • Restructuring/Insolvency

Café society

Serle Court prefers its own system of recruitment to Olpas. The application form is a chance to show off written advocacy skills and your capacity to be succinct. Around 30 make it to first interview and the best advice we can give is to 'get a good night's sleep before' and 'don't lapse into debate mode someone who declaims as if to a huge imaginary audience is a real turn-off.' CPE/GDL students will be at no disadvantage and the panel looks for people who 'take a healthy interest in legal issues in the world around them.'

Pupils are exposed to high and low-value work for clients ranging from banks, trust funds and companies to private individuals. They include both commercial and traditional Chancery, property and IP, but as one pupil's first piece of work on minority shareholders shows, there's no guarantee of encountering topics familiar from law school. The pupil in question took two extra days to complete the work because he had to give himself 'a crash course in company and insolvency law.' Luckily supervisors give their charges 'as long as they want' to carry out each assignment, and because pupils rarely carry out live work there are no external pressures. For some, this could be a potential downside: before tenancy is offered pupils do 'very little that is used and if it is, it's carefully checked.'

The general view is that 'you don't get the best out of people if they constantly feel under the cosh.' Accordingly, days usually begin around 8.30am and end around 6.30pm. There is morning coffee in the St George's Café and afternoon tea in chambers' library. Both are well attended and pupils are encouraged to join in the chat. Prospective pupils, however, should refrain from spying on these hallowed intervals. Pupils are welcome to join members for drinks at the Gaucho Grill or The Seven Stars, as well as for cricket, football and softball. When at 6pm members say they're 'popping out for a con, we know where they're going!' chuckled a clerk.

Been there, done that

Pupils share rooms with their supervisors, who monitor their work to ensure they gain a breadth of drafting experience. They are also farmed out to other members to experience other practice and interesting cases, perhaps to 'observe an expert cross-examination.' One pupil even carried out work on a criminal case at another set, assisting on the complicated trusts point it involved. Assessment is ongoing, although the first three months are 'quite heavily discounted.' At the end of each seat supervisors submit appraisal forms to the tenancy committee. There is at least one assessed advocacy exercise in which pupils play the same role, so their performances can be measured against each other. In April supervisors meet with the tenancy committee to discuss pupils' first sixes, following which feedback is given. In 2007, a sufficiently strong consensus was reached for the committee to reconvene and offer both pupils tenancy in May, at least a month earlier than usual. Serle Court has plenty of work and further room for expansion, so if a pupil meets the mark he or she will be offered tenancy, regardless of the fate of the other.

Anyone who is offered tenancy then spends the final three months shadowing juniors in the county courts, where 'everything is less smart and more chaotic' and it's 'common for the judge not to have had the papers in advance.' District Judges are not specialised, often doing 'family one minute, commercial the next,' so paradoxically, 'although they need more time, they get less.' It can be 'hard to anticipate what point they're going to seize on,' so the experience is invaluable for anyone on the verge of starting their own practice. Pupils also assist on bigger cases and devil for senior members. Juniors might be in court only five times a month, though this doesn't adversely impact on their earnings: in the first two years of tenancy at least £100K is 'guaranteed and often bettered.' There's a real sense of cohesion at Serle Court and the support network for juniors is excellent. 'Everyone is conscious of having been there before and we regularly trot into each other's rooms.'

And finally...

One thing you might not expect is a six-month secondment to the Cayman Islands just after taking tenancy. Sun, sea, sand and a constant flow of instructions after returning home it's not such a bad idea.

3/4 South Square

The facts

Location: Lincoln's Inn, London

Number of QCs/Juniors: 18/26 (7 women)

Applications: 120

Not in Olpas

Pupils per year: Up to 4

Seats: 6x6 weeks

Pupillage award: £42,500
(can advance £12,500 for the BVC)

This set is best known for its vast insolvency and corporate recovery practice. Its name is so synonymous with this area of law that solicitors suggest it is 'the IBM choice – why would you go anywhere else?'

Members of 3/4 South Square have left their mark on all the big corporate collapses and restructurings – BCCI, Maxwell, Lloyd's syndicates, Barings, Enron, Marconi, Parmelat, MyTravel, Metronet, the list goes on and on.

My word is my Bond

Chambers also has experts in fraud, banking and finance, commercial litigation, company law, insurance and reinsurance and arbitration. While the Insolvency Act is the 'lifeblood' of the set, a rough 60/40 split between insolvency law and broader commercial matters ensures that pupils will encounter interpretation of contract, property law, trusts, tort and EU law. 'If you can't handle EU law, don't come here,' advised one interviewee. Fraud is a 'sexy' area, not least because fraudsters range from the perplexingly normal to 'colourful, famous crooks.' Pupils say working in this area 'can be a bit like being in a Bond film.'

It's important to keep clients' business interests in mind at all times. Commercial awareness can be devilishly hard to define, not least when you're trying to show you have it. For a barrister, it's about looking at cases from a fresh perspective and maintaining an awareness of the commercial context. 'In every case you study at law school, and every textbook example, that context will be there, but it can be easily overlooked,' explained a pupil. Insolvency barristers receive instructions from specialist insolvency practitioners as well as solicitors, and at times they come into contact with some 'very aggressive and difficult' individuals at personal bankruptcy hearings. Having a real-world view on things is imperative. Equally as important is a healthy interest in raw legal principles, and as one pupil pointed out: 'The Insolvency Act is the second longest statute on the books after the Company Act 2006, which is the other one we specialise in.' There's no getting around it; if you want pupillage at 3/4 South Square, you're going to have to cover all the bases.

Island life

Supervision is a 'collaborative process' in which pupils are asked to identify the gaps in their knowledge, so that supervisors can fill them. In this intense year 'you really do hit the ground running.' 'Difficult stuff is thrown at you from an early stage' and 'people aren't going to hold your hand – you either sink or swim.' While pupils complete the same set pieces of work, doing them at different times avoids scrapping for books in the library. 'Chambers really wants you to find out how to work, so pupillage is geared towards letting you make your own decisions.' Time management, for example, is largely left to the individual. Supervisors will ensure they have access to interesting work, but it's up to them to decide whether they can take it on. 'Everyone makes mistakes,' but be reassured there are people to ask for advice and support, and 'pupils are never faced with someone being difficult for the sake of it.' It is the supervisors who pupils sit with after Christmas who take the most active role in the tenancy decision.

Chambers UK rankings

Banking & Finance • Chancery • Company • Restructuring/Insolvency

'This isn't the place to come if you want to be on your feet in the second six.' Advocacy skills aren't even formally assessed during pupillage (although it is important to give 'intelligent, lucid responses' when receiving feedback from supervisors). Adequate advocacy opportunities come in time, and until about eight years' call juniors spend roughly equal amounts of time representing clients alone and being led by seniors. After this, their role becomes more advisory.

Chambers and Partners Insolvency/Corporate Restructuring Set of the Year 2008

The set has a strong international practice, with associate members in Germany, Hong Kong, Singapore, the USA, Australia, South Africa, Scotland and Trinidad and Tobago. One pupil described a 'magical mystery island tour' taking in 'the British Virgin Islands, Mauritius, the Cayman Islands, the Seychelles, the Isle of Man, Jersey and Guernsey.' Needless to say, many cases have a trusts element.

Members' hours fluctuate dramatically – some arrive in the wee small hours to catch the Hong Kong traffic, while others work late to fit in with New York. Even for pupils 12-hour days are not unheard of; the average is 9am until 7pm. 'You'll write lots of long opinions and research notes and go through different drafts of one piece of work, but there's also a lot of time thinking about what you've read and staring into space.' It's important to be able to 'think creatively and logically in order to combat the complexity of the work.'

Tough cookies

After the first six 'no-hopers are told where they stand and given a choice about staying on or looking for a second six elsewhere.' The tenancy decision is made in July, when typically two make the cut. Indeed, in 2008 both pupils were successful. Technically, pupils don't compete for tenancy, but we sensed there was a 'combative' element to the process. As we interviewed them, the pupils engaged in a game of one-upmanship: one had been in court 11 times, visiting the Chancery Division, the Companies Court and the Privy Council. Another, who

had been in court only twice, pointed out that he'd written a chapter for a book and several articles during the same period.

Despite the picture we've painted, 3/4 South Square is by no means a macho set. There's a healthy number of female juniors, and from what we saw, wrap-around cardigans have more currency than sharp suits. At the hub of chambers is a strong administration team run by charismatic senior practice manager Paul Cooklin. 'If you have a technical problem, you go to Yvonne. If you have a pupillage query, you go to Alison. For broader chambers issues, there's Vicky… if you need something typed, you go to Jenny and Julie,' pupils willingly explained. In this set 'everybody knows your name' and juniors regularly go for drinks. 'People are very hard-working, but they still know when to take time off.'

You're advised to take the company law elective on the BVC and, if you're considering postgraduate study, the corporate insolvency paper on the BCL. Another new and developing area to consider is restitution law. Chambers takes into account that not everyone has studied that much law by the time they reach interview. 'We don't find setting legal problems very helpful; we prefer to start everyone with an ethics question, for which no prior knowledge is required.' Interestingly, one of the recruiters admitted: 'Their ethical approach matters quite a lot to us.' Anyone who impresses in an assessed mini-pupillage (chambers pays £500) is fast-tracked to a second-round interview. Most candidates go through two rounds, with third interviews used when the panel can't decide on someone, perhaps because they've underperformed due to nerves. Successful candidates are invited to a drinks party to meet more of the members.

Insolvency law is fast-paced and challenging, and with companies going bust and individuals teetering on the brink of bankruptcy, you need to be 'thick-skinned and resilient,' especially in situations that can be 'panicky and stressful for the client.' After meeting with these pupils, we sensed they were tough cookies.

And finally...

In this slick and ballsy set pupils learn their trade in a challenging and stimulating environment. If you're driven, focused and open-minded, there is every chance to shine; just be prepared for some firm handshakes at interview.

4 Stone Buildings

The facts

Location: Lincoln's Inn, London

Number of QCs/Juniors: 6/22 (3 women)

Applications: 107

Not in Olpas

Pupils per year: Up to 2

Seats: 4x3 months

Pupillage award: Up to £39,000 (can advance sum for BVC)

> While advisory work is a staple for some members, for most litigation is where it's at. As one member put it: 'I didn't come to the Bar to do the job of a solicitor.'

4 Stone Buildings, a small but self-assured set with a reputation for 'fighting with the heavyweights.' Members regularly appear in large commercial disputes, particularly those involving company law, and pride themselves on their 'business acumen, work ethic and amiability.'

On company business

Although company law has a reputation for being 'quite dry at times,' members appreciate that 'there's more to life' and their practices extend to 'more fun stuff' in the form of general commercial cases, fraud, asset tracing and insolvency. Cases range from the monumental (Equitable Life, Three Rivers) to 'short and snappy personal insolvency cases.' The Maxwell affair, in which media mogul Robert Maxwell took over £400m from his employees' pension funds to boost the company's share price, kept one member in court for 150 days. In the case of BCCI, the volume of paperwork gave one barrister an excuse to move into one of the largest rooms in chambers.

Not all litigation involves intriguing newspaper barons. As an eminent judge once said: 'A company is a *persona ficta*... it does not have a soul to be damned or a body to be kicked.' Yet dealing with the inhabitants of Companies House need not be without its human drama and there are personal relationships with clients. Liquidators, administrators, bankers, company directors and accountants are all busy professionals who 'want to know the answer and don't have time for flannel.' For them, litigation is 'an inherently financial thing,' an exercise in risk management, so legal advice must be tempered by commercial considerations. The closest you'll come to Joe Public is in shareholder disputes and Companies Act petitions, and even then 'it's likely to be a man who manages his own company, maybe turning over £50,000, maybe £20m.'

Pressure points

Pupils need to 'make the transition from academic life – where they will have excelled – to practical, real life.' The client will want to know 'should he sell his business today or wait until tomorrow?' and a good barrister must be able to convince him of the right answer, 'even if it means going against his gut instinct.' An approach that merely considers the relevant legal principles is unlikely to work because 'getting the legal answer is only half the battle.' If you're lucky enough to get a pupillage interview, bear this in mind when tackling the legal problem. 'We're looking for someone who can make the switch,' said one of the recruiters. This also means showing you have the 'raw materials' to argue in court. 'Making a nervous candidate more nervous doesn't serve much point,' so the panel won't pressurise candidates for the sake of it. 'If we're giving you a hard time, you're probably getting it right,' confided a source.

Chambers is home to some top QCs, among them Robert Hildyard, Robert Miles and head of chambers George

Chambers UK rankings

Banking & Finance • Chancery • Company • Financial Services Regulation • Fraud: Civil • Restructuring/Insolvency

Bompas. Jonathan Crow QC used to be First Treasury Devil and several juniors currently act as Treasury Counsel. We can't name every respected barrister here; it's enough to say that in a *Chambers UK* table measuring the ratio of individual rankings to size of set, 4 Stone Buildings took second place. So what's its like stepping into such a high-flying environment?

Firstly, pupillage is about 'being taught, not tested.' Supervisors are paternalistic towards their charges and there's a sense of being nurtured and coaxed into practice. As one pupil told us: 'There has definitely been an implicit understanding of how I work as an individual, and an effort to accommodate that.' Pupils sit with four different supervisors to experience a range of work. One supervisor's practice might be 'very company law-focused,' requiring the pupil to 'grapple with accounts;' another's might be 'centred around smaller contractual disputes;' and a third could be 'incredibly blue-chip, with the barrister instructed consistently by magic circle firms.' Assessment is 'informal and definitely not in your face,' but 'you get used to the feeling that your work is being looked at very carefully.' There are no 'artificially contrived' advocacy exercises or tests and all the work pupils do is real. Pupils carry out research and draft documents for their supervisors, often saving them time. In return, they give a lot back. One supervisor told us: 'Before a conference, I get the pupil to sit down with me and pretend to be me, while I pretend to be the client.' Pupils are given all the papers before accompanying a barrister to court and might also have a go at drafting the skeleton argument. After each court visit, pupil and supervisor sit down for post-match analysis.

In God we trust

Room sharing with supervisors works well. 'If I have a particularly poor conference, it's useful for the pupil to see how not to do it,' chuckled a source. Pupil advocacy is rare, although in the months just after taking tenancy 'you will pick up some of your own cases.' The pupils' work is 'very paper-heavy: you have to do a lot of fact handling and reading company accounts... so forensic skills are incredibly important.' Being farmed out to other members to 'see an interesting House of Lords case' or 'be exposed to a silk who needs some help' is important, as this allows pupils to meet every member of chambers at least before

the tenancy decision. Daily tea is another opportunity for pupils to get their faces known. The tenancy decision 'rests primarily on the supervisors' shoulders.' Usually one tenancy is awarded each year, occasionally two, in 2008 one out of two pupils was given tenancy.

A pupil's day generally runs from 9am to 6.30pm, although by January the workload keeps them pretty busy. At that stage 'I began to really enjoy the work and wanted to put in the hours,' one source explained. If things become too much to handle 'help is always there and you're not censured for availing yourself of it.' Clearly everyone works hard, but they also know when to stop. Fell running, skiing, sailing and flying are just some of the members' hobbies. George Bompas is a pilot, and after the BCCI case settled, one barrister upped sticks to South America for five months. Family life is clearly important, and many members have three or four children; each year the head of chambers likes to 'get the families together for a picnic in Lincoln's Inn Fields.' Senior clerk David Goddard – aka 'God' – is undoubtedly a father figure, having been with the set since 1983, before many of you were born. Suggestions that he has 'royal inroads' (members act as Attorney Generals to the Duchy of Lancaster and Prince Charles) only add to the aura of mystery surrounding him. Assurances to the contrary left us wondering who else could be responsible. The member whose wife was one of Princess Di's bridesmaids, perhaps?

And finally...

With a rock-solid core and 'consistency of quality throughout,' this set is 'a small SAS-type unit.' To us, 4 Stone Buildings combines a reputation for feisty court performances and very civilised behaviour back in chambers. It's one of those places where women are described as 'ladies' and a faint smell of cigar smoke pervades the air. As one source said: 'It feels like being a member of a rather select club.'

2 Temple Gardens

The facts

Location: Temple, London

Number of QCs/Juniors: 8/48 (18 women)

Applications: 200-250

Olpas: Summer season

Pupils per year: Up to 3

Pupillage: 3x4 months

Money: £35,000 + earnings (can advance £10,000 for BVC)

The set offers funded and unfunded mini-pupillages, but don't miss the deadlines for the former: 30 November for the winter season and 15 April for the summer season.

For the commercial and civil law multi-specialists of 2 Temple Gardens, breadth of experience is the name of the game.

From atomic testing to global warming

Chambers has occupied its bijou Temple Gardens residence ever since it was founded just after WWII. It has been a purely civil set since the 1960s, and today it adopts what it calls 'a multi-specialist, practice group approach.' This strategy was put in place about five years ago and has seen the set 'concentrate on core areas and grow others by a steady drip, drip accumulation.' As the senior clerk was quick to observe, any of the 50 or so members who now call 2tg home can 'belong to any of the groupings being in PI doesn't exclude you from media.'

The set's core areas are thriving under this approach. Its historically strong personal injury practice accounts for nearly 30% of annual revenue and strong relationships with a welter of top insurers means 'about 90% of our work is defendant.' That said, there's a willingness to 'grow our claimant side a little,' because 'the clients like barristers to have rounded experience.' One ongoing highlight is involvement in the 'Trigger litigation concerning asbestos cases that will probably go all the way to the House of Lords.' Members are also representing insurer clients in a Buncefield oil depot disaster claim and claimants in the Atomic Test Veterans case against the MoD arising out of 1950s testing. Members' proficiency in clinical and professional negligence also brings in regular instructions from the NHS Litigation Authority and professional bodies such as the Medical Defence Union and the Medical Protection Society. Then there's the growing commercial side, incorporating fraud, banking and finance and commodities cases. Additionally, an employment practice 'has really kicked on in the last few

years.' Having 'started out predominantly in claimant' the set is 'gradually getting work from big banks.' This might seem like breadth enough, but 2tg can also make credible claims to pronounced skills in public law, media and entertainment, and property. The latter involves a 'lot of subsidence, tree root and flooding claims from insurance clients, but also a good landlord and tenant practice.' With four members on the Treasury panel and ongoing involvement in the inquiry into the murder of a solicitor in Northern Ireland, public law is also buoyant. Meanwhile members in the media and entertainment team have recently acted for The Drifters in a royalty payments case and got involved when the showing of Al Gore's *An Inconvenient Truth* in UK schools became a political hot potato.

New York, Paris, Blackpool

'Breadth of opportunity was the hook' for our interviewees and a 2tg pupillage doesn't disappoint. Insurance, PI and banking had been the major experiences of one of our sources, but there is simply no set pattern. Two of the three allocated supervisors feature in the first six, the initial three-month stint being 'slightly more protected.' Handling the 'first drafts of court papers and research'

Chambers UK rankings

Clinical Negligence • Personal Injury • Professional Discipline • Professional Negligence

is the norm in the first six, as is accompanying supervisors to conferences, court and client seminars. The focus is on 'generating the skills needed to move into practice,' and as time goes by 'supervisors will notice pupils contributing more.' Looking back, juniors told us: 'When you do something complicated and your supervisor is able to use it in later months it is a fantastic feeling.' Once with their second supervisor, pupils can also expect to take on work for, or attend court with, other members 'to see new areas and different cases.' The pupil may be 'purely observing,' but the payoff is 'getting to chat on the train it helps expose you to more people before the tenancy decision.'

Feedback from supervisors comes on a 'piece-by-piece basis' and they also fill out an end-of-seat report. In the absence of set written assessments, making sure 'there's an organised paper trail' is important, and members who co-opt pupils to draft pleadings or advices will always fill out a feedback sheet. Once the second six starts pupils are faced with a flood of advocacy experience, usually requiring them to be in court three times a week. They are fed a diet of RTAs, small insurance cases and even fast-track claims. 'Variety is the greatest feature,' one pupil enthused, reflecting that 'RTAs help hone your cross-examination skills, while credit hire claims are more about legal analysis and argument.' The caseload also involves travel, albeit largely in and around London and the South East, with a few jaunts as far as Cardiff or Blackpool. 'Join the Bar, see the world,' laughed a clerk.

The tenancy decision is made by the end of June, after considering feedback forms, 'input from solicitors or evidence of repeat instructions,' and the results of several advocacy exercises. 2tg has an excellent record for making tenants, with as many as three a year kept on in the recent past. In 2008 the sole pupil was successful.

Garden parties

Around 40 pupillage applicants are invited to an appraisal day that includes groups activities and a debating exercise. Attendees are also treated to presentations by specialists from different practice areas, making it very much a two-way process. Said one member of the pupillage committee: 'We're aware we compete with other top sets for candidates and we want to show ourselves off.' Between ten and 15 progress to a more traditional second round for discussion of a legal problem given out half an hour beforehand. Surveying the genuine variety of university backgrounds and career histories of current tenants, the process clearly does successfully focus on 'intellect above all, an ability to persuade and ambition to succeed.' Displaying the 'maturity and presence to do well in court and with clients' is perhaps easier for second-careerers, of which there are many, but plenty of law graduates also manage to display such skills.

Commanding fine views of the eponymous gardens, 2tg is spread across multiple floors of its main building and a nearby annexe. Given the separation, you might imagine any sense of cohesion would suffer. Not a bit of it. 'We try to recognise that our members are our assets and it's a mistake not to use them,' said one tenant describing a 'co-operative ethos.' While things might be 'full-blooded if they face one another on a case,' at other times members are 'always available to give advice.' Said one source: 'Pupils are very much involved in extracurricular activities, we like them to feel they belong.' Weekly Friday drinks are a perfect time to catch up, and the Christmas party is well attended. If the 'glazed eyes and slow reactions' we encountered on our visit are anything to go by, the set certainly knows how to organise a knees-up. 'Not that we only do drink-related activities,' a junior hastened to assure us after recounting tales from the Scottish-themed party held the previous night to celebrate 'a High Court victory in a Scottish coal case.'

And finally...

Bursting with advocacy and more varied than a stick of rainbow rock, a 2tg pupillage is every flavour of commercial and civil law and a tasty prospect for it.

3 Verulam Buildings

The facts

Location: Lincoln's Inn, London
Number of QCs/Juniors: 16/41 (10 women)
Applications: 150
Olpas: Summer season
Pupils per year: 3-4
Seats: 4x3 months
Pupillage award: £42,500 (can advance £15,000 for BVC)

> The number of 3VB juniors ranked in our parent publication *Chambers UK* is exceptional. A dozen are ranked for commercial litigation alone, and there are ten ranked for banking and finance.

3 Verulam Buildings is an ambitious commercial set, motivated by the shared vision of a future in the magic circle. Its core work in banking and financial services has expanded to include insurance, fraud and insolvency, plus an interesting line in media and entertainment and a strong arbitration practice.

High hopes

Barristers frequently appear opposite members of other prestigious sets such as One Essex Court and Fountain Court, and it is 'in the same mould' as these giants that 3VB sees itself developing. Incremental changes to 3VB's profile, the calibre of instructions received and the size of its premises have made it a force to be reckoned with. We heard its name mentioned again and again during our tour of the Inns, and with silks from other chambers praising the quality of its juniors after leading them on big cases, the coming years are sure to bring further success.

Among the silks, Ali Malek QC stands out together with former general counsel to the FSA Michael Blair and popular head of chambers Christopher Symons. Tony Blair's brother Bill Blair QC has just been made a High Court judge. For recent major cases, look no further than the mammoth arbitration over Lloyd's New Central Fund (a case involving insurance brokers) or the $600m JPMorgan v Springwell litigation (relating to alleged mis-selling of Russian and other emerging market investments). Members have been involved in most major civil fraud cases over recent years (Maxwell, BCCI, Polly Peck), as well as a number of large insurance/reinsurance disputes rising out of 9/11, Equitable Life and the current 'spiral of personal injury claims.' In the much publicised bank charges litigation, 3VB has six members acting for various parties.

After extensive building work, the set now has a stunning admin area, conference rooms, seminar facilities and a waiting room. 'There's a real buzz about the place' and 'a feeling of going somewhere.' As senior practice manager Nick Hill proclaimed: 'Others inherit their name; we're out there earning ours.' There is, however, one very good reason why students might know 3VB's name – it offers the biggest pupillage award going. A huge amount of effort, as well as money, goes into making pupillage an attractive and viable entry point into the profession, 'especially for people who don't form part of the conveyor belt of white, Oxbridge-educated males on their way to the Bar.' Chambers says its aims are twofold: to find future tenants and (failing that) to make sure pupils are well placed to gain tenancy elsewhere.

Shadowy figures

Pupils change supervisors four times and also benefit from more junior 'shadow pupil supervisors'. The blend

Chambers UK rankings

Banking & Finance • Commercial (Dispute Resolution) • Financial Services Regulation • Fraud: Civil • Information Technology • Insurance • Media & Entertainment • Professional Negligence • Restructuring/Insolvency • Telecommunications

of 'big exciting cases' and 'small cases you can get to grips with and follow from start to finish' is one of the best things about this pupillage. Work from other members is permitted but 'rigidly controlled,' and pupils are given regular feedback. Said one: 'I always know where my work stands in terms of the required standard, and I also know what I need to do to get it to the required standard.' Supervisors take their role seriously. 'You can achieve so much more if you don't follow the traditional paradigm of sitting back, letting the pupil do the work and

Chambers and Partners Client Service Set of the Year 2008

then pointing out their mistakes afterwards.' Pupils and supervisors engage in regular dialogue, with pieces of work (research, drafting opinions, skeleton arguments, particulars of claim, defences and replies) the springboard for further discussion. Supervisors also go out of their way to elucidate 'areas of the Bar that can otherwise remain a mystery for years' and genuinely seem to enjoy sharing their rooms. 'Pupils are good companyit can be quite a lonely profession.'

Assessment is via written reports, and a handful of advocacy exercises are 'designed to remove any complacency and make pupils prepare carefully.' Said one: 'They give you a rough ride but you also get very thorough feedback.' On the insistence of pupillage committee head Andrew Onslow QC, a moderator is also present to 'make sure no confidence shattering goes on.' Second-six pupils are permitted to take their own cases – simple things like winding-up petitions and straightforward directions hearings. Such appearances are not regular and pupils are never sent out to take notes on long trials as 'frankly the way a pupil impresses his or her supervisor is by the quality of their written work and the way they interact in discussions, and those things happen in chambers.' The set's banking practice generates plenty of low-value instructions for baby juniors; think mortgage matters and 'endless cases over bank charges.' Remember, chambers represents one type of client in all of these cases, and it isn't the man on the street.

During a 3VB mini-pupillage everyone is expected to produce a piece of written work on which a report is writ-

ten and kept on file. A mini-pupillage is not compulsory for pupillage applicants, though it's certainly advisable. And if you have no debating or mooting experience, the recruiters will wonder: 'Why on earth are you thinking about the Bar?' Advocacy skills are important, but intelligence is even more so. You'll need to convince them you have energy, brains and practical common sense. Of the recruitment process, one source admitted: 'The hardest part is getting it down to the 40 we see at first interview.'

Survivor!

Plenty of space means the set is not constrained in how it grows. This is great for pupils as 'it's not like you're down in a pit with knives and a loin cloth, and one will survive.' Baby juniors have 'the best of both worlds,' working alone on cases to build up a following, and being led to 'buy that nice house in Islington.' Many new juniors complete a secondment to the FSA and short visits to firms of solicitors. The clerks take care that no one ever gets into the position where they 'emerge blinking into the sunlight after two years as fourth junior in the basement of a solicitors' office' (as is rumoured to happen at some well-known sets), and a mentor helps relieve the inevitable pressure of 'spending the first two years of practice in a constant state of panic.' In short, in no time at all you're a seasoned practitioner, taking on 'anything non-criminal with a lot of money involved.' 'Call me a knockabout commercial litigator,' chuckled one junior. In 2008 one of two pupils was awarded tenancy.

The atmosphere at 3VB is cordial and 'there's no 80s-macho, up-there-with-the-big-boys culture.' A group of juniors heads to the pub from time to time and there's also a tradition of pupils going for Friday lunch. Afternoon tea isn't quite 3VB's style, but members 'pop in and out of each other's rooms.' Other things to mention are an annual dinner, a summer party at Christopher Symons' house and the occasional cricket match. When it comes to decision making, tenants at all levels can participate through rolling membership of the management and practice development committees. 'We don't live by committee, but the ones we have work hard to make sure things happen.'

And finally...

There's no other way of saying it: this is a very nice set. It is sometimes more modest about its achievements than it need be, but maybe that's part of its charm.

Wilberforce Chambers

The facts

Location: Lincoln's Inn, London
Number of QCs/Juniors: 21/29 (11 women)
Applications: Up to 100
Not in Olpas
Pupils per year: 2
Seats: 6x2 months
Pupillage award: £40,000 (can advance £13,500 for BVC)

Lincoln's Inn-based Chancery giant Wilberforce Chambers is 50 in 2009, yet the set shows no sign of mid-life crisis.

Back in the 1980s, Wilberforce was one of the first sets to recognise the importance of establishing itself as a brand rather than just an address. Today, its name is synonymous with excellent legal advice and top-class litigation.

Lawyers' lawyers

While most Wilberforce barristers concentrate on Chancery Division cases, they also handle cases heard in the Queen's Bench Division. Among the set's best-known cases are Grupo Torras, Equitable Life, Charman v Charman (there was a heavy trusts element to this divorce) and the collapses of BCCI, the Mirror Group and Barings. Pensions are Wilberforce's playground. In 2005 members advised High Court judges threatening legal action over changes to their pensions. Very quickly a ministerial statement announced that the judges would be released from the controversial tax on their pension pots.

Certain members have very specialised practices, for example former Linklaters partner Anna Carboni is an IP lawyer. She was instructed on behalf of Simon Fuller in the dispute over the format of *X Factor,* and by Mars in its tussle with Nestlé, when it wanted to launch a competing chocolate bar called Have a Break. Wilberforce also receives numerous international instructions from places like Hong Kong and Singapore, as well as tax havens such as Bermuda, Jersey and the Cayman Islands. It's little wonder pupils seem in awe of the barristers and are keenly aware of the standards required of them. 'It is an incredibly able set,' remarked one, 'and some of the best people in the area are here.'

Over the past decade Wilberforce has outgrown its various buildings and annexes. With 50 members, eight clerks and various other members of staff including two house-keepers and a librarian, it's quite a family. Having identified an optimum number of about 50 members a decade ago, chambers is now considering whether bigger might be better. At the same time it also wants the entire set to be under one roof. Senior clerk Dannie Smilie doesn't rule out the idea of leaving the Inn altogether. 'Why not?' he asks, pointing out that even the Business Court of the RCJ is moving into a new building in Rolls Passage.

Strut your stuff

To succeed here you need to be commercially minded and have a good head for figures, particularly if you're thinking about messing around with tax cases. Chancery practice is a technical, rigorous, intellectually challenging discipline that requires barristers to unravel complex problems in such a way as to make them crystal-clear for a judge. Logic and precision are key, so you can't just sweep the court along with rhetoric. As one source put it, it is '[law] for the anally retentive.' Having 'a good, clear written style is imperative, as paper advocacy is just as important as standing up in court.' The majority of time is

Chambers UK rankings

Chancery • Charities • Fraud: Civil • Intellectual Property • Pensions • Professional Negligence • Real Estate Litigation

spent in chambers, although when cases do reach court, trials tend to run on.

Unashamed intellectual prowess is what pupils need. It's not just a case of being brainy, but knowing how to work your brain like it's on a catwalk. As one of the recruiters phrased it, you need 'inquisitiveness, sharpness and subtlety of mind.' Chambers tells us that having the required intelligence doesn't necessarily mean having a First, and it's fair to say that not everyone at Wilberforce does although those without are in the minority.

For an explanation of Chancery practice see page 849

The first-round pupillage interview is 'just a discussion about a topic of legal interest that's in the public eye and a more old-fashioned getting-to-know-you series of questions.' Smart candidates will have already done a mini-pupillage (three days, no formal assessment). The quality of a candidate's thinking is really tested during the second interview, when they must discuss a legal problem. 'The worst mistake is an un-thought-out mistake,' revealed a recruiter. To rehearse you could try and 'see both sides of an argument very quickly and outline the key points.' One thing worth taking into account is that 'it's absolutely not about cases; it's a knowledge and understanding of basic legal principles and common sense that we're looking for.'

Take your time

Pupils sit with three supervisors in their first six and three in the second. They are exposed to 'property, company insolvency, probate, trusts pretty much anything that comes the set's way.' All of the magic circle firms instruct, and lay clients range from multinationals to individuals. Pupils do work for people of all levels of seniority; and younger members, especially, 'remember the pitfalls' and happily offer advice. Be aware that advocacy is thin on the ground: 'I had a quiet time,' recalled one source, 'I wasn't in court amazingly frequently.'

There is ongoing informal assessment. 'In some chambers they mark specific pieces of work; here they want to gain an overall impression of you, so every individual piece of work counts.' In some ways this makes it more pressurised, 'but if you do let something slip, it's not game

over.' Pupils recommended taking the time to get things right rather than rushing to complete as much as possible: 'There's always time to get faster in this profession.' Hours 'depend totally on your supervisor as you tend to mimic them,' though 9am-6pm might be average. 'Almost all levels of seniority will work one day at the weekend,' commented a clerk, whose job it is to find a happy medium for barristers who 'moan when they're busy and moan when things are quiet.'

A lightness of touch

The tenancy decision is made in July, although 'you'll be given a good strong steer at six months as to whether you're on course.' One of the two pupils were successful in 2008. Does personality count? Undoubtedly. 'We do not want people who are too abrasive, even though they may make extremely good barristers,' said one source. And from another: 'We work as a group and a sort of team. A lot of us are very successful, hard-working and ambitious, but we're also fairly laid-backwe aim for a certain lightness of touch, while still doing the weighty work.' Said head of the pupillage committee John Furber QC: 'There are a lot of people like me who aren't home-grown, but the question is always asked, 'Will they fit in with the culture?'' A senior clerk commented: 'I certainly feel it's a tighter, happier ship than one or two of our competitors, who've found it difficult to break down some of the individual groups from the various banners they came under.'

A pupil described the Wilberforce culture as 'professional, inclusive, friendly and approachable.' The clerks are 'mostly on first-name terms' with barristers and there are no sirs or ma'ams here. On the social side, 'it's not the Criminal Bar where everyone's getting plastered every night,' but there are drinks and a monthly meal for all members (sadly, not pupils). Barristers regularly lunch together in Lincoln's Inn and juniors have impromptu nights out.

And finally...

You need to be a braniac to make an impression here, however people skills are just as essential for inspiring confidence in wealthy clients or company directors who are used to getting their own way. This is one of those sets where the barristers need to have it all.

- **Third time lucky:** Third-six pupillage vacancies are now listed on the Bar Council's website www.barcouncil.org.uk

A-Z of Barristers

Atkin Chambers

1 Atkin Building, Gray's Inn, London, WC1R 5AT
Tel: (020) 7404 0102   Fax: (020) 7405 7456
Email: clerks@atkinchambers.com
Website: www.atkinchambers.com

Chambers profile

Atkin Chambers was the first set to specialise in the law relating to domestic and international construction and engineering projects. It has a significant and growing international practice at all levels of seniority. Chambers success in this area has been recognised by the grant of the Queen's Award for Enterprise 2005 in the category of International Trade.

Type of work undertaken

Atkin Chambers is a leader in its field: technology and construction law. Members of Chambers have been involved in many of the largest high profile domestic and international disputes in the fields of construction, technology, power, energy computers and telecommunications of recent years, both in court and in international and domestic arbitration. Members of Chambers are regular participants as advocates, advisers or tribunals in all forms of alternative dispute resolution.

Pupil profile

Applicants for pupilage should have a first-class degree or a good 2.1 degree. Postgraduate qualifications are viewed favourably but are not essential. Applications from non-law graduates are welcome. Atkin Chambers is committed to applying equal opportunities good practice.

Pupillage

Atkin Chambers takes recruitment to pupillage and tenancy extremely seriously. The pupillage award (anticipated to be £47,500 for 2009/10 – equivalent to the sums paid by other much larger sets of chambers) reflects this.

The Pupillage year is structured to provide all of the Bar Council's training requirements and the additional training Chambers considers is necessary for successful entry into high-quality commercial work of its practice. Atkin Chambers provides its own advocacy training and assessment in addition to that provided by the Inns.

Full and up-to date details of the structure and goals of Atkin Chambers' pupilllage training programme may be reviewed on the website.

Mini pupillages

Six mini-pupillages are offered each year. Applications by letter with CV should be received by 30th November 2008. Mini-pupillages will be offered to candidates who have achieved or have clear potential to achieve the academic standards required for pupilage.

Sponsorship & awards

Three fully funded pupilages of £47,500 per pupil for 12 months are available. Funding for the BVC year by way of drawdown is available.

No of Silks	14
No of Juniors	24
No of Pupils	3
Contact	
Mr Andrew Burrows	
Email: aburrows@atkinchambers.com	
Method of application	
Pupillage: OLPAS (Summer)	
Mini-pupillage: CV and covering letter to contact	
Pupillages (p.a.)	
up to 3 funded	
Income	
(2009-10) expected to be £47,500	
Tenancies	
six in the last three years	

2 Bedford Row (William Clegg QC)

2 Bedford Row, London, WC1R 4BU
Tel: (020) 7440 8888   Fax: (020) 7242 1738
Email: clerks@2bedfordrow.co.uk
Website: www.2bedfordrow.co.uk

No of Silks **17**	
No of Juniors **47**	
No of Pupils **4**	
Graduate recruitment contact	
Tim Kendal	
020 7440 8888	
Method of application	
SUMMER OLPAS	
Pupillages (p.a.)	
12 months 4	
Tenancies offered according to ability	

Chambers profile

Widely regarded as one of the leading criminal sets in the UK, 2 Bedford Row continues to excel in the fields of crime, fraud and regulatory law. Chambers has been described by 'Chambers and Partners' 2008 as a "number-one criminal set" and many of its members are regarded as leaders in their fields.

Type of work undertaken

Chambers has a broad based criminal practice and its members have appeared in some of the most high profile criminal of recent years (in 2008, for example, R v Barry George, R v Levi Bellfield, R v Mark Dixie). In addition, members of Chambers have particular experience in the fields of confiscation/restraint, health and safety, financial services law, sports law and professional regulation/discipline. Members are frequently instructed to appear before regulatory bodies such as the GMC, the FA, the VAT tribunal and the Police Disciplinary Tribunal.

Pupil profile

Chambers recruits candidates from all backgrounds who display the highest intellectual ability, excellent advocacy skills, sound judgment and a real commitment to criminal law and its related fields. Candidates will also be well rounded individuals who are able to communicate effectively with a wide variety of people.

Pupillage

Chambers offers up to four 12 month pupillages each year. Each pupil will have two pupil supervisors in their first six and a different two in their second six. This ensures that pupils are provided with a thorough grounding in all aspects of Chambers' practice. Chambers also provides structured advocacy training throughout the pupillage year and will pay for pupils to attend the 'Advice to Counsel' and 'Forensic Accountancy' courses.

Mini pupillages

Chambers welcomes applications for mini-pupillage. Please see the website for details.

Funding

Chambers provides a grant of £10,000 to each pupil, paid monthly throughout the year. In addition, pupils can expect to earn in excess of £12,000 in their second six.

Blackstone Chambers (I Mill QC and T Beazley QC)

Blackstone House, Temple, London EC4Y 9BW   DX: 281
Tel: (020) 7583 1770 Fax: (020) 7822 7350
Email: pupillage@blackstonechambers.com
Website: www.blackstonechambers.com

Chambers profile
Blackstone Chambers occupies large and modern, premises in the Temple.

Type of work undertaken
Chambers' formidable strengths lie in its principal areas of practice: commercial, employment and EU, public law, human rights and public international law. Commercial law includes financial/business law, international trade, conflicts, sport, media and entertainment, intellectual property and professional negligence. All aspects of employment law, including discrimination, are covered by Chambers' extensive employment law practice. Public law incorporates judicial review, acting both for and against central and local government agencies and other regulatory authorities, all areas affected by the impact of human rights and other aspects of administrative law. EU permeates practices across the board. Chambers recognises the increasingly important role which mediation has to play in dispute resolution. Five members are CEDR accredited mediators.

Pupil profile
Chambers looks for articulate and intelligent applicants who are able to work well under pressure and demonstrate high intellectual ability. Successful candidates usually have at least a 2:1 honours degree, although not necessarily in law.

Pupillage
Chambers offers four (or exceptionally five) 12 month pupillages to those wishing to practise full-time at the Bar, normally commencing in October each year. Pupillage is divided into four sections and every effort is made to ensure that pupils receive a broad training. The environment is a friendly one; pupils attend an induction week introducing them to the Chambers working environment. Chambers prefers to recruit new tenants from pupils wherever possible. Chambers subscribes to OLPAS; applications should be made for the summer season.

Mini pupillages
Assessed mini pupillages are available and are an important part of the application procedure. Applications for mini pupillages must be made by 30 April; earlier applications are strongly advised and are preferred in the year before pupillage commences.

Funding
Awards of £42,500 per annum are available. The pupillage committee has a discretion to consider applications for up to £10,000 of the pupillage award to be advanced during the BVC year. Since Chambers insists on an accessed mini pupillage as part of the overall application procedure, financial assistance is offered either in respect of out of pocket travelling or accommodation expenses incurred in attending the mini pupillage, up to a maximum of £200 per pupil.

No of Silks 32
No of Juniors 41
No of Pupils 4 (current)

Contact
Miss Julia Hornor
Chambers Director

Method of application
OLPAS

Pupillages (p.a.)
12 months 4-5
Required degree grade
Minimum 2:1
(law or non-law)

Income
Award £42,500
Earnings not included

Tenancies
Junior tenancies offered
in last 3 years 58%
No of tenants of 5 years
call or under 11

Cloisters

Cloisters, 1 Pump Court, Temple, London, EC4Y 7AA
Tel: (020) 7827 4000 Fax: (020) 7827 4100
Email: clerks@cloisters.com
Website: www.cloisters.com

No of Silks 5
No of Juniors 45
No of Pupils 2

Contact
pupillage@cloisters.com

Method of application
via OLPAS

Pupillages (p.a.)
2 for 12 months

Chambers profile

Cloisters is a leading set with particular expertise in employment, equality, discrimination and human rights, personal injury and clinical negligence, media and sport, and public and regulatory law. Cloisters is known for its legal excellence, approachability, superb customer service and cost-effectiveness. It recruits only barristers who can offer these qualities.

Type of work undertaken

Cloisters acts for both claimants and respondents in all its practice areas.

Employment and discrimination: Cloisters continues to be at the forefront of this type of law. Recent high-profile cases include: Ahsan v. Watt (HL) – issue estoppel in tribunals, liability of political parties for discrimination; Cadman v. Health & Safety Executive (ECJ) – length of service pay increments; Coleman v. Attridge (ECJ) – discrimination by association.

Personal injury: Cloisters' personal injury team continues to appear in landmark cases and highly complex cases involving large sums. One of their specialisms is in cases involving occupational stress or bullying at work, which contain elements of both personal injury and employment law. Recent high-profile cases include: A v. Hoare (the Lotto Rapist) (HL) – limitation periods; Sarwar v. (1) Ali (2) MIB – highest-ever gross award in a personal injury case of £9.5m; Majrowski v. Guy's and St. Thomas' NHS Trust (HL) – employers' vicarious liability for harassment by employees to other employees at work.

Clinical negligence: In 2007 members of the PI and clinical negligence team and their instructing solicitors secured more than £100m for claimants. The set has the knowledge and experience to handle the full spectrum of work, right up to the multi-million pound catastrophic claims, and regularly appears on such instructions. They handle a full range of cases, including cases worth more than £10m. Recent major cases include: H v. Powys Health Board – highest-ever clinical negligence award of £10.7m.

Sport: Cloisters' sport practitioners handle disciplinary regulations, consultative work, litigation, non-professional sporting activity cases and matters arising from sports and entertainment cases, such as employment or contractual issues. For example, Cloisters has acted for Dwayne Chambers, Sam Allardyce, Status Quo and Frank Warren, among others.

Pupil profile

Chambers welcomes applications from outstanding candidates from all backgrounds and academic disciplines, including lawyers coming late to the Bar.

Pupillage

Chambers offers two twelve month pupillages to those wishing to practise full-time at the Bar, normally commencing in October each year. Each pupil is supervised and the supervisor changes every three months to show the pupil different areas of practice. Second six pupils will be allocated work by clerks subject to availability of work and pupil ability.

Internship programme

Cloisters offers twelve one week internship placements each year. All applicants must have completed at least their first year at university in any subject. The internships are unfunded, but we may pay travel costs in the event that an internee is asked to travel to court outside of London.

Funding

Cloisters offers two funded pupillages each year. Each pupil will receive an award (currently £30,000 per year). Pupils can also ask for an advance.

Crown Office Chambers

Head of Chambers: Antony Edwards-Stuart QC
2 Crown Office Row, Temple, London, EC4Y 7HJ
Tel: (020) 7797 8100   Fax: (020) 7797 8101
Email: mail@crownofficechambers.com
Website: www.crownofficechambers.com

No of Silks 14
No of Juniors 70
No of Pupils 2

Contact
Matthew Boyle

Method of application
Online application form,
downloadable from chambers
website

Pupillages (p.a.)
Up to three per year, 12
months
£42,500 plus earnings

Tenancies
No of tenancies offered in last
3 years 6

Chambers profile

Crown Office Chambers is one of the foremost sets of chambers specialising in civil common law work. The majority of members undertake at least some personal injury work, and some practise solely in that area. Chambers has an established reputation in other areas including construction, professional negligence, commercial contracts, insurance and product liability. It is not a 'pure commercial' set, and pupils will see a range of work during pupillage.

Pupil profile

Members pride themselves on their professionalism, an astute and business-orientated awareness of the practical needs of solicitors and lay clients, combined with an approachable and unstuffy attitude to their work. Chambers looks for the same in its pupils, all of whom are regarded as having strong tenancy potential. Pupils are expected to display the motivation, dedication and intelligence which are the hallmarks of a first-class barrister. Academically, they should have a first or upper second-class honours degree (not necessarily in law), a flair for oral and written advocacy, and a strong and committed work ethic.

Pupillage

Pupils rotate through three pupil supervisors during the course of the year. In their second six, pupils are briefed to attend County Court hearings on their own, probably at least two or three times per week. Generally these will be small personal injury cases. Pupils receive regular feedback on their work from pupil supervisors and other members of chambers. They also undertake a series of advocacy exercises in front of a panel of four members of chambers and receive extensive feedback after each exercise. There are also two assessed written exercises during the course of pupillage. Tenancy decisions are made in early July.

Mini-pupillage

Mini-pupillages available throughout the year – contact the Mini-Pupillage Administrator via online application form, downloadable from Chambers website.

One Essex Court

Chambers of Lord Grabiner QC, One Essex Court, Temple, London, EC4Y 9AR
Tel: (020) 7583 2000   Fax: (020) 7583 0118
Email: clerks@oeclaw.co.uk   Website: www.oeclaw.co.uk

No of Silks **22**	
No of Juniors **41**	
No of Pupils **4**	
Contact	
Joanne Huxley Secretary to the Pupillage Committee	
Method of application	
OLPAS	
Pupillages (p.a.)	
4-12 month	
Required degree grade	
Minimum 2:1	
(law or non-law)	
Income	
Award £45,000	

Chambers profile

One Essex Court is a pre-eminent set of barristers' chambers, specialising in commercial litigation. Members provide specialist advice and advocacy services worldwide, which include all areas of dispute resolution, litigation and arbitration.

Type of work undertaken

Chambers' work embraces all aspects of domestic and international trade, commerce and finance. Members of Chambers are recognised specialists in the many diverse fields characterised as commercial disputes, also regularly accepting nominations as arbitrators, mediators and experts. Chambers work includes, but is not limited to: arbitration, banking and finance, civil fraud, commercial litigation, company and insolvency, competition and EU, energy (oil, gas and utilities), financial services, insurance, IP, professional negligence and revenue law.

Pupil profile

Chambers has for many years maintained a policy of active recruitment and expansion and only offers pupillage to those who are thought capable of becoming tenants. Provided a candidate is proven to have the requisite ability, no distinction is drawn between candidates who do and those who do not have a law degree. Pupils at One Essex Court do not compete against one another for a predetermined maximum intake.

Pupillage

Four guaranteed 12 month pupillages are offered per year, each with substantial funding. From the beginning, pupils assist pupil supervisors with their papers, do legal research, draft opinions, pleadings and skeleton arguments. There are substantial opportunities for advocacy in the second six months of pupillage. Chambers subscribes to OLPAS.

Mini-pupillage

Mini-pupillages last for either one or two days. They are not assessed. A mini-pupillage is not a pre-requisite for pupillage although it is encouraged as it can provide a good opportunity both to see how Chambers works and to meet members of Chambers. Please visit Chambers' website for the application process and deadlines.

Funding

Chambers offers each pupil £45,000, supplemented by earnings in the second six. It is understood that this is amongst the highest, if not the highest, remuneration package available to pupils. An advance of the Award is available, upon request, during a prospective pupil's Bar Vocational Course ("BVC") year.

ONE ESSEX COURT

39 Essex Street

39 Essex Street, London, WC2R 3AT
Tel: 020 7832 1111   Fax: 020 7353 3978
Email: clerks@39essex.com
Website: www.39essex.com

No of Silks 24	
No of Juniors 55	
No of Pupils up to 3	
Contact	
Pupillage - Steven Kovats	
clerks@39essex.com	
020 7832 1111	
Method of application	
OLPAS	
Pupillages (p.a.)	
Up to three	

Chambers profile

39 Essex Street is a long established civil set. It currently has 79 members, including 24 QCs. Chambers has several members on each of the Attorney General's A, B and C Panels for civil litigation. Chambers prides itself on its friendly and professional atmosphere. Chambers is fully networked and its clerking and administrative services are of a high standard. Chambers works very hard but it also has extensive social, sporting and professional activities.

Type of work undertaken

Commercial law: commercial regulation; construction and engineering; corporate restructuring; employment; insurance and reinsurance; media, entertainment and sports; oil, gas and utilities; project finance.

Common law: clinical negligence; health and safety; insurance; material loss claims; personal injury; product liability; professional negligence; sports injuries; toxic torts.

Environmental and Planning: compulsory purchase; contaminated land; environmental civil liability; environmental regulation; international environmental law; licensing; marine environment; planning; nuisance; rating.

Public law: central and local government (including education, housing, immigration, prisons and VAT); European law; human rights; judicial review; mental health and community care; parliamentary and public affairs.

Regulatory and Disciplinary: medical; legal; social care and education; financial services; broadcasting, communications and media; sport; transport; health and safety; building and housing; local government standards; licensing.

Pupillage

Chambers takes up to three 12 month pupils a year. During the pupillage year, each pupil will be rotated among four pupil supervisors, covering a broad range of Chambers' work. The pupils will also do a number of assessed pieces of written work for other members of Chambers. There is an in-house advocacy course. Pupils work only 9.00 am to 6.00 pm, Monday to Friday.

Chambers is a member of OLPAS. Applicants should consult the OLPAS timetable.

Mini-pupillage

Mini-pupillage is an important part of Chambers selection process. It is encouraged that anyone who wishes to apply for pupillage at 39 Essex Street apply for mini-pupillage. Due to the limited number of places available, not all applicants will be successful. Applicants should be in their final year before undertaking the BVC, save in exceptional circumstances. Applications are made between 1 September and 30 November. Selection takes place between 1 December and 14 December. The deadline for acceptance of offers is mid-January. Mini-pupillages take place between mid-January until July.

Funding

Each 12 months pupillage comes with an award, currently £40,000. Of this, up to £8,000 may be drawn down during the year before pupillage commences. Awards and offers are all conditional upon passing the BVC. Junior tenants receive an interest free loan of £30,000, which is repaid out of earnings during the first 12 months.

ThirtyNine
ESSEX STREET

4-5 Gray's Inn Square

Gray's Inn, London, WC1 R 5AH
Tel: (020) 7404 5252   Fax: (020) 7242 7803
Email: clerks@4-5.co.uk
Website: www.4-5.co.uk

Pupillges funded 2/3
Tenants 47
Tenancies in last 3 years 6

Method of application
Apply through OLPAS summer
season, even if OLPAS exempt.
Candidates should see
Chambers' website for full
information

Pupillages (p.a.)
Up to three 12 month
pupillages

Annexes
None

Chambers profile

4-5 Gray's Inn Square is a leading set of chambers specialising in a wide range of work, including in particular public law and judicial review, planning and environmental law, commercial law, employment and human rights. A distinctive feature of Chambers is the large number of barristers who practise at the intersection of these various specialisms. Chambers believe its strong reputation owes a lot to this unusual diversity. Chambers is a large set, comprising 47 (11 QCs and 36 Juniors). and takes a modern and innovative approach to the changing market for legal services. It has well-established links with the academic world and has a number of leading lawyers and academics among its associate tenants. It is fully committed to the Bar's responsibilities as a profession and members of Chambers frequently undertake work in a pro bono capacity. Chambers prides itself on being not only a high-quality set, but a friendly one.

Type of work undertaken

General public law (including ,judicial review applications for and against local government and human rights challenges); planning and environmental law (including inquiries, statutory appeals and judicial review applications) on behalf of developers and planning authorities, and all aspects of domestic and EU environmental law: employment law (including unfair dismissal, sex, race, disability and other prohibited discrimination and trade union law); commercial law (including fraud, banking, shipping, regulatory work, insurance and reinsurance); professional negligence (including actions involving property, education and solicitors); education (including human rights and discrimination, special educational needs, admissions, exclusions and transport.)

Pupil profile

Chambers has a rigorous selection procedure for pupillage. To obtain a first interview, candidates must show first-class academic ability (though not necessarily a first-class degree) and strong evidence of advocacy potential. Successful interview candidates will be expected to demonstrate exceptional legal problem-solving and advocacy ability.

Pupillage

Pupils will receive a thorough training in the full range of Chambers' work during their pupillage. During the pupillage, pupils will generally be assigned to three or four different members of Chambers (pupil supervisors) to ensure they see the full range of work in which Chambers specialises. There may be some opportunity for pupils to gain advocacy experience by appearing in employment tribunals or in court, To gain additional advocacy experience pupils may take cases for the Free Representation Unit, which can be done both prior to and during pupillage. Chambers pays for all new tenants to attend the annual Advanced International Advocacy Course at Keble College in Oxford.

Mini pupillages

Chambers welcomes applications for mini-pupillages. Chambers also holds an annual open day and again full details can be found on our website.

Funding

Chambers normally offers up to three 12-month pupillages, each carrying an award of at least £36,500 (2009 figure) with the possibility to draw down up to £10,000 in the BVC year at Chambers' discretion.

4-5
Gray's Inn Square

2 Hare Court

2 Hare Court, Temple, London EC4Y 7BH
Tel: (020) 7353 5324 Fax: (020) 7353 0667
Email: clerks@2harecourt.com
Website: www.2harecourt.com

No of Silks 15	
No of Juniors 41	
No of Pupils 2	
Contact	
Jeremy Benson QC	
Method of application	
OLPAS (summer)	
Pupillages (p.a.)	
Up to 2 12 month pupillages	
Minimum degree 2:1	
Tenancies	
According to ability	
Annexes	
None	

Chambers profile

2 Hare Court has long been recognised as one of the UK's leading chambers specialising in criminal law and other related fields. It is described by Chambers and Partners Guide as being in "the top band for crime on the back of widespread approval for the way in which its practitioners conduct themselves in the big trials" and by the Legal 500 as "a set of choice for many solicitors for a range of general as well as high profile and complex crime". Its first rate reputation is based on a proven track record of high quality client care together with excellence in advocacy and trial management.

Type of work undertaken

The strength and depth of experience amongst its members enables this chambers to undertake all types of criminal work, particularly the more serious and complex matters such as murder, terrorism, serious fraud, corporate and financial crime, international drug trafficking, corruption and organised crime. The cases in which members of chambers have appeared read like a who's who of recent criminal litigation. Members are also regularly instructed in other related areas particularly in regulatory work before bodies as diverse as the General Medical Council, the Football Association, the Vat and Duties Tribunal, licensing and gaming, health and safety, environmental health, food and drugs,.

Pupil profile

Chambers select as pupils articulate and well motivated individuals of high intellectual ability who can demonstrate sound judgement and a practical approach to problem solving. Candidates should have at least a 2.1 honours degree.

Pupillage

Chambers offers up to two twelve month pupillages starting in September. The year is divided into two six month periods although pupils are assigned to a different pupil supervisor for each of the four months to ensure experience in different areas of crime. Chambers pays for the "Advice to Counsel" course and runs their own in-house advocacy training.

Mini pupillages

The programme runs throughout the year with one mini pupil taken each week and two each week in the summer except between mid-December and mid-January and throughout August. Applicants must be at least 18 years old and either be studying for Higher Education qualification or on or about to start CPE or BVC course. Please see the website for further details of the scheme, the application process and to download an application form.

Funding

12 month pupils will be sponsored through a combination of an award scheme, guaranteed earnings and additional earnings. No clerks' fees or deductions are taken from earnings.

Henderson Chambers

2 Harcourt Buildings, Temple, London EC4Y 9DB
Tel: (020) 7583 9020
Fax: (020) 7583 2686
Email: clerks@hendersonchambers.co.uk
Website: www.hendersonchambers.co.uk

Chambers profile

Henderson Chambers is a leading civil common law/commercial chambers. Chambers has acknowledged expertise in all of its principal areas of practice, and members of Chambers and its pupils are frequently involved in high profile commercial and common law litigation.

Type of work undertaken

Chambers has unrivalled expertise in product liability (which covers a wide range of commercial work including sale of goods and insurance disputes, multi-party pharmaceutical and medical device claims and regulatory and enforcement proceedings) and is consistently rated as the leading set of chambers in this area. Henderson Chambers is also widely recognised for the excellence of its health and safety work.

Members are also noted for their expertise and experience in areas including: employment law, regulatory and disciplinary proceedings, public law and judicial review, personal injury, property law, and technology and construction.

Pupil profile

Chambers looks for individuals who can demonstrate a first class intellect whether via the traditional route of an outstanding higher education record or via proof of success in other professions, in business or in employment. Henderson Chambers is friendly and sociable, and expect candidates to be able to show how they have both worked hard and played hard.

Pupillage

Pupillages are for 12 months, usually with two different pupil supervisors for six months each. Pupils have the opportunity to spend four weeks in Brussels at McDermott Will and Emery in order to experience European practice at first hand. Pupils will attend court regularly during their second six months.

Mini-pupillage

Chambers offer unassessed mini-pupillages. Applications are by way of a CV and covering letter, which should be addressed to Ross Fentem.

Funding

Chambers offer a maximum of three, and usually two, funded twelve-month pupillages with minimum remuneration of £42,500. This consists of an award of £35,000 and guaranteed earnings of £7,500 during the second six months.

No of Silks **8**
No of Juniors **32**
No of Pupils **2**

Contact
Adam Heppinstall (Recruitment Committee secretary)
aheppinstall@hendersonchambers.co.uk

Method of application
OLPAS

Pupillages (p.a.)
1-3 (usually 2) 12 month pupillages offered.
Remuneration for pupillage:
£42,500 for 12 months
(£35,000 award, £7,500 guaranteed earnings)

Tenancies
5 in the last 3 years.

Keating Chambers

15 Essex Street, London, WC2R 3AA
Tel: (020) 7544 2600
Fax: (020) 7544 2700

No of Silks **19**	
No of Juniors **30**	
No of Pupils currently **3**	
Contact	
ebrowne@keatingchambers.com	
Method of application	
OLPAS	
Pupillages (p.a.)	
Pupillages (p.a.): 4x12 month pupillages available	
Tenancies	
Not fixed but 5 offered in last 3 years.	

Chambers profile

Keating Chambers is a leading commercial set specialising in construction, technology and related professional negligence disputes. Disputes often relate to high-profile projects in the UK and overseas and typically involve complex issues in the law of tort, contract and restitution. Chambers is based in modern premises outside the Temple. In their first years of practice, tenants can expect earnings equivalent to those in other top sets of commercial chambers.

Type of work undertaken

Chambers is involved in disputes of all shapes and sizes: from residential building works to multi-million pound projects for the construction of airports, dams, power stations and bridges. Chambers has been instructed on projects such as Wembley Stadium, the "Gherkin", the Millenium Bridge, the London Eye and the Channel Tunnel. Much of Chambers' work now also includes developing areas such as IT, telecommunications and energy. Chambers acts as advocates in litigation and arbitration throughout the UK and internationally. Some are frequently appointed as mediators, arbitrators, and adjudicators.

Chambers' area of practice is dynamic and challenging. As leaders in the field Chambers are often in cases that are reported in the law reports. Chambers regularly publishes books, articles and journals.

Pupil profile

No specialist or technical knowledge of construction or engineering is required. A thorough understanding of principles of contract and tort law is essential. Criteria are listed on the website.

Pupillage

Pupils are allocated four supervisors over the course of the year ensuring that each pupil sees a variety of work of differing levels of complexity within Chambers. Comprehensive training is provided including a programme of advocacy exercises and provision for attendance at specialist seminars and lectures. For more details, see our website.

Mini pupillages

Chambers offers up to ten funded mini-pupillages lasting one week and 25 unfunded mini pupillages lasting three days. For further details, see website.

Funding

Awards of up to £42,500 are available. Of this, an advance of £15,000 is available during the BVC course.

7 King's Bench Walk

7 King's Bench Walk, Temple, London, EC4Y 7DS
Tel: (020) 7910 8300   Fax: (020) 7910 8464
Website: www.7kbw.co.uk

Chambers profile

7 King's Bench Walk is a leading commercial set of Chambers, with a reputation for excellence and intellectual rigour. The Legal 500 describes it as "One of the Bar's true elite".

Type of work undertaken

Chambers is at the forefront of commercial litigation, specialising in particular in the fields of insurance and reinsurance, shipping, international trade, professional negligence and private international law. Most of its work has an international dimension. Members regularly appear in the High Court (particularly the Commercial Court), the Court of Appeal and the House of Lords, as well as in arbitrations in London and overseas.

Pupil profile

Applicants must have at least a good 2:1, coupled with lively intelligence and strong advocacy skills (both oral and in writing). Chambers encourages applications from all outstanding candidates no matter what their background or academic discipline.

Pupillage

Chambers offers up to four (but typically two or three) twelve month pupillages each year. Pupils will sit with four pupillage supervisors prior to the tenancy decision in July. Pupils will assist their pupil supervisors with their work, and accompany them to hearings. Pupils will, particularly after completion of the first three months of pupillage, also do work for other members of Chambers.

Mini-pupillage

Mini-pupillages are unassessed, and last 3 days. They are offered in three separate periods throughout the year: 1 June to 30 September (excluding August), 1 October to 31 January and 1 February to 31 May. Applications for mini-pupillages during these periods must be received by 31 March, 31 July, and 30 November respectively. Application by way of a CV and covering letter should be made to the Secretary to the Mini-Pupillage Committee. Further details of how to apply may be found on Chambers' website.

Funding

A pupillage award of at least £43,000 will be available for the 2010/11 and 2011/2012 years, of which up to £10,000 may be drawn down during the BVC.

No of Silks 18
No of Juniors 28
No of Pupils up to 4

Contact
Emma Hilliard (pupillage secretary)
Pupillage@7kbw.co.uk

Method of application
OLPAS

Pupillages (p.a.)
Up to 4 12 month pupillages offered.
Required degree grade
Minimum 2:1 (law or non-law)
Remuneration for pupillage: at least £43,000

Tenancies
Junior tenancies offered in last 3 years: 6
No of tenants of 5 years call or under: 8

Littleton Chambers

3 King's Bench Walk North, Temple, London, EC4Y 7HR
Tel: (020) 7797 8600   Fax: (020) 7797 8699
Email: clerks@littletonchambers.co.uk
Website: www.littletonchambers.co.uk

No of Silks 12
No of Juniors 37
No of Pupils currently 2
Contact
Samantha Higgins, Chambers Administrator
Method of application
OLPAS
Pupillages (p.a.)
Pupillages (p.a.): 12 month 2 required degree level 2:1 (law or non law)
Tenancies
£40,000

Chambers profile

Littleton Chambers is acknowledged as being a top class set in each of its main practice areas. Its success is based upon both the desire to maintain high professional standards and a willingness to embrace change. It prides itself on the skills of its tenants, not only as advocates and advisers on the law, but also for their analytical and practical skills.

Type of work undertaken

Littleton Chambers specialises in commercial litigation, employment law and professional negligence.

Pupil profile

Chambers takes a considerable amount of care in choosing its pupils and prefers to recruit its tenants from persons who have completed a full twelve months of pupillage with Chambers. Chambers endeavors to take on pupils who not only have good academic skills, but who also show flair for advocacy and the ability to understand practical commercial issues.

Pupillage

Chambers generally offers pupillage to two people each year.

During your twelve month pupillage you will have the benefit of three pupil supervisors in succession. Your pupil supervisors will provide support and guidance to you throughout your pupillage, ensuring that you understand not only the nuts and bolts of a barristers work, but also the ethical constraints which are such a distinctive feature of Chambers professional life.

After six months pupillage, you will be entitled to take on your own work. Typically, pupils in Littleton Chambers have been briefed once or twice a week. Your pupil supervisor will provide assistance in the preparation of these briefs to ensure that your client receives the best possible service from you.

Mini-pupillage

Assessed mini-pupillage forms part of the pupillage application process. Mini-pupillages are not offered outside of this process.

Funding

Each pupillage is funded (currently £40,000 per year) and, if necessary, it is possible to draw down some of this funding during the year of Bar Finals.

Maitland Chambers

7 Stone Buildings, Lincoln's Inn, London WC2A 3SZ
Tel: (020) 7406 1200 Fax: (020) 7406 1300
Email: clerks@maitlandchambers.com
Website: www.maitlandchambers.com

Chambers profile

Chambers UK has rated Maitland as the pre-eminent commercial Chancery litigation set every year since 2001.

Type of work undertaken

Chambers is instructed on a very wide range of cases – from major international litigation to county court disputes. Much of the work is done in London, though the set frequently advises and appears for clients in other parts of the United Kingdom and abroad. Members are recommended as leaders in their field in commercial Chancery, company, charities, insolvency, media and entertainment, traditional Chancery, property litigation, partnership, pensions, banking, energy, tax, agriculture and professional negligence.

Pupil profile

Academically, Maitland Chambers looks for a first or upper second. Pupils must have a sense of commercial practicality, be stimulated by the challenge of advocacy and have an aptitude for and general enjoyment of complex legal argument.

Pupillage

Pupils sit with at least three different barristers but spend their first few months with one supervisor in order that the pupil can find his or her feet and establish a point of contact which will endure throughout the pupil's time in chambers. Pupils also undertake a structured advocacy training course which consists of advocacy exercises conducted in front of other members of chambers.

Mini pupillages

Applications are considered twice a year with a deadline of 30 April for the period June to November, and 15 November for December to May. Applications should be made with a covering letter and cv (listing undergraduate grades) to the Pupillage Secretary.

Funding

Chambers offers up to three, 12-month pupillages, all of which are funded (£40,000 for pupils starting in October 2008). Up to £10,000 of the award may be drawn down in advance during BVC year.

No of Silks 16
No of Juniors 47
No of Pupils up to 3

Contact
Valerie Piper
(Pupillage Secretary)
pupillage
@maitlandchambers.com

Method of application
See Chambers website from January 2009. Application deadline for pupillage in 2010-11 is 9 February 2008

Pupillages (p.a.)
Up to 3 funded

Income
£40,000 p.a.

Tenancies
5 in last 3 years

Four New Square

Four New Square, Lincoln's Inn, London, WC2A 3RJ
Tel: (020) 7822 2000   Fax: (020) 7822 2001
Website: www.4newsquare.com

No of Silks	14
No of Juniors	50
No of Pupils	4
Contact	
Catherine Culley	
Tel: (020) 7822 2000	
Email:	
c.culley@4newsquare.com	
Method of application	
Online: www.4newsquare.com	
Pupillages (p.a.)	
Up to 4	
Annexes	
3, London	

Chambers profile

Four New Square is a leading commercial and civil set of barristers comprising 63 members, of whom 14 are Queen's Counsel. Chambers acts as specialist advocates and advisers in a wide range of civil disputes and as expert advisers in non-contentious matters. Chambers has a particularly high reputation in the field of professional liability. The leading practitioners' work on the subject, Jackson & Powell on Professional Negligence, was written by Rupert Jackson QC (now Mr Justice Jackson) and John L Powell QC, and continues to be written and edited by members of chambers.

Type of work undertaken

Professional liability, product liability, chancery and commercial law, construction and engineering, insurance and reinsurance, financial services and banking.

Pupil profile

Chambers do not stream its pupils. Each has an equal prospect of securing a tenancy. Selection criteria: evidence of intellectual ability; potential as an advocate; personal qualities such as self-reliance, integrity, reliability and the ability to work effectively with colleagues and clients; motivation. Equal opportunities: Chambers observes a policy of equal opportunities in accordance with the Bar Code of Conduct. All applicants are required to complete the Bar Council Equality Code questionnaire. This is used for monitoring purposes only.

Pupillage

The first six months: You will go to court and attend conferences with your pupil supervisor. You will also assist your pupil supervisor with their written work: carrying out written advisory and drafting work on their current papers and undertaking detailed research on the law. The second six months: During your second six months, you will take on an increasing amount of your own court work. Chambers places a strong emphasis on advocacy and support its pupils in gaining valuable practical experience. You can expect to be in court on your own about once a week up to the tenancy decision and potentially on a more regular basis thereafter. Advocacy: You will also take part in an assessed moot during your first six months. Workshop training sessions are run to help you prepare for the moot, which usually takes place before a former member of Chambers who is now a High Court Judge. Environment: Chambers aims to provide a friendly and sociable atmosphere. Pupils are included in Chambers social events throughout the year.

Mini pupillages

Students considering applying to chambers in the next OLPAS round are encouraged to apply for one of 12 assessed mini pupillages. After an initial review of applications on paper, a number of applicants will be invited for a short interview with two members of chambers. The assessed mini will last for three days with an award of £500. Mini-pupils will be set a piece of assessed work and those judged to be of high calibre will be given an exemption from the first round OLPAS interviews should they apply. Chambers understands that not everyone seeking to apply for pupillage through OLPAS will be able to participate in the assessed mini-pupillage programme. Consequently chambers also offers unassessed mini-pupillages. Applications may be made at any time of the year. Unassessed mini-pupillages are granted after a review of an application form by two members of Chambers.

Funding

Funding: Chambers offers up to four 12-month pupillages with awards of £45,000 compromising an award of £37,500 (up to a third which may be drawn down during the BVC year) with further guaranteed second-six-month earnings of £7,500. Chambers also guarantees that the junior tenants will earn a minimum of £150,000 in total, net of Chambers' expenses, during their first three years of tenancy, in addition to their pupillage awards.

FOUR NEW SQUARE

XXIV Old Buildings

XXIV Old Buildings, 24 Old Buildings, Lincoln's Inn, London, WC2A 3UP
Tel: (020) 7691 2424   Fax: (0870) 460 2178
Website: xxiv.co.uk

No of Silks 7
No of Juniors 26
No of Pupils 2
Contact
Mrs Helen Galley, Secretary of the Pupillage Committee
Method of application
Letter and CV. Please see www.xxiv.co.uk for guidance
Pupillages (p.a.)
2 for 12 months
Tenancies
Usually 1-2 per year
Other offices
Geneva

Chambers profile

XXIV Old Buildings is a commercial Chancery chambers of 33 barristers based in Lincoln's Inn.

Members are instructed in a wide variety of commercial Chancery areas, with particular emphasis on business matters (both litigation and transactional matters, including mergers and acquisitions); company and financial services with related pension law aspects; insolvency; property; trusts and estates work; international and offshore – particularly in relation to trusts and offshore structures with the closely associated fields of fraud, breach of fiduciary duty and asset recovery. Professional liability is covered in all these fields, particularly in relation to solicitors, accountants, professional trustees and financial managers and advisors.

Type of work undertaken

The Set is particularly respected for its practice in the international and offshore fields, covering both traditional Chancery work as well as major commercial litigation.

The set also has a niche practice in aviation and travel law, specialising mainly in aircraft leasing and insurance/ reinsurance issues.

Pupillage

The set likes to recruit its junior members from those who have undertaken pupillage with the set. Chambers are therefore careful that its pupils acquire all the skills necessary to make them successful commercial Chancery barristers. During a 12 month pupillage, a pupil will have, on average, four pupil supervisors with whom they will spend the majority of their time. Each year the set is looking for two pupils with a first or 2:1 degree, though not necessarily in law, who have an enthusiasm for the type of work the set does, sound judgement and the application required to succeed in a very competitive and intellectually demanding environment. Applications for pupillages should be made by 16th March for pupillages commencing October of the following year.

Mini pupillages

The set is happy to consider applications for mini-pupillages. Please send a letter and CV to mini-pupillage@xxiv.co.uk

Funding

Each pupil will be paid £40,000.

Old Square Chambers

10-11 Bedford Row, London, WC1R 4BU D: 1046 Chancery Lane
Tel: (020) 7269 0300   Fax: (020) 7405 1384
Email: clerks@oldsquare.co.uk
Website: www.oldsquare.co.uk

No of Silks 10	
No of Juniors 57	
No of Pupils 2	
Contact	
Ben Cooper	
Felicity Schneider	
Method of application	
OLPAS (Summer)	
Pupillages (p.a.)	
2-12 month pupillages	
Income	
£30,000 (£22,000 award plus £8,000 guaranteed earnings) Plus additional earnings	
Tenancies	
4 in last 3 years	
Annexes	
Bristol	

Chambers profile

Old Square Chambers is recognised as a premier set in its core specialist areas of employment and discrimination, personal injury and environmental law. Chambers' defining quality is excellence, both in the specialist legal expertise it has to offer and in the customer-service which it provides. Members and staff have a reputation for being approachable and unstuffy. Many members hold part-time judicial positions, sit on specialist panels, act as mediators, and edit or contribute to leading practitioner texts.

Type of work undertaken

Chambers' strength lies in the depth of experience and expertise in its core practice areas. The Employment and Discrimination Group is widely regarded as one of the foremost in the UK. Work is in all aspects of employment and discrimination law. Clients range from individual employees and directors to major trade unions, private and public sector organisations. Personal Injury work covers all aspects of this wide-ranging and complex field, from employers' liability and road traffic claims to high value head, brain and spinal injury cases, with particular expertise in disaster litigation and multi-party actions. In environmental law, Chambers has been at the forefront of developing litigation in the area of toxic torts. Members appear in high-profile multi-party claims arising from pollution of various kinds. Alongside its core areas Chambers also has expertise in professional discipline, clinical negligence, product liability, public inquiries, health and safety and ADR.

Pupil profile

Chambers assesses candidates on intellectual ability (usually a first or upper second degree will be required), potential as an advocate, interest in Chambers' fields of practice, ability to cope with hard work and pressure and interpersonal skills.

Mini pupillages

Chambers runs a programme of mini-pupillages during the summer. Applications should be made through Chambers' website.

Funding

The current award is £30,000 (£22,000 award plus £8,000 guaranteed earnings). Pupils keep additional earnings from their second six.

Pump Court Tax Chambers

16 Bedford Row, London, WC1R 4EF
Tel: (0207) 414 8080   Fax: (0207) 414 8099
Email: clerks@pumptax.com
Website: www.pumptax.com

No of Silks 10
No of Juniors 19
No of Pupils 2-3 in any given year

Contact
Jonathan Bremner
pupils@pumptax.com

Method of application
CV and covering letter (non-OLPAS)

Pupillages (p.a.)
Up to 3 funded
Tenancies
4 in the last 3 years

Chambers profile

Pump Court Tax Chambers is the largest specialist set practising exclusively in tax.

Type of work undertaken

All areas of tax work (both contentious and non-contentious) are covered. On the corporate side, clients typically include the 'Big 4' accountants and 'magic circle' solicitors sending a wide variety of work such as M & A, reconstructions and demergers and structured finance. Chambers' private client work comes from a broad range of sources – city solicitors, accountants, regional firms, chartered tax advisors and IFAs, who act for private individuals, trustees and landed estates. Much of Chambers' work concerns large scale litigation (especially in the field of VAT) and members of chambers regularly appear in the Tax Tribunals, the High Court, the Court of Appeal, the House of Lords and the ECJ.

Pupil profile

Chambers looks for applicants who are intelligent, articulate and well-motivated. Successful candidates will have at least a 2:1 honours degree (although not necessarily in law). Prior experience of studying tax law is not required.

Pupillage

Chambers offers up to three 12 month pupillages (terminable after six months by either party) to those wishing to practise full-time at the Bar. Pupillage normally commences in October each year. Pupils will have at least three pupil supervisors and will also sit with other members of chambers so as to receive a broad training in all aspects of the work of chambers.

Mini pupillages

The programme runs throughout the year. Applications should be made via email to pupils@pumptax.com with accompanying CV and marked for the attention of the Pupillage Secretary.

Funding

Awards of up to £20,000 per six months (£40,000pa) are available. The pupillage committee has discretion to consider applications for up to £8,000 of the pupillage award to be advanced during the BVC year.

Quadrant Chambers (Nigel Teare QC)

Quadrant House, 10 Fleet Street, London EC4Y 1AU
Tel: (020) 7583 4444 Fax: (020) 7583 4455
Email: pupillage@quadrantchambers.com
Website: www.quadrantchambers.com

Chambers profile

Quadrant Chambers is one of the leading commercial chambers. Chambers offers a wide range of services to its clients within the commercial sphere specialising particularly in maritime and aviation law. Quadrant Chambers is placed in the first rank in both specialisms by Chambers Guide to the Legal Profession. In shipping law, seven silks and nine juniors were selected by Chambers, and Chambers concluded that 'these highly commercial barristers are at the forefront of the aviation field. In both these areas the set had more 'leaders in their field' selected than any other set of chambers. Quadrant Chambers advises on domestic and international commercial litigation and acts as advocates in court, arbitration and inquiries in England and abroad.

Type of work undertaken

The challenging and rewarding work of chambers encompasses the broad range of commercial disputes embracing arbitration, aviation, banking, shipping, international trade, insurance and reinsurance, professional negligence, entertainment and media, environmental and construction law. Over 70% of chambers work involves international clients.

Pupil profile

Quadrant Chambers seeks high calibre pupils with good academic qualifications (at least a 2.1 degree) who exhibit good written and oral skills.

Pupillage

Chambers offer a maximum of three funded pupillages of 12 months duration (reviewable at six months). Pupils are moved amongst several members of Chambers and will experience a wide range of high quality commercial work. Outstanding pupils are likely to be offered a tenancy at the end of their pupillage. Further information can be found on the website.

Mini pupillages

Mini pupillages are encouraged in order that potential pupils may experience the work of Chambers before committing themselves to an application for full pupillage. Please refer to Chambers' website for more details.

Funding

Awards of £40,000 p.a. are available for each funded pupillage – part of which may be forwarded during the BVC, at the Pupillage Committee's discretion.

No of Silks 10
No of Juniors 34

Contact
Secretary to Pupillage Committee

Method of application
Chambers' application form

Pupillages (p.a.)
1st 6 months 3
2nd 6 months 3
12 months
(Reviewed at 6 months)
Required degree
Good 2:1+

Income
1st 6 months
£20,000
2nd 6 months
£20,000
Earnings not included

Tenancies
Current tenants who served pupillage in Chambers 19
Junior tenancies offered in last 3 years 6
No of tenants of 5 years call or under 7
Income (1st year)
c. £50,000

Serle Court

Serle Court, 6 New Square, Lincoln's Inn, London WC2A 3QS
Tel: (020) 7242 6105 Fax: (020) 7405 4004
Email: pupillage@serlecourt.co.uk
Website: www.serlecourt.co.uk

No of Silks 13	
No of Juniors 35	
No of Pupils 2	
Contact	
Kathryn Barry	
Tel (020) 7242 6105	
Method of application	
Chambers application form, available from website or Chambers. Not a member of OLPAS	
Pupillages	
Two 12 month pupillages	
Tenancies	
Up to 2 per annum	

Chambers profile

'Commercial powerhouse of the Chancery Bar...' Chambers & Partners Guide to the UK Legal Profession 2006. Serle Court is one of the leading commercial chancery sets with 48 barristers including 13 silks. Widely recognised as a leading set, Chambers is recommended in 21 different areas of practice by the legal directories. Chambers has a stimulating and inclusive work environment and a forward looking approach.

Type of work undertaken

Litigation, arbitration, mediation and advisory services across the full range of chancery and commercial practice areas including: administrative and public law, banking, civil fraud, commercial litigation, company, financial services, human rights, insolvency, insurance and reinsurance, partnership, professional negligence, property, regulatory and disciplinary, trusts and probate.

Pupil profile

Candidates are well-rounded people, from any background. Chambers looks for highly motivated individuals with first class intellectual ability, combined with a practical approach, sound sensibility and the potential to become excellent advocates. Serle Court has a reputation for 'consistent high quality' and for having 'responsive and able team members' and seeks the same qualities in pupils.

Pupillage

Pupils sit with different pupil supervisors in order to experience a broad range of work. Two pupils are recruited each year and Chambers offers: an excellent preparation for successful practice; a genuinely friendly and supportive environment; the opportunity to learn from some of the leading barristers in their field; a real prospect of tenancy.

Mini-pupillages

About 30 available each year. Apply online at www.serlecourt.co.uk.

Funding

Serle Court offers awards of £45,000 for 12 months, of which up to £15,000 can be drawn down during the BVC year. It also provides an income guarantee worth up to £100,000 over the first two years of practice.

3-4 South Square

3-4 South Square, Gray's Inn, London WC1R 5HP
Tel: (020) 7696 9900 Fax: (020) 7696 9911
Email: pupillage@southsquare.com
Website: www.southsquare.com

No of Silks **18**	
No of Juniors **26**	
No of Pupils **3**	
Contact	
Pupillage Secretary	
Tel (020) 7696 9900	
Method of application	
CV with covering letter	
Pupillages (p.a.)	
Up to four, 12 month pupillages offered each year	

Chambers profile

Chambers is an established successful commercial set, involved in high-profile international and domestic commercial litigation and advice. Members of Chambers have been centrally involved in some of the most important commercial cases of the last decade including Barings, BCCI, Lloyds, Maxwell, Railtrack, TXU, Enron, Marconi, NTL and Global Crossing.

Type of work undertaken

3-4 South Square has a pre-eminent reputation in insolvency and restructuring law and specialist expertise in banking, financial services, company law, professional negligence, domestic and international arbitration, mediation, European Union Law, insurance/reinsurance law and general commercial litigation.

Pupil profile

Chambers seek to recruit the highest calibre of candidates who must be prepared to commit themselves to establishing a successful practice and maintaining Chambers' position at the forefront of the modern Commercial Bar. The minimum academic qualification is a 2:1 degree.

Pupillage

Pupils are welcomed into all areas of Chambers' life and are provided with an organised programme designed to train and equip them for practice in a dynamic and challenging environment. Pupils sit with a number of pupil supervisors for periods of six to eight weeks and the set looks to recruit at least one tenant every year from its pupils.

Mini pupillages

Chambers also offers funded and unfunded mini-pupillages – please see the set's website for further details.

Sponsorship & awards

Currently £42,500 per annum (reviewable annually).

4 Stone Buildings

4 Stone Buildings, Lincoln's Inn, London WC2A 3XT
Tel: (020) 7242 5524 Fax: (020) 7831 7907
Email: d.goddard@4stonebuildings.com

Chambers profile

An established friendly company/commercial set involved in high profile litigation and advice.

Type of work undertaken

4 Stone Buildings specialise in the fields of company law, commercial law, financial services and regulation and corporate insolvency.

Pupil profile

Candidates are expected to have first class, or good second class degrees. But mere intellectual ability is only part of it: a successful candidate must have the confidence and ambition to succeed, the common sense to recognise the practical advice a client really needs, and an ability to get on well with clients, solicitors and other members of Chambers - and the clerks.

Pupillage

The set aim to give all pupils the knowledge, skills and practical experience they need for a successful career at the Bar. They believe that it is important for all pupils to see as much as possible of the different kinds of work in Chambers. This enables pupils to judge whether their work suits them, and enables different members of Chambers to assess the pupils. Each pupil therefore normally spends time with two or more pupil-masters within any six month period. If other members of Chambers have particularly interesting cases in Court, pupils will be encouraged to work and attend Court with them. All pupils work in their pupil masters' rooms, read their papers, attend their conferences, draft pleadings and documents, write draft opinions and accompany their pupil supervisors to Court. Pupils are treated as part of Chambers, and are fully involved in the activities of Chambers while they are with 4 Stone Buildings.

Mini pupillages

Up to 20 mini-pupillages offered per year of up to a weeks duration. Application by letter and CV.

Sponsorship & awards

Up to £39,000 per 12 months.

Funding

As above.

No of Silks 6	
No of Juniors 22	
No of Pupils 2	
Contact	
David Goddard	
(020) 7242 5524	
Method of application	
On Chambers own application form	
Pupillages (p.a.)	
up to 2 x 12 months	
Tenancies	
On average 1 per year	
Annexes	
None	

2 Temple Gardens (Chambers of Benjamin Browne QC)

2 Temple Gardens, London, EC4Y 9AY   DX: 134 Chancery Lane
Tel: (020) 7822 1200   Fax: (020) 7822 1300
Email: clerks@2tg.co.uk
Website: www.2tg.co.uk

No of Silks **8**
No of Juniors **48**
No of Pupils **2**
Contact
Leanne McCabe
Pupillage Administrator
Method of application
OLPAS (Summer)
Pupillages (p.a.)
Up to three, 12 month pupillages
Award: £45,000

Chambers profile

2tg is regarded as one of the leading commercial and civil law barristers' chambers. Chambers specialises in professional negligence, insurance and personal injury and also has significant practices in banking, employment, technology and construction and clinical negligence, alongside strength in private international law.

Pupil profile

Academically, you will need at least a good 2.1 degree to be considered. Chambers look for applicants who work well in teams and have the ability to get on with solicitors, clients and other members of chambers.

Pupillage

Chambers offers one of the most generously funded, well structured and enjoyable pupillages at the Bar. It takes pupillage very seriously and aims to recruit the best applicants, and to ensure that its pupils have an excellent foundation from which to start a successful career at the Bar.

Pupils have three different pupil supervisors during pupillage, and will also do work for other members of chambers. Chambers' aim is for pupils to experience as much of chambers' work as possible during their pupillage year.

Mini pupillages

Chambers welcome 'mini-pupils'. Generally applicants will only be considered after their first year of a law degree or during CPE. Mini pupillages are a good way to experience life at 2tg first hand. Normally they last for one week. However, two or three day mini pupillages can be arranged. Chambers aims to provide you with a wide range of work during your week with us. Chambers offers an assessment at the completion of your mini pupillage and encourages you to give feedback too. Chambers also offers help with reasonable expenses (up to £50).

Mini pupillages are usually unfunded but a few funded mini pupillages (maximum £250 per person) are also available.

Funding

Chambers offers up to three, 12 month pupillages, all of which are funded. The pupillage award for pupils starting in 2009 is £45,000. This is made up of a grant of £35,000, of which up to £10,000 can be taken in the BVC year. The remainder of the grant will be paid in instalments in the first six months of pupillage with a guarantee of earnings during the second six months of £10,000.

3 Verulam Buildings (Christopher Symons QC/John Jarvis QC)

3 Verulam Buildings, Gray's Inn, London WC1R 5NT DX: LDE 331
Tel: (020) 7831 8441 Fax: (020) 7831 8479
Email: chambers@3vb.com
Website: www.3vb.com

Chambers profile

Sitting comfortably and spaciously in a newly refurbished and expanded row of buildings in Gray's Inn, 3VB is one of the largest and most highly regarded commercial sets, its members being involved in many of the leading cases, recent examples including the test case on overdraft charges, the Springwell professional negligence litigation, the Zambian fraud and vulture fund litigation, the Honeywell dispute, the Procol Harum bust-up, and the Rosemary Nelson enquiry in Northern Ireland.

Type of work undertaken

3VB's 16 silks and 39 juniors lead the field in banking and financial services, and are also among the top practitioners in the fields of professional negligence, civil fraud, insurance, arbitration, and company and insolvency. Chambers also has significant expertise in IT and telecommunications, energy, construction, and media and entertainment.

Pupil profile

Commercial practice is intellectually demanding and 3VB seeks the brightest and the best. The typical successful applicant will have a first or upper second class degree (not necessarily in law) from a good university, with good mooting experience and proven experience of the commercial bar (generally through mini-pupillages with us or elsewhere). Many have a Master's degree or other legal or commercial experience.

Pupillage

Chambers seeks to recruit three or four 12 months pupils each year through the OLPAS process. Chambers are committed to recruiting new tenants from its pupils whenever it can. Although tenancy is offered to all pupils who make the grade, on average two out of three pupils are successful in any one year.

Mini pupillages

Three day mini-pupillages are an important part of Chambers selection procedure and it is strongly encouraged that prospective applicants for pupillage apply for a mini-pupillage (e-mail James MacDonald at minipupillage@3vb.com, attaching a detailed CV).

Funding

For the year 2009/2010, the annual award will be at least £42,500, up to £15,000 of which may be drawn during the BVC year.

No of Silks 17
No of Juniors 40
No of Pupils 3

Contact
Mr Adam Kramer
(Pupillage)
Mr James MacDonald
(Mini Pupillage)

Method of application
OLPAS (Pupillage); CV & covering letter (Mini-pupillage)

Pupillages (p.a.)
12 months 3
Required degree grade
2:1

Income
In excess of £42,500 plus any earnings

Tenancies
Current tenants who served pupillage in Chambers Approx 41
Junior tenancies offered in last 3 years 4
No of tenants of 5 years call or under 11

Wilberforce Chambers

8 New Square, Lincoln's Inn, London WC2A 3QP
Tel: (020) 7306 0102   Fax: (020) 7306 0095
Email: pupillage@wilberforce.co.uk   Website: www.wilberforce.co.uk

No of Silks	21
No of Juniors	29
Method of application	
Online via website	
Pupillages (p.a.)	
2 x 12 months	
Mini-pupillages	
Total of 21 places	
Income	
£40,000 (2009/2010)	
Minimum qualification	
2:1 degree	
Tenancies in last 3 years	
4	

Chambers profile

Wilberforce Chambers is a leading Commercial Chancery set of Chambers and is involved in some of the most commercially important and cutting edge litigation and advisory work undertaken by the Bar today. Members are recognised by the key legal directories as leaders in their fields. Instructions come from top UK and International law firms, providing a complex and rewarding range of work for international companies, financial institutions, well-known names, sports and media organisations, pension funds, commercial landlords and tenants, and private individuals. Clients demand high intellectual performance and client-care standards but in return the reward is a successful and fulfilling career at the Bar. Chambers has grown in size in recent years but retains a united and friendly 'family' atmosphere.

Type of work undertaken

All aspects of traditional and modern Chancery work including property, pensions, private client, trust and taxation, professional negligence, general commercial litigation, banking, company, financial services, intellectual property and information technology, sports and media and charities.

Pupil profile

Chambers look to offer two 12 month pupillages. You should possess high intellectual ability, excellent communication skills and a strong motivation to do Commercial Chancery work. You need to be mature and confident, have the ability to work with others and analyse legal problems clearly, demonstrating commercial and practical good sense. Chambers look for people who have real potential to join as tenants at the end of their pupillage. Wilberforce takes great care in its selection process and puts effort into providing an excellent pupillage. There is a minimum requirement of a 2:1 degree in law or another subject, and Wilberforce has a track record of taking on CPE students.

Pupillage

Chambers operates a well-structured pupillage programme aimed at providing you with a broad experience of Commercial Chancery practice under several pupil supervisors with whom you will be able to develop your skills. Wilberforce aims to reach a decision about tenancy after approximately 9-10 months, but all pupils are entitled to stay for the remainder of their pupillage on a full pupillage award.

Mini-pupillages

Wilberforce encourages potential candidates for pupillage to undertake a mini-pupillage in order to learn how Chambers operates, to meet its members and to see the type of work that they do, but a mini-pupillage is not a prerequisite for pupillage. Wilberforce runs three separate mini-pupillage weeks (two in December and one in July). Please visit the website for an application form and for further information.

Funding

Wilberforce offers a generous and competitive pupillage award which is reviewed annually with the intention that it should be in line with the highest awards available. The award is currently £40,000 for 12 months and is paid in monthly instalments. A proportion of the award (up to £13,500) can be drawn down during the BVC year.

WILBERFORCE CHAMBERS